# Caribbean Islands

Ryan Ver Berkmoes
Amy C Balfour, Paul Clammer, Michael Grosberg, Scott
Kennedy, Richard Koss, Josh Krist, Tom Masters, Jens Porup,
Brandon Presser, Brendan Sainsbury, Ellee Thalheimer,
Karla Zimmerman

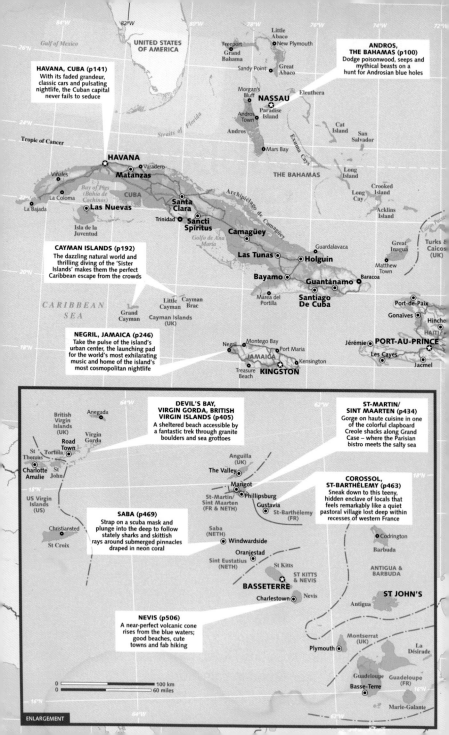

**HAVANA, CUBA (p141)**
With its faded grandeur, classic cars and pulsating nightlife, the Cuban capital never fails to seduce

**ANDROS, THE BAHAMAS (p100)**
Dodge poisonwood, seeps and mythical beasts on a hunt for Androsian blue holes

**CAYMAN ISLANDS (p192)**
The dazzling natural world and thrilling diving of the 'Sister Islands' makes them the perfect Caribbean escape from the crowds

**NEGRIL, JAMAICA (p246)**
Take the pulse of the island's urban center, the launching pad for the world's most exhilarating music and home of the island's most cosmopolitan nightlife

**DEVIL'S BAY, VIRGIN GORDA, BRITISH VIRGIN ISLANDS (p405)**
A sheltered beach accessible by a fantastic trek through granite boulders and sea grottoes

**ST-MARTIN/ SINT MAARTEN (p434)**
Gorge on haute cuisine in one of the colorful clapboard Creole shacks along Grand Case – where the Parisian bistro meets the salty sea

**COROSSOL, ST-BARTHÉLEMY (p463)**
Sneak down to this teeny, hidden enclave of locals that feels remarkably like a quiet pastoral village lost deep within recesses of western France

**SABA (p469)**
Strap on a scuba mask and plunge into the deep to follow stately sharks and skittish rays around submerged pinnacles draped in neon coral

**NEVIS (p506)**
A near-perfect volcanic cone rises from the blue waters; good beaches, cute towns and fab hiking

ENLARGEMENT

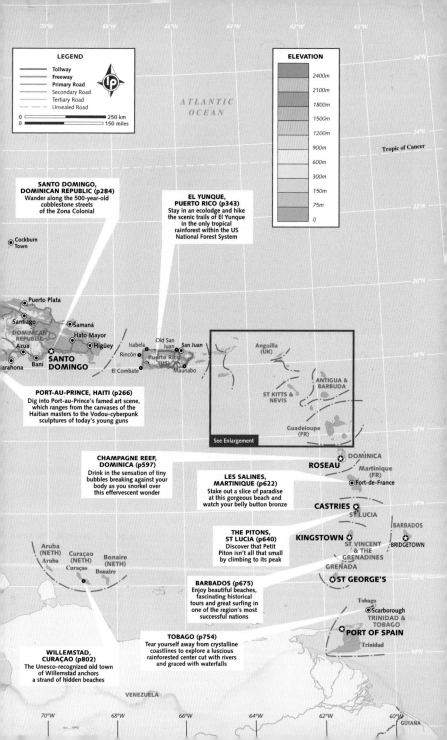

## LEGEND
- Tollway
- Freeway
- Primary Road
- Secondary Road
- Tertiary Road
- Unsealed Road

0 ___ 250 km
0 ___ 150 miles

### ELEVATION
2400m
2100m
1800m
1500m
1200m
900m
600m
300m
150m
75m
0

*ATLANTIC OCEAN*

Tropic of Cancer

**SANTO DOMINGO, DOMINICAN REPUBLIC (p284)**
Wander along the 500-year-old cobblestone streets of the Zona Colonial

**EL YUNQUE, PUERTO RICO (p343)**
Stay in an ecolodge and hike the scenic trails of El Yunque in the only tropical rainforest within the US National Forest System

Cockburn Town

Puerto Plata
Santiago
Samaná
DOMINICAN REPUBLIC
Hato Mayor
Azua
Higüey
Isabela
Rincón
Old San Juan
San Juan
Puerto Rico (US)
arahona
Bani
SANTO DOMINGO
El Combate
Maunabo

Anguilla (UK)

ANTIGUA & BARBUDA

ST KITTS & NEVIS

Guadeloupe (FR)

See Enlargement

**PORT-AU-PRINCE, HAITI (p266)**
Dig into Port-au-Prince's famed art scene, which ranges from the canvases of the Haitian masters to the Vodou-cyberpunk sculptures of today's young guns

**CHAMPAGNE REEF, DOMINICA (p597)**
Drink in the sensation of tiny bubbles breaking against your body as you snorkel over this effervescent wonder

**LES SALINES, MARTINIQUE (p622)**
Stake out a slice of paradise at this gorgeous beach and watch your belly button bronze

DOMINICA
ROSEAU
Martinique (FR)
Fort-de-France

CASTRIES
ST LUCIA

BARBADOS

**THE PITONS, ST LUCIA (p640)**
Discover that Petit Piton isn't all that small by climbing to its peak

KINGSTOWN
ST VINCENT & THE GRENADINES
BRIDGETOWN
GRENADA
ST GEORGE'S

Aruba (NETH)
Aruba
Curaçao (NETH)
Curaçao
Bonaire (NETH)
Bonaire

**BARBADOS (p675)**
Enjoy beautiful beaches, fascinating historical tours and great surfing in one of the region's most successful nations

Tobago
Scarborough
TRINIDAD & TOBAGO
PORT OF SPAIN
Trinidad

**TOBAGO (p754)**
Tear yourself away from crystalline coastlines to explore a luscious rainforested center cut with rivers and graced with waterfalls

**WILLEMSTAD, CURAÇAO (p802)**
The Unesco-recognized old town of Willemstad anchors a strand of hidden beaches

VENEZUELA

GUYANA

# On the Road

**RYAN VER BERKMOES**
Coordinating Author
It was late afternoon at the delightfully shabby and unvisited Fort James (p525) on Antigua. I had the place almost to myself: it was me, a dude singing to himself and a chicken. I looked out to sea then scanned my notes, trying to figure out if this gun had actually been used to shoot pirates. Verdict: maybe.

**PAUL CLAMMER** I'm near the end of my trip, in the clean air above Port-au-Prince (p266), wondering how that little notebook is going to be transformed into a guide, and trying to calculate how many more rum punches I can fit in before I head to the airport…

**AMY C BALFOUR** I'm bursting with latitudinal pride after finding the Tropic of Cancer Beach (p97). It's not well-marked, but the view is one-of-a-kind gorgeous. There's also a worn blue line on the ground signifying the Tropic of Cancer. The *Pirates of the Caribbean* II and III crew would load up here before boating south.

**MICHAEL GROSBERG** My girlfriend and I had just walked from Playa Bonita (p310) to Playa Coson and back; both are outside Las Terrenas on the Península de Samaná. We were both hungry because the fish shack we were counting on for lunch wasn't open, so I volunteered to get her a coconut. I failed.

**SCOTT KENNEDY** Cruising through St Vincent and the Grenadines (p650), it's hard *not* to feel a little like a pirate. Jumping on rickety old boats, floating from island to island, sailing from one adventure to the next, dolphins surfing the bow wave, Tobago Cays on the horizon – just another day on the road.

**RICHARD KOSS** My tour guide at Bob Marley's birthplace in Nine Mile (p238) was an intense Rasta whose solemnity about Bob's life was periodically broken by campy outbursts of song. Taking my photo in Marley's childhood home, he sang 'Is This Love,' pointing energetically at the single bed it mentions. I had a hard time maintaining a straight face.

**TOM MASTERS** I saw a 3m-long manatee swim by me shortly after this shot was taken. I'm cruising through the lagoon on my way to dive off the Isla de la Juventud (p160), where Cuba's very best (and most difficult to access!) diving is on offer.

**JOSH KRIST** Banging out a Rolling Stones tune in the music room at Cocoa Cottages (p594), near Trafalgar Falls. My guitar is what I missed most from home. You'll notice my notes on a pillow next to me – I was testing the guitar for research, I swear.

**BRANDON PRESSER** I didn't think it was possible for anything to be more beautiful than Saba's (p469) striking rugged peak, but lo and behold, the island's offshore reef system, 100ft underwater, is a magnificent kingdom of colorful coral patrolled by scores of slippery sharks.

**BRENDAN SAINSBURY** Cycling on the tropical island of Vieques (p343) can be hot work – especially when you've got human cargo fast asleep in the back seat. I'm drinking freshly squeezed lemonade just outside the gate to the now defunct US Navy military zone, a few miles north of the town of Esperanza.

**ELLEE THALHEIMER** Pure elation is what I feel when I discover a cycling jewel such as the out-and-back from Toco to Matelot (p749), a coastal ride that follows a hilly, remote road skirting a wild coastline that will drop your jaw.

**KARLA ZIMMERMAN** I was amazed by the Lind Point Trail (p372), which departs from Cruz Bay, St John. It left civilization fast in its wake, replacing it with yellow-bellied banana quits, wild donkeys nibbling shrubs, and beaches that were deserted except for the sea-grape trees (and this sign).

*For full author biographies see p855.*

# CARIBBEAN ISLANDS

Azure waters, white beaches, polychromatic culture – aren't the clichés of the Caribbean enough to make you want to visit? No? Well take the plunge with the following highlights. From volcanic peaks to extraordinary reefs, and from the luxe playgrounds of the wealthy to the heady salsas of local culture, you'll find something that will lure you to this diverse and surprising mixture of sea and land.

# Scenery

The Caribbean's stripes of white beaches and impossibly turquoise waters are beautiful enough to
make you weep. But save the tears as the region
has a lot more than just beaches: green volcanic
peaks rise out of the ocean, valleys are cleaved by
waterfalls, vast old forts guard the coasts, and palm
trees and flowers are everywhere you look.

### ❶ Mt Scenery, Saba

Rising dramatically out of the ocean, tiny Saba's volcanic peak, Mt Scenery (p476), can only be appreciated in person. Even the craftiest photographers can't correctly capture its ethereal beauty, which is particularly stunning at dusk, when the setting sun casts flickering shadows across the forested terrain.

### ❷ St-Barthélemy

It comes as no surprise that St-Barthélemy (p454) is the preferred retreat of the rich and famous – the stunning island fulfills every fantasy of a vacation in paradise. Head to Colombier, the most westerly lookout point, to truly appreciate the million-dollar views (literally).

### ❸ Cascada El Limón, Dominican Republic

Far from the golden beaches, the 165ft-high Cascada El Limón waterfall (p306) feels like a different Dominican Republic – rough, rugged and surrounded by forest-covered peaks.

### ❹ The Northern Range, Trinidad & Tobago

A chain of small coastal mountains, the Northern Range (p747) hosts rich rainforests and stunning beaches, creating extravagant stomping grounds for motorists, hikers, and cyclists.

### ❺ Dominica

Dominica (p580) doesn't have mountains – it *is* a mountain. The island has some of the most striking scenery in the Caribbean: a lake that literally boils, the aptly named Valley of Desolation and waterfalls splashing down everywhere.

### ❻ Northern Grande-Terre, Guadeloupe

Head to the northern part of Grande-Terre (p560) to see what many islands in this region must have looked like a hundred years ago. The biggest beach development here is likely to be a small snack shack.

### ❼ Brimstone Hill Fortress, St Kitts & Nevis

More than 8000 French troops fought with 1000 British troops for a month in order to seize Brimstone Hill Fortress (p505). This amazing Unesco World Heritage–listed fort has views north, west and south across the Caribbean – no doubt the soldiers wished they could see Britain or France.

# Activities

There's beauty above and below the water, but there's plenty to do as well. The biggest problem with diving is choosing a location – but you can also surf the waves, hike a volcano, mountain bike the trails and much more. You'll *almost* be too beat for a rum punch at the end of the day.

## ⑤ Hiking, Martinique

Go to the end of the line in Grand-Rivière and let the *syndicat d'initiative* arrange a hike (p623) along the base of the still-smoldering Mont Pelée, a volcano that wiped out Martinique's former capital in 1902.

## ① Diving, Saba

A hidden marine jungle of shining fluorescent coral lurks deep beneath Saba's offshore moorings. Protected by strict environmental laws, this pristine habitat (p478) teems with sharks, sea turtles, rays and plenty of barracuda.

## ② Surfing, Puerto Rico

West-coast Rincón (p350) is Puerto Rico's California. This tropical surfing town throws American expats among wacky locals in a laid-back wave riding scene that was once immortalized in a song by the Beach Boys.

## ③ Diving, Bonaire

Almost the entire coast of Bonaire (p799) is ringed by some of the healthiest coral reefs in the region. Sometimes it seems like half the population of the island are divers – and why shouldn't they be? The Unesco-recognized shore reefs can be reached right off the back pier at oodles of low-key diver-run hotels.

## ④ Diving, Guadeloupe

It's said that scuba divers will have good dives for the rest of their life if they pat the head of the Jacques Cousteau statue in the underwater reserve that bears his name (p565) in Guadeloupe. Whether that's true or not, the diving is incredible.

## ⑥ Hiking & Snorkeling, US Virgin Islands

Feral donkeys, ever nibbling a shrub, will watch as you hike along St John's trails (p372) to petroglyphs, sugar mill ruins, and beaches perfect for snorkeling with turtles, nurse sharks and spotted eagle rays.

## ⑦ Cycling, St Lucia

Who says you need to be in the mountains to go mountain biking? The purpose-built biking tracks (p641) on St Lucia are some of the best you'll find anywhere – as they should be, since they were designed by a former world champion.

## ⑧ Diving, Cayman Islands

The Bloody Bay Marine Park (p209) on Little Cayman is the pick of the dive spots in the Cayman Islands, although both Grand Cayman and Cayman Brac also have fantastic dives on offer, including plenty of exciting wrecks to explore.

## ⑨ Diving, Grenada

Tired of seeing the same old fish whenever you go scuba diving? Why not go for a swim in an underwater sculpture gallery? Beautiful sculptures sit below the surface at this spot in Molinière Bay (p710), which is visited by only a lucky few.

# Music

Reggae, calypso, salsa, soca and more – the Caribbean's music is as deeply ingrained in perceptions of the islands as beaches, blue water and fruity drinks. The difference is that music is the region's soul. Vibrant and ever changing, the Caribbean's beat is reason alone to make the trip.

①

**Author tip**

Want to know what's the hottest, latest music on almost any island? Hop on a public bus. On most islands these vans are owned and operated by their drivers, who lure crowds by playing the best mixes – and use the beat to set their speed.

### ❶ Steel Pan, Trinidad & Tobago

Electrifying, mesmerizing and embodying the creativity of Trinidad and Tobago, steel-pan music (p730) will infect every molecule of your being. Panorama, the pinnacle competition of steel bands, takes place during Carnival season and will keep your feet tapping long after you return home.

### ❷ Santiago de Cuba, Cuba

Santiago de Cuba (p178), Cuba's most Caribbean city, grinds to its own rhythm in its sweaty bars and open-air *trova* and rumba clubs. Start out at the Casa de la Trova and move on to the Patio Los Dos Abuelos and the Casa de las Tradiciones.

### ❸ Elvina's Bar & Restaurant, The Bahamas

Don't judge this pint-sized party shack by its sorry little sign. On Friday nights, rotating sets of roof-blowing jams turn Elvina's (p96), on Eleuthera, into the baddest banged-up toolshed east of Florida. Every surfer, yachtie and Eleutheran in a 50-mile radius is here or on the way.

### ❹ Aragorn's Studio, British Virgin Islands

When the sun sets and the moon waxes full, the fungi music begins at Aragorn's Studio (p402), on Tortola. Band members break out the washboards and ribbed gourds to lay down a beat for stilt walkers and fire jugglers.

### ❺ Santo Domingo, Dominican Republic

Test out your merengue moves with seriously talented dancers at one of the nightclubs along the Malecón in Santo Domingo (p293). The Dominican Republic's capital is a rollicking party that continues all night.

# Lifestyles of the Rich & Famous

Richard Branson inviting world leaders to his private island to discuss global warming over fine wine in his yoga pavilion is just one of the scenes you'll find in the islands from December to April, when the world's wealthy bring their yachts to these azure waters for a little sunshine and conspicuous consumption.

### ④ Anguilla

Ever since the first celebrity stepped ashore with their posse of thug bodyguards only to be greeted by indifference and disinterest, Anguilla (p419) has been the preferred retreat for those needing an escape from the spotlight. 'We even have the Brad and Jennifer breakup house,' said one local with a smirk and an eye roll.

### ① Harbour Island, The Bahamas

Air kisses, pashminas and strutting roosters? Ah yes, just another day of fabulousness on ever-so-chic Harbour Island (p93), where design maven India Hicks and her acolytes sell their island lifestyle at chichi boutiques – and wandering roosters clearly don't give a cluck.

### ⑤ Bitter End Yacht Club & Resort, British Virgin Islands

If ever there was a place where guys in blue blazers and white captain's hats sat around puffing cigars and clinking ice in their drinks after coming ashore from their tall-masted megayachts, it's the Bitter End Yacht Club & Resort on Virgin Gorda (p407).

### ② West Coast, Barbados

Rihanna, the queen of Barbadian music and a Grammy-winning international sensation, sings a merry tune at her beachside spread on the west coast (p688), which locals have renamed the 'Platinum Coast'. It's long been the refuge of rising-damp-afflicted posh Brits and is now discreetly welcoming some of the region's new rich.

### ⑥ Mustique, St Vincent & the Grenadines

How much could you possibly spend on a villa for the week? Shoot for the moon – and then double it. Mustique (p664) takes the prize for the most exclusive island around. Everything is exquisite – whether it's worth the $150,000 per week is up to you and your accountant.

### ③ English Harbour, Antigua & Barbuda

In 'the season,' Antigua's natural harbors are home to yachts that might better be called ships. English Harbour (p528) brims with swaying masts; you can see the perfectly protected waters and the hundreds of millions of dollars worth of watercraft from nearby Shirley Heights.

### ⑦ Pine Cay, Turks & Caicos

It just isn't fair that you have to share the island. Well, as long as the check clears, you can have your wish on Pine Cay (p123), the bastion of the wealthy, the famous and the infamous.

# Special Interests

It's not all sun, swimming, diving and dancing – there are myriad things to captivate you in the Caribbean's many islands. Whether it's the region's rich history, death-defying drinking spots or on-the-edge creations, there's something here to excite even the most offbeat tastes.

### ❶ History, Sint Eustatius

It's hard to believe that sleepy Sint Eustatius (p485) was once the busiest seaport in the world. Today the little island boasts over 600 unique archaeological sites and ruins, such as the synagogue in Oranjestad. It's one of the top spots in the region for colonial enthusiasts.

### ❷ Public Transportation, Haiti

Brightly colored taptap buses (p277) weave through the traffic of Port-au-Prince, embellished with extra bumpers and mirrors, and repainted until they look like a fairground ride. Decorations can be sacred or profane, with Biblical themes vying for attention with portraits of Ernest 'Che' Guevara and Tupac Shakur.

### ❸ Plane-Spotting, St-Martin/Sint Maarten

There you are, floating on your back in the gentle waves, when suddenly a 747 roars a few feet overhead, blasting hot exhaust in your face. This happens many times a day at the Sunset Beach Bar (p441), a wild place on the sliver of sand that divides the water from the end of the airport's runway.

### ❹ Rum, Jamaica

Of the many rums lurking in Jamaica's liquor cabinet, none is as potent as overproof (p221), a clear white rum that is 151 proof. It may come in a shot glass, but it's best enjoyed mixed with Ting, a local grapefruit drink.

# Contents

## On the Road 4

## Caribbean Islands 7

## Destination Caribbean Islands 24

## Getting Started 27

## Itineraries 33

## Snapshots 41

## Diving & Snorkeling 52

## The Bahamas 59

Highlights 60
Itineraries 60
Climate & When to Go 60
History 60
The Culture 61
Arts 61
Environment 61
Food & Drink 63
NEW PROVIDENCE 64
Nassau 66
Paradise Island 76
GRAND BAHAMA 77
Freeport & Lucaya 79
East of Freeport 86
West of Freeport 86
OUT ISLANDS 87
Abacos 87
Eleuthera 92
Exumas 96
Andros 100
DIRECTORY 102
TRANSPORTATION 106

## Turks & Caicos 111

Highlights 112
Itineraries 112
Climate & When to Go 112
History 113
The Culture 113
Arts 114

Environment 114
Food & Drink 114
TURKS ISLANDS 115
Grand Turk 115
Salt Cay 119
CAICOS ISLANDS 120
Providenciales 120
North Caicos 127
Middle Caicos 129
DIRECTORY 130
TRANSPORTATION 133

## Cuba 135

Highlights 136
Itineraries 136
Climate & When to Go 136
History 136
The Culture 139
Arts 140
Environment 140
Food & Drink 140
HAVANA 141
Information 141
Sights 144
Havana for Children 149
Tours 149
Sleeping 149
Eating 153
Drinking 155
Entertainment 155
Shopping 157
Getting There & Away 157
Getting Around 158
AROUND HAVANA 159
Parque Histórico Militar Morro-Cabaña 159
Playas del Este 159
PINAR DEL RÍO PROVINCE 160
Viñales 160
Península de Guanahacabibes 163
CENTRAL CUBA 164
Santa Clara 165
Remedios 168
Trinidad 169
EASTERN CUBA 173
Santiago de Cuba 173
Baracoa 180
Parque Nacional Alejandro de Humboldt 183
DIRECTORY 183
TRANSPORTATION 188

## Cayman Islands 192

| | |
|---|---|
| Highlights | 193 |
| Itineraries | 193 |
| Climate & When to Go | 193 |
| History | 193 |
| The Culture | 194 |
| Arts | 194 |
| Environment | 194 |
| Food & Drink | 195 |
| **GRAND CAYMAN** | **196** |
| George Town & Seven Mile Beach | 196 |
| West Bay | 204 |
| Bodden Town | 205 |
| East End | 205 |
| North Side | 205 |
| **CAYMAN BRAC** | **206** |
| History | 206 |
| Information | 206 |
| Sights & Activities | 206 |
| Sleeping | 207 |
| Eating & Drinking | 207 |
| Getting There & Around | 208 |
| **LITTLE CAYMAN** | **208** |
| Information | 209 |
| Sights & Activities | 209 |
| Sleeping & Eating | 210 |
| Getting There & Around | 210 |
| **DIRECTORY** | **210** |
| **TRANSPORTATION** | **213** |

## Jamaica 215

| | |
|---|---|
| Highlights | 216 |
| Itineraries | 216 |
| Climate & When to Go | 216 |
| History | 216 |
| The Culture | 218 |
| Arts | 219 |
| Environment | 220 |
| Food & Drink | 221 |
| **KINGSTON** | **221** |
| History | 222 |
| Orientation | 222 |
| Information | 222 |
| Dangers & Annoyances | 223 |
| Sights | 223 |
| Activities | 225 |
| Festivals & Events | 225 |
| Sleeping | 227 |
| Eating & Drinking | 228 |
| Entertainment | 229 |
| Shopping | 229 |
| Getting There & Away | 230 |

| | |
|---|---|
| Getting Around | 230 |
| **AROUND KINGSTON** | **230** |
| **THE BLUE MOUNTAINS** | **231** |
| **NORTHERN JAMAICA** | **232** |
| Port Antonio | 232 |
| Around Port Antonio | 233 |
| Ocho Rios | 235 |
| Around Ocho Rios | 238 |
| **MONTEGO BAY & AROUND** | **239** |
| Montego Bay | 239 |
| Around Montego Bay | 245 |
| **NEGRIL & THE WEST** | **246** |
| Negril | 246 |
| Around Negril | 250 |
| **SOUTHERN JAMAICA** | **250** |
| Treasure Beach | 250 |
| Black River | 251 |
| YS Falls | 252 |
| Appleton Rum Estate | 252 |
| **DIRECTORY** | **252** |
| **TRANSPORTATION** | **256** |

## Haiti 260

| | |
|---|---|
| Highlights | 261 |
| Itineraries | 261 |
| Climate & When to Go | 261 |
| History | 261 |
| The Culture | 264 |
| Arts | 265 |
| Environment | 265 |
| Food & Drink | 266 |
| **PORT-AU-PRINCE** | **266** |
| Information | 266 |
| Dangers & Annoyances | 266 |
| Sights | 267 |
| Sleeping | 268 |
| Eating | 268 |
| Entertainment | 268 |
| Shopping | 269 |
| Getting There & Around | 269 |
| **AROUND PORT-AU-PRINCE** | **270** |
| East of Port-au-Prince | 270 |
| North of Port-au-Prince | 270 |
| **SOUTHERN HAITI** | **270** |
| Jacmel | 270 |
| Les Cayes | 271 |
| Île-à-Vache | 272 |
| Port Salut | 272 |
| Parc National Macaya & Jérémie | 272 |
| **NORTHERN HAITI** | **272** |
| Cap-Haïtien | 272 |

| | |
|---|---|
| Beaches | 273 |
| The Citadelle & Sans Souci | 273 |
| **DIRECTORY** | **274** |
| **TRANSPORTATION** | **277** |

## Dominican Republic 278

| | |
|---|---|
| Highlights | 279 |
| Itineraries | 279 |
| Climate & When to Go | 279 |
| History | 279 |
| The Culture | 282 |
| Sports | 282 |
| Arts | 283 |
| Environment | 283 |
| Food & Drink | 284 |
| **SANTO DOMINGO** | **284** |
| Orientation | 284 |
| Information | 285 |
| Dangers & Annoyances | 285 |
| Sights & Activities | 285 |
| Santo Domingo for Children | 290 |
| Tours | 290 |
| Festivals & Events | 290 |
| Sleeping | 290 |
| Eating | 292 |
| Drinking | 293 |
| Entertainment | 293 |
| Shopping | 294 |
| Getting There & Away | 295 |
| Getting Around | 295 |
| **THE SOUTHEAST** | **296** |
| Bávaro & Punta Cana | 296 |
| **PENÍNSULA DE SAMANÁ** | **300** |
| Samaná | 300 |
| Las Galeras | 303 |
| Las Terrenas | 306 |
| Playa Bonita | 310 |
| **NORTH COAST** | **310** |
| Cabarete | 310 |
| **CENTRAL HIGHLANDS** | **313** |
| Jarabacoa | 314 |
| **DIRECTORY** | **318** |
| **TRANSPORTATION** | **321** |

## Puerto Rico 324

| | |
|---|---|
| Highlights | 325 |
| Itineraries | 325 |
| Climate & When to Go | 325 |
| History | 325 |
| The Culture | 327 |

Arts 327
Environment 327
Food & Drink 328
**SAN JUAN** **328**
Orientation 328
Information 329
Sights 329
Activities 333
San Juan for Children 333
Tours 333
Festivals & Events 333
Sleeping 334
Eating 337
Drinking 339
Entertainment 340
Shopping 340
Getting There & Away 341
Getting Around 341
**AROUND SAN JUAN** **342**
Bacardi Rum Factory 342
Arecibo Observatory 342
Parque de las
Cavernas del Río Camuy 342
**EASTERN PUERTO RICO** **342**
El Yunque 343
Luquillo 343
Vieques 343
Culebra 346
**SOUTHERN & WESTERN**
**PUERTO RICO** **347**
Ponce 348
Bosque Estatal de Guánica 350
Rincón 350
**DIRECTORY** **351**
**TRANSPORTATION** **354**

**US Virgin Islands** 357
Highlights 358
Itineraries 358
Climate & When to Go 358
History 358
The Culture 360
Arts 360
Environment 361
Food & Drink 362
**ST THOMAS** **362**
Charlotte Amalie 363
Red Hook & East End 368
**ST JOHN** **370**
Cruz Bay 371
North Shore 374
Coral Bay & Around 376
**ST CROIX** **377**
Christiansted 378

North Shore 381
Buck Island Reef
National Monument 381
Point Udall & Around 382
Frederiksted 382
Around Frederiksted 383
**DIRECTORY** **384**
**TRANSPORTATION** **387**

**British
Virgin Islands** 390
Highlights 391
Itineraries 391
Climate & When to Go 391
History 391
The Culture 393
Arts 393
Environment 394
Food & Drink 394
**TORTOLA** **395**
Road Town 395
Around Road Town 399
West End 399
Cane Garden Bay Area 400
East End 402
**VIRGIN GORDA** **403**
Spanish Town & the Valley 405
North Sound & Around 407
**JOST VAN DYKE** **407**
Great Harbour 408
White Bay 409
Little Harbour 409
**ANEGADA** **410**
West End 410
East End 411
**DIRECTORY** **412**
**TRANSPORTATION** **415**

**Anguilla** 419
Highlights 420
Itineraries 420
Climate & When to Go 420
History 420
The Culture 422
Arts 422
Environment 422
Food & Drink 422
**CENTRAL ANGUILLA** **422**
The Valley 422
Sandy Ground 424
Blowing Point 426
**WESTERN ANGUILLA** **426**
Meads Bay 426

West End 427
**EASTERN ANGUILLA** **428**
Shoal Bay East 428
Far East 429
**DIRECTORY** **430**
**TRANSPORTATION** **432**

**St-Martin/
Sint Maarten** 434
Highlights 435
Itineraries 435
Climate & When to Go 435
History 435
The Culture 436
Environment 437
Food & Drink 437
**SINT MAARTEN** **437**
Philipsburg 438
Simpson Bay 440
Maho & Mullet Bay 441
Cupecoy Beach 441
**ST-MARTIN** **441**
Marigot 442
Terres Basses 443
Sandy Ground &
Baie Nettlé 444
Friar's Bay 444
Pic Paradis 444
Grand Case 445
Anse Marcel 446
French Cul-de-Sac 446
Orient Beach
(La Baie Orientale) 447
Le Galion 447
Oyster Pond 448
**DIRECTORY** **448**
**TRANSPORTATION** **451**

**St-Barthélemy** 454
Highlights 455
Itineraries 455
Climate & When to Go 455
History 455
The Culture 457
Arts 457
Environment 457
Food & Drink 457
**GUSTAVIA** **458**
Information 458
Sights 458
Activities 458
Sleeping 458
Eating 459

Shopping 460
**AROUND GUSTAVIA** 460
**EASTERN
ST-BARTHÉLEMY** 460
St-Jean 460
Grand Cul-de-Sac 461
Lorient 462
Vitet 462
Anse de Gouverneur 463
Anse de Grande Saline 463
**WESTERN
ST-BARTHÉLEMY** 463
Corossol 463
Flamands 463
Anse de Colombier 464
**DIRECTORY** 464
**TRANSPORTATION** 467

# Saba 469

Highlights 470
Itineraries 470
Climate & When to Go 470
History 470
The Culture 472
Arts 472
Environment 472
Food & Drink 472
**SABA** 473
Flat Point 473
Hell's Gate 473
Windwardside 473
Mt Scenery 476
St John's 476
The Bottom 477
Well's Bay 477
Ladder Bay 477
Fort Bay 478
**DIRECTORY** 478
**TRANSPORTATION** 480

# Sint Eustatius 482

Highlights 483
Itineraries 483
Climate & When to Go 483
History 483
The Culture 485
Environment 485
Food & Drink 485
**SINT EUSTATIUS** 485
Information 486
Sights 486
Activities 488
Sleeping 490

Eating & Drinking 491
**DIRECTORY** 491
**TRANSPORTATION** 493

# St Kitts & Nevis 495

Highlights 496
Itineraries 496
Climate & When to Go 496
History 496
The Culture 498
Environment 498
Food & Drink 498
**ST KITTS** 499
Basseterre 499
Around Basseterre 502
Frigate Bay 502
Southeast Peninsula 504
Around Northern St Kitts 504
**NEVIS** 506
Charlestown 507
Pinney's Beach 509
Oualie Beach 509
South Nevis 510
**DIRECTORY** 512
**TRANSPORTATION** 515

# Antigua & Barbuda 517

Highlights 518
Itineraries 518
Climate & When to Go 518
History 518
The Culture 519
Sports 519
Arts 520
Environment 520
Food & Drink 520
**ANTIGUA** 521
St John's 523
Fort James 525
Runaway Bay 525
Dickenson Bay 525
North Shore 526
Five Islands 527
Jolly Harbour 527
Jolly Harbour to
Johnson's Point Beach 527
Fig Tree Drive 528
Falmouth Harbour 528
English Harbour 528
Half Moon & Nonsuch Bays 530
Long Bay 530
Betty's Hope 530
**BARBUDA** 531

Codrington 533
Codrington Lagoon 533
West & South Coasts 534
Caves 534
**DIRECTORY** 534
**TRANSPORTATION** 538

# Montserrat 540

Itineraries 541
Climate & When to Go 541
History 541
The Culture 541
Arts 541
Environment 542
Food & Drink 543
**MONTSERRAT** 543
Information 543
Sights & Activities 543
Sleeping & Eating 544
**DIRECTORY** 544
**TRANSPORTATION** 545

# Guadeloupe 546

Highlights 547
Itineraries 547
Climate & When to Go 547
History 547
The Culture 549
Arts 549
Environment 549
Food & Drink 549
**GRANDE-TERRE** 551
Pointe-à-Pitre 551
Gosier 555
Ste-Anne 556
St-François 557
Pointe des Châteaux 558
Le Moule 559
Northern Grande-Terre 560
**BASSE-TERRE** 561
Route de la Traversée 561
Northern Basse-Terre 561
South to
Capesterre-Belle-Eau 563
Chutes du Carbet 563
Trois-Rivières 564
La Soufrière 564
Basse-Terre 565
Plage de Malendure &
Pigeon Island 565
**TERRE-DE-HAUT** 566
Bourg des Saintes 567
Fort Napoléon 569

Baie du Marigot                     569
Baie de Pont Pierre                 569
East-Coast Beaches                  569
Southwest Beaches                   569
Le Chameau                          570
**TERRE-DE-BAS**                    **570**
**MARIE-GALANTE**                   **570**
Grand-Bourg                         571
St-Louis                            571
Capesterre                          572
**LA DÉSIRADE**                     **572**
Sleeping & Eating                   572
Getting There & Away                573
Getting Around                      573
**DIRECTORY**                       **573**
**TRANSPORTATION**                  **576**

## Dominica                         580

Highlights                          581
Itineraries                         581
Climate & When to Go                581
History                             581
The Culture                         583
Arts                                583
Environment                         583
Food & Drink                        584
**DOMINICA**                        **584**
Roseau                              584
Layou River Area                    589
Northern Forest Reserve             590
Portsmouth                          590
Portsmouth to Pagua Bay             592
Carib Territory                     592
Emerald Pool                        593
Trafalgar Falls                     594
Morne Trois Pitons
National Park                       595
Grand Bay                           596
South of Roseau                     596
**DIRECTORY**                       **597**
**TRANSPORTATION**                  **601**

## Martinique                       603

Highlights                          604
Itineraries                         604
Climate & When to Go                604
History                             604
The Culture                         606
Arts                                606
Environment                         606
Food & Drink                        607
**FORT-DE-FRANCE**                  **607**
Orientation                         607

Information                         607
Sights & Activities                 608
Tours                               610
Festivals & Events                  610
Sleeping                            610
Eating & Drinking                   611
Entertainment                       611
Shopping                            612
Getting Around                      612
**NORTHERN MARTINIQUE**             **612**
Fort-de-France to St-Pierre         612
St-Pierre                           613
St-Pierre to Anse Céron             614
Route de la Trace                   614
Basse-Pointe & Around               615
Grand-Riviére                       615
Basse-Pointe to Presqu'île
de Caravelle                        616
Presqu'île de Caravelle             616
Trinité                             617
**SOUTHERN MARTINIQUE**             **617**
Trois-Îlets                         618
Pointe du Bout                      618
Grande Anse                         619
Anse d'Arlet                        620
Diamant                             620
Ste-Luce                            620
Ste-Anne                            621
Les Salines                         622
**DIRECTORY**                       **622**
**TRANSPORTATION**                  **625**

## St Lucia                         628

Highlights                          629
Itineraries                         629
Climate & When to Go                629
History                             629
The Culture                         629
Arts                                631
Environment                         631
Food & Drink                        632
**CASTRIES**                        **632**
History                             632
Orientation                         632
Information                         632
Sights                              633
Activities                          634
Tours                               634
Festivals & Events                  634
Sleeping                            634
Eating                              634
Shopping                            634
Getting Around                      635
**NORTHERN ST LUCIA**               **635**

North of Castries                   635
Rodney Bay                          635
Gros Islet                          637
Pigeon Island National Park         638
**SOUTHERN ST LUCIA**               **638**
Marigot Bay                         638
Anse La Raye                        639
Soufrière                           639
Choiseul                            643
The South & East Coasts             643
**DIRECTORY**                       **644**
**TRANSPORTATION**                  **647**

## St Vincent & the
## Grenadines                       650

Highlights                          651
Itineraries                         651
Climate & When to Go                651
History                             651
The Culture                         652
Arts                                652
Environment                         653
Food & Drink                        653
**ST VINCENT**                      **654**
Kingstown                           654
Windward Highway                    659
Leeward Highway                     659
**BEQUIA**                          **660**
Port Elizabeth                      661
Lower Bay                           664
Friendship Bay                      664
**MUSTIQUE**                        **664**
Sleeping & Eating                   664
Getting There & Away                665
**CANOUAN**                         **665**
Activities                          665
Sleeping                            665
Eating                              666
Getting There & Away                666
**MAYREAU**                         **667**
Sleeping                            667
Eating                              667
Getting There & Away                667
**UNION ISLAND**                    **667**
Information                         668
Activities                          668
Sleeping & Eating                   668
Getting There & Away                668
Getting Around                      669
**OTHER ISLANDS**                   **669**
Tobago Cays                         669
Palm Island                         669
Petit St Vincent                    669
**DIRECTORY**                       **670**
**TRANSPORTATION**                  **673**

## Barbados 675

| | |
|---|---|
| Highlights | 676 |
| Itineraries | 676 |
| Climate & When to Go | 676 |
| History | 676 |
| The Culture | 677 |
| Sports | 678 |
| Arts | 678 |
| Environment | 678 |
| Food & Drink | 679 |
| **BRIDGETOWN** | **680** |
| Orientation | 680 |
| Information | 680 |
| Sights & Activities | 680 |
| Sleeping | 683 |
| Eating | 683 |
| Drinking | 684 |
| Entertainment | 684 |
| Shopping | 684 |
| Getting There & Away | 684 |
| Getting Around | 684 |
| **SOUTH COAST** | **684** |
| Hastings & Rockley | 685 |
| Worthing | 685 |
| St Lawrence Gap & Dover Beach | 686 |
| Oistins | 687 |
| Silver Sands | 687 |
| **SOUTHEAST COAST** | **688** |
| Crane Beach | 688 |
| **WEST COAST** | **688** |
| Paynes Bay | 688 |
| Holetown | 689 |
| North of Holetown | 689 |
| Speightstown | 690 |
| Shermans | 690 |
| **CENTRAL BARBADOS** | **690** |
| Speightstown to Bathsheba | 691 |
| Bridgetown to Belleplaine | 691 |
| Bridgetown to Bathsheba | 692 |
| **EASTERN BARBADOS** | **692** |
| Bathsheba | 692 |
| Bathsheba South to Christ Church Parish | 693 |
| **DIRECTORY** | **694** |
| **TRANSPORTATION** | **699** |

## Grenada 701

| | |
|---|---|
| Highlights | 702 |
| Itineraries | 702 |
| Climate & When to Go | 702 |
| History | 702 |
| The Culture | 704 |

| | |
|---|---|
| Arts | 704 |
| Environment | 704 |
| Food & Drink | 705 |
| **GRENADA ISLAND** | **706** |
| St George's | 707 |
| Grand Anse | 710 |
| Morne Rouge Bay | 712 |
| Point Salines & True Blue Bay | 712 |
| Lance aux Épines | 712 |
| La Sagesse Nature Centre | 713 |
| Grand Etang Road | 713 |
| Grenville | 715 |
| North of Grenville | 715 |
| Bathways Beach & Around | 715 |
| Levera Beach | 715 |
| Sauteurs | 716 |
| Victoria | 716 |
| Gouyave | 716 |
| Concord Falls | 716 |
| **CARRIACOU** | **716** |
| Hillsborough | 717 |
| North of Hillsborough | 718 |
| South of Hillsborough | 718 |
| Tyrrel Bay & the Nearshore Islands | 719 |
| **PETIT MARTINIQUE** | **719** |
| Sleeping & Eating | 719 |
| Getting There & Away | 720 |
| **DIRECTORY** | **720** |
| **TRANSPORTATION** | **723** |

## Trinidad & Tobago 726

| | |
|---|---|
| Highlights | 727 |
| Itineraries | 727 |
| Climate & When to Go | 727 |
| History | 727 |
| The Culture | 728 |
| Sports | 729 |
| Arts | 730 |
| Environment | 731 |
| Food & Drink | 731 |
| **TRINIDAD** | **732** |
| Port of Spain | 735 |
| Around Port of Spain | 744 |
| North Coast | 747 |
| Brasso Seco | 749 |
| West Coast | 750 |
| East Coast | 751 |
| Northeast Coast | 752 |
| **TOBAGO** | **754** |
| Crown Point | 756 |
| Buccoo | 760 |
| Leeward Road | 762 |
| Arnos Vale Road | 763 |

| | |
|---|---|
| Plymouth | 763 |
| Castara & Around | 763 |
| Parlatuvier | 764 |
| Scarborough | 765 |
| Windward Road | 766 |
| Speyside | 767 |
| Charlotteville | 768 |
| **DIRECTORY** | **769** |
| **TRANSPORTATION** | **774** |

## Aruba, Bonaire & Curaçao 777

| | |
|---|---|
| Highlights | 778 |
| Itineraries | 778 |
| Climate & When to Go | 778 |
| History | 778 |
| The Culture | 778 |
| Arts | 779 |
| Environment | 779 |
| Food & Drink | 780 |
| **ARUBA** | **780** |
| Oranjestad & the North | 781 |
| Northeast Coast | 789 |
| Arikok National Wildlife Park | 790 |
| San Nicolas | 791 |
| **BONAIRE** | **791** |
| Kralendijk | 792 |
| North of Kralendijk | 797 |
| East of Kralendijk | 798 |
| South of Kralendijk | 798 |
| **CURAÇAO** | **799** |
| Willemstad | 802 |
| South of Willemstad | 808 |
| North of Willemstad | 808 |
| **DIRECTORY** | **810** |
| **TRANSPORTATION** | **813** |

## Caribbean Islands Directory 815

| | |
|---|---|
| Accommodations | 815 |
| Activities | 817 |
| Books | 819 |
| Business Hours | 819 |
| Children | 819 |
| Climate Charts | 821 |
| Customs | 821 |
| Dangers & Annoyances | 821 |
| Embassies & Consulates | 822 |
| Festivals & Events | 822 |
| Gay & Lesbian Travelers | 822 |
| Holidays | 823 |
| Insurance | 823 |

Internet Access 823
Legal Matters 824
Maps 824
Money 824
Photography & Video 825
Post 826
Solo Travelers 826
Telephone 826
Time 827
Tourist Information 827
Travelers with Disabilities 827
Visas 828
Women Travelers 828
Work 828

## Caribbean Islands Transportation 829
GETTING THERE & AWAY 829
Entry Requirements 829
Air 829
Sea 830
GETTING AROUND 833

Air 833
Bicycle 834
Boat 834
Bus 835
Car & Motorcycle 836
Hitchhiking 836

## Health 837
BEFORE YOU GO 837
Insurance 837
Recommended Vaccinations 837
Medical Checklist 837
Internet Resources 837
Further Reading 838
IN TRANSIT 838
Deep Vein Thrombosis (DVT) 838
Jet Lag & Motion Sickness 838
IN THE CARIBBEAN ISLANDS 839
Availability & Cost of Health Care 839

Infectious Diseases 839
Traveler's Diarrhea 842
Environmental Hazards 842
Traveling with Children 843

## Language 844

## Glossary 853

## The Authors 855

## Behind the Scenes 859

## Index 863

## World Time Zones 879

## Map Legend 880

# Regional Map Contents

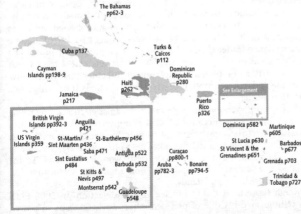

The Bahamas pp62-3
Cuba p137
Turks & Caicos p112
Cayman Islands pp198-9
Dominican Republic p280
Haiti p262
Jamaica p217
Puerto Rico p326
See Enlargement
British Virgin Islands pp392-3
Anguilla p421
Dominica p582
Martinique p605
US Virgin Islands p359
St-Martin/ Sint Maarten p436
St-Barthélemy p456
St Lucia p630
St Vincent & the Grenadines p651
Barbados p677
Saba p471
Antigua p522
Curaçao pp800-1
Grenada p703
Sint Eustatius p484
Barbuda p532
Aruba pp782-3
Bonaire pp794-5
St Kitts & Nevis p497
Trinidad & Tobago p727
Montserrat p542
Guadeloupe p548

# Destination Caribbean Islands

Pulsed by music, rocked by change, lapped by blue water, blown by hurricanes, the Caribbean is not a place anyone would call static. It's a lively and intoxicating profusion of people and places spread over 7000 islands (less than 10% are inhabited). But, for all they share, there's also much that makes them different. Forming a huge swath around the Caribbean Sea, the namesake islands contradict in ways big and small. Can there be a greater contrast than between socialist Cuba and its neighbor, the bank-packed Caymans? Or between booming British-oriented St Kitts and its sleepy, Dutch-affiliated neighbor St Eustatius, just across a narrow channel?

The diverse cultures of the region reflect the myriad influences that have washed over the islands through the centuries. Perhaps the greatest example of this ebb and flow can be found on St-Martin/Sint Maarten, which speaks French and is aligned with France on one half, and speaks Dutch and is aligned with the Netherlands (and calls itself Sint Maarten) on the other half. In one 30-minute drive across its minute 37 sq miles (96 sq km) you can change languages six times.

'The diverse cultures reflect the myriad influences that have washed over the islands'

Or there's Haiti and the Dominican Republic. Sharing one island, Hispaniola, the differences are stark – Haiti was once the stronger of the two but now it is the poorest country in the hemisphere. Across the border the Dominican Republic speaks Spanish and has a Hispanic culture that is much closer to pre-revolution Cuba than it is to French-speaking Haiti.

This tangle of colonial ties continues to unravel. The Netherlands Antilles, the ultimate hodgepodge of islands tossed into a basket by their colonial masters, finally came undone in 2008 as each island staked out an identity apart from the others. Although even here colonial ties proved compelling as Bonaire, Saba and St Eustatius decided to in effect become municipalities of the Netherlands (albeit warm ones) while Curaçao and Sint Maarten decided to follow the lead of Aruba, which had left the Netherlands Antilles for near independence in 1986.

The greatest political changes in the Caribbean have had nothing to do with old colonial powers, however. Ruling regimes are being sent packing across the islands, usually at the ballot box and usually peacefully. The old postcolonial regime of the Bird dynasty was shooed out of its Antiguan nest in 2004. But in 2006 St Lucia brought back its longtime pre-independence leader (before 1979!) John Compton (now in his 80s) for another go as prime minister. In 2007, Jamaicans ended the 18-year rule of one party and replaced it with another. Whether this will do anything for the endemic corruption or high murder rate is the number-one conversation starter.

Celebrity gossip even played a role in the Bahamas elections. The ruling party was tainted with allegations that it had given Anna Nicole Smith what was in effect rock-star treatment by granting her almost immediate residency. That she died shortly thereafter didn't help what was very messy situation. The result was the opposition party won the elections. To the south later that summer, the opposition won a landslide victory in elections on the British Virgin Islands.

Although typically it didn't involve an open election, in 2008 Fidel Castro relinquished his title of president after nearly 50 years in power,

## THE AUTHORS HAD FUN TOO (PART ONE)

Their experiences researching this book are informative, cautionary and entertaining.

### What Was Your Best Experience?

- Hanging out with Violet, the owner of the Miss Emily's Blue Bee Bar, and hearing stories about past customers while sipping a goombay smash. (Amy C Balfour, the Bahamas)
- I had two: doing a night dive with hyper nurse sharks off of Saba and hiking the Quill on Statia with five archaeologists taking the day off from work. (Brandon Presser, Saba and Sint Eustatius)
- Dancing at 3am in a Port-au-Prince club to RAM – the best Vodou rock & roots band out there. (Paul Clammer, Haiti)
- Several: wandering around Old San Juan, cycling on Vieques with my family, watching Rincon sunsets, visiting a coffee farm in the central mountains. (Brendan Sainsbury, Puerto Rico)
- My best experience was the festival J'ouvert and playing mas the next day. That's when the music truly made so much sense to me. (Ellee Thalheimer, Trinidad and Tobago)
- Seeing a 3m-long manatee swim past me while diving off the Isla de la Juventud in Cuba. (Tom Masters, Cuba)
- Being on Barbados for the election. It was the most civilized voting I have ever seen, yet it was a huge event: the party that had been in power for 15 years was voted out of office. Everyone was talking about it and yet there was none of the demonization of the opposition or the violence that happens elsewhere. (Ryan Ver Berkmoes, Antigua and Barbados)
- Sitting two rows back from the dugout on the first-base line at a baseball game in Santo Domingo. (Michael Grosberg, Dominican Republic).
- Honestly? Feeling like I really loved my girlfriend and proposing to her. (Josh Krist, Romantic)

### What Was Your Worst Experience?

- The overnight ferry to George Town, Exuma, from Nassau. We caught the fringes of Hurricane Stella. The crew decided to show the movie *The Holiday* with Cameron Diaz and Kate Winslet on a big TV, with the volume loud. Unfortunately, the disc would get periodically stuck and repeat portions. In the middle of the night the boat was heaving up and down, it was freezing, and the first six seconds of the movie's introductory music would play and then repeat every six seconds. This went on for hours. (Amy C Balfour, Bahamas)
- My hotel reservation was cancelled at a place in Guadeloupe and all the other places were full. Luckily, the guy at Ti Village Creole found a room for us at his place – he wanted to help travelers in trouble. (Josh Krist, Guadeloupe)
- Not organizing internal flights so I had to do the 12-hour bus trip from hell (Port-au-Prince to Jérémie) in both directions. (Paul Clammer, Haiti)
- Seeing how some quiet beaches I enjoyed on my last trip to Aruba are now backed by huge condo developments. The islands are growing incredibly fast. The desalinization plant makes me think of one of those old Looney Toons cartoons where an overtaxed machine would have smoke coming out the seams while rivets popped off. (Ryan Ver Berkmoes, Aruba, Bonaire and Curaçao)
- Getting totally chowed by mosquitoes upon arrival at a low-budget hotel in St Thomas. (Karla Zimmerman, US Virgin Islands)

and many wondered what was next for the sleeping giant of the Caribbean. Meanwhile over on Barbados, the conservative ruling party that had been in power for 15 years was ushered out in a landslide victory by the center-left opposition who ran under the theme of 'change.'

Change. It's probably one of the most clichéd political themes now but it lies at the heart of all the recent upsets in Caribbean elections. Voters no longer choose the party that makes the biggest promises. Too many murders and years of huge projects that only run up debt and produce little benefit have voters taking the longer view. (The African cliché of the huge hospital building without enough money for bedpans is also often true here.) 'Maybe if the government gives them less while spending more on basics like crime prevention, they'll have more in the future' is a popular line of thought.

Meanwhile the long-term issues for the islands are many, and first among them is tourism. Each year more and more people are arriving on the islands looking for their fun week in the sun. To places that have little more to offer than gorgeous waters, beautiful beaches and outgoing literate people this would seem to be an ideal situation. And in many ways it is. A poll in 2007 across several islands showed that more than 80% of people liked having tourists on their island. What would be the results of a similar poll in New York, London or Paris?

'A poll showed that more than 80% of people liked having tourists on their island'

But now the islands are beginning to realize that there may be limits to a good thing. Development is surging across the Caribbean, and new resorts and condos are appearing like mushrooms after the rain on formerly undeveloped coasts from Aruba to St Kitts to the Turks and Caicos. (After hotels had vacancies during Christmas 2007 many worried about who exactly would take all the new condos off developers' hands.)

But for islands that have never flourished on their own and where tourism represents the only hope after the collapse of commodity economies based on sugar, the question is: what else can they do? For even as discussions are beginning about limits on growth, it is continuing unabated. The region is not taking the lead environmentally although there is awareness. The report on the state of islands worldwide by *National Geographic Traveler* in 2007 got attention across the Caribbean, especially on the low-scoring Jamaica, and St Thomas in the US Virgin Islands. Even the top scorers took note: Bonaire publicized its tie for number 17 even as locals fretted over the line: 'poised for over-development.' (The top Caribbean scorers were Dominica and the Grenadines.)

Hurricanes are one thing that all the islands wish would go elsewhere. Two of the most powerful Category 5 storms roared across the region in 2007 and the trend is upward. Even comparatively minor tropical storms cause enormous damage as was seen in the Dominican Republic in 2007.

It's important to remember the good news. The region cheerfully acknowledged its British roots by successfully staging the Cricket World Cup in 2007 and things are looking up even for Haiti, where the UN has helped bring a peace that is allowing the Haitians to contemplate their future rather than fear it.

Questions and contradictions aside, the Caribbean is sure to continue as a place of strongly defined cultures unique to the planet. One need only attend Carnival on one of the islands to understand that blandness is *not* in their future.

# Getting Started

The Caribbean is not tough travel, it's delightful travel. Sure, you might miss a flight but it's a beautiful place to be stranded and the local vibe is the antithesis of the Type-A fretting over details. Relax, mon. The fun is deciding when and where to go. This chapter will help you decide on your type of trip and when you'll go.

Delving deeper, Itineraries (p33) will give you some ideas about destinations as will Snapshots (p41), which covers the cultural fabric of the Caribbean. For beginning to sort out details about activities, accommodation or a myriad of other questions, the Caribbean Islands Directory (p815) will guide you to the info you want in the individual island chapters. Caribbean Islands Transportation (p829) will do the same, helping you get to your chosen islands and showing you how to get around the region.

## WHEN TO GO

The most popular time for travel to the Caribbean has nothing to do with the weather there. It's all about the weather elsewhere. From mid-December to mid-April 'snowbirds' flee winter in North America and Europe for the balmy climes of the islands.

See p821 for climate charts.

During this high season, tourism is at its peak and indeed around Christmas, Easter and school holidays some islands simply sell out. Prices spike and places are crowded but its also the time when virtually everything is open.

You can enjoy a dramatically discounted 'summer' by visiting the islands during the lengthy low season, mid-April to mid-December. Prices at hotels fall by 40% or more, package deals are common and popular port towns don't look like a scene from a cattle call. The downside is that some resorts and attractions may simply close and your transport options will be reduced. In addition, the trade winds aren't as prevalent in summer, so the chance of encountering oppressively muggy weather is higher. Summer is also the hurricane season, particularly bad in August and September, when some hotels, restaurants and shops simply close for the month. If you're more interested in the culture of the islands as opposed to sleet-avoidance, this can be an ideal time to visit.

---

### DON'T LEAVE HOME WITHOUT...

The Caribbean islands are casual, so only bring light, comfy clothes: a bathing suit, T-shirt and shorts will be your wardrobe. Add long pants or a dress or skirt for swanky nights out. If you're coming from winter in Minneapolis or Montreal, don't be fooled into thinking you need a sweater. You don't! One long-sleeve shirt to prevent sunburn or mosquito bites will be plenty.

A few essentials you don't want to forget:

- basic medical kit
- strong mosquito repellent and sunscreen
- sun hat
- a small quick-dry towel, for those times when the whim to swim hits
- flashlight with batteries (nighttime reading with partner, blackouts)
- plastic resealable bags – essential for keeping things dry (eg camera, airline tickets, passports)
- Lonely Planet's *French Phrasebook* (for Guadeloupe, Martinique, St-Barthélemy, St-Martin and Haiti) and *Latin American Spanish Phrasebook* (for Cuba, Puerto Rico and Dominican Republic)

The authors of this book agree that the sweet spot for visiting the islands is November and early December. Rates are still low but the weather is good, except possibly where you live, thus giving you one more justification for the trip.

Another impetus for the timing of your trip might be one of the out-sized festivals that are the cultural events of the year on every island. For a few of our favorites, see p823.

## COSTS & MONEY

In general, traveling in the Caribbean islands is expensive, but costs can vary greatly depending on which islands you visit when, the type of accommodations you choose and how you travel.

'Hurricane' is derived from an old Taíno word for 'huge winds sent by the Goddess.' Damn woman.

Accommodations will generally be the heftiest part of your budget. St Vincent and the Grenadines, the Dominican Republic and Cuba are among the places where you can beat the averages. On islands such as Barbados and Trinidad, a conventional hotel room or apartment can be quite reasonable; on pricier islands such as Antigua, Aruba or Grand Cayman, a comparable room could easily cost twice as much. Places such as St-Barthélemy and the Virgin Islands are always much more expensive than average.

Of course the type of accommodations will also dictate cost – daily rates can vary from US$50 at a guesthouse to US$1000 at an exclusive resort. In

---

### THE AUTHORS HAD FUN TOO (PART TWO)

Their experiences researching this book are informative, cautionary and entertaining.

#### Best Advice for a Friend?

- Book your accommodations well in advance! (Brandon Presser, Anguilla, Saba, St-Barthélemy, Sint Eustatius and St-Martin/Sint Maarten)
- In Puerto Rico you've got to get off the main tourist track and scratch underneath the surface in order to uncover the intricacies (and beauty) of the local culture. What you see isn't always what you get. (Brendan Sainsbury, Puerto Rico)
- Don't go over Christmas, take your time to cruise through the Grenadines and take half as much stuff as you think you need. (Scott Kennedy, St Vincent and the Grenadines)

#### What About the Caribbean Challenged Your Preconceptions?

- Sint Eustatius and Saba: the strangest little slices of paradise I've ever seen. So quiet, down-to-earth, like no other islands in the region. (Brandon Presser, Saba and Sint Eustatius)
- French islands are not as expensive as you think. As my fiancée explained, the French take lots of vacations and they watch every centime – hoteliers and restaurants have to give good value for money if they want to stay alive. (Josh Krist, Dominica, Guadeloupe and Martinique)

#### What Was the Biggest Surprise or Lesson You Learned?

- The continuing interconnected relationship between the Dominican Republic and Haiti: how events of over 150 years ago are still very alive in the minds of many people, how the histories of the two countries are so intertwined, and the fact that the DR used to be the poorer, weaker relation. (Michael Grosberg, Dominican Republic)
- How friendly Haiti was, how safe it was and how easy it was to get around (as long as one remembers this is not a First World destination). (Paul Clammer, Haiti)
- How undeveloped parts were. St Lucia was full-on developing world, reminding me of Africa. It was much less polished almost everywhere and fewer tourists then I expected. (Scott Kennedy, St Lucia)

this book we've listed accommodations as follows: budget under US$100; midrange US$100 to US$200; and top end from US$200 up. These prices are for high season.

Food can be relatively expensive in the Caribbean. A great way to save money is to sample some of the local street food, which is usually both cheap and delicious. Seafood dinners in open-air seaside restaurants (always a treat) can be pricey, but savoring the same fare at a 'local' restaurant can cost half as much. Another good way to save costs is to rent a room or villa with a kitchen, shop at the colorful markets and cook for yourself. In this book, we've listed meal prices as follows: budget is under US$10; midrange is US$10 to US$25; and top end is anything more than that.

Transportation costs vary greatly. Car rentals generally cost between US$40 and US$80 a day. On the more developed islands, public buses provide a cheap way of getting around (plus a good dose of cultural immersion). Some island groups have cheap ferries, and if you make your plans in advance you can get decent-priced air tickets. See the Transportation chapter (p833) for details.

Note that irritating little costs can add up quickly, including local hotel taxes, departure taxes and hotel service charges (up to 25%).

## TRAVELING RESPONSIBLY

Since our inception in 1973, Lonely Planet has encouraged our readers to tread lightly, travel responsibly and enjoy the magic independent travel affords. International travel is growing at a jaw-dropping rate, and we still firmly believe in the benefits it can bring – but, as always, we encourage you to consider the impact your visit will have on both the global environment and the local economies, cultures and ecosystems.

Tourism pays the bills in most of the Caribbean, and the impact on the environment and the culture is huge. Most islands are still putting economic development ahead of the environment because poverty is so widespread. But you can do your part and make a difference. Here are a few pointers for minimizing your impact.

### Consume Less

- Do not waste water. Fresh water is an extremely precious commodity on all of the islands, where desalination plants work overtime converting saltwater to fresh.
- Many islanders depend only on rainwater collected in cisterns, so keep in mind that winter – peak tourism time – is the driest time of year.
- If the water is safe to drink, use it to fill containers, skipping bottled water and its transport and refuse costs.
- Travel globally; shop locally. Not only will buying local products infuse the local economy, it will also help to save you money. Local beer is always fresher than imported.
- Rarely is it so hot in the Caribbean that you need air-con at night; turn it off and let the breezes in.
- Never buy any souvenirs made of coral, seashell or turtle shell. Buying goods made with any of these only encourages environmental destruction and hunting.
- Ride the bus instead of renting a car. You immerse yourself in local culture while you save gas.
- If you rent a car, decide if you need it for your entire stay. You might just need it for a day or two of exploration.

Antigua is just daring someone to check its claim that it has 365 beaches – or one for every day of the year.

Countries in the Caribbean with Unesco World Heritage sites include Cuba (8), Dominica (1), Dominican Republic (1), Haiti (1), St Kitts and Nevis (1) and St Lucia (1).

## TRIP STYLE

There are as many ways to enjoy the Caribbean as there are islands. Here are some of the styles you might want to consider for your trip.

- Classic Island Holiday – You go to one place and you hang out there. Enjoy plenty of beach time and explore the towns and wilderness areas at your leisure.
- Islands by the Group – You go to one group of islands linked by ferries and you sample a few neighboring islands. There's no big travel drama and in the cases of near siblings like St Kitts and Nevis, the differences are greater than a few miles of water. See p834 for some of the island groups you could consider.
- Islands by the Dozen – Plan ahead, get cheap tickets, pack extra-light and experience a broad range of islands. See p34 for ideas.
- Cruise Control – Yes, the stereotypes of bloated tourists yakking about their raid on the buffet are often true. But there are also boats and ways to travel that reward the independent traveler. See p830 for ideas and details.
- Dirty Weekend – Find some gorgeous little beachside place and fly to that island direct. Skip a rental car and enjoy your weekend luxuriating, swimming, sunning, whatever!

## Show Respect

- Never litter – sure, you'll see many locals do it, but you definitely shouldn't. Almost everything discarded on land makes its way to the sea, where it can wreak havoc on marine life. Carry your trash off beaches, trails and campsites, and pick up a few extras left by others.
- Many people, especially vendors in the marketplaces, do not like to be photographed; ask first, and respect the wishes of those who refuse.

## Slow Down

- When driving on the islands, keep an eye out for pedestrians and stray dogs, chickens and goats, all of which meander aimlessly on the island roads.
- Take time for pleasantries. Always start with 'Good day,' 'buenos días' or 'bonjour' before launching into a conversation or abruptly asking questions; you'll find that a smile and a courteous attitude go a long way.

## Be Ecosmart

Although the image of the pirate ship flying the Jolly Roger skull and crossbones flag is iconic, in reality most flew the flags of their intended victims to better effect surprise. They were pirates after all.

- Look for hotels and resorts that carry an audited green certification. A good place to start your search is at **Eco-Index Sustainable Tourism** (www.eco-indextourism.org), which features businesses that have been recognized as environmentally and socially responsible.
- Ask your hotel about its green practices. Even if they have none, it'll tell them it matters to customers.
- Don't patronize swim-with-dolphins attractions. The practice has been condemned by environmental experts, and many of the mammals are caught in the wild and made captive for the enjoyment of tourists.
- When diving, snorkeling, boating or just playing in the water, remember that coral is a living organism that gets damaged with every touch, kick or step.

# READING UP

Reading books while lounging on some lovely beach is for many the perfect trip (in addition to a sublime rum punch, of course). One way to extend

## TOP BEACHES

These are classic places for Caribbean fun in the sun. Some offer big-time glitz with stylish bars and a full range of services. Others are hidden gems where you might find a beach bar in a shack and someone to rent you some snorkeling gear and a lounger. Or you might find nothing at all except beautiful sand lapped by azure waters.

- Dover Beach, Barbados (p686)
- Frigate Bay Beach, St Kitts (p502)
- Eleuthera, the Bahamas (p92)
- Shoal Bay East, Anguilla (p428)
- Les Salines, Martinique (p622)
- Long Bay, Jamaica (p247)
- Marigot Bay, St Lucia (p638)
- Morne Rouge Bay, Grenada (p712)
- Grace Bay Beach, Caicos (p121)
- Seven Mile Beach, Grand Cayman (p196)

## TOP WAYS TO GET SWEATY

There's a lot to see and do in the wilds of the islands. Whether it's ascending a volcano, hiking a wilderness area or seeing some of the legendary treasures beneath the surface, you'll start thinking about changing that ticket home.

- Hiking the volcano on Nevis (p513)
- Diving Bonaire's reefs (p799)
- Experiencing Barbuda's Codrington Lagoon (p533)
- Climbing the Quill on Sint Eustatius (p486)
- Swimming with sharks on Saba (p478)
- Diving Tobago's underwater canyons (p758)
- Hiking La Soufrière in the Parc National de la Guadeloupe (p564)
- Canyoning on Dominica (p594)
- Exploring the British Virgin Islands' RMS *Rhone* (p398)
- Hitting the trails at Virgin Islands National Park (p372)
- Hiking Cuba's Viñales (p160)

## TOP PLACES TO MAKE LIKE A PIRATE

Arrrgh! The Caribbean has a bounty of booty for pirate fans. Start with these ayyyye-deas.

- Old San Juan's two Unesco forts (p331)
- St Vincent, where *Pirates of the Caribbean* was filmed (p660)
- Pirates of Nassau museum, Bahamas (p69)
- Île-à-Vache, where Captain Morgan used to hang out on Haiti (p272)
- Jamaica's Port Royal (p230)
- Pirates Week on the Caymans (p212)

the joy is to start your Caribbean reading before you go. The following books will inform, entertain and inspire you before and during your trip. Books more relevant to the individual islands are listed under Books in the Directory of each chapter.

■ *The Pirate's Daughter* by Margaret Cezair-Thompson. In 1946 actor and rogue Errol Flynn was shipwrecked by a hurricane off Jamaica. This novel spins a yarn of mixed-race Flynn-spawn and their search for a place in white society.

■ *Dead Man in Paradise: Unraveling a Murder From a Time of Revolution* by JB MacKinnon. The author's uncle was murdered in the Dominican Republic in the 1960s. Plunging deep into the countryside, MacKinnon unravels stories of corruption and dictatorship.

■ *The Slave Ship: A Human History* by Marcus Rediker. Over three centuries, 12 million Africans were brought to the US and Caribbean as slaves. Few accounts survive, but using existing records Rediker constructs a complete and horrifying picture.

■ *The Republic Of Pirates* by Colin Woodard. By the 16th century no ship in the Caribbean was safe from pirates. Woodes Rogers was given the job of wiping them out. He did and Blackbeard lost his head.

■ *Banana: The Fate of the Fruit That Changed the World* by Dan Koeppel. Dictators, American marines and slaves helped make the banana the world's favorite fruit. Its impact on the Caribbean has been enormous and now it faces genetic extinction.

■ *A Caribbean Mystery* by Agatha Christie. The beach and Agatha Christie, can millions of vacationers be wrong? Here Miss Marple is shipped off to the Caribbean for her arthritis and corpses appear…

■ *Breath, Eyes, Memory* by Edwidge Danticat. Oprah loved this tale about a girl living a simple life in Haiti, who then goes to live with her mother in New York City. The descriptions of West Indies life are lyrical.

■ *Captive of My Desires* by Johanna Lindsey. Gabrielle is descended from pirates but loves strapping American sea captain Drew, who hates pirates. What's a girl to do? This bodice-ripping, best-selling beach read is a Caribbean fantasy ride.

> More than 50% of the population of St Vincent is involved in the cultivation of bananas.

## INTERNET RESOURCES

The Caribbean has scores of websites that will help travelers but most are specific to the scores of islands. Look in the Internet Resources section of each chapter's Directory for many good ones.

For regionwide info, a good place to start is lonelyplanet.com, where you'll find succinct summaries of the islands, plus the Thorn Tree online forum, which has a special branch devoted to Caribbean travel, another devoted to Cuba and a special worldwide Diving & Snorkeling branch.

The following should also help you get started:

**Caribbean Hurricane Network** (www.stormcarib.com) Hurricanes are blowing through at record levels and this fascinating site keeps track of all of them in real time.

**Caribbean Travel** (www.caribbeantravel.com) The official website of region-wide tourism authorities has a good section on tourism news across the region. A new parade in honor of a national hero? It's here.

**Caribbean Travel & Life** (www.caribbeantravelmag.com) The online version of this monthly magazine posts feature stories and planning tips for resort-style holidays.

**Caribseek** (www.caribseek.com) A good search directory with links to sites throughout the Caribbean.

**CBC** (www.cbc.bb) The Caribbean Broadcasting Corporation is the BBC of Barbados and its website has an excellent Caribbean news section.

**Cruise Critic** (www.cruisecritic.com) Offers profiles and frank reviews of cruise ships, cruise industry news and analysis, and it has the most active and candid discussion boards about all things connected to Caribbean travel.

**Pirate Jokes** (www.piratejokes.net) You'll be hooked by this site with thousands of jokes, most more profane than this family friendly one: Q: Why couldn't the pirates play cards? A: The captain was standing on the deck.

# Itineraries
## CLASSIC ROUTES

### A FERRY FANTASY    One Week / St-Martin/Sint Maarten to St-Barthélemy

Once off the plane in **St-Martin/Sint-Maarten** (p434), you can island-hop your way around some of the Caribbean's cutest islands by ferry and never see another plane until it's time to go home. St-Martin/Sint Maarten will be your hub.

Head to the French side of the island and hang out in **Grand Case** (p445). For beach time try the local favorite **Friar's Bay** (p444). Catch a ferry to **Saba** (p469), which has a volcano that acts as a beacon during the 90-minute trip. Explore the small town of **Windwardside** (p473), then head out into the bush for a rugged hike up the literally named **Mt Scenery** (p476). Rent some diving gear and explore submerged pinnacles that teem with nurse sharks. Head back to St-Martin/Sint Maarten, then make the 25-minute run to **Anguilla** (p419). Once there, choose between two beaches: popular **Shoal Bay East** (p428) or the quieter, windswept **Junk's Hole** (p429). The 45-minute ferry from St-Martin/Sint Maarten to **St-Barthélemy** (p454) is famous for being a wild ride. Have lunch at the gorgeous French village of **Gustavia** (p458), and then sun yourself on white-sand **Anse de Columbier** (p464).

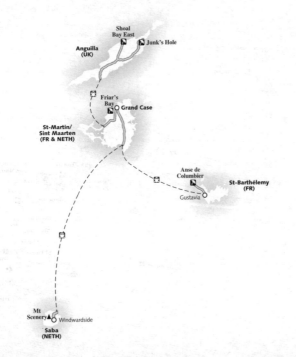

This itinerary takes advantage of the best network of ferries in the Caribbean. Cruise ships would seem to be the perfect way to get from one island to another but the companies absolutely refuse to consider one-way or partial passage between ports.

## ULTIMATE ISLAND-HOPPING  Three Weeks / Aruba to the Bahamas

You need your own yacht, your own plane or a handful of tickets to get around the Caribbean. Given that the full cost of the last one is still less than the monthly payment on the first two, it's probably the best option. Start in the resorts of **Aruba** (p780), then make the hop to **Curaçao** (p799) for old Willemstad. Now it's on to Port-of-Spain, **Trinidad** (p732), followed by a trip to the natural beauty of **Tobago** (p754). Next up is **Barbados** (p675), with its mix of luxury and historic beauty, then cut west and have a banana at its source on **St Vincent** (p654).

Island-hop your way north via the secluded coves of **St Lucia** (p628), *très Française* **Martinique** (p603), and the waterfalls and wilds of **Dominica** (p580). Now make the jump to **Antigua** (p521), from where you can take a 20-minute flight to isolated, beautiful **Barbuda** (p531 before making the 20-minute trip to **Montserrat** (p540) and its active volcano. Now it's on to the perfect cone of **Nevis** (p506), followed by a chance to get spray in your face on the quick ferry to **St Kitts** (p499). From here it's 30 minutes to **St-Martin/Sint Maarten** (p434), with its awesome runway beach and bar.

Turn west for the authentic charms of the US Virgin Islands' **St Croix** (p377), followed by the duty-free horror of **St Thomas** (p362). Pop over to **Tortola** (p395) for the British version of the Virgin Islands. Now go to the airline hub of **Puerto Rico** (p324) and walk round for a bit in the pre-air-travel streets of Old San Juan. Trade Spanish charm for reggae vibes on a flight to **Jamaica** (p215). After time on the beaches, go north to **Nassau** (p66) in the Bahamas, from where you can take a trip to the **Out Islands** (p87).

This itinerary includes 19 flights and one short ferry ride. With advance-purchase airfares you should be able to do this trip for under US$1500.

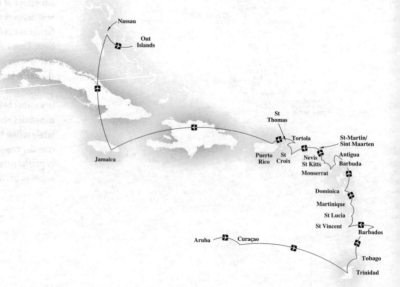

## CUBA & THE CAYMANS                    Three Weeks / Havana to Little Cayman

Why not combine one of the richest Caribbean countries with one of the poorest: a bastion of socialism with a citadel of capitalism? Think of it as economics 101 with beautiful beaches thrown in as extra credit.

Start your studies with architecture and music in **Havana** (p141), then head to **Santa Clara** (p165) and the venerable **Monumento Ernesto Che Guevara** (p165). Push on from here to **Trinidad** (p169), a Unesco World Heritage site. You can easily spend a week in this colonial town, hiking in **Topes de Collantes** (p170), horseback riding in **Valle de los Ingenios** (p170) or lazing at **Playa Ancón** (p170). Push east to **Santiago de Cuba** (p173) and its many attractions, including the **Castillo de San Pedro del Morro** (p175), the **Cuartel Moncada** (p174) and, of course, the vibrant music scene. Be sure to save at least two days for exploring in and around **Baracoa** (p180), one of Cuba's loveliest areas.

Return to Havana and fly to **Grand Cayman** (p196). You may have to connect through Montego Bay, Jamaica, but such are the vagaries of geopolitics. After flying into **George Town** (p196), base yourself at **Seven Mile Beach** (p196), which is backed by glitzy hotels and smart restaurants. After Cuba you may get a cultural hangover just being here. Go snorkeling at **Stingray City** (p199), where huge, fearless stingrays eat squid directly from your hands. Visiting **Cayman Brac** (p206) and **Little Cayman** (p208) require short flights. The former is the least visited of the Cayman Islands and by far the most dramatic, with great walking, bird-watching and diving. The latter has wonderful beaches and the best diving in the country.

**You can cover the 861km between Havana and Santiago de Cuba in 15 hours in a rental car. On the Caymans, you'll have some flights but can otherwise use taxis and buses.**

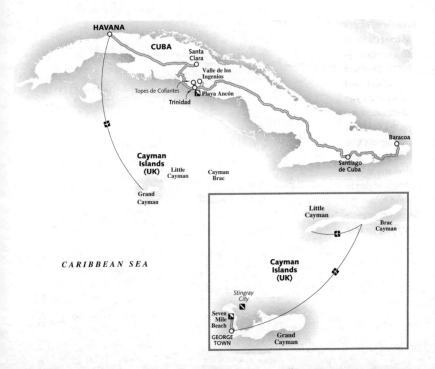

## A BAHAMAS WAY OF LIFE          Two to Four Weeks / Nassau to Eleuthera

Start off your Bahamian odyssey by spending three days in **Nassau** (p66), seeing sights such as **Cabbage Beach** (p76), before heading off to **Grand Bahama** (p77) for a few days of sandy pleasures. Go **diving** (p83) among the island's fish-filled coral reefs, or hike the mangrove trails in **Lucayan National Park** (p86).

Fly to Marsh Harbour on **Great Abaco** (p87), and relax on the exquisite beach on **Treasure Cay** (p89), before taking the ferry to **Green Turtle Cay** (p91) for a goombay smash at Miss Emily's Blue Bee Bar. On **Elbow Cay** (p90), wander streets lined with gingerbread fantasy houses, and admire the island's candy-striped lighthouse.

Fly to George Town on **Great Exuma** (p96) for some languid boat trips among the **Exuma Cays** (p98), a visit to **Stocking Island** (p97) and a snorkel around the captivating **Thunderball Grotto** (p98). Then head over to pretty **Long Island** (p102) for Gothic churches, lush greenery, blue holes and deserted beaches.

Finally, fly from Long Island's main settlement, Deadman's Cay, to Governor's Harbour on **Eleuthera** (p92) to see the beautiful people on chi-chi **Harbour Island** (p93), then head out to **Surfer's Beach** (p95) to watch the locals riding the waves while the sun goes down in the distance.

In under 900 miles of travel this trip takes you through the pleasures great and small of the vast series of islands known as the Bahamas. The big-city glitz of Nassau soon gives way to little towns of gingerbread houses and beaches of impossibly pure powder.

# ROADS LESS TRAVELED

## HUMPING HISPANIOLA    Three Weeks / Santo Domingo to Port-au-Prince

Fish-shaped Hispaniola combines the up-and-coming Spanish-cultured Dominican Republic and the finally-on-its-way-up French-speaking Haiti.

Explore **Santo Domingo** (p284). Start with the **Zona Colonial** (p285), wandering 500-year-old cobblestone backstreets that have changed little since the 16th century. Now, it's time for the beach: **Bávaro** (p296) and **Punta Cana** (p296) have miles and miles of beautiful beach and organized beachfront fun, and are good bases for independent travel. Head to **Samaná** (p300) for whale-watching, then take the plunge at **Playa Frontón** (p304) for undisturbed snorkeling around some of the best reefs in the country. Climb up to the central highlands for **Jarabacoa** (p314), and then go north to **Cabarete** (p310) for some adventure tours.

Back in Santo Domingo, you can catch a bus to Haiti – it will take a day of your trip and spans a good bit of Hispaniola. Start in chaotic **Port-au-Prince** (p266), with its vibrant art scene, pulsing music and urban Vodou culture. Now chill out in the decaying grand architecture of **Jacmel** (p270), Haiti's craft and Carnival center. Head to **Parc National La Visite** (p270), where the mountain hiking is as good as the views, then take a flight north from Port-au-Prince to Cap-Haïtien to visit the **Citadelle** (p273). This is *the* tropical-mountain fortress in the Caribbean, and Haiti's – literally – big must-see. Through the journey you will want some beach time and Haiti's are not exactly packed. Consider the ones near **Cap-Haïtien** (p272), **Côte des Arcadins** (p270) or **Île-à-Vache** (p272). You can get flights out of Port-au-Prince when your Haitian adventure is over or return to Santo Domingo.

You can explore the hills, valleys, coast and towns of the Dominican Republic and Haiti entirely by public transportation. Bring a book and maybe chicken-proof pants – you'll not only have long hours on the road but you're likely to be pecked by a seatmate or two.

## ISLANDS LESS VISITED                    Two to Three Weeks / Dominica to Grenada

Hopscotch your way south through some of the least-visited, least-developed Caribbean islands. Begin at **Dominica** (p580), which many people consider the wildest and most natural of the bunch. Start by getting on local time at the comfy properties of **Grand Bay** (p596). Then lose yourself in the rainforest at **Morne Trois Pitons National Park** (p595), a Unesco World Heritage site. Celebrate with a glass of bubbly – or at least the natural bubbles that tickle you while diving at **Champagne Reef** (p597).

It's a quick hop to **Martinique** (p603), where you should hit the beach at **Les Salines** (p622), followed by diving and drinking in the lively fishing village of **Ste-Luce** (p620).

Skip the airport and take the scenic ferry to **St Lucia** (p628), which emerges like a virescent monolith from the Caribbean as you home in. Stay in **Soufrière** (p639), which has a dramatic position on a bay that's shadowed by the iconic peaks of the Pitons. You can hike these in the morning and dive in the afternoon. For a jaunt, head over to **Marigot Bay** (p638), with its small beach and beautiful surrounds.

Endless views of bananas trees are the reward of your quick flight to **St Vincent** (p654) – as you'll see while walking the streets of **Kingstown** (p654, the all-business capital, the fruit is the mainstay of the economy. Take the boat to **Bequia** (p660), the center of beach fun and nightlife in the Grenadines, then take a day trip to the **Tobago Cays** (p669).

Your last jump lands you at **Grenada** (p701), where **St George's** (p707) is a welcome respite from stodgy main towns. Stroll the waterfront and enjoy the buzz, then head out to **Carriacou** (p716), a pint-sized sister island with beautiful beaches, quiet streets and genial locals.

These islands are what many people envision when they plan a Caribbean trip: lush tropical scenery, craggy peaks and ribbons of untrammeled beaches. Then they get conned into a trip to St Thomas. Here's your chance to realize the dream.

# TAILORED TRIPS

## QUICK GETAWAY

You've had it, you need a weekend away. It's got to be warm, have a beach and a good place to get a rum punch, but it can't cost so much that all the good karma will end in tears when you see the credit-card bills at the end. The following islands can all be reached by nonstop flights from North American cities; the snow hits your butt as you leave, and the sun hits your face as you arrive. Going from west to east, consider these sun-soaked places.

**Montego Bay** (p239), Jamaica's most famous resort town, has a huge range of places to stay on fun-filled beaches, while the old town of **San Juan** (p328), the capital of Puerto Rico, has forts and nearby beaches to explore by day, and lively bar-lined streets you can wander by night. The island of **St-Martin/Sint Maarten** (p434) gives you the choice of a French frolic or Dutch treat, but you can actually enjoy both as you beach-hop this crazy-shaped island. **St Kitts** (p499) has some of the region's most-fun beach bars on some of the least-crowded beaches, and you can take a fun ferry for a day trip to gorgeous **Nevis** (p506). **Antigua** (p521) offers fine seafood dining, a dose of history and a seemingly endless supply of sandy places to swim and snorkel, while **St Lucia** (p628) allows you to forget civilization among its lush foliage and hidden beaches.

## LUXE WEEK

There comes a time when the backpack needs to be forgotten, the bus saved for the airport parking lot and the only bubbles allowed in your glass must come from a cave in France. And the Caribbean is *the* place to do so. All easily reached from either North America or the UK, these are the spots for a sybaritic week amid the azure waters, blinding sands and every other Caribbean cliché that makes you tingle.

The **Cayman Islands** (p192) are among the most expensive islands in the Caribbean, and for good reason – there are a plethora of exclusive resorts here, ready to tend to your every whim. In the **Bahamas** (p59) you will find oodles of Boodles (the top brand of British gin) served at the kind of lavish places you see in swanky magazines that use thick paper, while **Tortola** (p395), in the British Virgin Islands, is the anchor – ha! – for the globe-trotting luxury-yacht set. The west coast of **Barbados** (p675), dubbed the 'Platinum Coast,' is lined with hidden resorts set in mansions previously owned by the fabulously wealthy expats who once wintered here. And, finally, **Mustique** (p664) in the Grenadines is the ultimate in posh – the few dozen lavish villas here are owned by the likes of Mick Jagger, but for the right price you can drop by.

## HIDDEN CARIBBEAN

While more than 90% of the Caribbean's 7000 islands are minute and uninhabited, there's a little club of islands that are *almost* uninhabited. These are tiny places well off the tourist track that offer the kind of escape many dream of but rarely realize. Expect an adventurous trip to reach these destinations, and be sure to bring a bag of books for your lazy days.

**Little Cayman** (p208) has a population that barely cracks three figures – and that's the iguanas. Come here for some of the world's best wall diving. The nicknames of **Anegada** (p410) say it all: 'Mysterious Virgin' and 'Ghost Cay.' It's a remote bit of sand in the British Virgin Islands. Frigate birds outnumber humans at least 10 to one on **Barbuda** (p531), an island that's happy to remain in the shadow of Antigua. Some comfy beach cottages can only be reached by boat. **La Désirade** (p572) is the place to bone up on your French, as little English is spoken in this outpost of Guadeloupe; there are, however, miles of beaches untrod by human foot. Grenada isn't exactly on the beaten path, and **Petit Martinique** (p719) is almost unknown. The little beach here is just 10 minutes by foot from the guesthouses serving the island.

## GREATER MOUNTAINS

The islands of the Dominican Republic, Haiti, Puerto Rico and Jamaica are part of the Greater Antilles (along with Cuba and the Caymans) and, among their few commonalities, is the fact that they share some of the Caribbean's most incredible mountains. On Puerto Rico, the 43-sq-mile Caribbean National Forest, more commonly known as **El Yunque** (p343) for its distinctive peak, has the island's only remaining virgin forest – some trees are more than 1000 years old. The Dominican Republic boasts a whopping 10 national parks, including **Parque Nacional Los Haitises** (p317) and Parque Nacional José del Carmen Ramírez, which is the home to **Pico Duarte** (p314), the Caribbean's tallest peak.

Neighboring Haiti has two mountain parks, **Parc National La Visite** (p270) and **Parc National Macaya** (p272), in which grows the country's remaining cloud forest.

Head west to Jamaica and you'll find the legendary **Blue Mountains** (p231), home to more than 500 species of flowering plants. The topography of the region is perfect for growing coffee beans, and the country's Blue Mountain coffee is often described as the best in the world.

# Snapshots

## HISTORY
### Ahoy Arawaks

The first Caribbeans arrived on the islands closest to South America around 4000 BC. These nomadic hunter-gatherers were followed by waves of Arawaks (a collective term for the Amerindian people believed to be from the Orinoco River Delta around Venezuela and Guyana) who moved north and west, beginning the great tradition of Caribbean island-hopping. Indeed, one of the Caribbean's recurrent themes, from pre-Columbian times until right now, has been movement of peoples.

Around AD 1200 the peaceable Arawaks were happily farming, fishing and minding their own business when the Caribs from South America started fanning out over the Caribbean. The Caribs killed the Arawak men and enslaved the women, triggering another wave of migration that sent the Arawaks fleeing as far west as Cuba and as far north as the Bahamas. When the Spanish explorers arrived, they dubbed the warfaring people they encountered 'cannibals' (a derivation of the word 'carital' or Carib), for their reputed penchant for eating their victims. Since the Arawaks had no written language, little of their culture survived, except – thankfully for weary travelers – the hammock.

*A Brief History of the Caribbean: From the Arawak and Carib to the Present* by Jan Rogonzinski is readable but the 'brief' part is debatable: it's 432 pages.

### Ahoy Columbus

Christopher Columbus led the European exploration of the region, making landfall at San Salvador in the Bahamas on October 12, 1492 – no matter that he thought he was in Asia. He too island-hopped, establishing the first European settlement in the Americas on Hispaniola, today shared by the Dominican Republic and Haiti. Discovering new lands gives glory, but what Columbus and subsequent explorers wanted was gold. Funny, though: despite four trips during which Columbus named and claimed much of the region for the Spanish crown, from Trinidad in the south to the Virgin Islands in the north, he never found much gold.

That's not to say there weren't riches: the land was fertile, the seas bountiful and the native population, after initial resistance by the toughest of the remaining Caribs, forcibly pliant. The conquistadores set to exploiting it all, violently. Focusing on the biggest islands promising the highest returns, they grabbed land, pillaged and enslaved, settling towns in Cuba, the Dominican Republic, Puerto Rico and Jamaica.

On tiny little Saba if someone's last name is Johnson or Hassel, they're Saban through and through as those were the names of the first European families to settle there in the 1600s.

Except for mineral-rich Trinidad, taken early by the Spanish, the Eastern Caribbean was left largely to its own devices until the English washed up on St Kitts in 1623, sparking domino-effect colonization of Barbados, Nevis, Antigua and Montserrat. Not to be outdone, the French followed, settling Martinique and Guadeloupe, while the Dutch laid claim to Saba, Sint Eustatius and St-Martin/Sint Maarten. Over the next 200 years the Europeans fought like children over these islands, and possession changed hands so often that a sort of hybridized culture developed; some islands, like St-Martin/Sint Maarten and St Kitts, were split between two colonial powers.

### Pirates & Forts

The Caribbean colonial story is largely one of giant agricultural interests – most notably sugar, but also tobacco, cattle and bananas – fueled by greed and slavery that promoted power struggles between landowners, politicians and the pirates who robbed them. The Bahamas, with hundreds of cays, complex shoals and channels, provided the perfect base for pirates such as Henry Jennings and 'Blackbeard' (Edward Teach) who ambushed treasure-laden boats headed for Europe. On the home front, Britain, Spain and France were embroiled in tiffs, scuffles and all-out war that allowed colonial holdings to change hands frequently. The English took Jamaica in 1655 and held Cuba momentarily in 1762, while the Spanish and French agreed to divide Hispaniola in 1731, creating the Dominican Republic and Haiti of today. The legacies of this period – Santo Domingo's Fortaleza Ozama (p288), the fortresses of Old San Juan (p331) and Havana (p144) and the vibrant mix of cultures – are among the most captivating attractions for travelers.

Except for the Eastern Caribbean, which has historically been more laid-back and easily controlled by its European overseers, colonial infighting had locals plotting rebellion and independence. Haiti was way in front of the curve in declaring independence in 1804, followed by the Dominican Republic in 1844 and Cuba in 1902. For some smaller islands – such as St Vincent and the Grenadines, and Barbuda and Antigua – the solution has been to band together. Other islands have opted to maintain strong neo-colonial ties to the parent country, as is the case with the French protectorates of St-Barthélemy, Martinique and Guadeloupe, and the commonwealth situation between Puerto Rico and the US. Independence on the one hand and statehood on the other has always had its champions in Puerto Rico, with statehood narrowly losing plebiscites in 1993 and 1998.

A different, but tenuous, alternative was forged by the Dutch holdings of Aruba, Curaçao, Bonaire, Sint Maarten, Sint Eustatius and Saba. In 1954 these holdings became an autonomous federation under Dutch rule known as the Netherlands Antilles, though the charter stipulated that each was to eventually become independent. After a long lag since Aruba split first in 1986, the others are doing that now (see boxed text, p779).

## A Rum-Punch Future

The last 100 years have been a mixed bag for the region. US intervention in countries seen as geostrategically important, particularly Haiti and Cuba, usually does more harm than good. Furthermore, monocrop agriculture – bananas in Jamaica, nutmeg in Grenada – means the islands are at the mercy of heavy weather and market fluctuations. At the same time, it polarizes societies into the rich who own the land and the poor who work it. This inevitably fosters socialist tendencies, including Fidel Castro, but also Maurice Bishop in Grenada (1979–83). Economic instability, especially, has given rise to dictators such as Rafael Leonidas Trujillo for 31 years in the Dominican Republic and the Duvaliers (Papa and Baby Doc) for 29 years in Haiti.

One thing all the islands have in common is tourism, which began taking hold when other sectors of the islands' economies began to crumble, particularly agriculture. Crop-leveling hurricanes (eg Gilbert in 1988, Hugo in 1989) spurred some islands to develop tourism industries, while the 1997 World Trade Organization ruling favoring Central American bananas over Caribbean ones forced St Vincent and Martinique to look at diversifying. Far from a panacea, unfettered tourism can wreak havoc on the environment (see p49) or give rise to societal woes like prostitution in Cuba. But overall the perception that tourism is a good source of jobs and revenue is widespread. In a recent poll, people in places as diverse as Trinidad and Barbados overwhelmingly said they not only liked tourists but said their presence made everybody's life better. Of course that poll may have been taken when Brobdingnagian cruise ships *weren't* in port.

Everyone on St-Barthélemy wears some sort of jewelry with the vaguely V shape of the island on it.

In the Bahamas, Junkanoo is a street parade with music that people prepare for all year. It happens between Boxing Day (December 26) and New Year's Day.

*The Banana Wars: United States Intervention in the Caribbean, 1898-1934* by Lester D Langley shows the cost of meddling in the region.

But like a sacking of an agrarian village by pirates, this summary makes short work of the Caribbean's complex story. Each island's particular history is more complex and nuanced; see individual chapters for the full scoop.

## PEOPLE

The stereotypical island slacker, swinging in a hammock with joint in hand, couldn't be further from the truth in today's Caribbean. On most islands, economic necessity or outright hardship means working in the fields, factory or hotel in a constant effort to make ends meet. Family is the hub on which life turns and interpersonal relationships make the day-to-day fun and purposeful. Gossiping is a major hobby. Casual with time and commitments, many islanders prefer to converse with a friend over one last beer than rush to catch a bus. In the villages away from big cities and on the small islands everyone knows each other.

Chivalrous at best, misogynistic at worst, machismo is a complex cultural phenomenon on many islands like Trinidad. Far from the simple domination of women – indeed, some social scientists argue, convincingly, that it's really the women holding the reins in these societies – machismo embraces many facets of the human condition including emotional vulnerability and virility. It can also manifest itself in homophobia, which has reached alarming, virulent proportions on some islands and especially Jamaica, where it is endemic and violent.

Health is a perennial challenge for the region. According to UNAIDS (the Joint United Nations program on HIV/AIDS), the Caribbean has the second-highest rate of adult HIV infection (2.3%) after sub-Saharan Africa. Although some countries including Barbados, the Bahamas and Cuba have had success in lowering infection rates, in other places such as Jamaica, rates of infection are reaching crisis proportions. For more information, see p840.

Another simmering issue is immigration: Dominicans sailing to Puerto Rico, boatfuls of Haitians alighting in the Bahamas and Cubans floating around the Florida Straits are common images. The land of opportunity, of course, is the US, which maintains a politically driven immigration policy that grants disgruntled Cubans automatic residency, but regularly turns away desperate Haitians. Those left behind on Haiti are poor but proud. They're well aware that most of the world thinks they're boat people from a land of dictators, chaos and zombies; so they're eager to show foreigners that the reality is far different.

Aside from the Carib reservation on Dominica of some 3000, little vestige of the original inhabitants remains in the Caribbean. Instead, there is the complex swirl of cultures and colors from all the people who came after: English, Spanish, French and Dutch mixed with Africans brought over as slaves. Once slavery was abolished, indentured laborers came from China, India and the Middle East, changing islands' identities. Regional immigration also adds to the mix: 'Bahatians' – Haitians born in the Bahamas – are recognized (and often discriminated against) as a separate group, and expats from the US have altered the makeup of some islands like the Caymans.

## SPORTS

You need only ask 'cricket or baseball?' to get your finger on the pulse. Closest to the US, baseball rules in Puerto Rico, the Dominican Republic and Cuba, with players by the dozens making the jump to the US big leagues. Catching a game in Cuba or the Dominican Republic is a window into the sport as a local passion.

Cricket is serious business in the Caribbean, where rivalries (and fans) are rabid and the sport attracts major dollars. Islands where cricket rules include

Arubans take their license plate motto seriously: 'One Happy Island.' They really believe it.

St-Martin/Sint Maarten is the Caribbean melting pot. Besides French and Dutch, the two-nation island has residents from over 80 other countries.

On Guadeloupe the Tour de Guadeloupe bicycle race is the Caribbean Tour de France.

## GET OUT OF YOUR SHELL

You can't begin to experience the Caribbean until you get to know its people. And that doesn't just mean the guy mixing the rum-punch or the woman handing you a conch fritter – although these folks are often fascinating in their own right. (People who run beach bars out of shacks on the sand easily have the highest average character quotient anywhere.)

Rather, to meet the locals you need to join the locals; something that often doesn't happen when you're in a whirlwind of package tours, resort-style ghettos and general frolic-filled days. Here are some simple, common-sense tips from the authors of this book for getting past the smiles of the tourist industry and experiencing the culture of the islands.

- Eat at lunch wagons or stalls. The food is cheap and you often get incredibly good local fare that hasn't been watered down for foreign palates. Plus you can break the ice just by asking what's what.

- Drop by a local bar for a drink. It's perhaps not best for single women, but rum shops on places like Aruba, Bonaire and Curaçao are the de facto community centers and you'll soon be part of the crowd.

- Be loyal. So many tourists blow through just once so if the folks in a café or bar think you're a regular (sometimes it takes but two visits), you'll be part of the crew.

- Look for community fish fries or barbecues. Typically held once a week, they're big street parties in the Eastern Caribbean, especially Barbados.

- Pick up people trudging along the road (hitchhiking is rare, so offer a lift to someone who needs it). We learned the drama-filled history of the sugar industry on St Kitts by giving a lift to a teacher late for class.

- Take the bus – locals love to show you their country and will go out of their way to show you things while you bounce down the road (and the jammed conditions of most buses mean you can't help but meet people).

- Be friendly, say hi. A no-brainer but why wait for others to welcome you? Icy resolve can melt when you make the first move.

For some of the world's most raucous baseball, catch a game in Santo Domingo and San Pedro de Macoris on the Dominican Republic.

Jamaica, the Leeward and Windward Islands, Barbados, and Trinidad and Tobago, and while there are no national clubs, the top players from these countries form the storied West Indies team. The 2007 Cricket World Cup was played across the Caribbean, with nations spending big sums on new and improved stadiums. Unfortunately for the West Indies team, it got as far as the Super 8, only to be eliminated in losses that included a brutal 103-run defeat by Australia. (Australia went on to win the cup.)

While volleyball (especially the beach variety) and soccer are popular in the Caribbean, basketball just seems to grow in popularity. Puerto Rico and Cuba have leagues and players regularly make the jump to the NBA, following in the size-15 footsteps of superstars Kareem Abdul-Jabbar (Trinidadian descent), Patrick Ewing (Jamaica) and Tim Duncan (Bahamas).

In the Olympics, you'll have noticed that folks from the Caribbean run *fast*. Tiny island countries regularly gain honors at the games through their runners. Famed sprinter Kim Collins, 'the Fastest Man on Earth,' hails from St Kitts, where you'll drive along Kim Collins Hwy.

Bone up on batsmen, bowlers and sticky wickets at www.windiescricket.com or www.caribbeancricket.com.

Windsurfing and board surfing have become part of the culture in Barbados, Bonaire and other places where the wind and waves allow for world-class competitions.

And yachts aren't just for the idle rich. Huge regattas draw teams of locals and foreigners in fierce competitions. Famous races include Sailing Week on Antigua, the Heineken Regatta on St-Martin/Sint Maarten, the Rolex Cup on St Thomas, USVI, the BVI Spring Regatta on Tortola and the Tour des

Yoles Rondes on Martinique. On Anguilla, local teams compete with their own home-grown designs.

## RELIGION

It's quite probable that every religion known to, well, God is practiced somewhere in the Caribbean. Nevertheless, Christian religions are still the classic forces on islands with a strong European heritage. Animist sects (obeah) have strongholds in Jamaica, the Bahamas and the Eastern Caribbean. Meanwhile evangelical sects are attracting scores with the promise of a peaceful afterlife that appeals to those fed up with the violence and destruction of the here and now.

Yet the islands are most closely identified with Afro-Caribbean religions like Vodou in Haiti and Santería in Cuba. These religions trace their roots to Africa, but were overlain and mixed with Christian trappings when the slaves were brought over. Masking tribal beliefs and traditions with those of the overseers ensured the survival of these religions. As they say on Haiti, the people are '80% Catholic, 20% Protestant and 100% Vodou.'

Rastafarianism was promulgated by Ethiopian Emperor Haile Selassie whom Rastas regarded as the Chosen One. The religion sprouted from Marcus Garvey's 'back to Africa' movement in the '30s, but gained worldwide exposure thanks to spliff-smoking, dreadlocked adherents like Bob Marley who believe that Africans are the 13th lost tribe of Israel and that they will be led from exile in Babylon (Jamaica) to Zion or the 'Promised Land' (Ethiopia) by Jah (God). In Jamaica, some 100,000 claim Rastafarianism as their religion and you'll find scores of Rastas throughout the islands.

From Cuba's all-male secret societies to the ganja-puffing rituals of Rastafarians, *Creole Religions of the Caribbean* by Margarite Fernández Olmos and Lizabeth Paravisini-Gebert is one of the most current and comprehensive treatments of the region's religions.

## ARTS

The list of Caribbean literary giants is so long, your on-the-road reading could comprise only local writers. See p30 for some notable examples; you'll also find more in the island chapters throughout this book.

You'll find a rich artistic culture on most of the islands, although you may have to peer past tourist-schlock to find it. Misunderstood Haiti is a perfect example. The Haitian Naive painters of the 1940s and 1950s (such as Hector Hyppolite) were internationally significant, changing Europe and America's idea of Caribbean and African art. The modern generation continues to build on those strong foundations and some of the best works you'll find in galleries on islands far away are by Haitian artists.

No matter the medium, Cuba is an artistic powerhouse: the paintings of Wilfredo Lam, the films of Tomás Gutiérrez Alea (*Death of a Bureaucrat; Memories of Underdevelopment*), the National Ballet of Cuba and the indelible images shot by Korda – including the Che you see peddled worldwide – are testament to artistic achievement. The Dominican Republic and Puerto Rico, both with arts schools, have a rich arts scene as well. Perhaps the most celebrated Caribbean painter is impressionist Camille Pissarro, born on St Thomas in 1803 and known for his landscapes.

Throughout the islands, you'll see clothes and costumes inspired by the flamboyance and sheer glitter that come from Carnival. It is the climax of the social calendar for rich and poor alike across the Caribbean.

The 'Lace Ladies' gather at the Eugenius Centre on Thursdays to do beautiful Saban stitching. These women are pushing 100 years old and are oh-so charming!

Many 'local' crafts sold in tourist areas are from China. Look for places like Festival Place in Nassau, where everything is Bahamian made.

## MUSIC

You're on a beach and you're listening to Bob Marley blaring out of the sound system of the bar that just sold you a cold one. You're in Jamaica, right? Maybe. In fact you could be on any warm beach on earth, so pervasive has Marley become around the world. It's been more than 25 years since he died but at any given moment his songs must be playing in thousands of sandy-floored beach joints worldwide.

That very image of laid-back reggae drives tourism on Jamaica and it's created a clichéd image of Caribbean torpor that is firmly stamped into the world's consciousness. But even as people sway to 'Could You Be Loved' they may have the sexy strains of Rihanna singing 'Umbrella' on their iPod or the jamming strains of Arrow's 'Hot Hot Hot' on the CD player in their traffic-bound car.

Although each island has its own musical style, all Caribbean music is percussion-based, born as a lingua franca from Africans confronting their new, nightmarish reality where music formed one of the few links to their mostly lost cultures (religion was the other). It's unsurprising that European and North American styles eventually began to infuse Caribbean rhythms. Thematically, sociopolitical commentary/criticism has always been a vital undercurrent but so too has sex – you'll hear lots of salacious rhythms and raunchy rhymes permeating the Caribbean airwaves.

## Calypso

Born in 19th-century Trinidad and Tobago among field hands who sang in French Creole to obscure the lyrics' meaning from the landowners, calypso continues to rely on clever wordplay (though now in English), and the Carnival competitions are a hot highlight. Calypso – too great a tradition to remain contained – eventually spawned soca, the high-energy mix of soul and calypso. These islands are also the birthplace of the steel drum.

## Reggae

With Jamaica as its fountainhead, reggae is driven by a kicking drum bass after-beat and is literally heard everywhere. Reggae lyrics traditionally addressed problems facing Jamaica's urban poor, including discrimination and marginalization, while also projecting self-affirmation. The reggae pantheon includes Peter Tosh and Bunny Livingston (with Marley, the original Wailers), Jimmy Cliff, the legendary producer Lee 'Scratch' Perry and Burning Spear.

## Newer Styles

Dancehall – a raw, cheap-to-produce genre that's like the bastard child of a Rasta and gangsta rapper – incorporates lewd lyrics with ghetto angst that created a whole new musical royalty in Jamaica including Yellowman, producers Sly & Robbie and Shabba Ranks (with his self-explanatory 'Hard and Stiff').

Salsa and its offshoots burn up dance floors from San Juan to Santo Domingo, which sizzle with salsa's up-tempo beat, sassy brass and smoking rhythm sections. It's hit big with Puerto Rican superstars such as Eddie Palmieri and Cuban bands like Los Van Van and NG La Banda.

And the scene, like a good Creole stew, just keeps changing as new forms blend old styles. Latino immigrants on Caribbean islands are creating a new soca/salsa twist, while Creole hip-hop is heard from New York to Rio. Dancehall, *the* style of local clubs throughout the region, has DJs adding vocals to raw rhythms. And reggaeton adds reggae strains to the driving dancehall beat.

## ENVIRONMENT
### The Land

You will see two main types of islands in the Caribbean: limestone and volcanic. This can directly affect your traveling experience. Limestone islands were formed by living coral forming layers of limestone that built up over

The classic reggae drama is *The Harder They Come*, starring Jimmy Cliff, but fans shouldn't miss *The Reggae Movie*, chock-full of concert footage from Burning Spear, Inner Circle, Ziggy Marley and more.

Dancehall Reggae (www .dancehallreggae.com) is the place to go for the latest on Jamaica's trendsetting music scene.

The film *Buena Vista Social Club* and its soundtrack continue to drive interest in 1950s Cuban dancehall music even as the island itself has moved far beyond in its tastes.

millions of years. In fact the islands look organic; one needs only see the Byzantine shapes of the Bahamas, the Virgin Islands, Anguilla, Antigua and Barbuda, Barbados, and Aruba, Bonaire and Curaçao to understand that these were formed by complex processes (St-Martin/Sint Maarten looks like something left by a bird). The islands have rolling interiors but their real allure is the crenellated coasts, which can provide ideal shelter for boats and which are lined with countless beaches with brilliant white or even pinkish sand from the coral.

Keep track of who is sleeping with whom and who is the latest reggaeton sensation at caribbeancelebrity.com.

Volcanic islands form a crescent from Saba to Grenada. Although most are dormant, there are still eruptions: Martinique (Mt Pelée, 1902), St Vincent (Soufrière volcano, 1979) and Montserrat, whose Soufrière Hills volcano has devastated much of the island in a series of eruptions since 1995. Volcanic islands typically have one or more tall cones that drop steeply down to flatter lands near the coast. The nearly perfect conical shape of Nevis is a good example. The upper reaches of the peaks often still have swaths of rainfor-

## CARIBBEAN GEOGRAPHY 101

You will often hear the Caribbean islands referred to in numerous ways – the Leewards, the Windwards, the West Indies etc. It can get confusing, so here's a quick primer in Caribbean geography.

- Caribbean islands – An archipelago of thousands of islands that stretch from the southeast coast of Florida in the USA to the northern coast of Venezuela. The largest island within the Caribbean Sea is Cuba, followed by the island of Hispaniola (shared by the nations of Haiti and the Dominican Republic), then Jamaica and Puerto Rico. The Bahamas, to the north, are technically outside of the Caribbean archipelago – although we have covered them in this book.

- Greater Antilles – Consists of the large islands such as Hispaniola, Cuba and Jamaica at the top of the Caribbean and goes east as far as Puerto Rico. It also includes the Cayman Islands, due to their western location.

- Lesser Antilles – The archipelago that extends east and southeastward from the Virgin Islands down to Trinidad and Tobago, just off the northern coast of Venezuela. Also called the Eastern Caribbean Islands, the Lesser Antilles are further divided into the Leeward Islands and the Windward Islands.

- Leeward Islands – From north to south: the US Virgin Islands (USVI), the British Virgin Islands (BVI), Anguilla, St-Martin/Sint Maarten, St-Barthélemy, Saba, Sint Eustatius (Statia), St Kitts and Nevis, Antigua and Barbuda, Montserrat, and Guadeloupe.

- Windward Islands – From north to south: Dominica, Martinique, St Lucia, St Vincent and the Grenadines, and Grenada. Barbados and Trinidad and Tobago are often geographically considered part of the Windwards, but do not belong to the Windward Islands geopolitical group.

The islands are further classified by their national sovereignty.

- British West Indies – Consists of Anguilla, Turks and Caicos, the Cayman Islands, Montserrat (an 'overseas territory') and BVI (a crown colony) due to their affiliation with the UK.

- French West Indies – Includes Guadeloupe, St-Martin, St-Barthélemy and Martinique due to their status as Départements d'Outre-Mer of France.

- Netherlands Antilles – Historically Aruba, Curaçao, Bonaire, Sint Maarten, Saba and Sint Eustatius. Aruba, Bonaire and Curaçao (often called the ABC Islands) are also known as the Leeward Netherlands Antilles. (The word 'former' was added to Netherlands Antilles in 2008; see p779.)

For our purposes, we've called the whole wonderful affair the Caribbean islands, but you'll see the other terms peppered throughout the text.

est that proved too difficult to clear during the plantation era. The coasts generally lack the intricate curves and inlets of the limestone islands, which means natural ports are uncommon. Beaches can be dark volcanic sand but also bright white from offshore reefs.

To understand your windward from your leeward and get a firm grasp of your Antilles, see the boxed text, p47.

*Treasure Island* supposedly was about BVI's Norman Island.

## Wildlife

### ANIMALS

Except for large iguana populations and tree rats on certain islands, land animals have largely been hunted to extinction. Responsibility is shared between humans and other introduced species including the mongoose, raccoons, cats, dogs and donkeys. Trinidad, home to 100 types of mammal, is the exception to the rule (see p731).

If you're anxious to behold the Caribbean's richest fauna, you're going to get wet. One of the world's most complex ecosystems is coral, a diminutive animal that lives in giant colonies that form over millennia. Fish pecking away at nutritious tidbits or hiding out in the reef include the iridescent Creole wrasse, groupers, kingfish, sergeant majors and angel fish. Hang – or float – around and you might see inflatable porcupine fish, barracudas, nurse sharks, octopus, moray eels and manta rays. See p52 for the region's best diving and below for details on the grave threats to reefs.

James Bond loves the Caribbean; films shot there include *Dr No* (Jamaica), *Thunderball* (Bahamas), *Live and Let Die* (Jamaica) *Golden Eye* (Puerto Rico) and *Casino Royale* (Bahamas). And Sean Connery lives in the Bahamas.

Other species you may see include pilot, sperm, blue and humpback whales, famous for their acrobatic breaching from January to March. Spinner, spotted and bottlenosed dolphins, and loggerhead, green, hawksbill and leatherback turtles are common sights for divers. Manatees or sea cows, herbivorous marine mammals so ugly they're cute, are found in waters around Cuba, the Dominican Republic, Jamaica and Puerto Rico. All of

---

### IMPERILED REEFS

More than half of the reefs in the Caribbean are dead or dying and the rest are severely threatened, according to a several recent scientific reports. The culprits are the usual suspects: global warming, population growth, overfishing and hurricanes. The findings explain the threats as follows:

- Global warming – The record temperatures of water across the Caribbean are killing beneficial types of algae that corals depend on symbiotically to survive, which results in the process called 'bleaching.' Higher carbon dioxide levels also deprive reefs of oxygen, and coral is highly susceptible to even slight reductions in oxygen.

- Population growth – Development along coasts increases the runoff of soil, which clouds the water and denies coral sunlight. Population growth also means increased agricultural activity – not only farms but also golf courses and other artificial plantings. Chemical runoffs contain poisons as well as nutrients that are used by harmful algae that destroy the reefs.

- Overfishing – While harmful algae have always been present in reefs, one of the forces keeping them in check were algae-eating fish. The greatly reduced numbers of fish in the region mean that harmful algae are thriving.

- Hurricanes – The record number of hurricanes are depriving the reefs of oxygen through turbulent waters that block sunlight; damage to land that increases soil runoff; and wave forces that already-weakened reefs cannot handle.

Experts familiar with Caribbean reefs say that it may already be too late save a lot of them but that with immediate action it might be possible. Although hard to calculate due to the sheer magnitude of the numbers, it's estimated that reefs provide over $4 billion in value to the Caribbean through shoreline protection and tourism, and as a habitat for sea creatures.

these animals are on the threatened or endangered species list – part of the reason the Bahamas and other islands like Curaçao are criticized for their captive dolphin facilities.

Hundreds of bird species, both endemic and migratory, frequent scores of islands. Look for iconic pink flamingos on the Bahamas and Bonaire. Common Caribbean seabirds include brown pelicans, white cattle egrets and herons. Hummingbirds and banana quits are always around, searching for something sweet.

## PLANTS

The Caribbean has thousands of plant species. The tropics in bloom feel like an epiphany and you'll see flowering trees such as the orange flamboyant, crimson African tulip (*spathodea*), white frangipani with its intoxicating scent, and the dark-blue blossoms of the lignum vitae, the hardest of all known woods. Hundreds of orchid species bejewel damper areas (best January to March), and vermilion bougainvillea, exotic birds of paradise, hibiscus of all colors and spiky crimson ginger pop up everywhere.

## Environmental Issues

The sheer popularity of the region as a destination creates or aggravates environmental problems. Specific sites suffering from overexposure include the reef around Tobago Cays off St Vincent and the Grenadines, a popular anchorage for sailors, and the reefs around the Virgin Islands, which have been damaged by careless snorkelers and divers.

Waste is a big problem. Mountains of garbage crowd Havana, acrid refuse burns from Vieques to Puerto Plata, and sewage needs somewhere to go – too often into the sea, unfortunately. St-Barthélemy is one island finding creative answers such as converting burning trash into energy.

Larger islands, in particular, have had difficulty inculcating a culture of conservation. Despite deforestation laws, only 10% of the Dominican Republic is forested. Neighboring Haiti – the most impoverished country in the western hemisphere – features in university environmental-management courses as a case study in how massive deforestation (95%) can destroy a country.

Overfishing is a major problem. The Bahamas outlawed long-line fishing in 1959, the first Caribbean island to do so, but now struggles with poachers; some communities have established marine preserves independently of the government to curb the abuse. In June 1997 an environmental scandal surfaced involving Grenada, St Kitts and Nevis, St Vincent, St Lucia, and Dominica, which were accused of taking bribes from Japan in exchange for helping block protection measures for endangered species.

Nevertheless, no legislation or vigilance can stop the environmental destruction wrought by a hurricane that indiscriminately uproots trees and clogs reefs, and the number of destructive hurricanes is growing. In 2007 two Category 5 hurricanes – the strongest – both made landfall in the region, a first.

## FOOD & DRINK

Caribbean cuisine blends fruits and rice, seafood and spice. And it blends influences from around the world. Indian, French, Italian, American and Asian influences are just some of the tastes and flavors you'll find. But don't expect every meal to be a feast of tropical flavors. Visitors can run into bland, dull food everywhere. From the hotel dining room slipping meat and two veg in front of you to bland buffets at all-inclusive resorts, there's plenty of reason to seek out the best of the region. It's not hard to find.

The sight of thousands of frigate birds puffing out their distinctive scarlet throat pouches in hopes of luring a mate on Barbuda is one of nature's great spectacles.

*Sweet Hands: Island Cooking from Trinidad and Tobago* by Ramin Ganeshram is a good cookbook specializing in TnT dishes.

A regionwide delicacy called 'mountain chicken' is no kind of fowl, but is actually a crapaud, a local species of frog with unusually large (and delicious) legs; it's a protected species and only to be caught between September and February.

## Staples & Specialties

A fish still dripping with salt water, thrown on the grill and spritzed with lime has made many a Caribbean travel memory. So too has a tasty lobster, grilled over colts and then drenched in garlic butter. Most islands have a pickled fish dish (*escovitched* or *escobeche*), a jazzy marinade of vinegar, lime and spices with a complexity belied by the simple ingredients. In the Bahamas, conch (pronounced 'conk') is so popular any which way – pounded, marinated and frittered, deep fried, grilled, in salad, chowders and stews – the animal is headed towards the threatened species list.

As for meat, there's the ubiquitous chicken. Mixed with rice it's found as *arroz con pollo* in the Spanish-speaking islands and as chicken *pelau* in Trinidad and St Vincent. The other omnipresent staple is pork, which is the star meat in Cuban and Puerto Rican sandwiches (*lechón asado*). Beef is not eaten widely, except in Jamaica. Goat is a staple on many of the Leeward Islands, including Montserrat, where it stars in a savory dish with an unsavory name: goat water.

Look for Creole food, the classic French-inspired spicy, tomatoey fare that is found on menus through the Eastern Caribbean and north all the way to New Orleans.

Rice flecked with black or red beans is a staple in the Bahamas, Cuba (*congrí*), Jamaica (rice and peas) and Trinidad, where aromatic basmati rice subs in for the traditional long grain. Cassava (yucca) is served with an addictive garlic sauce called *mojito* in Cuba and *ajili-mójili* in Puerto Rico. Plantains are a staple and accompany every meal fried as chips or as disks (*tostones*).

Tropical fruits are quintessential Caribbean icons. There are the usual pineapple, papaya, bananas, guava and mango, but mix it up some, sampling sugar apple in the Bahamas (*anon* in Cuba), a custardy fruit shot through with black pits, or *guinep* in Jamaica, a small lychee-like fruit.

The king and queen of Caribbean street snacks are the patty (flaky pastry pillows filled with meat) for which Jamaica is famous, and the roti, an eastern Indian creation of flatbread wrapped around curried meat or potatoes, served widely in the Caribbean, but particularly in Trinidad.

*Look for salted plantain chips sold in bags as snacks for bus journeys.*

*There are at least 12 kinds of mango widely sold through the Caribbean.*

### MEMORABLE EATING & DRINKING

Here are some of the more memorable experiences authors of this book had in pursuit of good food and fun.

- Curried shrimp – a local dish on Statia – at a place called Fruit Tree (p485), a hidden local haunt. (Brandon Presser, Sint Eustatius)
- Pataraj (p743) in Port of Spain has the most delicious shrimp roti served with pickled mango, pumpkin, and pepper. I'd go back for the tender sweet papaya flesh and the tangy pineapple from the markets that I cut into almost daily. (Ellee Thalheimer, Trinidad and Tobago)
- The jerk chicken and pork in Boston Bay (p234) was absolutely sensational – the seasoning fiery enough without overwhelming the meat. (Richard Koss, Jamaica)
- On Antigua at Coconut Grove (p526), for the first time in my life I enjoyed rock lobster when I wasn't flat on my back with my feet in the air barking like a dogfish to the B-52s. (Ryan Ver Berkmoes, Antigua and Barbuda)
- The awesome goombay smash at Miss Emily's Blue Bee Bar (p92), where it was created. Poured from a gallon jug into your cup, it is sneaky potent. (Amy C Balfour, the Bahamas)
- Getting nice and buzzed on my back porch with a friend in Dominica. We bought a bottle of cheap rum and some fruit juice, and went to town. (Josh Krist, Dominica)

**SUNNY, YUMMY, RUMMY** *Josh Krist*

If you could taste them, what would sunsets and long days at the beach taste like? Most likely, rum. In a daiquiri, by itself, or with sugar and a slice of lime, rum is *the* drink of the Caribbean.

In Puerto Rico, the Bacardi Rum Factory (p342) is a good introduction to rum production – fermenting mashed sugar cane or molasses in huge vats, capturing the alcohol through distillation, aging it in wooden casks in big hot warehouses – and there are free tastings.

Distillers explain that because of the warm Caribbean climate up to 15% of the rum evaporates every year during aging. This evaporation is called 'the angel's share' at distilleries around the world and usually averages closer to 5%. The angels in the Caribbean are living it up, apparently.

Sip a little something at the Cruzan Rum Distillery (p383); it has a pleasant 20-minute tour with tastings at the end.

Some say that Cuban rum is the best. Do some investigation at Havana's Museo del Ron (p145), where in addition to the usual tour and tasting there's a re-creation of a traditional distillery, complete with a model railway.

The Appleton Rum Estate (p252) has the largest and oldest distillery in Jamaica – it's been pumping out the good stuff since 1749. Appleton is probably the local favorite across the region.

Martinique is the epicenter of high-quality, pure-cane rums, which they call *rhum agricole*. There are many distilleries on this French island, but English speakers will learn the most at Musée du Rhum St James (p616).

Top rums include Bermudez Anniversario from the Dominican Republic, Haiti's Barbancourt Five Star and Mount Gay Extra Old from Barbados (see p683). The color of rum ranges from clear to honey brown. The darker the drink, the older, usually. Unlike Scotch, however, older does not necessarily equal better, especially considering that some distilleries add coloring and fresh product to the casks for 'aged rum' because of the thirsty angels.

Let taste be your guide; take a small sniff of straight rum with your mouth slightly open. This gives you an idea of the taste without being overwhelmed by the alcohol burn. In the better rums you might smell some vanilla, a hint of flowers, or even, oddly enough, cotton candy – it is just cooked sugar that soaked up the flavors of sun-warmed casks, after all.

On islands that see a fair number of visitors, like Barbados, the Caymans, Aruba and many more, look for wonderful restaurants run by creative chefs who are melding the region's foods and flavors with those of the world.

## Drinks

The Caribbean and drinks. Reasons to pack your bag now. Minty mojitos or lemony daiquiris in Cuba, sugary ti-punch in Martinique or the smooth and fruity goombay smash in the Bahamas. It's no surprise that all of these are rum drinks: the Caribbean makes the world's best rum, and while some venture no further than a regular old Cuba *libre* (rum and Coke) or piña colada, a highball of exquisite seven-year-old *añejo* over ice as the sun sets is liquid joy. See boxed text, above.

Beer is like bottled water, no it is the bottled water. Red Stripe from Jamaica and Carib from Trinidad and Tobago have earned global reputations. Numerous more regional lagers keep you cool during the hot days and nights.

Along with rum, the Caribbean produces some of the world's finest coffee. Jamaican Blue Mountain coffee needs no introduction, while Haitian Bleu (named for its color) is sought out for its dark roasted flavor and organic origins. Cuba also grows organic coffee, usually served strong, black and sweet or as silky, milky *café con leche,* which is also how they prefer it in Puerto Rico. Coconut water sipped fresh from the nut is refreshing and light – perfect on a hot day.

*Mamajuana* is a bottle filled with a variety of herbs and dried bark topped with rum, wine and a bit of honey, then allowed to steep for around a month. Most Dominican bars have a bottle somewhere.

Visitors from stodgier places are always amazed you can take your drink from a bar in a to-go cup on many Caribbean islands. Then they join right in.

# Diving & Snorkeling

Whether you're an ultraexperienced diver or a novice slapping on fins for the first time, you are in for a real treat. Few places in the world offer such perfect conditions for underwater exploration. The Caribbean Sea's consistently warm waters – year-round temperatures average a comfortable 80°F (27°C) – and spectacularly clear waters mean visibility can exceed 100ft (30m). Professional dive operators are as prolific as the postcard-worthy beaches and, whether you skim the surface or plunge far below, the colorful, active marine world delivers an amazing show.

The variety of islands – from lush and mountainous to arid and flat – mean the diversity of dive sites is almost endless. You'll find shallow fringing reefs that curve into protected bays, sheer walls and coral-covered pinnacles, exciting drift dives, and remnants of ancient shipwrecks that lie as historical relics on the sea floor.

You can come face-to-face with fish the size of small cars, or moray eels longer than your wingspan. You can peer into sea grass and find tiny seahorses, or watch translucent shrimp scratch along the coral. Caribbean waters harbor all sorts of colorful sponges, and both soft and hard coral, including wavering gorgonian fans and gemlike black coral.

At the end of the day, there's nothing better than sipping a cold beer while the sun licks the beads of water off your skin. You'll think about the turtle you just met – that's one traveling friend you will never, ever forget.

The Caribbean Sea is the world's fifth-largest body of water, just slightly bigger than the Mediterranean Sea.

## INFORMATION
### Books

Comprehensive guides that give good descriptions of both scuba diving and snorkeling sites, along with information on local dive operators, include the much-revered *Best Dives of the Caribbean* by Joyce Huber, and *The Complete Diving Guide: The Caribbean* series by Colleen Ryan and Brian Savage. Lonely Planet's Diving & Snorkeling series includes guides to Bonaire, Cayman Islands and the US Virgin Islands. Anyone curious about marine biology should check out Paul Humann's series on fish, coral and invertebrate identification. Titles include *Reef Fish Identification: Tropical Pacific* and *Reef Creature Identification: Florida Caribbean Bahamas*. Budding underwater naturalists will also want to arm themselves with *Scuba Dic.: Caribbean Sea*, a nifty underwater dictionary – printed on waterproof paper – detailing a variety of fish, plants and invertebrates, with corresponding photos.

### Dive Courses

With warm, calm, crystalline waters, the Caribbean is an excellent place to get scuba certified or further your training with specialized courses, such as night, wreck or deep diving, or digital underwater photography. Two reputable organizations are widely recognized as providing the best and most professional certification in the world: the Professional Association of Diving Instructors (PADI) and the National Association of Underwater Instructors (NAUI). Affiliation with either of these organizations means the dive shop adheres to high standards of safety and professionalism. Avoid unaffiliated operators; the lower cost can be alluring, but it often means dodgy service, old equipment and compromised safety.

If you want to experience diving for the first time, most operators offer a short beginner course for nondivers, commonly dubbed a 'resort course,' which includes brief instructions, followed by a shallow beach or boat dive.

## SAFETY GUIDELINES FOR DIVING

Before embarking on a scuba-diving, skin-diving or snorkeling trip, carefully consider the following points to ensure a safe and enjoyable experience.

- Possess a current diving certification card from a recognized scuba diving instructional agency (if scuba diving).
- Be sure you are healthy and feel comfortable diving.
- Obtain reliable information about physical and environmental conditions at the dive site (eg from a reputable local dive operation).
- Be aware of local laws, regulations and etiquette about marine life and the environment.
- Dive only at sites within your realm of experience; if available, engage the services of a competent, professionally trained dive instructor or divemaster.
- Be aware that underwater conditions vary significantly from one region, or even site, to another. Seasonal changes can significantly alter any site and dive conditions. These differences influence the way divers dress for a dive and what diving techniques they use.
- Ask about the environmental characteristics that can affect your diving and how local trained divers deal with these considerations.

The cost generally ranges from US$75 to US$125, depending on the operation and whether a boat is used.

For those who want to jump into the sport wholeheartedly, a number of operators offer full open-water certification courses. The cost generally hovers around US$400, equipment included, and the course takes the better part of a week. If you plan to be certified but don't want to spend your vacation in a classroom, consider a 'warm-water referral' program, where you take the classes at home, then complete your open-water dives in the Caribbean.

## Dive Operators

Excellent dive operators abound, offering everything from snorkeling rentals to full dive-certification courses. Reputable operators make safety a huge priority and they will help you determine the best sites to suit your experience and comfort level. Divemasters can also be excellent island resources, with information on everything from secret snorkel spots to the best beach bars. See the individual island chapters for listings of recommended dive operators.

## Dive Tours

Several companies offer dive trips that include all hotel and diving costs. Live-aboards are big yachts outfitted for a group of divers. Passengers sleep and eat meals on board, and spend days doing multiple dives. Both land-based dive tours and live-aboards offer a unique way to become immersed in the sport and meet other divers (who tend, incidentally, to be a social lot). Rates for week-long, land-based tours in the high season range from US$600 to US$1200. Live-aboard trips range from around US$1400 to US$2200 for seven nights. Prices are based on double occupancy and do not include airfare.

### LAND-BASED TOURS

**PADI Travel Network** ( ☎ 800-729-7234; www.padi.com) The PADI organization runs dive package tours at destinations throughout the Caribbean.

**Scuba Voyages** ( ☎ 800-544-7631; www.scubavoyages.com) These trips go to Bonaire, Dominica, Saba, St Lucia and Tobago.

Don't forget your C-card! If you are a certified diver, you'll be required to show proof before a reputable dive operator will rent you equipment or take you out on a dive. Your PADI, NAUI or other certification card will do the trick.

**World Dive Adventures** ( ☎ 800-433-3483; www.worlddive.com) These trips usually include a week's worth of hotels, meals and two dives per day. Destinations include the Bahamas; Aruba, Bonaire and Curaçao; St Lucia; Cayman Islands; and Turks and Caicos.

### LIVE-ABOARDS

**Aggressor** ( ☎ 800-348-2628; www.aggressor.com) With a fleet of live-aboards plying several of the world's waters, Aggressor has a great reputation. The 18-passenger *Cayman Aggressor IV* tours the Caymans and the 20-passenger *Turks & Caicos Aggressor II* tours – you guessed it – the Turks and Caicos.

**Explorer Ventures** ( ☎ 800-322-3577; www.explorerventures.com) These live-aboards include the 18-passenger MV *Caribbean Explorer I*, which travels the Bahamas, and the 18-passenger MV *Caribbean Explorer II*, which cruises to Saba, St Kitts and Nevis, Sint Eustatius and St-Martin/Sint Maarten. The 20-passenger MV *Turks & Caicos Explorer II* heads to those islands.

**Peter Hughes Diving** ( ☎ 800-932-6237; www.peterhughes.com) This long-respected company has week-long live-aboard tours of Tobago on the 18-passenger *Wind Dancer*.

Coral reefs are an integral part of a marine ecosystem, supporting life up and down the food chain. Like elsewhere in the world, Caribbean reefs are at risk. For details on the threats, see p48.

## Internet Resources

**Complete Diving Guides** (www.caribdiveguide.com) Dive site profiles with excerpts from *The Complete Diving Guide* series.

**Lonely Planet** (www.lonelyplanet.com) Click on the Thorn Tree's Diving & Snorkeling forum to chat with other new and experienced divers.

**Scuba Diving** (www.scubadiving.com) The website of *Scuba Diving* magazine offers articles on all the Caribbean destinations, with links to dive operators. Also has an active forum.

**Skin Diver Online** (www.skin-diver.com) The website for *Skin Diver* magazine has links to hundreds of articles about diving in each region.

**Sport Diver** (www.sportdiver.com) *Sport Diver* magazine is the official publication of the Professional Association of Diving Instructors (PADI) and this website, a tremendous resource, is the online version.

## Marine Conservation Organizations

Around the world, coral reefs and oceans face unprecedented environmental pressures. This is particularly true in the Caribbean, where vast episodes of coral bleaching threaten everything from fishing and culture, to land ecology and tourism. The following groups promote responsible diving practices, publicize environmental marine threats and lobby for better policies:

**Caribbean Environment Programme** (www.cep.unep.org) A conglomerate of Caribbean legislative bodies working to protect the coastal environment and promote sustainable development.

---

### RESPONSIBLE DIVING

Please consider the following tips when diving and help preserve the ecology and beauty of reefs.

- Never use anchors on the reef and take care not to ground boats on coral.

- Avoid touching or standing on living marine organisms or dragging equipment across the reef. Polyps can be damaged by even the gentlest contact. If you must hold on to the reef, touch only exposed rock or dead coral.

- Be conscious of your fins. Even without contact, the surge from fin strokes near the reef can damage delicate organisms.

- Practice and maintain proper buoyancy control. Divers descending too fast and colliding with the reef can cause major damage.

- Resist the temptation to collect or buy corals or shells or to loot marine archaeological sites.

- Ensure that you take home all your garbage and any litter you find. Plastics in particular are a serious threat to marine life.

- Do not feed fish and minimize your disturbance of marine animals.

### GOLD-STAR MARINE PARKS

Diving and snorkeling help keep Caribbean tourism thriving, and many islands recognize the need to protect their underwater resources. In recent years several marine parks have been established to reduce human pressure on the reef systems. While some are effective, others fail due to meager resources, poor management or lack of enforcement. Several marine parks get gold stars for their success at preservation, education and continued foresight.

**Bonaire Marine Park** (www.bmp.org) A Unesco World Heritage site, Bonaire's marine park was established in 1979, making the island one of the early leaders in reef preservation. It continues to be at the forefront of research and education, most of which is funded by a 'nature' fee levied on users ($25/10 scuba divers/snorkelers).

**Saba Marine Park** (www.sabapark.org) Established in 1987, the park encircles the entire island and has 36 permanent mooring buoys. Every diver pays a fee of US$4 that contributes to park maintenance.

**Statia Marine Park** (www.statiapark.org) Many of Statia's reefs have developed on the remains of an extinct volcano and boast incredible biodiversity. Established in 1996, the park encircles the island and includes two reserves where fishing and anchoring are prohibited. The park's 42 permanent mooring buoys help protect the reefs. Divers pay a $3 user fee.

**CORAL: The Coral Reef Alliance** (www.coralreefalliance.org) This global nonprofit organization works with coastal communities on protecting coral through education, ecosystem management and sustainable tourism.

**Ocean Futures Society** (www.oceanfutures.org) Jean-Michel Cousteau's organization focuses on the connection between human impact and the health of the world's oceans.

**Project AWARE Foundation** (www.projectaware.org) Has a mandate to conserve underwater environments through education, advocacy and awareness.

**Reef Environmental Education Foundation** (REEF; www.reef.org) An organization of scientists, divers and community leaders, dedicated to promoting conservation through research and education.

## DIVING

The following dive sites were picked as 'dream dives' for several reasons: they represent the Caribbean's wide diving variety, they are easily accessible with local dive operators, and they all offer fantastic diving *and* snorkeling.

### Bloody Bay Wall, Little Cayman

Little Cayman has some of the finest Caribbean wall diving, where sheer cliffs drop so vertically they make you gasp in your regulator. Little Cayman's Bloody Bay Marine Park encompasses some 22 mooring sites spanning both Bloody and Jackson's Bays. The shallow tops of the walls – some just 20ft (6m) below the surface – are nearly as incredible as their depths. The snorkeling here can be fantastic. The drop-offs sink quickly along this stretch of the island's north shore that's more than a mile (1.6km) long. Coral and sponges of all types, colors and sizes cascade downward as you slowly descend along the wall. Most dives here range from 40ft to 100ft (12m to 30m) deep.

- Dive type: wall
- Shore/boat: boat
- More info: www.bloodybaywall.com

While it's safe to dive soon *after* flying, your last dive should be completed at least 12 hours (some experts say 24 hours) *before* a flight to minimize the risk of decompression sickness caused by residual nitrogen in the blood.

### Keyhole Pinnacles, St Lucia

You wonder sometimes if Picasso came along with his paintbrush to coat St Lucia's corals with splashes of vibrant color. One of the best sites to see this display is the Keyhole Pinnacles, four underwater sea mountains that mimic the drama of St Lucia's famed Pitons. Rising up from 1000ft (305m) below sea level to just below the surface, the pinnacles are coated in colorful hard and soft corals, sea sponges and delightful fans. Underwater photographers flock here to snap brilliantly vivid shots.

- Dive type: pinnacle
- Shore/boat: boat

## Klein Bonaire

Since 1979, Bonaire's entire perimeter has been a protected marine park and its excellent administration has paid off. Dive boats are required to use permanent moorings and popular dive sites are periodically closed to let the reefs recover. One of Bonaire's best dive areas is off relatively uninhabited Klein Bonaire, where the gently sloping reef is positively festooned with hard and soft corals, sponges, gorgonians and a dizzying array of tropical fish. Look for unusual marine life like a brown long-snout seahorse or a yellow frogfish. Popular sites include Carl's Hill Annex, which, like most of the sites, is perfect for divers of all levels.

- Dive type: reef
- Shore/boat: boat

## Little Tobago

Situated on the South American Continental Shelf between the Caribbean and Atlantic, Tobago gets massaged by the Guyana and the North Equatorial currents. Also injected with periodic pulses of nutrient-rich water from the Orinoco River, Tobago's waters teem with marine life. The variety of corals, sponges and ancient sea fans make Tobago a top destination. Heart-pulsing drift dives swish you past large pelagic fish. Some of the world's largest brain corals grow around Little Tobago island, where manta rays swoop by for regular visits.

- Dive type: drift
- Shore/boat: boat
- More info: www.tobagodiveexperience.com

## RMS *Rhone*, British Virgin Islands

On a sun-washed October morning in 1867 the captain of the RMS *Rhone* thought the hurricane season was over. Built just two years earlier, the *Rhone* was one of a new class of British steamships, 310ft (94m) long and 40ft (12m) abeam.

Around 11am, the sky grew leaden, and hurricane-force winds began to blow. The *Rhone* struggled to pass Salt Island, but the waves and wind drove her ashore. The ship's boiler exploded, and only 23 of the 147 passengers survived.

The stern with its propeller now lies in 20ft to 40ft (6m to 12m) of water. The forward half lies nearby and intact about 80ft (24m) under. Divers salvaged copper, cotton, liquor and US$20,000 worth of money and gold. The BVI National Parks Trust moved in to preserve the wreck in the 1970s, long after divers had picked it clean. Today, it is one of the Caribbean's best wreck dives, for snorkelers, and novice and experienced divers.

- Dive type: wreck
- Shore/boat: boat
- More info: www.scubabvi.com

## Saba Marine Park

The world's only self-supporting marine park offers a little something for everyone. Well out of the paths of storm or anchor damage, a collection

'the gently sloping reef is positively festooned with corals, sponges and a dizzying array of fish'

of pinnacles – including Third Encounter, Twilight Zone, Outer Limits and Shark Shoals – peak at about 80ft (24m) below, offering a deep but spectacular dive. Snorkelers can explore a variety of structures at Well's Bay and Torrens Point, where large boulders and swim-throughs sit just beneath the surface.

- Dive type: pinnacles and reef
- Shore/boat: boat
- More info: www.sabapark.org

## Salt Cay, Turks & Caicos

Expect spectacular diving throughout the Turks and Caicos, where excellent visibility, unspoiled reefs, abundant marine life and vertical walls conspire to transport divers to an underwater utopia. Mostly uninhabited, Salt Cay is just south of Grand Turk and its north-shore wall is pocked with crevasses and grooves, overhangs and swim-throughs. The fish-watching is excellent and you'll often see spotted eagle rays, giant tiger grouper, and triggerfish. In the winter you have a good chance of spotting migrating humpback whales traversing the Turks Island Passage, the waterway separating the Turks from the Caicos Islands. Whales start to appear in late December and stick around through March. Just 16 miles (26km) south of Salt Cay is the wreck of the HMS *Endymion*, an 18th-century British warship. Nine ship anchors lie exposed in shallow water, making it a good wreck for snorkelers to explore too.

- Dive type: wall
- Shore/boat: shore and boat

## Scotts Head, Soufriere Bay Marine Reserve, Dominica

The highlight of Dominica diving is undoubtedly Soufriere Bay on the southwestern tip of the island. Formed and defined by the submerged crater of an underwater volcano, the dive sites reflect the volcanic action that created them – deep walls, pinnacles, massive boulders, chasms and gullies offer some of the Caribbean's most dramatic diving. The east edge of the crater is the shoreline, making for accessible shore dives and snorkeling, and the south edge is around Scotts Head, where you'll find a sheer drop-off whose many overhangs shelter healthy schools of fish, like barracuda and Bermuda chub. Soufriere Pinnacles is another popular spot, where three separate pinnacles reach up to almost break the surface. The swim out to the site passes over submerged hot springs and gas vents where tiny fish play in the bubbles.

- Dive type: wall and pinnacle
- Shore/boat: shore and boat
- More info: www.natureislanddive.com

## Sint Eustatius

Hard-core divers will appreciate Sint Eustatius' focus on its underwater bounty, along with the sheer variety of its dive sites. The island's last volcanic eruption was 1600 years ago, but you can still see evidence of the hardened lava-flow on the seabed, providing deep trenches and fissures. Vestiges of 18th-century colonial Sint Eustatius are found beneath the sea, such as portions of quay wall that slipped into the sea, and old ballast stones, anchors, canons and ship remains have become vibrant coral reefs. A series of newly sunk wrecks add diving variety. The island's waters are protected by the Statia Marine Park.

- Dive type: reef and wreck
- Shore/boat: boat

Of the world's 375 species of shark, only 30 have ever attacked humans. Since 1580, only 18 shark attacks have been reported in the Caribbean Islands.

## St Vincent & the Grenadines

The 32 cays and islands that compose the Grenadines stretch out in a bracelet of tropical jewels between St Vincent and Grenada. Long known as a yachters' haven, the sparsely inhabited islands and pristine bays shelter thriving offshore reefs. You'll find steep walls decorated with black coral around St Vincent, giant schools of fish around Bequia, a coral wonderland around Canouan and pure bliss in the Tobago Cays. The five cays are palm-studded deserted islands surrounded by shallow reefs that are part of a protected marine sanctuary, and offer some of the most pristine reef diving in the Caribbean.

- Dive type: wall and reef
- Shore/boat: boat

## SNORKELING

'the islands that compose the Grenadines stretch out in a bracelet of tropical jewels'

Donning a mask and snorkel allows you to turn the beach into an underwater aquarium. There are numerous sites throughout the Caribbean that offer splendid coral gardens, often teeming with colorful tropical fish including many varieties of wrasse, damselfish, sergeant majors, rainbow-colored parrotfish, angelfish, ballooning puffer fish and octopus. The best snorkeling is usually along rocky outcrops or on shallow reefs.

Some travelers bring along their own mask, snorkel and fins, but if you prefer to travel light you can usually rent equipment (about US$10 per day) at dive shops or beachside water-sports shacks. Having your own equipment can be enormously liberating, letting you jump in the water wherever you want.

The following is a list of some of the region's top snorkeling sites. Some are popular; others are off the beaten track. All of the dives listed in this chapter are great snorkeling sites too.

- Anse Chastanet, St Lucia (p640)
- The Baths, Virgin Gorda, British Virgin Islands (p405)
- Buccoo Reef, Tobago (p761)
- Buck Island, St Croix, US Virgin Islands (p381)
- De Palm Island, Aruba (p785)
- Exuma Cays Land & Sea Park, Bahamas (p98)
- Shoal Bay West, Anguilla (p427)
- Stingray City, Grand Cayman (p199)
- Wreck of the *Jettias*, Antigua (p535)

# The Bahamas

Scattered like dabs of possibility on an adventurer's palette, the Bahamas are ready-made for exploration. Just ask Christopher Columbus, he bumped against these limestone landscapes in 1492 and changed the course of history. But adventure didn't end with the *Niña*, the *Pinta* and the *Santa Maria*. From pirates to blockade dodgers to rum smugglers, wily go-getters have converged and caroused on the country's 700 islands and 2400 cays for centuries.

So what's in it for travelers? There's sailing to Abaconian villages. Diving Androsian blue holes. Kayaking Exumian cays. Lounging on Eleutheran beaches. Pondering pirates in Nassau. Indeed, there's a Bahamian island to match most every water-and-sand-based compulsion. Each of them framed by a backdrop of gorgeous, mesmerizing blue.

But every adventure has irritations, and here indifferent service, high prices and hungry no-see-ums take the lead. Nassau and Paradise Island are the prime troublemakers. But if casinos, Aquaventure and duty-free shopping don't top your to-do list, consider dropping off the grid for a bit in the Out Islands. Prices remain high but there's more bang for your Bahamian buck, with friendlier service, fewer crowds and, well, the pesky no-see-ums haven't gotten the memo. But don't wait long. Change is in the air and the Out Islands are blipping onto the radar screens of mega-developers and land grabbers the world over.

For now loaf, paddle, dive and après-snorkel. Paint your own adventure, the palette awaits.

## FAST FACTS

- **Area** Over 700 islands spread in a 760-mile (1206km) arc that add up to some 5363 sq miles (13,890 sq km) of land
- **Capital** Nassau, New Providence
- **Country code** ☎ 242
- **Departure tax** US$15. Normally included in ticket prices.
- **Famous for** Spectacular diving and snorkeling, Sir Sidney Poitier, James Bond films
- **Language** Bahamian Standard English
- **Money** Bahamian dollar (B$$); B$$1= US$1 = €0.64 = UK£0.51
- **Official name** Independent Commonwealth of the Bahamas
- **People** Bahamians
- **Population** 307,000
- **Visa** North American, UK and most Western European travelers don't require a visa; other nationalities need to get one in advance; see p106

## HIGHLIGHTS

- **Fish Fry** (p86) Debate the win-win choice between lobster or snapper at the Wednesday night fish fry at Smith's Point on Grand Bahama
- **Eleuthera** (p92) Navigate hidden turns and bumpy roads to find that perfect secluded beach
- **Exumas** (p96) Kayak through a stunning array of blues while exploring scores of lonely cays
- **Miss Emily's Blue Bee Bar** (p92) Hear engaging tales of the infamous goombay smash and the overserved cay-hoppers who left photos on the walls at Miss Emily's Blue Bee Bar on Green Turtle Cay
- **Andros** (p100) Hurtle off the platform above Captain Bill's Blue Hole, praying that the people-eating Lusca doesn't really exist

## ITINERARIES

- **Three days** Explore Pirates of Nassau, the Pompey Museum and Providence Square in downtown Nassau, grab a *jitney* for beach bar cocktails, wander shark-filled Predator's Lagoon then snooze on Cabbage Beach.
- **One week** Add a Bahamas Ferry ride to Harbour Island for pink sand shores and boutique browsing or ferry to Andros for mind-blowing dives to the Tongue of the Ocean and mysterious hikes to hidden blue holes.
- **Two weeks** Add a trip to the Abacos for cay-hopping or to the Exumas for kayaking, kitesurfing and adventuring.

## CLIMATE & WHEN TO GO

The Bahamas enjoy around 320 sunny days a year; and daytime temperatures during winter (December to April) average 70ºF (21ºC) and a perfect 80ºF (26ºC) in summer. In general, the islands are balmy year-round, with cooling, near-constant trade winds blowing by day from the east.

The so-called rainy season extends from late May to November and humidity in the northern islands is relatively high year-round, but declines from northwest to southeast across the archipelago. Hurricane season is June to November.

The high season typically runs from mid-December to mid-April, when hotel prices

---

**HOW MUCH?**

- Jitney bus ride US$1
- Two-tank dive US$99
- Kalik bottle US$5
- Conchy Joe Hot Sauce US$4.40
- Mid-sized book on pirates US$25

---

are highest. Some hotels are booked solid around Christmas and Easter. The rest of the year, many hotels reduce their rates significantly. Some Out Island hotels close for the low season, but tourist accommodations are always available.

## HISTORY

The original inhabitants of the Bahamas were a tribe of Arawaks, the peaceful Lucayans, who arrived near the turn of the 9th century. Christopher Columbus arrived in 1492 and soon after the Spanish began shipping out the Lucayans as slaves.

Pirates such as Henry Jennings and 'Blackbeard' (Edward Teach), who terrorized his victims by wearing flaming fuses in his matted beard and hair, took over New Providence, establishing a pirates' paradise that in 1666 was lined with brothels and taverns for 'common cheats, thieves and lewd persons.' With the aid of Woodes Rogers, the Bahamas' first Royal Governor and a former privateer, the British finally established order and an administration answerable to the English crown in 1718. The Bahamas' new motto was *Expulsis Piratis – Restituta Commercia* (Pirates Expelled – Commerce Restored).

Following the American Revolution, Loyalist refugees – many quite rich or entrepreneurial – began arriving, giving new vigor to the city. These wealthy landowners lived well and kept slaves until the British Empire abolished the slave trade in 1807. During the American Civil War the islands were an exchange center for blockade runners transferring munitions and supplies for Southern cotton.

While Nassauvians illicitly supplied liquor to the US during Prohibition, Yankees flocked to Nassau and her new casino. When Fidel Castro then spun Cuba into Soviet orbit in 1961, the subsequent US embargo forced revelers to seek their pleasures elsewhere; Nassau became *the* new hot spot.

Tourism and finance bloomed together. The government promoted the nascent banking industry, encouraging British investors escaping onerous taxes.

This upturn in fortunes coincided with the evolution of party politics and festering ethnic tensions, as the white elite and a growing black middle class reaped profits from the boom. Middle-class blacks' aspirations for representation coalesced with the pent-up frustrations of their impoverished brothers, leading to the victory of the black-led Progressive Liberal party and leader Sir Linden Pindling in 1967. On July 10, 1973, the Bahamas officially became a new nation; the Independent Commonwealth of the Bahamas, ending 325 years of British rule.

In 1984 it was revealed that Colombian drug barons had corrupted the new Bahamian government at its highest levels and the country's drug-heavy reputation tarnished its image abroad. Tourism and financial investment declined, so the government belatedly launched a crackdown led by the US Drug Enforcement Agency (US DEA). In response, the electorate voted in the conservative, business-focused Free National Movement (FNM) in 1992.

Devastating hurricanes ravaged various islands between 1999 and 2007, wreaking havoc on tourism. Despite these storms, the tourism juggernaut continues and massive resorts on New Providence, Grand Bahama and several Out Islands are chugging toward completion. Debates rage over whether these enclaves – many of them isolated from the primary settlements – will be a long-term boon or bust. Pick up a local paper on any island, flip to the editorials and you'll read a passionate range of opinions.

## THE CULTURE

Contemporary Bahamian culture still revolves around family, church and the sea, but the proximity of North America and the arrival of cable TV has had a profound influence on contemporary life and material values.

In Nassau and Freeport most working people are employed in banking, tourism or government work and live a nine-to-five lifestyle. The maturation of the banking and finance industries has fostered the growth of a large professional class, many of whom have become extremely wealthy.

The citizens inhabiting the islands outside of New Providence and Grand Bahamas, called the Out Islands or Family Islands, are a bit more neighborly as well as more traditional. Thus the practice of obeah (a form of African-based ritual magic), bush medicine and folkloric songs and tales still infuse their daily lives. Though tourism is bringing change to the Out Islands, many still live simple lives centered around fishing, catching conch and lobster and raising corn, bananas and other crops.

## ARTS

The Bahamas rocks to the soul-riveting sounds of calypso, soca, reggae and its own distinctive music that echoes African rhythms and synthesizes Caribbean calypso, soca and English folk songs into its own goombay beat.

Goombay – the name comes from an African word for 'rhythm' – derives its melody from a guitar, piano or horn instrument accompanied by any combination of goatskin goombay drums, maracas, rhythm sticks, rattles, conch-shell horns, fifes, flutes and cowbells to add a kalik-kalik-kalik sound.

Rake'n'scrape is the Bahamas' down-home, working-class music, usually featuring a guitar, an accordion, shakers made from the pods of poinciana trees and other makeshift instruments, such as a saw played with a screwdriver.

## ENVIRONMENT
### The Land

The Bahamian islands are strewn in a linear fashion from northwest to southeast. Several of them – Great Abaco, Eleuthera, Long Island and Andros – are more than 100 miles (160km) in length. Few, however, are more than a few miles wide. All are low lying, and the highest point in the Bahamas – Mt Alvernia on Cat Island – is only 206ft (62m) above sea level.

Virtually the entire length of these shores is lined by white or pinkish sand beaches – about 2200 miles (3540km) in all – shelving into turquoise shallows. The interiors are generally marked by scrub-filled forests, and on some of the more remote islands, the plants found here are still used in bush medicine remedies.

The islands are pocked by blue holes – water-filled circular pits that open to underground and submarine caves and descend as far as 600ft (182m).

# THE BAHAMAS

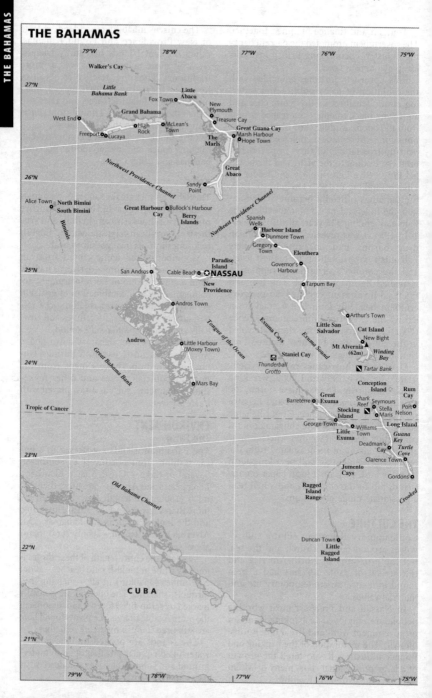

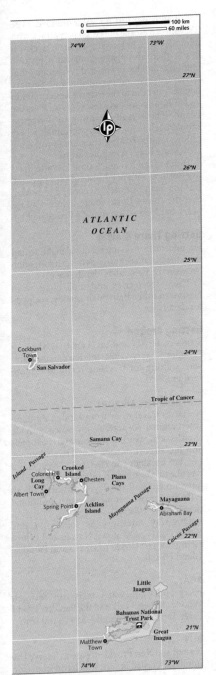

## Wildlife

The islands are a bird-watcher's paradise, with about 300 recorded species of birds. Only a few are endemic, including the Bahama swallow, the endangered Bahama parrot, and the Bahama woodstar hummingbird, a pugnacious bird weighing less than a US nickel. The West Indian (Caribbean) flamingo – the national bird – inhabits Crooked Island, Long Cay and the sanctuary of Great Iguana.

Iguanas inhabit some outlying isles and cays, and are protected. The archipelago's largest native land animal, they can reach 4ft (1.2m) in length.

The region's marine life is as varied as its islands and coral reefs. Depending on who you believe, the Bahamas has between 900 sq miles and 2700 sq miles (2330 sq km and 6992 sq km) of coral reef; it also has countless species of fish, such as bonito, stingrays, sharks, kingfish, jewelfish and deep-blue Creole wrasse.

Humpback whales pass through the waters windward of the Bahamas and blue whales are also frequently sighted.

## Environmental Issues

The Bahamas National Trust maintains 22 national parks and reserves, including large sections of the barrier reef, but outside of the national park system, inappropriate development, pollution and overexploitation increasingly threaten wildlife and marine resources. Although the Bahamas was the first Caribbean nation to outlaw long-line fishing, the islands' stocks of grouper, spiny lobster, and conch all face the consequences of overfishing. Commercial poaching, mostly by non-Bahamians, has also been a significant problem. In the late 1970s the problem stirred several island communities to establish their own nongovernmental reserves.

Today, local groups are leading the eco-charge. The Abacos' **Friends of the Environment** (www.friendsoftheenvironment.org) organizes communitywide projects and passes the ecomessage along in the schools. In Eleuthera, the **Eleuthera School** (www.islandschool.org) is earning kudos as an environmental learning center, drawing US high-schoolers, as well as adult 'students' looking to become environmentally engaged global citizens.

## FOOD & DRINK

Conch fritter? Conch ball? Conch salad? Cracked conch? Pronounced 'conk,' this

THE BAHAMAS

tough snail-like mollusk is a culinary celebrity. Served pounded, marinated, grilled, diced, 'soused' (stewed) and 'cracked' (battered and deep-fried), it's the Britney Spears of the Bahamas – try as you might, you just can't get away from its ubiquitous presence. And you're not entirely sure you want to. But there's a sad road ahead if the addiction isn't managed. Conch, as well as grouper, are being loved to death. Grouper populations are commercially extinct in much of the Caribbean and the Queen conch has been listed as endangered by the Convention on the Trade of Endangered Species of Flora and Fauna (CITES).

So what are the alternatives? Most food is imported, and vegetarian and vegan visitors will have a tough time of it. There are few fruit and vegetables, and conch, meat, fish, chicken and carbohydrates rule (much of the food is fried or baked). Colonial cultural hangovers include steak and kidney, bangers and mash and shepherd's pie, while main courses are served with coleslaw, slices of fried plantain, baked macaroni cheese and the ever-popular peas'n'rice.

The Bahamian beer Kalik is the perfect complement to any beach-bar sunset. If tropical cocktails are more your speed, the Green Turtle–originated goombay smash is a lethally easy-to-drink fruit juice and rum cocktail popular through the islands.

Most restaurants in the Bahamas now include an automatic 15% gratuity on the bill; many claim this addition has contributed to the country's notoriously bad restaurant service.

# NEW PROVIDENCE

**pop 212,500**

What New Providence lacks in size, it more than makes up for in energy, attitude and devil-may-care spirit. In fact, this 21 mile (33km) long powerhouse of an island is a perfect fit for the Type A tourist with money to burn. Plummet down a 50ft waterslide, puff on a hand-rolled stogie, place your bets on a high-stakes hand and party like a pirate into the wee hours – it's all there for the grabbing. Even rejuvenation is high-energy, with Paradise Island and Cable Beach boasting some of the liveliest beaches around. But who'd expect less on an island 007 calls home?

But all is not lost for value-minded Type B's, who can escape the go-go party track with minimal effort. In Nassau, just a few blocks off Bay St, there are engaging museums, historic buildings and locally owned restaurants that are crowd-free and personality-full. Scenery hounds can head to the island's western shores and hilltops as well as a few spots on Paradise Island. Those really wanting to disappear should beeline for the ferry terminals where sailing jaunts, fishing trips and snorkeling cruises are only an impulse away.

Don't spend too much time in contemplative isolation – it's not the island's strong point. Just ask Sean Connery. According to rumor, even he rouses from stodgy Lyford Cay for beach bar karaoke on the odd Friday night.

## Getting There & Away

For information on international flights to and from the Bahamas, as well as travel information between the Bahamian islands, see p106.

There are ferries and mail boats from Nassau to other Bahamian islands; see p108 for details.

## Getting Around

Scooters, ferries and taxis are parked along Woodes Rogers Walk, the harborside gateway, waiting for travelers ready to explore further afield.

### TO/FROM THE AIRPORT

No buses travel to or from Linden Pindling International Airport. A few hotels provide shuttles, and taxis line the forecourts of hotels and the airport outside the arrivals lounge. For **taxi bookings** ( ☎ 242-323-5111/4555), call a day ahead. Destination rates are fixed by the government and displayed on the wall; all rates are for two people and each additional person costs US$3.

One-way rates are as follows: Cable Beach US$15, downtown Nassau and Prince George Wharf US$22 to US$23 and Paradise Island US$30.

### BOAT

Ferry boats and water taxis run between Woodes Rogers Walk and the Paradise Island Ferry Terminal for about US$6 round trip.

### BUS

Nassau and New Providence are well served by minibuses, called *jitneys*, which run from 6am

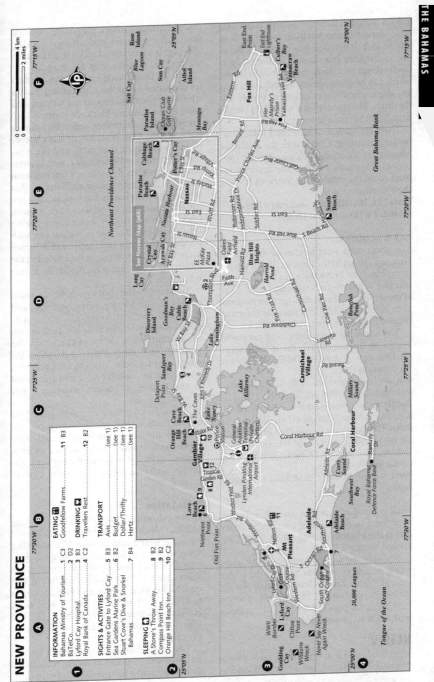

# NEW PROVIDENCE

**INFORMATION**
| Bahamas Ministry of Tourism | 1 C3 |
| BaTelCo | 2 D2 |
| Lyford Cay Hospital | 3 B3 |
| Royal Bank of Canada | 4 C2 |

**SIGHTS & ACTIVITIES**
| Entrance Gate to Lyford Cay | 5 B3 |
| Sea Gardens Marine Park | 6 B2 |
| Stuart Cove's Dive & Snorkel Bahamas | 7 B4 |

**SLEEPING**
| A Stone's Throw Away | 8 B2 |
| Compass Point Inn | 9 B2 |
| Orange Hill Beach Inn | 10 C2 |

**EATING**
| Goodfellow Farms | 11 B3 |

**DRINKING**
| Travellers Rest | 12 B2 |

**TRANSPORT**
| Avis | (see 1) |
| Budget | (see 1) |
| Dollar/Thrifty | (see 1) |
| Hertz | (see 1) |

See Nassau Map (p68)

to 8pm, although there are no fixed schedules. Buses depart downtown from Frederick St at Bay St and designated bus stops. No buses run to Paradise Island, only to the bridges. Destinations are clearly marked on the buses, which can be waved down. To request a stop anywhere when you're onboard, simply ask the driver. The standard bus fare is US$1 (children US$0.50) paid to the driver.

There are numerous buses and routes, but no central listing. Check with the Bahamas Ministry of Tourism Welcome Centre (opposite) for specifics, look at the destinations marked on the front of the *jitney*, or try one these common routes:

**Buses 10 & 10A** Cable Beach, Sandy Point & Lyford Cay
**Buses 1, 7 & 7A** Paradise Island Bridges

### CAR & SCOOTER

You don't need a car to explore downtown Nassau or to get to the beaches. If you intend to explore New Providence, it's worth saving taxi fare to and from Nassau by hiring a car at the airport. Collision damage waiver insurance costs about US$15 a day. For information on road rules, see p109.

The following companies have car-rental booths at the airport (Dollar is the cheapest, costing from around US$55 per 24 hours for economy):

**Avis** Cable Beach – Cumberland St ( ☎ 242-322-2889); Nassau International Airport (Map p65; ☎ 242-377-7121)
**Budget** Nassau International Airport (Map p65; ☎ 242-377-7405); Downtown Nassau ( ☎ 242-322-3321)
**Dollar/Thrifty** Nassau International Airport (Map p65; ☎ 242-377-8300); Cable Beach ( ☎ 242-677-6000; Sheraton); Nassau (Map p71; ☎ 242-325-3716; British Colonial Hilton Nassau);
**Hertz** (Map p65; ☎ 242-377-8684; Nassau International Airport)

Local companies may rent more cheaply. Ask your hotel to recommend a company or try **Orange Creek Rentals** (Map p68; ☎ 242-323-4967, 800-891-7655; West Bay St, Nassau).

Scooters are widely available and can be found outside most major hotels or the Prince George Wharf. **Knowles Scooter Rentals** (Map p71; ☎ 242-322-3415; Festival Pl, Nassau) rents scooters for US$50/day plus $15 for gas and insurance with a $20 returnable deposit.

## NASSAU

Who needs Red Bull when there's downtown Nassau? This cacophonous blur of bouncing *jitneys*, hustling cabbies, bargaining vendors, trash-talking pirates and elbow-knocking shoppers is a guaranteed pick-me up for even the sleepiest of cruise-ship day-trippers.

And it's been luring high-energy hustlers for centuries. From the 17th-century pirates who blew their doubloons on women and wine to the dashing blockade runners who smuggled cargo from the Confederacy during the American Civil War, the city has a history of accommodating the young and the reckless. The trend continues today, with bankers dodging between downtown's international banks as they manipulate millions on this offshore banking haven. But Nassau's not just for those wanting to earn or burn a quick buck. Banished royalty and camera-fleeing celebs have found refuge in Nassau too, with the disgraced Duke and Duchess of Windsor keeping tongues wagging in the 1940s and the ultimately tragic Anna Nicole Smith hiding out here in 2006.

Today, duty-free shops jostle for attention on Bay St with jewelry, coins, perfumes and rum cakes. Just east, historic Georgian-style government buildings glow like pink cotton candy confections. West of the wharf, the informative Pompey Museum describes the slaves' journey from Africa to the Caribbean while faux buccaneers set a rowdier mood at the Pirates of Nassau museum a few steps south.

Nassau has a grittier vibe than you might expect from a cruise-ship destination, but don't be put off by the initial hustle. Slow down, look around, then embrace its unabashed verve – it might be the perfect high-energy antidote to your lingering case of cabin fever.

## Orientation

Historic downtown Nassau is 10 blocks long and four blocks wide and faces north toward Paradise Island and Nassau Harbour. The town rises south to Prospect Ridge, a steep limestone scarp that parallels the entire north shore about 0.5 miles (800m) inland. A second, higher ridge – Blue Hill Heights – rises to 120ft (36m) and runs east to west along Nassau's southern border, 3 miles (4.8km) inland. The major residential areas lie between the ridges.

The main thoroughfare through town is Bay St, which runs east to the Paradise Island Bridge; beyond it follows the windward shore known as Eastern Rd. West of downtown, Bay St becomes West Bay St, which runs west to Cable Beach, past Lyford Cay and eventually joins Eastern Rd to complete an island loop.

Paradise Island is 4 miles (6km) long and 0.5 miles (800m) wide. Two road bridges (one to enter and the other to exit the island) link Paradise Island to New Providence. Both bridges have pedestrian walkways.

### MAPS
The free *Bahamas Trailblazer* foldout map for Nassau, Cable Beach and Paradise Island is a handy supplement to the maps in this guide. It includes emergency numbers, traffic rules and tourism-related coupons. Look for it in hotel lobbies.

## Information
### BOOKSHOPS
**Island Book Shop** (Map p71; ☎ 242-322-1011; Bay St, 2nd fl; ⏰ 9am-5:30pm Mon, 9am-6pm Tue, Fri & Sat, 9am-5pm Wed & Thu, 9am-3pm Sun) Magazines, current fiction and books on Bahamian travel and history.

### EMERGENCY
**Ambulance** ( ☎ 911, 919, 242-322-2881)
**Fire** ( ☎ 911, 919, 242-302-8404)
**Med-Evac** ( ☎ 242-322-2881)
**Police** ( ☎ 911, 919, 242-322-4444)
**Red Cross** ( ☎ 242-323-7370)

### INTERNET ACCESS
Expect to pay US$5 to US$10 per hour for internet services.
**Cyber Café** (Map p71; ☎ 242-322-3206; Prince George Plaza; ⏰ 9am-6pm Mon-Sat, until 4pm Sun)
**Internet Works** (Map p71; ☎ 242-323-1000; West Bay Hotel, West Bay St, Nassau; ⏰ 8am-9:30pm)
**Nassau Public Library & Museum** (Map p71; ☎ 242-322-4907; Shirley St; admission free; ⏰ 10am-8pm Mon-Thu, 10am-5pm Fri, 10am-2pm Sat)

### MEDICAL SERVICES
Pharmacies are located in all shopping malls, but keep mainly standard hours.
**Doctors Hospital** (Map p68; ☎ 242-322-8411, 242-302-4600; www.doctorshosp.com; cnr Shirley St & Collins Ave) Privately owned full-service hospital, provides emergency services and acute care.
**Princess Margaret Hospital** (Map p68; ☎ 242-322-2861/2/3/4; cnr Elizabeth Ave & Sands Rd) The main facility is this government-run, full-service hospital providing emergency services and acute care.

### MONEY
Banks cluster around Rawson Sq and Bay St. ATMs dispensing US and Bahamian dollars are found throughout Nassau and at banks like the Royal Bank of Canada (Map p71) and Scotiabank (Map p71).

### POST
**DHL Worldwide Express** (Map p68; ☎ 242-394-4040; Island Traders Bldg, East Bay St, Nassau)
**FedEx** (Map p71; ☎ 242-323-7611; www.fedex.com; Frederick St inside Norfolk House, Nassau)
**Main post office** (Map p71; ☎ 242-322-3025; cnr E Hill & Parliament Sts, Nassau; ⏰ 8:30am-5pm Mon-Fri)

### TELEPHONE
For telephone information and the services available in Nassau and New Providence, see p105.
**BaTelCo** East St (Map p71; ☎ 242-325-5661; ⏰ 7am-10pm); Festival Place (Map p71; ☎ 242-322-9001/2); John F Kennedy Dr (Map p65; ☎ 242-302-7000) All three locations have public phones.

### TOURIST INFORMATION
The Bahamas Ministry of Tourism is a government department with offices in Nassau and across the Bahamian islands (see p106). Information at its Nassau offices is surprisingly limited. Your best bet is to access the official Bahamas website and others listed under Internet Resources on p104. Tourist centers in Nassau can be located as follows:
**Bahamas Ministry of Tourism** (www.bahamas .com) Downtown (Map p71; ☎ 242-302-2000; George St; ⏰ 9am-5pm Mon-Fri); Nassau International Airport (Map p65; ☎ 242-377-6806; Airport Arrivals Terminal); Welcome Centre (Map p71; ☎ 242-323-3182/3; Festival Pl; ⏰ 9am-5pm Mon-Fri, 9am-7pm Sat & Sun) The Welcome Centre branch may stay open later on weekdays depending on cruise-ships schedules.

## Dangers & Annoyances
Crime was a hot topic in 2007. Local papers kept a close tally on the country's record high murder rate, which reached 79 by year's end. 60 of these murders occurred on New Providence. Although most criminal activity occurred in the 'Over-the-Hill' neighborhood outside of tourist-filled downtown, travelers should still take reasonable precautions during the day and extra care at night, as there has been recent spillover to the more touristed areas.

Watch for scams by taxi drivers. Rates are regulated and posted at the larger hotels, but

THE BAHAMAS

# NASSAU

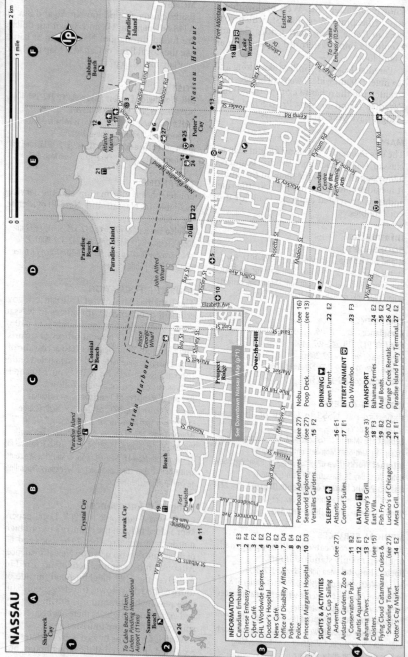

**INFORMATION**
Canadian Embassy....................1 E3
Chinese Embassy.......................2 F4
Cyber Café.................................3 F2
DHL Worldwide Express............4 E2
Doctor's Hospital........................5 D2
News Café.................................6 E2
Office of Disability Affairs............7 D4
Police.........................................8 E4
Police.........................................9 E2
Princess Margaret Hospital........10 D3

**SIGHTS & ACTIVITIES**
America's Cup Sailing
   Adventure.........................(see 27)
Ardastra Gardens, Zoo &
   Conservation Park................11 B2
Atlantis Aquariums...................12 E1
Bahama Divers..........................13 F2
Cloisters..............................(see 15)
Flying Cloud Catamaran Cruises &
   Snorkeling Tours................(see 27)
Potter's Cay Market.................14 E2
Powerboat Adventures............(see 27)
Seaworld Explorer...................(see 27)
Versailles Gardens....................15 F2

**SLEEPING** 🛏
Atlantis..................................16 E1
Comfort Suites.........................17 E1

**EATING** 🍴
Anthony's Grill.....................(see 3)
East Villa..................................18 F3
Fish Fry....................................19 B2
Luciano's of Chicago................20 D2
Mesa Grill................................21 E1
Nobu....................................(see 16)
Poop Deck................................22 E2

**DRINKING** 🍸
Green Parrot.............................23 F3

**ENTERTAINMENT** 🎭
Club Waterloo...........................24 E2

**TRANSPORT**
Bahamas Ferries........................25 E2
Mail Boats................................26 A2
Orange Creek Rentals................27 E2
Paradise Island Ferry Terminal....27 E2

To Cable Beach (1km);
Linden Pindling International
Airport (11km)

Shipwreck Cay

Saunders Beach

Crystal Cay

Arawak Cay

Fort Charlotte

Paradise Beach

Colonial Beach

Paradise Island Lighthouse

*Nassau Harbour*

Prince George Wharf

John Alfred Wharf

Prospect Ridge

See Downtown Nassau Map (p71)

**Over-the-Hill**

Cabbage Beach

Paradise Island

Atlantis Marina

Casino

Potter's Cay

*Nassau Harbour*

Fort Montagu

Lake Waterloo

To Chinese
Embassy (0.5ml)

Dundas Centre
for the Performing
Arts

the occasional driver will try to overcharge you. Avoid unlicensed drivers offering to give you a lift. All licensed taxi drivers will have a government ID badge.

## Sights
### DOWNTOWN NASSAU & BAY STREET
For those stepping off a quiet cruise-ship, Bay St may seem to teeter on the verge of absolute chaos. Scooters, trucks and *jitneys* hurtle through the center of town on this narrow artery, dodging trongs of tourists looking for duty-free deals. But there's more to downtown than liquor stores and T-shirt shops.

Don't even try to ignore the pirate pacing outside the **Pirates of Nassau** (Map p71; ☎ 242-356-3759; www.pirates-of-nassau.com; King St; adult/child US$12.50/6; ☑ 9am-6pm Mon-Fri, 9am-12:30pm Sat) museum. Like any seafaring ruffian worth his parrot and peg-leg, he had you in his sights the moment you turned the corner. But that's okay – with its partial recreation of a 130ft-long sailing ship, animatronic pirates and accessible exhibits on everything from marooning to pirate hall-of-famers, this museum provides the right mix of entertainment and history for kids, parents and students of piratology. Great gift shop, Plunder, next door.

It may be blasphemous to mention in this piratical context, but a dashing statue of pirate menace **Woodes Rogers** stands guard just across the street.

Named after a Bahamian slave who led an unsuccessful rebellion, the spare but moving **Pompey Museum** (Map p71; ☎ 242-356-0495; Vendue House; adult/child/senior US$3/1/2; ☑ 9:30am-4:30pm Mon-Wed, Fri & Sat, 9:30am-1pm Thu) traces the harrowing 'Middle Passage' slave voyages from Africa to the Caribbean and Americas. Stark exhibits – a 45lb ball-and-chain, a branding iron and slave collars – reinforce the horrors inflicted on millions of Africans between the 1500s and 1860s. The building is located on a former slave auction site.

A bustling warren of stalls at the corner of Bay and George Sts, **Straw Market** (Map p71) is worth a mention, but just barely. A maddening array of knock-off purses and cheap tee's obscure too few straw products. And even if you do find them, it's not always clear they're locally made. The decline of the market has been the subject of sincere hand-wringing in Bahamian newspapers but at press time their efforts appear to have made little difference.

For Bahamian-made products and straw goods, stay in Festival Place at the wharf.

**Parliament Square** (Map p71) is an oasis of gardens and government buildings that's seemingly unchanged from the 1800s. The pink-and-white Georgian buildings house the Leader of the Opposition (on the left), the House of Assembly (right) and the Senate (facing Bay St). **Queen Victoria's statue** (1905), perched in front of the Senate, is another reminder of the Bahamas' allegiance to the Crown.

A few yards south is the small **Garden of Remembrance** with a cenotaph honoring Bahamian soldiers killed in the two world wars.

For chills with your historical thrills, stop by the **Nassau Public Library & Museum** (Map p71; ☎ 242-322-4907; admission free; ☑ 10am-8pm Mon-Thu, 10am-5pm Fri, 10am-2pm Sat), the oldest government building downtown. This pink octagon, built in 1797, served as a jail in the 1800s but its cells are now crammed with books and dusty periodicals. There's a jumble of haphazardly marked artifacts – jars of corn, boxes of shells and a big animal skull – that presumably constitute the museum. Ask the librarian for the key to the tiny but creepy dungeon underneath the building. The dank walls bear scratches carved on their surface – a somber marking of days by prisoners long dead?

### WEST & EAST HILL STREETS
The Georgian **Government House** (1737; Map p71), residence to the Bahamas' Governor-General, sits atop Hill St like a pink candied topping. Below, the **statue of Christopher Columbus** (Map p71) has maintained a jaunty pose on the steps overlooking Duke St since 1830. Come here for the changing of the guard on alternate Saturdays at 10am. Call 242-322-1875 for specific dates.

Cigar aficionados and those who put up with them will enjoy the **Graycliff Cigar Co** (Map p71; ☎ 242-322-2795; West Hill St, Nassau; admission free; ☑ 9am-5pm Mon-Fri) just west of the Graycliff Hotel. At this tiny stogie factory visitors can watch a dozen Cubans roll pounded sheets of aromatic tobacco, supervised by a former personal roller for Fidel Castro.

### EAST & WEST OF DOWNTOWN
Hardscrabble **Potter's Cay market** (Map p68) lurks beneath the Paradise Island Exit Bridge. Locals gather here for fresh-off-the-boat seafood. For a cheap meal, stroll the wooden

stalls and see what strikes your fancy. It's a bit dodgy at night, but patrol cars cruise through regularly. The offices and docks for Bahamas Ferries and mail boats are just northwest and northeast of the market respectively. From downtown, grab eastbound buses labeled PI Bridge.

The conservation-minded **Ardastra Gardens & Zoo** (Map p68; ☎ 242-323-5806; www.ardastra.com; Chippingham Rd, Nassau; adult/child/under 4yr US$15/7.50/free; ⏰ 9am-5pm) houses nearly 300 mammals, birds and reptiles. Watch your step – many of the birds freely wander the premises. The zoo's highlight is the small regiment of marching West Indian flamingos, who strut their stuff at 10:30am, 2:10pm and 4:10pm daily.

**Cable Beach** (Map p65) is a curved stretch of white beach and sparkling turquoise sea west of downtown. Named for the undersea telegraphic cable that came ashore here in 1892, Cable Beach has for years been populated with nondescript resorts. Currently, these resorts and the casino are in the midst of a massive redevelopment project overseen by Baha Mar Resorts. Harrah's Entertainment made headlines in 2008 when it announced its intent to withdraw as a partner in the enterprise, raising concerns about the projects future development. Although the major hotels are open, by 2010 many of them will have been torn down or completely revamped as Starwood properties fitting within the theme and scheme of the new 1000-acre Vegas-style megaresort.

## Activities
### DIVING & SNORKELING
There's superb diving close to shore, including fantastic shallow reef, wall and wreck dives. The most noted sites lie off the southwest coast between Coral Harbour and Lyford Cay. Equipment can be rented from the operators listed below.

**Stuart Cove's Dive & Snorkel Bahamas** (Map p65; ☎ 242-362-4171, 800-879-9832; www.stuartcove.com; PO Box CB-13137, Nassau) offers Professional Association of Diving Instructors (PADI) certification (US$950, less if more than one person) as well as a bone-rattling shark wall and shark-feeding dive (US$145); a two-tank dive trip (US$99); and wall-flying – a two-tank underwater scooter adventure (US$145). Snorkeling trips are also available (adult/child US$55/30).

**Bahama Divers** (Map p68; ☎ 242-393-6054, 800-398-3483; www.bahamadivers.com; PO Box 5004, Nassau) offers

the Lost Blue Hole dive (famous for its sharks and schools of stingrays) and wrecks. A three-hour learn-to-dive course can be taken prior to PADI certification courses (US$449). A two-tank morning dive costs US$99, the two-tank blue hole dive is US$119 and half-day snorkeling trips are US$45.

Both companies include complimentary hotel pick-up and return.

### BOAT TRIPS
There's a jaunt for every type of adventurer in New Providence. Most vessels depart from the Woodes Rogers Walk area or the Paradise Island Ferry Terminal between the PI bridges.

**America's Cup Sailing Adventure** (Map p65; ☎ 242-363-1552; www.sailnassau.com; Paradise Island Ferry Terminal; adult/child US$95/65) Feel the rush of an America's Cup Race as a crew member on one of two 76ft sailboats that competed in the 1992 event. Since the two boats race, this trip is perfect for competitive families or big groups. Wannabe yachtsmen can take the helm or trim the sails while determined nonsailors are allowed to sit back and enjoy the ride.

**Bahamas Ferries** (Map p68; ☎ 242-323-2166; www.bahamasferries.com) offers a 'Harbour Island Day Away' excursion to shimmering Harbour Island just off the coast of northern Eleuthera. It departs from Potter's Cay, takes two hours each way and includes a golf cart, an island tour and choice of lunch at one of several restaurants (adult/child US$174/114).

---

#### PIRATE HUNTING
'It was a short life, but a merry one,' said Captain Bart Roberts about life as a wayfaring pirate. In downtown Nassau you can easily imagine pirates striding the gritty, narrow streets, looking for two-bit grog and a one-night girlfriend after a long few months at sea. Spend the night at gothic **Graycliff** (see p73), the hillside former home of Captain Graysmith, who plundered ships off the Spanish Main. Learn about marooning, parrots and peg-legs at the **Pirates of Nassau** (p69) then walk to the British Colonial Hilton to gaze upon the statue of pirate hunter **Woodes Rogers** (p69), who restored order to the city in 1718 and inspired the motto 'Expulsis Piratis, Commercia Restituta.'

# DOWNTOWN NASSAU

| | | 0 | 500 m |
| | | 0 | 0.3 miles |

### A    B    C    D

**INFORMATION**
Bahamas Ministry of Tourism............1  B3
Bahamas Ministry of Tourism.....(see 15)
BaTelCo............................................2  D4
BaTelCo......................................(see 15)
British Colonial Hilton Nassau..........3  B3
Cyber Café.......................................4  C3
FedEx..............................................5  C4
Internet Works.................................6  A3
Island Book Shop.............................7  C3
Main Post Office..............................8  C4
Royal Bank of Canada......................9  C3
Royal Bank of Canada....................10  C4
Scotiabank.....................................11  B3
Scotiabank (24-Hour ATM).............12  C3
UK Embassy....................................13  D4
US Embassy & Consulate................14  B4
Welcome Centre.............................15  C3

**SIGHTS & ACTIVITIES**
Garden of Remembrance................16  D4
Government House..........................17  B4
Graycliff Cigar Co.....................(see 35)
Nassau Public Library & Museum.....18  D4

Parliament Square..........................19  D4
Pirates of Nassau...........................20  B4
Pompey Museum............................21  C3
Queen Victoria's Statue..................22  D3
Seaworld Explorer..........................23  C3
Statue of Christopher Columbus.....24  B4
Statue of Woodes Rogers..........(see 3)
Straw Market.................................25  B3

**SLEEPING**
El Greco.........................................26  A3
Grand Central Hotel.......................27  C4
Graycliff Hotel & Restaurant...........28  B4
Mignon Guest House......................29  C4
Nassau Palm Resort........................30  A3
Quality Inn.....................................31  A3

**EATING**
Athena Café...................................32  C3
Café Matisse..................................33  D4
Café Skan's....................................34  C3
Humidor Churrascaria.....................35  B4
Ichiban Restaurant.........................36  A3
Imperial Cafeteria & Take-Away.....37  B4

Senor Frog's...................................38  B3
Taj Mahal.......................................39  C4

**ENTERTAINMENT**
Bambu...........................................40  C3
Palm Court................................(see 3)

**SHOPPING**
Coin of the Realm..........................41  C4
Colombian Emeralds.......................42  C3
Pasion Tea & Coffee
  Company...............................(see 15)
Perfume Shop & Beauty Spot..........43  C3
Plunder....................................(see 20)
Solomon's Mines............................44  C3
Tortuga Rum Cake..........................45  C3

**TRANSPORT**
Buses to Cable Beach & West..........46  C4
Buses to Paradise Island Bridge
  & East.........................................47  C3
Dollar/Thrifty...........................(see 3)
Knowles Scooter Rentals.................48  C3
Water Taxi to Paradise Island..........49  C3

**Flying Cloud Catamaran Cruises & Snorkeling Tours** (Map p68; ☎ 242-363-4430; www.flyingcloud .info; Paradise Island Ferry Terminal) offers half-day adventures that include a catamaran cruise, beach time and a bit of snorkeling (adult/child US$60/30). Sunday trips are five hours and include reef snorkeling and a BBQ on low-key Rose Island (adult/child US$75/37.50).

**Powerboat Adventures** (Map p68; ☎ 242-363-1466; www.powerboatadventures.com; Paradise Island Ferry Terminal) A custom-built powerboat roars 38 miles to the northern Exuma Cays on this high-octane day trip. Feed hungry stingrays, snorkel isolated reefs and mingle with iguanas of unusual size. All-you-can-eat lunch buffet and open bar are included (adult/child US$190/120).

**Seaworld Explorer** (Map p68; ☎ 242-356-2548; Paradise Island Ferry Terminal, Woodes Rogers Walk, Nassau; adult/child US$45/25), a 45-passenger semisubmarine with a window-lined hull, has a great 90-minute excursion above the fish-filled coral reefs of the Sea Gardens Marine Park off the north shore of Paradise Island.

### KITESURFING
Cross-Shore runs kitesurfing classes in southern New Providence; see p93 for details.

### NATURE TOURS
For guided birding tours, nature walks or off-road bikes trips, book a tour with **Bahamas Outdoors** ( ☎ 242-457-0329; www.bahamasoutdoors.com). For two or more, birding and nature trips cost $59 each and biking tours cost $99 each.

### FISHING
Nassau is a launch pad for fishing, with sites just 20 minutes away. Game species include blue marlin, sailfish, yellowfin tuna, mahi mahi and wahoo. Charters can be arranged at most major hotels or by calling a charter company. The following recommended companies charge two to six people about US$600/1200 per half/full day:

**Born Free Charter Service** ( ☎ 242-393-4144; www.bornfreefishing.com)

**Brown's Charter** ( ☎ 242-324-2061; www.browns charter.com)

**Chubasco Charters** ( ☎ 242-324-3474; www.chubasco charters.com)

## Festivals & Events
For information on Boxing Day's brilliant Junkanoo, see opposite. Otherwise contact the Bahamas Ministry of Tourism (p67) for events and dates or check www.bahamas.gov.bs. Following are two fun local events:

**Emancipation Day** Held on the first Monday of August, this holiday celebrates the abolition of slavery. Fox Hill features a very early morning 'Junkanoo Rush' followed by bands, dancing and shows.

**Police Band Annual Beat Retreat** In December, the Royal Bahamas Police Force Band celebrates the season with lively drill performances in Rawson Square.

## Sleeping
High prices, indifferent service and sad-sack furnishings seem to be the norm in Nassau. Ask about specials and remember that low-season (April to mid-December) rates drop between 25% to 60%. Surcharges and taxes can be hefty; quoted rates here do not include these additional charges, so inquire when making your reservation.

### DOWNTOWN NASSAU
The hotels listed here tend to be cheaper than those in Cable Beach and Paradise Island.

#### Budget
**Mignon Guest House** (Map p71; ☎ 242-322-4771; 12 Market St, PO Box N-786; s/d US$50/65; ✄ ) Six small but pleasant rooms with TV have been kept in top-notch shape for several decades by a friendly Greek couple. Bathrooms, microwave and fridge are shared, usually by an intriguing international crowd. Security is good and rates are inclusive. Don't be put off by initial language barriers or rigid house rules. This is a great bargain in the heart of downtown.

**Grand Central Hotel** (Map p71; ☎ 242-322-8356-8; www.grand-central-hotel.com; Bay & Charlotte Sts; s US$78; ✄ ) On first blush, the in-room sign reading, 'Please do not iron on the carpet' seems rather sad. On second blush, perhaps it's a reassuring indication that this lime-green, balconied hotel is doing what it can to maintain a whiff of decorum in an iron-on-the-carpet kind of world. Despite basic furnishings and worn fixtures, rooms are clean and serviceable. Not a bad deal considering its prime location near Bay Street. Ask for a room with a balcony. Rates are inclusive.

#### Midrange
The three properties below are across Bay St from tiny Junkanoo Beach. All are within a five-minute walk of both Arawak Cay (to the west) and downtown (east).

**Nassau Palm Resort** (Map p71; ☎ 242-356-0000; www.nassau-hotel.com; cnr West Bay & Nassau Sts; r US$108; ✄ ▢ ▣ ) Formerly the Holiday Inn Junkanoo Beach, this bustling 183-room property works best for on-the-go travelers looking for a simple home base at the end of a busy day. Bright tropical colors splash across bedspreads, brightening otherwise standard rooms. Each has a TV, hairdryer, iron and coffeemaker while some have a fridge. Wi-fi available in lobby (US$10 per hour). The front desk area can get congested, so plan ahead.

**Quality Inn** (Map p71; ☎ 242-322-1515; www.quality inn.com; cnr West Bay & Nassau Sts; r US$109; ✄ ▣ ) The six-story, 63-room Quality Inn is notable for its relatively low prices, fairly helpful staff and good views of incoming cruise-ships from

## JUMPING AT JUNKANOO

You feel the music before you see it…a frenzied barrage of whistles and horns overriding the ka-LICK-ka-LICK of cowbells, the rumble of drums and the joyful blasts of conch shells. Then the costumed revelers stream into view, whirling and gyrating like a kaleidoscope in rhythm with the cacophony. This is Junkanoo, the national festival of the Bahamas, a mass of energy, color and partying that starts in the twilight hours of Boxing Day.

Junkanoo is fiercely competitive and many marchers belong to 'shacks,' groups who vie to produce the best performance, costume, dancing and music. The most elaborately costumed performers are one-person parade floats, whose costume can weigh over 200lb (90kg) and depict exotic scenes adorned with a myriad of glittering beads, foils and rhinestones.

The name (junk-uh-noo) is thought to come from a West African term for 'deadly sorcerer.' Others say it's named for John Canoe, the tribal leader who demanded that his enslaved people be allowed to enjoy a festivity. Junkanoo, which had its origins in West African secret societies, evolved on the plantations of the British Caribbean among slaves who were forbidden to observe their sacred rites and hid their identity with masks.

In Nassau the first 'rush,' as the parade is known, is on Boxing Day (December 26); the second occurs New Year's Day and the third in summer, when teams practice. Parades begin at about 3am. Elbow into a viewing spot along Shirley or Bay Sts, where crowds can be thick and rowdy. For a less-hectic bleacher seat, contact the Ministry of Tourism for information on obtaining tickets.

its upper floors. The few-frills, yellow rooms sport wooden furnishings more functional than fancy. In fact, dresser handles serve as handy bottle openers for impromptu Kaliks. Don't leave food sitting out – the lack of an in-room fridge exacerbates a Bahamas-wide ant problem.

**El Greco** (Map p71; ☎ 242-325-1121; cnr W Bay & Augusta Sts; s/d US$129/189; ✻ ❑ ) The hotel's name may be evocative of a divey, beans-and-rice joint, but don't be dissuaded by first impressions. With its bougainvillea-draped balconies, bright monochromatic doors and cute central courtyard, this compact, two-story hotel is a welcome respite from the clatter of nearby Bay St. The sin of slightly worn furniture is forgiven once you discover the lobby phone – free calls for guests to the US and Canada. Upstairs rooms are larger, have balconies and offer a little more light.

### Top End

**Graycliff Hotel & Restaurant** (Map p71; ☎ 242-322-2796/97; www.graycliff.com; 8-12 W Hill St, Nassau; r/ste US$325/450; ✻ ❑ ❑ ) Nassau's most discreet and character-laden hotel is this slightly spooky 260-year-old home built by a wealthy pirate. Hidden above town on West Hill St, the Georgian-style main house is reminiscent of a gothic mansion, filled with high-ceilinged rooms, musty antiques, marble bathrooms and intriguing nooks and corners begging further exploration. Huge gardenside cot-

tages are equally alluring. The hotel's common rooms feature unique Cuban art, comfortably faded and eclectic furnishings, a smoking room and a library resplendent with the rich aroma of Cuban cigars, an astonishing wine cellar and a five-star restaurant beloved by deep-pocketed gourmands. Former guests include Sir Winston Churchill, the Beatles and LL Cool J.

### WEST OF DOWNTOWN

**ourpick Orange Hill Beach Inn** (Map p65; ☎ 242-327-7157, 888-399-3698; www.orangehill.com; W Bay St, Orange Hill Beach; s/d/cottage US$110/125/150; ✻ ❑ ❑ ) If Fido would just bring your slippers, you'd swear you never left home. Low-key Orange Hill is a welcoming way station for those wanting distance from downtown or a nice place close to the airport. Rustic-style furniture covers clean, tiled floors in fairly spare rooms; some of the 36 units come with kitchenettes. An international crowd mingles around the inviting lobby (which has free wi-fi) and dining room. Diver friendly, and locals recommend it to their friends.

**A Stone's Throw Away** (Map p65; ☎ 242-327-7030; www.astonesthrowaway.com; West Bay St, Nassau; r US$200-290, ste US$290; ✻ ❑ ❑ ) If blockade runner Rhett Butler strode through the door at this gorgeous, plantation-style B&B, one would hardly be surprised. Inviting balconies, well-appointed sitting rooms and a fine honor bar enhance the glow of Southern-minded

THE BAHAMAS

hospitality. The stone-blasted entranceway and sweeping ocean views add a melodramatic flair, making it hard to believe this delectable getaway is only four years old. The 10 rooms and suites boast wooden floors, bright quilts and rustic vintage furnishings. Wi-fi is available.

**Compass Point Inn** (Map p65; ☎ 242-327-4500; www.compasspointbeachresort.com; West Bay St, Gambier Village, Nassau; r US$300-500; ✷ ▢ ☎ ) With a color scheme best described as jellybean Junkanoo, this jumble of vibrantly colored huts is an automatic mood enhancer. Rooms are on the small side, but hip furniture, cute porches and astounding views make up for tight quarters. And who's staying inside when Love Beach and a sweet beach bar are steps away? On Friday nights, keep an ear out for karaoke-singing Sean Connery, who's been known to drop in from Lyford Cay. There's free wi-fi access.

## Eating

### DOWNTOWN NASSAU

**Imperial Cafeteria & Take-Away** (Map p71; ☎ 242-322-4522; Marlborough St, Nassau; mains US$5-10; ☯ breakfast, lunch & dinner) Ignore the grubby yellow walls and worn red booths, this busy number consistently offers the best-value takeout in Nassau. Beloved of many Nassauvians and guests of the lordly British Colonial Hotel opposite, its Bahamian highlights include fried chicken, cracked conch and souse.

**Café Skan's** (Map p71; ☎ 242-322-2486; cnr Bay & Frederick Sts, Nassau; mains US$7-23; ☯ breakfast, lunch & dinner) Typically stretched to its deep-fried seams, this down-home diner bustles with office workers, moms with babies, and the occasional hungry cop. If the happy hordes and friendly service don't pull you in, the tiered dessert case by the door should close the deal. Fried daily specials look to be most popular.

**Athena Cafe** (Map p71; ☎ 242-322-8833; Bay & Charlotte Sts; mains US$10-25; ☯ breakfast & lunch 8:30am-6pm Mon-Fri, to 4pm Sun) Locals have a love-hate affair with this cozy Greek café perched tightly over the bustling Bay and Charlotte Sts intersection. The authentic Greek food may be scrumptious, but $15 for a gyro? Pass the ouzo, take another bite and blame the just-off-the-boat cruise-ship crowd. Enter through the jewelry store.

**Senor Frog's** (Map p71; ☎ 242-323-1777; Woodes Rogers Walk; mains US$11-18; ☯ lunch & dinner) Snubbed by locals and most gourmets, this raucous tourist trap is actually, er, kind of fun if your mood's right. Down-and-dirty Mexican grub, cheesy pop tunes, bad frog puns and colorful tropical cocktails – it's tacky, it's wacky and don't tell anyone we sent you.

**Ichiban Restaurant** (Map p71; ☎ 242-326-7224; W Bay St, Nassau; mains US$14-32; ☯ lunch Tue-Sun, dinner Tue-Sat) *Pad thai, kung pao* chicken and spicy tuna handrolls crowd the menu at this welcoming Pan-Asian restaurant across from Junkanoo Beach. Warm ambience, good food and reasonable prices – a rare Nassau triple play.

**ourpick Café Matisse** (Map p71; ☎ 242-356-7012; Bank Lane, Nassau; mains US$15-26; ☯ lunch & dinner Tue-Sat) Tucked in the shadows of historic buildings and leafy palms, this casually elegant bistro just off Parliament Sq is a delightful escape from the cruise-ship-and-Bay-St mob scene. Savor top-notch pastas, pizzas and seafood dishes on the inviting back patio where you'll be served by crisp-shirted waiters to the sounds of cool world beats. If you don't opt for wine, try the refreshing ginger lemonade.

**Taj Mahal** (Map p71; ☎ 242-356-3004; 48 Parliament St, Nassau; mains US$16-38; ☯ lunch Mon-Sat, dinner daily) British expats claim that wood-paneled Taj Mahal serves the city's best Indian food. Lucky they didn't have to move from their bar stools to find it – the restaurant assumed the dark, clubby space formerly known as Green Shutters Restaurant & Pub, a very English watering hole. Look for tandoori dishes, curries and rice specialties.

**Humidor Churrascaria** (Map p71; ☎ 242-322-2796 ext 301; W Hill St; mains US$40; ☯ dinner Mon-Sat) Machismo hangs in the smoky air at this wood-paneled Brazilian steakhouse where slow-roasted tenderloins are delivered with gauchoed flair. The *prix-fixe* menu includes a salad bar stuffed with seafood apps, veggies and pastas. Conclude with a fine Graycliff stogie, hand rolled at the cigar factory next door.

### EAST & WEST OF DOWNTOWN

**Luciano's of Chicago** (Map p68; ☎ 242-323-7770; 701 E Bay St; lunch US$9-28, dinner US$14-36; ☯ lunch Mon-Fri, dinner daily) Bring your love to Luciano's and improve your odds of getting lucky. This Italian restaurant may be part of a chain, but its gorgeous harbor-side patio sets an easy stage for romance. Dishes include shrimp-and-scallop tossed fettuccini in a light cream sauce, fresh pan-seared salmon and eggplant parmigiana.

**East Villa** (Map p68; ☎ 242-393-3377; E Bay St; mains US$11-29; ⓨ lunch Sun-Fri, dinner daily) Superb, lightly seasoned Chinese dishes are the draw at this popular restaurant east of the Pardise Island bridges.

**our pick Goodfellow Farms** (Map p65; ☎ 242-377-5000; Nelson Rd, Mt Pleasant; mains US$14; ⓨ lunch 11am-3pm Mon-Sat, 11am-2pm Sun, market 9am-4pm Mon-Sat, 10am-3pm Sun) This inviting gourmet market and deli proves the power of strong word of mouth. From humble beginnings as a small purveyor of homegrown produce, 'the Farm' has rapidly become a fave of yachties, picnickers and Lyford Cayers who lunch. Relax at umbrella-ed tables just steps from the fields. The chalkboard menu changes daily but most salads and sandwiches are can't miss.

**Poop Deck** (Map p68; ☎ 242-393-8175; E Bay St; lunch US$15-26, dinner US$17-50; ⓨ lunch & dinner) It's a pick-your-lobster kind of place where old salts ogle fresh snappers at the been-there-forever front bar. On the back deck, locals and tourists select from a seafood menu heavy on Bahamian favorites – conch, grouper, mahi mahi – that's complemented by scenic views of the harbor. Second location in Sandyport ( ☎ 242-327-3325; W Bay St).

For fresh seafood with a daiquiri, try the colorful jumble of shacks at Arawak Cay (Map p68), also known as 'the Fish Fry.' Locals advise that those trying the tasty coconut-and-gin concoction sold here, known as Sky Juice, keep an eye out for, er, nearby bathrooms as the popular drink has sudden diuretic properties.

## Drinking

Nassau has several fantastic outdoor beach bars accessible by *jitney* or short taxi ride.

**Travellers Rest** (Map p65; ☎ 242-327-7633; W Bay St, Gambier Village) For laid-back ocean views framed by palm trees, hop aboard bus 10 heading west.

**Compass Point Inn** (Map p65; ☎ 242-327-4500; W Bay St, Gambier Village, Nassau) You're three times cooler than you used to be the moment you step onto the inn's thatched deck. Here, a stylish crowd sips potent cocktails with the deep blue sea as a backdrop. Stunning.

**Green Parrot** (Map p68; ☎ 242-322-9248; E Bay St) The beloved original at PI's Hurricane Hole is slated for closure – another victim of Atlantis' continued expansion. This new

outpost, overlooking Nassau Harbour west of the Paradise Island entrance bridge, keeps the cocktails-and-Kalik crowd satisfied with its happy central bar, hearty apps and twinkling harborside views.

## Entertainment

Check hotel lobbies for flyers blaring theme nights and admission specials. Most action starts after 10pm. Downtown, join the sweaty, dancing masses at stylish **Bambu** (Map p71; ☎ 242-326-6627; Prince George Dock), the newest club on the block, which keeps its doors open late for the cruise-ship crowds; perennial favorite **Club Waterloo** (Map p68; ☎ 242-393-7324; E Bay St; admission Fri & Sat US$20), east of the PI bridges near Fort Montagu, keeps spring-breakers happy with several bars and dance areas.

**Palm Court** (Map p71; ☎ 242-322-3301; British Colonial Hilton Nassau, Bay St, Nassau) is a lower key spot, and offers jazz on Tuesday, Wednesday and Thursday nights.

## Shopping

The masses flock to Bay St for duty-free liquor, jewelry, perfume and cigars, but savings are not guaranteed. Check prices at home before your trip. Most stores close at night and on Sunday, even when the cruise-ships are in port. Bahamian-made products are sold at booths throughout Festival Place. The Straw Market? Not necessarily.

### CIGARS

Premium Cuban cigars are relatively inexpensive in Nassau. Too bad Uncle Sam prohibits US citizens from importing them.

**Graycliff Cigar Co** (Map p71; ☎ 242-302-9150; W Hill St, Nassau; ⓨ 9:30am-7pm Mon-Fri) Castro's own cigar roller, Avelino Lara, oversees fellow Cubans hand-rolling these award-winning cigars; see also p69. Since they're not made with Cuban tobacco, they're permitted by US customs.

### DUTY-FREE GOODS

Designer clothing, leather, linen and perfume outlets blanket Bay St and its offshoots.

**Colombian Emeralds** (Map p71; ☎ 242-322-2230; Bay St, Nassau) Bright sparkling emeralds and much more.

**Perfume Shop & Beauty Spot** (Map p71; ☎ 242-322-2375; cnr Bay & Frederick Sts, Nassau) Fragrances to the left, cosmetics to the right.

**Solomon's Mines** (Map p71; ☎ 242-356-6920; Bay St, Nassau) This jewelry and luxury goods powerhouse first opened in 1908.

## PLUNDER, RUM CAKE & TEA

**Coin of the Realm** (Map p71; ☎ 242-322-4497; Charlotte St, Nassau) Salvaged Spanish doubloons are the coolest find at this busy coin and jewelry shop.

**Pasion Tea & Coffee Company** (Map p71; ☎ 242-327-7011; www.pasionteas.com; Festival Place, Nassau) Look for tropically flavored gourmet teas, created by Bahamian Julie Hoffer, at its stall in Festival Place and at shops throughout town. Hot pepper tonics, spices and bush-medicine-inspired remedies are sold too.

**Plunder at Pirates of Nassau** (Map p71; ☎ 242-356-3759; King & George Sts, Nassau; ☒ 9am-6pm Mon-Sat, 9am-12:30pm Sun) Eye patches, black flags, pirate tees and a good selection of pirate lit for buccaneering bookworms.

**Tortuga Rum Cake** (Map p71; Charlotte St) Tasty yes, local no. Tortuga's treats are made in the Cayman Islands. But the samples are delish.

# PARADISE ISLAND

Paradise Island (PI) glitters off the northern coast of Nassau like a gorgeous siren, luring travelers with easy promises of glistening shores, decadent restaurants and one mind-blowing water park. But tread carefully. Like a true mythological beast, she'll shred the soul of the unprepared visitor – dashing vacation dreams against the rocky shores of outrageous pricing, pre-fab blandness and infuriating indifference.

But she can sure be fun if you know what you're getting into. Known for years as 'Hog Island' – for the pigs once raised there – PI took steps toward respectability in 1939 when Dr Axel Wenner-Gren, a Swedish industrialist, developed his own Shangri-La here. He spruced up his holdings – creating the sweeping 35-acre Versailles Gardens – before selling them to the equally wealthy Huntington Hartford. Hartford developed a golf resort and marina, simultaneously persuading Bahamians to rename the property Paradise Island. Resorts and property here passed though the hands of several more developers, with the majority of it landing in the hands of billionaire Sol Kerzner in 1994. His company South African International owns the ever-expanding Atlantis resort and casino.

Today, two arcing bridges connect the island to Nassau, the first constructed in 1967, the second in 1998. The western bridge leads northbound traffic onto the island while the eastern span leads visitors back to Nassau. The cost to enter is $1. See p64 for details of transportation from Nassau.

## Information

**Cyber Café** (Map p68; ☎ 242-363-1253; Casino Dr, Paradise Island Shopping Plaza; per hr US$10; ☒ 10am-6pm Mon-Sat, until 5pm Sun) Has high-speed internet access.

**News Café** (Map p68; ☎ 242-363-4684; Harbour Dr, Hurricane Hole Plaza; per min US$0.20; ☒ 24hr) Great indie spot for newspapers, magazines, computers and coffee – at least until the rumored Atlantis expansion consumes it. It's US$3 sign-on plus US$0.20 per minute for internet access.

## Sights

### ATLANTIS AQUARIUMS & AQUAVENTURE

Strolling through a clear glass tunnel while sharks glide overhead is, simply put, awesome. This underwater thrill is found in the Predator's Lagoon, one of the 'exhibits' in the **Discover Atlantis Tour** (Map p68; ☎ 242-363-3000; adult/hotel guest/child US$32/free/22; ☒ 9am-5pm), a popular walking tour meandering past big-windowed aquariums and predator-filled lagoons. Buy tickets outside the Dig, a faux archaeological site on the lower level of the Royal Towers lobby. Look for manta rays, spiny lobsters, striped Nemos, translucent jellyfish and thousands of other underwater creatures – 250 species and 70,000 fish to be specific.

Arrive early to beat oppressive crowds. Since the biggest windows lack any fish-identifying signage, join one of the regularly departing guided tours but stick close to the guide – they move fast and can be hard to hear. See the desk for tour times.

And then there's the Atlantis' astounding **Aquaventure** (Map p68; adult/hotel guest/child US$105/free/75). No matter how much you despise 'imagineered' reality, the resort's newly enhanced 63-acre water park is likely to change your mind. Plummet down a 50ft waterslide, bob over 4ft waves on a mile-long river ride, or float through a shark-filled lagoon from the safety of a long clear tube. It's 20 million gallons of liquid fun – almost enough to make you forget how expensive it all is. You can purchase tickets at Guest Services inside Royal Towers.

### BEACHES

You don't have to overnight at a posh seaside resort to enjoy the gorgeous white sand of **Cabbage Beach** (Map p65) – though it helps. For nonguests, there's a public access path through the pines east of RIU Hotel on

Casino Dr. This 2-mile beach is perfect for people-watching, indolent lounging and water sports. Another beauty, **Paradise Beach** (Map p68), curves around the northwest side of the island. With the recent completion of the sleek Cove hotel at Atlantis, however, a bit of this paradise has been lost.

### GARDENS

Paradise Island Dr runs through **Versailles Gardens** (Map p68). Developed as a hideaway by industrialist Axel Wenner-Gren in 1939 and modeled on Versailles, this lovely sweeping 35-acre (14-hectare) tiered garden is lined with fountains and classical statues depicting the millionaire's heroes.

At the southern crest is **Cloisters** (Map p68), a romantic gazebo overlooking the harbour. This genuine 14th-century cloister was purchased by newspaper magnate William Randolph Hearst from an Augustine estate in France.

Visitors are welcome to wander the gardens but don't dare place a toe onto the restricted One & Only Ocean Club next door. Security is on high alert for peasants at this uberexclusive resort, with the Club clearly forgetful of the fates of the cake-eating denizens of the original Versailles.

### Activities

See p70 for details of activities. Many outfitters depart the Paradise Island Ferry Terminal underneath the PI Exit Bridge.

### Sleeping

**Comfort Suites** (Map p68; ☎ 242-363-3680, 1-800-228-5150; www.comfortsuites.com; Casino Dr; r incl breakfast US$350; 🐾 🖳 🛋 ) Occupants of this all-suites hotel enjoy full guest privileges at neighboring Atlantis, typically at a much better rate. The rooms are slightly bigger than average, with a sitting area, and include a refrigerator and safe. The continental breakfast, served by the pool, is substantial. There's also a guest laundry. Wi-fi is US$5 per hour.

**Atlantis** (Map p68; ☎ 242-363-3000; www.atlantis .com; Atlantis Resort, Paradise Island; r US$425-495; 🐾 🖳 🛋 ) If Disneyland, Vegas and Sea World birthed a lovechild, this watery wonderland would be its overpriced but oddly irresistible spawn. The newest addition to this busy multitowered megaresort is the stylish, all-suites the Cove, catering to adults and children over 12. Prices vary, with costs

typically increasing as you move west from the Beach Tower toward the Cove. The resort boasts 20 restaurants and lounges (not including those in adjacent Marina Village), three shopping areas, a kid's club and a library; and an entertainment complex with a casino, comedy club and theater. Check for resort packages. Give your patience a workout before your stay – staff can be surprisingly unhelpful. See opposite for information on Aquaventure.

### Eating & Drinking

**Anthony's Grill** (Map p68; ☎ 242-363-3152; Casino Dr, Paradise Island Shopping Center; mains US$9-29; 🕑 breakfast, lunch & dinner) Burgers, pasta, nachos and a few Bahamian specialties crowd the menu at this family-friendly, reasonably priced spot that's off the Atlantis compound.

**Nobu** (Map p68; ☎ 242-363-3000 ext 29; Royal Towers, Atlantis; mains $14-49) Trendy Zen decor complements top-notch sushi and high-grade celebs. Try the black cod with miso or the yellowtail sashimi.

**Mesa Grill** (Map p68; ☎ 242-363-6925; 1 Casino Dr W, The Cove at Atlantis; mains US$32-60; 🕑 5:30-10pm) Sip cocktails on cattle-print chairs at Bobby Flay's latest, a southwestern rendezvous inside the ever-so-chic Cove. The spice-rubbed-pork is popular and the *dulce de leche* crepes are *dulce*-delicious for dessert.

# GRAND BAHAMA

**pop 47,000**

In the Bahamas family of islands, Grand Bahama is the scrappy middle kid – usually overlooked, occasionally knocked down and ultimately misunderstood. The one-two punch for this 85-mile-long isle came in 2004 and 2005 when hurricanes ripped across its low-lying shores, ravaging hotels, restaurants and businesses. While the island was shaking off its daze, its once shy siblings, the Out Islands, charged ahead, establishing distinct personalities and snapping up glossy headlines and ever-so-fickle celebs.

But who needs glitz and glamour when you've got fish-filled reefs, tree-lined nature walks, kayak-friendly creeks and dolphins ready for kisses? Grand Bahama is slowly realizing its nature-minded strengths and poised to strut its stuff as the best Bahamian bet for outdoor adventure and ecotravel. It just needs to spread the word – and quick –

# GRAND BAHAMA

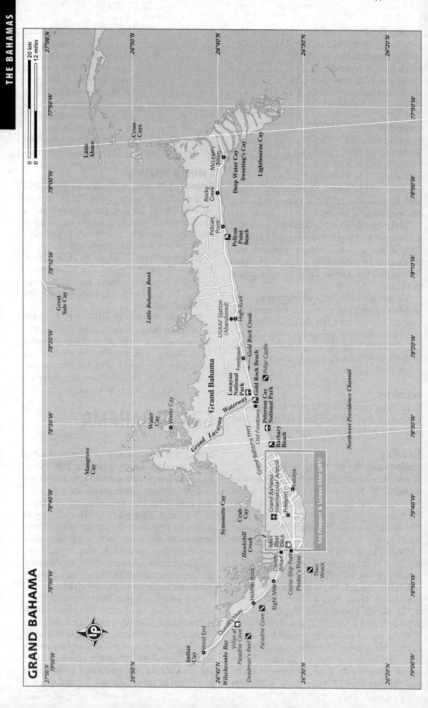

0          20 km
0          12 miles

27°00'N
26°50'N
26°40'N
26°30'N
26°20'N

77°50'W
78°00'W
78°10'W
78°20'W
78°30'W
78°40'W
78°50'W
79°00'W

**Little Abaco**

Cross Cays

McLean's Town

Deep Water Cay
Sweeting's Cay
Lighbourne Cay

Rocky Creek

Pelican Point
Pelican Point Beach

**Little Bahama Bank**

Great Sale Cay

USAAF Station (Abandoned)
High Rock
Gold Rock Creek

Freetown
Pillar Castle
Gold Rock Beach

**Grand Bahama**

Lucayan National Park

Water Cay
Water Cay

Peterson Cay National Park

**Grand Lucayan Waterway**

Barbary Beach

Mangrove Cay

Old Freetown
Grand Bahama Hwy

Symonette Cay
Crab Cay

Grand Bahama International Airport
Freeport
Lucaya

See Freeport & Lucaya Map (p81)

Hawksbill Creek
Wall
Boat
Dock

Holmes Rock
Eight Mile
Caribe Wharf

Cruise-Ship Ports
Pinder's Point
Theo Wreck

**Northwest Providence Channel**

Indian Cay
West End
Wilschombe Bay
Villas at Paradise Cove
Deadman's Reef
Paradise Cove
Queen's Hwy

before the megaresorts swoop in, gobble up the goodies and ruin it all. Which is a distinct possibility now that Ginn sur Mer, a massive hotel-condo-marina complex, is rumbling toward completion on the western shore.

For now, take the nature tour, kayak under the mangroves, ride a horse along the sand – prices are right and the best views still open to the public. At times the island can be frustrating – unexplained closings, indifferent customer service – but if you take time to see what's under the surface, you'll probably like what you find. Best of all, it's only 95 miles from Ft Lauderdale.

## Getting There & Away
### AIR
For international and regional flight information, see p107 and p108.

### BOAT
For information on mail boats to/from Nassau, see p109.

Pinder's Ferry runs a small boat – maximum 20 people – from MacLean's Town, Grand Bahama, to Crown Haven, Abaco.

## Getting Around
### TO/FROM THE AIRPORT
**Grand Bahama International Airport** (Map p81; ☎ 242-352-6020) lies 2 miles (3.2km) north of Freeport. There's no bus service to or from the airport. However, car-rental booths are based in the arrivals hall and taxis meet each flight. Displayed fares are set by the government. Taxi rides for two people to/from the airport to Freeport are US$11, and US$20 to/from Lucaya. Each additional passenger costs US$3.

### BUS
A handful of private minibuses operate as 'public buses' on assigned routes from the bus station in Freeport at the City Market parking lot (formerly Winn Dixie Plaza), traveling as far afield as West End and McLean's Town. Buses are frequent and depart when the driver decides he has enough passengers. The bus stop in Freeport is at the parking area behind the International Bazaar; and the bus stop in Lucaya is on Seahorse Dr, 400 yards (365m) west of Port Lucaya Marketplace.

The eastern end of the island is known as the 'East End' and the western part as the 'West End.' Fares from Freetown include Port Lucaya Marketplace (US$1), East End (US$8, twice daily) and West End (US$4, twice daily).

A bus usually runs twice daily, morning and afternoon, from downtown's City Market to McLean's Town on Grand Bahama's eastern edge, timed in conjunction with the Pinder's Ferry departure to Crown Haven, Abaco. Ask drivers at City Market which of them is running that route.

Buses will occasionally drop you in taxi-designated city areas for US$2.

Free shuttles also run from most downtown hotels to the beach and town.

### CAR & SCOOTER
The following companies have car-rental agencies inside or close to the airport. Rentals cost from US$50 to US$95 per 24 hours. Collision waiver damage insurance is about US$17 to US$18 a day.
**Avis** ( ☎ 242-352-7666) A quarter of a mile from airport. Look for the shuttle.
**Brad's** ( ☎ 242-352-7930)
**Dollar** ( ☎ 242-352-9325)
**Hertz** ( ☎ 242-352-9277) Across the street from airport. Look for the shuttle.
**KSR Rent A Car** ( ☎ 242-351-5737)

Scooters are available for rent from the parking lot in front of the Port Lucaya Resort & Yacht Club for US$50 per day, plus a hefty cash deposit.

### TAXI
You'll find taxis at the airport and major hotels. If you like your driver, ask for his or her card. Some can be quite helpful with trip planning. Fares are fixed by the government for short distances.

You can call for a radio-dispatched taxi from **Freeport Taxi** ( ☎ 242-352-6666) or **Grand Bahama Taxi Union** ( ☎ 242-352-7101). **Buddy's Mobile Transportation Service** ( ☎ 242-646-7287) plans to add a wheelchair lift to its van later this year. **G Cooper's Taxi-Cab Service** ( ☎ 242-646-3336) was also reliable.

## FREEPORT & LUCAYA
pop 33,000
Freeport and its southeastern suburb Lucaya are the primary settlements on Grand Bahama, dominating the economic, cultural and tourism landscape. Freeport is the sun-parched, slightly sprawling business

center buzzing with banks, insurance companies, the hospital, the library and several tasty Bahamian restaurants. Budget travelers should start their lodging search here, realizing that loss of beach proximity is the trade-off for $100 rooms. Most hotels provide complimentary shuttles, however, and $1 *jitneys* regularly bounce back and forth between downtown and the beach.

The party vibe picks up in Lucaya, with yachties, beach bums, divers and gamblers wandering their way into Port Lucaya Marketplace to shop, eat, or hire an outdoor outfitter. Located within steps of Unexso (Underwater Explorers Society), several hotels and Bell Channel Bay, the complex is the hub of the social scene, where you can savor coffee in the morning then knock back a tropical cocktail after a day on the water. And if crowds aren't your thing, try a sunset stroll on gorgeous Lucayan Beach – it's just across the street.

## Information

Free copies of the *Grand Bahamas Trailblazer Map* are stacked in hotel lobbies and tourist shops.

### BOOKSTORES
**H&L Bookstore** (Map p85; ☎ 242-373-8947; Port Lucaya Marketplace, Lucaya) Books, magazines and Bahamian maps and history books. Second location across from City Market downtown (Map p82; ☎ 242-352-5470; Freeport).

### EMERGENCY
**Ambulance** ( ☎ 242-352-2689)
**Police** ( ☎ 911)

### INTERNET ACCESS
**Charles Hayward Library** (Map p82; ☎ 242-352-7048; East Mall Dr, Freeport; ☎ 10am-5pm Mon-Fri, 10am-2pm Sat) Fantastic used bookstore in back that's popular with yachties. Internet access for $2.50 per hour.
**Cyber Café** (Map p85; ☎ 242-225-0460; Port Lucaya Marketplace; per 30min US$5; ☼ 8am-8pm Mon-Sat, 10am-8pm Sun) For long-distance calls and internet access, although rates are expensive.

### MEDICAL SERVICES
**LMR Drugs** (Map p82 ☎ 242-352-7327; 1 West Mall Dr, Freeport; ☼ 8am-8pm Mon-Sat, 8am-3pm Sun)
**Lucayan Medical Centre East** (Map p81; ☎ 242-373-7400; East Sunrise Hwy, Freeport)

**Rand Memorial Hospital** (Map p82; ☎ 242-352-6735; East Atlantic Dr, Freeport) Entrance on East Mall Dr.
**Sunrise Medical Centre & Hospital** (Map p82; ☎ 242-373-333; E Sunrise Hwy, Lucaya)

### MONEY
**Royal Bank of Canada** Freeport (Map p82; ☎ 242-373-8628; East Mall Dr); Lucaya ( ☎ 242-352-6631; Port Lucaya Marketplace)
**Scotiabank** (Map p82; ☎ 242-352-6774; Regent Centre, Explorers Way, Freeport)

### POST
**FedEx** (Map p82; ☎ 242-352-3402; www.fedex.com; Seventeen Centre, cnr Woodstock St & Bank Lane, Freeport)
**Post office** (Map p82; ☎ 242-352-9371; Explorers Way, Freeport)

### TELEPHONE
**BaTelCo** (Map p82; ☎ 242-352-6220; Pioneer's Way, Freeport) Public phones can be found here.

### TOURIST INFORMATION
**Grand Bahama Island Tourism Board** (Map p82; ☎ 242-352-8044; www.grand-bahama.com; Poinciana Dr, Freeport)
**Tourism information booth** (Map p81; ☎ 242-352-2052; Grand Bahama International Airport)

## Dangers & Annoyances

At night use caution downtown near City Market and west of Freeport at Pinder's Point and Eight Mile. Post hurricanes there have been problems with street lighting in some of these areas and there have been some reports of drug-related violence.

## Sights

### PORT LUCAYA MARKETPLACE & MARINA COMPLEX

A 12-acre (4.8-hectare) shopping, dining and entertainment area, **Port Lucaya Marketplace** (Map p85; ☎ 242-373-8446; www.portlucaya.com) fronts the Port Lucaya Marina. Together they form an integrated yacht basin and waterfront tourism area, much more appealing than the International Bazaar. At its heart beats **Count Basie Sq**, where everything from church choirs to Junkanoo bands perform on weekends.

### BEACHES

In Port Lucaya, the best beaches include **Silver Point** (Map p81) and **Lucayan Beach** (Map p85). For a nice sunset stroll, start at

# FREEPORT & LUCAYA

**INFORMATION**
Lucayan Medical Centre East.....................1 C3
Tourist Information Booth..........................2 B2

**SIGHTS & ACTIVITIES**
Pinetree Stables........................................3 C3
Rand Nature Center...................................4 C2

**EATING** 🍴
Georgie's Restaurant & Lounge................5 E2
Smith's Point Fish Fry...............................6 E3

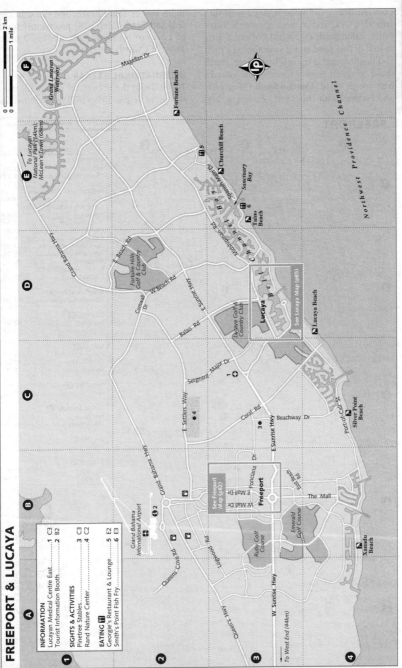

Lucayan Beach and walk west. Crowds thin and views expand as you approach Silver Point. **Taino Beach** (Map p81) offers a long stretch of fine sand and if your timing's right you might stumble upon a beachfront conch stand allegedly selling some of the island's best conch salad. **Churchill Beach** (Map p81) and **Fortune Beach** (Map p81) extend several

miles east of Taino Beach; and the stunning **Gold Rock Beach** (Map p78) preens just south of Lucayan National Park, about 20 miles away. It's worth the trip.

## INTERNATIONAL BAZAAR
If you doubt the strength of your soul, avoid this pit of despair (Map p82). Abandoned res-

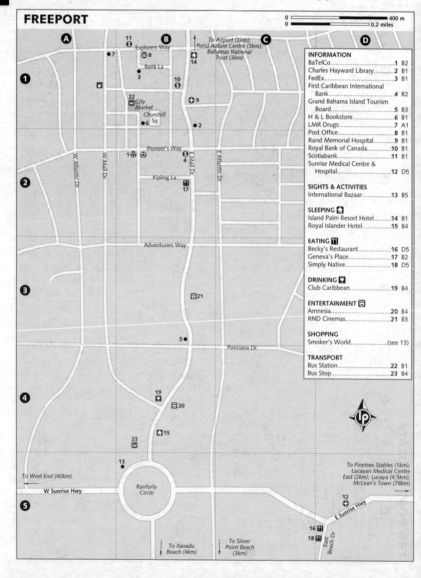

# FREEPORT

0 |————————| 400 m
0 |————————| 0.2 miles

**INFORMATION**
BaTelCo...........................................1 B2
Charles Hayward Library.............2 B1
FedEx.............................................3 B1
First Caribbean International
    Bank..........................................4 B2
Grand Bahama Island Tourism
    Board.........................................5 B3
H & L Bookstore...........................6 B1
LMR Drugs....................................7 A1
Post Office....................................8 B1
Rand Memorial Hospital..............9 B1
Royal Bank of Canada...............10 B1
Scotiabank..................................11 B1
Sunrise Medical Centre &
    Hospital...................................12 D5

**SIGHTS & ACTIVITIES**
International Bazaar....................13 B5

**SLEEPING**
Island Palm Resort Hotel..........14 B1
Royal Islander Hotel..................15 B4

**EATING**
Becky's Restaurant....................16 D5
Geneva's Place...........................17 B2
Simply Native............................18 D5

**DRINKING**
Club Caribbean..........................19 B4

**ENTERTAINMENT**
Amnesia......................................20 B4
RND Cinemas..............................21 B3

**SHOPPING**
Smoker's World....................(see 13)

**TRANSPORT**
Bus Station.................................22 B1
Bus Stop.....................................23 B4

taurants, empty alleyways, suspicious shop-keepers, Japanese *torii* gates to nowhere – it's a wonder this 'marketplace' still adorns every tourist map. If dragged here against your will, the Straw Market, Smoker's World and China Arts & Handicraft are worth a brief look.

## Activities

### BIRD-WATCHING & NATURE WALKS
**Rand Nature Centre** (Map p81; ☎ 242-352-5438; www .thebahamasnationaltrust.org; adult/child US$5/3; ☉ 9am-4:30pm Sun-Fri) Bird-watchers and nature hikers can spend a tranquil hour or two exploring tree-canopied trails and meditating by a quiet pond at this 100-acre reserve run by the Bahamas National Trust. This nonprofit conservation agency manages the country's 25 national parks and has its local head-quarters here. An exhibit area in the main building has loads of books on Bahamian flora and fauna as well as handouts on en-dangered Bahamian species. Don't miss the peacocks and red-tailed hawk just outside the main building. Hour-long tours depart on Tuesday and Thursday at 10:30am.

### DIVING & SNORKELING
Diving is excellent here. One prime site is the *Theo* wreck, a 230ft-long (73m) sunken freighter with safe swim-through areas; and East End Paradise, an underwater coral range. Another good spot is Deadman's Reef, off Paradise Cove; see p87 for details.
**Pat & Diane Fantasia Tours** (Map p85; ☎ 242-373-8681; www.snorkelingbahamas.com; behind Port Lucaya Resort) Offers half-day snorkeling trips on a double deck catamaran (adult/child US$40/20) to a shallow coral reef.
**Seaworld Explorer** ( ☎ 242-373-7863; adult/child US$45/25) Ogle tropical fish in their natural habitat from the comfort of a 'semi-submarine' – a 49ft boat with a glass-bottom hull. Trip includes 30 minutes of snorkeling. It provides a courtesy van to and from your hotel.
**Underwater Explorers Society** (Unexso; Map p85; ☎ 242-373-1244; www.unexso.com; Port Lucaya Marina) One of the biggest draws on the island, Unexso offers a full range of dive programs, including a two-tank dive to the *Theo* wreck (US$89), a shark dive (US$89) and a night dive (US$70). The Open Ocean Dolphin Experience allows interaction with trained dolphins in their natural element, the open sea, for US$199.

### FISHING
The Gulf Stream, off the west coast of Grand Bahama, teems with game fish. The Northwest Providence Channel drops to 2000ft (609m)

just 400 yards (365m) off the south shore, where snapper and barracuda are prevalent. Bonefishing is superb on the flats of the Little Bahama Bank to the north and east of the island.

**Reef Tours Ltd** (Map p85; ☎ 242-373-5880; Port Lucaya Marina) offers 3¼-hour bottom-fishing tours (adult/child US$50/35) that travel about two miles out. Bait and tackle included. For deep-sea fishers, there's a half-day trip (adult/spectator US$110/50) going six miles out. Prey can include mahi mahi, barracuda, wahoo and yellow-fin tuna.

### HORSEBACK RIDING
**Pinetree Stables** (Map p81; ☎ 242-373-3600; www .pinetree-stables.com; Beachway Dr, Freeport) offers two-hour horseback rides (US$85) through pine forests and along a southern beach. Guides provide ecominded information on local woodlands and birds.

### KAYAKING
**Grand Bahama Nature Tours** ( ☎ 242-373-2485; www .gbntours.com) Enthusiastic, knowledgeable guides lead a variety of active ecotrips outside Freeport. Kayak through a mangrove forest (US$79), paddle across the sea to a gorgeous cay (US$79), bike along the beach (US$79) or bounce through the backcountry in an open-top jeep (US$99). The kayaking tour includes an interesting stop at the caves in Lucayan National Park and a picnic lunch on Gold Rock Beach where a Disney-esque family of raccoons begs for scraps.

### WATER SPORTS & BOAT TRIPS
**Lucaya Watersports & Tours** (Map p85; ☎ 242-373-4677; www.lucayawatersports.com; Seahorse Rd, Port Lucaya) offers a variety of trips and rentals for water rats of every age and courage level, most leaving from Flamingo Bay Marina at Taino Beach. Trips include a 90-minute waverunner island tour (US$120 for two-seater), a banana boat ride (adult/child $15/10) and parasail-ing (US$60). There's also a two hour sunset cruise offering unlimited Bahama Mamas (US$45). Kayak and waverunner rentals also available.

## Festivals & Events
For information on these festivals and events and many others, contact the **Grand Bahama Island Tourism Board** (Map p82; ☎ 242-352-8044; www .grand-bahama.com; Poinciana Dr, Freeport).

**THE BAHAMAS**

### PIRATE HUNTING

Like any self-respecting Bahamian island, Grand Bahama has a pirate-filled past, though evidence tends toward the celluloid variety. In 2005 an infusion of Hollywood cash boosted the economy when *Pirates of the Caribbean II* and *III* spent several months filming at Gold Rock Creek. The massive shell of a faux-ship from the movie now glowers like a nautical Ozymandias from a sandy grave just east of Lucayan National Park. To get there, take the first major dirt road on your right after passing the park (a few hundred yards), drive toward the beach and thar she lays, visible through the fencing.

**Conch Cracking Contest** In October, sleepy McLean's Town, at the east end of the island, hosts this contest. It's not much fun for the conch, but a great day for the humans.

**Junkanoo Parade** Held on Boxing Day and New Year's Day. For more details, see the boxed text, p73.

## Sleeping

Budget options are hard to find. However, nearly all accommodations reviewed here offer great specials, even in high season. Expect heavy additional taxes and daily service charges nonetheless.

### FREEPORT

**Island Palm Resort** (Map p82; ☎ 242-352-6648; http://bahamasvg.com/islandsisters.html; East Mall Dr, Freeport; r US$89; 🔀 🖳 🕿 ) Pastels and palm trees give this 143-room property a beachy feel, even though it's nowhere close to the ocean. This carefree vibe continues inside the mid-sized, slightly spare rooms where tropical bedspreads and bright pictures keep things festive. An inviting L-shaped pool attracts sun-loving guests not up for a ride on the courtesy beach shuttle. Five minutes from the airport.

**Royal Islander Hotel** (Map p82; ☎ 242-351-6000; www.royalislanderhotel.com; East Mall Dr, Freeport; r US$100; 🔀 🖳 🕿 ) Bold floral-print bedspreads, colorful pictures and faux rattan furniture keep things bright at this well-traveled property. Mid-sized rooms surround a courtyard pool and come with in-room safe, cable TV and phone. Late-night partiers will appreciate the proximity of two popular clubs, Amnesia and Club Caribbean. Wi-fi access costs US$10 per day.

### LUCAYA

**Port Lucaya Resort & Yacht Club** (Map p85; ☎ 242-373-6618; www.portlucayaresort.com; Bell Channel Rd; r/ste US$112/196; 🔀 🕿 ) The word 'resort' might be stretching it, but the 10 brightly painted buildings here are a convenient, serviceable option for families, divers and budget-minded groups. Red-tiled floors, lots of mirrors and beds sporting green-and-blue jungle-flora prints distract from slightly shabby, not-entirely-chic furniture. All rooms have a patio or balcony. It's adjacent to Port Lucaya Marketplace.

**Flamingo Bay Hotel & Marina** (Map p85; ☎ 242-373-5640; www.tainobeach.com/flamingo; Jolly Roger Drive; r US$120; 🔀 🖳 🕿 ) If you don't mind a short water shuttle ride to get to the action, this three-story hotel on the east side of Bell Channel is a reasonably priced alternative to the larger resorts near the marketplace. Guests enjoy full use of the pool, beach and business center at Taino Resort, the hotel's sister property and have easy access to several small outfitters docked out back. Bright, mid-sized rooms include a small kitchenette and there's a laundry on site. Service can be a bit nonchalant.

**Sheraton & Westin Grand Bahama Island Our Lucaya Resort** (Map p85; ☎ Sheraton 242-373-1444, Westin 242-373-1333; www.starwoodhotels.com; Seahorse Rd, Port Lucaya; Sheraton r US$129, Westin r US$279; 🔀 🖳 🕿 ) Incorporating two hotels, the Sheraton and Westin, this perfectly coiffed beachfront complex hogs the best views of stunning Lucayan Beach. The resort sits on 7.5 acres (2.8 hectares) and incorporates numerous restaurants, bars, a casino, three fabulous swimming pools, kids' facilities, the Port Lucaya Marketplace & Village promenade of boutiques, cafés, bars and shops and two 18-hole golf courses, all linked by a 0.75-mile (1.2km) boardwalk. The ambience at the pricier Westin is a bit more sophisticated and low-key. Don't miss the towering palms in the two-story lobby. Rates seem to have actually gone down in the last few years. Free wi-fi access is available in the lobbies.

**Pelican Bay at Lucaya** (Map p85; ☎ 242-373-9550, 800-600-9192; www.pelicanbayhotel.com; Seahorse Rd, Port Lucaya; r US$179; 🔀 🖳 🕿 ) A burbling pineapple fountain greets guests at this upscale retreat where crisp, monochromatic buildings stand in secluded attention between Port Lucaya Marketplace and Bell Channel. The beach chic allure continues inside the 182 rooms, with wicker furniture and bold green bedspreads enlivening standard rooms. Three pools and proximity to Unexso round out the appeal.

**Villas at Paradise Cove** ( ☎ 242-349-2677; www.dead mansreef.com; r per week US$1400; ⧉ ) Rebuilt after the recent hurricanes, the two oceanfront cottages here have a relaxed, beachy style incorporating white wicker furniture, ceiling fans and a screened porch with a view. Best part? Unbeatable access to one of the island's top snorkeling spots at Deadman's Reef. Telephone, TV and full kitchen in both villas. Nightly rentals also available.

## Eating & Drinking

Downtown restaurants and the Wednesday night fish fry serve up the best traditional Bahamian meals. Most restaurants are open 'until' – meaning until the last person goes home. For a variety of cuisines, stick to Port Lucaya Marketplace. Live music and dancing often feature at Count Basie Sq here on Thursday nights and weekends.

### FREEPORT

For Bahamian cooking in town, consider these recommended spots:

**Simply Native** (Map p82; ☎ 242-352-5003; East Beach Dr; mains US$6-12; ⧖ from 8am) Hands-down best grits we have had in ages. If you want to try chicken souse, johnnycakes and other traditional Bahamian dishes – and eat where locals eat – ditch Port Lucaya and come here. Hanging baskets of flowers don't go far in sprucing up the dim, wood-railed dining room but who cares, just pass the grits.

**Geneva's Place** (Map p82; ☎ 242-352-5085; cnr East Mall Dr & Kipling Lane; mains US$6-17; ⧖ from 7am) Don't be deterred by the shale-strewn lawn and the it's-not-clear-I'm-open exterior. The ambience improves inside with friendly waitresses, colorful murals and lots of open space. Peas-and-rice accompany every main at this long-popular spot where cracked conch and stew fish are most requested.

**Becky's Restaurant** (Map p82; ☎ 242-352-5247; East Beach Dr; mains US$6-18; ⧖ breakfast, lunch, dinner) Simply Native's popular neighbor is also good, and serves American dishes as well as Bahamian.

### LUCAYA

The following eateries and bars are located in the Port Lucaya Marketplace or across the street at the Sheraton & Westin complex.

**Zorba's** (Map p85; ☎ 242-373-6137; mains US$7-26; ⧖ breakfast, lunch & dinner) Savor souvlaki and spanakopitas beneath a canopy of grapevines and pink bougainvillea at this reasonably priced and commonly recommended Greek diner in the heart of the marketplace.

**Pub at Port Lucaya** (Map p85; ☎ 242-373-8450; mains US$10-22; ⧖ lunch & dinner) There's a choice for every palate at this busy corner spot beside Count Basie Square and the marina. Staples are burgers, grilled fish and a few British dishes including shepherd's pie.

**La Dolce Vita** (Map p85; ☎ 242-373-8652; mains US$13-29; ⧖ dinner) For a 'sexy' meal, locals recommend La Dolce Vita, a romantic bayside rendezvous where fine Italian dishes are

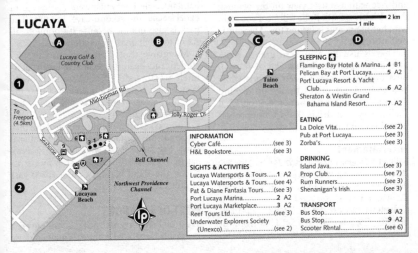

**LUCAYA**

0 —————— 2 km
0 —————— 1 mile

**SLEEPING** ⧉
Flamingo Bay Hotel & Marina....**4** B1
Pelican Bay at Port Lucaya.........**5** A2
Port Lucaya Resort & Yacht
  Club..................................**6** A2
Sheraton & Westin Grand
  Bahama Island Resort...........**7** A2

**EATING**
La Dolce Vita..........................(see 2)
Pub at Port Lucaya..................(see 3)
Zorba's...................................(see 3)

**DRINKING**
Island Java..............................(see 3)
Prop Club................................(see 7)
Rum Runners...........................(see 3)
Shenanigan's Irish...................(see 3)

**TRANSPORT**
Bus Stop..................................**8** A2
Bus Stop..................................**9** A2
Scooter Rental.........................(see 6)

**INFORMATION**
Cyber Café...............................(see 3)
H&L Bookstore.........................(see 3)

**SIGHTS & ACTIVITIES**
Lucaya Watersports & Tours......**1** A2
Lucaya Watersports & Tours......(see 4)
Pat & Diane Fantasia Tours......(see 3)
Port Lucaya Marina....................**2** A2
Port Lucaya Marketplace...........**3** A2
Reef Tours Ltd..........................(see 3)
Underwater Explorers Society
  (Unexco)...............................(see 2)

Lucaya Golf & Country Club

Midshipman Rd

To Freeport (4.5km)

Seahorse Rd

Midshipman Rd

Taino Beach

Jolly Roger Dr

Bell Channel

Northwest Providence Channel

Lucayan Beach

served under twinkling lights. Settle in on the plantation-style porch or the brick-lined patio for yacht-filled marina views.

For coffee or cocktails, consider:

**Island Java** (Map p85; ☎ 242-373-6137) Linger over lattes and pastries at batik-covered patio tables at this brand new Java joint. Friendly staff are a bonus.

**Rum Runners** (Map p85; ☎ 242-373-7233) Follow the laughter and crowds to Rum Runners, a jovial watering hole overlooking Count Basie Sq.

**Shenanigan's Irish Pub** (Map p85; ☎ 242-373-4734) For Guinness and lively conversation.

**Prop Club Beach Bar** (Map p85; ☎ 242-373-1333; Sheraton Hotel) At sunset, walk straight past the propellers and wingnut decor. Grab a stool on the patio. Order a cocktail. Repeat as needed.

### TAINO BEACH

If you're exasperated by indifferent service and high prices in town, these friendly outposts will re-affirm your faith in Bahamian hospitality.

**Smith's Point Fish Fry** (Map p81; Taino Beach; mains US$10-22; ☺ from 6pm Wed) Smitty's is the place to be on Wednesday nights. Locals and tourists alike queue for grouper, lobster and snapper, all fried up under a bustling beachfront shack.

**ourpick Georgie's Restaurant & Lounge** (Map p81; ☎ 242-373-8513; Mather Town off Mid-shipman Rd; mains $10-24; ☺ lunch & dinner) Formerly Club Caribe, Georgie's is owned by friendly George Gibson – who might just pick you up from your hotel if you need a ride. Complement an order of can't-miss cracked conch and peas-and-rice with a sunset view on the wooden deck. Waitress Faith Rolle will steer you right with her menu and traveling tips. Live music on Saturdays.

There's usually a line, so grab a Kalik at the **Outrigger Beach Club** ( ☎ 242-373-4811) next door then make a few friends while you wait. A DJ mixes things up around 7:30pm – a reggae version of 'Cotton-Eyed Joe'? Every taxi driver knows how to get here. Recommended.

## Entertainment

**Galleria 5 Cinemas** (Map p82; ☎ 242-351-9190; RND Plaza, East Atlantic Mall Dr, Freeport; admission adults/children US$7/3) Five-screen cinema showing mainstream hits.

**Amnesia** (Map p82; ☎ 242-351-2582; East Mall Dr, Freeport; ☺ 9pm-late Thu, Fri & Sat) This tropical-themed nightclub has a state-of-the-art light-and-sound system blending reggae, soca, goombay and hip-hop. Hours and admission fees vary, so check beforehand.

The resorts offer in-house entertainment, while the **Port Lucaya Marketplace** (Map p85; ☎ 242-373-8446; www.portlucaya.com) hosts live music Thursday to Sunday. This is a great open-air setting, with a stage and dance floor surrounded by open bars and cafés.

## EAST OF FREEPORT

East of the Grand Lucayan Waterway (a 7.5-mile, or 12km, canal), the Grand Bahama Hwy runs parallel to the shore to the east end of the island. Side roads lead to the south shore's talcum-powder-soft beaches.

### Peterson Cay National Park

This 1.5-acre (0.6-hectare) park is the only cay on Grand Bahama's south shore. It's a popular getaway, busy with locals' boats on weekends. Coral reefs provide splendid snorkeling and diving. You can hire a boat from any marina in Freeport and Lucaya. Take snorkel gear and a picnic. Also try Grand Bahama Nature Tours (p83).

### Lucayan National Park

This 40-acre (16-hectare) park is Grand Bahama's finest treasure. About 25 miles east of Ranfurly Circle, the park is known for its underwater cave system, which is one of the longest in the world. Visitors can easily check out two of the caves via a short footpath. Bones of the island's earliest inhabitants, the Lucayans, were discovered in **Burial Mound**, the second cave, in 1986. The park is also unique because it's home to all six of the Bahamas' vegetation zones.

Mangrove trails spill out onto the secluded and beautiful **Gold Rock Beach**, definitely worth a stop if you're out this way. Watch your food at the picnic area near the beach, the raccoons are unabashed – but harmless – beggars.

For park entry conditions and further information contact the **Bahamas National Trust** ( ☎ 242-352-5438; www.thebahamasnational trust.org; E Settlers Way, Freeport) or stop by its office at the Rand Nature Center (p83) east of downtown.

## WEST OF FREEPORT

West of Freeport, a slender, scrub-covered peninsula, separated from the 'mainland' by

Freeport Harbour Channel, extends north-west to West End.

The channel opens to **Hawksbill Creek**, named for the once-common marine turtles that now only infrequently come ashore. There's good diving offshore, especially at Deadman's Reef at **Paradise Cove** ( ☎ 242-349-2677; www.deadmansreef .com). This mini-resort sits on one of the few beaches on the west coast, about 15 miles west of downtown Freeport, and it's a fun place to spend a beach day. Snorkeling here is great for newbies and pros alike, just walk into the surf then kick your way to the reefs for an assortment of tropical fish. Not a snorkeler? Lounging on the beach, kayaking, playing vol-leyball and enjoying a burger and Kalik at the resort's tiny Red Bar are also on tap. Word to the wise, irritating the fry cook may result in momentary unpleasantness. Snorkel Tour A includes lunch and hotel pick-up (adult/child US$35/23). There's a small access fee if you don't take the tour.

# OUT ISLANDS

Just when the glossy mags started tout-ing the Out Islands as 'in,' the Ministry of Tourism slapped a new label on them and confused the issue. In order to highlight the slower pace and small-town values of the is-lands scattered beyond New Providence and Grand Bahama, they're now also marketed as 'the Family Islands.' Whatever you call them, it's hard to deny the allure of the quiet rhythms and unspoiled views that make the Out Islands the best of the Bahamas for off-the-beaten-path exploring.

## ABACOS
pop 13,200
Though the Out Islands might rightly be described as sleepy, the Abacos will be the first to shake off the snooze. Yachtsmen and divers flock to this glittering crescent of islands and cays – stretching south for 200 miles just east of Grand Bahama – for stellar sailing, spectacular reef diving and sunny ports-of-call.

The main island is 130-mile-long Abaco, with most Abaconians living in bustling Marsh Harbour. Home to the Out Islands' only stoplight – a lone beacon of either progress or doom depending on who's got your ear – this marina-crammed community is a prime launch pad for exploring the sur-

rounding cays and reefs. The Loyalist Cays – Elbow, Great Guana, Man O' War and Green Turtle – beckon offshore just a short ferry ride away. Named after the 18th-century settlers who came here to avoid prosecution during the American Revolution, they're an inviting collection of clapboard homes, narrow streets and chock-a-block museums. The Great Abaco Barrier Reef, allegedly the third largest in the world, lures divers and snorkelers alike, with some of the best snor-keling just a short kick from shore.

But it's not all fish and history. The Abacos may be most fondly known for their fantastic island bars – Miss Emily's Blue Bee and Nippers to name two – which make this lovely chain the best Bahamian spot for a yacht crawl.

### GETTING THERE & AWAY
#### Air
For information on air travel to the Abacos, see p106 and p108.

#### Boat
**Bahamas Ferries** ( ☎ 242-323-2166; www.bahamas.com) runs between Sandy Point, Great Abaco and Nassau. There was no bus service at press time between Marsh Harbour and Sandy Point, which is 60 miles south of the city. This means that savings garnered from the ferry may be lost on cab fare – which is about $120. Scaredy-cat flyers won't care.

There's also a ferry between Grand Bahama and Little Abaco and a mail boat between Nassau and Abaco (see p108 for details).

### GETTING AROUND
#### Boat
Ferry schedules can be found on maps, in the *Abaconian,* or on the websites for Abaco and Albury's ferries. You can set your watch by the latter. Get there on time.

**Abaco Ferry** ( ☎ 242-367-3277; www.abacoferry .com; round trip adult/under 6yr/child US$20/free/10) The new kid on the block offers prices slightly cheaper than Albury's. Its dock is the sec-ond one on the right as you approach the end of Bay St. They travel to Hopetown and White Sound.

**Albury's Ferry Service** ( ☎ 242-367-0290; www .alburysferry.com; round trip adult/under 6yr/child US$22/ free/11) operates scheduled daily water taxis to Elbow (Hope Town), Man O' War and Great

Guana Cays. The dock for Elbow and Man O' War ferries is first on your right at the east end of Bay St; the dock for Guana Cay is at Conch Inn Marina. One-way tickets are $16 for adults, $8 for kids.

**Green Turtle Ferry** ( ☎ 242-365-4166; round trip tickets adult/child US$15/8) departs from the ferry dock just south of Treasure Cay airport and arrives at the New Plymouth ferry dock on Green Turtle Cay 12 minutes later. One-way tickets are US$10 for adults, US$5 for children.

### Bus
Call the **Abaco Ministry of Tourism** ( ☎ 242-367-3067) for the latest information on who, if anyone, is running bus service between Crown Haven and Marsh Harbour. Otherwise pray for a cab or hitch. This trip can be an adventure if ill-prepared.

### Car, Motorcycle & Golf Cart
**Rental Wheels** ( ☎ 242-367-4643; Bay St, Marsh Harbour; ☷ 8am-5pm Mon-Fri, 9am-1pm Sat & Sun) has rental rates as follows: bicycles US$10/45 per day/week and cars US$65/300 per day/week. You need a motorcycle license for the motorbikes, which cost US$45/200 per day/week. The economy cars book fast, so call ahead.

Golf carts can be hired on the cay docks for around US$50 per day.

### Taxi
Taxi fares are pre-established. A ride between Marsh Harbour's airport and most hotels is US$12 for two people. Taxis run up and down Bay St and are easy to flag down. Also try the Curly Tails parking lot at the ferry dock. **Knowles Taxi Service** ( ☎ 242-359-6270) has two vans.

The cab ride from Marsh Harbor to Treasure Cay and the Green Turtle ferry dock can cost $60 one way – for a 17-mile trip! It's cheaper to rent a car for the day.

## Marsh Harbour
Home to the Abacos' one stoplight and countless curly-tailed lizards, Marsh Harbour is the place to stock up on supplies, check emails, get cash and take advantage of culinary diversity. Many hotels and restaurants cluster around the Conch Inn & Marina on Bay St, just east of Don McKay Blvd. Traffic here and downtown has gotten heavy surprisingly quickly and the flow of trucks filled with construction workers seems constant during daylight hours.

Like many communities in the Bahamas, Marsh Harbour is facing potentially long-term problems resulting from ill-planned development, absentee homeowners and environmental degradation. Just read the editorial page of the *Abaconian* and its letters to the editor for a summary of the conflicts. Prominent locals have taken the initiative environmentally through **Friends of the Environment** (www.friendsoftheenvironment.org), which highlights key eco-issues through education and communitywide projects.

The ferry docks for Elbow Cay and Man O' War are at the eastern end of Bay St. and the Guana Cay ferry stops beside the Conch Inn. For Treasure Cay, follow the Bootle Hwy 17 miles north from Marsh Harbour. The Green Turtle Cay ferry dock is a few miles further north off the Bootle.

### INFORMATION
Public telephones can be found at BaTelCo and the Conch Inn & Marina, and scattered throughout downtown. The Abacos' free and helpful weekly, *The Abaconian,* provides ferry schedules, taxi cab fares and phone numbers for restaurants, fishing guides and rental companies. The websites www.go-abacos.com, www .abacolife.com and www.abacomessageboard .com are also helpful.

Abaco Life sells the informative *Map of the Abacos* (US$3), which has helpful drawings of Great Abaco, Marsh Harbour and the busiest cays, plus ferry schedules. The free, bright yellow Abaco maps are also good, if not quite as comprehensive.

**Bahamas Family Market** ( ☎ 242-367-3714; cnr Queen Elizabeth Dr & Don McKay Blvd) Enjoy a homemade meat pie while internet surfing at this popular local market. It's US$2 for 10 minutes.

**Bahamas Ministry of Tourism** ( ☎ 242-367-3067; Memorial Plaza, Queen Elizabeth Dr; ☷ 9am-5pm Mon-Fri)

**Hospital clinic** ( ☎ 242-367-2510)

**Out Island Internet** ( ☎ 242-367-3006; Queen Elizabeth Dr) Offers wi-fi packages for those cruising the cays, starting at $US10 for 12 hours. On-site internet rates are US$5 for 20 minutes then US$0.25 for each additional minute.

**Police** ( ☎ 242-367-2560; 911 emergencies)

**Post office** ( ☎ 242-367-2571)

**Royal Bank of Canada** ( ☎ 242-367-2420) ATM.

**Scotiabank** ( ☎ 242-367-2141) ATM.

### SIGHTS & ACTIVITIES
Most outfitters in Marsh Harbour are clustered on Bay St east of Don McKay Blvd. A

few sights and tour companies are based in Treasure Cay, about 17 miles north.

### Beaches
**Treasure Cay Beach** is the pin-up girl of the Abacos. Located about 17 miles north of Marsh Harbour, her white sand and turquoise shallows garner kudos from travel magazines as well as one reality TV family – the Roloffs, whose popular Learning Channel show *Little People, Big World* followed them here in 2007.

### Diving & Snorkeling
Wade in and try the snorkeling at Mermaid Reef on the north side of the city.

**Bahamas Underground** ( ☎ 242-359-6128; www .bahamasunderground.com; Marsh Harbour) is best for advanced divers who want to explore underwater caves and blue holes. Guide and co-owner Brian Kakuk is a local diving legend with more than 17 years' experience exploring the region's intricate cave systems. Call for details.

**Dive Abaco** ( ☎ 242-367-2787; www.diveabaco.com; Conch Inn Resort & Marina, Marsh Harbour) has two-tank dives (US$100), two-tank shark dives (US$135) and night dives (US$100), as well as wreck and inland blue-hole trips. Daily and weekly rentals also available.

### Boat Trips & Fishing
Sailboats and motorboats can be rented at most marinas. Demand often exceeds supply, so reserve early. See the Visitors' Guide in the weekly *Abaconian* for a full listing of rental companies.

**Blue Wave Boat Rentals** ( ☎ 242-367-3910; www .bluewaverentals.com; Harbour View Marina, Bay St) charges US$200 per day, US$500 for three days and US$1000 per week for its 21ft boats.

**CJ's Abaco Dorado Boat Rentals** ( ☎ 242-367-1035; www.abacodoradoboatrentals.com; Conch Inn Marina, Bay St) rents 22ft (6.7m) boats for US$200 a day, US$1085 a week. Newly available are 26ft (8m) boats with GPS navigation systems for $350 per day or $1400 per week.

**Captain Justin Sands** ( ☎ 242-367-3526; www.baha masvg.com/justfish.html) is a highly recommended bonefishing guide who will prepare and price tailor-made trips for you.

### SLEEPING
Marsh Harbour is a good central base for those day-tripping to the various cays. The occasional brief electrical outage seems to be a common problem.

**Conch Inn Marina & Hotel** ( ☎ 242-367-4000; www .go-abacos.com/conchinn; Bay St; r US$130; 🛜 🏊 ) Yachties, divers and cay hoppers inevitably buzz past this queen bee during extended Abaco vacations. Adjacent to a busy marina, Curly Tails restaurant, Dive Abaco and the Guana Cay dock, it's a well-situated gateway for exploring. Mid-sized rooms have white tile floors, wicker-style furniture, a fridge and a coffee maker. A few rooms have occasional hot water problems, so ask before you book.

**Lofty Fig Villas** ( ☎ 242-367-2681; www.loftyfig.com; Bay St; r US$176; 🛜 🖥 🏊 ) This minivillage of canary-bright duplexes works well for budget-minded travelers wanting to be close to, but not in the middle of, the harbor-side action. Rooms are big, bright, airy and clean; and each has a small kitchen, wi-fi access and screened porch. Rooms don't have phones, but the office does. Don't doubt any helpful tips provided by the Fig's friendly owner, Sid. The man knows Abaco and if he says it's cheaper to rent a car than hire a taxi to get to Treasure Cay, believe him.

### EATING & DRINKING
Marsh Harbour has the Abacos' widest array of choices, from fast food to fine dining, while the cays offer a mix of beach bars and mom-and-pop joints – most with ocean or marina views.

**Jamie's Place** ( ☎ 242-367-2880; Bay St; mains US$6-13; ☻ breakfast, lunch, dinner) It's T-shirts, ball caps and flip flops at this sparely decorated diner where locals greet each other by name and Bahamian and American dishes are served up piping hot. For a hearty breakfast, try the scram special, a mix of eggs, onions, garlic and mushrooms.

**Curly Tails Restaurant & Bar** ( ☎ 242-367-4444; Bay St; lunch US$9-25, dinner US$18-39; ☻ breakfast, lunch & dinner) Named for the island's ubiquitous curly-tailed lizard, this is the see-and-be-seen spot for upscale noshing. Fancy wraps, gourmet burgers and international dishes *du jour* are best enjoyed on the breezy marina-side patio where day-trippers queue for the Guana Cay ferry.

**our pick Snappa's** ( ☎ 242-367-2278; Bay St; mains US$11-28; ☻ lunch & dinner) We love Snappa's for its awesome grilled seafood – which can be darn hard to find on the Out Islands. The thick, grilled mahi mahi sandwich is superb

**LIVING THE GOOD LIFE**

Penny Turtle is an Abaco good-life connoisseur. She was the local film liaison during *Thunderball* and *Help!*, and has been a Bahamas resident since 1959.

**How did you assist with Help!?**

I was a den mother to the Beatles, protecting them from girls hiding in the bushes and up in trees.

**Any stories from the Bond film Thunderball?**

We did a shark scene at a friend's house. They kept the sharks in a pool with transparent fiberglass down the center of the pool. Sharks were on one side, Sean on the other. There was a gap…and the shark came around the corner and Sean came out of the pool muttering an expletive.

**Where do those-in-the-know hang out on weekends in Marsh Harbour?**

The Jib Room is great fun on a Saturday night. They have a band and the head bartender is the lead singer.

**Best beach spot?**

Nippers has one of the most special beaches. It has two pools and a beautiful view.

**Any misconceptions about your name?**

Everyone thought I ran Green Turtle Cay.

**What's your favorite thing about living here?**

The people I meet.

and with a splash of Conchy Joe's Pepper Sauce you might just nibble into heaven. Live music is the evening draw at this marina-side mecca Wednesday through Saturday, with the biggest party crowds descending on Friday.

**Jib Room Restaurant & Bar** ( ☎ 242-367-2700; Pelican Shores Rd; lunch US$10-15, dinner US$25; ⏰ lunch Wed-Sat, dinner Wed & Sat) Got the post-snorkel munchies? After a morning at Mermaid Reef, order a salad or sandwich on the Jib's harborside deck and tell fish tales as the yacht's pull in. On Saturday nights, everyone's here for steaks, live music and dancing.

For java, pastries and local art, try friendly **Java of Abaco** ( ☎ 242-367-5523; Bay St; ⏰ 8am-1pm).

## Elbow Cay

The Queen's 'Highway' isn't much more than a sidewalk through parts of Hope Town – the heart of Elbow Cay – but that's not unexpected in a gingerbread town guarded by a candy-stripe lighthouse. Beyond the impossible cuteness of clapboard houses and flower-lined streets, you'll find plenty of historical attractions that highlight the adversities faced by the Loyalists and their descendants. The ferry, which takes about 20 minutes, stops at three Hope Town docks – the lower dock, the government/post office dock and the Harbour Lodge dock. To visit the lighthouse, located across the channel from the lower dock, tell the ferry driver you'd like to stop. He'll drop you off then pick you up on his next loop.

**INFORMATION**

Public restrooms and a slim-pickings tourist information board are across from the Government Dock.

The **Post office** ( ☎ 242-366-0098; Queen's Hwy) is above the tourist information board.

**SIGHTS & ACTIVITIES**

The island's signature attraction, the candy-striped **Elbow Cay Lighthouse**, was an object of community-wide loathing when built in 1863. Many here supplemented their incomes by salvaging loot off ships that crashed against the cay's treacherous reefs – usually one a month. An 89ft lighthouse was the last thing these 'wreckers' needed. Today, you can check out views from the top. There's no admission, just follow the signs, walk up 101 steps and – if you dare – push your way through a small trap door to panoramic views from a scare-your-mother balcony.

In Hope Town, the engaging exhibits at the **Wynnie Malone Museum** ( ☎ 242-366-0293; Back St; adult/family US$3/5; ⏰ 10am-3pm Mon-Sat, closed Aug-Oct) examine the island's Loyalist roots and its maritime history. Downstairs, check out a 1783 *New York Post* article calling for a meeting for all Tories intending to move to the Abacos. Upstairs, look for the exhibit discussing the aforementioned wreckers as well as an account of the wreck of the *Athel Queen*, an Italian tanker torpedoed off the coast here in 1942.

Take in tranquil ocean views from the small gazebo at the **Byrle Patterson Memorial Garden**. Just north on Back Street is a small dune fronted by a white picket fence. This is the **Cholera Cemetery** where victims of an 1850s cholera epidemic are buried. At the top of the dune is a moving **monument** overlooking the ocean. Erected in 2007, it's dedicated to the souls lost at sea off the Elbow Cay Reef with a bronze plaque memorializing the three lost men from the M/V *Athel Queen*.

### Cycling
Rent bikes at **Sundried T's** ( ☎ 242-366-0616), located beside the Government Dock, for US$10 per day.

### Diving & Snorkeling
**Froggies Out Island Adventures** ( ☎ 242-366-0431; www.froggiesabaco.com) offers one-/two-tank dives (US$95/105) as well as half- and full-day snorkeling trips (US$55/45 per half/full day, children are $15 less). Tanks rentals are US$10 per day, and mask and fin rentals are also US$10 per day.

### Surfing
The offshore waters boast several good surfing breaks on the south Atlantic shore, especially in the winter. Try Rush Reef or the reef off Garbanzo Beach for some of the Bahamas' best surfing. Rent boards for US$30/day at **Sundried T's** ( ☎ 242-366-0616), located beside the Government Dock.

### SLEEPING & EATING
**Hope Town Harbour Lodge** ( ☎ 242-366-0095; www .hopetownlodge.com; Back Street; r/cottage US$175/275; ☒ ☐ ☒ ) With her white picket fence and frosting-blue balconies, this hilltop charm-cake will have you at hello; palm-framed harbor views will keep you from saying good-bye. Orange bedspreads, island prints and inviting balconies enhance smallish rooms in the main house. For more space and a kitchenette, try one of the cottages.

**Cap'n Jack's** ( ☎ 242-366-0247; Queen's Hwy; mains US$7-17; ☺ breakfast, lunch & dinner) If *Cheers'* bar-flies Norm and Cliff drank beer in Abaco, this wood-planked watering hole is where you'd likely find them. Locals linger over burgers, salads and fish sandwiches at tight booths inside while tourists opt for marina views on the waterside deck. Everyone heads here for Monday night bingo and Thursday night trivia.

## Green Turtle Cay
If you've got time for only one cay, make it Green Turtle. By far the friendliest island in the Abacos, if not the Bahamas, the inhabitants are more than willing to point you in the right direction for hearty dining, primo diving and Loyalist-minded sight-seeing. And being the birthplace of the goombay smash isn't such a shabby distinction either. The northernmost of the four Loyalist cays, it takes a little more effort it get here, but only the most determined curmudgeons will leave unhappy.

The compact town of New Plymouth is easily explored on foot though golf carts are for rent near the ferry dock at **Kool Karts** ( ☎ 242-365-4176; per day US$50). Note that many shops and businesses close for lunch.

In sum? The roosters here are so darn jazzed, they crow about it all day long.

### INFORMATION
The **police station** ( ☎ 242-365-4450, 911) and **post office** ( ☎ 242-365-4242) are located inside an old pink-and-white building on Parliament Street.

### SIGHTS
Take a left off the ferry dock, walk to Mission St and turn right. Miss Emily's Blue Bee is on your right. You'll be stopping here later. Just past the Blue Bee are the pink ruins of **Ye Olde Jail**. Diagonally across the intersection is a small, windswept **cemetery** where the headstones have sweeping views of Great Abaco.

Every small town needs a musty, knick-knack filled repository and the 1826 **Albert Lowe Museum** ( ☎ 242-365-4095; Parliament & King Sts, Loyalist Rd; admission US$5; ☺ 9am-11:45pm Mon-Sat), serves this purpose admirably. Once home to future Prime Minister Neville Chamberlain, the museum now boasts a fine collection of locally crafted model ships and black-and-white photographs highlighting the cay's history. Ask to see the collection of old liquor bottles excavated from the outhouse.

At the **Loyalist Memorial Sculpture Garden** you'll discover that the inspirational can sometimes be creepy. Here, 24 busts of notable Bahamian loyalists and slaves all gaze in dead-eyed wonder at bronze statues of two girls, one holding a conch and the other a Union Jack.

## ACTIVITIES
**Brendal's Dive Center** ( ☎ 242-365-4411; www.brendal.com; White Sound), winner of the Bahamas Tourism Cacique Award in 2006 for Sustainable Tourism, offers one-/two-tank dives (US$82/102) as well as half-day snorkeling trips (US$70), island-hopping tours (US$80) and a variety of family and group-oriented adventure packages. Kayaks and bikes also available for rent.

## EATING & DRINKING
**McIntosh Restaurant & Bakery** ( ☎ 242-365-4625; Parliament St; mains US$10-25; ☺ breakfast, lunch & dinner) Leave your willpower at the door at this homey spot where hearty fried Bahamian dishes, fresh breads and decadent squares of cheesecake are more than happy to ruin all dietary resolutions. Also worth a savor are the cracked conch sandwich and the key lime pie.

**ourpick** **Miss Emily's Blue Bee Bar** ( ☎ 242-365-4181; Victoria St, New Plymouth; mains $6-10; ☺ lunch & dinner) From the walls slathered with business cards, photographs and personal messages to the convivial customers who return year after year, it's clear this bar is truly loved. A portrait of the original owner, Miss Emily, perches high above the front counter, a perfect vantage point for watching over the happy hordes enjoying her signature drink, the goombay smash. Created for a thirsty customer decades ago, the potent concoction is poured straight from a plastic gallon jug into your cup – the exact ingredients still a secret.

Miss Emily's charming daughter Violet Smith runs the bar today. After years of watching guests leave to grab meals at neighboring restaurants, she opened her own at the Blue Bee on Thanksgiving Day 2007. It's a hit and her plate-filling fried chicken, cracked lobster and burgers are earning kudos beyond the tiny cay.

So what's the record for goombay smashes consumed in one evening? One male imbiber drank 29 and played golf the next day. And for women? According to Violet, one lady consumed 19 and claimed she felt fine, although she no longer drinks.

## Great Guana Cay
Everyone's here for one reason. Maybe two. But trust me, if you ask your ferry mates if they're heading to **Nippers Beach Bar & Grill** ( ☎ 242-365-5143; www.nippersbar.com; mains lunch US$11-

US$16, mains dinner US$20-US$30; ☺ lunch & dinner), it's almost guaranteed they'll say yes. This candy-bright beachside Shangri-La is a forget-your-cares kind of place where Kaliks taste better, your sweetie looks cuter and everyone in sight is your new best friend. The Sunday afternoon pig roast is legendary, drawing party-hearty locals and intrepid tourists from across the Abacos. The timid need not stay home. There's 5½ miles of stunning white sand for those itching to slip the crowds. Other distractions include tasty burgers, a gift shop, inviting pools and an Australian owner who looks like Russell Crowe. To get here, take a right off the ferry dock, walk a bit, then follow the signs. The no-see-ums can be pesky so bring spray.

The second big draw? Awesome **snorkeling** off the Great Abaco Barrier Reef. It's a short beach stroll and a few strong kicks from the bar. Forget your gear? No worries, Nippers has some for the borrowing.

# ELEUTHERA
### pop 8200
So what do you do in Eleuthera, a 100-mile-long wisp curving east like an archer's bow? According to literature, research and dependable local gossips, most people come here to do…absolutely nothing. That's right. While shoppers, kiteboarders and divers might find themselves graciously indulged, the beach bum is the true king here, his every do-nothing need met by a slew of obliging shores.

The first non-native settlers to land here were a bit more industrious. These forward thinkers, the Eleutheran Adventurers, arrived in 1648 to establish a community where 'Freedom of Conscience' in the practice of religion would be a guiding tenet. Though most Adventurers eventually left due to the hardships of island life, religion has flourished, and according to one count, 112 churches stretch from north to south.

For those looking for more than a suntan, Eleuthera offers a number of high energy distractions. Wreck divers can explore the Devil's Backbone; fashionistas can wander the upscale boutiques of Harbour Island; and seasoned kitesurfers can skip across waves off eastern shores.

Hotels across Eleuthera and Harbour Island are typically pricey with a handful of exceptions. To save money, avoid high season from mid-December through mid-April and time your visit for early summer or late fall.

### GETTING THERE & AROUND
For flights to Eleuthera, see p107 and p108.

Ferries and mail boats run to Harbour Island and Governor's Harbour from Nassau; see p108 for details. One-day vacation packages are also available; see p70.

From Harbour Island, water taxis run between the Government Dock and North Eleuthera (US$10).

## Harbour Island
This 3-mile speck has done such a great job touting itself as the chichi home of supermodel Elle MacPherson and style maven India Hicks that you're vaguely disappointed when they fail to greet you at the dock with muffins and scented candles. In fact, glossies tout 'Briland's' charming mix of rustic and chic to such a nauseating degree that it's hard not to hate the place on sight – an inclination abetted by knowledge that Masters of the Universe are snapping up the island's best parcels as quick as they can.

But ignoring these facts for a moment – as well as the island's less-than-captivating golf carts, pain-in-the-ass roosters and snooty boutiques – the shimmering pink sand beach here does glow with a soul-replenishing beauty. One that's frustratingly hard to hate. Another plus? Thrill-seeking kiteboarders, recently drawn to the island's superb mix of shallows, wind and crowd-free beaches, have added a 'Hey bro' friendliness to the trendy mix. And divers continue to descend for pristine reefs and ancient wrecks.

In sum, supermodels, scented candles and land-grabbing moguls are the price one pays for gorgeous sand and surf. And according to local rumor, MacPherson has already left the building.

### INFORMATION
Harborside Dunmore Town is the island's administrative center and dates back 300 years. The commonly seen appellation 'Briland,' is a local slurring of Harbour Island.

**Arthur's Bakery & Café** ( ☎ 242-333-2285; ⏰ 8am-2pm, closed Sun) Internet access is US$7.50 per 30 minutes.
**Bahamas Ministry of Tourism** ( ☎ 242-333-2621; Dunmore St; ⏰ 9am-5pm Mon-Fri)
**Harbour Island Medical Clinic** ( ☎ 242-333-2227; Colebrook St)

**Police** ( ☎ 242-333-2111, for emergencies 333-2919; Gaol St)
**Post office** ( ☎ 242-333-2215; Gaol St)
**Royal Bank of Canada** ( ☎ 242-333-2250; Dunmore St)

### SIGHTS & ACTIVITIES
One of the finest examples of Loyalist architecture is the **Loyalist Cottage** (Bay St), west of Princess St, dating back to 1797.

The funky side of things is to be found at the corner of Dunmore and Clarence Sts, where a mish-mash of signs, international license plates and driftwood relics are displayed, painted with humorous limericks and aphorisms.

The wide and stunning length of **Pink Sands Beach** shimmers with a pink glow that's a faint blush by day and a rosy red when fired by the dawn or sunset.

Harbour Island is surrounded by superb snorkeling and dive sites, highlighted by the Devil's Backbone. The pristine reefs are littered with ancient wrecks. **Valentine's Dive Center** ( ☎ 242-333-2080; www.valentinesdive.com; Bay St) offers a two-tank dive (US$75), a one-tank night dive (US$85) and snorkeling (US$45). Fishers can charter boats for US$750/950 per half/full day. Kayaks are US$30/45 per half/full day. Kayaks are also available at Michael's Cycles (p95) for US$20/40 per half/full day. At the southern end of town, try the 28-year veteran **Ocean Fox** ( ☎ 242-333-2323; www.oceanfox.com). Two-tank dives are US$110.

Kitesurfing is 'taking off' here, with internationally known pros dropping in for perfect – but unforgiving – gust-and-wave combos off Harbor Island. Beginners can take lessons on the shallow shores of nearby Spanish Wells with **Cross-Shore** ( ☎ 242-393-3261; www.cross-shore.com) run by friendly Aussie AJ Watson. Currently, two-day beginner lessons cost US$450. Cross-Shore also offers lessons off the southern coast of New Providence.

### SLEEPING
**Royal Palm Hotel** ( ☎ 242-333-2738; Chapel St; r US$90; ❄ ) Rooms could be cleaner, but units are bright and spacious. Deluxe rooms come with a kitchenette. The hotel is comprised of several two-story buildings scattered along Dunmore St. The lobby is at the corner of Dunmore and Clarence Sts. Golf carts available for US$47/day.

**Bahama House Inn** ( ☎ 242-333-2201; www.bahamahouseinn.com; cnr Dumore & Hill Sts; r US$160; ❄ ) Outdoor decking connects cool and comfy living areas at this welcoming inn where rooms are furnished with eclectic colonial furniture. Rooms have private baths and overlook a large garden and patio deck. No children under 12. Full breakfasts provided.

**Rock House** ( ☎ 242-333-2053; www.rockhouse bahamas.com; Chapel St; r US$380; 🗙 🖳 🖭 ) Thatch-covered cottages, bamboo walls, flickering torches – it's a tiki-chic cocktail at this hilltop retreat where shimmering harbor views recharge a stylish but friendly crowd. Steep stone steps lead from Bay St to Rock House's nine rooms, decorated in crisp earth tones discreetly splashed with tropical color. Bright pillows distract from sometimes smallish digs – though you do get your own private poolside cabana. It has a full gym and wi-fi by the pool. Visitors flock to the bar and restaurant for poolside cocktails or a late-night 'hokey pokey' – homemade vanilla ice cream with honeycomb.

**Pink Sands Resort** ( ☎ 242-333-2030; www.pinksands resort.com; Chapel St; r US$750; 🗙 🖳 🖭 ) Sweeeet! Luxurious cottages dot tropical gardens like private minikingdoms, but perky conch shell 'fences' do much to keep pretension at bay. Inside, envision throw rugs on rough-cut marble-like floors, uniquely crafted beds and decor seamlessly merging Asian and Caribbean designs with flat-screen modern functionality. This is where bad-boy celebs tumble from oceanfront decks and supermodels snooze past noon. Mayhem is discreet but indulged. Even if you're not a guest, stop by the infamous Blue Bar for a seaside cocktail. There's wi-fi for guests.

### EATING

**ourpick Arthur's Bakery & Café** ( ☎ 242-333-2285; mains under US$10; 🕑 8am-2pm Mon-Sat) One of the friendliest spots in town, this cornerside nook is the place to catch up on gossip, gather travel advice and relax over warm fresh bread and coffee. Sandwiches available for lunch.

**Ma Ruby's** ( ☎ 242-333-2161; Tingum Village Hotel & Bar; breakfast & lunch mains up to US$20, dinner mains US$8-40; 🕑 breakfast, lunch & dinner) Alleged home of Jimmy Buffett's 'Cheeseburger in Paradise.'

**Sip Sip** ( ☎ 242-333-3316; Court Rd; mains US$15-30; 🕑 lunch, closed Tue, closed Tue & Wed Jun-Aug) Treat yourself to a little taste of fabulous at this chichi lime box preening at the end of Court Rd. Gourmet fusion lunches – lobster quesa-

dillas, conch chili – are best nibbled on the crisp white deck. Here you can enjoy pink sand views while indulging in a little 'sip sip' – the local term for gossip. US$15 hotdogs may leave you murmuring as well.

**Aqua Pazza** ( ☎ 242-333-3240; Harbour Island Marina; mains lunch US$15-20, mains dinner US$20-38; 🕑 lunch & dinner) Tucked between a haunted house and the harbor, the new kid on the block is earning raves for its Italian cuisine. The wine list, marina views and romantic ambience are impressive; the service, alas, a smidge less so. But ah, those views and that pasta.

For gourmet deli sandwiches and fancy sides, try **Dunmore Deli** ( ☎ 242-333-2644; King St; 🕑 breakfast & lunch Mon-Sat)

Some of the island's best meals are served at the shacks lining Bay St north of the harbor. There's always a line for Bahamian fare at Harry O's and people risk missing the ferry for a fresh, tart bowl of conch salad at Queen Conch.

### DRINKING

**Vic Hum Club** ( ☎ 242-333-2161; cnr Barrack & Munnings Sts; 🕑 11am-late) For ramshackle good times, park your putter at this late night party shack and abandon all reserve at the door. From kick-back natives to Aussie kiteboarders to yacht crews on shore leave, it's a funky, rum-fueled bazaar where a basketball court doubles as a dance floor. Miss it and forever rue the day. Pronunciation is key: Viccum.

Late night, try **Gusty's Bar** ( ☎ 242-333-2165; 🕑 9:30pm-1am) on Coconut Grove Ave where Jimmy Buffett's been known to jam.

### SHOPPING

Harbour Island's not kidding around when it comes to boutiques, even earning kudos from *Travel + Leisure* in 2007 as the best Caribbean island for shopping. Try the blue-shuttered **Blue Rooster** ( ☎ 242-333-2240; King & Dunmore Sts) for stylish sun dresses, wraps and accessories; and **The Sugar Mill Trading Company** ( ☎ 242-333-3558; Bay St) for unique gifts and island-minded merchandise. The most fun may be had at boldly bright, non-boutiquey **Dilly Dally** ( ☎ 242-333-3109), unabashedly jam-packed with flip-flops, bikinis, Briland tees and Bahamian books. Most stores are closed on Sunday.

### GETTING AROUND

Briland is a mini-LA – no one walks if they can help it. For golf carts, try **Dunmore Rentals**

(☎ 242-333-2372) on Bay St by the Government Dock (US$50) or **Ross Rentals** (☎ 242-333-2122) on Colebrook St just past Alice St (US$45). If you find sputtering golf carts non-charming, **Michael's Cycles** (☎ 242-333-2384) rents bikes for US$12/day.

## Gregory Town

Quiet six nights out of the week, this low-key village is 25 miles north of Governor's Harbour and five miles south of the Glass Window Bridge, where the island narrows dramatically to a thin span straddling the divide between pounding Atlantic waves and the tranquil green shoals of the Bight of Eleuthera. A hurricane destroyed the natural bridge that was once there, so a narrow man-made substitute is now the only thing connecting north and south Eleuthera.

Gregory Town, once famous for its thriving pineapple industry, sits above a steep cove on a sharp bend in the Queen's Hwy. Just before the bend, stop at the **Island Made Gift Shop** (☎ 242-335-5369; Queen's Hwy) for Bahamian-made hot sauces, prints, candles and batik

clothing. Just south – at the bend – is a colorful, snapshot-worthy **mileage marker**. Surfer's Beach is two miles south (see below). To get there, creep up the axle-testing road at **Surfer's Haven** (☎ 242-333-3282; www.surfershavenbahamas.com; r $US25), a laid-back, hostel-style retreat five minutes' walk from the beach. Rooms are inside or attached to the main house, with full use of the den, kitchen and large wooden deck with sea views. The apartment (US$75) has a kitchenette. Owner Tom Glucksmann runs ecominded kayaking, snorkeling and nature trips with his company **Bahamas Out-island Adventures** (☎ 242-335-0349; www.bahamasadventures.com; half/full day US$59/99). The man knows his birds and is a passionate advocate for preserving lonely Lighthouse Point at the southern tip of the island.

The towering stone silos dotting the skyline as you continue south once held cow feed. Just past these are the brightly painted, octagonal cottages of the **Rainbow Inn** (☎ 242-335-0294; www.rainbowinn.com; r US$140; 🖳 🖳 ), another good lodging choice. The nautical-themed restaurant's popular for supper on Friday Steak Nights.

### BEACHES

The island's secluded shores are some of the best in the Bahamas for lounging, loafing, lollygagging and maybe, just maybe, a little beachcombing. For beach hunters, there's the helpful *The Elusive Beaches of Eleuthera*, by Geoff and Vicky Wells (US$25.95), which is sold at Haynes Library and The Island Made Gift Shop. The Tarbox map (US$10) sold at the Rainbow Inn is also good. Here are a few of the best starting from the north:

■ Pink Sands Beach – The sand really does glow a light shade of pink. Follow Chapel St or Court St to public access paths to the Atlantic side shores.

■ Surfer's Beach – Windswept bluffs are a primo perch for watching surfers catching waves below. Follow the trail down to the protected beach. Two miles south of the Island Made Gift Shop in Gregory Town, take the rutted dirt road at the Surfer's Haven sign on the Atlantic side and follow the occasional marker to the bluffs and a small parking area.

■ Club Med Beach – Majestic pines sway beside a softly curving shore at this beautiful beach, one of the prettiest in the Bahamas. Known for years as Club Med Beach, for the resort that once stood here, the shores will probably be renamed after the French Leave Resort opens, probably in 2008. For now, drive toward the Atlantic on Haynes Ave, passing the Quality Inn on your left. Turn right at the T, drive about an eighth of a mile to a dirt pull-off.

■ Ten Bay – South of Palmetto Point, this quiet, palm-shaded alcove borders Savannah Sound on the Caribbean side. Great for beachcombing, its shallows hold starfish and tiny conch shells. Heading south on Queen's Hwy, drive 3.5 miles past the Palmetto Point junction then turn right at the telephone pole with red reflectors that's next to the white sale-pending sign. Yes, slightly vague, but that's Eleuthera.

■ Lighthouse Beach – It's a drive, but the dazzling 6 miles of rosy-pink beach at the southern tip of the island are inspiring. Bring snorkel gear, a picnic and your soulmate. And hurry – developers are circling.

THE BAHAMAS

And about that not-so-quiet seventh George Town night? Fridays are Jam Night at **Elvina's Bar & Restaurant** ( ☎ 242-335-5032), just south of the bend. By 9:30pm this old-school party shack – don't count on getting food – is rumblin' to the rafters with half-hour sets by natives and visiting musicians. You might just see local landowner Lenny Kravitz strolling through the upbeat crowd of low-key locals, over-served yachties, sun-dried surfers and befuddled tourists – who can't figure out where all these people came from. Everyone's here or on the way.

## Governor's Harbour

The sleepy island 'capital' overlooks a broad harbor that runs west along a peninsula to Cupid's Cay, apparently the original settlement of the Eleutheran Adventurers in 1648. Centrally located, this is a great home base for exploring the rest of the island.

### INFORMATION

**Bahamas Ministry of Tourism** ( ☎ 242-332-2142; Queen's Hwy; ⏰ 9am-5pm Mon-Fri)
**Governor's Harbour Medical Clinic** ( ☎ 242-332-2774; Queen's Hwy)
**Haynes Library** ( ☎ 242-332-2877) Housed in a two-story building constructed in 1897, the library has about a dozen computers. Internet US$5 per hour.
**Police** ( ☎ 242-332-21117)
**Post office** ( ☎ 242-332-2060; Haynes Ave)

### SIGHTS & ACTIVITIES

**Clearwater Dive Shop** ( ☎ 242-332-2146) rents tanks for US$12/day and snorkel gear for US$10/day, both requiring a US$50 deposit. The shop doesn't run its own dive or snorkel trips.

### SLEEPING

**Laughing Bird Apartments** ( ☎ 242-332-2012; Queen's Hwy; 1-2 person apt US$100; ☒ ) Just steps from the beach, these beautifully landscaped apartments are a great deal, with the clean, cozy units boasting kitchenettes and palm-framed ocean views. The British owner is absolutely delightful but won't get in your way. Lots of returning international guests.
**Duck Inn** ( ☎ 242-332-2608; www.theduckinn.com; Queen's Hwy; d US$110, 3 night min; ☒ ) This 200-year-old colonial complex, set amid an orchid garden, incorporates three comfortable, fully equipped cottages. Perfect for couples, Cupid's Cottage offers harbor views, while the four-bedroom Flora Cottage works well for large families. A local map and the *Elusive Beaches of Eleuthera* are found in every cottage.
**Quality Inn Cigatoo** ( ☎ 242-332-3060; www.choicehotels.com; Haynes Ave; r US$120; ☒ ☒ ) This spot is also good; it has bright, mid-sized rooms and an on-site restaurant.

### EATING

Friday night, try fresh fish and live music on the waterfront at the **Fish Fry** (mains US$10-20; ⏰ 6pm-midnight) just past Haynes Library. Tourists start showing up around 7pm, locals a little later. Almost too cool for it own good, **Tippy's** ( ☎ 242-332-3331; Banks Rd; mains US$8-21; ⏰ lunch & dinner, bar open until last person goes home) is an upscale beach shack that's the current darling of visiting celebs, the *New York Times* and a host of fawning travel mags. Tippy's specializes in gourmet seafood dishes – lobster wraps, shrimp pizzas, conch fritters with chili mayo – prepared with Bahamian flair. In sum? Delicious food, great views and service a whiff shy of the hoopla.

To create your own fresh dishes, **Island Farm Fresh Produce** (Palmetto Pt, Queen's Hwy; ⏰ 9am-4pm Mon-Sat) offers a variety of fresh fruits and vegetables as well as locally made jams and hot sauces. Try extra-hot Pirates' Revenge.

### GETTING AROUND

**North Eleuthera S/S Car Rental** ( ☎ 242-335-1128) Located at the Shell station just west of the ferry dock and airport; cars rent for about $US80 and require a US$100 deposit. Staff will pick you up at the dock.

## EXUMAS

**pop 3600**

Life's a little snappier in the Exumas. Whether kayaking, kiteboarding or trimming a sail, a crisp palette of ocean blues sharpens every adventure. And with 365 cays unspooling over more than 100 miles, there's a lot of adventure to go around. Wannabe Robinson Crusoes can wander lonely isles in Exuma Cays Land & Sea Park. Lifetime-To-Do-Listers can paddle shimmering Moriah Cay. Determined bonefishers can track wily prey on glass-clear shallows. And that's without mentioning the gregarious yachtsmen who can mix their way to the perfect on-deck cocktail during the festive Family Island Regatta.

Landlubbers have distractions too, with the 62-mile Queen's Highway winding past historic ruins, hidden beaches and convivial beach bars on Great Exuma and Little Exuma, the two largest islands in the chain. In fact, the biggest thrill in Exuma may be the hair-raising one-lane bridge that connects them.

The launch pad for exploring is George Town, the bustling administrative center of Great Exuma that sits on the western shore of the sail-dotted blue waters of Elizabeth Harbour. Bordering the harbor to the east is Stocking Island, a sliver of land best known for its soft white sand and the infamous Chat & Chill Sunday pig roast.

## Information

There are public telephone booths in all the main centers.

**Bahamas Ministry of Tourism** ( ☎ 242-336-2430; Queen's Hwy, George Town)

**BaTelCo** ( ☎ 242-336-2011; Queen's Hwy, George Town) Sells phone cards and SIM cards.

**Exuma Business Centre** ( ☎ 242-336-2091; Queen's Hwy, George Town) Inside Seascape Real Estate; internet access is US$0.20 per minute.

**Government Medical Clinic** ( ☎ 242-336-2088; George Town)

**Police** ( ☎ 242-336-2666, emergency 919; George Town)

**Post office** ( ☎ 242-347-3546; George Town)

**Royal Bank of Canada** (242-336-3251; Queen's Hwy)

**Scotiabank** ( ☎ 242-336-2651; Queen's Hwy)

## Sights

### GEORGE TOWN

The sugar-pink and white neoclassical **Government Administration Building** houses the post office and jail. Just south, the small **Straw Market** sells Bahamian made straw goods. Stock up here instead of Nassau, although you'll still find the ubiquitous Kalik T-shirts. Just north of town is the serene white-stoned **St Andrew's Anglican Church**, which sits atop a bluff above Lake Victoria. For a great photo-op, stop by the rainbow-colored **city mileage markers** stacked high at the southern junction of the Queen's highway and the city loop.

### SOUTH OF GEORGE TOWN
#### Historic Attractions

The Queen's Highway rolls south of George Town to Rolle Town and Little Exuma, offering an engaging half-day mix of sight-seeing, sunning and seafood noshing.

The first major settlement is **Rolle Town**. Follow the main road of Queen's Hwy to the town's hilltop crossroads. Here, turn north and drive along a short ridge for panoramic views – you might see a parasailer catching gusts off Man O' War Cay. South of the crossroad, follow the signs a short distance to the **Rolle Town Tombs**. Here lie a few solitary 18th-century tombs, one dated 1792 and shaped like a stone double bed. The plaque notes that the young wife of a Scottish overseer, Captain Alexander McKay, slumbers there with an infant child. The captain died the following year, some said from a broken heart.

Next up is a keep-on-your-toes one lane bridge linking Great and Little Exuma islands at the town of **Ferry**. After passing through Forbes Hill, you'll soon arrive at lonely Williamstown. Just past Santana's, follow the sign road to the overgrown ruins of the **Hermitage Estate**, a cotton plantation once run by a prominent Loyalist family. They also sold salt drawn from nearby salt ponds.

### Beaches

Two stunning beaches await south of George Town. For solitary sunning, drive south on the Queen's Hwy, cross the one-lane bridge at Ferry and pass through Forbes Hill. After passing the 'Leaving Forbes Hill' sign, there's a dangerous curve then a beach access sign on your left (sometimes these disappear). Park anywhere – all four wheels off the highway – then follow the dirt track past an old stone building and an overturned jeep to the glimmering, usually shallow, turquoise water.

Next up is **Tropic of Cancer Beach**. About 2½ miles past the Leaving Forbes Hill sign is a series of dirt roads on the left. Take one of them – if you get to the 'Lonesome Conch' cottage on Queen's Hwy you've gone too far. These 'roads' lead to poorly-marked Ocean Rd running parallel to the beach. Turn right on Ocean Rd and follow it to a wooden beachside hut with a small parking area. Stand on the Tropic of Cancer – there's a faded blue line marking the spot. The *Pirates of the Caribbean II* and *III* crew loaded gear onto boats here before heading to southern cays.

### STOCKING ISLAND

This 600-acre (240-hectare) slip of an island beckons about a mile off the coast, separated from George Town by the turquoise beauty of Elizabeth Harbour. For a day-trip appealing to adventurers and beach bums alike, grab one of the two daily ferries departing

Club Peace & Plenty (10am & 1pm, US$10) to Hamburger Beach on the northern side of the island. Here you can snorkel, stroll over talcum-fine beaches, or bushwack up a nature 'trail' to the island's highest point. Don't miss the short hike across the island to the Atlantic for more deep blue views.

Order a hamburger or conch burger at **Peace & Plenty Beach Club** (mains under US$10; ☼ lunch). American germ freaks be warned – friendly but scratched-up feral cats leap onto the counter and table tops with no apparent regard for your silly health codes.

There are no roads on the island and all access is by boat. For a cocktail at the popular **Chat & Chill Bar & Grill** ( ☎ 242-336-2700; www.chatnchill .com) on the other end of the island, call Elvis at **Exuma Water Taxi** ( ☎ 242-464-1558) for a shuttle (one way/round trip US$10/12) that will pick you up at Club Peace & Plenty. You can also look for a water taxi on the government dock. Your taxi driver or hotel can also call the bar. The Chat & Chill's Sunday afternoon pig roast (US$19 per person) is a don't-miss affair.

### EXUMA CAYS

The cays begin at the barren Sail Rocks, 40 miles southeast of New Providence and offer a variety of sights and experiences as they unspool to the south. A highlight of any visit to **Staniel Cay** is a snorkel or dive trip into **Thunderball Grotto**. The cavern, named for its inclusion in the Bond movie *Thunderball*, is lit by shafts of light pouring in from holes in the ceiling that sear through the water, high-lighting the fish darting blow. This crystalline grotto was also used for scenes in *Splash* and another Bond movie *Never Say Never Again*. The current here can be dangerous.

The first marine 'replenishment nursery' in the world, created in 1958, the **Exuma Cays Land & Sea Park** boasts 112,640 acres (175 sq miles) of protected islands and surrounding seas. All fishing and collecting is banned – this includes plants and shells. **Hawksbill Cay** has marked trails that lead to the ruins of a Loyalist Plantation. **Little Hawksbill Cay** is a major nesting sight for ospreys.

## Activities

Exuma offers a plethora of activities, including diving, snorkeling, boat trips, fishing, kayak-ing and kitesurfing. Call or stop by Exuma's Ministry of Tourism Office (p97) for a list of bonefishing guides.

A day of snorkeling? Blue hole explora-tion? Sunset cruising? Call Steve at **Off Island Adventures** ( ☎ 242-524-0524; www.offislandadventures .com) to customize your own adventure. Charters for up to eight people are per half/full day US$400/700.

**Minn's Water Sports** ( ☎ 242-336-3483; www.mws boats.com; Queen's Hwy) rents 15ft Boston whal-ers for $US120/day and 19ft Powercats for US$210/day. Snorkel gear also available for rent for US$10/day with a US$50 deposit.

**Fish Rowe Charters** ( ☎ 242-357-0870; www.fish rowecharters.com) offers deep-sea fishing on a 40ft boat, from which you can hunt for wahoo, mahi mahi and kingfish (half/full day US$800/1600).

**Dive Exuma** ( ☎ 242-336-2893; www.dive-exuma. com) offers two-tank wreck-and-reef dives (US$175) and a one-tank blue hole dive (US$125). To get there, turn off the Queen's Hwy at February Point Estates, take first right, first left, second right and go downhill through the stone gate to the bright blue building.

**Starfish** ( ☎ 242-336-3033; www.kayakbahamas .com; George Town) hosts a variety of activities, including four-hour guided kayak trips (adult/child US$85/68), a snorkeling trip (adult/child US$70/56) and three-hour Eco Boat trips (adult/child US$70/56) that tour the harbor and include a nature hike on Stocking Island. Single/double kayaks can be hired for US$50/60 a day. A three-hour boat charter with a captain is available for US$500.

**Exuma Watersports** ( ☎ 242-336-3422; www.exuma watersports.com) charters a variety of trips from February Point Marina including a four-hour Eco-Safari Tour with snorkeling, hiking and sightseeing (US$100/person) and a deserted cay drop-off (US$500/group up to eight, then US$50/per extra person). Parasailing (US$85) and charters are also offered (half/full day US$500/900).

You'll be skipping across waves in no time with **Exuma Kitesurfing** ( ☎ 242-345-0359; www.exuma kitesurfing.com; 3-day course US$925), a high-octane outfitter that 'launches' guests from some of the Exumas' most scenic cays. The action shots on its website will have you grabbing for your credit card.

## Festivals & Events

For a full listing, contact the Ministry of Tourism (p97).

During the **Family Island Regatta**, held in the last week of April, hundreds of yachts from near and far congregate in Elizabeth Harbour for racing, socializing and general mayhem. The premier regatta in the Bahamas, it's an excuse for the hoi polloi and yachting elite to mingle and party.

## Sleeping

**Club Peace & Plenty** ( ☎ 242-336-2551; www.peaceand plenty.com; r US$175; ✗ 💻 ) Best for social butterflies and those without a car, this busy, 32-room hotel is also a way station for day-trippers hopping the Stocking Island ferry. Vacation-minded themes – African, English, Beach, Island – enliven slightly worn furnishings, but it's hard not to look tired next to the piercing harbor blues glistening out the window. The inn's restaurant and bar hum with crowds throughout the week. Check out the bathtub views from Rooms 28 and 32. There's complimentary wi-fi and computer in the lobby.

**Coral Gardens B&B & Apartments** (www.coralgar densbahamas.com; Hooper's Bay; r US$95; ✗ 💻 ) With rooms under US$100, this two-story B&B 3 miles northwest of George Town is a gobsmackingly good deal. British expats Peter and Betty Oxley keep the three comfortable bedrooms with private baths in tip-top shape. A fiction-filled bookcase, satisfying breakfasts and a porch with a sweeping island view round out the appeal. But perhaps most memorable are the English charm, resourcefulness and can-do-itiveness of the owners. You'll be tossing off British-isms in no time. Two adjacent apartments are also available. Due to cell phone audibility issues, email for reservations through the website. There's free wi-fi.

**Peace & Plenty Bonefish Lodge** ( ☎ 242-345-5555; www.ppbonefishlodge.com; Queen's Hwy; r US$242; ✗ ) Adventure feels nigh in this clubby lodge where fishermen trade tall tales in the lounge while the proprietress feeds sharks by hand in the backyard lagoon. Green patchwork bedspreads brighten the lodge's eight rooms, all coming with two queen beds and ocean views. Snorkels and kayaks available for guests. Not a great option for kids, but adults will appreciate the softening bursts of bougainvillea. Its restaurant is open for lunch and dinner (closed Tuesday) and serves seafood and steaks for dinner (mains US$20 to US$50).

**Palm Bay Beach Club** ( ☎ 242-336-2787; www .palmbaybeachclub.com; Queen's Hwy; studio/ste US$250/359; ✗ 💻 🐾 ) Individually owned and decorated, the Palm Bay's 80+ oceanfront cottages and

### PIRATE HUNTING

The cast and crew of the second and third *Pirates of the Caribbean* movies filmed on Sandy Cay, which is the chain's southernmost isle and, according to the tourism brochure, Keira Knightley's favorite shooting island. Equipment was loaded at Tropic of Cancer Beach (see p97) and next to Santana's Grill Pit (see below).

But celluloid pirates weren't the only ones to grace the Exumas' shores. Kidd's Cove, just off the Government Dock, is named for another infamous pirate, Captain Kidd, who ruled these shores…as harbor master.

hillside villas are typically bright and airy with tile floors and wooden ceilings. Starfish Activity Center, and Splash bar and grill are on site. Complimentary wi-fi.

## Eating & Drinking

**Edgewater Eddie's** ( ☎ 242-336-2050; Queen's Hwy; lunch mains US$7-13, dinner mains US$10-36; ✗ breakfast, lunch & dinner Mon-Sat) On Tuesdays, don't be distracted by the bright murals or the men drinking beer (unless you want one) at this scruffy watering hole known for its Bahamian dishes. You're here for the okra stew – potatoes, corn, onion and okra all chunked together for your slurping delight. Monday night's rake'n'scrape draws crowds.

**Club Peace & Plenty** ( ☎ 242-336-2551; Queen's Hwy) The bar scene and harbor views are superb, the high-priced restaurant a little less so. Master mixologist and local legend Lermon 'Doc of Libations' Rolle stirs things up on the poolside patio starting at 11am. Everyone's here at some point.

**Splash at Palm Bay Beach Club** ( ☎ 242-336-2787; Queen's Hwy, mains US$10-37; ✗ breakfast, lunch & dinner) You'll find pub fare here as well as tasty versions of the usual Bahamian suspects – conch, lobster, grouper – but the biggest draw is the convivial beach-shack bar scene. Sports-filled TV screens lure sports-minded locals and tourists alike.

**ourpick Santana's Grill Pit** ( ☎ 242-345-4102; Williamstown; US$14-25; ✗ lunch & dinner Tue-Sat) Sit on the bar stools of pirates at this popsicle-bright beach shack south of Georgetown, where Keira, Orlando and Johnny spent faux-pirate downtime before boating to outlying cays. Husband and wife team Denise and Edgar

THE BAHAMAS

will fry up your lobster on the central grill while you sip Kaliks with your counter-mates. From Venetian bonefishermen to BaTelCo workers to traveling families, it's a diverse but convivial crew. Ask to see the photo albums; they're stuffed with snapshots of the cast of *Pirates of the Caribbean II* and *III*. The crew loaded equipment onto boats just past the grill before heading south to Sandy Cay.

**Cocoplums Beach Bar & Grill** ( ☎ 242-554-3358; Rolleville; mains US$20-25) Kick off your flip-flops and stay awhile at this gourmet beach hut where the food is as tasty as the views. Jade curry shrimp and coconut lobster are touted by the locals; the prices are bumped by the Four Seasons – whose wealthy guests sleep a few miles south.

For the Exumas' most famous conch salad, swing by **Big D's Conch Spot** ( ☎ 242-358-0059; conch salad US$10; ⏱ noon-midnight Mon-Sat) in Steventon just off the Queen's Hwy.

The Fish Fry, just northwest of town, is a bright cluster of beach shacks and takeaways that open at sunset and on weekends. Names change with some regularity, so follow your nose or the crowds.

## Getting There & Away

For air travel information to the Exumas, see p107 and p108. For information on transport by ferry or mail boat, see p108.

## Getting Around
### TO/FROM THE AIRPORT

Taxis await the arrival of all flights to the airport and cost US$28 to George Town. However, two good car-rental agencies are based at the airport.

### BOAT

Ferries (US$10 round trip, 10am and 1pm) to Stocking Island currently depart from Peace & Plenty Bonefish Lodge's dock.

### CAR

**Don's Rent A Car** ( ☎ 242-345-0112; Exuma Airport; ⏱ 6:30am-7pm) rents excellent air-con vehicles from US$70 per day.

### TAXI

**Exuma Transit Services** ( ☎ 242-345-0232) and **Luther Rolle Taxis** ( ☎ 242-345-5003) and **Leslie Dames** ( ☎ 242-357-0015) offer taxi service around the island. The rate from the airport to Club Peace & Plenty is about US$35.

# ANDROS
pop 7900

Those wanting adventure when they fall off the grid have no better choice than Andros. At 2300 sq miles Andros is the largest of the Bahamian islands, but its unique geographic features and rich cultural traditions have protected this lonely outpost from the reckless overdevelopment common to its neighbors.

Divers and bonefishermen have been in on its charms for years, the former flocking here to peek into the Tongue of the Ocean – a 6000ft abyss just past the world's third-largest barrier reef – while the latter fly in to cast for bonefish on miles of secluded flats. Andros' rich folkloric traditions stem from the island's unusual foundation, a limestone base that's filled with swampy mangrove swashes and thick pine forests above and caverns and blue holes below. A perfect breeding ground for monsters and legends.

In the last few years, the island's boutique resorts – Tiamo and Small Hope Bay Lodge – have garnered kudos as true leaders in the ecotourism craze, not just talking the talk but walking…the garbage. Yep, guests might be asked to carry off the recycling or otherwise help in making sustainable tourism a reality. Recycling aside, empty beaches and tasty cocktails abound, with ecofriendly attitudes just frosting on the tropical paradise cake.

## GETTING THERE & AROUND

For information on flights to Andros, see p107 and p108. There are mail boats and ferries to Andros; for details, see p108.

Taxis meet arriving flights and ferries. Arrangements can also be made through your hotel. Try **Adderly's Rent-A-Car** ( ☎ 242-357-2149) or **Steve & Hyacinth Hanna** ( ☎ 242-368-6140) for car rentals which run at about US$85/day.

## Fresh Creek Area

Just a two-hour ferry ride from Nassau, Fresh Creek is a convenient weekend destination for divers, bonefishers and hikers with a sense of adventure. Andros Town and Coakley Town make up the Fresh Creek Township. A giant plastic crab greets visitors at Coakley Town on the north side of the creek while taxis greet visitors at Andros Town on the south side as they step from the ferry at the dock. Small Hope Bay Lodge is the area's friendly diving and adventure hub that becomes a convivial social center in the evenings.

## INFORMATION

**Bahamas Ministry of Tourism** ( ☎ 242-368-2286; Andros Town) Stop by for maps of Andros and Fresh Creek.

**Government Medical Clinic** ( ☎ 242-368-2038) On the north side of the Fresh Creek Bridge.

**Police** ( ☎ 242-368-2626, emergencies 911 or 919)

**Post Office**( ☎ 242-368-2012)

**Royal Bank of Canada** ( ☎ 242-368-2071) Just north of town on the Queen's Hwy; the bank has an ATM.

## SIGHTS & ACTIVITIES

The famous Androsian batiks of **Androsia Ltd** ( ☎ 242-368-2020; www.androsia.com; �9am-4pm Mon-Fri, 8am-1pm Sat) are sold throughout the Bahamas. Melding age-old wax techniques and island motifs, workers at the small factory create a wide range of bright clothing. A guide will show you around and there's a factory outlet.

Two relatively short hikes off of the Queen's Hwy north of Small Hope Bay Lodge lead through thick pine forests to inland blue holes. Look out for the island's mythical beasts: the three-toed chickchamie, which likes to hang upside down from trees, or the half-dragon, half-octopus Lusca, which whirlpools its victims to a watery death. You'll find a platform and rope swing at **Captain Bill's Blue Hole**, located off the dirt road beside the Department of Environmental Health. For a look at Androsian flora and fauna, try the marked, slightly spooky **nature trail** to the Rainbow Blue Hole further north, just past telephone pole number 209. Look for the wooden sign.

Guests at Small Hope have the use of complimentary bicycles. You can also bring bikes from Nassau on the Bahamas Ferry. There's an easy, scenic 6-mile ride along the Queen's Hwy from the ferry dock to the Small Hope area and the blue holes further north.

**Small Hope Bay Lodge** ( ☎ 242-368-2013/4; www .smallhope.com; Calabash Bay), highly acclaimed by divers, offers one-/two-tank dives (US$60/80), night dives (US$70) and shark dives (US$85), as well as snorkeling safaris (adult/child US$45/25). Ask about specialty trips including blue hole dives and wall dives to 185ft.

The lodge also leads half- and full-day bonefishing, reef fishing and deep-sea trips. Call for prices.

## SLEEPING & EATING

A handful of small hotels of varying quality cluster around Fresh Creek. Small Hope is about six miles north on Queen's Hwy.

---

**TWIST MY ARM: THE SPOTS THE AUTHORS WANTED TO KEEP SECRET**

A sultry pink sun dips low on the horizon. Calm seas lap the shore. Empty hammocks sway between lazy palms. Unattainable paradise? Not in Andros, where the view from Room 12 at the Small Hope Bay Lodge (below) is just a phone call, a puddle jump and two-and-a-half Benjamins away.

---

**Andros Lighthouse Yacht Club & Marina** ( ☎ 242-368-2305; www.androslighthouse.com; Andros Town; r US$120; ⛽ 🏊 ) Bright, spacious rooms, an on-site restaurant and proximity to the Government Dock make this an attractive option for a short stay. The island's 116-year-old lighthouse is nearby. Complimentary wi-fi in the lobby.

**Small Hope Bay Lodge** ( ☎ 242-368-2013/4; www .smallhope.com; Calabash Bay; cottage per person US$209; 💻 ) If you've dreamt of joining an Explorers' Club but weren't sure you had the goods, let this convivial adventure den provide that first little push. Though a famous dive destination for decades, the lodge is newbie-friendly, offering a supportive beginner's dive class. Beyond diving, the lodge provides kayaks, snorkel gear, bikes and trail maps for its guests and leads nature and bird-watching tours through neighboring forests. Children's activities are also offered. The central lodge is strewn with couches and throw pillows, and the low-slung building incorporates a library, game room and an open-bar that's hewn from half a dinghy. Coral-stone cottages look directly onto a stunning hammock-and-palm-lined beach and offer king-sized beds, screened windows and Androsian batik fabrics. No TV or phone. The rate is all inclusive, with guests enjoying hearty family-style buffets three times a day. Nonguests can come for meals (breakfast/lunch/dinner US$10/15/30) but reservations are recommended. Notably, Small Hope is leading the way environmentally, educating the staff and guests on their wide array of ecoconscious practices.

**Hank's Place Restaurant & Bar** ( ☎ 242-368-2447; Fresh Creek; mains US$8-25; �dinner) A shady deck overlooks the creek at laid-back, nautical-minded Hank's which lures 'em in with pub grub, Bahamian seafood specialties and booze.

Also recommended is **Love at First Sight** ( ☎ 242-369-6082; www.loveatfirstsight.com; dinner mains US$25-40; ☼breakfast, lunch & dinner) in Staniard Creek, about 20 miles north of Fresh Creek.

This locally touted restaurant serves native and gourmet seafood dishes in a romantic, very pink, setting.

## South Andros

**Tiamo Resort** ( ☎ 242-357-2330; www.tiamoresorts .com; South Andros; r per person US$415; 🖳 ) Take the recycling with me? Most guests would be offended if asked to lug a load of trash, but not at Tiamo, where ecosavvy travelers support sustainable tourism. Open since 2001, Tiamo is a leader in the ecotourism movement. But the resort knows ecosavviness isn't enough to lure guests; that's the role of the 11 luscious beachfront cottages – screened-in hideaways set back from the beach – and the delicious meals. Beyond top-notch accommodations and dining, the resort provides sail boats, snorkel gear and local ecotours.

# DIRECTORY

## ACCOMMODATIONS

The Bahamian islands offer a range of lodging that includes cottages, inns, condos, hotels and resorts. Prices tend to be high, often unjustifiably, for the level of service and quality of amenities. Taxes and imaginative surcharges are often used to hike up your bill by around 20% to 30%. Check prior to booking that quoted rates are inclusive of all these additional costs.

Nearly all hotels and inns change their rates at least twice a year between low and high season. While this guide quotes high-season rates, be aware that some hotels charge even higher prices from Christmas Eve through to New Year's Day. The good news? The low season (or summer) extends for most of the year from mid-April to mid-December. During this period accommodations prices drop between 20% and 60%, so although this region is pricy, it is possible to find value-for-money lodgings.

Weekly rentals and all-inclusive resorts are also options on many islands. Camping, however, is not: it's illegal on the beaches and there are no official campsites, even in wilderness areas.

## ACTIVITIES

Diving, snorkeling, fishing, kayaking, sailing and swimming – with or without dolphins – are all on the menu in the Bahamas. Hiking's not bad for landlubbers, though trails are usually short.

### Diving & Snorkeling

Wrecks, reefs, blue holes and sharks are the name of the underwater game. On New Providence several dive operators rent equipment and run trips. On Grand Bahama and the larger Out Islands and cays, you'll typically find one, possibly two, operators per island. For the greatest variety – peeking at the Tongue of the Ocean and plunging into

---

**THE BEST OF THE REST**

The heart of traditional Bahamian culture still beats on **Cat Island**, one of the islands least touched by tourism. Obeah and bush medicine are still practiced. Cat has several interesting historic sites, including plantation ruins and the Mt Alvernia Hermitage.

The island's second-largest settlement is **Arthur's Town**, 30 miles (48km) north of New Bight, the island's governmental administrative center. The hamlet's main claim to fame is that it was the boyhood home of Sir Sidney Poitier, the Academy Award–winning actor. Sadly his childhood home is now derelict.

On top of **Mt Alvernia** (206ft; 62m), or Como Hill, as it is called by locals, is a blanched-stone church, built by the hermit Father Jerome, with a bell tower that looks like something Merlin might have conjured up in the days of King Arthur. You can enter the small chapel, tiny cloister and a guest cell the size of a large kennel. It's reached by a rock staircase hewn into the side of the hill. From the top, there's a spiritually reviving 360-degree view. Try to make it at sunrise or sunset.

**Long Island** is one of the most scenic Out Islands, stretching almost 80 miles south – only 4 miles at the widest – past stunning white and sky blue churches, lush greenery, bougainvillea-draped villages and pastel-colored schoolyards. The lone highway leads to magnificent bays, blue holes and miles of empty beach. Hurricane Noel caused extensive flooding in the fall of 2007, but the island is bouncing back and is ready for business.

a blue hole – consider Andros (p100), only a 2½-hour ferry ride form Nassau.

Some of the Bahamas' best reef snorkeling awaits just a few swift kicks from the beach. For operators and dives, see the activities section for each destination.

## Fishing
The fighting bonefish lures determined fishermen to Bahamian sandbanks from around the world.

Deep sea fishers can charter boats for about $600/half day for trips off the coast of New Providence, Grand Bahama and some of the larger Out Islands. It's strictly regulated. Depending on the season, prey include mahi mahi, tuna and wahoo. See individual destination listings for guides.

## Kayaking
With their clear blue shallows and typically calm harborside waters, the Bahamian islands are a kayaker's nirvana. For low-key inland kayaking and informative ecotrips, try Grand Bahama (p83) and Eleuthera (p95). For cay-hopping and stunning blue water, there's the Exumas (p98 ). Many resorts and lodges provide complimentary kayaks for guests. The larger islands have a handful of rental companies.

## Kitesurfing
Kitesurfing is taking off, with newbies heading to Spanish Wells (p93) and Exuma (p98) and pros heading to the pink sands of Harbor Island, Eleuthera – where it's do it yourself at the moment.

## Surfing
The Bahamas best surf spots are off Elbow Cay in Abaco (p91) and at Surfer's Beach just south of Gregory Town, Eleuthera (p95).

## BUSINESS HOURS
**Banks** 9am or 9:30am to 3pm Monday to Thursday, 9am or 9:30am to 4:30pm Friday
**Businesses & Shops** 9am to 5pm Monday to Friday, 10am to 5pm Saturday
**Supermarkets** 8am-7pm

Exceptions are noted in specific listings. Banks on smaller Out Islands and cays may be open only once or twice a week.

## CHILDREN
The Bahamas pursues the family traveler aggressively and the larger hotels compete by providing good facilities for children. Many have a babysitter or nanny service and large resorts, such as Atlantis, have a full range of activities for children. Children under 12 years normally room with their parents for free.

## DANGERS & ANNOYANCES
Murder rates reached a record high in 2007, with 79 reported throughout the Bahamas. These incidents, however, typically occurred in specific neighborhoods in larger cities or involved random disputes between citizens. Before you travel, however, check the country specific link at the website of the **US State Department** (http://travel.state.gov/travel) for the latest updates.

Note that the main thoroughfare on many Out Islands, typically the ubiquitous Queen's Hwy, is usually shoulderless and poorly lit. For walkers and those not used to driving on the left, the highway experience can be quite thrilling – or terrifying. Along these lines, you won't find many signs with street names either, so keep this guide and local maps handy.

**THE BAHAMAS**

As for annoyances, pesky sand flea–like bugs, called no-see-ums, can drive one to distraction on some of the prettiest beaches. Carry repellant.

## EMBASSIES & CONSULATES

Most countries are represented by honorary consuls. All listings below are located in Nassau, New Providence.

**Canada** ( ☎ 242-393-2123; Shirley St)
**China** ( ☎ 242-393-1415: Office Village Rd)
**UK** (Map p71; ☎ 242-325-7471/3)
**USA** (Map p71; ☎ 242-322-1181/2/3; http://nassau .usembassy.gov/overview.html; 42 Queen St, Nassau, New Providence) For emergencies call 242-328-2206.

## FESTIVALS & EVENTS

See individual island listings, the Junkanoo boxed text (p73) or check the **Bahamas Ministry of Tourism website** (www.bahamas.com) for information on festivals and events in the Bahamas.

## GAY & LESBIAN TRAVELERS

The pink dollar isn't particularly welcome in the Bahamas and there's not much public support for Bahamian gay and lesbian populations across the islands. Discretion is the better part of affection here. Antigay protesters met a gay-family-values cruise with placards and protests in 2004 and many gay-themed cruises now avoid Nassau. For more information, contact the gay-rights group **Rainbow Alliance of the Bahamas** ( ☎ 242-455-7242; http://bahamianglad.tripod.com).

## HOLIDAYS

Bahamian national holidays that fall on Saturday or Sunday are usually observed on the previous Friday or following Monday. The Bahamas has the following national holidays:

**New Year's Day** January 1
**Good Friday** Friday before Easter
**Easter Monday** Monday after Easter
**Whit Monday** Seven weeks after Easter
**Labour Day** First Friday in June
**Independence Day** July 10
**Emancipation Day** First Monday in August
**Discovery Day** October 12
**Christmas Day** December 25
**Boxing Day** December 26

## INTERNET ACCESS

Internet cafés are scattered throughout New Providence and Grand Bahamas and you can usually find a library or coffee shop with access on the larger Out Islands. Don't assume your hotel has a computer – check first. More hotels are providing wi-fi, if not in rooms, typically in the lobby or by the pool.

## INTERNET RESOURCES

Helpful Bahamian-oriented websites include the following:

**Bahama Pundit** (www.bahamapundit.com) Provides informative, sometime quirky, essays by Bahamian columnists on cultural, environmental and political topics.
**Bahamas – Tourist Guide** (www.geographia.com/ bahamas) Information about the country, its history and present culture.
**Government of the Bahamas** (www.bahamas.gov.bs) Government website with official contact information.
**Islands of the Bahamas** (www.bahamas.com) The official tourism website of the Bahamas is a good starting point and provides packages, but it's not comprehensive.
**Nassau Guardian** (www.thenassauguardian.com) The newspaper's site is a good starting point to find out about issues key to the country.
**Out Islands of the Bahamas** (www.myoutislands.com) This helpful sight from the Out Island Promotions Board provides information on beaches, landmarks and a fair number of hotels – reviews being promotionally positive of course. Fairly comprehensive event calendar.

## MAPS

See listings for each destination.

## MEDICAL SERVICES

Many of the Out Islands are serviced by small government clinics, usually found off the Queen's Hwy in the major settlements. Listings for local hospitals and medical clinics are listed for each destination.

## MONEY

The Bahamian dollar (BS$) is linked one-to-one with the US dollar, so you can use US currency everywhere. The major commercial banks maintain branches throughout the islands, although in the Out Islands they are thin on the ground.

There are ATMs in the leading tourist centers. Most accept Visa, MasterCard and Amex via international networks, such as Cirrus and PLUS. Bring extra cash for small meals, sundries and tips when heading to the far reaches of the Out Islands or hopping between cays where ATMS are few and far between.

Major credit cards are widely accepted throughout the islands. Credit cards are *not* widely accepted for general transactions in the more remote Out Islands. You can use your credit card to get cash advances at most commercial banks.

## POST

The cost for an intra-island and interisland surface mail stamp is US$0.25 per ounce; 1oz air mail letters interisland are US$0.35. Air mail rates for 0.5oz letters/postcards to the US are $US0.75/0.65; to Europe and Central and South America, US$0.80/0.65; and to Africa, Asia and Australia US$0.90/0.65.

## TELEPHONE

The Bahamian country code is ☎ 242. You need to dial this when making interisland calls. When dialing within an island, you just need to dial the seven-digit local number. The country code has been included in the Bahamian phone listings in this chapter. To call the Bahamas from the US and Canada, dial ☎ 1-242 then the local number. From elsewhere, dial your country's international access code then ☎ 242 then the local number.

The government-owned **Bahamas Telecommunications Corporation** (BaTelCo; Map p65; ☎ 242-302-7000; www.btcbahamas.com; John F Kennedy Dr, Nassau, New Providence) has an office on most Bahamian islands. Even the smallest settlement usually has at least one public phone. Many booths require phone cards, issued in denominations of US$5, US$10 and US$20.

Hotel rates are typically very expensive. Many hotels also charge for an unanswered call after the receiving phone has rung five times.

If traveling in the Bahamas for an extended period and making lots of local calls, consider buying a SIM card upon arrival at a cell phone shop for about US$15. Make sure your cell is unlocked by your provider or pay to have it unlocked at the store. Cell phones can also be rented for local use for about US$10/day plus a phone card and security deposit.

### Cell Phones

You can bring your own cell phone into the Bahamas, but you may be charged a customs fee upon entry (refunded upon exit). Some phones may not operate on BaTelCo's cellular system until you rent temporary use of a 'roaming' cellular line. Many will have no problems and will roam without registration. Check this with your service provider

before leaving. Roaming fees here can be very expensive.

### Domestic Calls

Local calls are free of charge, although hotels will charge US$0.75 to US$1 per call.

### International Calls

Many Bahamian phone booths and all BaTelCo offices permit direct dial to overseas numbers. It is usually cheaper to call direct from a phone booth than to call from your hotel via an operator. In some hotels, however, you can dial a local pre-paid calling card access number and then pay the hotel only the cost of the local call.

Before your trip, call your cell phone provider to check for plans offering lower rates for calls from the Bahamas. US iPhone owners should note that due to the iPhone's roaming superpowers, you could come home to an astronomical bill. Keep the phone in the right travel mode or ask about disabling the dataport prior to leaving.

Many national companies also offer a service for their subscribers, issuing international charge cards and a code number. Costs for calling home are then billed directly to your home number. Check with you provider.

### Phone Cards

The majority of Bahamian public telephones accept only prepaid phone cards issued by BaTelCo, available at stores and other accredited outlets near phone-card booths. The phone cards are sold in denominations of US$5, US$10, US$20 and US$50.

## TRAVELERS WITH DISABILITIES

Disabled travelers will need to plan their vacation carefully, as few allowances have been made for them in the Bahamas. For a listing of transportation options and services, start with the government's **Office of Disability Affairs** ( ☎ 242-325-2252/3). In Grand Bahama there's also the **Northern Bahamas Council for the Disabled** ( ☎ 242-352-7720; Freeport).

**THE BAHAMAS**

## TOURIST INFORMATION

The Bahamas Ministry of Tourism can be reached at ☎ 242-302-2000; for comprehensive information and reservations, visit www.bahamas.com. For information on the Out Islands, visit www.myoutislands.com.

Most large towns have tourist offices; see individual destinations for details.

## VISAS

Citizens of the US, Canada, the EU and Commonwealth countries do not currently need a visa for stays of up to eight months. Check with the Bahamian embassy for specific requirements. Citizens of most Central and South American countries, including Mexico, do not require a visa for stays up to 14 days. Visas are required for all visitors staying longer than eight months.

Citizens from the following countries require passports and visas for stays of any duration: Dominican Republic, Haiti, South Africa, all communist countries and many Asian countries. Citizens from all other countries should check the current entry requirements at the nearest Bahamian embassy or with the **Department of Immigration** ( ☎ 242-322-7530; PO Box N-831, Hawkins Hill, Nassau). There are also offices for Immigration at Nassau International Airport and at Prince George Wharf. Keep trying the number, they can be slow to pick up. See below for passport information.

## WORK

It is very difficult for non-Bahamians to obtain a work permit, the rule being that no expatriate may be offered a job that a qualified Bahamian can do. Employers must advertise locally and if the job is unfilled, a fairly exhaustive amount of paperwork is then required by the Department of Immigration.

# TRANSPORTATION

## GETTING THERE & AWAY
### Entering the Bahamas

All visitors must carry a valid passport and a return or onward ticket as well as sufficient funds to support their stay. This requirement will be extended to sea travel for US citizens; check for updates before you leave.

This section addresses transportation to the Bahamas from other countries. See p108 for information on travel between the islands.

### Air

The departure tax of US$15 is typically included in the ticket price. For a brief summary of airlines and flight schedules by island, check www.bahamas.com. The two largest airports are Nassau International Airport and Grand Bahama International Airport. A few airlines fly directly to airports on the larger Out Islands, but the majority of flights arrive in Nassau or Freeport where passengers will connect to another flight before continuing to the Out Islands.

The national airline **Bahamasair** ( ☎ 242-377-5505, in Freeport 242-352-8341; www.bahamasair.com) has an unblemished safety record and its pilots have an excellent reputation (see www.airsafe.com for details). Delays, however, are regular occurrences and flights are canceled without warning. Bahamians say 'If you have time to spare, fly Bahamasair.'

The listings below include international cities offering direct flights to the destination; keep in mind, however, that this information changes regularly.

#### ABACOS

Abacos has two airports: **Marsh Harbour International Airport** (MHH; ☎ 242-367-3039; Marsh Harbour, Abacos) and **Treasure Cay International Airport** (TCB), located 25 miles north of Marsh Harbour. Taxis between Treasure Cay and Marsh Harbor can run US$60, so pick the right airport when making reservations.

The following airlines fly into Marsh Harbour:

**American Airlines** ( ☎ 800-433-7300; www.aa.com) Miami

**Bahamas Air** ( ☎ 242-367-2095, 800-222-4262; www.bahamasair.com) West Palm Beach, Nassau

**Continental Connection/Gulfstream International** ( ☎ 242-367-3415, 800-231-0856; www.continental.com/ www.gulfstreamair.com) Fort Lauderdale, Miami, West Palm Beach

**Twin Air** ( ☎ 242-367-0140, 954-359-8266; www.flytwinair.com) Fort Lauderdale

**Vintage Props & Jets** ( ☎ 242-367-4852, 800-852-0275; www.vpj.com) Daytona, Fort Lauderdale, Melbourne

**Yellow Air Taxi** ( ☎ 242-367-0033, 888-935-5694; www.flyyellowairtaxi.com) Fort Lauderdale; charters also available

Continental flies directly from Ft Lauderdale and West Palm Beach to Treasure Cay. Island Express, **Twin Air** (☎ 242-365-8660), Vintage Props & Jets and Yellow Air Taxi fly into Treasure Cay from the same departure points listed above.

## ANDROS

There are four airports on Andros. Be sure to choose the correct one based on your lodging. The **Andros Town Airport** (☎ 242-368-2724) in Central Andros is currently serviced by **Continental Connection/Gulfstream International** (☎ 242-377-5486, 800-231-0856; www.continental.com, www.gulfstreamair.com), which has flights from Fort Lauderdale, Nassau, West Palm Beach.

## ELEUTHERA

In 100-mile-long Eleuthera, try to fly into the airport closest to your destination. **North Eleuthera International Airport** (ELH; ☎ 242-335-1242; North Eleuthera) is close to the ferry dock across the sound from Harbour Island. Governor's Harbor is in the middle of the island and Rock Sound is further south.

All airlines listed below also fly into Governor's Harbor from Fort Lauderdale.
**Continental Connection/Gulfstream International** (☎ 800-231-0856; www.continental.com/www.gulfstreamair.com) Fort Lauderdale, Miami
**Lynx** (☎ 954-772-9808, 888-596-9247; www.lynxair.com) Fort Lauderdale
**Twin Air** (☎ 242-335-1696; www.flytwinair.com) Fort Lauderdale

## EXUMAS

Located a few miles north of George Town, **Exuma International Airport** (GGT; George Town, Exuma) offers a handful of car rental agencies and a restaurant. Taxis meet most flights.
**American Airlines/American Eagle** (☎ 242-345-0124, 800-433-7300; www.aa.com) Miami
**Bahamas Air** (☎ 800-222-4262; www.bahamasair.com) Nassau
**Continental Connection/Gulfstream International** (☎ 800-525-0280; www.continental.com, www.gulfstreamair.com) Fort Lauderdale
**Lynx Air** (☎ 954-772-9808, 888-596-9247; www.lynxair.com) Fort Lauderdale
**United Airways** (☎ 800-622-1015) Charlotte, Philadelphia, Boston and New York seasonally

## GRAND BAHAMA

Just north of downtown, **Grand Bahama International Airport** (FPO; ☎ 242-352-6020; Freeport, Grand Bahama) is served by the following airlines:

**American Airlines/American Eagle** (☎ 800-433-7300; www.aa.com) Miami
**Bahamas Air** (☎ 242-352-8341, 800-222-4262; www.bahamasair.com) Fort Lauderdale, Nassau
**Continental Connection/Gulfstream International** (☎ 800-525-0280; www.continental.com, www.gulfstreamair.com) Fort Lauderdale, Miami, Orlando, West Palm Beach
**Delta Connection** (☎ 800-221-1212; www.delta.com) Atlanta
**US Airways** (☎ 800-622-1015; www.usairways.com) Charlotte

## NEW PROVIDENCE

New Providence's main airport is **Lynden Pindling International Airport** (NAS; ☎ 242-377-7281; Nassau, New Providence), called the Nassau International Airport until 2008. This hub services international and domestic flights, with most interisland flights originating and returning here. New US and international terminals are due for completion in 2011. In the meantime, you'll find a couple of ATMs, a few cafés and a bunch of duty-free shops.

The following airlines fly into the airport:
**Air Canada** (☎ 242-377-8220, 888-247-2262; www.aircanada.com) Montreal, Toronto
**Air Jamaica** (☎ 800-523-5585; www.airjamaica.com) Montego Bay
**American Airlines/American Eagle** (☎ 800-433-7300; www.aa.com) Chicago, Dallas, Fort Lauderdale, Miami
**Bahamasair** (☎ 242-377-8451, 800-222-4262; www.bahamasair.com) Fort Lauderdale, Miami, Orlando, West Palm Beach
**British Airways** (☎ 242-377-2338; www.ba.com) London
**Continental Connection/Gulfstream International** (☎ 800-231-0856; www.continental.com, www.gulfstreamair.com) Fort Lauderdale, Miami, Newark, West Palm Beach
**Delta** (☎ 242-377-1053, 800-221-1212; www.delta.com) Atlanta, Cincinnati, Fort Lauderdale, New York, Orlando, Tampa
**Jet Blue** (☎ 242-377-1174; www.jetblue.com) Boston, New York
**Spirit Airlines** (☎ 242-377-0152; www.spiritair.com) Fort Lauderdale, New York, Orlando
**United** (☎ 800-864-8331; www.united.com) Washington DC
**US Airways** (☎ 242-377-8886/7; 800-622-1015; www.usairways.com) Charlotte; flights from Boston, New York, Philadelphia, Washington available seasonally

## Sea

### CRUISE-SHIP

Numerous cruise ships dock in Nassau and Grand Bahama. Most originate in Florida.

Please see p830 for more information on the various type of cruises available.

### FERRY

**Discovery Cruise Line** ( ☎ 800-259-1579; www.discoverycruiseline.com) runs daily between Fort Lauderdale, Florida, and Freeport, Grand Bahama (US$140). It departs Florida at 8am, returning at 10pm. Rates include three buffet meals and a Las Vegas–style casino.

### YACHT

The sheltered waters of the 750-mile-long archipelago attract thousands of yachters each year. Winds and currents favor the passage south. Sailing conditions are at their best in summer, though hurricanes can be a threat throughout the season.

## GETTING AROUND

Perusing a map, it's tempting to think that island-hopping down the chain is easy. Unfortunately, it's not – that is, unless you have your own boat or plane. Interisland air is centered on Nassau. Getting between the islands without constantly backtracking is a bit of a feat. Even the mail boats are Nassau-centric.

## Air

Interisland flights offer the only quick and convenient way to travel within the Bahamas and islanders ride airplanes like Londoners use buses. Private charter flights can be an economical option for those traveling in a group.

**Bahamasair** ( ☎ 242-377-5505, in Freeport 242-352-8341; www.bahamasair.com) The dominant airline in the Bahamas operates on a hub-and-spoke system, so to fly between adjacent islands, such as Cat and Long Islands, you'll have to first return to Nassau. If you do a lot of island-hopping, you'll feel like a yo-yo and may need to overnight in Nassau between flights; budget accordingly. Bahamasair flies to Freeport, Marsh Harbour, Treasure Cay, North Eleuthera, Governor's Harbour, Rock Sound, George Town and several southern islands including Cat Island and Long Island.

Most flights to the Out Islands are during the day since the smaller airports are not properly lighted for night flights. A few smaller interisland airlines and charters, are listed below:

**Abaco Air** ( ☎ 242-367-2266; www.abacoaviationcentre.com) Flies from Marsh Harbour to Nassau and North Eleuthera. Charters also available.

**Southern Air** ( ☎ 242-323-7217; www.southernaircharter.com) Flies from Nassau to Governor's Harbour and North Eleuthera in Eleuthera, as well as Stella Maris and Deadman's Cay on Long Island.

**Western Air** ( ☎ 242-377-222; www.westernairbahamas.com) Flies from Nassau to Andros Town, Bimini, Grand Bahama and Exuma.

## Bicycle

Cycling is cheap, convenient, healthy, environmentally sound and typically fun. Just make sure your seat has padding – most bikes are heavy, have one speed and can be a bit worn out. Major resort hotels rent bicycles for about US$20 daily. See local listings for specific rental companies.

## Boat
### FERRY

The primary ferry operation in the islands is **Bahamas Ferries** (Map p68; ☎ 242-323-2166/8; www.bahamasferries.com), a high-speed ferry linking Nassau to Andros, Abacos, Eleuthera and the Exumas.

### Nassau to Abacos

Bahamas Ferries makes the four-hour run (one way/round trip US$60/100) between Sandy Point, Great Abaco and Nassau twice a week.

### Nassau to Eleuthera

Bahamas Ferries also currently makes a daily two-hour run from Potter's Cay in Nassau to Harbour Island (one way/round trip US$75/115) at 8am, returning at 3:55pm Mon-Fri and 1pm Sun. It also runs a ferry (one way/round trip US$70/80) from Potter's Cay to Governor's Harbour on Tuesdays, Thursday and Fridays and returns on the same days.

### Nassau to Exumas

A not-so-fast ferry departs the Bahamas Ferries dock at Potter's Cay for the overnight journey to the Exumas. The scheduled 12-hour trip can stretch closer to 14 depending on the weather. It's a 'sleep in your seat' deal so pack a blanket and a toothbrush, dress comfortably and expect to wake up several times during the night. It provides a snack bar and a movie.

## Nassau to Andros

There's a two-hour ferry run by Bahamas Ferries from Nassau to Fresh Creek on Andros on Wednesday, Fridays and Saturdays, returning on the same day.

## Grand Bahama to Abacos

**Pinder's Ferry** ( ☎ 242-353-3093, 242-557-6624; round trip/one way $US90/45, children half price) A small boat runs twice a day between McLean's Town, Grand Bahama and Crown Haven on Little Abaco.

## MAIL BOAT

About 20 mail boats sail under government contract to most inhabited islands. They regularly depart Potter's Cay in Nassau for Grand Bahama and the Out Islands. Traditionally sailing overnight, journeys last five to 36 hours. Simple meals are typically included but you might want to bring back-up. This is the quintessential slow boat – expect delays – but it's also a great way to meet locals and soak up the island lifestyle. Call the **Dockmaster's Office** ( ☎ 242-393-1064) for up-to-date schedules and fares. Some information also available on the **Bahamas Ministry of Tourism** (www.bahamas.com) website.

## Nassau to Abacos

The *Captain Gurth Dean* departs Nassau for the Abacos at 11pm Tuesday and returns Friday at 5am; it's a seven-hour trip (US$40 one way).

## Nassau to Eleuthera

The *Eleuthera Express* (US$30 one way) departs Nassau's Potter's Cay on Monday and Thursday, returning from Harbour Island on Tuesday and Sunday.

## Nassau to Exumas

The *Grand Master* ($US45 one way) departs Potter's Cay in Nassau on Tuesdays at 2pm and arrives in George Town in the Exumas 14 hours later. It returns Thursday at 10am. Call the boat's owner directly ( ☎ 242-393-1041) for an updated schedule and fare.

## Nassau to Andros

Currently, MV *Lady D* departs Nassau for Fresh Creek on Andros on Thursday, returning on Sunday.

## WATER TAXI

Water taxis ply between Nassau and Paradise Island. Several other offshore islands and their neighboring cays are served by private water taxis.

## Bus

Nassau and Freeport have dozens of *jitneys* (private minibuses) licensed to operate on pre-established routes.

There's no public transportation on the Out Islands or at airports, as the taxi drivers' union is too powerful. Likewise, few hotels are permitted to operate their own transfer service for guests. A number of adventure outfitters and tours, however, will send courtesy shuttles to your hotel before and after reserved trips.

## Car & Golf Cart

Bahamians are generally cautious and civilized drivers and main roads are usually in good condition. Side roads? Not so much. Believe any Bahamian who warns you that a road is bad. Lighting is also poor on main roads and side roads on the Out Islands, so night driving can be a bit of challenge when looking for unfamiliar destinations.

### DRIVER'S LICENSE

To drive in the Bahamas you must have a current license from your home country or state. A visitor can drive on his or her home license for three months.

### RENTAL

Several major international car-rental companies have outlets in Nassau and Freeport, along with smaller local firms. In the Out Islands there are some very good local agencies. Ask your hotel for recs, or look for display boards at the airport.

Renters must be 21 (some companies rent only to those 25 or older). Collision damage waiver insurance is US$15 a day. Local companies may not offer insurance.

You usually rent for a 24-hour period, with rates starting at US$70 (from around US$80 in Nassau and from US$65 for smaller islands).

Golf carts can be rented on the smaller islands and cays for US$50 per day.

### ROAD RULES

Always drive on the *left*-hand side. At traffic circles (roundabouts), remember to circle in a clockwise direction, entering to the left. You must give way to traffic already in the circle. It's compulsory to wear a helmet when riding a motorcycle or scooter.

## Taxi

There's no shortage of licensed taxis in Nassau and Freeport, where they can be hailed on the streets. Taxis are also the main local transportation in the Out Islands, where they

meet all incoming planes and ferries in the larger settlements.

All taxi operators are licensed. Taxi fares are fixed by the government according to distance: rates are usually for two people. Each additional person is charged a flat rate of US$3. Fixed rates have been established from airports and cruise terminals to specific hotels and major destinations. These rates should be displayed in the taxi.

# Turks & Caicos

The Turks and where? That's the reaction most people have when you mention these tropical isles. Like all great Shangri-Las, this one is hidden just under the radar. Be glad that it is, as this tropical dream is the deserted Caribbean destination you've been looking for. And the best part – it's only 90 minutes by plane from Miami; this slice of paradise is just around the corner.

So why would you want to go there? How about white-sand beaches, clear blue water and a climate that defines divine. Secluded bays and islands where you'll see more wild donkeys than other travelers. Historic towns and villages that look like something out of a pirate movie, where life creeps along at a sedate pace.

Divers and beach aficionados will rejoice at the quality of the sea here. Clear warm water teem with sea life, yet are devoid of crashing waves. Even the most ardent land lover can't help but be mesmerized by the azure water and golden sand.

Islands like Grand Turk – set in a time long since past, with its dilapidated buildings, salt ponds and narrow lanes – contrast with the ever expanding Providenciales. While development is on the rise, all one has to do is dig a bit deeper, catch a boat to the next island over and the solace of solitude returns

## FAST FACTS

- **Area** Over 40 islands together add up to 430 sq miles of land
- **Capital** Cockburn Town, Grand Turk
- **Country code** ☎ 649
- **Departure tax** US$35 (normally included in ticket prices)
- **Famous for** Diving, whale-watching, tax evasion, pristine beaches
- **Language** English
- **Money** US dollar (US$); US$1 = €0.65 = UK£0.51
- **Official name** Turks and Caicos Islands
- **People** Belongers, residents
- **Phrase** Alright, alright (a common way of saying 'hello')
- **Population** 30,000
- **Visa** Not required by North American, British and most Western European travelers. Other nationalities need to get them in advance; see p133.

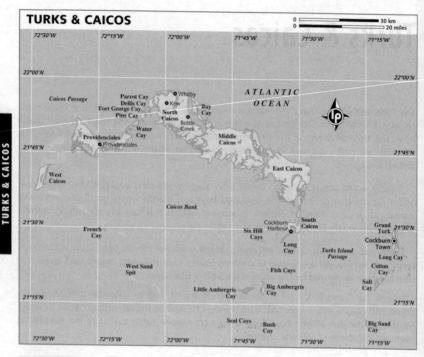

## HIGHLIGHTS

- **Diving** (p116) Believe the hype – the diving here is as good as it gets; get wet on Grand Turk where the fish are plenty and the reef pristine

- **Grace Bay Beach** (p121) Spend a day lounging on this white, wide and wonderful beach

- **Grand Turk** (p115) Step back in time on this beautiful sun-kissed island. Historic buildings, salt ponds and top-shelf beaches

- **Middle Caicos** (p129) Seek out Mudjin Harbor and discover one of the best beach entrances anywhere

- **Whale-Watching** (p119) Look out for the graceful gods of the sea – humpback whales – on Salt Cay

## ITINERARIES

- **Three Days** Spend the day admiring Grace Bay on Providenciales then wake up the next day to go for a snorkeling trip to French Cay and hand feed some stingrays. Finally on the last day rent a bike and explore the island under your own steam.

- **One Week** Add a trip to the islands of North Caicos and Middle Caicos and discover what solitude is really all about.

- **Two Weeks** Complete the trip by heading to Grand Turk to explore the town, do some great diving and spend a day or two on Salt Cay – the best-kept secret in the country.

## CLIMATE & WHEN TO GO

The Turks and Caicos' climate is a beach lover's dream, with temperatures rarely getting excruciatingly hot or anything approaching cool. Temperatures average 77°F (25°C) in winter and 90°F (32°C) in summer. The hottest months are August to November, and average humidity is 35%. Average annual rainfall is 21in and it's wettest in summer.

The winter season is most definitely the peak season for visitors. Hotel availability plummets and the prices soar from December through to April. Despite increasing popularity, even at the height of the high season, rooms to fit most budgets are generally available. A good option for travelers is to visit during the low season, when there are bargain rooms aplenty, deserted beaches and months of weather better then wherever you live.

## HISTORY

Recent discoveries of Taíno (the indigenous population) artifacts on Grand Turk have shown that the islands evolved much the same indigenous culture as did their northern neighbors. Locals even claim that the islands were Christopher Columbus' first landfall in 1492.

The island group was a pawn in the power struggles between the French, Spanish and British, and remained virtually uninhabited until 1678, when some Bermudian salt rakers settled the Turks islands and used natural *salinas* (salt-drying pans) to produce sea salt. These still exist on several islands.

Fast forward to the mid-20th century: the US military built airstrips and a submarine base in the 1950s, and John Glenn splashed down just off Grand Turk in 1962, putting the islands in the international spotlight.

Administered through Jamaica and the Bahamas in the past, the Turks and Caicos became a separate Crown colony of Great Britain in 1962 then an Overseas Territory in 1981. In 1984 Club Med opened its doors on Providenciales (Provo), and the Turks and Caicos started to boom. In the blink of an eye, the islands, which had lacked electricity, acquired satellite TV.

The Turks and Caicos relied upon the exportation of salt, which remained the backbone of the British colony until 1964. Today finance, tourism and fishing generate most income, but the islands could not survive without British aid. The tax-free offshore finance industry is a mere minnow compared with that of the Bahamas, and many would be astonished to discover that Grand Turk, the much-hyped financial center, is just a dusty backwater in the sun.

The per capita GDP in 2002 was estimated at US$11,500. Illegal drug trafficking, a major problem in the 1980s, has also been a source of significant revenue for a few islanders.

Relations between islanders and British-appointed governors have been strained since 1996, when the incumbent governor's comments suggesting that government and police corruption had turned the islands into a haven for drug trafficking appeared

in the *Offshore Finance Annual,* and opponents accused him of harming investment. Growing opposition threatened to spill over into civil unrest. The issue created a resurgence in calls for independence, calls that still continue today.

While some pine for more autonomy, there are calls for closer ties with Canada, of all nations. Recently there have been moves to join the northern nation as an official province. The drive is for economic spillover, better trade relations and a more prominent international voice. Whether this comes to pass is still up in the air, but if it does the influx of frostbitten patriots would certainly change the current population landscape.

## THE CULTURE

The culture of the Turks and Caicos is that of a ship that is steadied by a strong religious keel. There is a strong moral fiber to these islands, and the populace is friendly, welcoming and a bit sedate. Native Turks and Caicos islanders, or 'Belongers' as they are locally known, are descended from the early Bermudian settlers, Loyalist settlers, slave settlers and salt rakers.

There are a few expats lurking about calling the Turks home; Americans because of the proximity, Canadians because of the weather and Brits because of the colonial heritage. Some have come to make their fortunes, some to bury their treasure like the pirates of old and others to escape the fast-paced life that permeates nearly everywhere else in the world.

More recently hundreds of Haitians have fled their impoverished island and landed on the Turks and Caicos Islands; for some this is only a port of call on their way to America, while others are happy to stay. Some Belongers resist this invasion, some have sympathy and others seem not to notice. Time will tell how these impoverished fresh arrivals are treated in the long term.

---

### HOW MUCH?

- **Turks Head beer** US$3
- **Two-tank dive** US$75
- **Midrange double room** US$110
- **Cracked conch and fries** US$14
- **Gallon of gas** US$5.50

Nightlife in the Turks and Caicos is of the mellow variety for the most part. There are a few night spots in Provo, and some beachside bars on the outer islands. Those seeking a roaring party of a holiday should look elsewhere – having said that, the local rake'n'scrape music can really get the crowd going. For those not in the know, rake'n'scrape or ripsaw (as it is locally known) is a band fronted by someone playing a carpenter's saw by rhythmically scraping its teeth with the shaft of a screwdriver.

## ARTS

The art scene in the Turks and Caicos is slowly evolving. Traditional music, folklore and sisal weaving evolved during colonial days, and have been maintained to this day. Paintings depicting the scenery are popular and the quality appears to be improving. The Haitian community has had a strong influence on the Turks and Caicos art scene.

There are a few shops in Provo that have a good selection of locally produced art; unfortunately, except for a few choice locations, most of the art that's available outside Provo is tourist crap, made in China and slapped with a T&C sticker.

## ENVIRONMENT
### The Land

Much of the Turks and Caicos can be described as flat, dry and barren. The salt industry of the last century saw fit to remove much of the vegetation from Salt Cay, Grand Turk and South Caicos. Low-lying vegetation now covers the uninhabited sections of these islands. The larger islands are in a much more pristine state, with vegetation and a higher degree of rainfall prominent on North, Middle and East Caicos. Small creeks, inland lakes – often home to flamingos – and wetlands make up the interior of these larger land masses.

On Providenciales the most common sight on land is not anything natural but the explosive degree of development. Everywhere you look, there seems to be another new property and resulting heap of building garbage. The scrubby landscape is still visible among the fresh buildings – but for how long?

All the islands are rimmed with stunning beaches. Most are great and some are exceptional – truly world-class stretches of sand worthy of every accolade and hyperbolic description of sun, sand and gentle surf.

## Wildlife

Walking down a dusty laneway and coming upon a donkey is a quintessential T&C experience. Their forebears once carried 25lb burlap bags of salt from the ponds to the warehouses and docks. Having earned their rest, they were set free.

Iguanas once inhabited much of the Turks and Caicos until they lost their lives to introduced dogs and cats, and their habitats to development. Now Little Water Cay, Fort George Cay and the Ambergris Cays are all protected iguana reserves.

The waters are favored by four species of turtle: hawksbills (an internationally endangered species, although sadly not recognized in this region), green, loggerheads and, occasionally, leatherbacks.

Countless species of seabirds and waders have been sighted, both migratory and nonmigratory. Ospreys are numerous and easily spotted, as are sparrow hawks and barn owls. Flamingos – once numerous throughout the chain – are now limited to West, North and South Caicos, where you may also see Cuban herons.

A flourishing population of bottle-nosed dolphins lives in these waters. Also, some 7000 North Atlantic humpback whales use the Turks Island Passage and the Mouchoir Banks, south of Grand Turk, as their winter breeding grounds between January and March. Manta rays are commonly seen during the spring plankton blooms off of Grand Turk and West Caicos.

## FOOD & DRINK

You can't come to the Turks and Caicos and not try the local delicacy – conch (pronounced conk). The chewy sea creature lives in the amazing spiraled shells that are often found on the beach. The meat is liberally tenderized, seasoned with Cajun spices and grilled to perfection. There are some issues elsewhere in the Caribbean with declining conch numbers, but the heavily regulated local fishing industry and the Conch Farm on Provo ensure there is plenty of grilled gastropod to go around.

Jamaican flavors such as jerk are a heavy influence on local cuisine, meaning that beans and rice are a stalwart dinnertime side dish. With a growing number of upper-end establishments an air of sophistication is creeping into mealtime. French, Italian and other continental specialties are popping up – mixing the local seafood with classic dishes to fuse the best of both worlds.

Turks Head beer is a good local drop on a hot day and the ever-present rum punch always seems to be on offer at the bar. There is some local rum worth tasting such as Spicy Gosling. Do beware of some of the lower-end varieties of rum – though the cheap price point may be enticing, it's first cousin to paint thinner.

# TURKS ISLANDS

The Turks group comprises Grand Turk and its smaller southern neighbor, Salt Cay, in addition to several tiny cays. The islands lie east of the Caicos Islands, separated from them by the 22-mile-wide (35km) Turks Island Passage.

## Getting There & Away
For flight information, see p133.

## Getting Around
### TO/FROM THE AIRPORT
Taxis meet incoming flights; to Cockburn Town (1 mile north of the airport) costs US$8. There are no buses, but pre-booked rental cars will meet your plane.

### BICYCLE
Most, if not all, hotels on Grand Turk provide bikes for their guests as they are the perfect way to get around the tiny island. On Salt Cay, **Trade Winds Guest Suites** ( ☎ 946-6906; www .tradewinds.tc; Victoria St, Salt Cay) will get you pedaling for US$10 per day.

### BOAT
A ferry runs biweekly from Grand Turk to Salt Cay (US$12 round-trip). Contact **Salt Cay Charters** ( ☎ 231-6663; piratequeen3@hotmail.com). Whale-watching boat trips with this bunch cost US$75. Arrangements can also be made with any of the Grand Turk dive companies to take you over to Salt Cay; costs vary depending on numbers, but expect to pay about $60.

### CAR & SCOOTER
You're hardly likely to need a car in town, but do pay attention anyway to the one-way system along Duke and Front St. You can rent cars from **Tony's Car Rental** ( ☎ 231-1806; Airport Rd), located at the airport.

### TAXI
Taxis are an inexpensive and reliable way to get around Grand Turk. A taxi from the airport to town will cost you about US$8, but be sure to settle on a price before you head out as the cabs are unmetered. Your hotel can easily sort you a cab, or call **Carl's Taxi Service** ( ☎ 241-8793)

## GRAND TURK
Happily lacking the modern development that has enveloped Provo, Grand Turk is a step back in time. At just 6.5 miles long, this dot amid the sea is a sparsely populated, brush-covered paradise.

Cockburn Town, the main settlement, is still the capital of the country and is lined with buildings that date back to colonial times. Narrow streets are frequented by wild donkeys and the odd local cruising by.

Where salt was once the main industry, tourism has taken over and you are blessed with a slew of charming guesthouses to choose from. Beaches rim the land and calm blue water invites you in for a refreshing swim. There is a quiet peace to the island and a feel among the locals, discovered long ago, that this is the place to be.

## Cockburn Town
### pop 5500
Without knowing beforehand you'd be hard pressed to guess that sleepy Cockburn is the capital city of the Turks and Caicos. What it lacks in polish and sophistication it more than makes up for in rustic charm. The town itself is comprised of two parallel streets that are interconnected with narrow laneways. Colonial-era houses line the tiny streets, looking not dissimilar to how they would have a century ago. Former salt storage sheds connect back to a bygone era of dusty roads and donkey-filled lanes. Like a time capsule to a gentler age, walking among the architectural relics is a love letter to a bygone era.

### ORIENTATION
The heart of town is sandwiched between the ocean and the salt pond named Red Salina. Front St runs one way, along the waterfront, then narrows and becomes Duke St three blocks south of the government plaza.

Pond St runs parallel 50yd to the east, along Red Salina. To the north, Pond St divides: Hospital St runs north to the hospital;

Lighthouse Rd runs northeast to the lighthouse at Northeast Point, then divides to follow the waterfront to Governor's Beach and the dock, or southeast to the airport.

## INFORMATION

Businesses and government offices close at 3pm on Friday. Some businesses open from 9am to 1pm on Saturday. Public phones can be found at most central places.

**Cable & Wireless** ( ☎ 946-2200; www.cwcaribbean.com /turkscaicos; Front St) Offers internet access.
**Federal Express** ( ☎ 231-6097)
**General Post Office** ( ☎ 946-1334; Front St)
**Grand Turk Hospital** ( ☎ 946-2333; Hospital Rd)
**Police** ( ☎ 946-2299; Hospital Rd)
**Scotiabank** ( ☎ 946-2507; Front St)
**Turks & Caicos Islands Tourist Board** ( ☎ 946-2321; www.turksandcaicostourism.com; Front St)

## SIGHTS

The Turks & Caicos Island Tourist Board, the museum and most hotels have free Heritage Walk pamphlets.

### Front St

The stretch of road along the waterfront has some magnificent buildings. The salt air and the rough treatment of time have not been kind to many of these structures. Some have begun the slip into dilapidation. But there are still highlights here, and a walk among the architecture is recommended.

The **General Post Office** is a relic of a forgotten era, and still shines brightly. Nearby, four large cannons point to sea, guarding the site that Columbus supposedly set foot upon land – the reality of that claim is still up for grabs, but it does make for a nice photo. The fringing coral reef just offshore is protected within the confidently named **Columbus Landfall National Park**.

The little **Turks & Caicos National Museum** ( ☎ 946-2160; www.tcmuseum.org; Front St; admission nonresidents US$5; ☺ 9am-4pm Mon, Tue, Thu & Fri, to 6pm Wed, to 1pm Sat) boxes above its weight with a great selection of displays. Everything from shipwrecks to messages in bottles and crash-landing spacecraft are covered. The new curator is full of enthusiasm and expansion ambitions – be sure to ask to see the cabinet of cannons.

### Duke St

South of the heart of downtown, Duke St narrows off to form a twisting lane of old buildings. Even the most jaded of futurists will be left enchanted by the colonial-era structures.

### Around Town

The long and pothole-covered road to Northeast Point is the way to get to the old cast-iron **lighthouse**. It's open when cruise ships are in port and offers a good vantage of the crashing waves.

**Corktree** and **Pillory Beaches** are good for bathing and enough out of the way that you'll likely have the sand to yourself.

Lovely pine-shaded **Governor's Beach** lies 1.5 miles south of town, and is a popular place for a picnic, a dip in the sea or an impromptu party.

**Waterloo** (1815) is the official Governor's residence. The island's dock is here, and the old US missile-tracking station sits as a reminder of the Cold War. In 1962 Grand Turk was briefly put on the world stage when astronaut John Glenn splashed down in his Mercury spacecraft off the coast of the island. He made landfall at this dock and was debriefed at the missile-tracking post.

Dirt roads lead south to **White Sands Beach** for snorkelers and east to three prime **bird-watching spots**: Hawkes Pond Salina, Hawkes Nest Salina, and South Creek National Park, which protects the mangroves and wetlands along the island's southeast shore.

### ACTIVITIES

The magnificent diving off of Grand Turk and Salt Cay is not only popular with travelers but with the local community. These operations will take you snorkeling if you're not a diver, and run courses if you want to learn, and all have good equipment for rent.

### Diving & Snorkeling

**Oasis Divers** ( ☎ 946-1128; www.oasisdivers.com; Duke St) will take you down on a two-tank dive (US$75), a single tank in the afternoon (US$50) or a night dive (US$55). It rents out gear at good rates and has a great reputation for service and professionalism. It also runs trips to Gibbs Cay, where you can hand-feed stingrays (US$60 plus diving rates).

Local legendary divemaster Smitty has started up **Grand Turk Diving Co** ( ☎ 946-1559; www.gtdiving.com; Duke St). There are two-tank dives for $75 and singles for $55 and night dives for $60. This new company's reputation is already building as a first-class dive operation.

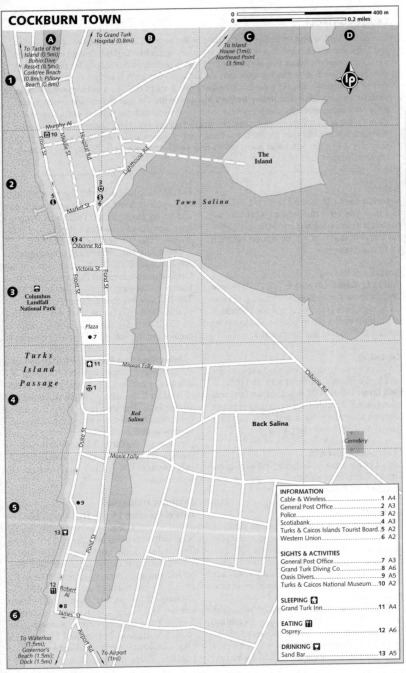

# COCKBURN TOWN

0 ——————— 400 m
0 ——————— 0.2 miles

To Grand Turk Hospital (0.8mi)

To Island House (1mi); Northeast Point (3.5mi)

To Taste of the Island (0.5mi); Bohio Dive Resort (0.5mi); Corktree Beach (0.8mi); Pillory Beach (0.8mi)

Murphy Al
Front St
Middle St
Hospital Rd
Lighthouse Rd

The Island

Town Salina

Market St

Osborne Rd

Victoria St
Front St
Pond St

Columbus Landfall National Park

Plaza

Turks Island Passage

Mission Folly

Duke St

Red Salina

Back Salina

Osborne Rd

Cemetery

Moxie Folly

Pond St

Robert Al

James St

To Waterloo (1.5mi); Governor's Beach (1.5mi); Dock (1.5mi)

To Airport (1mi)

Airport Rd

**TURKS & CAICOS**

| INFORMATION | |
|---|---|
| Cable & Wireless | 1 A4 |
| General Post Office | 2 A3 |
| Police | 3 A2 |
| Scotiabank | 4 A3 |
| Turks & Caicos Islands Tourist Board | 5 A2 |
| Western Union | 6 A2 |

| SIGHTS & ACTIVITIES | |
|---|---|
| General Post Office | 7 A3 |
| Grand Turk Diving Co | 8 A6 |
| Oasis Divers | 9 A5 |
| Turks & Caicos National Museum | 10 A2 |

| SLEEPING | |
|---|---|
| Grand Turk Inn | 11 A4 |

| EATING | |
|---|---|
| Osprey | 12 A6 |

| DRINKING | |
|---|---|
| Sand Bar | 13 A5 |

### CRUISE CONTROL?

Grand Turk used to be a forgotten oasis of quiet in the eastern Caribbean, devoid of overtourism and huge visitor numbers. That was until a few years ago, when Carnival Cruise Lines dredged out a harbor on the south end of the island so that it could park its ships up for the day. More than just a simple jetty, the complex that the company has built is a sight to see. Like some sort of pre-molded, plastic, pseudo-Caribbean port, it sticks out like a palm tree on a plain. Included in the madness is **Jimmy Buffet's Margaritaville** – a sort of Disneyland with booze. It's a fascinating place for people-watching as newlyweds and nearlydeads get drunk in the swim-up bar and scoff down their cheeseburger in Paradise. Local reaction to this development is mixed, but the fact that it's miles from town and is now a major employer is a help. On a busy day, two ships will be in port – offloading nearly 7000 people, suddenly outnumbering the residents of Grand Turk.

## Fishing

**Screaming Reels** ( ☎ 231-2087) will take you out and help you land the big one. Charters are based on a per boat basis and start at US$500 per day, but that cost can be shared between up to eight people.

## Horseback Riding

**Chukka Caribbean Adventures** ( ☎ 232-1339; www .chukkacaribbbean.com; adult/child $65/46) is a great one for horse lovers as there is the added bonus of swimming in the ocean while still atop your noble steed – good fun for families.

## Kayaking

If you're looking to get out and explore the ocean in a bit of a different way, the folks at **Oasis Divers** ( ☎ 946-1128; www.oasisdivers.com) will take you for a guided sea-kayaking mission through the mangrove forest. The half-day trip costs US$45 including your gear.

## FESTIVALS & EVENTS

See p131 for a list of festivals and events on Grand Turk, most of which happen in and around Cockburn Town.

## SLEEPING

There are several accommodations options in both downtown Cockburn and elsewhere on the island. Everything is close enough that staying on one end of the island doesn't preclude you from enjoying the other. Bikes are often provided to guests and are a great way to get around.

**our pick** **Island House** ( ☎ 946-1388; www.island house-tci.com; d US$112; 🅿 🖳 🖵 ) Walking through the doors at Island House you'll be met with Mediterranean-influenced architecture, whitewashed walls and arched doorways.

Further in you'll discover the inviting pool and opulent courtyard. The rooms are airy and nicely put together. There's wi-fi, guests have free use of a car while staying and there are bikes too, if you're feeling energetic.

**Grand Turk Inn** ( ☎ 946-2827; www.grandturkinn .com; Front St; ste US$300; 🐾 ) You can't get a better Caribbean endorsement than the place where Jimmy Buffet stays when he's in Grand Turk. The Balinese bamboo furniture sets the tone in this classic old house that just celebrated its 160th birthday. There are full kitchens in each of the five suites and its central location in Cockburn Town is hard to beat.

**Bohio Dive Resort & Spa** ( ☎ 946-2135; www.bohio resort.com; Front St; s/d per 3 nights US$360/600; 🐾 🖵 ) Boasts a prime location on a stunning stretch of sand, in-house dive packages and a friendly atmosphere. The staff here is top notch and the rooms are pleasant and clean. There are kayaks, sailboats, snorkeling gear and even yoga classes available. The only downside is the restaurant, which is overpriced and decidedly average. The resort is just north of the town center.

## EATING & DRINKING

**Taste of the Island** ( ☎ 946-2112; West St; mains from US$10; 🕑 lunch & dinner) Come to this locals' beachside restaurant and bar to have a great feed and work on your Creole. The food is simple, fresh and cheap. It can get loud, boisterous and a little crazy, a real taste of the island. It's just north of the town center.

**Osprey** ( ☎ 946-2666; Duke St; mains from $15; 🕑 lunch & dinner) Make sure you drop by on Sunday night for the legendary BBQ. Amazing seafood, poultry and beef grilled before your eyes, bombarded with salads and served up poolside. There are great ocean views and the band gets going after dinner so you can dance off that desert.

**our pick** **Sand Bar** ( ☎ 946-1111; Duke St; ☺ noon-1am) This small yet lively bar is a popular hot spot with locals, expats and tourists alike. It has yummy burgers if you've got the munchies, and the potential for spotting the green flash (a Caribbean phenomenon where you can see a green flash as the sun sets into the ocean) is great, especially if you've had a few Turk's Heads first.

### SHOPPING
The best shopping to be found on the island is in the street stalls that open up on Duke Street when the cruise ships are in port. There is a good variety of locally made goods, Haitian artwork and hand-drawn maps. Conversely if you are seeking cheap T-shirts, snow globes and shot glasses, head to the cruise-ship center where you will be inundated with an ocean of cheap rubbish.

## SALT CAY
If you can't quite envision what the Turks would have been like in the 19th century, take a trip to Salt Cay. Like stepping into a time machine, this picturesque island is the sort of hideaway that you search your whole life to discover. A few dusty roads interconnect the handful of structures, and donkeys wander aimlessly through the streets intermixed with friendly locals. While the land is quiet, the sea surrounding the island is awash with life. Turtles, eagle rays and the majestic humpback whale all frequent the waters. Hard to get to and even harder to leave, this place is a true haven for scuba divers and for those seeking an escape from the modern world.

---

### A WHALE OF A TALE
Salt Cay could very well be one of the best places on earth to see whales – by the thousands. Every winter the gentle giants make their annual pilgrimage to the warm seas of the Caribbean to mate and give birth. From the sandy shores of Salt Cay your can watch the majestic beauties of the sea saunter past from February to March. They are plain to see from the beach but you can also get among it on a whale-watching trip or dive trip organized from either Grand Turk or Salt Cay.

---

### Activities
**Salt Cay Divers** ( ☎ 946-6906; www.saltcaydivers.tc) is a one-stop dive shop. The owner is a long-term local who has her finger in most pies on the island. The staff can take you out for a dive ($40 per tank), and sort you out with accommodation and a hearty meal too. The annual humpback whale migration (January to March) is a big draw, and this operation takes pride in showing off the whales yet not disturbing them (whale-watching trips $75).

### Sleeping
**our pick** **Pirate's Hideaway Guesthouse** ( ☎ 946-6909; www.pirateshideaway.com; Victoria St; r US$165; ✖ ☎ ) Some places have pirate names and that's as deep as the theme goes; Nick, who runs the Pirate's Hideaway, *is* a pirate. Nearly as colorful as the establishment, he goes out of his way to make you feel at home. Recent renovations have changed things up a fair bit with an 'infinity bed' in the crow's-nest room and a new freshwater pool to cool you off. You can see the whales from the upstairs rooms as they pass by, or just hang out with the parrots – it is a pirate's place after all.

**Trade Winds Guest Suites** ( ☎ 946-6906; www.tradewinds.tc; Victoria St; r US$187; ✖ ) Right on the beach, just a few steps from town. Trade Winds is a great spot to base yourself for an extended stay: there are weekly rates and the location is tops. There are complimentary bikes and dive packages available too. The rooms are tidy, ocean facing and good value.

### Eating & Drinking
**Green Flash Cafe** ( ☎ 649-6977; mains from $10; ☺ lunch & dinner) Right off the main dock and the perfect vantage point to watch out for its namesake. Nothing pretentious here, just simple food enjoyed on picnic tables in a beautiful setting. Great burgers, conch and cold beer – what more could you want?

**Island Thyme Bistro** ( ☎ 649-6977; mains from $20; ☺ breakfast, lunch & dinner) This little restaurant and bar is set to be the big memory of your Salt Cay stay. The food is great and is prepared and presented with a sense of fun; there's even wi-fi. Ever wanted to get behind the grill in a proper restaurant? Well here's your chance – they have a guest chef night, where you get to strut your stuff in

---

**THE KEY TO SALT CAY**

Porter Williams is one of those iconic members of the Salt Cay community that you'd struggle *not* to meet on your visit. For the last eight years he's called the tiny island home. In that time he's opened up two restaurants, become the driving force in promoting Salt Cay to the outside world, and even managed to relax on the beach from time to time.

**So how has Salt Cay changed in the time that you've been here?**

Salt Cay has become a world-class destination for those looking to escape the rigors of our modern world. In the past it was primarily a dive destination, but now is a destination for those looking to return to a simpler time and place where they can be absorbed into the community and culture.

**Has that increase in tourism affected life here in Salt Cay?**

No, Salt Cay is still the island time forgot, the Caribbean of yesteryear. We aren't affected by cruise ships here so things are staying pristine, just how we like it.

**Are people in Salt Cay, and Turks and Caicos for that matter, thinking about climate change?**

Salt Cay is proposed to be a Green Island, the first in the Caribbean. There is an emphasis on keeping the population density low and we're striving to maintain the historical character of the island. So far climate change hasn't affected the annual humpback whale migration; in fact there have been more sightings this year than in the past.

**So what does the future hold for Salt Cay?**

Salt Cay is going to develop over time. However, the emphasis is on preserving the beauty, heritage and the pristine nature of the island. It's a wonderful place, nothing on Salt Cay is world class in itself but the total experience is world class.

---

the kitchen. Friday is pizza night and the restaurant prides itself on a flexible menu – so what do you feel like tonight?

# CAICOS ISLANDS

The fan of islands that form the main landmass of this nation are the Caicos Islands. West Caicos, Providenciales (the main tourist gateway), North Caicos, Middle Caicos, East Caicos, and South Caicos, plus numerous other tiny islands both inhabited and deserted.

## PROVIDENCIALES
pop 8900

It wasn't too long ago that Providenciales, or Provo as it's known locally, was a sleepy little corner of the Caribbean. But unlike the rest of the islands in the T&C, the secret is out. Everywhere you look there is a new hotel sprouting from the ground and the promise of more to come.

The upside to all this development is that finding a room beachside isn't a mission – there are stacks to choose from. But that's one of the few positives – hotels are getting taller and the rate of development is staggering. One must wonder where all the tourists are going to come from? For the moment, rooms are

easy to come by, deals are simple to find and the beach is still quiet.

Provo is home to Grace Bay Beach, one of the best beaches in the country – the whiter than white sand draws visitors from around the globe. Despite the explosive growth there is an unhurried feel to Provo – people walk slow, talk slow and sail through life at a relaxed pace.

### Orientation

The main highway, Leeward Hwy, runs east from downtown Providenciales along the island's spine, ending near Bird Rock. A coastal highway, Grace Bay Rd, parallels Grace Bay.

A separate coast road runs northwest from downtown to Blue Hills and Wheeland settlements, beyond which it turns into a dirt track to Northwest Point. A fourth road runs south from downtown to Sapodilla Bay.

### Information
**EMERGENCY**
**Fire** ( ☎ 946-4444)
**Police** ( ☎ 946-4259; Old Airport Rd)

**MEDICAL SERVICES**
**Associated Medical Practices Clinic** ( ☎ 946-4242; Leeward Hwy) Has several private doctors. The clinic has a recompression chamber.

**Provo Discount Pharmacy** (☎ 946-4844; Central Sq Plaza, Leeward Hwy; ☼ 8am-10pm)

## MONEY
**First Caribbean** (☎ 946-4245; Butterfield Sq, Leeward Hwy)
**Scotiabank** (☎ 946-4750; Cherokee Rd) Has a 24-hour ATM.
**Western Union** (☎ 946-5484; Butterfield Sq, Leeward Hwy)

## POST
**DHL Worldwide Express** (☎ 946-4352; Butterfield Sq, Leeward Hwy)
**Federal Express** (☎ 946-4682; www.fedex.com; Center Complex, Leeward Hwy)
**Post office** (☎ 946-4676; Old Airport Rd; ☼ 8am-noon & 2-4pm Mon-Thu, 8am-12:30pm & 2-5:30pm Fri) Next to the police station.

## TELEPHONE
There are public phone booths at several roadside locations. You dial ☎ 111 to place credit-card calls.
**Cable & Wireless** (☎ 111; Leeward Hwy) Make calls here; has telephone information and can sort you out with a cell phone.

## TOURIST INFORMATION
**Tourist information booth** (Arrivals Hall, Providenciales International Airport)
**Turks & Caicos Tourism** (☎ 946-4970; www.turksand caicostourism.com; Stubbs Diamond Plaza, Provo; ☼ 9am-5pm Mon-Fri)

## Sights
The biggest attraction on the island is the world-famous **Grace Bay Beach**. This stunning stretch of snow white sand is perfect for relaxing, swimming and evening up your sunburn. Though it's dotted with hotels and resorts, its sheer size means that finding your own square of paradise is a snap.

If you feel inclined to tear yourself away from the beach and see some sights, there are a few worth taking in. Though the options are limited, there are some historic points that should perk scholarly interest. Check out the ruins of **Cheshire Hall** (Leeward Hwy), a plantation house constructed in the 1790s by British Loyalists.

If you've got a rental car that can handle a bit of dirt road, be sure to check out the lighthouse at **Northwest Point**. Caution is the word as the road has been known to swallow cars whole.

Once you get all that history out of your system go for an anti-intellectual cleanse and seek out the sparkling beach at **Malcolm Roads**. From the settlement of Wheeland, northwest of downtown, a rough dirt road leads to this top-notch sandy spot.

Protecting reefs off of Provo's west shore, Northwest Point Marine National Park also encompasses several saline lakes that attract breeding and migrant waterfowl. The largest is **Pigeon Pond**, inland. This part of the park is the Pigeon Pond & Frenchman's Creek Nature Reserve. Other ponds – notably **Northwest Point Pond** and **Frenchman's Creek** – encompass tidal flats and mangrove swamps along the west coast, attracting fish and fowl in large numbers. You'll have to hike here, and come equipped with food and water.

### CHALK SOUND NATIONAL PARK
The waters of this 3-mile-long (5km) bay, 2 miles southwest of downtown, define 'turquoise.' The color is uniform: a vast, unrippled, electric-blue carpet eerily and magnificently studded with countless tiny islets.

A slender peninsula separates the sound from the sea. The peninsula is scalloped with beach-lined bays, notably **Sapodilla Bay**. A horribly potholed road runs along the peninsula; although it is accessible, drive carefully! Unfortunately, large vacation homes line both sides of the peninsula from top to toe, which clip the views and hinder some public access from the roads to the water and beaches.

At the far eastern end of the Sapodilla Bay peninsula, a rocky hilltop boasts **rock carvings** dating back to 1844. The slabs of rock are intricately carved with Roman lettering that records the names of sailors apparently shipwrecked here and the dates of their sojourns. The carvings are reached via a rocky trail that begins 200yd east of the Mariner Hotel; it leads uphill 200yd to the summit, which offers wonderful views over the island and Chalk Sound.

If you want to see what you've been chowing down on, head to the northeast corner of Provo and have a look at **Caicos Conch Farm** (☎ 946-5643; tour adult/child US$6/3; ☼ 9am-4pm). Slightly ramshackle and a little strange, it has a speedy 20-minute tour to show you how they grow the Caribbean Queens. Feels a bit like visiting a turkey farm – you leave there a little bit disturbed, and a little bit hungry.

# PROVIDENCIALES

**TURKS & CAICOS**

**A** | 72°20'W | **B** | **C** | 72°15'W | **D**

**INFORMATION**
Associated Medical Practices Clinic....**1** D5
Cable & Wireless..................................**2** D5
DHL Worldwide Express................(see 11)
Federal Express...................................**3** C5
First Caribbean..................................**4** E1
Police Station.....................................**5** E2
Post Office.........................................**6** E2
Provo Discount Pharmacy..................**7** D5
Scotiabank.........................................**8** E5
Scotiabank (24-Hour ATM)................**9** E1
Turks & Caicos Tourism....................**10** E5
Western Union..................................**11** E1

**SIGHTS & ACTIVITIES**
Art Pickering's Provo Turtle Divers..(see 21)
Caicos Conch Farm...........................**12** F5
Catch the Wave Charters................(see 30)
Cheshire Hall....................................**13** F1
Dive Provo......................................(see 26)
J&B Tours.......................................(see 30)

Ocean Vibes..................................(see 30)
Rock Carvings..................................**14** B6
Turtle Parasail................................(see 30)
Undersea Explorer Semi Submarine..(see 21)
Windsurfing Provo.........................(see 18)

**SLEEPING** 🏠
Airport Inn.......................................**15** C5
Comfort Suites.................................**16** E5
Miramar Resort.................................**17** D5
Ocean Club West..............................**18** E5
Sands...............................................**19** E5
Sibonné Hotel & Beach Club............**20** E5
Turtle Cove Inn................................**21** D5

**EATING** 🍴
Baci Ristorante..................................**22** D5
Big Bamboo....................................(see 26)
Calico Jack's...................................(see 26)
Coyaba............................................**23** D5
Danny Buoy's Irish Pub & Restaurant.**24** E5

Grace's Cottage.............................(see 19)
Island Scoop Ice–Cream................(see 24)
Magnolia Restaurant & Wine Bar...(see 17)
O'Soleil............................................**25** D5
Tiki Hut..........................................(see 21)

**SHOPPING** 🛍
Marilyn's Crafts.............................(see 26)
Night & Day Boutique....................(see 26)
Ports of Call Plaza...........................**26** E5
Tattooed Parrot.............................(see 26)
Town Centre Mall ...........................**27** E1

**TRANSPORT**
Budget.............................................**28** C5
Budget...........................................(see 27)
Hertz................................................**29** C5
Hertz..............................................(see 28)
Leeward Marina................................**30** F4
Scooter Bob's................................(see 21)
Turtle Cove Marina.......................(see 21)

*Caicos Passage*

**3** 🏕 Northwest Point Marine National Park

Northwest Point

*Northwest Point Pond*

21°50'N
**4** 🏖 Malcolm Roads
• *Tiki Hut*

*Pigeon Pond*

**Wheeland** 🏕

**Blue Hills**

Pigeon Pond & Frenchman's Creek Nature Reserve

🏕 Princess Alexandra National Park

**5**

See Enlargement

**Downtown Providenciales**

Airport Rd

28 ● | 15
29 ● | 🏕
Providenciales International Airport

3 ●
21 🏕 | 22 🏕 | **Turtle** | 23 🏕 | 25
🏕 17 | **Cove** | 🏕 2
1 | 7

*Venetian Rd*

*Juba*

*Frenchman's Creek*

*Chalk Sound*

🏕 Chalk Sound National Park

*Silly Cay*

*Five Cays Bay*

● South Side Marina

*Cooper Jack Bight*

**6**
*Proggin' Bay*

*South Bluff*

*Taylor Bay*

*Stubb's Creek*

*Sapodilla Bay* 14 ●

Five Cays

72°20'W                   South Dock          72°15'W

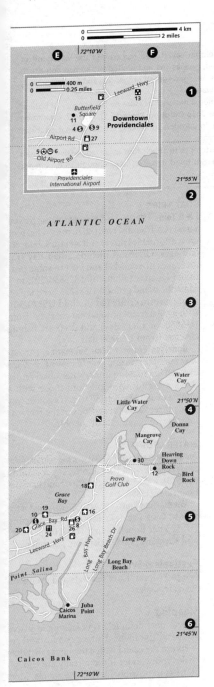

## THE CAYS
### French Cay
Shiver me timbers, this old pirate hideaway is now more frequented by migrating birds than swashbuckling scoundrels. Uninhabited and a permanent wildlife sanctuary, this small island 15 miles south of Provo is home to a staggering number of bird species. Just offshore the waters are teeming with stingrays who use the calm waters as a nursery. Nurse sharks gather here in summer where they feed, breed and scare swimmers. You can snorkel among the menagerie of sea life on a day trip from Provo; just remember the sharks are more scared of you – well, almost.

### Little Water Cay
Northeast of Provo and separated from it by the 400yd-wide channel, Little Water Cay is a nature reserve within Princess Alexandra National Park and is the home of about 2000 endangered rock iguanas. Please don't feed or touch the iguanas. Also keep to the trails to avoid trampling their burrows and the ecologically sensitive plants. Look out for Curious Iguana, so-named for obvious reasons!

### Pine Cay
Some cays are rife with seabirds, some are teeming with iguanas. Pine Cay's primary residents are celebrities. The 2 miles of ocean separating it from the northeast edge of Provo is plenty of moat to keep the riffraff out. You can visit this 800-acre private island by prior arrangement, just be sure to say hi to Denzel Washington, Bill Cosby and Jimmy Buffet for me – they all call the island home for at least part of the year.

### Fort George Cay
Close enough that you could lob a champagne cork from neighboring Pine Cay, Fort George Cay is home to the remnants of an 18th-century British built fort built back in the day to protect the islands. Now the only invaders are divers and snorkelers there to inspect the gun emplacements slowly becoming one with the sea bottom. The site is protected within Fort George Land & Sea National Park.

### Dellis Cay
Oh the irony – Dellis Cay has some of the best shells around, but being in the park precludes you from taking them home. Perhaps that's why it has the best shells around.

TURKS & CAICOS

---

### JOJO: A NATIONAL TREASURE

Since the mid '80s a 7ft bottle-nosed male dolphin called JoJo has cruised the waters off of Provo and North Caicos. When he first appeared, he was shy and limited his human contact to following or playing in the bow waves of boats. He soon turned gregarious and has become an active participant whenever people are in the water.

JoJo is now so popular that he has been named a national treasure by the Ministry of Natural Resources. This treasure is protected through the **JoJo Dolphins Project** ( ☎ 941-5617; www.marine wildlife.org; PO Box 153, Providenciales, Turks & Caicos). In addition to looking out for JoJo, it educates and raises awareness of issues affecting the ocean.

JoJo, as with any wild dolphin, interprets attempts to touch him as an aggressive act, and will react to defend himself, so please bear that in mind if you're lucky enough to experience his playfulness and companionship for a while.

---

## Activities

### DIVING & SNORKELING

All the dive operators offer a range of dive and snorkel options, from introductory 'resort courses' to Professional Association of Diving Instructors (PADI) certification (US$350 to US$395).

Most offer free hotel pickup and drop-offs. Dive sites include the other Caicos islands and cays.

**Art Pickering's Provo Turtle Divers** ( ☎ 946-4232; www.provoturtledivers.com; Turtle Cove Marina) has been going strong for 35 years now; it offers two-tank/night dives for US$112/80. Visits all the major dive sites – the company is all about service.

**Dive Provo** ( ☎ 946-5040; www.diveprovo.com; Ports of Call plaza, Grace Bay Rd) has two-tank/night dives (US$115/80) at sites around the island, plus photo and video services.

**Ocean Vibes** ( ☎ 231-6636; www.oceanvibes.com; Leeward Marina) is the only dive operation on the island run by Belongers. It specializes in small groups and an intimate feel to its aquatic adventures. Two-tank dives are US$110 and a useful refresher course costs US$125.

### FISHING

A plethora of boat charters and trips can be arranged from Leeward and Turtle Cove Marinas (see right). Try the following:

**Catch the Wave Charters** ( ☎ 941-3047; www.catch thewavecharters.com; Leeward Marina) runs a variety of boat charters to suit your taste. Fishing costs US$500 for half a day. Deep-sea/bottom fishing is US$750 for a half-day rental of a boat that will fit four fishers.

**Bite Me Sportfishing** ( ☎ 231-0366; biteme@tciway .tc) is not just a great name, but a good group of folks to help you land the big one.

### BOAT TRIPS

**J & B Tours** ( ☎ 946-5047; www.jbtours.com; Leeward Marina) is a friendly team that runs a heap of great affordable trips to suit all tastes, budgets and ages. Offerings include a half-day trip that takes in a snorkel and visit to some protected iguanas (adult/child US$50/30), to a romantic island getaway (US$225 per couple), or glowworm cruise (adult/child US$70/50). Also available are power-boat charters (from US$650 for a half day) and deep-sea fishing charters (from US$250 half-day)

**Undersea Explorer Semi Submarine** ( ☎ 231-0006; www.caicostours.com; Turtle Cove Marina; adult/child US$50/40) is a moving underwater observatory that's a big hit with kids and those with a phobia of actually getting wet. It's a neat way to see three different sections of the reef – as long as you're not claustrophobic.

### WATER SPORTS

**Turtle Parasail** ( ☎ 941-0643; www.captainmarvins parasail.com; Leeward Marina) offers parasailing (US$70), wake boarding (US$60) and banana-boat rides (US$25).

**Windsurfing Provo** ( ☎ 241-1687; www.windsurfing provo.tc; Ocean Club, Grace Bay) has windsurfing (US$25 per hour), sailing (US$100 per day) and kayaking (US$15 per hour) on offer.

## Festivals & Events

See p131 for a list of festivals and events on Providenciales.

## Sleeping

Provo most definitely isn't lacking in places to spend the night. Hotels, condos and resorts dot the island with a frequency that may make you wonder if there really are enough tourists to possibly fill all these rooms. Most

**GO FLY A KITE**

The steady winds that buff the coastline of the Turks and Caicos mixed with the reef-sheltered shoreline are the perfect combination for the snowboarding of the aquatic world – kitesurfing. The bastard child of stunt kite flying, wakeboarding and windsurfing, this sport is going off right now. Imagine flying the biggest kite you've ever seen, strapping yourself onto a wakeboard and holding on for dear life. Depending on how much sugar you like in your tea, it either sounds terrific or terrifying. The warm T&C waters are already on the radar of the sport's elite – but don't be put off, it's also a great place to learn. Chat to Mike at **Windsurfing Provo** ( ☎ 241-1687; www .windsurfingprovo.tc; Ocean Club, Grace Bay) to get hooked up with the how-to (US$150 for a two-hour lesson). Who said all there is to do in the Caribbean is lie on the beach?

budgets are accommodated for, but there is a skew to the higher end so those with deeper pockets will be spoilt for choice. At present, supply outnumbers demand so there are some good deals to be found, especially in the low season.

Browse the following websites: www.where whenhow.com, www.provo.net and www.tci mall.tc/villas. Also check the hotels' websites listed here for some great discounts.

### DOWNTOWN & TURTLE COVE
**Airport Inn** ( ☎ 941-3514; airportinn@tciway.tc; Airport Plaza; s/d US$99/110; ❄ ) Sporting unencumbered views of the runway, the Airport Inn isn't the sort of place to spend your holiday. But it is a perfect option for those catching an early flight or on a very tight budget. It's steps from the airport and at time of research was undergoing some renovations in the rooms, bringing them up a notch. There are plenty of eating options nearby, all with a local flavor.

**Turtle Cove Inn** ( ☎ 946-4203; www.turtlecovehotel .com; Turtle Cove Marina; d US$105; ❄ ⍰ ) If you're here to dive and lounge by the pool, this older property in the heart of the Turtle Cove Marina is a good option. Nothing too flashy, and it's getting a bit worn, but it puts you in a great location. There are numerous restaurants a few steps away, and dive boats, fishing charters and rental cars all leaving from the doorstep.

**Miramar Resort** ( ☎ 946-4240; www.miramarresort.tc; Turtle Cove; d US$145; ❄ ⍰ ⍰ ) Has bright, clean and spacious rooms with patios, fridges and good views of Turtle Cove from the hill above. It does lack a bit of character and there are some quirks to the place. It's also a fair trek from the beach. But it has a pool, tennis courts and a gym to keep you busy, plus wi-fi, and there is the excellent Magnolia Restaurant in the adjacent building so, all up, it's a winner.

### GRACE BAY & EAST PROVIDENCIALES
**Comfort Suites** ( ☎ 946-8888; www.comfortsuitestci.com; Grace Bay; r incl breakfast US$170; ❄ ⍰ ⍰ ) If you're searching for an affordable resort and are willing to accept that it isn't beachfront, this is a great option. Clean and spacious rooms stack in three stories above the pool and chilled poolside bar. Couches in the rooms, free wi-fi and chilled-out staff are thrown in. There are even designated chairs on the beach for guests. Nothing too special, but if you're here to dive, lie on the beach or not liquidate your finances, this is the place to stay.

**Sibonné Hotel & Beach Club** ( ☎ 946-5547; www .sibonne.com; Grace Bay; r US$185; ❄ ⍰ ) Deservedly popular and occupying a divine stretch of sand on Grace Bay, Sibonné is a real anti-resort. While some of its neighbors are big and flashy, the focus here is small and intimate. Trees dominate the courtyard with plenty of shade for when that sun gets to be flammable. Hammocks dot the property and are prime real estate with the relaxed set. The rooms are basic and a few years old now, but Sibonné still holds it own.

**Ocean Club West** ( ☎ 946-5880; www.oceanclub resorts.com; Grace Bay; r US$260; ❄ ⍰ ⍰ ) With a great location in the heart of Grace Bay, the OC is a safe bet. The enchanting pool is complete with an arch-bridge-appointed 'river' and the requisite swim-up bar. Rooms are a bit cramped, but the kitchenettes and balconies more than make up for it. There's also wi-fi.

**Sands** ( ☎ 946-5199; www.thesandstc.com; Grace Bay; d US$275; ❄ ⍰ ⍰ ) A great family option with a kiddy pool, and kitchenettes in every room. The recent renovations have yielded rooms with clean lines and an elegant design. There are tiki huts on the beach for the sun worshipers and the excellent Hemingway's Bar and Grill on site. Offers wi-fi.

## Eating & Drinking

Outside influences have helped to create an abundance of eclectic dining options in Providenciales. Those on a budget or wishing for a simple meal have the choice of some great pubs and family-style restaurants. Conversely, if you want to spend it up and have a truly memorable meal there are more than a few venues that will fit the bill to a delicious tee.

### DOWNTOWN & TURTLE COVE

**Tiki Hut** ( ☎ 941-5341; Turtle Cove Inn, Turtle Cove Marina; mains from US$10; ☺ breakfast, lunch & dinner) Many a salty sea dog has spun a fish story or two under the umbrellas at the Tiki Hut. Set right on the wharf at Turtle Cove Marina, this is where you can sit with a cold beer and spy the boats as they return to port. There are cheap burgers that hit the spot, pizzas to share, daily specials and enough local cred to keep it real.

**Baci Ristorante** ( ☎ 941-3044; Harbour Towne Plaza, Turtle Cove; mains from US$20; ☺ lunch & dinner) Maritime chic at its best with wrought-iron scrollwork lining the ceilings, all with an authentic Italian-infused flavor. The bronzed mermaids keep watch as you dine on nice cuts of veal, fresh pasta and other delightful dishes. There are choice views of the marina and an upscale feel at this classy Turtle Cove eatery.

**Magnolia Restaurant and Wine Bar** ( ☎ 941-5108; mains from US$25; ☺ dinner) Sitting on the hill overlooking Turtle Cove, Magnolia is a real find – the view is almost as delicious as the food. The fairy-light-rimmed balcony is the perfect setting for the signature dish, a cracked-pepper and sesame-encrusted rare-seared tuna. It's so tender it melts in your mouth. The restaurant has an ample wine list to choose from and the service is impeccable. Book ahead to get a table with a good view – it's worth it in every way.

### GRACE BAY & EAST PROVIDENCIALES

There is a plethora of dining options in this neck of the woods. The Ports of Call shopping plaza has a stack of midrange options and most of the hotels have some form of restaurant too.

**Island Scoop Ice-cream** ( ☎ 241-4230; Grace Bay Plaza, Grace Bay Rd; ice cream US$3; ☺ 10am-9pm) When the sun is shining and it's all starting to get just a bit too hot, slide into Island Scoop for the

therapy you need. Twenty-four flavors of goodness to choose from piled into homemade waffle cones. Go on, make it a double – you're on holiday!

**Calico Jack's** ( ☎ 946-5120; upstairs, Ports of Call plaza; mains from US$10; ☺ dinner) Comes with a generous helping of nautical paraphernalia and is named after a pirate named Jack – no not *that* pirate named Jack. Nightly drink specials, Spanish-armada-sized portions and a friendly atmosphere make it a locals' favorite. The conch is awesome, and be sure to swing by on a Thursday when the place really hops to the sounds of live music.

**Danny Buoy's Irish Pub and Restaurant** ( ☎ 946-5921; Grace Bay Rd; mains from US$10; ☺ lunch & dinner) This lively little pub is a slice of the emerald isle, in a place about as far from Dublin as you can get. Traditional Irish fare mixed with Caribbean classics makes for an odd sort of fusion – the Guinness is good and if you have enough of them, you might just be convinced you're in the old country.

**O'Soleil** ( ☎ 946-5900; The Somerset, Princess Dr; mains from US$25; ☺ dinner) Fresh seafood is the specialty in this stylish eatery. The Mediterranean-influenced architecture is the perfect backdrop for the culinary designs created in the kitchen. Be sure to try the Turks and Caicos chowder; it's loaded with fresh seafood and the secret ingredient that makes it nearly irresistible – Caribbean rum.

**our pick** **Grace's Cottage** ( ☎ 946-8147; www.pointgrace.com; Point Grace; mains from US$25; ☺ dinner) If you're looking for a romantic setting to drop to one knee and pop the question, or perhaps just in the mood for an amazing meal, Grace's is the place. Tables are spread out among the foliage in a fan of private patios, and crisp white linen tablecloths adorn the surfaces, creating a visual feast. And that's before you try the food – fresh fish, poultry and beef all cooked to perfection, topped off with a fine selection of wine. What more could you want in a place to eat dinner?

**Big Bamboo** ( ☎ 946-5832; Ports of Call plaza, Grace Bay Rd; mains US$25-30; ☺ lunch & dinner) If you want to hang out with some Belongers and sample some great authentic Caribbean delicacies, this is the place to do it. The staff is superfriendly and the feel is relaxed and inviting. Tuck into some beans and rice and a serve of the jerk chicken. You'll feel right at home – irie mon!

**Coyaba** ( ☎ 946-5186; www.coyabarestaurant.com; Paradise Inn; mains from US$35; ☺ dinner) Off Grace

Bay Rd, Coyaba somehow treads the line of fine dining while retaining a relaxed atmosphere. The food is a clever fusion of Caribbean flavors and faithful classics. The legendary chef shows his skills with daily specials that outnumber the menu standards. This is a real food-lovers' paradise. Be sure to make a reservation – word's out about this one.

## Shopping
A large selection of beachy items, casual clothing and batiks is offered at **Tattooed Parrot** ( ☎ 946-5829), Marilyn's Crafts and the Night & Day Boutique, all in the Ports of Call plaza.

## Getting There & Around
### AIR
For flight information to and from the Caicos Islands, see p133.

There is no bus service from Providenciales International Airport. A taxi from the airport to Grace Bay costs US$20 one way for two people; each extra person costs US$5. Some resorts arrange their own minibus transfers.

### BICYCLE
**Scooter Bob's** ( ☎ 946-4684; scooter@provo.net; Turtle Cove Marina Plaza) rents out mountain bikes for US$20 per day.

### BOAT
A plethora of boat charters and trips can be arranged to the islands and cays from Leeward and Turtle Cove Marinas (see p124).

### BUS
Sporadic buses run routes to some of the settlements out of town; if you see one of the small vans, flag it down. There is also a tourist-oriented bus called the **Gecko Bus** ( ☎ 232-7433; US$4); get tokens at most hotels and they'll call for a pick-up. The schedule is on island time and only runs when needed.

### CAR & MOTORCYCLE
You'll find the following rental agencies on the island:
**Budget** ( ☎ 946-4079; www.budget.com; Providenciales International Airport)
**Hertz** ( ☎ 941-3910; www.hertztci.com; Providenciales International Airport)
**Rent-a-buggy** ( ☎ 946-4158; www.rentabuggy.tc) Specializes in 4x4 rentals.
**Scooter Bob's** ( ☎ 946-4684; scooter@provo.net; Turtle Cove Marina Plaza) Rents out cars and 4WDs from US$70 per

day and scooters from US$50 per day. It also rents out bicycles for US$20 per day and snorkeling gear for US$15 per day.

### TAXI
Taxis are a popular way of getting around the island. Most are vans and although unmetered the pricing is consistent. It's best not to be in a hurry as they often take forever to come pick you up. You hotel can arrange a taxi for you and they meet all flights at the airport. Here are a couple of good options:
**Nell's Taxi Service** ( ☎ 941-3228)
**Provo Taxi & Bus Group** ( ☎ 946-5481)

# NORTH CAICOS
pop 1500
There was a time a century ago when bountiful North Caicos, with its lush farmland and bustling towns, was the center of action in the island chain. But those times have long since passed. These days there are only stone ruins and a few small towns to show for these early expansions. But don't despair; there remains a pristine tropical isle that is a joy to visit.

There are a few tiny settlements, more groups of dwellings than towns – but that is where the charm lies. There is a distinctive lost-world feel to this island. As you wander along the empty roads, shell-strewn beaches and green interior you have the feeling that you've discovered something new, something that not many people are lucky enough to see. And isn't that the whole point?

## Information
There's a post office in Kew, and Bottle Creek has a small public library. The nearest hospital is in Provo (p120). In an emergency, dial ☎ 911.
**Government clinic** Bottle Creek ( ☎ 946-7194); Kew ( ☎ 946-7397)
**Police** Bottle Creek ( ☎ 946-7116); Kew ( ☎ 946-7261)

## Sights & Activities
The Kew area has several historic ruins, including the interesting **Wades Green Plantation**, granted to a British Loyalist by King George III. The owners struggled to grow sisal and Sea Island cotton until drought, hurricanes and bugs drove them out. The plantation lasted a mere 25 years; the owners abandoned their slaves and left. It's a sobering place to visit and worth the effort.

Beaches include **Pumpkin Bluff**, **Horsestable** and most importantly, **Whitby Beach**. On any

---

**THE CLOCK IS TICKING**

For as long as everyone can remember North Caicos has always been the ultraquiet neighbor to Provo. But times are a changing – there is an unprecedented amount of development underway on the island. Granted, it's not going to look like Miami Beach any time soon, but there are quite a few new projects under way. The new ferry has increased numbers and there's a deep-water harbor under construction that will make bringing building materials to the island much easier. This translates into more people, and soon more options for places to stay, eat and drink. Sadly it does signal the end of a very quiet era on North Caicos; the days when you got the beaches all to yourself are numbered. So if you want to see NC the way it's supposed to be – quiet as a mouse – you better get here ASAP.

---

one, yours will be the only Robinson Crusoe footprints. Pumpkin Bluff beach is especially beautiful and the snorkeling is good, with a foundered cargo ship adding to the allure.

**Cottage Pond**, a 150ft-deep (45.7m) blue hole on the northwest coast, attracts waterfowl such as West Indian whistling ducks, grebes and waders. Bellfield Landing Pond, Pumpkin Bluff Pond and Dick Hill Creek also attract flamingos, as does a large brine lake, **Flamingo Pond**, which floods the center of the island. Here the gangly birds strut around in hot pink. The ponds are protected as individual nature reserves.

A series of small cays off the northeast shore are protected within **East Bay Islands National Park**, and a trio of cays to the northwest form **Three Mary Cays National Park**, another flamingo sanctuary and an osprey nesting site. The **snorkeling** is good at Three Mary Cays and further west at Sandy Point Beach.

## Sleeping

Generally accommodation on North Caicos is set up with self-catering in mind. All the options listed here come standard with kitchenettes, except for the Pelican Beach Hotel, which cooks for you. The best website displaying the island's accommodation and rentals is www.tcimall.tc.

**our pick Ocean Beach Hotel** ( ☎ 946-7113; www.turksandcaicos.tc/oceanbeach.com; s/d US$115/130) Popular with families and often full of returning guests, Ocean Beach is a treat. Beautifully maintained with simple homely touches, it feels like you're staying at a friend's cottage – with the best view money can buy. There are rooms here to accommodate every type of group; big or small they'll sort you into the right spot. Ocean Beach has been a trendsetter in sustainability from its inception: the 'so simple it's clever' solar-heated rooftop water-collection system provides all the water for the hotel, and it doesn't stop there – compact fluorescent lighting, room orientation to take advantage of the wind and avoid air-con use, and a commitment to reducing linen and towel washing. Big hotels around the world could learn a lot from this little inn on North Caicos.

**Pelican Beach Hotel** ( ☎ 946-7112; www.pelicanbeach.tc; r US$160) For those looking for a relaxed, back-to-basics place to stay, this is an excellent option. Suzie and Clifford's place is getting a bit old and tired, but the old-school feel adds to the experience. There is nothing fancy here; plain TV-less rooms sit in a row only a few feet from the beach. There is the option to have breakfast and dinner included, which is available to nonguests on a limited basis too. This option is hard to beat – Suzie is a legend in the kitchen!

**St Charles** ( ☎ 946-7042; www.stcharlesnc.com; r from US$180; 🞖 🖵 🞖) The future has arrived in North Caicos in the form of the St Charles. Dominating the skyline, this five-story resort is by far the tallest building on the island. With all the appointments you'd expect in a high-end resort, it doesn't disappoint. Beautifully designed and furnished rooms all come standard with stunning views. The penthouse suite has the best view on the island – but the $3000 per night rate will prohibit most from getting to see it. There's an aesthetically pleasing pool with a swim-up bar and a nice stretch of beach out front too. Has wi-fi.

**Hollywood Beach Suites** ( ☎ 231-1020; www.hollywoodbeachsuites.com; ste from $260; 🞖 🖵) With a maximum capacity of a whopping eight guests, finding space on the beach won't be an issue. The rooms are tidy, modern and well set up for a relaxing holiday, with couches, TVs and DVD players for when the stress of sun worshiping just gets to be too much. There are complimentary kayaks and bikes for guests. Your dinner is cooked for you the first night of your stay too – go for the lobster!

## Eating

**Wharf Restaurant** ( ☎ 946-7042; www.stcharlesnc.com; mains US$6-20; ✷ breakfast, lunch & dinner) Situated just off the pool at the St Charles, this casual restaurant is a great place to grab a bite and watch the sun set. Island fare is intertwined with burgers, sandwiches and fish and chips. Very stylish and tasty too.

**Silver Palm** ( ☎ 946-7113; Ocean Beach Hotel; mains US$8-15; ✷ breakfast, lunch & dinner) Lobster and conch are the specialties here – all of course sourced locally. Informal and friendly, small and intimate, this place epitomises the North Caicos experience: simple and delicious.

You can buy produce and groceries at KH's Food Store in Whitby and at Al's Grocery in Bottle Creek.

## Getting There & Around

For information on getting to/from the island by air or boat, see p134. A taxi from the airport to Whitby costs US$10 or about US$40 from the ferry landing, one way. Mac of **M&M Tours** ( ☎ 231-6285) will pick you up; be sure to prebook.

Most hotels and condos offer complimentary bikes to their guests. Ask around at Al's Rent A Car; it should be able to track one down for about US$20 per day.

Car rental costs around US$75 per day. Try the following options:

**Al's Rent A Car** ( ☎ 946-7232)
**Pelican Car Rentals** ( ☎ 241-8275)

## MIDDLE CAICOS

**pop 300**

If you're really looking to get away from it all, treat yourself by checking out Middle Caicos. With an area the size of North Caicos and a population of only 300 you'll be lucky to see *anyone*. The topography is much the same as North Caicos, with a green, lake-filled interior surrounded by white-sand beach and azure water. Recently a causeway has been completed connecting North and Middle, making the visiting process a whole lot easier. There are few places to stay on the island and even fewer places to eat, so those not intending on a self-catered, pre-arranged stay would do well to plan a day trip. But for those who do decide to stay, your efforts will most certainly be rewarded – this is the way the Caribbean used to be.

There are a few tiny settlements dotted along the island; Conch Bar and Bambara are the largest, but there still isn't much to them.

## Information

There are few services to speak of on the island, save the odd seemingly abandoned gas pump (which may or may not have gas) and a few phone booths that have seen better days. The proximity to North Caicos dictates that traveling over to the neighboring island is the way to go if you want to buy groceries or head out for a meal.

## Sights & Activities

The aim of the game on Middle is to relax – but if you're keen to get the blood flowing a bit there are a few options worth checking out. Directly in front of Blue Horizon Resort is **Mudjin Harbor** – the rocky shore rears up to form a bit of rare elevation. Walking along the cliff top you'll be surprised to see a staircase appear out of nowhere, leading into the earth. Take it down through the cave and emerge on a secluded cliff-lined beach. Looking seaward you'll be entertained by the waves crashing into the offshore rocks in spectacular fashion.

A great way to get a feel for the island is to go for a walk on the **Crossing Place Trail**. Hugging the northern edge of Middle Caicos and crossing into North Caicos, this easy-to-follow and straightforward track supports

---

**TWIST MY ARM: THE SPOTS THE AUTHORS WANTED TO KEEP SECRET**

A beach is a beach, right? Wrong – there are beaches and then there are *beaches*. And this one is most definitely the latter. **Bambara beach** on the far northeast corner of Middle Caicos is the Caribbean beach that you've been dreaming about. Impossibly white sand, robin-egg blue water and not a soul around. On the quiet end of a blissfully uninhabited island, this beach sees little traffic of any sort. If there just so happens to be somebody else there, just go for a walk – seclusion is only a few steps away.

TURKS & CAICOS

---

**BEST OF THE REST**

If you really want an adventure and want to escape from any sort of tourist infrastructure, then all you have to do is head to either South or East Caicos. These islands are a paradise for those with a phobia of development, tourism or other people.

**East Caicos** is the least inhabited island on the chain. There is a Haitian immigrant community on the island but little else. The beaches are renowned and odds are you will have them all to yourself.

**South Caicos** is the place to go for unspoilt scuba diving. The waters are pristine and prized for the effort required to get there. The land itself is a windswept wasteland of sand and scrub. The towns are microscopic and you really will find more donkeys than people here. Each May things spark up a bit for the annual **Big South Regatta** – but don't worry, this is still way off the radar of most T&C visitors.

---

good ocean views and bird-watching opportunities. It's easily picked up from Mudjin Harbor or from other points along the main road – keep an eye open for the signs.

## Sleeping

At present there are only a few sleeping options on the Middle Caicos. The emphasis is on longer term stays where self-catering is a must.

**Blue Horizon Resort** ( ☎ 946-6141; http://bhresort .com; cabins from $450; ❄ ) The distinctive blue roofs are the iconic landmarks of this beautiful property. The five cabins are spread out among the greenery, all with prime ocean views. The decor is simple and muted with a pastel theme that harks back to the '80s. But the views and the seclusion more than make up for the slightly dated sense of style. The units all have kitchens and you can provide a shopping list so the cupboards are full for you when you arrive. The best part is the location, sitting atop a cliff overlooking one of the best views in the T&C.

**ourpick** **Dreamscape Villa** ( ☎ 946-7112; www .middlecaicos.com; per week US$2000) You might just think you're dreaming when you walk into this stunningly situated villa. It's beautifully maintained and on a pristine section of land, only a few yards from the sea. The house itself has three bedrooms and is set up to sleep four comfortably. It has all the modern conveniences and is perfectly arranged for a week of relaxation. There are bikes and sea kayaks to keep you busy, and great snorkeling, right out front, if the mood strikes. Nice touches like an outdoor shower, hammocks and BBQ add up to make Dreamscape a perfect little oasis in the heart of paradise.

# DIRECTORY

## ACCOMMODATIONS

Accommodation in the Turks and Caicos is mostly in hotels, resorts and the odd smaller establishment. On Provi you'll mostly find larger resorts, but as you head out to the less populated islands the establishments get more intimate.

The **Turks & Caicos Hotel Association** (www.turks andcaicoshta.com) has a useful website, while the following agencies arrange villa rentals:

**Coldwell Banker** ( ☎ 946-4969; fax 946-8969)

**Grace Bay Realty** ( ☎ 941-4105; info@gracebay realty.com)

**Prestigious Properties** ( ☎ 946-4379; www.prestigious properties.com)

**Turks & Caicos Realty** ( ☎ 946-4474; www.tcrealty.com)

## ACTIVITIES

The most popular activities are diving and snorkeling, fishing and boating.

Diving highlights include Salt Cay (p119) where you can dive with humpback whales during their annual migration. Grand Turk (p116) has pristine reefs and spectacular wall diving, while the exceptional diving on rarely visited South Caicos (above) is worth the hassle of getting there. And then there is diving off Provo (p124), where you might just get the chance to share the sea with JoJo the dolphin. See p57 for more on diving here.

In Caicos, a two-tank dive typically costs around US$100 and a half-day snorkeling trip is around US$65. Fishing can cost US$400 to US$800 per half-/full day, while windsurfing is US$25 per hour.

A two-tank dive in the Turks typically costs from US$40 to US$80 and snorkeling around US$50 per half-day. Fishing is around US$300 to US$400 per half-/full day.

## BOOKS

The *Turks & Caicos Islands – Beautiful by Nature* by Julia and Phil Davies is a beautiful coffee-table book.

*Water and Light* by Stephen Harrigan is a splendid memoir by a Texan who spent several months diving off of Grand Turk.

The *Turks & Caicos Islands: Land of Discovery* by Amelia Smithers covers the history and idiosyncrasies of these charming islands.

Charles Palmer, a 'Belonger,' as those born on the islands describe themselves, depicts island living and the changes from the early 1950s to the current day in *Living in the Turks & Caicos Islands: From Conch to the Florida Lottery*.

## BUSINESS HOURS

The following are standard business hours on the islands; exceptions are noted in individual reviews. Expect limited hours away from Provo or touristy areas.

**Bars** ☾ to 1am or 2am
**Businesses** ☾ 9am to 5pm Monday to Saturday
**Restaurants** ☾ breakfast from 8am, lunch from noon, dinner 6:30pm to 9pm

## CHILDREN

The Turks and Caicos is a fantastic kid-friendly destination although you will struggle to find specific programs and activities aimed at younger travelers. Crime is low, traffic is sparse, waves are tiny and the locals are friendly. Some hotels are specifically non-kid-friendly so it's a good idea to check with your hotel beforehand.

## DANGERS & ANNOYANCES

There are few real worries on the islands. Crime is nearly unheard of, but normal precautions are advised like not leaving valuables on the beach unattended.

## EMBASSIES & CONSULATES

There are no foreign embassies or consulates in the Turks and Caicos. Contact the relevant officials in Nassau, New Providence (see p104).

## FESTIVALS & EVENTS

**Big South Regatta** Held on South Caicos in late May, this regatta is a classic for the sea dogs.
**Annual Music and Cultural Festival** Held in July and August, this annual event is the islands' biggest party – good times and hangovers guaranteed.
**Grand Turk Game Fishing Tournament** Held end July/early August. I once caught a fish that was this big…
**Marathon Run** December. Why relax when you can run 26.2 miles?
**Christmas Tree Lighting Ceremony** Grand Turk hosts this special event in mid-December for kids of all ages.

## GAY & LESBIAN TRAVELERS

As in most Caribbean destinations, the attitude towards gay and lesbian travelers in the Turks and Caicos is sadly behind the times. Gay men in particular will find they aren't

---

**PRACTICALITIES**

- **Newspapers & Magazines** There are two newspapers in the Turks and Caicos: the biweekly *Free Press* and the weekly *Turks & Caicos News*.

- **Radio & TV** The official Turks and Caicos government radio station is Radio Turks and Caicos (106FM) on Grand Turk. There are several private stations. For contemporary light rock, try 92.5FM; country and western 90.5FM; easy listening 89.3FM; and classical music 89.9FM. WPRT at 88.7FM is a religious and public announcement channel, as is WIV at 96.7FM. Multichannel satellite TV is received from the USA and Canada. The islands have one private TV station.

- **Video Systems** VHS is the standard, and tapes can be purchased from photo-supply shops.

- **Electricity** Hotels operate on 110V (60 cycles), as per the USA and Canada. Plug sockets are two- or three-pin US standard.

- **Weights & Measures** The British Imperial and metric systems are both in use. Liquids are generally measured in pints, quarts and gallons, and weight in grams, ounces and pounds.

welcomed with open arms. Having said that, some of the cruise ships that enter port are gay and lesbian cruises so there is some degree of acceptance.

## HOLIDAYS

Turks and Caicos national holidays:

**New Year's Day** January 1
**Commonwealth Day** March 13
**Good Friday** Friday before Easter
**Easter Monday** Monday after Easter
**National Heroes' Day** May 29
**Her Majesty The Queen's Official Birthday** June 14 (or nearest weekday)
**Emancipation Day** August 1
**National Youth Day** September 26
**Columbus Day** October 13
**International Human Rights Day** October 24
**Christmas Day** December 25
**Boxing Day** December 26

## INTERNET ACCESS

Internet access in the Turks is getting easier all the time. Wireless internet is offered free of charge in many hotels, and internet terminals are popping up everywhere. Connections are generally fast and the computers are good quality.

## INTERNET RESOURCES

**North Caicos** (www.northcaicos.tc) Lots of great info about North Caicos, including maps, updates on the goings-on and accommodation links.
**Providenciales** (www.provo.net) This site concentrates on the tourism aspects of Providenciales and provides some good links to the island's activities.
**Salt Cay** (http://saltcay.org) Everything you wanted to know about Salt Cay, but were afraid to ask.
**TCI Mall** (www.tcimall.tc) Lots of general information and a good gateway into everything TCI.
**Times of the Island** (www.timespub.tc) This online magazine gets under the surface of the islands and gives the skinny on what's up.
**Turks & Caicos Islands Tourist Board** (www.turksand caicostourism.com) The official site of the Turks and Caicos tourism board; great general information and a good place to start.
**Turks & Caicos National Museum** (www.tcmuseum .org) A plethora of online information on the history of the islands.

## MAPS

Tourist maps of Provo and Grand Turk are easily acquired from the tourist offices, the arrivals hall in the airport and at most hotels. The tourist offices have some substandard maps of the less populated islands, but finding one with any sort of detail is a challenge.

## MEDICAL SERVICES

There are small hospitals on Provo and on Grand Turk. There are clinics on the smaller islands and a recompression chamber in Provo.

## MONEY

The Turks and Caicos are unique as a British-dependent territory with the US dollar as its official currency. The treasury also issues a Turks and Caicos crown and quarter. There are no currency restrictions on the amount of money that visitors can bring in.

The country is pricey. Credit cards are readily accepted on Provo and Grand Turk, as are traveler's checks. Elsewhere, you may need to operate on a cash-only basis. Foreign currency can be changed at banks in Provo and Grand Turk, which can also issue credit-card advances and have ATMs. Major credit cards are widely accepted in the Caicos and Grand Turk. However, credit cards are not widely accepted for small transactions in the more remote cays and islands.

Traveler's checks are accepted in the Caicos and Grand Turk, but you may be charged a transaction fee of 5%.

If you find yourself in need of an emergency cash injection, you can arrange a telegraphic or mail transfer from your account in your home country via **Western Union** (Grand Turk ☎ 946-2324; Dots Enterprises, Pond St; Providenciales ☎ 941-5484; Butterfield Sq, Leeward Hwy).

## POST

Post offices can be found on Provo, Grand Turk and North Caicos. To send a postcard to the US will cost US$0.50; a letter is US$0.60.

## TELEPHONE

The Turks and Caicos country code is ☎ 649. To call from North America, dial ☎ 1-649 + the local number. From elsewhere, dial your country's international access code + ☎ 649 + the local number. For interisland calls, dial the seven-digit local number. We've included only the seven-digit local number in Turks and Caicos listings in this chapter.

Phone calls can be made from **Cable & Wireless** ( ☎ 1800-804-2994), which operates a digital network from its offices in Grand Turk and Provo.

Public phone booths are located throughout the islands. Many booths require phone cards (see below).

Hotels charge US$1 per local call. Frustratingly, some also charge for unanswered calls after the receiving phone has rung five times.

Following are some useful telephone numbers:

**Directory Assistance** ( ☎ 118)
**International Operator Assistance** ( ☎ 115)
**Local operator** ( ☎ 0)

## Cell Phones

Most cell phones will work in the Turks and Caicos; you can either set your phone up for global roaming prior to leaving home or purchase a SIM card for it once you get here. Global roaming is easy and more expensive; be sure to check rates with your phone company prior to dialing. If you have a GSM phone that is unlocked you can purchase a new SIM card for it ($10 from Cable and Wireless). This gives you a local number to call from and is much cheaper in the long run.

## Phone Cards

Phone cards cost US$5, US$10 or US$15, and can be bought from Cable & Wireless outlets, as well as from shops and delis.

You can also bill calls to your Amex, Discover, MasterCard or Visa card by dialing ☎ 1-800-744-7777 on any touchtone phone and giving the operator your card details (there's a one-minute minimum).

## TOURIST INFORMATION

**Turks & Caicos Islands Tourist Board** ( ☎ 946-2321; www.turksandcaicostourism.com; Front St, Cockburn Town, Grand Turk)
**Turks & Caicos Tourism** ( ☎ 946-4970; www.turksand caicostourism.com; Stubbs Diamond Plaza, Providenciales)

## TRAVELERS WITH DISABILITIES

Some of the larger hotels have rooms that are wheelchair accessible, but it's best to enquire before arriving.

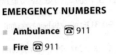

**EMERGENCY NUMBERS**

- **Ambulance** ☎ 911
- **Fire** ☎ 911
- **Police** ☎ 911

## VISAS

No visas are required for citizens of the US, Canada, UK and Commonwealth countries, Ireland and most Western European countries. Citizens from elsewhere require visas, which can be obtained from British representation abroad.

## WOMEN TRAVELERS

The Turks and Caicos is a relatively safe place to travel and no special precautions are required for women travelers.

## WORK

Those wishing to work in the Turks and Caicos will need to get a work permit from the immigration department. See www.immi gration.tc for more information.

# TRANSPORTATION

## GETTING THERE & AWAY
### Entering Turks & Caicos

All visitors, including US citizens, need a valid passport to enter the country. Proof of onward transportation is required upon entry.

### Air

There are three airports handling international traffic to Grand Turk and Provo, but most international flights arrive at Provo. The Provo airport has a tourist info booth in arrivals, a restaurant and not much else. Other islands have local airstrips.

**Grand Turk International Airport** (GDT; ☎ 946-2233)
**Providenciales International Airport** (PLS; ☎ 941-5670)
**South Caicos International Airport** (XSC; ☎ 946-4255)

There are limited flights to elsewhere within the Caribbean from Turks and Caicos; those planning on island-hopping may find themselves backtracking to Florida before delving deeper into the region. The following airlines fly into Turks and Caicos:

**American Airlines** ( ☎ 1-800-433-7300; www.aa.com) Miami, New York

**Bahamas Air** ( ☎ 941-3136; www.bahamasair.com) Nassau

**British Airways** ( ☎ 1-800-247-9297; www.ba.com) London

**Delta Airlines** ( ☎ 1-800-221-1212; www.delta.com) Atlanta

**Spirit Air** (www.spiritair.com) Fort Lauderdale

**US Airways** ( ☎ 1-800-428-4322; www.usairways.com) Charlotte

## GETTING AROUND

### Air

Following are airlines flying within the Turks and Caicos:

**Air Turks & Caicos** ( ☎ 941-5481; www.airturksand caicos.com) Flies from Providenciales to Grand Turk six times daily, North Caicos three times daily, Middle Caicos four times per week, and Salt Cay daily. It also flies from Grand Turk to Salt Cay daily.

**Skyking** ( ☎ 941-5464; wwwskyking.tc) Flies from Providenciales to South Caicos three times daily, Grand Turk eight times daily, and from Grand Turk to South Caicos three times daily.

### Bicycle

Cycling is a cheap, convenient, healthy, environmentally sound and above all fun way to travel. Bicycles are complimentary to guests at many hotels or can be rented at concessions for around US$20 per day.

### Boat

**TCI Ferry Service** ( ☎ 946-5406) is a new ferry operation taking passengers from the Leeward Marina on Providenciales to North Caicos (US$25, $40 round-trip same day), eliminating the need for the expensive and inconvenient flight. There are four departures each way daily.

A ferry runs biweekly trips from Grand Turk to Salt Cay (US$12, round-trip). Contact **Salt Cay Charters** ( ☎ 231-6663; piratequeen3@hotmail .com). Whale-watching boat trips with this company cost US$75.

### Bus

The **Gecko Shuttle** ( ☎ 232-7433) is a privately run bus service on Provo. One ride is $4 or you can buy a day pass for $11. There isn't a regular schedule; when you purchase tickets from a hotel desk they'll call the bus for you.

### Car, Motorcycle & Scooter

Taxis get expensive in the long run so renting a car makes sense if you plan to explore Provo or Grand Turk. The local companies are very good, and may be cheaper than the internationals. Rentals are around $80 per day and the cars are generally in good nick; most rental companies offer free drop-off and pickup. A government tax of $15 is levied on car rentals ($8 on scooter rentals). Mandatory insurance costs $15. A minimum age of 25 years may be required.

Driving is on the left-hand side. At roundabouts (traffic circles), remember to circle in a clockwise direction, entering to the left, and give way to traffic already on the roundabout.

Speed limits in the Turks and Caicos are 20mph (around 32km/h) in settlements and 40mph (around 65km/h) on main highways.

Please refer to island destinations for rental companies.

#### DRIVER'S LICENSE

To rent a car, citizens of the US, Canada, and the UK and Commonwealth countries are required to have a valid driver's license for stays of up to three months. Everyone else requires an International Driving Permit. You must get this permit before you arrive on the Turks and Caicos Islands.

#### FUEL

Gas stations are plentiful and usually open from 8am to 7pm. Some close on Sunday. Gasoline costs about US$5.50 per US gallon – luckily most destinations are pretty close. Credit cards are accepted in major settlements. Elsewhere, it's cash only, please!

### Taxi

Taxis are available on all the inhabited islands. Most are minivans. They're a good bet for touring, and most taxi drivers double as guides. Be sure to negotiate an agreeable price before setting out as the cabs are unmetered.

# Cuba

Dogs sleep on the motorway as a Russian Lada roars past, brightly painted in the incongruous colors of the tropics. Behind it a 1954 Cadillac belches black from its impossibly large and beautifully contoured frame. The two Cold War classics coexist here so naturally that it's curious to imagine that this is the motoring equivalent of seeing a penguin and a polar bear on the same ice floe. After a century split evenly between US and Russian influence, Cuba is slowly rousing itself as the Cuban Revolution moves on to its next stage.

With Fidel having shuffled off stage left, Cuba's boundless energy threatens to burst at any moment. Yet, until it does, 1950s Americana overlaid with a generous layer of 1970s Sovietica lives on in a glorious and unique time warp. Whatever your opinion of this most divisive of nations, there's never been a better time to visit.

As well as having the usual Caribbean attractions in abundance – from white sand and palm-fringed beaches to dramatic mountain scenery, Cuba has one of the world's most exciting (and bloody) histories, extraordinary musical and dance traditions all of its own and a rich national architecture that never ceases to astound.

Yes, it's harder work than most of its neighbors, and yes, the government is cashing in on every penny you spend, but the reason people come to Cuba again and again, rife as it is with contradictions and intrigue, is that there's simply nowhere else like it on earth.

## FAST FACTS

- **Area** 110,860 sq km
- **Capital** Havana
- **Country code** ☎ 53
- **Departure tax** CUC$25 (cash only)
- **Famous for** Cigars, rum, Fidel Castro, salsa, classic cars
- **Language** Spanish
- **Money** Cuban convertible peso (CUC$) and Cuban peso (CUP; also known as *moneda nacional*, MN); CUC$1 = US$1.04 = €0.67 = UK £0.53
- **Official name** Republic of Cuba
- **People** Cubans
- **Phrase** *Queué bolá assure?* (What's up, brother?); *ciao/ciaocito* (goodbye/bye)
- **Population** 11.2 million
- **Visa** All visitors require a tourist card (CUC$15), which is usually issued with your plane ticket or can be bought at airports; see p187

CUBA

## HIGHLIGHTS

- **Havana** (p141) Revel in the gorgeous colonial architecture, the dramatic sea-whipped Malecón and the steamy nightlife of Cuba's thrilling capital, which brings new meaning to the words 'faded grandeur'
- **Santiago de Cuba** (p173) Discover Cuba's beguiling second city, a place shot through with revolutionary history, great music and much charm
- **Viñales** (p160) Drink in some of the Caribbean's most extraordinary landscapes and join the ranks of climbers, hikers and nature lovers discovering this unique Unesco World Heritage site
- **Península de Guanahacabibes** (p163) Explore this fantastic iguana-heavy national park, which has two good resorts on superb beaches; you'll find the mainland's best diving here
- **Las Parrandas, Remedios** (p168) Head to tiny colonial backwater Remedios on Dec 24 for Cuba's most exciting street party, before spending Christmas on the beach

## ITINERARIES

- **One Week** While seven days can easily be spent soaking up Havana's rich brew of culture, history and nightlife, an overnight trip to Viñales, Santa Clara or Trinidad is a great way to see a little more of the country.
- **Two Weeks** After several days in Havana, either head west to the Península de Guanahacabibes via Viñales or east to Trinidad, Santa Clara and the beaches at Playa Ancón or Cayo Santa María.
- **Three Weeks** Follow the two-week itinerary on the eastern route and then head east to Santiago de Cuba and Baracoa on the very eastern tip of the island.
- **One Month** Follow the three-week itinerary, but take the time at explorer pace, with hiking thrown in: Topes de Collantes or Parque Nacional Alejandro de Humboldt. Keen divers might want to consider a side trip to Isla de la Juventud.

## CLIMATE & WHEN TO GO

Peak times for travelers are Christmas, Easter, July and August. Overbooking and price hikes are the disadvantages at these times, especially during July and August, when it's also un-pleasantly hot throughout much of the country. The ideal time to visit is January to May, when it's warm but uncrowded and there's no threat of hurricanes (which can be a problem on the coasts from June to November). Festivals happen all year round (see p185).

## HISTORY
### European Arrivals

When Christopher Columbus neared Cuba on October 27, 1492, he described it as 'the most beautiful land human eyes have ever seen.' Spanish conquistadors, led by Diego Velázquez de Cuéllar, agreed: they came, they saw, they conquered and enslaved – despite resistance by indigenous chiefs Hatuey and Guamá. The native population was decimated, and by 1550 only about 5000 survivors remained from a population of around 120,000. The Spanish then began using Africans as slaves.

By the 1820s Cuba was the world's largest sugar producer and the US was sweet on it. So important was Cuban sugar that the US offered – twice – to buy Cuba from Spain. The slave trade continued furiously and by the 1840s there were some 400,000 Africans in Cuba, forever altering the country's makeup.

### The Road to Independence

Fed up with the Spanish power structure, landowners plotted rebellion. On October 10, 1868, sugar baron Carlos Manuel de Céspedes launched the uprising by releasing his slaves and asking them to join his independence struggle. This began the First War of Independence, which extended into a Ten Years' War, costing some 200,000 lives before a pact improving conditions in Cuba – but not granting independence – was signed with the Spanish in February 1878. Around this time, some Cuban landowners began advocating annexation by the US.

### HOW MUCH?

- **Room in casa particular** CUC$20 to CUC$30
- **Dinner in casa particular** CUC$7
- **Bus ticket Havana–Santiago** CUC$51
- **Concert ticket** CUC$10
- **Internet per hour** CUC$6

CUBA

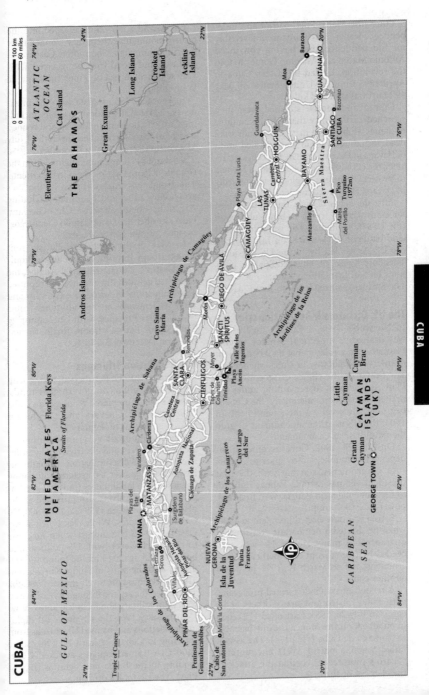

CUBA

0   100 km
0   60 miles

*GULF OF MEXICO*

*ATLANTIC OCEAN*

UNITED STATES OF AMERICA

Florida Keys

*Straits of Florida*

Tropic of Cancer

THE BAHAMAS

Eleuthera

Cat Island

Great Exuma

Long Island

Crooked Island

Acklins Island

Andros Island

Archipiélago de Camagüey

Playa Santa Lucia

Baracoa

Moa

GUANTÁNAMO

Baconao

SANTIAGO DE CUBA

Guardalavaca

HOLGUÍN

BAYAMO

Sierra Maestra

Pico Turquino (1972m)

Marea del Portillo

Manzanillo

LAS TUNAS

Carretera Central

CAMAGÜEY

CIEGO DE ÁVILA

Morón

Cayo Santa María

SANCTI SPÍRITUS

Remedios

Meyer

Valle de los Ingenios

Playa Ancón

Topes de Collantes

Trinidad

Archipiélago de los Jardines de la Reina

SANTA CLARA

CIENFUEGOS

Archipiélago de Sabana

Cárdenas

Varadero

Carretera Central

Autopista Nacional

Ciénaga de Zapata

Cayo Largo del Sur

MATANZAS

Playas del Este

HAVANA

Surgidero de Batabanó

Las Terrazas

Soroa

Autopista Habana–Pinar del Río

Viñales

Los Colorados

Archipiélago de los Canarreos

NUEVA GERONA

Isla de la Juventud

Punta Frances

PINAR DEL RÍO

Península de Guanahacabibes

Cabo de San Antonio

María la Gorda

*CARIBBEAN SEA*

Little Cayman

Cayman Brac

CAYMAN ISLANDS (UK)

Grand Cayman

GEORGE TOWN

Enter José Martí. Poet, patriot and independence leader, Martí organized feverishly for independence and, having convinced Antonio Maceo and Máximo Gómez to lead the revolution, landed in eastern Cuba in April 1895 from the United States: on May 19 Martí was shot and killed.

Gómez and Maceo stormed west in a scorched-earth policy that left the country in flames. Cuba was a mess: thousands were dead, including Antonio Maceo, killed south of Havana in December 1896. On February 15, 1898, the US battleship *Maine,* sent to Havana to 'protect US citizens,' exploded unexpectedly in Havana Harbor, killing 266 US sailors.

After the *Maine* debacle, the US scrambled for control, even trying to buy Cuba again (for US$300 million). The only important land battle of the war was on July 1, when the US Army, led by future US president Theodore Roosevelt, attacked Spanish positions on San Juan Hill in Santiago de Cuba. The Spaniards surrendered on July 17, 1898.

## The US, Dictators & Revolutionaries

In November 1900, a Cuban constitution was drafted. Connecticut senator Orville Platt attached a rider giving the US the right to intervene militarily in Cuba whenever it saw fit. Given the choice of accepting this Platt Amendment or remaining under US military occupation indefinitely, the Cubans begrudgingly accepted the amendment; in 1903, the US used the amendment to grab the naval base at Guantánamo.

On May 20, 1902, Cuba became an independent republic, led by a series of corrupt governments, starting with the first president, Tomás Estrada Palma, right up to dictator Fulgencio Batista, who first took power in a 1933 coup.

Batista was duly elected president in 1940, when he drafted a democratic constitution guaranteeing many rights. He was succeeded by two corrupt and inefficient governments, and on March 10, 1952, he staged another coup.

A revolutionary circle formed in Havana, with Fidel Castro and many others at its core. On July 26, 1953, Castro led 119 rebels in an attack on the Moncada army barracks in Santiago de Cuba (see p174). The assault failed when a patrol 4WD encountered Castro's motorcade, costing the attackers the element of surprise.

Castro and a few others escaped into the nearby mountains, where they planned their guerrilla campaign. Soon after, Castro was captured and stood trial; he received a 15-year sentence on Isla de Pinos (now Isla de la Juventud).

In February 1955 Batista won the presidency and freed all political prisoners, including Castro, who went to Mexico and trained a revolutionary force called the 26th of July Movement ('M-26-7'). On December 2, 1956, Castro and 81 companions alighted from the *Granma* at Playa Las Coloradas in the Oriente. The group was quickly routed by Batista's army, but Castro and 11 others (including Argentine doctor Ernesto 'Che' Guevara, Fidel's brother Raúl, and Camilo Cienfuegos) escaped into the Sierra Maestra.

In May of the next year, Batista sent 10,000 troops into the mountains to liquidate Castro's 300 guerrillas. By August, the rebels had defeated this advance and captured a great quantity of arms. Che Guevara and Camilo Cienfuegos opened additional fronts in Las Villas Province, with Che capturing Santa Clara. Batista's troops finally surrendered on December 31, 1958.

## The Revolution Triumphs

On January 1, 1959, Batista fled, taking with him US$40 million in government funds. Castro's column entered Santiago de Cuba that night and Guevara and Cienfuegos arrived in Havana on January 2.

The revolutionary government immediately enacted rent and electricity reductions, abolished racial discrimination and nationalized all holdings over 400 hectares, infuriating Cuba's largest landholders (mostly US companies). Many Cubans also protested at the new policies: between 1959 and 1970, 500,000 Cubans said *adios*. While clearly left-wing, Castro was no communist when he came to power. However, with US political and business will against him, he found himself driven into the arms of Nikita Khrushchev. The Soviet Union massively invested in Cuba and helped the regime through its early years with both military and technical know-how.

In January 1961 the US broke off diplomatic relations and banned US citizens from traveling to Cuba. On April 17, 1961, some 1400 CIA-trained émigrés attacked Cuba, landing in the Bahía de Cochinos (Bay of Pigs). The US took a drubbing.

After this defeat the US declared a full trade embargo (known as the *bloqueo*). In April 1962, amid rising Cold War tensions, Khrushchev secretly installed missiles in Cuba, sparking the Cuban Missile Crisis and bringing the world to the brink of nuclear war. Six days later, after receiving a secret assurance from Kennedy that Cuba would not be invaded, Khrushchev ordered that the missiles be dismantled. Castro was excluded from the deal-making.

Marked by inconsistency and bureaucracy, the Cuban economy languished despite massive injections of Soviet aid. Conversely, educational advances were rapid, particularly the 1961 literacy campaign that taught every Cuban to read and write. Meanwhile, Cuba started supporting revolutionary efforts in Latin America and Africa.

## The Wall Falls & the Special Period

When the Eastern bloc collapsed in 1989, US$5 billion in annual trade and credits to Cuba vanished, forcing Castro to declare a five-year *período especial* (special period) austerity program, technically ongoing. Rationing and rolling blackouts were instituted and food was scarce. Cubans share their survivor stories of this time willingly.

In August 1993 the US dollar was legalized to provide much-needed liquidity. Class differences re-emerged as people with dollars gained access to goods and services not available in CUP (Cuban pesos); touts (known as *jinteros*, or jockeys) and prostitutes (*jineteras*) reappeared.

When it comes to sore subjects, US immigration policy runs a close second to the embargo. The Cuban Adjustment Act (1966) grants residency to any Cuban arriving on US shores. This has sparked immigration crises, including the *Mariel* boatlift in 1980 when 125,000 people left and the 1994 *balsero* crisis when some 35,000 people on makeshift rafts struggled across the Florida Straits; many died.

In recent years under George W Bush the US policy, which had softened somewhat under Bill Clinton, became far stricter and travel for Americans to Cuba became far more zealously prosecuted.

## Life After Fidel

On February 18, 2008, in a letter to daily Communist newspaper *Granma,* Fidel Castro announced to the world that he would not 'aspire or accept' a further term as president and commander in chief. The announcement may have been a surprise (most observers were expecting Fidel to die in office) but there was no revelation about Castro's fitness; his brother and closest ally Raúl Castro had been running the country since Fidel was struck down by serious illness in 2006.

Raúl Castro was duly elected President on February 24, 2008, and is expected to run Cuba for the next few years before passing power onto a younger generation of politicians groomed by Fidel to carry on his legacy.

All bets are currently off about what will happen here in the near future. Many believe that, once Fidel dies, cautious reform will be instituted by Raúl, who is believed to be far less of a dogmatist than Fidel, as well as less anti-American. Indeed, in his first months as president, Raúl Castro has repealed some of Cuba's most backward laws, including bans on cell phones and computers for individual citizens. He has also signaled a further shift from state-run to private agriculture, abandoning the disastrously inefficient state farms that dominate the sector at present. Perhaps even more significantly, he has announced the first Communist Party congress since 1997. It will convene in 2009, and will likely plot the future of Cuba for the next decade and beyond. Once Raúl – who is only seven years younger than Fidel – relinquishes power, the scramble for control of the Caribbean's largest island and one of the last communist states on earth will begin. Whatever the outcome, these will be interesting times for Cuba.

## THE CULTURE

In Cuba, money is a consuming topic because hard currency rules: there are places you can go and things you can buy with CUCs (Cuban convertible pesos) but not with CUP. This double economy has reinvigorated the class system that the revolution has worked to neutralize, and the re-emergence of haves and have-nots is among the most ticklish issues confronting Cuba today.

Though housing is free, acute shortages mean even four generations may live under one roof. This cramps love-lives and Cubans will tell you it's why the country has one of the world's highest divorce rates.

Most homes don't have a phone or computer, infinitesimally few have internet access, and disposable income – disposable anything –

is an oxymoron. These factors combine to make recycling and repurposing a national pastime – one foreigners seem to think is much more charming than locals do.

## ARTS

The Buena Vista Social Club with their take on *son* may have put Cuban music on the map, but today you'll only hear these now rather tired-sounding songs played in joyless tourist bars. The rest of the country is busy listening to thumping, angry reggaeton – the Panamanian combination of hip-hop, dancehall and reggae – the perfect soundtrack to a frustrated country yearning for change.

If you have the chance, check out some live reggaeton performances, as they are likely to be memorable (the sheer energy and enthusiasm is impressive), although you'll need to go looking for them – a reggaeton group won't pitch up at your hotel during cocktail hour.

Of course if *son*, salsa, jazz or hip-hop are more your thing, you'll have plenty of chance to see them too. Respected founders of *son* include Ñico Saquito, Trio Matamoros and Arsenio Rodríguez. In the 1940s and '50s, *son* bands grew, playing rumba, *chachachá* (cha-cha) and mambo. The reigning mambo king was Benny Moré (1919–63), known as 'El Bárbaro del Ritmo' (Barbarian of Rhythm). You will still hear his voice floating out from bars.

Jazz, considered music of the enemy in the revolution's most dogmatic days, has always seeped into Cuban sounds. Jesus 'Chucho' Valdés' band Irakere, formed in 1973, broke the Cuban music scene wide open with its heavy Afro-Cuban drumming laced with jazz and *son*. Havana remains the best place for seeing jazz live (p156 ).

## ENVIRONMENT
### The Land

Cuba is the largest island in the Caribbean, a long, thin country with 5746km of coastline. Though more prone to winter cold fronts, the north shore has the Caribbean standard powdery sands and turquoise sea. The southern coast is more rocky, bedeviled by *diente de perro* (jagged rocks that line the shore), but has good fishing and unexplored pockets with some lovely beaches too.

Over millions of years, Cuba's limestone bedrock has been eroded by underground rivers, creating interesting geological features like the 'haystack' hills of Viñales. Cuba has several important mountain ranges providing good hiking opportunities, including the Sierra del Escambray in the center of the country (see p170) and the Sierra Maestra in the Oriente, featuring Pico Turquino (1972m), Cuba's highest peak.

At present, more than 14% of the country is protected in some way. There are six national parks: Parque Nacional Península de Guanahacabibes and Parque Nacional Viñales, in Pinar del Río; the Gran Parque Natural Montemar (aka Parque Nacional Ciénaga de Zapata) in Matanzas; Parque Nacional Desembarco del Granma in Granma and Gran Parque Nacional Sierra Maestra (straddling Granma and Santiago de Cuba Provinces); and Parque Nacional Alejandro de Humboldt in Guantánamo.

### Wildlife

Cuba hosts 350 varieties of birds, including the toothpick-sized *zunzuncito* (bee hummingbird), the world's smallest bird. Cuba also boasts the world's smallest toad, the *ranita de Cuba* (Cuban tree toad, 1cm).

Land mammals have been hunted almost to extinction, except for the indigenous *jutía* (tree rat), a 4kg edible rodent. Marine fauna is more inspiring: manatees frequent Punta Frances on the Isla de la Juventud and the coastline around the Parque Nacional Alejandro de Humboldt in Guantánamo, and whale sharks swim around María la Gorda (August to November). Leatherback, loggerhead, green and hawksbill turtles also frequent Cuban seas. Iguanas are a common sight in the Parque Nacional Península de Guanahacabibes in Pinar del Rio Province.

There are 90 types of palm, including the *palma real* (royal palm); the national tree, it figures prominently in Cuba's coat of arms and the Cristal beer logo (you'll see plenty of those!). Reforestation programs have been a priority for the Cuban government, which has planted over three million trees since 1959.

## FOOD & DRINK

With easily the worst food in the Caribbean, Cuban cuisine is likely to be the bugbear of your trip. If you have high cholesterol or are a non-fish-eating vegetarian or, heaven help you, a vegan, you may want to consider your need to travel to Cuba carefully.

Standard meals are fried pork or chicken with *congrí* (rice flecked with red or black beans), fried plantains and a 'salad' meaning whatever raw vegetables are available. Standards soar when you eat in casas particulares (private homes renting out up to two rooms) and paladares (private restaurants), but inconsistently so. Some towns inexplicably have dreadful restaurants and poor paladares (Santiago de Cuba is one), while in other towns it's easy to eat well (Baracoa, for example).

Drinking in Cuba is a much better experience than eating. The two main beers, Cristal (light) and Bucanero (heavier and with more of a kick) are both good for cooling down, but Cuban cocktails are where things become truly sublime. Excellent mojitos, daiquirís and Ron Collins are easy to find almost anywhere. To be safe, drink bottled water *(agua natural)* or boil it (the local method).

# HAVANA

pop 2.2 million / ☎ 7

Perhaps the Caribbean's most beguiling city, Havana (La Habana) gets under your skin quickly and stays with you for years – its filthy but vibrant streets, crumbling but breathtaking buildings and the good-humored *habaneros* all combine to form an unforgettable Hispanic–Afro-Caribbean vibe you'll be sad to leave.

Unlike many other Caribbean capitals, Havana remains remarkably true to its colonial design and has suffered surprisingly little damage in two centuries of turbulent history. The original heart of the city, Habana Vieja, a Unesco World Heritage site and the finest colonial complex in the Americas, has been reinventing itself during the past decade with painstaking restoration work. Now many of its abandoned churches and fine mansions have been restored to their former glory after a century of neglect – all you have to do is take a look at some of the buildings not yet tackled to see the scale of the ruination.

Recently the focus of restoration efforts has moved from Habana Vieja to the Malecón, the beautiful but desperately crumbling city seafront. Now blighted by scaffolding, in a few years the Malecón will hopefully be the jewel in the crown of Havana once again.

# INFORMATION
## Emergency
**Ambulance** ( ☎ 106, 55-11-85, 55-21-85)

## Internet Access
Havana is the most internet-friendly place in the country, but access is still not cheap anywhere and computers can be slow. Those with their laptops can head to the NH Parque Central and use the wi-fi there (CUC$8 per hour).
**Cibercafé Capitolio** (Map pp142-3; ☎ 862-0485; Prado & Teniente Rey; per 30min/hr CUC$3/5; ☉ 8am-8pm) Inside the main entrance of Capitolio Nacional, this is the cheapest access in town.
**Etecsa** Habana Vieja (Map pp142-3; ☎ 860-4477; Habana 406 cnr Obispo; ☉ 9am-6pm); Vedado (Map pp146-7; cnr Calles 23 & O, Centro de Prensa Internacional; ☉ 8am-7pm) Access is CUC$6 per hour at all branches.
**Servicio de Internet** (Map pp146-7; ☎ 831-1321; Calle 15 No 551 btwn Calles C & D; per 1/2/5 hr CUC$6/10/20; ☉ 9am-6pm Mon-Fri) Havana's most unusually located cybercafé is inside a mathematical institute.

## Medical Services
**Clinica Central Cira García** (Map pp146-7; ☎ 204-2811; www.cirag.cu; Calle 20 No 4101, Playa)
**Hospital Nacional Hermanos Ameijeiras** (Map pp146-7; ☎ 877-6053; www.hha.sld.cu; San Lázaro No 701) Enter below the parking lot off Padre Varela (ask for 'CEDA' in Section N).
**Tryp Habana Libre Pharmacy** (Map pp146-7; ☎ 834-6100; Calle L btwn Calles 23 & 25, Vedado) A well-stocked pharmacy in Havana's largest hotel.

## Money
The following are the main banks and currency exchange places in Havana. Banks can be crowded and have long queues, so those in a hurry should head to a Cadeca, where exchange rates are a little worse and traveler's checks and cash advances are a little more expensive, but where you're usually dealt with quickly.
**Banco de Crédito y Comercio** Habana Vieja (Map pp142-3; ☎ 862-5006; Aguiar No 310; ☉ 8:30am-1:30pm Mon-Fri) Near Obispo; Vedado (Map pp146-7; ☎ 870-2684; Calle 23) In the Airline Building.
**Banco Financiero Internacional** Centro Habana (Map pp146-7; ☎ 873-6496; Av Salvador Allende); Habana Vieja (Map pp142-3; ☎ 860-9369; cnr Oficios & Teniente Rey); Vedado (Map pp146-7; ☎ 55-44-29; Calle L btwn Calles 23 & 25) In Tryp Habana Libre.
**Banco Metropolitano** Calle M (Map pp146-7; ☎ 55-33-16/17/18; Línea & Calle M); Paseo (Map pp146-7; ☎ 830-1962; Línea off Paseo); Vedado (Map pp146-7; ☎ 879-2074; Av de la Independencia) In the post office.

CUBA

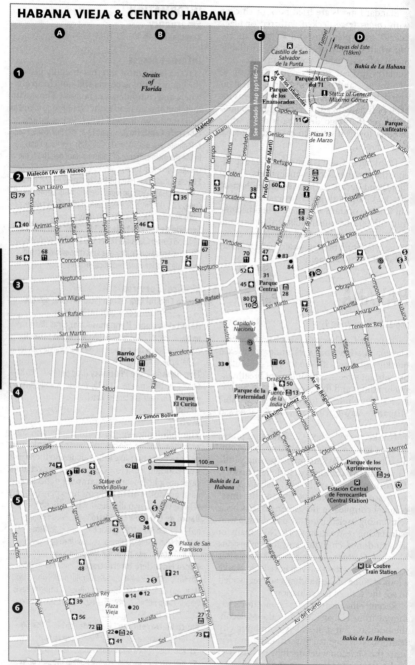

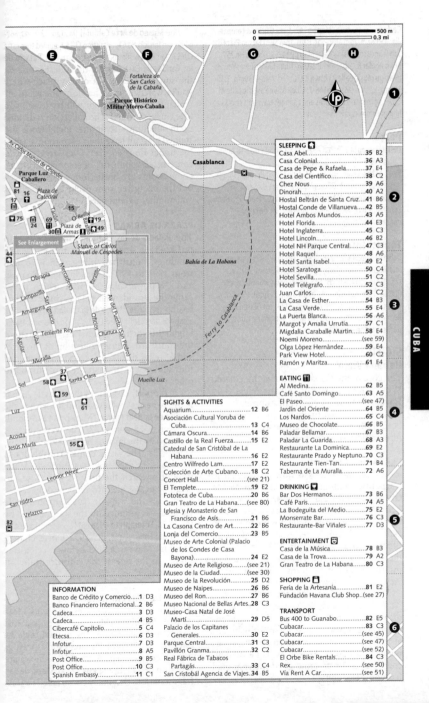

**CUBA**

## SLEEPING 🏠
| | |
|---|---|
| Casa Abel | **35** B2 |
| Casa Colonial | **36** A3 |
| Casa de Pepe & Rafaela | **37** E4 |
| Casa del Científico | **38** C2 |
| Chez Nous | **39** A6 |
| Dinorah | **40** A2 |
| Hostal Beltrán de Santa Cruz | **41** B6 |
| Hostal Conde de Villanueva | **42** B5 |
| Hotel Ambos Mundos | **43** A5 |
| Hotel Florida | **44** E3 |
| Hotel Inglaterra | **45** C3 |
| Hotel Lincoln | **46** B2 |
| Hotel NH Parque Central | **47** C3 |
| Hotel Raquel | **48** A6 |
| Hotel Santa Isabel | **49** E2 |
| Hotel Saratoga | **50** C4 |
| Hotel Sevilla | **51** C2 |
| Hotel Telégrafo | **52** C3 |
| Juan Carlos | **53** C2 |
| La Casa de Esther | **54** B3 |
| La Casa Verde | **55** E4 |
| La Puerta Blanca | **56** A6 |
| Margot y Amalia Urrutia | **57** C1 |
| Migdalia Caraballe Martin | **58** E4 |
| Noemi Moreno | (see 59) |
| Olga López Hernández | **59** E4 |
| Park View Hotel | **60** C2 |
| Ramón y Maritza | **61** E4 |

## EATING 🍴
| | |
|---|---|
| Al Medina | **62** B5 |
| Café Santo Domingo | **63** A5 |
| El Paseo | (see 47) |
| Jardín del Oriente | **64** B5 |
| Los Nardos | **65** C4 |
| Museo de Chocolate | **66** B5 |
| Paladar Bellamar | **67** B3 |
| Paladar La Guarida | **68** A3 |
| Restaurante La Dominica | **69** E2 |
| Restaurante Prado y Neptuno | **70** C3 |
| Restaurante Tien-Tan | **71** B4 |
| Taberna de La Muralla | **72** A6 |

## DRINKING 🍷
| | |
|---|---|
| Bar Dos Hermanos | **73** B6 |
| Café París | **74** A5 |
| La Bodeguita del Medio | **75** E2 |
| Monserrate Bar | **76** C3 |
| Restaurante-Bar Viñales | **77** D3 |

## ENTERTAINMENT 🎭
| | |
|---|---|
| Casa de la Música | **78** B3 |
| Casa de la Trova | **79** A2 |
| Gran Teatro de La Habana | **80** C3 |

## SHOPPING 🛍
| | |
|---|---|
| Fería de la Artesanía | **81** E2 |
| Fundación Havana Club Shop | (see 27) |

## TRANSPORT
| | |
|---|---|
| Bus 400 to Guanabo | **82** E5 |
| Cubacar | **83** C3 |
| Cubacar | (see 45) |
| Cubacar | (see 47) |
| Cubacar | (see 52) |
| El Orbe Bike Rentals | **84** C3 |
| Rex | (see 50) |
| Vía Rent A Car | (see 51) |

## SIGHTS & ACTIVITIES
| | |
|---|---|
| Aquarium | **12** B6 |
| Asociación Cultural Yoruba de Cuba | **13** C4 |
| Cámara Oscura | **14** B6 |
| Castillo de la Real Fuerza | **15** E2 |
| Catedral de San Cristóbal de La Habana | **16** E2 |
| Centro Wilfredo Lam | **17** E2 |
| Colección de Arte Cubano | **18** C2 |
| Concert Hall | (see 21) |
| El Templete | **19** E2 |
| Fototeca de Cuba | **20** B6 |
| Gran Teatro de La Habana | (see 80) |
| Iglesia y Monasterio de San Francisco de Asís | **21** B6 |
| La Casona Centro de Art | **22** B6 |
| Lonja del Comercio | **23** B5 |
| Museo de Arte Colonial (Palacio de los Condes de Casa Bayona) | **24** E2 |
| Museo de Arte Religioso | (see 21) |
| Museo de la Ciudad | (see 30) |
| Museo de la Revolución | **25** D2 |
| Museo de Naipes | **26** B6 |
| Museo del Ron | **27** B6 |
| Museo Nacional de Bellas Artes | **28** C3 |
| Museo-Casa Natal de José Martí | **29** D5 |
| Palacio de los Capitanes Generales | **30** E2 |
| Parque Central | **31** C3 |
| Pavillón Granma | **32** C2 |
| Real Fábrica de Tabacos Partagás | **33** C4 |
| San Cristobál Agencia de Viajes | **34** B5 |

## INFORMATION
| | |
|---|---|
| Banco de Crédito y Comercio | **1** D3 |
| Banco Financiero Internacional | **2** B6 |
| Cadeca | **3** D3 |
| Cadeca | **4** B5 |
| Cibercafé Capitolio | **5** C4 |
| Etecsa | **6** D3 |
| Infotur | **7** D3 |
| Infotur | **8** A5 |
| Post Office | **9** B5 |
| Post Office | **10** C3 |
| Spanish Embassy | **11** C1 |

Map labels:

Fortaleza de San Carlos de la Cabaña

Parque Histórico Militar Morro-Cabaña

Casablanca

Av Carlos Manuel de Céspedes

Parque Luz Caballero

Plaza de Catedral

O'Reilly

Plaza de Armas

See Enlargement

Statue of Carlos Manuel de Céspedes

Bahía de La Habana

Obrapía

Mercaderes

Baratillo

Lamparilla

San Ignacio

Oficios

Av del Puerto (San Pedro)

Amargura

Teniente Rey

Cuba

Churruca (San Pedro)

Aguiar

Muralla

Sol

Muelle Luz

Sol

Santa Clara

Luz

Acosta

Jesús María

Leonor Pérez

San Isidro

Velazco

Ferry to Casablanca

0    500 m

0    0.3 mi

**Cadeca** Habana Vieja (Map pp142-3; cnr Oficios & Lamparilla; 8am-7pm Mon-Sat, 8am-1pm Sun) Facing Plaza de San Francisco; Habana Vieja (Map pp142-3; Obispo No 257 btwn Aguiar & Cuba; 8:30am-10pm) ATMs here; Vedado (Map pp146-7; Calle 23 btwn K & L; 7am-2:30pm, 3:30-10pm); Vedado (Map pp146-7; Línea btwn Paseo & Calle A) Cadeca gives cash advances and changes traveler's checks at higher commissions than banks.

## Post

**DHL** (Map pp146-7; 832-2112; Calzada No 818 btwn Calles 2 & 4; 8am-5pm Mon-Fri)
**Post office** Centro Habana (Map pp142-3; Prado); Habana Vieja (Map pp142-3; Oficios No 102, Plaza de San Francisco); Vedado (Map pp146-7; Línea & Paseo; 8am-8pm Mon-Sat); Vedado (Map pp146-7; Av de la Independencia; 24hr)

## Tourist Information

**Infotur** Airport ( 266-4094; Terminal 3 Aeropuerto Internacional José Martí; 8:30am-5:30pm); Habana Vieja (Map pp142-3; 863-6884; www.infotur.cu; cnr Obispo & San Ignacio; 10am-1pm, 2-7pm); Habana Vieja (Map pp142-3; /fax 866-3333; cnr Obispo & Bernaza) Arranges tours, sells maps and phone cards, has transportation schedules.

# SIGHTS
## Habana Vieja

The core of the Cuban capital is the Unesco World Heritage site of Habana Vieja (Old Havana), a fantastic cluster of stunning buildings and churches, many of which have been beautifully restored from near ruins to their former glory over the past decade.

### PLAZA DE CATEDRAL

'Music set in stone' was how novelist Alejo Carpentier eulogized the **Catedral de San Cristóbal de la Habana** (Map pp142-3; cnr San Ignacio & Empedrado; 10:30am-3pm; admission free, to climb tower CUC$1), and its baroque double towers do exude lyrical ambience, especially at night. Elevated to a cathedral in 1788, it's one of the oldest in the Americas, even though its interior is rather ho-hum. There are great views from the tower.

The excellent **Centro Wilfredo Lam** (Map pp142-3; 861-2096; San Ignacio No 22 cnr Empedrado), which displays work by one of Cuba's leading modern painters, was closed for refurbishment at the time of research, but should be opening again in 2009. As well as its permanent collection, it hosts some good international temporary exhibits.

The **Museo de Arte Colonial** (Map pp142-3; 862-6440; San Ignacio No 61; admission CUC$2, guided tour extra CUC$1; 9am-6:30pm), housed in the **Palacio de los Condes de Casa Bayona**, the oldest house on the square (1720), is a quirky place where you're watched like a hawk by the room attendants (most of whom will try to sell you Che Guevara coins). The collection is divided up by medium – sculpture, metal work and stained glass all have their own rooms, while the upper floor is given over largely to reconstructed rooms full of colonial furniture. Some rooms are borderline surreal – check out the one given over exclusively to chairs and another to cupboards.

### PLAZA DE ARMAS

The **Palacio de los Capitanes Generales** (Map pp142–3) is one of Cuba's most majestic buildings. Construction began in 1776, and from 1791 to 1902 it was home to Spanish and US power players, after which it became the presidential palace. Since 1968 it has housed the **Museo de la Ciudad** ( 861-6130; admission unguided/guided CUC$3/4; 8:30am-5:45pm). Highlights include peacocks strutting about the courtyard, a large collection of carriages and a stellar display of weaponry. A guided tour allows you to visit areas off-limits to other visitors.

On the northeast side of the Plaza de Armas is the Americas' oldest colonial fortress, the **Castillo de la Real Fuerza** (Map pp142–3), built between 1558 and 1577. The west tower is crowned by the famous bronze weather vane **La Giraldilla**. The saucy dame probably looks familiar – she's the Havana Club logo. At the time of research the fortress was closed to visitors but was likely to reopen soon.

In 1519 the Villa de San Cristóbal de la Habana was founded on the spot marked by the 1828 **El Templete** (Map pp142-3; admission CUC$1; 8:30am-6pm), a neoclassical Doric chapel. The first Mass was held below a ceiba tree similar to the one at the entrance (touch it for good luck).

### PLAZA DE SAN FRANCISCO

Another of Havana's picturesque plazas, Plaza de San Francisco (Map pp142–3) is a real beauty distinguished by the domed **Lonja del Comercio** (1909), now Havana's most prestigious office space. The south side of the square is dominated by the **Iglesia y Monasterio de San Francisco de Asís**. Originally constructed in 1608 and rebuilt between 1719 and 1738, today it's a **concert hall** (concerts CUC$10; ☺ performances 8pm) hosting classical recitals and the **Museo de Arte Religioso** ( ☎ 862-3467; admission CUC$2, guided tour extra CUC$1; ☺ 8:30am-6pm), with access to Havana's tallest church tower (closed for restoration during our last visit) and a surprisingly large religious art collection housed in two adjacent colonial mansions. There are often excellent temporary photographic exhibits in the 3rd-floor gallery.

On the water, two blocks south of here, is the **Museo del Ron** (Map pp142-3; ☎ 862-3832; Av del Puerto No 262; admission CUC$7; ☺ 9am-5pm Mon-Thu, 9am-4pm Fri & Sat, 10am-4pm Sun). This is a great place to learn about the brewing process if you're unable to visit a *ron* (rum) factory while you're in Cuba. The tour takes you through the process from cane cutting to finished product (you'll get to quaff amber Añejo Reserva in the tasting room). The scale model of the Central La Esperanza distillery (complete with functioning train) is especially cool.

### PLAZA VIEJA

The Plaza Vieja (Map pp142–3), dating from the 16th century, is the much-loved heart of Habana Vieja and is now almost complete after the restoration of nearly all its buildings. There's a slight feel that many of the 'sights' here have been purpose-built to keep the tourist groups occupied. A case in point is the **Cámara Oscura** ( ☎ 866-4461; admission CUC$2; ☺ 9am-5:20pm), providing live, 360-degree city views from atop a 35m-tall tower. Frankly you'd be better off having a cocktail on a Parque Central hotel roof. Next door is **Fototeca de Cuba** ( ☎ 862-2530; Mercaderes No 307; admission free; ☺ 10am-5pm Tue-Sat), a photo gallery where contemporary photography is showcased. At the time of research a planetarium was being built next door as well.

A much more genuine sight is the eccentric **Museo de Naipes** (Map pp142-3; Muralla No 101; admission by donation; ☺ 8:30am-5pm Tue-Sat, 9am-1pm Sun), a museum of playing cards. The surprisingly good display of over 2000 different decks includes ones portraying Mussolini, Scooby Doo and U Thant. Next door is **La Casona Centro de Arte** (Map pp142-3; ☎ 861-8544; Muralla No 107; admission free; ☺ 8:30am-5:30pm Mon-Sat), with quality art exhibits in a fantastic colonial palace.

### MUSEO-CASA NATAL DE JOSÉ MARTÍ

Located in front of Havana's wonderful main train station, the **Museo-Casa Natal de José Martí** (Map pp142-3; ☎ 861-3778; Leonor Pérez No 314; admission CUC$1; ☺ 8:30am-6:30pm) is the birthplace of Cuba's national hero and an important sight for Cubans. Martí was born in this humble dwelling on January 28, 1853, and while there are a few mildly interesting documents, photos and trinkets on display, the Spanish-only exhibit may leave some people rather cold.

## Centro Habana
### CAPITOLIO NACIONAL & AROUND

Havana's signature architectural sight is the very impressive **Capitolio Nacional** (Map pp142-3; ☎ 863-7861; admission unguided/guided CUC$3/4; ☺ 9am-6:30pm), which is similar to the US Capitol Building, but richer in detail.

Initiated in 1929, the Capitolio took 5000 workers three years, two months and 20 days to build at a cost of US$17 million. Everything is monumental here, from the huge bronze doors to the 49-tonne, 17m statue of the republic, the third-largest indoor bronze statue in the world (only the Buddha in Nava, Japan, and the Lincoln Memorial in Washington, DC, are bigger). Below the Capitolio's 62m-high dome, a 24-carat diamond replica is set in the floor. Inside there is an internet club, a café and a selection of arts and crafts stalls.

Behind the Capitolio is the **Real Fábrica de Tabacos Partagás** (Map pp142-3; ☎ 867-6657; Industria No 520 btwn Barcelona & Dragones; admission CUC$10; ☺ tours every 15min 9:30-11am & noon-3pm), a cigar factory built in 1845 and, at the time of writing, the only Havana cigar factory it's possible to visit with any ease. A tour here is a fascinating insight into both Cuba's most famous export and, perhaps even more so, into the lives of ordinary Cubans working in a factory. Few people leave unimpressed by the level of quality control that goes on here. Starting on the ground floor where the leaves are unbundled and sorted, the tour moves to the upper floors to watch the tobacco being rolled, pressed, banded and boxed. The tours (in English, French or Spanish) culminate in a visit to the well-stocked cigar shop.

Across the Prado the **Asociación Cultural Yoruba de Cuba** (Map pp142-3; ☎ 863-5953; www .nnl-cuba.org/obinibata; Prado No 615; admission CUC$10; ☺ 9am-5pm) would be an interesting introduction to the Afro-Caribbean religious tradition of Santería were it not so overpriced.

CUBA

# VEDADO

**INFORMATION**
| | |
|---|---|
| Banco de Crédito Comercio | (see 62) |
| Banco Financiero Internacional | **1** G4 |
| Banco Financiero Internacional | (see 34) |
| Banco Metropolitano | **2** C3 |
| Banco Metropolitano | **3** E2 |
| Banco Metropolitano | **4** E5 |
| Cadeca | **5** E3 |
| Cadeca | (see 2) |
| Clínica Central Cira García | **6** A5 |
| DHL | **7** C3 |
| Etecsa | (see 43) |
| French Embassy | **8** A5 |
| German Embassy | **9** D3 |
| Hospital Nacional Hermanos | |
| Ameijeiras | **10** G2 |
| Immigration Office | **11** D6 |
| Netherlands Embassy | **12** A4 |
| Post Office | **13** C3 |
| Post Office | (see 4) |
| Servicio de Internet | **14** D3 |
| Tryp Habana Libre Pharmacy | (see 34) |
| US Interests Section | **15** E2 |

**SIGHTS & ACTIVITIES**
| | |
|---|---|
| Anfiteatro Parque Almendares | (see 45) |
| Bosque de la Habana | **16** B6 |
| Cubanacan | **17** F2 |
| Cubatur | **18** D2 |
| El Focsa | **19** E2 |
| Memorial José Martí | **20** E5 |
| Ministry of the Interior | **21** E5 |
| Parque Almendares | **22** B6 |
| Parque Lennon | **23** C4 |
| US Interests Section | (see 15) |

**SLEEPING**
| | |
|---|---|
| Ana Livia Grimany Rojo | **24** D4 |
| Casa Silvia | **25** D4 |
| Hotel Mélia Cohiba | **26** C2 |
| Hotel Nacional | **27** F2 |
| Hotel St Johns | **28** F2 |
| Hotel Vedado | **29** F2 |
| Hotel Victoria | **30** E2 |
| Iris y Felipe | **31** F3 |
| José A García | **32** D4 |
| Melba Piñeda Bermúdez | **33** C3 |
| Tryp Habana Libre | **34** F3 |

**EATING**
| | |
|---|---|
| Coppelia | **35** F2 |
| Decameron | **36** C3 |
| El Conejito | **37** F2 |
| La Roca | **38** F2 |
| Paladar Los Amigos | **39** F2 |
| Pan.com | **40** C4 |
| Trattoria Maraka's | **41** F2 |

*Straits of Florida*

*Boca de la Chorrera*

**Miramar**

**Vedado**

*Socialist Revolution Plaque*

**Necropolis Cristóbal Colón**

*San Antonio Chiquito*

**Nuevo Vedado**

To Canadian Embassy (500m); UK Embassy (750m)

To Tropicana Nightclub (2km); Marianao (2.5km)

**19 de Noviembre Train Station**

To Viazul Terminal (3km)

CUBA

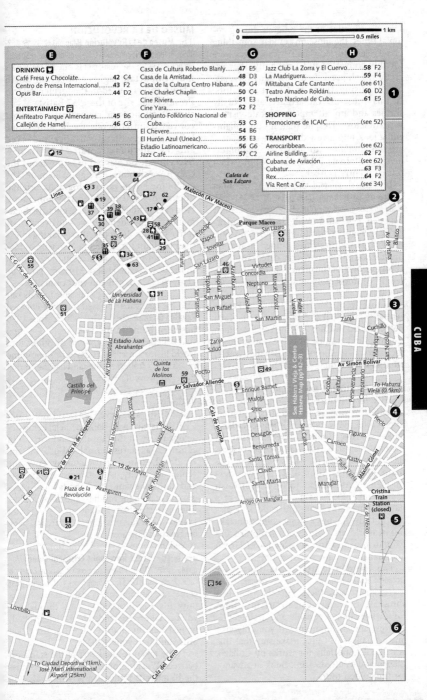

**DRINKING** 🍷
Café Fresa y Chocolate...................**42** C4
Centro de Prensa Internacional.......**43** F2
Opus Bar...........................................**44** D2

**ENTERTAINMENT** 🎭
Anfiteatro Parque Almendares.........**45** B6
Callejón de Hamel.............................**46** G3

Casa de Cultura Roberto Blanly.......**47** E5
Casa de la Amistad............................**48** D3
Casa de la Cultura Centro Habana....**49** G4
Cine Charles Chaplin.........................**50** C4
Cine Riviera.......................................**51** E3
Cine Yara............................................**52** F2
Conjunto Folklórico Nacional de
  Cuba...............................................**53** C3
El Chevere..........................................**54** B6
El Hurón Azul (Uneac)......................**55** E3
Estadio Latinoamericano..................**56** G6
Jazz Café...........................................**57** C2

Jazz Club La Zorra y El Cuervo.........**58** F2
La Madriguera....................................**59** F4
Mittabana Cafe Cantante...............(see 61)
Teatro Amadeo Roldán......................**60** D2
Teatro Nacional de Cuba...................**61** E5

**SHOPPING**
Promociones de ICAIC.....................(see 52)

**TRANSPORT**
Aerocaribbean.................................(see 62)
Airline Building.................................**62** F2
Cubana de Aviación.........................(see 62)
Cubatur.............................................**63** F3
Rex.....................................................**64** F2
Vía Rent a Car..................................(see 34)

CUBA

Like the practice of the religion during colonial times, the museum is today something
of a Trojan Horse; when African slaves were
forcibly converted to Christianity, they secretly worshipped their own gods (orishas)
by disguising them as Christian saints.
In this 'museum' the artifacts are actually
shrines and any attempt to educate visitors
is perfunctory. Despite that, it's an enlightening look into a very different world. There
are free *tambores* (drum jams/ceremonies)
here on alternate Fridays at 4:30pm (when
museum entry is free).

Just north of the Capitolio is the **Gran
Teatro de La Habana** (Map pp142-3; ☎ 861-3077;
Prado No 458; guided tours CUC$2; ⌚ 9am-5pm). Built
between 1907 and 1914, this is an outrageously beautiful building inside and out.
As well as visiting for a guided tour during the daytime, you can catch some of
Havana's best performances here (CUC$20;
see p156), most notably the National Ballet
of Cuba.

Across from the Gran Teatro is **Parque
Central** (Map pp142-3) and the very first Martí
statue erected in Cuba (1905). You'll see men
laughing and arguing near the statue; this is
the famous *esquina caliente*, where baseball
fanatics debate their favorite teams.

## MUSEO NACIONAL DE BELLAS ARTES
Cuba's largest and most impressive art
collection is housed in two striking buildings, collectively called the **Museo Nacional
de Bellas Artes** (Map pp142-3; ☎ 863-9484; www
.museonacional.cult.cu; admission one/both buildings
CUC$5/8; ⌚ 10am-6pm Tue-Sat, 10am-2pm Sun). The
main building, housed in the wonderful Centro Asturianas (a former Spanish
social club), looks every bit the part of a
national art collection and it doesn't dis-
appoint, displaying a huge collection taking in world art from Greek sculpture and
Roman mosaics to canvases by El Greco
and Gainsborough.

The **Colección de Arte Cubano** (Map pp142-3;
Trocadero btwn Agramonte & Av de las Misiones; guided
tours in Spanish/English CUC$2/7) up the road is a
showcase of purely Cuban art in a new,
fully wheelchair-accessible and architectur-
ally distinguished building. If you only visit
one art gallery in Cuba, make sure that this
is it. Look especially for works by Collazo,
Blanco and Wilfredo Lam. Book in advance
for the guided tours.

## MUSEO DE LA REVOLUCIÓN
The **Museo de la Revolución** (Map pp142-3; ☎ 862-
4092; Refugio No 1; admission CUC$5, guided tour in Spanish
per person CUC$2; ⌚ 10am-5pm) is one of Havana's
most important sights and is well worth
a few hours. Housed in the former Palacio
Presidencial, site of the 1957 Batista assassination attempt and where Castro's cabinet
convened until the '60s, the building alone
is fascinating, with several offices preserved
and the interiors decorated by Tiffany's.
Everything you wanted to know about the
Cuban Revolution is here, and a lot more. The
exhibition boasts rare photographs, original
documents and revolutionary ephemera.
However, while individual events are documented in huge detail, there's no overall nar-
rative linking them together, making it less
than brilliant for newcomers to Cuban history. There are often good temporary exhibits
in the downstairs Hall of Mirrors. You'll be
charged extra to bring in your camera.

From the museum it's possible to walk out
into the backyard and visit the glass-encased
**Pavillón Granma** (Map pp142-3), which since 1976
has been home to the 18m 'yacht' *Granma*
that ushered Fidel Castro and 81 others into
world history in 1956. Today this is one of the
revolution's holiest shrines and has the eternal
flame to prove it.

## Vedado
Vedado ('forest reserve') is a world away from
Centro Habana and Habana Vieja, being developed only in the late 19th and early 20th
centuries as a residential suburb for the
wealthy. Despite that, it's in many senses the
center of the city, with its most vibrant arts
and cultural scenes, and the favored playground of both the business and political elite.
The main streets of Vedado are Calle 23 and
Línea – both full of shops, restaurants, bars,
cinemas and theaters.

Vedado's most obvious attraction to travelers is the huge **Necrópolis Cristóbal Colón** (Map
pp146-7; ☎ 830-4517; entrance cnr Calzada de Zapata &
Calle 12; admission CUC$1; ⌚ 9am-5pm), Cuba's largest
cemetery, famous for its elaborate mausole-
ums. It's very pleasant to stroll through, or
you can take a free guided tour (tip expected)
or just buy the map (CUC$1) at the ticket
office and find your own way.

To be taken to the heart of the stand-off
between Washington and Havana don't miss
the **US Interests Section** (Map pp146-7; ☎ 833-3551;

Calzada btwn Calles L & M, Vedado), which has been at the center of Cold War–style wrangling ever since it first opened in 1977. In recent years lots of drama has surrounded this building, especially since the US decision in 2006 to broadcast messages and news through an electronic billboard. In retaliation the Cuban government has built an 'anti-imperialism park' outside with hundreds of flagpoles to obscure the billboard. Unsurprisingly the area is thick with propaganda and police.

Beatles fans should visit **Parque Lennon** (Map pp146-7; Calles 15 & 17 btwn Calles 6 & 8) with its rather unusual (and none too flattering) bronze statue of John lounging on a bench. Every December 8 there are musical vigils here commemorating his life.

Running along the Río Almendares below the bridge on Calle 23, **Parque Almendares** (Map pp146-7) is a wonderful oasis in the heart of chaotic Havana. Benches line the river promenade, plants grow profusely and there are many facilities here, including an antiquated **miniature golf course**, the Anfiteatro Parque Almendares (p156) and a **playground**.

Most people are surprised to learn that the vast **Plaza de la Revolución** (Map pp146-7), ultimate symbol of Castro's revolution, was actually built under Batista to commemorate national hero José Martí. On important occasions, Fidel Castro addressed up to 1.2 million supporters from in front of the star-shaped, 142m-high **Memorial José Martí** (☎ 859-2347; admission museum & tower adult/student CUC$5/3.50; ☉ 9:30am-5pm Mon-Sat) and 17m Martí statue. Join the crowd on May 1 if you want to experience it yourself. There's a thoughtful museum dedicated to José Martí inside the memorial; ride the elevator to the enclosed 129m-high viewpoint. If you go late in the afternoon you'll get some fantastic close-up views of circling vultures enjoying the updrafts.

The **Ministry of the Interior** (Map pp146-7) on the plaza's north side is easily identifiable by its huge 'Che' mural. Be careful walking around here, it's a very sensitive center of government and lots of officious guards are intent on blowing whistles if you stop in the wrong place.

Havana has become synonymous with **Malecón** (Map pp146-7), its 8km seawall that was constructed in 1901. Though you've probably seen many photos of this seaside scene, the pastiche of architectural gems in Havana's unrivaled afternoon light is enchanting.

Two blocks off the Malecón at Calle M is **El Focsa** (Map pp146-7), the monstrous green-and-yellow architectural wonder (or blunder, depending on your viewpoint) that is Cuba's tallest building.

## HAVANA FOR CHILDREN

Havana is not an obvious place to bring children and the combination of the heat and the lack of things to do may dismay some younger travelers. Kids will enjoy a trip to the **Fortaleza de San Carlos de la Cabaña** (Map pp142-3; admission CUC$5; ☉ 9am-6pm) for the chance to clamber around an old fortress and get a taste of the city's rich history. There's also the freshwater **Aquarium** (Map pp142-3; ☎ 863-9493; Calle Teniente Rey No 9 btwn Mercaderes & Oficios; admission CUC$1; ☉ 9am-5pm Mon-Sat, 9am-1pm Sun) and the beach at Playas del Este (p159).

## TOURS

Havana tours can be convenient if you've got little time or inclination to see the city alone, but they're definitely not necessary. While tours of Habana Vieja (CUC$18, half a day) can be very enlightening and a great introduction to the city, it's probably the more further flung attractions that tours are useful for, such as day trips to megaresort Varadero (from CUC$40, including lunch and open bar) and the out-of-town Tropicana Nightclub (starting at CUC$80). Other options include tours to Viñales (CUC$50) and a Trinidad–Cienfuegos overnight (CUC$140). The following arrange similar tours:

**Cubanacán** (Map pp146-7; ☎ 833-4090; www .cubanacan.cu; Calle 23 No 156 btwn Calles O & P, Vedado)
**Cubatur** (Map pp146-7; ☎ 835-4155; www.cubatur.cu; Calle F No 157, Vedado)
**San Cristóbal Agencia de Viajes** (Map pp142-3; ☎ 861-9171/2; www.viajessancristobal.cu; Calle de los Oficios No 110 bajos btwn Lamparilla & Amargura)

## SLEEPING

You are much, much better off staying in a casa particular than a hotel anywhere in Havana, unless you're planning to splash out on a five-star experience. There are a few hotel exceptions where service is good, but on the whole you'll be paying far more for far less.

### Habana Vieja
#### CASAS PARTICULARES
**Ramón y Maritza** (Map pp142-3; ☎ 862-3303; maritza mirabal@yahoo.es; Calle Luz No 115 btwn San Ignacio &

Inquisidor; r CUC$25; 🔀 ) Two rooms in a gorgeous colonial house, highly recommended for atmosphere.

**Olga López Hernández** (Map pp142-3; ☎ 867-4561; olgarene@hotmail.com; Cuba No 611, Apt 1 btwn Luz & Santa Clara; s/d incl breakfast CUC$25/30; 🔀 ) A very pleasant, well furnished and quiet colonial apartment. Both rooms share a bathroom, living room and balcony.

**La Puerta Blanca** (Map pp142-3; ☎ 867-2736; mer cyvlady@yahoo.es; Cuba No 505 btwn Teniente Rey & Muralla; r CUC$30; 🔀 ) A charming colonial house with two rooms opening onto an interior patio, one with private balcony, the other with air-con. The rooms share a bathroom, but each has a refrigerator. There's a great roof terrace and the house is safe and friendly.

**Chez Nous** (Map pp142-3; ☎ 862-6287; cheznous@ ceniai.inf.cu; Teniente Rey No 115 btwn Cuba & San Ignacio; r CUC$30; 🔀 ) Huge rooms with tiled floors, fridge, TV, en suite bathroom and high ceilings are supplemented by a vast roof terrace (if you're brave enough to climb up the rickety stairs). There's one room on the terrace, which is our favorite. Meals available. French spoken.

**Noemi Moreno** (Map pp142-3; ☎ 862-3809; Cuba No 611, Apt 2 btwn Luz & Santa Clara; r CUC$30; 🔀 ) Noemi's tasteful apartment is a mirror image of Olga López Hernández's casa next door. There are two rooms available, each with fantastic bathroom and pleasant furnishings, and it has a sitting room and an open-air patio to boot.

**Migdalia Caraballe Martin** (Map pp142-3; ☎ 861-7352; www.casamigdalia@yahoo.es; Santa Clara No 164, Apt F btwn Cuba & San Ignacio; r CUC$30; 🔀 ) Migdalia's house is large and attractive and its three rooms all have high ceilings. One has its own bathroom and the other two share one. It's excellently located and faces the Santa Clara convent.

**La Casa Verde** (Map pp142-3; ☎ 862-9877; fabio .quintana@infomed.sld.cu; San Ignacio No 656 btwn Jesús María & Merced; r CUC$30; 🔀 ) The most over-the-top colonial house in Havana, this place should be avoided by minimalists. It is, however, a great option, friendly and full of atmosphere. The two rooms have private bathrooms and fridges and share access to a superb roof terrace. English spoken.

**Casa de Pepe & Rafaela** (Map pp142-3; ☎ 862-9877; San Ignacio 454 btwn Sol & Santa Clara; r CUC$30; 🔀 ) The parents of Fabio, the owner of La Casa Verde, rent three good rooms with smart private bathrooms in a similarly styled colonial mansion stuffed with antiques and decorated with Moorish tiles.

## HOTELS

**Hostal Beltrán de Santa Cruz** (Map pp142-3; ☎ 860-8330; www.habaguanex.com; San Ignacio No 411 btwn Sol & Muralla; s/d/ste incl breakfast CUC$80/130/150; 🔀 🖳 ) This atmospheric colonial courtyard hotel has just 11 beautifully appointed rooms decked out with antiques. It's extremely popular, so book well ahead and request one of the bigger rooms overlooking the courtyard. There's a fantastic bar-restaurant in the courtyard and staff are charming.

**Hotel Florida** (Map pp142-3; ☎ 862-4127; www .habaguanex.com; Obispo No 252; s/d/ste incl breakfast CUC$95/160/200; 🔀 🖳 ) A real Havana classic, the Florida has it all – a fantastic location, beautiful façade, attractive rooms and a classy atmosphere. The two-tier arched and colonnaded courtyard will impress anyone – book ahead.

**Hotel Ambos Mundos** (Map pp142-3; ☎ 860-9530; www.habaguanex.com; Obispo No 15; s/d/ste CUC$95/160/200; 🔀 🖳 ) Not nearly the museum piece you might expect it to be (Hemingway partially wrote *For Whom the Bell Tolls* in room 511, which is still accepting visitors at CUC$2 a pop), the Ambos Mundos feels like the throbbing heart of Old Havana. The rooms are decent – generally large and airy, if unremarkable – and there's a good rooftop bar and restaurant with superb views.

**Hotel Conde de Villanueva** (Map pp142-3; ☎ 862-9293; www.habaguanex.com; Mercaderes No 202; s/d/ste incl breakfast CUC$95/160/200; 🔀 🖳 ) This tiny hideaway is fantastically atmospheric, with only nine rooms surrounding a verdant colonial courtyard in the heart of the old town. Six of the rooms have balconies, and all have good facilities and are attractively furnished although, in the spirit of most Cuban hotels, the cheap bathroom fixtures are already in need of a refit.

**Hotel Raquel** (Map pp142-3; ☎ 860-8280; www.haba guanex.com; cnr Amargura & San Ignacio; s/d/ste incl breakfast CUC$115/200/240; 🔀 🖳 ) The glorious marble-pillared lobby and wonderful stained-glass atrium on the upper floor are reasons enough to stay here, one of Havana's most beautifully restored hotels. Rooms are well appointed, many with balconies, mosaic floors and high ceilings. However, reports on the staff vary enormously, so don't count on the best standards of service.

**Hotel Santa Isabel** (Map pp142-3; ☎ 860-8201; www .habaguanex.com; Baratillo No 9 btw Obispo & Narciso López; s/d/ste incl breakfast CUC$190/240/340; ✷ ▣) Despite its enviable location on the quiet side of the Plaza de Armas, the Santa Isabel feels somehow out of the melee of Habana Vieja, a cool, calm oasis of luxury. Its 27 rooms, 20 of which overlook the plaza, all have balconies and feature iron-framed beds, large bathtubs, TV, phone and minibar.

## Centro Habana
### CASAS PARTICULARES

**our pick Casa Abel** (Map pp142-3; ☎ 863-4033; www .havana-house.webcindario.com; Blanco No 111 btwn Ánimas & Trocadero; r CUC$20; ✷) A superb deal here at Abel's colonial house above a lively *agropecuario* (free-enterprise vegetable market) in Centro Habana. Two good rooms with private bathrooms are supplemented by motherly love from Abel's wife and excellent meals. One of the best places in town.

**Dinorah** (Map pp142-3; ☎ 864-5683; Animas No 766 btwn Gervasio & Beloscaín; r CUC$20-25; ✷) With four rooms in a beautiful colonial house stuffed with antiques and what we'll charitably call knick-knacks, the Museo Dinorah (as her husband calls it) is a fantastic, eccentric place – look out for the car parked in the living room. The rooms are spacious and very well appointed with antique furniture and private bathrooms.

**Juan Carlos** (Map pp142-3; ☎ 863-6301; Crespo No 107 btwn Colón & Trocadero; r CUC$20-25; ✷) A traditional Havana colonial home, Juan Carlos' bright, super-clean house is a great deal with an excellent location just moments from the Prado and the Malecón. The cheapest room shares a bathroom, the other has its own private facilities.

**Casa Colonial** (Map pp142-3; ☎ 862-7109; orixl@yahoo .com; Gervasio No 216 btwn Concordia & Virtudes; r CUC$25; ✷) This repeatedly reader recommended charmer is in the heart of Centro and is well removed from the tourist crowds. The two comfortable rooms are both quiet, with new fittings such as fridge and air-con. Each has its own private en suite bathroom and Cary and Nilo, the hosts, are warm and welcoming. Meals available.

**La Casa de Esther** (Map pp142-3; ☎ 863-0401; es thercv2551@cubarte.cult.cu; Aguila No 367 btwn Neptuno & San Miguel; r CUC$25-30, tr CUC$45) This excellent artistic hangout enjoys a prime position, great rooms, stylish décor and a superb roof terrace.

Superclean bathrooms are shared and breakfast is excellent.

**Margot y Amalia Urrutia** (Map pp142-3; ☎ 861-7824; Apt A, 7th fl, Prado No 20; r CUC$25-35; ✷) The only thing Centro Habana about this superb option is the address, situated as it is in an elite high-rise apartment block moments from the Malecón. With stunning views from the large terrace, this makes for a memorable introduction to the city. Of the two rooms, the larger has an en suite bathroom and goes for CUC$35, while the smaller (CUC$25) is cheaper, but lacks the views.

### HOTELS
**Hotel Lincoln** (Map pp142-3; ☎ 862-8061; Av de Italia; s/d incl breakfast CUC$39/46; ✷) Despite its fantastic exterior, the Lincoln is a mediocre place, although staff try their best to be helpful. Rooms are basic, but fine, with cable TV, telephone and bathroom. Use the safe and leave your high expectations at the door.

**Casa del Científico** (Map pp142-3; ☎ 862-1607, 862-1608; Prado No 212; s/d with shared bathroom CUC$45/55; ✷ ▣) Housed in a gorgeous colonial building complete with marble columns, sweeping stairways and a roof terrace overlooking the Prado, the once forlorn Casa del Científico is in the process of refurbishing its 11 rooms (four were complete at the time of research), making this an excellent option. All rooms have private facilities. Staff members, while not speaking English, are helpful and friendly.

**Park View Hotel** (Map pp142-3; ☎ 861-3293; www .hotelparkview.cu; cnr Calle Colón & Morro; s/d CUC$52/86; ✷ ▣) Unexpected good value here – the Park View has none of the history or grand style of other nearby hotels, but its clean, comfortable rooms, many with good views and balconies, are excellent value.

**Hotel Inglaterra** (Map pp142-3; ☎ 860-8595; www.grancaribe.cu; Prado No 416; s/d/tr CUC$84/120/168; ✷ ▣) This historic hotel, built in 1875, is not the prime place to stay that it once was (noisy rooms, swarming hustlers etc). The rooftop La Terraza bar has excellent views.

**Hotel Telégrafo** (Map pp142-3; ☎ 861-1010, 861-4741; Prado No 408; s/d CUC$90/150; ✷ ▣) With a stylish lobby, enviable location and modern rooms, the Hotel Telégrafo, a recent refit of a classic late-19th-century hotel, is a winner and gets strong recommendations from those who've stayed here. Enjoy a cocktail on the terrace and watch the crowds go by. Has wi-fi.

**Hotel Sevilla** (Map pp142-3; ☎ 860-8560; fax 860-8582; Trocadero No 55 btwn Prado & Agramonte; s/d incl breakfast CUC$102/142; ✖ 🖳 ☎ ) Fantastically atmospheric and immortalized as the site of a key scene in Greene's *Our Man in Havana*, the elegant Moorish Sevilla has played host to everyone from Fidel Castro to Al Capone. With pleasant, airy rooms and a large outdoor swimming pool overlooking the Prado, this is a fantastic way to get to know Havana.

**Hotel Saratoga** (Map pp142-3; ☎ 868-1000; www .hotel-saratoga.com; Prado No 603; s/d from CUC$200/275, ste CUC$330-670; ✖ 🖳 ☎ ) Havana's finest hotel opened in 2005. It is slap bang in the center of the city and boasts every possible convenience, from free wi-fi internet access in each room to a stunning rooftop pool, bar, gym and restaurant with incredible city views. The rooms are spacious, stylish and comfortable, and include huge bathrooms, DVD players and gorgeous views of the Capitolio.

**Hotel NH Parque Central** (Map pp142-3; ☎ 860-6627; www.hotelnhparquecentral.com; Neptuno btwn Agramonte & Prado; s/d CUC$205/270, ste CUC$330-550, all incl breakfast; ✖ 🖳 ☎ ) The Saratoga may have the edge over the NH nowadays, but this pioneering five-star place remains hugely popular for its high standards of service and supreme location, even if it's almost a pastiche of the sterile five-star international hotel with its large but bland rooms. Views from the 9th-floor bar are spectacular, however, and you could do far, far worse. Offers wi-fi access.

## Vedado

### CASAS PARTICULARES

**Iris y Felipe** (Map pp146-7; ☎ 873-5286; www.irisweb .freeservers.com; Calle Mazón No 4 btwn Neptuno & San Miguel; r CUC$25; ✖ ) This excellent, easy-going and friendly house just by Havana's university is a safe and reliable option. Iris offers two rooms, both with private bathrooms, a great breakfast (CUC$5 extra) and a huge roof terrace. Both rooms have an independent entrance.

**Ana Livia Grimany Rojo** (Map pp146-7; ☎ 830-4311; anagrimany@yahoo.es; Calle 23 No 1103 btwn Calles 8 & 10; r CUC$25-30; ✖ ) This large, beautifully understated but interesting apartment hosted by two young architects is a great place to kick back in the heart of arty Vedado. The two rooms both have private bathrooms, and while one is bigger, the other has a private terrace.

**José A García** (Map pp146-7; ☎ 830-9367; joseve dado1003@yahoo.es; Calle 23 No 1003 btwn Calles 4 & 6; r incl breakfast CUC$25-30) This thoroughly extraordinary place is one of the biggest and most beautiful casas in town. The house has two large rooms with private bathrooms, and while there's no air-con, it's naturally cool with its vast corridors and high ceilings. A fantastic, atmospheric option.

**Melba Piñeda Bermúdez** (Map pp146-7; ☎ 832-5929; lienafp@yahoo.com; Calle 11 No 802 btwn Calles 2 & 4; r CUC$30; ✖ ) A very friendly house on a quiet and leafy Vedado backstreet with two rooms available. One has a private terrace, both have private bathrooms and access to a large communal balcony.

**Casa Silvia** (Map pp146-7; ☎ 833-4165; silviavidal602@ yahoo.es; Paseo No 602 btwn Calles 25 & 27; r CUC$30-35; ✖ ) This unbelievably palatial home has two rooms with fridges and private bathrooms. There's also an independent cabaña next door complete with kitchen for long-term rentals. All rooms have refrigerators and discounts for singles are available. Look no further for style and atmosphere.

### HOTELS

**Hotel Vedado** (Map pp146-7; ☎ 836-4072; www .gran-caribe.com; Calle O No 244 btwn Calles 23 & 25; s/d incl breakfast CUC$67/80; ✖ 🖳 ☎ ) This large Vedado block houses 203 average rooms. There are some good views to be had, and TV and phone in each room, but overall it's a bit of a damp squib, although a decent pool and a good location for central Vedado compensate somewhat.

**Hotel Victoria** (Map pp146-7; ☎ 833-3510; www .hotelvictoriacuba.com; Calle 19 No 101 & Calle M; s/d/tr incl breakfast CUC$80/100/138; ✖ 🖳 ☎ ) Much preferable to its bigger neighbors, the intimate 1920s-built Victoria has rooms that, while not luxurious or large, have plenty of character and some excellent views. It's quiet too, but within easy walking distance of downtown Vedado.

**Hotel Nacional** (Map pp146-7; ☎ 836-3564; www .hotelnacionaldecuba.com; Calles O & 21; s/d/tr CUC$120/170/238; ✖ 🖳 ☎ ) Cuba's most famous hotel, this stunner soars above the Malecón on its own hillside, boasting superb views and unbeatable gardens. Indeed, the entire place is more of a museum than a hotel, with its old-world elevators and general air of splendor and privilege, to the point that the dull and rather worn rooms seem an afterthought. The 6th (executive) floor has its own reception, fax, meeting rooms, secretarial staff and higher room rates (single/double/triple CUC$150/210/278).

**Hotel Mélia Cohiba** (Map pp146-7; ☎ 833-3636; www.solmelia.com; Paseo btwn Calles 1 & 3; r from CUC$170; 🞰 🖫 🞱 ) This is a good choice for business or just comfort if you've hit your tolerance threshold for 'five star' Cuban hotels elsewhere in the country – this is the real thing. While it won't win any beauty contests, Havana's business hotel of choice boasts very comfortable rooms, excellent service, good restaurants and friendly staff.

**Tryp Habana Libre** (Map pp146-7; ☎ 834-6100; www .solmelia.com; Calle L btwn Calles 23 & 25; r/ste CUC$200/300; 🞰 🖫 🞱 ) This vast white elephant is Havana's biggest hotel, and even though it's far nicer inside than its exterior would suggest, you still wonder who comes to Cuba and stays somewhere so sterile. The rooms are large (and many have extraordinary views) but the furnishings are dated and some just plain old. This is where many package groups end up – you've been warned.

# EATING
Havana's eating scene, while it has its moments, is on the whole a microcosm of that throughout the country – gems are out there, but they're extremely few and far between.

## Habana Vieja
**Museo de Chocolate** (Map pp142-3; ☎ 866-4431; cnr Mercaderes & Amargura; 🕾 10am-5:45pm Tue-Sun) This 'museum' is really just a café, but it serves up an incredibly tempting range of chocolate-based goodies, from steaming cups of hot chocolate to delicious on-site made chocolates. It's popular with tourist crowds and can be busy, but it's worth braving.

**Jardín del Oriente** (Map pp142-3; ☎ 860-6686; Amargura btwn San Ignacio & Mercaderes; mains CUC$1-3; 🕾 10am-11pm) This rightly popular place is in the heart of Habana Vieja, but avoids much of the tourist crowd by being hidden away in a charming garden. With food at rock-bottom prices, it's worth the wait when it's busy for a choice of Cuban and international staples.

**Café Santo Domingo** (Map pp142-3; Obispo No 159 btwn San Ignacio & Mercaderes; snacks CUC$2.50-3.50; 🕾 24hr) Tucked away upstairs beyond a good bakery is this café hideaway. The sandwiches and pizzas are big and tasty, plus there are eggs and bacon for breakfast.

**Restaurante La Dominica** (Map pp142-3; ☎ 860-2918; O'Reilly No 108; pizzas CUC$4.50-9.50, mains CUC$5-15; 🕾 noon-midnight) There's no disguising that it's almost exclusively tourists who come to La Dominica, either to sit inside the plush, fiercely acclimatized main dining room, or to be strummed at by Buena Vistas outside. Despite that, the food's pretty good, with a full Italian menu that includes several vegetarian options, tasty pizza, lobster and seafood pasta.

**Taberna de la Muralla** (Map pp142-3; ☎ 866-4453; cnr San Ignacio & Muralla; mains CUC$4.50-12.50; 🕾 11am-midnight) Havana's first (and as yet, only) microbrewery is a magnet for both tourists and locals on one side of the Plaza Vieja, drawn by the great-smelling barbecue, endless glasses of cold beer, and live music that goes on all day. Go inside for peace and quiet in the high-ceilinged main room, or join the crowds on the square for beers and kebabs.

**Al Medina** (Map pp142-3; ☎ 867-1041; Oficios 12 btwn Obrapía & Obispo; mains CUC$5-10; 🕾 noon-11pm) Middle Eastern food in Havana? Surprisingly so. Al Medina has a large selection of dishes, from delicious tagines to mezze platters serving up specialties such as hummus and dolmades. Of course these are all very Cuban versions of familiar dishes, but it's still a pleasant space set in a charming courtyard in the middle of the old town.

## Centro Habana
**Restaurante Prado y Neptuno** (Map pp142-3; ☎ 860-9636; cnr Prado & Neptuno; appetizers CUC$4-7, mains CUC$4-9; 🕾 noon-midnight) Dubbing itself rather fancifully as 'the best Italian restaurant in the Caribbean' (ha!), Prado y Neptuno nevertheless does pretty decent Italian food and has a warm and friendly atmosphere untypical of most state-run restaurants. Try the good pizza or the house lasagna.

**Restaurante Tien-Tan** (Map pp142-3; ☎ 861-5478; Cuchillo No 17 btwn Zanja & San Nicolás; mains CUC$4-15; 🕾 11am-11pm) The touts working at other restaurants on this strip will try to waylay you, but keep walking until you get here, by far the best of the Chinese restaurants on Cuchillo. The sizzling beef platter (CUC$10) and sweet-and-sour pork (CUC$6.50) are highly recommended, as is the wonton soup. The upstairs dining room is better.

**Los Nardos** (Map pp142-3; ☎ 863-2985; Prado No 563 btwn Teniente Rey & Dragones; mains CUC$4.50-10; 🕾 noon-midnight) Chef Ángel Ochoa works away in a bright kitchen with glass walls in sharp contrast to the dark, wood-heavy dining area at Los Nardos, one of Havana's most innovative restaurants. The menu is strong on fish and seafood and has enough veggie choice in the starters at least to make it one of Centro's few good choices for non-carnivores.

**Paladar Bellamar** (Map pp142-3; ☎ 861-0023; Virtudes No 169 near Amistad; dishes CUC$6-8; ☾ noon-10pm) This family-run place never seems to change – its cooking can hardly be called exciting, but it's perfectly tasty and there's usually a variety of home-cooked Cuban standards, from pork and *congrí* to freshly caught fish. The family sits around watching soap operas while you enjoy the food in their front room.

**our pick** **Paladar La Guarida** (Map pp142-3; ☎ 866-9047; www.laguarida.com; Concordia No 418 btwn Gervasio & Escobar; mains CUC$10-16; ☾ noon-4pm, 7pm-midnight) Gorgeously decorated and bedecked in stills from '90s cult movie *Fresa y Chocolate* (filmed in the building), Paladar La Guarida is Centro Habana's – and some would say the whole city's – best paladar. Inventive starters (rabbit lasagna with black-olive tapenade, eggplant stacks with quail) are followed by more traditional main courses served with a twist. Dessert is sublime, English is spoken and service is remarkably friendly. While you'll always need to reserve ahead for the evenings, you can usually pop in unannounced for lunch.

**El Paseo** (Map pp142-3; ☎ 860-6627; Neptuno btwn Prado & Agramonte, NH Parque Central; mains CUC$16-33; ☾ dinner) This smart restaurant, the smartest on offer from the NH Parque Central, is a rare place to enjoy a sophisticated atmosphere on the tourist-choked Parque. With its silver service and quiet atmosphere, the place maintains the highest international standards to match the gourmet menu.

## Vedado

**Coppelia** (Map pp146-7; ☎ 832-6184; Calles 23 & L; ☾ 11am-10:30pm Tue-Sun) This classic Havana ice-cream mecca draws crowds from morning until closing time – look no further for your authentic experience of the capital than here, across the street from student favorite Cine Yara. Enter the *divisa* (CUC) part on Calle 23 or wait in line for the real deal and pay peanuts in pesos.

**Pan.com** (Map pp146-7; cnr Callea 17 & 10; sandwiches CUC$2-4; ☾ 11am-11pm Mon-Fri, noon-midnight Sat & Sun) The TV may have inane slapstick comedy blaring out all day and service might border

on the rude, but pan.com is one of Havana's best places for sandwiches and burgers. The fries are good too, and the place attracts a relaxed student crowd just around the corner from Parque Lennon.

**La Roca** (Map pp146-7; ☎ 834-4501; Calle 21 No 102; specials CUC$3-8; ☾ midday-12:30am) This fiercely air-conditioned space is an old Havana classic although, like most things classic in the city, it's a rather faded version of its former self. Still, you can enjoy a cocktail in the small bar, or dine on *langosta mariposa* (butterfly lobster; CUC$18) in the main stained-glass salon, attended by liveried staff.

**El Conejito** (Map pp146-7; ☎ 832-4671; Calle M No 253; rabbits CUC$4-7; ☾ noon-11pm) El Conejito is a very smart 'English-style tavern,' moodily lit and decked out in dark wood fittings and red tablecloths. Oh yes, and it's all about rabbit, as its Spanish name might suggest. Delicious specialties include Creole rabbit, rabbit in Burgundy sauce, rabbit in aioli sauce… you name it, they've got a rabbit dish for it. There's also a good selection of seafood and fish dishes for those uncomfortable eating little Thumper.

**Paladar Los Amigos** (Map pp146-7; ☎ 830-0880; Calle M No 253; mains CUC$5-6; ☾ noon-midnight) This pleasant little place is tucked away at the back of a colonial house in one of the smarter parts of Vedado. It won't win any awards, but the Cuban cuisine the kitchen cooks up is remarkably popular, so you should book ahead.

**Trattoría Maraka's** (Map pp146-7; ☎ 833-3740; Calle O No 260 btwn Calles 23 & 25; pizzas CUC$6-7, mains CUC$8-12; ☾ noon-11:45pm) This handy place looks like it would be deeply average, but it actually serves up very good pizza in a useful location just off Vedado's main strip. You'll have to work hard to get the staff's attention, but if you do, try the Greek salad, gooey lasagna or spinach cannelloni.

**Decameron** (Map pp146-7; ☎ 832-2444; Línea No 753 btwn Paseo & Calle 2; appetizers CUC$3.50-5.50, mains CUC$9-16; ☾ noon-11pm) It's easy to miss on the outside, but you'll be glad you made the effort to come here once inside. The quirkily decorated dining rooms are bedecked with everything from musical instruments to antique clocks and are often full of diners. The real high point is the food – it's all delicious, from the large selection of imaginative starters to grills, pizzas, fresh fish and a good wine list.

# DRINKING
## Habana Vieja & Centro Habana

**Bar Dos Hermanos** (Map pp142-3; ☎ 861-3436; San Pedro No 304; ✌ 24hr) Once Lorca propped the bar up here (in a spot with a good view of the sailors across the road) and it's still a brilliant place, with good cocktails and a friendly crowd, even if the majority of people here are on the tourist trail.

**La Bodeguita del Medio** (Map pp142-3; ☎ 867-1374; Empedrado No 207; ✌ 11am-midnight) Havana's most famous bar, La Bodeguita may have been a Hemingway favorite but today feels rather like a tourist trap. Despite that, it's still a fun and atmospheric place for a tipple.

**Monserrate Bar** (Map pp142-3; ☎ 860-9751; Obrapía No 410; ✌ 10am-midnight) On Havana's most popular bar strip, next door to the horrendously over-priced and charmless La Floridita, here drinks are half the price in a far more enjoyable atmosphere. This is our favored place for a daiquiri, even if there are no Hemingway connections.

**Restaurante-Bar Viñales** (Map pp142-3; cnr O'Reilly & Compostela; ✌ 10am-midnight) For local atmosphere, you can't beat this big, open place featuring strong cocktails and colorful characters.

**Café Paris** (Map pp142-3; Obispo No 202; ✌ 10am-midnight) This unexpectedly excellent hot spot right in the heart of Habana Vieja is a gem – every night things get busy here with impromptu concerts, a packed bar and lots of regular characters keeping things lively.

## Vedado

**Opus Bar** (Map pp146-7; ☎ 836-5429; Calzada & Calle D; ✌ 3pm-2am) This Havana time warp, on the top floor above the prestigious Teatro Amadeo Roldán, is quirky and you certainly don't need to worry about it being overrun by tourists. With great views, good cocktails and comfy cream leather-effect chairs, this is a great out-of-the-way spot. Unusually for Havana, the entire place is nonsmoking.

**Centro de Prensa Internacional** (Map pp146-7; Calles 23 & 0; ✌ 9am-7pm) The basement bar here is favored by journalists and is a good place generally to pick up the buzz, and make contacts and expat friends.

**Café Fresa y Chocolate** (Map pp146-7; ☎ 826-3629; cnr Calles 23 & 12; ✌ 10am-10pm Mon-Wed, noon-midnight Thu-Sun) An arty crowd patronizes this place, named after the cult '90s Cuban movie nominated for an Oscar. It adjoins the ICAIC film institute and attracts a solid crowd of actors, directors and theater folk.

# ENTERTAINMENT
## Live Music
### TRADITIONAL & SALSA MUSIC

**Casa de la Amistad** (Map pp146-7; ☎ 830-3114; Paseo No 406; admission Mon, Wed & Fri/Tue, Thu & Sat free/CUC$5; ✌ noon-11pm Mon, Wed & Fri, noon-1am Tue & Thu, noon-2am Sat) This superb venue, housed in a stunning colonial mansion in the heart of Vedado, is the place to come in Havana for quality salsa, Cuban jazz and other live music. While on Monday, Wednesday and Friday it's just a great place for a drink or dinner in a refined atmosphere, on Tuesday, Thursday and Saturday the place comes alive with music performed outside. Performances start at 9pm and dancing continues until the early hours.

**Casa de la Música** Centro Habana (Map pp142-3; ☎ 878-4727; Av de Italia; 4pm matinee CUC$5, night CUC$15-25); Miramar ( ☎ 202-6147; Calle 20 No 3308; admission CUC$15-20; ✌ 8pm-2am Tue-Sat, shows 10pm) Of the two Casas de la Música in Havana, the outpost in distant Miramar is reckoned by locals to be the superior by far. It's probably worth swallowing the cab fare to get out here and enjoy a much more authentic program of music in a less touristy atmosphere, although the slightly divey Centro Habana club of the same name can be a lot of fun too.

**Casa de la Trova** (Map pp142-3; ☎ 879-3373; San Lázaro No 661; admission free; ✌ 6pm-midnight Tue-Sun) Headquarters of Havana's *son* sound it may be, but the Casa de la Trova has been looking like one of the city's less essential music joints of late. While some excellent Cuban bands play here on a regular basis, it's always best to call ahead and see what's on.

**El Hurón Azul** (Map pp146-7; ☎ 832-4551; Calles 17 & H; admission CUC$1-5) This excellent place is the social club of the Unión Nacional de Escritores y Artistas de Cuba (Uneac; National Union of Cuban Writers & Artists), the once much reviled state-run center of artistic and intellectual life in Cuba. Head here for an Afro-Cuban *peña* (musical performance or get-together) on Wednesday, boleros from 10pm to 2am Saturday, or jazz and *trova* (traditional poetic singing) from 5pm Thursday.

**Casa de Cultura Roberto Blanly** (Map pp146-7; ☎ 881-0722; Calles 37 No 262; admission CUP20-50) Formerly counter-cultural Mecca Patio de María, this peso-charging house of culture hosts excellent salsa concerts with lots of dancing every Saturday from 8pm. A great place to meet locals.

**Conjunto Folklórico Nacional de Cuba** (Map pp146-7; ☎ 830-3060; Calle 4 No 103 btwn Calzada & Calle 5; admission CUC$5; ☻ from 3pm Sat) This place has a steamy Sábado de Rumba – audience participation is encouraged.

**Callejón de Hamel** (Map pp146-7; Callejón de Hamel btwn Aramburu & Hospital; admission by donation; ☻ from 11am) Another recommended rumba happens at this wild place.

### JAZZ

**Jazz Club La Zorra y El Cuervo** (Map pp146-7; ☎ 66-24-02; Calles 23 & 0, Vedado; admission CUC$10; ☻ 9pm-2am) Havana's most famous jazz club is in a funky underground cavern on Vedado's main drag. As with most jazz clubs around the world, the kind of night you'll have here depends entirely on who's playing. Get a timetable from the entrance and ask around for who's hot. It's a dark, smoky space shared between local jazz aficionados and curious tourists. Make a beeline here for jams held during the International Jazz Fest, where you may find some true jazz greats on the stage.

**Jazz Café** (Map pp146-7; ☎ 55-33-02; Calle 1 & Paseo, Galerías de Paseo; drink minimum CUC$10; ☻ noon-late) This upscale supper club overlooking the Malecón is perfect for sunset cocktails. At night, the club swings into action with jazz, *timba* (contemporary salsa) and salsa, although the dance floor is tiny. You'll get some of Havana's best jazz combos on stage here.

### ROCK, REGGAE & RAP

**La Madriguera** (Map pp146-7; ☎ 879-8175; Quinta de los Molinos, cnr Calzada de Infanta & Salvador Allende; admission CUP40; ☻ 9am-7pm Mon-Wed, 9am-midnight Thu-Sat) Home of the youth wing of Uneac, the Asociación Hermanos Saíz, this is the place to come to experience Cuba's best reggaeton. There are also good rap and rumba groups performing here.

**Anfiteatro Parque Almendares** (Map pp146-7; Calle 23 & Río Almendares; admission CUP2-5) This riverside amphitheater hosts terrific concerts by the likes of Frank Delgado and Interactivo. Regular *peñas* (musical performances or get-togethers) include reggae at 8pm on Friday and rap at 8pm on Saturday.

### Nightclubs

**Mi Habana Cafe Cantante** (Map pp146-7; ☎ 879-0710; Paseo & Calle 39; admission CUC$5-10; ☻ 10pm-2am Tue-Sat) This subterranean club next door to the Teatro Nacional de Cuba in Vedado's hauntingly empty Plaza de la Revolución is incongruously lively, with nightly salsa and *son* acts and good DJs. Locally famous band Síntesis performs here regularly. There's a 'no shorts and T-shirts' dress code.

**El Chevere** (Map pp146-7; ☎ 204-5162; Calles 49-A & 28-A in Parque Almendares; admission CUC$10-15; ☻ midnight-4am) One of Havana's hottest discos, this place hosts a good mix of locals and tourists in a large complex by the beautiful Parque Almendares at Vedado's furthest end.

## Cabarets

**Tropicana Nightclub** ( ☎ 267-0110; Calle 72 No 4504, Marianao; admission from CUC$70-90; ☻ box office 10am-4pm, show 10pm) This Havana institution is the place to head for high-kicking scantily clad dancers who have been doing their rather dated thing since the '30s. It's horrendously overpriced (and you'll be charged extra to bring a camera), but Greene fans (yes another key scene in *Our Man in Havana* happens here) and those wanting some old-style Cuban glitz will not leave disappointed.

## Theater

**Gran Teatro de La Habana** (Map pp142-3; ☎ 861-3077; Prado & San Rafael; admission CUC$10; ☻ box office 9am-6pm Mon-Sat, 9am-3pm Sun) This magnificent theater is closely associated with its most famous resident: the acclaimed Ballet Nacional de Cuba and its founder Alicia Alonso.

**Teatro Nacional de Cuba** (Map pp146-7; ☎ 879-6011; Paseo & Calle 39; per person CUC$10; ☻ box office 9am-5pm & before performances) This modern theater on the Plaza de la Revolución hosts landmark concerts, foreign theater troupes, La Colmenita children's company and the Ballet Nacional de Cuba. It was being refurbished at the time of research, but should be open again during the lifetime of this book.

**Teatro Amadeo Roldán** (Map pp146-7; ☎ 832-4522; Calzada & Calle D; admission CUC$10) This modern, 886-seat theater is the best place for classical music in Havana and is the seat of the Orquesta Sinfónica Nacional (performing at 11am on Sunday, in season). Try to catch master Leo Brouwer conducting.

## Cinemas

Havana has a vibrant cinema scene, with some 200 theaters citywide. Movie tickets cost CUC$2; most theaters show Cuban movies

---

**IN THE BLOOD**   *As related to Brendan Sainsbury*

Regla Yurisán Pentón Hernández is a pianist who lives in Habana Vieja.

**Could you sum up Havana in one sentence?**
It is a place where everyone in the world wants to be.

**How has Havana changed in the last 10 years?**
Thanks to the restoration work of city historian Eusebio Leal, *habaneros* [inhabitants of Havana] have been able to rediscover their culture.

**What, in your opinion, is the finest Cuban cigar and why?**
Populares, for their aroma and taste.

**What is your favorite Havana night out?**
The Casa de la Música in Galiano [Av de Italia], Bar Monserrate, and Café París in Calle Obispo.

**Why are Cubans such skillful dancers?**
It's a tradition born out of the union between Indians, Spanish and Africans. It's in our blood. If a Cuban can't sing, they dance; if they can't dance, they sing.

**How can the inquisitive traveler find the 'real' Cuba?**
Get on a *camello* [metro bus]; go to an *agropecuario* [free-enterprise vegetable market]; visit a school, hospital, theater or cinema; experience a festival; see an exposition of art; or come to Habana on May 1 and witness a parade.

**What do people talk about on the Malecón?**
They discuss work or school; they talk about their dreams; they drink rum; and they talk about love.

---

and a surprising amount of mainstream fare flowing from Hollywood.

**Cine Yara** (Map pp146-7; ☎ 832-9430; Calles 23 & L) Havana's most famous cinema also has the best popcorn. Admission to its varied program of movies costs CUC$2.

**Cine Riviera** (Map pp146-7; ☎ 830-9564; Calle 23 No 507 near Calle G) Also hosts quality rock and pop concerts on occasion (admission CUC$10).

**Cine Charles Chaplin** (Map pp146-7; ☎ 831-1101; Calle 23 No 1157 btwn Calles 10 & 12) The theater of the Instituto Cubano del Arte e Industria Cinematográfico (ICAIC) has special screenings (premieres, foreign films, festivals etc) and Dolby surround sound.

## Sports

**Estadio Latinoamericano** (Map pp146-7; ☎ 870-6526; Zequiera No 312; admission CUP3) Baseball games happen at 8:30pm Monday to Saturday and 1:30pm on Sunday at this 58,000-seat stadium in Cerro, just south of Centro Habana, from October to April (and beyond if Havana's Industriales make the play-offs).

## SHOPPING

**Fería de la Artesanía** (Map pp142-3; Tacón btwn Tejadillo & Chacón; 9am-6pm Wed-Sat) While this won't be the cheapest crafts market you'll find in Cuba, and it can be over-run with tour groups, there's still a good selection of paintings,

*guayaberas* (pleated, buttoned men's shirts), woodwork, Che everything, jewelry and more. Haggling is both expected and essential.

**Fundación Havana Club Shop** (Map pp142-3; ☎ 861-1900; Av del Puerto; 9am-9pm) Come to the Fundación Havana Club for cool Havana Club gear, such as martini glasses (CUC$6) or mojito glasses (CUC$2).

**Promociones de ICAIC** (Map pp146-7; ☎ 832-9430; Calles 23 & L) A fabulous selection of original Cuban movie posters (CUC$10) are on offer here, in Cine Yara, making fantastic souvenirs. There are also film-themed T-shirts (CUC$7) and classic Cuban films on video and DVD. Another outlet is inside Café Fresa y Chocolate (corner Calles 23 and 12).

## GETTING THERE & AWAY
### Air

**José Martí International Airport** (☎ 649-5666, 649-0410) is at Av de la Independencia, 25km southwest of Havana. For information on flights to Havana, see p188 and p188.

To book a flight, take a number at **Cubana de Aviación** (Map pp146-7; ☎ 834-4446; www.cubana.cu; Airline Bldg, Calle 23 No 64; 8:30am-4pm Mon-Fri, 8:30am-noon Sat). **Aerocaribbean** (Map pp146-7; ☎ 879-7524/25; www.aero-caribbean.com; Airline Bldg, Calle 23 No 64) is located a couple of doors down. Most other airlines that have offices in Havana are located on this strip.

CUBA

## Bus

The **Víazul** ( ☎ 881-1413; www.viazul.com; Calle 26 & Zoológico, Nuevo Vedado) terminal is located 3km southwest of Plaza de la Revolución. Infotur (p144) and **Cubatur** (Map pp146-7; cnr Calles 23 & L) sell tickets. There's also a Víazul ticket office in the arrivals area of Terminal 3 at José Martí Airport, and several others scattered around town. See below for bus services. Those bound for Santa Clara should buy a ticket on any Santiago de Cuba service, or the 8:40am service to Holguín (CUC$18).

## Car

The following offices deal with car hire. You're often better off going directly to hotel representatives than calling the operators.
**Cubacar** Hotel Inglaterra (Map pp142-3; ☎ 866-6218); Hotel NH Parque Central (Map pp142-3; ☎ 866-6507); Hotel Telégrafo (Map pp142-3; ☎ 863-8990); Plaza Hotel (Map pp142-3; ☎ 866-8915)
**Rex** Airport ( ☎ 642-60-74); Hotel Saratoga (Map pp142-3; ☎ 868-1000 ext 1302); Vedado (Map pp146-7; ☎ 835-6830; Línea & Malecón)
**Vía Rent a Car** Hotel Sevilla (Map pp142-3; ☎ 206-9791); Tryp Habana Libre (Map pp146-7; ☎ 838-4954)

## Taxi

Taxis at the **Víazul** (Calle 26 & Zoológico, Nuevo Vedado) bus terminal offer fares for up to four people to Varadero (CUC$50), Santa Clara (CUC$75) Cienfuegos (CUC$94) and Trinidad (CUC$100).

## Train

Most trains depart from Havana's **Estación Central de Ferrocarriles** (Map pp142-3; ☎ 861-7651, 862-1920; Av de Bélgica & Arsenal). The smaller, more modern La Coubre terminal, used by certain arrivals and departures, is a short walk down the road. See opposite for train services.

## GETTING AROUND
### To/From the Airport

For all practical purposes, there is no public transportation from the airport to the city center, and taxi drivers work this to their full advantage. A taxi should cost CUC$20 (or CUC$15 from the city to the airport), but you'll be told CUC$25; bargain hard. You may also find yourself sharing a taxi with another traveler or two – this is perfectly normal, although make sure you're definitely not paying over CUC$20 in this case. A taxi between any of the terminals costs CUC$5 per person – bargaining doesn't seem to be an option on this one.

## Bicycle

**El Orbe** (Map pp142-3; ☎ 860-2617; Av de las Misiones; ⊗ 9am-4:30pm Mon-Sat) rents out beat-up cruisers for CUC$2 per hour or CUC$12 for 24 hours. You have to leave identification as deposit; there's a parts and service store on site. It's always best to reserve ahead, as there's a limited number of bikes available. The locks provided are risible so, if you want to be able to leave the bike somewhere, bring your own lock.

## Buses

Havana's public transportation system is a misery that locals have to deal with every day. Long waits for horribly overcrowded buses make for excessively long journey times and we don't recommend taking the plunge. Cheap taxis, bici-taxis (see below) and walking are the best way to get around town.

## Taxis

Bici-taxis (two-seater taxis powered by a bicyclist) are available throughout Habana Vieja and Centro Habana and are great for short hops (CUC$1 to CUC$2). Agree on the price first. Coco-taxis are the yellow eggs-on-wheels you will see zipping all over town; they carry three people and cost CUC$0.50 per kilometer.

**Panataxi** ( ☎ 55-55-55) has the cheapest official taxis. Fancier taxis can be ordered from **TaxiOK** ( ☎ 204-0000) and **Transgaviota** ( ☎ 267-1626).

| SERVICES FROM HAVANA'S VÍAZUL BUS TERMINAL | | | | |
| --- | --- | --- | --- | --- |
| **Destination** | **One-way fare (CUC$)** | **Distance (km)** | **Duration (hr)** | **Schedule** |
| Santiago de Cuba | 51 | 861 | 15 | 3pm, 6:15pm, 10pm |
| Trinidad | 25 | 335 | 5¾ | 8:15am, 1pm |
| Varadero | 10 | 140 | 3 | 8am, noon, 6pm |
| Viñales | 12 | 189 | 3½ | 9am, 2pm |

| SERVICES FROM HAVANA'S ESTACIÓN CENTRAL & LA COUBRE | | | | |
|---|---|---|---|---|
| **Destination** | **One-way fare (CUC$)** | **Distance (km)** | **Duration (hr)** | **Schedule** |
| Santa Clara | 10 | 276 | 4 | 6:20am*, 2pm, 3:15pm, 4:45pm, 7pm, 8:25pm*, 9:45pm* |
| Santiago de Cuba | 32 (regular)<br>70 (especial) | 861 | 13-16 | 3:15pm (regular) alternate days & 7pm (especial) alternate days |

\* from La Coubre.

# AROUND HAVANA

There's plenty to explore in the vicinity of the Cuban capital, although most travelers head straight for Trinidad or Santiago. The wonderful Parque Histórico Militar Morro-Cabaña, which includes the protective fortress that has guarded the Bahía de la Habana for centuries, is a must-see day trip, while the Playas del Este are the most obvious place to make an easy escape to beautiful beaches for the day.

## PARQUE HISTÓRICO MILITAR MORRO-CABAÑA

One of Havana's must-see sights is the impressive Parque Histórico Militar Morro-Cabaña (Map pp142–3), across the Bahía de la Habana from the city's port. The complex makes for a great half-day trip, and the views of Havana to be had from here are outstanding.

The **Castillo de los Tres Santos Reyes Magnos del Morro** ( ☎ 863-7941; admission incl museum CUC$4; ☺ 8am-8pm) was erected between 1589 and 1630 on an abrupt limestone headland to protect the entrance to the harbor. In 1762 the British captured El Morro by attacking from the landward side and digging a tunnel under the walls. In 1845 the first lighthouse in Cuba was added to the castle (admission CUC$2). There is also a **maritime museum**.

The **Fortaleza de San Carlos de la Cabaña** ( ☎ 862-0617; admission CUC$4; ☺ 8am-11pm) was built between 1763 and 1774 to deny attackers the long ridge overlooking Havana. It's one of the largest colonial fortresses in the Americas, replete with grassy moats, ancient chapel and cobblestone streets. Dictators Gerardo Machado y Morales and Batista used the fortress as a military prison, and Che Guevara established his revolutionary headquarters here. Be sure to visit the creative Havana skyline **mirador** (viewpoint) on the other side of the **Museo de Comandancia del Che** here.

Nightly at 9pm a cannon is fired on the harbor side of La Cabaña by a squad attired in 19th-century uniforms, a hold-over from Spanish times when these shots signaled that the city gates were closing. The **cañonazo** (admission CUC$6) begins at 8:30pm, followed by a concert by Moncada, a geriatric rock band.

To get here, take the ferry from Muelle Luz (Map pp142–3) to Casablanca (CUC$1, every 15 to 30 minutes dawn to dusk), from where it's an easy walk to the Parque Histórico Militar Morro-Cabaña.

## PLAYAS DEL ESTE

Havana's pine-fringed Riviera, Playas del Este (off Map pp142–3), begins at Bacuranao, 18km east of Havana, and continues east through **Santa María del Mar** (the nicest of the beaches here) to Guanabo, 27km from the capital. These beaches provide an effortless escape from Havana should you need it, and there are many casas particulares in Guanabo (look for the green triangle).

The beach is lined with **rentals** including windsurfers (per hour CUC$6), catamarans (per hour CUC$12) and beach chairs (per three hours CUC$2). Several simple fish restaurants line the beach.

Bus 400 to Guanabo leaves hourly from the rotunda at Desamparados near the train station in Habana Vieja. Bus 405 runs between Guanabacoa and Guanabo.

A taxi from Playas del Este to Havana will cost around CUC$20.

**CUBA**

### ISLA DE LA JUVENTUD – THE CARIBBEAN'S BEST DIVING?

True diving fanatics should look no further than the incredible Punta Frances on the Isla de la Juventud, a short internal flight south of the Cuban mainland. Most famous for being where Fidel Castro spent several years imprisoned in the 1950s, the island is generally considered to have the best diving in the Caribbean.

The **Hotel Colony** ( ☎ 46-398-181; fax 46-398-428; r half board CUC$108; ⊠ 🖳 🖳 ) is the place to stay for divers. It's a remote place with excellent rooms and very bad food, which you have to grin and bear, as staying here gives you relatively easy access to the fantastic diving. The hotel is a 30 minute, CUC$20 taxi ride from Nueva Gerona Airport. There is absolutely nothing out here, so there's no alternative to eating in the hotel unless you're lucky enough to hire one of the island's very scarce rental cars and want to drive to Nueva Gerona each evening. From the hotel you're just a short bus ride from the **International Diving Center** ( ☎ 46-398-282) where every day a boat makes the trip to the Punta Frances diving site for a two-tank dive, with plenty of beach time between on a gorgeous, pristine strip of white sand. Manatees, sharks, lots of fish and rays, huge lobsters and crabs, plenty of wrecks, dramatic cliffs and bright coral combine to make this Cuba's most exciting diving.

Flights to the island's administrative center, Nueva Gerona, are operated several times daily by **Cubana de Aviación** (Map pp146-7; ☎ 834-4446; www.cubana.cu; Airline Bldg, Calle 23 No 64, Havana; ⏰ 8:30am-4pm Mon-Fri, 8:30am-noon Sat) and cost CUC$86 return.

For more information, see Lonely Planet's *Cuba* guide.

# PINAR DEL RÍO PROVINCE

The Western flank of Cuba extends from Havana Province to the narrow Yucatán Channel separating Cuba from Mexico. This lush part of the island is home to endless tobacco plantations, pine trees, sugarcane and rice fields and is one of Cuba's most scenic. With rock climbing, caving, diving and birding sprinkled throughout two Unesco Biosphere Reserves and one World Heritage site, this is Cuba's outdoor adventure hub. Beyond the uninteresting city of Pinar del Río, the countryside becomes breathtaking, as well as extremely rural.

Whether you go north to stunning Viñales, famous for its vast limestone hills, or continue heading west to the Península de Guanahacabibes, where superb diving, pristine beaches, and exciting hikes await you, you'll be guaranteed a rewarding trip.

Pinar del Río Province is also home to San Juan y Martínez and the Vuelta Abajo plantations, where the world's finest tobacco thrives in the sandy soil. The majority of export-quality tobacco comes from here. The best time to visit is at harvest time, from January to March.

If you're driving from Havana, the roads are generally good all the way to Viñales (via Pinar, the northern coastal route is far worse) and the main challenge will be finding your way onto the Autopista Habana-Pinar del Río from the capital.

## VIÑALES

**pop 27,000 / ☎ 048**

Quite unlike anywhere else in Cuba, Viñales is a nature-lover's paradise and well deserving of its Unesco World Heritage site status. Tucked within the Sierra de los Órganos is Parque Nacional Viñales, at the end of a stunning and often white-knuckle road from the south. The name Viñales refers to both this area of extraordinary limestone cliffs as well as the quiet and generally unremarkable town at its center, which nevertheless enjoys one of the most dramatic settings in the Caribbean. With its famous *mogotes*, bizarrely mammoth limestone extrusions that pepper the otherwise flat but lush landscape, Viñales has become a center for climbers, walkers and anyone who enjoys a good sunset. Indeed, the government has now set up an official climbing center here; until recently all climbers were effectively breaking the law. Viñales itself is a sleepy place but one well-adapted for travelers, with plenty of activities on offer.

## Information

**Banco de Crédito y Comercio** ( ☎ 79-31-30; Salvador Cisneros No 58; ⏰ 8am-3pm Mon-Fri)

**Cadeca** ( ☎ 79-63-34; Salvador Cisneros & Adela Azcuy; ⏱ 8:30am-6pm Mon-Sat) Gives cash advances and changes traveler's checks at higher commissions than banks.
**Cubanacán** ( ☎ 79-63-93; Salvador Cisneros No 63C; internet per hr CUC$6; ⏱ 8:30am-12:30pm & 1:30-9pm)
**Etecsa** (Ceferino Fernández No 3) Internet access and international calls.
**Post office** ( ☎ 79-32-12; Ceferino Fernández No 14; 9am-6pm Mon-Sat)
**Viñales Visitor Center** ( ⏱ 8am-6pm) On the main road into town from Pinar del Río before Hotel Los Jazmines. Guided tours can be booked (CUC$8, 2½ hours).

## Sights

The stand-out attractions of Viñales are its *mogotes* and the fascinating cave complex of Santo Tomás, a 20km drive from town. The town itself has a few mildly diverting sights, but it's really about kicking back and drinking in the scenery here. Across from the Cupet gas station in the town center, look for a funky gate hung with fresh fruit. This is the **Jardín de las Hermanas Caridad** (Salvador Cisneros No 5; admission by donation; ⏱ 8am-5pm), a sprawling, nearly 100-year-old garden. Cascades of orchids bloom beside plastic doll heads, lilies grow in soft groves and turkeys run amok.

Just past the baseball stadium – look for the giant T-Rex and teeny Martí – is the **Mundo Prehistórico Museo Parque** (Adela Azcuy Norte No 6; admission by donation; ⏱ 9am-6pm), an outdoor labyrinth of local natural history created by Jesús Arencibia. His explanations of the fossils and endemic plants are peppered with humor, poetry and lore.

The **Museo Municipal Adela Azcuy Labrador** ( ☎ 79-33-95; Salvador Cisneros No 115; admission CUC$1; ⏱ 9am-10pm Mon-Sat, 9am-4pm Sun) occupies the former home of independence heroine Adela Azcuy (1861–1914). The small, but earnest, collection focuses on the history of Viñales, replete with reconstructed cave. Hikes set out from here (see right).

About 4km west of Viñales is the **Mural de la Prehistoria** (admission CUC$1; ⏱ 8am-7pm), a 120m-long painting on the side of Mogote Dos Hermanas. Designed in 1961, it took 15 people five years to complete. Ponder the psychedelic/horrific spectacle with a drink at the bar. **Horseback riding** (per 15min/1hr CUC$1/5) is available. For phenomenal valley views, hike the **Sendero Al Mural** at the base of the cliff to the top of the *mogote*; allow an hour, round-trip.

The stand-out sight of the area is **Gran Caverna de Santo Tomás** (admission CUC$10; ⏱ 8:30am-4pm) is not to be missed. Tours leave at half past the hour from 8:30am. With over 46km of galleries on eight levels, it's Cuba's largest cave system. Tours are given by friendly, if eccentric guides in both Spanish and English. Wear sturdy shoes, not sandals, as there's a fair bit of clambering to be done, over often slippery surfaces. Headlamps are provided for the 1km, 90-minute tour that takes in surreal formations including giant stalagmites and stone percussive pipes that the guide will 'play'. The cavern is at El Moncada, off the road to Minas de Matahambre, 15km from Viñales. A cab there and back including waiting time will cost CUC$15.

For an idyllic **beach**, head north to **Cayo Jutías** (admission incl 1 drink CUC$5). The *pedreplén* (causeway) begins 4km west of Santa Lucía. **Restaurante Cayo Jutías** ( ⏱ 9am-5pm) is here. The fastest, prettiest route is via El Moncada and Minas de Matahambre. Two private rooms are available for rent in Santa Lucía or you can camp.

## Activities

### HIKING

The Museo Municipal (left) offers five excellent **walking tours** (tours CUC$5; ⏱ 9am & 3pm) that make a great introduction to the area, taking in everything from tobacco farming to local traditions, coffee plantations and visits to the more accessible *mogotes*. Tours last from one to four hours and are expertly led in Spanish, English or French. Longer hikes can be arranged.

The **Maravillas de Viñales trail** (admission CUC$1) is a 5km signposted hike beginning 2km before El Moncada, 13km from the Dos Hermanas turn-off (admission fee payable at the trailhead). This makes a good three-hour hike with endemic plants and orchids lining the trail; it's not quite a loop and leaves you about 500m downhill from the trailhead.

### ROCK CLIMBING

Viñales has finally arrived as one of the Caribbean's top climbing draws. After years of being tolerated by default, it was finally made fully legal with a permit system as of early 2008. Amateur local climbers and a smattering of professionals from around the world have collectively mapped over 300 routes. Climbers should check www.cubaclimbing.com for exhaustive information and background essential for planning.

As the government was just getting the permit process ready at the time of research, those heading to climb in Viñales should contact either Oscar Jaime Rodriguez who runs Casa Oscar (below), a casa favored by climbers, or Edgar Rivery Ricardo at Casa El Cafetal (below) for information and help with obtaining permits. In general, climbing is still in its infancy here, so it's a good idea to bring your own gear and to be generous about leaving as much of it as you can here with locals keen to help the industry grow. October to April is the preferred climbing season.

## Sleeping

### CASAS PARTICULARES

**Villa Nelson** ( ☎ 01-52-23-90-68; Cienfuegos No 4; r CUC$15-20; ✺ ) Look out for the unnervingly well reproduced Lonely Planet sign at this good casa run by a friendly young couple, a block from the main road. It offers two basic rooms; one has air-con, the other a fan and a small private kitchen. Excellent meals can be organized for nonguests as well as guests.

**Villa El Mojito** ( ☎ 01-52-23-90-24; Adela Azcuy Norte No 43; r CUC$15-20; ✺ ) The owner of this friendly casa, a short walk from the main road, is a former barman and a daily mojito is included in the price. There are two decent rooms in the back yard, and the daughter speaks English.

**Casa El Cafetal – Martha Martínez** ( ☎ 01-52-23-89-13; villaelcafetal@correodecuba.cu; Adela Azcuy Norte Final; r CUC$20) Set in a charming garden at the end of a road off the main street, you're almost in the countryside here, beneath a looming *mogote*. Martha rents out one super-clean room with a private bathroom. Meals available. Her son, Edgar, is a leading local climber who speaks good English and can provide a wealth of information.

**Casa Campo** ( ☎ 01-52-23-89-13; Adela Azcuy Norte Final; r CUC$20) Beyond Martha's (and sharing the same telephone) is another charmer in the same rural style. There's one bedroom here with a private bathroom and access to a gorgeous garden.

**Casa Oscar** ( ☎ 79-33-81, 69-55-16; leydisbel040610@yahoo.es; Adela Azcuy Sur No 43; r CUC$20; ✺ ) This buzzing two-room casa is the favorite place for visiting climbers to stay. Host Jaime (Oscar Jaime Rodriguez) is a mine of information and this is a good first port of call for those interested in climbing. There are two rooms here, both with private bathroom. The upstairs room has a private roof terrace, while the one downstairs has a small patio and is larger.

**Villa Yudy y Emilio** ( ☎ 69-51-68; Sergio Dopico 32; r CUC$20; ✺ ) Another delightfully bucolic-feeling house. The two large bedrooms here both have private bathrooms. There are great views towards a nearby *mogote*, at the end of the village. From the center of town, pass Restaurant Don Tomás and take the first right. When the road splits follow the left fork and it's the last house.

**Villa Tinquillo** ( ☎ 69-51-58; Sergio Dopico 30; r CUC$20; ✺ ) Two houses before Yudy y Emilio, this small place is very cozy, offering one room with a private bathroom. It's a breezy and calm place, run by an old lady.

### HOTELS

**Hotel Rancho San Vicente** ( ☎ 79-62-01; s/d incl breakfast CUC$44/61; ✺ 🛋 ) With its lovely setting beneath the hillside, Rancho San Vincente is less about the views and more about being surrounded by nature. Make sure you get one of the excellent newer rooms (6 to 43) as the older ones aren't great. The breakfast is dreadful – give it a miss. Instead enjoy the onsite sulfur baths and massages.

**Los Jazmines** ( ☎ 79-62-05; s/d incl breakfast CUC$48/71; ✺ 🛋 ) Forget the fact that this state-run place is a little rough around the edges and that the paint is peeling; come here for one of the most extraordinary views in the country, available from nearly every room. The pink Jazmines, in its coveted hilltop position, is visible for miles around, and while its rooms are smallish, there's nothing better than sitting back on the patio and watching the sun go down with a cocktail.

**La Ermita** ( ☎ 79-60-71; s/d incl breakfast CUC$58/74; ✺ 🛋 ) The best option to be had in Viñales is La Ermita, with its stunning views, sweet cabin-style rooms and friendly staff. Poolside mojitos are highly recommended. Horseback riding (CUC$5 per hour) is available. This is the only hotel within easy walking distance of town.

## Eating & Drinking

Viñales, second only to Santiago de Cuba, has some of the poorest food on offer in the country. There simply aren't any decent paladares in town, so your best bet is to eat in a casa (nearly all will do an evening meal even if you aren't a guest; just call ahead).

**El Estanco II** (Carretera de Puerto Esperanza; mains CUC$2-4; ⏰ 11am-10pm) This pleasant open-air pizza and pasta place serves up basic meals at a slow pace. Don't come wanting to eat in a hurry, but otherwise it's fine, with agreeably low prices, a local vibe and a cigar shop as well. It's 1km north of town on the road to Cueva del Indio, a nearby cave.

**Restaurante Las Magnolias** ( ☎ 79-60-62; mains CUC$3-8; ⏰ 8am-4pm) With what is probably the best food to be had in town, Las Magnolias is a cozy and friendly spot outside the town center across from Cueva del Indio. Sink into the complete lunch (CUC$8) in the attractive patio here and enjoy the views of the surrounding countryside.

**Restaurante San Tomás** ( ☎ 79-63-00; mains CUC$6-10; ⏰ 10am-9:30pm) This wonderful colonial house in the center of town could be superb, but sadly it's afflicted with ever worsening food and rude service. Any night of the week it's busy with tourists eating and drinking in the picturesque garden, but standards have been dropping for a decade and it's currently hard to recommend.

**Ranchón y Finca San Vincente** ( ☎ 79-61-10; mains CUC$8; ⏰ noon-5pm) This beautifully located restaurant is unquestionably touristy, but still serves up decent food in its huge al fresco dining room. Still, unless a tour group comes in, the place can feel eerily empty.

## Entertainment

The Casa de la Cultura, situated on the main square, has a full program of cultural activities. Don't miss the annual Viñales festival in mid-December; it's a fun weekend of music and drinking attended by thousands. For the rest of the year there are two decent bars, although there's often some sort of nightlife at the three big hotels.

**Patio del Decimista** ( ☎ 79-60-14; Salvador Cisneros No 102; admission free; ⏰ 7pm-midnight) Serves live music nightly from 9pm and cold beers on its patio.

**El Viñalero** (Salvador Cisneros No 105; ⏰ 7:30am-midnight) Across the street from Patio del Decimista, this place also has live music and sidewalk tables.

## Getting There & Around

There are two routes to Viñales from Havana – the slightly quicker one on the highway via Pinar del Río and the more adventurous back route via Bahía Honda. Both roads as they approach Viñales are dramatic and somewhat vertiginous.

### BUS

**Víazul** (Salvador Cisneros No 63A; ⏰ 8am-noon & 1-3pm) is opposite Viñales' main square. The two daily Havana departures are at 8am (CUC$12, 3¼ hours via Pinar del Río) and 2pm (CUC$12, 3½ hours via Las Terrazas).

### CAR

The following agencies rent out wheels:
**Cubanacán** (Salvador Cisneros No 63C; ⏰ 9am-7pm) Has scooters (per day CUC$25) and bicycles (per day/week CUC$6/20).
**Havanautos** ( ☎ 79-63-90) At the Cupet; rents out scooters.

### TAXI

Taxis parked alongside the square will take you to Pinar del Río (CUC$10) or Gran Caverna de Santo Tomás (CUC$15, round-trip).

# PENÍNSULA DE GUANAHACABIBES
☎ 048

The far western tip of Cuba is made up of the large Península de Guanahacabibes, a national park and Unesco Biosphere Reserve. It's a long, attractive drive around 150km southwest of Pinar del Río through the lush tobacco plantations and pretty villages for which Pinar del Río Province is famed.

However, the peninsula itself is very different – a semiwilderness made up of huge forests, mangrove swamps and more than its fair share of stunning white beaches – this is a nature-watcher's and diver's paradise, with two decent hotels to choose between. Anyone with a car should take the road towards Cabo de San Antonio, where the local population of iguanas can be seen basking on the rocks throughout the day. Edible tree rats (*jutías*), white-tail deer and a huge population of varied birds are other attractions that can be seen on this road.

## Sights & Activities

Well within the entrance to the park is the **Estación Ecológica Guanahacabibes** ( ☎ 75-03-66; ⏰ 9am-2pm) where a multilingual group of guides offer tours in Spanish, English and Italian to Cabo de San Antonio. They also run guided hikes along two **hiking trails**, Cuevas las Perlas (CUC$8, three hours, 3km) is superior, highlighted by dense forest and **Pearl Cave**, a multigallery cave system of which 300m is accessible. Much of the Del Bosque al Mar 'hike' (CUC$6, 1½ hours, 1.4km) is on hot tarmac.

CUBA

Its saving grace is the terrific shoreline cenote filled with tropical fish.

The peninsula has two large areas full of **dive sites** with incredible concentrations of fish. The long-established sites are around María la Gorda and number over 30, including El Valle de Coral Negro, a 100m-long black-coral wall, and El Salón de María, a 20m-deep cave with feather stars and Technicolor corals. The second concentration, around Punta El Cajón beyond Cabo de San Antonio, remains almost totally unknown to divers, as the diving center only opened here in 2008.

The **Puertosol International Dive Center** ( ☎ 77-81-31; per dive CUC$35, equipment CUC$7.50; ☼ courses 9am & 3pm) at Hotel María la Gorda offers certification and introductory courses and night dives. Snorkelers can ride along for CUC$12.

The **Cabo de San Antonio Dive Center** ( ☎ 75-01-18) opened in 2008 and had not published price information at the time of research. It's located by the Cabo de San Antonio Marina, 3km beyond the hotel Villa Cabo de San Antonio.

### Sleeping & Eating

Accommodation on the peninsula is limited to one of two state-run beach resorts on the far side of the national park. Both are above average and are a world away from the package-tourist scene.

**Hotel María la Gorda** ( ☎ 77-81-31, 77-30-72; co mmercial@mlagorda.co.cu; s/d/tr incl breakfast CUC$44/68/98, full board extra per person CUC$26; ☒ ) This long-established resort enjoys idyllic isolation on its own gorgeous palm-fringed bay. The accommodations are divided up into uninspiring two-story blocks on the beach, or far better wooden cabins scattered among the woods behind the main hotel. Go for these, as they're newer, less crowded together and full of charm, even if they aren't right on the beach. Most people come here for the excellent diving, although it's a great place for nondivers too with a water-sports center and an excellent beach. Isolated as you are out here, you're better off not taking the full-board option as the buffet is pretty mediocre, and there's a better *á la carte* restaurant next to reception with tasty pizzas and other meals. Credit cards are accepted here and the diving is of fantastic quality.

**Villa Cabo de San Antonio** ( ☎ 75-76-55, 75-76-54; www.gaviota-grupo.com; s/d incl breakfast CUC$56/76, s/d half board CUC$64/92; ☒ ) This relatively new property is the best option on the peninsula. With just 14 spacious, beautifully designed, dark-wood rooms moments from a stunning white beach, this really is about as isolated as it's possible to get on mainland Cuba, a good 1½ hours' drive beyond María La Gorda. There's a decent restaurant (where absurdly formal waiting prevails – check out the tongs used to serve packets of butter!) and a couple of kilometers up the road there is a new marina, a dive center and a second restaurant. Watch the mosquitoes.

### Getting There & Around

There is a daily bus service in both directions connecting Havana with María La Gorda. The Transgaviota bus (CUC$60/100 one way/return, five hours) collects travelers from hotels in Havana according to demand (call the main hotel number to book a seat), leaving at 8am. The bus then returns to Havana at 2pm from the resort. There is at present no public transport to Cabo de San Antonio. Any car can make the journey easily, although drivers should be aware that the road deteriorates to a dirt track halfway between the Estación Ecológica and the hotel. There is a gas station at the Marina Cabo de San Antonio.

# CENTRAL CUBA

What central Cuba lacks in dramatic scenery it makes up for with a host of gorgeous colonial towns, including the single most-visited place on the island, the utterly lovely Trinidad. While the beauty of Trinidad remains incontestable, there's also a good choice of far less visited gems in central Cuba such as cultural Santa Clara and gorgeous backwater Remedios.

Of course central Cuba is also home to the mother lode of Cuba's tourist industry, the megaresort town of Varadero, which, while not covered in this book, is still where approximately half the tourists arriving in Cuba are heading. There are excellent stretches of beaches across the north coast, as well as some good pockets in the south. You'll also find good hiking in Topes de Collantes and important historic monuments including Che Guevara's solemn last resting place in Santa Clara. So central Cuba shouldn't just be seen as a region to get through on the way to Oriente –

stop off as much as you can and you'll be amply rewarded.

By car or bicycle, you have the choice of the Autopista, a multilane highway that makes for fast driving, or the Carretera Central. While the latter is certainly more scenic, the driving can be laborious as you dodge horse carts, goats and tractors. From Havana there are daily **Víazul** (www.viazul.cu) buses to Trinidad, Santiago de Cuba (stopping in Santa Clara) and Remedios. There's also a service between Trinidad and Santiago de Cuba.

## SANTA CLARA
pop 210,700 / ☎ 42

Wonderful Santa Clara is synonymous with an Argentinean doctor-turned-revolutionary who never spent much time here. 'El Che' made this his adopted home due to the town being the site of his most famous military victory. While he died in Bolivia at the hands of the CIA in 1967 and was cremated, his remains were returned to Cuba and buried here in 1997. As a result Santa Clara is official home to the extraordinary Che cult, although those coming here for the city's revolutionary history alone might leave disappointed. Santa Clara is instead much better enjoyed as a progressive, friendly city with a large student population and a lively cultural scene.

### Information
**Banco Financiero Internacional** ( ☎ 20-74-50; Cuba No 6 & Rafael Trista)

**Bandec** ( ☎ 21-81-15; Rafael Tristá & Cuba; ☒ 8am-2pm Mon-Fri, 8-11am Sat) Banking services.

**Cadeca** ( ☎ 20-56-90; Rafael Tristá & Cuba on Parque Vidal; ☒ 8:30am-6pm Mon-Sat, 8:30am-12:30pm Sun) For cash advances and cashing traveler's checks.

**DHL** ( ☎ 21-49-69; Cuba No 7 btwn Rafael Tristá & Eduardo Machado; ☒ 8:30am-4pm Mon-Fri, 8am-2pm Sat, 8am-noon Sun)

**Dino's Pizza** (Marta Abreu No 10; per hr CUC$5; ☒ 9am-10:30pm Mon-Fri, 9:30am-10:30pm Sat & Sun) This place has a couple of terminals with sketchy internet access.

**Etecsa Telepunto** (Marta Abreu No 55 btwn Máximo Gómez & Villuendas; per hr CUC$6; ☒ 8:30am-7:30pm) The most reliable internet access in town.

**Post office** (Colón No 10; ☒ 8am-6pm Mon-Sat, 8am-noon Sun)

### Sights
The **Monumentos a Ernesto Che Guevara** and **Tren Blindado** are within walking distance of the

Parque Vidal if you have good legs; otherwise catch a taxi or horse carriage.

### MONUMENTO ERNESTO CHE GUEVARA
Santa Clara's premier site is a semireligious monument, mausoleum and museum in honor of Ernesto 'Che' Guevara. The **complex** (Av de los Desfiles; admission free; ☒ 9am-5:30pm Tue-Sat, 9am-5pm Sun) is just outside the town center and can be seen for miles around with its tall Che statue. The statue was erected in 1987 to mark the 20th anniversary of Guevara's murder in Bolivia, and the mausoleum below contains 38 stone-carved niches dedicated to the guerillas killed in that failed revolutionary attempt. In 1997 the remains of 17 of them, including Guevara, were recovered from a secret mass grave in Bolivia and reburied here. Fidel Castro lit the eternal flame on October 17, 1997. The adjacent museum contains a large number of Che photographs – the great poser playing golf and eating what appears to be a hamburger are two of the less expected shots. Other ephemera include guns, letters, medical equipment and a rare late picture of Che shorn and looking uncannily like Brando in *The Godfather*.

### MONUMENTO A LA TOMA DEL TREN BLINDADO
This rather eccentric train wreck (literally) is a reconstruction of Che's greatest military victory, when he led 18 men into a ridiculously brave ambush of a 22-car armored train containing 408 heavily armed Batista troops. Amazingly, this battle on December 29, 1958, only lasted 90 minutes. The **museum** (admission CUC$1; ☒ 9am-5:30pm Mon-Sat), east on Independencia just over the Río Cubanicay, is contained within the very boxcars Che ambushed. Events are painstakingly documented, and it's a great spot simply to see how well everything has been reconstructed.

### PARQUE VIDAL & AROUND
Parque Vidal is the charming central Plaza of Santa Clara, around which the city is clustered. Any weekend evening you'll find live music here, whether impromptu or planned, small scale or large.

Buildings of note include the 1885 **Teatro La Caridad** (Máximo Gómez; performances CUC$2), in the northwest corner of Parque Vidal, with frescoes by Camilo Zalaya. The **Museo de Artes Decorativas** ( ☎ 20-53-68; Parque Vidal No 27; admission

CUC$2; 9am-6pm Mon, Wed & Thu, 1-10pm Fri & Sat, 6-10pm Sun), just east of Teatro La Caridad, is an 18th-century building packed with period furniture and treasures. The inner patio is a treat.

West of the park is the **Casa de la Ciudad** ( 20-55-93; Independencia & JB Zayas; admission CUC$1; 8am-noon Mon, 8am-noon & 1-5pm Tue-Sun), showing the history of Santa Clara, hosting contemporary art exhibitions and functioning as a general meeting place for the city's intellectuals. Check here for nighttime cultural activities.

A glimpse inside the town's **Cigar Factory** ( 20-22-11; Calle Maceo 181 btwn Julio Jover & Berenguer; admission CUC$3; 9-11am & 1-5pm Mon-Sat) is a fascinating experience, not least because it's relatively unvisited by tourists and as authentic a Cuban experience as can be had. Annoyingly you can't buy tickets there, but have to buy them from the **Havanatur office** ( 20-40-01; Maximo Gomez 9B) near Independencia.

## Sleeping
### CASAS PARTICULARES
**Vivian y José Rivero** ( 20-37-81; Maceo No 64 btwn Martí & Independencia; r CUC$20; ) Two spacious, well-appointed rooms both with private bathroom in a pleasant colonial house with a large terrace and courtyard. Granny's love of loud TV somewhat detracts from the colonial vibe, but otherwise this is a great place.

**El Castillito** ( 29-26-71; Céspedes No 65A btwn Maceo & Pedro Estévez; r CUC$20; ) Run by an extremely friendly couple, El Castillito has just one very comfortable room with a double bed, safe, well-stocked fridge, TV and a private roof terrace moments from Parque Vidal. Some English is spoken and meals are offered.

**ourpick Hostal Florida Center** ( 20-81-61; Maestra Nicolasa Este No 56 btwn Colón & Maceo; r CUC$20-25; ) One of the most lovely places to stay in Cuba, this casa-cum-paladar has two beautiful guest rooms stuffed full of Art Deco furnishings. Each enjoys a private bathroom, fridge, TV and access to the gorgeous verdant courtyard, also home to an aviary, a speedy tortoise and the world's cutest chow-chow. Superb meals are on offer as well, and the knowledgeable, warm-hearted, English- and French-speaking owner, Ángel, is keen to help.

**Héctor Martínez** ( 21-74-63; Rolando Pardo No 8 btwn Maceo & Parque Vidal; r CUC$20-25; ) Charming Héctor offers two lovely rooms in his large colonial house just off the main square. Both have private facilities and share access to an attractive courtyard.

**Hostal Casa Mercy** ( 21-69-41; Eduardo Machado No 4 btwn Cuba & Colón; r CUC$20-25) Two super-clean rooms with private bathrooms, fridges and shared access to a large airy terrace are available at this central location. A washing service and guarded parking are also offered by the kindly, multilingual hosts.

**Olga Rivera Gómez** ( 21-17-11; zaidabarreto2006@ yahoo.es; Evangelista Yanes No 20 btwn Máximo Gómez & Carolina Rodríguez; r CUC$25; ) Friendly Olga has two lovely rooms in a big colonial house on a quiet square a five-minute walk from the center. Ask for the bright room overlooking the church, which enjoys both views and light. Each room has private bathroom, fridge and access to a huge roof terrace.

**Zaida Barreto García** ( 29-48-44; zaidabarreto2006@ yahoo.es; Berenguer No 11 btwn Máximo Gómez & Carolina Rodríguez; r CUC$25; ) Olga's sister has two similar rooms in a connecting house backing onto Olga's, making it possible for groups of eight or so to share the two houses.

### HOTELS
**Hotel Santa Clara Libre** ( 20-75-48; fax 68-63-67; Parque Vidal No 6; s/d incl breakfast CUC$22/29; ) There's no real reason to stay in this deeply mediocre hotel when Santa Clara has some of the friendliest and most charming casas in the country on offer, but at least it's a cheap option and the staff are friendly. The rooms are small and many suffer from damp, but there are good views from the 11th-floor bar. The hotel facade is bullet-pocked from one of the revolution's final battles.

## Eating & Drinking
There's a busy stretch of bars and cafés on the pedestrian strip of Independencia, just north of Parque Vidal. While they're all pretty similar, the most popular, with al fresco tables and a good atmosphere, are La Cubana and Europa.

**El Castillo** (9 de Abril No 9 btwn Cuba & Villuendas; noon-11pm) Unlike almost every state-run peso canteen in Cuba, this is a little gem. Friendly staff serve up large, good quality portions of pork, chicken, congrí and salad for peanuts at an impressive marble bar. Look no further to make local friends and hear people discuss the news and sports.

**Dino's Pizza** (Marta Abreu No 10; pizzas CUC$3-7; 9am-10:30pm Mon-Fri, 9:30am-10:30pm Sat & Sun) A carbon copy of the many Dino's around Cuba, this version remains a decent place for pizza, and there's internet access to boot (CUC$5 per hour).

**La Concha** ( ☎ 21-81-24; cnr Carretera Central & Danilito; mains CUC$4-10; ☻ 11am-11pm) While La Concha's premises are a rather sterile arrangement of tables in a glass-fronted unit (on the main road out of the center towards the Che Memorial), it's often hard to get a table simply because the pizza here is so prized by locals. Seafood specialties and meaty mains are also on offer.

**El Sabor Latino** ( ☎ 40-65-39; Esquerra No 157 btwn Julio Jover & Berenguer; set meal CUC$12-15; ☻ noon-midnight) This relaxed paladar offers a huge range of Creole cooking. It's not cheap, although it can be if you go for the soups or salads rather than the voluminous all-inclusive meal deals, which, while slightly overpriced, are delicious.

## Entertainment

**Club Mejunje** (Marta Abreu No 107; ☻ 4pm-1am Tue-Sun) If you're here on Saturday night, come along to Cuba's only openly gay club, which is remarkably straight-friendly and attracts everyone from local stars of drag to young gangs of toughs. Set in the ruins of an old building, this is the heart of the city's alternative culture. There's usually dancing or theater every other night of the week, and there's nowhere else in Cuba quite like it.

**El Bar Club Boulevard** ( ☎ 21-62-36; Independencia No 2 btwn Maceo & Pedro Estévez; admission CUC$2; ☻ 10pm-2am Tue-Sun) A fun cocktail lounge with comedy acts and live music.

Villa Clara ('La Villa,' aka Las Naranjas) are the arch rivals of Havana's Industriales; catch a baseball game at Estadio Sandino, east of the center via Av 9 de Abril.

## Shopping

Stroll 'El Bulevar,' Independencia, between Maceo and Zayas for good secondhand clothes and consignment shops.

**La Veguita** ( ☎ 20-89-52; Calle Maceo No 176A btwn Julio Jover & Berenguer; ☻ 9am-6pm Mon-Sat) This excellent specialist shop opposite the cigar factory unsurprisingly sells cigars, and boasts an excellent humidor and smoking room, as well as offering coffee and a range of rums to take home. There's a friendly bar-café at the back where you'll get the best coffee in town.

**Fondo Cubano de Bienes Culturales** (Luis Estévez Norte No 9 btwn Parque Vidal & Independencia) Sells Cuban handicrafts.

**ARTex** ( ☎ 21-43-97; Colón No 16 btwn Machado & Rafael Tristá; ☻ 9am-5pm Mon-Sat, 9am-noon Sun) Cuba's reliable musical and clothing outlet has CDs, souvenirs and a range of T-shirts and other gifts. There's a second, smaller outlet on the south side of Parque Vidal.

## Getting There & Away

The **Nacionales Bus Station** ( ☎ 22-25-23) is 2.5km out on the Carretera Central toward Matanzas, 500m north of the Che monument. Tickets for Víazul are sold in the Víazul office on your right in the main hall. For daily departures see below.

The **intermunicipal bus station** (Carretera Central), just west of the center via Marta Abreu, has three daily buses to Remedios (CUC$1.45, approximately one hour, 6:40am, 9:05am and 2:35pm,).

The **train station** ( ☎ 20-28-95) is straight up Luis Estévez from Parque Vidal on the north side of town. The **ticket office** (Luis Estévez Norte No 323) is across the park from the station. In theory, trains serve the destinations shown in the boxed text, p168.

## Getting Around

Local transportation is mostly by *coche* (horse cart), with an important route along Marta Abreu toward the bus stations and Che monument (CUP1). From the train station to the center, catch the 'Materno' (CUP2).

**SERVICES FROM SANTA CLARA NACIONALES BUS STATION**

| Destination | One-way fare (CUC$) | Distance (km) | Duration (hr) | Schedule |
| --- | --- | --- | --- | --- |
| Havana | 18 | 276 | 4 | 8am, 5:30pm, 3:10am |
| Santiago de Cuba | 33 | 590 | 12 | 7:30pm, 7:25am, 1:15pm, 6:45pm, 12:55am, 1:45am |
| Trinidad | 8 | 88 | 3½ | 11:30am |

**CUBA**

**SERVICES FROM SANTA CLARA TRAIN STATION**

| Destination | One-way fare (CUC$) | Distance (km) | Duration (hr) | Schedule |
| --- | --- | --- | --- | --- |
| Havana | 10 | 276 | 6 | 9:30am daily |
| Santiago de Cuba | 20 (slow train) 41 (fast train) | 590 | 8-10 | 8:24am (slow train) alternate days, midnight (fast train), alternate days |

Scooters are rented from **Cubatur** ( ☎ 422-20-85-34; Marta Abreu No 10; ✆ 9am-8pm) for CUC$18 per day.

Taxis in front of the national bus station and around Parque Vidal charge CUC$8 to Remedios, CUC$50/80 one way/round trip to Cayo Santa María and CUC$45 to Havana, or call **Cubataxi** ( ☎ 20-25-80).

# REMEDIOS
pop 46,500 / ☎ 42

Dreamy Remedios, less than an hour east of Santa Clara, is a wonderful place to escape the tourists and relax into everyday Cuban life in a *jintero*(tout)-free, tranquil town set around a brightly painted square full of traditional colonial houses. Come here to escape the megaresorts of the coast and the busy towns more emblazoned on the bus tour trail – you'll find some of the island's most beautiful and welcoming casas and will still enjoy easy access to the beaches at Cayo Santa María if you have your own car. For many, the real reason to come here is to see the tranquility shattered every December 24 for **Las Parrandas**, a night of mind-blowing fireworks, street dancing and general chaos as the tiny town descends into one of Cuba's most raucous street parties.

## Sights & Activities

The town is built around the 18th-century **Parroquia de San Juan Bautista de Remedios** (Camilo Cienfuegos No 20 on Parque Martí; ✆ 9-11am Mon-Sat), a rather faded beauty famous for its gilded altar. The pregnant Inmaculada Concepción (with charming pearl teardrops) is said to be unique in Cuba. It's not always possible to visit, but ask around and someone will usually be able to let you in. Which of the church's two chapels you live nearest to determines your affiliation as the town splits into two groups for its ultimate spectacle, the Las Parrandas fireworks and street party.

Visiting the **Museo de las Parrandas Remedianas** (Máximo Gómez No 71; admission CUC$1; ✆ 9am-6pm Mon-

Sat, 9am-noon Sun), two blocks off Parque Martí, is the next best thing to partying here on December 24. It has a photo gallery, scale models of floats and graphic depictions of how the fireworks are made. Another room is jammed with the feathers, headdresses and tassels from the previous year.

You can escape to **Cayo Santa María**, 65km from Remedios, for a day on central Cuba's most brilliant beach. You'll have to pay for a day pass to one of the very smart resorts (CUC$25 to CUC$50 per person including unlimited food and drink). The prettiest stretches are alongside Villa las Brujas and at the end of the Meliá resorts' access road. The cay is accessed via the *pedreplén* (CUC$2 toll; sadly no Cubans allowed).

## Sleeping
### CASAS PARTICULARES

**Hostal El Patio** ( ☎ 39-52-20; aile@uclv.edu.cu; José A Peña No 72 btwn Hermanos García & A Romero; r CUC$20-25; ✖ ) One very pleasant room is on offer at the back of this centrally located colonial house. Private bathroom and fridge are included and meals are available.

**our pick** **La Paloma** ( ☎ 39-54-90; Balmaseda No 4 btwn Máximo Gómez & Capablanca; r CUC$20-25; ✖ ) Right on the main square, this excellent casa oozes charm with two large rooms, both with big marble bathrooms, and two attentive and friendly young hosts. If offers a shared communal terrace and antiques aplenty – a great choice for atmosphere and location.

**La Casona Cueto** ( ☎ 39-53-50; amarelys@capiro.vcl.sld.cu; Alejandro del Río No 72; r CUC$20-25; ✖ ) Few places feel as properly colonial as this large family home just off the main square. It offers three rooms, all with good private bathrooms, although the upstairs room has no air-con. It has a fantastic courtyard and a gorgeous roof terrace, and the house is full of pets.

**Villa Colonial** ( ☎ 39-62-74; www.villacolonial.de.ki; Maceo No 43 btwn General Carrillo & Fe del Valle; r CUC$20-25; ✖ ) Staying here effectively means you have your own four-room house, complete with antiques, huge high ceiling and a friendly family next door on hand to help. English is spoken, and dinners are available. Stay here for privacy, atmosphere and style.

**Hostal La Estancia** ( ☎ 39-55-82; amarelys@capiro.vcl .sld.cu; Cienfuegos No 34 btwn Brigadier González & Maceo; r CUC$25-30; ✷ ) This is one of Cuba's finest casas, a gorgeous rambling house stuffed full of antiques, built around a large shady courtyard containing a pool. The two rooms both have large private bathrooms and pretty tilled floors. Meals available.

### HOTELS

**Hotel Mascotte** ( ☎ 39-51-45; Parque Martí; r incl breakfast CUC$49; ✷ ) Remedios only has one hotel, but it's a charmer and not a bad alternative to a casa. All 10 rooms have TV, phone and rather shabby bathrooms, but it's a fantastic *grande dame* of a building, dating from 1869 and overlooking the main square. If you have the choice rooms 1 to 5 all have balconies overlooking the square, of which 1 and 5 are the most spacious. Room prices go up to CUC$80 for Las Parrandas.

### Eating & Drinking

As usual the best food is available in casas particulares, although there are a couple of other options.

**Driver's Bar** (José Peña No 65; mains CUP10-15; ☿ noon-2:45pm & 6-9:45pm) An atmospheric peso option, this is a local favorite comprising a busy bar and a popular restaurant where steaks, fried chicken and pork are served up for next to nothing.

**Las Arcadas** ( ☎ 39-51-45; Parque Martí; mains CUC$5-10) The Hotel Mascotte restaurant serves up very standard Cuban dishes and enjoys the smartest setting in town.

**El Louvre** (Máximo Gómez No 122; ☿ 8am-10pm) For morning coffee and evening drinks head here. This place has been serving refreshments since 1866 from a long stone bar, opposite the church.

### Getting There & Away

The bus station marks the beginning of the old town, a short distance after the entrance to town on the first major road left. There are three daily services to Santa Clara (CUC$1.45, one hour) at 5am, 7:10am and 4:30pm and Havana (CUC$8, 6½ hours,

7:15pm daily and an extra service at 7pm on alternate days). For services to the rest of the country, change in Santa Clara.

## TRINIDAD

### pop 65,000 / ☎ 41

Cuba's worst kept secret, Trinidad is almost unbearably gorgeous with its large pastel-painted colonial mansions, horse-drawn carriages rattling down cobbled streets and the distant mountains providing a suitably dramatic setting. Sadly the gem that originally attracted backpackers in the mid-'90s has been overwhelmed by bus tours, day-trippers and the inevitable *jinteros* (touts) who now dominate the town, to the point that you should look elsewhere for your authentic small-town Cuban experience. (For more on *jinteros*, see p184)

However, to miss out would be a shame – there's a bevy of superb, atmospheric casas here, plus a great beach at nearby Playa Ancón and the lush hills of the Topes de Collantes and Valle de los Ingenios (the latter is a Unesco World Heritage site, along with Trinidad's old town). So disregard the touts and the fact that most of the year there are just as many foreigners as locals here, and prepare to love Trinidad in spite of it all.

### Information

#### INTERNET ACCESS

**Cafe Internet Las Begonias** (Antonio Maceo No 473; per hr CUC$6; ☿ 7:30am-1am) Good place to meet other travelers.

**Etecsa** ( ☎ 99-41-29; General Lino Pérez No 274; per hr CUC$6; ☿ 8:30am-7:30pm) On Parque Céspedes.

#### MEDICAL SERVICES

**Servimed Clínica Internacional Cubanacán** ( ☎ 99-62-40; General Lino Pérez No 103; ☿ 24hr) Consultations before/after 4pm CUC$25/30. Has an on-site pharmacy.

#### MONEY

**Banco de Crédito y Comercio** ( ☎ 99-24-05; José Martí No 264)

**Banco Financiero Internacional** ( ☎ 99-61-07; cnr Camilo Cienfuegos & José Martí; ☿ 8am-3pm Mon-Fri) Cash advances; ridiculously long lines.

**Cadeca** ( ☎ 99-62-63; Martí No 164 btwn Lino Pérez & Camilo Cienfuegos)

**CUBA**

**POST**

**Post office** (Antonio Maceo No 420 btwn Colón & Zerquera)

**TRAVEL AGENCIES**

**Cubanacán** ( ☎ 99-61-42; www.cubanacan.cu; cnr José Martí & Zerquera)

**Cubatur** ( ☎ 99-63-14; www.cubatur.cu; cnr Calle Maceo & Bolívar)

**Havanatur** ( ☎ 99-61-83; www.havanatur.com; Lino Pérez No 336, btwn Maceo & Codania)

## Sights & Activities

Trinidad has two main centers – the Plaza Mayor, home to many of the bigger tourist sites, and the far more 'real' Parque Céspedes, a short walk away down José Martí. Head to the latter and beyond if you want to get a feeling for the 'real' Trinidad. In general the town has no unmissable sites – coming here is really about drinking the whole place in – but there are plenty of moderately interesting things to do for those so inclined. Most of the more substantial things to see and do are outside the town.

Near Plaza Mayor is the impressive **Museo Histórico Municipal** (Casa Cantero; ☎ 99-44-60; Simón Bolívar No 423; admission CUC$2; 🕙 9am-5pm Sat-Thu), the town's single most impressive museum, where the ill-gotten wealth of slave trader Justo Cantero is displayed in the stylish, neoclassical rooms. The view from the top of the tower alone is worth the admission price.

Near to the church is the **Museo Romántico** ( ☎ 99-43-63; Echerri No 52; admission CUC$2; 🕙 9am-5pm Tue-Sat, 9am-1pm Sun) in the Palacio Brunet, built between 1740 and 1808. The mansion-turned-museum collects 19th-century furnishings, china and such. As with most old houses, the kitchen and bathroom are the most interesting rooms.

Housed in the former San Francisco de Asís convent, the photogenic **Museo Nacional de la Lucha Contra Bandidos** ( ☎ 99-41-21; Echerri No 59; admission CUC$1; 🕙 9am-5pm Tue-Sat, 9am-1pm Sun) is distinguished by its yellow campanile, the only part of the original building remaining. The collection relates to the struggle against counter-revolutionary bands in the Sierra del Escambray (1906–65). Climb the tower for good views.

For a bird's-eye view of Trinidad, walk up Simón Bolívar, between the Iglesia Parroquial and the Museo Romántico, to the ruined 18th-century **Ermita de Nuestra**

**Señora de la Candelaria de la Popa**. From here, it's a 30-minute uphill hike to 180m-high **Cerro de la Vigía**, which delivers broad vistas of Trinidad, Playa Ancón and beyond.

**Playa Ancón**, 12km south of Trinidad, is an inviting ribbon of white beach lapped by tranquil blue waters – perfect for a day cycling trip. There's an excellent reef for snorkeling and scuba diving offshore. The seven-hour **snorkeling tour** (per adult/child incl lunch & open bar CUC$40/30) to Cayo Blanco, departing at 9am, gets rave reviews; black coral and bountiful marine life are highlights. All the Trinidad agencies arrange these trips, or you can go to **Cubanacán Náutica Trinidad** ( ☎ 99-47-54), a few hundred meters north of Hotel Ancón, which also offers sailboat charters.

Dozens of crumbling 19th-century *ingenios* (sugar mills) dot **Valle de los Ingenios**. The royal palms, waving cane and rolling hills are timelessly beautiful, especially seen from the saddle (see below). The valley's main sight is the 1750 **Manaca Iznaga** (admission CUC$1), 16km east of Trinidad, a 44m-high tower with exquisite 360-degree views. The tourist train stops here; it's an hour's walk from the local train station at Meyer (see p172).

**Topes de Collantes**, the rugged 90km-long Sierra del Escambray mountain range some 20km northwest of Trinidad, has some of Cuba's best unguided hiking. The **Carpeta Central information office** ( ☎ 99-02-31; 🕙 8am-5pm) sells a topographical map of the area (CUC$2.50), and offers camp sites (CUC$10) and guides. The most popular hike is the 2.5km, 2½-hour round-trip trek to the **Salto del Caburní** (per person CUC$6.50), a 62m waterfall cascading into cool swimming holes. It's difficult to get here without a car.

## Tours

Cubatur and Cubanacán (left) sell the same excursions, including the popular Valle de los Ingenios **sugar train tour** (adult/child CUC$10/5), which starts at 9:30am), **horseback riding** tours to the Cascada El Cubano (CUC$18 including transportation, park entrance fee, lunch and guide) and **day hikes** (adult/child CUC$29/20) to Topes de Collantes.

Freelance guides lead **horseback riding** (per person 3/6hr CUC$7/15) trips to the Valle de los Ingenios or Cascada El Cubano (add a CUC$6.50 park entry fee for the latter). A tour to the Guanajara National Park and its waterfall is also on offer (CUC$55 per person).

# Sleeping

## CASAS PARTICULARES

**Carmelina de la Paz** ( ☎ 99-32-94; Piro Guinart No 239 btwn Suyama & Independencia; r CUC$15-20) Wow! This huge old house really is something – look no further for somewhere memorable to stay. Two vast bedrooms both have private bathrooms, and the one at the front of the house has sole access to an equally large terrace. High ceilings, good food and a warm welcome make this a great place to bed down.

**Yolanda** ( ☎ 99-63-81; yolimar56@yahoo.com; Piro Guinart No 227 btwn Suyama & Independencia; r CUC$15-20; ✴ ) Yolanda has four excellent rooms on offer, each with private facilities and a fridge. Go for the upstairs room, which has both air-con and a terrace with wonderful views. The other rooms surround a leafy colonial courtyard and Baby Jesus sleeps on the sitting room sofa.

**Orlando Rodríguez Ramon** ( ☎ 99-21-10; Antonio Guiteras No 229 btwn Calzada & País; s CUC$15-20, d CUC$20-25; ✴ ) Offers a private upstairs apartment with a double and single bed, large terrace and living room with fridge. Excellent for privacy although the bathroom is a bit makeshift. Some English is spoken.

**Familia Gil Lemes** ( ☎ 99-31-42; carlosgl3142@yahoo .es; José Martí No 263 btwn Rosario & Colón; s CUC$15-20, d CUC$20-25; ✴ ) Another fantastic colonial place. The Gil Lemes family rents one room with its own bathroom down the corridor. There's also a garage where cars can be parked safely.

**Aracelys Reboso** ( ☎ 99-35-97; bernatdad@yahoo.com; Lino Perez No 207 btwn Frank País & Calzada; r CUC$20-25; ✴ ) Aracelys, a retired English teacher, speaks very good English and her two excellent rooms, both with private bathroom, share a sitting room and two gorgeous terraces. Meals are available, and her son Francisco Peterssen also rents No 179 (CUC$15 to CUC$20), a comfortable, quiet room with large bathroom leading to a sunny patio.

**Gustavo Cañedo** ( ☎ 99-66-16; gustavocanedo13@ yahoo.es; Piro Guinart No 216 btwn Maceo & Izquierdo; r CUC$20-30) Another huge house with high ceilings and tiled floors. Two communicating rooms share a bathroom.

**Casa Muñoz** ( ☎ 99-36-73; http://casa.trinidadphoto .com; José Martí No 401 btwn Olvido & Claro; r CUC$25-30; ✴ ) Being refurbished at the time of research, this charming house will soon be even better. There are two rooms both with private bathrooms. The house is a colonial stunner run by a photographer and his wife.

**Casa Arandia** ( ☎ 99-66-13; eloely2006@htdad.ssp.sld .cu; Maceo No 438 btwn Colón & Zerquera; r CUC$25-30; ✴ ) Another great place to stay is this friendly casa, which offers two rooms (one of which was about to be redone at last pass) with private bathrooms and fridges. Go for the upstairs room, though, which is self-contained and has access to a private roof terrace. Meals available.

## HOTELS

**Casa de la Amistad** ( ☎ 99-38-24; Zerquera btwn Martí & País; r CUC$25; ✴ ) This tiny hotel has just six humble but comfortable rooms, all with private bathroom. Favored by fellow travelers of the Cuban government, the place is nonetheless open to all, although it's best to call ahead.

**Iberostar Grand Hotel Trinidad** ( ☎ 99-60-70; www .iberostar.com; Martí No 262; s/d CUC$125/150; ✴ ☐ ) Trinidad's star hotel does not disappoint and is well worth the splurge if you fancy some pampering. The beautiful and unobtrusively designed five-star property is in the heart of town and manages to pull off both a traditional design and thoroughly modern touches, from a gorgeous lobby centered on a fountain to free internet access and a fantastic restaurant and cocktail bar. The 40 rooms are very smart and spacious, with large bathrooms and comfortable fittings.

# Eating

The stretch of Martí around Lino Pérez and Camilo Cienfuegos is crowded with peso stalls, selling pizza, *cajitas* (takeout meals that come in small boxes) and snacks.

**Cremería Las Begonias** ( ☎ 99-64-04; Antonio Maceo No 473; burgers CUC$3-4; ⏰ 7:30am-1am) Hide out in the back patio with a milkshake, ice cream or coffee. Across the street there's Cafeteria Las Begonias, another branch of this popular café, which has a Cubatur office and internet access, as well as snack food.

**Trinidad Colonial** ( ☎ 99-64-73; Antonio Maceo No 402; mains CUC$4-20; ⏰ 11:30am-10pm) The Trinidad Colonial is inside a suitably grand historic villa with tables outside as well as in. Avoid it at lunch times when it's the preferred realm of the tour-bus crowd, but come in the evening when the fish and seafood menu is best enjoyed. Try the shrimp in chili sauce.

**Mesón del Regidor** ( ☎ 99-64-56; Simón Bolívar No 424; mains CUC$5-12; ⏰ 10am-10pm) Just down from the Plaza Mayor, this popular but firmly tourist-

CUBA

oriented eatery does a mean line in grilled meats, but gets crowded at lunch with tour groups. There's live music here as well, which can sometimes be excellent.

**Paladar Sol y Son** (Simón Bolívar No 283 btwn Frank País & José Martí; mains CUC$6-10; ⏰ noon-3pm & 7-10pm) This atmospheric 1830s mansion with tables sprinkled throughout the back garden is definitely the place to head for romance. There's friendly service and the food is largely excellent – try the superb side of pork and clean your palate with a killer daiquiri.

**Paladar Estela** (☎ 99-43-29; Simón Bolívar No 557; meals CUC$8-10; ⏰ 7-10pm Mon-Fri) Trinidad's second-choice paladar (after Paladar Sol y Son) is also good, serving up a straightforward menu of Cuban dishes based around chicken, pork and *congrí* in a pleasant back garden a short distance from the Plaza Mayor. Set meals include side dishes and dessert.

## Entertainment

**Casa de la Música** (☎ 99-34-14; admission free; ⏰ 4pm-midnight) This enormous place is spread over a steep set of outdoor steps and is the busiest place in town, with a packed after-dinner crowd for the main show at 10pm nightly. As well as the main performance and the several bars, there are sometimes salsa concerts in the rear courtyard (admission CUC$2).

**Casa de la Trova** (☎ 99-64-45; Echerri No 29; admission CUC$1; ⏰ 10pm-1am) Housed in a pretty old mansion with a smart colonial vibe, this place has a changing schedule of local live music – it can be pot luck, but is sometimes surprisingly good.

**Palenque de los Congos Reales** (cnr Echerri & J Menéndez; admission CUC$1; ⏰ 1:30pm-midnight Sun-Fri, 1:30pm-1am Sat) Offers energetic salsa and *son*, heavy on the Afro-Cuban beat with live shows nightly at 10pm.

**Las Ruinas del Teatro Brunet** (Antonio Maceo No 461 btwn Simón Bolívar & Zerquera; cover CUC$1) Hosts an athletic Afro-Cuban show at 10pm from Tuesday to Friday, and a Cuban folklore show from 10pm Saturday, in a crumbling colonial patio. The cover charge is added to the cost

of your drink. Check here for drumming and dance classes.

## Shopping

There's a decent **arts and crafts market** (Jesús Menéndez) in front of the Casa de la Trova. This is a good place for (pricey) shopping, especially for its elaborate lace designs, though do avoid the black coral and turtle-shell items.

You can buy locally produced artwork at the **Casa de la Cultura Julio Cueva Díaz** (Zerquera No 406). **Yami Martínez** (☎ 99-30-17; Maceo No 413 btwn Zerquera & Colón) creates funky sculptures that you can buy directly from her home studio.

Head to **Casa del Habano** (cnr Zerquera & Maceo) for all your rum and cigar needs. If it's CDs and musical instruments you're after, it's the **Casa de la Música**, up the stairway beside the Iglesia Parroquial.

## Getting There & Away

### BUS

The **bus station** (Piro Guinart No 224), accessed via Gustavo Izquierdo, has a left-luggage room. See below for services.

### CAR

The quickest route to Trinidad from Havana is via Santa Clara and Manicaragua, offering beautiful mountain scenery. The coastal route from Cienfuegos, though slower, is lined with little beaches and fishing villages. Both roads are decent. You can organize car hire at **Cubatur** (☎ 99-63-14; www.cubatur.cu; cnr Calle Maceo & Bolívar).

### TAXI

For trips to Havana (CUC$60) or Cienfuegos (CUC$40), **Cubataxi** (☎ 419-2214) can be contracted at the bus station.

### TRAIN

While there is a risibly small, pink **terminal** (☎ 99-42-23, 99-33-48) here, Trinidad's trains are strictly local and do not connect with the rest of the country's stellar network.

| SERVICES FROM TRINIDAD'S BUS STATION | | | | |
|---|---|---|---|---|
| Destination | One-way fare (CUC$) | Distance (km) | Duration (hr) | Schedule |
| Havana | 25 | 335 | 6 | 7:30am & 5pm |
| Santa Clara | 8 | 88 | 3 | 9am & 3:30pm |
| Santiago de Cuba | 33 | 581 | 11½ | 8am |

There's one train a day in each direction along a pretty branch line through the Valle de los Ingenios, departing Trinidad at 9:30am and stopping at Iznaga and Condado before terminating in Meyer, 19km north of Trinidad (CUC$10, 80 minutes). It returns to Trinidad from Meyer at 1:30pm, giving you a few hours to explore the valley. You can also hop on the return train at Condado or Iznaga. It arrives back in Trinidad at 2:50pm.

### Getting Around

You can rent bicycles (per day CUC$3) beside **Cubataxi** ( ☎ 99-22-14) at the bus station. There's also a regular bus between Trinidad and Playa Ancón that leaves from outside the Havantur office. A coco-taxi costs around CUC$4 to Playa Ancón.

**Transtur** ( ☎ 99-61-10; cnr Maceo & Zerquera) at Cubatur rents out scooters (per day/week CUC$20/126).

# EASTERN CUBA

You can't claim to have really seen Cuba without a visit to 'El Oriente', as the eastern half of the island is known. Here, things move more slowly (the motorway peters out somewhere around Ciego de Ávila, as if to make a point) and a more simple yet exotic way of life prevails. This is Cuba's Caribbean heart – dramatic, steamy and moving to its very own unpredictable rhythm.

At the end of the island, of course, cultural heavyweight and second city Santiago de Cuba is the center of its own world, providing relief from Havana's domination of everything else in the country. The region also includes the infamous Guantánamo Bay US Naval Base, as well as one of the country's most stunning drives – between Guantánamo and Baracoa, the charming town right on the eastern tip of the island, which is a great place to chill out off the beaten track.

### Getting There & Away

Santiago de Cuba's Aeropuerto Antonio Maceo receives a smattering of international flights, mainly from elsewhere in the Caribbean. Domestic flights connect Santiago to Havana. Baracoa also has an airport that connects it to Havana.

Train travel, though slow, is a possibility between Havana and Santiago de Cuba. However, most people either take the bus (12 hours) or drive the distance themselves, often stopping over in friendly Camagüey to break up the journey.

### Getting Around

Bus connections center on Santiago, and are limited, especially from Baracoa. The road network is fine, and it is possible to drive a loop from Santiago to Holguín via Baracoa, although the road is in bad repair for much of the journey beyond Baracoa. Despite that, it's easily doable in a normal car. The only local transportation up this way is by truck.

## SANTIAGO DE CUBA

pop 495,000 / ☎ 22

There's magic in the air of Santiago, Cuba's second city and the much needed counterweight to Havana in music, politics and culture. With its beguiling setting on the mouth of a large bay surrounded by mountains, its plethora of beautiful buildings and a brightly painted old town located on a precipitous hillside, it's unlike almost anywhere else in the country. The city looks firmly to its Caribbean neighbors in a way Havana never has done, and as a result there are far more pronounced Haitian, African and Hispanic influences to be felt here. Take your time to enjoy Santiago and you'll find it soon enchants you.

### History

Founded in 1514, Santiago de Cuba was the first Cuban capital (1515–1607). After the capital shifted to Havana and Santiago's gold reserves and indigenous labor started giving out, the city lost prominence; despite being the 'cradle of the revolution,' it still nurses an inferiority complex.

On July 26, 1953, Fidel Castro and his companions stole away from the Granjita Siboney farm 20km southeast of Santiago and unsuccessfully attacked the Moncada Barracks, an embarrassingly badly planned attack now talked up as a key part of Castro's revolutionary myth. At his trial here Castro made his famous 'History Will Absolve Me' speech, which became the basic platform of the Cuban Revolution.

### Information
#### EMERGENCY
**Police** ( ☎ 106; cnr Mariano Corona & Sánchez Hechevarría)

CUBA

## INTERNET ACCESS

**Etecsa** (per hr CUC$6; ☼ 8:30am-7:30pm) Heredia (cnr Heredia & Félix Peña); Tamayo Fleites (cnr Tamayo Fleites & Hartmann)

## MEDICAL SERVICES

**Clínica Internacional Cubanacán Servimed** ( ☎ 64-25-89; cnr Av Raúl Pujol & Calle 8, Vista Alegre; consultations CUC$30; ☼ 24hr) Some English-speaking staff, plus a dentist.

**Farmacia Cubanacán** ( ☎ 64-25-89; cnr Av Raúl Pujol & Calle 8; ☼ 24hr) Best pharmacy. Another is in the Meliá Santiago de Cuba, open from 8am to 6pm.

**Farmacia Las Américas** (Av Victoriano Garzón No 422; ☼ 24hr)

**Hospital Provincial Saturnino Lora** ( ☎ 64-56-51; Av de los Libertadores; ☼ 24hr)

## MONEY

**Banco de Crédito y Comercio** ( ☎ 62-80-06; Felix Peña No 614) ATM on Heredia.

**Banco Financiero Internacional** ( ☎ 62-20-73; Felix Peña No 565; ☼ 8am-4pm Mon-Fri)

**Cadeca** ( ☎ 68-61-76; Aguilera No 508; ☼ 8:30am-6pm Mon-Sat, 8:30am-noon Sun) Others are in the Meliá Santiago de Cuba and Hotel Las Américas.

## POST

**Post office** (Aguilera No 519)

## TRAVEL AGENCIES

**Cubatur** ( ☎ 62-31-24, 62-87-37; Av Garzón No 364 btwn Calle 3 & 4; ☼ 8am-8pm)

**Havanatur** ( ☎ 68-72-80; Calle 8 No 54 btwn Calle 1 & 3, Vista Alegre; ☼ 8am-5pm)

## Sights

### PARQUE CÉSPEDES & AROUND

The heart of Santiago is **Parque Céspedes**, a large square dominated by the five-nave **Catedral de Nuestra Señora de la Asunción**, situated on the south side of the park. Cuba's first cathedral was built here in the 1520s; the present cathedral with its coffered ceiling, dome and graceful archangel was completed in 1922.

The square is named for Carlos Manuel de Céspedes, the man who freed his slaves and declared Cuban independence in 1868; a bronze bust stands here in his honor. Some of Santiago's most impressive buildings ring this park, including the 1522 **Casa de Diego Velázquez** (Felix Peña No 602), the oldest house still standing in Cuba. This Andalusian-style showpiece now houses the **Museo de Ambiente Histórico Cubano** ( ☎ 65-26-52; admission CUC$2; ☼ 9am-1pm,

2-5pm Mon-Thu & Sat, 2-5pm Fri, 9am-9pm Sun), with its collection of period furnishings.

Two blocks downhill from the park is the **Balcón de Velázquez** (Bartolomé Masó & Mariano Corona; admission with/without camera CUC$1/free; ☼ 9am-7pm Tue-Sun), the site of an old Spanish fort with lovely harbor views. Three long blocks downhill on Bartolomé Masó is the **Fábrica de Tabacos César Escalante** ( ☎ 62-23-66; Av Jesús Menéndez No 703; admission CUC$5; ☼ 9-11am & 1-3pm), a working cigar factory open for visits.

Pio Rosado, the alley running alongside the Museo del Carnaval, leads up to the quite fabulous neoclassical building housing the **Museo Municipal Emilio Bacardí Moreau** ( ☎ 62-84-02; admission CUC$2; ☼ 9am-4:15pm). Founded in 1899 by famous rum distiller and first mayor of Santiago de Cuba, Emilio Bacardí y Moreau (1844–1922), this is one of Cuba's oldest functioning museums and features exhibits relating to the 19th-century independence struggles, as well as European and Cuban paintings.

Eight blocks northwest of Parque Céspedes is the important **Museo-Casa Natal de Antonio Maceo** ( ☎ 62-37-50; Los Maceos No 207; admission CUC$1; ☼ 9am-4:30pm Mon-Sat), where the independence war general was born on June 14, 1845. During the 1895 war he was second in command, after Máximo Gómez, and died fighting in western Cuba in 1896. This museum exhibits highlights of Maceo's life, including the tattered flag flown in battle.

### CUARTEL MONCADA (MONCADA BARRACKS)

The **Parque Histórico Abel Santamaría** (General Portuondo & Av de los Libertadores) is the home to the hospital that was occupied by revolutionary forces on July 26, 1953, during the attack on the adjacent Moncada Barracks.

The **Cuartel Moncada** (Moncada Barracks) is where more than 100 revolutionaries led by Fidel Castro attacked Batista's troops on July 26, 1953. At the time, this was Cuba's second-most-important military garrison. The revolutionaries had hoped the assault would spark a general uprising throughout Cuba, but things went awry and the armed struggle was put on hold for another 3½ years.

A major **museum** ( ☎ 62-01-57; admission CUC$2; ☼ 9:30am-5:30pm Mon-Sat, 9:30am-12:30pm Sun) can be visited through gate No 3 (on General Portuondo near Moncada), where the main attack took place. The outer walls here are still bullet-pocked. The museum outlines the history of Cuba, with heavy emphasis on the revolution. A scale model of Moncada illustrates the 1953 assault.

### CEMENTERIO SANTA IFIGENIA

A visit to the 1868 **Cementerio Santa Ifigenia** (☎ 63-27-23; Av Crombet; admission CUC$1; ☼ 7am-5pm), 2km north of the city center, is a stroll through history. Many of the giants of Cuban history are found among the 8000 tombs here, including Cuba's national hero, José Martí (1853–95). The Martí Mausoleum (1951) is flanked by the muses and there's a dramatic changing of the guard every half-hour. Buried here are those who died during the 1953 attack on the Moncada Barracks, and Carlos Manuel de Céspedes (1819–74), the father of Cuban independence.

### CASTILLO DE SAN PEDRO DEL MORRO

This dazzling excursion is a must on any trip to Santiago. A Unesco World Heritage site and the best preserved 17th-century Spanish military complex in the Caribbean, the **Castillo de San Pedro del Morro** (☎ 69-15-69; admission CUC$4, photos CUC$1; ☼ 8am-8pm) perches dramatically on a 60m-high promontory, 10km southwest of town via Carretera del Morro. Built between 1633 and 1693, El Morro guards the entrance to the Bay of Santiago and the views are extraordinary.

A taxi here from Parque Céspedes with a 30-minute wait costs between CUC$10 and CUC$15, depending on your negotiating skills.

## Sleeping

### CASAS PARTICULARES

#### Casco Histórico

**Andres y Ramona Gamez** (☎ 65-43-49; Corona No 371 Altos btwn General Portuondo & Máximo Gómez; r CUC$15-20; ☒ ) This friendly couple offer one very independent room with a double and single bed, complete with kitchen, dining area, bathroom and patio. There's an extra room in the host's sister's house downstairs.

**La Terraza Azul** (☎ 65-29-88; Aguilera No 615 btwn Barnada & General Serafín Sánchez; r CUC$20; ☒ ) There are three different rooms on offer at this sprawling colonial pile just off the Plaza de Marte. The best of the lot are upstairs on the blue terrace for which the casa's named – both have basic kitchens and private bathrooms.

**Ana Delia Villalón Pérez** (☎ 65-11-91; Bartolomé Masó No 172 btwn Corona & Padre Pico; r CUC$20, apt CUC$25; ☒ ) There are sublime views from this old blue-painted house that faces the Balcon Velazquez. Both rooms have private facilities but the apartment has its own kitchen so is more expensive. The roof terrace is superb.

**our pick El Mirador** (☎ 65-21-95; mariangelcuba@hotmail.com; Pío Rosado No 412 btwn Sagarra & Hechavarría; r CUC$20-25; ☒ ) This excellent casa has two rooms available, both with private bathrooms and a fully stocked fridge. If you can, book the upstairs room on the roof terrace in advance, as it's by far the best. The food here is excellent too, and the young host family is charming.

**Casa Mundo** (☎ 62-40-97; Heredia No 308 btwn Pío Rosado & Porfirio Vallente; r CUC$20-25; ☒ ) An excellent location in an antique-stuffed colonial home with two fairly basic but spotless rooms, both with private facilities.

**Casa Colonial** (☎ 62-27-47; ali@ucilora.scu.cu; José A Saco No 516 btwn Mayía Rodríguez & San Agustín; r CUC$20-25; ☒ ) This busy family home offers two attractive rooms, both with fridge and private bathroom. The upstairs room comes complete with roof terrace and is the best.

**Ylia Deas Díaz** (☎ 65-41-38; Hartmann No 362 btwn General Portuondo & Máximo Gómez; r CUC$20-30; ☒ ) This pretty casa has one room with a double and single in it as well as a fridge and a private bathroom. It's in a charming neighborhood a short walk from Parque Céspedes.

**Nena Acosta Alas** (☎ 65-41-10; botin@medired.scu.sld .cu; Hechavarría No 472 btwn Pío Rosado & Porfirio Vallente; r CUC$25; ☒ ) This highly recommended atmospheric colonial home is decked out in antiques and boasts a lovely dog. There's currently only one room available, but another is planned. It has a private bathroom, a fridge and access to a beautiful garden.

#### Vista Alegre

**Marcía Segares Vives** (☎ 64-42-32; Calle 17 No 2; r CUC$20; ☒ ) Two rooms, both with large private bathrooms, one of which has a tub and access to a small patio. Both have fridges. The house is old and atmospheric.

**Angela Casillo** (☎ 64-15-51; Calle 8 No 60 Altos btwn Calle 1 & 3; r CUC$20; ☒ ) Two big rooms off a giant terrace in a modern house; there are also rooms available with the neighbor downstairs.

**Rosa Coutín** (☎ 64-12-42; Calle 10 No 54 btwn Calles 3 & 5; r/apt CUC$20/25; ☒ ) Two rooms in a small modern house on a quiet side street. Both rooms have independent entrances and are

CUBA

# SANTIAGO DE CUBA

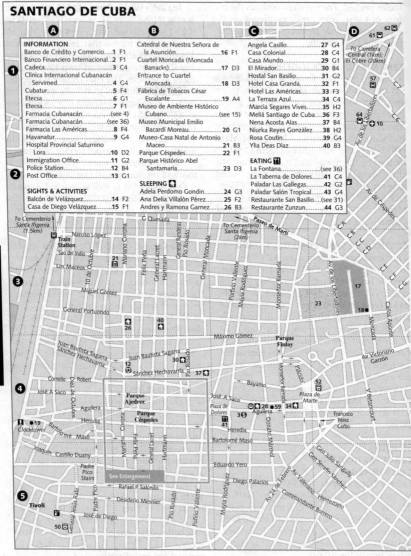

**INFORMATION**
Banco de Crédito y Comercio.....1 F1
Banco Financiero Internacional..2 F1
Cadeca...................................3 C4
Clinica Internacional Cubanacán
Servimed.............................4 G4
Cubatur................................5 F4
Etecsa.................................6 G1
Etecsa.................................7 F1
Farmacia Cubanacán..............(see 4)
Farmacia Cubanacán.............(see 36)
Farmacia Las Américas...........8 F4
Havanatur.............................9 G4
Hospital Provincial Saturnino
Lora..................................10 D2
Immigration Office.................11 G2
Police Station......................12 B4
Post Office..........................13 G1

**SIGHTS & ACTIVITIES**
Balcón de Velázquez..............14 F2
Casa de Diego Velázquez........15 F1

Catedral de Nuestra Señora de
la Asunción.........................16 F1
Cuartel Moncada (Moncada
Barracks)............................17 D3
Entrance to Cuartel
Moncada..............................18 D3
Fábrica de Tabacos César
Escalante.............................19 A4
Museo de Ambiente Histórico
Cubano.............................(see 15)
Museo Municipal Emilio
Bacardí Moreau....................20 G1
Museo-Casa Natal de Antonio
Maceo................................21 B3
Parque Céspedes...................22 F1
Parque Histórico Abel
Santamaría..........................23 D3

**SLEEPING**
Adela Perdomo Gondin...........24 G3
Ana Delia Villalòn Pèrez..........25 F2
Andres y Ramona Garnez........26 B3

Angela Casillo.......................27 G4
Casa Colonial........................28 C4
Casa Mundo..........................29 G1
El Mirador............................30 B4
Hostal San Basilio..................31 G2
Hotel Casa Granda.................32 F1
Hotel Las Américas................33 F3
La Terraza Azul.....................34 C4
Marcia Segares Vives.............35 H2
Meliá Santiago de Cuba..........36 F3
Nena Acosta Alas..................37 B4
Niurka Reyes González............38 H2
Rosa Coutin.........................39 G4
Ylia Deas Diaz......................40 B3

**EATING**
La Fontana........................(see 36)
La Taberna de Dolores............41 C4
Paladar Las Gallegas..............42 G2
Paladar Salón Tropical............43 G4
Restaurante San Basilio......(see 31)
Restaurante Zunzun...............44 G3

---

simple and airy; they also include a fridge and private bathroom.

**Adela Perdomo Gondin** ( ☎ 64-16-21; Calle 10 No 201; r CUC$20-25; ❄ ) This modern and breezy house has one large room on offer with a decent-sized private bathroom.

**Niurka Reyes González** ( ☎ 64-42-42; Calle 4 No 407 bajos; r CUC$20-25; ❄ ) This stunner of a 1940s

mansion has to be seen to be believed. With two gorgeous rooms with excellent private bathrooms, a shared back terrace and tons of style, this is a great suburban retreat.

## HOTELS
**Hostal San Basilio** ( ☎ 65-17-02; Bartolomé Masó No 403; r CUC$49; ❄ ) This is the best all-round deal in

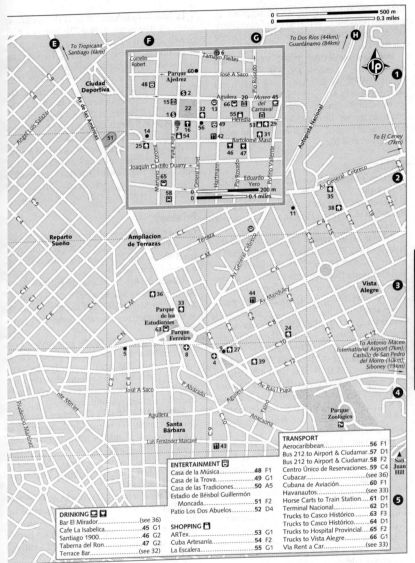

**DRINKING**
Bar El Mirador........................(see 36)
Cafe La Isabelica......................**45** G1
Santiago 1900..........................**46** G2
Taberna del Ron.......................**47** G2
Terrace Bar............................(see 32)

**ENTERTAINMENT**
Casa de la Música.....................**48** F1
Casa de la Trova.......................**49** G1
Casa de las Tradiciones..............**50** A5
Estadio de Béisbol Guillermón
  Moncada..............................**51** F2
Patio Los Dos Abuelos................**52** D4

**SHOPPING**
ARTex.................................**53** G1
Cuba Artesanía.......................**54** F2
La Escalera..........................**55** G1

**TRANSPORT**
Aerocaribbean.........................**56** F1
Bus 212 to Airport & Ciudamar.....**57** D1
Bus 212 to Airport & Ciudamar.....**58** F2
Centro Único de Reservaciones....**59** C4
Cubacar.............................(see 36)
Cubana de Aviación..................**60** F1
Havanautos..........................(see 33)
Horse Carts to Train Station.......**61** D1
Terminal Nacional...................**62** D1
Trucks to Casco Histórico..........**63** F3
Trucks to Casco Histórico..........**64** D1
Trucks to Hospital Provincial......**65** F2
Trucks to Vista Alegre.............**66** G1
Via Rent a Car......................(see 33)

town – book ahead and stay in one of the eight comfortable rooms in this boutique-ish old mansion. Excellent location, a good restaurant and immunity from tour groups are other advantages.

**Hotel Las Américas** ( ☎ 64-20-11, 68-72-25; comerc@ hamerica.hor.tur.cu; Av de las Américas & Av General Cebreco; s/d incl breakfast CUC$53/69; ) This motel-style place is a decent option between the city center and Vista Alegre. There are 70 decent rooms, a good pool and various eating and drinking options.

**Hotel Casa Granda** ( ☎ 65-30-21/22/23/24; www .grancaribe.cu; Heredia No 201; s/d incl breakfast CUC$98/152; ) This grand place on Parque Céspedes may have made it into Graham Greene's *Our*

*Man in Havana,* but today it's a disappointing place to bed down. With dark and often dirty rooms, it's a deeply mediocre place trading on its past.

**Meliá Santiago de Cuba** ( ☎ 68-70-70; www.solmelia cuba.com; Av de las Américas & Calle M; r CUC$115, ste CUC$145-165; ⊠ 🖳 �ℛ ) Santiago's best hotel will never win any awards for unobtrusive architectural blending, but despite its unattractive exterior the rooms are of international business standard, and it has a good pool, restaurant and bar.

## Eating

Santiago's main drawback is its food, which is probably the worst in Cuba – no meager achievement. Ask around for any new paladares, but in general eating in a casa particular is your best bet.

**Paladar Salón Tropical** ( ☎ 64-11-61; Fernández Marcané No 310, Reparto Santa Barbara; mains CUC$3-8; ⍥ noon-midnight) This well-established paladar feels far more like a private venture than the other paladar in town, as it's located on the roof of a far-flung family home with great views across the city. Try the large selection of *brochetas extravagantes* (literally 'extravagant kebabs'; various meats on a skewer) or the many different types of fresh fish.

**La Fontana** ( ☎ 68-70-70; Mélia Santiago de Cuba, Calle M; mains CUC$6-12; ⍥ noon-11pm) This breezy and surprisingly decent Italian restaurant is located within the unbecoming carapace of Santiago's poshest hotel, but its quality pizza, antipasti, pasta and fresh fish dishes don't disappoint.

**Restaurante Zunzun** ( ☎ 64-15-28; Av Manduley No 159; mains CUC$6-21; ⍥ noon-10pm) This Vista Alegre mansion is about the most glamorous setting in town. The food is decent too – try the seafood enchilada or the crustacean medallion, and enjoy the translation of *ropa vieja* as 'old rope' (it's actually shredded beef). Ask for a table on the terrace or book a private room to escape the bus parties. Staff are friendly and there's a passable selection of wines available.

**Restaurante San Basilio** ( ☎ 65-17-02; Bartolomé Masó No 403; mains CUC$7-9; ⍥ midday-2:30pm & 7-10:30pm) This charming Italian place oozes informal style, tucked away in one room of Santiago's most boutique hotel. The menu is a lot more inventive and interesting than most 'Italian' places in Cuba, and the fresh seafood is especially good.

**La Taberna de Dolores** ( ☎ 62-39-13; Plaza Dolores; mains CUC$7-10; ⍥ noon-11:45pm) The best of a bad bunch on Plaza de Dolores, a square given over almost entirely to tourists, La Taberna is housed in a fantastic colonial house over two floors and has very friendly service. The menu will hold no surprises, but there are sometimes barbecues here too in addition to the standard Cuban mains on the menu.

**Paladar Las Gallegas** (Bartolomé Masó No 305; mains CUC$8-10; ⍥ 1-10:45pm) This is Santiago's best-established private restaurant, occupying a potentially attractive space upstairs in a colonial building in the Casco Histórico. The food is fine, but unexciting, while service can be sloppy and rude. Try to get a table on the balcony.

## Drinking

**Cafe La Isabelica** (Aguilera & Porfirio Valiente; ⍥ 7am-11pm) This little charmer is a great place to meet locals and share strong peso coffee in a smoky atmosphere.

**Taberna del Ron** (Pío Rosado btwn Bartolomé Masó & Duany; ⍥ 10am-10pm) This small hideaway in one side of the Museo del Ron is a great place to sample numerous different styles and types of rum.

**Terrace Bar** (Heredia No 201; admission nonguests CUC$2; ⍥ 10am-1am) The rooftop of the Hotel Casa Granda has great views but a compulsory entry fee now means that the only Cubans here will be serving your drinks. Entry includes a mojito or soft drink.

**Santiago 1900** ( ☎ 62-35-07; Bartolomé Masó No 354; ⍥ noon-midnight) We're only including this as it's so bad you should be warned. Potentially fabulous, this gorgeous old Bacardí palace sums up everything wrong with Cuban tourist venues: rude service, strip lighting, loud music and bad cocktails.

**Bar El Mirador** (Av de las Américas & Calle M; ⍥ 9pm-2am) You get top-notch cocktails served up here in a refined and businesslike atmosphere. There are great views from up here – it's on the 15th floor of the Meliá Santiago de Cuba.

## Entertainment

**Casa de la Trova** ( ☎ 65-26-89; Heredia No 208; admission CUC$2; ⍥ 11am-3pm & 8:30-11pm Tue-Sun) Santiago's hottest spot, the large Casa de la Trova is home to *nueva trova* and is still a big center of innovation. Sadly though, it's an unpredictable place – some nights it's excellent, while others you can be overwhelmed by tour groups.

**Patio Los Dos Abuelos** ( ☎ 62-33-02; Francisco Pérez Carbo No 5; admission CUC$2; ◷ 10am-2am) You have to search this place out, but if you do so you won't be disappointed. Friendly staff serve drinks in the main bar, while there are live performances of everything from *son* to reggaeton in the breezy back garden. Tuesday is *trova* night, while Sunday is *oriental típico* (music typical of the Oriente region of Cuba).

**Casa de las Tradiciones** (Rabí No 154; admission CUC$1; ◷ from 8:30pm) This place is a good opportunity to escape the tourist crowds. Located in the edgy (and hilly!) Tivolí district, this intimate but great fun venue attracts some fantastic caliber musicians. Friday is traditional *trova* night.

**Casa de la Música** ( ☎ 65-22-27; Corona btwn José A Saco & Aguilera; admission CUC$5; ◷ 10pm-2:30am) This semi-swanky place features live salsa, followed by taped disco. It gets rowdy after midnight.

**Estadio de Béisbol Guillermón Moncada** ( ☎ 64-26-40; Av de las Américas; admission CUP1) The stadium's on the northeastern side of town about 1km north of Hotel Las Américas; catch a game with some of the country's most rambunctious baseball fans – they're even more so since Santiago won the national championship in 2007. Games start at 7:30pm Tuesday, Wednesday Thursday and Saturday, and at 1:30pm on Sunday.

## Shopping

**La Escalera** (Heredia No 265 btwn Pío Rosado & Hartmann; ◷ 9am-9pm) Eddy Tamayo's wonderful antique bookshop shouldn't be missed. The fascinating collection includes some very rare gems and Eddy is a mine of information on what he sells.

**ARTex** (Heredia No 304 btwn Pío Rosado & Porfirio Valiente) The standard range of handicrafts, music, books, novelty gifts and a superior selection of postcards are available here. There's a small café out the back as well.

**Cuba Artesanía** (Felix Peña No 673; ◷ 9am-9pm) Souvenir hunter heaven: a huge range of quality handicrafts and other knick-knacks are on offer here.

## Getting There & Away
### AIR
**Antonio Maceo International Airport** (SCU; ☎ 69-86-14) is 7km south of Santiago de Cuba, off the Carretera del Morro.

For flight information, see p188.

Some airline offices:

**Aerocaribbean** Airport ( ☎ 69-40-00); Town Center ( ☎ 68-72-55; www.aero-caribbean.com; General Lacret No 701; ◷ 9am-noon & 1-4:30pm Mon-Fri, 9am-noon Sat)
**Cubana de Aviación** Airport ( ☎ 69-12-14); Town Center ( ☎ 65-15-77/78/79; Saco & General Lacret; ◷ 8:15am-4pm Mon, Wed & Fri, 8:15am-6:30pm Tue & Thu, 8:15am-11pm Sat)

### BUS
**Terminal Nacional** (National Bus Station; cnr Av de los Libertadores & Calle 9) is 3km northeast of Parque Céspedes. For **Víazul** ( ☎ 62-84-84) services see below.

### TRAIN
Santiago's deeply ugly but relatively efficient new **train station** ( ☎ 62-28-36; Av Jesús Menéndez), northwest of the center, has daily trains to Havana. The 'regular' service (CUC$30, 17 hours, 861km, 9:50pm alternate days) is even longer than the still slow 'especial' service (CUC$72, 16 hours, 861km, 5:35pm alternate days). Both trains also stop in Santa Clara (regular/especial CUC$20/42, 10 hours, 590km).

You can buy tickets more centrally at **Centro Único de Reservaciones** ( ☎ 65-21-43; Aguilera No 565 bajos; ◷ 7am-7pm Mon-Fri, 7-11am Sat & Sun). For day-of-departure tickets, you have to go to the 'última hora' window outside the train station; arrive by 8am.

## Getting Around
### TO/FROM THE AIRPORT
A taxi to the airport costs CUC$5. Taxis congregate in front of the Meliá Santiago de Cuba

### SERVICES FROM SANTIAGO DE CUBA'S NATIONAL BUS STATION

| Destination | One-way fare (CUC$) | Distance (km) | Duration (hr) | Schedule |
| --- | --- | --- | --- | --- |
| Baracoa | 15 | 234 | 5 | 7:45am |
| Havana | 51 | 861 | 16 | 9am, 3:15pm, 6pm & 10pm |
| Santa Clara | 33 | 590 | 11½ | 9am, 3:15pm, 6pm & 10pm |
| Trinidad | 33 | 581 | 11½ | 7:30pm |

and around Parque Céspedes. Elsewhere call **Cubataxi** ( ☎ 65-10-38/39).

Buses 212 and 213 (40 centavos) travel to the airport; 212 is faster for going to the airport, while 213 is faster coming from the airport.

### CAR & SCOOTER

There are dire shortages of hire cars in Santiago – even worse than in the rest of the country. Even if you have a reservation it may just be down to luck if there's something available.

**Cubacar** Airport ( ☎ 69-41-95); Meliá Santiago de Cuba ( ☎ 68-71-77)

**Havanautos** Airport ( ☎ 68-61-61); Hotel Las Américas ( ☎ 68-71-60; ◷ 8am-10pm) Hotel Las Américas has scooters (rent for CUC$27 per day).

**Rex** Airport ( ☎ 68-64-44)

**Vía Rent a Car** Airport ( ☎ 68-70-18); Hotel Las Américas ( ☎ 22-68-72-90)

### HORSE CART

To get into town from the train station, catch a southbound horse cart (CUP1) to the clock tower at the north end of Alameda Park, from which Aguilera (to the left) climbs steeply up to Parque Céspedes. Horse carts between the Terminal Nacional bus station (they'll shout 'Alameda') and the train station (CUP1) run along Av Juan Gualberto Gómez and Av Jesús Menéndez, respectively.

### TRUCK

*Camiones* (trucks) run from the city center to the Moncada Barracks and the Hospital Provincial (near the Terminal Nacional); hop on along Corona one block west of Parque Céspedes or on Aguilera. Trucks for Vista Alegre also travel along Aguilera; there's a stop facing the Etecsa building. From the Hotel Las Américas to the Casco Histórico (the city's historic center), trucks stop at the Parque de los Estudiantes rotary.

## BARACOA

**pop 82,000 / ☎ 121**

Baracoa is a delightful backwater fast attracting the attention of travelers who, hearing rumors of a new Trinidad as yet untouched and unspoiled, are heading out this way. Sadly the rumors aren't strictly true – and while there's lots to recommend Baracoa, including plenty of pretty colonial buildings, Trinidad this isn't. Yet the traveler presence is minimal compared to Cuba's other big draws, and with a charming setting, a laid-back vibe and some fantastic beaches and hiking in the vicinity, Baracoa is definitely somewhere to head for if you'd like to spend some time buried deep in El Oriente.

## Information

**Banco de Crédito y Comercio** ( ☎ 64-27-71; Antonio Maceo No 99; ◷ 8am-3pm Mon-Fri, 8-11am Sat)

**Cadeca** ( ☎ 64-53-46; José Martí No 241) Gives cash advances and changes traveler's checks.

**Clínica Internacional Baracoa** ( ☎ 64-10-38; Calle Martí 237 btwn Reyes &Sánchez; ◷ 24hr) This excellent new clinic has English-speaking doctors on call and the best pharmacy in town.

**Cubatur** ( ☎ 64-53-06; cubaturbaracoa@enet.cu; Calle Martí No 181) Tours in English, Italian and German.

**Etecsa** (cnr Antonio Maceo & Rafael Trejo, Parque Central; Internet access per hr CUC$6; ◷ 8:30am-7:30pm)

**Farmacia Principal Municipal** (Antonio Maceo No 132; ◷ 24hr)

## Sights & Activities

Founded in December 1511 by Diego Velázquez, Baracoa was the first Spanish settlement in Cuba. It served as the capital until 1515, when Velázquez moved the seat of government to Santiago de Cuba.

Two fortresses, one at either end of town, are reminders of Baracoa's strategic significance – Fuerte de la Punta is at the end of the peninsula and now houses a decent restaurant, while the Fuerte Matachín at the far end of José Martí houses a mildly diverting **Museo Municipal** ( ☎ 64-21-22; cnr Martí & Malecón; admission CUC$1; ◷ 8am-6pm) containing pre-Hispanic pottery, copies of Columbus' diary and some impressive colonial weapons. Check out the huge cannons out back.

A more engaging museum is the **Museo Arqueológico Cueva del Paraíso** (admission CUC$2; ◷ 8am-5pm). It's a steep walk from town; head up the steps from Coroneles Galano and turn left on the dirt track at the top. Among the stalactites are spatulas for vomiting, pipes for smoking hallucinogens, and the remains of what may prove to be indigenous rebel Guamá. The expert docents here also lead **cave tours**.

The charming triangular town square, Parque Central, is dominated by the collapsing squat pile of the restoration-due **Catedral de Nuestra Señora de la Asunción** (Antonio Maceo No 152; admission by donation; ◷ Mass 6pm daily plus 9am Sun), which dates from 1883 and houses the Cruz de La Parra; experts agree that this is the last remaining cross out of some two dozen that the original Spaniards settlers erected throughout Latin America (the one in Santo Domingo is a copy). If the church is closed, knock on the last door on Calle Maceo to gain access.

Facing the cathedral is a bust of Taíno chief **Hatuey**, who was burned at the stake by the Spanish in 1512 for leading anti-Spanish guerillas. Famously, before his death at the stake, a priest asked him if he'd like to go to heaven. 'Are there people like you there?' he asked. 'Yes' came the reply, to which Hatuey answered that he wanted nothing to do with a god that allowed such evil deeds to be carried out in his name.

For a pleasing day trip, hike southeast of town, past the stadium and along the beach for about 20 minutes to a bridge crossing the Río Miel. After the bridge, turn left at the fork; after 15 minutes you reach **Playa Blanca** (admission CUC$2), an idyllic picnic spot. Head right at the fork and after about 45 minutes you will come to the blue and yellow **homestead of Raudeli Delgado**. For a donation (per person CUC$3 to CUC$5), Raudeli will lead you on a 30-minute hike into a lush canyon and to the **Cueva del Aguas**, a cave with a freshwater swimming hole.

Stunning 569m **El Yunque** dominates the landscape around town and can be climbed on an enjoyable and exciting half-day hike with a guide. To climb the mountain take the road towards Moa for 6km and then turn left at the signposted spur. The trailhead is 4km further on. The 10km, four- to five-hour **hike** (☎ 64-27-18; per person CUC$13) is hot; bring plenty of water and good shoes, but the crystal currents of the Río Duaba and a 7m waterfall provide relief. It costs CUC$8 per person for the 2.5km, one-hour walk just to the waterfall. On the way you should see rare frogs, butterflies, endangered giant snails and tree lizards.

For a taste of hidden Cuba, where early morning rainbows arch over the sea and women carry burdens on their heads, take a road trip through the palm-studded valley to **Playa Bariguá**, 17km from Baracoa. A further 4km along, you come to Boca de Yumurí, where there's a **black sand beach** and **boat trips** (CUC$2) up the jungle-fringed river.

You won't find a prettier beach up here than **Playa Maguana**, an idyllic, white-sand beauty 22km northwest of Baracoa. Grab yourself some shade under a palm and a cold beer from the snack bar and try to figure out how to tweak your itinerary to stay here for a while. Check if one of the four rooms at Villa Maguana is available.

## Sleeping

### CASAS PARTICULARES

**our pick** **El Mirador** ( ☎ 64-36-71; Maceo No 86 btwn 24 de Febrero & 10 de Octubre; r CUC$15-20; ) This excellent casa, housed in a wonderful colonial house, offers two good rooms for rent, with access to a fantastic balcony over one of Baracoa's main streets. Both rooms have private bathrooms and share access to a kitchen.

**Casa de Huesped Colonial** ( ☎ 64-25-94; Maceo No 80 btwn 24 de Febrero & Coliseo; r CUC$15-20; ) Two rooms in an atmospheric and welcoming colonial home, with one further room in the flat above, looked after by the hostess' daughter. All rooms have private facilities and share a roof terrace with fantastic bay views.

**Casa Tropical** ( ☎ 64-34-37, 64-37-30; Martí No 175 btwn Ciro Frias & Céspedes; r CUC$15-20; ) This charming paladar also has two good rooms with private bathrooms out the back overlooking the small garden courtyard. Rooms are simple but cool and airy.

**Casa Bella Vista** ( ☎ 64-38-83; c.bellavista@yahoo.com; Calixto García No 55; r CUC$15-20; ) A two-room house with good views over the bay from the front balcony. Both rooms have bathrooms and fridges and are presided over by friendly hosts.

**Casa Sofi** ( ☎ 64-21-84; sofi@toa.gtm.sld.cu; Maceo No 27 btwn Castillo Duany & Peraljo; r CUC$15-20; ) Pretty blue and white wooden house with a grand front porch for people-watching. One comfortable room with private bathroom. Excellent food served. The owners' son also rents at Casa La Marina on Calixto García.

**La Terraza** ( ☎ 64-25-29; Ciro Frias No 40 btwn Calixto García & Rubert López; r CUC$20-25; ) A friendly and well-run place, La Terraza affords some privacy and is ideal for a group of friends. The two rooms both have private bathrooms and share access to a kitchen, dining room and the eponymous terrace.

### HOTELS

**Hotel El Castillo** ( ☎ 64-51-06; www.hotelelcastillocuba.com; Loma del Paraíso; s/d CUC$42/58; ) The view alone from this former Spanish fort is worth the trip up the steep hillside. The best of the three properties around Baracoa owned

CUBA

by state-run tourism company Gaviota, El Castillo has 34 rooms full of character and complete with fridge, TV, phone, safe and bathroom. Sadly not much is made of the views from the rooms themselves, but these are best enjoyed from the large pool area anyway. It's a 10-minute walk from town up the steps on Frank País or Calixto García.

**Hostal La Habanera** ( ☎ 64-52-73/4; www.hostalla habanera.com; Maceo No 68; r incl breakfast CUC$49; ✖ ▢ ) There's lots to recommend Baracoa's surprisingly good main hotel, housed in a wonderful colonial building that was refitted in 2003. The combination of old and modern works here and you can't beat rooms 1, 8, 9 and 10 for their direct access to a huge, shared walk-out balcony overlooking the town's main square.

## Eating & Drinking

Baracoa has two local specialties worth a try – the street snack *cucurucho* (grated coconut mixed with sugar served in cones) and hot chocolate, made with chocolate from Baracoa's famous factory.

**Casa del Chocolate** (Antonio Maceo No 123; snacks CUC$1; ✖ 7am-11pm) An astonishing number of flies and grumpy service don't seem to deter locals from this place, where hot chocolate and chocolate ice cream (from the local chocolate factory) are the seriously delicious treats of choice. Don't miss it.

**1511** ( ☎ 64-15-11; Martí No 167; mains CUC$1-3; ✖ 7:30-9:30am, noon-2pm & 6-9:40pm) Look no further for the local scene. You may feel conspicuous as a tourist coming in here but, if you have a smattering of Spanish, you may well make friends quickly with gregarious locals who use this place as a canteen. Food is not Michelin-starred, but it's fine.

**Cafetería Piropo** (Antonio Maceo No 142; light meals CUC$1-3; ✖ 24hr) This Palmares venture on Parque Central is unmissable (in fact you can hear it from several blocks away most of the time). Come here to catch up with the local teen and 20s crowd who pack it out for live music, flowing drinks and fast food. The poorer kids hang out on the square in front.

**Casa Tropical** ( ☎ 64-34-37; Martí No 175; mains CUC$5-7; ✖ 11am-11pm) This friendly paladar and casa particular is a great place for a meal, with seating inside and out. The menu is heavy in grilled fish and shrimp, but also does a mean line in soups and chicken dishes.

**Restaurante La Punta** ( ☎ 64-14-80; Fuerte de la Punta; mains CUC$6-9; ✖ 9am-11pm) Atmospherically set within the walls of one of the town fortresses (what a pity the outside tables are cheap and plastic! – the setting could so easily be stunning), this is a formal state-run concern with fancy tablecloths and a menu of unexciting but decent Cuban cooking. Book a table on the outside terrace.

**Bar Restaurante La Colonial** ( ☎ 64-53-91; Martí No 123; mains CUC$9-12; ✖ 10am-11pm) With its charming colonial setting and good food, this paladar is a winner, even if it did rather seem to be resting on its laurels on our last visit. The English-speaking staff are friendly and the food is generally very good for rural Cuba. Try the fresh coconut shrimp.

## Entertainment

**Casa de la Trova Victorino Rodríguez** (Antonio Maceo No 149A; admission in evenings CUC$1; ✖ 7am-midnight, shows 9pm-midnight) Lively live *trova* and *son* are played every night at this old favorite on Parque Central. It's also open for coffee and drinks all day and is a popular meeting place.

**El Ranchón** (admission CUC$1; ✖ 10pm) Up 146 steep stairs at the western end of Coroneles Galano, El Ranchón has a great hilltop setting with superb views over the town and sea. However, this is a pretty rough bar favored by locals. It's rowdy and can be fun, but proceed with caution.

Baseball games are held at Estadio Manuel Fuentes Borges from October to April. It's southeast from Fuerte Matachín.

## Getting There & Away

Planes and buses out of Baracoa are sometimes fully booked, so avoid coming here on a tight schedule without an outbound reservation.

**Cubana de Aviación** Airport ( ☎ 64-25-80; Calle Martí No 181 ☎ 64-21-71; ✖ 8am-noon & 1-3pm Mon-Sat) flies in both directions between Havana and Baracoa (CUC$130, 2½ hours one way) every Thursday and Sunday.

The **National Bus Station** ( ☎ 64-38-80; Av Los Mártires & José Martí) has daily Víazul departures to Santiago de Cuba (CUC$15, five hours, 234km), leaving at 2:15pm. This is the only bus in and out available to foreigners at the time of writing – so reserve your return ticket ahead of time.

The **Intermunicipal Bus Station** (Galano & Calixto García) has daily trucks to Moa, passing Parque Nacional Alejandro de Humboldt

(CUP5, 1½ hours, 78km), with departures from 5am, and Yumurí (CUP1, one hour, 28km), with departures at 8am and 3pm.

## Getting Around
There is a **Cubacar** (☎ 64-53-43/4) office at the airport and a **Vía Rent a Car** (☎ 64-51-55) inside the adjacent Hotel Porto Santo. Scooters can be rented from Vía Rent a Car for CUC$14/18/24 per four/eight/24 hours, though they must be picked up from the Hotel El Castillo where they are stored. A taxi to Boca de Yumurí is CUC$5.

## PARQUE NACIONAL ALEJANDRO DE HUMBOLDT
A Unesco World Heritage site 40km northwest of Baracoa, this beautiful **national park** perched above the Bahía de Taco should serve as a paradigm for Cuba's protection efforts. The 60,000 hectares of preserved land includes pristine forest, 1000 flowering plant species and 145 ferns, making it the Caribbean's most diverse plant habitat. As for fauna, it's the home to the world's smallest frog and the endangered manatee, both of which you can see while hiking here.

Hikes are arranged at the **visitors center** (hikes per person CUC$5-10; ✆ 9am-6pm). The three hikes currently offered are the challenging 7km Balcón de Iberia loop, with a 7m waterfall, El Recrea, a 3km bayside stroll and the Bahía de Taco boat tour (with a manatee-friendly motor developed here); December to February is the best time to see these elusive beasts.

You can arrange a tour through Cubatur in Baracoa or get here independently on the Moa-bound truck.

# DIRECTORY

## ACCOMMODATIONS
Cuba has a huge range of accommodations, mostly substandard due to being state-run. By far the best accommodations in the country are in casas particulares, or private homes, a '90s innovation that allowed Cubans to rent out one or two rooms in their house to independent travelers. Casas particulares are cheaper, cleaner and friendlier than hotels, and in general they offer a better standard of accommodations, although this of course varies tremendously.

All those listed in this guide are recommended. Accommodations are rented by the room (CUC$15 to CUC$30; bargaining possible); by law, casas can only rent out two rooms, with a maximum of two people per room (parents with children excepted). Some casas break this rule, but it's rare.

Hotels, with the exception of some four- and five-star foreign-managed joint ventures, are generally disappointing by comparison. In Havana and big beach resorts there are some excellent options, though. Prices quoted here are for the high season; low-season prices are 10% to 25% cheaper. Prearranging accommodations here is difficult; never pay for anything up front. Cubans are not allowed in hotel rooms.

## ACTIVITIES
### Diving & Snorkeling
With its huge coastline Cuba is known for all things aquatic, including diving and snorkeling. There are over 30 dive centers throughout Cuba. Most equipment is older than that you'll be used to diving with and safety standards (Briefing? What briefing?) are much lower than elsewhere in the Caribbean. Dives cost around CUC$35, while certification courses are CUC$300 to CUC$350, and introductory courses cost CUC$35 to CUC$50.

The most popular diving area covered in this book is María la Gorda (p164). The best diving in the country is at Punta Frances on the Isla de la Juventud (see p160), while a brand new area has recently been opened up with some 30 pristine sites off the Península de Guanahacabibes at Cabo de San Antonio.

### Hiking
Top hikes include the Cuevas las Perlas stroll (p163) on the Península de Guanahacabibes, summiting flat-topped El Yunque (p181) and exploring Parque Nacional Alejandro de Humboldt (left), the latter two both a short distance from Baracoa.

There are lamentably few independent hikes. Try the Salto del Caburní trail (Topes de Collantes, p170), or the various hikes around Viñales (p161).

### Rock Climbing
The Viñales valley (p161) has over 300 routes (at all levels of difficulty, with several 5.14s) in one of Cuba's prettiest settings. Word is well and truly out among the international

**CUBA**

climbing crowd, so much so that it's now recognized as a sport and regulated by the government who started issuing climbing permits in 2008.

Due to the heat, the climbing season is from October to April. For more information, visit the website of **Cuba Climbing** (www .cubaclimbing.com).

## BOOKS

Required reading for any trip are Graham Greene's silly classic thriller *Our Man in Havana*, an amusing story of a vacuum salesman falling into spying circles during the last days of the Batista regime; Reinaldo Arenas' *Before Night Falls*, a heartbreaking tale of a gay writer's struggle to fit into Castro's brave new world in 1960s and '70s Cuba; and *The Dirty Havana Trilogy* by Pedro Juan Gutiérrez, a more contemporary account of life in the troubled Cuban capital.

Covering the First War of Independence to the present, *Cuba: A New History*, by Richard Gott, is the latest, broadest history of the island. A slew of Castro biographies has graced the shelves in recent years, although arguably the true story will only be told some time from now.

Taking a frank but reverent look at the revolution is *Cuba: Neither Heaven Nor Hell*, by María López Vigil. For a traveler's point of view on this confounding island, *Enduring Cuba*, by Zoë Bran is highly recommended.

## BUSINESS HOURS

The following are the standard business hours used in this chapter; exceptions are noted in individual reviews. All businesses shut at noon on the last working day of each month.

**Banks** ☽ 9am to 3pm Monday to Friday
**Restaurants** ☽ 10:30am to 11pm Monday to Sunday
**Shops** ☽ 9am to 5pm Monday to Saturday, 9am to noon Sunday

## CHILDREN

Children are integrated into all parts of Cuban society: at concerts, restaurants, church, political rallies and parties. Travelers with children will find this embracing attitude heaped upon them, too.

One aspect of local culture parents (and children) may find unusual is the physical contact that is so typically Cuban: strangers ruffle kids' hair, give them kisses or take their hands with regularity.

---

> **PRACTICALITIES**
>
> - **Newspapers** *Granma, Juventud Rebelde* and *Trabajadores* are the three national papers.
> - **Radio & TV** There are over 60 local radio stations and five TV channels; most midrange and top-end hotels have some cable.
> - **Electricity** The most common voltage is 110 volts, 60 cycles, but you'll also find 220 volts; sockets are suited to North American–style plugs with two flat prongs.
> - **Weights & Measures** The metric system is used, except in some fruit and vegetable markets.

Shortages of diaper wipes, children's medicine, formula etc, can be a challenge, but Cubans are very resourceful: ask for what you need and someone will help you out.

Children travel for half price on trains, buses and flights. Most hotels offer room discounts. For ideas on fun kids' stuff in Havana, see p149.

## CUSTOMS

Travelers can bring in personal belongings (including cell phones, cameras, binoculars, recording devices, radios, computers, tents and bicycles), but no GPS equipment or satellite phones. Canned, processed and dried foods are no problem. You can export 50 cigars without a receipt. Cash up to US$5000 or its equivalent need not be declared. A helpful leaflet in English is available on arrival at José Martí International Airport documenting all the dos and don'ts.

## DANGERS & ANNOYANCES

'You wanna buy cigar, my fren?' – this refrain will follow you throughout the country. Welcome to the land of the *jintero* or tout, a profession raised to an art form by the Cubans, who, in their defense, have very few other ways to make money. Learn quickly to ignore them, don't make eye-contact, say 'no thank you' clearly but firmly, never stop walking, and when you're asked where you're from, choose somewhere obscure (this avoids a rehearsed and interminably cutesy patter about your *jintero*'s sister working as a nurse in Liverpool or studying in Toronto). Harsh? Yes, but *jintero*ism is any traveler in Cuba's single biggest annoyance so getting to grips with it will improve your holiday vastly.

Cigar selling is not the only racket the *jinteros* work. They will also offer to take you to a casa or paladar (they'll get CUC$5 from the owners usually – which comes from hiked prices for your accommodation or meal), find you a 'beautiful woman,' get you a taxi or take you out dancing. Unless you're at your wits' end, never go with them.

Cuba is not a dangerous destination, although Centro Habana is the most likely spot in the country that you'll get mugged (a rarity, but just be aware at night). Apart from this and other small opportunistic crimes such as pickpocketing, you have almost nothing to be afraid of. Never leave valuables in any room, and use the safe if there's one provided.

## EMBASSIES & CONSULATES

**Canada** Embassy ( ☎ 204-2516; www.havana.gc.ca; Calle 30 No 518, Miramar); Consulate ( ☎ 45-61-20-78; fax 45-66-73-95; Calle 13 No 422, Varadero) Also represents Australia.

**France** Embassy (Map pp146-7; ☎ 201-3131; www.amba france-cu.com; Calle 14 No 312 btwn Avs 3 & 5, Miramar)

**Germany** Embassy (Map pp146-7; ☎ 833-2460; alema nia@enet.cu; Calle 13 No 652, Vedado)

**Italy** Embassy ( ☎ 204-5615; ambitcub@cubacel.net; Av 5 No 402, Miramar)

**Netherlands** Embassy (Map pp146-7; ☎ 204-2511; http://cuba.nlambassade.org; Calle 8 No 307 btwn Avs 3 & 5, Miramar)

**Spain** Embassy (Map pp142-3; ☎ 866-8025; emb.laha bana@mae.es; Cárcel No 51, Centro Habana)

**UK** Embassy ( ☎ 204-1771; www.britishembassy.gov.uk/ cuba; Calle 34 No 702, Miramar) Also represents New Zealand.

**US Interests Section** (Map pp146-7; ☎ 833-3551/52/53, out of hr 834-4400; http://havana.usinterest section.gov; Calzada btwn Calles L & M, Vedado)

## FESTIVALS & EVENTS

**Liberation & New Year's Day** Big street parties countrywide on January 1; outdoor concerts in Havana.

**Baseball playoffs** Two weeks of top ball in late April; location varies.

**Día de los Trabajadores** Massive rallies on May day, May 1, in Plazas de la Revolución countrywide.

**Festival del Caribe, Fiesta del Fuego** In the first week of July, Santiago de Cuba holds a raucous week-long festival celebrating Caribbean dance, music and religion.

**Day of the National Rebellion** In a different province each year, July 26 is the celebration of the 1953 attack on the Moncada Barracks.

**Carnaval, Santiago de Cuba** Held in the last week of July, this is the country's oldest and biggest.

**Festival de Rap Cubano Habana Hip Hop** Everyone's bustin' rhymes in this wildly successful international event in mid-August.

**Festival Internacional de Ballet** Tremendous biennial event packed with performances; held in mid-October in even-numbered years.

**Festival Internacional de Jazz** Straight ahead, be-bop, Latin, far out or funkified jazz happens in the first week of December.

**Festival Internacional del Nuevo Cine Latino-Americano** This prestigious film festival features hundreds of screenings in the first week of December.

**Las Parrandas** Extravagant fireworks and floats in one of Cuba's most outrageous festivals, on December 24 (Remedios).

## GAY & LESBIAN TRAVELERS

Despite the bad old days of communist persecution, things have changed massively in the past two decades and Cuba is now a surprisingly gay-friendly place (by pitiful Caribbean standards at least). The two main factors for this are the hit 1994 movie *Fresa y Chocolate*, which sparked a national dialogue about homosexuality, something that had previously been taboo, and, in more recent times, the campaigning efforts of Mariela Castro, daughter of President Raúl Castro and director of the National Center for Sex Education. Castro has campaigned for tolerance towards all sexualities, she has advocated AIDS education and even speaks out for gender reassignment rights – something utterly unheard of in the Caribbean before.

Despite this, gay life remains hidden from public view. With the exception of one progressive club in Santa Clara (Club Mejunje, p167) there are no openly gay clubs and gay life revolves heavily around internet contacts, cruising and private *fiestas de diez pesos* (private parties charging CUC$2 cover). These mostly gay parties are moving shindigs held on Friday and Saturday nights in Havana from around midnight; head to gay meeting spot Cine Yara (p157) and chat up the crowds of partygoers to find out where that night's party is happening.

In general, foreigners are treated as a breed apart by Cubans, so gay travelers requesting a double bed won't shock most people. Still,

CUBA

for your own safety it's good to remain discreet at street level by avoiding public displays of affection.

## HOLIDAYS

There are only a few holidays that might affect your travel plans, when shops close and local transportation is erratic.

**January 1** Triumph of the Revolution; New Year's Day.

**May 1** International Worker's Day; no inner-city transportation.

**July 26** Celebrates start of the revolution on July 26, 1953.

**October 10** Start of the First War of Independence.

**December 25** Declared an official holiday after the Pope's 1998 visit.

## INTERNET ACCESS

Access to the internet is provided in all sizeable towns by Etecsa (per hour CUC$6) from small and often slow internet cafés. You may be asked to show your passport or give your passport number when purchasing access cards. Laptop connections in hotels are getting better – there's a smattering of wi-fi places in Havana, although none are free even for guests, with the exception of the Saratoga (p152), which has free connections in each room. Despite not officially being allowed, some casas particulares have internet access, which you will usually be charged to use by your host family.

## MEDICAL SERVICES

Cubans famously enjoy far better free health care than their far-wealthier US neighbors, and continue to set high standards for developing nations with excellent hospitals and doctors throughout the country. Most medication is available in Cuba, although you should bring anything you know you'll need. You should also have insurance covering you during your stay. In large cities and places where many tourists visit there are usually clinics designed for foreigners, with English-speaking doctors and better supplies than elsewhere. Charges are made for treatment, but are tiny compared to treatment in Western private hospitals. The free health care in normal Cuban hospitals should only be used when there are no private clinics available.

## MONEY

Two currencies circulate throughout Cuba – Cuban convertible pesos (CUC) and Cuban pesos (CUP), also called *moneda nacional*

(MN). Most prices in this chapter are quoted in convertible pesos (CUC$) and nearly everything tourists buy is in this currency, although you can often buy street food and drinks in CUP, making it a good idea to change CUC$10 to CUC$20 for such sundries at a Cadeca.

Convertible pesos can only be bought and sold in Cuba with euros, British pounds, Canadian dollars and Swiss francs; these currencies are exchanged at the global exchange rate for the dollar, plus an 8% tax tacked on by the Cuban government. US dollars are also convertible, but with a huge 18% tax. Therefore bring one of the four accepted currencies to avoid giving more than is inevitable of your holiday funds to the Cuban government.

Convertible pesos are useless outside Cuba; you can reverse-exchange currency at the airport before you pass through immigration. Do not change money on the street as scams are rampant and there's no benefit to you.

ATMs have become much more reliable in recent years, but should only ever be taken for granted in Havana and Santiago. Elsewhere imagine their working as a useful bonus, but never count on it. Credit cards are also charged at an 8% commission, so their use will not save you any money, sadly. Generally, using them in better hotels and resorts is trouble-free, but again, never rely on them. Visa is the most widely accepted credit card. Due to embargo laws, no credit card issued by a US bank or subsidiary is accepted in Cuba.

While they add security, traveler's checks are a hassle in Cuba. In addition to commissions, cashing them takes time, and smaller hotels don't accept them. They're virtually useless in the provinces. If you insist on carrying them, get Thomas Cook checks.

## TELEPHONE

Cuba's country code is ☎ 53. To call Cuba from North America, dial ☎ 1-53 + the local number. From elsewhere, dial your country's international access code, then Cuba's country code ☎ 53 + city or area code + local number. In this chapter, the city or area code is given in the statistics at the start of each section and only the local number is given in the listings.

To call internationally from a Cuban payphone, dial ☎ 119 + country code + area code and the number. To the US, just dial ☎ 119-1 + area code and the number.

To place a collect call (reverse charges, *cobro revertido*) through an international operator, dial ☎ 012. This service is not available to all countries. You cannot call collect from public phones.

To call between provinces, dial ☎ 0 + area code + number. To call Havana from any other province, you just dial ☎ 7 + number.

## Cell Phones

Cuba's cell phone monopoly is **Cubacel** (www.cubacel.com), which has good coverage throughout the country. Most cell phones (with the obvious exception of US ones!) will roam quite happily onto the local Cubacel network, although this is an expensive way to communicate.

Anyone using their phone regularly can buy a SIM card from any Etecsa office and put it in their cell phone providing it has been unlocked. You have to buy prepaid cards, plus pay CUC$3 line rental per day. You are charged for both incoming *and* outgoing local calls (from CUC$0.52 to CUC$0.70 per minute). International rates are CUC$2.70 per minute to the US and CUC$5.85 per minute to Europe. Only 900 MHz, unlocked phones work here; you can rent one for CUC$7 per day.

## Phone Cards

Etecsa is where you buy phone cards, use the internet and make international calls. Blue public Etecsa phones (most broken) are everywhere. Phone cards (magnetic or chip) are sold in convertible-peso denominations of CUC$5, CUC$10 and CUC$20, and *moneda nacional* denominations of CUP3, CUP5 and CUP7. You can call nationally with either, but you can only call internationally with convertible-peso cards.

## Phone Rates

Local calls are CUP0.05 per minute, while interprovincial calls cost from 35 centavos to CUP1 per minute.

International calls made with a card cost CUC$2.45 per minute to North America and CUC$5.85 to Europe/Oceania. Operator-assisted calls cost CUC$3.71 and CUC$8.78, respectively.

## TOILETS

Toilets are plentiful – if rather smelly – throughout the country. It's customary to tip 5 to 10 centavos per visit to the bathroom

> **EMERGENCY NUMBERS**
> ■ **Fire** ☎ 105
> ■ **Police** ☎ 106

when there's an attendant. Cuban sewer systems are not designed to take toilet paper and every bathroom has a small wastebasket beside the toilet for this purpose. Except in top-end hotels and resorts, you should discard your paper in this basket or risk an embarrassing backup.

## TOURIST INFORMATION

Despite tourism being all-pervasive, the tourist infrastructure in Cuba is nowhere near as good as in neighboring Caribbean nations. The national tourism portal is www.cuba travel.cu, although it carries little information you can't find in a guidebook or elsewhere online. Tourist offices in Cuban towns usually serve the dual functions of providing promotional materials for local restaurants and hotels, and selling tours and excursions. While English is usually spoken, the practical use of tourist information offices is extremely limited.

## VISAS

Visitors initially get four weeks in Cuba with a *tarjeta de turista* (tourist card) issued by their airline or travel agency. Unlicensed US visitors buy their tourist card at the airline desk in the country through which they're traveling to Cuba (US$25); they are welcomed in the country like any other tourist. You cannot leave Cuba without presenting your tourist card (replacements cost CUC$25).

The 'address in Cuba' line should be filled in with a hotel or legal casa particular, if only to avoid unnecessary questioning.

Business travelers and journalists need visas. Applications should be made through a consulate at least three weeks in advance, preferably longer.

Obtaining an extension is easy: go to an immigration office and present your documents and CUC$25 in stamps (obtainable at local banks). You'll receive an additional four weeks, after which you'll need to leave Cuba and re-enter anew if you need to stay longer. Attend to extensions at least a few business days before your visa is due to

**CUBA**

expire. The following cities covered in this book all have immigration offices:

**Baracoa** (Antonio Maceo No 48; ⊗ 8am-noon & 2-4pm Mon-Fri)

**Havana** (Map pp146-7; ☎ 206-0307; cnr Calle Factor al final & Santa Ana, Nuevo Vedado)

**Santa Clara** (cnr Av Sandino & Sexta; ⊗ 8am-noon & 1-3pm Mon-Thu)

**Santiago de Cuba** (Map pp176-7; Calle 13 near Av General Cebreco, Vista Alegre; ⊗ 8am-5pm Mon, Tue, Thu & Fri)

**Trinidad** (Julio Cueva Díaz off Paseo Agramonte; ⊗ 8am-5pm Tue-Thu)

**Viñales** (cnr Salvador Cisneros & Ceferino Fernández; ⊗ 8am-5pm Mon-Fri)

# TRANSPORTATION

## GETTING THERE & AWAY
### Entering Cuba

For a country with such a fearsome reputation as a communist prison, Cuba's a very straightforward place to enter. The key thing is to have your passport, onward ticket and tourist card (see p187), and know where you're staying (at least for your first night). Ensure you've filled out your tourist card before you arrive at the immigration counter, and if you don't know where you'll be staying make something up.

### Air

Despite the best efforts of the US to isolate Cuba, the island remains well connected throughout the Caribbean and beyond.

Cuba's national airline is **Cubana de Aviación** (www.cubana.cu). Its modern fleet flies major routes and its fares are usually the cheapest. Still, overbooking and delays are nagging problems and it charges stiffly for every kilo above the 20kg luggage allowance.

**José Martí International Airport** (☎ 649-5666, 649-0410; Av de la Independencia) is 25km southwest of Havana. Terminal 1, southeast of the runway, handles domestic Cubana flights. A few kilometers away on Av de la Independencia is Terminal 2, which receives direct charter flights from the US. Most international flights use the excellent Terminal 3, a modern facility 2.5km west of Terminal 2. Aerocaribbean and Aerogaviota use Terminal 5 (aka the Caribbean Terminal).

Jamaica is a major transportation hub to Cuba. Cubana flies from Kingston and Montego Bay to Havana daily, as does Air Jamaica.

Cubana also flies twice a week to Havana from Guadeloupe, Martinique, Santo Domingo and Puerto Príncipe. The latter two flights stop in Santiago de Cuba first. From the Bahamas, Cubana flies daily between Nassau and Havana; Bahamasair flies three times a week. US citizens cannot purchase Nassau–Havana tickets online or anywhere in the US.

The following airlines fly to/from Cuba:

**Aerocaribbean** (☎ 833-3621; www.aero-caribbean.com)

**Aeroflot** (☎ 204-3200; www.aeroflot.com) Moscow

**Air Canada** (☎ 836-3226/27; www.aircanada.com) Toronto

**Air France** (☎ 833-2642; www.airfrance.com) Paris

**Air Jamaica** (☎ 833-3636; www.airjamaica.com) Montego Bay

**Air Transat** (☎ 204-3802/04; www.airtransat.com) Toronto

**Bahamasair** (☎ 833-3114; www.bahamasair.com) Nassau

**Cayman Airways** (www.caymanairways.com) Grand Cayman

**Copa Airlines** (☎ 204-1111; www.copa air.com) Panama City

**Cubana de Aviación** (☎ 834-4949; www.cubana.cu) London, Mexico City, Montego Bay, Montreal, Paris, Santo Domingo, Toronto, plus other destinations

**Iberia Mexicana de Aviación** (☎ 204-3454; www .iberia.com) Cancún, Mexico City

**TACA** (☎ 833-3114; www.taca.com) San Salvador

**Virgin Atlantic** (☎ 7-207-0747; www.virginatlantic.com) London

### Sea

Marinas around Cuba accepting foreign vessels include María la Gorda, Cabo de San Antonio, Marina Hemingway (Havana), Cienfuegos, Varadero, Trinidad and Santiago de Cuba. Harbor anchorage fees are CUC$10 per day or 45 centavos per foot for a pier slip with water and electric hookups. There are no scheduled ferry services to Cuba.

## GETTING AROUND
### Air

Internal flights are well provided for by national carrier **Cubana de Aviación** (☎ 834-4949; www.cubana.cu) and **Aerocaribbean** (☎ 833-3621; www.aero-caribbean.com). Both connect Havana to Santiago de Cuba (CUC$219 return),

> **TRAVEL BAN PENALTIES**
>
> Together with the embargo against Cuba, the US government enforces what is known as a 'travel ban,' preventing its citizens from visiting Cuba. Technically a treasury law prohibiting US citizens from spending money in Cuba, it has largely squelched leisure travel for over 40 years.
>
> The 1996 Helms-Burton Bill imposes fines of up to US$50,000 on US citizens who visit Cuba without government permission. It also allows for confiscation of their property. In addition, under the Trading with the Enemy Act, violators may also face up to US$250,000 in fines and up to 10 years in prison. The authors and publisher of this guide accept no responsibility for repercussions suffered by US citizens who decide to circumvent these restrictions. You are strongly encouraged to visit www.democracyinamericas.org to inform yourself of the latest legislation on Capitol Hill, and to review the Office of Foreign Assets Control regulations limiting travel (www .treas.gov/ofac).

Baracoa (CUC$259 return) and Nueva Gerona (CUC$86 return) on the Isla de la Juventud. One-way tickets are half the price of round-trip.

## Bicycle

Cuba is legendary among cyclists and you'll see more bicycle enthusiasts here than divers, climbers and hikers put together. Cuba's status with cyclists dates from the mid-'90s when it first opened up to tourism, when cars were still few and far between. Sadly, conditions aren't quite as good as they once were: as driving becomes more affordable for many Cubans, the roads are getting busier with ancient Soviet lorries and 1950s American cars belching out plumes of pollution wherever they go. However, Cuba is a largely flat country, with a driving population used to sharing the road.

Spare parts are difficult to find; *poncheras* fix flat tires and provide air. Bring your own strong locks as bicycle theft is rampant. Try to leave your bike at a *parqueo* – bicycle parking lots costing CUP1, located wherever crowds congregate (markets, bus terminals etc). Riding after dark is not recommended. Trains with baggage carriages (*coches de equipaje* or *bagones*) take bikes for CUC$20. These compartments are guarded, but take your panniers with you and check over the bike when you arrive. Víazul buses also take bikes.

## Bus

Bus travel is a dependable option with **Víazul** (☎ 881-1413, 881-5652, 881-1108; www.viazul.cu; Calle 26 & Zoológico, Nuevo Vedado), which has punctual, air-con coaches to destinations of interest to travelers. Sadly it's not possible for foreigners to travel on Astro buses, which cover the

country far more comprehensively, meaning that if you want to get off the beaten path you're pretty much forced to hire a car or ride a bike. Bus reservations are advisable during peak travel periods (June to August, Christmas and Easter) and on popular routes (Havana–Trinidad, Trinidad–Santa Clara and Santiago de Cuba–Baracoa). See individual Getting There & Away sections for information about bus connections to and from other towns in Cuba.

Very crowded, very steamy, very Cuban *guaguas* (local buses) can be useful in bigger cities. There is always a line at *paradas* (bus stops). Shout '*el último?*' ('the last?') to determine who is last in line. You 'give' *el último* when the next person arrives, thereby knowing exactly where you fall in line. Buses cost from 40 centavos to CUP1. You must always walk as far back in the bus as possible and exit through the rear. Make room to pass by saying '*permiso*,' and watch your bag.

## Car

Renting a car in Cuba follows the predictable pattern of so much of Cuban life. It's pretty straightforward, but resign yourself to paying over the odds for a badly maintained and usually pretty crappy machine.

To rent a car, you'll need your passport, your home driver's license and a refundable CUC$200 deposit (in cash or with non-US credit card). You can rent a car in one city and drop it off in another for a reasonable fee. The cheapest cars start at CUC$50 per day for a Hyundai Atos and climb steeply to around CUC$70 per day minimum during the high season.

Another bugbear is that (especially in Havana and Santiago) cars are in such short

190 TRANSPORTATION •• Getting Around

supply that reservations are pretty much meaningless. Usually the best thing to do is call around the car-hire places the day you want a car, then go straight there if they have something available. The hotel outlets are often better bets than the main offices. In Havana, those around Parque Central are often the best places to ask; try the Plaza, NH Parque Central, Sevilla, Telégrafo and the Inglaterra, all within easy walking distance of each other.

Contracts for three days or more come with unlimited kilometers. As if things weren't idiotic enough, your car comes with only a tiny bit of gas in it to allow you to drive to the gas station to fill up. You're expected to return it empty, but don't risk running out just to save a few CUCs. Drivers under 25 pay a CUC$5 fee; additional drivers on the same contract pay a CUC$15 surcharge.

Check over the car carefully before driving off as you'll be responsible for any damage or missing parts. Make sure there is a spare tire of the correct size, a jack and lug wrench. Check that there are seatbelts, all the lights work, and all the doors lock properly. Some cars are in a shocking state. It's worth complaining and trying to swap if the engine sounds strange. Take the optional CUC$10 per day insurance.

We have received many letters about poor or nonexistent customer service, bogus spare tires, forgotten reservations and other car-rental problems. The more Spanish you speak and the friendlier you are, the more likely problems will be resolved to everyone's satisfaction (tips to the agent may help).

### FUEL & SPARE PARTS

Cupet and Oro Negro *servicentros* (gas stations) selling hard-currency gas are nearly everywhere. Gas is sold by the liter and is either regular (per liter CUC$0.80) or *especial* (per liter CUC$0.95). Either works equally well, although car hire companies ask you to put *especial* in your car.

### ROAD CONDITIONS

The Autopista and Carretera Central are generally in good repair. While motorized traffic is refreshingly light, bicycles, pedestrians, tractors and livestock can test your driving skills. Driving at night is not recommended due to variable roads, crossing cows, poor lighting and drunk drivers (an ongoing

problem despite a government educational campaign). Signage, though improving, is still sadly appalling. Particularly bad is the signage around Havana – getting out of the city and finding *any* roads from the ring road is a complete nightmare. Allow plenty of extra time and ask repeatedly to check you're going the right way.

### ROAD RULES

Seatbelts are required and speed limits are technically 50km/h in the city, 90km/h on highways and 100km/h on the Autopista.

There are some clever speed traps along the Autopista. Speeding tickets start at CUC$30 and are noted on your car contract (deducted from your deposit when you return the car). However, in practice most police will ignore hire cars going too fast, but do slow down to the speed instructed for the ubiquitous 'control zones'.

## Horse Cart

Many provincial cities have *coches* (horse carts) that trot on fixed routes.

## Taxi, Bici-taxi & Coco-taxi

Car taxis are metered and cost CUC$1 to start, CUC$0.75 per kilometer thereafter. Cabbies usually offer foreigners a flat, off-meter rate that works out close to what you'll pay with the meter.

Bici-taxis are big tricycles with two seats behind the driver. Tourists pay CUC$1 to CUC$2 for a short hop; agree on the price beforehand. You'll be mobbed all over the country in tourist spots by the ubiquitous cry of 'taxi' from these guys.

So-called coco-taxis are egg-shaped motorbike taxis that hold two to three people and are mainly seen in Havana. Locals often refer to them as *huevitos* (literally 'little eggs'). Agree on a price before getting in.

## Train

Public railways operated by Ferrocarriles de Cuba serve all the provincial capitals and are a great way to experience Cuba if you have time and patience, but a nightmare if you're keen to make progress and move about efficiently! Departure information provided in this chapter is purely theoretical. Getting a ticket is usually no problem – tourists will be charged in CUC$, though Spanish-speaking travelers frequently travel on trains for the local peso price. The most useful routes for travelers are Havana–Santiago de Cuba and Havana–Santa Clara. The bathrooms are foul. Watch your luggage and bring food.

## Truck

*Camiones* (trucks) are a cheap, fast way to travel within or between provinces. Every city

has a provincial and municipal bus stop with *camion* departures.

This is the most basic and least comfortable way to travel. In most cases there's standing room only, and there are no toilet facilities. Departures are scheduled,g though, and prices are ridiculously cheap. This is definitely a great way to experience local life.

# Cayman Islands

Three tiny islands make up the British Overseas Territory of the Cayman Islands, balanced precariously one side of the enormous Cayman Trench, the deepest part of the Caribbean. While synonymous worldwide with banking, tax havens and beach holidays, there's much more to this tiny, proud nation, even if you do need to look quite hard to find it.

What's so surprising about the Caymans at first is how un-British they are – it would be hard to design a more Americanized place than Grand Cayman, where the ubiquitous SUVs jostle for space in the parking lots of large malls and US dollars change hands as if they were the national currency. Only the occasional portrait of the Queen or a fluttering Union Jack ever begs to differ. This contradiction is just the first of many you'll discover while getting to know these islands.

The key to understanding what makes the Caymans tick is getting away from the crowded commercialism of Grand Cayman's long western coastline and exploring the rest of the island. Better still, leave Grand Cayman altogether and visit the charming 'sister islands' of Cayman Brac and Little Cayman. Here life runs at a slower pace and the natural delights that see people coming back again and again – from bird-watching and hiking to diving and snorkeling – are never far away.

The Caymans may lack the dramatic scenery and steamy nightlife of much of the rest of the Caribbean, but in their place you'll find a charming, independent and deeply warm people spread over three islands boasting many of life's quieter charms.

**FAST FACTS**

- **Area** 100 sq miles
- **Capital** George Town, Grand Cayman
- **Country code** ☎ 1345
- **Departure tax** CI$20 (usually included in the price of your air ticket)
- **Famous for** Diving, banking and iguanas
- **Language** English
- **Money** Cayman Islands dollar (CI$); US dollars accepted everywhere; CI$1 = US$1.25 = €0.78 = UK£0.62
- **Official name** Cayman Islands
- **People** Caymanians
- **Population** 52,000
- **Visa** Not required for nationals of the USA, Canada, UK, EU members prior to 2004 and most Commonwealth countries; see p213.

# HIGHLIGHTS

- **Diving** (p199) Explore some of the very best diving in the Caribbean, with sites such as legendary Bloody Bay Wall on Little Cayman and the *Captain Keith Tibbets* wreck dive on Cayman Brac
- **Seven Mile Beach** (p196) Enjoy swimming, sunbathing and water sports galore on Grand Cayman's superb stretch of white sand, which is backed onto by glitzy hotels, smart restaurants and laid-back beach bars
- **Snorkeling at Stingray City** (p199) Have the amazing experience of huge, fearless stingrays eating squid directly from your hands as you snorkel in so-called Stingray City – the most famous attraction of this tiny island nation
- **Cayman Brac** (p206) Discover the Brac, the least visited of the Cayman Islands and by far the most dramatic, with great walking, bird-watching and diving
- **Little Cayman** (p208) Take life at a slower pace on the smallest of the three Cayman islands, which is packed with quiet charm, some great beaches and the best diving in the country

# ITINERARIES

- **Three Days** Join the crowds on wonderful Seven Mile Beach, shop yourself into oblivion in George Town and experience the extraordinary Stingray City.
- **One Week** After several days in and around George Town, explore some of Grand Cayman's lesser-known attractions. Try the Botanic Park and Rum Point, and get some diving in.
- **Two Weeks** Add on Cayman Brac and Little Cayman for some nature hikes, superb diving, secluded beaches and a wonderful taste of the traditional Caribbean.

# CLIMATE & WHEN TO GO

The best time to visit is from December to April, when the temperature averages a pleasant 75°F (23.9°C) and humidity is at its lowest. During the off-season, temperatures average 83°F (28.3°C) with July and August usually being uncomfortably hot. During these times crowds dissipate, particularly on Cayman Brac and Little Cayman, bringing lodging rates down by as much as 40%. Rainfall is

---

**HOW MUCH?**

- **Taxi from Owen Roberts International Airport to George Town** US$15
- **Guided snorkeling trip** US$35
- **Stingray City dive/snorkel trip** US$50/30
- **Meal of fresh fish in a touristy restaurant** US$30
- **Meal of fresh fish in a local restaurant** US$15

---

highest from mid-May through to October, with frequent afternoon showers that clear as quickly as they arrive.

# HISTORY

For the first century after Christopher Columbus happened upon the Caymans in 1503, the islands remained uninhabited by people – which may explain why multitudes of sea turtles were happy to call the place home, giving the islands their original Spanish name, Las Tortugas. The sun-bleached landscape languished in a near-pristine state, undisturbed but for the occasional intrusion of sailors stopping in to swipe some turtles and fill up on fresh water.

No permanent settlers set up house until well after the 1670 acquisition of the islands – and its turtles – by the British Crown, which has held dominion over the three islands ever since. Once settlers started trickling in from Jamaica in the early 18th century, Caymanians quickly established their reputation as world-class seafarers. From the 1780s the Caymanian shipbuilding industry produced schooners and other seacraft used for interisland trade and turtling.

By 1800 the population numbered less than 1000 – of whom half were slaves. After the Slavery Abolition Act was read at Pedro St James (near Bodden Town on Grand Cayman) in 1835, most freed slaves remained, and by 1900 the Caymans' population had quintupled.

Until the mid-20th century, the economy remained tied to the sea with fishing, turtling and shipbuilding as the main industries. Divers put the Cayman Islands on the international tourist map as early as the 1950s; islanders were understandably protective of

**CAYMAN ISLANDS**

their little slice of paradise and were slow to relinquish their isolation. By the next decade, however, Caymanians had begun fashioning the tax structure that's made Grand Cayman an economic powerhouse – and designing an infrastructure that's made it a capital of Caribbean tourism.

In September 2004, Hurricane Ivan gave Grand Cayman a body blow, causing such widespread destruction that tourism was halted and a curfew enforced for several months to prevent looting. Fortunately, Cayman Brac and Little Cayman did not receive a direct hit and damage to the smaller islands was limited. Repairs are largely complete now and the future looks bright for the Caymans, where tourism is making ever greater steps into even the remote 'sister islands.' At the time of writing an international airport was being built on Little Cayman, the smallest of the Caymans – a controversial move that has divided the local population and even the country at large.

## THE CULTURE

For centuries, the Caymans had been left to simmer undisturbed in their own juices as the rest of the world rushed headlong into modernity. As recently as 40 years ago (aside from a few adventurers and fishing nuts) there were few tourists. Electric power was provided solely by noisy generators, and most islanders did without it. What has occurred between then and now constitutes a Caymanian cultural revolution. With the advent of large-scale tourism and big business banking, life on the islands has changed so rapidly that cultural discourse has turned to measuring what's been gained and lost.

Historically, the population is an amalgamation with Jamaican, North American, European and African roots, but contemporary Cayman has become even more multifaceted. For better or worse, a large influx of expatriate workers – representing 78 countries and growing ever greater in number in the aftermath of Hurricane Ivan – has caused Caymanians to become a minority in their own country. The upside is that the Cayman Islands have a remarkably rich social fabric that truly celebrates diversity. At stake, however, is the cultural legacy of this religious, seafaring nation. Borrowing a theme from the islands' traditional folk songs, which regularly feature the laments of sailors longing to return

home, many islanders speak with nostalgia of the old ways.

## ARTS

While the art scene in the Caymans may fail to scintillate visiting urbanites, it is gathering steam. The National Gallery in George Town, Grand Cayman, was opened in 1996 to promote and encourage the embryonic art scene of the islands. An art collective known as Native Son, comprising homegrown artists Wray Banker, Al Ebanks, Luelan Bodden and Horatio Estaban has exhibited locally and internationally, while late-blooming visionary artist 'Miss Lassie' has become well known abroad in 'outsider art' circles. (Her death in 2003 was cause for spontaneous national mourning.) Unsurprisingly, underwater photography is widely practiced in the Caymans, most notably by Cathy Church, whose Underwater Photo Centre & Gallery at Sunset House (p202) provides a focal point.

## ENVIRONMENT
### The Land

Located approximately 150 miles south of Cuba and 180 miles west of Jamaica, the Cayman Islands consist of Grand Cayman and two smaller islands – Cayman Brac and Little Cayman – 75 miles to the northeast and 5 miles apart. All three islands are low-lying, flat-topped landmasses, although Cayman Brac does have a 140ft cliff, by far the most dramatic scenery in the country. In fact, the Caymans are the tips of massive submarine mountains that just barely emerge from the awesome Cayman Trench, an area with the deepest water in the Caribbean.

Encircling all three of the islands are shallow waters and a reef system harboring one of the world's richest accumulations of marine life. At Bloody Bay Wall, on the north shore of Little Cayman, the seafloor ends abruptly at a depth of only 18ft to 25ft, dropping off into a 6000ft vertical cliff. Along its sheer face grows an astonishing variety of corals, sponges and sea fans and thousands of mobile creatures going about their daily business as the occasional diver looks on, agog.

### Wildlife

The Caymans' dry land is not quite as exciting as its waters, but it still gives nature lovers plenty to do and see. With nearly 200 native winged species, the islands offer outstand-

---

**CAYMAN CRUISING: SOME MORE WELCOME THAN OTHERS?**

In one of the most homophobic regions of the world it's hard to pinpoint which country is a worse offender and why, although in terms of sheer violence Jamaica usually leads the way. Yet the Caymanians have also made a pretty good case for themselves in recent years. The controversy started back in 1998 when a gay cruise ship was told it was not welcome to weigh anchor here. This rather sad piece of discrimination discredited the Cayman Islands massively in the eyes of tourists around the world, and as a result the Caymans saw a drop off in cruise ships of all kinds.

With a change of administration came a change of heart, though, and – ever sensitive to the tourist dollar – in 2001 the Cayman government reversed the policy when it introduced antidiscrimination legislation.

Five years passed before another gay cruise attempted to land in the Caymans, but in 2006 the *Navigator of the Seas* made a one-day visit without incident. Despite the move being very unpopular with much of the Caymanian population, it seems as if the Cayman Islands have finally – officially, at least – embraced diversity, although the detainment of one young American in 2008 for embracing his partner in a nightclub caused more embarrassment for the tourism department. Despite progressive intentions, there's still a long way to go.

---

ing bird-watching. Keep your eyes open and you'll spot parrots, boobies, yellow-bellied sapsuckers, herons and egrets. Reptiles include celebrities such as green sea turtles and blue iguanas, and plenty of common geckos and lizards (the latter sometimes making an appearance in the baths of luxury hotels). The islands have a remarkably well protected ecology – driving on beaches is against the law due to the harm this can do to turtle habitats, iguanas have the right of way and there are plentiful marine replenishment zones where fishing is not permitted. For more about the fascinating and still endangered blue iguanas, see the website of the **Blue Iguana Recovery Program** (www.bluei guana.ky).

The Caymans aren't lush, but they do support a fair swag of plant life. Mahogany was once abundant but has been mostly logged. Poisonous species include maiden plum (a weed with rash-causing sap), lady's hair or cowitch (a vine with fiberglass-like barbs) and the vicious manchineel tree, which produces a skin-blistering sap. Take care not to shelter under a manchineel in the rain! Other indigenous plants are cochineel, used as a shampoo as well as eaten, and pingwing, whose barbed branches were once fashioned into a natural fence.

## FOOD & DRINK

You'll eat superbly almost anywhere in the Caymans – the combination of a large international community and plenty of cash sloshing about means that no effort is spared to import excellent fresh food and specialties from around the world. Just don't be horrified to see turtle on the menu – it remains the national dish and any restaurant serving it will be using ecologically sound farm-raised turtles to make your steak, stew or soup. It's surprisingly delicious.

As in the Bahamas, conch is a popular item on restaurant menus. This large pink mollusk is cooked with onion and spices in a stew, fried up as fritters, or sliced raw and served with a lime marinade. **Cayman Sea Sense** (www.na tionaltrust.org.ky/seasense.html) is a fantastic program designed to let diners know when restaurants are sourcing all their fish and seafood sustainably. See the website for a full list of restaurants that have met the exacting standards. Sadly it's as yet only a small number of eateries that reach the required standard, but among them are some of the very best.

For dessert, try 'heavy cake,' a dense confection made from starchy ingredients such as grated cassava, cornmeal, yam and liberal quantities of brown sugar, or the classic Tortuga Rum Cake, which is available in a number of flavors and makes a great gift to take home.

Wash it all down with a 'jelly ice,' chilled coconut water sucked from the shell, or perhaps a bottle of Stingray Beer, the local brew. Or, if you can handle a thousand extra calories, slurp a mudslide, the creamy cocktail – a potent concoction of Kahlua, Baileys and vodka – invented on Rum Point. Alcohol is generally expensive and can only be bought from liquor stores.

CAYMAN ISLANDS

# GRAND CAYMAN

**pop 37,000**

To most of the world, Grand Cayman *is* the Cayman Islands, a glitzy shopping mecca and global financial centre where five-star hotels line the fabulous white-sand Seven Mile Beach and the wealthy from around the world spend time sipping cocktails and discretely playing with their millions.

Yet beyond George Town and Seven Mile Beach the island does have its own quiet charm and Caribbean life still leaves its mark on what, in many places, could otherwise be mistaken for suburban Florida – whether it's the island-wide cockerels crowing at dawn or the impromptu parties that take place at a moment's notice. The island is crowded, no doubt, and it's far from being an idyllic Caribbean hideaway, but with its excellent restaurants, shopping, activities and things to see and do, Grand Cayman is certainly not a place to be bored.

## Getting There & Away

For information on getting to (and from) Grand Cayman, see p213.

## Getting Around

### TO/FROM THE AIRPORT

There's a taxi queue just outside the airport building. Fares are set by the government, based on one to three people sharing a ride.

Sample fares from the airport:

**East End** US$60
**George Town, Southern Seven Mile Beach** US$12.50
**Northern Seven Mile Beach** US$25
**Rum Point/Cayman Kai** US$70

All of the major car-rental agencies have offices across the road from the terminal. Unfortunately, there is no bus service to the airport, and hotels are not permitted to collect guests on arrival.

### BICYCLE & SCOOTER

With its flat terrain and always stunning views of the sea, Grand Cayman is a pleasure for cyclists (many hotels make bikes available to guests). Renting a scooter will enable you to easily access the far reaches of the island.

**Cayman Cycle Rentals** ( ☎ 945-4021; Coconut Place Shopping Center, West Bay Rd, Seven Mile Beach; per day mountain bikes/scooters US$15/30) rents both bicycles and scooters.

### BUS

The public **bus terminal** ( ☎ 916-1293), located adjacent to the public library on Edward St in downtown George Town, serves as the dispatch point for buses to all districts of Grand Cayman. The system uses color-coded logos on the buses to indicate routes.

The main routes:

**West Bay** (fare US$2.50; ☽ 6am-11pm Sun-Thu, 6am-midnight Fri & Sat) Every 15 minutes. Served by Route 1 (yellow) and Route 2 (lime green) buses.

**Bodden Town** (fare US$2.50; ☽ 6am-11pm Sun-Thu, 6am-midnight Fri & Sat) Every 30 minutes. Served by Route 3 (blue) buses.

**East End** (fare US$2.50; ☽ 6am-9pm Sun-Thu, 6am-midnight Fri & Sat) Hourly. Served by Route 4 (purple) and Route 5 (red) buses. Via Bodden Town.

**North Side** (fare US$2.50; ☽ 6am-9pm Sun-Thu & Sat, 6am-midnight Fri) Hourly. Served by Route 5 (red) buses. Passes the entrance to Queen Elizabeth II Botanic Park.

### CAR

During the peak season, rates for a compact car start at around US$40 per day; rentals during the low season may be 25% less. The following are the main rental suppliers.

**Andy's Rent-a-Car** ( ☎ 949-8111; www.andys.ky; Owen Roberts International Airport; ☽ 6am-10pm)

**Avis** ( ☎ 949-2468; www.aviscayman.com; Owen Roberts International Airport) Other branches are at the Ritz Carlton, Marriott Hotel and Westin.

**Budget** ( ☎ 949-5605; www.budgetcayman.com; Owen Roberts International Airport)

**Cayman Auto Rentals** ( ☎ 949-1013; www.cayman autorentals.net; West Bay Rd)

**Coconut Car Rentals** ( ☎ 949-4037; www.coconutcar rentals.com) Offices at Owen Roberts International Airport and Coconut Place, Seven Mile Beach.

**Economy Car Rental** ( ☎ 949-9550; www.economycar rental.com.ky; Owen Roberts International Airport)

### TAXI

Taxis are readily available at Owen Roberts International Airport, from all resorts and from the taxi stand at the cruise-ship dock in George Town. They offer a fixed rate per vehicle or per person to all points on Grand Cayman. A sign with current rates is posted at the dock.

## GEORGE TOWN & SEVEN MILE BEACH

**pop 21,000**

George Town is the supremely wealthy but surprisingly modest capital of the Caymans. While no doubt cosmopolitan, with more than its fair share of excellent restaurants,

**GRAND CAYMAN FOR CHILDREN**

Most kids will love the Caymans (just try to stop them visiting the turtle farm, snorkeling at Stingray City or enjoying the beach at Rum Point!) but there's little better suited to intergenerational interaction than the fantastic **Kids Sea Camp** ( ☎ 1-803-419-2556, from within the USA 800-934-3483; www.kidseacamp.com). This inventive travel package is designed to bring families closer together, underwater. Organized excursions to a number of great dive and snorkeling sites, combined with access to age-appropriate instruction, make this a good option for families that want to push the active vacation envelope. Kids Sea Camp is hosted by Divetech at Cobalt Coast Resort & Suites (p204) in July and August each year.

bars and shopping, there's something terribly unassuming about the place as well – it's tiny, tidy and easy to walk around, and there's often little going on, especially at weekends when much of the worker population stays at home outside the town. The obvious flip side to this is when the cruise ships come into port and thousands of passengers descend en masse to buy anything in sight.

North of the harbor and town center is Seven Mile Beach, a gorgeous stretch of unbroken white sand where Grand Cayman's tourist industry is concentrated. Despite being very built up with condos, big hotels, malls and restaurants, the beach is stunning, and you'll usually find it busy with locals and visitors alike any day of the week.

Most of Grand Cayman's hotels, restaurants and shopping complexes line the island's busiest thoroughfare, West Bay Rd, which travels alongside Seven Mile Beach.

## Information
### BOOKSTORES
**BookNook** ( ☎ 949-7392; Anchorage Centre, Harbour Dr, George Town) Limited stock of general interest titles, including regional travel guides. Find it under Margaritaville.
**Hobbies & Books** ( ☎ 949-0707; Piccadilly Centre, Elgin Ave, George Town) Another book shop with a large selection of magazines and newspapers.

### EMERGENCY
**Police** (RCIP; ☎ 949-4222; Elgin Ave, George Town)

### INTERNET ACCESS
**Café del Sol Internet Coffee House** ( ⊙ 7am-7pm Mon-Sat, 8am-7pm Sun) George Town ( ☎ 946-3322; www.cafedelsol.ky; Aqua World Duty Free Mall, South Church St, George Town; 30min/1hr US$3/5); Seven Mile Beach ( ☎ 946-2233; cnr West Bay Rd & Lawrence Blvd, Seven Mile Beach) The cheapest access in the most comfortable surroundings. The George Town branch has

wi-fi only, the Seven Mile Beach branch has both terminals and wi-fi.
**Computer Geeks** ( ☎ 949-4335; Queen's Court, Seven Mile Beach; 30min US$2; ⊙ 10am-3am Mon-Fri)

### MEDICAL SERVICES
**Cayman Islands Hospital** ( ☎ 949-8600; Hospital Rd, George Town) Houses a state-of-the-art recompression chamber: phone ☎ 555 (24 hours).

### MONEY
George Town, it seems, has nearly as many banks as people. Filling your wallet with the brightly colored currency is optional if you're flush with greenbacks: US currency is accepted everywhere at a standard island exchange rate of CI$0.80 to US$1.

### POST
**Main post office** ( ☎ 949-2474; cnr Edward St & Cardinal Ave, George Town; ⊙ 8:15am-5pm Mon-Fri, 9-12:30pm Sat)

### TOURIST INFORMATION
**Department of Tourism** ( ☎ 949-0623; www.cayman islands.ky) The Cayman Islands' tourism department operates information booths that are located at the Owen Roberts International Airport and at the North Terminal cruise-ship dock at George Town harbor. The booth at the airport is open when flights arrive; the booth at the dock is only open when cruise ships are in port.

## Sights
There is nothing you can't miss in George Town – it's pleasant enough to stroll around, eat and shop in, but the sights are of negligible interest. The best of the lot is the **Cayman National Museum** ( ☎ 949-8368; www.museum.ky; cnr Harbour Dr & Sheddon Rd, George Town), which at the time of research was being restored after damage inflicted by Hurricane Ivan in 2004. When it reopens the museum collection – a variety of exhibits on the islands' cultural and natural

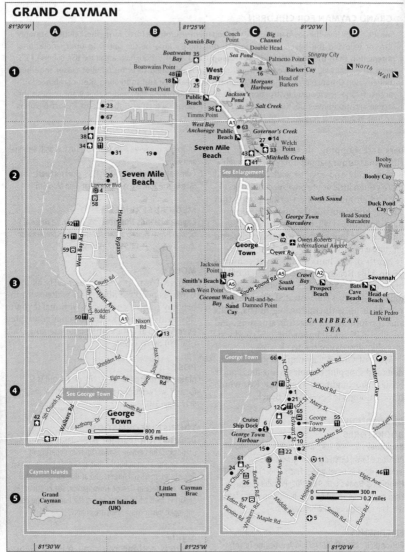

history and an engaging audiovisual presentation, will again be on display in George Town's oldest building.

At the **National Gallery of the Cayman Islands** ( ☎ 945-8111; www.nationalgallery.org.ky; ground fl, Harbour Pl, South Church St, George Town; admission free; ☑ 9am-5pm Mon-Fri, 11am-4pm Sat), located somewhat incongruously in a mall devoted to duty-free

shopping, you can see the work of local artist Margaret Barwick alongside a few other imports. While certainly not to all tastes, there are some pretty and evocative island scenes.

Further north in Seven Mile Beach is the **Butterfly Farm** ( ☎ 946-3411; www.thebutterflyfarm.com; Lawrence Blvd, Seven Mile Beach; admission adult/child US$10/5; ☑ 8:30am-4pm, last tour 3:30pm), a popular excursion

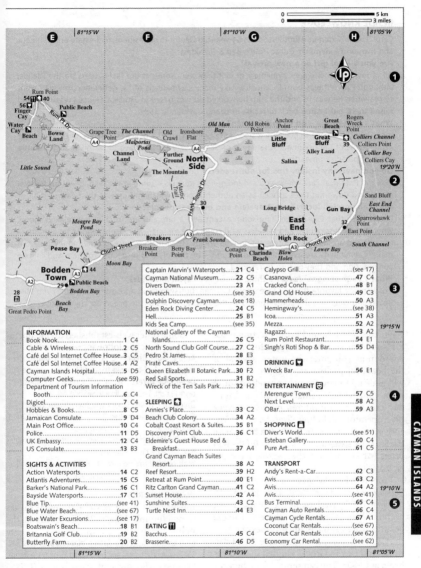

0 _____ 5 km
0 _____ 3 miles

| INFORMATION | |
|---|---|
| Book Nook | 1 C4 |
| Cable & Wireless | 2 C5 |
| Café del Sol Internet Coffee House | 3 C5 |
| Café del Sol Internet Coffee House | 4 A2 |
| Cayman Islands Hospital | 5 D5 |
| Computer Geeks | (see 59) |
| Department of Tourism Information Booth | 6 C4 |
| Digicel | 7 C4 |
| Hobbies & Books | 8 C5 |
| Jamaican Consulate | 9 D4 |
| Main Post Office | 10 C4 |
| Police | 11 D5 |
| UK Embassy | 12 C4 |
| US Consulate | 13 B3 |

| SIGHTS & ACTIVITIES | |
|---|---|
| Action Watersports | 14 C2 |
| Atlantis Adventures | 15 C5 |
| Barker's National Park | 16 C1 |
| Bayside Watersports | 17 C1 |
| Blue Tip | (see 41) |
| Blue Water Beach | (see 67) |
| Blue Water Excursions | (see 17) |
| Boatswain's Beach | 18 B1 |
| Britannia Golf Club | 19 B2 |
| Butterfly Farm | 20 B2 |

| | |
|---|---|
| Captain Marvin's Watersports | 21 C4 |
| Cayman National Museum | 22 C5 |
| Divers Down | 23 A1 |
| Divetech | (see 35) |
| Dolphin Discovery Cayman | (see 18) |
| Eden Rock Diving Center | 24 C5 |
| Hell | 25 B1 |
| Kids Sea Camp | (see 35) |
| National Gallery of the Cayman Islands | 26 C5 |
| North Sound Club Golf Course | 27 C2 |
| Pedro St James | 28 E3 |
| Pirate Caves | 29 E3 |
| Queen Elizabeth II Botanic Park | 30 F2 |
| Red Sail Sports | 31 B2 |
| Wreck of the Ten Sails Park | 32 H2 |

| SLEEPING 🏠 | |
|---|---|
| Annies's Place | 33 C2 |
| Beach Club Colony | 34 A2 |
| Cobalt Coast Resort & Suites | 35 B1 |
| Discovery Point Club | 36 C1 |
| Eldemire's Guest House Bed & Breakfast | 37 A4 |
| Grand Cayman Beach Suites Resort | 38 A2 |
| Reef Resort | 39 H2 |
| Retreat at Rum Point | 40 E1 |
| Ritz Carlton Grand Cayman | 41 C2 |
| Sunset House | 42 A4 |
| Sunshine Suites | 43 C2 |
| Turtle Nest Inn | 44 E3 |

| EATING 🍴 | |
|---|---|
| Bacchus | 45 C4 |
| Brasserie | 46 D5 |

| | |
|---|---|
| Calypso Grill | (see 17) |
| Casanova | 47 C4 |
| Cracked Conch | 48 B1 |
| Grand Old House | 49 C5 |
| Hammerheads | 50 A3 |
| Hemingway's | (see 38) |
| Icoa | 51 A3 |
| Mezza | 52 A2 |
| Ragazzi | 53 A2 |
| Rum Point Restaurant | 54 E1 |
| Singh's Roti Shop & Bar | 55 D4 |

| DRINKING 🍷 | |
|---|---|
| Wreck Bar | 56 E1 |

| ENTERTAINMENT 🎭 | |
|---|---|
| Merengue Town | 57 C5 |
| Next Level | 58 A2 |
| OBar | 59 A3 |

| SHOPPING 🛍 | |
|---|---|
| Diver's World | (see 51) |
| Esteban Gallery | 60 C4 |
| Pure Art | 61 C5 |

| TRANSPORT | |
|---|---|
| Andy's Rent-a-Car | 62 C3 |
| Avis | 63 C2 |
| Avis | 64 A2 |
| Avis | (see 41) |
| Bus Terminal | 65 C4 |
| Cayman Auto Rentals | 66 C4 |
| Cayman Cycle Rentals | 67 A1 |
| Coconut Car Rentals | (see 67) |
| Coconut Car Rentals | (see 62) |
| Economy Car Rental | (see 62) |

**CAYMAN ISLANDS**

for visitors, who are taken around on a tour and introduced up close to many beautiful butterflies native to the Caymans.

## Activities
### DIVING & SNORKELING

Many people coming to Grand Cayman are coming for one thing alone, the great diving.

While arguably better, more pristine sites are available on Cayman Brac and Little Cayman, the diving around Grand Cayman should not be discounted. As well as over 160 dive sites there's the superb **Stingray City**, often considered to be one of the best shallow dives in the world and an undoubted highlight of any trip. This stretch of sandy seafloor in Grand

---

**INSIDE KNOWLEDGE**

Carol 'Tootie' Eldemire-Huddleston is a 64-year-old Georgetown resident, real-estate entrepreneur and owner of Eldemire's Guest House Bed & Breakfast.

**Are you a local girl or a new arrival?**

All of my ancestors were Caymanian. In fact they were some of the first settlers on the islands, although I myself was born in Jamaica. Like many Caymanians of his generation, my dad went to sea when he was 16 and the ship he worked on was based in Jamaica. Hence I was born and raised there but I came back to reside in Grand Cayman in 1987.

**What's it like to live on Grand Cayman?**

It's a delightful place to live with a slow, easy island pace. The beaches, sunsets and crystal clear azure colors of the ocean are what really makes it a very special place to be. All in all, it's a little piece of paradise on earth.

**Do you have any insider tips for our readers?**

Visit the Botanical Park where you see indigenous iguanas – some in the wild, beautiful tropical plants and flowering trees as well as an authentic old Caymanian home at the heart of it all.

**How can you tell locals from travelers and business people?**

Locals have that Caymanian 'sing-song' accent and a tan, and are usually in a relaxed mood, whereas business people and travelers who come here for financial reasons tend to be a bit more uptight and are not really interested in who we are. Their main focus is on the money they can make. Caymanians are extremely kind though – be friendly and respectful to them and initiate conversation and they're sure to respond.

**What's your personal favorite thing about the Cayman Islands?**

I have many favorite things I love about Cayman, but swimming and snorkeling off Seven Mile Beach and watching the sun setting over the striking colors of the ocean are my favorites…

---

Cayman's North Sound is the meeting place for southern stingrays hungry for a meal. As soon as you enter the water, several of the beautiful prehistoric-looking creatures will glide up to you to suck morsels of squid from your tentative fingers. Half- and full-day excursions are offered by nearly every dive operator, including **Divers Down** ( ☎ 949-6796; www.diversdown.net; Coconut Pl, West Bay Rd, Seven Mile Beach; dive/snorkel trip US$65/35) and **Off the Wall Divers** ( ☎ 945-7525; www.otwdivers.com; dive/snorkel trip US$45/20).

From **Eden Rock Diving Center** ( ☎ 949-7243; www.edenrockdive.com; 124 South Church St, George Town; 1-/2-tank dive US$55/85), overlooking the George Town harbor, it's an easy matter to shore dive to the beautiful caves, tunnels and grottoes of two of the Caymans' most celebrated dive sites: Eden Rocks and Devil's Grotto. Guided shore dives begin at US$55. You can snorkel from here for free, although there's a locker fee.

**Red Sail Sports** ( ☎ 949-8745; www.redsailcayman.com; Grand Cayman Beach Suites Resort, West Bay Rd, Seven Mile Beach; 1-/2-tank dive US$70/110) is the largest and best-known of the diving providers, offering excursions island-wide and numerous outlets across Grand Cayman, including at Rum Point for access to the North Wall.

Some other well-established diving operations include the following:

**Ambassador Divers** ( ☎ 916-1046; www.ambassadordivers.com; 1-/2-tank dive US$65/95)

**Deep Blue Divers** ( ☎ 947-0116; www.deepbluediverscayman.com; 1-/2-tank dive US$65/90)

**Divetech** ( ☎ 946-5658; www.divetech.com; Cobalt Coast Resort & Suites, West Bay; 1-/2-tank dive US$60/110) Located near the awesome North Wall.

**Sun Divers** ( ☎ 916-0862; www.sundivers.ky; Boatswains Bay; 1-/2-tank dive US$60/90)

**Wall to Wall Diving** ( ☎ 916-6408; www.walltowalldiving.com; 1-/2-tank dive US$60/90)

### WATER SPORTS

Independent paddlers will find rental kayaks (single/double US$20/25 per hour) at the public beach at Seven Mile Beach. They are also available from **Action Watersports** ( ☎ 548-3147; www.ciactionmarine.com; Grand Caymanian Resort, Safe Haven), who also rent waverunners (US$65 per 30 minutes) and can organize catamaran hire. Parasailing is possible at Seven Mile Beach through **Blue Water Beach** ( ☎ 525-5400; www.bwbcayman.com; Royal Palms Beach Club).

### FISHING

The clear, warm waters of the Caymans are teeming with blue marlin, wahoo, tuna and mahimahi. Charter a boat (half-day charters US$500 to US$600, full-day charters US$700 to US$1200) with an experienced Caymanian captain and hook some real action.

**Bayside Watersports** ( ☎ 949-3200; www.bayside watersports.com; Batabano Rd, Morgan's Harbour) True Caymanian hospitality and fishing expertise.

**Blue Water Excursions** ( ☎ 925-8738; www.bluewater excursions.ky; Morgan's Harbour) Local fisherman Capt Richard Orr is at the helm of his 32ft vessel *Trouble Maker*.

**Captain Marvin's Watersports** ( ☎ 949-3200; www .captainmarvins.com; Waterfront Centre, North Church St, George Town) In business since 1951.

### GOLF

Plenty of great sunshine and three world-class courses make the Caymans a prime destination for golf nuts.

**Britannia Golf Club** ( ☎ 949-8020; Grand Cayman Beach Suites Resort, West Bay Rd, Seven Mile Beach), designed by Jack Nicklaus, this course is reminiscent of legendary Scottish courses with its traditional 'links' layout.

The superb **North Sound Club Golf Course** ( ☎ 947-4653; www.northsoundclub.com; Safehaven Dr, Seven Mile Beach) closed after Ivan and has now reopened with new management. The new 18-hole course is championship level and in a stunning location, interwoven with the canals off the North Sound.

A Greg Norman–designed nine-hole course belonging to the new Ritz-Carlton hotel, **Blue Tip** ( ☎ 815-6500; www.ritzcarlton.com; West Bay Rd, Seven Mile Beach) is the latest addition to Grand Cayman's golf scene. Adjacent to the North Sound Club, many of the holes are over water.

### HORSEBACK RIDING

While Grand Cayman lacks the dramatic scenery of much of the Caribbean, horseback riding is still very popular here. The following places are recommended.

**Nikki's Beach Rides** ( ☎ 916-3530, 945-5839). Well regarded for its engaging tours led by the amiable Caymanian owner. Small groups of up to six ride along the beach and through scenic inland wetlands.

**Pampered Ponies** ( ☎ 945-2262; www.ponies.ky) Offers dawn riding down deserted beaches for experienced riders, romantic sunset rides and awesome full moon ones as well. The small groups are all led by professionals.

## Tours

It's possible to visit the underwater world without even mussing up your hair on an **Atlantis Adventures** ( ☎ 949-7700; www.atlantis adventures.com; 32 Goring Ave, George Town; adult/child/teen US$79/59/69) submarine expedition. The *Atlantis XI* submarine takes groups to a depth of 100ft, for which tours leave every hour Monday through Sunday. Children under 3ft tall cannot join the fun. Other trips are available, including spooky nighttime descents.

## Sleeping

Flying down Seven Mile Beach as you approach the airport, you could be forgiven for thinking that the whole of Grand Cayman is covered in luxury condos, guesthouses and sprawling hotel complexes. It isn't, but most of the coast is, and there's a huge choice here, as long as you're not looking for a youth hostel. Most hotels are midrange and top end, although there are a few budget-friendly places.

**Eldemire's Guest House Bed & Breakfast** ( ☎ 916-8369; www.eldemire.com; Glen Eden Rd, George Town; r US$110-135, 1-/2-bedroom ste $145/225; ✷ ▢ ) This guesthouse is the favorite of independent travelers and provides a large range of accommodations, from very basic rooms for seasonal workers to very smart and spacious suites. The suites have their own kitchens while room guests in the main block share a spacious and well-equipped common kitchen. All guests have access to laundry facilities. There's free wi-fi throughout the complex and rental bikes are available (per day US$15). Take South Church St from downtown and the turn off is signposted.

**Annie's Place** ( ☎ 945-5505; www.anniesplace.ky; 282 Andrew Dr, Snug Harbour; s/d US$110/140; ✷ ) Annie Multon has opened up her home as a charming B&B just a few blocks back from Seven Mile Beach. The well-decorated bungalow has a great garden, and all bedrooms have private bathrooms and cable TV. This is a great place to feel local – you'll rarely see tourists down here. Annie's has a three-night minimum stay during the summer (April to September), and a seven-night minimum stay during the winter season (October to March).

**Sunshine Suites** ( ☎ 949-3000; www.sunshinesuites .com; Peninsula Ave, Seven Mile Beach; r incl breakfast from US$175; ✷ ▢ ☒ ) This complex of 131 studios and apartments offers a good half-way house between hotel and condo. Because it's set back from the beach (though only a short walk away), rates are lower than for waterfront places. The smart, fully serviced accommodations come complete with a buzzing bar-restaurant and a good pool. Each unit is equipped with a full kitchen, making self-catering an easy option.

**Discovery Point Club** ( ☎ 945-4724; www.discovery pointclub.com; West Bay Rd, Seven Mile Beach; r with/without sea view from US$300/210, 2-bedroom ste US$345-525; ❄ 🖥 🐀 ) This excellent condo complex has been totally renovated since Ivan and is recommended for a family beach holiday. Right on stunning Seven Mile Beach, all suites have superb views, balconies or patios and self-catering facilities. The smaller one-bed studios don't have kitchens but share the excellent hotel facilities including the tennis courts, pool, spa and wi-fi.

**Sunset House** ( ☎ 949-7111; www.sunsethouse .com; 390 South Church St, George Town; courtyard/ocean view/apt US$200/250/345; ❄ 🖥 🐀 ) Just south of George Town, this divers' haven is a great spot, although the weekly packages work out far more economically than the higher per night rates. As you'd expect, the whole operation revolves around diving, with a dive school boasting specialized guides as well as a famed underwater photography center. The rooms are clean and comfortable.

**Beach Club Colony** ( ☎ 949-8100; bchclub@candw .ky; West Bay Rd, Seven Mile Beach; s/d from US$290/440; ❄ 🖥 🐀 ) This all-inclusive resort has 41 rooms right on the beach in the heart of Seven Mile Beach. Guest rooms are bright and cheerful, and interconnecting rooms are available on request. Weekly packages make a stay here work out much cheaper.

**Grand Cayman Beach Suites Resort** ( ☎ 949-1234, in the US 888-591-1234; www.grand-cayman-beach-ste.com; West Bay Rd, Seven Mile Beach; r/ste from US$499/849; ❄ 🖥 🐀 ) This former Hyatt, which lost its prestigious name in 2008 but retained its impressive $80m refit following Hurricane Ivan, may now play second fiddle to the Ritz-Carlton, but it's still an excellent property. All rooms are large and beautifully set out, including kitchens, large bathrooms and balconies. The resort has a gym, golf course, three restaurants, a stunning beach and an excellent diving center.

**Ritz-Carlton Grand Cayman** ( ☎ 943-9000; www .ritzcarlton.com; West Bay Rd, Seven Mile Beach; r/ste from US$879/2530; ❄ 🖥 🐀 ) The newest and certainly the largest luxury resort in Grand Cayman is this vast 365-room property located on both sides of West Bay Rd, the two buildings connected by an enclosed pedestrian bridge. Given the incredible price tags these rooms attract, they tend to feel sterile and somewhat *nouveau riche*. Despite this, it's undeniably a great place to stay with two stunning pools, a beautiful stretch of beach, a magnificent spa, a nine-hole golf course (p201), tennis courts and a host of superb bars and restaurants.

## Eating & Drinking

You'll eat extraordinarily good food on Grand Cayman. From super-smart restaurants catering to the leisurely rich to simpler cafés producing excellent fresh meals, it's hard to go wrong here, although there are very few bargains to be had! **Cayman Islands Restaurants** (www.caymanrestaurants.com) is a good resource for further listings.

### GEORGE TOWN

**Singh's Roti Shop & Bar** ( ☎ 946-7684; cnr Doctor Roy's Dr & Shedden Rd; mains US$7-10; �} lunch & dinner, closed Sun) This is one of George Town's best bargains. In a city where dinner often means a three-figure check, this cheerful hole-in-the-wall is a great place for some tongue-searing roti (curry filling, often potatoes and chicken, rolled inside flat bread).

**Hammerheads** ( ☎ 949-3080; North Church St; mains US$10-20; �} lunch & dinner) This is a great spot to meet locals who come in droves for sundowners and satisfying diner fare out on the large deck with great sea views. Burgers, fried chicken and some seriously good sandwiches are the main offerings – as well as killer cocktails. There's also tarpon feeding on the deck every evening at 9pm.

**Casanova** ( ☎ 949-7633; www.casanova.ky; 65 North Church St; mains US$17-30; �} lunch Mon-Fri, dinner daily) This relatively affordable Italian restaurant overlooking the sea is a great spot for a quality dinner. Reserve a table with a view out on the veranda. The pizzas are good, as are the fresh fish and seafood dishes.

**Grand Old House** ( ☎ 949-9333; South Church St; mains US$20-36; �} lunch Mon-Fri, dinner daily) This seriously establishment stunner is probably the island's best-known restaurant, housed in a beautiful white plantation house that, on a delightfully eccentric note, also serves as the honorary Austrian consulate each morning. The menu is traditional Caribbean, including farm-raised turtle steaks and a superb wine list. Reservations and smart dress are recommended.

**Brasserie** ( ☎ 945-1815; www.brasseriecayman.com; Cricket Sq; mains US$22-40) This excellent place enjoys the patronage of many of the political and business elite in George Town, and while there's a rarified air and not a cruise ship passenger in sight, there's nothing snooty or unwelcoming here. The beautifully attired dining rooms are great for a flash evening out. The international menu is impressive and beautifully realized.

**Bacchus** ( ☎ 949-5757; www.bacchus.ky; Fort St; mains US$27-38; ☾ 10am-1am Mon-Thu, 10am-2am Fri, 11am-midnight Sat) This cozy place is an award winner as much for being a great wine bar as for its sublime food. The sophisticated and interesting menu has something for everyone – there are plenty of vegetarian options as well as a host of more traditional dishes from lobster thermidor to yellowfin tuna steaks.

### SEVEN MILE BEACH

**Ragazzi** ( ☎ 945-3484; Buckingham Sq, West Bay Rd; pizzas US$10-17, mains US$15-35; ☾ 11:30am-11pm) This much-loved Italian place is far more than the pizzeria it bills itself as. Even though the pizza here is excellent, there's plenty more of interest besides, with a rich list of antipasti, pasta and mains. Try *scaloppine limone* or Maryland crab ravioli for something different. The wine list is excellent and service charming.

**our pick** **Icoa** ( ☎ 945-1915; www.icoacayman.com; Seven Mile Shops, West Bay Rd; mains US$12.50-20; ☾ 7am-6pm Mon-Thu, 7am-11pm Fri & Sat, 8am-3pm Sun) Located in an unprepossessing shopping mall, Icoa, a café, deli, takeaway and full restaurant, is perhaps our single favorite find in the Cayman Islands. Always busy with locals in the know, this fanatically run place has, quite simply, never served up a bad dish. The menu is deceptively simple – seared scallops or Moroccan lamb spiced stew, for example – but the resulting dish is always memorable. Great for breakfast, weekend brunch, takeout sandwiches and more – don't miss this slice of heaven.

**Mezza** ( ☎ 946-3992; West Bay Rd; mains US$19-32; ☾ 11:30am-3pm & 5-10pm Mon-Fri, 5-10pm Sat) This exclusive, buzzing bar-restaurant is the hangout of well-connected locals and is a top Seven Mile Beach pick. The menu is made up of simple American-led standards at lunchtime, but becomes markedly more ambitious in the evenings, when specialties such as jerk chicken fettuccine, red snapper curry and black-tea–dusted yellowfin appear. Desserts are sublime. Reservations advised.

**Hemingway's** ( ☎ 945-5700; Grand Cayman Beach Suites Resort, West Bay Rd, Seven Mile Beach; mains US$26-38; ☾ lunch & dinner) This exceptional restaurant is far from being just another hotel eatery and so, while it's the flagship restaurant of the Grand Cayman Beach Suites Resort, it's also a favorite with Grand Cayman high society. Its menu's gimmick is that each dish relates to Papa somehow, and even if that sometimes feels a bit labored ('Hemingway feasted on fresh lobster regularly at his home in Key West'), the food is superb. Try paella Valencia, tenderloin of beef, or just brunch and coffee on the terrace overlooking the beach. Reservations advised.

## Entertainment

People don't come to the Caymans for the nightlife, although there's a clutch of decent nightclubs around George Town and Seven Mile Beach – the only ones in the country.

The legal drinking age is 18. As a result of draconian laws, all clubs and bars close at midnight on Saturday. As a result Thursday and Friday are the big nights to go out.

**OBar** ( ☎ 943-6227; Queens Court Plaza, West Bay Rd, Seven Mile Beach; ☾ 10pm-3am Mon-Fri) Still the best place in town, this unpretentious nightclub and lounge has great resident DJs, fantastic cocktails and occasional live performances.

**Merengue Town** ( ☎ 949-6833; Boilers Rd, George Town; ☾ 10pm-3am Mon-Fri) This steamy club has become a hugely popular dance place recently, playing a range of Caribbean rhythms from merengue to rumba and reggaeton. You'll meet a very local crowd determined to party here.

**Next Level** ( ☎ 946-6398; www.nextlevelcayman .com; West Bay Rd, Seven Mile Beach; ☾ 8pm-3am Mon-Fri) The smartest club on the island gets the best DJs and a young and friendly crowd as its regulars. Monday is 'All You Can Drink Monday,' Wednesday is for hip-hop and dancehall, while Friday is the biggest night on the island – R&B, hip-hop and retro music prevails. Ladies enter free before 11pm most nights.

## Shopping

At the malls clustered around the waterfront, savings are significant for consumer goods such as watches, jewelry, sunglasses, designer clothing, cameras, crystal, spirits and cosmetics as there are no sales taxes here. You will also encounter a plethora of local treasures, including shell jewelry, thatch work, wood carvings, crocheted items, pepper sauces, tropical fruit jams, honey and caymanite (Cayman's semiprecious stone) figurines. Most of it is tat.

Some of the better shops:

**Diver's World** ( ☎ 949-8128; Seven Mile Shops, Seven Mile Beach; ☺ 10am-6pm Mon-Sat) This fantastic diving shop is the Cayman's biggest. Knowledgeable staff will help you get what you need.

**Esteban Gallery** ( ☎ 946-2787; ground fl, AAL Trust Bank Bldg, North Church St, George Town; ☺ 10am-5pm Mon-Sat) The place for Caymanite sculptures by noted local artist Bracker Horacio Esteban.

**Pure Art** ( ☎ 949-9133; South Church St, George Town; ☺ 9am-5pm Mon-Sat) Head here for locally made arts and crafts.

## WEST BAY

North of George Town, West Bay is quietly suburban and home to the excellent turtle farm, the quaint township of Hell and the more remote Barkers National Park – the first national park in the Caymans.

### Sights

**Boatswain's Beach** ( ☎ 949-3894; www.boatswains beach.ky; North West Point Rd; general admission adult/child US$55/25, turtle farm only adult/child US$18/9; ☺ 8:30am-4:30pm) is the closest thing the Caymans have to Disney Land – and a firm favorite with kids. If you balk at the exorbitant prices then the turtle farm remains the best part of the visit and is well worth coming for alone at a much lower price.

The **turtle farm** is a unique hatchery where green sea turtles are raised from hatchlings to behemoths averaging over 300lb. While protecting wild populations by meeting market demand for turtle products, the farm has, over the years, also released more than 31,000 hatchlings into the waters surrounding the Cayman Islands. Visitors can peer into tanks filled with specimens ranging from babies to massive adults moshing about in their breeding pond.

Elsewhere in the complex for those paying the full price you have a huge swimming pool, complete with two waterfalls, a shark and predator tank (feeding time is always fun), a bird aviary, a butterfly grove and

a 'Caymanian Street,' a ye olde Caribbean street where fishermen and craftsmen magically flown in from 'yesteryear' tell stories to anyone unable to run away fast enough.

Opposite Boatswain's Beach a rather controversial dolphinarium, **Dolphin Discovery Cayman**, is due to open in 2008, offering patrons the chance to swim with dolphins, a practice that is widely condemned by environmentalists. The local campaigning group, **Keep Dolphins Free** (http://dolphinfreecayman.org) has bitterly opposed the development.

The tiny village of **Hell** attracts gawpers with very little to do indeed. Comprised primarily of a post office, a gift shop and, tellingly, an Esso Station, Hell is for the cruise ship crowd and anyone who wants to send a postcard from Hell.

A far better way to spend the afternoon is to have a ramble in the **Barkers National Park**. Dedicated in 2004, it's the first land in the Caymans to be set aside for such a purpose. Leave your car and wander along the isolated beaches. There was no visitor center nor any facilities here at the time of research.

### Sleeping & Eating

**Cobalt Coast Resort & Suites** ( ☎ 946-5656; www.cobalt coast.com; r US$240, ste from US$280; ☒ ☐ ☒ ) Over 80% of the guests at this resort, located on a pleasantly isolated strip beyond Boatswains Bay, are here to dive. The setting is dramatic, with crashing waves and a small, ever growing white-sand beach that you have to clamber over rocks to get to. It's a friendly place with great rooms – very spacious and modern. Divetech (p200) is the in-house dive center.

**Cracked Conch** ( ☎ 945-5217; www.crackedconch .ky; Northwest Point Rd; mains US$12-48; ☺ lunch & dinner) This oceanfront stunner of a restaurant has been open for 25 years, and despite sounding like a beach bar, it's all white tablecloths and sublime service. Totally refitted since Hurricane Ivan, the Conch guarantees you a memorable meal. The lunch menu is simpler and less expensive – including a popular turtle burger, while dinner pulls out all the stops – try green plantain crusted grouper fillet or pink snapper with coconut shrimp.

**Calypso Grill** ( ☎ 949-3948; www.calypsogrillcayman .com; Morgan's Harbour, West Bay; mains US$18-38; ☺ lunch & dinner Tue-Sun) Few restaurants on Grand Cayman come as warmly recommended by locals as the excellent Calypso Grill, tucked away on Morgan's Harbour away from the crowds of Seven Mile Beach. Mains range from simple fresh fish cooked as you ask to more explorative and inventive dishes such as Wahoo Escoveitch (wahoo strips deep fried and served in Jamaican hot pepper and onion vinaigrette) and Crispy Mango Shrimp.

## BODDEN TOWN
### pop 5000

Historic Bodden Town (the surname Bodden will soon be a familiar one if you spend much time in the Caymans!) was the capital of the Cayman Islands until George Town scooped that honor in the mid-19th century. It's a bit of a backwater today, and took the brunt of Hurricane Ivan back in 2004, which destroyed many of the island's oldest buildings and wreaked havoc on the beach, where there's still a large number of fallen trees today.

The main draw for visitors is **Pedro St James** in nearby Savannah. An imposing Caribbean great house dating from 1780, 'Pedro's Castle' has served over the years as everything from jail to courthouse to parliament before making the transition to **museum** ( ☎ 947-3329; www.pedrostjames.ky; Pedro Rd, Savannah; adult/child US$10/free; ☷ 9am-5pm), quite recently. Touted as the Caymans' 'birthplace of democracy,' it was here in 1831 that the decision was made in favor of a public vote for elected representatives. Just as momentously, this is where the Slavery Abolition Act was read in 1835. The grounds showcase native flora, and there's a multimedia presentation evoking 18th-century Cayman.

Another family favorite is the **Pirate Caves** ( ☎ 947-3122; admission adult/child US$8/5; ☷ 9am-6pm) on the coast in Bodden Town. This is a big hit with kids, as you can explore caves where pirates apparently hid their treasures in the past, along with a mini-zoo, a petting pool for freshwater sting rays and displays of various pirate ephemera. Some of the caves are eerily beautiful even if the treasure hidden here remains elusive!

Few people stay around here, but one place is worth considering.

**our pick** **Turtle Nest Inn** ( ☎ 947-8665; www.turtlenestinn.com; r from US$99-179, ocean view apt US$129-229, beachfront apt US$159-279; ☷ ☐ ☷ ) is a breath of fresh air. Prices are low, and week-long packages work out even better and include a free rental car. Located right on the beach, the hotel has trouble keeping up with demands from repeat customers. Other thoughtful pluses are free wi-fi,

great phone rates, cable TV, free snorkeling equipment and self-catering facilities. The hotel is also leading local efforts to replant the hurricane-devastated beach.

## EAST END

The East End is the place to head if you want a feel for traditional Caymanian life and don't have the time to visit the sister islands. Here, at the furthest point on the island from the commercial and tourism centers of George Town and Seven Mile Beach, open space, quiet hamlets and dramatic shoreline are the main features. To the east of the village itself is the **Wreck of the Ten Sails Park**, commemorating the spot where a legendary shipwreck occurred in 1794.

Away from the village itself the main attraction on this part of the island is the excellent **Queen Elizabeth II Botanic Park** ( ☎ 947-3558; Frank Sound Dr; adult/child US$10/6; ☷ 9am-5pm), a veritable treasure trove for anyone wanting to experience the island's native species. The park is home to orchids (in bloom late May through June), iguanas (elusive) and parrots, as well as other birds.

The nearby **Mastic Trail** meanders through the old-growth forest that once supplied early settlers with timber. The 2-mile-long trail gives hikers the chance to experience a fascinating exploration deep into the old-growth forest of Grand Cayman's wild interior. To get here, rent a car or take the North Side/East End bus from the George Town library (US$2.50). Ask the driver to drop you at the visitors center, and arrange to be picked up.

One of the most remote yet more fun places to base yourself on the island is the **Reef Resort** ( ☎ 947-0100; www.thereef.com; Collier's Bay; studio/ste/villa from US$220/385/390; ☷ ☐ ☷ ), which gets high praise from travelers. All the 110 rooms face the sea along the very long, gorgeous beach and the standard of accommodations is very high indeed, with large, attractive rooms complete with all comforts and in great condition. There's good snorkeling and diving nearby, and local musical hero Bare Foot Man performs his risqué set here a couple of times a week.

## NORTH SIDE
### pop 1100

Geographically isolated from the rest of the island, and the last district to be settled, North Side's earliest residents were freed slaves in search of unclaimed land. Today, the district is windswept and uncrowded, providing a direct link to Grand Cayman's past.

The highlight of the area is beautiful **Rum Point**, where swinging in hammocks and snorkeling are the main activities. A ferry service here from Seven Mile Beach no longer runs, making this quite a quiet spot, although travelers still drive here from all over the island to spend a day on the beach. There's a shuttle bus service (p214) from Seven Mile Beach.

The **Retreat at Rum Point** ( ☎ 947-9135; www .theretreat.com.ky; North Side/Rum Point; 1-/2-bedroom condo US$325/395, deluxe/oceanfront condo US$495/630; ✂ 🖳 ☰ ) has a fantastic beach and an exclusive feel. The privately owned condos here are let out for their owners and each apartment (from one to three bedrooms) is fully equipped. Amenities include a tennis court, gym, sauna, racquetball court and laundry facilities.

Beach bars don't come much more friendly than the **Wreck Bar** ( ☎ 947-9412; ✹ 10am-5pm Mon-Sat, 10am-6pm Sun) despite the sarcastic list of questions 'not to ask' posted on the wall outside. Watched over by the cantankerous Alpha, a squawking, biting parrot, enjoy a famous mudslide cocktail with the sea views right on the beach. Good bar food and small meals are served here too (mains US$9 to US$12). The much loved Rum Point Restaurant next door had still not reopened at the time of writing following damage from Ivan but renovations were about to begin, so it should be back in service soon.

# CAYMAN BRAC

**pop 1822**

Named after the 'brac' or 'bluff' that makes up much of this cheese wedge of an island, the most easterly of the Cayman Islands is markedly different from both Grand and Little Cayman. The simple reason is that, unlike their cousins, the majority of locals do not work in the tourism industry and life here goes on much as it always has. With just one hotel of any size here, head to the Brac to escape the crowds and to engage with nature – the Brac boasts by far the most varied landscapes in the entire country.

The 14 sq mile Brac is dominated by the Bluff, a dramatic limestone formation that rises gently from the flatlands of the west end to a height of 140ft, traveling the length of the island before plunging into the sea. The road to the top passes through the National Trust Parrot Reserve, a nesting ground for the islands' endangered emerald green native species, and ends at a lighthouse at the blustery Northeast Point.

The island's four main settlements – West End, Stake Bay, Watering Place and Spot Bay – are on the western or northern ends. Resorts and beaches are clustered along the southern tip, including the peaceful expanses of the public beach.

## HISTORY

Cayman Brac's first settlers were boat builders, turtlers and fishers who started arriving from Grand Cayman in 1833. Trading relations were established between the tiny island and Jamaica, Cuba and Central America; exports mainly comprised turtle shell, jute rope, coconut and cows. By 1932 the Brac sustained a population of 1200. That same year a hurricane brought death and much damage to the isolated island, and islanders took shelter in caves as many houses were washed out to sea. Electricity, along with the first wave of tourists, did not make it to Cayman Brac until the 1960s.

## INFORMATION

**Cayman National Bank** ( ☎ 948-1551; West End Cross Rd; ✹ 9am-4pm Mon-Thu, 9am-4:30pm Fri) Has an ATM and currency exchange.

**Faith Hospital** ( ☎ 948-2243; Stake Bay) This modern hospital serves both the Brac and Little Cayman.

**It's Yours To Explore** (www.itsyourstoexplore.com) Excellent official website of the sister islands.

**Nature Cayman** (www.naturecayman.com) Website that covers both the Brac and Little Cayman. Packed with information on everything from bird to marine life.

**Post office** ( ☎ 948-1422; West End; ✹ 8:30am-5pm Mon-Fri) Internet access is available in the lobby (per 30 minutes/hour US$4/8).

**Tourist office** ( ☎ 948-1649; www.caymanislands.ky; North Bay Rd; ✹ 8:30am-5pm Mon-Fri) Hidden away just east of the airport adjacent to the West End Community Park, this is a good resource for lodging and activities information. Free island tours can be given by the local government ( ☎ 948-2222) by arrangement. Ask for Chevala Burke.

## SIGHTS & ACTIVITIES

The **Cayman Brac Museum** ( ☎ 948-2222; Stake Bay; admission free; ✹ 9am-noon & 1-4pm Mon-Fri, 9am-noon Sat) is housed in a pretty white-and-blue painted colonial house on the coastal road to Stake Bay. It's not very clear that it's a museum from the road, but it's just in front of the island administration buildings. The charming collection details life for early settlers on the island during a time when it was largely cut off from the rest of the world.

The **Bluff** is a must. The best way to explore it is to walk along the trail that runs along the edge (don't get too close!) giving incredible views and allowing you to see the varied bird life such as brown boobies and frigate birds gliding in the updrafts. There's no circular trail, so you'll need to drive or cycle to the starting point at the **lighthouse** and then double back on yourself. Another trail crosses the Brac at the middle through the **National Trust Parrot Reserve**, where you should have no trouble spotting one of the 350 remaining Cayman Brac parrots who are slowly re-establishing themselves. Pick up the useful *Heritage Sites & Trails* leaflet, which includes a good map, from any hotel, the airport or the tourist office.

Bird-watchers should also head for the **Westerly Ponds** at the western tip of the island, where there are over 100 species of birds to be seen nesting around the wetlands and helpful viewing platforms have been built. Down the road beyond the airport runway there's also **Salt Water Pond**, where a large colony of least tern can be seen in residence from April to August.

With crystal waters affording superb visibility and 41 permanent dive moorings, Cayman Brac attracts its share of **diving** and **snorkeling** enthusiasts. Of particular interest is the wreck of a 315ft Russian frigate now named the *Captain Keith Tibbetts*. It was purchased from Cuba and intentionally sunk offshore off the northwest of the island to serve as a dive attraction.

Two well-run dive providers operate on the western end of the island:

**In Depth** ( ☎ 329-6348; www.indepthwatersports.com; West End; 2-tank dive US$150, snorkeling trips US$35) A new outfit based in the former Divi Tiara Resort; a two-tank dive goes out every day at 10am.

**Reef Divers** ( ☎ 948-1642; www.reefdivers.ky; West End; 1-/2-tank dive US$55/120) Based at the Brac Reef Beach Resort, Reef Divers is the longest-established dive operator on the island. Priority is given to resort guests, but nonguests are welcome too.

The Brac is home to Caymanian fishing captains **Edmund Bodden** ( ☎ 948-1288) and **Lemuel Bodden** ( ☎ 948-1314), both of whom offer bone, tarpon, reef and deep-sea fishing excursions.

## SLEEPING

Accommodations range from casual Caymanian guest houses and private condos to the main resort, Brac Reef, which caters to diving enthusiasts. Lodging prices are cheaper here than elsewhere in the Caymans.

**Walton's Mango Manor** ( ☎ 948-0518; www.waltonsmangomanor.com; Stake Bay; d incl breakfast US$105-130, villa US$180-210; ✹ ) This whimsical place is one of the more unusual guesthouses in the Caymans. Guests are accommodated in the five-bedroom main house decorated with traditional antiques, including a banister made from the mast of an old sailing schooner. All rooms have private facilities and those upstairs have balconies. The lush garden runs down to the beach, where there's also a two-bedroom villa, as well as the only synagogue in the Caymans!

**Brac Reef Beach Resort** ( ☎ 948-1323; www.bracreef.com; West End; r US$140; ✹ ▢ ☎ ) If this is as close to a resort as the Brac gets, then that's a great sign – Brac Reef is a supremely relaxed and friendly diving hotel on a charming stretch of beach. The 40 rooms are spread out around a pool and Jacuzzi, each with either a small patio or balcony. It offers free wi-fi in the lobby and there's a firm focus on diving through the excellent in-house operators Reef Divers. Bicycles and kayaks are available for guests. Meal and diving packages are offered but food is nothing special so you might be better off not taking a full-board package.

**Carib Sands & Brac Caribbean** ( ☎ 948-1121; www.caribsands.com; West End; 1-/2-/3-bedroom apt US$185/245/305; ✹ ) These two condo complexes next to each other and right on the beach are managed by the same company. Both have great sea views and a pool, and offer a large choice of serviced, comfortably furnished apartments with balconies.

## EATING & DRINKING

**our pick** **Aunt Sha's Kitchen** ( ☎ 948-1581; West End Rd; mains US$9-15; ⊙ 8am-11pm) This Brac favorite (it seems that everybody on the island comes in for takeout lunch at least once a week) is now located on the north coast after Hurricane Ivan devastated the previous premises. The new place is charming and the famously good Caymanian home cooking as delicious as ever – fresh fish, goat curry, grilled tuna and chicken stew are all specialties.

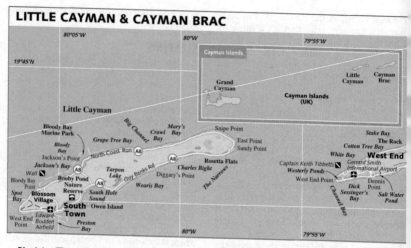

## LITTLE CAYMAN & CAYMAN BRAC

**Biggie's** ( ☎ 948-2449; West End Rd; mains US$10-35; ☺ breakfast, lunch & dinner Mon-Sat, 10:30am-2:30pm Sun) This newcomer to the island's eating scene is a winner. It has a fantastic lunch takeout deal for US$8.50 and an all-you-can-eat buffet for US$19. Caymanian cuisine is served up with an international slant. There's a great vegetarian selection, as well as burgers, Caribbean quesadillas and delicious fresh seafood and fish.

**Captain's Table** ( ☎ 948-1418; West End; mains US$14-32; ☺ lunch & dinner) The restaurant of the small Brac Caribbean resort, this is good option, especially if you can get a table outside by the pool. The food is Caribbean and international. Try the conch fritters, supposedly the best on the island.

**Edd's Place** (West End; ☺ noon-1am Mon-Sat, noon-midnight Sun) This dark and very loud bar is patronized by a largely male crowd. It's not the most inviting place, but it's definitely a good way to meet the locals.

## GETTING THERE & AROUND

Flights from Grand Cayman to Cayman Brac's **Gerrard Smith International Airport** ( ☎ 948-1222) are offered daily by Cayman Airways Express.

There's no public transportation on Cayman Brac, but the negligible crime rate – and the amiability of the locals – makes hitchhiking safe and easy. The mere sight of a visitor marching down the roadway often results in ride offers by passing motorists. Bicycles may be rented or borrowed from the resorts and are available from many guesthouses. Taxis are few; it's a good idea to book in advance for your ride from the airport. Lodging providers will pick you up by prior arrangement. Renting a car is the best way to enjoy the island.

**B&S Motor Ventures Ltd** ( ☎ 948-1646; www.bandsmv.com) Hires scooters, jeeps and bikes as well as cars.

**Brac Rent-A-Car** ( ☎ 948-1515; www.bracrentals.com; Stake Bay)

**CB Rent-A-Car** ( ☎ 948-2329; www.cbrentacar.com; Gerrard Smith International Airport) Right outside the terminal.

**Elo's Taxi** ( ☎ 948-0220)

**Four D's** ( ☎ 948-1599, 948-0459) Free pick-up and drop-off at the airport offered.

**Hill's Taxi** ( ☎ 948-0540)

# LITTLE CAYMAN

**pop 115**

Tiny Little Cayman (the clue is indeed in the name) is a joy. With more iguanas resident than humans, this delightful island is the place to head for solitude, tranquility and the odd spot of extraordinary diving. Because, despite its small size, Little Cayman is firmly established on the world map of great diving sites for its extraordinary Bloody Bay Marine Park, where you'll find some of the best wall diving anywhere in the world.

As your twin-prop plane swoops down over the vivid turquoise sea and onto the grass landing strip of the tiny airport, you'll know that you have arrived at one of the Caribbean's most unspoiled and untrammeled destinations. Yet things are changing here. A new

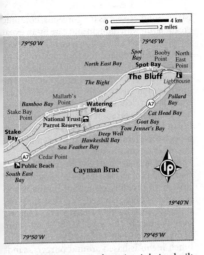

airport that can receive large jets is being built and inevitably more development will follow, meaning that you should grab this chance to visit Little Cayman before it goes the way of Grand Cayman and the Brac. Until then, you should feel like you have the island pretty much to yourself.

## INFORMATION

Public phones can be found at the airport, near the clinic and at the Hungry Iguana restaurant. Most hotels have wi-fi.

**Cayman National Bank** ( ☎ 948-0051; Guy Banks Rd, Blossom Village; ⊙ 9am-2:30pm Mon & Thu) There is no ATM on Little Cayman, and this bank is only open two days each week, so plan accordingly.

**Little Cayman Clinic** ( ☎ 948-1051; Blossom Ave, Blossom Village; ⊙ 9am-1pm Mon, Wed & Fri, 1-5pm Tue & Thu) The clinic is normally staffed by nurses, but a doctor visits on Wednesday afternoon.

**McLaughlin Enterprises** ( ☎ 948-1619; per 15min US$6.50) Found next door to Village Square Store and the airport. You can get online here (albeit not cheaply).

**Post office** ( ☎ 948-0016; Blossom Village; ⊙ 8-11am & 1-3pm Mon-Fri) This tiny post office is located next to the airfield.

**Village Square Store** ( ☎ 948-1069; Guy Banks Rd, Blossom Village; ⊙ closed Sun) Phone cards can be purchased here. This is also the only shop of any size on the island.

## SIGHTS & ACTIVITIES

The sights of Little Cayman are almost entirely natural, whether they be the birds that nest in the wetlands, the iguanas that bask by the road or the marine life on the reef.

A good place to start is the tiny **Little Cayman Museum** ( ☎ 948-1033; Guy Banks Rd, Blossom Village; admission free; ⊙ 3-5pm Thu & Fri) containing local artifacts and beach treasures. The main reason to visit is to see the resident wild – yet remarkably fearless – iguanas that hatch out their young under the building. If you'd like to visit outside the rather restricted opening hours, call Nelvie Eldemire ( ☎ 948-2999) and she'll usually be happy to open it up for you.

Across the road is the **National Trust Visitors Centre** ( ☎ 948-1107; ⊙ 9am-noon & 2-6pm Mon-Sat), which is a combination of shop, café with free wi-fi, information center and viewing platform. Backing onto the **Booby Pond Nature Reserve**, home to one of the hemisphere's largest breeding populations of red-footed boobies and a large colony of swooping frigate birds, the veranda also has telescopes available for visitors.

The main draw on the island is the excellent diving and snorkeling. The **Bloody Bay Marine Park** is legendary among divers, who come from all over the world for a truly exhilarating experience. Here, near the shore and at a depth of only 18ft, the Bloody Bay wall plummets vertically into aquamarine infinity as the divers hovering over the abyss wonder whether they are hallucinating (for more information on diving in this area, see p55).

Little Cayman has 57 dive sites marked with moorings. Snorkelers and shore divers find plenty of satisfaction at many well-known sites.

Recommended diving outfitters:

**Conch Club Divers** ( ☎ 948-1033; www.conchclub.com; Guy Banks Rd; 1-/2-tank dive US$55/85)

**Pirates Point Resort** ( ☎ 949-1010; www.piratepoint resort.com; Guy Banks Rd; 1-/2-tank dive US$50/80)

**Reef Divers** ( ☎ 948-1040; www.reefdivers.ky; Little Cayman Beach Resort; 1-/2-tank dive US$65/95)

**Sam McCoy's Diving & Fishing Lodge** ( ☎ 948-0026; www.mccoyslodge.com.ky; North Coast Rd; 1-/2-tank dive US$45/75)

**Southern Cross Club** ( ☎ 948-1099; www.southern crossclub.com; Guy Banks Rd; 1-/2-tank dive US$65/95)

Little Cayman's shallow coastal waters and flats offer **fishing** action year-round. In the grassy flats and sandy bottoms are wily bonefish, and tarpon are frequently caught in the aptly named **Tarpon Lake**. A short distance offshore beyond the drop-off, anglers find action from blue marlin and other game fish. Southern Cross Club (p210) provides excursions.

Perfect for shipwreck fantasies, **Owen Island** is a short kayak ride or swim across a narrow channel from Southern Cross. The beach here is unspoiled and the vegetation thick and unexplored. Make a day of it with a picnic.

## SLEEPING & EATING

For such a small island there's no shortage of resorts here. Most offer favorable diving packages when booked in advance. Most prefer week-long bookings.

**Blue Lagoon** ( ☎ 945-8096; Guy Banks Rd; r US$100, apt US$125; ⊠ ) This is the cheapest hotel on the island, and for your money you get spotless rooms in a couple of charming colonial-style buildings right on the beach. There's also a pleasant little restaurant on site for simple meals. The apartments come with small kitchens and use of a shared laundry room.

**Little Cayman Beach Resort** ( ☎ 948-1033; www .littlecayman.com; Guy Banks Rd; r per person half board from US$175; ⊠ ☐ ☎ ) By far the largest resort on the island, this popular place is somewhat anomalous with the general Little Cayman vibe. Its 80 rooms are in the process of being renovated, but are all a good size and comfortable. The Beach Nuts bars hosts a very popular karaoke night each Friday, which brings folks from all over the island. The resort also manages two blocks of condos further down the road, both of which can be reserved through the website.

**Paradise Villas** ( ☎ 948-0001; www.paradisevillas .com; Blossom Village; s/d/tr US$175/195/210; ⊠ ☐ ☎ ) You can practically step off the airplane and into your room here – but these smart and comfortable cottages are right on the beach and are idyllic with verandas and hammocks coming as standard. Free wi-fi is included.

**Pirates Point Resort** ( ☎ 948-1010; www.pirates pointresort.com; Guy Banks Rd; r per person from US$199-260; ⊠ ☐ ) This friendly and quirky diving place seemingly casts spells on its guests, as 80% of guests are repeat visitors! Fantastically located on a pretty beach in a corner of the island, there are 10 rooms here, all different and strikingly individual, with mosquito nets, large bathrooms and plenty of books to read. There are no TVs, but there's a busy club house–style bar and restaurant (with the only all-inclusive alcohol deal on Little Cayman) and it never closes. Kids under five are not allowed.

**ourpick Southern Cross Club** ( ☎ 948-1099; www .southerncrossclub.com; Guy Banks Rd; cottage US$335-400; ⊠ ☐ ☎ ) Definitely the classiest place on the island, Southern Cross is a gorgeous, boutique creation run with thought and care by an expat couple. Of the 12 bungalows, go for the newer ones built to replace the four destroyed by Hurricane Ivan – these are right on the beach, with outdoor showers and bright decor. The green credentials here are impressive – 'gray' water is recycled, solar panels provide power and biodiesel will soon be powering the dive boats. Free wi-fi, bikes and kayaks, excellent food, a top diving operator and friendly staff are other reasons to stay.

**Hungry Iguana** ( ☎ 948-0007; Blossom Village; lunch mains US$10-15, dinner mains US$24-37; ☺ lunch & dinner) Just about the only restaurant on the island is a real winner. Housed in a charming old building just by the airstrip and looking over the beach, the main, dark wood room is divided between bar and restaurant. The lunch menu is based around burgers, sandwiches and pasta, while dinner is more elaborate: conch chowder, black bean soup, jerk chicken and pork combo are all delicious. This is also the best place to come for a drink.

Head to **Village Square Store** ( ☎ 948-1069; Guy Banks Rd, Blossom Village; ☺ closed Sun) for groceries, beer and other basic necessities.

## GETTING THERE & AROUND

Flights from Grand Cayman to Little Cayman's **Edward Bodden Airfield** ( ☎ 948-0144) are offered several times a day by Cayman Airways Express. See p213 for more information. The controversial new airport will begin construction and possibly even operation during the lifetime of this book.

Cycling is the preferred mode of transportation on the island, and nearly every hotel makes bicycles available for guests. If you'd prefer to drive, **McLaughlin Rentals** ( ☎ 948-1000; Guy Banks Rd) provides jeeps and mopeds from its office next door to the Village Square Store in Blossom Village.

# DIRECTORY

## ACCOMMODATIONS

Accommodations aren't cheap in the Caymans, but are usually of a very high standard. Budget travelers should head for guesthouses where they exist, and try their best to travel outside of high season, when savings everywhere can be huge. A few resorts cater specifically to divers and include excursions and equipment rentals in their prices, as well as food. Always see if there's a self-catering and non-diving option to get a lower rate. Those on a top-end budget can expect to shell out upwards of US$350 per person each day for accommodations and basic meals, and then more on top of that for diving, water sports, car or boat hire.

The midrange for lodging is around US$200 and if you hope to travel on a shoestring, you might want to sit down before reading further: the lowest-priced accommodations start at around US$100. It's unrealistic to budget less than this per night.

Rates quoted are for walk-ins during the high season (mid-December through mid-April) and do not include the 10% government tax and 10% to 15% service tax. Many places will also expect a gratuity for staff. Low-season rates are as much as 40% cheaper.

## ACTIVITIES
### Bird-Watching
On Little Cayman, the Booby Pond Nature Reserve, which dominates the southwestern coast, is a big draw for bird-watching enthusiasts (p209). Over the three islands, some 200 winged species including boobies, frigate birds, and the endangered Cayman Brac parrot keep bird-watchers blissfully busy.

### Diving & Snorkeling
The most popular activity in the Caymans is diving. An extensive marine-park system and endlessly fascinating dive sites make it perfect for all skill levels. With 265 moored sites, and plenty of shore diving and snorkeling possibilities, the only question is where to start. All three islands have fine-tuned dive operations ready to submerse you, although Little Cayman (p209) is the place to head for true world-class dives.

### Fishing
Those who love fishing love the Caymans for the large numbers of bonefish, blue marlin, tuna and wahoo. Plenty of guides and charter companies can lead you to the best action, both from shore and in deep waters. Grand Cayman has a small fleet of modern, well-equipped sport fishing boats available, and smaller charter boats and excellent local captains are available in Cayman Brac and Little Cayman.

---

### PRACTICALITIES

■ **Newspapers & Magazines** *Caymanian Compass, Cayman Observer, Cayman Net News, Cayman Activity Guide, What's Hot*

■ **Radio** Radio Cayman – 89.9FM & 105.3FM

■ **Video Systems** NTSC

■ **Electricity** 110V, 60Hz; US-style three-pin plugs are used

■ **Weights & Measures** Imperial

---

### Hiking
Hiking is a very popular pursuit on Grand Cayman's Mastic Trail (p205) and on Cayman Brac's many well-marked trails (p207).

### Other Activities
The reef-protected shorelines are ideal for sea kayaking, and the breezy east end of Grand Cayman offers excellent windsurfing.

On Grand Cayman, three excellent golf courses (p201) draw repeat visitors year after year. And if you've ever dreamed of horseback riding on the beach (p201), the Caymans are a great place to do this.

## BUSINESS HOURS
The following are standard business hours across the islands. Exceptions are noted in specific listings.
**Banks** ⏰ 9am to 3:30pm Monday to Friday
**Restaurants** ⏰ noon to 11pm
**Shops** 9am to 6pm Monday to Saturday

## CHILDREN
Families with children couldn't hope for a better travel destination than the Cayman Islands. Kids of most ages will appreciate Boatswains Bay Turtle Farm (p204), the Bodden Town Pirate Caves (p205) and the Butterfly Farm (p198) in Seven Mile Beach.

Most hotels have plenty of rooms that sleep four people or more, and many offer babysitting services and activity programs. The gentle sandy beaches provide a very safe playground for kids of all ages, and older kids can accompany the adults and enjoy the many water sports activities. Kids of all ages can attend Kids Sea Camp (p197) on Grand Cayman. Most diving and water-sports operators offer programs for kids as well.

## EMBASSIES & CONSULATES

**Jamaica** ( ☎ 949-9526; Rankin Plaza, Eastern Ave, PO Box 431, George Town)

**UK** ( ☎ 244-2434; Governor's Office, 4th fl, AALL Bldg, North Church St, George Town)

**US** ( ☎ 945-8173; Mirco Center, 2nd fl, 222 North Sound Way, George Town) For after-hours emergencies US citizens should contact the embassy in Kingston, Jamaica (p254).

## FESTIVALS & EVENTS

The following events all take place on Grand Cayman, with the exception of Pirates Week, which is celebrated on all three islands.

**Cayman Islands International Fishing Tournament** (www.fishcayman.com) This high-stakes fishing tournament in mid-April is the premier angling event of the western Caribbean. There are other fishing tournaments organized March through October by the Cayman Islands Angling Club.

**Batabano** (www.caymancarnival.com) The Cayman Islands' Carnival is a colorful parade of costumes, music and dancing in early May.

**Pirates Week** (www.piratesweekfestival.com) A wildly popular family-friendly extravaganza is kicked off with a mock pirate invasion from the sea. For 10 days in late October, music, dances, costumes, games and controlled mayhem fill up the streets. However, just remember to book your transportation and lodgings well in advance.

## GAY & LESBIAN TRAVELERS

Homosexuality is legal between two consenting adults in the Caymans. However, the islands remain extremely conservative and so discretion is key. Most hotels will happily accommodate same-sex couples, but it's a good idea to check in advance. There are no gay bars or clubs in the Cayman Islands; most local gay contacts are made through the internet. See also boxed text, p195.

## HOLIDAYS

**New Year's Day** January 1
**National Heroes' Day** Fourth Monday in January
**Ash Wednesday** Late February
**Easter** (Good Friday to Easter Monday inclusive) March/April
**Discovery Day** Third Monday in May
**Queen's Birthday** Second Monday in June
**Constitution Day** First Monday in July
**Remembrance Day** Third Monday in November
**Christmas Day** December 25
**Boxing Day** December 26

## INTERNET ACCESS

The Caymans has good web access. Most hotels will offer wi-fi, although in most cases it's still charged for some reason. Smaller, more independent guesthouses tend to offer free wi-fi. There are web cafés in and around George Town and Seven Mile Beach, but they are few and far between elsewhere. Quite a few hotels offer terminals to access the web as well. Other than that, your best bets are the Cable & Wireless hotspots, which you have to pay for in advance. You'll find these at both Owen Roberts International Airport and Gerrard Smith Airport as well as at numerous hotels and many places in George Town.

## MEDICAL SERVICES

There are excellent medical facilities in the Cayman Islands. For minor illnesses, nearly all hotels will have a doctor on call or will be able to help you find assistance. In more serious cases there is a good hospital on Grand Cayman (p197), and a smaller one on Cayman Brac (p206); anyone who falls ill on Little Cayman will usually be flown to the latter hospital. All visitors to the Caymans should have comprehensive medical insurance as no reciprocal health-care agreements exist with other countries.

## MONEY

The official currency is the Cayman Islands dollar (CI$), permanently fixed at an exchange rate of CI$0.80 to US$1 (US$1 equals CI$1.25). Cayman dollars and US dollars are accepted throughout the islands, although you'll usually get change in CI$ even if you pay with US$. The local currency comes in CI$1, 5, 10, 25, 50 and 100 notes. All major currencies can easily be changed at any bank. ATMs are easy to find across Grand Cayman. There's one on Cayman Brac and none on Little Cayman.

## TELEPHONE
### Cell Phones

Cell phones compatible with 800MHz or TDMA networks can roam in the islands. **Cable & Wireless** ( ☎ 949-7800; www.cw.ky; Anderson Sq, George Town) and **Digicel** ( ☎ 945-3494; www.digicel cayman.com; Royale Plaza, George Town) both sell local SIM cards (which can be put directly into any unlocked set) and a cheap pay-as-you-go service. They can also rent out handsets from their main offices.

### Phone Cards

Cable & Wireless prepaid calling cards in denominations of CI$5 and CI$10 are available throughout the islands. Rates to the US, UK, Canada and Caribbean destinations (excluding Cuba) average US$0.50 per minute; other destinations cost US$1.25 per minute.

## TOURIST INFORMATION

The tourism infrastructure of the Cayman Islands is second to none, with the entire country geared toward visitors. There is a very helpful desk at Owen Roberts International Airport where you can stock up on maps, as well as a booth in George Town that's open whenever cruise ships are visiting; see p197 for details. There is also a tourist office (p206) on Cayman Brac. The website for the **Department of Tourism** (www.cay manislands.ky) is a very useful place to start.

## VISAS

Visas are not required by nationals of the UK, Canada, USA, Australia, New Zealand, South Africa and most Commonwealth and Western European countries. However, holders of passports from Ireland and most Eastern Europeans do require visas. Visas are not required by any cruise-ship passengers, regardless of nationality.

Tourist visas are valid for 30 days and can be extended for up to three months. They can be obtained from any British consulate or embassy for a varying fee.

# TRANSPORTATION

## GETTING THERE & AWAY
### Entering the Cayman Islands

All visitors are required to have a valid passport and a return ticket.

### Air

The main passenger airport in the Cayman Islands, **Owen Roberts International Airport** (GCM; ☎ 949-8052), is located 1.5 miles east of George Town on the island of Grand Cayman. Cayman Brac is served by **Gerrard Smith International Airport** (CYB; ☎ 948-1222). On Little

Cayman, flights to **Edward Bodden Airfield** (LYB; ☎ 948-0144) land on a grass airstrip, although a new airport with a longer asphalt runway was being constructed at the time of writing.

The following airlines provide international services to the Cayman Islands:

**Air Canada** ( ☎ 949-8503; www.aircanada.com) Toronto

**Air Jamaica** ( ☎ 949-2300; www.airjamaica.com) Kingston, Montego Bay

**American Airlines** ( ☎ 949-0666; www.aa.com) Miami

**British Airways** ( ☎ 1-800-247-9297, 949-8200; www .ba.com) London, Nassau

**Cayman Airways** ( ☎ 949-8200; www.cayman airways.com)

**Continental Airlines** (www.continental.com) Houston, New York

**Delta Airlines** (www.delta.com) Atlanta

**Northwest Airlines** ( ☎ 949-2955; www.nwa.com) Detroit, Minneapolis

**US Airways** ( ☎ 949-7488; www.usairways.com) Boston, Charlotte, Philadelphia

### Sea

Numerous cruise-ship lines drop anchor in George Town from Monday to Saturday, unloading passengers for a few hours of duty-free shopping, diving and snorkeling, or lounging on nearby Seven Mile Beach.

Most cruises from the US last one to two weeks and include other western Caribbean destinations such as Cozumel and Progreso, Mexico; Key West and Miami, Florida; and Montego Bay and Ocho Rios, Jamaica. See p830 for more information on cruises.

Those entering Cayman waters by private yacht should display the red ensign version of the Cayman flag and report to the port authority in George Town to clear customs and immigration.

## GETTING AROUND
### Air

Flights from Grand Cayman to the 'sister islands,' Cayman Brac and Little Cayman, are offered daily by Cayman Airways Express. Island Air offers charter flights only and no longer has scheduled connections.

**Cayman Airways Express** ( ☎ 949-8200; www.cayman airways.com) This subsidiary of Caymans Airways provides the only scheduled services between Grand Cayman and Cayman Brac. There are several flights each day in both directions. All flights usually call in at both sister islands on their way to and from Grand Cayman.

**Island Air** ( ☎ 949-5252; www.islandair.ky) Offers charter flights and private hire to Grand Cayman, Cayman

CAYMAN ISLANDS

Brac and Little Cayman via 19-passenger turboprop Twin Otter aircraft.

## Bicycle

Bikes are readily available on all three islands and are often included as part of an accommodations package. Flat terrain, relatively light traffic and near-constant sea access make bicycling a pleasure on the 'sister islands,' although the heavy traffic in and around George Town and Seven Mile Beach makes this a less attractive mode of transportation on Grand Cayman.

## Bus

A fleet of beige-and-white minibuses serves all districts of Grand Cayman. The **bus terminal** (☎ 945-5100) is next to the public library on Edward St in downtown George Town and serves as the dispatch point for all eight routes. Fares are from US$2.50 to US$5.00. There's a **shuttle bus** (☎ 928-1333) from the major Seven Mile Beach hotels (Ritz, Westin, the two Marriotts and the Grand Cayman Beach Suites) to Rum Point for those who fancy a day on a more isolated beach. On Sunday, Monday, Wednesday and Friday the bus picks up around 9:30am and leaves Rum Point at 3:30pm.

There are no bus services available on Cayman Brac and Little Cayman.

## Car & Motorcycle
### DRIVER'S LICENSE

Visitors must obtain a temporary driver's license from the police station or, more normally, their car-rental agency (US$5 to $10 depending on who issues it); you'll need to show a valid international driver's license or one from your home country.

## RENTAL

Driving is an essential part of life on the islands, with limited public transport and much of the island given over to parking. While traffic on the islands is light compared to big cities, it can still be surprisingly heavy in and around George Town and Seven Mile Beach, especially during rush hour. Driving on the sister islands is a joy as cars are very few and far between.

All rentals are automatics, although rental 4WDs and vans have left-hand stick shift. A variety of models at competitive rates are available in Grand Cayman. On Cayman Brac, there are a limited number of cars, with fewer still on Little Cayman.

You must be aged at least 21 to rent a car in the Cayman Islands, and some rental agencies' insurance will not cover renters under 25; check with your rental company in advance.

Scooter and motorcycle rentals are available on all three islands.

## ROAD RULES

Driving is on the left-hand side of the road in the Cayman Islands, as in the UK – although you're just as likely to get a left-hand as a right-hand drive car. The wearing of seat belts is mandatory and speed limits are very low. The whole of Little Cayman has a 25mph limit, and much of Cayman Brac is the same. Traffic moves faster on Grand Cayman, but only marginally so. One quirk of the Caymans is the four-way – a crossroads where the right of way changes as each car turns. Basically wait until you have been waiting there the longest and then proceed with caution! On the sister islands iguanas have right of way.

# Jamaica

Despite its location almost smack in the center of the Caribbean Sea, the island of Jamaica doesn't blend easily with the rest of the Caribbean archipelago. Sure, it boasts the same addictive sunrays, sugary sands and pampered resort life as most of the other islands, but it is set apart historically and culturally.

Nowhere else in the Caribbean is the connection to Africa as keenly felt. Kingston was the major nexus in the New World for the barbaric triangular trade that brought slaves from Africa and carried off sugar and rum to Europe; and the Maroons (runaways who took to the hills of Cockpit Country and the Blue Mountains) safeguarded many of the African traditions – and introduced jerk seasoning to Jamaica's singular cuisine. Marcus Garvey founded the back-to-Africa movement of the 1910s and '20s; Rastafarianism took up the call a decade later, and reggae furnished the beat in the '60s and '70s. Little wonder many Jamaicans claim a stronger affinity for Africa than for neighboring Caribbean islands.

And less wonder that today's visitors will appreciate their trip to Jamaica all the more if they embrace the island's unique character. In addition to the inherent African-ness of its population, Jamaica boasts the world's best coffee, world-class reefs for diving, offbeat bush medicine hiking tours, congenial fishing villages, pristine waterfalls, cosmopolitan cities, wetlands harboring endangered crocodiles and manatees, unforgettable sunsets – in short, enough variety to comprise many different and utterly distinct vacations.

## FAST FACTS

- **Area** 11,391 sq km
- **Capital** Kingston
- **Country code** ☎ 876
- **Departure tax** US$22 (usually included in ticket price)
- **Famous for** Reggae, Rastas, rum
- **Language** English, patois
- **Money** Jamaican dollar (J$); J$100 = US$1.41 = €0.90 = UK£0.71
- **Official name** Jamaica
- **People** Jamaicans
- **Phrase** Everyt'ing irie? (a greeting that literally means 'everything alright?'); respect
- **Population** 2.7 million
- **Visa** Not required for residents of the EU, US, Commonwealth countries, Mexico, Japan and Israel. For other nationalities, see p256

## HIGHLIGHTS

- **Long Bay, Negril** (p247) Hang loose or party hard on this 11km stretch of beach, where the fiery sunsets never fail to live up to their hype
- **Blue Mountain Peak** (p231) Set out before dawn for Jamaica's greatest – and most natural – high
- **Bob Marley Museum** (p225) Delve into the life of Jamaica's most revered contemporary hero at his former home and studio
- **Red Stripe Reggae Sumfest** (p242) Dance into the wee hours at Jamaica's world-class midsummer reggae festival
- **Black River Great Morass** (p251) Travel by boat deep into river country that's teeming with crocodiles

## ITINERARIES

- **Three Days** Lounge around on the beach in Negril, explore the reefs, catch some live reggae, watch the sun set…and then do it again.
- **One Week** Add on a journey to the mellow, less-touristed town of Treasure Beach, taking in nearby YS Falls, Black River and the Appleton Rum Estate.
- **Two Weeks** Precede the above itineraries with an energetic visit to cosmopolitan Kingston (the heartbeat of Jamaica), followed by a jaunt into the high Blue Mountains.
- **Three Weeks** After Kingston and the Blue Mountains, press on to Portland parish for some rafting on the Rio Grande and surfing in Boston Bay. Continue with the one-week itinerary.

## CLIMATE & WHEN TO GO

Jamaica is a year-round destination: coastal temperatures average 26°C (79°F) to 30°C (86°F) year-round. Temperatures fall with increasing altitude but even in the Blue Mountains average 18°C (64°F).

The rainy season extends from May to November, with peaks in May and June and in October and November. Rain usually falls for short periods (normally in the late afternoon), and it's quite possible to enjoy sunshine for most of your visit during these months. In Portland parish, however, it can rain for days on end.

The tourist high season runs from mid-December to mid-April, when hotel prices are highest. Many hotels also charge peak-season rates during Christmas and Easter.

## HISTORY
### Columbus & the Spanish Wave

Jamaica's first tourist was none other than Christopher Columbus, who landed on the island in 1494. At the time there were perhaps 100,000 peaceful indigenous Arawaks, who had settled Jamaica around AD 700. Spanish settlers arrived from 1510 and quickly introduced two things that would profoundly shape the island's future: sugarcane production and slavery. By the end of the 16th century the Arawak population had been entirely wiped out, worn down by hard labor, ill-treatment and European diseases.

### The English Invasion

In 1654 an ill-equipped and badly organized English contingent sailed to the Caribbean. After failing to take Hispaniola, the 'wicked army of common cheats, thieves and lewd persons' turned to weakly defended Jamaica. Despite the ongoing efforts of Spanish loyalists and guerilla-style campaigns of freed Spanish slaves (cimarrones – 'wild ones' – or Maroons), England took control of the island.

### Slavery

New slaves kept on arriving, and bloody insurrections occurred with frightening frequency. The last and largest of the slave revolts in Jamaica was the 1831 Christmas Rebellion, inspired by Sam Sharpe, an educated slave who incited passive resistance. The rebellion turned violent, however, as up to 20,000 slaves razed plantations and murdered planters. When the slaves were tricked into laying down arms with a false promise of abolition – and then 400 were hanged and hundreds more whipped – there was a wave of revulsion in England, causing the British parliament to finally abolish slavery. See p244, for more.

The transition from a slave economy to one based on wage labor caused economic chaos, with most slaves rejecting the starvation wages offered on the estates and choosing to fend for themselves. Desperation over conditions and injustice finally boiled over in the Morant Bay Rebellion.

### The Road to Independence

A banana-led economic recovery was halted by the Great Depression of the 1930s, and then

# JAMAICA

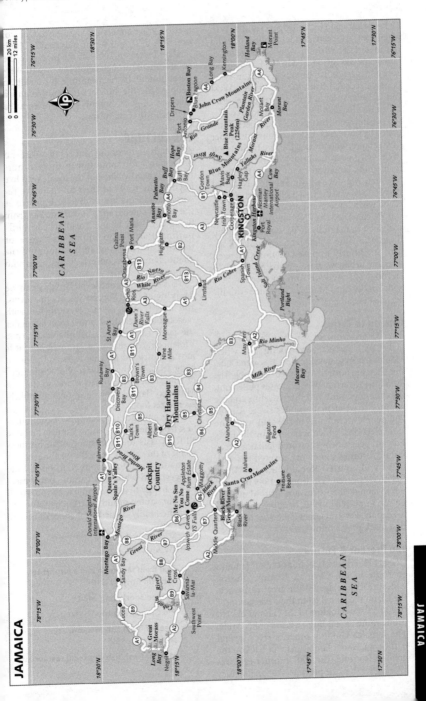

kick-started again by the exigencies of WWII, when the Caribbean islands supplied food and raw materials to Britain. Adult suffrage for all Jamaicans was introduced in 1944, and virtual autonomy from Britain was granted in 1947. Jamaica seceded from the short-lived West Indies Federation in 1962 after a referendum called for the island's full independence.

Post-independence politics have been dominated by the legacy of two cousins: Alexander Bustamante, who formed the first trade union in the Caribbean just prior to WWII and later formed the Jamaican Labor Party (JLP), and Norman Manley, whose People's National Party (PNP) was the first political party on the island when it was convened in 1938. Manley's son, Michael, led the PNP toward democratic socialism in the mid-1970s, causing a capital flight at a time when Jamaica could ill afford it. Bitterly opposed factions engaged in open urban warfare preceding the 1976 election, but the PNP won the election by a wide margin and Manley continued with his socialist agenda.

### Coming to Terms

The US government was hostile to the socialist path Jamaica was taking and, when Manley began to develop close ties with Cuba, the CIA purportedly planned to topple the Jamaican government. Businesses pulled out, the economy went into sharp decline and the country lived virtually under siege. Almost 700 people were killed in the lead-up to the 1980 elections, which were won by the JLP's Edward Seaga. Seaga restored Jamaica's economic fortunes somewhat, severed ties with Cuba and courted Ronald Reagan's USA. Relatively peaceful elections in 1989 returned a reinvented 'mainstream realist' Manley to power; he retired in 1992, handing the reins to his deputy, Percival James Patterson, Jamaica's first black prime minister.

### The Present & Future

In 2004 Hurricane Ivan bounced off Jamaica en route to the Cayman Islands, causing widespread damage. With great resilience, the island recovered from the devastation. In 2007, Bruce Golding of the JLP was elected prime minister, ending 18 years of PNP rule. The Jamaica Golding inherits faces several battles, and most Jamaicans will tell you the greatest is crime (the 2007 murder rate was 17% higher than the previous year's). Illiteracy

is also a grave concern (according to Unesco, over 90% of 15-to-24-year-olds couldn't both read and write in 2004) as are threats to the environment through deforestation and over-development. In the meantime, the Jamaican people face the future with resolve and a measure of good humor – they've endured so much worse in the past.

## THE CULTURE

Although many of the tourists that descend on Jamaica for some fun in the sun nurture packaged visions of the locals who live beyond the walls of their all-inclusive resorts, Jamaicans are as diverse a people as the island's geography is varied. Far from being confined to the dreadlocked, spliff-puffing Rastafarian vibing to reggae or the violent 'rude boy' (armed thug) of the ghetto, Jamaicans comprise many social and demographic strata.

To be sure, street-level Jamaica can be daunting at first. Poverty blights the towns, and tourists mean money. Nevertheless, with reasonable precaution, you'll soon fall under the spell of Jamaica's inimitable charms. Violence rarely impinges on foreigners; it is mostly restricted to drug wars and political gang feuds in the claustrophobic ghettoes of Kingston, Spanish Town and sections of Montego Bay where you're highly unlikely ever to set foot.

What emerges is a panoply of communities: from the sleepy fishing hamlets that line all the coasts to the cosmopolitan business sector of the capital, from the bustling market towns to the autonomous Maroon hillside villages. And while you can of course meet Rastas happy to smoke ganja with you, you'll also encounter proud matriarchs presiding over the family-owned rum shop; dancehall

---

**HOW MUCH?**

- Taxi from Montego Bay's airport to the 'Hip Strip' US$10
- Guided snorkeling trip US$30
- Rio Grande raft trip US$60
- Meal of fresh fish in a touristy restaurant US$15
- Meal of fresh fish in a local restaurant US$6

enthusiasts delighted to take you to the local sound-system party; bush medicine doctors who can explain the benefits of every local root, herb and flower; or students who know as much about your own country as you do.

You'll learn to greet strangers with the local salutation 'blessed,' and by the time you leave Jamaica, you'll realize you have been.

The nation's motto, 'Out of Many, One People,' reflects the diverse heritage of Jamaica. Tens of thousands of West Africans, plus large numbers of Irish, Germans and Welsh, arrived throughout the colonial period, along with Hispanic and Portuguese Jews and those whom Jamaicans call 'Syrians' (a term for all those of Levantine extraction). In 1838, following emancipation, Chinese and Indian indentured laborers arrived from Hong Kong and Panama.

Jamaica's population is currently estimated at a little over 2.7 million, of which about 750,000 live in Kingston. At least another two million live abroad, generally in the US, the UK or Canada. Some 91% of the population are classified as being of pure African descent; 7.3% are of Afro-European descent; the remainder are white (0.2%), East Indian and Middle Eastern (1.3%), and Afro-Chinese and Chinese (0.2%).

Jamaica professes to have the greatest number of churches per sq km in the world, with virtually every imaginable denomination represented. Although most foreigners associate the island with Rastafarianism, more than 80% of Jamaicans identify themselves as Christian.

Rastafarians, or Rastas, with their uncut, uncombed hair grown into long sun-bleached tangles known as 'dreadlocks' or 'dreads,' are as synonymous with the island as reggae. There are perhaps as many as 100,000 Rastafarians in Jamaica. A faith not a church, Rastafarianism has no official doctrine or dogmatic hierarchy and is composed of a core of social and spiritual tenets that are open to interpretation.

All adherents, however, accept that the African race is one of God's chosen – one of the Twelve Tribes of Israel descended from the Hebrews and displaced. Moreover, Africa is regarded as the black race's spiritual home to which it's destined to return, Haile Selassie, Ethiopian emperor from 1930 to 1975, is believed to be a divine being and the black messiah.

## ARTS

Jamaica has evolved a powerful artistic and cultural expression rooted in African traditions, while quintessentially Jamaican styles have evolved across the spectrum of the arts. In addition, Jamaica's crafts industry supports tens of thousands of artisans, who offer a cornucopia of leatherwork, ceramics, shell art, beadwork, woodcarving and basket-weaving.

### Cinema

Jamaica has produced some excellent films (often pronounced 'flims' in Jamaica), most notably cult classic *The Harder They Come* (1973), starring Jimmy Cliff as a 'rude boy' in Kingston's ghettoes. *Rockers* (1978) is another music-propelled, socially poignant fable with a cast of reggae all-stars.

Rick Elgood's emotionally engaging 1997 film *Dancehall Queen* found an international audience for its tale of redemption for a struggling middle-aged street vendor, who escapes the mean streets of Kingston through the erotic intoxication of dancehall music. Jamaica's highest-grossing film of all time is Chris Browne's 2000 drama *Third World Cop*, in which old friends straddling both sides of the law must come to terms with each other.

### Literature

Through the years Jamaican literature has been haunted by the ghosts of slave history and the ambiguities of Jamaica's relationship to Mother England. The classic novels tend to focus on survival in a grim colonial landscape and escape to Africa, which often proves to be even grimmer. Best known, perhaps, is Herbert de Lisser's classic *White Witch of Rose Hall*. This plantation-era tale – now an established part of Jamaican lore – tells of Annie Palmer, the wicked mistress of Rose Hall who supposedly murdered three husbands and several slave lovers. The truth is less lurid.

Perry Henzell's *Power Game* is a tale of power politics based on real events in the 1970s, told by the director of the movie *The Harder They Come*. The poignant novel of that name, written by Michael Thewell, recounts the story of a country boy who comes to Kingston, turns into a 'rude boy' and becomes fatally enmeshed in the savage drug culture. The mean streets of Kingston are also the setting for the gritty novels of Roger Mais, notably *The Hills Were Joyful Together* and *Brother Man*. Orlando Patterson's *The Children of Sisyphus* mines the same bleak terrain from a Rastafarian perspective.

In recent years a number of Jamaican female writers have gained notice: they include Christine Craig *(Mint Tea)*, Patricia Powell *(Me Dying Trial)*, Michelle Cliff *(Abeng, Land of Look Behind)* and Vanessa Spence *(Roads Are Down)*.

## Music

Music is everywhere – and it's loud! The sheer creativity and productivity of Jamaican music has produced a profound effect around the world. As reggae continues to attract and influence a massive international audience, Jamaica's sound system–based dancehall culture continues to inform contemporary rap, rave and hip-hop cultures.

Reggae is the heartbeat of Jamaica, and it is as strongly identified with the island as R&B is with Detroit or jazz with New Orleans. But reggae is actually only one of several distinctly Jamaican sounds, and the nation's musical heritage runs much deeper. Inspired by the country's rich African folk heritage, music spans mento (a folk calypso), ska, rock-steady, 'roots' music and contemporary dancehall and ragga. Kingston is the 'Nashville of the Third World,' with recording studios pumping out as many as 500 new titles each month.

The legacy of reggae superstar Bob Marley continues to thrive, as witnessed in the month-long celebration held in Ethiopia in early 2005 marking the 60th anniversary of his birth. There's long been talk about elevating Marley to National Hero status, a mantle reserved only for the nation's most pivotal figures.

The term dancehall, although used to mean a sound-system venue, is also used specifically to refer to a kind of Caribbean rap music that focuses on earthly themes dear to the heart of young male Jamaicans, principally 'gal business,' gunplay and ganja. This is hardcore music, named for the loosely defined outdoor venues at which outlandishly named 'toasters' (rapper DJs) set up mobile discos with enormous speakers, and singers and DJs pumped-up with braggadocio perform live over instrumental rhythm tracks.

## ENVIRONMENT

No less a world traveler than Columbus described Jamaica as 'the fairest isle that eyes beheld; mountainous…all full of valleys and fields and plains.' Much of the coast is still fringed by coral reefs harboring an astonishing array of marine life. Visitors can forsake sandals for hiking boots and follow mountain trails, shower in remote waterfalls, and shoot birds through the lens of a camera. Several areas have been developed as ecotour destinations, most notably the Black River Great Morass, a swampland penetrated by boat.

The Rio Grande Valley is a premier destination for hiking. The Blue Mountains have been opened up in recent years; for a taste of these rugged heights try a climb up Blue Mountain Peak (2256m). Negril's Great Morass is being developed as an eco-attraction protecting fabulous birdlife and wetland ecosystems.

## The Land

At 11,425 sq km (about equal to the US state of Connecticut, or 5% of the size of Great Britain) Jamaica is the third-largest island in the Caribbean and the largest of the English-speaking islands. It is one of the Greater Antilles, which make up the westernmost of the Caribbean islands.

Jamaica is rimmed by a narrow coastal plain except in the south, where broad flatlands cover extensive areas. Mountains form the island's spine, rising gradually from the west and culminating in the Blue Mountains in the east, which are capped by Blue Mountain Peak at 2256m. The island is cut by about 120 rivers, many of which are bone dry for much of the year but spring to life after heavy rains, causing great flooding.

Two-thirds of the island's surface is composed of soft, porous limestone (the compressed skeletons of coral, clams and other sea life), in places several kilometers thick and covered by thick red-clay soils rich in bauxite (the principal source of aluminum). Coastal mangrove and wetland preserves, montane cloud forests and other wild places are strewn across Jamaica. Most travelers stick to beach resorts, however. Those who do get close to nature are as yet poorly served by wildlife reserves.

## Wildlife

The island has more than 255 bird species. Stilt-legged, snowy-white cattle egrets are ubiquitous, as are 'John crows' (turkey vultures), which are feared in Jamaica and are the subject of several folk songs and proverbs. *Patoo* (a West African word) is the Jamaican name for the owl, which many islanders superstitiously regard as a harbinger of death. Jamaica has four of the 16 Caribbean species of hummingbird. The crown jewel of West Indian hummingbirds is the streamertail, the national bird, which is indigenous to Jamaica.

Coral reefs lie along the north shore, where the reef is almost continuous and much of it is within a few hundred meters of shore. Over 700 species of fish zip in and out of the exquisite reefs and swarm through the coral canyons: wrasses, parrotfish, snappers, bonito, kingfish, jewelfish and scores of others. Barracudas, giant groupers, tarpon and nurse sharks are frequently seen. Further out, the cobalt deeps are run by sailfish, marlin and manta rays. Last but not least, three species of endangered marine turtles – the green, hawksbill and loggerhead – lay eggs on Jamaica's beaches.

## FOOD & DRINK

Dining in Jamaica ranges from wildly expensive restaurants to humble roadside stands where you can eat simple Jamaican fare for as little as US$1. Most hotels incorporate Jamaican dishes in their menus. Food bought at grocery stores is usually expensive, as many of the canned and packaged goods are imported. Cheap fresh fruits, vegetables and spices sell at markets and roadside stalls islandwide.

Jamaica's homegrown cuisine is a fusion of many ethnic traditions and influences. The Arawaks brought callaloo (a spinach-like green), cassava (a root vegetable), corn, sweet potatoes and several tropical fruits to the island. The Spanish adopted native spices, which were later enhanced by spices brought by slaves from their African homelands. Immigrants from India brought hot and flavorful curries, often served with locally made mango chutney. Middle Eastern dishes and Chinese influences have also become part of the national menu. And basic roasts and stews followed the flag during three centuries of British rule, as did Yorkshire pudding, meat pies and hot cross buns.

Jamaica's most popular dish is jerk, a term that describes the process of cooking meats smothered in tongue-searing marinade. Jerk is best served hot off the coals wrapped in

paper. You normally order by the pound (US$4-worth should fill you up).

Naturally, there's a strong emphasis on seafood. Snapper and parrotfish are two of the more popular species. A favorite is escoveitched fish, which is pickled in vinegar then fried and simmered with peppers and onions.

Many meals are accompanied by starchy vegetables ('breadkinds') such as plantains and yam, or other bread substitutes such as pancake-shaped cassava bread (*bammy*) and johnnycakes (delicious fried dumplings, an original Jamaican fast food).

No island produces a wider variety of rum than Jamaica, ranging from the clear and light white rums, flavored rums, brain-bashing overproof rums (rum over 151 proof) and the deep dark rums such as Myers to the rare amber nectar of the finest premium rums. Rum has come a long way since the rowdy days of the early 17th century when it was a foul, powerful concoction called 'kill devil' for its exorcist qualities. Red Stripe is the beer of Jamaica. Crisp and sweet, it's perfectly light and refreshing.

# KINGSTON

**pop 750,000**

As Jamaica's one true city, Kingston is something of an island within the island. Its pace and pulse are alien to the rest of Jamaica, for which it's the governmental, commercial and cultural hub. Most visitors to the island skip it – the crime, traffic, crowds and shantytowns of the capital are simply too volatile to mix into the average vacationer's dream Jamaican cocktail. Give the capital more than a once-over, however, and you'll be hooked. Launching pad for some of the world's most electrifying music, the city by no means trades on its reputation, and its spirited clubs, bustling record stores and riotous street-system parties attest to the fact that the beat is alive and bumping.

Kingston divides neatly into downtown and uptown. The former is in a state of perpetual decay yet still boasts a scenic waterfront, Jamaica's greatest art museum and most of Kingston's historic buildings, complemented by a frenetic street life with street preachers and mix-tape hawkers vying for the attentions of the human parade.

**JAMAICA**

Uptown holds the city's hotels, restaurants and nightlife, largely confined to the pocket of New Kingston. In addition to the city's most essential sight, the Bob Marley Museum, the capital's diplomatic and commercial status assures uptown a definite cosmopolitan suaveness – not to mention security.

Sadly, security *does* require mention – the threat of crime in Kingston can never be dismissed. Pockets of the west Kingston shantytowns are as dangerous as any place on the planet, and their volatility can spill over onto the downtown streets after dark. Be sure to follow safety directives, ask your hotel for guidance and keep your wits about you.

## HISTORY

Kingston was founded in 1693 by survivors of the devastating earthquake that flattened nearby Port Royal. Though whacked repeatedly by more earthquakes and hurricanes, the port city prospered throughout the 18th century, becoming one of the most important trading centers in the western hemisphere and an important transshipment point for slaves destined for the Spanish colonies.

In 1872 Kingston supplanted Spanish Town as Jamaica's capital. In spite of an early-20th-century economic boom, the city's slow physical decline seemed assured as sprawling shantytowns put down roots around the old city's perimeter.

In 1907 a violent earthquake leveled much of the city, killing 800 people and rendering tens of thousands homeless. The aftermath witnessed a transformation as modern buildings replaced the ruins and damaged edifices were given new life.

In the 1960s the Urban Development Corporation reclaimed the waterfront. Several historic landmarks, including Victoria Market, were razed to make way for a complex of gleaming new structures, including the Bank of Jamaica and the Jamaica Conference Centre. About the same time, Kingston's nascent music industry was beginning to gather steam, lending international stature and fame to the city. This, in turn, fostered the growth of New Kingston, an uptown area of multistory office blocks, banks, restaurants, shops and hotels.

## ORIENTATION

The city overlooks the seventh-largest natural harbor in the world, with the waterfront on its southern border. It spreads out in a fan shape from the harbor and rises gently toward the foothills and spur ridges of the Blue Mountains.

Downtown, the historic area fanning north of the waterfront, is arranged on a grid system and forms the city center. Some 3km north, New Kingston, or 'uptown,' is defined by several major roads, including Knutsford Blvd, Half Way Tree Rd and Hope Rd.

## INFORMATION

### Bookstores

**Bookland** (Map pp224-5; ☎ 926-4035; 53 Knutsford Blvd) A good selection on island history, folklore and culture.

### Emergency

**Police** Headquarters (Map pp226-7; ☎ 922-9321; 11 East Queen St); Half Way Tree (Map pp224-5; 142 Maxfield Ave); Cross Roads (Map pp224-5; Brentford Rd)

### Internet Access

Most upscale hotels along Knutsford Blvd provide in-room dial-up internet access and have business centers with internet service.
**Café What's On** (Map pp224-5; ☎ 929-4490; Devon House courtyard, Hope Rd; per 15min $1) Adjacent to the historic Devon House, this is a pleasant place to get online.
**Innovative Superstore** (Map pp224-5; ☎ 978-3512; Sovereign Centre, 106 Hope Rd; per 30min US$2.50; ⏰ 9am-5pm Mon-Sat) Overly air-conditioned but efficient.

### Laundry

**Express Laundromat** (Map pp224-5; ☎ 978-4319; 30 Lady Musgrave Rd)

### Medical Services

**Ambucare Ambulance Service** ( ☎ 978-2327) Private service.
**Bellevue Hospital** (off Map pp224-5; ☎ 928-1380; 6-1/2 Windward Rd, Kingston 2) Public hospital, 24-hour emergency ward.
**Kingston Public Hospital** (Map pp226-7; ☎ 922-0210; North St) Downtown public hospital with emergency department.

### Money

Uptown, you will find more than a dozen banks located along Knutsford Blvd. Most have foreign-exchange counters as well as 24-hour ATMs.
**Scotiabank** (Map pp226-7; ☎ 922-1000; cnr Duke & Port Royal Sts) Has its main foreign-exchange center immediately east of the Jamaica Conference Centre. There's another branch at 35 King St.

**Western Union** (Map pp224-5; ☎ 926-2454, 888-991-2056; 7 Hillcrest Ave) Has about 20 agencies throughout Kingston.

## Post
**FedEx** (Map pp224-5; ☎ 960-9192; 75 Knutsford Blvd)
**Post office** Main (Map pp226-7; ☎ 922-2120; 13 King St); New Kingston (Map pp224-5; ☎ 926-6803; 115 Hope Rd)

## Tourist Information
**Jamaica Tourist Board** (JTB) Airport ( ☎ 924-8024); Headquarters (Map pp224-5; ☎ 929-9200; fax 929-9375; 64 Knutsford Blvd; ☷ 8:30am-5:30pm Mon-Fri) The headquarters in New Kingston maintains a small research library.

## DANGERS & ANNOYANCES
The island averages just over four murders per day, and 75% of these occur in Kingston. Most of the murders are drug-related or politically inspired and occur in the shantytowns of West Kingston. Although the level of general violence and crime has escalated frighteningly in recent years, visitors can enjoy the city's sights and sounds in reasonable safety so long as a few commonsense guidelines are followed.

Avoid Kingston entirely during periods of tension, when localized violence can spontaneously erupt. If you're in town when street violence flares up, definitely avoid downtown, and adhere to any curfews that police may impose.

Stick to the main streets – if in doubt ask your hotel concierge or manager to point out the trouble areas. If you need a taxi, ask the front desk to call one from a service known to them, rather than flagging one down. Avoid West Kingston (especially Trench Town, Jones Town, Greenwich Town and Tivoli), particularly west of the Parade, downtown.

Foreigners, especially white tourists, will stand out from the crowd. Fortunately, visitors to Kingston are not hassled by hustlers and touts to anywhere near the degree they are in the north-coast resorts.

## SIGHTS
### Downtown
Some visitors – particularly those who've just arrived in Jamaica – find the intense urban environment of downtown Kingston a bit daunting. As long as you keep your eyes open and are selective in choosing your friends, a visit to the city's historic center can be enjoyed in relative safety.

---

**KINGSTON IN...**

**Two Days**
Visit the **Bob Marley Museum** (p225) and **Devon House** (below), tour the **National Gallery** (below), and take in a meal to remember at **Up on the Roof** (p229) or the **Red Bones Blues Café** (p229).

**Four Days**
Add on an excursion to **Port Royal** (p230) for a peek into Jamaica's distant past, and head into the Blue Mountains for Sunday brunch at **Strawberry Hill** (p231).

---

For several blocks, the waterfront is paralleled by the breeze-swept, 365m-long harborfront **Ocean Blvd**, marked by the iconic **Negro Aroused statue** (Map pp226–7). Nearby, the **National Gallery** (Map pp226-7; ☎ 922-1561; www.galleryjamaica.com; Roy West Bldg, 12 Ocean Blvd; admission US$1.50; ☷ 10am-4:30pm Tue-Thu, 10am-4pm Fri, 10am-3pm Sat) makes an impressive case for the vitality of Jamaican art with a coherent and moving collection of works by John Dunkley, Albert Huie, Edna Manley and other big names in the Jamaican artistic pantheon.

Half a block north, the **African Caribbean Heritage Centre** (Map pp226-7; ☎ 922-4793; Orange St; ☷ 8:30am-4:30pm Mon-Thu, 8:30am-3:30pm Fri) houses a library and a small yet informative gallery that is dedicated to the history of the Middle Passage and a socio-cultural exploration of the African Diaspora.

At the national mint and treasury is the small but fascinating **Museum of Coins & Notes** (Map pp226-7; ☎ 922-0750; cnr Nethersole Pl & Ocean Blvd; admission free; ☷ 9am-4pm Mon-Fri), displaying Jamaican currency through the centuries.

Just 800m up King St from the waterfront you reach the **Parade**, the streets surrounding William Grant Park at the bustling heart of the downtown mayhem. Notable buildings include the historic **Kingston Parish Church**, dating from 1699, and the stately **Ward Theatre** (Map pp226–7).

### Uptown
The beautiful **Devon House** (Map pp224-5; ☎ 929-6602; 26 Hope Rd; admission US$5; ☷ 9am-5pm Tue-Sat), built in 1881, is a classic Jamaican 'great house' that will delight antique lovers and history buffs. The shaded lawns attract couples on weekends. The former carriage house and courtyard are home to two of Jamaica's more

# UPTOWN KINGSTON

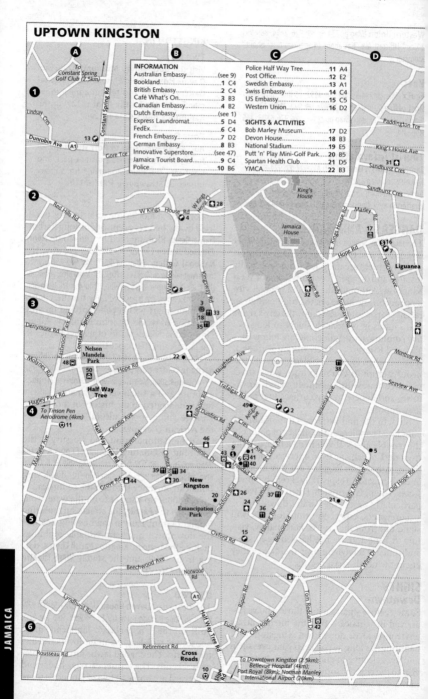

**INFORMATION**

| | |
|---|---|
| Australian Embassy | (see 9) |
| Bookland | 1 C4 |
| British Embassy | 2 C4 |
| Café What's On | 3 B3 |
| Canadian Embassy | 4 B2 |
| Dutch Embassy | (see 1) |
| Express Laundromat | 5 D4 |
| FedEx | 6 C4 |
| French Embassy | 7 D2 |
| German Embassy | 8 B3 |
| Innovative Superstore | (see 47) |
| Jamaica Tourist Board | 9 C4 |
| Police | 10 B6 |
| Police Half Way Tree | 11 A4 |
| Post Office | 12 E2 |
| Swedish Embassy | 13 A1 |
| Swiss Embassy | 14 C4 |
| US Embassy | 15 C5 |
| Western Union | 16 D2 |

**SIGHTS & ACTIVITIES**

| | |
|---|---|
| Bob Marley Museum | 17 D2 |
| Devon House | 18 B3 |
| National Stadium | 19 E5 |
| Putt 'n' Play Mini-Golf Park | 20 B5 |
| Spartan Health Club | 21 D5 |
| YMCA | 22 B3 |

JAMAICA

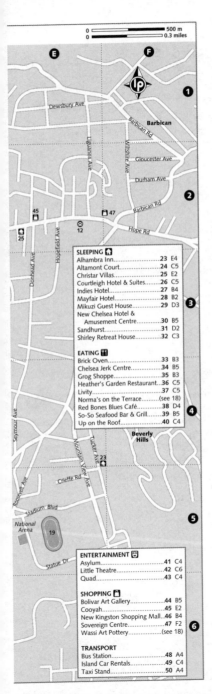

SLEEPING
Alhambra Inn......................23 E4
Altamont Court....................24 C5
Christar Villas.....................25 E2
Courtleigh Hotel & Suites.......26 C5
Indies Hotel.........................27 B4
Mayfair Hotel......................28 B2
Mikuzi Guest House...............29 D3
New Chelsea Hotel &
   Amusement Centre.............30 B5
Sandhurst...........................31 D2
Shirley Retreat House............32 C3

EATING
Brick Oven..........................33 B3
Chelsea Jerk Centre..............34 B5
Grog Shoppe.......................35 B3
Heather's Garden Restaurant...36 C5
Livity.................................37 C5
Norma's on the Terrace..........(see 18)
Red Bones Blues Café............38 D4
So-So Seafood Bar & Grill.......39 B5
Up on the Roof....................40 C4

ENTERTAINMENT
Asylum...............................41 C4
Little Theatre.......................42 C6
Quad.................................43 C4

SHOPPING
Bolivar Art Gallery................44 B5
Cooyah..............................45 E2
New Kingston Shopping Mall...46 B4
Sovereign Centre..................47 F2
Wassi Art Pottery.................(see 18)

TRANSPORT
Bus Station..........................48 A4
Island Car Rentals.................49 C4
Taxi Stand...........................50 A4

famous restaurants, Norma's on the Terrace and Grog Shoppe. Admission includes a guided tour.

The most-visited site in Kingston is the **Bob Marley Museum** (Map pp224-5; ☎ 927-9152; 56 Hope Rd; adult/child/student US$8.50/3.50/6.75; ⏰ 9:30am-4pm Mon-Sat). An Ethiopian flag flutters above the gate of the red-brick manse that Marley turned into his Tuff Gong Recording Studios. Dominating the forecourt is a gaily colored statue of the musical legend. The hour-long tour offers fascinating insights into Marley's life. The highlight is his simple bedroom, left just as it was, with star-shaped guitar by the bedside. The former recording studio out back is now an exhibition hall and theater, where the tour closes with a fascinating film of his final days. No cameras or tape recorders are permitted.

## ACTIVITIES

A favorite spot for runners is the well-kept **Emancipation Park** (Map pp224–5) in New Kingston, which has a 1.6km track; it's a social place used by Kingstonians in large numbers at dawn and dusk.

Built in the 1920s and one of Jamaica's oldest courses, **Constant Spring Golf Club** (off Map pp224-5; ☎ 924-1610; 152 Constant Spring Rd) has a par-70 course and boasts a swimming pool and bar, as well as tennis, squash and badminton courts.

**Spartan Health Club** (Map pp224-5; ☎ 927-7575; 9 Lady Musgrave Rd; nonmembers US$15) is a modern gym. You can have a swim at the **YMCA** (Map pp224-5; ☎ 926-0801; 21 Hope Rd; pool use US$2)

**Putt 'n' Play Mini-Golf Park** (Map pp224-5; ☎ 906-4814; 78 Knutsford Blvd; adult/child & senior US$8/4; ⏰ 5-11pm Mon-Thu, 5pm-midnight Fri, 11am-midnight Sat & Sun), next to the Liguanea Golf Club, is an 18-hole miniature golf course complete with miniature waterfalls, meandering streams, ponds, sand traps and natural obstacles.

## FESTIVALS & EVENTS

**Carnival** (www.jamaicacarnival.com) Kingston's week-long Easter Carnival brings costumed revelers into the streets in droves. There's reggae and calypso, of course, but soca is king. Carnival ends with the Road March, when the two camps parade through the streets in carnival costume.
**Bob Marley Birthday Bash** ( ☎ 927-9152; www.bob marley.com) Brings reggae fans to the Bob Marley Museum on February 6.
**Jamaica Coffee Festival** ( ☎ 922-4200) Jamaica's world famous coffee is something to celebrate at this family-friendly festival in October.

# DOWNTOWN KINGSTON

To New Kingston (3.5km)

To New Kingston (3.5km)

National Heroes Park

Trench Town

Ministry of Education

North Ave

Lockett Ave

Gleaner Building

To Washington Blvd (6km); Spanish Town (23km)

Jones Town

To Spanish Town Rd

Tivoli Gardens

William Grant Park

North Parade

Sutton Rd

W Queen St

E Queen St

South Parade

Marcus Garvey Ave

Barry St

To Tinson Pen Airport (3km); Causeway (6km); Portmore (10km)

Water La

Tower St

Water St

Harbour St

Port Royal St

Nethersole Pl

Ocean Blvd

Derelict Wharves

Kingston Harbour

JAMAICA

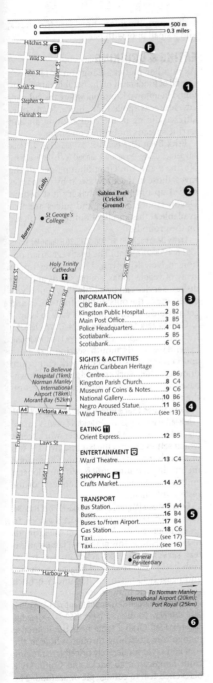

INFORMATION
CIBC Bank.............................1 B6
Kingston Public Hospital.........2 B2
Main Post Office....................3 B5
Police Headquarters...............4 D4
Scotiabank............................5 B5
Scotiabank............................6 C6

SIGHTS & ACTIVITIES
African Caribbean Heritage
  Centre...............................7 B6
Kingston Parish Church...........8 C4
Museum of Coins & Notes.......9 C6
National Gallery....................10 B6
Negro Aroused Statue...........11 B6
Ward Theatre...................(see 13)

EATING 🍽
Orient Express.......................12 B5

ENTERTAINMENT 🎭
Ward Theatre........................13 C4

SHOPPING 🛍
Crafts Market........................14 A5

TRANSPORT
Bus Station...........................15 A4
Buses...................................16 B4
Buses to/from Airport............17 B4
Gas Station...........................18 C6
Taxi...............................(see 17)
Taxi...............................(see 16)

**Fireworks on the Waterfront** ( ☎ 922-4200) Ring in the New Year on the Kingston waterfront with 100,000 others (December 31).

## SLEEPING

Most hotels are in uptown and New Kingston. The pickings are virtually nonexistent downtown. Rates are usually the same year-round.

**Sandhurst** (Map pp224-5; ☎ 927-8244; 70 Sandhurst Cres, Kingston 6; s US$40, d US$45-50, d with air-con US$50; ❌ ♨ ) This eccentric favorite in the quiet, residential, Liguanea neighborhood has spotlessly kept pale-blue rooms with black-and-white tile floors, utility furniture and an air of Miami in the 1960s. Some have TV and telephone and private veranda. A dining terrace has views toward the Blue Mountains.

**Mayfair Hotel** (Map pp224-5; ☎ 926-1610; www.in-site.com/mayfair; 4 W Kings House Close; r US$58-70, ste s/d US$88/128; ❌ ♨ ) A popular option with Jamaican travelers, this hotel sports a columned portico entrance that hints at grandeur within, but the 32 rooms in eight individual houses are fairly basic, with utility furniture and phone, though all are clean and well lit. Its best feature is the view toward the Blue Mountains. A buffet is hosted poolside on Wednesday and Saturday nights.

**Indies Hotel** (Map pp224-5; ☎ 926-2952, 926-0989; www.indieshotel.com; 5 Holborn Rd; s/d/tr US$58/64/77, d fan only US$41; ❌ 💻 ) Providing perhaps the best value in Kingston, this well-run operation is highly rated for its cheerful ambience and accommodating atmosphere. The 15 rooms each have TV and phone and overlook a garden patio complete with fishpond; take an upstairs room for sunlight. There's wi-fi.

**New Chelsea Hotel & Amusement Centre** (Map pp224-5; ☎ 926-5803; fax 929-4746; 5 Chelsea Ave; r US$60; ❌ ) It's a stretch to call this basic option amusing, but it does provide an economical stay in New Kingston. Older rooms are dark; modern rooms in an annex are slightly better. All feature air-con, hot water and cable TV. A fifth night is free. It has a pool hall and an amusement center, plus a disco and a rooftop bar.

**Shirley Retreat House** (Map pp224-5; ☎ 927-9208, 946-2678; 7 Maeven Rd, Kingston 10; r incl breakfast US$65-75; ❌ ) A pleasant option operated by the United Church of Jamaica, this unique place offers four simply furnished, well-lit rooms with hardwood floors, pleasant fabrics, fans, and private bathroom with hot water. Two rooms have small TVs, and one has air-con. Meals are cooked on request.

JAMAICA

**ourpick** **Mikuzi Guest House** (Map pp224-5; ☎ 978-4859, cell 813-0098; www.mikuzijamaica.com; 5 Upper Montrose Rd; d/ste US$80/125; ✿ 🖳 ) Not far from the Bob Marley Museum, this welcoming guesthouse offers 14 comfortable rooms, several with kitchenettes, in a handsome home. The guesthouse's two highest-priced suites are decked out with art and antiques, and are more like small apartments. There's also one cheaper room (US$35). Few restaurants are nearby, however, so if you lack wheels you'll have to hoof it at mealtime. It offers wi-fi access.

**Alhambra Inn** (Map pp224-5; ☎ 978-9072; 1 Tucker Ave; r from US$85-105; ✿ 🖳 🖵 ) Across from the National Stadium, this is an attractive, two-story property with 20 air-con rooms in Spanish style. It's designed to lure convention business and offers gracious furnishings, cable TV, wi-fi, phones and spacious bathrooms. Upstairs rooms have lofty ceilings and king-size beds. Facilities include a restaurant, two bars and a pool in the courtyard.

**Christar Villas** (Map pp224-5; ☎ 978-3933; www.christarvillashotel.com; 99A Hope Rd; r US$93, studio US$125, 2-bedroom ste US$180-275; ✿ 🖵 ) Just east of the Bob Marley Museum, this is the pick of the self-catering options. You can choose from modern, pleasantly furnished studio apartments and one- and two-bedroom suites with satellite TVs, full kitchen and comfy beds. Upper-story suites tend to get hot. You can cool off in the pool, and there is a self-service laundry, a restaurant and a gym. Airport transfer is available on request.

**Courtleigh Hotel & Suites** (Map pp224-5; ☎ 929-9000; www.courtleigh.com; 85 Knutsford Blvd; s/d US$115/125, ste US$190-200, office ste US$190, penthouse US$145-435; ✿ 🖵 🖵 ) This is a splendid contemporary option with deluxe rooms and one-bedroom suites featuring four-post beds and tasteful mahogany furnishings, plus cable TV, direct-dial phone, hair dryer and a work desk. The suites have kitchenettes. There's a pool bar with live music on Friday, a small gym, and a coin-operated laundry. Rates include continental breakfast.

**Altamont Court** (Map pp224-5; ☎ 929-4497, 929-5931; www.altamontcourt.com; 1 Altamont Cres; r US$125, ste US$160; ✿ 🖵 🖵 ) Rather soulless though centrally located mid-size hotel with 55 modern, clean one-bedroom studios and suites – each equipped with phone, wi-fi, cable TV, safe, and basic furnishings. Facilities include the Mango Tree, an attractive restaurant offering complimentary breakfast for guests, and a small pool with bar.

## EATING & DRINKING

As in other matters, Kingston is Jamaica's capital of food; most of the notable eateries are found in uptown Kingston, where the culinary adventurer is spoiled for choice. Many offer alfresco dining in the cool evening air and terrific spreads for brunch on Sunday.

**Brick Oven** (Map pp224-5; ☎ 968-2153; 26 Hope Rd; patties US$1; ☽ lunch & dinner) While nearby Norma's and the Grog Shoppe get all the raves, those in the know swear by the patties served up in this small bakery just behind Devon House. Pastries and juices are also available at this excellent option for a picnic on the grounds.

**Livity** (Map pp224-5; ☎ 906-5618; 30 Haining Rd; mains US$2-6; ☽ lunch & dinner) The best vegetarian option in New Kingston, Livity serves up an array of veggie fajitas, soups, salads and tofu dishes. Service can be a little slow, but if you order one of the outstanding fruit juices and get an outdoor seat, the wait's easy to bear.

**Chelsea Jerk Centre** (Map pp224-5; ☎ 926-6322; 7 Chelsea Ave; mains US$3-10; ☽ 11am-midnight) Legendary for its mouth-searing jerk pork and chicken, this congenial jerk emporium draws the after-work crowd as well as uptown-based visitors grateful for a chance to get off the main drag.

**So-So Seafood Bar & Grill** (Map pp224-5; ☎ 968-2397; 4 Chelsea Ave; mains US$5-12; ☽ lunch & dinner) A casual place, known for its mellow after-work scene, which settles around the bar and two TV sets or sprawls into its outdoor patio. The seafood menu, divided into conch, shrimp, lobster and fish sections, belies the modesty of the restaurant's name.

**Grog Shoppe** (Map pp224-5; ☎ 968-2098; 26 Hope Rd; mains US$8-28; ☽ lunch & dinner Mon-Sat, brunch Sun) In an atmospheric brick edifice on the grounds of Devon House, this grand old Jamaican eatery serves dishes like ackee crepes, baked crab backs, and roast suckling pig with rice and peas. It's known for its Sunday brunch (US$17). Come hungry.

**Heather's Garden Restaurant** (Map pp224-5; ☎ 926-2826, 960-7739; 9 Haining Rd; mains US$9-24; ☽ lunch & dinner Mon-Sat) Grab a table near the immense mango tree stretching through a hole in the roof and savor moderately priced fare ranging from Jamaican crab backs and Cajun-style blackened fish to cottage pie or seafood. The bar scene gets increasingly raucous as the evening progresses.

**our pick Up on the Roof** (Map pp224-5; ☎ 929-8033; 73 Knutsford Blvd; mains US$9-36; ☺ lunch & dinner Mon-Thu, dinner Sat) Above the bustle of New Kingston's main drag, this atmospheric rooftop terrace is popular with locals and a terrific starting point before a night on the town. The marlin salad and shrimp with garlic jerk mayo stand out in a menu of Jamaican standards. There's a sporadic calendar of jazz events and poetry readings; on Saturdays, the bar mixes cocktails until the last patron leaves.

**our pick Red Bones Blues Café** (Map pp224-5; ☎ 978-8262; 21 Braemar Ave; mains US$20-40; ☺ 11am-1am Mon-Fri, from 7pm Sat) The in crowd is in at this former colonial house, now a beehive of cultural and culinary activity. Stellar dishes include chicken breast stuffed with callaloo and jerked cheddar in a white wine sauce, or the seafood trio of shrimp, mussels and salmon sautéed in a spicy coconut sauce served on a bed of pasta. Opt for patio dining overlooking the gardens or the handsome bar.

**Norma's on the Terrace** (Map pp224-5; ☎ 968-5488; 26 Hope Rd; mains US$22-55; ☺ 10am-10pm Mon-Sat, closed public holidays) This lovechild of Jamaica's leading food emissary Norma Shirley is Kingston's most celebrated restaurant. The seasonal menu explores Caribbean-fusion food with great finesse. Recent gems include the smoked pork loin in teriyaki sauce, red snapper encrusted in herbs in a thyme-and-caper sauce and an exquisite seafood lasagna. Even if a meal is beyond your budget, it's well worth having a drink on the candlelit terrace.

## ENTERTAINMENT
### Nightclubs
**Quad** (Map pp224-5; ☎ 754-7823; 20-22 Trinidad Tce; admission US$10) This complex comprises four clubs with distinct personalities: on the main floor is Christopher's Jazz Club, a tasteful jazz bar where the city's movers and shakers gather nightly. In the basement is Taboo, a naughty gentleman's club featuring pole dancers. On Wednesday, Friday and Saturday, two clubs open on the top floor: Voodoo Lounge, which draws an older, more urbane crowd, and Oxygen, which attracts a 20-something set ready to get sweaty until 4am. The US$10 admission will get you into Christopher's, Voodoo Lounge and Oxygen; Taboo charges a separate US$10 admission.

**Asylum** (Map pp224-5; ☎ 929-4386; 69 Knutsford Blvd) Still *the* happening scene, packing in crowds Tuesday through Sunday. Tuesday is ladies' night, with free admission until 11pm, and on Thursday the inimitable Stone Love sets up their legendary sound system.

### Theater
**Little Theatre** (Map pp224-5; ☎ 926-6129; 4 Tom Redcam Dr) Puts on plays, folk concerts, pantomimes and modern dance throughout the year. The main season is July through August, and a 'mini season' is held each December.

**Ward Theatre** (Map pp226-7; ☎ 922-0453; North Pde) This is home to the National Dance Theater Company, known for its rich repertoire, which combines Caribbean, African and Western dance styles.

### Sports
**Sabina Park** (Map pp226-7; ☎ 967-0322; South Camp Rd) Renovated for the 2007 World Cup, this is *the* place for cricket in Jamaica. The 30,000-seat arena hosted its first test match in 1929 and has been a focal point for the sport ever since. Attending a match – particularly an international test – is a must.

**National Stadium** (Map pp224-5; ☎ 929-4970; Arthur Wint Dr) Hosts track-and-field events and matches by the Reggae Boyz, Jamaica's football (soccer) team that surprised the world by reaching the World Cup finals in 1998.

## SHOPPING
Several modern shopping malls are concentrated on Constant Spring and Hope Rds. Two of Kingston's largest are **Sovereign Centre** (Map pp224-5; 106 Hope Rd) and **New Kingston Shopping Mall** (Map pp224-5; Dominica Dr).

In an old iron building on the waterfront, the **Crafts Market** (Map pp226-7; Pechon & Port Royal Sts; ☺ Mon-Sat) has dozens of stalls selling wickerwork, carvings, batiks, straw hats and other crafts. Watch your wallet!

Works by Jamaica's leading artists, fine books, antiques and maps can be found at **Bolivar Art Gallery** (Map pp224-5; ☎ 926-8799; 1D Grove Rd). **Wassi Art Pottery** (Map pp224-5; ☎ 906-5016; Devon House, 26 Hope Rd) sells marvelous vases, planters, plates, bowls etc, each hand-painted and signed by the artist.

**Cooyah** (Map pp224-5; ☎ 978-9215; cooyahdesign@jamweb.net; 96 Hope Rd) is the place to go for licensed reggae T-shirts and assorted tops and dresses.

## GETTING THERE & AWAY
### Air
**Norman Manley International Airport** (KIN; off Map pp226-7; ☎ 924-8546; www.manley-airport.com .jm) handles international flights. Domestic flights land at **Tinson Pen Aerodrome** (off Map pp224-5; ☎ 924-8452; Marcus Garvey Dr) in west Kingston. See p257 for information on international flights, and p257 for domestic flights.

### Bus
Buses, coasters and route taxis run between Kingston and every point on the island. They arrive and depart from the **bus station** (Map pp226-7; Beckford & Pechon Sts), five blocks west of the Parade; see below for details. The terminal adjoins Trench Town, and travelers should exercise caution when passing through.

A smaller number of buses arrive and depart from the preferable Half Way Tree junction, where it's a snap to jump a local bus into New Kingston.

### Car
**Island Car Rentals** ( ☎ 929-5875, in the USA 866-978-5335, in Canada 416-628-8885; www.islandcar rentals.com; 17 Antigua Ave) has its main office in New Kingston, plus an outlet at Norman Manley International Airport. Other companies with offices at Norman Manley airport are **Avis** ( ☎ 924-8293; www.avis.com), **Budget** ( ☎ 759-1793; www.budget.com) and **Hertz** ( ☎ 924-8028; www.hertz.com).

## GETTING AROUND
### To/From the Airport
Norman Manley International Airport is located midway along the Palisadoes, about 27km southeast of downtown Kingston. The bus stop is opposite the airport police station. Bus 98 operates about every 30 minutes between the airport and the west side of the Parade (US$1). Route taxis also operate between the airport and West Parade (US$1.75).

A taxi between the airport and New Kingston will cost about US$20. From Tinson Pen Aerodrome a taxi costs about US$8 to New Kingston, and a bus to the Parade, downtown, is about US$0.25.

### Bus
The main downtown termini for local buses is at North and South Parade and Half Way Tree junction. Kingston's **bus system** (JUTC; ☎ 749-3196; ⌚ 5am-10pm) runs Mercedes-Benz and Volvo buses, including buses for the disabled; fares are US$0.35 to US$0.50.

### Taxi
Taxis are numerous in Kingston except when it rains, which is when demand skyrockets. Use licensed cabs only (they have red PPV license plates). Taxis wait outside most major hotels. Taxi companies are listed in the Yellow Pages. Fares from New Kingston to downtown are about US$10. There is a taxi stand uptown at the south side of Nelson Mandela Park.

# AROUND KINGSTON

**Port Royal** is a dilapidated, ramshackle place of tropical lassitude, replete with important historical buildings collapsing into dust. Today's funky fishing hamlet was once the pirate capital of the Caribbean. Later, it was the hub of British naval power in the West Indies, but the remains give little hint of the town's former glory.

The English settled the isolated cay in 1656. They called it 'Cagway' or 'the Point' and built Fort Cromwell (which was renamed Fort Charles after the Restoration in 1660). Within two years, General William Brayne was able to report that 'there is the faire beginning of a town upon the poynt of this harbor.' A massive earthquake in 1692 put an end to Port Royal's ascension as survivors crossed the harbor to settle on the firmer ground of what would become Kingston.

The town has many fascinating historic sites, including old **Fort Charles** ( ☎ 967-8438; adult/

| SERVICES FROM KINGSTON BUS STATION | | | | |
| --- | --- | --- | --- | --- |
| **Destination** | **One-way fare (US$)** | **Distance (km)** | **Duration (hr)** | **Schedule** |
| Montego Bay | 8 | 191 | 4 | Four daily |
| Ocho Rios | 4 | 87 | 2 | Four daily |
| Port Antonio | 4 | 98 | 2 | Four daily |

JAMAICA

child US$5/2; 9am-5pm, closed Good Friday, Christmas Day & New Year's Day) itself, a terrific **Maritime Museum** (Fort Charles) and the 1725 **St Peter's Church**. An excellent map called 'Port Royal: A Walking Tour' is included in *Port Royal* by Clinton V Black, which you can buy in the gift store of Morgan's Harbour Hotel.

**Lime Cay**, a picture-perfect uninhabited island with white sand and accessible snorkeling, is 15 minutes by boat from Port Royal. Boats run from Morgan's Harbour Hotel, or they can be obtained by asking local fishermen at the pier (US$5). On weekends there are food stalls; at other times bring a picnic.

**Morgan's Harbour Hotel** ( 967-8075; www .morgansharbour.com; s/d US$130/142, ste US$197-206; ) is an atmospheric though overpriced hotel within the grounds of the old naval dockyard. It has 63 spacious air-con rooms with terra-cotta tile floors and French doors opening onto balconies.

Bus 98 runs from the Parade in downtown Kingston several times daily (US$1.25). A route taxi from the Parade in Kingston costs about US$1.50; a licensed taxi costs about US$35 one way. Morgan's Harbour Hotel offers free airport transfers to guests. Otherwise, it's about US$15 for the five-minute taxi ride.

# THE BLUE MOUNTAINS

Looming majestically over the eastern half of the island, the Blue Mountains throw the rest of Jamaica into sharp relief. Barely an hour from Kingston, their slopes and crags are a world away from the capital's gritty streets. And where better to take a break from the beach than to rise 2000m above sea level and luxuriate in the cool of a fern forest?

Home to the celebrated Blue Mountain coffee, the region is a hiker's dream. For many, a trip to Jamaica would be incomplete without a ritual ascent of Blue Mountain Peak, from which you can get a superb panorama of the whole island (weather permitting).

The **Blue Mountains–John Crow National Park** covers the forest reserves of the Blue and John Crow Mountain Ranges. Many stalwart hikers make the journey here to scale **Blue Mountain Peak**, Jamaica's highest mountain at 2256m.

The ramshackle village of Hagley Gap is the gateway to Blue Mountain Peak. The road forks in the village, where a horrendously denuded dirt road for Penlyne Castle begins a precipitous ascent. **Penlyne Castle** is the base for the 11km, 915m ascent to the summit. Most hikers stay overnight at one of three simple lodges near Penlyne Castle before tackling the hike in the wee hours. The most popular is **Wildflower Lodge** ( 929-5395; r with shared/private bathroom US$13/33, cottage US$55), 360m east of the ridge crest at Penlyne Castle. **Guides** (half/full day US$30/50) can be hired locally at Hagley Gap, Penlyne Castle or from the lodge.

**our pick** **Strawberry Hill** ( 944-8400; www.straw berryhillresort.com; r/ste/villa US$595/695/895; ) is a luxury retreat just north of Irish Town. Gaze at Kingston and the harbor 950m below from a deckchair by the infinity pool, or roam the bougainvillea-draped grounds. The Caribbean-style cottages range from well-appointed mahogany-accented studio suites, each with canopied four-poster beds, to a four-bedroom, two-story house built into the hillside. A sumptuous breakfast is included in the rates, as are transfers. Birding, hiking and other tours are offered and Strawberry Hill also hosts a calendar of special events throughout the year. No children are allowed.

The friendly **Jah B Guest House** ( 377-5206; farmhillcoffee@yahoo.com; dm/r US$14/30; ), run by a family of Bobo Rastas, has a basic but cozy wooden guesthouse providing several rooms with four bunks apiece, plus a shared shower and flush toilet; there are also four private rooms. Wi-fi access is available in the communal areas. Jah B himself cooks I-tal meals (about US$8) amid a cloud of ganja smoke and a nonstop volley of friendly banter. His son Alex now runs the outfit and offers transfers from Kingston in his beat-up Land Rover and will guide you up Blue Mountain Peak for US$55.

To get here from Kingston, simply follow Hope Rd uphill to Papine, a market square and bus station, where Gordon Town Rd leads into the mountains. At the Cooperage, the B1 (Mammee River Rd) forks left steeply uphill for Strawberry Hill and Newcastle. Gordon Town Rd continues straight from the Cooperage and winds east up the Hope River Valley to Gordon Town, then steeply to Mavis Bank and Hagley Gap. It is possible to catch an inexpensive route taxi from Papine.

JAMAICA

# NORTHERN JAMAICA

The northeast coast is Jamaica's windward corner, where surf rolls ashore into perfect beach-lined coves and waves chew at rocky headlands. Colonial-era edifices are relatively few, though beautiful pocket-size beaches line the shore. You'll also find several unspoiled fishing villages where budget travelers can ease into a laid-back local lifestyle.

Beautiful Portland parish, presided over by the sleepy town of Port Antonio, is the least developed resort area in Jamaica – a fact that endears it to many. Further west, the bustling port of Ocho Rios provides a convenient staging ground for excursions to some of Jamaica's most popular attractions, including the incomparable Dunn's River Falls.

## PORT ANTONIO
### pop 13,000

Cupping an unruffled bay and backing into the sleepy Rio Grande Valley, Port Antonio is the perfect capital for Portland. The parish's only sizeable town is largely untarnished by the duty-free, tourist-overfriendliness of Ocho Rios or Montego Bay, its streets, squares, quayside and market inviting leisurely strolls – invitations that are freely accepted by the town's dog and goat populaces. It's an ideal base for exploring Portland's hidden treasures.

### Information

**D-Tech** ( ☎ 993-4184; upstairs, 3 West St; internet access per 30min US$1.25; ☼ 9am-7pm Mon-Sat)
**Jamaica Tourist Board** ( ☎ 993-3051; fax 993-2117; City Centre, Harbour St; ☼ 8:30am-4:30pm Mon-Fri) Operates a poorly stocked office that's barely worth a visit.
**Port Antonio Hospital** ( ☎ 993-2646; Nuttall Rd) Above town on Naylor's Hill, south of West Harbour.
**Portland Parish Library** ( ☎ 993-2793; 1 Harbour St; internet access per 30min US$1; ☼ 9am-6pm Mon-Fri, 9am-1pm Sat) Near the entrance to the marina.
**Post office** ( ☎ 993-2651) On the east side of the town square.
**RBTT Bank** ( ☎ 993-9755; 28 Harbour St)
**Scotiabank** ( ☎ 993-2523; 3 Harbour St)
**www.portantoniojamaica.com** This website is a good starting point for tourist information.

### Sights

Port Antonio's heart is the main square at the junction of West and Harbour Sts. It's centered on a **clock tower** and backed by a handsome red-brick Georgian **courthouse** topped by a cupola. From here walk 45m down West St to the junction of William St, where the smaller Port Antonio Sq has a cenotaph honoring Jamaicans who gave their lives in the two world wars.

On the west side of the square is the clamorous and colorful **Musgrave Market**. To the north is the imposing façade of the **Village of St George**, a beautiful three-story complex with an exquisitely frescoed exterior in Dutch style; inside, you'll find an assortment of high-end shops.

Fort George St leads to the Titchfield Peninsula, where you'll find several dozen Victorian-style gingerbread houses, notably **DeMontevin Lodge** (21 Fort George St), an ornate rust-red mansion. Continue north to the remains of **Fort George** at the tip of the peninsula, dating from 1729. Several George III–era cannons can still be seen mounted in their embrasures in 3m-thick walls.

### Activities

**Lady G'Diver** ( ☎ 715-5957, 844-8711; ladygdiver@cwjamaica.com; 2 Somerstown Rd) is a full-service dive shop at Port Antonio Marina; dive boats leave at 11am and 2pm daily.

**Grand Valley Tours** ( ☎ 993-4116, 858-7338; www.portantoniojamaica.com/gvt; 12 West St) offers guided hikes in the Rio Grande Valley, plus horseback riding, bird-watching, caving and other trips of interest to ecotourists.

The **San San Golf Course & Bird Sanctuary** ( ☎ 993-7645; 9/18 holes US$50/70; ☼ 8am-5pm), 13km east of town, is an 18-hole course laid out along valleys surrounded by rainforest. It has a clubhouse, a small pro shop and bistro dining.

### Festivals & Events

**Portland Jerk Festival** ( ☎ 715-5465) A food festival in July for folks in love with the hot and spicy.
**International Marlin Tournament** ( ☎ 927-0145) Anglers rejoice at this time-honored fishing tournament in October.

### Sleeping

Visitors to Port Antonio and environs enjoy some of the most economical lodging on the island. For a good overview, visit the website of **Port Antonio Guest House Association** (www.go-jam.com).

**DeMontevin Lodge** ( ☎ 993-2604; 21 Fort George St; r US$30-140; ☒ ) This venerable Victorian guesthouse boasts a homey ambience and a blend of modern kitsch and antiques reminiscent of granny's parlor. The 13 simple bedrooms (six with private bathrooms) are timeworn, but as clean as a whistle. Behind the lodge is an ancillary building with small budget doubles.

**Ocean Crest Guest House B&B** ( ☎ 993-4024; 7 Queen St; s/d US$35/70; 🚗 ) Somewhat dark and a little loud, this B&B is a favorite with the backpacker crowd. The lounge has a large-screen TV. Four bright new deluxe rooms were recently unveiled on the top floor, with balconies and a stunning view of Port Antonio and its picturesque bay.

**Hotel Timbamboo** ( ☎ 993-2049; http://hoteltimbamboo.com; 5 Everleigh Park Rd; s US$50-70, 1-/2-/3-bedroom ste US$85/150/200; 🚗 🖳 🛋 ) The centrally located Timbamboo has spacious, sunny rooms with modern furniture, carpeted floors and cable TV. Suites have sizeable kitchens, while some rooms have balconies with views of the Blue Mountains. The hotel's sun deck is a great placed to unwind. Common areas have wi-fi.

**Jamaica Heights Resort** ( ☎ 993-3305; www.jamaicaheights.net; Spring Bank Rd; d US$75-125, cottages US$175; 🛋 ) This splendid hilltop plantation home is set amid lush gardens with incredible views. The six rooms and two cottages are tastefully furnished with white wicker and antiques, plus four-poster beds. A spa offers massage and treatments, and there's a beautiful plunge pool plus a nature trail.

### Eating & Drinking
**Norma's at the Marina** ( ☎ 993-9510; Ken Wright Pier; mains $11-20; 🕑 lunch & dinner) Fronting a lovely white-sand beach, this quality restaurant can be a forlorn place – but some might find the solitude blissfully peaceful. Steaks, chops and fish prepared in the continental style are served at outdoor tables overlooking the Errol Flynn Marina.

**Anna Bananas Restaurant & Sports Bar** ( ☎ 715-6533; 7 Folly Rd; breakfast US$4, seafood dinners US$12-16; 🕑 breakfast, lunch & dinner) Overlooking a small beach on the southern lip of the harbor, this breezy restaurant-bar specializes in jerk or barbecued chicken and pork and, for dinner, large plates of conch and lobster. The curried goat is particularly good. There are two pool tables, darts and friendly service.

**our pick Dicky's Best Kept Secret** ( ☎ 809-6276; breakfast/dinner US$12/25; 🕑 breakfast & dinner) Almost too well kept a secret for its own good, Dicky's – an unsigned hut on the A4, less than 1km west of Port Antonio – offers enormous five-course meals in two small rooms perched over the sea. Dicky and his wife promise to cook anything you want (provided they have the ingredients). Invariably, the meal begins with a palate-cleansing fruit plate followed by soup and a callaloo omelet. Dicky's has only a few tables, so reservations are essential.

**Club La Best** (5 West St; 🕑 9:30-till the last person leaves) The newest, liveliest spot in Port Antonio, La Best assumes a different identity depending on the evening. Dancehall throbs into the wee hours on Fridays; Sundays groove to a mellow blend of reggae and old-school R&B; ladies' nights are on Fridays; and periodic live shows occur on Saturdays.

### Getting There & Around
**Ken Jones Aerodrome** ( ☎ 913-3173), 9.5km west of Port Antonio, accepts charter flights.

A **transportation center** (Gideon Ave) extends along the waterfront. Buses, coasters and route taxis leave regularly for Port Maria (where you change for Ocho Rios) and Kingston.

**Eastern Rent-a-Car** ( ☎ 993-3624, 993-2562; 16 West St) offers car rentals, while **JUTA** ( ☎ 993-2684) has taxi transfers from Montego Bay (US$250) and Kingston (US$225) airports.

## AROUND PORT ANTONIO
### Rio Grande Valley
The Rio Grande rushes down from the Blue Mountains through a deeply cut gorge to the sea. The region is popular for **hiking**, but trails are confusing and demanding and should not be attempted without a guide.

**Rafting** is also a big draw. Passengers make the three-hour, 9.5km journey on poled bamboo rafts from Grant's Level or Rafter's Village, just east of Berridale, all the way to St Margaret's Bay. En route, you'll pass through Lovers Lane, a moss-covered narrow stream where you're supposed to kiss and make a wish. Try **Rio Grande Experience Ltd** ( ☎ 913-5434; Berridale; per raft US$60; 🕑 9am-5pm).

To enter the valley, take Red Hassell Rd south from Port Antonio to Fellowship.

### Frenchman's Cove
This small cove, near the town of Drapers 8km east of Port Antonio, boasts one of the prettiest beaches for a long way. A stream winds lazily to a white-sand **beach** (admission US$5; 🕑 closed Tue) that shelves steeply into the water. Bring insect repellent. There's a snack bar and a secure parking lot. A route taxi from Port Antonio costs US$1.

JAMAICA

**ourpick Drapers San Guest House** ( ☎ 993-7118; www.go-jam.com/drapersan-e; Hwy A4, Drapers; s US$27, d US$48-52, all incl breakfast; ☒ ) is an agreeable guesthouse above Frenchman's Cove comprising two cottages with five doubles and one single room (two share a bathroom), all with fans and louvered windows. It has a lovely lounge and communal kitchen. A minimum two-night stay is required.

The trek up a winding dirt road to the romantic, 'eco-chic' 10-room property **Hotel Mocking Bird Hill** ( ☎ 993-7267; www.hotelmocking birdhill.com; Mocking Bird Hill Rd; r US$165-255, ste US$305-450; ☒ ☐ ☐ ☒ ), in the hills above Frenchman's Cove, is well worth it. All rooms are lovingly appointed with well-chosen fabrics and modern art and appliances. Most boast ocean views from private balconies. Facilities include a Caribbean-bright lounge, wi-fi in common areas, and a sublime restaurant. Trails lead through the lush hillside gardens…fabulous for birding!

## Blue Lagoon

The waters that launched Brooke Shields' movie career (and the site of a less-famous Jacques Cousteau dive), the Blue Lagoon, 11km east of Port Antonio, is by any measure one of the most beautiful spots in Jamaica. The 55m-deep 'Blue Hole' (as it is known locally) opens to the sea through a narrow funnel, but is fed by freshwater springs that come in at about 40m deep. Its color changes through every shade of jade and emerald during the day, and you're welcome to take a dip.

The lagoon is public property and accessible from the road. Tours may demand an entrance 'donation,' but J$200 should assuage them. At last visit, the restaurant adjacent to the lagoon, which had closed following Hurricane Ivan, was under construction, and should be completed by the time you read this.

## Fairy Hill & Winnifred Beach

The small clifftop hamlet of Fairy Hill is 13km east of Port Antonio. A dirt road leads steeply downhill to Winnifred Beach – up until recently a great place to hang with 'real' Jamaicans. The turn-off to the beach is opposite the Jamaica Crest Resort. You can catch a route taxi here from Port Antonio (US$1.50).

Only a short ramble away from the now-closed Winnifred Beach, the economical **Mikuzi Vacation Cottages** ( ☎ 978-4859; www.mikuzi.com; Hwy A4, Fairy Hill; 1-bedroom cottage US$25-30, 2-bedroom cottage US$75), set in pleasingly landscaped grounds, provides a perfect hideaway. Two tastefully appointed cottages and a small house are presided over by a warm and attentive caretaker. The cheaper garden cottage lacks a kitchen.

## Boston Bay

The pocket-sized beach of Boston Bay, 14.5km east of Port Antonio, shelves into jewel-like turquoise waters. High surf rolls into the bay, making this perhaps the best **surfing** spot in Jamaica; surfboards in various states of decay are available for rent on the beach.

Boston Bay is known for highly spiced jerk chickens and pork sizzling away on smoky barbecue pits along the roadside. Some contend that jerk was invented here. Also on the scene is the Maroon Prophet, a roots bush doctor selling his handmade tonic and blood cleanser, made from roots and bushes according to tradition.

One of the most unusual accommodations in Jamaica, **Great Huts** ( ☎ 993-8888; www.greathuts .com; Boston Beach Lane; African-style tent per person US$60-139, tree house US$157; ☐ ) perches on a scenic crag overlooking Boston Bay, it consists of nine tents or huts, each decorated with distinctive and imaginative Afrocentric design, and two spacious 'tree houses.' These two-story open-air structures have verandas, bamboo-walled bedrooms, Jacuzzi baths and kitchenettes. If you can tear yourself from your room, check out the Cliff Bar, featuring excellent pizzas and superlative views of the sea, and the hotel's own beach on the rocks below. Wi-fi is available in the common area.

A route taxi from Port Antonio will cost you US$1.50.

## Long Bay

Once Negril lost its patina of countercultural credibility, free spirits began looking to Long Bay to assume the mantle of Jamaica's hippest hideaway. Set in a dramatic 1.5km-wide bay, the hamlet appeals to budget travelers and surfers, and has drawn a number of expats who have put down roots and opened guesthouses. At the time of research, however, Long Bay was recovering from Hurricane Dean, whose impact (in August 2007) it felt more keenly than any other place on the island.

The fare to Long Bay from Port Antonio by route taxi is about US$3.

# OCHO RIOS
pop 16,500

Wrapped around a small bay with postcard-worthy snugness, Ocho Rios is a former fishing village that the Jamaica Tourist Board earmarked for tourism in the mid-1980s. Whatever character Ocho Rios had, it lost when the local nets were redirected from fish to the tourist dollar. Its streets today are lined with interchangeable duty-free shopping plazas and fast-food emporia, persistent higglers and a palpable air of waiting for something.

That something is cruise ships – after Montego Bay, this is the island's premier port of packaged call. When the floating resorts pull in, their human cargo streams into town to meet the local traffic in souvenirs untainted by memories; the full frontal hustle is on.

Yet if you're looking for a central base for exploring the north coast, this is it. A terrific reggae museum, a lively nightlife scene, a trio of serene hillside gardens and an abundance of fine hotels and guesthouses make Ochi a good place to pause.

## Information

**Bryan's Bookstores Ltd** ( ☎ 795-0705; Shop 12-15, Island Plaza) Has a wide range of titles about Jamaica, including maps.

**Cable & Wireless** ( ☎ 974-9906; Shop 13-15, Island Plaza) Offers long-distance calling.

**CIBC** ( ☎ 974-2824; 29 Main St) Has foreign exchange facilities and ATM.

**Internet Jungle** ( ☎ 974-9906; Shop 13-15, Island Plaza; internet access per 15min/30min/1hr/all day US$2.50/5/10/20) In the Cable & Wireless office.

**Police station** ( ☎ 974-2533) Off DaCosta Dr, just east of the clock tower.

**Post office** (Main St; ☼ 8am-5pm Mon-Sat) Opposite the Ocho Rios Craft Park.

**St Ann's Bay Hospital** ( ☎ 972-2272) In St Ann's Bay, about 11km west of Ocho Rios. Your hotel's front desk can arrange a doctor's visit.

**Scotiabank** ( ☎ 974-2081; Main St) Has foreign exchange facilities and an ATM.

**Tourism Product Development Co** (TPDCo; ☎ 974-7705, 974-3866; Shop 3, Ocean Village, Main St; ☼ 8:30am-5pm Mon-Thu, 8:30am-4pm Fri) Represents the Jamaica Tourist Board. While it doesn't offer much in the way of literature, staff will spend time helping you suss out Ochi's transportation, lodging and attractions options. TPDCo also operates two information booths on Main St when cruise ships are in port.

## Dangers & Annoyances

Ocho Rios' biggest annoyance is the persistent entreaties of hustlers, who are especially thick around the clock tower and DaCosta Dr.

Avoid the area immediately behind the market south of the clock tower. Use caution at night anywhere, but particularly on James St, a poorly lit street with several nightspots and a hangout strip of ill repute.

## Sights

To visit Jamaica and not climb **Dunn's River Falls** ( ☎ 974-2857; www.dunnsriverfallsja.com; adult/child US$15/12; ☼ 8:30am-4pm Sat-Tue, 7am-5pm Wed-Fri), on the A3, about 3km west of town, is like visiting Paris without seeing the Eiffel Tower. Join hands in a daisy chain at the bottom and clamber up the tiers of limestone that step 180m down to the beach in a series of cascades and pools. The water is refreshingly cool and the falls are shaded by a tall rainforest.

Swimwear is essential. There are changing rooms and lockers (US$5) on the beach, as well as an orchid garden, children's playground, a crafts market, jerk stalls, snack bars and a restaurant. A warning: expect to be given the hard sell here by professional hustlers. Plan to arrive before 10am, when the tour buses arrive, or around 4pm after they depart. Also try to visit when the cruise ships aren't in town (usually Saturday to Tuesday).

Public minibuses and route taxis (US$1) head west to Dunn's River Falls and beyond from Main St; it's simple to flag one down.

The main beach is the long crescent of Ocho Rios Bay Beach, locally known as **Turtle Beach** (adult/child US$1/0.50; ☼ 6am-6pm), stretching east from Turtle Towers condominiums. There are changing rooms, watersport concessionaires, and palms for shade. **Island Village Beach** (admission US$3; ☼ 6am-6pm), at the west end of Main St, is a peaceful, smaller beach with a complete range of water sports. **Mahogany Beach**, 1km east of the town center, is a small and charming beach with no admission charge.

**Reggae Xplosion** ( ☎ 675-8895; Island Village; admission US$7; ☼ 9am-5pm Mon-Fri, 10am-5pm Sat) offers an excellent presentation of the grand lineage of Jamaican music, from ancient African drumming to the futuristic digital rhythms of dancehall. The self-billed 'interactive reggae experience' is divided into mento, ska, reggae, dancehall and other sections, including one commemorating Bob Marley.

JAMAICA

**Shaw Park Gardens** ( ☎ 974-2723; Shaw Park Rd; admission US$10; ⏰ 8am-5pm) is a tropical fantasia of ferns and bromeliads, palms and exotic shrubs, spread out over 10 hectares and centered on an 18th-century great house. Trails and wooden steps lead past waterfalls that tumble in terraces down the hillside. A viewing platform offers a bird's-eye vantage over Ocho Rios. It has a bar and a restaurant. The gardens are signed from opposite the public library on the A3.

## Activities

Virtually the entire shoreline east of Ocho Rios to Galina Point is fringed by a reef, and it's great for diving and snorkeling. You can arrange dives and snorkeling at most resorts or at **Watersports Enterprise** ( ☎ 974-2244; Turtle Beach; 1-/2-/4-tank dive US$45/70/140).

If you're after a round of golf, head to **Sandals Ocho Rios Golf & Country Club** ( ☎ 975-0119; Bonham Spring Rd; green fees US$100; ⏰ 7am-5pm), 6.5km southeast of town, signed from the A3.

## Tours

**Chukka Caribbean Adventure Tours** ( ☎ 927-2506; www.chukkacaribbean.com/jamaica; tours US$50-100) offers an invigorating menu of quality excursions including horseback ride 'n' swim, river tubing, 4WD safari, the Zion Bus Line Tour to Nine Mile and a forest canopy tour.

**Hooves** ( ☎ 972-0905; www.hoovesjamaica.com; tours US$55-100) leads several interesting horseback tours, including Heritage Beach Trail, Bush Doctor Mountain Trail and Rainforest River Trail.

**Blue Mountain Bicycle Tours** ( ☎ 974-7075; www.bmtoursja.com; adult/child US$89/65) leads excellent full-day biking tours from Ocho Rios to the Blue Mountains, featuring a hair-raising mountain descent and a dip at a waterfall.

## Festivals & Events

**Carnival** (www.jamaicacarnival.com) Street parties and soca music all night long in March and April.

**Ocho Rios Jazz Festival** ( ☎ 927-3544; www.ochoriosjazz.com) Top names in jazz, under the stars in June.

**Hi Pro High Goal Family Tournament** ( ☎ 952-4370; shane@tobyresorts.com; St Ann Polo Club) Features Jamaica's best polo families in an August competition.

## Sleeping

Ocho Rios and environs offers everything from simple guesthouses to opulent resorts.

**Mahoe Villa and Guesthouse** ( ☎ 974-6613; 11 Shaw Park Rd; r with shared bathroom US$20-30, r with private bathroom US$40-75) If you've been looking high and low for a decent US$20 room, this is it. On the road to Shaw Park Garden is this brilliantly priced guesthouse with 11 spic-and-span, fan-cooled rooms of varying size. The large house has polished wood floors and is replete with original works of art. It also has a communal kitchen, cable TV, and several hammocks strung up in the yard.

**Ocean Sands Resort** ( ☎ 974-2605; www.caribbeancoast.com/nhotels/oceansands; 14 James St; s/d US$50/70; ⊠ ⚟ ) This attractive property has an oceanfront setting and its own pocket-size beach, with coral, at your doorstep. A tiny restaurant sits at the end of a wooden wharf. The 35 pleasant rooms have French doors that open onto private balconies. Rates include breakfast.

**Little Shaw Park Guest House** ( ☎ 974-2177; www.littleshawparkguesthouse.com; 21 Shaw Park Rd; r/apt US$50/60; ⊠ ) Providing a restful retreat, this trim place is set among 0.6 hectares of beautifully tended lawns and bougainvillea with a gazebo and hammocks. There's a room in the owner's house, plus seven spacious (though dark) cabins boasting homey decor. Also on offer are well-lit studio apartments with kitchens, cable TV and hot water. Meals are available by request.

**Crane Ridge** ( ☎ 974-8050, 866-277-6374; www.craneridge.net; 17 DaCosta Dr; ste US$110, deluxe 1-/2-bedroom ste US$168/240; ⊠ ⚟ ) Offering a breezy hilltop location on the west side of town, this modern, all-suite resort features 119 suites in six three-story structures. Some rooms have loft bedrooms. An airy restaurant on stilts looms over a large pool. There's a shuttle service to the hotel's private beach and to Shaw Park Gardens and Dunn's River Falls.

**ourpick** **Cottage at Te Moana** ( ☎ 974-2870; www.harmonyhall.com; cabin US$120; ⊠ ) With its small clifftop garden overhanging a reef, this exquisite reclusive rental offers a delightful alternative to Ochi's resort hotels. The clifftop bedroom is reached via an external staircase and has a king-size bed and ceiling fan, and a magnificent artist's aesthetic. Steps lead down to a coral cove good for snorkeling, and kayaks are available.

**Hibiscus Lodge** ( ☎ 974-2676; www.hibiscusjamaica.com; 83 Main St; r US$140-152; ⊠ ▣ ⚟ ) A well-run hotel perched on a breezy clifftop setting amid lush grounds, this hotel offers spacious but modestly furnished rooms. There's a small clifftop pool, wi-fi, an atmospheric bar, plus a fine restaurant.

**Sandcastles Resort** (☎ 974-5626; www.sandcastle sochorios.com; 120 Main St; r/ste US$149/230; 🌂 🔄 ) A large centrally located option that's a beach-ball's throw from Turtle Beach, this well-refurbished resort has bright studios and one- and two-bedroom suites in various configurations. All have cable TV and modern furnishings. There's also a sports bar, and wi-fi access is available in common areas.

**Royal Plantation** (☎ 974-5601; www.royalplantation.com; r US$605-1245; 🌂 🔄 🔄 ) While luxury can be found across Jamaica, its lap is surely on this 3-hectare spot nestled around two private beaches. From the Neoclassical lobby decked in Victorian furnishings to the C Bar (Jamaica's only caviar and champagne bar), the Royal Plantation goes the extra mile. All 74 rooms face the sea and feature marble bathrooms, and there are three gourmet restaurants. An array of water sports is available, while cigar-rolling displays and an artist in residency program help make this one of the most unique hotels on the island.

## Eating

As a major resort, Ochi offers a satisfying variety of restaurants from simple but hearty vegetarian fare to haute cuisine. The following restaurants are all within walking distance of downtown.

**World of Fish** (☎ 974-1863; 3 James Ave; US$3-8; 🕐 11am-1am) Popular with locals, this casual and economical eatery serves fresh seafood, including lobster, shrimp and conch. In keeping with the Jamaican capacity for making juice from just about anything that grows, sweet nectars of june plum, ginger and soursop are served.

**Michelle's Pizzeria** (☎ 974-4322; Pineapple Hotel, Main St; US$6-8; 🕐 lunch & dinner) In addition to four styles of pizza (including a 'Hawaiian' with pineapple), this causal spot serves an array of pastas and hero sandwiches to be eaten on a small patio.

**Bibibips Bar & Grill** (☎ 974-8759; 93 Main St; mains US$6-28; 🕐 10am-midnight) This popular, touristy oceanfront bar and restaurant with a porch overlooking Mahogany Beach serves up a range of seafood, jerk and barbecue dishes that don't quite live up to their pricing.

**Coconuts** (☎ 795-0064; Fisherman's Point; US$7-25; 🕐 breakfast, lunch & dinner) Whether you stop in

for a *ménage à trois* plate (coconut shrimp, conch and chicken samosas) or have a jerk chicken quesadilla, the terrace here invariably keeps you here longer than you intended. And why not? The view of the bay is stellar, and the drink specials ease you into the evening, when Coconuts becomes a lively bar.

**Passage to India** (☎ 795-3182; Soni's Plaza, 50 Main St; US$9-25; 🕐 lunch & dinner Tue-Sun, lunch Mon) On the rooftop of a duty-free shopping center, Passage to India offers respite from the crowds below in addition to very good northern Indian fare. The naan is crisp, the curries sharp, and the menu divided into extensive chicken, mutton, seafood and vegetarian sections. Tandoori options are also on offer.

**ourpick Toscanini** (☎ 975-4785; Harmony Hall; mains US$10-24; 🕐 lunch & dinner Tue-Sun) One of the finest restaurants on the island, this roadside spot is run by two gracious Italians who mix local ingredients into recipes from the motherland. The daily menu ranges widely, encompassing appetizers such as prosciutto with papaya or marinated marlin, and mains such as lobster pasta, or shrimp sautéed with garlic and Appleton rum. Leave room for desserts such as strawberry tart or apple and plum strudel. Go on, treat yourself!

**Ruins at the Falls** (☎ 974-8888; 17 DaCosta Dr; lunch buffet US$14, mains US$9-24; 🕐 breakfast & lunch) Set amid a tropical garden with a lovely bridal-veil waterfall and pools, this Jamaican-Chinese restaurant has one-of-a-kind ambience. The all-inclusive lunchtime buffet features beverages, live entertainment and a garden tour.

## Drinking

**Coconuts** (☎ 795-0064; Fisherman's Point) The potent cocktails and omnipotent US$20 all-you-can drink hard liquor special make the terrace here an excellent vantage point for watching the cruise ships pull out from the dock across the street.

**Jimmy Buffett's Margaritaville** (☎ 675-8800; Island Village; nightclub admission US$10-20) This ostentatious behemoth offers a boozy good time with its three bars, rooftop whirlpool tub and an endlessly entertaining water slide.

**Ruins Pub** (☎ 974-9712; 17 DaCosta Dr) This classy joint offers a peaceful environment for enjoying a quiet drink.

JAMAICA

## Entertainment

**Amnesia** ( ☎ 974-2633; 70 Main St; admission US$5; ☽ Wed-Sun) A classic Jamaican dancehall, this remains the happening scene. Theme nights include an oldies jam on Sunday, ladies' night on Thursday and an after-work party on Friday. This is all leading up to Saturday's dress-to-impress all-night dance marathon.

**Little Pub** ( ☎ 795-1831; 59 Main St) This touristy pub is an old favorite, with sports TV and the occasional eclectic floor show to amuse you while you sit at the bar. A resident band plays here six nights per week. The entertainment schedule changes night by night, and includes an Afro-Caribbean musical, karaoke, and a weekly cabaret on Friday.

**Roofe Club** ( ☎ 974-1042; 7 James Ave; admission US$3) The gritty Roofe sends earth-shattering music across the roofs of town; it's the place to get down and dirty with the latest dancehall moves.

## Shopping

Shopping is big business in Ocho Rios. There is a wide variety of duty-free shops located on Main St.

**Wassi Art** ( ☎ 974-5044; www.wassiart.com; Bougainvillea Dr; ☽ closed Sun) Here you'll witness scores of rising and established Jamaican masters creating exquisite works of art. To get here, take Milford Rd (A3) and watch for the signs.

**Island Village** (cnr Main St & DaCosta Dr) Has more than a dozen pleasant stores with carefully chosen merchandise. These include several beachwear shops, duty-free stores, an outlet for film and photography needs, and upscale outlets for quality paintings, carvings and crafts.

## Getting There & Away

**Boscobel Aerodrome** ( ☎ 975-3101) is 16km east of town. No international service lands here; see p257 for domestic-flight details.

Buses, coasters and route taxis arrive at and depart Ocho Rios from the **Transportation Center** (Evelyn St); direct services to Montego Bay and Port Antonio operate throughout the day. For a route taxi to Kingston, take the short ride to Fern Gully bus yard and transfer there. If you're coming from the east, you will be deposited at the taxi stand near One Love Park, up the hill from the harbor.

**JUTA** ( ☎ 974-2292) is the main taxi agency catering to tourists. A licensed taxi costs about US$90 per person between Montego Bay and Ocho Rios, and about US$80 between Ocho Rios and Kingston (US$100 to the airport).

Car rental rates are cheaper in Ocho Rios than elsewhere on the island, averaging US$50/300 for the day/week.

**Island Car Rentals** ( ☎ 974-2334; www.islandcarrentals.com; Main St)

**Salem Car Rentals** ( ☎ 974-0786; www.salemcarrentals.com; 7 Sand Castles Complex)

## Getting Around

Ocho Rios has no bus service within town. Coasters and route taxis ply Main St and the coast road (US$1 for short hauls; US$4 to Boscobel Aerodrome).

Government-established licensed taxi fares from downtown include Dunn's River US$25, Firefly US$65, Prospect Plantation US$32 and Shaw Park Gardens US$22.

# AROUND OCHO RIOS
## Nine Mile

Despite its totally out-of-the-way location 64.5km south of Ocho Rios, the village of Nine Mile is firmly on the tourist map for pilgrimages to Bob Marley's birth site and resting place. At the **Nine Mile Museum** ( ☎ 999-7003; http://ninemilejamaica.com; admission US$15; ☽ 8am-5:30pm), Rastafarian guides given to sudden outbursts of song lead pilgrims to the hut – now festooned with devotional graffiti – where the reggae god spent his early years. Another highlight is the Rasta-colored 'rock pillow' on which he laid his head when seeking inspiration. Marley's body lies buried along with his guitar in a 2.5m-tall oblong marble mausoleum inside a tiny church of traditional Ethiopian type.

Getting to Nine Mile is no simple matter. The site is extremely secluded, but all cab drivers know the route (haggle hard for a reasonable fare; US$75 is common). A far easier way to visit is via 'Zion Bus Line' tour, run by **Chukka Caribbean Adventure Tours** ( ☎ 927-2506; www.chukkacaribbean.com/jamaica), which departs from Ocho Rios.

If you are driving, be sure to pull up right outside the museum compound and honk your horn to get someone to open the gate. The alternative is to park on the street and pay any number of locals to watch the vehicle.

## Firefly

About 32km east of Ocho Rios, **Firefly** ( ☎ 997-7201, 994-0920; admission US$10; ☽ 9am-5pm Mon-Fri) was the home of Sir Noël Coward, the English playwright, songwriter, actor and wit. The cottage, set amid wide lawns high on a hill with tremendous views of the coastline below, is a museum, looking just as it did on Sunday February 28, 1965, the day the Queen Mother visited. Coward lies buried beneath a plain white marble slab on the wide lawns where he entertained so many illustrious stars of stage and screen. Firefly is well signed along three different routes from the A3.

# MONTEGO BAY & AROUND

Montego Bay is the second-largest city on the island and Jamaica's most important tourist resort. The region boasts a greater concentration of well-preserved colonial houses than any other, some of which are working plantations that offer guided tours. Several championship golf courses, horse stables and the island's best shopping add to the region's appeal.

## MONTEGO BAY
### pop 110,000

A bustling town with a turbulent history, a thriving port and a hopping 'hip strip,' Montego Bay (MoBay) is Jamaica's most charged city. While spring-breakers from the US descend on MoBay each year for bouts of ritualized raucousness, being host to the island's busiest airport and cruise-ship port assures the town a steady stream of visitors, many of whom pop down from North America for long weekends.

Many never make it off Gloucester Av, which has attained the wince-inducing title of 'hip strip.' Most of the hotels, restaurants, bars and souvenir emporia line this parade, which runs parallel to the beach; everything is here – and a loose confederacy of hustlers patrols the strip ready to offer guidance (and other services) should you find it all over-whelming. Despite its gaudiness, the strip boasts some of the best eating options on the island.

Street life of another, more genuine, order courses through downtown, which features a selection of decaying Georgian buildings that hint at earlier prosperity and the excellent Museum of St James, which bears poignant testament to the city's brutal slave history.

## Information

**Cornwall Regional Hospital** ( ☎ 952-5100; Mt Salem Rd) Has a 24-hour emergency room.

**Cyber Café** ( ☎ 971-8907; Gloucester Ave; per 15min/hr US$2/7.50; 🕙 8am-8:30pm) At Doctor's Cave Beach, with a wireless network serving the beach.

**Exchange bureau** ( 🕙 24hr) In the arrival hall at Sangster International Airport.

**Fire** ( ☎ 952-2311)

**FX Trader** ( ☎ 952-3171; 37 Gloucester Ave) At the Pelican restaurant; one of a number of money exchange bureaus downtown.

**Jamaica Tourist Board** Airport ( ☎ 952-3009); Cornwall Beach ( 🕙 8:30am-4:30pm Mon-Fri, 9am-1pm Sat); Gloucester Ave ( ☎ 952-4425; fax 952-3587) Opening hours are variable.

**Official Visitors Guide** (www.montego-bay-jamaica .com) An up-to-date online resource for info on MoBay and environs.

**Post office** Gloucester Ave ( ☎ 979-5137; 🕙 8am-5pm Mon-Fri); Downtown ( ☎ 952-7016; Fort St)

**Sangster's Bookshop** ( ☎ 952-0319; 2 St James St) The largest bookstore in town, albeit only modestly stocked.

## Dangers & Annoyances

Montego Bay has a reputation for harassment of tourists by hustlers. Visitors can expect to be approached in none-too-subtle terms by locals offering their services, and the barrage of young men selling drugs is a wearying constant. Uniformed members of the Montego Bay Resort Patrol police the strip. Downtown is not patrolled; it's safe to walk in the historic center during daylight hours but stick to the main streets and stay alert.

## Sights

The bustling, cobbled **Sam Sharpe Sq** is named for national hero the Right Excellent Samuel Sharpe (1801–32), the leader of the 1831 Christmas Rebellion (see the boxed text, p244). At the square's northwest corner is the **National Heroes Monument**, an impressive bronze statue of Paul Bogle and Sam Sharpe, Bible in hand, speaking to three admirers. Also on the northwest corner is the **Cage**, a tiny cut-stone and brick building built in 1806 as a lockup, now a small souvenir shop.

At the southwest corner is the copper-domed **Civic Centre**, a handsome colonial-style cut-stone building on the site of the ruined colonial courthouse. It contains the small yet highly informative **Museum of St James** ( ☎ 971-9417; admission US$3; 🕙 9:30am-4:30pm Tue-Thu, 9:30am-3:30pm Fri, 10:30am-2:30pm Sat) with relics and other

**JAMAICA**

**JAMAICA**

# MONTEGO BAY

**INFORMATION**
| | |
|---|---|
| Canadian Embassy | 1 C4 |
| Cornwall Regional Hospital | 2 F6 |
| Cyber Café | 3 C3 |
| FX Trader | (see 29) |
| Jamaica Tourist Board | 4 C4 |
| Jamaica Tourist Board | 5 C2 |
| Post Office | 6 E5 |
| Post Office | 7 C3 |
| Sangster's Bookshop | 8 E6 |
| US Embassy | 9 C2 |

**SIGHTS & ACTIVITIES**
| | |
|---|---|
| Aquasol Theme Park | 10 E5 |
| Cage | (see 14) |
| Civic Centre | (see 14) |
| Montego Bay Marine Park Trust | 11 D6 |
| Museum of St James | (see 14) |
| National Heroes Monument | (see 14) |
| Rhapsody Cruises | 12 F2 |
| St James Parish Church | 13 E6 |
| Sam Sharpe Sq | 14 E5 |

**SLEEPING**
| | |
|---|---|
| Altamont West | 15 C4 |
| Buccaneer Beach | 16 E2 |
| Caribic House | 17 C3 |
| Gloucestershire Hotel | 18 C3 |
| Knightwick House | 19 C3 |
| Linkage Guest House | 20 E6 |
| Richmond Hill Inn | 21 F5 |
| Royal Decameron Montego Beach Resort | 22 C2 |
| Sandals Montego Bay | 23 D3 |

**EATING**
| | |
|---|---|
| El Campay Gallo | 24 C3 |
| Houseboat Grill | 25 C8 |
| Marguerite's | 26 B3 |
| Native Restaurant & Bar | 27 C4 |
| Nyam 'n' Jam | 28 E6 |
| Pelican | 29 B4 |
| Pork Pit | 30 C4 |
| Town House by the Sea | 31 B3 |

**DRINKING**
| | |
|---|---|
| Jamaican Bobsled Café | 32 C3 |
| Jimmy Buffett's Margaritaville | 33 B3 |
| MoBay Proper | 34 E5 |

**ENTERTAINMENT**
| | |
|---|---|
| Blue Beat Jazz & Blues Bar | 35 B3 |
| Coral Cliff Gaming Lounge | 36 B3 |

**SHOPPING**
| | |
|---|---|
| Craft Market | 37 E6 |
| Gallery of West Indian Art | 38 E8 |
| Tafara Products | 39 E6 |

**TRANSPORT**
| | |
|---|---|
| Montego Bay Metro Line | 40 E5 |
| Taxi Stand | 41 E5 |
| Taxi Stand | 42 C3 |
| Transportation Station | 43 E6 |

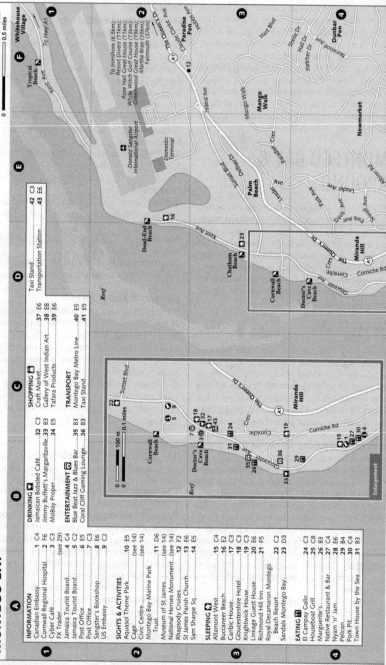

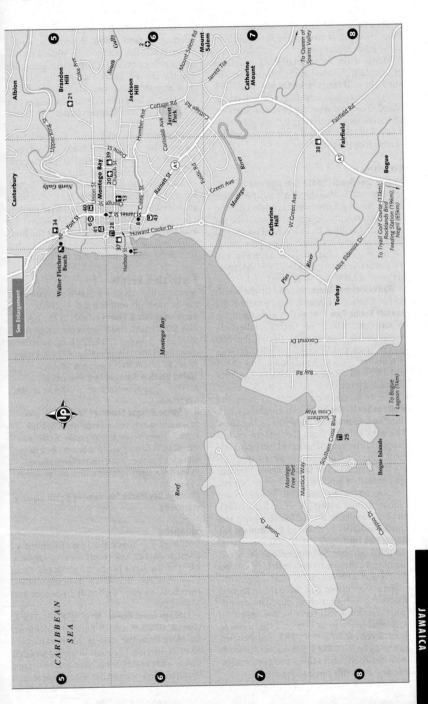

exhibits tracing the history of St James Parish from Arawak days through the slave rebellions to the more recent past.

Many of the most interesting buildings in town are clustered along Church St. The highlight is **St James Parish Church** ( ☎ 952-2775; Church St), regarded as the finest church on the island. You can view the beautiful interior, which contains a stunning stained-glass window behind the altar and a number of notable marble monuments.

## Activities

**Doctor's Cave Beach** ( ☎ 952-2566; adult/child US$5/2.50; ⏱ 8:30am-6pm) is Montego Bay's most excellent beach. It can get obscenely crowded during the winter months, so arrive early to stake out your turf. Facilities include a food court, grill bar, internet café and water sports, plus changing rooms. You can rent shade umbrellas and inflatable air mattresses (lilos) for US$5, snorkel gear for US$5 and chairs for US$4.

**Walter Fletcher Beach**, located at the south end of Gloucester Ave, is the venue for the **Aquasol Theme Park** ( ☎ 940-1344; adult/child US$5/3; ⏱ 9am-10pm), which has netball, volleyball, tennis courts, water sports, the MoBay 500 go-cart track and Voyage Sports Bar & Grill. It rents out lockers, beach mats, and chairs and umbrellas. Reggae parties are a regularly scheduled attraction.

Nature-lovers won't want to miss the **Montego Bay Marine Park** for its coral reefs, rich flora and fauna, and shoreline mangroves. The park extends from the eastern end of Sangster International Airport westward (almost 9.5km) to the Great River, encompassing the mangroves of **Bogue Lagoon**. You can set out with a guide to spot herons, egrets, pelicans and waterfowl, while below, in the tannin-stained waters, juvenile barracudas, tarpon, snapper, crabs and lobsters swim and crawl. Authority is vested in the **Montego Bay Marine Park Trust** (MBMPT; ☎ 971-8082; www.montego-bay-jamaica.com/mbmp; Pier 1, off Howard Cooke Dr), which maintains a meager **resource centre** ( ⏱ 9am-5pm Mon-Fri) with a library on the vital ecosystem.

Here you will also find first-rate diving and snorkeling with a variety of sites. These range from teeming patch reefs to awe-inspiring walls that begin in as little as 11m of water. **Resort Divers** ( ☎ 953-9699, 940-1183; www.resortdivers .com; Holiday Inn, Rose Hall Rd; 4-/5-dive package US$140/180, certification US$395) offers dives and certification courses, and rents out equipment.

The waters off of Jamaica's north coast offer spectacular **game fishing**. Beyond the north-shore reefs, the ocean floor plummets for thousands of meters. Deep-water game fish use the abyss – known as 'Marlin Alley' – as a migratory freeway. Half- and full-day charters can be booked through hotels, at Pier 1 Marina, or from **Rhapsody Cruises** ( ☎ 979-0102; Shop 204, Chatwick Plaza).

Rhapsody also offers three-hour **chartered cruises** (US$60; ⏱ 10am-1pm & 3-6pm) with an open bar and a snorkeling stop in the marine park. A bus will pick you up at your hotel.

Montego Bay is world-renowned for **golf**; three championship courses are east of town in Ironshore. Jamaica's two most famous courses, **Tryall Golf Course** ( ☎ 956-5660) and the **White Witch Golf Course** ( ☎ 953-2800) at the Ritz-Carlton Rose Hall, are world-class links that lure enthusiasts from all over the world.

## Festivals & Events

Montego Bay's most celebrated annual events are its two high-profile music festivals.

**Air Jamaica Jazz & Blues Festival** ( ☎ 888-359-2475, 800-523-5585; www.airjamaica.com; 1-night pass US$75-80, 2-/3-day pass US$150/225) Brings internationally acclaimed acts to Cinnamon Hill near Rose Hall in late January for three nights of music under the stars.

**Spring Break** In March and April, thousands of American college students descend on MoBay for all-night bacchanalia.

**Red Stripe Reggae Sumfest** ( ☎ 953-4573; www .reggaesumfest.com; weekend/event pass US$52/160) Jamaica's premier reggae festival typically includes more than 50 world-class reggae artists. Held in July, it starts with a beach party on Walter Fletcher Beach, followed by four theme nights, including a 'street jam' on Gloucester Ave.

**Montego Bay Marlin Tournament** Big fish, big party in September.

## Sleeping

Montego Bay boasts the largest number of guest rooms of any resort area in Jamaica. Most of the Bay's hotels are clustered along Gloucester Ave; deluxe resorts nestle on their own beaches east of town at Ironshore and Mahoe Bay.

**Linkage Guest House** ( ☎ 952-4546, 979-0308; 32 Church St; s US$18-25, d US$25) Located downtown far away from the strip is this backpackers favorite offering 15 rooms in an old wooden house. They're simple but clean and have fans, louvered windows, and hot water in the shared bathrooms. Meals are served. The owners also offer Maroon heritage tours (US$50).

**Caribic House** ( ☎ 979-6073; fax 979-0322; 69 Gloucester Ave; standard s US$45-59, d US$51-69; ❤ ) This compact no-frills option across the street from Doctor's Cave Beach (and right above the Jamaica Bobsled Café) is a favorite of the budget-minded. It has 17 basic rooms with fridges and large bathrooms, including one 'superior' room with kitchen, dining room and three beds.

**ourpick Knightwick House** ( ☎ 952-2988; tapas 45@hotmail.com; Corniche Rd; s US$45, d US$65-70; ❤ ) Behind and above the Coral Cliff Hotel, this wonderful B&B is close to the action without being submerged by it. Run by a charming couple, the colonial structure – boasting terra-cotta floors, wrought-iron railings and abundant artwork – has three modest yet appealingly furnished bedrooms with one, two and three beds. All are well-lit and airy, and each has a balcony.

**Buccaneer Beach** ( ☎ 952-6489; fax 979-2580; 7 Kent Ave; s/d US$69/89; ❤ ❢ ) A small, modest property with a homey feel. Rooms have tile floors, phone, cable TV and safety box, plus large balconies. There's a plunge pool in each of the front and back courtyards, plus a piano bar with large-screen TV. Its reclusive location at the end of Kent Ave is a five-minute walk from Gloucester Ave.

**ourpick Richmond Hill Inn** ( ☎ 952-3859; www .richmond-hill-inn.com; Union St; s/d US$85/115, ste US$189; ❤ ❢ ) Gazing out over the town and the bay, this charming hotel, built of limestone and molasses and chock-full of antiques, is far removed from the Montego Bay bustle. The rooms have cable TV and modest furnishings. It's noted for its restaurant, which has attracted many of the great and famous. There's also a six-person penthouse suite (US$450).

**Altamont West** ( ☎ 952-9087; www.altamontwest hotel.com; 33 Gloucester Ave; s/d US$90/120, ste US$280-420; ❤ ▭ ❢ ) For guests who can't rouse themselves to cross the street for Walter Fletcher Beach, this MoBay newcomer offers a sundeck as well as an outdoor pool. Rooms are modern and gold-accented and come with cable TV, wi-fi, radio and hairdryers. Children under 12 stay for free.

**Glousterhire Hotel** ( ☎ 952-4420; in North America 877-574-8497, in the UK 0800-169-7103; www.gloustershire .com; Gloucester Ave; s US$110-125, d US$115-130, ste US$125-130; ❤ ▭ ❢ ) A faded, service-oriented 95-room hotel across the street from Doctor's Cave Beach, this MoBay veteran nestled against the cliff offers rooms with direct-dial phones, safes, wi-fi, satellite TV and a pastel decor that could use some attention. Most rooms feature a balcony. It has a pool deck with Jacuzzi, a restaurant and a helpful tour desk.

**Royal Decameron Montego Beach Resort** ( ☎ 952-4340, 888-790-5264; 2 Gloucester Ave; d all-inclusive US$130; ❤ ▭ ❢ ) This resort gets high marks in the all-inclusive section. A welcoming low-rise beachfront resort, it has 128 rooms with lively tropical decor and its own private beach overlooked by a competent restaurant. Rooms all have ocean views and balconies. The range of activities include tennis, golf and water sports. Offers wi-fi.

**Sandals Montego Bay** ( ☎ 952-5510; www.sandals .com; N Kent Ave; d all-inclusive US$590-1550; ❤ ▭ ❢ ) This place takes up 8 hectares of splendid beachfront north of the airport and is a superb all-inclusive, couples-only resort for rekindling that honeymoon sparkle while snorkeling, sailing and sunning to your heart's content. It has 245 rooms and suites in 10 categories, all with vibrant plantation-style furniture. There are four pools, four whirlpools, five restaurants, four bars and top-notch entertainment. Wi-fi access is available in common areas.

## Eating

Montego Bay has the most cosmopolitan cuisine scene in Jamaica, with everything from roadside jerk chicken to nouvelle Jamaican dining. Most restaurants double as bars, encouraging guests to make a night of it.

### BUDGET

**Pork Pit** ( ☎ 952-1046; 27 Gloucester Ave; meals US$4-8; ❤ lunch & dinner) Searing tongues for decades, this jumping jerk joint is MoBay's best. Eat at open-air picnic tables shaded by a gargantuan silk-cotton tree that the chef reckons to be 300 years old. Finger-lickin' jerk chicken, pork, fish and shrimp are ordered by the pound, with yams, festival (sausage-shaped fried biscuit) and sweet potatoes as sides.

**Nyam 'n' Jam** ( ☎ 952-1922; 17 Harbour St; mains US$5-9; ❤ breakfast, lunch & dinner) This local fave has real-deal Jamaican fare and daily specials including standards such as jerk meat, and callaloo and salt fish, but also more esoteric choices such as cow mouth, cow foot and oxtail.

---

**PREACHING RESISTANCE**

The week-long Christmas Rebellion that began on December 27, 1831, was the most serious slave revolt to rock colonial Jamaica. Its impact and the public outcry over the terrible retribution that followed were catalysts for the British Parliament passing the Abolition Bill in 1834.

The instigator of the revolt was Samuel Sharpe (1801–32), the slave of a Montego Bay solicitor. A deacon of Montego Bay's Burchell Baptist Church, Sharpe used his forum to encourage passive rebellion.

In 1831 Sharpe counseled slaves to refuse to work during the Christmas holidays. Word of the secret, passive rebellion spread throughout St James and neighboring parishes. The rebellion turned into a violent conflict when the Kensington Estate was set on fire. Soon, plantations and great houses throughout northwest Jamaica were ablaze, and Sharpe's noble plan was usurped by wholesale violence. Fourteen colonists were murdered before authorities suppressed the revolt. Swift and cruel retribution followed.

More than 1000 slaves were killed. Day after day for six weeks following the revolt's suppression, magistrates of the Montego Bay Courthouse handed down death sentences to scores of slaves, who were hanged two at a time, among them 'Daddy' Sam Sharpe. He was later proclaimed a national hero.

---

**Pelican** ( ☎ 952-3171; Gloucester Ave; mains US$6-12; ✆ 7am-11:30pm) You shouldn't be fooled by the roadside-diner appearance of this good-value local favorite. Its menu of Jamaican dishes is simply outstanding; a highlight is red snapper in parchment paper, cooked in wine and béchamel sauce. Other dishes include stew peas with rice and stuffed conch with rice and peas, but the Pelican also serves sirloin steaks and seafood. The Sunday buffet is US$12.

**El Campay Gallo** ( ☎ 531-0637; 47 Gloucester Ave; mains US$7-14; ✆ lunch & dinner) You'll be warmly welcomed as if you're one of the family. This exuberant family-run place serves traditional Cuban dishes such as *empanadillas* (meat-filled pastry) and potent cocktails. If you're lucky, the owner will display his considerable talent as a jazz violinist.

**ourpick Native Restaurant & Bar** ( ☎ 979-2769; mains US$8-25; 29 Gloucester Ave; ✆ breakfast, lunch & dinner) An excellent place to learn about Jamaican cuisine – try 'goat in a boat' (curried goat in a pineapple half) or 'yard man fish' (whole fish escoveitched or steamed). If you're really hungry, consider the 'Boonoonoonoos' sampler (composed of ackee and salt fish, jerk chicken, curried goat, escoveitched fish, plantains and pineapple) – it's like taking a crash course in Jamaican food.

**Marguerite's** ( ☎ 952-4777; Gloucester Ave; meals US$12-33; ✆ dinner) Adjoining Margaritaville, Marguerite's is a great place to watch the sunset over cocktails, followed by dinner on the restaurant's elegant clifftop patio. The pricey menu edges toward nouvelle Jamaican, but also includes sirloin steak and a seafood platter (US$33).

**Town House by the Sea** ( ☎ 952-2660; Gloucester Ave; mains US$14-35; ✆ lunch & dinner) This elegant dining room overlooking the beach takes food seriously, so come seriously hungry. If you've been craving snails – and who hasn't? – you'll find escargot with a Jamaican twist. Equally rich is the stuffed lobster, red snapper or filet mignon. If you're merely peckish, choose from the pasta, curry and Jamaican dishes. The smoked marlin is one of the best on the island.

**ourpick Houseboat Grill** ( ☎ 979-8845; houseboat@ cwjamaica.com; Southern Cross Blvd; meals US$15-30; ✆ dinner Tue-Sun) Anchored in Bogue Bay at Montego Bay Freeport is Houseboat Grill, one of Jamaica's top-notch restaurants, which offers a changing menu of eclectic Caribbean fusion cuisine that includes dishes such as spicy conch fritters with a rémoulade dipping sauce or honey-soy glazed grilled tenderloin of beef with Chinese oyster sauce. You can dine inside, or reclusively out on the sundeck. Reservations are recommended on weekends.

## Drinking

**Jimmy Buffett's Margaritaville** ( ☎ 952-4777; Gloucester Ave; admission after 10pm US$5) This wildly popular place claims to have 'put the hip into the Hip Strip'…who woulda thunk that anything to do with Jimmy Buffett could obtain a cachet of cool? Four open-air bars, 15 big-screen TVs, and dance floors on decks overhanging the water offer plenty of diversion.

**MoBay Proper** ( ☎ 940-1233; Fort St) Attracting a young local crowd, this exuberant bar serves libations on the terrace and has decent Jamaican cooking. The pool table generates considerable heat, while dominoes are the rage with an older crowd out on the patio. On Friday night there's a fish fry and vintage reggae.

**Jamaican Bobsled Café** ( ☎ 952-1448; 69 Gloucester Ave; ☺ 10am-2am) This watering hole makes a good-natured attempt to capitalize on everybody's favorite fish-out-of-water story – the Jamaican bobsled team immortalized in the film *Cool Runnings*, which is in a perpetual loop on a corner screen.

## Entertainment

**Blue Beat Jazz & Blues Bar** ( ☎ 952-4777; Gloucester Ave) Montego Bay's first martini jazz and blues bar offers sophisticated entertainment and Asian-Caribbean fusion cuisine. It's next to Marguerite's restaurant.

**Coral Cliff Gaming Lounge** ( ☎ 952-4130; Gloucester Ave; ☺ 24hr) This medium-size gamblers' haunt has over 100 video-slot machines, big-screen TVs and free drinks, with fashion shows, cabarets and/or live jazz nightly.

## Shopping

MoBay's streets spill over with stalls selling wooden carvings, straw items, jewelry, ganja pipes, T-shirts and other touristy items.

**Craft Market** (Harbour St) For the largest selection of the above items, head to this downtown market, which extends for three blocks between Barnett and Market Sts.

**Tafara Products** ( ☎ 952-3899; 36 Church St) An African/Rastafarian cultural center selling books, arts and crafts, and natural foods.

**Gallery of West Indian Art** ( ☎ 952-4547; www.galleryofwestindianart.com; 11 Fairfield Rd) In the suburb of Catherine Hall, this is a quality gallery that sells arts and crafts from around the Caribbean including Cuban canvases, hand-painted wooden animals, masks and handmade jewelry.

## Getting There & Around

**Donald Sangster International Airport** (MBJ; ☎ 979-1034, 979-1035; www.mbjairport.com) is about 3km north of Montego Bay. For info regarding international flights, see p257; for domestic flights, see p257.

Buses, coasters and route taxis arrive and depart from the **transportation station** (Barnett St), at the south end of St James St.

**Montego Bay Metro Line** ( ☎ 952-5500; 19A Union St) links MoBay with suburbs and outlying towns; the fare is US$0.50.

Taxi stands are on Gloucester Ave opposite Doctor's Cave Beach, downtown at the junction of Market and Strand Sts, and by the transportation station. The fare from the airport to Gloucester Ave is US$8.

These rental car companies have offices at Donald Sangster:
**Avis** ( ☎ 952-0762; www.avis.com)
**Budget** ( ☎ 952-3838; www.budget.com)
**Dollar** (953-9100; www.dollar.com)
**Hertz** ( ☎ 979-0438; www.hertz.com)
**Island Car Rentals** ( ☎ 952-5771; www.islandcarrentals.com)

## AROUND MONTEGO BAY
### Rose Hall Great House

This **mansion** ( ☎ 953-2323; adult/under 12yr US$20/10; ☺ 9am-6pm), with its commanding hilltop position 3.2km east of Ironshore, is the most famous great house in Jamaica. Most of the attraction is the legend of Annie Palmer, the 'White Witch of Rose Hall,' a multiple murderer said to haunt the house. Her bedroom upstairs is decorated in crimson silk brocades. The cellars now house an old-English-style pub and a well-stocked gift shop. There's also a snack bar.

To get to Rose Hall, take a charter taxi (US$25), or a route taxi from the Barnett St Transportation Station in Montego Bay (US$2) and walk 1.6km up from the main road. Alternatively, you can arrange a tour at any hotel.

### Greenwood Great House

This marvelous **estate** ( ☎ 953-1077; www.greenwoodgreathouse.com; admission US$14; ☺ 9am-6pm) sits high on a hill 8km east of Rose Hall, and is a far more intimate property. Construction began on the two-story stone-and-timber structure in 1780 by the Honorable Richard Barrett, whose family arrived in Jamaica in the 1660s and amassed a fortune from its sugar plantations.

Remarkably, Greenwood survived the slave rebellion of Christmas 1831 unscathed. Among the highlights is the rare collection of musical instruments, containing a barrel organ and two polyphones, which the guide is happy to bring to life. The view from the front balcony down to the sea is quite stunning.

Buses traveling between Montego Bay and Falmouth will drop you off anywhere along the A1; ask to be let off across from the Total gas station on the sea side of the road and take the road up the hill. It's a good 20-minute slog to the top.

### Falmouth

Few other towns in Jamaica have retained their original architecture to the same degree as Falmouth, which has a faded Georgian splendor. The city, 37km east of Montego Bay, has been the capital of Trelawny parish since 1790. On weekends, farmers come from miles around to sell their produce, recalling the days when Falmouth was Jamaica's major port for the export of rum, molasses and sugar.

Route taxis leave for Falmouth from the Barnett St Transportation Station in Montego Bay (US$2) several times each day.

### Martha Brae

Most visitors come to this small village, 3km due south of Falmouth, for the exhilarating 1½-hour **rafting** trip on the Martha Brae River. Long bamboo rafts poled by a skilled guide cruise down the river and stop at 'Tarzan's Corner' for a swing and swim in a calm pool. Trips begin from Rafter's Village, about 1.5km south of Martha Brae. A raft trip costs US$60 per raft (one or two people). Contact **River Raft Ltd** ( ☎ 952-0889; www.jamaicarafting.com). Remember to tip your raft guide.

Route taxis make the 10-minute ride from Falmouth to Martha Brae during daylight hours on a continuous basis (US$0.75). There are also regular buses.

### Rocklands Bird Feeding Station

You don't have to be a bird nerd to love **Rocklands** ( ☎ 952-2009; admission US$10; ☺ 9am-5pm), where hummingbirds, saffron finches and many other birds come to feed from your hand. You can visit through a hotel-sponsored tour, or by private cab or rental car. The 800m road leading to the sanctuary is rough. The turn-off from the B8 is 180m south of the signed turn-off for Lethe.

# NEGRIL & THE WEST

If the popular tourist image of Jamaica is sun, beach life, rum, sun, sea, sun, scuba diving and sunsets, chances are the popular tourist is thinking of Negril – or thinking in particular of Jamaica's longest swathe of sugary white-sand beach at Long Bay (also known as Seven Mile Beach). It also boasts superb coral reefs that make for excellent scuba diving, and a large swamp area – the Great Morass – that is an ecotour haven.

## NEGRIL
### pop 4400

In the 1970s Negril lured hippies with its offbeat beach-life to a countercultural Shangri-la where anything went. To some extent, anything still goes here, except the innocent – they left long ago.

To be sure, the gorgeous 11km-long swathe of sand that is the beach at Long Bay is still kissed by the serene waters into which the sun melts evening after evening in a riot of color that will transfix even the most jaded. And the easily accessible coral reefs offer some of the best diving in the Caribbean. At night, an array of rustic beachside music clubs keep the reggae beat going without the watered-down-for-tourist schmaltz that so often mars the hot spots of Montego Bay and Ocho Rios.

Yet these undeniable attractions have done just that: attract. In the last three decades, Negril has exploded as a tourist venue, and today the beach can barely be seen from Norman Manley Blvd for the intervening phalanx of beachside resorts. And with tourism comes the local hustle – you're very likely to watch the sunset in the cloying company of a ganja dealer or an aspiring tour-guide-cum-escort.

### Orientation

Negril is divided in two by the South Negril River, with Long Bay to the north and West End to the south. The apex is Negril Village, which lies immediately south of the river and is centered on a small roundabout – Negril Sq – from which Norman Manley Blvd leads north, West End Rd leads south and Sheffield Rd goes east and becomes the A2, which leads to Savanna-la-Mar, 31km away.

## Information

**Easy Rock Internet Café** ( ☎ 957-0671; West End Rd; per hr US$5) The most pleasant and personable place to surf the digital wave.

**Jamaica Tourist Board/TPDCo** ( ☎ 957-4803, 957-9314; Times Sq Plaza; ☼ 9am-5pm Mon-Fri)

**Negril Beach Medical Center** ( ☎ 957-4888; fax 957-4347; Norman Manley Blvd; ☼ 9am-5pm, doctors on call 24hr)

**Police station** ( ☎ 957-4268; Sheffield Rd)

**Post office** ( ☎ 957-9654; West End Rd) Between A Fi Wi Plaza and King's Plaza.

**Scotiabank** ( ☎ 957-4236) About 45m west of Negril Plaza; has foreign exchange service and an ATM.

**Top Spot** ( ☎ 957-4542) In Sunshine Village, is well stocked with international publications.

## Sights & Activities

The blindingly white, world-famous 11km-long beach of **Long Bay** is Negril's main claim to fame. The beach draws gigolos and hustlers offering everything from sex to aloe massages and, always, 'sensi' (drugs). 'Pssst! Bredda, you want ganja? Negril de place to get high, mon!' Tourist police now patrol the beach, but by law all Jamaican beaches must permit public access, so the hustlers are free to roam. Water-sports concessions line the beach. By night, this section is laden with the blast of reggae from disco bars.

**Booby Cay** is a small and lovely island 800m offshore from Rutland Point in Long Bay. The island is named for the seabirds that nest there, but the beautiful coral beach is the main draw. Water-sports concessionaires can arrange boats for about US$25 round trip.

Five kilometers south of Negril Village, the gleaming-white, 20m-tall **Negril Lighthouse** (West End Rd; admission free; ☼ 9am-sunset) illuminates the westernmost point of Jamaica. Wilson Johnson, the superintendent, will gladly lead the way up the 103 stairs for a bird's-eye view of the coast.

The waters off Negril are usually mirror-calm – ideal for all kinds of **water sports**. Numerous concessions along the beach rent out jet skis (about US$40 for 30 minutes), plus sea kayaks, sailboards and Sunfish (about US$20 per hour). They also offer waterskiing (US$25 for 30 minutes) and banana-boat rides (using an inflatable banana-shaped raft towed by a speedboat; US$15).

Negril offers extensive offshore reefs and cliffs with grottoes. The shallow reefs are perfect for **diving** and **snorkeling**. Visibility often exceeds 30m and seas are dependably calm. Most dives are in 10.5m to 22.5m of water. Expect to pay about US$5 an hour for masks and fins from concession stands on the beach. Try one of the branches of the **Negril Scuba Centre** (www.negrilscuba.com; 1-/2-tank dive US$40/70; Mariner's Negril Beach Club ☎ 957-4425, 957-9641; Norman Manley Blvd; Negril Escape Resort & Spa ☎ 957-0392; West End Rd; Sunset @ the Palms ☎ 383-9533; Bloody Bay Beach).

Negril's waters are teeming with tuna, blue marlin, wahoo and sailfish and provide excellent action for sport-fishing enthusiasts. **Stanley's Deep Sea Fishing** ( ☎ 957-0667; deepsea fishing@cwjamaica.com) offers custom fishing trip charters (up to four people for a half/full day costs US$400/800).

The Negril Hills provide excellent terrain for rip-roaring mountain biking. **Rusty's X-Cellent Adventures** ( ☎ 957-0155; rustynegril@hotmail .com) offers guided bike tours; it's US$25 if you have your own bike, or US$35 if you want to borrow one of the company's.

**Negril Hills Golf Club** ( ☎ 957-4638; Sheffield Rd), about 5km east of Negril, has a delightful setting by the Great Morass swampland. And should your ball land in the water, best leave it as a souvenir for one of the resident crocodiles.

## Festivals & Events

**Negril Music Festival** ( ☎ 968-9356) A beach bash in mid-March featuring leading Jamaican and international reggae stars, calypso artists and other musicians.

**Spring Break Jamaica Beachfest** Negril is thronged for this mid-April exercise in Bacchanalian excess.

**Negril Jerk Fest** ( ☎ 782-9990) Jerk chefs come from far and wide to face off at Three Dives Jerk Centre in November.

## Sleeping

As with Montego Bay, Negril boasts a stunning array of accommodations. Budget travelers are particularly spoiled for choice with scores of places charging less than US$75 per night and many half that sum. Many hotels enjoy a beach location, but up on the cliffs of the West End are Negril's most remarkable digs.

### LONG BAY

**Westport Cottages** ( ☎ 957-4736, 307-5466; s/d US$15/20) This offbeat place is popular with the laid-back backpacking crowd (amiable owner Joseph Mathews says it is approved for 'smoke-friendly heartical people'). Joseph has 17 very rustic huts with well-kept outside toilet and cold shower, plus mosquito nets and fans. Newer rooms to the rear are preferred. A well-equipped communal kitchen is available; bicycles (US$5 per day) and snorkeling equipment are provided.

**Negril Yoga Centre** ( ☎ 957-4397; www.negrilyoga .com; Norman Manley Blvd; d US$46-75; 🏊 ) The eight rustic yet quite atmospheric rooms and cottages – most with refrigerators and fans – surround an open-air, thatched, wood-floored yoga center set in a garden. Options range from a two-story, Thai-style wooden cabin to an adobe farmer's cottage; all are pleasingly if modestly furnished. Yoga classes are offered (guests/nonguests US$10/15), as is massage (US$60). There's a communal kitchen.

**our pick Rondel Village** ( ☎ 957-4413; www.rondel village.com; d US$95-150, 1-/2-bedroom villa US$210/245; 🏊 ⬜ 🏊 ) A highly affable and efficient hotel graced by walkways lined with an array of indigenous fruit trees, the family-owned Village offers well-appointed studios and beachfront rooms clustered around a small pool and Jacuzzi. You can also choose octagonal one- and two-bedroom villas that sleep up to six and feature marble floors, French doors, satellite TV, DVD players fully equipped kitchenettes and Jacuzzi.

**Negril Tree House** ( ☎ 957-4287; www.negril-tree house.com; r US$150-170, ste US$275-350; 🏊 ⬜ 🏊 ) This unpretentious resort is a favorite for its 16 octagonal bungalows and oceanfront villas nudging pleasingly up to the beach. Each has a TV and a safe. More elegant one- and two-bedroom suites each feature kitchenette, king-size bed and a Murphy bed in the lounge, which opens onto a wide veranda. The beachside bar is popular. Water sports are offered, and the resort has a tour desk, gift store, masseuse and manicurist. Wi-fi is available in the common areas.

### WEST END

**Blue Cave Castle** ( ☎ 957-4845; www.bluecavecastle.com; s/d US$75/120; 🏊 ) Providing perhaps the best view of Long Bay from the West End, this atmospheric, all-stone concoction attracts nudists, travel junkies and freethinkers. The 14 bedrooms are cavelike, but in a good way. Each is equipped with a CD player, ceiling fan and refrigerator; tower rooms open to the sea and superior rooms include air-con and cable TV. Stairs from the castle lead down to a blue cave.

**Xtabi** ( ☎ 957-0120; www.xtabi-negril.com; r US$83-90, cottages US$210, extra person US$25; 🏊 ⬜ 🏊 ) This chic and casual hotel bills itself as 'the meeting place of the gods.' Its clientele is decidedly human, but the setting is truly divine. You can choose from rooms, simple garden cottages or quaint octagonal seafront bungalows perched atop the cliff. The bar is lively and the restaurant appealing. It has sunning platforms built into the cliff. Children under the age of 15 stay free. Massage is offered (US$40 per hour).

**Catcha Falling Star** ( ☎ 957-0390; www.catcha jamaica.com; 1-/2-bedroom cottage US$135/250; ⬜ ) In the inimitable West End style, these pleasant fan-cooled cottages – including several with two bedrooms – sit on the cliffs. Each is named for an astrological sign and comes with microwave oven, fridge, bar and double beds draped in mosquito netting. A tiered cliff affords easy access to the sea, where clothing-optional bathing can be enjoyed in a private cove. Popular masseuse Oya Oezcan offers her services here (US$70 per hour).

**our pick Rockhouse** ( ☎ 957-4373; www.rockhouse hotel.com; r/studio/villa US$150/175/325; 🏊 ⬜ 🏊 ) One of the West End's most beautiful and well-run hotels, with 13 thatched rondavels (two are 'premium villas') of pine and stone, plus 15 studios dramatically clinging to the cliffside above a small cove. Each cabin has a ceiling fan, refrigerator, safe, minibar, alfresco shower and wraparound veranda. Catwalks lead over the rocks to an open-sided, multilevel dining pavilion (with one of the best restaurants around) overhanging the ocean. A dramatically designed pool sits atop the cliffs.

## Eating & Drinking

Negril has plenty of upscale, elegant restaurants and just as many economical local-flavored joints serving vegetarian food, pasta, seafood and jerk chicken for a song.

### LONG BAY

**Bourbon Beach** ( ☎ 957-4405; mains US$2-7) Though it's best known for its live reggae concerts, those in the know swear by its jerk chicken. The sauce is thick and pastelike, and well-complemented by a Red Stripe as you wait for a show.

**Jamaica Tamboo** ( ☎ 957-4282; Jamaica Tamboo; mains US$6-24; ☻ breakfast, lunch & dinner) Near Kuyaba, this is a bamboo-and-thatch two-story restaurant (lit by brass lanterns at night) with a varied menu that includes a breakfast of 'pigs in a blanket' (pancakes and sausage) and a fruit platter with ice cream. It also has snack foods such as deep-fried lobster nibblets, sandwiches and pizzas.

**our pick Lobster House** ( ☎ 957-4293; Sunrise Club; mains US$8-22; ☻ breakfast, lunch & dinner) Renowned for its pink gnocchi in a parmesan cream and its signature lobster dishes, this congenial outdoor spot also has a brick oven that's brought it the status of best pizzeria in town – if you need proof, try the Queen Aragosta pizza with lobster tails. Many, however, come for a cup of what is arguably the best espresso on the island, made from the proprietor's vintage 1961 Faema espresso machine.

**Norma's on the Beach at Sea Splash** ( ☎ 957-4041; Sea Splash Resort; mains US$13-28; ☻ dinner) This Negril branch of Norma Shirley's celebrated Jamaican culinary empire seems to have escaped the hype around her Kingston flagship, but the 'new world Caribbean' food at this stylish beach restaurant is just as adventurous. Expect to find the likes of lobster, Cornish game hen, jerk chicken and pasta as well as tricolored 'rasta pasta.'

**WEST END**

**our pick 3 Dives Jerk Centre** ( ☎ 957-0845; quarter/half chicken US$4/7; ☻ noon-midnight) It's no small tribute to 3 Dives that its jerk overshadows its reputation for lengthy waits (sometimes over an hour). Fortunately, the chefs are more than happy to let you peek into the kitchen, where there's bound to be a pile of super-hot Scotch bonnet peppers threatening to spontaneously combust, and you can sip cheap Red Stripe on the cliffs at the end of a small garden. This is the site of the annual Negril Jerk Festival.

**Royal Kitchen Vegetarian Café** ( ☎ 775-0386; West End Rd; mains US$4-7; ☻ breakfast, lunch & dinner) This welcoming roadside I-tal eatery is popular with local Rastafarians and those who come to collect their pearls of wisdom. The fare – strictly vegetarian – is served on simple tables where you are sure to make friends with inquisitive passersby. The juices are especially good.

**Hungry Lion** ( ☎ 957-4486; mains US$12-30; ☻ dinner) Renovated in late 2007, this bright-painted spot serves intricate fare from a changing menu of largely fish and vegetarian dishes, like vegetarian shepherd's pie or que-

sadillas stuffed with shrimp and cheese. The alfresco rooftop dining room is tastefully decorated with earth tones and original art. The music is trancelike, and the bar serves an extensive menu of cocktails and juices.

**Rockhouse Restaurant & Bar** ( ☎ 957-4373; mains US$15-30; ☻ breakfast, lunch & dinner) Lamplit at night, this pricey yet relaxed cliffside spot boasts outstanding nouvelle Jamaican treats such as vegetable tempura with lime and ginger, specialty pastas and daily specials like watermelon spare ribs and blackened mahimahi with mango chutney. At the very least, stop by for a sinful bananas Foster.

## Entertainment

Negril's reggae concerts are legendary, with performances every night in peak season, when there's sure to be some big talent in town. A handful of venues offer weekly jams, and they have a rotation system so that they all get a piece of the action. Big-name acts usually perform at **MXIII** (West End Rd) in the West End, and at **Roots Bamboo** ( ☎ 957-4479; ☻ Wed & Sun) on Long Bay. You'll see shows advertised on billboards and hear about them from megaphone-equipped cars.

The **Jungle** ( ☎ 957-4005; ☻ 4pm-late) is a classic nightclub on Long Bay Beach, with a thronged and sweaty dance floor downstairs and a pleasant deck with pool tables.

## Getting There & Away

Negril Aerodrome is at Bloody Bay, about 11km north of Negril Village. See p257 for information on domestic charters.

Dozens of coasters and route taxis run between Negril and Montego Bay. The two-hour journey costs about US$6. You may need to change vehicles in Lucea. Be prepared for a hair-raising ride. Minibuses and route taxis also leave for Negril from Donald Sangster International Airport in Montego Bay (the price is negotiable, but expect to pay about US$10).

A licensed taxi between Montego Bay and Negril will cost about US$60.

## Getting Around

Negril stretches along more than 16km of shoreline, and it can be a withering walk. Coasters and route taxis cruise Norman Manley Blvd and West End Rd. You can flag them down anywhere. The fare between any two points should never be more than about

JAMAICA

US$2. Tourist taxis display a red license plate. Fares run about US$3 per 3km.

Some rental options:

**Jus Jeep** ( ☎ 957-0094; fax 957-0429; West End Rd)

**Vernon's Car Rentals** ( ☎ 957-9724, 957-4354; fax 957-4057) At Fun Holiday Beach Resort and Shop 22, Negril Plaza.

## AROUND NEGRIL

No, the name **Great Morass** doesn't refer to the legions of drunken college students who descend on Negril for spring break. This virtually impenetrable 3km-wide swamp of mangroves stretches 16km from the South Negril River to Orange Bay. The swamp is the island's second-largest freshwater wetland system and forms a refuge for endangered waterfowl. American crocodiles still cling to life here and are occasionally seen at the mouth of the Orange River.

The easiest way to get a sense of the Great Morass is at the **Royal Palm Reserve** ( ☎ 957-3115; www.royalpalmreserve.com; adult/child US$10/5; ⏰ 9am-6pm). Wooden boardwalks make a 1.5km loop. Three distinct swamp forest types are present: the royal palm forest, buttonwood forest and bull thatch forest – home to butterflies galore as well as doctorbirds, herons, egrets, endangered black parakeets, Jamaica woodpeckers and countless other birds. Two observation towers provide views over the tangled mangroves.

If you're driving, take Sheffield Rd east of the roundabout for 10 minutes and turn left after the golf course. Otherwise, **Caribic Vacations** ( ☎ 957-3309; Norman Manley Blvd, Negril) and other local tour operators run trips to the reserve. To explore the Great Morass outside the Royal Palm Reserve, negotiate with villagers who have boats moored along the South Negril River (just northeast of Negril Village), or with fishermen at Norman Manley Sea Park, at the north end of Bloody Bay. It should cost approximately US$35 for two hours.

# SOUTHERN JAMAICA

Untrampled by the lockstep march of the resort-catered hordes, the southern coast serves up an irresistible slice of the unspoiled Jamaica. The area is awash with natural splendor – majestic rivers, lugubrious swamps, gorgeous waterfalls, looming mountains, ominous cliffs and sandy beaches. It's one of the island's great ironies that a region so unsullied by mass tourism is so packed with sights and activities.

## TREASURE BEACH

Treasure Beach is the generic name given to four coves – Billy's Bay, Frenchman's Bay, Calabash Bay and Great Pedro Bay – with rocky headlands separating lonesome, coral-colored sand beaches. Calabash Bay is backed by the Great Pedro Ponds, which is a good spot for birding.

You'll be hard-pressed to find a more authentically charming and relaxing place in Jamaica. The sense of remoteness, the easy pace and the graciousness of the local farmers and fisherfolk attract travelers seeking an away-from-it-all, cares-to-the-wind lifestyle. Many have settled here – much to local pride.

It's said that Scottish sailors were shipwrecked near Treasure Beach in the 19th century, accounting for the preponderance of fair skin, green eyes and reddish hair.

---

### CALICO JACK'S LAST STAND

Before you park yourself on the sand at Bloody Bay, consider the plight of '**Calico' Jack Rackham**, a pirate who dallied a little too long on the beach. In 1720, Calico Jack, so named for his fondness for calico underwear, and his buccaneers paused in Bloody Bay after a particularly satisfying plundering spree. He and his band of merry men got a little too merry on the local rum, and in the course of their beach party were taken unaware by the British Navy, which overwhelmed them after a struggle worthy of the bay's name.

After the battle, the British were shocked to find that two of Calico Jack's cohorts were actually women: Mary Read and Anne Bonny, who had been his mistress. Rackham was executed and his body suspended in an iron suit on what is now called Rackham Cay, at the harbor entrance at Port Royal, as an example to other pirates. The lives of Read and Bonny were spared because they were pregnant, although Read died in jail.

For more details on Read and Bonny, see p361.

## Information

The nearest bank is in Southfield, 16km east of Treasure Beach.

**Jake's Place** (☎ in the USA 965-3000, 800-688-7678, in the UK 020-7440-4360; www.jakeshotel.com) is an unofficial tourist information source. Here you can book boat rides along the coast and into the Great Morass, plus fishing trips and mountain-bike tours (US$30 to US$35 per person). Also visit **TreasureBeach.Net** (www.treasurebeach.net), a good starting point for information.

The post office is on a hillside beside the **police station** (☎ 965-0163), between Calabash Bay and Pedro Cross.

## Sleeping & Eating

**Ital Rest** (☎ 863-3481, 421-8909; r US$40) An atmospheric out-of-the-way place with two exquisite (if rustic), clean, all-wood thatched cabins with showers, toilets and solar electricity. An upstairs room in the house has a sundeck. Kitchen facilities are shared.

**Calabash House** (☎ 382-6384; www.calabashhouse.com; r/cottage US$75/275; 🔆) A highly congenial spot run by an American expat, the Calabash House offers airy rooms with private bathrooms each adorned with its own distinctive mosaic as well as secluded beachside cottages with hammocks.

our pick **Jake's Place** (☎ in the USA 965-3000, 800-688-7678, in the UK 020-7440-4360; www.jakeshotel.com; r US$95-195, cottages US$195-325; 🖳 🐾) The most glistening gem in Treasure Beach's chest, this rainbow-colored retreat wins the award for the 'chicest shack' between Negril and Kingston. There are 13 single rooms (many perched over the sea), four two-bedroom cottages, a three-bedroom villa (rooms can be rented separately) like a mini-Moroccan *ksar,* and a one-up/one-down house that features an exterior spiral staircase, and exquisite handmade beds. The gorgeous pool – lamplit at night – is shaded by a spreading tree. Wi-fi is available in common areas.

our pick **Jack Sprat Café** (mains US$6-12; 🕑 7am-midnight) An excellent barefoot beachside eatery affiliated with Jake's, this appealing joint features vintage reggae posters and an old jukebox as well as a lively bar scene that spills onto the tree-shaded patio. Jack Sprat warms to any crowd or time of day, and offers a diverse menu of sandwiches, salads, crab cakes, smoked marlin and lobster as well as excellent jerk or garlic shrimp.

**Pelican Bar** (☎ 354-4218; Caribbean Sea; 🕑 morning-sunset) Built on a submerged sandbar 1km out to sea, this thatch-roofed eatery on stilts provides Jamaica's – and perhaps the planet's – most enjoyable spot for a drink. Getting there is half the fun: hire a local boat captain (you can book passage from Jake's for US$30). In between Red Stripes, or perhaps before your meal of lobster, shrimp or fish, feel free to slip into the salubrious waters for a dip.

## Getting There & Around

There is no direct service to Treasure Beach from Montego Bay, Negril or Kingston. Take a coaster or route taxi to Black River (US$3), then connect to Treasure Beach (US$1.75).

**Jake's Place** (☎ in the USA 965-3000, 800-688-7678, in the UK 020-7440-4360; www.jakeshotel.com) arranges transfers from MoBay for US$100 (up to four people), car and motorcycle rental, and transfers by taxi.

## BLACK RIVER

Though capital of St Elizabeth and the parish's largest town, Black River has a transient feel to it. Most visitors who come here are less interested in the town than in exploring what is beyond. Its namesake river, on whose western banks it rests, spirits day-trippers off to the southern half of the **Great Morass** to see crocodiles and eat at waterside jerk shacks.

The waters, stained by tannins and dark as molasses, are a complex ecosystem and a vital preserve for more than 100 bird species. The morass also forms Jamaica's most significant refuge for crocodiles; about 300 live in the swamps. Locals take to the waters in dugout canoes, tending funnel-shaped shrimp pots made of bamboo in the traditional manner of their West African forebears.

A number of companies in Black River offer Great Morass boat tours. **South Coast Safaris** (☎ 965-2513, 965-2086; US$20, with lunch & visit to YS Falls US$33; 🕑 tours 9am, 11am, 12:30pm, 2pm & 3:30pm), on the east side of the bridge, offers 60- to 75-minute journeys aboard the *Safari Queen.* The trips leave from the old warehouse on the east bank of the river.

You can also hire a guide to take you upriver in his canoe or boat for about US$15 to US$25, round trip. Ask near the bridge in town.

Midday tours are best for spotting crocodiles; early and later tours are better for birding. Take a shade hat and mosquito repellent.

## YS FALLS

Among Jamaica's most spectacular falls, this series of eight **cascades** ( ☎ 997-6055; adult/child US$15/6; ☼ 9:30am-3:30pm Tue-Sun, closed last 2 weeks Oct) fall 36.5m and are separated by cool pools that are perfect for swimming. The falls are hemmed in by limestone cliffs and are surrounded by towering forest.

The falls are on the YS Estate, 5.5km north of the A2 (the turn-off is 1.5km east of Middle Quarters). The entrance is just north of the junction of the B6 toward Maggotty.

Buses travel via YS Falls from the Shakespeare Plaza in Maggotty. On the A2, buses, coasters and route taxis will drop you at the junction to YS Falls, from where you can walk (it's about 3.2km) or catch an Ipswich-bound route taxi.

## APPLETON RUM ESTATE

You can smell the yeasty odor of molasses wafting from the **Appleton Rum Estate** ( ☎ 963-9215; factory tour & rum tasting US$12; ☼ Mon-Sat), well before you reach it, 1km northeast of Maggotty in the middle of the Siloah Valley. The largest distillery in Jamaica, it has been blending the famous Appleton brand of rums since 1749.

The 45-minute tour of the factory details how molasses is extracted from sugarcane, then fermented, distilled and aged to produce rum, which you can taste in the 'John Wray Tavern.' Several dozen varieties – including the lethal Overproof – are available for sampling, and the gift shop does brisk business with tipsy visitors who just can't get enough.

A motor-coach excursion, the Appleton Estate Rum Tour (US$85) departs MoBay daily, and from Ocho Rios and Negril several times each week. Contact **Caribic Vacations** ( ☎ Montego Bay 953-9878, Negril 957-3309, Ocho Rios 974-9106) or Jamaica Estate Tours Ltd at the Appleton Rum Estate itself.

# DIRECTORY

## ACCOMMODATIONS

From the lazy, beach-oriented playgrounds of the resort centers to the offbeat, atmospheric towns of the western and southern coasts, Jamaica offers a compelling range of accommodations for every budget and style. If you're traveling on a shoestring, head to a simple guesthouse; in the midrange category there's a wide range of choice in appealing small hotels, many with splendid gardens, sea views or both. If traveling with your family or a group, consider one of the hundreds of villas available to rent across the island. And if you've decided to splurge on something sumptuous, Jamaica's luxury hotels rank among the finest in the world.

For worse or better, Jamaica was the spawning ground for the all-inclusive resort. At chains like **Sandals** (www.sandals.com), **Couples** (www.couples.com) and **SuperClubs** (www.superclubs.com), guests pay a set price and (theoretically) pay nothing more once setting foot inside the resort.

Jamaica boasts hundreds of private houses for rent, from modest cottages to lavish beachfront estates. These arrangements are very cost-effective if you're traveling with family or a group of friends. Many include a cook and maid. Rates start as low as US$400 per week for budget units with minimal facilities. More-upscale villas begin at about US$850 weekly and can run to US$10,000 or more for a sumptuous multibedroom estate. **Holiday Solutions** (www.rentjamaica.com) lists scores of economical short-term accommodations, or try **Jamaican Association of Villas & Apartments** (JAVA; ☎ 974-2508; www.villasinjamaica.com).

Rates quoted are for the high season (mid-December to April), unless otherwise noted. At other times rates can be 20% to 60% lower.

## ACTIVITIES
### Diving & Snorkeling

Jamaica's shores are as beautiful below the surface as they are above. Waters offer tremendous visibility and temperatures of around 27°C year-round, and treasures range from shallow reefs, caverns and trenches to walls and drop-offs just a few hundred meters offshore.

Most diving occurs in and around the Montego Bay and Negril marine parks, in proximity to a wide range of licensed dive operators offering rental equipment and group dives. The main draws around Montego Bay are the Point, a dive wall renowned for its dense corals, fish, sharks and rays, and Airport Reef, which boasts masses of coral canyons, caves and tunnels, and even a DC-3 wreck. See p242 for operators.

Around Negril, the caves off the West End have tunnels and the occasional hawksbill turtle. Among the area's highlights are the Throne, a cave with sponges, plentiful corals,

---

**PRACTICALITIES**

- **Newspapers & Magazines** The *Jamaica Gleaner* is the most respected newspaper; its rival is the *Jamaica Observer*.

- **Radio & TV** There are 30 radio stations and seven TV channels; most hotels have satellite.

- **Electricity** The voltage used is 110V, 50Hz. Sockets are usually two- or three-pin – the US standard.

- **Video Systems** NTSC is the system used in Jamaica.

- **Weights & Measures** Jamaica is still transitioning from imperial to metric; distances are measured in kilometers, and gas in liters, but coffee is strictly by the pound.

---

nurse sharks, octopuses, barracuda and stingrays; Deep Plane, which holds the remains of a Cessna airplane lying at 21m underwater; and Sands Club Reef, which lies in 10m of water in the middle of Long Bay. See p247 for more information.

Visitors to the north coast will find excellent diving along the reef that is aligned with the shoreline between Ocho Rios and Galina Point; see p236 for more.

By law, all dives in Jamaican waters must be guided, and dives are restricted to a depth of 30m. (See p54 for ways to protect the reef.) If you spend enough time in the water, you're practically guaranteed to see parrotfish, angelfish, turtles, eels and the odd barracuda.

Dives cost US$50/80 for one-/two-tank dives. A snorkeling excursion, which generally includes equipment and a boat trip, costs US$25 to US$50. 'Resort courses' for beginners (also called 'Discover Scuba') are offered at most major resorts (about US$80), which also offer Professional Association of Diving Instructors (PADI) or National Association of Underwater Instructors (NAUI) certification courses (US$350 to US$400) and advanced courses.

## Fishing

Jamaica's waters are a pelagic playpen for schools of blue and white marlin, dolphin fish, wahoo, tuna and dozens of other species. Deepwater game fish run year-round

through the deep Cayman Trench that begins just 3.2km from shore.

Charters can be arranged for around US$400/600 per half/full day through hotels or directly through operators in Montego Bay, Negril, Ocho Rios and Port Antonio. A charter includes captain, tackle, bait and crew. Most charter boats require a 50% deposit.

For a more 'rootsy' experience, local fishermen will take you out in 'canoes' (narrow longboats with outboards) using hand lines.

## Golf

Jamaica has 12 championship golf courses – more than any other Caribbean island. All courses rent out clubs and have carts. Most require that you hire a caddy – an extremely wise investment, as they know the layout of the course intimately.

The two most famous courses can be found near Montego Bay (p242). For those enticed by scenic links, try the Negril Hills Golf Club (p247). For more information on the island's links, contact the **Jamaica Golf Association** ( ☎ 925-2325; www.jamaicagolfassociation.com; Constant Spring Golf Club, PO Box 743, Kingston 8).

## Surfing

Although Jamaica is little known as a surfing destination and board rentals on the island can be difficult to come by, the east coast is starting to attract surfers for its respectable waves coming in from the Atlantic. Boston Bay, 14.5km east of Port Antonio, is a well-known spot, as is Long Bay, 16km further south. The southeast coast, including the Palisadoes Peninsula, also gets good surf.

**Surfing Association of Jamaica/Jamnesia Surf Club** ( ☎ 750-0103; www.geocities.com/jamnesiasurfclub; PO Box 167, Kingston 2) provides general information about surfing in Jamaica, and operates a surf camp at Bull Bay, located 13km east of Kingston.

**Jah Mek Yah** ( ☎ 435-8806, in the US 954-594-9619; www.theliquidaddiction.com/jaspots.html; Morant Bay, St Thomas) is a surf lodge in Jamaica's unspoiled eastern corner offering relaxed, rootsy surf packages.

## BUSINESS HOURS

The following are standard hours for Jamaica; exceptions are noted in reviews.
**Bars** ☽ until the last guest leaves
**Businesses** ☽ 8:30am to 4:30pm Monday to Friday

JAMAICA

**Restaurants** ⊗ breakfast dawn to 11am, lunch noon to 2pm, dinner 5:30pm to 11pm
**Shops** ⊗ 8am or 9am to 5pm Monday to Friday, to noon Saturday

## CHILDREN

Some all-inclusive resorts cater specifically to families and have an impressive range of amenities for children. Most hotels also offer free accommodations or reduced rates for children staying in their parents' room. Many hotels provide a babysitter or nanny by advance request.

## DANGERS & ANNOYANCES

If you don't like reggae music (you can't escape it!), can't cope with poverty or power outages, and hate being hustled, Jamaica is definitely not for you. Moreover, if you prize efficient service, this place is liable to drive you nuts. To savor Jamaica properly, to appreciate what makes people passionate about the place, it pays to take things in stride and try to 'get' Jamaica. If you can handle that, and if you like travel with a raw edge, you'll love it.

Jamaica has the highest murder rate for any country not in the throes of war (the nation had a record 1574 murders in 2007, a 17% rise on the previous year), and Kingston and Spanish Town have the worst reputations in the Caribbean for violent crime. Although the vast majority of violent crimes occur in ghettoes far from tourist centers, visitors are sometimes the victims of robbery and scams. Crime against tourists has dropped in recent years, however, and the overwhelming majority of visitors enjoy their vacations without incident.

Drugs – particularly ganja (marijuana) – are readily available in Jamaica, and you're almost certain to be approached by hustlers selling them. Possession and use of drugs in Jamaica is strictly illegal and penalties are severe. Roadblocks and random searches of cars are common. If you *do* buy drugs in Jamaica, don't be foolish enough to take any out of the country. If you get caught in possession, you will *not* be getting on your plane home, however small the amount. A night (or a lengthy sentence) in a crowded-to-bursting Jamaican lock-up is dangerous to your health!

The traveler's biggest problem in Jamaica is the vast army of hustlers who harass visitors, notably in and around major tourist centers. Hustlers walk the streets looking for potential buyers of crafts, jewelry or drugs, or to wash cars, give aloe vera massages or offer any of a thousand varieties of services. If you as much as glance in their direction, they'll attempt to reel you in like a flounder.

## EMBASSIES & CONSULATES

More than 40 countries have official diplomatic representation in Jamaica. Except for a couple of Montego Bay consulates, all are located in Kingston. If your country isn't represented in this list, check 'Embassies & High Commissions' in the yellow pages of the Greater Kingston telephone directory.

**Australia** (Map pp224-5; ☎ 926-3550, 926-3551; 64 Knutsford Blvd, Kingston 5)
**Canada** High Commission (Map pp224-5; ☎ 926-1500; 3 West Kings House Rd, Kingston); Consulate (Map pp240-1; ☎ 952-6198; 29 Gloucester Ave, Montego Bay)
**France** (Map pp224-5; ☎ 978-0210; 13 Hillcrest Ave, Kingston 6)
**Germany** (Map pp224-5; ☎ 926-6728; 10 Waterloo Rd, Kingston 10)
**Netherlands** (Map pp224-5; ☎ 926-2026; 53 Knutsford Blvd, Kingston 5)
**Sweden** (Map pp224-5; ☎ 941-3761; Unit 3, 69 Constant Spring Rd, Kingston 10)
**Switzerland** (Map pp224-5; ☎ 978-7857; 22 Trafalgar Rd, Kingston 10)
**UK** High Commission (Map pp224-5; ☎ 510-0700, 926-9050; bhckingston@cwjamaica.com; 28 Trafalgar Rd, Kingston); Consulate ( ☎ 912-6859, Montego Bay)
**US** Embassy (Map pp224-5; ☎ 929-4850, after hr 926-6440; kingstonacs@state.gov; Life of Jamaica Bldg, 16 Oxford Rd, Kingston); Consulate (Map pp240-1; ☎ 952-0160, 952-5050; usconsagency.mobay@cwjamaica.com; St James Plaza, 2nd fl, Gloucester Ave, Montego Bay)

## FESTIVALS & EVENTS

Throughout the year you'll find festivals in various towns around Jamaica celebrating anything from jazz to jerk. Kingston is the place for New Year's Eve fireworks. See the Festivals & Events sections for each destination in this chapter for details. Other notable events include the following:

**A Fi Wi Sinting** ( ☎ 715-3529; www.fiwisinting.com; Buff Bay) A festival in late February featuring traditional music, song, dance and a marketplace.
**Trelawny Yam Festival** ( ☎ 610-0818; Albert Town) Yam-balancing races, the crowning of the Yam King and Queen – how can you resist? Held in late March.
**Carnival** (www.jamaicacarnival.com; Kingston & Ocho Rios) Street parties and soca music all night long in March-April.

**Calabash International Literary Festival** ( ☎ 922-4200; www.calabashfestival.org; Treasure Beach) This highly innovative literary festival in late May draws voices from near and far.

## GAY & LESBIAN TRAVELERS

Jamaica is an adamantly homophobic nation. Sexual acts between men are prohibited by law and punishable by up to 10 years in prison and hard labor. Some reggae dancehall lyrics by big-name stars seem intent on instigating violence against gays. Law enforcement in most cases looks the other way, and gay-bashing incidents are almost never prosecuted.

Most Jamaican gays are still in the closet. Nonetheless, many hoteliers are tolerant of gay visitors, and you should not be put off from visiting the island. Just don't expect to be able to display your sexuality openly without an adverse reaction.

**Purple Roofs** (www.purpleroofs.com/caribbean/jamaica.html) lists gay-friendly accommodations in Jamaica.

## HOLIDAYS

Public holidays:

**New Year's Day** January 1
**Bob Marley Day** February 6
**Ash Wednesday** Six weeks before Easter
**Good Friday, Easter Monday** March/April
**Labour Day** May 23
**Emancipation Day** August 1
**Independence Day** August 6
**National Heroes' Day** October 19
**Christmas Day** December 25
**Boxing Day** December 26

## INTERNET ACCESS

Although wi-fi has made its first appearances in Jamaican hotels, in-room, dial-up access for laptop computers is still sporadic. Even some of the most upscale establishments only offer access in communal lobby, bar or pool areas. Most town libraries now offer internet access (US$1 for 30 minutes), though you may find there's only one or two terminals and waits can be long. Most towns also have at least one commercial entity where you can get online.

## INTERNET RESOURCES

**Afflicted Yard** (http://afflictedyard.com) Edgy culture site with entertainment listings.
**Dancehall Reggae** (www.dancehallreggae.com) The place to go for *the* latest on the island's music scene.

**Jamaica Gleaner** (www.jamaica-gleaner.com) Best news source from the island's most reliable newspaper.
**Jamaica National Heritage Trust** (www.jnht.com) Excellent guide to Jamaica's history and heritage.
**Jamaica Yellow Pages** (www.jamaicayp.com) Handy online presentation of the Jamaican phone directory.
**Lonely Planet** (www.lonelyplanet.com) Succinct summaries on travel in Jamaica, plus the popular Thorn Tree bulletin board, travel news and a complete online store.
**Visit Jamaica** (www.visitjamaica.com) The tourist board's presentation of Jamaica to travelers, with plenty of destination, attractions and lodging information.
**What's On Jamaica** (www.whatsonjamaica.com) Calendar-based event and entertainment listings.

## LANGUAGE

Officially, English is the spoken language. In reality, Jamaica is a bilingual country, and English is far more widely understood than spoken. The unofficial lingo is patois (*pa-twah*), a musical dialect with a staccato rhythm and cadence, laced with salty idioms and wonderfully and wittily compressed proverbs.

Patois evolved from Creole English and a twisted alchemy of the mother tongue peppered with African, Portuguese and Spanish terms and, in the last century, Rastafarian slang. Linguists agree that it is more than simplified pidgin English, and it has its own identifiable syntax.

Patois is deepest in rural areas, where many people do not know much standard English. Although it is mostly the lingua franca of the poor, all sectors of Jamaica understand patois, and even polite, educated Jamaicans lapse into patois at unguarded moments.

Most Jamaicans vary the degree of their patois depending on who they're speaking to.

## MEDICAL SERVICES

Acceptable health care is available in most major cities and larger towns throughout Jamaica, but may be hard to locate in rural areas. To find a good local doctor, your best bet is to ask the management of the hotel where you are staying or to contact your embassy in Kingston or Montego Bay.

Many doctors expect payment in cash, regardless of whether or not you have travel health insurance. If you do develop a life-threatening medical problem, you'll probably want to be evacuated to a country with state-of-the-art medical care. Since this may cost tens of thousands of dollars, be sure you have insurance to cover this before you depart.

JAMAICA

Many pharmacies are well supplied, but important medications may not be consistently available. Be sure to bring along adequate supplies of all prescriptions.

## MONEY

The unit of currency is the Jamaican dollar, the 'jay,' which uses the same symbol as the US dollar ($). Jamaican currency is issued in bank notes of J$50, J$100, J$500 and J$1000. The official rate of exchange fluctuates daily. Prices for hotels and valuable items are usually quoted in US dollars, which are widely accepted.

Commercial banks have branches throughout the island. Those in major towns maintain a foreign exchange booth. Traveler's checks are widely accepted in Jamaica, although some hotels, restaurants and exchange bureaus charge a hefty fee for cashing them. Most city bank branches throughout Jamaica now have 24-hour ATMs linked to international networks such as Cirrus or Plus. In more remote areas, look for ATMs at gas stations.

## TELEPHONE

Jamaica's country code is ☎ 876. To call Jamaica from the US, dial ☎ 1-876 + the seven-digit local number. From elsewhere, dial your country's international dialing code, then ☎ 876 and the local number.

For calls within the same parish in Jamaica, just dial the local number. Between parishes, dial ☎ 1 + the local number. We have included only the seven-digit local number in Jamaica listings in this chapter.

Jamaica has a fully automated, digital telephone system operated by **Cable & Wireless Jamaica** ( ☎ 888-225-5295; www.cwjamaica.com), which has offices islandwide where you can make direct calls.

Major hotels have direct-dial calling; elsewhere you may need to go through the hotel operator, or call from the front desk. Hotels add a 15% government tax, plus a service charge, often at ridiculous rates.

### Cell Phones

You can bring your own cellular phone into Jamaica (GSM or CDMA), but if your phone is locked by a specific carrier, don't bother. Another option is to purchase an inexpensive cellular phone (from US$35) at a **Digicel** ( ☎ 888-344-4235; www.digiceljamaica.com) or **bMobile** ( ☎ 888-225-5295; www.cwmobile.com/jamaica) outlet

and purchase a prepaid phone card. These are sold in denominations of up to J$1000, and you'll find them at many gas stations and stationery shops.

### Phone Cards

Public phones require a prepaid phone card, available from Cable & Wireless Jamaica offices, retail stores, hotels, banks, and other outlets displaying the 'Phonecards on Sale' sign. The card is available in denominations of J$20 to J$500. For international calls, you can also buy WorldTalk calling cards, good for use on any phone, including public call boxes and cellular phones.

## TOURIST INFORMATION

The **Jamaica Tourist Board** (JTB; www.visitjamaica.com) has offices in key cities around the world, where you can request maps and literature, including hotel brochures; however, they do not serve as reservation agencies.

In Jamaica, the JTB has offices in Kingston (p223), Montego Bay (p239) and Port Antonio (p232).

## VISAS

For stays of six months or less, no visas are required for citizens of the EU, the US, Commonwealth countries, Mexico, Japan and Israel. Nationals of Argentina, Brazil, Chile, Costa Rica, Ecuador, Greece and Japan don't need a visa for stays of up to 30 days.

All other nationals require visas (nationals of most countries can obtain a visa on arrival, provided they are holding valid onward or return tickets and evidence of sufficient funds).

# TRANSPORTATION

## GETTING THERE & AWAY

### Entering Jamaica

All visitors must arrive with a valid passport. US citizens must show a valid US passport when traveling from the Caribbean in order to re-enter the US (see the boxed text, p830).

Immigration formalities require every person to show a return or ongoing airline ticket when arriving in Jamaica.

---

**EMERGENCY NUMBERS**

- Ambulance ☎ 011
- Fire ☎ 110
- Police ☎ 119

---

## Air

The majority of international visitors to Jamaica arrive at Montego Bay's **Donald Sangster International Airport** (MBJ; ☎ 979-1034, 979-1035; www.mbjairport.com). In Kingston, **Norman Manley International Airport** (KIN; ☎ 924-8452, 888-247-7678; www.manley-airport.com.jm), around 11km southeast of downtown, handles international flights. The following airlines serve these airports:

### KINGSTON

**Air Jamaica** ( ☎ 888-359-2475; www.airjamaica.com) Atlanta, Baltimore, Chicago, Curaçao, Fort Lauderdale, Grand Cayman, Havana, London, Miami, New York, Orlando, Philadelphia, Toronto

**American Airlines** ( ☎ 800-433-7300; www.aa.com) Boston, Fort Worth, Miami, New York

**British Airways** (www.ba.com) London, Miami

**Continental Airlines** ( ☎ 800-523-3273; www.continental.com) Newark

**Delta** ( ☎ 800-221-1212; www.delta.com) New York

### MONTEGO BAY

**Air Canada** ( ☎ 888-247-2262; www.aircanada.com) Toronto

**Air Jamaica** ( ☎ 888-359-2475; www.airjamaica.com) Atlanta, Baltimore, Barbados, Bonaire, Chicago, Curaçao, Fort Lauderdale, Grenada, London, Miami, Nassau, New York, Orlando, Philadelphia, St Lucia, Toronto

**American Airlines** ( ☎ 800-433-7300; www.aa.com) Boston, Fort Worth, Miami, New York

**British Airways** ( ☎ 800-247-9297; www.ba.com) Miami

**Continental Airlines** ( ☎ 800-523-3273; www.continental.com) Newark

**Delta** ( ☎ 800-221-1212; www.delta.com) Atlanta

**Northwest** ( ☎ 800-225-2525; www.nwa.com) Detroit, Minneapolis

**US Airways** ( ☎ 800-428-4322; www.usair.com) Charlotte, Philadelphia

**Virgin Atlantic** ( ☎ 800-821-5438; www.virgin-atlantic.com) London

## Sea

Jamaica is a popular destination on the cruising roster, mainly for passenger liners but also for private yachters.

If all you're after is a one-day taste of Jamaica, then consider arriving by cruise ship. Port visits usually take the form of one-day stopovers at either Ocho Rios or Montego Bay. See p830 for more information on cruises.

Many yachters make the trip to Jamaica from North America. Upon arrival in Jamaica, you *must* clear customs and immigration at Montego Bay, Kingston, Ocho Rios or Port Antonio.

In addition, you'll need to clear customs at *each* port of call.

# GETTING AROUND
## Air

There are four domestic airports: **Tinson Pen Aerodrome** ( ☎ 924-8452; Marcus Garvey Dr) in Kingston, **Boscobel Aerodrome** ( ☎ 975-3101) near Ocho Rios, **Negril Aerodrome** and **Ken Jones Aerodrome** at Port Antonio. Montego Bay's **Donald Sangster International Airport** (MBJ; ☎ 979-1034, 979-1035; www.mbjairport.com) has a domestic terminal adjacent to the international terminal.

**Air Jamaica Express** ( ☎ 922-4661, in the USA 800-523-5585; www.airjamaica.com/express.asp) Operates a scheduled service between Kingston, Montego Bay and Ocho Rios on a daily basis.

**TimAir** (www.timair.net) Montego Bay ( ☎ 952-2516, 979-1114); Negril ( ☎ 957-5374) This air taxi service serves Montego Bay, Negril, Ocho Rios, Port Antonio, Kingston and Mandeville.

## Bicycle

Mountain bikes and 'beach cruisers' can be rented at most major resorts (US$15 to US$30 per day). However, road conditions are hazardous, and Jamaican drivers are not very considerate to cyclists. For serious touring, bring your own mountain or multipurpose bike. You'll need sturdy wheels to handle the potholed roads.

## Bus

Traveling by public transportation could be the best – *or worst!* – adventure of your trip to Jamaica. The island's extensive transportation network links virtually every village and comprises several options that range from standard public buses to 'coasters' and 'route taxis.' These depart from and arrive at each town's transportation station, which is usually near the main market. Locals can direct you to

JAMAICA

the appropriate vehicle, which should have its destination marked above the front window (for buses) or on its side.

## COASTER

'Coasters' (private minibuses) have traditionally been the workhorses of Jamaica's regional public transportation system. All major towns and virtually every village in the country is served.

Licensed minibuses display red license plates with the initials PPV (public passenger vehicle) or have a Jamaican Union of Travelers Association (JUTA) insignia. JUTA buses are exclusively for tourists. They usually depart their point of origin when they're full, often overflowing, with people hanging from the open doors. Guard your luggage carefully against theft.

## PUBLIC BUS

Kingston and Montego Bay have modern municipal bus systems. Throughout the island, bus stops are located at most road intersections along the routes, but you can usually flag down a bus anywhere (except in major cities, where they only pause at designated stops). When you want to get off, shout 'One stop!' The conductor will usually echo your request with, 'Let off!' The following fares apply to public buses: Kingston metropolitan region US$1; Montego Bay licensed area US$0.50; and rural areas US$0.25 flat rate, plus US$0.05 per kilometer.

## ROUTE TAXI

These communal taxis are the most universal mode of public transportation, reaching every part of the country. They operate like coasters (and cost about the same), picking up as many people as they can squeeze in along their specified routes. A 30-minute ride typically costs about US$2; a one-hour ride costs about US$3.

Most are white Toyota Corolla station wagons marked by red license plates. They should have 'Route Taxi' marked on the front door, and they are not to be confused with identical licensed taxis, which charge more.

## Car

Despite the hazards of driving, exploring by rental car can be a joy. There are some fabulously scenic journeys, and with your own wheels you can get as far off the beaten track

as you wish, discovering the magic of Jamaican culture beyond the pale of the touristy areas.

A paved coastal highway circles the entire island; in the southern parishes it runs about 32km inland. Main roads cross the central mountain chains, north to south, linking all of the main towns. A web of minor roads, country lanes and dirt tracks provides access to more-remote areas.

## DRIVER'S LICENSE

To drive in Jamaica, you must have a valid International Driver's License (IDL) or a current license for your home country or state, valid for up to six months. You can obtain an IDL by applying with your current license to any Automobile Association office.

## FUEL & SPARE PARTS

Many gas stations close after 7pm or so. In rural areas, stations usually close on Sunday. At time of research, gasoline cost about US$3 per liter.

## RENTAL

Several major international car-rental companies operate in Jamaica, along with dozens of local firms. Rates begin at about US$45 per day and can run as high as US$125, depending on the vehicle. Some companies include unlimited mileage, while others set a limit and charge a fee for excess kilometers driven. Most firms require a deposit of at least US$500, but will accept a credit card imprint. Renters must be 21 years of age (some companies will rent only to those 25 years of age or older).

There are rental companies in large towns, including Kingston (p230), Montego Bay (p245), Ocho Rios (p238) and Negril (p250).

## ROAD CONDITIONS

The main roads are usually in reasonable condition, despite numerous potholes. Many secondary roads (B-roads) are in appalling condition and are best tackled with a 4WD. Most roads are narrow, with frequent bends.

## ROAD HAZARDS

Driving in Jamaica is dangerous. Licenses can be bought without taking a driving test, and the roads are governed by an infatuation with speed completely incongruous with the rest of Jamaican life. Look out for people along the roads or animals that might dash in front of you, and pay extra attention at roundabouts, where driving on the left is not always adhered to. Pedestrians should beware of the many drivers who would as soon hit you as slow down.

## ROAD RULES

Always drive on the left. Remember: 'Keep left, and you'll always be right.' Here's another local saying worth memorizing: 'De left side is de right side; de right side is suicide!'

The speed limit is 30mph (about 50km/h) in towns and 50mph (around 80km/h) on highways. Jamaica has a compulsory seatbelt law for passengers in the front seat.

## Taxi

Fares are expensive, but you can share the cost with other passengers. Meters are generally not used. It is possible to negotiate a fare that is less than the stated price; agree on a fare before getting into a taxi. Rates are posted at some hotels. Only use taxis with red license plates bearing a PPV designation.

Don't be misled by drivers who may want to take you somewhere other than where you want to go. Some drivers receive incentives from establishments for delivering customers.

# Haiti

Let's not kid ourselves: Haiti has an image problem. Say the name and you're likely to invoke a sad litany of coups and boat people, tinged with lurid clichés of voodoo sacrifices. As both failed state and media whipping boy, Haiti has long played the dark shadow to the bright sunlight of the rest of the Caribbean. But banish those thoughts, because we believe that Haiti may just be one of the most exciting countries in the world in which to travel.

Haiti saw the only successful slave revolution in colonial history, with the result that it clung on to its African roots more than any other Caribbean country. These roots have evolved into a wholly unique culture. The most famous result is Vodou, which informs many aspects of life, from the rhythms of *racines* music to the exuberance of Haitian painting.

Port-au-Prince is a frenetic city where you'll find plenty of good food, music and art. In the north is the Citadelle, a truly mind-blowing fortress high in the tropical mountains. In the south, Jacmel is the country's handicrafts capital, and hosts one of the best Carnival parades around. And between the two there are plenty of deserted beaches.

Getting around can sometimes be a little tough, but you certainly shouldn't believe all the scare stories. Haitians are enormously welcoming and proud, and desperate to show visitors the reality behind the screaming headlines. As the country moves out of the turmoil of recent years towards a cautious stability, now just may be the time to visit.

## FAST FACTS

- **Area** 27,750 sq km
- **Capital** Port-au-Prince
- **Country code** ☎ 509
- **Departure tax** None (paid for in air ticket)
- **Famous for** Vodou
- **Language** Creole, French
- **Money** Haitian gourde (HTG); HTG100 = US$2.62 = €1.69 = UK£1.33
- **Official name** Republic of Haiti
- **People** Haitians
- **Phrase** *bonjou/bonswa* (good morning/good afternoon); *mèsi anpil* (thank you); *orevwa/babay* (goodbye); *se konbyen kob li koute?* (how much is it?)
- **Population** 8.7 million
- **Visa** None needed; see p276

## HIGHLIGHTS

- **Port-au-Prince** (p266) Explore the unparalleled arts and music scene of Haiti's vibrant and sometimes chaotic capital city
- **Jacmel** (p270) Chill out in this laid-back southern port, the country's handicrafts and Carnival center
- **Citadelle** (p273) Want a tropical mountaintop fortress? We challenge you to find a better one in the Caribbean
- **Vodou** (p264) Dispel your fear of zombies by lifting the lid on this misunderstood but deeply spiritual religion
- **Cornier Plage and Plage Labadie** (p273) Catch some waves on the golden sands of Haiti's dramatic north coast

## ITINERARIES

- **One Week** Stay a couple of days in Port-au-Prince, then spend two more in Jacmel before taking a flight north to visit the Citadelle.
- **Two Weeks** Follow the itinerary above at a more relaxed pace, and add on Parc National La Visite and some beaches near Cap-Haïtien, Côte des Arcadins or Île-à-Vache.
- **One Month** You can see the whole of Haiti in a month, with time for scuba diving, and more out-of-the-way destinations like Jérémie or Parc National Macaya.

## CLIMATE & WHEN TO GO

There's no season for visiting Haiti. April to November are generally the wetter months, and hurricane season (August/September) can cause transport problems due to mudslides. If you plan to visit during Carnival (usually celebrated in February), book well in advance as a good hotel may be hard to find. Otherwise, hotel prices generally don't fluctuate through the year.

## HISTORY

Hispaniola's earliest inhabitants arrived around 2600 BC in huge dugout canoes, coming from what is now eastern Venezuela. They were called the Taínos, and by the time Christopher Columbus landed on the island in 1492, they numbered some 400,000. However, within 30 years of Columbus' landing, the Taínos were gone, wiped out by disease and abuse.

The Spanish neglected their colony of Santo Domingo, and through the 17th century it became a haven for pirates and, later, ambitious French colonists. In 1697 the island was formally divided, and the French colony of St-Domingue followed soon after. The French turned St-Domingue over to sugar production on a huge scale. By the end of the 18th century it was the richest colony in the world, with 40,000 colonists lording it over half a million black slaves.

Following the French Revolution in 1789, free mulattos (offspring of colonists and female slaves) demanded equal rights, while the slaves themselves launched a huge rebellion. Led by the inspiring slave leader Toussaint Louverture, the slaves freed themselves by arms and forced France to abolish slavery.

### World's First Black Republic

French treachery dispatched Toussaint to a prison death, but in May 1803 his general, Jean-Jacques Dessalines, took the French tricolor flag and, ripping the white out of it, declared he was ripping the white man out of the country. The red and blue were stitched together with the motto *Liberté ou la Mort* (Liberty or Death), creating Haiti's flag.

Dessalines won a decisive victory against the French at the Battle Vertières, near Cap-Haïtien, and on January 1, 1804, at Gonaïves, Dessalines proclaimed independence for St-Domingue and restored its Taíno name, Haiti, meaning 'Mountainous Land.'

Dessalines crowned himself Emperor of Haiti and ratified a new constitution that granted him absolute power. However, his tyrannical approach to the throne inflamed large sections of society to revolt – his death in an ambush at Pont Rouge in 1806 marked the first of many violent overthrows that would plague Haiti for the next 200 years.

Dessalines' death sparked a civil war between the black north, led by Henri Christophe, and the mulatto south, led by Alexandre Pétion. Christophe crowned himself king, while Pétion became president of the southern republic. It took both their deaths (Christophe by suicide) to reunite the country, which happened in 1820 under new southern leader Jean-Pierre Boyer, who established a tenuous peace.

During his reign Boyer paid a crippling indemnity to France in return for diplomatic recognition. The debt took the rest of the century to pay off and turned Haiti into the first Third World debtor nation. Boyer also

# HAITI

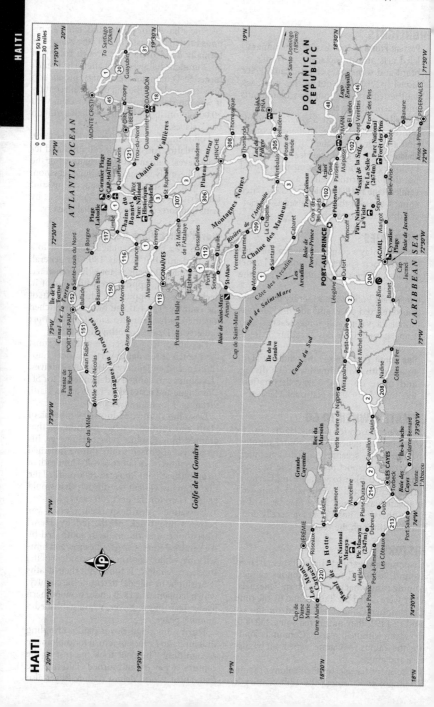

sought to unify Hispaniola by invading Santo Domingo. The whole of the island remained under Haitian control until 1849, when the eastern part proclaimed independence as the Dominican Republic.

The next half-century was characterized by continued rivalry between the ruling classes of wealthy mulattos and blacks. Of the 22 heads of state between 1843 and 1915, only one served his full term in office; the others were assassinated or forced into exile.

## US Intervention

By the beginning of the 20th century the US had begun to recognize that Haiti's proximity to the Windward Passage gave the country strategic importance. The stretch of sea between Haiti and Cuba was an important shipping route from the newly opened Panama Canal to the eastern coast of the US.

When Haitian President Vilbrun Guillaume Sam was killed by an angry civilian mob in 1915, the Americans took it as their chance to invade Haiti, in theory aiming to stabilize the country. The occupation furthered the economic interests of the US in Haiti, who rewrote the constitution in favor of American corporations and introduced forced labor gangs to build infrastructure. The occupation brought predictable resistance, with the Cacos peasant rebellion led by Charlemagne Péralte from 1918 to 1920. Its brutal suppression cost the lives of about 2000 Haitians, and is still bitterly remembered in the country today. The occupation proved costly and the US finally pulled out in 1934.

## The Duvaliers & Aristide

Haiti's string of tyrannical rulers reached its zenith in 1956 with the election of François Duvalier, whose support came from the burgeoning black middle class and the politically isolated rural poor. But he knew where the dangers lay and within months acted swiftly to neutralize his opponents.

Duvalier consolidated his power by creating the notorious Tontons Macoutes. The name refers to a character in a Haitian folk story, Tonton Macoute (Uncle Knapsack), who carries off small children in his bag at night. The Tontons Macoutes were a private militia who could use force with impunity in order to extort cash and crops from a cowed population. In exchange for this privilege, they afforded Duvalier utmost loyalty and protection.

---

### HOW MUCH?

- Taxi from Port-au-Prince to Pétion-ville US$10
- Meal in a touristy restaurant US$9
- Snickers bar US$1.20
- Bottle of five-star Haitian rum US$15
- Double room in a midrange hotel US$75

---

'Papa Doc' died on April 21, 1971, and was succeeded by his son Jean-Claude 'Baby Doc' Duvalier. Periodic bouts of repression continued until major civil unrest forced Baby Doc to flee to France in February 1986.

Control changed hands between junta leaders until finally the Supreme Court ordered elections for December 1990. A young priest named Father Jean-Bertrand Aristide, standing as a surprise last-minute candidate with the slogan 'Lavalas' (Flood), won a landslide victory.

Aristide promised radical reforms to aid the poor, but after just seven months he was pushed out of office. An alliance of rich mulatto families and army generals, worried about their respective business and drug interests, staged a bloody coup, with General Raoul Cédras as their front man. Despite international condemnation, an embargo against the junta was barely enforced, and thousands of Haitians fled political repression in boats to the USA. After four years a joint US-UN plan saw Cédras leave for exile in Panama, and Aristide finally back as president. In return, Aristide was forced to implement harsh free-trade economic reforms.

### Haiti Today

After a period in opposition, Aristide returned as president in 2001. His opponents boycotted the elections and disputed the results, leading to several years of political instability. Things came to a head in early 2004, soon after Haiti marked the 200th anniversary of independence. With violence rife from all sides, an armed revolt forced Aristide back in to exile in February 2004. His supporters claim that US agents effectively kidnapped him (a claim the US denies).

The accession of pro-US Gerard Latortue did little to quell the violence, and the devastation of Tropical Storm Jeanne, which killed 3000, did little to improve matters. A UN peacekeeping mission, Minustah, was sent to the island, but it took until 2006 before the country appeared to have turned the corner. On the political front, largely peaceful elections returned René Préval as president, while a controversial military campaign by Minustah tackled the gang problem head-on, drastically reducing the violence and kidnappings that had become endemic.

Haiti remains the poorest country in the western hemisphere. A shattered economy, corruption, low life expectancy and high illiteracy rates are only the tip of the challenges facing the nation. In spring 2008, street protests about rising goods prices turned briefly violent and led to the sacking of the prime minister. But whenever conditions have allowed, Haitians have shown themselves able to start building for the future. The continuing attention of the UN will hopefully allow such a breathing space to occur.

## THE CULTURE

Haiti is predominantly made up of peasants who live a subsistence lifestyle in rural areas. Traditionally, the men plant and harvest the crops, while the women care for the children, prepare meals and sell surplus crops at the market.

Their small, usually two-room wooden houses have no electricity, and food preparation takes place outside on a charcoal fire. If faced with difficult and arduous work, the men work together on one piece of land in a communal work team called a *kombit*. Neighbors work for free and are compensated by a feast at the end of the day. In the evenings after eating, the group often relaxes by playing *Krik? Krak!*, an oral game of riddles.

As the growing population's demands on the land have reached breaking point, many peasants have sought a better life in the capital. But the mass exodus from the land has created teeming slums, such as Cité Soleil. Here much of the communal spirit of the countryside is lost in the everyday grind as about 200,000 people occupy 5 sq km of land, mainly reclaimed sea swamp, in some of the harshest conditions imaginable.

Another life altogether prevails in the cool hills above Port-au-Prince. The country's elite, the 1% of society that has nearly half the wealth, lives in mansions surrounded by high walls, in and above Pétionville.

Haiti is home to almost nine million people, of whom 80% are rural. People of African origin make up about 95% of Haiti's population. The other 5% is made up of mulattos,

### VODOU

It's hard to think of a more consistently maligned and misunderstood religion than Vodou, with many thinking it less a religion than a mass of superstitions based on fear and ignorance. This negative portrayal comes partly from lurid Hollywood movies, but also from Haiti's isolation and demonization during the 19th century following its impertinence in casting off colonial rule with its successful slave revolution.

Vodou (the Creole spelling is preferred locally over the anglicized 'Voodoo') is not an animist religion that worships spirits. Followers worship God, who they call Gran Met, but believe he is distant from the physical plane, so lesser spirit entities called lwa are approached in ceremonies as interlocutors. Lwa are summoned through prayer, song and drumming. The lwa possess Vodou initiates, and manifest and identify themselves by singing, dancing, healing the sick and offering advice. There are several 'families' of lwa, including the Rada and Géde (associated with death), and families connected to Vodou's African forbears such as the Kongo and Ibo.

Haitian Vodou is unique. It's a mix of the traditional religions brought by slaves from West and Central Africa, blended with residual rituals from the Taíno along with Catholicism inherited from the plantation owners. While conversion to Christianity was encouraged, many saw in the icons of Catholic saints their own African spirits, represented in new forms and ideas, and appropriated the images as their own. Each lwa in the Vodou pantheon has its own surrogate Catholic saint, and Vodou altars are rich blends of African and Christian iconography.

Vodou has had a conflicted relationship with Haitian power. It played a key role in both the inspiration and organization of the struggle for independence, has also been outlawed at various times, with regular Catholic-led 'anti-superstition' campaigns. In 1991 Vodou was officially recognized as a Haitian religion, coexisting and (mostly) tolerated by the Church.

Middle Easterners and people of other races. Members of the mulatto class, which constitutes half of the country's elite and controls most of the economy and political life, are the descendants of African slaves and French plantation owners.

A popular maxim has it that Haiti is 80% Catholic, 20% Protestant, but 100% Vodou. This uniquely Haitian religion, blending many traditional African religions with Catholic elements permeates the country (see boxed text, opposite).

Catholicism dominates public life, and has frequently found itself swimming in the murky currents of Haitian politics. Papa Doc Duvalier exiled many Catholic orders and created his own loyal clergy, who remembered him in their prayers and stayed silent over the regime's excesses. On a grassroots level, the Ti Legliz (Little Church) movement took inspiration from the 1980s Latin American liberation theologists, and was instrumental not only in ousting the Duvaliers but sweeping Father Jean-Bertrand Aristide into power in 1991.

Protestantism is a relatively new import into Haiti, arriving in an evangelical wave in the 1970s. Many churches from North America, mainstream and otherwise, continue to pour missionaries and money into the country, and own many radio stations. Evangelicals are usually fiercely opposed to Vodou, often claiming that Haiti's myriad problems are punishment by God for the sins of following Vodou.

## ARTS

For its size and population, Haiti has an abundance of artists – they are predominantly painters, but also metalworkers and Vodou flag makers. Much of Haitian art has been classified as 'naïve' or 'primitive,' partly due to its simple style and avoidance of classical perspective.

The major factor contributing to the singular vision of Haiti's artists is their inextricable link with Vodou. Artists serve the lwa (Vodou spirits) by painting murals to decorate the walls of temples and making elaborate sequined flags for use in ceremonies.

Hector Hyppolite, now considered Haiti's greatest painter, was a Vodou priest. Other great naïves include Rigaud Benoît and Philomé Obin. The murals of Ste Trinité Episcopalian Cathedral (p267) in Port-au-Prince are the best showcase of this classic period of Haitian art.

Musical expression in Haiti reflects both the fusion of cultural influences and, more recently, popular resistance and struggle in Haitian politics. Vodou ceremonies have always been accompanied by music, song and dance. *Rara* is a Vodou performance ritual held during the weeks before Easter, when temple ceremonies are taken to the streets.

*Racines* (roots) music grew out of the Vodou jazz movement of the late 1970s. Vodou jazz was a fusion of American jazz with Vodou rhythms and melodies. Two of the best *racines* bands are RAM and Boukman Eksperyans. *Compas,* a Haitian form of merengue, is very popular in dance clubs.

In the years since independence, intellectual Haitians have created a strong school of indigenous literature to counter prevailing concepts of Haiti as a nation of primitive savages. The most important cultural flowering was in response to the US occupation of 1915–34, from which grew the Noirisme movement, and its artistic counterpart Indigénisme. Both positively embraced Haiti's unique identity and African heritage. The leading Noiriste writers were Jean Price-Mars and Jacques Roumain, author of *Les gouverneurs de la rosée* (Masters of the Dew), considered to be Haiti's finest work of literature. Some of the best current Haitian writers are those of the diaspora, including novelist Edwidge Danticat, author of *Breath, Eyes, Memory,* and *The Farming of Bones.*

On the architectural front, little remains of the colonial period, although a number of independence-era forts can be visited, including the stupendous Citadelle (p273). In the late 19th century, Parisian style met the requirements of tropical living in Haiti's so-called gingerbread houses and mansions, characterized by their graceful balconies, detailed wooden latticework and neo-Gothic designs. Many fine examples can still be seen in Port-au-Prince and Jacmel.

## ENVIRONMENT
### The Land

Haiti occupies the mountainous western third of Hispaniola, sharing a 388km border with the Dominican Republic. About the size of the US state of Maryland, the country is cut by hundreds of rivers and streams, many of which bring torrential flood waters and eroded soil during the hurricane season. Rising above these river valleys are four mountain chains;

HAITI

Haiti's tallest mountain is 2674m Pic La Selle, located in the southeast of the country. Haiti's largest drainage system, the Artibonite river, extends 400km through the center of the country. The river was dammed in its upper reaches in 1956, forming the Lac de Péligre behind Haiti's major hydroelectric facility. Its delta, south of Gonaïves, is a key rice-producing area.

## Wildlife

Haiti is rich in birdlife, with 220 species, including the palmchat and the La Selle thrush. The gray-crowned palm tanager is a species unique to Haiti. Water birds include American flamingos and the black-capped petrel, a seabird that nests in the high cliffs of Massif de la Selle and the Massif de la Hotte.

Despite major habitat destruction, some endemic animals remain, including a small population of manatees in the coastal waters. Of the four types of sea turtle here, the largest is the leatherback, which can weigh up to 600kg. Reptiles include iguanas and American crocodiles, which can be seen at Étang Saumâtre.

## Environmental Issues

Haiti is a popular university case study in environmental degradation and disaster, perhaps equaled only by Madagascar and the more devastated parts of the Amazon rainforest. Unchecked clearing of the land for food production and fuel wood has depleted massive tracts of broadleaf forest. Only a small portion of virgin forest survives, including on the Massif de la Selle and the cloud forests of Massif de le Hotte.

The destruction of the forests for firewood and farmland has caused an untenable amount of soil erosion, as well as trapping Haiti's peasants in a cycle of subsistence farming with ever-diminishing returns. The bare hillsides can prove lethal during hurricane season, when rainfall easily causes terrible mudslides and floods. Neighboring Dominican Republic with its intact forest cover comes out of the same storm systems in much better shape.

## FOOD & DRINK

You'll frequently eat at bar-restos, cheap eating places that double up as drinking holes in the evening. Most offer a plat complet, with diri ak pwa (rice and beans), bannann peze (fried plantain), salad and meat – usually poule (fried chicken), tasso (jerked beef), griyo (fried pork) or kabri (goat). The dish can be served with sòs Kreyol (tomato-based Creole sauce), ti malice (onion and chili sauce) or a sòs vyann (meat sauce). Seafood is widely available, including lobster, and is very reasonably priced.

Haiti has a prize-winning beer, Prestige, and is the only Caribbean country that makes rum direct from sugarcane rather than molasses. The Haitian rum company is called Barbancourt, and both its three- and five-star varieties are excellent. Also look out for clairin, a cheap cane spirit. There's also wonderful local coffee, including Haitian Blue that's produced mainly for export.

# PORT-AU-PRINCE

**pop 3 million**

Port-au-Prince is the picture of a chaotic developing-world city. It has a reputation for impoverished chaos, and its infrastructure can seem permanently on the point of collapse. Yet behind this lies one of the most vibrant and exciting cities in the Caribbean, with a fantastic arts scene, good restaurants and live music and an irrepressible spirit.

The center of the city is compact and manageable on foot, while on the hillsides above you'll find the rich suburb of Pétionville, where many of the best hotels and restaurants are based.

## INFORMATION

If you are changing US$ cash, all supermarkets have change counters.

**Companet Cyber Café** (Rue Lamarre, Pétionville; per hr US$1.20; ⏱ 9am-7pm)

**DNS Computer** (Rue Capois; per hr US$0.80; ⏱ 8am-9pm)

**Hôpital du Canapé Vert** ( ☎ 2245-0984/85; 83 Rte de Canapé Vert) Has a 24-hour emergency department. It's 1.5km east of the center.

**Post office** ( ⏱ 8am-4pm Mon-Sat); Pétionville (Place St Pierre); Port-au-Prince (Rue Bonne Foi, Bicentenaire)

**Scotiabank** (cnr Rues Geffrard & Louverture, Pétionville) Has an ATM.

**Sogebank** Pétionville (Rue Lamarre; Pétionville); Port-au-Prince (Delmas 30) Both have ATMs.

## DANGERS & ANNOYANCES

Port-au-Prince is a lot calmer than preconceptions would have you believe. But street

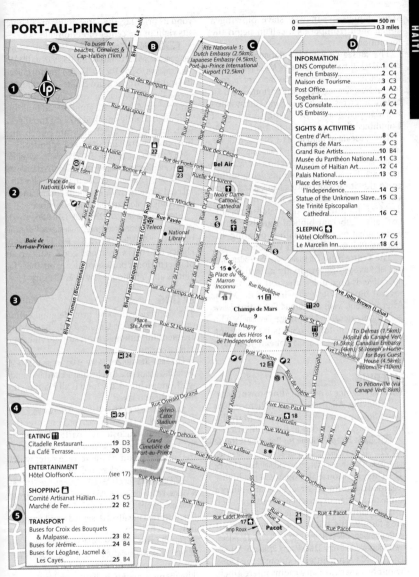

## PORT-AU-PRINCE

0 — 500 m
0 — 0.3 miles

**INFORMATION**
DNS Computer..........................1 C4
French Embassy........................2 C4
Maison de Tourisme...................3 C3
Post Office................................4 A2
Sogebank.................................5 C2
US Consulate.............................6 C4
US Embassy...............................7 A2

**SIGHTS & ACTIVITIES**
Centre d'Art..............................8 C4
Champs de Mars........................9 C3
Grand Rue Artists.....................10 B4
Musée du Panthéon National....11 C3
Museum of Haitian Art.............12 C4
Palais National.........................13 C3
Place des Héros de
  l'Independence......................14 C3
Statue of the Unknown Slave...15 C3
Ste Trinité Episcopalian
  Cathedral..............................16 C2

**SLEEPING**
Hôtel Oloffson.........................17 C5
Le Marcelin Inn........................18 C4

**EATING**
Citadelle Restaurant.................19 D3
La Café Terrasse......................20 D3

**ENTERTAINMENT**
Hôtel OloffsonX..................(see 17)

**SHOPPING**
Comité Artisanat Haïtian..........21 C5
Marché de Fer.........................22 B2

**TRANSPORT**
Buses for Croix des Bouquets
  & Malpasse............................23 B2
Buses for Jérémie....................24 B4
Buses for Léogâne, Jacmel &
  Les Cayes..............................25 B4

crime isn't unknown, so don't be ostentatious or keep your cash in your back pocket as the pickpockets are skillful. It's very unwise to walk around after dark, even around areas such as Champs de Mars. Avoid visiting the slum areas, such as Cité Soleil off Rte Nationale 1 and Cité Liberté off Blvd Harry Truman.

## SIGHTS

The main area for sightseeing is within and around the **Champs de Mars**, the large park built in 1953. Here you'll find a couple of museums and the **Palais National**. The **Place des Héros de l'Independence**, east of the palace, contains the statues of the founders of independent Haiti. The *Statue of the Unknown*

HAITI

*Slave* depicts a runaway slave blowing a conch-shell trumpet as a call to begin the revolution.

The **Musée du Panthéon National** (Mupanah; ☎ 2222-8337; Place du Champs de Mars; adult/student US$1.40/0.70; ⏰ 8am-4pm Mon-Thu, 8am-5pm Fri, noon-5pm, Sat 10am-4pm Sun) contains various items of historical interest, including King Christophe's suicidal pistol and the rusting anchor of Columbus' flagship, the *Santa María*.

The **Museum of Haitian Art** (☎ 2222-2510; Rue Légitime; admission US$1.40; ⏰ 10am-5pm Mon-Sat, to 4pm Sun) has a large collection of Haitian naïve art. For an even more inspiring setting go to the **Ste Trinité Episcopalian Cathedral** (cnr Ave Mgr Guilloux & Rue Pavée), just north of Champs de Mars. Its interior is decorated with fantastically exuberant biblical murals painted by the great masters of Haitian painting, including Philomé Obin and Wilson Bigaud.

The **Centre d'Art** (58 Ruelle Roy; ⏰ 9:30am-5pm Mon-Fri, 9am-3pm Sat), originally an artists' co-operative, is on a quiet street off Rue Capois several blocks south of Champs de Mars. Alternatively, visit the **Grand Rue artists** (www.atis-rezistans.com; 622 Blvd Jean-Jacques Dessalines), who turns scrap and found objects into startling Vodou sculpture – a Caribbean junkyard gone cyber-punk.

## SLEEPING

The main choice is heading downtown, or up to Pétionville. All places reviewed here, except Doux Sejour Guest House and Le Marcelin Inn, have wi-fi included in the room price.

**our pick** **St Joseph's Home for Boys Guest House** (☎ 2257-4237; sjfamilyhaiti@hotmail.com; 3rd street on right, Delmas 91; shared r per person incl half-board US$35; 💻) This guesthouse also operates as a highly regarded home for ex–street boys, and offers a fantastic Haitian experience. Meals are taken communally, making you feel part of the 'St Joe's family.' It's 4.5km east of the center.

**Doux Sejour Guest House** (☎ 2257-1533, 2257-1560; www.douxsejourhaiti.com; 32 Rue Magny, Pétionville; s/d from US$40/50; ❄) A fun little guesthouse, the Doux Sejour has a series of airy rooms interestingly laid out and a good restaurant.

**Le Marcelin Inn** (☎ 2221-8233, 2221-9445; www.marcelin.com; 29 Rue Marcelin; r US$76-86; ❄ 🍴) A good-value modern hotel that's been pleasingly 'gingerbreadized' to inject some character

**Hotel Kinam** (☎ 2257-0462, 2257-6525; www.hotelkinam.com; Place Saint-Pierre, Pétionville; s/d/ste from US$76/112/120; ❄ 💻 🍴) Offering quality be-

yond its price tag, this large gingerbread hotel sits right in the center of Pétionville.

**our pick** **Hôtel Oloffson** (☎ 2223-4000/02; oloffsonram@aol.com; 60 Ave Christophe; s/d US$80/92, ste US$130-146, bungalows US$101-118; ❄ 💻 🍴) Immortalized in Graham Greene's novel *The Comedians*, a stay at the Oloffson is an iconic Port-au-Prince experience. A beautiful gingerbread building (although slightly knocked around the edges), with a terrace for lunch and rum punch, and live music every Thursday (see opposite).

**La Villa Creole** (☎ 2257-1570, 2257-0965; www.villacreole.com; Rte El Rancho, Pétionville; s/d/ste from US$132/165/185; ❄ 💻 🍴) Top-end service marries well with a relaxed air here, with excellent rooms and an exceedingly pleasant bar and pool area.

**Hotel Montana** (☎ 2229-4000, 3510-9495; www.htmontana.com; Impasse Cardozo, Ave Panaméricaine, Pétionville; s/d/ste from US$133/165/330; ❄ 💻 🍴) The hotel of choice for Haiti's great and good, with an air of international professionalism, business facilities and a famous view over the city.

## EATING

The sleeping listings all provide good eating options. For quick Creole food, 'bar-restos' are plentiful, although most stop serving food early evening.

**Citadelle Restaurant** (4 Rue St Cyr; mains US$1-3.50; ⏰ lunch & dinner) In a lovely dilapidated red-and-white gingerbread, the food is all Haitian, the atmosphere relaxed.

**La Café Terrasse** (☎ 2222-5648; 11 Rue Capois; lunches around US$4-9; ⏰ 10am-4pm Mon-Fri) You enter this café on Rue Ducoste. It's particularly good for salads and crepes; you can eat in either the upstairs salon or the terrace café, which is designed for quick refueling.

**our pick** **Anba Tonel** (☎ 2257-7560; cnr Rues Clerveaux & Vilatte, Pétionville; mains US$6; ⏰ 5-11pm, closed Mon-Wed) Excellent Creole food, including *kibby* (fried stuffed meatballs), served amid wonderfully kitsch decor.

**Fior di Latte** (☎ 2256-8474; Choucoune Plaza, Rue Lamarre, Pétionville; mains US$6-11; ⏰ lunch & dinner Mon-Sat) Very popular for extended lunch breaks. The menu is mainly Italian, with homemade ice cream for dessert.

**Papaye** (☎ 3513-9229; 48 Rue Métellus, Pétionville; mains around US$18-28; ⏰ noon-2:30pm & 7-11pm, closed Sun & Mon) 'Caribbean fusion' isn't a term that should work, but here it's carried off with aplomb, taking Creole dishes and jamming them up against Asian, European and other culinary influences.

# ENTERTAINMENT

Many bar-restaurants host live music, and serve booze well after the food runs out. Look out for billboards posted on major junctions advertising forthcoming concerts.

Several bands play regular concerts; they generally start between 11pm and midnight. Foremost is RAM at the **Hôtel Oloffson** ( ☎ 2223-4000/02; oloffsonram@aol.com; 60 Ave Christophe) every Thursday (see below). Also worth checking out is the troubadour band Macaya at the **La Villa Creole** ( ☎ 2257-1570, 2257-0965; www.villacreole.com; Rte El Rancho, Pétionville) There's no cover charge for these shows, but you'll have to pay to get into **Xtreme** ( ☎ 2257-0841; 64 Rue Grégoire, Pétionville) to see Orchestre Super Choucoune, a big band playing *compas* and merengue on Saturdays.

# SHOPPING

**Marché de Fer** (Iron Market; cnr Blvd Jean-Jacques Dessalines & Rue des Fronts Forts) This is *the* Port-au-Prince shopping experience, a huge Arabian Nights–style hall that's both a food and craft market, selling everything from baskets of dried mushrooms to various Vodou ephemera. It's open daily. Be prepared for plenty of bustle, and a little hustle too.

**Comité Artisanat Haïtien** (29 Rue 3) This craft-makers' cooperative has worked to promote Haitian crafts and provide fair wages for its artisans. The shop is strong on well-priced metalwork, sculptures, and painted boxes and miniature taptaps (local Haitian buses).

For paintings, try the Centre d'Art (opposite) or the upscale galleries in Pétionville.

# GETTING THERE & AROUND

For more information on international and domestic air travel to and from Port-au-Prince, see p277 and p277 respectively. A taxi to the airport costs around US$20.

Buses for southwest Haiti, including Jacmel (US$2.70, three hours) and Les Cayes (US$8, four hours), depart from the junction of Rue Oswald Durand and Blvd Jean-Jacques Dessalines (Grand Rue). For Cap-Haïtien (US$12, seven hours) and points north, go to Estation O'Cap, at the corner of Grand Rue and Blvd La Saline, 1.5km north of the center.

To get around, taptaps run set routes along the major roads, including Grand Rue, Delmas, Ave John Brown (Lalue) and Canape Vert. The last three all go to Pétionville. Fares are HTG5 (US$0.15). *Publiques* (collective taxis) cost HTG25 (US$0.40).

---

## VODOU ROCK & ROOTS

Every Thursday night between 11 and midnight, crowds gather at the Hôtel Oloffson to dance until the small hours to the Vodou rock 'n' roots music of RAM. A potent blend of African rhythms, *rara* horns, guitar and keyboards, the shows have an irresistible atmosphere. At the center of everything is band leader (and Oloffson owner) Richard A Morse. We caught up with him after a show:

**How would you describe RAM's music?**

When Haiti became independent, half the population had been born in Africa. Because it was a slave revolt, the surrounding countries ostracized Haiti to try to keep the revolution from spreading. That isolation kept Haiti's roots intact. We take those African roots as a starting point to our music, hence the word *racines* or 'roots.'

**RAM's music often has a strong political element, and you've had some run-ins with the authorities in the past...**

Well, I've been grabbed by authorities and some band members were once arrested during a show. If I get into more detail, perhaps we'll lose our 'tourist' audience!

**Do you really play every single Thursday at the Oloffson?**

We sometimes take the month of October off before starting up again in November. But the party here on Thursdays is always new and fresh. People join in, people dance, some are off in the corners making deals or exchanging stories. Sometimes I can't believe I'm in the middle of it. When I read Quincy Jones' description of a 'Juke Joint,' I thought, 'I live in a Juke Joint!'

**We heard you bought the Oloffson in a slightly unorthodox manner.**

I was coming back from a friend's house one Saturday morning with a *houngan* (Vodou priest) I had met. He asked me, 'Do you want the hotel?' to which I replied 'No.' Once again he asked me, 'Do you want the hotel?' and once again I said 'No.' His eyes were getting wider and he was getting more excited as he said 'Say yes! Say yes! Do you want the hotel??' To which I resigned myself and said 'Okay, I want the hotel' and he snapped back, 'GIVE ME TWENTY DOLLARS!...'

# AROUND PORT-AU-PRINCE

The clamor of Port-au-Prince can tire even the most die-hard traveler after a while – luckily there are several worthwhile sights within striking distance of the capital.

## EAST OF PORT-AU-PRINCE

The market town of **Croix des Bouquets** (taptaps US$1, 30 minutes from Carrefour Trois Mains near Port-au-Prince airport) is famous for its iron workers, who hammer out incredible decorative art from flattened oil drums and vehicle bodies. It's great fun to wander around the Noailles districts watching the artisans and looking for souvenirs. There's a complete absence of hard sell.

East of Croix des Bouquets, the main road reaches **Lac Azuei**, Haiti's largest saltwater lake. The lake supports over 100 species, including flamingos and American crocodiles. If you have time, it's worth making a detour to also visit **Trou Caïman**, an excellent place for spotting waterfowl.

Kenscoff, above Pétionville, is the entry point for **Parc National La Visite**. A hike from here across the western section of Massif de la Selle to Seguin, overlooking the Caribbean, takes six to eight hours, and is one of the most spectacular walks in Haiti. Start your trek at Carrefour Badyo just beyond Kenscoff, and be prepared for unexpected rain and chill as well as strong sun. Once you reach Seguin, you can sleep overnight in the cozy **Auberge de la Visite** ( ☎ 2246-0166, 2257-1579; tiroyd@yahoo.com; r with full board US$50), before descending to Marigot and catching transport to Jacmel.

## NORTH OF PORT-AU-PRINCE

Rte Nationale 1 is the main highway to Cap-Haïtien via Gonaïves. It skirts the coast, called the Côte des Arcadins, for most of the first 80km between Cabaret (the former Duvalierville satirized in Greene's *The Comedians*) and St-Marc. It is here that most of the country's beach resorts are situated, packed out at weekends. **Kaliko Beach Club** ( ☎ 3513-7548; www.kalikobeachclub.com; Km 61, Rte National 1; s/d with full board US$110/150, day pass US$25; 🏊 🖥 🌊 ) is an attractive resort and also home to dive operators **Pegasus** ( ☎ 3624-9486, 3624-9411,

3624-4775; nicolemarcelinroy@yahoo.com), which can arrange charters for qualified divers.

If you wish to take public transportation catch a bus or taptap in Port-au-Prince from Estation O'Cap, beside the Shell gas station at the confluence of Blvd Jean-Jacques Dessalines (Grand Rue) and Blvd La Saline. Return transport is a lot more hit and miss, as you're reliant on flagging down passing buses – don't leave it too late in the afternoon.

# SOUTHERN HAITI

Haiti's south is all about taking it easy. Pulling out of Port-au-Prince, the urban hustle is soon replaced by a much more relaxed air and rightly so – you're heading towards the Caribbean Sea.

## JACMEL
pop 40,000

Jacmel is a 120km drive southwest of Port-au-Prince, via one of the best roads in the country. A busy coffee port at the turn of the 20th century, it retains much of its late-Victorian grace with wide streets lined by elegant town houses. It's an easy town to be charmed by. Famed as Haiti's handicrafts capital, much of its creativity can be seen in the fantastic papier-mâché masks made for the Carnival festivities.

### Information

**Associations des Micro-Enterprises Touristiques du Sud'Est** (AMETS; ☎ 2288-2840; amets_service@yahoo.fr; 40 Rue d'Orléans; 🕑 8am-4pm Mon-Fri, 8am-2pm Sat) Has maps of Jacmel, and can arrange car and horse hire.

**Banque Nationale de Crédit** (Grand Rue)

**Jacmel Cybernet** (Ave Baranquilla; per hr US$1.10; 🕑 7am-10pm Mon-Sat, 9am-10pm Sun) Has good electricity supply.

**Philippe Agent de Change** (Ave Baranquilla) Changes euros and Canadian dollars

**Post office** (Rue du Commerce; 🕑 8am-4pm Mon-Sat)

### Sights & Activities

Close to the seafront, Rue du Commerce has many fine examples of 19th-century warehouses; at the eastern end of the street are the **customs house**, an old 18th-century **prison** and the **wharf**. There are **merchants' mansions** strewn all over town in varying states of lecay, including the Manoir Alexandre, a ickety old hotel, and **Salubria Gallery**.

East of Place d'Armes, the town square, is a red-and-green baroque **Marché de Fer** built in 1895, which resembles a scaled-down version of the grand iron market in Port-au-Prince. The pretty 19th-century **Cathédrale de St Phillippe et St Jacques** (Rue de l'Eglise) is close to the market.

The closest beach to town is **La Saline**, a 30-minute walk from the center past the cemetery (US$0.40 by moto-taxi), a small cove with crystal-clear water. The best beach is at **Cyvadier Plage**, 10km east of town.

Around 12km inland from Jacmel, reached on horseback or on foot, is **Bassins-Bleu**, a spectacular grotto of cascades and cobalt blue pools.

There are many guides in Jacmel who will, for a fee, take you on the journey by horse, which takes about two hours each way. It is advisable to negotiate the full price before you set off to avoid endless squabbling en route. Consider paying about US$20 per person, but you may have to pay more. A broad hat and sunblock are recommended.

## Sleeping & Eating

**Guy's Guesthouse** ( ☎ 2288-2569, 2288-9646; Ave de la Liberté; s US$25-40, d US$40-50, tr US$55, all incl breakfast; ✖ 🖳 🕭 ) Popular with NGO workers, Guy's is a welcoming place, and although bathrooms are shared, everything is kept very clean. Breakfasts are huge, and the restaurant out front is a good place for lunch or dinner.

**Hôtel de la Place** ( ☎ 2288-3769; 3 Rue de l'Eglise; r US$45; ✖ ) A pleasant old building overlooking Place Toussaint L'Ouverture, and a good place to enjoy Carnival. Some rooms are a little on the small side; most manage a view. The ground-floor terrace bar seems designed for hours of people-watching.

**Cyvadier Plage Hôtel** ( ☎ 2288-3323; www.hotel cyvadier.com; Route de Cyvadier; s US$61-72, d US$82-104, tr US$158; ✖ 🖳 🕭 ) Off the main highway, this is the furthest of the beach hotels from the center of Jacmel, but also one of the best. Rooms in a cluster of buildings face the excellent terrace restaurant and the private cove of Cyvadier Plage.

**Hôtel Florita** ( ☎ 2288-2805; www.hotelflorita.com; 29 Rue du Commerce; r US$66; ✖ ) A converted mansion, the Florita oozes charm. There are polished floorboards, period furniture and comfy chairs aplenty, while rooms are whitewashed

and airy (extra rooms at the back are a bit more cramped).

**Petit Coin Restaurant** ( ☎ 2288-3067; Rue Bourbon; mains around US$7; ✖ noon-11pm) A cozy little restaurant, with a hint of French bistro. Three tables on a tiny terrace allow you to catch the last of the day's sun and to people-spot, before retiring to the interior.

**Eritaj Café** (50 Ave Barranquilla; fish US$7-12; ✖ lunch & dinner) On the main drag, the Eritaj has a shady courtyard with bright murals on the wall. Fish is the order of the day, but there are some interesting pasta dishes also on offer.

## Shopping

Jacmel is a souvenir-buyer's paradise. Handicrafts include hand-painted placemats and boxes, wooden flowers, and models of taptaps, jungle animals and boats. Prices are cheap, starting at a couple of dollars for the smallest items, and the atmosphere is very relaxed. Most of the shops can be found on Rue St-Anne in the vicinity of the Hôtel la Jacmelienne sur Plage.

## Getting There & Around

**Caribintair** ( ☎ 2250-2031) has a daily flight to Port-au-Prince (US$80, 15 minutes). Buses to Port-au-Prince (US$2.70, three hours) leave from the Bassin Caïman station just outside of town. Some taptaps (US$3, 2½ hours) also leave from Marché Geffrard closer to the center. If you want to travel west, get off at Carrefour Duffort and flag down passing buses; there are no direct buses west from Jacmel.

## LES CAYES
### pop 46,000

You'd be hard pressed to find a sense of urgency in this old rum port, as it's lulled into a sense of torpor by the gentle Caribbean breeze. More popularly known as Aux Cayes, it's sheltered by a series of reefs that have sent many ships to their graves. Though there's little here for visitors, it's the jumping off point for nearby Île-à-Vache.

The **Concorde Hôtel** ( ☎ 2286-0079; Rue Gabions des Indigenes; s/d with fan US$40/47, with air-con US$45/57; ✖ 🕭 ) is the best option, set in large, pleasant gardens. The **Nami Restaurant** ( ☎ 286-1114; 15 Rue Nicholas Geffrard; mains US$5-7; ✖ breakfast, lunch & dinner) surprises with Chinese, continental and Creole dishes.

Buses, including to Port-au-Prince (US$8, four hours), leave from near Carrefour des Quatre Chemins. For travel to and from Jacmel, take a Port-au-Prince bus and change at Léogâne. Taptaps to Port Salut (US$1; 45 minutes) are plentiful.

## ÎLE-À-VACHE

About 15km off the coast of Les Cayes, the Île-à-Vache makes a good tropical getaway, complete with rural houses, mangroves, the odd Arawak burial ground and some great beaches. Its history is tied closely with that of Captain Morgan, the famous buccaneer who was based here for a while.

Two equally excellent upmarket resorts make up the accommodation options: **Abaka Bay Resort** ( ☎ 3721-3691; www.abakabay.com; s/d US$98/195; ❄ ▯ ) and **Port Morgan** ( ☎ 921-0000; www.port-morgan.com; s/d with full board from US$225/420, 2 night minimum; ❄ ▯ ☆ ). The former has the best beach, the latter the better food. Both offer transfers for guests, otherwise boats leave from Les Cayes wharf several times a day (US$2, 30 minutes).

## PORT SALUT

An excellent new road leads west from Les Cayes to Port Salut, a one-street town strung for several miles along the coast. The main reason to come here is the beach: miles of palm-fringed white sand with barely a person on it, and the gorgeously warm Caribbean to splash around in.

The series of chalets that is **Hôtel du Village** ( ☎ 3779-1728; portsaluthotelduvillage@yahoo.fr; r with fan/air-con US$40/65; ❄ ) was getting a facelift when we visited. The rooms are airy, although you're not likely to spend much time inside since your front door opens straight onto the beach.

Stylish and immaculate rooms are the order of the day at **Auberge du Rayon Vert** ( ☎ 3713-9035; aubergedurayonvert@yahoo.fr; s/d US$79/112; ❄ ), with locally made furniture and very modern bathrooms, and the beach seconds away. The restaurant-bar is the best in Port Salut.

A decent bar-resto, **Chez Guito** (mains US$4-9; ✹ lunch, dinner), opposite Hôtel du Village, is the place to head for fish, a cold Prestige and a sweet *compas* soundtrack.

There are regular taptaps to Les Cayes (US$1, 45 minutes).

## PARC NATIONAL MACAYA & JÉRÉMIE

The cloud forest–covered mountains of Parc National Macaya contain a number of rough trails that cut through some beautiful terrain. The most challenging trek, taking four days round-trip, is to the top of Pic Macaya.

There are no facilities, and you'll need to be self-sufficient. If you're planning a trip we advise getting in touch with **Philippe Bayard** (pbayard@societeaudubonhaiti.org), president of the Société Audubon Haïti, who can advise on logistics.

Over the mountains (the road is terrible but spectacular) is the isolated port of Jérémie. It has a sleepy charm about it, and the beaches of Anse d'Azur nearby. The lovely **Auberge Inn** ( ☎ 3727-9678, 465-2207, aubergeinn@netscape.net; 6 Ave Emile Roumer; s US$45-54, d US$72-84, tr US$90-108, all incl breakfast; ❄ ▯ ) is more home than guesthouse.

Buses leave every afternoon for Port-au-Prince (US$14, 11 hours). There's also a ferry every Friday but it's very creaky and often dangerously overloaded. The quickest way out is the heavily subscribed daily flight to Port-au-Prince (US$85, 45 minutes).

# NORTHERN HAITI

If you're interested in how Haiti came to be how it is today, head for the north coast: it all happened here, and there are still many monuments left to mark out the path of history.

## CAP-HAÏTIEN
### pop 130,000

Known simply as 'Cap', Haiti's second city is a laid-back place to base yourself in to explore the north. Its streets are laid out in a grid system that makes it difficult to get lost, and the architecture of high shop fronts and balconies make it a pleasant place to wander. The faded grandeur hides the fact that under the French this was the richest port in the Caribbean.

### Information

Streets parallel to the sea are lettered A through Q, while those perpendicular are numbered 1 through 24. The wide avenue running the length of the seafront is simply called Boulevard.

There's a useful cluster of banks along Rue 10-11A. When the banks are closed, you can change money on the street outside the Universal Hotel.

**Discount Cybercafé** (Rue 14H; per hr US$1.15; ☺ 8am-8pm)

**Hôpital Justinien** ( ☎ 2262-0512, 2262-0513; Rue 17Q) Cap-Haïtien's main hospital.

**Post office** (Rue 16-17A)

**Teleco office** (Rue 17) Between Rue A and the Boulevard.

## Sights

Cap-Haïtien has few sights, although it's fun exploring the streets between the central **Place d'Armes** with the Notre Dame Cathedral, and the busy **Marché de Fer** (Iron Market; ☺ Mon-Sat). There are a few interesting gingerbread houses tucked away on Rues 15 and 16.

If you follow Boulevard north past the suburb of Carenage, you'll come across three French fort sites. The foundations of **Fort Etienne Magny** are marked by a group of cannons, followed by **Fort St Joseph**, on the edge of the cliff. If you continue north until the road peters out at Plage Rival, then continue along the sand for 400m, you'll reach **Fort Picolet**. The fort is ruined, but some quite large walls and staircases still stand, along with an array of cannons. It's a peaceful place to watch the sunset, although it's a dark walk home.

## Sleeping & Eating

All hotels listed also have good restaurants.

**Universal Hotel** ( ☎ 2262-0254; Rue 17B; r with shared bathroom US$18, with private bathroom US$22$-30; ☺ ) A large hotel with several terraces, this is definitely one of the better budget options. Rooms here are simple and clean. The management is helpful and pious too: Bible passages remind guests that the meek shall inherit the earth.

**Beau Rivage Hôtel** ( ☎ 2262-3113; beaurivage@yahoo.com; 25 Blvd de Mer; s/d US$60/80; ☺ ⌨ ) The Beau Rivage is a good recent addition to Cap's sleeping options. If some rooms are little on the small and boxy side, they're all well appointed with modern fixtures and fittings (including wi-fi).

**Hôtel Mont Joli** ( ☎ 2262-0300; www.hotelmontjoli.com; Rue B, Carenage; s/d US$78/96; ☺ ⌨ ☎ ) On a hill overlooking Cap, the Mont Joli easily has the best views in the city, and is good value for the price. Rooms are generously sized, and the hotel has an exceedingly pleasant pool and terrace to chill out on.

**Hostellerie du Roi Christophe** ( ☎ 2262-0414; Rue 24B; s/d/ste US$96/120/132; ☺ ⌨ ☎ ) This French colonial building has something of the Spanish hacienda about it. Set within lush gardens, there's an elegant central courtyard with a bar, and breezy comfortable rooms. There's wi-fi.

**Lakay** ( ☎ 2262-1442; Blvd de Mer; mains from US$8; ☺ dinner) One of the busiest restaurants in Cap-Haïtien, and it's not hard to see why. Eat alfresco and load up on generous plates of Creole food, plus a few pizzas. The atmosphere is lively, and at weekends there are often live bands (a cover charge of US$4 applies).

## Getting There & Away

For more information on international and domestic flights to and from Cap-Haïtien, see p277.

The bus station for destinations south including all points on the way to Port-au-Prince (US$12, seven hours) is at Barriére Bouteille on Rue L. If you're heading to Port-au-Prince, leave early as it's not advisable to arrive in the area of La Saline, where buses terminate, after dark. Taptaps to Milot leave from Rue Lapont; those for Cormier Plage from Rue 21Q.

## BEACHES

The road west out of Cap-Haïtien winds through the hills to the northwest of the cape. Here you'll find some of the most beautiful coastal scenery in Haiti, with lush forested hills tumbling into the Atlantic Ocean.

The road hits the north coast of the cape near the lovely beach of **Cormier Plage** and ends on the western edge of **Plage Labadie**, a small walled-off peninsula and the only place in Haiti where cruise ships visit.

**Cormier Plage Resort** ( ☎ 3528-1110; cormier@hughes.net; s/d with half board US$106/168; ☺ ⌨ ) is one of Haiti's best resorts, with a renowned seafood restaurant. A short boat-taxi hop from Labadie is **Norm's Place** (www.normsplacelabadee.com; r per person US$25; ☺ ⌨ ☎ ), a restored fort-cum-guesthouse.

Taptaps from Cap-Haïtien (US$0.75, 30 minutes) travel through Cormier Plage and terminate at Labadie.

## THE CITADELLE & SANS SOUCI

Henri Christophe's twin triumphs, the Citadelle and Sans Souci palace, are a short taptap ride from Cap-Haïtien, on the edge of the town of Milot (US$0.45, one hour).

Built in 1813 as a rival to the splendors of Versailles in France, Christophe's elegant palace of **Sans Souci** has lain abandoned since an earthquake ruined it in 1842. The years of neglect have left it partially reclaimed by the tropical environment, creating a wonderfully bizarre and evocative monument.

From Sans Souci, it's a 5km walk to the Citadelle, situated in the Parc Nationale Historique La Citadelle. If you have a vehicle, you can drive another 3.5km to a parking area at the foot of the Citadelle.

It took Christophe 15 years to build the World Heritage–listed **Citadelle**, a vast mountaintop fortress, constructed to combat another invasion by the French. It is one of the most inspiring sights in the Caribbean. The astounding structure was completed in 1820, having employed up to 20,000 people, many of whom died during the arduous task. With 4m-thick walls that reach heights of 40m, the fortress was impenetrable. The views are breathtaking.

Combined entrance tickets (US$5) are sold from an office close to Sans Souci. If you wish to ascend by horse, the rate is US$10 per horse. The sight of a foreigner invariably attracts a throng of would-be guides and horse-wranglers eager for your custom so be prepared for some hassle.

In Milot, the **Lakou Lakay** ( ☎ 2262-5189, 3667-6070; meals US$10) cultural center is building accommodation, and welcomes lunch guests (call ahead) with drumming, dancing and a huge Creole feast.

# DIRECTORY

## ACCOMMODATIONS

Accommodations aren't fantastic value in Haiti. There are few budget hotels aimed at foreigners, and those at the cheapest end frequently double up as brothels. A decent budget hotel weighs in at around US$40; a midrange hotel should cost about US$70, for which you should get hot water, air-con and a decent electricity supply. Room standards can be highly variable. Port-au-Prince has the best choice, from good international standard hotels to cheap Christian-run guesthouses that can be excellent value.

Many hotels add an electricity surcharge of US$5 to US$10 to the daily rate, included in the prices listed here. Midrange and top-end rates also include the 10% government tax added to the bill.

## ACTIVITIES

While not as developed as in other parts of the Caribbean, Haiti still has some great opportunities for snorkeling and scuba diving. The Côte des Arcadins has the best sites, including Amani, near St-Marc, where a wall descends to the home of the elephant's ear, believed to be the world's largest sea sponge. On the north coast, sites near the beach resort of Cormier Plage also offer rich diving possibilities.

Haiti's mountainous terrain lends itself well to hiking. A short drive from Port-au-Prince, the Parc National La Visite (p270) offers good trekking country, with superb views and cool pine forests to explore, along with many high-altitude bird species. Birders will also be amply rewarded by a visit to Trou Caïman (p270) and the wild Parc National Macaya (p272).

## BOOKS

*Libeté: A Haiti Anthology*, edited by Charles Arthur and Michael Dash, is an excellent primer on Haitian history, society, culture and politics, collecting writings on the country from Colombus to the present day.

Full of vivid detail and meticulous portraits, Ian Thomson's *Bonjour Blanc* covers the author's often hair-raising travels through Haiti during the turmoil of the early 1990s.

Almost every visitor to Haiti reads Graham Greene's *The Comedians* at some stage. Set in Haiti during the reign of Papa Doc Duvalier, it's a somber and acid potrayal of life under a dictatorship.

## BUSINESS HOURS

Banks are usually open from 8:30am to 1pm weekdays, with larger branches also open from 2pm to 5pm weekdays. Shops and offices usually open at 7am and close at 4pm weekdays, often closing earlier on Friday; most shops are also open on Saturday. Government offices are open 7am to 4pm weekdays, closing for an hour at midday.

Local restaurants open for food around 8am, with lunchtime being the busy period; they generally close around 9pm. More expensive restaurants keep more traditional hours; they often close in the afternoon, but are open as late as 11pm. Many restaurants are closed on Sundays.

## DANGERS & ANNOYANCES

Haiti has rarely enjoyed a good media image abroad. Poverty and regular political turmoil play their part, and many governments currently advise against travel to the country.

The presence of UN soldiers has done much to bring stability to Haiti, especially in dealing with the gang and kidnapping problem. But always keep your ear to the ground for current developments before traveling – trouble generally occurs around elections, although it's incredibly rare for foreigners to get caught up in it. Avoid demonstrations, and if you come across one, turn in the opposite direction.

A weak state and high poverty levels can foster street crime. Take advantage of hotel safes and don't carry anything you're not willing to lose (or money in your back pocket).

For all this, the main annoyance travelers are likely to face are the poor electricity supply and crazy traffic. Beggars can be persistent in some places, and at tourist spots such as the Citadelle expect persistent attention from faux guides. Try to discourage them before you set off – their only function seems to be to tell you how much tip you're going to have to pay at the end – as it's very hard to not pay them after they've run up a mountain alongside you.

Finally, while taking care to be sensible, it's important not to get too hung up on Haiti's bad name. Many travelers fear the worst and avoid the country; those who do make it here are more likely to come away with positive impressions rather than horror stories.

## EMBASSIES & CONSULATES

All the embassies and consulates listed here are in Port-au-Prince or Pétionville. Australia, New Zealand and Ireland do not have diplomatic representation in Haiti.

**Brazil** ( ☎ 2256-6206; fax 2256-6206; 168 Rue Darguin, Place Boyer, Pétionville)

**Canada** ( ☎ 2249-9000; fax 2249-9920; between Delmas 75-76, Rte de Delmas, Port-au-Prince)

**Cuba** ( ☎ 2256-3811; fax 2257-8566; 3 Rue Marion, Pétionville)

**Dominican Republic** ( ☎ 2257-9215; fax 2257-0568; 121 Ave Pan Américaine, Pétionville)

**France** ( ☎ 2222-0951; fax 2223-9858; 51 Rue Capois, Port-au-Prince)

**Germany** ( ☎ 2256-4131; fax 2257-4131; 2 Impasse Claudinette, Bois Moquette, Pétionville)

**Japan** ( ☎ 2245-5875; fax 2245-834; 2 Impasse Tulipe, Croix Desprez, Port-au-Prince)

**Netherlands** ( ☎ 2222-0955; fax 2222-0955; Rue Belleville, Parc Shodecosa, Port-au-Prince) Off Rte Nationale 1.

**Spain** ( ☎ 2245-4411; fax 2245-4410; 54 Rue Pacot, Port-au-Prince)

**UK** (Hotel Montana, Rue F Cardoza, Port-au-Prince) Currently closed, but may be reopened during the lifetime of this book. It's off Ave Pan Américaine.

**USA** Rue Oswald Durand ( ☎ 2223-0989, 2223-8853, 2223-9324, 2223-7011; fax 2223-5515; 104 Rue Oswald Durand, Port-au-Prince); Blvd Harry Truman ( ☎ 2222-0220/69; fax 2223-1641; Bicentenaire, Blvd Harry Truman, Port-au-Prince),

**Venezuela** ( ☎ 2222-0971; fax 2222-3949; 2 Cité de l'Exposition, Blvd Harry Truman, Port-au-Prince)

## FESTIVALS & EVENTS

Carnival is huge in Port-au-Prince. The Jacmel celebrations are equally popular, and are held a week before to avoid clashing. Also watch out for the following Vodou festivals:

**Soukri** Held on January 6 near Gonaïves.

**Souvenance** Held on Good Friday near Gonaïves.

**Saut d'Eau pilgrimage** Held on July 16 at Ville-Bonheur.

**Fet Gédé** Late at night, in cemeteries across the country, on November 1 and 2.

## HOLIDAYS

The following are public holidays in Haiti:

**Independence Day** January 1

**Ancestors' Day** January 2

**Carnival** January/February (three days before Ash Wednesday)

**Good Friday** March/April

**Agriculture and Labor Day** May 1

**Flag and University Day** May 18

**Anniversary of Jean-Jacques Dessalines' Death** October 17

HAITI

**Anniversary of Toussaint Louverture's Death**
November 1
**Anniversary of the Battle of Vertières** November 18
**Christmas Day** December 25

## INTERNET ACCESS

Getting online isn't a problem, and internet cafés open and close with reckless abandon. Prices range from US$0.80 to US$3 per hour. Cheap places don't run generators, making them highly susceptible to the regular power cuts. If you're bringing a laptop, top-end (and some midrange) hotels often provide wi-fi access.

## INTERNET RESOURCES

**Haiti Info** (www.haiti-info.com) Has Haitian resources and a good news wire service.
**Haiti Innovation** (www.haitiinnovation.org) Runs an interesting commentary on the state of development and aid in Haiti.
**Haiti Support Group** (http://haitisupport.gn.apc.org) A good place to start for Haitian resources

## LANGUAGE

The language of law, government and culture is French, although only 10% of the population speak it; everyone else speaks Creole, a blend of European and West African languages evolved from Haiti's slave past. Much Creole vocabulary is borrowed from French.

## MEDICAL SERVICES

Port-au-Prince has the best medical facilities and a few international-standard hospitals, but there are decent pharmacies across the country. A foreign-aid program means that there are many Cuban doctors in Haiti.

## MONEY

The official currency is the gourde, and there are 100 centimes to 1 gourde. US dollars are also widely accepted for large purchases. The gourde used to be tied to the US dollar at a rate of one to five, with the result that HTG5 is universally known as one Haitian dollar. When buying something, always check whether people are quoting the price in gourdes or Haitian dollars.

Don't bother bringing traveler's checks as they're near impossible to change. There are ATMs in Port-au-Prince, but they can be unreliable (those in Pétionville tend to be better), so always make sure you have some US dollars as backup. Large businesses, most midrange and all top-end hotels will accept credit cards.

## TELEPHONE

Haiti's country code is ☎ 509, but you just dial the eight-digit local number in Haiti. To call from overseas, dial your country's international dialing code + ☎ 509 + the local calling number. We've included only the eight-digit local number in Haiti listings in this chapter. To reach an international operator, dial ☎ 00; for information on international calls, dial ☎ 00-09.

Landlines in Haiti can be very unreliable and everyone uses cell (mobile) phones; a GSM SIM card for networks like Digicel and Voila will cost around US$20. You can make calls from Teleco offices, or the ubiquitous phone 'stands' – usually a youth on the street with a cell phone that looks like a regular desk phone.

## TOURIST INFORMATION

Haiti's moribund tourist industry offers no useful information to visitors. The official **Maison de Tourisme** ( ☎ 2222-8659; Rue Capois, Champ de Mars, Port-au-Prince) was closed when we visited, with no known plans to reopen it.

## TOURS

Two excellent operators offer countrywide tours and professional fixer services:
**Tour Haiti** ( ☎ 3510-2223; www.tourhaiti.net; 115 Rue Faubert, Pétionville)
**Voyages Lumière** ( ☎ 2249-6177, 3557-0753)

## VISAS

Unless you're a citizen of the Dominican Republic, Colombia, Panama or China, no visa is needed to visit Haiti, just a passport valid for six months and a return ticket. Your entry stamp entitles your to stay for up to 90 days. You'll also be given a green entry card to be produced on departure from Haiti - don't lose this.

---

**EMERGENCY NUMBERS**

- **Ambulance** ☎ 118
- **Fire** ☎ 117
- **Police** ☎ 114

# TRANSPORTATION

## GETTING THERE & AWAY

### Entering Haiti

All foreign visitors must have a valid passport to enter Haiti. Be sure you have room for both an entry and exit stamp, and that your passport is valid for at least six months beyond your planned travel dates.

### Air

Haiti's main hub is **Aéroport International Toussaint Louverture** (PAP; ☎ 2250-1120) in Port-au-Prince, although a few flights also connect Cap-Haïtien to Florida. Horror stories about hassles and bribery at Port-au-Prince's airport are a thing of the past, although arrivals can sometimes be a little chaotic.

The main airlines flying into Haiti:

**American Airlines** ( ☎ 2246-0100, 3510-7010; www.aa.com) Miami, Fort Lauderdale, New York

**Air Canada** ( ☎ 2250-0441/2; www.aircanada.ca) Montreal.

**Air France** ( ☎ 2222-1078, 2222-4262; www.airfrance.com) Miami, Paris, Pointe-à-Pitre

**Lynx Air** ( ☎ 3513-2597, 2257-9956; www.lynxair.com) Fort Lauderdale

**Spirit Airlines** ( ☎ 800-772-7117; www.spiritair.com) Fort Lauderdale

### Land

There are three points where you can cross from Haiti into the Dominican Republic. One is near Malpasse/Jimaní in the south, on the road that links Port-au-Prince to Santo Domingo. A second crossing point is near Ouanaminthe/Dajabón in the north; it's on a road that connects Cap-Haïtien and Santiago. The third border crossing is at Belladère/Elías Piña. These crossings close at 6pm.

**Caribe Tours** ( ☎ 2257-9379; cnr Rues Clerveaux & Gabartt, Pétionville) and **Terra Bus** ( ☎ 2257-2153; Ave Pan Américaine, Pétionville) have daily coach departures to Santo Domingo in the Dominican Republic (US$40, nine hours). From Cap-Haïtien, **Ayido Tours** ( ☎ 3729-8711, 3556-3082) runs a direct coach service to Santiago in the Dominican Republic every Wednesday and Saturday from the Hôtel Mont Joli.

## GETTING AROUND

### Air

**Caribintair** ( ☎ 250-2031/2; caribintair@accesshaiti.com), **Tortug Air** ( ☎ 2250-2555/6; tortugair@yahoo.com) and **Tropical Airways** ( ☎ 2256-3626/7) link Port-au-Prince to several departmental capitals, including Cap-Haïtien, Les Cayes, Jacmel and Jérémie. Haiti's size means that flights are short (just 15 minutes to Jacmel), saving hours on bad roads. The planes are small and demand can be high, so book as far in advance as possible. One-way tickets usually cost around the US$85 mark.

### Boat

There are quite a few islands and remote areas around Haiti accessible only by ferry. Routes include Port-au-Prince to Jérémie and Côte des Arcadins to Île de la Gonâve. Boats are rarely comfortable and often dangerously overcrowded. In some areas, such as Labidie and Île-à-Vache, small boats operate as water taxis. Fix the price before you board, as the owner may try to charge for the whole boat.

### Bus & Taptap

Haiti's buses are big and seemingly indestructible affairs, and they need to be. They're cheap too – even the longest 12-hour trip gives change from US$15. There are no timetables; buses leave when filled. A taptap is more likely to be a minibus or pickup truck, used for travel within cities, or hopping between towns. Bus and taptap stations are sprawling conglomerations of vehicles and people and market stalls: Haiti in microcosm.

### Car & Motorcycle

Driving in Haiti is an adventure sport. Roads can be terrible, traffic signs are rare, and 'might is right' is the main rule. If you do drive, you will need an International Driving Permit or a current license from your home country.

There are rental companies in Port-au-Prince, mostly near the airport. Fees are around US$70 per day for a saloon, and US$150 per day for a 4WD, the latter being better able to cope with the road conditions.

### Taxi

Port-au-Prince and Cap-Haïtien have collective taxis called *publiques*, which run along set routes and charge around HTG25 (US$0.75) per trip. You can spot them by the red ribbon on the mirror – if the driver takes it off he's treating you as a private commission, and you'll have to negotiate the fee.

There a motorcycle taxis (moto-taxis) everywhere, with a trip rarely costing more than about HTG20 (US$0.60).

# Dominican Republic

The Dominican Republic (DR) is a land of contrasts – the physical kind, like the highest peak and the lowest point in the Caribbean, and the more metaphorical kind, like that between the urban street life of Santo Domingo and the rural villages only a short drive away.

Santo Domingo, or 'La Capital' as it's typically called, is to Dominicans what New York is to Americans, a collage of cultures; or what Havana is to Cubans, a vibrant beating heart that fuels the entire country. It's also a living museum, offering the sight of New World firsts scattered around the charming cobblestone streets of the Zona Colonial.

The DR is also famous for the large all-inclusive resorts that dominate much of the country's prime beachfront real estate. However, the result is less like the high-rise congestion of Cancun or Miami and more like low-slung retirement communities, albeit ones populated by families, couples and singles of all ages looking for a hassle-free holiday. Beyond the gated luxury enclaves, the roads lead inland past vast sugar plantations and through small villages.

To get away from the get-away, travelers head to the Península de Samaná, where the European vibe is as strong as an espresso, and where escape is the operative word. Cabarete on the North Coast has winds which draw adrenaline junkies from around the world. And for the anti-Caribbean experience head to the popular mountain retreats of Jarabacoa and Constanza – places where bathing suits are out and sweaters are in.

## FAST FACTS

- **Area** 48,717 sq km
- **Capital** Santo Domingo de Guzmán
- **Country code** ☎ 809
- **Departure tax** Air: up to US$20 depending on length of stay; land: US$20
- **Famous for** Baseball, cockfighting, merengue, cigars, Columbus landing here first
- **Language** Spanish
- **Money** Dominican Republic peso (RD$); RD$100 = US$2.96 = €1.90 = UK£1.50
- **Official name** República Dominicana
- **People** Dominicans
- **Phrase** Siempre a su orden (you're welcome); gua-gua (bus)
- **Population** 9 million
- **Visa** Issued on arrival; see p320

# HIGHLIGHTS

- **Zona Colonial** (p285) Wander the 500-year-old cobblestone backstreets of the Zona Colonial in Santo Domingo – not much different from the 16th-century version of the city
- **Bávaro & Punta Cana** (p296) Enjoy the miles and miles of beautiful beach and organized beachfront fun
- **Whale-watching** (p301) Feel small – very small – after witnessing the majesty of 30-ton humpbacks breaching and diving on a whale-watching trip from Samaná
- **Kitesurfing** (p311) Strap yourself to the board and pray – for good winds and your safety – and get swept up in the thrill of skimming full speed across the waves
- **Playa Frontón** (p304) Snorkel undisturbed around some of the best reefs the country has to offer

# ITINERARIES

- **Five Days** Spend a day in Santo Domingo before zipping up to Samaná for whale-watching, and spend some beach time at Las Galeras.
- **Ten Days** First follow the five-day itinerary, spending a couple of days in Santo Domingo. Then head to Jarabacoa and Cabarete for some adventure tours and Los Haitises National Park for a tour of ancient cave paintings.
- **Two Weeks** Do the 10-day tour, then end your stay with three or four days at an all-inclusive in Bávaro or Punta Cana.

# CLIMATE & WHEN TO GO

Except in the central mountains, temperatures don't vary much in the Dominican Republic, averaging a summery 81°F (28°C) to 87°F (31°C) in most places for much of the year. Tropical humidity can make the temperatures feel higher, though sea breezes help mitigate the effect. The rainy season is May to October, though in Samaná and on the north coast it can last until December. August and September constitute hurricane season.

The main foreign tourist seasons are December to February and July to August and Semana Santa (the week before Easter). Expect higher prices and more crowded beaches at these times – Semana Santa is especially busy. February has great weather and you can enjoy Carnaval and the whales in Samaná. November is good, too – you'll miss the whales but catch baseball season.

# HISTORY
## First Arrivals
Before Christopher Columbus arrived, the indigenous Taínos (meaning 'Friendly People') lived on the island now known as Hispaniola. Taínos gave the world sweet potatoes, peanuts, guava, pineapple and tobacco – even the word 'tobacco' is Taíno in origin. Yet the Taínos themselves were wiped out by Spanish diseases and slavery. Of the 400,000 Taínos that lived on Hispaniola at the time of European arrival, fewer than 1000 were still alive 30 years later. None exist today.

## Independence & Occupation
Two colonies grew on Hispaniola, one Spanish and the other French. Both brought thousands of African slaves to work the land. In 1804, after a 70-year struggle, the French colony gained independence. Haiti, the Taíno name for the island, was the first majority-black republic in the New World.

In 1821 colonists in Santo Domingo declared their independence from Spain. Haiti, which had long aspired to unify the island, promptly invaded its neighbor and occupied it for more than two decades. But Dominicans never accepted Haitian rule and on February 27, 1844, Juan Pablo Duarte – considered the father of the country – led a bloodless coup and reclaimed Dominican autonomy. The country resubmitted to Spanish rule shortly thereafter, but became independent for good in 1864.

The young country endured one disreputable *caudillo* (military leader) after the other. In 1916 US President Woodrow Wilson sent the marines to the Dominican Republic, ostensibly to quell a coup attempt, but they ended up occupying the country for eight years. Though imperialistic, this occupation succeeded in stabilizing the DR.

## The Rise of the Caudillo
Rafael Leonidas Trujillo, a former security guard and the eventual chief of the Dominican national police, muscled his way into the presidency in February 1930 and dominated the country until his assassination in 1961. He implemented a brutal system of repression, killing and imprisoning political opponents. Though he was himself partly black, Trujillo

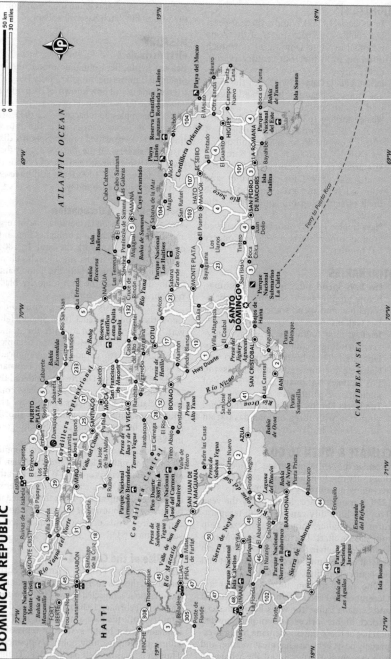

# DOMINICAN REPUBLIC

was deeply racist and xenophobic. In October 1937 he ordered the extermination of Haitians along the international border. In a matter of days some 20,000 Haitians were hacked to death with machetes and their bodies dumped into the ocean.

During these years Trujillo used his government to amass a personal fortune by establishing monopolies that he and his wife controlled. By 1934 he was the richest man on the island. To this day there are many Dominicans who remember Trujillo's rule with a certain amount of fondness and nostalgia, in part because Trujillo did develop the economy. Factories were opened, a number of grandiose infrastructure and public works projects were carried out, bridges and highways were built and peasants were given state land to cultivate.

## Caudillo Redux

Joaquín Balaguer was Trujillo's puppet president at the time of Trujillo's assassination. Civil unrest and another US occupation followed Trujillo's death, but Balaguer eventually regained the presidency, to which he clung fiercely for the next 12 years. And like his mentor, Balaguer remained a major political force long after he gave up official control. In 1986 he became president again, despite frail health and blindness. He was as repressive as ever and his economic policies sent the peso tumbling.

Dominicans whose savings had evaporated protested and were met with violence from the national police. Many fled to the USA. By the end of 1990, 12% of the Dominican population – 900,000 people – had moved to New York.

After rigging the 1990 and 1994 elections, the military had grown weary of Balaguer's rule and he agreed to cut his last term short, hold elections and, most importantly, not run as a candidate. But it wouldn't be his last campaign – he would run once more at the age of 92, winning 23% of the vote in the 2000 presidential election. Thousands would mourn his death two years later, despite the fact that he prolonged the Trujillo-style dictatorship for decades. His most lasting legacy may be the Faro a Colón (see p289), an enormously expensive monument to the discovery of the Americas that drained Santo Domingo of electricity whenever the lighthouse was turned on.

### HOW MUCH?

- Taxi from Las Américas airport to Santo Domingo US$25 to US$35
- Liter of bottled water US$1
- Day of diving in Las Terrenas (gear included) US$35 to US$45
- Meal of fresh fish in a touristy restaurant US$10 to US$17
- Gallon of gas US$4.50 to US$5.50

## Breaking with the Past

The Dominican people signaled their desire for change in electing Leonel Fernández, a 42-year-old lawyer who grew up in New York City, as president in the 1996 presidential election; he edged out three-time candidate José Francisco Peña Gómez in a runoff. But would too much change come too quickly? Shocking the nation, Fernández forcibly retired two-dozen generals, encouraged his defense minister to submit to questioning by the civilian attorney general and fired the defense minister for insubordination – all in a single week. In the four years of his presidency, he oversaw strong economic growth, privatization and lowered inflation, unemployment and illiteracy – although endemic corruption remained pervasive.

Hipólito Mejía, a former tobacco farmer, succeeded Fernández in 2000 and immediately cut spending and increased fuel prices – not exactly the platform he ran on. The faltering US economy and World Trade Center attacks ate into Dominican exports as well as cash remittances and foreign tourism. Corruption scandals involving the civil service, unchecked spending, electricity shortages and several bank failures, which cost the government in the form of huge bailouts for depositors, all spelled doom for Mejías' reelection chances.

Familiar faces appear again and again in Dominican politics and Fernandez returned to the national stage by handily defeating Mejía in the 2004 presidential elections. Though he's widely considered competent and even forward thinking, it's not uncommon to hear people talk about him rather unenthusiastically as a typical politician beholden to special interests. The more cynical claim that the Fernandez administration is allied with corrupt business and government officials who perpetuate a patronage system different from Trujillo's rule in name only. In 2007 the faltering US economy, the devastation wrought by Tropical Storm Noel, the threat of avian bird flu and continued tension with Haiti provided challenges to Fernandez's reelection campaign.

## THE CULTURE

History is alive and well in the Dominican Republic. With a past filled by strong-arm dictators and corrupt politicians, the average Dominican approaches the present with a healthy skepticism – why should things change now? Whether it's the Santo Domingo taxi driver's outspoken disbelief that the metro will ever function or the local fisherman's acceptance that the new resort marina is going to take away his livelihood, Dominicans have learned to live through hardships. What is extraordinary to the traveler is that despite this there's a general equanimity, or at the very least an ability to look on the bright side of things. Sure, people complain, they know unfairness and exploitation when they see it, but on the whole they're able to appreciate the good things: family, togetherness, music and laughter. It's not a cliché to say that Dominicans are willing to hope for the best and expect the worst – with a fortitude and patience that isn't common.

In general an accepting and welcoming culture, Dominicans' negative attitudes towards Haitian immigration has only become more pronounced as the country has received more and more international criticism over its treatment of the nearly one million Haitians in the DR. 'If the country could just solve the "Haiti problem" things would work out' is not an unusual sentiment to hear. By the end of 2007 there were 200 UN soldiers, mostly from other Caribbean countries, to help buttress the DR army's attempts to stop the flow of drugs and arms across the Haitian border. In early 2008 there were increased tensions along the border over accusations of cattle rustling and reprisals; and Dominican chickens being turned away because of fears over avian flu.

Almost a quarter of Dominicans live in Santo Domingo, which is without question the country's political, economic and social center. But beyond the capital, much of the DR is distinctly rural and a large percentage of Dominicans still live by agriculture (or by fishing, along the coast). This is evident if you drive into the DR's vast fertile interior, where you'll see cows and horses grazing alongside the roads, tractors ploughing large fields and trucks and *burros* (donkeys) loaded down with produce.

Dominican families, typical of the stereotypical Latin American kind, are large and very close-knit. Children are expected to stay close to home and help care for their parents as they grow older. That so many young Dominicans go to the United States creates a unique stress in their families. While Americans and Europeans commonly leave home to live and work in another city, this is still troubling for many Dominicans, especially in the older generation – it's no surprise that Dominicans living abroad send so much money home.

The DR is a Catholic country, though not to the degree practiced in other Latin American countries – the churches are well maintained but often empty – and Dominicans have a liberal attitude toward premarital and recreational sex. This does not extend to homosexuality, though, which is still fairly taboo. Machismo is strong here but, like in merengue dancing, many Dominicans experience the traditional roles of men and women as more complementary than confrontational, as naturally separate spheres of influence. And the physical, mainly in the way a woman looks or dances, is appreciated unashamedly by both sexes.

## SPORTS
### Baseball

This national pastime is in season from October to January. There are six professional teams – Licey and Escojido, both from Santo Domingo; the Águilas from Santiago; the Gigantes from San Francisco; the Estrellas from San Pedro de Macoris; and the Azuqueros from La Romana – and an untold number of formal and semiformal teams around the country. Many Dominican players are stars in the US major leagues, which Dominican fans also follow religiously. The official website for the professional **Dominican winter league** (www .lidom.com) contains game schedules and news from around the league.

### Cockfighting

Cockfighting rings (*galleras*) look like mini sports arenas or ancient coliseums, which is appropriate since Dominicans approach these brutal contests between specially bred roosters as events worthy of the same enthusiasm. There are around 1500 official *galleras* throughout the country, but by far the most prestigious – and safe – is the Coliseo Gallístico Alberto Bonetti Burgos (p294), which regularly hosts international competitions. Gambling on fights is part of the sport, all conducted under a strict honor code. That said, some rings are decidedly seedy and tourists should be alert for trouble.

Perhaps it is no surprise that cockfighting – specifically the roosters' intensity and willingness to fight to the death – would resonate in a country that has endured so much civil strife and outside manipulation. Indeed, the fighting cock is the symbol of a number of political parties and social organizations. For those reasons, many travelers see cockfighting as a window into Dominican culture. Others cannot reconcile a night at the *gallera* with the concept of responsible tourism. It is impossible to argue that cockfighting is not a form of cruelty to animals – after all, the point is for one animal to kill the other, sometimes slowly and agonizingly, for the sake of entertainment and monetary gain. Both are justifiable points of view.

## ARTS
### Literature
Only a few Dominican novels have been translated into English. Viriato Sención's *They Forged the Signature of God* follows three seminary students in the DR suffering oppression at the hands of both the state and the church. Ten years after publishing the short story collection *Drown,* Junot Diaz received critical acclaim for his 2007 novel *The Wondrous Life of Oscar Wao,* a stylistically inventive story of a self-professed Dominican nerd in New Jersey and the tragic history of his family in the DR. Less well known than Diaz's novel, but maybe a more devastating picture of the Dominican diaspora's rejection of the conventional American Dream is Maritza Pérez's *Geographies of Home. In the Time of the Butterflies* is an award-winning novel by Julia Álvarez about three sisters slain for their part in a plot to overthrow Rafael Trujillo. Also by Álvarez is *How the García Girls Lost Their Accents* describing an emigrant Dominican family in New York. Other well-known contemporary Dominican writers include José Goudy Pratt, Jeannette Miller and Ivan García Guerra.

### Music
Merengue is truly the national music and from the moment you arrive you'll hear it being played on the bus, at the beach, in the taxi, everywhere – and usually at high volume. Top Dominican merengue groups include Los Hermanos Rosario, Coco Band, Milly y Los Vecinos and, perhaps the biggest name of all, Juan Luis Guerra.

If merengue is the DR's urban sound, *bachata* is definitely its 'country.' This is the music of breaking up and losing out, working hard and playing even harder. Top performers include Raulín Rodríguez, Antony Santos, Luis Vargas and Leo Valdez.

## ENVIRONMENT
### The Land
If a nation's wealth could be measured by its landscape, the Dominican Republic would be the richest country in the Caribbean. Here you can reach the Caribbean's highest point – Pico Duarte at 3087m – and its lowest – Lago Enriquillo at 40m below sea level. Bisecting the country is the mighty Cordillera Central mountain range, which makes up one-third of Hispaniola's landmass. In the lowlands are a series of valleys filled with plantations of coffee, bananas, cacao, rice, tobacco and many other crops. Almost 1000 miles of coastline includes bountiful coral reefs, multitudes of tiny islands and sheltered banks where humpback whales gather to breed.

### Wildlife
Over 250 species of bird have been found in the Dominican Republic, including numerous endemics and the country is known for its humpback whales, manatees and other marine mammals. Among a rich variety of reptiles, the most interesting of all has to be the Jaragua lizard, found in 1998, which is the world's smallest terrestrial vertebrate – adults measure only 25mm.

### Environmental Issues
The Dominican Republic can easily see, in Haiti, the effects of deforestation – lack of trees and ground cover were largely to blame for the severity of flooding and mudslides that killed more than 1000 Haitians during Tropical Storm Jeanne in September 2004. The Dominican Republic has set aside large areas of forest as national parks and

scientific reserves, but illegal logging remains a problem.

The large-scale tourist development along the coast is another potential environmental problem. While a few resorts have adopted eco-friendly practices, like limited use of plastic cups and not using bleach in laundry – they are the exception, not the rule. Heavy boat traffic – not to mention the construction of piers suitable for large ships – can damage fragile coral reefs.

## FOOD & DRINK

The basis of most meals here is rice and beans, which are served separately or mixed together. Bananas and yucca are other popular starches – both are served boiled, though you will also see bananas sliced and fried (tostones) or mashed up into a dish called mangú (or mofongo if it's mixed with pork rind).

As on any island, seafood figures prominently in the national diet. Grouper and snapper are the most common dinner fish and are usually served baked or grilled with a sauce – al coco (in coconut sauce) or a la diabla (a spicy tomato-based sauce) are favorites. Other seafood dishes include a type of ceviche typically made with octopus and called pulpo a la vinaigrette.

Beef, chicken and pork are also part of Dominican cuisine, though the preparations are generally less creative than in other countries. One exception is guinea hen broiled with red wine, a popular dish in the central highlands.

Street food is limited mostly to empanadas and pastelitos (meat- or cheese-filled pastries), which are sold from carts or bus-station snack shops.

The Dominican Republic makes great fruit drinks. Batidas (smoothies) consist of crushed fruit, water, ice and several tablespoons of sugar and sometimes they also contain a little milk. Popular batidas include batida de piña (pineapple) and morir soñando (literally, 'to die dreaming'), an unlikely combination of milk and orange juice.

Other popular nonalcoholic Dominican drinks include limonada (lemonade) and mabí, a delicious drink made from the bark of the tropical liana vine.

It's tough to beat Dominican ron (rum) for quality. Dozens of local brands are available, but the big three are Brugal, Barceló and Bermudez, which all come in blanco (clear), dorado (golden) and añejo (aged) varieties.

There are a handful of locally brewed beers including Presidente, Quisqueya, Bohemia and Soberante. It's customary for friends to share a Presidente Grande – a 40oz (1.2L) bottle – that's brought to tables in a wood or plastic container with small glass cups.

# SANTO DOMINGO

**pop 2.9 million**

This is a deeply Dominican city – an obvious statement but no less true. It's where the rhythms of the country are on superdrive, where the sounds of life – domino pieces slapped on tables, backfiring mufflers and horns from chaotic traffic, merengue and bachata blasting from corner colmados – are most intense. At the heart of the city is the Zona Colonial, which contains several New World firsts – the oldest church, the oldest street, the oldest surviving fortress, and so on and so on. Amid the cobblestone streets, reminiscent of the French Quarter in New Orleans, it would be easy to forget Santo Domingo is on the Caribbean – if it weren't for the heat and humidity.

But this is an intensely urban city, home not only to colonial-era relics but to hot clubs packed with trendy 20-somethings, museums and cultural institutions (the best of their kind in the DR), and business people taking long lunches at elegant restaurants. Santo Domingo somehow manages to embody the contradictions central to the Dominican experience: a living museum; a metropolis crossed with a seaside resort; and a business, political and media center with a laid-back casual spirit.

## ORIENTATION

For travelers, the Zona Colonial (Hotel Zone) is the heart of Santo Domingo, where most of the museums, churches and other historical sites are located, as well as hotels, restaurants and services. El Conde, the pedestrian mall running the length of the Zona Colonial, is the modern commercial center of the neighborhood. Just west of the Zona Colonial is Gazcue, a residential area where the hotels are better value but the location less ideal. South of Gazcue, the Malecón (officially called Av George Washington) is the broad waterfront avenue where Santo Domingo's high-rise hotels, nightclubs and casinos are located.

## Maps
**Mapas GAAR** ( ☎ 809-688-8004; www.mapasgaar.com
.do; Espaillat; ☺ 8:30am-5:30pm Mon-Fri) This is Santo
Domingo's best map store, located on the
3rd floor of an aging office building near
El Conde.

# INFORMATION
## Bookstores
**Editorial Duarte** ( ☎ 809-689-4832; cnr Arzobispo
Meriño & Mercedes; ☺ 8am-7pm Mon-Fri, 8am-6pm Sat)
This dusty shop in the Zona Colonial has a good selection of
Spanish-language fiction books, foreign-language
dictionaries and maps.
**Librería Cuesta** ( ☎ 809-473-4020; www.cuestalibros
.com; cnr Av 27 de Febrero & Abraham Lincoln; ☺ 9am-
9pm Mon-Sat, 10am-3pm Sun) This modern, two-story
Dominican version of Barnes & Noble is easily the nicest
and largest bookstore in the city.

## Cultural Centers
**Casa de Teatro** ( ☎ 809-689-3430; www.arte-latino.com/
casadeteatro; Arzobispo Meriño 110; admission varies;
☺ 9am-6pm, 8pm-3am Mon-Sat) Housed in a renovated
colonial building, this fantastic arts complex features a gallery with rotating exhibits by Dominican artists, an open-air
bar and performance space.
**Centro Cultural Español** (Spanish Cultural Center;
☎ 809-686-8212; www.ccesd.org in Spanish; cnr Av
Arzobispo Meriño & Arzobispo Portes; admission free;
☺ 10am-9pm Tue-Sun) This institute regularly hosts art
exhibits, film festivals and musical concerts.

## Emergency
**Politur** (Tourist Police; ☎ 809-689-6464; cnr El Conde &
José Reyes; ☺ 24hr)

## Internet Access, Telephone & Fax
**Abel Brawn's Internet World** ( ☎ 809-333-5604;
Plaza Lomba, 2nd fl; per hr US$1; ☺ 9am-9pm Mon-Sat,
10am-4pm Sat) Fast internet access as well as international
phone and fax service.
**Caribae** ( ☎ 809-685-2142; General Luperón 106; per hr
US$1.40; ☺ 9am-9pm Mon-Sat) Quiet internet café.
**Centro de Internet** ( ☎ 809-238-5149; Av Independencia 201; per hr US$1; ☺ 8:30am-9pm Mon-Sat, 8:30am-
3pm Sun) Internet and call center in Gazcue.
**Codetel Centro de Comunicaciones** ( ☎ 809-221-
4249; El Conde 202; ☺ 8am-9:30pm) Large call center
and has internet (per hr US$1) to boot.

## Medical Services
**Clínica Abreu** ( ☎ 809-688-4411; cnr Av Independencia
& Burgos; ☺ 24hr) Widely regarded as the best hospital
in the city.

**Farmacia San Judas** ( ☎ 809-685-8165; cnr Av Independencia & Pichardo; ☺ 24hr) Free delivery.
**Hospital Padre Billini** ( ☎ 809-221-8272; Av Sánchez
btwn Arzobispo Nouel & Padre Billini; ☺ 24hr) The closest
public hospital to the Zona Colonial.

## Money
**Ban Reservas** (cnr Isabel la Católica & Las Mercedes)
**Banco Popular** (cnr Av Abraham Lincoln & Gustavo Mejia
Ricart)
**Banco Progreso** (cnr Av Independencia & Socorro Sánchez)
**Scotiabank** (cnr Isabel la Católica & Las Mercedes)

## Post
**Post office** (Isabel la Católica; ☺ 8am-5pm Mon-Fri,
9am-noon Sat) Facing Parque Colón.

## Tourist Information
**Tourist office** ( ☎ 809-686-3858; Isabel la Católica 103;
☺ 9am-3pm Mon-Fri) Limited selection of brochures and
maps at this office, which faces Parque Colón. English and
French spoken.

## Travel Agencies
**Colonial Tour & Travel** ( ☎ 809-688-5285; www
.colonialtours.com.do; Arzobispo Mériño 209; ☺ 8:30am-
1pm & 2:30-5:30pm Mon-Fri, 8:30am-noon Sat)
**Giada Tours & Travel** ( ☎ 809-686-6994, 809-264-
3704; giada@verizon.net.do; Hostal Duque de Wellington,
Av Independencia 304; ☺ 8:30am-6pm Mon-Fri,
9am-2pm Sat)

# DANGERS & ANNOYANCES
The Zona Colonial is generally very safe to
walk around, day or night, though be alert
for pickpockets in crowded areas. On the
Malecón be extra cautious if you've been
drinking or are leaving a club or casino especially late. Like in any big city, stick to
well-lit and well-trafficked areas as much
as possible and be inconspicuous with your
cash, jewelry, cameras etc.

# SIGHTS & ACTIVITIES
Most of Santo Domingo's historical and interesting sites are in the Zona Colonial and are
easily explored on foot. Sites further afield,
like the Faro a Colón and Jardín Botánico,
are best reached by taxi.

## Zona Colonial
For those fascinated by the origin of the 'New
World,' by the dramatic and complicated
story of the first encounter between native
people of the Americas and Europeans, the

**DOMINICAN REPUBLIC**

# CENTRAL SANTO DOMINGO (ZONA COLONIAL)

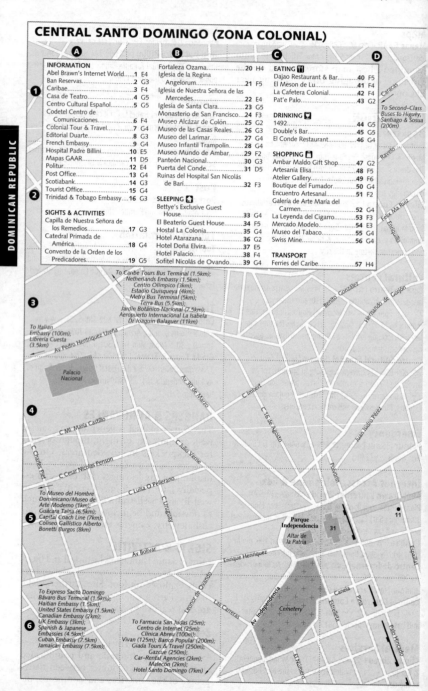

**INFORMATION**
Abel Brawn's Internet World......1 E4
Ban Reservas...........................2 G3
Caribae...................................3 F4
Casa de Teatro........................4 G5
Centro Cultural Español............5 G4
Codetel Centro de
   Comunicaciones....................6 F4
Colonial Tour & Travel..............7 G4
Editorial Duarte.......................8 G3
French Embassy.......................9 G4
Hospital Padre Billini.............10 E5
Mapas GAAR........................11 D5
Politur................................12 E4
Post Office...........................13 G4
Scotiabank..........................14 G3
Tourist Office.......................15 G4
Trinidad & Tobago Embassy...16 G3

**SIGHTS & ACTIVITIES**
Capilla de Nuestra Señora de
   los Remedios......................17 G3
Catedral Primada de
   América.............................18 G4
Convento de la Orden de los
   Predicadores......................19 G5

Fortaleza Ozama......................20 H4
Iglesia de la Regina
   Angelorum..........................21 F5
Iglesia de Nuestra Señora de las
   Mercedes............................22 E4
Iglesia de Santa Clara.............23 G5
Monasterio de San Francisco...24 F3
Museo Alcázar de Colón.........25 G2
Museo de las Casas Reales.....26 G3
Museo del Larimar..................27 G4
Museo Infantil Trampolín........28 G4
Museo Mundo de Ambar.......29 F2
Panteón Nacional...................30 G3
Puerta del Conde...................31 D5
Ruinas del Hospital San Nicolás
   de Bari..............................32 F3

**SLEEPING**
Bettye's Exclusive Guest
   House................................33 G4
El Beaterío Guest House.........34 F5
Hostal La Colonia..................35 G4
Hotel Atarazana.....................36 G2
Hotel Doña Elvira..................37 E5
Hotel Palacio........................38 F4
Sofitel Nicolás de Ovando.......39 G4

**EATING**
Dajao Restaurant & Bar..........40 F5
El Meson de Lu.....................41 F4
La Cafetera Colonial...............42 F4
Pat'e Palo............................43 G2

**DRINKING**
1492...................................44 G5
Double's Bar.........................45 G5
El Conde Restaurant...............46 G4

**SHOPPING**
Ambar Maldo Gift Shop..........47 G2
Artesanía Elisa......................48 F5
Atelier Gallery.......................49 F6
Boutique del Fumador............50 G4
Encuentro Artesanal...............51 F2
Galería de Arte María del
   Carmen..............................52 G4
La Leyenda del Cigarro..........53 F3
Mercado Modelo...................54 E3
Museo del Tabaco.................55 G4
Swiss Mine...........................56 G4

**TRANSPORT**
Ferries del Caribe..................57 H4

To Caribe Tours Bus Terminal (1.5km);
Netherlands Embassy (1.5km);
Centro Olímpico (3km);
Estadio Quisqueya (4km);
Metro Bus Terminal (5km);
Terra Bus (5.5km);
Jardín Botánico Nacional (7.5km);
Aeropuerto Internacional La Isabela
Dr Joaquín Balaguer (11km)

To Italian
Embassy (100m);
Librería Cuesta
(3.5km)

Av Pedro Henríquez Ureña

Palacio
Nacional

Caracas

To Second–Class
Buses to Higüey,
Santiago & Sosua
(200m)

Ravelo

Félix Ma. Ruiz

Enriquillo

Benito González

Hernando de Gorjón

Av 30 de Marzo

C Imbert

C 15 de Agosto

Juan Isidro Pérez

C Ml. María Castillo

C Jullo Verne

C Charles Pier

C Cesar Nicolás Penson

To Museo del Hombre
Dominicano/Museo de
Arte Moderno (1km);
Guácara Taína (6.5km);
Capital Coach Line (7km);
Coliseo Gallístico Alberto
Bonetti Burgos (8km)

C Luisa O Pellerano

C Uruguay

Padorín

Parque
Independencia

Altar de
la Patria

Av Bolívar

Enrique Henríquez

To Expreso Santo Domingo
Bávaro Bus Terminal (1.5km);
Haitian Embassy (1.5km);
United States Embassy (1.5km);
Canadian Embassy (2km);
UK Embassy (3km);
Spanish & Japanese
Embassies (4.5km);
Cuban Embassy (7.5km);
Jamaican Embassy (7.5km);

Leonor de Ovando

Las Carreras

Canela

Cemetery

Pina

Estrelleta

To Farmacia San Judas (25m);
Centro de Internet (25m);
Clínica Abreu (100m);
Vivan (125m); Banco Popular (200m);
Giada Tours & Travel (250m);
Gazcue (250m);
Car–Rental Agencies (2km);
Malecón (2km);
Hotel Santo Domingo (7km)

Av Independencia

El Número

Palo Hincado

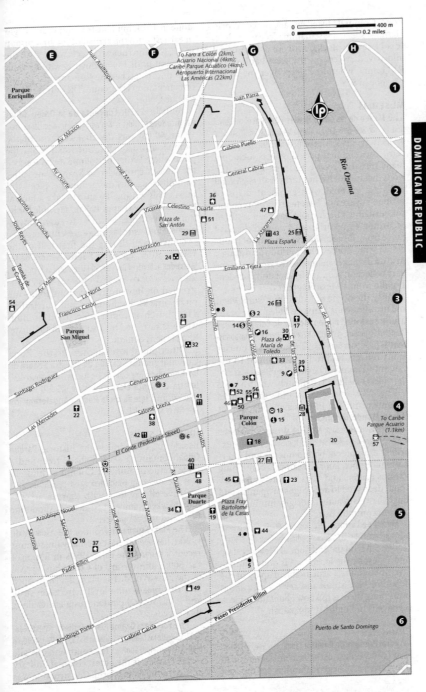

Zona Colonial, listed as a Unesco World Heritage site, is a fascinating place to explore. It is 11 square blocks, a mix of cobblestoned and paved streets on the west bank of the Rí Ozama, where the deep river meets the Caribbean Sea.

## MUSEUMS

The **Museo de las Casas Reales** (Museum of the Royal Houses; ☎ 809-682-4202; Calle de las Damas; adult/student US$1/0.15; ☼ 9am-5pm Tue-Sun), near Plaza España, showcases colonial-period objects including many treasures recovered from Spanish galleons that foundered in nearby waters. Several walls are covered with excellent maps of various voyages of European explorers and conquistadors. Each room has been restored according to its original style and displays range from Taíno artifacts to dozens of hand-blown wine bottles and period furnishings. Also on display is an impressive antique weaponry collection acquired by dictator-president Trujillo from a Mexican general.

Once the home of Columbus' son Diego and his wife, Doña María de Toledo, the beautifully restored **Museo Alcázar de Colón** (Museum Citadel of Columbus; ☎ 809-682-4750; Plaza España; admission US$2; ☼ 9am-5pm Tue-Sat, 9am-4pm Sun) houses many objects said to have belonged to the Columbus family. The building itself – if not the objects inside – is definitely worth a look.

The DR is one of the world's top sources of amber and the impressive collection at **Museo Mundo de Ambar** ( ☎ 809-682-3309; www.amberworldmuseum.com; Arzobispo Mériño 452; admission US$2; ☼ 9am-6pm Mon-Sat, 9am-1pm Sun) includes excellent examples of both domestic and international amber. Look for samples containing various critters and bugs – there's an entire room dedicated to ants. Signs in Spanish and English explain amber's origin, mining process and common uses.

**Museo de Larimar** ( ☎ 809-689-6605; www.larimarmuseum.com; Isabel la Católica 54; admission free; ☼ 8:30am-6pm Mon-Sat) is on the 2nd floor of a jewelry shop and – despite the location – is quite impressive. It contains a remarkable display of the beautiful blue stone and relates just about everything there is to know about the subject. Signage is in English and Spanish.

## CHURCHES

**Catedral Primada de América** (admission free; ☼ 9am-4pm) is the oldest cathedral in operation in the Américas. Diego Columbus set the first stone in 1514, but construction didn't begin in earnest until the arrival of the first bishop in 1521. Numerous architects worked on the cathedral until 1540, which is why its vault is Gothic, its arches are Romanesque and its ornamentation is baroque. The entrance faces Parque Colón.

Built in 1510, **Convento de la Orden de los Predicadores** (Hostos & Padre Billini; admission free; ☼ irregular hrs) was the first convent of the Dominican order in the Americas. It is also the place where Father Bartolomé de las Casas – the famous chronicler of Spanish atrocities committed against indigenous peoples – did most of his writing. Be sure to take a look at the vault of the chapel; it is remarkable for its stone zodiac wheel, which is carved with mythological and astrological representations.

Constructed during the first half of the 16th century, **Iglesia de Nuestra Señora de las Mercedes** (Church of Our Lady of Mercy; cnr Las Mercedes & José Reyes; admission free; ☼ irregular hrs) was reconstructed on numerous occasions following pirate attacks, earthquakes and hurricanes. The church is remarkable for its pulpit, which is sustained by a support in the shape of a serpent demon.

Other notable churches in the Zona Colonial include **Capilla de Nuestra Señora de los Remedios** (cnr Calle de las Damas & Las Mercedes), **Iglesia de Santa Clara** (cnr Padre Billini & Isabel la Católica) and **Iglesia de la Regina Angelorum** (cnr José Reyes & Padre Billini).

## HISTORIC SITES

Beside the cathedral is the historic **Parque Colón**, containing several shade trees and a large statue of Admiral Columbus himself. It is the meeting place for area residents and it's alive all day long with tourists, townsfolk, hawkers, guides, taxi drivers, shoeshine boys and tourist police.

The **Plaza España**, in front of the Alcázar de Colón, has been made over many times, most recently during the early 1990s in honor of the 500th anniversary of Columbus' arrival in the New World. The plaza is a large, open area that makes for a lovely afternoon stroll and it has several outdoor restaurants along its west edge.

The **Fortaleza Ozama** (Ozama Fortress; ☎ 809-686-0222; Calle de las Damas; admission US$1; ☼ 9am-6:30pm Mon-Sat, 9am-4pm Sun), at the south end of Calle de las Damas, is the oldest colonial military edifice in the New World. Construction was commenced in 1502 and it served as a military garrison and prison until the 1970s, when it was opened to the public for touring. **Torre del Homenaje** (Tower of Homage) is the main structure, with 6ft-thick (1.8m) walls containing dozens of riflemen's embrasures and offering great rooftop views. Near the door there are several guides whose knowledge of the fort is generally quite impressive. A 20-minute tour should cost around US$3.50 per person.

Originally constructed in 1747 as a Jesuit church, the **Panteón Nacional** (National Mausoleum; Calle de las Damas; admission free; 🕑 9am-5pm Tue-Sun) was also a tobacco warehouse and a theater before dictator Trujillo restored the building in 1958 as the final resting place of the country's most illustrious persons. The mausoleum is next to Plaza de María de Toledo. Shorts and tank tops are discouraged.

The **Monasterio de San Francisco** (Monastery of St Francis; Hostos, btwn Emiliano Tejera & Restauración), the first monastery in the New World, belonged to the first order of Franciscan friars who arrived to evangelize the island. Dating from 1508, the monastery was set ablaze by Sir Francis Drake in 1586, rebuilt, devastated by an earthquake in 1673, rebuilt, ruined by another earthquake in 1751 and rebuilt again. From 1881 until the 1930s it was used as an insane asylum – portions of the chains used to secure inmates can still be seen – until a powerful hurricane shut it down for good.

The ruins of the New World's first hospital, **Ruinas del Hospital San Nicolás de Barí** (Hostos), near Las Mercedes, remain in place as a monument to Governor Nicolás de Ovando, who ordered it built in 1503. So sturdy was the edifice that it survived centuries of attacks by pirates, earthquakes and hurricanes. It remained virtually intact until 1911, when, after being damaged by a hurricane, much of it was knocked down so that it wouldn't pose a threat to pedestrians. Today, visitors can still see several of its high walls and Moorish arches. Note that the hospital's floor plan follows the form of a Latin cross.

The **Puerta del Conde** (Gate of the Count; Calle El Conde) owes its name to the Count of Peñalba, Bernardo de Meneses y Bracamonte, who in 1655 led the successful defense of Santo Domingo against an invading force of 13,000 British troops. The gate is the supreme symbol of Dominican patriotism because right beside it, in February 1844, a handful of brave Dominicans executed a bloodless coup against occupying Haitian forces; their actions resulted in the creation of a wholly independent Dominican Republic. It also was atop this gate that the very first Dominican flag was raised. The gate is at the west end of Calle El Conde.

## Other Neighborhoods

Santo Domingo has a number of interesting sites outside of the Zona Colonial. For most, it's easiest to get to them by taxi.

Resembling a cross between a Soviet-era apartment block and a Las Vegas version of an ancient Mayan ruin, the **Faro a Colón** (Columbus Lighthouse; ☎ 809-592-1492, ext 251; Parque Mirador del Este; admission US$2.25; 🕑 9am-5:15pm Tue-Sun) is worth visiting for its controversial and complicated history. The Faro's massive cement flanks stretch nearly a block and stand some 10 stories high, forming the shape of a cross. High-powered lights on the roof can project a blinding white cross into the sky, but are rarely turned on because doing so causes blackouts in surrounding neighborhoods. At the intersection of the cross's arms is a guarded tomb that purportedly contains Columbus' remains. However, Spain and Italy dispute that claim, both saying that *they* have the admiral's bones. Inside the monument a long series of exhibition halls display documents (mostly reproductions) relating to Columbus' voyages and the exploration and conquest of the Americas.

The lush grounds of the **Jardín Botánico Nacional** (National Botanical Garden; ☎ 809-385-2611; Av República de Colombia; admission US$1.25; 🕑 9am-6pm) cover 2 sq km and include vast areas devoted to aquatic plants, orchids, bromeliads, ferns, endemic plants, palm trees, a Japanese garden and much more. An open-air trolley takes passengers on a pleasant half-hour turn about the park (US$1.25, departures every 30 minutes until 4:30pm) and is especially enjoyable for children.

Several of the country's best museums are clustered on the Plaza de la Cultura; the most extensive of these is the **Museo del Hombre Dominicano** (Museum of the Dominican Man; ☎ 809-689-4672; admission US$0.75; 🕑 10am-5pm Tue-Sun). Highlights here are an impressive collection of Taíno artifacts, including stone axes and intriguing urns. Other displays focus on slavery, the colonial period and Carnaval. The explanations are all in Spanish and the displays are very old-fashioned. English-speaking guides can be requested at the entry – the service is free, but small tips are customary.

The permanent collection at the **Museo de Arte Moderno** (Museum of Modern Art; admission US$3; 10am-6pm Tue-Sun) includes paintings and a few sculptures by the Dominican Republic's best-known modern artists, including Luís Desangles, Adriana Billini and Martín Santos, but the temporary exhibits tend to be fresher and more inventive.

## SANTO DOMINGO FOR CHILDREN

Santo Domingo isn't particularly kid friendly. Outside of the Zona Colonial, it's not a pedestrian friendly city, there are no beaches and few parks, or at least ones that are well maintained and shady. **Parque Colón** (cnr El Conde & Isabel la Católica) and **Parque Duarte** (cnr Padre Billini & Av Duarte) in the Zona Colonial are basically flagstone plazas where you can sit on a bench and feed pigeons. There are, however, several sights meant to keep youngsters occupied.

**Museo Infantil Trampolín** ( ☎ 809-685-5551; www .trampolin.org.do in Spanish; Calle de las Damas; adult/ child US$3.50/1.75; 9am-6pm Tue-Fri, 10am-7pm Sat & Sun) is a high-tech, hands-on natural history, biology, science, ecology and social museum all wrapped into one. Enthusiastic guides (most are Spanish speaking) lead kids through the touchy-feely exhibits: the earthquake machines and volcano simulations are big hits, less so the exhibit on children's legal rights.

If the kids aren't going to have a chance to snorkel and see underwater creatures in their natural habitat, then the **Acuario Nacional** (National Aquarium; ☎ 809-766-1709; Av España; admission US$1; 9:30am-5:30pm Tue-Sun) can substitute. It's quite run-down in parts, however, and algae often covers the viewing windows. That being said, the long, clear underwater walkway where you can watch sea turtles, stingrays and huge fish pass on the sides and overhead can be exciting. Signs in Spanish only. Across the street is **Caribe Parque Acuario** (Av España; adults/children US$6/4.50; 11am-7pm Wed-Sun), a not-very-well-taken-care-of water park. It's a lot of concrete and safety probably isn't the best but…

Restaurants in general are probably more relaxed and kid-friendly than elsewhere. Hotels with pools, such as all those along the Malecón (see p292), allow you and the kids to take a break from the sightseeing for several relaxing hours.

## TOURS

Interesting and informative walking tours of the Zona Colonial are offered daily by a number of official guides – look for men dressed in khakis and light blue dress shirts but always ask to see their official state tourism license. Tours cover the most important buildings in the zone and can be tailored to your specific interests. Walks typically last 2½ hours and cost between US$20 and US$30 depending on the language that the tour is given in (ie Spanish and English are less expensive). To find a guide, head to Parque Colón – you'll find a number of them hanging out under the trees. Also be sure to agree upon a fee before setting out.

## FESTIVALS & EVENTS

**Carnaval** (or Carnival in English) Celebrated throughout the country every Sunday in February, culminating in a huge blowout in Santo Domingo the last weekend of the month or first weekend of March. Av George Washington (the Malecón) becomes an enormous party scene all day and night. Central to the celebration are the competitions of floats and costumes and masks representing traditional Carnaval characters.

**Latin Music Festival** Held at the Olympic Stadium every October, this huge three-day event attracts the top names in Latin music – jazz, salsa, merengue and *bachata*. Jennifer Lopez and Marc Anthony have performed in the past.

**Merengue Festival** The largest in the country, a two-week celebration of the DR's favorite music held every year at the end of July and beginning of August. Most of the activity is on the Malecón, but there are related events across the city.

## SLEEPING

The Zona Colonial is the most distinctive part of the city and therefore where most travelers prefer to stay. All of the sights and restaurants are within walking distance and there's an excellent choice of midrange and top-end hotels, some in attractive restored colonial-era buildings. Gazcue (p292 ), a quiet residential area southwest of Parque Independencia, has several hotels in the midrange category, though there are far fewer eating options. The high-rise hotels on the Malecón (p292) are best if you're looking for resort-style amenities.

### Zona Colonial
#### BUDGET
**Bettye's Exclusive Guest House** ( ☎ 809-688-7649; bettyemarshall@hotmail.com; Isabel la Católica 163; dm/r US$22/44; ) Look for the nondescript

iron doorway opening onto Plaza de María de Toledo around the corner from Isabel la Católica. Don't be discouraged by the messy gallery space; there's some method to the madness. The owner, originally from Tennessee, hopes to attract travelers who appreciate the eclectic, laid-back vibe. There are several dorm rooms (only one has a fan) with five to six beds, a mash of antiques and colorful modern art. There's wi-fi, plus access to a common kitchen. For those seeking privacy but not quiet, there's a private room that opens directly onto Isabel la Católica.

**Hostal La Colonia** ( ☎ 809-221-0084; hostallacolonia@ yahoo.com; Isabel la Católica 110-A; s/d US$50/60; ✖ ) Ideally located just around the corner from Parque Colón, newly opened La Colonia is a good choice. In addition to shiny, polished floors and large rooms with cable TV and refrigerators, each of the three floors has its own spacious street-side sitting area and balcony with armchairs.

### MIDRANGE

**Hotel Atarazana** ( ☎ 809-688-3693; www.hotel-atarazana .com; Vicente Celestino Duarte 19; s/d with fan US$50/70, s/d with air-con US$70/90, all incl breakfast; ✖ 🖳 ) A newly opened boutique hotel for the design conscious only a few feet away from Plaza España. Housed in a beautifully renovated building from the 1860s, all six rooms sport custom-made furniture along with high-concept fixtures and textiles. Each of the light and airy rooms has a balcony. The breakfast buffet is served in a secret patio shaded by lush vegetation; there's even a small Jacuzzi to relax in and the rooftop has fabulous views. High-speed internet access in rooms.

**our pick El Beaterío Guest House** ( ☎ 809-687-8657; elbeaterio.fr; Av Duarte 8; s/d US$50/60, s/d with air-con US$60/70, all incl breakfast; ✖ 🖳 ) Take thee to this nunnery – if you're looking for austere elegance. It's easy to imagine the former function of this 16th-century building: the heavy stone façade, the dark and vaulted front room – now a beautiful reading room and dining area – giving way to a lush and sunny inner courtyard, all inspire peacefulness and tranquility. Each of the 11 large rooms is sparsely furnished but the wood-beamed ceilings and stone floors are truly special; the bathrooms are modern and well-maintained. There's also wi-fi.

**Hotel Doña Elvira** ( ☎ 809-221-7415; www.dona -elvira.com; Padre Billini 209; loft US$70; r US$85-95, ste US$105, all incl breakfast; ✖ 🖳 ) Tucked away on a quiet block far from the bustle around Parque Colón, the Doña Elvira is housed in a renovated colonial building, which is a plus. Unfortunately, much of the character seems to have been renovated out as well; the cramped loft room especially is in bad shape. There are 13 rooms in total, most are fairly modern looking, though the exposed stone walls and tile floors in the suite are attractive. You can hang out in the inner courtyard, take a dip in the pool (it's too small for swimming), lounge on the rooftop solarium, use the wi-fi, or read in the lobby-cum-dining-area.

### TOP END
**Hotel Palacio** ( ☎ 809-682-4730; www.hotel-palacio .com; Av Duarte 106; s US$78-88, d US$88-98; ✖ 🖳 ) Cross colonial with a little touch of medieval and you have the Palacio, a mazelike hotel occupying a 17th-century mansion only a block north of the El Conde pedestrian mall. Service is exceptional and you'll need it to find your way past the charming nooks and crannies, which include reading areas, a small bar, a lush interior courtyard and stone-walled walkways. Room design is strictly German-conquistador – that is, minimalist with a few large imposing pieces of furniture. An additional wing and a rooftop pool were under construction at the time of research. There's wi-fi.

**Sofitel Nicolás de Ovando** ( ☎ 809-685-9955; www .sofitel.com; Calle de las Damas near Plaza de María de Toledo; s US$220-336, d US$238-354, all incl breakfast; ✖ 🖳 ☎ ) Even heads of state must thrill when learning they're sleeping in the former home of the first Governor of the Americas. Oozing character, old, old world charm and a historic pedigree tough to beat, the Nicolás de Ovando is as far from a chain hotel as you can get. The 107 rooms are definitely 21st century – flat screen TVs, recessed Jacuzzi, internet cable hookup, luxurious boutique-style fixtures and linens. However, all this modernity is offset by beautifully crafted wood and stone interiors, cobblestone walkways and lushly shaded courtyards – the fabulous pool probably didn't exist during the governor's time. An excellent buffet breakfast is included in the rate; the hotel's superb and elegant restaurant, La Residence has a separate entrance down the street. IT's open for lunch and dinner and mains are about US$17 to US$35.

## Gazcue

**Hotel La Danae** ( ☎ 809-238-5609; www.hoteldanae .com; Danae 18; r US$24-30; ❄ ) Dominican-owned La Danae is the best of a number of similar small hotels located on this quiet residential street. Choose from the older, cheaper rooms in the front building and the newer, more modern ones in the back annex. The former have higher ceilings but are subject to what street noise there is. All have cable TV and there's a kitchen area for common use.

**Hotel Residencia Venezia** ( ☎ 809-682-5108; www .residence-venezia.com; Av Independencia 45; s/d US$45/58; ❄ 🖳 ) Within walking distance of the Zona Colonial and the Malecón, the Venezia is a logical and good value option if you choose to stay in Gazcue. Rooms here are immaculate and have large bathrooms; a couple of suites come with balconies and kitchenettes and obviously get more sunlight than the somewhat dim standard rooms. A pleasant surprise is a tiny bistro-bar off the 1st-floor lobby. Two internet-ready computers are available for guests.

**Hostal Duque de Wellington** ( ☎ 809-682-4525; www.hotelduque.com; Av Independencia 304; s/d US$45/90; ❄ 🖳 ) Room furnishings and decor at this hotel try terribly to be tasteful but are in the end fairly dowdy. Rooms on the 2nd floor have higher ceilings, and more expensive rooms have balconies, which provide more light. Guests can access the internet (per hour US$2) from an old computer in the lobby. There's a travel agency on the 1st floor and it's a short walk to the Malecón.

## Malecón

**Hotel InterContinental** ( ☎ 809-221-0000; www.inter continental.com/santodomingo; Av George Washington 218; r from US$120; ❄ 🖳 ☒ ) Other than the Hilton, the InterContinental has the plushest lobby of the hotels on the Malecón and an even more hip bar-lounge area. Like all the big hotels on the waterfront, the hotel also has a pool, spa, tennis courts and a casino, popular both with tourists and the Dominicans on weekends.

**Hilton Santo Domingo** ( ☎ 809-685-0000; www .hiltoncaribbean.com/santodomingo; Av George Washington 500; r from US$130; ❄ 🖳 ☒ ) Easily the nicest of the luxury hotels on the Malecón, the Hilton is part of a huge complex including a casino, movie theaters and several restaurants (although much of it remains vacant). The highest of the high-rises, it's a long elevator ride in the atrium to the top. Rooms here are nicer and newer than its nearby competitors, and it has a bar and restaurant with stunning ocean views.

# EATING

Santo Domingo has a good selection of restaurants in various price ranges. The ones in the Zona Colonial are usually the most convenient.

## Zona Colonial

**La Cafetera Colonial** ( ☎ 809-682-7122; El Conde btwn Av Duarte & 19 de Marzo; mains US$2-5; ❄ breakfast, lunch & dinner) Everyone knows everyone else's name here. That can seem intimidating at first, especially because the narrow entranceway means new customers can't pull up a stool at the long lunch counter unnoticed. It's a classic greasy spoon menu: eggs and toast, simple sandwiches and super strong espresso.

**El Meson de Lu** (Hostos; mains US$5-13; ❄ lunch & dinner) This simple and unpretentious restaurant has loyal locals lining up at the small bar or sitting in the open-air dining room for filling plates of seafood and meat. Even though service isn't with a smile it's a good choice, especially at dinnertime when it's not uncommon for a trio of musicians to serenade your table.

**Dajao Restaurant & Bar** ( ☎ 809-686-0712; Arzobispo Nouel 51; mains US$9-20; ❄ lunch & dinner) There are two Dajaos – a sleek, small, modern side, resembling a European café; and an older, basic side, much like an ordinary *comedor*. The former outshines the latter, not only in terms of style but also in its menu: it serves specials such as conch meat croquettes (US$10), shrimp crêpes (US$9) and grilled octopus (US$10).

**our pick Pat'e Palo** ( ☎ 809-687-8089; Calle la Atarazana 25; mains US$12-22; ❄ 4:30pm to late Mon-Thu & 1:30pm to late Fri-Sun) Another one of Plaza España's eateries, Pat'e Palo is for gourmands and anyone tired of the same old bland pasta and chicken. Everything here is special but a personal recommendation is the grilled Angus rib eye with *rugula* and parmesan cheese with potato fricassee, mushrooms and bacon.

## Gazcue

**Ananda** ( ☎ 809-682-7153; Casimiro de Moya 7; mains US$3-10; ❄ lunch & dinner Mon-Sat, lunch Sun) Hard-core vegetarians will want to try out this cafeteria-style restaurant-cum-yoga-center run by the 'International Society of Divine Realization.'

They may not find the offerings enlightening; Dominican dishes such brown rice and roast beans outnumber the Indian meals.

**L'Osteria de Charly y Christian** ( ☎ 809-333-6701; Av George Washington 47; mains US$6-12; ☷ noon-midnight) A favorite hangout for local expats and Dominicans alike, L'Osteria is a casual open-air restaurant on the Malecón. Aging, albeit with character, it's as much a good place for a drink as a serving of homemade pasta or other Italian and French standards.

**Restaurant Train Steak House** ( ☎ 809-686-5961; Calle Pasteur 100; mains US$12; ☷ 11:30am-midnight Tue-Sun) Not quite a chop house, not quite a sports bar, this restaurant combines a little of both. In the front bar there are several TVs tuned to international sporting events, while uniformed waiters and the enthusiastic owner hustle about the brick walled dining room serving delicious cuts of meat as well as grilled seafood and tapas.

## DRINKING

**El Conde Restaurant** ( ☎ 809-688-7121; mains US$3-16; Hotel Conde de Peñalba, cnr El Conde & Arzobispo Meriño; ☷ breakfast, lunch & dinner) Hands down, the best place for an afternoon drink. As much a restaurant as a café, El Conde's appeal isn't its large varied menu of decent food, but its commanding location at the busiest corner in the Zona Colonial.

**Double's Bar** (Arzobispo Meriño; ☷ 6pm to late) Good-looking 20-somethings grind away to loud pop and Latin music at Double's. Others lounge around in groups downing bottles of Presidente, while the classic long wood bar is better for conversation.

**1492** ( ☎ 809-686-6009; Arzobispo Meriño 105; ☷ Tue-Sat) Aptly named, since it feels like a discovery, 1492's horseshoe-shaped wood bar is conducive to conversation, the dim lighting is flattering and the barkeep/owner is friendly.

## ENTERTAINMENT
### Nightclubs

**Guácara Taína** ( ☎ 809-533-0671; Av Mirador del Sur 655; admission US$10) Still a popular spot for ravers and electronica fans, this giant club-cum-batcave does see tourist groups fresh off the bus but live acts, especially merengue and salsa, draw Dominican partygoers. The club is difficult to find, but every taxi driver in the city knows where it is. Gets going after midnight from Thursday to Sunday.

The hotels on the Malecón have Santo Domingo's largest and most popular night clubs: the Jubilee at the **Renaissance Jaragua** ( ☎ 809-221-2222; Av George Washington 367) and the club at the **InterContinental** ( ☎ 809-221-0000; Av George Washington 218) draw crowds, especially on weekends. Discos operate from Tuesday through Saturday and open around 9pm, but things don't get hopping until 11pm or later. Admission is US$3 to US$5 when there's a DJ (most nights), US$10 when there's a band. The clubs attract the capital's wealthiest and hippest and they dress up when they go dancing.

### Gay & Lesbian Venues

Much like the straight scene, gay and lesbian venues in Santo Domingo don't tend to last for too long. However, the following were open at the time of research.

**Amazonia** ( ☎ 809-412-7629; Dr Delgado 71; ☷ 8pm-late Fri-Sun) A mostly lesbian bar in Gazcue.

**CHA** (Av George Washington 165, btwn Maximo Gomez & Lincoln; ☷ 6pm-3am Fri & Sat, 6pm-1am Sun) A fun place with good music and shows.

**Esedeku** ( ☎ 809-869-6322; cnr Las Mercedes 341 & Santome) Only a block from El Conde, Esedeku is an intimate bar with a huge selection of cocktails; not for hustlers.

### Casinos

There are casinos at most of the large hotels on the Malecón, including the **Hotel Santo Domingo** ( ☎ 809-221-1511; cnr Avs Independencia & Abraham Lincoln) and **El Napolitano** ( ☎ 809-687-1131; Av George Washington 101). They generally open at 4pm and close at 4am.

### Sports
#### BASEBALL

The boys of summer play in the winter here, in this *béisbol*-mad city. Soon after the US major league season ends in October, the 48-game Dominican season kicks off. From mid-November until early February, the top players from the DR with a handful of major and minor leaguers from the US compete all over the country. One of the better places to see a game and experience the madness is the **Estadio Quisqueya** ( ☎ 809-540-5772; cnr Av Tiradentes & San Cristóbal; tickets US$2-18; ☷ game times 5pm Sun, 8pm Tue, Wed, Fri & Sat), home field for two of the DR's six professional teams, **Licey** (www.licey.com) and **Escogido** (www.escogido.com). Asking for the best seats available at the box office will likely run

**DOMINICAN REPUBLIC**

you US$18 and put you within several feet of either the ballplayers or the between-innings dancers. Scalpers also congregate along the road to the stadium and at the entrance.

### COCKFIGHTING

The Madison Square Garden of the Dominican cockfighting world, the **Coliseo Gallístico Alberto Bonetti Burgos** ( ☎ 809-565-3844; Av Luperón; admission US$7-17.50; ☾ matches 6:30pm Wed & Fri, 3pm Sat) is where the best and the fiercest roosters are brought to fight. If you have any interest in experiencing this traditional Dominican spectator sport (for more about cockfighting see p282), this *gallera* (cockfighting ring) is a good choice. Matches are held Wednesday and Friday at 6:30pm and Saturdays at 3pm from November to June, but December to April is the busiest season (the roosters' plumage is fullest then). A match could have 30 or 40 fights and last into the wee hours; betting on cockfights is an intense and complex art. Fights are to the death – some are quick, others are tortuous bloody affairs that can last up to 15 minutes (the official limit before a fight is called off) and so obviously aren't appropriate for everyone.

## SHOPPING
### Amber & Larimar

Considered national treasures, amber and larimar are sold widely throughout Santo Domingo. For a sure thing, try one of the following.

**Swiss Mine** ( ☎ 809-221-1897; El Conde 101; ☾ 9am-6pm Mon-Fri, 10am-4pm Sat) This shop, on Parque Colón, sells some of the finest-quality amber and larimar around; the design work is also unsurpassed. English, French, Italian and German are spoken.

**Ambar Maldo Gift Shop** ( ☎ 809-688-0639; Calle La Ataranza; ☾ 10am-5pm Mon-Sat) With an eclectic selection of amber and larimar jewelry, this makes a great stop if you like to hunt for unique pieces. Prepare to bargain hard – prices have been marked up in anticipation of the ritual.

### Art

Santo Domingo's galleries tend to offer more and better Dominican art than Haitian, though you can find good examples of both in the following shops.

**Atelier Gallery** ( ☎ 809-688-7038; Arzobispo Portes 120; ☾ 10am-8pm Mon-Sat) Art sold here is of the type you would expect to see in any fine modern-art museum; traditional work – paintings, sculpture, pottery – is top tier and experimental pieces are the norm. Quite impressive.

**Galería de Arte María del Carmen** ( ☎ 809-682-7609; Arzobispo Mériño 207; ☾ 9am-7pm Mon-Sat, 10am-1pm Sun) Specializing in paintings, this gallery has been in business long enough to attract a wide range of talented Dominican artists.

### Cigars

If you want to sample some of the finest *tabacos* around, drop by the **Boutique del Fumador** ( ☎ 809-685-6425; El Conde 109; ☾ 9am-7pm Mon-Sat, 10am-3:30pm Sun) or the **Museo del Tabaco** ( ☎ 809-689-7665; El Conde 101; ☾ 9:30am-8pm). Both are located on Parque Colón and are owned by the same tobacco company – Monte Cristi de Tabacos. At either shop you can watch as two workers roll cigars in the shop window. Montecristo, Cohiba and Caoba brand cigars are sold at both shops. Prices vary from US$2 to US$6 per cigar and boxes cost up to US$110.

**La Leyenda del Cigarro** ( ☎ 809-686-5489; Hostos 402 at Mercedes) is a small shop with a good selection of premium cigars and the helpful staff are more than willing to answer the naïve questions of cigar novices.

### Handicrafts

**Encuentro Artesanal** ( ☎ 809-687-1135; Arzobispo Meriño 407; ☾ 10am-8pm Mon-Sat) At this urban-chic shop, you'll find beautiful woodwork, paintings, kitchenware, hip clothing and unique jewelry. Hands down, the best all-around selection of high-end handicrafts in the Zona Colonial.

**Artesanía Elisa** ( ☎ 809-682-9653; Arzobispo Nouel 54; ☾ 9am-6pm Mon-Sat) Specializing in traditional faceless dolls, you'll find hundreds of handcrafted porcelain beauties here; all figurines are dressed in late-18th-century garb and are priced according to the size and detail of each (US$10 to US$550).

### Markets

**Mercado Modelo** (Av Mella btwn Tomás de la Concha & Del Monte y Tejada; ☾ 9am-5pm) Bargain hard at this local market, which sells everything from love potions to woodcarvings and jewelry. Housed in an aging two-story building just north of the Zona Colonial near a neighborhood of Chinese restaurants and stores. It's best not to dress too sharply or wear any fine jewelry yourself, in part to get a fair deal and in part because this isn't the best neighborhood to wander around especially after dark.

## GETTING THERE & AWAY
### Air
Santo Domingo has two airports: the main one, **Aeropuerto Internacional Las Américas** (SDQ; ☎ 809-549-0081), is 22km east of town. The smaller **Aeropuerto Internacional La Isabela Dr Joaquin Balaguer** (JBQ, Higuero; ☎ 809-567-3900), north of the city, handles mostly domestic carriers and air taxi companies. **Aerodomca** (☎ 809-826-4141/4242), **Caribair** (☎ 809-542-6688) and **Take Off** (☎ 809-552-1333; www.takeoffweb.com) service both airports.

For details on international air travel to and from the Santo Domingo area, see p321.

### Bus
Santo Domingo has no central bus terminal. Instead, the country's two main bus companies – **Caribe Tours** (☎ 809-221-4422; www.caribetours.com.do; cnr Avs 27 de Febrero & Leopoldo Navarro) and **Metro** (☎ 809-227-0101; www.metroservicioturisticos.com; Francisco Prats Ramírez) – have individual depots west of the Zona Colonial. Caribe Tours has the most departures and covers more of the smaller towns than Metro does; a taxi is the most convenient way to reach either station.

**Expreso Santo Domingo Bávaro** (☎ 809-682-9670; cnr Juan Sánchez Ruiz & Máximo Gómez); Bávaro (☎ 809-552-0771) has a direct 1st-class service between the capital and Bávaro, with a stop in La Romana. Departure times in both directions are 7am, 10am, 2pm and 4pm (US$9, four hours).

There also are four **2nd-class bus depots** near Parque Enriquillo in the Zona Colonial. All buses make numerous stops en route. Because the buses tend to be small, there can be a scrum for seats, especially for destinations with one to a few departures a day.

To get to Haiti, **Capital Coach Line** (☎ 809-530-8266; www.capitalcoachline.com; 27 de Febrero 455), **Caribe Tours** (☎ 809-221-4422; www.caribetours.com.do; cnr Avs 27 de Febrero & Leopoldo Navarro) and **Terra Bus** (☎ 809-531-0383; Plaza Lama, Avs 27 de Febrero & Av Winston Churchill) offer daily bus services to Port-au-Prince.

### Car
Numerous international and domestic car rental companies have more than one office in Santo Domingo proper and at Las Américas International Airport – the majority have a booth in a small building just across the street from the arrivals exit.

**Advantage Rent-a-Car** airport (☎ 809-549-0536); Av Independencia (☎ 809-685-4000; Av Independencia btwn José Ma Heredia & Socorro Sánchez)

**Avis** airport (☎ 809-549-0468); Av Abraham Lincoln (☎ 809-535-7191; cnr Avs Abraham Lincoln & Sarasota)

**Budget** airport (☎ 809-549-0351); Av John F Kennedy (☎ 809-566-6666; cnr Avs John F Kennedy & Lope de Vega)

**Dollar** airport (☎ 809-549-0738); Av Independencia (☎ 809-221-7368; Av Independencia 366)

**Europcar** airport (☎ 809-549-0942); Av Independencia (☎ 809-688-2121; Av Independencia 354)

**Hertz** airport (☎ 809-549-0454); Av José Ma Heredia (☎ 809-221-5333; Av José Ma Heredia 1)

**National/Alamo** Av Independencia (☎ 809-221-0805; cnr Av Independencia & Máximo Gómez; airport (☎ 809-549-8303)

## GETTING AROUND
### To/From the Airport
There are no buses to or from Aeropuerto Internacional Las Américas or Aeropuerto Internacional La Isabela Dr Joaquin Balaguer. From Las Américas, a taxi into town costs US$25 to US$35, with little room for negotiation. The fare from Herrera is US$10 to US$15 – there's no permanent taxi stand, but a couple of cabs meet every flight.

### Bus
City buses (US$0.25) tend to follow major thoroughfares, including Av Independencia (eastbound) and Av Bolivar (westbound), both of which intersect with Parque Independencia in the Zona Colonial.

### Car
Driving can be difficult in Santo Domingo due to traffic and aggressive drivers, especially those of taxis and buses. Many midrange and top-end hotels have parking with 24-hour guards. Otherwise you'll probably have to leave your rental on the street. Do not leave any valuables inside in either case.

### Público
More numerous than buses are *públicos* – mostly beat-up minivans and private cars that follow the same main routes but stop anywhere that someone flags them down (US$0.35). Be prepared for a tight squeeze – drivers will cram seven or even eight passengers into an ordinary four-door car.

## Taxi

Taxis in Santo Domingo don't have meters, so you should always agree on the price before climbing in. The standard fare is US$4, less within the Zona Colonial. Taxi drivers don't typically cruise the streets, but you can always find one at Parque Colón and Parque Independencia. You can also call a cab; try **Apolo Taxi** (☎ 809-537-7771), **Super Taxi** (☎ 809-536-7014) or **Taxi Express** (☎ 809-537-7777).

# THE SOUTHEAST

This iconic region, synonymous with sun, sand and binge eating, is rightly popular with the hundreds of thousands of visitors who make the southeast the economic engine of the tourism industry in the Dominican Republic. Sprawling resort developments, some like city-states unto themselves, line much of the beachfront from Punta Cana to Bávaro.

The fishing village of Bayahibe is the departure point for trips to the nearby islands in the Parque Nacional del Este. North of Bávaro is Playa Limón, an isolated stretch of beach backed by palm trees but also more unusually, a lagoon and several mountain peaks. Those committed to carrying on west to Sabana de la Mar are rewarded with the Parque Los Haitises, a protected maze of caves and mangroves.

## BÁVARO & PUNTA CANA

Ground zero of DR tourism. The epicenter of the all-inclusive. Where buffet items seem to outnumber grains of sand. If you were to tell a Dominican anywhere in the world that you visited their country, this is where they would assume you came. Deservedly popular because its beaches rival those anywhere else in the Caribbean, both for their soft, white texture and their warm aquamarine waters, a trip here nevertheless involves as much a love for swim-up pool bars and rubbing suntanned elbows with like-minded people.

## Orientation

Most of Bávaro's services are located in one of several outdoor plazas (malls) just north of El Cortecito, the small one-road enclave where there's another cluster of shops and tour companies.

Punta Cana actually refers to the area just east and south of the airport. It's much more isolated than Bávaro as there is really only one coastal road that eventually peters out further south and doesn't connect with the highway to Higüey. There are few services here and no towns in the immediate area.

## Information

### EMERGENCY
**Politur** (Tourist Police; ☎ 809-686-8227) Next to the bus terminal in Bávaro and at Plaza Bolera in Punta Cana.

### INTERNET ACCESS & TELEPHONE
**Cone Xion.com** (Plaza Punta Cana, Bávaro; per hr US$2; ⏰ 8am-11pm Mon-Sat, 9am-11pm Sun) A small dual internet/call center.
**Cyber Cafe** (Plaza Riviera/Estrella, Bávaro; per hr US$2; ⏰ 10am-10pm) Towards the back of Plaza Estrella; a call center as well.
**Tricom/Cyber Beach** (El Cortecito; per hr US$3; ⏰ 8am-11pm) Along the main beach road in Cortecito proper.

### LAUNDRY
Most hotels offer laundry service but you pay by the piece, which can make washing your clothes more expensive than the clothes themselves.
**Laundry Euro** (☎ 809-552-1820; Plaza Riviera/Estrella, Bávaro; ⏰ 8am-8pm Mon-Sat, 8am-5pm Sun) Charges by the piece with same-day service if you drop off in the morning.

### MEDICAL SERVICES
Every all-inclusive hotel has a small on-site clinic and medical staff, which can provide first aid and basic care.
**Centro Médico Caribe Bávaro** (☎ 809-552-1415; www.caribeasistencia.com/cmcb; Plaza las Brisas, Bávaro; ⏰ 8:30am-6pm) Open 24 hours for emergencies.
**Centro Médico Punta Cana** (☎ 809-552-1506; btwn Plaza Bávaro & the bus terminal, Bávaro) The name notwithstanding, this is the main private hospital in Bávaro, with a multilingual staff, a 24-hour emergency room and an in-house pharmacy.
**Farmacia Estrella** (☎ 809-552-0344; Plaza Estrella, Bávaro; ⏰ 8am-10pm)
**Hospitén Bávaro** (☎ 809-686-1414; bavaro@hospiten .com; btwn airport & turn-off to Bávaro) Best private hospital in Punta Cana, with English-, French- and German-speaking doctors and a 24-hour emergency room.
**Pharma Cana** (☎ 809-959-0025; Plaza Bolera, Punta Cana; ⏰ 9am-10pm Mon-Sat, 8am-11pm Sun) Punta Cana's main pharmacy.

**MONEY**

**Banco BHD** (Plaza Caney 1, Bávaro)

**Banco Popular** (Plaza Bávaro, Bávaro; ☻ 9am-4pm Mon-Fri)

**Banco Progreso** El Cortecito supermarket ( ☻ 9am-9pm Mon-Sat); Plaza Bolera, Bávaro ( ☻ 9am-4pm Mon-Fri)

**Scotiabank** (Plaza Las Brisas, Bávaro; ☻ 9am-5pm Mon-Fri, 9am-1pm Sat)

## Sights

**BEACHES**

Superlatives to describe the beaches here are bandied about like free drinks at a pool bar but they're mostly deserved.

Public access is ingrained in the law so you can stroll from less exclusive parts like **Playa El Cortecito**, which tends to be crowded with vendors, to nicer spots in front of resorts. Playa El Cortecito, though, is a good place to **parasail** (12-15min US$40) or to find a boat operator to take you fishing or snorkeling.

North of El Cortecito is Playa Arena Gorda, lined with all-inclusives and their guests. A further 9km north of here is **Playa del Macao**, a gorgeous stretch of beach best reached by car. It's also a stop-off for a slew of ATV (All-Terrain Vehicle) tours that tear up and down the beach every day.

In the other direction, south of Bávaro and El Cortecito, is **Playa Cabo Engaño** – an isolated beach you'll need a car, preferably an SUV, to reach.

### PARQUE ECOLÓGICO PUNTA CANA

A half-kilometer south of Punta Cana Resort and Club, the **Punta Cana Ecological Park** ( ☎ 809-959-8483; www.puntacana.org; ☻ 8am-4pm) covers almost 2000 acres of protected coastal and inland habitat and is home to some 80 bird species, 160 insect species and 500 plant species. Visitors can take very worthwhile 1½-hour **guided tours** (adult/child US$10/5) through a lush 45-acre portion of the reserve known as Parque Ojos Indígenas (Indigenous Eyes Park), so named for its 11 freshwater lagoons all fed by an underground river that flows into the ocean. **Horseback riding tours** (1-/2hr tour US$20/30) through the park and along the coast can also be arranged with advance notice. Unfortunately, there is no hotel pick-up service; a cab here will cost around US$25 each way from Bávaro or El Cortecito.

## Activities

Virtually every water activity is available, but involves a long commute to the actual site. Every hotel has a tour desk offering snorkeling, diving and boat trips to destinations such as Isla Saona, a large island with picturesque beaches off the southeastern tip of the DR. Parasailing is done from the beach all over Punta Cana and Bávaro.

**La Cana Golf Course** ( ☎ 809-959-2262; www.punta cana.com; Punta Cana Resort & Club, Punta Cana; ☻ 7:30am-6pm) is one of Punta Cana's top golf courses and is located at the area's top resort. Green fees are guest/nonguest US$115/156 for 18 holes or guest/nonguest US$71/96 for nine, including a golf cart. A new Tom Fazio–designed course is scheduled to open the summer of 2008.

If you'd like to get in a round of golf but La Cana is somewhat rich for your blood, the **Catalonia Bávaro Resort** ( ☎ 809-412-0000; Cabeza de Toro; ☻ 8:30am-5pm) has a decent nine-hole par-three course that costs US$45 for one round and US$60 for two. Carts are US$25 for 18 holes and US$20 for nine and club rental just US$10.

**DOMINICAN REPUBLIC**

---

**TWIST MY ARM: THE PLACES THE AUTHORS WANTED TO KEEP SECRET**

The drive alone justifies the trip. Hwy 104 passes through rolling mountain scenery and past bucolic ranches, where any unrecognized vehicle is sure to turn the heads of locals walking with friends or on horseback; it practically qualifies as an event in the sleepy villages along the way. **Playa Limón** itself, about 20km east of Miches and just outside the hamlet of El Cedro, is a 3km-long, isolated beach lined with coconut trees leaning into the ocean, coveted property that you're likely to have to yourself for much of the day.

There's a saying in the mountains of the Dominican Republic: 'God is everywhere, but he lives in Constanza.' Set at 1200m in a fertile valley and walled in by towering mountains, you can see why – it's a breathtaking spot. **Constanza** makes a fine weekend getaway but during the week you're likely to be the only one there. There isn't a whole lot do here, though, and the tourist attractions are of far less interest than the cooler climate and the sheer remoteness of it all.

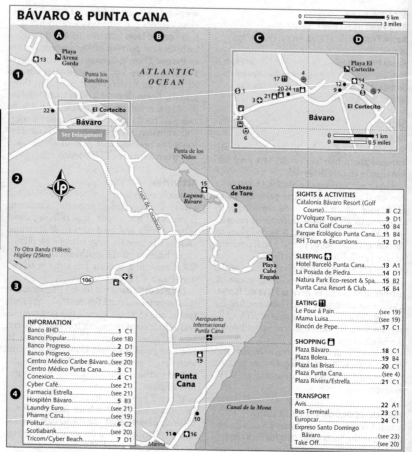

## BÁVARO & PUNTA CANA

**SIGHTS & ACTIVITIES**
| | |
|---|---|
| Catalonia Bávaro Resort (Golf Course) | 8 C2 |
| D'Volquez Tours | 9 D1 |
| La Cana Golf Course | 10 B4 |
| Parque Ecológico Punta Cana | 11 B4 |
| RH Tours & Excursions | 12 D1 |

**SLEEPING**
| | |
|---|---|
| Hotel Barceló Punta Cana | 13 A1 |
| La Posada de Piedra | 14 D1 |
| Natura Park Eco-resort & Spa | 15 B2 |
| Punta Cana Resort & Club | 16 B4 |

**EATING**
| | |
|---|---|
| Le Pour á Pain | (see 19) |
| Mama Luisa | (see 19) |
| Rincón de Pepe | 17 C1 |

**SHOPPING**
| | |
|---|---|
| Plaza Bávaro | 18 C1 |
| Plaza Bolera | 19 B4 |
| Plaza las Brisas | 20 C1 |
| Plaza Punta Cana | (see 4) |
| Plaza Riviera/Estrella | 21 C1 |

**TRANSPORT**
| | |
|---|---|
| Avis | 22 A1 |
| Bus Terminal | 23 C1 |
| Europcar | 24 C1 |
| Expreso Santo Domingo Bávaro | (see 23) |
| Take Off | (see 20) |

**INFORMATION**
| | |
|---|---|
| Banco BHD | 1 C1 |
| Banco Popular | (see 18) |
| Banco Progreso | 2 D1 |
| Banco Progreso | (see 19) |
| Centro Médico Caribe Bávaro | (see 20) |
| Centro Médico Punta Cana | 3 C1 |
| Conexion | 4 C1 |
| Cyber Café | (see 21) |
| Farmacia Estrella | (see 21) |
| Hospitén Bávaro | 5 B3 |
| Laundry Euro | (see 21) |
| Pharma Cana | (see 19) |
| Politur | 6 C2 |
| Scotiabank | (see 20) |
| Tricom/Cyber Beach | 7 D1 |

## Tours

Every resort has a separate tour desk that can arrange all variety of trips, from snorkeling and deep-sea fishing to the popular Isla Saona trip. A handful of locals set up on El Cortecito beach offer **snorkel trips** (2½hr trip per person US$20-25) and **glass-bottom boat rides** (2hr trip per person US$25-30) to a nearby reef. Most also offer **deep-sea fishing trips** (min 4 people, per person US$80-90).

If you're looking to explore the region, **D'Volquez Tours** ( ☎ 809-552-1861, 776-3823; El Cortecito) and **RH Tours and Excursions** ( ☎ 809-552-1568; www.rhtours.com; El Cortecito; ✆ 9am-7pm) offer a number of decent day trips. Popular excursions include exploring Parque Nacional Los Haitises (US$88), boat trips to Isla Saona

(US$79) and tours of Santo Domingo's Zona Colonial (US$58).

## Sleeping

For resorts in the area, walk-in-guests are about as common as snowstorms; if you can convince the suspicious security guards that your intentions are innocent and make it to the front desk, you'll be quoted rates that absolutely nobody staying at the resort is paying. Instead, book all-inclusive vacations online or through a travel agent, as they can offer discounts of up to 50% off rack rates. Bear in mind that most resorts cater to a particular niche, whether it's families, honeymooners, golfers or the spring-break crowd.

## BÁVARO

**La Posada de Piedra** ( ☎ 809-221-0754; www.laposada depiedra.com; El Cortecito; r with shared/private bathroom US$25/45) The only budget accommodation with a beachfront location, this privately owned stone house is smack in the middle of busy Cortecito. Those with only primitive needs will be happy in one of the two beachfront cabanas. Inside the owner's home are two comfortable rooms with private bathrooms and a shared balcony with views of the ocean. Breakfast, drinks and sandwiches are served at a few small tables set up on the street in front of the house.

**Hotel Barceló Punta Cana** ( ☎ 809-476-7777; www .barcelopuntacana.com; Playa Arena Gorda; r from US$150; 🔀 💻 🖳 ) Ideally located at the end of a strip of all-inclusives but only a short drive from the commercial plazas of Bávaro, this resort (also known as Barceló Premium) is a good choice considering the reasonable rates. A mix of young families and singles, the Premium exudes a Club Med–like atmosphere. Some of the bathrooms of this huge complex could stand an update but the rooms are comfortable nevertheless – each has a balcony. Wireless access is per day US$10. Don't confuse this with the several other Barceló resorts in the area or with the fact that it's not in Punta Cana despite the name.

**Natura Park Eco-Resort & Spa** ( ☎ 809-221-2626; www.blau-hotels.com; Cabeza de Toro; d per person US$150; 🔀 💻 🖳 ) Located midway between Bávaro and Punta Cana, Natura Park has a narrow beach outside the village of Cabeza de Toro. This is an isolated area nowhere near busy El Cortecito and Bávaro so not the best choice for people looking to hop in and out of different resort clubs at night. Egrets and flamingos wander the property, which has won awards for its efforts to reduce its environmental impact. Large glass doors open out onto balconies or terraces. The pool is a bit small, but the beach quite nice.

## PUNTA CANA

**Punta Cana Resort & Club** ( ☎ 809-959-2262; www.punta cana.com; Punta Cana; d incl breakfast US$140; 🔀 💻 🖳 ) Famous for its part time residents like Julio Iglesias, Oscar de la Renta and Mikhail Baryshnikov, this resort is also notable for its environmental efforts, especially the associated ecological park across the street from the entrance to the resort. Newly opened Tortuga Bay, an enclave of 15 luxurious villas is part of the main resort property of 15,000-acres and 400 rooms. Three-story buildings line a beautiful beach and there are nine restaurants to choose from, though unlike the typical resort lunch, dinner and drinks aren't included. It's a low-key resort for people happier to read a book on the beach rather than do aqua-aerobics to loud disco music in the pool.

## Eating

Most visitors are hardly hungry after gorging themselves at their resort's buffets but there are enough condos, villas and locals to support a handful of eateries. Most are in various shopping centers in the area.

**Le Pour á Pain** (Plaza Bolera, Bávaro; mains US$6; 🕙 10am-10pm) This small, pleasant café with outdoor patio seating is in Plaza Bolera, not exactly picturesque but a good spot if you're in town. Good coffee as well as crêpes (US$6), salads (US$8) and sandwiches (US$6) are served.

**Mama Luisa** ( ☎ 809-959-2013; Plaza Bolera; mains US$8-15; 🕙 lunch & dinner Mon-Sat) The food and service at this friendly and pleasant restaurant outshine its prosaic setting – it's in a mini-mall a half-kilometer west of the airport. Pastas (US$8) of course are good but the paella for two (US$35) is especially recommended.

**Rincón de Pepe** ( ☎ 809-552-0603; Bávaro shopping center; mains US$8-15; 🕙 lunch & dinner Mon-Sat) A classy but low-key restaurant that serves quality Spanish food at sunny outdoor tables or inside an airy, hot-pink dining area. You may even forget you're in a mall.

## Getting There & Away

### AIR

The **Aeropuerto Internacional Punta Cana** is on the road to Punta Cana about 9km east of the turn-off to Bávaro.

**American Airlines** ( ☎ 809-959-2420), **Air France** ( ☎ 809-959-3002), **LAN** ( ☎ 809-959-0144) all have offices at the airport. Other international airlines serving the Punta Cana airport include US Airways, Air Canada, Air France, Continental, Northwest, Corsair, LTU, Iberworld and USA3000.

For domestic air connections, check out the airline/travel agency **Takeoff** ( ☎ 809-552-1333; www.takeoffweb.com; Plaza las Brisas; 🕙 6am-8pm).

None of the international rental car agencies have booths here; a representative will pick you up upon arrival if reservations are made in advance.

DOMINICAN REPUBLIC

Resort minivans transport the majority of tourists to nearby resorts; however, taxis are plentiful. Fares between the airport and area resorts and hotels range from US$10 to US$35 depending on the destination.

### BUS

The bus terminal is located at the main intersection in Bávaro near the Texaco gas station, almost 2km inland from El Cortecito.

**Expreso Santo Domingo Bávaro** (Bávaro ☎ 809-552-1678; Santo Domingo ☎ 809-682-9670; cnr Juan Sánchez Ruiz & Máximo Gómez) has services between Bávaro and the capital, with a stop in La Romana. Departure times in both directions are 7am, 10am, 2pm and 4pm (US$9, four hours).

For other destinations, take a local bus (marked Sitrabapu) to Higüey and transfer there. *Caliente* buses to Higüey leave Bávaro's main terminal (US$2.50, 1½ hours, every 20 minutes), as does the express service (US$3, 1¼ hours, every hour).

## Getting Around

Local buses pass all the outdoor malls on the way to El Cortecito. Buses have the drivers' union acronym – Sitrabapu – printed in front and cost US$0.75. They are supposed to pass every 15 to 30 minutes, but can sometimes take up to an hour.

Day time traffic is sometimes gridlocked between the resorts clustered just north of Bávaro and El Cortecito. Despite the stop-and-go pace of driving, renting a car for a day or two is recommended if you prefer to see the surrounding area independently. Rental agencies include **Avis** ( ☎ 809-688-1354; Plaza Caney, Carretera Arena Gorda) and **Europcar** ( ☎ 809-686-2861; near Plaza Punta Cana, Bávaro).

Otherwise, there are numerous taxis in the area – look for stands at El Cortecito, Plaza Bávaro and at most all-inclusives. You can also call a cab – try **Arena Gorda taxi** ( ☎ 809-552-0786). Fares vary depending on distance, but are typically US$5 to US$35.

# PENÍNSULA DE SAMANÁ

The Península de Samaná (Samaná Peninsula) is only a sliver – just 40km long and 15km wide – of rolling mountains, a sea of hillocks pushing their way to a long coastline of protected beaches and picturesque coves. A new international airport and a new highway to the capital, either ominous signs of development or economic lifelines to the rest of the country and the world, suggest that Samaná's character, defined in part by its relative inaccessibility, is trending more to the mainland and the mainstream. However, for now it's still a place where the stereotypical image of a vacation in the Dominican Republic need not apply, where French and Italian are at least as useful as Spanish and it's only a short *moto-concho* ride from a luxurious second home to an open-air disco pumping merengue.

Tens of thousands of tourists follow the migratory pattern of the North Atlantic humpback whale, busing and flying in to Samaná from mid-January to mid-March, seeing little else of the peninsula – though if there's time for only one thing, this is definitely it. Las Terrenas, the most developed in terms of tourism, is the place to base yourself if you crave a lively social scene; and Las Galeras, a sleepy one road town, boasts several of the best beaches in the DR, their beauty enhanced by the effort it takes to get there.

## SAMANÁ

### pop 50,000

For much of the year, Samaná follows the slow daily rhythms of an ordinary Dominican town – it's a compact place built on a series of bluffs overlooking Bahía de Samaná. In fact, it remained an isolated fishing village until 1985, when the first whale-watching expedition set out. Because North Atlantic humpbacks find the bay water particularly suitable for their annual version of speed dating from mid-January to mid-March, Samaná is transformed by tens of thousands of tourists who flock here to go on a whale-watching tour, a natural spectacle with few equals.

## Orientation

Arriving in town from the direction of El Limón or Sánchez, the main street, Av Malecón or Av la Marina, is about a kilometre downhill past the municipal market (where the *gua-gua* station is). Most of the restaurants, banks and bus stations are located on the main street. The port is across the street from a small shady park near where the buses leave from.

## Information

**Banco Popular** (Av Malecón; ☻ 8:15am-4pm Mon-Fri, 9am-1pm Sat)

**BanReservas** (Santa Barbara; 8am-5pm Mon-Fri, 9am-1pm Sat)

**CompuCentro Samaná** ( 809-538-3146; cnr Labandier & Santa Barbara; per hr US$2.10; 9am-midday, 3-6pm Mon-Fri)

**Farmacia Giselle** ( 809-538-2303; cnr Santa Barbara & Julio Labandier; 8am-10pm Mon-Sat, 8am-noon Sun)

**Hospital Municipal** (San Juan; 24hr) A very basic hospital near the Palacio de Justicia.

## Sights & Activities
### WHALE-WATCHING

For sheer awe-inspiring 'the natural world is an amazing thing' impact, a whale-watching trip is hard to beat. Around 45,000 people travel to Samaná every year from January 15 to March 15 to see the majestic acrobatics of these massive creatures. Try to avoid coming here during Carnaval, a holiday for Dominicans, making it the busiest day of the year. Most of the companies have a morning and afternoon trip. There are around 43 vessels in total, eight companies, all owned or at least partly owned by Dominicans from Samaná and around 12 independent operators. See A Whale of a Time (p302) for more about the whales.

**Victoria Marine** ( 809-538-2494; www.whalesamana.com; cnr Mella & Av Malecón; adult/under 5yr/5-10yr US$55/free/30; 9am-1pm, 3-6pm) is Samaná's most-recommended whale-watching outfit. **Moto Marina** ( 809-538-2302; motomarina@yahoo.com; Av la Marina 3; 8am-6pm) and **Samaná Tourist Service** ( 809-538-2848; samana.tour@codetel.net.do; Av la Marina 6; 8:30am-12:30pm & 2:30-6pm Mon-Fri, 8:30am-12:30pm Sat) can also arrange trips for independent travelers.

### CAYO LEVANTADO

Only the western third of this lush island 7km from Samaná is open to the public; the eastern two-thirds is now occupied by a five-star hotel development. The public beach here is gorgeous, with white sand and turquoise waters, but don't expect much peace and quiet. Large cruise ships dock here regularly and the facilities include a restaurant and bar – and 2000 lounge chairs. Boatmen at the pier make the trip for US$10 to US$15 per person round-trip; if you have a group of six to eight people you can negotiate the round-trip for US$60.

### CASCADA EL LIMÓN

A trip to this 50m **waterfall**, a short distance from the town of El Limón, is a chance to revel in some breathtaking mountain scenery. Travel agencies in Samaná offer trips there for around US$45, including transport, horses, guide and lunch. However, it's perfectly easy and much cheaper to do the trip yourself by taking a *gua-gua* to El Limón. See p306 for more details.

## Sleeping

**Hotel Chino** ( 809-538-2215; San Juan 1; s/d US$60/75; ) Located on top of a Chinese restaurant on top of a hill, Hotel Chino's rooms have balconies with fantastic views of town and the waterfront. And while the rooms are shiny and clean with cable TV and air-con, it's of questionable value considering there's no lounge area or other amenities and no beach within walking distance.

There are two resorts in the Bahía Principe area. **Gran Bahía Principe Cayacoa** ( 809-538-3131; www.bahiaprincipeusa.com; per person US$100; ) is the older of the two, and is perched on a cliff 6km east of Samaná with spectacular views of the bay and maybe even of humpbacks during whale season. Food and rooms however are mediocre.

The other resort is **Gran Bahía Principe Cayo Levantado** ( 809-538-3131; www.bahiaprincipeusa.com; Cayo Levantado; r from US$200; ). If the beach at Cayacoa (which is accessed from an outdoor elevator) isn't to your liking, there are free daily shuttles to this new five-star resort, which is situated on a beautiful beach. It's a step above the Cayacoa in every category including cuisine and room decor; the downside is you're on an island and need to take a boat to get there (provided by the hotel). Well, that's the upside too.

## Eating & Drinking

The majority of restaurants are along Av Malecón. The following are fairly interchangeable in terms of menu and cost.

**Restaurant Mate Rosada** (Av Malecón; mains US$4-11; lunch & dinner)

**Cayacoa Restaurant** (Av Malecón; mains US$6-12; lunch & dinner)

**L'Hacienda Restaurant** (Calle Santa Barbara; mains US$3-12; breakfast, lunch & dinner)

Beginning around 6pm and lasting until the early hours of the morning, you can also get cheap eats at a series of food stands that line Av Malecón near Calle Maria Trinidad Sánchez.

**A WHALE OF A TIME**

Canadian Kim Beddall, a marine mammal specialist since 1983 and the pioneer of the whale-watching industry in the Dominican Republic, has devoted herself to maintaining a healthy environment for the whales and a healthy living for the people of Samaná.

**How many North Atlantic humpbacks come to these waters every year?**

The estimated population is 10,000 to 12,000 and almost all these whales spend part of the winter in Dominican waters. During the peak months here from January to March, there are maybe 200 to 300 whales in the bay itself but they don't hang out in large groups, they're spread out and others are in transit.

**Why do the humpbacks come to these waters?**

It's like the world's largest singles bar, they come to mate and calve – we see an average of 12 new calves a year in Samaná Bay. We think humpbacks come specifically to Samaná because they like certain depths, around 60ft to 80ft; within 2km outside the bay it drops to 600m to 700m. The wind conditions are right, as is the salinity of the bay mouth.

**Are the humpbacks found in other waters around the DR?**

Samaná Bay is part of the National Marine Mammal Sanctuary of the Dominican Republic, approximately 27,000 sq km and one of the largest in the world, which includes Silver Bank, Navidad Bank and Samaná Bay. Silver Bank is around 70 miles north of Puerto Plata and Navidad Bank is 45 miles northeast of Cape Samaná. The rest of the year these whales can be found feeding anywhere from the eastern seaboard of the US to the Arctic Circle, including Greenland and all the way to Norway. We are the sister sanctuary to Stellwagon Bank, in front of Boston, and are the first sanctuaries in the world to protect humpbacks on both ends of an annual migration.

**What is the DR's official position concerning the whale-watching industry?**

The DR has no whaling history, and promotes responsible whale-watching as an economic alternative to whaling in the wider Caribbean. The country is in the process of becoming a proconservation member of the International Whaling Commission (IWC). To date, six countries vote with

## Getting There & Away

### AIR

The nearest airport in regular operation is Aeropuerto Internacional El Portillo, just outside of Las Terrenas. Aeropuerto El Catey is another option and receives some international flights. See p321 and p322 for information on domestic and international flights.

### BOAT

**Transporte Marítimo** ( ☎ 809-538-2556; Av Malecón) provides the only ferry service – passengers only, no vehicles – across the Bahía de Samaná to Sabana de la Mar (US$4.25, one hour plus, four daily at 7am, 9am, 11am and 3pm). From there, it's possible to catch *gua-guas* to several destinations in the southeast and then on to Santo Domingo.

### BUS

Facing the pier, **Caribe Tours** ( ☎ 809-538-2229; Av Malecón) offers services to Santo Domingo at 7am, 8:30am, 10am, 1pm, 2:30pm and 4pm (US$8.50, 4½ hours, daily). The same bus stops along the way at Sánchez (US$2, 30 minutes), Nagua (US$2.15, one hour) and San Francisco de Macorís (US$3, 1½ hours). A block west, **Metro** ( ☎ 809-538-2851; cnr Av Malecón & Rubio y Peñaranda) offers a similar service (US$8, 4½ hours, twice daily, 7:30am and 3:30pm). Like its competitor, it stops at Sánchez (US$2.30, 30 minutes), Nagua (US$2.30, one hour) and San Francisco de Macorís (US$3.50, 1½ hours). Tickets are sold in the Western Union office next door to Caribe Tours.

For direct service to Puerto Plata 210km to the west, there are two options: **El Canario** ( ☎ 809-291-5594; Av Malecón) buses leave at 10am (US$7, 3½ to four hours) beside the Banco Popular; while **Papagayo** ( ☎ 809-970-2991) has a service at 1:30pm from under the mango tree on the eastern side of the little park next to Banco Popular on the *malecón*.

For service to towns nearby, head to the **gua-gua terminal** (Av Malecón) at the *mercado municipal*, 90m west of the Politur station near Angel Mesina. From here, trucks and minivans head to Las Galeras (US$2, 45 minutes to one hour, every 15 minutes, 6am to 6pm), El Limón (US$3, 30 minutes,

Japan in favor of reinstating commercial whaling: Antigua, St Lucia, St Kitts, St Vincent and the Grenadines, Commonwealth of Dominica and Grenada. These countries' waters are part of the general migratory area for North Atlantic humpbacks. These countries receive economic assistance from Japan – the assumption of many people is they are being rewarded for their vote. Starting in 1982 there was a 10-year moratorium on whale hunting, and this was extended in 1992 but there's no real way to enforce the ban other than through voluntary compliance.

**What's the most immediate threat to the health of the North Atlantic humpback population?**

Considering that humpbacks are coastal species and so brush up against humans and everything that comes with us, they are surprisingly tolerant and resilient animals, but are still classified as a vulnerable species by the Convention on International Trade in Endangered Species (CITES). Being coastal animals, they like to occupy shallow waters close to shore, areas of intense human activity. Entanglement in fishing gear, ship strikes, contamination of feeding and reproductive habitats, uncontrolled coastal development with resulting erosion affecting water quality, solid and liquid waste, high concentrations of vessel traffic, unregulated whale-watching and the rapidly developing cruise-ship market in the Caribbean, along with sound contamination, may all have impacts on humpbacks that we do not yet fully understand. Global warming and climate change may effect migratory routes, feeding and reproductive grounds, forcing species to move to other areas they previously have not occupied.

**What's your advice for tourists?**

Whale-watch responsibly everywhere you go on vacation; only in this way can you give local communities an economic alternative to whaling. Only whale-watch with permitted vessels. Here in Samaná, all have numbered yellow flags from the Ministry of the Environment and a permit they can show you. Learn what the regulations are and ask your captain to comply. Ask if there is a naturalist on board, and also just ask as many questions as possible to reinforce the idea that tourists are concerned and they want people with expertise.

every 15 minutes, 6am to 6pm) and Sánchez (US$1.75, 45 minutes, every 15 minutes, 6am to 4:30pm).

## Getting Around

Samaná is walkable but if you're carrying luggage *motoconchos* are everywhere. 4WD vehicles are your only option in terms of car rental – roads on the peninsula are bad enough to warrant the extra expense. Rates run from US$70 to US$90 per day (tax and insurance included). Try **Xamaná Rent Motors** ( ☎ 809-538-2380; Av Malecón; ☼ 8am-noon & 2-6pm).

# LAS GALERAS

The road to this small fishing community 28km northeast of Samaná ends at a fish shack on the beach. So does everything else, metaphorically speaking. Las Galeras, as much as anywhere else on the peninsula, offers terrestrial and subaquatic adventures for those with wills strong enough to ignore the pull of inertia. Or you can do nothing more than lie around your bungalow or while away the day at a restaurant watching others do the same.

## Orientation

The road coming from Samaná winds along the coast and through lovely, often-forested countryside before reaching the outskirts of Las Galeras. There's one main intersection in town (about 50m before the highway dead-ends at the beach) and most hotels, restaurants and services are walking distance from there.

## Information

Most of the relevant services are located on or around the main intersection, a short walk from the beach.

**Consultoria Las Galeras** ( ☎ 829-918-3233; Plaza Lusitania; ☼ 8:30am-noon & 3-6pm Mon-Fri, 3-6pm Sat)

**Plaza Lusitania Internet & Call Center** (internet per hr US$2.50; ☼ 8:30am-8pm Mon-Sat)

## Sights

### PLAYA RINCÓN

Playa Rincón is a pitch-perfect beach. Stretching uninterrupted for almost 3km of nearly white, soft sand and multihued water good for swimming, the beach even has a small stream at its far western end, great for

**DOMINICAN REPUBLIC**

a quick freshwater dip at the end of a long, sunny day. Rincón is large enough for every day tripper to claim their own piece of real estate. A thick palm forest provides the backdrop. Several small restaurants serve mostly seafood dishes and rent beach chairs, making this a great place to spend the entire day. Most people arrive by boat. The standard option is to leave around 9am and boats return to pick you up at 4pm – it's around 20 minutes each way. If you join up with other beachgoers, it costs per person about US$12 to US$15. You can also drive there, though the last kilometer or so is too rough for small or midsize cars. A taxi to Rincón should cost US$55 round-trip.

### PLAYITA

Better than the beach in town, Playita (Little Beach) is easy to get to on foot or by *motoconcho*. It's a swath of tannish sand, with mellow surf, backed by tall palm trees. There are two informal outdoor restaurants, basically thatched-roof shelters, where you can get grilled fish or chicken. On the main road just south of Las Galeras, look for signs for Hotel La Playita pointing down a dirt road headed west.

### PLAYAS MADAMA & FRONTÓN

Preferred by some locals over Playa Rincón, 750m-long Playa Frontón boasts some of the best snorkeling in the area. Playa Madama is a small beach framed by high bluffs; keep in mind there's not much sunlight in the afternoon.

The trail to both begins at the far east end of the Casa Marina Bay beach, about 200m past the resort's entrance, near a private house which most people know as 'La Casa de los Ingleses' (House of the English) after its original owners. Coming from town, the house and the trail will be on your right. There are several turn-offs that are easy to miss; it's much simpler to take a boat to either of these beaches for around US$15 per person round-trip, with a pick-up in the afternoon.

### BOCA DEL DIABLO

'Mouth of the Devil' is an impressive vent or blowhole, where waves rush up a natural channel and blast out of a hole in the rocks. Car or motorcycle is the best way to get there – look for an unmarked dirt road 7km south

of town and about 100m beyond the well-marked turnoff to Playa Rincón. Follow the road eastward for about 8km, then walk the last 100m or so.

## Activities

### DIVING & SNORKELING

For experienced divers, Cabo Cabrón (Bastard Point) is one of the north coast's best dive sites. Other popular sites in the area include Piedra Bonita, a 50m stone tower that's good for spotting jacks, barracudas and sea turtles; Cathedral, an enormous underwater cave opening to sunlight; and a sunken 55m-container ship haunted by big green morays. Several large, shallow coral patches, including Los Carriles, a series of small underwater hills, are good for beginner divers. Playa Frontón has excellent snorkeling.

**Grand Paradise Samaná Dive Center** (Dive Samaná; ☎ 809-538-2000; www.lacompagniadeicaraibi.com; Grand Paradise Samaná resort; ⏲ 7am-6pm) is located at the far end of Casa Marina Bay's beach. One-/two-tank dives are, including all equipment, US$60/114 (US$5 to US$12 less if you have your own). Also on offer are snorkeling trips (US$12).

### HORSEBACK RIDING

The Belgian owners of Bungalows Karin y Ronald offer well-recommended **horseback riding tours** (from US$52) to various spots around Las Galeras, including Boca del Diablo, El Punto lookout and Playas Madama and Frontón. Casa Marina Bay resort offers similarly priced but somewhat less-personalized horseback tours as well.

### WATER SPORTS

**Grand Paradise Samaná Dive Center** (Dive Samaná; ☎ 809-538-2000; www.lacompagniadeicaraibi.com; Grand Paradise Samaná resort; ⏲ 7am-6pm) has windsurf and sailboat rental and instruction (US$10 to US$15 per hour), all available to guests and nonguests alike.

## Tours

You can visit many of the beaches and sights on your own or hire a *motoconcho* driver to act as your chauffeur and guide. Organized tour operators include **ATM-Tours** ( ☎ 809-324-1696; Calle Principal), **R-azor Tours** ( ☎ 809-538-0218; www.azortour.eu; Calle Principal) and **Grand Paradise Samaná Dive Center** (Dive Samaná; ☎ 809-538-2000; www.lacompagniadeicaraibi.com; Grand Paradise Samaná resort; 7am-6pm). The numerous day trips on offer include whale-watching in Bahía de Samaná (per person US$80), trips to Playa Rincón (US$10), land and boat excursions through Parque Nacional Los Haitises (per person US$70) and hikes to the area's isolated beaches (per person US$20). Village tours that include a cock fight, and stops in a typical home and primary school, and overnight trips further afield can also be arranged.

## Sleeping

### BUDGET

**Bungalows Karin y Ronald** ( 829-878-0637; www.larancheta.com; r US$30, bungalow US$54) Buried in the lush jungle 2.5km east of the main intersection is this unique hotel with a number of funky and simple two-storied bungalows that can accommodate four to six people comfortably. Semioutdoor rustic kitchens lend an eclectic, if not cabin-in-the-woods, feel to this out-of-the-way hotel. Take full advantage of Karin's knowledge – she's an expert tour guide who leads day and overnight hiking and horseback trips to out of the way beaches and mountain tops (opposite).

**Casa Por Qué No?** ( /fax 809-712-5631; s/d incl breakfast US$32/45; ) Pierre and Monick, the charming owners of this bed and breakfast, rent out two rooms on either side of their cozy home – each has a separate entrance and hammock. Only 25m or so north of the main intersection on your right as you're walking towards the beach, the house is fronted by a long, well groomed garden where delicious breakfasts are served (US$6 breakfast for nonguests). Open from November to the end of April.

### MIDRANGE

**Plaza Lusitania Hotel** ( 809-538-0093; www.plazalusitania.com; r US$60; 1-bedroom apt US$75-100, all incl breakfast; ) This hotel *is* downtown Las Galeras – it's situated on the main intersection on the 2nd floor of a tiny mall, complete with an internet and telephone center, good Italian restaurant, medical office and shop. A stay at Plaza Lusitania is as urban as Las Galeras gets, which is to say not at all. Rooms are large and extremely comfortable and even boast small balconies and kitchenettes.

**Todo Blanco** ( 809-538-0201; www.hoteltodoblanco.com; r US$75; ) In a wash of white, Todo Blanco, a well-established inn run by a cheerful Dominican–Italian couple, sits atop a small hillock a short walk from the end of the main drag in Las Galeras. The multi-leveled grounds are nicely appointed with gardens and a gazebo and wrap-around porches, all with views of the ocean. The rooms are large and airy, with high ceilings and private terraces. A homey living room area has a TV and DVD player and wi-fi internet access. Meals can be provided if ordered and arranged ahead of time.

### TOP END

**Villa Serena** ( 809-538-0000; www.villaserena.com; r without/with air-con US$140/150, all incl breakfast; ) A cross between a Victorian manor home and a Caribbean villa, this hotel, 300m east of the main intersection, has gorgeous ocean views and is probably the nicest place in Las Galeras. That being said, the room furnishings are a little worn and kitsch. Each has a balcony, some face the ocean directly and others open on to the meticulously landscaped garden and swimming pool area. Off the main lobby, where there is a free wi-fi signal, is a peaceful terrace with rocking chairs.

## Eating

**El Kiosko** (Calle Principal; mains US$5-7; 7am-midnight) Chow down on freshly caught fish, seafood and grilled meats at this basic thatch-roofed restaurant on the beach at the end of the main road.

**Plaza Lusitania Italian Restaurant** ( 809-538-0093; Calle Principal; mains US$6-12; breakfast, lunch & dinner Tue-Mon, dinner only May-Oct) Easily the nicest restaurant in town both in terms of cuisine and ambience, Plaza Lusitania has a varied menu of Italian dishes, an extensive selection of pastas, excellent large pizzas, grilled fish and even a Chinese dish or two (chicken fried rice US$8). A fruit shake (US$3) and a banana split (US$4.25) can round out a nice meal.

**Grigiri** (Calle Principal; mains US$5.75-11; breakfast, lunch & dinner) and **Chez Denise** ( 809-538-0219; Calle Principal; mains US$4-14; 9am-10pm Mon-Sat), two other restaurants located at the main intersection, have similar menus including crepes with various toppings. Grigiri is a better value than Chez Denise where service can be very slow.

## Getting There & Around

*Gua-guas* head to Samaná (US$2, 45 minutes, every 15 minutes, 7am to 5pm) from the beach end of Calle Principal but also cruise slowly out of town picking up passengers. There's also a daily 5:30am bus with service to Santo

Domingo (US$8, six hours). Locals refer to it as the Bluebird Express, though it's neither blue nor express.

You can pretty much walk everywhere in Las Galeras proper. For outlying areas, a *motoconcho* ride costs around US$0.50 to US$1 – consider arranging with the driver to pick you up if you know when you'll be returning.

**Taxis** (☎ 829-380-0775) are available as well; some sample fares are Aeropuerto Catey (US$85), Las Terrenas (US$85), Samaná (US$30) and Santo Domingo (US$200).

Renting a car is an excellent way to explore the peninsula on your own. **Caribe Fun Rentals** (☎ 809-912-2440; ◷ 9am-1pm & 3-6:30pm Mon-Sat, 9am-noon Sun) and **Xamaná Rent Moto** (☎ 809-538-0208; per day US$25; ◷ 9am-noon & 3-6pm Mon-Fri, 9am-noon Sat & Sun), 50m west of the intersection, rent motorcycles as well.

## LAS TERRENAS
**pop 15,000**

No longer a rustic fishing village, today Las Terrenas is a cosmopolitan town, seemingly as much French and Italian as Dominican. It's a balancing act between locals and expats, one that has produced a lively mix of styles and a social scene more vibrant than anywhere else on the peninsula. Either way you walk along the beach road leads to beachfront scattered with hotels, high palm trees and calm aquamarine waters.

### Orientation

The main road in town, Av Duarte (also known as Calle Principal), begins at the beach, and passes several small shopping plazas, restaurants, stores, banks etc before leaving the resort area. Calle del Carmen, a dirt road version of Av Duarte, runs parallel to the latter until it too ends at the beach and veers left to Pueblo de los Pescadores (Fishermen's Village), a collection of beachside bars and restaurants. Turning east at the intersection of Av Duarte and Calle 27 de Febrero or Carretera a Portillo takes you past another cluster of restaurants, bars and hotels and eventually leads to the airport, a large all-inclusive resort, El Limón and finally Samaná.

### Information

**Banco Leon** (Av Duarte) Has a 24-hour ATM.
**Banco Popular** (Av Duarte; ◷ 9am-5pm Mon-Fri, 9am-1pm Sat) Has a 24-hour ATM.

**Centro de Especialidades Medicas** (☎ 809-240-6817; Av Duarte; ◷ 24hr) Small private hospital.
**Internet café & call center** (internet per hr US$2.25; ◷ 9am-1pm & 2-9pm Mon-Sat) Next door to Lavandería Tu Net.
**Internet Point** (Plaza Taína, Av Duarte; ◷ 8:30am-1pm & 3-7pm Mon-Sat, 9am-1pm Sun) Fast internet connections.
**Lavandería Tu Net** (Lavandería Pat y Memo; ☎ 809-848-1661; Centro Colonial, Calle del Carmen; ◷ 8am-6pm Mon-Fri, 8am-3pm Sat) Wash and dry US$1.50 per 1lb.

### Sights & Activities
#### CASCADA EL LIMÓN

Tucked away in surprisingly rough landscape, and surrounded by peaks covered in lush greenery, is the 52m-high **El Limón Waterfall**. A beautiful swimming hole is at the bottom. The departure point for the falls is the small town of El Limón, only a half-hour from Las Terrenas.

Just about everyone who visits does so on horseback and almost a dozen *paradas* (horseback riding operations) in town and on the highway toward Samaná offer tours. (It is not recommended that you hire someone off the street, as there's little saving and the service is consistently substandard.) All outfits offer essentially the same thing: a 30- to 60-minute ride up the hill to the waterfalls, 30 to 60 minutes to take a dip and enjoy the scene and a 30- to 60-minute return trip, with lunch at the end. Your guide – who you should tip, by the way – will be walking, not riding, which can feel a little weird but is the custom.

Otherwise it's a minimum 40-minute walk, sometimes up a very steep trail over rough terrain with even a river or two to ford. It's not especially difficult to follow the path once you find it, especially if there are groups out on the trail.

Spanish-owned **Santí** (☎ 809-452-0776; limonsanti@terra.es; per person without/with lunch US$14/23; ◷ 8am-7pm), at the main intersection in El Limón, is the most popular of the *paradas* and also the most expensive. The lunch is excellent and the guides and staff (all adults) are better paid than elsewhere. If you book with a tour company in Las Terrenas, transportation to/from El Limón is not included (*gua-gua* US$1.50). Typically it costs per person from US$22 to US$24. Most other operators charge without/with lunch around US$7/14.

## LOCATION, LOCATION, LOCATION

Because of Bahía de Samaná's fortuitous geography – its deep channel, eastward orientation and easy-to-defend mouth, perfect for a naval installation – the Peninsula de Samaná has been coveted and fought over and bought several times over.

Founded as a Spanish outpost in 1756, Samaná was first settled by émigrés from the Canary Islands but the political turmoil of Hispaniola – the sale of the island to the French, a Haitian revolution and two British invasions – kept Samaná town's population growing and changing. It was deemed a prize even as early as 1807 during the brief French possession of Hispaniola – France's commander in Santo Domingo, an ambitious leader no doubt, proposed building a city named Port Napoleon in Samaná but France was dispossessed of the island before the plan could move forward.

After its independence from Spain, the DR was taken over by Haiti, which controlled Hispaniola from 1822 to 1844. During this period Haiti invited more than 5000 freed and escaped slaves from the US to settle on the island. About half moved to the Samaná area. Today, a community of their descendents still speak a form of English.

During Haitian rule, France pressured its former colony to cede the Península de Samaná in return for a reduction in the debt Haiti owed it. Incredibly, Haiti had been forced to pay restitution to France for land taken from French colonists in order to gain international recognition. Of course, France never paid restitution to former slaves for their ordeal.

After Dominican independence from Haiti in 1844, the new Dominican government feared Haiti would reinvade and sought foreign assistance from France, England and Spain. The Dominican Republic eventually resubmitted to Spanish rule in 1861 and Spain immediately sent a contingent of settlers to the Samaná area and reinforced the military installations on Cayo Levantado, a large island (and the site of a luxury resort today) near the mouth of the bay.

Even after independence in 1864, the Península de Samaná remained a tempting prize for other countries. Beginning in 1868 the US, under President Ulysses S Grant, sought to purchase the peninsula from the DR in order to build a naval base there. Dominican president and strongman Buenaventura Baéz agreed to the sale in order to obtain the money and weapons he needed to stay in power. However, the US Senate, under pressure from Dominican exile groups and strong opposition from France and the UK, rejected the proposal in 1871. A year later, Baéz arranged to lease the area to the US-based Samaná Bay Company for 99 years. To the relief of most Dominicans, the company fell behind on its payments and Baéz's successor, Ignacio María González, rescinded the contract in 1874. The US revisited the idea of annexing Samaná in 1897 as the Spanish-American War loomed, but decided to build its Caribbean base in Guantanamo Bay, Cuba, after it quickly defeated Spain.

## DIVING & SNORKELING

Las Terrenas has reasonably good diving and snorkeling and at least three shops in town to take you out. Favorite dive spots include a wreck in 28m of water and Isla Las Ballenas, visible from shore, with a large underwater cave. Most shops also offer special trips to Cabo Cabrón (p304) near Las Galeras and Dudu cave near Río San Juan. Standard one-tank dives average US$45 with equipment, around US$35 if you have your own. Two-tank Cabo Cabrón and Dudu trips run from about US$80 to US$100, including gear, lunch and transport.

Snorkelers also go to Isla Las Ballenas, which has good shallow coral flats (one hour; per person US$20). A popular full-day snorkel trip is to Playa Jackson, several kilometers west of town, reached by boat with stops in two or three locations along the way (per person including lunch, minimum six people US$60).

**Stellina Dive Center** ( ☎ 809-868-4415; www.stellina diving.com; Kari Beach Hotel; ☺ 9am-noon)

**Las Terrenas Divers** ( ☎ 809-889-2422; www.lt-divers .com; Hotel Bahía las Ballenas, Playa Bonita; ☺ 9am-noon) Well respected German-run operation.

## WATERSPORTS

Second to Cabarete, Las Terrenas is nevertheless a good place to try out a windsport in the DR. The beach at Punta Popy, only a kilometer or so east of the main intersection, is a popular place for kitesurfers and windsurfers. Two recommended outfits,

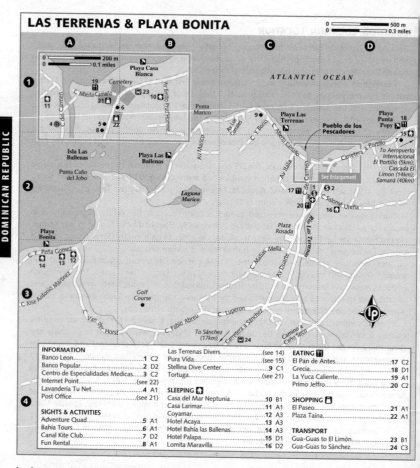

# LAS TERRENAS & PLAYA BONITA

| INFORMATION | | EATING |
|---|---|---|
| Banco Leon..................................**1** C2 | Las Terrenas Divers..................(see 14) | El Pan de Antes........................**17** C2 |
| Banco Popular............................**2** D2 | Pura Vida...................................(see 15) | Grecia.......................................**18** D1 |
| Centro de Especialidades Medicas..**3** C2 | Stellina Dive Center....................**9** C1 | La Yuca Caliente......................**19** A1 |
| Internet Point..........................(see 22) | Tortuga.....................................(see 21) | Primo Jeffro.............................**20** C2 |
| Lavandería Tu Net.....................**4** A1 | | |
| Post Office..............................(see 21) | SLEEPING | SHOPPING |
| | Casa del Mar Neptunia................**10** B1 | El Paseo....................................**21** A1 |
| SIGHTS & ACTIVITIES | Casa Larimar.............................**11** A1 | Plaza Taína...............................**22** A1 |
| Adventure Quad.......................**5** A1 | Coyamar....................................**12** A3 | |
| Bahía Tours..............................**6** A1 | Hotel Acaya...............................**13** A3 | TRANSPORT |
| Canal Kite Club.........................**7** D2 | Hotel Bahía las Ballenas.............**14** A3 | Gua-Guas to El Limón................**23** B1 |
| Fun Rental...............................**8** A1 | Hotel Palapa..............................**15** D1 | Gua-Guas to Sánchez................**24** C3 |
| | Lomita Maravilla.........................**16** D2 | |

both near each other and Punta Popy, are the long-established **Pura Vida** ( ☎ 809-878-6640; www.puravidacaraibes.com; Hotel Palapa, Calle 27 de Febrero; 🕙 10am-5:30pm) and **Canal Kite Club** ( ☎ 809-240-6556, 829-933-9325; www.canalkite.com; Calle 27 de Febrero). Both rent windsurf boards, body boards, surfboards, kitesurfing equipment and provide lessons for all these activities.

## Tours

Along with booking airline tickets and hotels, and arranging car rentals, the full-service travel agency **Bahía Tours** ( ☎ 809-240-6088; www .bahia-tours.com; Av Duarte 237; 🕙 9am-1pm & 3:30-7pm Mon-Fri, 9:30am-1pm & 4:30-6:30pm Sat) organizes many tours in the area. Popular day trips include whale-watching in Bahía de Samaná

(per person US$70), excursions to Los Haitises National Park (per person US$60), jeep tours to El Rincón beach (per person US$70) and horseback riding to El Limón waterfalls (per person US$25).

There are several other recommended tour companies in town:

**Adventure Quad** ( ☎ 809-657-8766; aventurequad@ hotmail.com; Calle Principal 165) Half-day excursions one four-wheel for two people US$80.

**Fun Rental** ( ☎ 809-240-6784; www.funrental.fr; Calle Principal 258, Plaza Creole) Quad rentals (per day US$55) and trips to Los Haitises (US$58).

**Tortuga** ( ☎ 829-808-2233; tropicodoelsol@yahoo.fr; El Paseo) In addition to trips to Los Haitises, Tortuga offers catamaran excursions to Playa Rincon, Playa Jackson and elsewhere.

## Sleeping

**Casa del Mar Neptunia** ( ☎ 809-240-6617; www.casas-del-mar-neptunia.com; Av Emilio Prud'Homme; s/d incl breakfast US$35/45; ✱ ) This whitewashed hotel is equally homey and quiet with 12 large, airy rooms. Maybe the only downside is that each of the little porches faces a lush interior garden and so lacks privacy and views. Breakfast can be served here or in the comfortable lounge area in front.

**Casa Larimar** ( ☎ 809-240-6539; www.casa-larimar.com; Pueblo de los Pescadores; r incl breakfast US$50-55; ▢ ✱ ) This French-owned hotel, the first you come to walking west along the path in Pueblo de los Pescadores, is more notable for its spectacular rooftop patio and Jacuzzi and charming little garden pool than for its rooms. The latter is sparsely furnished with concrete floors. Cable TV and wi-fi are included. Not much Spanish is spoken so bring your French dictionary.

**Hotel Palapa** ( ☎ 809-240-6797; www.palapabeach.com; cnr Calle 27 de Febrero & Av España; r US$65, q US$85, all incl breakfast; ▢ ✱ ) Across the road from Punta Popy, the Palapa is especially good for families and groups because the rooms are large and have loft spaces serving as an extra bedroom. Mostly everything is white, other than the thatched roofs of the bungalows, which surround a little pond – in the far back is a peaceful pool area. Look for the hotel behind Pura Vida, the water-sports company.

**our pick Lomita Maravilla** ( ☎ 809-240-6345; www.lomitamaravilla.com; Salome Ureña; villas US$100, with private Jacuzzi US$150, with private pool US$200; ✱ ▢ ✱ ) A short walk down a dirt road – often muddy – off Av Duarte, you'll find one of the gems of Las Terrenas. This European-inspired boutique hotel consists entirely of thatched-roof private bungalows set along palmed paths and around a swimming pool. Rooms verge on swanky, with TVs, DVD players and fully loaded kitchens ready for a make-it-yourself Caribbean meal. Offers wi-fi access.

## Eating & Drinking

Most of the restaurants along Pueblo de Pescadores are fairly interchangeable – a mix of pizza, pasta, fish, grilled meats and a sprinkling of Dominican specials. And most have bars and stay open well after the kitchen has closed.

**El Pan de Antes** ( ☎ 809-994-3282; Calle del Carmen; ⏱ 8am-7pm Tue-Sat, 8am-5pm Sun) Delicious pastries are made fresh daily at this French owned *patisserie*. Croissants go fast on Sunday mornings.

**Primo Jeffro** ( ☎ 829-352-7654; Calle del Carmen 143; mains US$2-7; ⏱ breakfast, lunch & dinner) For a change of pace, both in terms of cuisine and decor, head to this no-nonsense American-owned Mexican eatery. The open-air dining room couldn't be simpler, and unpretentious but the hearty tacos (US$1.25), burritos and *chimichangas* hit the spot. *Almuerzos* (US$4) and combo dinners (US$4.75) are great deals.

**Grecia** (Punta Popy, Carretera a Portillo; mains US$10; ⏱ breakfast, lunch & dinner) This restaurant-café-bar by the beach is popular with Dominicans and expats and it's no wonder – there's even a shower and faucet to clean off the sand after a dip in the ocean. Sandwiches and grilled meats and fish are served to diners on picnic tables.

**La Yuca Caliente** ( ☎ 809-240-6634; Calle Libertad 6; mains US$10-23; ⏱ lunch & dinner) A stand-out along Las Terrenas' restaurant row, Spanish-themed La Yuca Caliente combines professional service, a sophisticated ambience and a conversation-friendly sound system. Tables are set out on the beach, a romantic and serene spot for a late night meal. It's a wi-fi hot spot.

## Getting There & Away

### AIR

The Península de Samaná is now more easily accessible because of the new **Aeropuerto Internacional El Catey** (AZS; ☎ 809-338-0094), which receives international flights from San Juan, Puerto Rico (American Eagle), and various cities in Europe (Air Comet, Condor, LTU, CanJet, Corsair, Skyservice, Neos, Sunwing and Air Transat). Located 8km west of Sánchez and a 35-minute taxi ride (US$50) from Las Terrenas, this airport will likely transform tourism on the peninsula.

Domestic airlines service **Aeropuerto Internacional El Portillo** (EPS; ☎ 809-248-2289), a one-strip airport located a few kilometers east of Las Terrenas.

**Takeoff** ( ☎ 809-552-1333, 809-481-0707; www.takeoffweb.com; El Paseo, Las Terrenas) and **Aerodomca** ( ☎ 809-240-6571, in Santo Domingo 809-567-1195; www.aerodomca.com) operate propeller planes between El Portillo and Santo Domingo.

There are minivan taxis (US$9) waiting at El Portillo for arriving flights.

### BUS

Las Terrenas has two *gua-gua* stops at opposite ends of Av Duarte. *Gua-guas* headed

DOMINICAN REPUBLIC

DOMINICAN REPUBLIC

to Sánchez (US$1.40, 30 minutes, every 25 minutes, 7am to 6pm) take on passengers at a stop 500m south of Calle Luperón. From Sánchez you can connect to an El Caribe bus to Santo Domingo.

Those going to El Limón, 14km away (US$1.75, 20 minutes, every 15 minutes, 7am to 5pm), leave from the corner of Av Duarte and the coastal road.

### Getting Around

You can walk to and from most places in La Terrenas, though getting from one end to the other can take a half-hour or more. Taxis charge US$10 each way to Playa Bonita and US$15 to US$20 to El Limón. *Motoconchos* are cheaper – US$1.75 to Playa Bonita – but are less comfortable.

## PLAYA BONITA

A get-away from a get-away, this appropriately named beach only a few kilometers west of Las Terrenas is a better alternative for those seeking a more peaceful, reclusive vacation. The half-moon shaped beach is fairly steep and narrow and parts are strewn with palm tree detritus. However, backed by a handful of tastefully landscaped hotels, many with well-manicured lawns that rival the beach in terms of attractiveness, this is an enticing spot.

**Las Terrenas Divers** ( ☎ 809-240-6066; www.lt-divers .com; Hotel Bahía Las Ballenas; ☉ 9:30am-noon, 3-5pm) offers dive trips and courses (one tank US$34, equipment US$7, five tanks US$155), and snorkel trips to Isla Ballenas (US$15, one hour) and Playa Jackson (per person US$25 to US$30, minimum three people).

### Sleeping & Eating

**Coyamar** ( ☎ 809-240-5130; www.coyamar.com; cnr Calles F Peña Gomez & Van der Horst; s/d US$45/60; ☒ ) Located at the corner of Calle Van der Horst and the beach road, Coyamar is the least luxurious of the Playa Bonita hotels. The vibe is casual and friendly, especially good for families, and the restaurant near the front of the property and the pool are good places to hang out. Batiks and bright colors rule the day here and there.

**Hotel Acaya** ( ☎ 809-240-6161; www.hotelacaya.com; Calle F Peña Gomez; r US$65-85; ☒ ☐ ) Evocative of times gone by, this sophisticated French-owned hotel is a rebuke to the big box all-inclusives. Rooms in the two-story colonial building are simple and comfortable and everything is tastefully done, from the ceiling fans (air-con

available for US$10 extra) to the lounge/restaurant in front. Offers wi-fi access.

**our pick Hotel Bahía las Ballenas** ( ☎ 809-240-6066; www.bahia-las-ballenas.net; Calle José Antonio Martínez; d US$95-130; ☐ ☒ ) Spread out over a meticulously landscaped property, the Bahía las Ballenas has huge airy villas – all unique and some with interesting touches like roofless bathrooms. All have large wooden decks looking out over the lawn and garden and there's a large well-maintained pool lined with towering palm trees.

### Getting There & Away

By car, Playa Bonita is reachable by a single dirt road that turns off from the Sánchez–Las Terrenas highway. A taxi ride here is US$10, a *motoconcho* around US$1.75.

# NORTH COAST

Within two hours drive of Puerto Plata airport you'll find all the best the North Coast has to offer – watersports and beach nightlife in Cabarete, mountain biking in the coastal hills, the celebrated 27 waterfalls of Damajagua, sleepy little Dominican towns where it's still possible to escape the tourist hordes and mile after mile of that famous Caribbean sand.

## CABARETE

pop 15,000

Cities gentrify; surf towns grow up. So it's been here in Cabarete – this one-time farming hamlet is now the adventure-sports capital of the country, booming with condos and new development. You'll find a sophisticated, grown-up beach town, with top-notch hotels and a beach dining experience second to none (not to mention the best winds and waves on the island).

### Orientation

Cabarete is a one-street town, built up around the highway that runs right through the middle. Virtually all hotels, restaurants and shops are on the main drag, making it a congested, though easy-to-navigate place.

### Information

**All City** ( ☎ 809-571-0112; per hr US$1; ☉ 9am-9pm Mon-Sat, 10am-6pm Sun) Fast internet, headphones. Also a call center.

**Banco Progreso** Right in the center of town.

**Servi-Med** ( ☎ 809-571-0964; ☯ 24hr) Highly recommended clinic.

## Sights

Cabarete's beaches are its main attractions and not just for sun and sand. They're each home to a different water sport and are great places to watch beginner and advanced athletes alike.

**Playa Cabarete**, the main beach in front of town, is the best place for watching windsurfing, though the very best windsurfers are well offshore at the reef line. Look for them performing huge high-speed jumps and even end-over-end flips.

**Bozo Beach** is the western downwind side of Playa Cabarete and so named because of all the beginner windsurfers and kitesurfers who don't yet know how to tack upwind and so wash up on Bozo's shore. There are more kitesurfers at Bozo and the surf here is better for boogie boarding.

**Kite Beach**, 2km west of town, is a sight to behold on windy days, when scores of kiters of all skill levels negotiate huge sails and 30m lines amid the waves and traffic. On those days, there's no swimming here, as you're liable to get run over.

**Playa Encuentro**, 4km west of town, is the place to go for surfing, though top windsurfers and kitesurfers sometimes go there to take advantage of the larger waves. The beach itself is OK, but the strong tide and rocky shallows make swimming here difficult.

**La Boca**, at the mouth of the Río Yasica, 7km east of town, is an ideal spot for wakeboarding – more than 2km of straight, flat river water to practice your latest trick.

## Activities

### KITESURFING

Cabarete is one of the top places in the world to kitesurf and the sport has eclipsed windsurfing as the town's sport *du jour*. Kite Beach has ideal conditions for the sport, which entails strapping yourself to a modified surfboard and a huge inflatable wind foil then skimming and soaring across the water. A number of kitesurfing schools offer multi-day courses for those who want to learn – just to go out by yourself you'll need at least three to four days of instruction (two to three hours instruction per day).

Expect to pay US$50 to US$70 per hour for private instruction, or roughly US$400 to US$500 for a three- to four-day course.

About half of the schools are on Kite Beach.

**Kite Club** ( ☎ 809-571-9748; www.kiteclubcabarete.com) This well-run club is at the top of Kite Beach.

**Kitexcite** ( ☎ 809-571-9509; www.kitexcite.com; Kite Beach) Award-winning school uses radio helmets and optional off-shore sessions to maximize instruction.

**Laurel Eastman Kiteboarding** ( ☎ 809-571-0564; www.laureleastman.com) Friendly, safety-conscious shop located on Bozo Beach and run by one of the world's top kitesurfers.

### WINDSURFING

The combination of strong, steady winds, relatively shallow water and a rockless shore creates perfect conditions for windsurfing here.

Board and sail rentals cost US$30 to US$35 per hour, US$60 to US$65 per day or US$280 to US$300 per week. Renters are usually required to purchase damage insurance for an additional US$50 per week. Private lessons cost around US$50 for an hour, US$200 for a four-session course, with discounts for groups.

**Carib Bic Wind Center** ( ☎ 809-571-0640; caribwind .com) With more than 20 years of experience, the Bic Center is the oldest in town. It also rents bodyboards and Lasers (for those of you who prefer an actual boat attached to your sail).

**Happy Surfpool** ( ☎ 809-571-0784; www.happycaba rete.com; Villa Taína Hotel) This friendly shop also sells quality windsurfing equipment.

**Vela Windsurf Center** ( ☎ 809-571-0805; velacabarete .com; main beach) One of the best choices for windsurfing in Cabarete. It uses excellent gear and can also rent sea kayaks (US$10 to US$15 per hour).

### SURFING

Some of the best waves for surfing on the entire island – up to 4m – break over reefs 4km west of Cabarete on Playa Encuentro. Several outfits in town and on Playa Encuentro rent surfboards and offer instruction. Surfboard rental for a day is around US$25 to US$30; a three-hour course costs US$45 to US$50 per person and five-day surf camps costs US$200 to US$225 per person. All the surf schools have small offices on Playa Encuentro.

**Ali's Surf Camp** ( ☎ 809-571-0733; alissurfcamp.com) Part of the hotel of the same name. Frequent shuttle service from Cabarete to Encuentro for surfers.

**No Work Team** ( ☎ 809-571-0820; www.noworkteam cabarete.com) In the center of town. Also has a surf school on Encuentro.

**Take Off** ( ☎ 809-963-7873; www.321takeoff.com; Playa Encuentro) The German owner also organizes the Master of the Ocean competition.

**DOMINICAN REPUBLIC**

## DIVING

**Northern Coast Diving** ( ☎ 809-571-1028; www.north erncoastdiving.com) This well-respected Sosúa-based dive shop has a representative in the offices of Iguana Mama and can organize excursions from Río San Juan in the east to Monte Cristi in the west.

You're better off, though, popping over to Sosúa to compare prices and services.

## Tours

**Iguana Mama** ( ☎ 809-571-0908; www.iguanamama .com) In a class of its own, Iguana Mama is the leading adventure-sports tour operator on the north coast. Its specialties are mountain-biking (easy to insanely difficult, US$65) and cascading. It is the only operator that takes you to the 27th waterfall at Damajagua (US$85) and it's pioneered a new cascading tour to Ciguapa Falls. There's also a variety of hiking trips, including one to Pico Duarte; the trek is expensive, but handy if you want transportation to and from Cabarete (US$450 per person). It can also arrange a number of half-day and full-day canyoning opportunities in the area (US$90 to US$125).

## Festivals & Events

**Master of the Ocean** ( ☎ 809-963-7873; www.master oftheocean.com) is a triathlon of surfing, wind-surfing and kitesurfing held the final week of February. From the beach you can watch some spectacular performances.

The last week of February sand sculpture enthusiasts convene in Cabarete for the **International Sand Castle Competition**.

Held in Santiago and Cabarete in early November, the **Dominican Jazz Festival** (www .drjazzfestival.com) attracts top musical talent from around the country and even abroad. A large stage and beer tent is set up at the western end of the beach and the players trumpet jazz into the night.

## Sleeping

**Ali's Surf Camp** ( ☎ 809-571-0733; alissurfcamp.com; s/d US$29-44/33-66, apt US$75-120; ⊠ ▢ ▣ ▣ ) The closest thing Cabarete has to a backpackers, this place rocks – the German owner serves up great portions of barbecued meat for dinner, where guests sit at picnic tables and, as he put it, 'are forced to make friends.' The rooms are rustic, there's no air-con and you'll want to use the

mosquito net provided (it's south of town adjacent to the lagoon). Surf school on site.

**Kite Beach Hotel** ( ☎ 809-571-0878; www.kitebeach hotel.com; Kite Beach; s/d US$60/66, studio s/d US$70/80, apt US$90-240, penthouse US$450-600, all incl breakfast; ⊠ ▢ ▣ ) This oceanfront hotel boasts well-appointed rooms with gleaming tile floors, good-sized bathrooms and satellite TV. All suites and apartments have balconies that afford at least partial ocean views. The laid-back pool area makes a great place to watch the action in the sky and on the water. An extensive breakfast buffet is included.

**Agualina Kite Resort** ( ☎ 809-571-0787; www.agua lina.com; Kite Beach; r US$70, studio US$85, apt US$150; ⊠ ▢ ▣ ) Opened in 2004, this is the most comfortable lodging on Kite Beach. Studios and apartments have stylish, well-equipped kitchens – stainless steel refrigerators are an especially nice touch – and large modern bathrooms with glass showers and gleaming fixtures. Offers wi-fi access.

**our pick** **Natura Cabañas** ( ☎ 809-571-1507; www .naturacabana.com; s/d/tr/q US$120/160/210/240; ▢ ▣ ) Buried at the end of a McMansion subdivision just west of Cabarete, these marvellous eco-themed bungalows (think exposed freestone bathrooms) are right on the beach. Even if you aren't staying here, come for its day spa – yoga and massage are both on offer. The Chilean owners also serve excellent seafood in the on-site restaurant (mains US$15 to US$30).

## Eating

Dining out on Cabarete's beach is the quintessential Caribbean experience – paper lanterns hanging from palm trees, a gentle ocean breeze and excellent food (even if it does cost the same you'd pay back home). You can also find good, cheap Dominican set meals on the main street.

**Panadería Repostería Dick** ( ☎ 809-571-0612; breakfast US$4-7; ⏰ 7am-3pm, closed Wed) The undisputed champion of breakfast in Cabarete, Dick serves large set breakfasts with juice and strong coffee. Its bakery does whole wheat bread and mind-blowing vanilla-cream Danishes.

**Hexenkessel** ( ☎ 809-571-0493; mains US$5-14; ⏰ 24hr) After a night of debauchery, nothing hits the spot like a monstrous schnitzel (US$5) at this never-closes German eatery. Clients sit side by side at picnic tables and other house specialties include potato pancakes with ground beef (US$6.50) and fried Bavarian bratwurst (US$4).

---

**TWENTY-SEVEN WATERFALLS**

Travelers routinely describe the tour of the waterfalls at Damajagua as 'the coolest thing they did in the DR.' We agree. Guides lead you up, swimming and climbing through the waterfalls. To get down you jump – as much as 5m – into the sparkling pools below.

These days it's mandatory to go with a guide and wear a helmet and life jacket, but there's no minimum group size, so you can go by yourself if you wish. You'll need around four hours to make it to the 27th waterfall and back. The falls are open 8:30am to 4pm, but go early, before the crowds arrive and you might just have the whole place to yourself.

To get to the falls, go south from Imbert on the highway for 3.3km until you see a sign on your left with pictures of a waterfall. From there it's about 1km down to the visitors center. Alternatively, take a *gua-gua* from Puerto Plata and ask to get off at the entrance.

You can go up to the 7th, 12th, or 27th waterfall. Most 'jeep safari' package tours only go to the 7th waterfall. You should be in good shape and over the age of 12. The entrance fee varies depending on your nationality and how far you go. Foreigners pay US$8 to the 7th waterfall, US$10 to the 12th and US$14 to the highest waterfall.

US$1 of every entrance fee goes to a community development fund – plans are underway to build a library for the local school, fix a local church and build foot bridges over a nearby river.

---

**Casanova** ( ☎ 809-571-0806; mains US$12-25; ⓨ breakfast, lunch & dinner) This Asian-decorated restaurant has Buddha statues about the place and plays funky house music. The food is the best you'll find directly on the beach – the usual suspects like surf-n-turf, but also a goat's cheese salad and some mighty fine pizza, too.

**our pick** **Otra Cosa** ( ☎ 809-571-0607; La Punta; mains US$15-35; ⓨ dinner, closed Tue) This French-Caribbean restaurant, just across from Velero and with marvellous sea breezes at dusk, does some of the choicest food in town. *Foie gras* ($20) – features prominently on the menu, as does filet mignon with duck liver, morels and cognac ($33). There's good fish, lobster and steak dishes, too. It has wi-fi access.

## Drinking

**Lax** (http://lax-cabarete.com; ⓨ 9am-1am) This mellow bar and restaurant serves food until 10:30pm. In many ways it's the social headquarters of Cabarete. Try the *chinola mojito* – surprisingly good.

**Onno's** ( ☎ 809-571-0461; ⓨ 9am-late) This edgy, foreign-owned restaurant and nightclub serves some of the cheapest food on the beach – a basic breakfast goes for just US$2. At night a DJ spins a decent set and the party spills out onto the beach.

**Bambú** ( ⓨ 6pm-late) Just 100m west of Onno's, this bar and disco plays loud house music and reggaeton, and the crowd spills out onto the beach until it merges with those at Onno's.

## Getting There & Around

None of the main bus companies offers service to Cabarete – the closest bus depots are in Sosúa, where you can get a *gua-gua* (US$0.30, 20 minutes) or taxi (US$12) to Cabarete. Heaps of *gua-guas* ply this coastal road, including to Río San Juan (US$2.25, one hour) and Puerto Plata (US$1.75, one hour).

Transportation in town is dominated by *motoconchos*; a ride out to Encuentro should cost US$1.50 but will probably cost more like US$3.

A popular option for the many visitors who stay a week or longer is to rent a scooter or motorcycle. Expect to pay around US$10 to US$15 per day.

The motorcycle-shy can call a **taxi** ( ☎ 809-571-0767), which will charge you US$8 to Encuentro, US$20 to the airport and US$35 to Puerto Plata.

# CENTRAL HIGHLANDS

Even the most die-hard beach fan will eventually tire of sun and sand, and when you do, the cool mountainous playground of the Central Highlands is the place to come. Here you'll find the popular mountain retreat of Jarabacoa (500m) – the Cabarete of the interior – a tourist town and the center of a booming adventure-tour trade. Here you can go white-water rafting, visit waterfalls on horseback and still party till the sun comes up, if you've a mind to do so. Economic life in the area revolves around Santiago, the DR's second-largest city and the capital of a vast tobacco and sugarcane-growing region.

## JARABACOA
pop 57,000

Nestled in the low foothills of the mountains at 500m, Jarabacoa likes to call itself the 'City of Eternal Spring.' This may be an exaggeration – you can still happily tan poolside if you wish – but in the evenings the climate is noticeably cooler. More importantly, Jarabacoa is the outdoor capital of the Central Highlands, a place to go white-water rafting, horseback riding or canyoning and the base most people use to hike to Pico Duarte.

There's some excellent value hotels in Jarabacoa and a couple of good restaurants. Those wanting to party hearty can join the locals in the many *colmados* that ring Parque Central, or practice your merengue steps in the handful of nightclubs in town.

## Orientation

Av Independencia and Calle María N Galán one block over, are Jarabacoa's main north-south streets – Parque Central is at one end of Av Independencia and the Caribe Tours bus terminal at the other. The city's major east–west street is Calle El Carmen, which borders Parque Central.

## Information

**A&G Servicios Multiples** ( ☎ 809-574-4044; genaotours @hotmail.com; Av Independencia 43; ☼ 8am-10pm) This travel agency doubles as telephone center.
**Banco Popular** (Av Independencia near Herrera)
**Banco Progreso** (Calle Uribe near Av Independencia)
**Clínica Dr Terrero** ( ☎ 809-574-4597; Av Independencia 2-A)
**New York Net Café** (Plaza Ramirez; US$0.75/hr; ☼ 8am-12midnight) Best hours and prices in town.
**Politur** ( ☎ 809-754-3216; cnr José Duran & Mario Galán) Behind the Caribe Tours terminal.

## Sights & Activities

White-water rafting is the star of the show here, followed closely by visiting the three

---

### CLIMBING PICO DUARTE

Pico Duarte (3087m) was first climbed in 1944 to commemorate the 100th anniversary of Dominican independence. These days about 3000 people a year ascend Pico Duarte.

For all the effort involved to summit the mountain, there actually isn't a great deal to see. Up to around 2000m you travel through rainforest, passing foliage thick with ferns and some good bird life. You quickly pass above this limit, however, and spend most of the trip in a wasteland; numerous forest fire have left the landscape barren and the only animals you're likely to see are marauding bands of cawing crows.

There are **ranger stations** (admission Dominicans/foreigners US$1.50/3; ☼ 8am-5pm) near the start of the major trails into the parks – at La Ciénaga, Sabaneta, Mata Grande, Las Lagunas and Constanza. As a safety precaution, everyone entering the park, even for a short hike, must be accompanied by a guide.

While the average temperature ranges between 12°C and 20°C most of the year, lows of -5°C are not uncommon, especially in December and January. Rainstorms can happen at any time during the year. While the soil is sandy and drains well, you'll still want a good raincoat plus sturdy shoes or boots.

#### Routes to the Top

There are two popular routes up Pico Duarte.

The shortest and easiest route (and by far the most utilized) is from **La Ciénaga**, reached via Jarabacoa. It is 23km in each direction and involves approximately 2275m of vertical ascent en route to the peak. It's recommended to do this route in three days – one long day to arrive at the La Compartición campground, one easy day to summit and enjoy the views and one long day back out again. Consider also adding a fourth day to your trip to do the side-trip to the **Valle de Tetero**, a beautiful valley at the base of the mountain.

The second most popular route is from **Mata Grande**. It's 45km to the summit and involves approximately 3800m of vertical ascent, including going over La Pelona, a peak only slightly lower

waterfalls nearby. You can also go can-yoning and there are a few short hikes in the area. See p316 for tour information.

## WHITE-WATER RAFTING
The Río Yaque del Norte is the longest river in the country and rafting a portion of it can be a fun day trip. The rapids are rated two's and three's (including sections nicknamed 'Mike Tyson' and 'the Cemetery') and part of the thrill is the risk your raft may turn over, dumping you into a rock-infested river.

## WATERFALLS
So picturesque are the waterfalls near Jarabacoa that an opening scene of the movie *Jurassic Park* was filmed here, using **Salto Jimenoa Uno** as the backdrop. It's definitely the prettiest, a 60m waterfall that pours from a gaping hole in an otherwise solid rock cliff. (A lake feeds the waterfall via a subsurface drain.) There's a nice swimming hole, but the water is icy cold. The trail to the waterfall is 7.1km from the Shell station in Jarabacoa along Calle El Carmen, the road to Constanza.

**Salto de Jimenoa Dos** is a 40m cascade with an appealing bathing pool – but don't, the currents are sometimes quite strong. The turnoff to the falls is 4km northwest of Jarabacoa on the road to Hwy Duarte and a portion of the trail includes walking over a series of narrow suspension bridges and trails flanked by densely forested canyon walls.

**Salto de Baiguate** is also in a lush canyon but isn't nearly as impressive as the others, nor is the pool as inviting. To get there, take Calle El Carmen east out of Jarabacoa for 3km until you see a sign for the waterfalls on the right-hand side of the road. It's a pleasant walk from town, if you're not in a hurry.

The falls are easy to visit if you've got your own transportation. If not, a *motoconcho* tour to all three falls will cost around US$15 to US$20 and a taxi US$60 to US$80. Either way you'll have to pay the park entrance fee (Dominicans/foreigners US$0.60/1.50).

## HIKING
There's a number of half-day and full-day walks you can take in the area. The best day

than Pico Duarte itself. You'll spend the first night at the Río La Guácara campground and the second at the Valle de Bao campground. You can walk this route return in five days, but far more interesting is to walk out via the Valle de Tetero and La Ciénega (also five days).

### Tours & Guides
The easiest way to summit Pico Duarte is to take an organized tour. Prices vary widely and depend on how many people are going and for how long. Expect to pay roughly US$80 to US$100 per person per day. Be sure to book at least a month in advance.

Rancho Baiguate (p316) is the best overall choice for non-Spanish speakers, as it is based in Jarabacoa and also offers the detour through Valle de Tetero. Iguana Mama (see p312) in Cabarete is good if you're in a hurry and want transportation to and from the north coast.

Your other option – assuming you speak good Spanish and you're not in a hurry – is to go to the trailhead in person and organize mules, food and a guide on your own. Mules and muleteers go for around US$10 per day each and the lead guide around US$15 per day (minimum one guide for every five hikers). Guides can organize basic provisions for you.

Attempting to summit Pico Duarte without mules is neither possible nor desirable – you can't enter the park without a guide and a guide won't go without mules. Plus walking with a full pack in this heat would drain whatever enjoyment you might get from the walk. Mules are also essential in case someone gets injured.

### Sleeping
There are approximately 14 campgrounds in the parks, each with a first-come first-served cabin that hikers can use for free. Each cabin holds 20 or more people and consists of wood floors, wood walls and a wood ceiling (and rats), but no beds, mats or lockers – if you have a tent, consider bringing it along so you can avoid using the cabins altogether. Most of the cabins also have a stand-alone 'kitchen': an open-sided structure with concrete wood-burning stoves.

walk is to **El Mogote**, a short peak just 2km west of town. To get there, hop a *motoconcho* (US$3) or taxi (US$7) to the entrance. Just past the entrance you'll encounter a Salesian monastery; from here it's a stiff 2½- to three-hour walk to the summit. It's a slippery walk, nay, slide, down from the top.

## Tours

Jarabacoa's biggest and best tour operator, **Rancho Baiguate** ( ☎ 809-574-6890; www.ranchobaiguate .com; Carretera a Constanza) dominates the stage, leaving but crumbs for the rest. While its main clientele are Dominican groups from the capital and foreign guests from the all-inclusives near Puerto Plata, independent travelers are always free to join any of the trips (call as far in advance as possible).

Prices are as follows: rafting (US$50), canyoning (US$50), mountain biking (US$25), all with breakfast and lunch included. It also offers horseback/jeep tours to the waterfalls (US$16 to US$21 with lunch). Its Pico Duarte trips range in price depending on the number of people and the side trips you take; a group of four people for three days with no side trips pay US$300 per person.

## Sleeping

**Hotel Brisas del Yaque II** ( ☎ 809-574-2100; Independencia 13; d/tw US$45/75; 🅿 ) Although it shares the same ownership and has a similar name with another hotel in town, this newer version has 20 comfortable and modern rooms. The twin rooms have two bathrooms, one for each guest. Ask for a mountain-facing room, if only to avoid the noisy street-side market.

**Hotel Gran Jimenoa** ( ☎ 809-574-6304; www .granjimenoa.com; Av La Confluencia; s/d/tr/ste incl breakfast US$50/74/95/117; 🅿 🖥 🏊 ) Set several kilometers from Jarabacao directly on the roaring Río Jimenoa, this is easily the best hotel in town. It may be neither on the beach nor an all-inclusive, but you could easily spend a week here without leaving the grounds (the restaurant is excellent). A new wing was under construction when we were there.

**Rancho Baiguate** ( ☎ 809-574-6890; www.rancho baiguate.com; Carretera a Constanza; s US$77-107, d US$126-163, tr US$170-220, q US$252; 🖥 🏊 ) A cross between

---

### RESERVA CIENTÍFICA LOMA QUITA ESPUELA

The 'Mountain of the Missing Spur' – a reference to the dense underbrush that ripped boot spurs from cowboys, not the 'espuela' or fighting claw of a cock (also frequently removed) – is a remote and lovely (and definitely off the beaten track) national park. The NGO **Fundación Loma Quita Espuela** ( ☎ 809-588-4156; www.flqe.org.do; Urbanización Almánzar, cnr Calle Luis Carrón & Av del Jaya; 🕐 8am-noon & 2-5pm) runs the national park on behalf of the government and is actively involved in developing sustainable ways for the local farmers to use this natural resource.

Many of the local, small cocoa growers whose land borders the national park now produce organic cocoa and the foundation helps them achieve organic certification. A beekeeping project is also encouraging locals to keep bees in the national park – more bees helps the endemic plants fertilize better and it's extra income for the locals at minimal cost to the environment.

The national park contains the largest rainforest on the island and is full of endemic species, both plant and animal, that are on the point of extinction. Additionally, more than 60 streams flow from these mountains and provide water to the cities and towns surrounding, making the foundation's efforts critical to the survival not only of the park but also the hundreds of thousands of people who live nearby.

Visiting Quita Espuela makes a pleasant day trip from Santiago or Santo Domingo. The foundation offers a number of tours, including the hike to the top of **Loma Quita Espuela** (942m, 2½ hours), where an observation tower commands excellent views out over the Valle de Cibao. A guide is mandatory (Spanish-only) and can explain the flora and fauna you see along the way. The tour costs US$12 for a group of up to 15 people. You'll also have to pay the park entrance fee (Dominicans/foreigners US$0.60/1.50).

For those less actively inclined, there's a shorter walk that tours several cocoa plantations, where you can buy *bola de cacao* – crude chocolate balls the local housewives grate and sweeten to make hot chocolate. The tour ends at a local *balneario*, where you can swim.

The entrance to Loma Quita Espuela is 14km (30 minutes) northeast of San Francisco de Macorís on a rough road that gets progressively worse. Don't try this without a good 4WD.

a summer camp and an all-inclusive resort, Rancho Baiguate offers plain but comfortable accommodations on its 72-sq-km complex about 5km east of town. Three meals are included in the price. An on-site veggie garden supplies the competent Dominican cook, and a worm farm and grey-water treatment plant reduce its impact on the environment. Bring mosquito repellent. Staff can pick you up from town.

## Eating

**Restaurant Del Parque Galería** ( ☎ 809-574-6749; cnr Duarte & Mirabal; mains US$8-15; ☺ breakfast, lunch & dinner) Overlooking Parque Central, this open-air restaurant-bar serves up traditional Dominican meals as well as international favorites. This is a great place to people watch – feel free to just order a drink and check out the goings-on in the park.

**Restaurante El Rancho** ( ☎ 809-574-4557; Calle Independencia 1; mains US$8-15; ☺ breakfast, lunch & dinner) Part of the Baiguate empire, El Rancho offers a varied menu of chicken and beef dishes, sushi-style wraps and excellent pizzas. The walls of this semi-dressy, open-sided restaurant are graced with handsome local paintings although the *motoconcho* traffic outside detracts somewhat from the setting.

**Hotel Gran Jimenoa** ( ☎ 809-574-6304; www .granjimenoa.com; Av La Confluencia; mains US$14-35; ☺ 7am-11pm) Jarabacoa's best hotel also offers one of the town's most unique dining experiences. The restaurant here occupies an open-air deck, perched right alongside the roaring Río Jimenoa. Dishes are fairly standard, though well-prepared; try the local Jarabacoa specialty, chicken breast stuffed with cream cheese.

## Getting There & Away

**Caribe Tours** ( ☎ 809-574-4796; Calle Duran near Av Independencia) offers the only 1st-class bus service to Jarabacoa. Four daily departures to Santo Domingo (US$5.40, three hours, 7am, 10am, 1:30pm and 4:30pm) include a stop in La Vega (US$2.30, 1½ hours).

Next door a **gua-gua terminal** (Av Independencia at Duran) provides service to La Vega (US$1.40, 45 minutes, every 10 to 30 minutes, 7am to

**DOMINICAN REPUBLIC**

---

**BEST OF THE REST**

**Bayahibe**, originally founded by fishermen from Puerto Rico in the 19th century, is like an actor playing many roles in the same performance. In the morning it's the proverbial tourist gateway, when busloads of tourists from resorts further east hop into boats bound for Isla Saona. But once this morning rush hour is over it turns back into a drowsy village. Another buzz of activity when they return and then after sunset another transformation. What sets Bayahibe apart is that it manages to maintain its character despite the continued encroachment of big tourism

Meaning 'Land of the Mountains,' **Parque Nacional Los Haitises** (admission US$3.50; ☺ 7am-8pm) is a 1375-sq-km park at the southwestern end of the Bahía de Samaná containing scores of lush hills jutting some 30m to 50m from the water and coastal wetlands. The knolls were formed one to two million years ago, when tectonic drift buckled the thick limestone shelf that had formed underwater. The area receives a tremendous amount of rainfall, creating perfect conditions for subtropical humid forest plants such as bamboo, ferns and bromeliads. In fact, Los Haitises contains over 700 species of flora, including four types of mangrove, making it one of the most highly bio-diverse regions in the Caribbean. Los Haitises also is home to 110 species of bird, 13 of which are endemic to the island. The park also contains a series of limestone caves, some of which contain intriguing Taíno pictographs.

With its scores of tiny, jungly islands and thick mangrove forests, the park makes for great exploring by boat. Victoria Marine (p301) and other tour outfits in Samaná offer trips here for around US$45 per person, including guide and transportation to, and inside, the park.

Fortunately, the area around the park has one of the more special places to stay anywhere in the DR. A stay at **Paraíso Caño Hondo** ( ☎ 809-248-5995; www.paraisocanohondo.com in Spanish; r US$48) couldn't be further from the typical beach resort experience. The Jivales River, which runs through the property, has been channeled into 10 magical waterfall-fed pools, perfect for a soak any time of the day. Rooms are large and rustic, made mostly of wood, though extremely comfortable. Signs from the center of Sabana de la Mar direct you to the turn-off for the hotel – the same one as for the entrance to Parque Los Haitises.

6pm). If you prefer to hire a cab to La Vega, the ride costs around US$22.

**Públicos to Constanza** (cnr Deligne & El Carmen) leave from in front of the Shell gasoline station at around 9am and 1pm daily (US$2.80, two hours). It's a scenic but rough ride in the back of a pickup truck.

### Getting Around
The town of Jarabacoa is easily managed on foot but to get to outlying hotels and sights you can easily flag down a *motoconcho* on any street corner during the day. If you prefer a cab, try Taxi Jarabacoa ( ☎ 809-574-7474) or just catch a cab at the corner of José Duran and Av Independencia.

# DIRECTORY

## ACCOMMODATIONS
Compared to other destinations in the Caribbean, lodging in the Dominican Republic is relatively affordable. That being said, there is a dearth of options for independent travelers wishing to make decisions on-the-fly and for whom cost is a concern. All the room rates listed in this book are for the high season, which varies slightly from region to region. More so than other destinations, hotel rooms booked a minimum of three days in advance on the internet are shockingly cheaper (especially at the DR's famous all-inclusive resorts), than if you book by phone or, worst case scenario, simply show up without a reservation. Much of the prime beachfront property throughout the country is occupied by all-inclusives. The largest concentrations are at Bávaro–Punta

Cana in the east and Playa Dorada in the north, though their numbers are growing in areas around Bayahibe, Río San Juan, Sosúa and Luperón.

## ACTIVITIES
### Cycling
Several tour operators – like Iguana Mama in Cabarete (p312) – offer highly recommended mountain-bike tours ranging from half-day downhill rides to 12-day cross-country excursions.

### Diving & Snorkeling
On the southern coast, warm Caribbean waters and abundant tropical fish make for fun, easy dives. On the north coast, the Atlantic waters are cooler and less transparent but the terrain includes more canyons, swim-throughs, caverns and rock outcrops; Sosúa is the north coast's dive capital, and excursions can be organized from there to all points along the coast. A variety of underwater sights around Las Galeras (p304) are popular.

### Hiking
The town of Jarabacoa is the jumping-off point for ascents of the Caribbean's tallest peak, Pico Duarte at 3087m. Hiking through the Valle de Tétero, a beautiful valley with rivers and indigenous petroglyphs, makes a rewarding side trip.

### Golf
Known as one of the premier golf destinations in the Caribbean, the Dominican Republic has more than two dozen courses to choose from.

---

**PRACTICALITIES**

- **Newspapers & Magazines** You'll find *Listín Diario, Hoy, Ultima Hora, Siglo* and *Nacional*, plus *International Herald Tribune, New York Times* and *Miami Herald* in many tourist areas.

- **Radio & TV** There are some 150 radio stations, most playing merengue and *bachata* (the DR's 'country'-style music); there are also seven local TV networks, though cable and satellite programming is very popular for baseball, movies and American soap operas.

- **Electricity** The Dominican Republic uses the same electrical system as the USA and Canada (110V to 125V AC, 60Hz, North American–style plugs). Power outages are common but many hotels and shops have backup generators.

- **Video Systems** NTSC

- **Weights & Measures** The metric system is used for everything except gasoline, which is in gallons and at laundromats, where pounds are used.

Signature courses by high-profile designers are being built at a steady pace. The majority are affiliated with (or located nearby) the top all-inclusive resorts, but are open to guests and nonguests alike.

## Whale-Watching
From mid-January to mid-March, thousands of humpback whales congregate in and around the Bay of Samaná, making it one of the best whale-watching spots in the world.

## Windsurfing & Kitesurfing
The DR is one of the top places in the world for windsurfing and kitesurfing. The wind blows hardest in Cabarete, a town on the north coast given over almost wholly to the two sports. Cabarete has numerous schools for those interested in either. Las Terrenas on the Península de Samaná is a growing destination for both sports.

## BOOKS
Lonely Planet's *Dominican Republic & Haiti* has more information on traveling in the DR. Baseball fans should pick up *Sugarball: The American Game, the Dominican Dream*. For more on the DR's music, try *Bachata: A Social History of Dominican Popular Music*, by Deborah Pacini Hernandez and *Merengue: Dominican Music and Dominican Identity*, by Paul Austerlitz. *Why the Cocks Fight*, by Michele Wucker, examines Dominican-Haitian relations through the metaphor of cockfighting. *Death in Paradise* by JB Mackinnon is perhaps the best contemporary account of the DR; it's also an investigation into the Trujillo regime.

## BUSINESS HOURS
The following hours are standard for the DR. Exceptions are noted in individual listings.
**Banks** ☯ 8am to 4pm Monday to Friday, 9am to 1pm Saturday
**Government offices** ☯ 7:30am to 2:30pm Monday to Friday
**Restaurants** ☯ 9am to 10pm Monday to Saturday; most close between lunch and dinner
**Shops** ☯ 9am to 7:30pm Monday to Saturday
**Supermarkets** ☯ 8am to 10pm Monday to Saturday
**Tourist attractions** ☯ 9am to 6pm; many museums and galleries close one day per week (usually Monday)

Liquor licensing laws, and hence bar opening and closing times, were in flux at the time of research. However, expect bars, nightclubs and casinos to be open from 6pm to late.

## CHILDREN
All-inclusive resorts can be a convenient and affordable way for families to travel, as they do away with decisions on when and where to eat, what to do and where to stay. For independent-minded families, the DR has plenty of family-friendly beaches and outdoor activities.

There are few kid-specific parks or attractions, however.

## DANGERS & ANNOYANCES
Some guests at all-inclusive resorts report having items stolen from their rooms. As in any hotel, don't leave money or valuables in plain view.

Use the room safe (if one is available) or lock items in an inside pocket of your suitcase.

## EMBASSIES & CONSULATES
For the contact information of all Dominican embassies and consulates, check out the website of the **Secretaría de Estado de Relaciones Exteriores** (www.serex.gov.do). When it's functioning, it's a good resource.
**Canada** ( ☎ 809-685-1136; sdgo@dfai-maeci.gc.ca; Av Eugenio de Marchena 39)
**Cuba** ( ☎ 809-537-2113; Calle FP Ramírez 809)
**France** ( ☎ 809-687-5270; www.ambafrance-do.org; Calle de las Damas 42 btwn Luperón & El Conde)
**Germany** ( ☎ 809-542-8949; 16th fl, Torre Piantini, cnr Avs Gustavo A Mejía Ricart & Abraham Lincoln)
**Haiti** ( ☎ 809-686-5778; cnr Calle Juan Sánchez Ramírez 33 & Av Máximo Gómez)
**Italy** ( ☎ 809-682-0830; Calle Rodríguez Objío 4)
**Japan** ( ☎ 809-567-3365; 8th fl, Torre BHD office bldg, cnr Calle Luís Thomen & Av Jiménez Moya)
**Netherlands** ( ☎ 809-565-5240; Mayor Enrique Valverde)
**Spain** ( ☎ 809-535-6500; 4th fl, Torre BHD office bldg, cnr Calle Luís Thomen & Av Jiménez Moya)
**Trinidad & Tobago** ( ☎ 809-687-1202; Isabel La Catolica 171)
**UK** ( ☎ 809-472 7111; cnr Av 27 de Febrero 233 & Av Máximo Gómez)
**USA** ( ☎ 809-221-2171; www.usemb.gov.do; cnr Av César Nicolás Penson & Av Máximo Gómez)

## FESTIVALS & EVENTS
If there's any generalization to be made about Dominicans, it is that they take holidays and celebrations very seriously.
**Carnaval** (February) Celebrated with great fervor throughout the country every Sunday in February, culminating in

a huge blowout in Santo Domingo the last weekend of the month or the first weekend of March. Masks and costumes figure prominently in every town's celebration – Santiago even hosts an international Carnaval mask competition.

**Independence Day** (February 27) On this day in 1844 the Dominican Republic gained independence from Haiti, which had occupied the DR shortly after the latter declared independence from Spain. The day is marked by street celebrations and military parades.

**Semana Santa** 'Holy Week,' in March, is the biggest travel holiday in the country and much of Latin America. Everyone heads to the water – expect crowded beaches, innumerable temporary food stands and music day and night.

**Santo Domingo Merengue Festival** Santo Domingo hosts the country's largest and most raucous merengue festival. For two weeks at the end of July and beginning of August, the world's top merengue bands play for the world's best merengue dancers.

## HOLIDAYS

**New Year's Day** January 1
**Epiphany/Three Kings Day** January 6
**Our Lady of Altagracia** January 21
**Duarte Day** January 26
**Independence Day** February 27
**Holy Thursday, Holy Friday, Easter Sunday**
March/April
**Pan-American Day** April 14
**Labor Day** May 1
**Foundation of Sociedad la Trinitaria** July 16
**Restoration Day** August 16
**Our Lady of Mercedes** September 24
**Columbus Day** October 12
**UN Day** October 24
**All Saints' Day** November 1
**Christmas Day** December 25

## MONEY

The Dominican monetary unit is the peso, indicated by the symbol RD$. There are one- and five-peso coins, while paper money comes in denominations of 10, 20, 50, 100, 500 and 1000 pesos.

### ATMs

Banco Popular, Banco Progreso, Banco de Reservas, Banco León and Scotiabank all have ATMs that accept most foreign debit cards.

### Black Market

Moneychangers will approach you in a number of tourist centers, but you get equally favorable rates and a much securer transaction at an ATM, bank or exchange office.

### Credit Cards

Visa and MasterCard are accepted widely (Amex a little less so), especially in areas frequented by tourists. Some businesses add a surcharge for credit card purchases (typically 16%).

### Taxes & Tipping

There are two taxes on food and drink sales: a 16% sales tax (ITBIS) and a 10% service charge. The latter is supposed to be divided among the wait and kitchen staff; some people choose to leave an additional 10% tip for exceptional service. There's a 23% tax on hotel rooms – ask whether the listed rates include taxes.

## TELEPHONE

The Dominican Republic country code is ☎ 809, and you need to dial this number even when making calls with the DR. To call from North America, dial ☎ 1-809 + the local number. From elsewhere, dial you country's international dialing code + ☎ 809 + the local number. We've included the full 10-digit number in the DR listings in this chapter.

Call centers are the easiest and cheapest way to make international phone calls (average rates per minute to USA US$0.20; per minute to Europe US$0.50; per minute to Haiti US$0.50).

Phone cards are available at many hotels and mini-marts; follow the Spanish/English instructions printed on the back.

Mobile phones are very popular and travelers with global roaming–enabled phones can often receive and make cell phone calls – be aware that per-minute fees can be exorbitant. If you have a GSM phone that you can unlock you can use a SIM card bought from Orange or Claro (prepaid startup kit US$10). New cell phones can be bought at Orange with a prepaid SIM card for less than US$30.

## VISAS

Tourist cards, available upon arrival for US$10, are issued to foreign visitors from Argentina, Australia, Austria, Belgium, Brazil, Canada, Chile, Denmark, France, Germany, Greece, Ireland, Israel, Italy, Japan, Mexico, Netherlands, Portugal, Russia, Spain, Sweden, Switzerland, South Africa the UK and USA, among many others.

**EMERGENCY NUMBERS**

- Ambulance ☎ 911
- Fire ☎ 911
- Police ☎ 911

# TRANSPORTATION

## GETTING THERE & AWAY
### Entering the Dominican Republic
All foreign visitors must have a valid passport to enter the Dominican Republic. A tourist card is purchased on arrival – see opposite.

At airports, neither immigration nor customs officials pay much attention to tourists carrying an ordinary amount of luggage. Border officials may be more vigilant.

### Air
Santo Domingo's **Aeropuerto Internacional Las Américas** (SDQ; ☎ 809-549-0081) is easily the largest and most modern airport in the country; however, **Aeropuerto Internacional Punta Cana** (PUJ; ☎ 809-959-2473), serving Bávaro and Punta Cana, actually handles more passengers. Puerto Plata's **Aeropuerto Internacional Gregorio Luperón** (POP; ☎ 809-586-1992) and Santiago's **Aeropuerto Internacional Cibao** (STI; ☎ 809-581-8072) also handle a good number of international flights.

The following airports also service international flights:

**Aeropuerto Internacional El Catey** (AZS; ☎ 809-338-0094) New airport 40km west of Samaná that handles international flights from various European cities and San Juan, Puerto Rico.

**Aeropuerto Internacional La Romana** (LRM, Casa de Campo; ☎ 809-689-1548) Modern airport near La Romana and Casa de Campo; handles primarily charter flights from the US, Canada and Europe.

The following airlines service the DR:

**Aeropostal** ( ☎ 809-549-8067; www.aeropostal.com) Caracas

**Air Canada** ( ☎ 809-541-2929; www.aircanada.ca) Toronto

**Air Europa** ( ☎ 809-683-8020; www.aireuropa.com) Mallorca

**Air France** ( ☎ 809-686-8432; www.airfrance.com) Paris

**Air Jamaica** ( ☎ 809-872-0080; www.airjamaica.com) Kingston

**American Airlines** ( ☎ 809-542-5151; www.aa.com) New York, San Juan

**Condor** ( ☎ 809-689-9625; www.condor.com) Munich

**Continental Airlines** ( ☎ 809-262-1060; www.continental.com) Newark

**COPA Airlines** ( ☎ 809-472-2672; www.copaair.com) Havana, Kingston, Panama City, Port of Spain

**Cubana Air** ( ☎ 809-227-2040; www.cubana.cu) Havana

**Delta** ( ☎ 809-200-9191; www.delta.com) Atlanta

**Iberia** ( ☎ 809-508-7979; www.Iberia.com) Madrid

**Jet Blue** ( ☎ 809-549-1793; www.jetblue.com) New York, Orlando

**Lan Chile** ( ☎ 809-689-2116; www.lan.com) Santiago

**LTU** ( ☎ 809-586-4075; www.ltu.com) Dusseldorf

**Lufthansa** ( ☎ 809-689-9625; www.lufthansa.com) Frankfurt

**Martinair Holland** ( ☎ 809-621-7777; www.martinair.com) Amsterdam, Frankfurt

**Mexicana** ( ☎ 809-541-1016; www.mexicana.com) Mexico City

**Spirit Airlines** ( ☎ 809-381-4111; www.spiritair.com) Fort Lauderdale

**US Airways** ( ☎ 809-540-0505; www.usair.com) Philadelphia

**Varig** ( ☎ 809-563-3434; www.varig.com) São Paolo

### Land
#### BORDER CROSSINGS
There are three main border crossings between the Dominican Republic and Haiti: Jimaní/Malpasse in the south on the road between Port-au-Prince and Santo Domingo; in the north at Dajabón/Ouanaminthe between Cap-Haïtien and Santiago; and further south at Elías Piña/Belladère. Borders open 8am to 6pm but it is always a good idea to arrive early.

When leaving the Dominican Republic, travelers will be asked to produce their passports and tourist cards. From Haiti, you must have your passport and the yellow entry card you received upon arrival.

#### BUS
If you want to travel to Haiti, **Capital Coach Line** ( ☎ 809-530-8266; www.capitalcoachline.com; 27 de Febrero 455), **Caribe Tours** ( ☎ 809-221-4422; www.caribetours.com.do; cnr Avs 27 de Febrero & Leopoldo Navarro) and **Terra Bus** ( ☎ 809-531-0383; Plaza Lama, cnr Avs 27 de Febrero & Winston Churchill) offer daily bus services to Port-au-Prince. Capital Coach Line has one departure daily at 10am and Caribe and Terra at 11am and 11:30am, respectively. All three use comfortable, air-con coaches and the trip takes from six to nine hours and costs US$40.

DOMINICAN REPUBLIC

## Sea

**Ferries del Caribe** ( ☎ in Santo Domingo 809-688-4400, in Santiago 809-724-8771, in Mayagüez 787-832-4400, in San Juan 787-725-2643) offers the DR's only international ferry service, connecting Santo Domingo and Mayagüez, Puerto Rico. The ticket office and boarding area are on Av del Puerto opposite Fortaleza Ozama in Zona Colonial. The ferry departs Santo Domingo Sunday, Tuesday and Thursday at 8pm and returns from Mayagüez on Monday, Wednesday and Friday at 8pm. The trip takes 12 hours and costs around US$129/189 one-way/return in an airplane-style seat, or around per person single/double US$182/311 one-way or single/double US$295/474 return in a private cabin with an exterior window.

## GETTING AROUND

### Air

Along with the airports listed previously (p321), the following airports handle domestic flights:

**Aeropuerto Internacional Arroyo Barril** (ABA; ☎ 809-248-2718) West of Samaná. Used mostly during whale-watching season (January to March) and handles only propeller aircraft. Serves Santiago and the interior.

**Aeropuerto Internacional El Portillo** (EPS) Airstrip only a few kilometers from Las Terrenas, used mostly for domestic flights and gets busiest during whale-watching season.

**Aeropuerto Internacional La Isabela** (JBQ, Dr Joaquín Balaguer; ☎ 809-567-3900) Located 16km north of Santo Domingo in Higuero, this airport services domestic airlines.

**Aeropuerto Internacional María Montez** (BRX; ☎ 809-524-4144) Five kilometers from Barahona; does not have a regular commercial passenger service.

The main domestic carriers and air taxi companies:

**AeroDomca** ( ☎ 809-567-1195; www.aerodomca.com) Scheduled flights between La Isabela outside Santo Domingo to El Portillo near Las Terrenas (US$75). Charter flights can be booked to almost any airport.

**Air Century** ( ☎ 809-826-4222; www.aircentury.com) Charter flights from La Isabela outside Santo Domingo.

**Take Off** ( ☎ 809-552-1333; www.takeoffweb.com) Offers the widest selection of scheduled flights, including Santo Domingo to El Portillo ($80). There's a small, efficient office with English speakers in the Plaza Brisas in Bávaro.

## Bicycle

The DR's under-maintained highways are not well suited for cycling, though mountain biking on back roads can be rewarding. There are a number of recommended tours available from Jarabacoa (p316) and Cabarete (p312 ).

## Bus

### FIRST-CLASS SERVICE

First-class buses are comfortable, have air-con, and often also have TVs and a movie. Fares are low – the most expensive is less than US$10. Reservations aren't usually necessary.

The following companies have 1st-class services:

**Caribe Tours** ( ☎ in Santo Domingo 809-221-4422; cnr Avs 27 de Febrero & Leopoldo Navarro) The most extensive bus line, with service everywhere but the south east.

**Expreso Santo Domingo Bávaro** ( ☎ in Santo Domingo 809-682-9670; cnr Juan Sánchez Ruiz & Máximo Gómez) Connects Santo Domingo and Bávaro with a stop in La Romana.

**El Canario** ( ☎ 809-291-5594) Not exactly 1st-class vehicles, but the only daily direct service between Puerto Plata and Samaná (US$7, 3½ to 4 hours, with stops in Nagua and Sánchez).

**Metro** ( ☎ in Santo Domingo 809-566-7126; Calle Francisco Prats Ramírez) Located behind Plaza Central Mall in Santo Domingo, Metro serves nine cities, mostly along the Santo Domingo–Puerto Plata corridor.

**Terra Bus** ( ☎ 809-531-0383; Plaza Lama, cnr Avs 27 de Febrero & Winston Churchill) Air-con service from Santo Domingo to Port-au-Prince, Haiti.

### GUA-GUAS

*Gua-guas* vary in size, from minivans to midsize buses with room for around 30 passengers. They don't have toilet facilities and only occasionally have air-con. Unlike regular buses, *gua-guas* stop all along the route to pick up and drop off passengers. Wherever long-distance buses don't go, you can be sure a *gua-gua* does. *Gua-guas* rarely have signs, so ask a local if you're unsure which one to take. Most pass every 15 to 30 minutes and cost US$1 to US$2. Simply wave to be picked up.

### LOCAL BUS

Large cities like Santo Domingo have public bus systems that operate as they do in most places around the world. However, *públicos* (see opposite) pass much more frequently.

## Car & Motorcycle

### RENTAL

Renting a car is a great way to see the country without wasting time waiting for buses.

Prices range from US$40 to US$100 per day. Motorcycles can also be rented, but only experienced drivers should do so because of poor road conditions. If you bust a tire – the most common car trouble here – a *gomera* is a tire repair and retail shop.

You must have a valid driver's license and be at least 25 years old to rent a car. You will be required to show a major credit card or leave your passport as a deposit. Be sure to ask about the 'deductible' (the amount you pay out-of-pocket before insurance kicks in) and whether the insurance covers damage to your tires or windows.

### ROAD HAZARDS
Roads in the DR range from excellent to awful, sometimes along the same highway over a very short distance. Be alert for potholes, speed bumps and people walking along the roadside, especially near populated areas. On all roads, large or small, watch for slow-moving cars and especially motorcycles. Be particularly careful when driving at night, better yet, *never drive at night*. Even the most skilled person with the reflexes of a superhero will probably end up in a ditch by the side of the road.

### ROAD RULES
First rule is there are none. In theory, road rules in the DR are the same as for most countries in the Americas and the lights and signs are the same shape and color you find in the US or Canada. Seatbelts are required at all times. That said, driving in the DR is pretty much a free-for-all, a test of one's nerves and will, a continuous game of chicken where the loser is the one who decides to give way just before the moment of impact.

### Motoconchos
Cheaper and easier to find than taxis, *motoconchos* (motorcycle taxis) are the best and sometimes only way to get around in many towns. An average ride should cost you no more than US$1.50. However, a high number of riders have been injured or killed in *motoconcho* accidents; ask the driver to slow down (*¡Más despacio por favor!*) if you think he's driving dangerously. Avoid two passengers on a bike since not only is the price the same as taking separate bikes but the extra weight makes most scooters harder to control. For longer trips, or if you have any sort of bag or luggage, *motoconchos* are usually impractical and certainly less comfortable than the alternatives.

### Públicos
These are banged-up cars, minivans or small pickup trucks that pick up passengers along set routes in towns. *Públicos* (also called *conchos* or *carros*) don't have signs but the drivers hold their hands out the window to solicit potential fares. They are also identifiable by the crush of people inside them – up to seven in a midsize car! To flag one down simply hold out your hand – the fare is around US$0.30. If there is no one else in the car, be sure to tell the driver you want *servicio público* (public service) to avoid paying private taxi rates.

### Taxis
Dominican taxis rarely cruise for passengers – instead they wait at designated *sitios* (stops), which are located at hotels, bus terminals, tourist areas and main public parks. You also can phone a taxi service (or ask your hotel receptionist to call for you). Taxis do not have meters – agree on a price beforehand.

# Puerto Rico

Puerto Rico is where the easy-going Caribbean collides with the slick efficiency of modern America. The result is a colorful, diverse and culturally unique island that is often as confusing as it is cosmopolitan. Hip funky restaurants nestle next to 15th-century Spanish forts; sprawling shopping malls encroach upon fecund tropical rainforests; and glitzy casinos lie juxtaposed against some of the most stunning beaches in the Caribbean.

History is another draw card. While the United States struggles to emulate the erstwhile glories of 'old world' Europe, Puerto Rico gets out its killer trump card: beguiling Viejo San Juan, one of the oldest and best-preserved colonial cities in the Americas. Cocooned in what was the crucible of Spain's once-illustrious colonial empire, neighborly pensioners recline languidly in creaking rocking chairs; *bomba* drums light up the somnolence of a diminutive baroque plaza; and the walls of two great military forts rise like wizened sentinels above the depths of the untamed Atlantic.

Racing headlong into the 21st century, contemporary Puerto Rico can sometimes present a bewildering picture to culture-seeking visitors. Decades of unchecked American-style development have meant that, despite significant economic advances, the modern world has stamped its ugly mark on the idyllically named *Isla del Encanto* (Island of Enchantment). But purists can take heart. In Puerto Rico what you see isn't always what you get. Scratch under the surface and the soul of island will serendipitously reveal itself. Hop on a local bus, disappear off into the central mountains, or pedal your way around the beautiful island of Vieques; just be sure to tear up any cast-iron itineraries and let the open road lead you where it will.

## FAST FACTS

- **Area** 3500 sq miles
- **Capital** San Juan
- **Country code** ☎ 787
- **Departure tax** US$14.10 (normally included in the ticket price)
- **Famous for** Rum, salsa, baseball
- **Language** Spanish, English
- **Money** US dollar (US$); US$1 = €0.65 = UK£0.51
- **Official name** Puerto Rico
- **People** Puerto Ricans
- **Phrase** *Qué pasa?* What's happening? *Esta todo hablado.* It's all understood.
- **Population** 3.9 million
- **Visa** Unnecessary for most countries; see p354

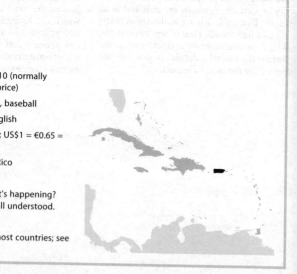

## HIGHLIGHTS

- **Old San Juan** (p329) Uncover the city's soul where over 500 years of history gets crammed into just seven square blocks
- **Vieques** (p343) Roam through a newly appointed wildlife refuge where the sound of exploding US navy shells has been replaced by the somnolence of over a dozen deserted beaches
- **El Yunque** (p343) Fall asleep to a chorus of frogs and wake up to a mug of locally grown coffee in El Yunque, Puerto Rico's dripping tropical rainforest
- **Ponce** (p348) Find out why Puerto Ricans are aficionados of salsa at an open-air music festival in Plaza Las Delicias in Puerto Rico's most colonial city
- **Parque de las Cavernas del Río Camuy** (p342) Head underground among stalagmites and stalactites in the island's cavernous karst country

## ITINERARIES

- **Three Days** Discover the wonders of Old San Juan, with its museums, galleries, monuments and forts. After dark, jump back into the 21st century and bar hop along Fortaleza. Take a trip to the rum factory in Cataño and hit the municipal beaches of Condado and Ocean Park.
- **One Week** Follow the three-day itinerary and on day four take an ecotour to El Yunque for hiking and river swimming. Check out Playa Luquillo, then head west to the Camuy caves and the Arecibo Observatory.
- **Two Weeks** Follow the one-week itinerary, lingering in karst country at the Casa Grande Mountain Retreat before heading east to Fajardo. Take the ferry to Vieques and visit the bioluminescent bay before heading over to Culebra. Check out Playa Flamenco and spend the night at Mamacitas. After a mid-morning ferry ride back, drive to Ponce and use that as a base to check out Guánica forest, then move up the coast to Rincón.

## CLIMATE & WHEN TO GO

The best time to visit Puerto Rico is mid-December through late-April. The upside of visiting at this time is the weather, which is sunny (but not too hot) and free from the threat of hurricanes. The downside is that prices get hiked up and crowds are generally heavier. Skirt the edges of the high season (ie November and May) and you could get lucky with both the weather and cut-price rates.

The Caribbean hurricane season runs from June to November, with the highest storm risk in September and October. Every year is different, however, and booking your trip around the weather can be a bit of a lottery.

Temperatures – aside from in the Central Mountains – rarely fall below 60°F (16°C). Generally it's 80°F (27°C) and sunny. Rains last from June to November and can be heavy with wash-outs occurring frequently.

## HISTORY

Indigenous peoples are thought to have arrived – via a raft from Florida – around the 1st century AD, quickly followed by groups from the Lesser Antilles. The Taínos created a sophisticated trading system on the island they named Borinquen and became the reigning culture, although they were constantly fighting off Carib invaders.

All that changed forever in 1508, when Juan Ponce de León came back for a second and closer look at the island he had glimpsed from one of Christopher Columbus' ships. Driven by a desire for gold, Spanish *conquistadores* enslaved, murdered, starved and raped natives with impunity. Virtually wiped out by war, smallpox and whooping cough, a few remaining Taínos took to the mountains. Soon Dutch and French traders became frequent visitors, dropping off human cargo from West Africa. By 1530 West African slaves – including members of the Mandingo and Yoruba tribes – numbered about half the population of 3000 in Puerto Rico.

And so it went for several generations. The Spanish-American War of 1898 finally pried Puerto Rico out from under the yoke of the Spanish empire, but it established the small island as a commonwealth of the United States – Borinquen was liberated from Spain, but not quite free.

Operation Bootstrap poured money into the island and set up highways, post offices, supermarkets and a few military posts. Puerto Ricans have accepted the US economic and military presence on their island, with varying degrees of anger, indifference and satisfaction, for more than 100 years now – and the strong *independentista* movement that wanted to cut all ties with the US in the 1950s has mostly receded into the background. The biggest

# PUERTO RICO

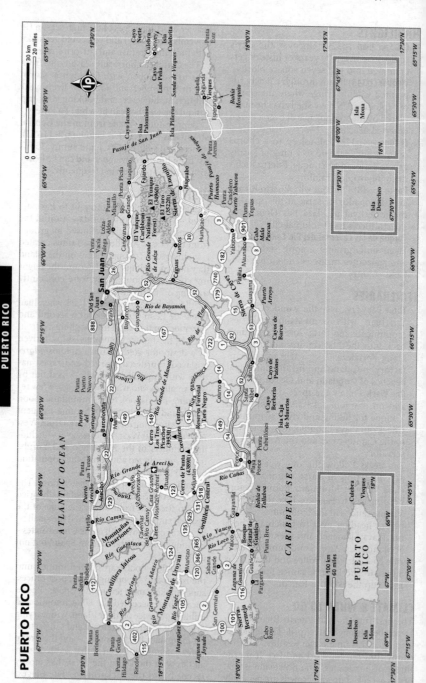

question for Puerto Ricans – a passionately political people who muster at least a 90% voter turnout on election days – is whether to keep the 'status quo' or become, officially, America's 51st state.

In May 2006 a stalemate between Governor Aníbal Acevedo and the Puerto Rican legislature led to a massive budgetary crisis that forced the government to literally 'shut down' after it ran out of funds to pay over 100,000 public sector employees. The crisis lasted two weeks before a grudging compromise was reached, but it made a laughing stock out of the Puerto Rican government and drew intense criticism from business leaders, Puerto Rican celebrities and the general public. In March 2008 Acevedo was indicted by the US on corruption charges after a two-year grand jury investigation. He has denied any wrongdoing and faces up to 20 years in prison if convicted.

## THE CULTURE

As a predominantly Catholic country (albeit widely mixed with African and indigenous practices), Puerto Ricans treasure family values and family pursuits and often have three or more generations living in the same home. But they don't interpret 'family-friendly' as being closed-minded. They are fiercely and justifiably proud of their mixed European, African and indigenous ancestry – in a country where skin tones range from the darkest coal to freckled white (sometimes even in the same family), it's no mean feat to have created a culture where all are welcome.

## ARTS

Abundant creative energy hangs in the air all over Puerto Rico (maybe it has something to do with the Bermuda Triangle) and its effects can be seen in the island's tremendous output of artistic achievement. Puerto Rico has produced renowned poets, novelists, playwrights, orators, historians, journalists, painters, composers and sculptors. The island's two most influential artists are considered to be rococo painter José Campeche and impressionist Francisco Oller. As well as being a groundbreaking politician, Puerto Rican governor Luís Moñez Marín was also an eloquent poet. In the world of entertainment, Rita Morena is the only Puerto Rican to have won an Oscar, a Grammy, a Tony and an Emmy, while the island's hottest new film talent is actor Benicio

del Toro, star of Steven Soderbergh's recent two-part biopic of Che Guevara.

While it's known for world-class art in many mediums, music and dance are especially synonymous with the island.

## ENVIRONMENT
### The Land

At 100 miles long and 35 miles wide (161km x 56km), Puerto Rico is clearly the little sister of the Greater Antilles (Cuba, Jamaica and Hispaniola). With its four principal satellite islands and a host of cays hugging its shores, Puerto Rico claims approximately 3500 sq miles (9060 sq km) of land, making the commonwealth slightly larger than the Mediterranean island of Corsica or the second-smallest state in the USA, Delaware.

Puerto Rico has more than a dozen well-developed and protected wilderness areas, most of which are considered *reservas forestales* (forest reserves) or *bosques estatales* (state forests). The best known is the 43-sq-mile (111-sq-km) Caribbean National Forest, generally referred to as El Yunque, which dominates the cloudy yet sun-splashed peaks at the east end of the island. Bosque Estatal de Guánica, on the southwest coast, is home to a tropical dry forest ecosystem.

National forest campground and reservation information can be obtained by calling ☎ 800-280-2267.

### Wildlife

Endangered sea turtles, such as the hawksbill, green and leatherback, nest on Puerto Rican beaches, particularly on the island of Culebra. Puerto Rico's vast coral reefs are the nurseries and feeding grounds for hundreds of species of tropical fish. It offers some of the best places in the world for divers to come face-to-face with large barracudas, manta rays, octopuses, moray eels and nurse sharks.

**PUERTO RICO**

---

**HOW MUCH?**

- **San Juan–Fajardo taxi** US$80
- **San Juan–Fajardo público** US$5
- **Liter of gas** US$0.85
- **Bottle of beer** US$2
- **Cheapest hotel room** US$60

El Yunque is home to more than 60 species of bird, including the greenish-blue, red-fronted Puerto Rican parrot, which is on the edge of extinction. The coastal dry forest of Guánica features more than 130 bird species, largely songbirds.

Snakes are everywhere, but remember that none of them are poisonous, including the Puerto Rican boa, which grows to more than 7ft (2.1m).

Keep your eyes peeled for small-boned Paso Fino horses, brought to the island by the Spanish conquistadors. In many places, but particularly in Vieques, they roam freely across the roads in untamed herds.

## FOOD & DRINK

Thanks to a full-on culinary revolution, Puerto Rico now offers the best selection of food in the Caribbean, and restaurants in cities such as San Juan could confidently compete with their stateside counterparts in New York. But, though many of the island's menus popularly describe their food as 'fusion' or 'eclectic,' most owe more than a passing nod to Puerto Rico's real deal – comida criolla. The irony, for food lovers, is that comida criolla is itself a fusion of numerous international influences, from the indigenous natives to the colonizing Spanish. The mélange can be traced back to the pre-Columbian Taínos who survived on a diet of root vegetables, fish and tropical fruits. With the arrival of the Spanish came an infusion of more European flavors such as olive oil, rice, peppers, beef, pork and spices like cilantro and cumin. Slavery brought African influences to Puerto Rico including yams, plantains and coffee and a style of cooking that favored deep-fried food and stews. The US influence in Puerto Rican food is reflected more in the fast food boom than in comida criolla per se, though the Americans did introduce corn oil (for cooking), sausages and various fruits such as papaya, tomatoes and avocados.

A typical comida criolla dish today can consist of many different ingredients, though roast pork, rice, beans, deep-fried plantains and yucca are all popular staples.

# SAN JUAN

pop 442,447

Take note New York! Modern America started here. Well, almost. Established in 1521, San Juan is the second-oldest European-founded settlement in the Americas (after Santo Domingo) and the oldest under US jurisdiction. Shoehorned onto a tiny islet that guards the entrance to San Juan harbor, the atmospheric 'Old City' juxtaposes historical authenticity with pulsating modern energy. Surreal sounds and exotic sights resonate everywhere. A stabbing salsa stanza in sonorous San Sebastián, timid cats scurrying under winking lanterns in Plaza de San José; and the omnipresent roar of Atlantic breakers battling mercilessly with the sturdy 500-year-old fortifications of El Morro.

But beyond its 15ft-thick walls, San Juan is far more than a dizzying collection of well-polished colonial artifacts. To get the full take on the capricious capital, visitors must first run the gamut of its distinct but ever-changing neighborhoods. There's seen-it-all Condado, where Cuba's 24-hour gambling party got washed up in the early 1960s; tranquil Ocean Park, with its gated villas and strategically located B&Bs; and swanky Isla Verde, awash with luxurious resort hotels and kitschy casinos.

Choked by crawling traffic and inundated with nearly five million annual tourists, parts of San Juan can leave you wondering if you took a wrong turn at Miami airport and never left North America. But the confusion rarely lingers. Cultural borrowing has long been this city's pragmatic hallmark. For every gleaming office block you'll stumble upon a colorful Spanish fiesta, a strange African religious ritual, a delicate native woodcarving and architecture that could quite conceivably been ripped out of Seville, Cartegena, Buenos Aires, or even Paris.

## ORIENTATION

Starting at the westernmost tip of the city and working backward toward the Aeropuerto Internacional de Luis Muñoz Marín (LMM), you've got Old San Juan, the tourist center and most visually appealing part of town.

Next comes Condado, flashy and full of big buildings and hotels along Av Ashford and then Miramar and Santurce, a little south of the beach and mostly filled with working-class families. Ocean Park is a private community (with gates) lying along the water between Condado and Isla Verde; its main street is Av McLeary. The final stop in the city is Isla Verde (although technically it is in Carolinas, a suburb of San Juan). Av Isla Verde is a long stretch of hotels and casinos along a narrow but pretty white beach. Its drawback is the proximity of the airport. Large jets thunder overhead every 20 minutes or so for most of the day.

## Maps

Travelers will find tourist maps of Old San Juan, Condado and Isla Verde readily available through the tourist information offices run by the Puerto Rico Tourism Company (right). The standard complimentary map can also be found online at www.travelmaps.com.

# INFORMATION
## Bookstores

**Bell, Book & Candle** (Map pp334-5; ☎ 728-5000; 102 Av José de Diego, Condado) Pulls in the vacation crowd and offers a wide range of English titles.

## Emergency

In *any* kind of emergency, just call ☎ 911. Beware: you may find that the telephone directory and tourist publications list nonfunctioning local numbers for emergency services.

**Fire** ( ☎ 722-1120)
**Hurricane Warnings** ( ☎ 253-4586)
**Isla Verde Police** ( ☎ 449-9320)
**Medical** ( ☎ 754-2222, 343-2550)
**Rape Crisis Hotline** ( ☎ 877-641-2004)
**Río Piedras Police** ( ☎ 765-6439)
**Tourist Zone Police** ( ☎ 911, 726-7020; ☯ 24hr) English spoken.

## Internet Access

**Cybernet Café** (Map pp334-5; ☎ 724-4033; 1128 Av Ashford; per hr US$5-6; ☯ 9am-11pm)
**Internet@active** (Map p330; ☎ 289-0345; JA Corretjer; per 15min US$4)

## Medical Services

**Ashford Memorial Community Hospital** (Map pp334-5; ☎ 721-2160; 1451 Av Ashford) This is probably the best-equipped and most convenient hospital for travelers to visit.

## Money

**Banco Popular** LMM airport ( ☎ 791-0326; Terminal C); Old San Juan (Map p330; ☎ 725-2635; cnr Tetuán & San Justo) Near the cruise ship piers and Paseo de la Princesa; Condado (Map pp334-5; Av Ashford).

## Post

Greater San Juan has about 20 post offices.
**Old San Juan Post Office** (Map p330; ☎ 723-1281; 100 Paseo de Colón; ☯ 8am-4pm Mon-Fri, 8am-noon Sat) The one likely to be most convenient for travelers.

## Tourist Information

Puerto Rico Tourism Company (PRTC) distributes information in English and Spanish at two venues in San Juan, the LMM airport and La Casita in Old San Juan.

**Departamento de Recursos Naturales y Ambientales** (DRNA; Department of Natural Resources; ☎ 999-2200; www.drna.gobierno.pr in Spanish; Km 6.3, Rte 8838, Sector El Cinco, Río Piedras) For information on camping, including reservations and permits, contact this department or visit its office.

**Puerto Rico Tourism Company** (PRTC; ☎ 800-223-6530, 721-2400; www.prtourism.com) LMM airport ( ☎ 791-1014; ☯ 9am-5:30pm); Old San Juan (Map p330; ☎ 722-1709; La Casita, Comercio & Plaza de la Darsena near Pier 1)

# SIGHTS

Most of San Juan's major attractions, including museums and art galleries, are in Old San Juan. Be aware that most museums are closed on Mondays.

## Old San Juan

Old San Juan is a colorful kaleidoscope of life, music, legend and history and would stand out like a flashing beacon in any country, let alone one as small as Puerto Rico. Somnolent secrets and beautiful surprises await everywhere. From the blue-toned cobblestoned streets of Calle San Sebastián to the cutting-edge gastronomic artistry of SoFo, you could spend weeks, even months, here and still only get the smallest taste.

### CASA BLANCA

First constructed in 1521 as a residence of Puerto Rico's pioneering governor, Juan Ponce de León (who died before he could move in), the **Casa Blanca** (White House; Map p330; ☎ 724-4102; adult/child US$2/1; ☯ 9am-noon & 1-4:30pm Tue-Sun, guided tours Tue-Fri by appointment) is the oldest continuously occupied house in the western hemisphere. Today it is a historic monument containing a museum, secluded grounds, a chain of fountains and an Alhambra-style courtyard. The interior rooms are decked out with artifacts from the 16th to the 20th century. An animated guide can give you a theatrical complementary tour.

### CATEDRAL DE SAN JUAN

Noticeably smaller and more austere than other Spanish churches, the city **cathedral** (Map p330; ☎ 722-0861; 153 Calle del Cristo; admission

PUERTO RICO

# OLD SAN JUAN

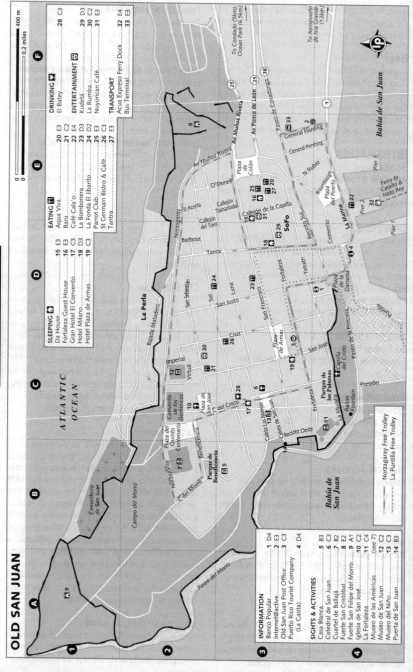

0 _____ 400 m
0 _____ 0.2 miles

**SLEEPING**
Da House...........................15 E3
Fortaleza Guest House...........16 E3
Gran Hotel El Convento..........17 C3
Hotel Milano......................18 D3
Hotel Plaza de Armas............19 C3

**EATING**
Aqua Viva...........................20 E3
Baru.................................21 C2
Café Cala'o.........................22 E4
La Bombonera.......................23 D3
La Fonda El Jibarito..............24 D2
Parrot Club.........................25 E3
St Germain Bistro & Café.........26 C3
Tantra..............................27 E3

**DRINKING**
El Batey............................28 C3

**ENTERTAINMENT**
Kudeta..............................29 D3
La Rumba...........................30 C2
Nuyorican Café......................31 E3

**TRANSPORT**
Acua Expreso Ferry Dock.........32 E4
Bus Terminal.......................33 E3

**INFORMATION**
Banco Popular......................1 D4
Internet@active....................2 E3
Old San Juan Post Office..........3 C3
Puerto Rico Tourist Company
(La Casita)........................4 D4

**SIGHTS & ACTIVITIES**
Casa Blanca.........................5 B3
Catedral de San Juan..............6 C3
Cuartel de Ballajá................7 B2
Fuerte San Cristóbal..............8 E2
Fuerte San Felipe del Morro......9 A1
Iglesia de San José...............10 C2
La Fortaleza.......................11 C4
Museo de las Américas.............12 C2
Museo de San Juan.................(see 7)
Museo del Niño.....................13 C3
Puerta de San Juan................14 B3

Norzagaray Free Trolley
La Puntilla Free Trolley

To Condado (5km);
Ocean Park (6.5km)

To Aeropuerto
de Isla Grande
(13km)

Ferry to
Cataño &
Hato Rey

*ATLANTIC
OCEAN*

*Bahía de San Juan*

*Bahía de
San Juan*

---

### SAN JUAN IN...

#### Two Days

Find a midrange hotel or apartment in Old San Juan. Explore the historical sights of the colonial quarter and dine along **Fortaleza** (p337 ) before heading to **La Rumba** (p340) or **Nuyorican Café** (p340) after dark for mojitos and salsa music. Wander over to **Condado** (p332) on day two for some solitary sunbathing or beachside water sports.

#### Four Days

Add a walking tour around **Old San Juan** (p333) and throw in a visit to the Cataño **Bacardi Rum Factory** (p342). Find an ecotour company to run you out to **El Yunque** (p343) for a day. Finally, scour the nightclubs of the big hotels in **Condado** (p336 ) and Isla Verde, or dine in one of the beautiful restaurants in **Gran Hotel El Convento** (p335).

#### One Week

Head into the 'burbs for Santurce's **Museo de Arte de Puerto Rico** (p332) or head further south to the **Mercado de Río Piedras** (p332) in Río Piedras. Rent a bike from **Hot Dog Cycling** (p333) and pedal out to Piñones for the beach kiosks and laid-back Puerto Rican ambience. Round up by hiring some beach toys on **Playa Isla Verde** (p332).

---

free; 8am-4pm) nonetheless retains a simple earthy elegance. Founded in the 1520s, the first church on this site was destroyed in a hurricane in 1529. A replacement was constructed in 1540 and, over a period of centuries, it slowly evolved into the Gothic-neoclassical–inspired monument seen today. Most people come to see the marble tomb of Ponce de León and the body of religious martyr St Pio displayed under glass.

### FUERTE SAN FELIPE DEL MORRO

A six-level fort with a gray, castellated lighthouse, **El Morro** (Map p330; Fuerte San Felipe del Morro; San Felipe Fort; ☎ 729-6960; www.nps.gov/saju/morro .html; adult/child US$3/free; 9am-5pm Jun-Nov, 9am-6pm Dec-May, free tours at 10am & 2pm in Spanish, 11am & 3pm in English) juts aggressively over Old San Juan's bold headlands, glowering across the Atlantic at would-be conquerors. The 140ft walls (some up to 15ft thick) date back to 1539 and El Morro is said to be the oldest Spanish fort in the New World. The National Park Service (NPS) maintains this fort and the small military museum on the premises. It was declared a Unesco World Heritage site in 1983. Pay US$5 and you also gain entry to Fuerte San Cristóbal.

### FUERTE SAN CRISTÓBAL

San Juan's second major fort is **Fuerte San Cristóbal** (San Cristóbal Fort; Map p330; ☎ 729-6777; www.nps.gov/saju/sancristobal.html; adult/child US$3/free; 9am-5pm Jun-Nov, 9am-6pm Dec-May), one of the largest military installations the Spanish built in the Americas. In its prime, San Cristóbal covered 27 acres with a maze of six interconnected forts protecting a central core with 150ft walls, moats, booby-trapped bridges and tunnels. The fort was constructed to defend Old San Juan against land attacks from the east via Puerta de Tierra. It became a National Historic site in 1949 and a Unesco World Heritage site in 1983. Facilities include a fascinating museum, a store, military archives, a reproduction of a soldiers' barracks and prime city views. There are also regular historical reenactments.

### IGLESIA DE SAN JOSÉ

This **church** (Map p330; ☎ 725-7501; admission free; 8:30am-4pm Mon-Sat, Mass noon Sun) in the Plaza de San José is the second-oldest religious building in the Americas, after the cathedral in Santo Domingo in the Dominican Republic. Established in 1523 by Dominicans, this church with its vaulted Gothic ceilings still bears the coat of arms of Juan Ponce de León, whose family worshipped here; a striking carving of the Crucifixion; and ornate processional floats. For 350 years the remains of Ponce de León rested in a crypt here before being moved to the city's cathedral, down the hill.

### LA FORTALEZA

Also known as El Palacio de Santa Catalina, **La Fortaleza** (The Fortress; Map p330; ☎ 721-7000 ext 2211 or 2358; admission free; 9am-3:30pm Mon-Fri) is the oldest executive mansion in continuous use in the western hemisphere and dates from 1533. Once the original fortress for the young colony, La Fortaleza eventually yielded its military pre-eminence to the city's newer and larger forts and was remodeled and expanded to domicile island governors for more than three centuries. If you are dressed in respectful attire, you can join a free guided tour.

### MUSEO DE LAS AMÉRICAS
Built in 1854 as a military barracks, the **Cuartel de Ballajá** (Map p330; off Norzagaray) is a three-story edifice with large gates on two ends, ample balconies, a series of arches and a protected central courtyard that served as a plaza and covers a reservoir. It was the last and largest building constructed by the Spaniards in the New World. Facilities included officers' quarters, warehouses, kitchens, dining rooms, prison cells and stables. Now its 2nd floor holds the **Museo de las Américas** (Museum of the Americas; Map p330; ☎ 724-5052; admission free; ☽ 10am-4pm Tue-Fri, 11am-5pm Sat & Sun, guided tours available weekdays 10:30am, 11:30am, 12:30pm & 2pm), which gives an excellent overview of cultural development in the New World.

### MUSEO DE SAN JUAN
Located in a Spanish colonial building overlooking the ocean on Calle Norzagaray, this **museum** (Map p330; ☎ 724-1875; 150 Norzagaray; donations accepted; ☽ 9am-4pm Tue-Fri, 10am-4pm Sat & Sun) is the definitive take on the city's 500-year history. The well laid out exhibition showcases pictorial and photographic testimonies from the Caparra ruins to modern-day shopping malls. There's also a half-hour TV documentary about the history of San Juan.

### PASEO DE LA PRINCESA
Emanating a distinctly European flavor, the **Paseo de la Princesa** (Walkway of the Princess; Map p330) is a 19th-century esplanade just outside the city walls. Lined with antique street lamps, trees, statues, benches, fruit vendors' carts and street entertainers, this romantic walkway culminates at the magnificent **Raíces Fountain** (Map p330), a stunning statue-cum-water-feature that depicts the island's Taíno, African and Spanish heritage.

### PUERTA DE SAN JUAN
Spanish ships once anchored in the cove just off these ramparts to unload colonists and supplies, all of which entered the city through a tall red portal known as **Puerta de San Juan** (San Juan Gate; Map p330). This tunnel through the wall dates from the 1630s. It marks the end of the Paseo de la Princesa and stands as one of three remaining gates into the old city. Turn right after passing through the gate and you can follow the **Paseo del Morro** northwest, paralleling the city walls for approximately three-quarters of a mile.

## Santurce
While the Old Town's historic attractions are universally famous, fewer people are aware that San Juan boasts one of the largest and most celebrated art museums in the Caribbean. The **Museo de Arte de Puerto Rico** (MAPR; Map pp334-5; ☎ 977-6277, for tours ext 2230 or 2261; www.mapr.org; 299 Av José de Diego, Santurce; adult/child/senior US$6/3/3; ☽ 10am-5pm Tue & Thu-Sat, to 8pm Wed, 11am-6pm Sun) opened in 2000 and rapidly inserted itself as a important nexus in the capital's vibrant cultural life. Housed in a splendid neoclassical building that was once the city's Municipal Hospital, MAPR is located in the city's revived Santurce district and boasts 18 exhibition halls spread over an area of 130,000 sq ft.

## Río Piedras
If you like the smell of fish and oranges, the bustle of people and trading jests in Spanish as you bargain for a bunch of bananas, the **Mercado de Río Piedras** (Paseo de Diego; ☽ 9am-6pm) is for you. As much a scene as a place to shop, the market continues the colonial tradition of an indoor market that spills into the streets.

## Beaches
San Juan has some of the best municipal beaches this side of Rio. Starting a kilometer or so east of the Old Town, you can go from rustic to swanky and back to rustic all in the space of 12 kilometers.

**Balneario Escambrón** (Map pp334-5) is a sheltered arc of raked sand with decent surf breaks, plenty of local action and a 17th-century Spanish fort shimmering in the distance.

Hemmed in by hotel towers and punctuated by rocky outcrops, visitors to the **Condado** beaches can expect splashes of lurid graffiti, boisterous games of volleyball and plenty of crashing Atlantic surf.

Resort pluggers will tell you that **Playa Isla Verde** is the Copacabana of Puerto Rico with its legions of tan bodies and dexterous beach bums flexing their triceps around the volley-ball net. Other more savvy travelers prefer to dodge the extended families and colonizing spring break hedonists that stake space here and head west to **Ocean Park**.

## ACTIVITIES
### Diving & Snorkeling
While Puerto Rico is well known for its first-class diving, San Juan is not the best place for it. Strong winds often churn up the water. Condado has an easy dive that takes you through a pass between the inner and outer reefs into coral caverns, over-hangs, grottoes and tunnels.

**Eco-Action Tours** ( ☎ 791-7509; www.ecoaction tours.com; tours US$40-130) can do just about any tour imaginable, from rappelling to nature walks. It operates out of a van and comes to you. Check out the website or phone the company. The guides are knowledgeable and very accommodating.

**Caribe Aquatic Adventures** (Map pp334-5; ☎ 281-8858; snorkel/dive US$50/135) operates out of the Normandie Hotel in Puerta de Tierra and offers dives near San Juan but also fur-ther afield: eg the islands off the coast of Fajardo (Icacos for snorkeling and Palomino and Palominito for diving). The company's shore dives from the beach behind the hotel are said to be some of the best in the Caribbean. Cruise passengers love utilizing this place.

### Kayaking
**Ecoquest** ( ☎ 616-7543; www.ecoquestpr.com) offers a great three-hour long trip to Piñones and its adjacent lagoon. The excursion includes information on local flora and fauna, a one-hour kayak on the lagoon and traditional food from one of the local fish restaurants. Prices start at US$69 per person.

### Fishing
**Benitez Fishing Charters** (Map pp334-5; ☎ 723-2292; San Juan Bay Marina, Miramar) is captained by the celebrated Mike Benitez who has carried the likes of former US President Jimmy Carter. If you want to trade White House gossip while fishing for dolphin, tuna, wahoo and white and blue marlin, book a space on his deluxe 45' boat for some serious deep-sea fishing. Prices start at US$185 per person for a four-hour excursion.

### Cycling
Forget the notorious traffic-jams. Cycling in San Juan can actually be good fun, as long as you know where to go. In fact, it is perfectly feasible to work your way along the coast from Old San Juan out as far as Carolina and the bike paths of Piñones.

In Isla Verde, **Hot Dog Cycling** ( ☎ 791-0776; www.hotdogcycling.com; 5916 Av Isla Verde; 10am-5pm) rent excellent 21-speed mountain bikes from US$25 per day. These guys are handily situated near the start of the designated Isla Verde–Piñones bike route. You can also ask about its bike tours.

## SAN JUAN FOR CHILDREN
Puerto Ricans love children – it doesn't mat-ter who they belong to. And they love fam-ily. So traveling with youngsters is rarely a hassle, because the Puerto Ricans are doing it too.

In and around San Juan there are several attractions that children really enjoy. The **Museo del Niño** (Children's Museum; Map p330; ☎ 722-3791; 150 Calle del Cristo; adult/child US$5/7; 9am-5pm Tue-Fri, 11:30-5:30pm Sat & Sun) is always a big hit, as is the **Luis A Ferré Parque de Ciencias** (Science Park; ☎ 740-6868; Hwy 167; adult/child/senior US$5/3/3, parking US$1; 9am-4pm Wed-Fri, 10am-6pm Sat & Sun) in Bayamón. Isla Verde is the most child-friendly beach with safe swimming and plenty of beach toys,

## TOURS
**Legends of Puerto Rico** ( ☎ 605-9060; www.legendsofpr .com) The perennially popular 'Night Tales in Old San Juan' and 'Legends of San Juan' walk-ing tours (from US$30 to US$35 per person) fill up fast, so book ahead. Bus trips are also available, as are special discounts for families with children and wheelchair-accessible tours (advance booking required).

## FESTIVALS & EVENTS
**Noches de Galerías** (Gallery Nights; first Tuesday of every month: February to May; September to December) Art galleries stay open late to showcase special exhibitions and present up-and-coming talent.

**Festival San Sebastián** (Mid-January) Held in the old city's famous party street, Calle San Sabastián. For a full week in mid-January it hums with semi-religious proces-sions, music, food stalls and larger-than-ever crowds.

**Fiesta de San Juan Bautista** (June 24) Celebration of the patron saint of San Juan and a summer solstice party Latin style in Old San Juan.

**PUERTO RICO**

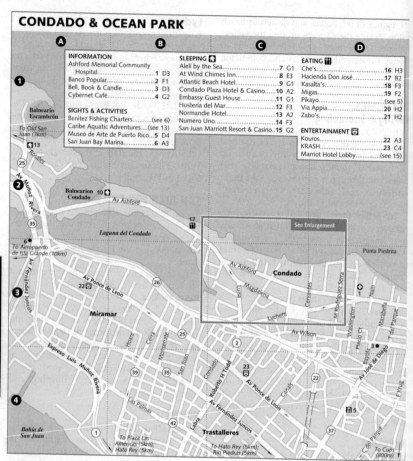

## CONDADO & OCEAN PARK

**INFORMATION**
Ashford Memorial Community
  Hospital..............................................**1** D3
Banco Popular........................................**2** F1
Bell, Book & Candle...............................**3** D3
Cybernet Café........................................**4** G2

**SIGHTS & ACTIVITIES**
Benitez Fishing Charters..................(see 6)
Caribe Aquatic Adventures.........(see 13)
Museo de Arte de Puerto Rico.....**5** D4
San Juan Bay Marina.........................**6** A3

**SLEEPING** 🏠
Aleli by the Sea......................................**7** G1
At Wind Chimes Inn.............................**8** E3
Atlantic Beach Hotel...........................**9** G1
Condado Plaza Hotel & Casino.....**10** A2
Embassy Guest House.......................**11** G1
Hosteria del Mar.................................**12** F3
Normandie Hotel................................**13** A2
Numero Uno.........................................**14** F3
San Juan Marriott Resort & Casino.....**15** G2

**EATING** 🍴
Che's.........................................................**16** H3
Hacienda Don José...............................**17** B2
Kasalta's.................................................**18** F3
Migas.......................................................**19** F2
Pikayo...............................................(see 5)
Via Appia...............................................**20** H2
Zabo's......................................................**21** H2

**ENTERTAINMENT** 🎭
Kouros......................................................**22** A3
KRASH......................................................**23** C4
Marriot Hotel Lobby......................(see 15)

---

**Culinary Festival** (November) SoFo's alfresco culinary festival is a moveable feast where local restaurateurs set up their tables in the street and rustle up their best dishes.

## SLEEPING

You'll find ample accommodations in San Juan for every price range except one – budget traveling. Outside of a few affordable guest houses, it's slim pickings for those watching their money. Aside from that, San Juan is wide open. Upscale, midscale, boutique or B&B: take your pick.

### Old San Juan

**Fortaleza Guest House** (Map p330; ☎ 721-7112; 361 Fortaleza; r with shared bathroom per week from US$65; 🌊 ) Budget accommodation in Old San Juan is not for the fussy. For this price you get a tiny room with air-con and not a lot else – except for perhaps a few multilegged creatures skittering by (ants, not roaches). Phone ahead, as this place books up fast.

**Da House** (Map p330; ☎ 977-1180; 312 San Francisco; r US$80; 🌊 🖥 ) Make no mistake; da House is da place. Old San Juan's newest and funkiest hotel is also one of its best bargains with 27 boutique-style rooms kitted out with chic furnishings and decorated with eye-catching contemporary art. For the musically inclined, one of San Juan's best salsa bars, the Nuyorican, is situated downstairs; for the less enamored (or the sleep-deprived), the reception staff will ruefully give out ear plugs.

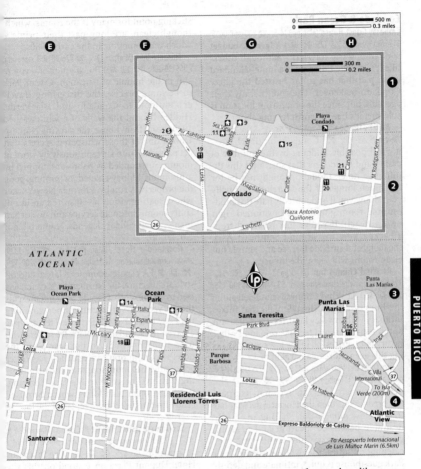

PUERTO RICO

**Hotel Plaza de Armas** (Map p330; ☎ 722-9191; www.ihphoteles.com; 202 Calle San Jose; r US$90-175; ❄ ) Location, location, location – but not a lot else. The Plaza de Armas is a rather characterless hotel situated in San Juan's most character-loaded quarter. Run by the Howard Johnson chain, the lobby has some funky modern touches but upstairs the rooms are a little worn.

**Hotel Milano** (Map p330; ☎ 729-9050; www .hotelmilanopr.com; 307 Fortaleza; r incl breakfast US$95-185; ❄ 🖥 ) Sandwiched into the happening hub of Fortaleza, the Milano is a safe, reliable, if slightly austere option. Rooms are clean but unexciting, there's wi-fi in the lobby and up on the roof there's an open-to-the-elements restaurant with peek-a-boo views of the harbor. Beware of some closetlike rooms lacking windows.

**ourpick Gran Hotel El Convento** (Map p330; ☎ 723-9020; www.elconvento.com; 100 Calle del Cristo; r US$235-420; ❄ 🖥 🏊 ) Historic monument, tapas restaurant, meeting place, coffee bar and evocative colonial building…without a doubt El Convento is Puerto Rico's most complete, atmospheric and multifaceted hotel. Built in 1651 as the New World's first Carmelite convent, this sturdy baroque beacon oozes with priceless old world relics and subtle 'Siglo de Oro' charm. El Convento's 58 rooms and six suites are gorgeously decorated with Andalusian tiles, mahogany and thick rugs, plus the service from the bar to the front desk is impeccable. Oh – and there's no casino!

## Condado & Ocean Park

**Embassy Guest House** (Map pp334-5; ☎ 800-468-0615; 1126 Sea View; r US$65-125; ⚄ ⚄ ) A favorite budget spot among gay travelers – although others like it too – the Embassy is a motel-standard crash pad that has so far resisted the glitzy Condado makeover. The rooms show their age a bit, but since the oceanfront location is sublime, it's hardly worth fussing about.

**Alelí by the Sea** (Map pp334-5; ☎ 725-5313; 1125 Sea View; r US$65-100; ⚄ ) Condado on the cheap – it's still possible. Judging by the number of cranes and bulldozers that surround this diminutive hotel, though, it might not be for too much longer. If the Marriot's normally your thing, you'll undoubtedly hate this modest nine-room guesthouse positioned right on the beach. If you've just returned from a backpacking trip around Southeast Asia, the delightful surfside terrace and simple but clean rooms will seem like luxury.

**At Wind Chimes Inn** (Map pp334-5; ☎ 800-946-3244; www.atwindchimesinn.com; 53 Taft; r US$80-155; ⚄ ⚄ ⚄ ) At Wind Chimes is modeled along the lines of a Spanish-style villa that mixes intimacy with low-key luxuries. It's a pleasant antidote to the resort feel of Condado's other luxury piles. Prices fall in the low season, making this even more of a bargain.

**Hostería del Mar** (Map pp334-5; ☎ 727-3302; hosteria@caribe.net; 1 Tapia; r US$89-199; ⚄ ⚄ ) If the nearby Número Uno can live up to its priceless premier tag, then the Hostería del Mar has to be a close *número dos*. Sharing an equally desirable beachside location and greeting guests with an artsy water feature and eye-catching antiques, this whitewashed Ocean Park guesthouse is quiet, intimate and definitively Caribbean. There is no pool, but there is an excellent restaurant in an enclosed gazebo overlooking the beach. Rooms are furnished with a simple rattan-inspired elegance.

**Atlantic Beach Hotel** (Map pp334-5; ☎ 721-6900; www.atlanticbeachhotel.net; 1 Vendig; r US$90-170; ⚄ ) This place is regularly held up as the nexus of the Caribbean's gay community, though in recent years many visitors have derided it for its dingy rooms and lackluster service. It all depends on your expectations. Wedged up against the beach at the end of one of Condado's tattier streets, the Atlantic certainly has a great oceanside location and, with a buzzing bar scene, rooftop Jacuzzi and famous Sunday drag shows, it's a good place to hang out and meet other gay travelers. The

sticking point for many is the rooms, which, though clean, are long past their prime – which was sometime in the early 1980s.

**Número Uno** (Map pp334-5; ☎ 726-5010; 1 Santa Ana; r US$130-200; ⚄ ⚄ ⚄ ) Pinch yourself – you're still in the middle of San Juan, Ocean Park to be more precise, the discerning traveler's antidote to Condado and Isla Verde. Hidden behind the walls of a whitewashed 1940s beachfront house, the glowing Número Uno is one of those whispered secrets that get passed around surreptitiously by word of mouth. Surrounded by palms and topped by a luminous kidney-shaped swimming pool, the property is run by a former New Yorker whose soaring vision has inspired an inn of spiffy rooms, intimate service and one of San Juan's newest culinary legends, Número Uno? Not far off.

**Normandie Hotel** (Map pp334-5; ☎ 729-2929; www.normandiepr.com; Av Muñoz Rivera; r US$200-325; ⚄ ⚄ ⚄ ) A classic example of late art deco-style architecture, the Normandie is characterized by its minimalist façade, which represents the curved bows of a cruise liner guarding the busy entrance to Puerta de Tierra. Once a haven for scandalous 1950s jet setters who used to cavort nude in the rear pool, the hotel's contemporary incarnation has fewer accessories but more soul than the neighboring Caribe. The centerpiece is a towering, if austere, open plan lobby where bemused cruise liner refugees have replaced the lounge lizards of lore.

**San Juan Marriott Resort & Casino** (Map pp334-5; ☎ 722 7000; www.marriotthotels.com; 1309 Av Ashford; r incl breakfast US$265-525; ⚄ ⚄ ⚄ ) The infamous Hotel Dupont Plaza once stood on this site before an arson attack burnt it to the ground, claiming 97 lives, in 1986. Rising in its place a decade later, Marriot has turned a den of notoriety into a pretty beachfront property, with two pools and 525 units. A lot more personable than other resorts in its class, the Marriott boasts enviably modern rooms, a lavish breakfast buffet and some mean salsa entertainment where even the staff join in.

**Condado Plaza Hotel & Casino** (Map pp334-5; ☎ 721-1000; 999 Av Ashford; r US$300-1350; ⚄ ⚄ ⚄ ) Guarding the entrance to Condado like a sparkling concrete sentinel, the Condado Plaza straddles the thin wedge of land that separates the area's eponymous *laguna* from the Atlantic Ocean. Housed in two concrete towers connected by an overhead walkway above Ashford Ave, the hotel offers the best of both worlds with stunning views extending in both directions. A swanky lobby hints at luxury, and guests in the newly renovated oceanfront rooms generally aren't disappointed.

## Isla Verde

**El Patio Guesthouse** ( ☎ 726-6298; 87 Calle 3; r US$69-90; ❄ ▣ ) Your average Isla Verde visitor probably wouldn't poke a stick at this place, but in the cheaper price bracket it's not a bad bet – although gamblers will be disappointed to know that there's no casino onsite. A little villa close to the beach and other amenities, it is run by a little old lady who'll bend over backwards to make sure that your rooms are spick-and-span.

**Coquí Inn** ( ☎ 726-4330; 36 Mar Mediterraneo; r US$89-119; ▣ ▣ ) Bisected by a major expressway, Isla Verde has its ugly side and you'll get a face full of it here. But location aside, the Coquí Inn is quite the bargain. Expect clean, modern, but simple rooms with kitchenettes and plenty of handy extras, such as wi-fi, free coffee and pastries, morning newspapers, cable TV and maid service.

**Water & Beach Club** ( ☎ 728-3610; 2 Tartak; r US$150-650; ❄ ▣ ▣ ) Breaking the resort ubiquity of Isla Verde, the Water Club is one of Puerto Rico's most celebrated 'boutique' hotels. With a reception area straight out of *Architectural Digest* and elevators that sport glassed-in waterfalls, this is probably the closest San Juan comes to emulating South Beach, Florida. Rooms are minimalist, but artfully designed and benefit from spectacular beach views. There's also a chicer-than-chic swimming pool on the roof.

**El San Juan Hotel & Casino** ( ☎ 800-468-2818; www.elsanjuanhotel.com; 6063 Av Isla Verde; r US$325-450; ❄ ▣ ▣ ) Dimly lit, frigidly air-conditioned and decked out in throwback 1970s furnishings, the lobby of the El San Juan is redolent of a Roger Moore–era James Bond movie. You half expect to see the dapper 007 lounging around in his tux at the baccarat table. Renowned for its flashy casino and rollicking nightlife, El San Juan does its best to recreate 'tourist brochure paradise' among the Isla Verde skyscrapers. If you want decent rooms, unlimited water features, classy restaurants, Starbucks coffee and a heaving nightlife all in one big happy package, this is the place for you.

**InterContinental San Juan Resort & Casino** ( ☎ 800-443-2009; www.intercontinental.com; 187 Av Isla Verde; r US$399-539; ❄ ▣ ▣ ) Probably the least interesting of Isla Verde's craning tourist piles, the Intercontinental is, nonetheless, opulent with all of the usual gadgets and marketing ploys you'd expect in a well-appointed four star. An expensive refurbishment a few years back was designed to bring it onto a par with the El San Juan next door but, although the rooms and facilities are spiffy enough, the latter still wins first prize for character and panache.

# EATING

Most would agree that San Juan offers the best eating in the Caribbean. The latest craze is fusion cuisine – expect to see all sorts of creative combinations: Asian-Latino, Puerto Rican–European, Caribbean with a Middle Eastern twist. When in doubt, head to SoFo around Fortaleza in Old San Juan, the eclectic heart of San Juan's 21st-century gastronomic revolution.

## Old San Juan

**Café Cala'o** (Map p330; ☎ 724-4607; Pier 2; muffins US$2) Smooth, earthy coffee straight from Puerto Rico's Central Mountains and staff who confect it like trained experts; this is the best coffee on the island, hands down. The muffins aren't bad either.

**La Bombonera** (Map p330; ☎ 722-0658; 259 San Francisco; mains US$5-10; ☺ 8am-4pm) The old-fashioned coffee machine hisses like a steam engine, career waiters in black trousers appear like royal footman at your table and a long line of seen-it-all *Sanjuaneros* populate the lengthy row of bar stools catching up on the local breakfast gossip. It shouldn't take you long to work out that La Bombonera is a city institution – it's been around since 1902 and still sells some of the best cakes in town.

**St Germain Bistro & Café** (Map p330; ☎ 725-5830; 156 Sol; dishes US$7-15; ☺ closed Mon) Kudos to the chef for transforming the main course salads – so often the dullest dish on the menu – into something fresh, tasty and filling. Then there's the aromatic Puerto Rican coffee, the delicious paninis and the homemade cakes, which can only be described as melt-in-your-mouth heavenly.

**La Fonda El Jibarito** (Map p330; ☎ 725-8375; 280 Sol; dishes US$8-22) El Jibarito is the kind of salt-of-the-earth, unpretentious place that you

## SMALL ISLAND, WORLD-CLASS COFFEE

Erica Reyes Ocasio is the founder of Old San Juan's Café Cala'o (p337).

**What kinds of coffee are produced in Puerto Rico?**

In Puerto Rico the focus is on gourmet and specialty coffees. Because we are a small island there's a tendency to go for quality rather than quantity. At certain points in our history, our economy has been dominated by coffee and the product has often been in great demand in places such as Italy and Japan. In the past, Puerto Rican coffee was even drunk in the Vatican.

**What's the concept behind Café Cala'o?**

We're trying to promote specialty coffee, which is a new concept for many people in Puerto Rico. Because coffee demand exceeds supply, the island has traditionally had to import well over half its beans and quality has suffered as a result. At Café Cala'o we want to educate people about Puerto Rican coffee and combine great beans with great confection. Good beans are often ruined by people who don't know how to transfer them into the cup. All my staff members are trained; they're professionals in the coffee-making process.

**What brands do you sell?**

We sell local brands made from Arábica beans that are grown in Puerto Rico's central mountains. These include Jayauya, Utuado, Adjuntas, Maricao (one of the best) and Yauco (one of the island's oldest blends, dating from 1758).

**How do Puerto Ricans traditionally take their coffee?**

We drink it as a *pocillo*, that is, a small 4oz cup of coffee with milk. Coffee here is traditionally strong and because, in the past, the quality has often been poor, we usually spike it with sugar.

should reserve to sample your first *mofongo* (fried balls of mashed plantains mixed with pork rind and spices) or *arroz con habichuelas* (rice and beans). A favorite of local families, in-the-know tourists and passing *New York Times* journalists, the meals are simple but hearty with good pork and prawns, or plantains smashed, mashed and fried just about any way you want.

**Baru** (Map p330; ☎ 977-7107; 150 San Sebastián; dishes US$13-30; ☺ 6pm-midnight) Very popular with food-lovers and martini drinkers, Baru doubles as a nightspot as well as a trendy restaurant. Dishes include 'yuccafongo' (yucca made like a *mofongo*) with shrimp, beef *carpaccio* with basil essence or the mahi-mahi topped with crispy onions.

**Tantra** (Map p330; ☎ 977-8141; 356 Fortaleza; dishes US$18-27; ☺ noon-midnight) For purists, eating *masala dosa* in Puerto Rico is probably about as incongruous as chomping on *mofongo* in Madras, but for those willing to drop the cultural blinkers, Tantra's adventurous 'Indo-Latin fusion' cuisine is actually rather authentic. Enjoy it in Asian-inspired surroundings that host nightly belly-dancing shows.

**Parrot Club** (Map p330; ☎ 725-7370; 363 Fortaleza; dishes US$20-32; ☺ noon-3pm, 6-11pm) The menu's in Spanglish, the decor's a lurid mix of orange, blue and yellow and the waitress could quite conceivably be sporting a pink wig.

Welcome to the Parrot Club, where Puerto Rican politicians wind down and enamored gringos live it up. SoFo's original restaurant is now well into its second decade and the menu continues to win kudos with its eclectic crab-cake *caribeños*, pan-seared tuna and vegetarian 'tortes.'

**Aqua Viva** (Map p330; ☎ 722-0665; 364 Fortaleza; dishes US$30-40; ☺ 6-11pm Mon-Wed, 6pm-midnight Thu-Sat, 4-10pm Sun) Designed with an arty water-slash-sea-life theme and specializing in seafood, Aqua Viva is often packed to the rafters. This SoFo restaurant was invented with the word 'hip' in mind – everything from the open-view kitchen to the catwalk clientele is slavishly stylish. But the real test is the food: fresh oysters, calamari filled with shredded beef and dorado with lightly grilled bell peppers. It has been voted one of the top 75 restaurants in the world.

## Condado & Ocean Park

**Hacienda Don José** (Map pp334-5; ☎ 722-5880; 1025 Av Ashford; dishes US$3-12; ☺ 7am-11pm) Condado on the cheap; it can still be done. Indeed, the Don José is more redolent of a Mexican beach bar than a plush tourist trap. Waves lash against the rocks within spitting distance of your pancakes and *huevos rancheros* and busy waitresses shimmy around the tiled tables and colorful murals.

**Kasalta's** (Map pp334-5; ☎ 727-7340; 1966 McLeary; dishes US$4-10; ☒ 6am-10pm) Wake up with a jolt at Kasalta's, a popular early morning breakfast haunt and the sort of authentic Puerto Rican bakery and diner that you will find yourself crossing town to visit. Tucked into Ocean Park's residential enclave, the coffee here is as legendary as the sweets that fill a long glass display case and include everything from Danish pastries to iced buns.

**Via Appia** (Map pp334-5; ☎ 725-8711; Av Ashford; pizzas US$7-14) The good thing about Condado is that it still retains a smattering of family-run jewels among all the Starbucks and 7-Elevens. Via Appia is one such gem, a no-nonsense Italian restaurant where the pizza is classic and the gentlemanly waiters could quite conceivably have walked off the set of *The Godfather*. Munch on garlic bread or feast on meatballs alfresco, as the multilingual mélange of Av Ashford goes strolling by.

**Zabó** (Map pp334-5; ☎ 725-9494; 14 Candina; dishes US$12-30; ☒ 6-11pm Tue-Sat) Over in condo land, this older colonial-style villa hints at something different. The variations continue inside in an intimate restaurant-cum-bar where trendsetters sup on martinis and gastronomes tuck into creative dishes such as mango and curry rice and rosemary pork chops with garlic merlot sauce. There's music some nights, everything from Latin jazz to Flamenco.

**Migas** (Map pp334-5; ☎ 721-5991; 1400 Magdalena; dishes US$15-35; ☒ 6-11pm Mon-Wed, 6pm-midnight Thu-Sat) A newish boutique restaurant on Magdalena, Migas is high on the list of bar-hopping *sanjuaneros*. Some come for drinks (champagne mainly) and others for the food – miso-glazed salmon, classic French steak frites, spicy duck with orange glaze. Real lounge lizards, meanwhile, arrive just to hang out amid the sleek elegance and fashionable buzz.

**Pamela's** (Map pp334-5; ☎ 726-5010; 1 Santa Ana; dishes US$20-30; ☒ noon-10:30pm) Right on the beach and right on the money, Pamela's is encased inside the elegant Numero Uno. Diners sup wine and munch on scallops beside a teardrop-shaped swimming pool while the ocean crashes just feet away. The menu specializes in fresh ingredients plucked from the nearby sea – think jalapeño-ginger shrimp and seafood chowder – though there are surprise twists. The place is tucked away, but that hasn't prevented it from becoming an open secret. Reserve ahead.

### Santurce

**Pikayo** (Map pp334-5; ☎ 721-6194; 299 Av José de Diego; dishes US$25-40; ☒ 6-11pm Mon & Sat, noon-3pm & 6-11pm Tue-Fri) Wilo Benet is the island's very own Gordon Ramsey (without the expletives), a celebrity chef par excellence who has uncovered the soul of Caribbean cooking by infusing colonial-era Puerto Rican cuisine with various African and Indian elements. Adding atmosphere to authenticity, Pikayo, Benet's showcase restaurant is situated inside San Juan's stunning Museo de Arte de Puerto Rico (p332), where diners can watch the action in the kitchen on closed-circuit TVs.

### Isla Verde

**Edith Café** (☎ 253-1281; Km 6.3, Av Isla Verde; dishes US$6-15; ☒ 24hr) No frills, no formalities, just good food – and it's open 24 hours, though you'd think it wasn't operating at all looking at the heavily tinted windows. Come here for breakfast after one of those exuberant all-night parties and nip your hangover in the bud with two fried eggs, bacon and ham washed down with a strong cup of coffee.

**Che's** (Map pp334-5; ☎ 726-7202; 35 Caoba; dishes US$12-24; ☒ lunch & dinner) Che T-shirts aren't too common in Puerto Rico, where the man who promised to 'create two, three…many Vietnams' in the Americas is regarded with a certain degree of suspicion. That said, you might see the odd red-starred beret in here tucking into *churrasco* and *parrillada* (grilled, marinated steak), or veal chops with a kind of revolutionary zeal. Che's is situated in the neighborhood of Punta Las Marías at the far western end of Av Isla Verdé.

**Metropol** (☎ 791-5585; Av Isla Verde; dishes US$12-26; ☒ dinner) You can't miss this place – it's right next to the cockfighting arena. It's a neighborhood favorite well-known for the plentiful portions and simple (but not plain) Spanish fare. Wandering tourists are sometimes lured out of their upscale resorts and into its inviting fold.

## DRINKING

There are plenty of drinking options in Old San Juan, primarily along San Sebastián and Cristo. The bohemian **El Batey** (Map p330; 101 Calle del Cristo; ☒ 3pm-late) is where you'd find Hunter S Thompson if he were still alive and living in Puerto Rico. **Wet & Liquid** (☎ 728-3666; Water & Beach Club, 2 Tartak) is a far trendier duo of bars

PUERTO RICO

## GAY & LESBIAN SAN JUAN

San Juan is considered to be the most gay-friendly destination in the Caribbean. One of the oldest gay meeting spots is the bar at the Atlantic Beach Hotel (p336) in Condado. More mixed venues include Número Uno (p336) in Ocean Park and the delectable Gran Hotel El Convento (p335) in the heart of the Old City.

High energy nightspots to look out for are **KRASH** (Map pp334–5; ☎ 722-1131; 1257 Av Ponce de León; ☼ 10pm-late) for men, **Cups** (off Map pp334–5; ☎ 268-3570; 1708 San Mateo; ☼ 10pm-late) for women and **Kouros** (Map pp334–5; ☎ 977-0771; 1515 Av Ponce de León; ☼ 10pm-late Sat & Sun) for a good mix of both.

situated in Isla Verde's Water & Beach Club. Here you'll encounter the beautiful people, perched on zebra-striped stools or lounging on strategically positioned sofas, martinis in hand.

## ENTERTAINMENT

Old San Juan is the G-spot of the city's nightlife, hosting what is popularly considered to be the hottest and hippest entertainment scene in the Caribbean. For a condensed late-night scene, hit San Sebastián with its dive bars and musical clubs, or Fortaleza with its trendy yet undeniably tasty restaurants.

Isla Verde is an alternative nexus with most of the action confined to a trio of international-class hotels. Further west, resurgent Condado plays hosts to one of the Caribbean's biggest gay scenes. Down-at-heel Santurce also has a handful of late-night dance clubs that you'll need a taxi or car to get to.

**Nuyorican Café** (Map p330; ☎ 977-1276; 312 San Francisco; ☼ 7pm-late) Now this is more like it. If you came to Puerto Rico in search of authentic salsa music, you'll find the legend still lives on at the Nuyorican Café. San Juan's hottest nightspot is a congenial hub of live Latino sounds and hip-gyrating locals that easily matches its famous New York namesake. Stuffed into an alley off Fortaleza, opposite a nameless drinking hole, here you'll get everything from poetry readings to six-piece salsa bands that barely jam onto the stage. Things usually get interesting here around 11pm-ish.

**La Rumba** (Map p330; ☎ 725-4407; 152 San Sebastián; ☼ 11pm-late) This is what you came to Puerto Rico for – a club so packed with people of all races and ages that it matters not if you are an expert twirler or a rank neophyte who can't even spell syncopation. It won't get busy until after 11pm, when the live bands start warming up, but soon enough the

trickle of people through the door will turn into a torrent and you'll be caught up in a warm tropical crush of movement. Expect salsa, samba, reggaeton, rock and, of course rumba music.

**Kudetá** (Map p330; ☎ 721-3548; 314 Fortaleza ☼ 10pm-5am) In the snakes and ladders of San Juan nightlife, Kudetá (coup de etat – geddit?) is a precocious newcomer. It is also part of an emerging new trend: a Pan-Asian restaurant that metamorphoses after hours into a hip club with a hidden upstairs lounge where diners can disappear to dance off their Indonesian barbecued baby-back ribs and Cuba Libre–cured salmon-roll salad.

**Marriot Hotel Lobby** (Map pp334–5; ☎ 722 7000, 1309 Av Ashford) Salsa springs up in the unlikeliest of places, including in the lobby of this international hotel chain. But this is no standard tourist show. Indeed the authenticity and variety of the music here is something to behold – and people dance too (including the staff). Thursday through Saturday is salsa and merengue dancing; Wednesday is Nueva Trova with a Cuban influence; and Sunday through Tuesday is a live salsa sextet.

## SHOPPING

There are several beautiful boutiques and clothing stores lining Av Ashford in Condado. For arts and crafts, the shopping is in Old San Juan. Calles San Francisco and Fortaleza are the two main arteries in and out of the old city and both are packed cheek-by-jowl with shops. Running perpendicular at the west end of the town, Calle del Cristo is home to many of the old city's most chic establishments.

If you can't live without your mall fix, head out to the **Plaza Las Américas** (☼ 9am-9pm Mon-Sat, 11am-5pm Sun) in Hato Rey, the largest mall in the Caribbean with over 200 stores.

PUERTO RICO

# GETTING THERE & AWAY

## Air

International flights arrive at and depart from San Juan's Aeropuerto Internacional de Luis Muñoz Marín (LMM), about 8 miles (12.8km) east of the old city center. See p354 for details of flights.

Private aircraft, charter services and the bulk of the commuter flights serving the islands of Culebra and Vieques arrive at and depart from San Juan's original airport at Isla Grande, on the Bahía de San Juan in the city's Miramar district. See p355 for details.

## Público

There is no island-wide bus system. *Públicos* (taxis) form the backbone of public transportation in Puerto Rico and can provide an inexpensive link between San Juan and other points on the island, including Ponce (US$8) and Mayagüez (US$12). *Públicos* are generally shared taxis in the form of minivans that pick up passengers along predetermined routes.

In San Juan the major *público* centers include the LMM airport, two large *público* stations in Río Piedras (Centro de Públicos Oeste and Centro de Públicos Este) and – to a lesser extent – the Plaza de Colón in Old San Juan.

# GETTING AROUND
## To/From the Airport

The bus is the cheapest option. Look for the 'Parada' sign outside the arrivals concourse at LMM airport. The B40 bus will get you from the airport to Isla Verde or Río Piedras. From Isla Verde you can take bus A5 Old San Juan and Condado. From Río Piedras you can take bus A9 to Santurce and Old San Juan.

There are also airport shuttle vans or limousine kiosks on the arrivals concourse. Chances are you can join some other travelers headed your way. Once the van fills, you'll pay around US$7 to Isla Verde, US$9 to Condado and US$12 to Old San Juan.

Taxis to/from LMM airport to San Juan are generally fixed rate to the following destinations: Isla Verde (US$10), Condado (US$14) and Puerta de Tierra/Old San Juan (US$19).

## Bus

The **Autoridad Metropolitana de Autobuses** (AMA; Metropolitan Bus Authority & Metrobus; ☎ 767-7979) has a main bus terminal (Map p330) in Old San Juan near the cruise-ship piers. These are the routes taken most often by travelers (bus numbers are followed by associated route descriptions):

**A5** Old San Juan, Stop 18, Isla Verde.
**B21** Old San Juan, Condado, Stop 18 (Santurce), Plaza Las Américas.
**B40** LMM Airport, Isla Verde, Piñones and Río Piedras.
**C10** Hato Rey, Stop 18, Condado, Isla Grande.
**M1 & M9** Old San Juan, Río Piedras via various routes.

In Old San Juan there is a handy free trolley bus that plies a route around the old quarter (see Map p330). The trolley starts and finishes just outside the main bus terminal, but you can get on and off at any one of two dozen designated stops.

## Car

Traffic, parking, the maze of thoroughfares and the danger of being carjacked make having and using a rental car in the city a challenge. And with an excellent public transport system it is largely unnecessary. For car hire see p355.

## Ferry

A commuter ferry service called the **Acua Expreso** (Map p330; ☎ 788-1155; US$0.50; 6am-9pm) connects the east and west sides of Bahía de San Juan, Old San Juan and Cataño every 30 minutes. In Old San Juan the ferry dock is at Pier 2, near the Sheraton Old San Juan.

## Metro

The brand new **Tren Urbano** ( ☎ 866-900-1284), which opened in 2005, connects Bayamón with downtown San Juan as far as Sagrado Corazón on the south side of Santurce. Efficient trains run every five minutes in either direction between 5:30am and 11:30pm. Bicycles are permitted with a special permit. The 16 super-modern stations are safe, spacious and decked out with acres of eye-catching art and polished chrome. The line, which is a mix of sky-train and underground, charges US$1.50 one-way or US$3 return for any journey, regardless of length.

## Taxi

Meters – when or if they do go on – charge US$1.75 initially and US$1.90 per mile or part thereof. You'll also pay US$1 per piece of luggage. There's a US$5 reservation charge; add a US$1 surcharge after 10pm.

Taxis line up at the south end of Fortaleza in Old San Juan; or you can book at your

---

**TWIST MY ARM: THE PLACES THE AUTHORS WANTED TO KEEP SECRET**

Ah…serenity has arrived. Materializing like a leafy apparition out of Puerto Rico's crenellated karst country, the **Casa Grande Mountain Retreat** ( ☎ 888-343-2272; www.hotelcasagrande.com; Km 0.3, Hwy 612; r US$90-135; ☒ ) ought to be on the prescription list of Caribbean doctors as an antidote for stress, hypertension and rat-race burnout. Nestled in its own steep-sided valley and run efficiently by an ex-New York lawyer, the Casa is an ecologically congruous 'green' hotel that stops you in your tracks, forcing you to slow down and take it easy. While there are no TVs or phones in any of the 20 jungle-esque rooms, there are daily yoga classes, a scrumptious onsite restaurant and every available excuse to sit around all day and do – absolutely nothing. Try it, you might just get addicted.

---

hotel. Elsewhere, try **Metro Taxi Cabs** ( ☎ 787-725-2870) or **Rochdale Radio Taxi** ( ☎ 787-721-1900).

# AROUND SAN JUAN

In a place as small as Puerto Rico you can be three-quarters of the way across the island and still be within an hour or two's drive of San Juan (traffic permitting). Day trips from the capital can thus take you almost anywhere in the commonwealth. If you're keen to probe deeper, it's worthwhile traveling slower and making at least one overnight stop.

## BACARDI RUM FACTORY

Called the 'Cathedral of Rum' because of its six-story pink distillation tower, the **Bacardi plant** ( ☎ 788-8400; Hwy 888, Bayamón; admission free; ☒ 8:30am-4:30pm Mon-Sat) covers 127 acres (51 hectares) and stands out like a petroleum refinery across from Old San Juan, near the entrance to the bay. The world's largest and most famous rum-producing family started their business in Cuba more than a century ago, but they began moving their operation to this site in 1936. Today the distiller produces some 100,000 gallons of rum per day and ships 21 million cases per year worldwide.

To get to the factory, take the US$0.50 ferry from Old San Juan to Cataño followed by a US$3 *público* from the ferry terminal along the waterfront on Palo Seco (Hwy 888).

## ARECIBO OBSERVATORY

The Puerto Ricans reverently refer to it as 'El Radar.' To everyone else it is simply the largest radio telescope in the world. Resembling an extraterrestrial spaceship grounded in the middle of karst country, the

**Arecibo Observatory** ( ☎ 878-2612; www.naic.edu; adult/child/senior US$4/2/2; ☒ noon-4pm Wed-Fri, 9am-4pm Sat, Sun & most holidays) looks like something out of a James Bond movie – probably because it is; 007 aficionados will recognize the saucer-shaped dish and craning antennae from the 1995 film *Goldeneye*.

In reality, this 20-acre 'dish' set in a sinkhole among clusters of haystack-shaped mogotes, is planet earth's ear into outer space. Involved in the SETI (Search for Extraterrestrial Intelligence) program, the telescope, which is supported by 50-story cables weighing more than 600 tonnes, is used by onsite scientists to prove the existence of pulsars and quasars, the so-called 'music of the stars.'

## PARQUE DE LAS CAVERNAS DEL RÍO CAMUY

This **park** ( ☎ 898-3100; adult/child US$12/6; ☒ 8am-3:45pm Wed-Sun & holidays) is home to one of the largest cave systems in the world and is definitely worth a stop (but call ahead if it's been raining – too much water causes closures).

Trolleybus trips and ample walking among stalagmites and stalactites make this a fun trip for the whole family. If you come early enough you can do the caves in the morning and the observatory in the afternoon. They are a 30-minute drive apart.

# EASTERN PUERTO RICO

The East Coast is Puerto Rico shrink-wrapped; a tantalizing taste of almost everything the island has to offer squeezed into an area not much larger than Manhattan. Here in the foothills of the Sierra de Luquillo the sprawling suburbs of San Juan blend caustically with the jungle-like quietness of El Yunque National Forest, the commonwealth's giant green lungs and biggest outdoor attraction.

Separated from mainland Puerto Rico by a 7-mile stretch of choppy ocean, the two islands of Culebra and Vieques sport unsullied beaches and unblemished countryside that glimmers invitingly with nary a resort, golf course or casino to break the natural vista.

# EL YUNQUE

Covering some 43 sq mile of land in the Luquillo mountains, this verdant, tropical rainforest is impressively healthy and bountiful and some of the island's old trees still remain (1000 years and growing!). The views of the valleys, the Atlantic, the Caribbean and the eastern islands are inspiring; the temperatures are cool; the hiking is heart-pounding; and the streams and waterfalls are rejuvenating. The first place of note that most people stop at is **El Portal Visitor's Center** ( ☎ 888-1880; www.southernregion.fs.fed.us/caribbean; Hwy 191, adult/under 5yr/child/senior US$3/free/1.50/1.50; ☼ 9am-5pm, closed Christmas Day). Built in 1996, El Portal is the key for visitors who want to understand more about El Yunque, and pick up details about its hikes.

**ourpick** **Casa Cubuy Ecolodge** ( ☎ 874-6221; www.casacubuy.com; Km 22 from Naguabo, Hwy 191; r US$90-115; ☒ ☒ ) If listening to a frog symphony and relaxing on a shady balcony within hammock-swinging distance of a mystical tropical rainforest has you dashing for your jungle apparel, then this could be your place. Cocooned atop the winding Hwy 191 on El Yunque's wild and isolated southern slopes, Casa Cubuy Ecolodge's 10 cozy rooms offer a welcome antidote to the modern Puerto Rico of crowded beaches and spirit-crushing traffic.

You can get here from San Juan on an organized trip or by driving along Hwy 3 to the junction with Hwy 191 just past the settlement of Río Grande.

# LUQUILLO

Luquillo is synonymous with its *balneario* (public beach), the fabulous **Playa Luquillo** (admission free, parking US$2; ☼ 8:30am-5:30pm). Set on a calm bay facing northwest and protected from the easterly trade winds, the public part of this beach makes a mile-long arc to a point

of sand shaded by evocative coconut palms. Although crowds converge here at weekends and during holidays, Luquillo has always been more about atmosphere than solitude. With its famous strip of 50-plus food kiosks congregated at its western end it's also a great place to sample the local culinary culture. There is a bathhouse, a refreshment stand, a security patrol and well-kept bathrooms.

## Sleeping & Eating

**Luquillo Sunrise Beach Inn** ( ☎ 889-1713; A2 Costa Azul; d US$95-135; ☒ ☒ ) Filling a gap in the midrange market, the newly opened Sunrise Beach Inn is caressed by cooling Atlantic sea breezes in each of its spiffy 14 ocean-facing rooms. There's a communal patio and all upper-floor rooms have large balconies overlooking the beach. Luquillo plaza is two blocks away and the famous *balneario* and food kiosks a 30-minute stroll along the beach

**ourpick** **Rosa's Seafood** ( ☎ 863-0213; 536 Tablazo; dishes US$14-25; ☼ 11am-10pm Thu-Tue) Frustrated ferry passengers mix with loyal locals at this much vaunted seafood salon situated within anchor-dropping distance of Fajardo docks. You'll walk through a gauntlet of rusting cars and snarling canines to get here, but enter the bright yellow building at road's end and the smell of fresh fish and the sound of sizzling onions will soon have you forgetting about your ferry delays.

## Getting There & Away

*Públicos* run from San Juan (US$4) to and from the Luquillo plaza. Aside from that, you'll need your own wheels.

# VIEQUES
## pop 10,000

With a name stamped in infamy, Vieques was where Puerto Rico's most prickly political saga was played out in the public eye. For over five decades the US navy used more than two-thirds of this lusciously endowed Spanish Virgin Island for military target practice.

These days Vieques teeters precariously between undiscovered tropical nirvana and the Caribbean's next 'big thing' although, to date, a tight community of US expats have managed to jealously guard their largely untainted Viequense paradise against the braying bulldozers. Protected via a newly established wildlife refuge and receiving only 3% of Puerto

Rico's five million annual visitors, the tranquility remains – at least for the time-being

## Information

Unless otherwise noted, all of these addresses are in Isabella Segunda.

It's a good idea to carry cash on the island (but watch out for petty thieves) as the ATMs have been known to run dry.

**Banco Popular** ( ☎ 741-2071; Muñoz Rivera; ☼ 8am-3pm Mon-Fri) Has one of two ATMs in Isabella Segunda.

**Post office** ( ☎ 741-3891; Muñoz Rivera 97; ☼ 8:30am-4:30pm Mon-Fri, 8am-noon Sat) Across from the Banco Popular, this is the island's only post office. It will take general-delivery letters.

**Puerto Rico Tourism Company** (PRTC; ☎ 741-0800; www.gotopuertorico.com; Carlos LeBrun 449; ☼ 8am-5pm)

## Sights
### ORCHID, RED, GARCIA, SECRET & BLUE BEACHES

All these south-shore beaches, which used to be on navy land, can be reached by entering the Garcia Gate on Hwy 997.

Red Beach usually has a few *cabanas* up to shade bathers from the sun. Garcia Beach and Secret Beach are the next coves along the road. Blue Beach, at the east end of the Camp Garcia road, is long, open and occasionally has rough surf. Orchid Beach, at the eastern tip of the US Fish & Wildlife Reserve, is often deserted, with wide, deep blue waters (not good for children).

### BAHÍA MOSQUITO

This bioluminescent bay – a designated wildlife preserve about 2 miles east of Esperanza – has one of the highest concentrations of phosphorescent dinoflagellates in the world. Indeed, it's also known as Phosphorescent Bay – and it's magnificent.

An evening trip through the lagoon is nothing short of psychedelic, with hundreds of fish whipping up bright-green contrails below the surface as your kayak or electric boat passes by (don't ever accept a ride in a motorized boat – the engine pollution kills the organisms that create phosphorescence). But the best part is when you stop to swim: it's like bathing in the stars.

The best way to see the bay is with an organized trip. **Island Adventures** ( ☎ 741-0720; www.biobay .com; Km 4.5, Rte 996) offers ecofriendly 90-minute tours (US$30) in an electric boat just about every night, except when there's a full moon.

## Activities

**Blue Caribe Kayaks** ( ☎ 741-2522; http://enchanted-isle.com/bluecaribe; Flamboyán, Esperanza; trips US$23-30) rents out kayaks to individuals (US$10/25 for one/four hours) and offers trips through the bioluminescent bay (US$30) with a swim stop included.

**Blackbeard Sports** ( ☎ 741-1892; 101 Muñoz Rivera, Isabella Segunda) is the island's main dive operator and offers two-tank dives from US$100. It also rents out North American standard bicycles from its store in Isabel Segunda for US$25 per day including helmet. Ask about the fantastic bike tours.

Fishing is sublime in Vieques where you can access isolated stretches of coastline in the former naval zone. For a good local operator try **Caribbean Fly-fishing Company** ( ☎ 741-1337; www.caribbeanflyfishingco.com).

## Sleeping
### ESPERANZA

**Bananas** ( ☎ 741-8700; www.bananasguesthouse.com; Flamboyán; r US$65-80; 🞖 ) This is where it all started. Bananas is Esperanza's original cheap guesthouse/restaurant and it's a classic, in the mold of a backpacker's hostel in Thailand or a beach bar in Jamaica. Seasoned travelers will know the deal here: great prices, a lively downstairs bar, a funky and relaxed atmosphere, and basic but adequate rooms that receive the odd nightly visitor from the insect kingdom.

**Trade Winds** ( ☎ 741-8666; Flamboyán; r US$70; 🞖 ) Another vintage Vieques abode (vintage meaning since 1984). Situated on the far west end of the *malecón,* this popular guesthouse and inn has 10 rooms, most with air-con, including three terrace rooms that have a harbor view and catch the breeze. The biggest feature is probably the fabulous open-air deck where meals are served – it offers splendiferous views of the ocean.

### ISABELLA SEGUNDA

**Ocean View** ( ☎ 741-3696; 751 Plinio Peterson; r US$75-100; 🞖 🞖 ) Vieques' old dockside stalwart is centrally located, convenient and ...well, that's about it. Don't expect a plethora of home comforts in this faded and rather bleak town center hotel. For the unfussy, however, the Ocean View does have friendly staff, a swimming pool and – surprise, surprise – a lovely ocean view.

**Bravo Beach Hotel** ( ☎ 741-1128; www.bravobeach hotel.com; North Shore Rd 1, Bravos de Boston; r US$190-300, villa US$550; 🖂 💻 🔊 ) Up above the lighthouse, in the burgeoning Bravos de Boston neighborhood, Vieques is fast creating its very own Beverley Hills. The trend is epitomized in the Bravo Beach Hotel, a former sugar merchant's hacienda whose gorgeous 'Viejo San Juan'–style exterior looks like it's been lifted straight off the front cover of *Travel & Leisure* magazine. Nine fantastical guest rooms are set in lush tropical grounds with ample verandahs and two mesmerizing swimming pools.

### ELSEWHERE ON THE ISLAND

**La Finca Caribe** ( ☎ 741-0495; www.lafinca.com; Hwy 995; r from US$85; 🔊 ) Finca Caribe is Vieques personified. Sitting high up on a mountain-ridge seemingly a million miles from anywhere (but only actually 3 miles from either coast), it's the kind of rustic haven stressed-out city slickers probably dream about. Despite its back-to-nature facilities – outdoor communal showers, shared kitchen and hippy-ish decor – it has a religious following and has inspired gushing reviews from numerous top newspapers and magazines.

**ourpick Inn on the Blue Horizon** ( ☎ 741-3318; www.innonthebluehorizon.com; r US$200-400; 🖂 💻 🔊 ) Small is beautiful. The Inn on the Blue Horizon was surely invented with such a motto in mind. With only nine rooms harbored in separate bungalows wedged onto a stunning ocean-side bluff a few clicks west of Esperanza, the sense of elegance here – both natural and contrived – is truly breathtaking. The luxury continues inside the restaurant and cozy communal lounge, which overlook an Italianate infinity pool fit for a Roman emperor.

## Eating
### ESPERANZA

**Belly Button's** (Flamboyán; dishes US$5-11; 🕑 7am-2pm Wed-Sun) Make a beeline for breakfast at Belly Button's and bring a good appetite. Your belly will be more than happy after you've heroically demolished the three Frisbee-sized pancakes that appear rather magically on your plate here.

Bananas and Trade Winds both have popular restaurants onsite.

### ISABELLA SEGUNDA

**La Viequense Deli** ( ☎ 741-8213; Antonio Mellado; dishes US$5-12; 🕑 6am-6pm Mon-Sat, 6am-2pm Sun) If it's breakfast you're after, this is the place to come for your 6am pancakes or hangover-curing

coffee. If you miss the 11am cut-off you can feast instead on decent baked goods, tortillas and sandwiches. Service is no nonsense and fast and the clientele local with a smattering of in-the-know tourists.

**Topacio** ( ☎ 741-1179; Carlos Lebrun; mains US$17-24; 🕑 lunch & dinner) The newly opened Topacio has already cemented a strong reputation among those with a penchant for delicious seafood served Caribbean style. On an outside patio underneath colorful lights you can sample the generous paella, fish in a Creole sauce, seafood *mofongo* and lobster cooked in garlic.

**Café Media Luna** ( ☎ 741-2594; 351 Antonio G Mellado; mains US$18-30; 🕑 dinner) Romance is not dead in Vieques' original 'posh' restaurant where candle-lit tables and a tiny streetside balcony add panache to any meal. And there's more. Isabel II's music scene more or less begins and ends in this attractive colonial building where smooth live jazz accompanies lamb chops, seared tuna and rather authentic pizza.

**Blue Macaw** ( ☎ 741-1147; Antonio Mellado; dishes US$24-32; 🕑 dinner) No birds here, but plenty of fancy metal curves and elaborate downlighting. One of a trio of plush new eating houses that could quite easily have been plucked straight out of San Juan's SoFo neighborhood, the Blue Macaw's menu is as delicious as the decor is plush. Try the scampi, the lamb tenderloin or the tempura trout and leave room for a lavish dessert.

## Getting There & Away
### AIR

There are a good 10 flights a day to/from San Juan's Isla Grande and LMM airports and approximately half a dozen between Fajardo and the island with **Vieques Air Link** ( ☎ San Juan-Vieques flights 888-901-9247, 787-741-8331, for Fajardo-Vieques flights 741-3266). **Isla Nena Air Service** ( ☎ 863-4447) links Vieques with Culebra. Round-trip prices start at US$165 (25 minutes) from LMM, US$90 from Isla Grande and US$45 (10 minutes) from Fajardo. Phone for more up-to-date information.

### BOAT

Call the **Puerto Rican Port Authority** ( ☎ 863-0705, 800-981-2005; 🕑 8-11am & 1-3pm Mon-Fri) for vehicle reservations (required) or call the **Vieques office** ( ☎ 741-4761; 🕑 8-11am & 1-3pm Mon-Fri) at the ferry dock in Isabella Segunda. For ferry schedules see p355.

## Getting Around

Vieques is a small island and renting a bike (p344) is a great way to get around. *Públicos* and taxis congregate at the ferry terminal, the airport and on 'the strip' in Esperanza.

Reliable car-rental places include **Island Car Rentals** ( ☎ 741-1666) and **Maritza's Car Rental** ( ☎ 741-0078).

# CULEBRA

pop 2000

Welcome to Culebra – the island that time forgot; mainland Puerto Rico's weird, wonderful and distinctly wacky smaller cousin that lies glistening like a bejeweled Eden to the east.

Situated 17 miles to the east of mainland Puerto Rico, but inhabiting an entirely different planet culturally speaking, the island is home to an offbeat mix of rat-race dropouts, earnest idealists, solitude seekers, myriad eccentrics and anyone else who can't quite get their heads around the manic intricacies of modern life. Long feted for its diamond dust beaches and world-class diving reefs, there's but one binding thread – the place is jaw-droppingly beautiful.

## Information

**Banco Popular** ( ☎ 742-3572; Pedro Márquez; 8:30am-2:30pm Mon & Wed-Fri) There's an ATM here.

**Post office** ( ☎ 742-3862; Pedro Márquez; 8:30am-4:30pm Mon-Fri, 8:30am-noon Sat) Right in the center of town.

**Tourist office** ( ☎ 742-3116; Pedro Márquez; 8:30am-3:30pm Mon-Fri) Good islandwide information can be found at this booth outside the Alcaldía (town hall) on the main street 200 yards from the ferry terminal.

## Sights

### PLAYA FLAMENCO

Stretching for a mile around a sheltered, horseshoe-shaped bay, Playa Flamenco is not just Culebra's best beach; it is also generally regarded as the finest in Puerto Rico and quite possibly the whole Caribbean. Backed by low scrub and equipped with basic amenities, it is also the only public beach on the island and a good place to camp. To get there walk, bike or drive 2.5 miles north of the main settlement of Dewey.

### PLAYA BRAVA

The beauty of Brava lies in the fact that there is no road here; you *have* to hike – make that bushwhack – along a little-used trail

that is often overgrown with sea grape and low scrub. The rewards are immense when you finally clear the last mangrove and are confronted with an isolated but stunning swathe of sand that glimmers with a fierce but utterly enchanting beauty.

Leatherback sea turtles use isolated Brava as a nesting site from April to June. To witness this amazing sight you can volunteer for a turtle watch with the **US Fish & Wildlife Service** ( ☎ 742-0115; www.fws.gov; 7am-4pm Mon-Fri), which maintains an office on the island.

### ISLA CULEBRITA

If you need a reason to rent a kayak or take a boat trip, Isla Culebrita is it. This small islet just a mile east of Playa Zoni is part of the wildlife refuge. With its abandoned lighthouse, six beaches, tide pools, reefs and nesting areas for seabirds, Isla Culebrita has changed little in the past 500 years.

## Activities

Culebra retains some of Puerto Rico's most amazing dive spots, including sunken ships, coral reefs, drop offs and caves. Good snorkeling can be accessed from Playas Carlos Rosario, Tamarindo and Melones.

**Culebra Divers** ( ☎ 742-0803; www.culebradivers.com) across from the ferry dock rents snorkel gear for about US$10 to US$12 and offers one-/two-tank dive trips for US$65/90.

**Ocean Safaris** ( ☎ 379-1973) offers half-day guided kayak trips to places such as Isla Culebrita or Cayo Luis Peña from US$45.

The **Tanama Glass Bottom Boat** ( ☎ 501-0011; trips US$25-40) offers some really fantastic two-hour harbor cruises in and around the various reefs and trips out to Culebrita.

## Sleeping & Eating

**Flamenco Campground** ( ☎ 742-0700; campsites US$20) The only place you can legally camp in Culebra is just feet from the paradisiacal Playa Flamenco. Report to the office at the entrance and you will be assigned a spot. Six people maximum per tent. There are outdoor showers with water available between 4pm and 7pm; bathrooms are open 24/7.

**Hotel Kokomo** ( ☎ 742-0683; r US$45-85; ) If you're anxious to dump your bags in the first visible crash pad in order to get out exploring, then Hotel Kokomo, the bright yellow building right on the ferry dock, is just the ticket. New management has given this old place a second lease on life and rooms, while still basic, are clean and cheery enough.

**Mamacita's** ( ☎ 742-0090; www.mamacitaspr.com; r US$85-110; ❀ ) Screaming lurid pink and pastel purple, Mamacita's is the raffish Caribbean crash pit you've been dreaming about. Although the water's invariably cold and the reception staff will have probably gone home by the time your boat arrives, there's something strangely contagious about this old Culebra stalwart with its simple rooms and legendary onsite restaurant.

**Posada La Hamaca** ( ☎ 742-3516; www.posada .com; r US$92-146) Rooms here (all with private bathrooms) are basic but comfortable and overlook the canal, while location-wise you're right in the heart of Dewey with plenty of eating options within walking distance. The front desk is a good font of local information.

**Palmetto Guesthouse** ( ☎ 742-0257; r US$95-115; ❀ ) Set up in Barrianda Clark, this new business is a super friendly and accommodating escape run by two ex–Peace Corps volunteers from New England. Five guestrooms with private bathrooms have the run of two kitchens, a deck, a handy book exchange and a sporty magazine pile.

**Bahía Marina** ( ☎ 742-3112; www.bahiamarina.net; r US$150-300; ❀ ❀ ) One of the island's newest accommodations is also one of its most luxurious – in fact, it's Buckingham Palace by Culebra standards. Abutting a 100-acre nature preserve, this condo resort has 16 well-integrated apartments with modern kitchenettes and cable TV; the resort also has a pool, restaurant-grill and live music at weekends.

**Juanita Bananas** ( ☎ 742-3855; Harbor Villas; dishes 12-24; ❀ 5:30-10pm Fri-Mon) Opened in 2004, this revolutionary restaurant gives new meaning to the words 'fresh' and 'sustainable.' Sporting it very own greenhouse and garden, almost all of the fruit, vegetables and herbs listed on the menu will have traveled only a few hundred yards before hitting your plate. The seafood is also local and fished using sustainable methods. Specialties include tasty soups, fruity desserts and the famous *sofrito* sauce. Reservations are necessary.

**Dinghy Dock** ( ☎ 742-0581; mains US$13-28) If you can brave the gauntlet of cigarette-smoking expats that requisition the steps nightly, you'll find the DD to be something of a culinary revelation. Fish is the obvious specialty here, with fresh catches like swordfish and snapper done in Creole sauces. The busy bar is a frenzy of expats nursing Medalla beers that acts as the unofficial island grapevine. If you haven't heard it here first, it's not worth hearing.

## Getting There & Away

### AIR
Culebra gets excellent air service from San Juan and Fajardo on the commuter carriers that also serve Vieques; see p345 for details. **Isla Nena Air Service** ( ☎ 812-5144; www.islanena.8m .com) can be chartered for flights to St Thomas and **Air St Thomas** ( ☎ 791-4898; www.airstthomas.com) does charter flights to St Croix, St Thomas and many other Caribbean islands, with stopovers at Vieques or Culebra on demand.

### BOAT
If you need to confirm the ferry schedule, call the **Fajardo Puerto Rican Port Authority office** ( ☎ 863-0705, car reservations 800-981-2005; ❀ 8-11am & 1-3pm Mon-Fri); Culebra office ( ☎ 742-3161; ferry dock, Dewey; ❀ 8-11am & 1-3pm Mon-Fri). For ferry schedules, see p355.

## Getting Around
It's not always necessary to hire a car in Culebra (there are too many cars on the island as it is). The Dewey area is all walkable, Flamenco beach is a not unpleasant 30-minute hike and everywhere else can be easily reached by *público*, bus, taxi or, if you're energetic, bicycle. **Dick & Cathy** ( ☎ 742-0062) rent bikes or, if you really can't be parted from your four wheels, contact **Thrifty Car Rental/JM Scooter Rentals** ( ☎ 742-0521).

*Público* vans run between the ferry dock and Playa Flamenco for US$2. Some local entrepreneurs double as taxi drivers.

**Willy's** ( ☎ 742-3537, 396-0076) generally meets every ferry and also arrives on your door when booked. If he's busy and you're stuck for a ride, try **Romero** ( ☎ 378-0250).

# SOUTHERN & WESTERN PUERTO RICO

A stunning change of scenery awaits you along the southern coast – particularly west of the main city, Ponce. The central mountains tumble down to denuded plains that once were full of sparse bushes – everything was cleared away to make room for sugar plantations in the 1800s. Now there's little to catch the eye – outside of the colonial charms of Ponce – until you arrive at Bosque Estatal de Guánica, a fabulous 'dry forest' that brings to mind the deserts of southern Arizona. Unbelievably, it's little more than an hour's drive from El Yunque's fecund greenery.

# PONCE

## pop 194,636

Given its fiercely proud, poetic history as the historic center of Puerto Rico's south; it's little wonder that Ponce is the subject of so many lofty declarations. From the mouths of Puerto Rican statesmen to the inscriptions on public fountains, Ponce is 'a city of initiative, understanding and heart' (Eugenio María de Hostos), a place that 'does not repeat history, but improves it' (Rafael Pon Flores) and a 'land of Camelot: ideal, legendary, dreamlike and real' (Antonio Gautier). The locals put it a bit more succinctly. '*Ponce es Ponce,*' they proudly claim and the rest of Puerto Rico is one great big parking lot.

## Information

Banks line the perimeter of Plaza Las Delicias, so finding a cash machine is no problem.

**Post office** (Atocha; �} 7:30am-4:30pm Mon-Fri, 8:30am-noon Sat) Three blocks north of Plaza Las Delicias, this is the most central of the city's four post offices.

**Puerto Rico Tourism Company** (PRTC; ☎ 284-3338; www.letsgotoponce.com; Parque de Bombas, Plaza Las Delicias; �} 9am-5:30pm) You can't miss the big red-and-black structure in the middle of the park, where friendly, English-speaking members of the tourist office are ready with brochures, answers and suggestions.

## Sights & Activities

### PLAZA LAS DELICIAS

The soul of Ponce is its idyllic Spanish colonial plaza, within which stands two of the city's landmark buildings, the red-and-black striped Parque de Bombas and Catedral Nuestra Señora de Guadalupe. At any hour of the day a brief stroll around the plaza's border will get you well acquainted with Ponce – the smell of *panderias* follows churchgoers across the square each morning; children squeal around the majestic **Fuente de Leones** (Fountain of Lions) under the heat of midday; and lovers stroll under its lights at night. Even as the kiosks of lottery tickets and trinkets, commercial banks and fast food joints encroach at the edges,

reminders of the city's proud history dominate the plaza's attractions, including marble statuary of local *danza* icon Juan Morel Campos and poet/politician Luis Muñoz Marín, Puerto Rico's first governor. The **Catedral Nuestra Señora de Guadalupe** (Our Lady of Guadalupe Cathedral; ☎ 842-0134; admission free; �} 6am-1pm Mon-Fri, 6am-noon & 3-8pm Sat & Sun) was built in 1931 in the place where colonists erected their first chapel in the 1660s, which (along with subsequent structures) succumbed to earthquakes and fires.

Facing Plaza Las Delicias on the south side of the plaza, Ponce's **Casa Alcaldía** (City Hall; ☎ 284-4141; admission free; �} 8am-4:30pm Mon-Fri) started life in the 1840s as a general assembly house and was later a jail.

### PARQUE DE BOMBAS

Poncenos will claim that the eye-popping **Parque de Bombas** (☎ 284-3338; admission free; �} 9:30am-5pm) is Puerto Rico's most frequently photographed building – not too hard to believe while you stroll around the black-and-red-stripped Arabian-styled edifice and make countless unwitting cameos in family albums. Originally constructed in 1882 as an agricultural exhibition hall, the space later housed the city's volunteer fire fighters, who are commemorated in a small, tidy exhibit on the open 2nd floor. Since 1990 the landmark has functioned as a tourist information center (left).

### MUSEO DEL ARTE DE PONCE

With an expertly presented collection, this commanding **art museum** (☎ 848-0505; www.museoarteponce.org; 2325 Av Las Américas; adult/child/student/senior US$5/1/2/2; �} 10am-5pm) in the vibrant heart of the city's artistic community is easily among the best fine arts centers in the Caribbean and itself worth the trip from San Juan. Set across from Universidad Católica the museum's expertly curated collection contains some 850 paintings, 800 sculptures and 500 prints representing five centuries of Western art.

### PASEO TABLADO LA GUANCHA

Ponce built this great half-mile (0.8km) boardwalk in the mid-1990s to overlook the town's yacht harbor and *club náutico*. Today there is a seaside concert pavilion with dozens of bars and restaurants, often great live salsa,

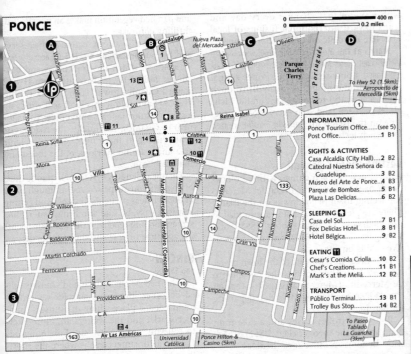

# PONCE

**INFORMATION**
Ponce Tourism Office......(see 5)
Post Office........................**1** B1

**SIGHTS & ACTIVITIES**
Casa Alcaldía (City Hall)....**2** B2
Catedral Nuestra Señora de
  Guadalupe.....................**3** B2
Museo del Arte de Ponce.**4** B3
Parque de Bombas...........**5** B1
Plaza Las Delicias.............**6** B2

**SLEEPING**
Casa del Sol......................**7** B1
Fox Delicias Hotel............**8** B1
Hotel Bélgica....................**9** B2

**EATING**
Cesar's Comida Criolla....**10** B2
Chef's Creations..............**11** B1
Mark's at the Meliá..........**12** B2

**TRANSPORT**
Público Terminal..............**13** B1
Trolley Bus Stop..............**14** B2

**PUERTO RICO**

an obligatory observation tower and a well-maintained public beach.

## Sleeping

**Hotel Bélgica** ( ☎ 844-3255; 122 Villa; r US$50–75; 🅿 ) A travelers' favorite for years, the Bélgica is just off the southwest corner of Plaza Las Delicias, a 20-room hotel with European-style high ceilings and wrought iron balconies. Rooms near the front allow you to stare out over the plaza from a private balcony, but be prepared for noise on weekend nights.

**Casa Del Sol Guest House** ( ☎ 812-2995; www.casadel solpr.com; 97 Union; r incl breakfast US$60–75; 🅿 🖳 🖥 ) Situated just north of the plaza, this nine-room guesthouse is the city's best deal, offering pleasant rooms and a welcoming staff within steps of the plaza. Shared balconies look over the busy street and it offers free wi-fi, a basic continental breakfast and a private terrace out back that has a small hot tub.

**Fox Delicias Hotel** ( ☎ 290-5050; www.foxdeliciashotel .com; 6963 Reina Isabel; r US$85–250; 🅿 🖳 🖥 ) The Fox family refitted an old building on the corner of the plaza with a modern hotel. Opened in 2005, its plaza-facing rooms are a

favorite among sophisticated *sanjuaneros*. The cocktail lounges swell at the high season and during festivals, but off-season amenities are limited and the place is pretty sleepy.

**Ponce Hilton & Casino** ( ☎ 259-7676; www.hilton .com; 1150 Av Caribe; r US$210–280; 🅿 🖳 🖥 ) The most deluxe place in town, the 153-room Hilton has well-manicured grounds, on-site golf, a nightclub, restaurants and a casino. Sun-pink golfers and wealthy Americans are wont to gripe about their last round and the quality of the buffet, but the live music and ocean views give a touch of local flavor.

## Eating

**Cesar's Comida Criolla** (cnr Mayor & Cristina; dishes US$2–14; 🕐 lunch) The ultimate hole in the wall for *comida criolla* (traditional Puerto Rican cuisine), this humble joint might be rough around the edges, but the savory piles of pork, chicken and seafood (most served with rice and beans) is the city's best home cookin'.

**Chef's Creations** ( ☎ 848-8384; Reina 100; mains US$6–12; 🕐 lunch). On first level of a former residence, this place exudes casual elegance, with a menu that changes every day and leans toward international fusions of local fare, like the delicious *paella con tostones*.

**Mark's at the Meliá** ( ☎ 842-0260; www.marksatthemelia.net; Hotel Meliá, 2 Cristina; mains US$14-26; ☺ dinner) Long regarded as Ponce's final word in fine dining, the cozily lit (though somewhat stuffy) restaurant within the Meliá Hotel has been lauded in every foodie magazine on the island for *comida criolla* treated to French technic.

## Getting There & Around

A nice, new *público* garage is three blocks north of the plaza near Plaza del Mercado connecting to all major towns on the island. There are plenty of long-haul vans headed to Río Piedras in San Juan (about US$20) and Mayagüez (about US$10), and an inexpensive café is on site.

Four miles (6.4km) east of the town center off Hwy 1 on Hwy 5506 is the Aeropuerto de Mercedita (Mercedita Airport). **Cape Air** ( ☎ 848-2020) has five flights a day departing for San Juan.

Ponce has trolley buses and a fake train that runs on the roads (tickets US$2). Check with the tourism office for schedules.

Car rental agencies include **Avis** ( ☎ 842-6184), **Dollar** ( ☎ 843-6940) and **Hertz** ( ☎ 842-7377); and taxi companies include **Cooperativa de Taxis** ( ☎ 848-8248) and **Ponce Taxi** ( ☎ 642-3370).

## BOSQUE ESTATAL DE GUÁNICA

The immense 10,000 acres of the Guánica Biosphere Reserve is one of the island's great natural treasures and a blank slate for the outdoor enthusiast. Trails of various lengths and difficulty make loops from the visitors center, lending themselves to casual hikes, mountain biking, bird-watching and broad views of the Caribbean.

The remote desert forest is among the best examples of subtropical dry forest vegetation in the world – a fact evident in the variety of extraordinary flora and fauna that is present around every corner. Scientists estimate that only 1% of the earth's dry forest of this kind remains and the vast acreage makes this a rare sanctuary. It's crossed by 30-odd miles of trails that lead from the arid, rocky highlands, which are covered with scrubby brush, to over 10 miles of remote, wholly untouched coast. Only a two-hour drive from the humid rainforests of El Yunque, the crumbling landscape

and parched vegetation makes an unexpected, thrilling contrast.

To get to the eastern section of the reserve and the **ranger station** ( ☎ 821-5706; admission free; ☺ 9am-5pm), which has trail maps and brochures, follow Hwy 116 south from Hwy 2 toward Guánica town. Turn left (east) onto Hwy 334 and follow this road as it winds up a steep hill through an outlying *barrio* (suburb) of Guánica. Eventually, the road crests a hill ending at the ranger station, a picnic area and a scenic overlook of the forest and the Caribbean.

Guánica's lengthy system of hypnotic trails offer a million surprises and although none of the foliage is particularly dense and getting lost isn't easy, be safe and bring water, sunscreen and bug repellent; the sun is unrelenting any time of year and there's little shade.

## RINCÓN

pop 15,000

Shoehorned far out in the island's most psychedelic corner, Rincón is Puerto Rico at its most unguarded, a place where the sunsets shimmer scarlet and the waiters are more likely to call you 'dude' than 'sir.' For numerous California dreamers this is where the short-lived summer of love ended up. Arriving for the Surfing World Championships in 1968 many never went home. Hence Rincón became a haven for draft-dodgers, alternative lifestylers, back-to-the-landers and people more interested in catching the perfect wave than bagging US$100,000 a year in a Chicago garden suburb.

Not surprisingly, Rincón's waves are often close to perfect. Breaking anywhere from 2ft to 25ft, the names are chillingly evocative: Domes, Indicator, Spanish Wall and Dogman's. The crème de la crème is Tres Palmas, a white-tipped monster that is often dubbed the 'temple' of big-wave surfing in the Caribbean.

## Activities

### DIVING & SNORKELING

Located inside the little marina on the north side of town, **Taíno Divers** ( ☎ 823-6429; www.tainodivers.com; Black Eagle Marina; 2-tank dive US$109, snorkeling US$75) is probably the best outfit on the west coast. Guides are responsible, professional and very environmentally aware. It does almost daily runs to Isla Desecheo (8am to 2pm), an almost uninhabited island off the coast that has very clear water and some of Puerto Rico's best diving. It also does shorter trips to nearby reefs (8am to noon).

## SURFING

Downtown on the Plaza de Recreo you will find the **West Coast Surf Shop** ( ☎ 823-3935; www .westcoastsurf.com; 2E Muños Rivera). Aside from selling all the appropriate gear, the owners have great local knowledge and can organize lessons for any standard or age at short notice.

## Sleeping & Eating

**Rincón Surf & Board** ( ☎ 823-0610; dm US$20, d US$55-65, ste US$85-95) In the Sandy Beach area north of town, this inn advertises basic apartments 'over the jungle.' It's a favorite haunt of the 'surf trolls' who show up to ride the waves all winter and the guesthouse offers 10 to 15% discounts if you stay a week or more.

**Beside the Pointe** ( ☎ 823-8550; www.besidethepointe .com; r US$75-125; 🗙 ) Right on Sandy Beach, this guesthouse also has a very popular après-surf restaurant, known as Tamboo Tavern, which attracts a fun crowd. Rooms are actually like small apartments, with cooking facilities and mini-kitchens. If you just want somewhere to rest your surfboard while you hit the beach bars, this could be the place.

**our pick Lazy Parrot Inn** ( ☎ 823-5654; www.lazy parrot.com; Km 4.1, Hwy 413; r US$110-155; 🗙 🖵 🖭 ) Claiming the middle ground between high quality and high quirky, the Lazy Parrot captures the unique essence of Rincón without scrimping on the home comforts. A venerable inn crammed with all kinds of parrots, it occupies the high country above Rincón Pueblo and offers peek-a-boo glimpses of the sparkling ocean. Rooms are comfortable, but not flash, there's a sublime pool and onsite Smilin' Joe's restaurant is a culinary corker.

**Hotel Villa Cofresí** ( ☎ 823-2450; www.villacofresi .com; Km 12.3, Hwy 115; r US$115-160; 🗙 🖭 ) Away from the plusher resorts, the Villa Cofresí is the down-to-earth place down the road that places fabulous customer service over fabulous art, and wicker furniture over wood. Standard rooms have king-sized beds and some come with kitchenettes; the property also has a pool, restaurant, bar and watersports concession.

**Pancho Villa** ( ☎ 823-8226; Plaza de Recreo; dishes US$10-12; 🕒 11am-3pm, 5-10pm Tue-Sun) If you have long grown bored of lukewarm enchiladas or unpalatable refried beans, this modest place in Rincón's main square could quite easily reignite your taste buds for all things Mexican. Though the decor's nothing fancy and the service only so-so, the Rancho Villa delivers the goods where it matters: the food's damn tasty.

## Entertainment

**our pick Calypso Tropical Café** ( ☎ 823-4151; 🕒 noon-midnight) Wall-to-wall suntans, svelte girls in bikini tops, bare-chested blokes nursing cold beers and syncopated reggae music drifting out beneath the sun-dappled palm trees; the Calypso is everything you'd expect a beach-side surfer's bar to be – and perhaps a little more. On the leafy road to the El Faro light-house, Calypso hosts the oldest pub scene in Rincón and regularly books live bands to cover rock, reggae and calypso classics.

## Getting There & Around

Rincón doesn't have an airport, but there are two in the area: Mayagüez and Aguadilla.

The *público* stand is situated just off the town plaza on Nueva. Expect to pay about US$4 if you are headed north to Aguadilla or US$1.50 to go south to Mayagüez (you can access San Juan from either of these cities).

The easiest way to approach the town is via the valley roads of Hwy 402 and Hwy 115, both of which intersect Hwy 2 south of the Rincón peninsula.

You will pay US$20 or more for a taxi from either the Aguadilla or Mayagüez airport and you may prefer a car to move around to the various attractions in Rincón. There are rental-car sites at both the Mayagüez and Aguadilla airports.

# DIRECTORY

## ACCOMMODATIONS

There are no hostels in Puerto Rico and very few dorm-style accommodations near local universities. Most options are guesthouses, inns, hotels and *paradores* (midrange to high-end hotels that get regular surprise visits from the tourism board). Rentals are a good idea for long-term guests or big groups. Most hotels rates are for a room where you specify what type of bed you want (double versus twin). If you have more than two to a room you'll be charged more, but solo travelers mostly aren't given any price break.

# ACTIVITIES

Puerto Rico's tropical climate and variety of land- and seascapes make the island a mecca for outdoor activities.

The semiprotected waters off the east end of Puerto Rico, which include the islands of Culebra and Vieques, provide the setting for racing and cruising aboard sailboats. You can count on the trade winds blowing 12 to 25 knots out of the east almost every day. A number of marinas meet sailors' needs in the Fajardo area. The largest is the **Puerto del Rey Marina** (☎ 860-1000), with 750 slips and room for vessels up to 200ft (79m) long.

There are plenty of good diving operators scattered around the island. In San Juan, check out Eco-Action Tours and Caribe Aquatic Adventures (p333). In Rincón, call by at Taíno Divers (p350). Out east, try Culebra Divers (p346) on the island of Culebra, and Blackbeard Sports (p344) in Isabella Segunda on Vieques.

Among both tourists and islanders, the most popular hiking area in Puerto Rico is the national rainforest at El Yunque (p343). All the commonwealth's *reservas forestales* offer good hikes, as does the dry forest in Guánica (p350).

Since the 1968 world surfing championships at Rincón, surfers the world over have known that Puerto Rico ranks with a few sites in Mexico and Costa Rica as some of the biggest and best winter surfing in all of the Americas. If you stay close to San Juan, you will find the surfers' scene at the beaches eastward from Isla Verde. But for the big stuff, you need to make a pilgrimage west to Rincón and Isabela, which host numerous important competitions each year.

Puerto Rico played host to the Ray Ban Windsurfing World Cup in 1989 and the sport has been booming here ever since. Hotdoggers head for the surfing beaches at Isla Verde or, better yet, the rough northwest coast.

## BUSINESS HOURS

The following are standard hours in Puerto Rico. Exceptions are noted in individual listings.

**Banks** ⊗ 9am to 5pm Monday to Friday

**Restaurants** ⊗ breakfast 7am to 10am, lunch noon to 3pm, dinner 7:30pm to 11pm

**Shops** ⊗ 10am or 11am to 7pm or 8pm Monday to Friday, 11am to 8pm Saturday and Sunday

---

**PRACTICALITIES**

■ **Newspapers & Magazines** *San Juan Star* (www.sanjuanstar.com) is a bilingual daily newspaper and *Puerto Rico Breeze* is a biweekly paper on gay nightlife in San Juan. *Que Pasa!* is a bimonthly magazine published by the PR Tourism Office.

■ **Radio & TV** US TV is broadcast across the island. The English-language radio station is WOSO San Juan, at 1030AM. Elsewhere, radio is mostly in Spanish.

■ **Video Systems** Puerto Rico uses VHS for videos.

■ **Electricity** Puerto Rico has the 110V AC system used in the USA.

■ **Weights & Measures** Puerto Rico follows the US system with two exceptions: all distances you see on road signs are in kilometers and gas is pumped in liters.

---

# CHILDREN

Puerto Ricans love children – it doesn't matter who they belong to – and even more, they love family. So traveling with youngsters is rarely a hassle. There are some hotels that won't take children under a certain age but it's very rare. Several museums and hotels offer child rates or discounts. If renting a car, make sure that the rental agency has a car seat for you and if taking a taxi any long distance, bring one with you. Children should carry some form of ID in case of an emergency.

# DANGERS & ANNOYANCES

Although street crime is a serious issue in urban areas, visitors need not be obsessed with security. A few commonsense reminders should help keep you secure.

Always lock cars and put valuables out of sight. If your car is bumped from behind in a remote area, it's best to keep going to a well-lit area or service station. Never allow yourself to get in a conflict with another driver on Puerto Rican roads: 'road rage' is common here and more than a few antagonized drivers have been known to retaliate with gunfire.

One type of daylight mosquito carries dengue fever although the risk of contracting it is extremely low. Nonetheless, bring some repellent and use it.

## EMBASSIES & CONSULATES

The following official buildings are located in San Juan.

**Austria** ( ☎ 766-0799; Plaza Las Américas, Río Piedras)
**Canada** ( ☎ 790-2210; 107 Cereipo Alturas, Guaynabo)
**Mexico** ( ☎ 764-0258; Bankers Finance, Hato Rey)
**Netherlands** ( ☎ 759-9400; Mercantil Plaza, Hato Rey)
**Spain** ( ☎ 758-6090; Mercantil Plaza, Hato Rey)
**UK** ( ☎ 727-1065; 1509 Lopez Landron, Santurce)
**Venezuela** ( ☎ 766-4255; Mercantil Plaza, Hato Rey)

## FESTIVALS & EVENTS

**Carnaval, Ponce** (February) Laid-back Ponce gets pretty wild during this week, in the six days preceding the beginning of Catholic Lent, with *vejigante* masks (colorful paper maché masks depicting often-scary characters from African and European mythology).

**Coffee Harvest Festival, Maricao** (mid-February) A celebration of Maricao's principal product, with lots of caffeine-fueled dancing.

**Cinco Días con Nuestro Tierra** (second week in March) Held in Mayagüez, this is one of the island's agricultural/industrial fairs, featuring local produce.

**Festival de Mavi, Juana Diaz** (April) *Mavi*, or *mabi* in Spanish, is a fermented drink invented by Taínos that uses local bark as its primary ingredient. This festival is as much about honoring Taíno heritage as it is about drinking *mavi*.

**Fiesta Nacional de la Danza, Ponce** (mid-May) This is a perfect opportunity to learn about the old-fashioned *danzas* that were practiced during colonial times.

**Festival Casals, San Juan** Internationally renowned, the Casals festival brings musicians from around the world to remember Pablo Casals, who lived most of his adult life in Puerto Rico.

**Fiesta de Santiago Apostal, Loíza Aldea** (end of July) The place to come for an African-influenced party – parades, fabulous drum ensembles, *vejigante* masks and colorful costumes.

**Hatillo Masks Festival, Hatillo** (December 28) The island's third major festival of masks features masked devils prowling the streets.

See also p333 for festivals in San Juan.

## GAY & LESBIAN TRAVELERS

Puerto Rico is probably the most gay-friendly island in the Caribbean. San Juan has a well-developed gay scene, especially in the Condado district, for Puerto Ricans and visitors. Other cities, such as Ponce, have gay clubs and gay-friendly accommodations as well. Vieques and Culebra have become popular destinations for an international mix of gay and lesbian expatriates and travelers.

## HOLIDAYS

**New Year's Day** January 1
**Three Kings Day (Feast of the Epiphany)** January 6
**Eugenio María de Hostos' Birthday** January 10; honors the island educator, writer and patriot
**Martin Luther King Jr Day** Third Monday in January
**Presidents' Day** 3rd Monday in February
**Emancipation Day** March 22; island slaves were freed on this date in 1873
**Palm Sunday** Sunday before Easter
**Good Friday** Friday before Easter
**Easter** Sunday in late March/April
**Jose de Diego Day** April 18
**Memorial Day** Last Monday in May
**Independence Day/Fourth of July** July 4
**Luis Muñoz Rivera's Birthday** July 18; honors the island patriot and political leader
**Constitution Day** July 25
**Jose Celso Barbosa's Birthday** July 27
**Labor Day** First Monday in September
**Columbus Day** Second Monday in October
**Veterans' Day** November 11
**Thanksgiving Day** Fourth Thursday in November
**Christmas Day** December 25

## INTERNET ACCESS

Finding a good internet café outside of San Juan and the main resorts can be difficult, although most public libraries have computers with internet access. Free wi-fi access is increasingly available in the better hotels, although whether it is working is another matter.

## INTERNET RESOURCES

Good general websites include the following:
**El Boricua** (www.elboricua.com)
**Escape to Puerto Rico** (http://escape.topuertorico.com)
**Puerto Rico Tourist Company** (www.gotopuertorico.com)
**Welcome to Puerto Rico** (http://welcome.topuertorico.org)

## LANGUAGE

Both English and Spanish are official languages in Puerto Rico, although Spanish is far more widely spoken. You'll get by OK in the major urban centers with English alone, though a smattering of Spanish will always win kudos from the locals. If you're venturing to the island's more remote corners, take a Spanish phrasebook.

## MAPS

Rand McNally publishes fold-out maps of San Juan/Puerto Rico that include a detailed overview of the metro area. This map is widely available from most bookstores and drugstores in San Juan for about US$5. The Puerto Rican Tourist Company gives out excellent free maps of the island (with San Juan on the reverse).

## MEDICAL SERVICES

For emergencies in Puerto Rico, call ☎ 911. Excellent medical facilities are available on the island. A number of hospitals offer emergency rooms.

Pharmacies in Puerto Rico are known as *farmacias*, and they are generally well stocked with medications up to North American standards.

## MONEY

Puerto Rico uses US currency. ATMs are called ATHs in Puerto Rico (for *a todos horas* – at all hours) and are common in most shopping areas and even in many small-town banks.

## POST

You'll find a **US post office** ( ☎ 800-275-8777; www.usps.gov) in almost every Puerto Rican town, providing familiar postal services such as parcel shipping and international express mail.

## TELEPHONE

The Puerto Rican area code is ☎ 787. To call from North America, dial ☎ 1-787 + the seven-digit local number. From elsewhere, dial your country's international access code followed by ☎ 787 + the local number. To call within Puerto Rico, just dial the local number. We have included only the local number for Puerto Rico listings in this chapter.

## TOURIST INFORMATION

The **Puerto Rico Tourism Company** (PRTC; www .gotopuertorico.com) is the commonwealth's official tourist bureau and maintains offices in San Juan (p329), Ponce (p348) and Vieques (p344).

## TRAVELERS WITH DISABILITIES

Puerto Rico is surprisingly compliant with the *American Disabilities Act*. Most modern hotels have at least one room set up for special needs clients. All the ferries to Culebra and Vieques are wheelchair-accessible and

Playa Luquillo has a wheelchair-accessible stretch of sand.

## VISAS

US residents don't need visas to enter Puerto Rico; however, if they are planning to work or study they should check on the latest regulations with their embassy. Canadians don't need visas for stays of up to 180 days, as long as they aren't working or studying during that period. Citizens of most European countries, Australia and New Zealand can waive visas through the Visa Waiver program. All non-US and Canadian travelers planning to stay for longer than 90 days need a visa: contact the closest US embassy and be prepared to pay US$100.

## WOMEN TRAVELERS

Puerto Rican women crisscross the island all the time by themselves, so you won't be the only solo woman on the ferry or public bus. But as a foreigner, you will attract a bit more attention. If you don't want the company, most men will respect a firm but polite 'no thank you.'

# TRANSPORTATION

## GETTING THERE & AWAY
### Entering Puerto Rico

US nationals need proof of citizenship (such as a driver's licence with photo ID) to enter Puerto Rico, but should be aware that if they're traveling to another country in the Caribbean (other than the US Virgin Islands, which, like Puerto Rico, is a US territory), they must have a valid passport in order to re-enter the US. Visitors from other countries must have a valid passport to enter Puerto Rico.

### Air

**Aeropuerto Internacional de Luis Muñoz Marín** (SJU; ☎ 749-5050; www.lmm.150m.com) – commonly shortened to LMM – in San Juan is a major Caribbean hub. Chances are that you will be arriving and departing from the airport in San Juan, but Aguadilla's **Aeropuerto Rafael Hernández** (BQN; ☎ 891-2286), at the former Base Ramey on the island's northwest tip, has some scheduled international flights. Ponce and Mayagüez each has a small air-

**EMERGENCY NUMBERS**

■ **Ambulance** ☎ 911

■ **Fire** ☎ 911

■ **Police** ☎ 911

port for domestic flights. San Juan's original airport at Isla Grande, on the Bahía de San Juan in the Miramar district, services private aircraft and the bulk of the commuter flights to the Puerto Rican islands of Culebra and Vieques.

The following airlines fly to/from Puerto Rico:

**Air St Thomas** ( ☎ 800-522-3084; www.airstthomas.com) British Virgin Islands, US Virgin Islands

**Air Sunshine** ( ☎ 888-879-8900; www.airsunshine.com) St Croix, St Thomas, Tortola, Virgin Gorda

**American Airlines** ( ☎ 800-433-7300; www.aa.com) Chicago, Dallas, Miami, New York

**American Eagle** ( ☎ 800-433-7300; www.aa.com) Chicago, Dallas

**Cape Air** ( ☎ 800-352-0714; www.flycapeair.com) St Croix, St Thomas, Tortola

**Continental Airlines** ( ☎ 800-525-0280; www.continental.com) Houston, New York

**COPA** ( ☎ 722-6969; www.copaair.com) Guayaquil

**Delta** ( ☎ 800-221-1212; www.delta.com) Atlanta, New York

**LIAT** ( ☎ 800-468-0482; www.liatairline.com) Antigua, Barbados, St Lucia, Trinidad

**Seaborne Airlines** ( ☎ 888-359-8687; www.seaborneairlines.com) St Croix, St Thomas

**United Airlines** ( ☎ 800-538-2929; www.united.com) Chicago

**Vieques Air Link** ( ☎ 888-901-9247; www.vieques-island.com/val) St Croix, St Thomas

## Sea
### CRUISE SHIP

San Juan is the second-largest port for cruise ships in the western hemisphere (after Miami). More than 24 vessels call San Juan their home port or departure port and every year new cruise ships either originate sailings from San Juan or make San Juan a port of call. The ships dock at the piers along Calle La Marina, which are just a short walk from the cobblestone streets of Old San Juan.

### FERRY

**Transportation Services Virgin Islands** ( ☎ 340-776-6282) run an irregular ferry between Puerto Rico and the US Virgin Islands leaving Fajardo twice a month.

**Ferries Del Caribe** ( ☎ 787-832-4800; www.ferriesdelcaribe.com) runs the massive M/S *Caribbean Express* between Mayagüez in Puerto Rico and Santo Domingo in the Dominican Republic. The trip takes 12 hours and one way tickets start at US$115.

## GETTING AROUND
### Air

In an island the size of Yellowstone National Park, getting around by airplane is pretty superfluous (and not particularly environmentally friendly). The bulk of Puerto Rico's domestic air traffic links San Juan to the offshore islands of Culebra and Vieques. Fares to Vieques are one way/round-trip US$45/90; fares to Culebra are about US$50/90.

**Air Flamenco** ( ☎ 724-6464; www.airflamenco.net) Flies from San Juan to Culebra and Vieques.

**Isla Nena Air Service** ( ☎ 742-0972; www.islanena.8m.com) Flies from San Juan and Fajardo to Culebra and Vieques.

**Vieques Air Link** ( ☎ San Juan-Vieques 888-901-9247, San Juan-Culebra 722-3736; www.viequesisland.com/val) Flies from San Juan to Culebra and Vieques.

### Boat

The **Puerto Rican Port Authority Office** ( ☎ 800-981-2005, 863-0705) handles the solid and safe ferry service from Fajardo to Vieques and Culebra. Reservations are required to take a car on a transport ferry (a bit of a hassle). Passenger ferries run three to four times daily. A round-trip is US$4.50. Schedules:

**Fajardo-Culebra Passenger Ferry** ( ☒ 9:30am & 3pm Mon-Fri, 9am, 2:30pm & 6:30pm Sat & Sun) Schedule varies on holidays.

**Fajardo-Culebra Cargo Ferry** ( ☒ 3:30am, 4pm & 6pm Mon-Fri, also 10am Wed & Fri)

**Fajardo-Vieques Passenger Ferry** ( ☒ 9:30am, 1pm & 4:30pm Mon-Fri, 9am, 3pm & 6pm Sat & Sun & holidays)

**Fajardo-Vieques Cargo Ferry** ( ☒ 4am & 1:30pm & 6pm Mon-Fri)

### Car

Car rental costs about US$45 to US$65 per day, depending on availability. Several good highways now link San Juan to just about every other major point with a drive of less than two hours. Scooters are available for rent on Culebra and Vieques (about US$40 per day) – they are not safe to ride on any major roads.

**PUERTO RICO**

If you rent a car, take all the insurance options unless you already have good coverage on your credit card. Be aware that if you rent a car and then take it on the ferry to Vieques or Culebra (not an easy feat to get a reservation, by the way) the rental agency will not cover any damage. In fact, they will tell you it's against their policy to take the cars to the islands. Nobody will stop you if you take the chance, but if you have an accident, no tow truck's coming to get you. You'll be liable for the whole auto.

### DRIVING LICENSE

A valid driver's license issued from your country of residence is all that's needed to rent a car.

### FUEL & SPARE PARTS

Garages and gas stations are few and far between in Puerto Rico. It's a good idea to carry extra fuel in the trunk if you are doing heavy driving. Be aware that gas is sold in liters on the island.

### ROAD RULES

Basically, there are none. Watch your back, don't tailgate and ignore the general craziness of local drivers. Drive on the right-hand side of the road. On major highways, using a turn signal to indicate a lane change seems to amuse drivers – if you give them advance warning of where you're going, it just makes it easier for them to cut you off.

## Público

*Públicos* – large vans that pick up and drop off passengers with great frequency and little haste – run between a few of the major cities, but it's a very slow (although cheap) way to travel. You'd better have a lot of time if you choose this method of transportation.

# US Virgin Islands

You can almost hear the three main islands squabbling at the family dinner table:

'I can't believe you sold out to the cruise ships,' St John says to St Thomas.

'Of course I did. But I did what I had to so my inhabitants would be prosperous. You can't feed an island on hippie idealism and ecotents,' St Thomas retorts.

'Pipe down,' says St Croix, covering its ears.

'What do you care? Tourism isn't your main source of income,' the other two shoot back.

So it goes in the US Virgin Islands' household, where St Thomas, St John and St Croix were all raised by Uncle Sam, but each grew up to have a very different personality.

St John is the greenest island, literally and figuratively. It cloaks two-thirds of its area in parkland and sublime beaches, ripe for hiking and snorkeling. It also leads the way in environmental preservation, with limited development and several low-impact tent-resorts for lodging. Dizzying cruise-ship traffic and big resorts nibbling its edges make St Thomas the most commercialized island. St Croix is the odd island out, located far from its siblings and offering a mix of rainforest, sugar plantations, old forts and great scuba diving. Its economy is *not* based on tourism, which makes it feel even more off-the-beaten path.

While the islands are American territories (and a favorite of American tourists since they don't require a passport), West Indian culture remains their strongest influence. Calypso and reggae rhythms swirl through the air, and curried meats, callaloo soup and mango-sweetened microbrews fill the tables.

## FAST FACTS

- **Area** 136 sq miles
- **Capital** Charlotte Amalie, St Thomas
- **Country code** ☎ 340
- **Departure tax** None
- **Famous for** Duty-free shopping, Virgin Islands National Park, Cruzan rum
- **Language** English
- **Money** US dollar (US$); US$1 = €0.65 = UK£0.51
- **Official name** US Virgin Islands
- **People** US Virgin Islanders
- **Phrase** Wind at your back, mon (a parting comment that means 'I hope you have an easy day'); limin' (pronounced '*lime*-in'; means 'relaxing').
- **Population** 108,448
- **Visa** Unnecessary for most countries; see p386

## HIGHLIGHTS

- **Virgin Islands National Park** (p372) Trek to petroglyphs, sugar mill ruins, and isolated beaches rich with marine life.
- **Christiansted** (p378) Sip microbrews, explore a Danish fort and dive 'the wall' at nearby Cane Bay
- **Leinster Bay and Waterlemon Cay** (p376) Snorkel with barracudas, turtles, spotted eagle rays and nurse sharks
- **Cruzan Rum Distillery** (p383) Drink the islands' favorite attitude adjuster at its fragrant source
- **Virgin Islands Ecotours** (p369) Kayak through a twisted mangrove lagoon

## ITINERARIES

- **One Day** What? Only 24 hours in the USVIs? Make it Cruz Bay, St John, where hiking trails with wild donkeys and beachside mojito bars are steps from the ferry arrival dock.
- **One Week** Spend a couple of days eating and beaching around Charlotte Amalie, then ferry over to St John to hike, snorkel and kayak.
- **Two Weeks** Island hop: spend a few days in Charlotte Amalie, then seaplane to St Croix to dive and hang out for four days. Hike and snorkel through St John's natural bounty for five days, then sail onward to the nearby British Virgin Islands. It's an easy return from there to Charlotte Amalie.
- **Go Green** For those watching their eco-footprint, you can rest easy at the VI Campground near St Thomas; at Maho Bay, Cinnamon Bay and Concordia tent-resorts on St John; and at Mt Victory Campground and Northside Valley on St Croix. To learn more about the islands' rich ecosystems, take a tour with Friends of the VI National Park and or an eco-hike on St Croix.

## CLIMATE & WHEN TO GO

The balmy temperature averages 78°F (25°C) in winter (December through March) and 83°F (28°C) in summer (June through August). Easterly trade winds keep the humidity lower than on most other Caribbean islands. The wettest months are August through November; rain usually comes in brief tropical showers. Hurricane season peaks in August and September. High season is December 15 to April 30; those willing to risk a little rain will find much better hotel deals outside this period. November, early December and May are particularly good times to visit.

## HISTORY

### Pirates, Sugar and Powerbrokering

Folks have been living on the islands from as early as 2000 BC. The Taínos ruled the roost for a while, but the ruthless, seafaring Caribs eventually wiped them out.

Around this time Christopher Columbus sailed up to Salt River Bay (p381) during his second trip to the Caribbean. It was 1493, and he gave the islands their enduring name: Santa Ursula y Las Once Mil Vírgenes, in honor of a 4th-century princess and her 11,000 maidens. Mapmakers soon shortened the mouthful to 'The Virgins.'

The islands remained under Spanish control until the English defeated the Spanish Armada in 1588. England, France and Holland were quick to issue 'letters of marque,' which allowed 'privateers' the rights to claim territory and protect those claims.

One king's privateer became every other king's pirate. Blackbeard (Edward Teach) operated in the Virgin Islands before 1720, with a collection of other rascals such as 'Calico' Jack Rackham, lover of colorful clothes and female pirate partners (see p361).

The Danes and English bickered over the islands, while each built vast sugar and tobacco plantations. The English held colonies on islands east of St John, while the Danes held St Thomas to the west. St John remained disputed territory. Finally, in 1717 the Danes sent a small but determined band of soldiers to St John and drove the British out. The Narrows, between St John and Tortola in the British Virgin Islands, became the border that has divided the eastern (first Danish, now US) Virgins from the British Virgins for more than 250 years.

### Slavery & Liberation

The West Indies grew rich producing sugar and cotton for Europe. In pursuit of profits, the Danish West India and Guinea Company declared St Thomas a free port in 1724, and purchased St Croix from the French in 1733. By the end of the century, the number of African slaves on the islands exceeded 40,000.

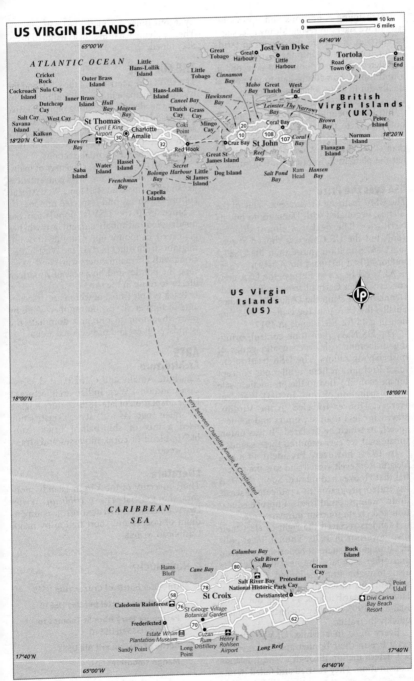

# US VIRGIN ISLANDS

0 ————— 10 km
0 ————— 6 miles

*ATLANTIC OCEAN*

65°00'W

Cricket Rock

Cockroach Island
Sula Cay

Dutchcap Cay

Salt Cay
Savana Island
West Cay

Kalkun Cay

Outer Brass Island

Inner Brass Island

Little Hans-Lollik Island

Hans-Lollik Island

*Hull Bay*
*Magens Bay*

**St Thomas**
Cyril E King Airport
**30**
**Charlotte Amalie**

*Brewers Bay*

Saba Island

Water Island
*Hassel Island*

*Frenchman Bay*

**32**

Red Hook

*Secret Harbour*
*Bolongo Bay*
Little St James Island

*Capella Islands*

Dog Island

Coki Point

Mingo Cay

*Caneel Bay*
Thatch Cay
Grass Cay
*Hawksnest Bay*

Great Tobago

Little Tobago

*Cinnamon Bay*
*Maho Bay*

Great Thatch

Great Harbour

Little Harbour

**Jost Van Dyke**

West End

*Leinster Bay*
*The Narrows*

**10**

**Cruz Bay** **St John**
**108**
**107**

Coral Bay

*Coral Bay*

*Reef Bay*

*Salt Pond Bay*

Ram Head

*Hansen Bay*

Great St James Island

**Tortola**
Road Town

East End

**British Virgin Islands (UK)**

*Brown Bay*

Flanagan Island

Norman Island

Peter Island

64°40'W

18°20'N                                                                                   18°20'N

**US Virgin Islands (US)**

18°00'N                                                                                   18°00'N

*Ferry between Charlotte Amalie & Christiansted*

*CARIBBEAN SEA*

Hams Bluff

*Cane Bay*

**80**

*Columbus Bay*

Salt River Bay

Salt River Bay National Historic Park

**St Croix**

**58**

**78**

**Caledonia Rainforest**

**76**

St George Village Botanical Garden

**Frederiksted**

**70**

Estate Whim Plantation Museum

Sandy Point

Long Point

Cruzan Rum Distillery

Henry E Rohlsen Airport

Protestant Cay

**Christiansted**

Green Cay

Buck Island

**62**

*Long Reef*

Point Udall

Divi Carina Bay Beach Resort

65°00'W

17°40'N                                                                                   17°40'N

64°40'W

**US VIRGIN ISLANDS**

Harsh living conditions and oppressive laws drove slaves to revolt. Meanwhile, sugar production in Europe and American tariffs on foreign sugar cut into the islands' profits. The deteriorating economy put everyone in a foul mood. Something had to give and it finally did in 1848, when black people on St Croix forced the legal end to slavery.

But black people remained in economic bondage. Life in the islands was dismal. Average wages for field workers were less than US$0.15 a day. A series of labor revolts left the plantation infrastructure in ruins.

### USA Eyes the Prize

The USA, realizing the strategic value of the islands, negotiated with Denmark to buy its territories. The deal was almost done in 1867, but the US Congress choked at paying US$7.5 million (more than the US$7.2 million it had just paid for Alaska).

As WWI began in Europe, the USA grew concerned that German armies might invade Denmark and claim the Danish West Indies. Finally, the USA paid the Danes US$25 million in gold for the islands in 1917.

The US Navy then took control, bringing draconian rule, racism and gangs of misbehaving sailors. The USA tried to enforce Prohibition here, a hilarious concept for an economy tied to the production, sale and distribution of rum. In 1931 President Herbert Hoover traveled to the Virgins, stayed for less than six hours and made a speech in which he declared, 'It was unfortunate that we ever acquired these islands.'

In 1934, however, President Franklin Delano Roosevelt visited and saw the potential that Hoover had missed. Soon, the USA instituted programs to eradicate disease, drain swamps, build roads, improve education and create tourism infrastructure.

Islanders received the right to elect their own governor in 1970. Though local politics brought its share of nepotism, cronyism and other scandals, the next four decades also brought unprecedented growth in tourism and raised the standard of living. Hurricane Marilyn took a chunk out of the islands in 1995, but they got back to business quickly thereafter.

Every once in a while, USVIs citizens get a bee in their bonnet and seek greater self-determination through a Virgin Islands Constitution. They've tried and failed to rat-ify it four times during the last half century. They're giving it a fifth shot as we go to press. Stay tuned.

## THE CULTURE

The USVIs are a territory of the USA, and the islands participate in the political process by sending an elected, nonvoting representative to the US House of Representatives. All citizens of the USVIs are US citizens (and have been since 1927) with one exception: they cannot vote in presidential elections.

Though the USVIs wear a veneer of mainstream American culture, with conveniences like shopping malls and fast food, West African culture is a strong and respected presence.

Since 1970 the USVIs' population has quadrupled, although current growth has plateaued. Economic opportunities draw immigrants from other parts of the West Indies, along with US mainlanders who come to escape the politics and busyness of American life, or to retire in the sun.

Black people (most of whom are descendants of former slaves) outnumber white by more than four to one and dominate the islands' political and professional arenas.

## ARTS
### Architecture

Charlotte Amalie and Christiansted showcase traditional West Indian architecture, a loose adaptation of late-18th-century English Georgian (neoclassical) style. Construction used a mix of ship-ballast brick, 'rubble' (a blend of coral, molasses and straw) and wood.

### Literature

The University of the Virgin Islands sponsors the journal *The Caribbean Writer* (www.thecaribbeanwriter.org), a compendium of poems and short fiction by major Caribbean writers.

---

**HOW MUCH?**

- **One-liter bottle of Cruzan rum** US$9
- **Snorkel gear rental per day** US$10
- **Passenger ferry from St Thomas to St John** US$5 to US$10
- **Bottle of Blackbeard Ale** US$3
- **Mango smoothie** US$6

## AVAST! LADIES OF PLUNDER

Boatloads of pirates sailed through the Virgin Islands in the early 1700s. Most were indistinguishable in their eye patches and wooden legs, except for two buccaneers: Anne Bonny and Mary Read.

Anne was the daughter of a respectable Charleston, South Carolina family, who showed her wild ways early by marrying James Bonny against her father's wishes. Bonny was a small-time pirate working out of Nassau and, while he was out cavorting, he wanted Anne to stay home and cook for him. Instead, she began a series of affairs.

'Calico' Jack Rackham ultimately won her heart. 'Come sail away with me,' the sharp-dressed scalawag presumably said.

Anne disguised herself in men's clothing (women on ships were considered bad luck), and wielded her pistol and cutlass so fiercely no one questioned her gender. Well, one pirate did, and she stabbed him through the heart.

The thing that finally gave her away was pregnancy. Jack dropped her off in Cuba to have the baby, which died shortly after birth.

After Anne returned she discovered another woman on board. Mary Read also donned men's garb as a disguise. Anne walked in on her getting dressed and found out the truth. The two became pals.

The good times ended in 1720. The governor of Jamaica sent his troops to capture Jack's gang. They waited until the pirates were drunk and celebrating a recent ship-taking. The only crew left sober to defend the ship? Anne and Mary. They tried their best, but were outgunned.

The crew was condemned to hang, except for Anne and Mary, who were both pregnant. Mary died in jail. Anne was ransomed by her rich father and returned to Charleston. Some stories say she became a respectable society lady and lived to age 84. Others say she went back to life on the high seas.

## Music

Reggae and calypso tunes blast from vehicles and emanate from shops, restaurants and beach bars. *Quelbe* and fungi (*foon*-ghee, also an island food made of cornmeal and fish) are two types of folk music. *Quelbe* blends jigs, quadrilles, military fife and African drum music, with *cariso* lyrics (often biting satire) from slave field songs. Fungi uses homemade percussion like washboards, ribbed gourds and conch shells to accompany a singer. The best time to experience island music is during the 'jump up' parades and competitions associated with major festivals like Carnival on St Thomas and St John, or at St Croix's Cruzan Christmas Fiesta; see p385 for festival info.

## Painting

The most celebrated painter to come from the USVIs is Camille Pissarro. Born in St Thomas in 1830 as Jacob Pizarro, the son of Spanish Jews, young Jacob grew up on Main St in Charlotte Amalie. He eventually moved to Paris, changed his name and became known as the 'Father of Impressionism.' His original home is now a gallery (p368) that includes historical information about the family.

## ENVIRONMENT
### The Land

The USVIs consist of about 50 islands, 40 miles east of Puerto Rico. They are the northernmost islands in the Lesser Antilles chain and, along with the British Virgin Islands, form an irregular string of islands stretching west to east. The one exception to this string is the USVIs' largest island, St Croix, which lies 40 miles south.

St Thomas is the second-largest island. St John is east of St Thomas, the last of the USVIs.

As with almost all of the islands ringing the Caribbean Basin, the USVIs owe their existence to a series of volcanic events that built up layers of lava and igneous rock, creating islands with three geographical zones: a coastal plain, coastal dry forests and a high ridge of central mountains.

The mountain slopes are dense subtropical forests. All of the timber is second or third growth; the islands were stripped for sugar, cotton and tobacco plantations in the colonial era. There are no rivers and very few freshwater streams. Coral reefs of all varieties grow in the shallow waters near the seashores.

## Wildlife

Very few of the land mammals that make their home in the Virgin Islands are natives; most mammal species have been accidentally or intentionally introduced to the island over the centuries. Virtually every island has a feral population of goats and burros, and some islands have wild pigs, white-tailed deer, cattle, horses, cats and dogs. Other prevalent land mammals include mongooses and bats.

The islands are home to a few species of snake (none of which are poisonous), including the Virgin Island tree boa.

More than 200 bird species – including the official bird, the banana quit – inhabit the islands.

## Environmental Issues

The USVIs have long suffered from environmental problems, including deforestation, soil erosion, mangrove destruction and a lack of fresh water. During the 18th century logging operations denuded many of the islands to make room for plantations. The demise of the agricultural economy in the late 19th century allowed the islands to reforest, and in recent years locals (especially on St John) have begun several forest conservation projects.

But population growth and rapid urbanization continue to pose grave threats. If not for the desalination plants (which make fresh water out of sea water) the islands couldn't support even a quarter of their population, let alone visitors. When a hurricane strikes, power and diesel facilities shut down. Islanders with enough foresight and money keep rainwater cisterns for such emergencies, but folks without suffer.

Rising sea temperatures from global warming are another topic of concern, as they impact local reefs and cause coral bleaching (see p48). In 2005 a particularly 'hot' period killed about half of the USVIs' coral.

Prior years of overfishing have put conch (a local shellfish) in a precarious situation. Currently, conch fishing is not allowed from July through September so stocks can replenish.

The past decade has seen an increase in the level of awareness, resources and action dedicated to conservation efforts. The following groups are working toward environmental preservation:

**Friends of the Virgin Islands National Park**
( ☎ 779-4940; www.friendsvinp.org)

**National Marine Fisheries Law Enforcement Division** ( ☎ 774-5226; www.nmfs.noaa.gov/ole/se_south east.html)
**University of the Virgin Islands Conservation Data Center** ( ☎ 693-1020; http://cdc.uvi.edu)
**USVI Department of Planning & Natural Resources** ( ☎ 774-3320; www.vifishandwildlife.com)

## FOOD & DRINK

Soups and stews are staples in West Indian cooking. Many use root vegetables and fruits to add texture, taste and vitamins. *Dasheen* (taro root) tastes like potato. Its green leaves are a primary ingredient in the islands' famous callaloo soup, which also mixes in one or more types of meat, okra, spices and hot peppers.

*Pate* (*paw*-tay) is the islands' most popular finger food. It's a fried pastry of cassava (yucca) or plantain dough stuffed with spiced goat, pork, chicken, conch, lobster or fish. Plain, unfilled fried dough is called a johnnycake, often served as a side dish. Another popular food is roti, flatbread envelopes stuffed with curried meat, fish or poultry. Island cooks often serve fungi (*foon*-ghee), which is made from cornmeal, with fish and gravy.

Meat dishes are primarily curried or barbecued with tangy spices. *Daube* meat is pot roast spiced with vinegar and native seasonings. Fish and shellfish are common, and cooks will bake, grill, stew or boil whatever is the daily catch. Conch (pronounced 'conk') is often fried into crispy fritters. Be aware that commercial fishing of conch is halted from July through September (see left) so you're less likely to find it on menus then.

While tap water is usually safe, visitors with a sensitive stomach might want to stick to bottled water. 'Bush tea' is made from the aromatic leaves of indigenous plants.

Blackbeard Ale and mango-tinged VI Pale Ale are the slurpable local microbrews. Cruzan rum is served everywhere and is, literally, cheaper than the juice with which to mix it. You have to be 18 or over to legally consume booze. Open-container laws do not exist in the USVIs, so you can drink on the streets.

# ST THOMAS

**pop 51,000**

Most visitors arrive to the USVIs via St Thomas, and the place knows how to strike a first impression. Jungly cliffs poke high in the sky, red-hipped roofs blossom over the hills, and all around the turquoise, yacht-dotted sea laps. Unfortunately, once you disembark from your plane or boat, you'll find you're sharing this scene with 20,000 tourists who've just piled off the seven cruise ships docked in the harbor.

Years ago, St Thomas made a bargain with the devil: provide us with a good and steady source of income and we'll give you your innocence and our environment. And so it became the darling of the cruise-ship industry and its two million passengers. In 2007 St Thomas ranked last in the 'world's most beautiful islands' survey by National Geographic, which called it 'totally spoiled' and 'one big ugly jewelry store.'

That's true…to an extent. Most of the mob-fest happens in Charlotte Amalie. Visitors who make the effort to move deeper into the 30-sq-mile island will find opportunities for surfing, kayaking through mangrove swamps and getting face-to-face with sea turtles.

## Orientation

Charlotte Amalie, St Thomas' main town and the USVIs capital, lies on the island's south shore, 2.5 miles east of the airport. The bulk of St Thomas' resorts and attractions lie along the island's East End, where Red Hook anchors the main business district and hosts the busy St John ferry terminal. The northwest coast has a string of spectacular bays, including world-renowned Magens Bay.

## Getting There & Away

See the p387 for details on airline, seaplane and ferry travel to and from St Thomas.

## Getting Around
### TO/FROM THE AIRPORT

Taxis (ie multipassenger vans) are readily available. The fare for one passenger going between the airport and Charlotte Amalie is US$7; it's US$15 to/from Red Hook. Per-person fares come down a bit if two or more passengers share the taxi. Luggage costs US$2 extra per piece.

### BUS

**Vitran** ( ☎ 774-5678; fare US$1) operates buses over the length of the island. Look for the bus stop signs on Rtes 30 and 38. 'Dollar' buses (aka 'safaris') also stop along the routes. These vehicles are open-air vans that hold 20 people. They look like taxis, except they're filled with locals instead of sunburned tourists. Flag them down by flapping your hand, and press the buzzer to stop them when you reach your destination. The fare is US$2.

### CAR

Most of St Thomas' rental agencies have outlets at the airport and resort hotels. Prices start around US$60 per day.

**Avis** ( ☎ 800-331-1084; www.avis.com)

**Budget** ( ☎ 776-5774, 800-626-4516; www.budgetstt.com)

**Dependable Car Rentals** ( ☎ 800-522-3076; www.dependablecar.com)

**Discount Car Rentals** ( ☎ 776-4858, 877-478-2833; www.discountcar.vi)

**Hertz** ( ☎ 800-654-3131; www.hertz.com)

### TAXI

Territorial law requires taxi drivers to carry a government-set rate sheet, and prices are listed in the readily available free tourist guide *St Thomas/St John This Week*.

Many taxis are vans that carry up to 12 passengers. These service multiple destinations and may stop to pick up passengers along the way, so their rates are usually charged on a per-person basis. The following table shows current per-person rates for popular destinations from Charlotte Amalie. Note the price drops a few dollars when more than one passenger goes to the destination.

| Destination | Cost |
| --- | --- |
| Frenchtown | US$4 |
| Havensight | US$6 |
| Magens Bay | US$10 |
| Red Hook | US$13 |

## CHARLOTTE AMALIE

Brace yourself: every morning thousands of cruise-ship passengers arrive and flood the streets of Charlotte Amalie (a-*mall*-ya). Sure, you can let the scene overwhelm you, but why not take a deep breath and focus on the town's lip-licking West Indian cuisine, Frenchtown wine bars and proximity to white-sand beaches?

## Orientation

Charlotte Amalie stretches about 1.5 miles around St Thomas Harbor from Havensight on the east side (where cruise ships dock) to

US VIRGIN ISLANDS

Frenchtown on the west side. Around the peninsula from Frenchtown lies Crown Bay, another cruise-ship-filled marina.

Upscale shops line the alleys between Waterfront Hwy (aka Veterans Dr) and Dronningens Gade (Main St). Street signs are labeled with original Danish names. North St, for example, is Norre Gade (*gaa*-da, which is 'street' in Danish).

## Information

There is no official tourist office in town, but the free *St Thomas/St John This Week* magazine has maps and everything else you'll need; it's available at most businesses. FirstBank, Scotiabank, Banco Popular and other banks are on Waterfront Hwy.

**Beans, Bytes & Websites** (☎ 776-7265; 5600 Royal Dane Mall; per half hr US$3; ⊙ 7am-6pm Mon-Sat, to 1pm Sun) Connect with your electronic mailbox at the 12 or so terminals, plus wi-fi and data ports for laptops.

**Dockside Bookshop** (☎ 774-4937; Havensight Mall; ⊙ 9am-5pm Mon-Sat, 11am-3pm Sun) Excellent bookstore in Havensight, with plenty of regional titles.

**Main post office** (☎ 774-3750) On the west side of Emancipation Garden. There are several satellite post offices, including one west of the Marine Terminal (at Frenchtown's entrance), and one in the Havensight Mall. Most are open 7:30am to 4:30pm Monday to Friday and 8:30am to noon Saturday.

**ParadiseGate** (☎ 714-1400; ⊙ 9am-7pm) In Havensight at the south end of the cruise ship dock, this multiuse facility has a 30 internet terminals (US$2 per 15 minutes), free wi-fi, a gym (day pass US$10), bar, restaurant and Western Union office. You also can burn digital photos onto a CD (US$3).

**Roy Schneider Community Hospital** (☎ 776-8311; 48 Sugar Estate Rd at Rte 313; ⊙ 24hr) On the east side of Charlotte Amalie, this full-service hospital has an emergency room, recompression chamber and doctors in all major disciplines.

## Dangers & Annoyances

Charlotte Amalie has some big-city issues including drugs, poverty, prostitution and street crime. Waterfront Hwy and Main St in the town center are fine at night, but move a few blocks away and the streets get deserted quickly. Avoid the Savan area, a red-light district that surrounds Main St west of Market Sq and north of the Holiday Inn Windward Passage hotel; this is where the island's underworld takes root. In general, savvy travelers who take reasonable precautions should have no problems.

## Sights
### EMANCIPATION GARDEN & AROUND

Emancipation Garden is where town officials read the emancipation proclamation after slaves were freed on St Croix in 1848. Carnival celebrations and concerts take place here, but mostly folks kick back under shade trees with a cold fruit smoothie from the **Vendors' Plaza**, where sellers also hawk batik dresses, souvenir T-shirts and Prada knock-offs under blue-canopied stalls.

Red-brick **Fort Christian** (☎ 776-4566; donation US$1; ⊙ 8:30am-4:30pm) is the oldest colonial building in the USVIs, dating back to 1666. Over the years, the fort has functioned as a jail, governor's residence and Lutheran church; currently it serves as a local history museum. At press time, the fort was closed and undergoing renovations. Its reopening date had not been determined.

Nearby, the **Frederik Lutheran Church** (Norre Garde; admission free) is one of Charlotte Amalie's architectural gems. During the 19th century the church had segregated congregations – one West Indian, the other Danish. The church is open on Saturday and you can attend services on Sunday.

### GOVERNMENT HILL

**Blackbeard's Castle** (☎ 776-1234; admission US$12; ⊙ 9am-3pm) watches over town from atop Government Hill. In the 18th century this five-story masonry watchtower was said to be the lookout post of pirate Edward Teach, alias Blackbeard. Actually, historians don't lend much credence to the tale. What's known for certain is that the tower was built by colonial Danes as a military installation in 1678.

The admission fee includes use of the three pools on the grounds, photos with the myriad pirate statues that dot the property, and entrance to Villa Notman, Britannia House and Haagensen House – three colonial homes furnished with West Indian antiques. But unless you're a real history buff, it's kind of a hefty price without much payoff.

A better idea is to attack Government Hill from below and ascend the steep set of stairs – the so-called **99 Steps** – that lead from the commercial district near Kongens Gate up into a canopy of trees. These steps, of which there are actually 103 (though you'll be too out of breath to count), were constructed using ship-ballast brick in the mid-18th cen-

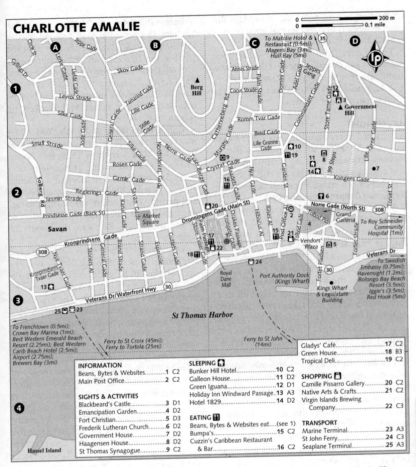

## CHARLOTTE AMALIE

| INFORMATION | |
|---|---|
| Beans, Bytes & Websites | 1 C2 |
| Main Post Office | 2 C2 |

| SIGHTS & ACTIVITIES | |
|---|---|
| Blackbeard's Castle | 3 D1 |
| Emancipation Garden | 4 D2 |
| Fort Christian | 5 D3 |
| Frederik Lutheran Church | 6 D2 |
| Government House | 7 D2 |
| Haagensen House | 8 D2 |
| St Thomas Synagogue | 9 C2 |

| SLEEPING | |
|---|---|
| Bunker Hill Hotel | 10 C2 |
| Galleon House | 11 D2 |
| Green Iguana | 12 D1 |
| Holiday Inn Windward Passage | 13 A3 |
| Hotel 1829 | 14 D2 |

| EATING | |
|---|---|
| Beans, Bytes & Websites eat | (see 1) |
| Bumpa's | 15 C2 |
| Cuzzin's Caribbean Restaurant & Bar | 16 C2 |
| Gladys' Café | 17 C2 |
| Green House | 18 B3 |
| Tropical Deli | 19 C2 |

| SHOPPING | |
|---|---|
| Camille Pissarro Gallery | 20 C2 |
| Native Arts & Crafts | 21 C2 |
| Virgin Islands Brewing Company | 22 C3 |

| TRANSPORT | |
|---|---|
| Marine Terminal | 23 A3 |
| St John Ferry | 24 C3 |
| Seaplane Terminal | 25 A3 |

tury. At the top of the 99 Steps, and about halfway up to the watchtower, you'll see **Haagensen House**, which you can sometimes peek in for free. Explore the area in the cool of the morning, before the cruise-ship crowds arrive.

Also on the hill is the grand white **Government House** ( ☎ 774-0001; 21-22 Kongens Gade; admission free; ⏰ 9am-noon & 1-5pm Mon-Fri), where the territorial governor has his offices. It was built between 1865 and 1867, and restored in 1994. You can walk around the first floor, though there's not much to see.

### ST THOMAS SYNAGOGUE
The second-oldest Hebrew temple in the western hemisphere (the oldest is on the island of Curaçao), peaceful **St Thomas Synagogue** ( ☎ 774-4312; http://onepaper.com/synagogue; 16A&B Crystal Gade; admission free; ⏰ 9:30am-4pm Mon-Fri) is a National Historic Landmark. The current building dates from 1833, but Jews have worshipped here since 1796, from Sephardic Jews from Denmark to today's 110-family Reform congregation. The temple floor is made of sand to symbolize the flight of the Israelites out of Egypt and across the desert. There's a tiny museum in the back room.

### FRENCHTOWN
The island's 'Frenchies,' aka Huguenots, who immigrated to St Thomas from St-Barthélemy during the mid-19th century, populated this community of brightly painted frame houses

US VIRGIN ISLANDS

on the harbor's western side. Nowadays the quiet neighborhood has several good restaurants that overlook the water.

To get here from town, take a taxi (per person US$4), or walk west past the Seaplane Terminal and turn left just past the post office. The 1.25-mile walk takes about 25 minutes from Emancipation Garden.

### HAVENSIGHT

A hundred years ago, the area on the east side of St Thomas Harbor (known today as Havensight) was a bustling steamship wharf and coaling station. Today it's still busy, but with behemoth cruise ships that tie up to the **West Indian Company Cruise Ship Dock**.

When passengers disembark, they find **Havensight Mall**, a compound with dozens of shops and restaurants. They also find the **Paradise Point Skyride** ( ☎ 774-9809; www.stthomas skyride.com; adult/child US$19/9.50; ☷ 9am-5pm Mon & Thu-Sun, to 7pm Tue, to 9pm Wed Nov-Apr). From a base station across the street from the mall, gondolas whisk visitors 700ft up Flag Hill to a scenic outlook; the ride takes seven minutes. At the top you'll find a restaurant, bar, gallery of shops, cheesy tropical bird show and a short nature trail. From May to October, the Skyride is open only when a cruise ship is in port.

The **Butterfly Farm** ( ☎ 715-3366; www.thebutter flyfarm.com; adult/child US$15/9; ☷ 8:30am-5pm) lies at the cruise-ship dock's far south end. Amid the garden full of fluttering beasties, you'll learn about metamorphosis during a 25-minute guided tour. Wear bright colors and perfume if you want the butterflies land on you.

Taxis travel to and from Havensight regularly (US$6 per person).

## Sleeping

The rates listed are for the high season and do not include 18% tax. Some places require a two- or three-night minimum stay in high season.

**Galleon House** ( ☎ 774-6972, 800-524-2052; www .galleonhouse.com; 31 Kongens Gade; r incl breakfast US$85-155; ☒ ☐ ☲ ) The 'harbor view' rooms are the winners at friendly Galleon House, with wood doors that open onto a balcony overlooking the waterfront. The 'shared bathroom' and 'interior private bathroom' rooms are confining and not recommended unless you're truly strapped for dough. The veranda and pool are good for hanging out and munching breakfast. Offers wi-fi access.

**Bunker Hill Hotel** ( ☎ 774-8056; www.bunkerhill hotel.com; 7A Commandant Gade; d/ste incl breakfast US$98/129; ☒ ☐ ☲ ) You're gonna get what you pay for: the 16 rooms are cheap, but they're also relatively dark, shabby and mosquitoey. Each unit does have a big bathroom; some have patios, and the sunny deck and cooked breakfast are nice touches. Still, Bunker Hill is basic to the bone.

**ourpick** **Hotel 1829** ( ☎ 776-1829, 800-524-2002; www.hotel1829.com; 30 Kongens Gade; r incl breakfast US$125-260; ☒ ☲ ) Built in 1829, this classy, 15-room inn blends the atmosphere of a Victorian gentlemen's club and a colonial villa. Exposed rubble walls, beamed ceilings and period West Indian furnishings characterize the rooms. The result is a romantic, Old World island vibe. Be aware the 'moderate' rooms are tiny.

**Green Iguana** ( ☎ 776-7654; www.thegreeniguana.com; 1002 Blackbeard's Hill; r US$135-165; ☒ ☐ ) Way the heck up the hill behind Blackbeard's Castle, this homey place is set in lush gardens and overlooks St Thomas Harbor. The nine rooms come in several configurations, but all have private bathrooms, wi-fi access, microwaves, refrigerators and bright, welcoming decor; some also have fully equipped kitchens. It's great value if you don't mind the steep walk.

**Inn at Villa Olga** ( ☎ 715-0900; www.villa-olga-inn .com; r US$150-175; ☒ ☐ ☲ ) Villa Olga offers 12 motel-like rooms off the beaten path in Frenchtown. While the rooms are a bit faded, they are spacious and scattered over pretty, palm-shaded grounds. The bonus here is free access to the beach and water-sports equipment at Bolongo Bay Beach Resort, Olga's sister property. Also offers wi-fi access.

**Mafolie Hotel** ( ☎ 774-2790, 800-225-7035; www .mafolie.com; 7091 Estate Mafolie; r incl breakfast US$150-200; ☒ ☲ ) On Mafolie Hill, 850ft above town, the eponymous hotel offers a dramatic vista, the feel of a Danish colonial villa and a popular alfresco restaurant. The good points: killer harbor views and relatively low prices for such views. The not-so-good points: Spartan rooms and a location far from town.

**Holiday Inn Windward Passage** ( ☎ 774-5200, 800-524-7389; www.holidayinn.st-thomas.com; Waterfront Hwy; r US$245-275; ☒ ☐ ☲ ) The four-story Holiday Inn is primarily a business hotel. It's useful for those seeking in-room wi-fi internet access, a fitness center, on-site eateries and quick taxi access. It's less beneficial to those seeking good value, since the peach-colored, cookie-

## TOP THREE OUTLYING BEACHES

To reach the sweetest stretches of sand, you'll need to motor beyond Charlotte Amalie.

### Magens Bay

The sugary mile that fringes heart-shaped Magens Bay, 3 miles north of Charlotte Amalie, makes almost every travel publication's list of beautiful beaches. The seas here are calm, the bay broad and surrounding green hills dramatic, and tourists mob the place to soak it all up. The **beach** (admission US$4; ⏲ 6am-6pm) has picnic tables, changing facilities, food vendors and water-sports operators renting kayaks and sailboats (US$20 to $35 per hour). Alas, it's the only beach on St Thomas to charge an admission fee. A taxi from Charlotte Amalie costs US$8 per person. On the road down, stop for a milkshake (alcohol-spiked if you want) at **Udder Delite Dairy Bar** ( ☎ 777-6050; ⏲ 1pm-6:30pm Mon, 10am-6:30pm Tue-Sat, 11:30am-6:30pm Sun), part of a working farm.

### Hull Bay

Also on the north coast and just west of Magens Bay, Hull Bay is the island's most popular surfing beach and usually a gem of solitude when Magens is overrun. The shady strand lies at the base of a steep valley and has a restaurant, bar and changing facilities. **Homer's** ( ☎ 774-7606, 866-719-1856; www.nightsnorkel.com; ⏲ 10am-5pm, closed Mon mid-Apr–mid-Dec) rents surfboards (US$50 per half-day) and kayaks (US$40 per half-day) and conducts raved-about night snorkel tours (US$38 per person). Taxis are scarce, so you'll need a car to get here.

### Brewers Bay

This beach, located behind the University of the Virgin Islands, is beloved by students, local families and shell collectors alike. There are no facilities other than snack vans serving *pates* and cold Heineken beers. It gets deserted fast come nighttime. Brewers is right by the airport and accessible by taxis and public buses.

cutter rooms are overpriced. However, when other hotels are booked, there's usually room at the Inn. It's at the edge of downtown near the Marine Terminal, away from the town's restaurant core.

**Bolongo Bay Beach Resort** ( ☎ 775-1800, 800-524-4746; www.bolongobay.com; 7150 Bolongo Bay; r US$300-330; ⧢ 🏊 ) Family-owned Bolongo is a fun, casual resort. Its public facilities are its strength: a beach with a full array of free water sports (kayaks, sailboats, snorkel gear etc), tennis courts, a pool and fitness center. All 75 rooms and 20 villas have ocean views and private patios. The interiors won't win any awards for size or decor, but who cares? You'll be outside enjoying fun in the sun. It's about 3.5 miles east of town.

Some recommended beachfront properties by the airport:

**Best Western Carib Beach Hotel** ( ☎ 774-2525, 800-792-2742; www.caribbeachresort.com; 70C Lindbergh Bay; r US$159-179; ⧢ 🏊 ) As close as you'll get to the airport, just 0.25 miles away. Rooms are fine but nothing special.

**Best Western Emerald Beach Resort** ( ☎ 340-777-8800; 800-233-4936; www.emeraldbeach.com; 8070 Lindbergh Bay; r US$279; ⧢ 🖥 🏊 ) A step up from

the Carib, this is a full-on resort. Rooms are snazzier, with private beachfront balconies.

For local villa and condo rentals try **Calypso Realty** ( ☎ 774-1620; www.calypsorealty.com) or **Paradise Properties** ( ☎ 779-1540, 800-524-2038; www.st-thomas.com/paradiseproperties).

## Eating & Drinking

### CHARLOTTE AMALIE

**Beans, Bytes & Websites** ( ☎ 777-7089; 5600 Royal Dane Mall; sandwiches US$4-6; ⏲ breakfast & lunch) This chic little cyber-bistro has yummy coffee, bagels and toasted sandwiches.

**Tropical Deli** ( ☎ 776-7777; Garden St; mains US$6-10; ⏲ breakfast & lunch) To eat Cuban pork sandwiches, oxtail stew or burgers and drink ginger beer or bush tea with locals, pull up a chair at one of the six bare-bone tables.

**Bumpa's** ( ☎ 776-5674; Waterfront Hwy; mains US$8-13; ⏲ breakfast & lunch) Climb the stairs to the second floor, order at the counter, then carry your hearty, homemade oatmeal pancakes, pumpkin muffin, veggie burger, chicken *pate* or grilled fish wrap to the small patio overlooking the street.

**Iggie's** ( ☎ 775-1800; Bolongo Bay Beach Club; mains US$8-14; ⏰ lunch & dinner) Beachside at Bolongo Bay, good-time Iggie's serves top-notch sandwiches, burgers and seafood mains, plus a kids' menu. Things kick up at night, when the place grooves to a festive bar atmosphere.

**ourpick** **Gladys' Café** ( ☎ 774-6604; Royal Dane Mall; mains US$9-17; ⏰ breakfast & lunch) With the stereo blaring beside her, Gladys belts out Tina Turner tunes while serving some of the best West Indian food around. There is no view here, but the bistro setting, art-covered walls and fun, breezy atmosphere make up for it. This is a great place to come for a full breakfast or a bowl of callaloo soup. Buy a bottle of Gladys' famous hot sauce for US$5.

**Green House** ( ☎ 774-7998; cnr Store Tvaer Gade & Waterfront Hwy; mains US$11-20; ⏰ lunch & dinner) Cavernous, open-air Green House overlooks the harbor and rocks hard during happy hour (from 4:30pm to 7pm, when drinks are two for the price of one) and evenings after 10pm. The cuisine is predictable American pub fare, but the menu is extensive, with burgers, pizzas and seafood.

**Cuzzin's Caribbean Restaurant & Bar** ( ☎ 777-4711; 7 Back St; mains US$14-24; ⏰ lunch Mon-Sat, dinner Tue-Sat) With exposed brick walls, burnished wood furnishings and red-clothed tables, classy-but-casual Cuzzin's is everybody's favorite stop for West Indian cuisine. Try the conch (curried, buttered or Creole style) or the 'Ole Wife' fish alongside fungi, johnnycakes and a Blackbeard Ale.

**Mafolie Restaurant** ( ☎ 774-2790; 7091 Estate Mafolie; mains US$19-25; ⏰ dinner, closed Tue) Sitting high above the bay at the Mafolie Hotel, the dining patio here offers incredible alfresco dining. Cool breezes, candle light and striking vistas complement the Caribbean and Creole-infused seafood, such as seared tuna, crab and lobster, and coconut-crusted chicken and BBQ ribs. An extensive wine list offers choices in all budgets, and the friendly staff can help you pick the perfect meal.

### FRENCHTOWN

The following restaurants huddle around the parking lot in Frenchtown.

**Frenchtown Deli** ( ☎ 776-7211; mains US$4-8; ⏰ 8am-7pm Mon-Fri, to 5pm Sat, to 4pm Sun) The deli is a popular stop for breakfast and lunch. Order at the counter, then plop down in a booth with an egg sandwich, bagel or good ole cup of coffee. Lunch is all about thick-cut sandwiches.

**Hook, Line & Sinker** ( ☎ 776-9708; mains US$13-25; ⏰ lunch & dinner Mon-Sat, brunch Sun) This open-air, mom-and-pop operation feels like a real sea shack, where you smell the salt water, feel the ocean breeze and see sailors unload their boats dockside. The menu mixes sandwiches, salads, pastas and seafood mains, such as the almond-crusted yellowtail, with plenty of beers to wash it down.

**Epernay Wine Bar & Bistro** ( ☎ 774-5348; mains US$19-28; ⏰ lunch Mon-Fri, dinner Mon-Sat) Epernay is a great place to meet fellow hipsters while hanging out at the bistro's bar, or to settle at a shadowy table. Delicious starters such as steamed mussels (US$11) complement mains such as sesame-crusted tuna or seared salmon.

## Shopping

Jewelry is the big deal in town. Shops fill the alleys between Waterfront Hwy and Main St, west of Emancipation Garden. US citizens can leave with up to US$1600 in tax-free, duty-free goods.

The Vendors' Plaza (p364) is interesting to wander, as are the following places.

**Camille Pissarro Gallery** ( ☎ 774-4621; 14 Dronningens Gade) Located in Pissarro's boyhood home (a display case outside summarizes the family's history), the gallery sells a few reproductions of the famous impressionist's St Thomas scenes, but mostly focuses on works by contemporary artists.

**Native Arts & Crafts** ( ☎ 777-1153; Tolbod Gade) This is the place to buy spices, straw dolls and painted gourd bowls made by island craftspeople, as well as books by local authors.

**Virgin Island Brewing Company** ( ☎ 714-1683; 1C Royal Dane Mall) It's good for pirate-logoed T-shirts, ball caps and other souvenirs, plus Blackbeard Ale samples.

## RED HOOK & EAST END

The East End holds the bulk of the island's resorts. Red Hook is the only town to speak of, though it's small and built mostly around the St John ferry dock and American Yacht Harbor marina.

## Sights & Activities

### CORAL WORLD

This 4.5-acre **marine park** ( ☎ 775-1555; www.coral worldvi.com; 6450 Estate Smith Bay; adult/child US$18/9;

**WATER ISLAND**

Do the Charlotte Amalie crowds have you frustrated, and pining for peace and seclusion? Water Island is your answer. Sometimes called the 'Fourth Virgin,' it floats spitting distance from town. But with only about 100 residents and very few cars or shops, it feels far more remote.

At 2.5 miles tip to tip, it doesn't take long to walk the whole thing. Honeymoon Beach offers fine swimming and snorkeling. If you want to spend the night, Water Island has only one option, but it's an eco-winner: the **Virgin Islands Campground** ( ☎ 776-5488, 877-502-7225; http://virgin islandscampground.com; cottages US$135; 💻 ). Each wood-frame-and-canvas cottage has beds, linens, electrical outlets and a table and chairs inside. Guests share the communal bathhouse, cooking facilities and hot tub, plus there's wi-fi access through the grounds. Captured rainwater runs through the sinks and showers; solar energy heats it.

The **Water Island Ferry** ( ☎ 690-4159; one way US$5) departs every few hours from outside Tickle's Dockside Pub at Crown Bay Marina. The journey takes 10 minutes. Taxis from downtown to the marina cost US$5 per person.

---

9am-5pm), at Coki Point, is the most popular tourist attraction on St Thomas. Pick up a schedule when entering – staff feed the sea creatures and give talks about marine biology and conservation throughout the day, and it's during these times that you'll engage in behaviors you never thought possible, such as petting baby nurse sharks, touching starfish and feeding raw fish right into a stingray's mouth. Many of the park's creatures have been rescued (ie the sea turtles were orphans; the sea lions were in harm's way in Uruguay, where fishermen were shooting them as pests). Pay an extra US$25 to US$80, and you can swim with the sharks, turtles or sea lions.

The site has restaurants and gift shops, along with changing rooms if you want to visit nearby Coki Beach. Look for Coral World discount coupons in the free tourist guides.

### EAST END BEACHES

**Coki Bay**, right at the entrance to Coral World, is a protected cove with excellent snorkeling, but beware – the small, festive beach can get very crowded.

A west-facing beach in front of the eponymous resort, **Secret Harbour** could hardly be more tranquil. It is protected from breezes as well as waves, and the water remains shallow a long way offshore. It's an excellent place to snorkel or to learn to windsurf with equipment rented from the resort's water-sports operation.

To reach **Vessup Beach**, a long, broad strand overlooking St John, follow a dirt road around the south side of the harbor at Red Hook until you reach Vessup Bay

Marina. Serious windsurfers love this spot. Beachfront **West Indies Windsurfing** ( ☎ 775-6530; 10am-5pm Sat & Sun, by appointment Mon-Fri) rents equipment and provides lessons.

**Sapphire Beach Resort**, just off Rte 38, is perhaps the most welcoming of all the island's resorts to transient beach visitors. The volleyball games here can get spirited, as can the party scene on Sunday afternoon, when the resort brings in live bands.

### DIVING & SNORKELING

St Thomas features several premier dive sites, and most island resort hotels have a dive service on the property. Dive centers charge about US$75 for a one-tank dive, or US$105 for two. They also rent snorkeling gear for about US$10. Recommended dive shops are:

**Chris Sawyer Diving Center** ( ☎ 775-7320, 877-929-3483; www.sawyerdive.vi) The retail center is at American Yacht Harbor. It offers mostly boat dives out of the Wyndham Sugar Bay Resort, also night dives and trips to the British Virgin Islands' wreck RMS *Rhone*.

**Coki Beach Dive Club** ( ☎ 775-4220; www.cokidive.com; closed Sun) Just steps away from Coki Beach, offers shore and night dives, plus Professional Association of Diving Instructors (PADI) courses.

**Dive In!** ( ☎ 777-5255, 866-434-8346; www.diveinusvi.com; Sapphire Beach Resort) Mostly boat dives, plus PADI certification courses.

### KAYAKING

**Virgin Islands Ecotours** ( ☎ 779-2155, 877-845-2925; www.viecotours.com; 2.5hr tours adult/child US$65/35; 9am & 1pm) offers a guided kayak-and-snorkeling expedition where you'll paddle through a mangrove lagoon to a coral rubble

US VIRGIN ISLANDS

beach. Tours depart just east of the intersection of Rtes 30 and 32, at the entrance to the Inner Mangrove Lagoon Sanctuary. There's also a three-hour tour (adult/child US$75/35) that adds hiking to the mix.

### BOAT TRIPS

Expect to pay US$70 per person for a four-hour trip and about US$125 for a full-day adventure. The trips generally include a catered lunch, free drinks and snorkel gear, and depart from American Yacht Harbor in Red Hook. The **Winifred** ( ☎ 775-7898; www.sailwinifred.com; full-day tour US$125), helmed by Captain Sharon Allen, wins raves. You also can organize fishing trips at the yacht harbor.

## Sleeping

Resorts are the East End's only option.

**Pavilions and Pools** ( ☎ 775-6110, 800-524-2001; www.pavilionsandpools.com; 6400 Estate Smith Bay; r incl breakfast US$260-360; 🐾 🖥 🐾 ) The cool thing about this small hotel is that each of the 25 suites has its own pool – yeah, you read that right! Suites have full kitchens, wi-fi access and separate bedrooms with sliding doors that open to your own pool. You can spend days here and never put on a stitch of clothing. When you're ready to get dressed, the friendly staff will shuttle you to nearby Sapphire Beach.

**Point Pleasant Resort** ( ☎ 775-7200, 800-524-2300; www.pointpleasantresort.com; 6600 Estate Smith Bay; r US$300-550; 🐾 🐾 ) On a steep hill overlooking Water Bay, the property has lots of charm though the rooms are somewhat dated (in a flowery way, akin to your grandma's 1980 Florida condo). The 128 suites are in multi-unit cottages tucked into the hillside forest. Each unit has a full kitchen, separate bedroom and large porch. The grounds have walking trails, three pools and a beach.

These Mondo family favorites offer lots of beachfront and water activities:
**Sapphire Beach Resort & Marina** ( ☎ 775-6100, 800-524-2090; www.sapphirebeachresort.com; 6720 Estate Smith Bay; d US$335-495; 🐾 🐾 )
**Wyndham Sugar Bay Resort** ( ☎ 777-7100, 800-996-3426; www.wyndhamsugarbayresort.com; 6500 Estate Smith Bay; d from US$350; 🐾 🐾 )

## Eating & Drinking

**Señor Pizza** ( ☎ 775-3030; slice US$2.50-3.25, large pizza US$21; 🕑 lunch & dinner) Next door to Red Hook

Plaza, this place serves the island's best pizza. It can get busy with takeout orders in the evening.

**Burrito Bay Deli** ( ☎ 775-2944; American Yacht Harbor; sandwiches US$7-12; 🕑 breakfast & lunch) Longing for healthy-leaning sandwiches, wraps or breakfast foods (including tofu and vegetarian options)? Burrito Bay is your place.

**Duffy's Love Shack** ( ☎ 779-2080; 650 Red Hook Plaza; mains US$9-16; 🕑 lunch & dinner) It may be a frame shack in the middle of a paved parking lot, but Duffy's creates its legendary atmosphere with high-volume rock and crowds in shorts and tank tops. The food is classic, burger-based pub fare. The big attractions here are the people-watching and killer cocktails.

**Molly Malone's** ( ☎ 775-1270; American Yacht Harbor; mains US$10-22; 🕑 breakfast, lunch & dinner) A recreation of a friendly Irish pub, Molly's has a huge menu, from omelets to shepherd's pie to veggie lasagna. It's a great place to watch sports on overhead TVs, or cool off with a brew at the bar.

You'll find two excellent restaurants at the Point Pleasant Resort, including the highly respected **Agavé Terrace & Bar** ( ☎ 775-4142; mains US$30-50; 🕑 dinner only), whose deck hangs out in thin air over a steep slope, giving diners a breathtaking view of St John and the British Virgin Islands. It specializes in fish, lobster and crab legs. Also here is **Fungi's on the Beach** ( ☎ 775-4142; meals from US$13; 🕑 lunch & dinner), a fun, waterside place to try local dishes.

# ST JOHN

pop 4300

Outdoor enthusiasts and ecotravelers: welcome to your island. Two-thirds of St John is a protected national park, with gnarled trees and spiky cacti spilling over its edges. There are no airports or cruise-ship docks, and the usual Caribbean resorts are few and far between. Instead, the island hosts several tent-resorts (aka campgrounds with permanent canvas structures), keeping costs reasonable and the environment intact.

Hiking and snorkeling are the big to-dos. Trails wind by petroglyphs and sugar-mill ruins, and several drop out onto beaches prime for swimming with turtles and spotted eagle rays. Add to the scene mystical mojito bars, wild donkeys and goodtime happy hours, and you've found paradise.

## Orientation

At 9 miles long and 5 miles wide, St John rises above the surrounding sea like a peaked green cap. All but the extreme east and west ends of the island lie within the borders of the national park and will remain forever wild. Cruz Bay at the West End is St John's port of entry, with constant ferry traffic and most of the island's shops, restaurants and pubs.

The settlement of Coral Bay at the East End is the sleepy domain of folks who want to feel like they're living on a frontier. Centerline Rd (Rte 10) scales the island's heights and proceeds east–west along the mountain ridges to connect St John's two communities. The North Shore Rd (Rte 20) snakes along the north coast and connects the most popular beaches, bays and campgrounds.

St John floats just 3 miles from St Thomas.

## Getting There & Away

Passenger ferries between Charlotte Amalie and Cruz Bay run about every two hours and cost US$10 one way. Ferries run almost every hour between Red Hook and Cruz Bay, costing US$5 one way. For more information, see p388.

Ferries also travel to the British Virgin Islands, departing for Tortola three times daily and to Jost Van Dyke on Friday, Saturday and Sunday; see p387 for details.

## Getting Around

### BUS

**Vitran** (☎ 774-5678; fare US$1) operates air-con buses over the length of the island via Centerline Rd. Buses leave Cruz Bay in front of the ferry terminal at 6am and 7am, then every hour at 25 minutes after the hour until 7:25pm. They arrive at Coral Bay about 40 minutes later.

### CAR

St John has a handful of rental agencies. Most provide Jeeps and SUVs to handle the rugged terrain. Costs hover near US$75 per day. The following agencies have outlets in Cruz Bay near the ferry terminals:

**Cool Breeze Jeep/Car Rental** (☎ 776-6588; www .coolbreezecarrental.com)

**Delbert Hill Car Rental** (☎ 776-6637; www.delbert hillrental.com)

**O'Connor Car Rental** (☎ 776-6343; www.oconnorcar rental.com)

**St John Car Rental** (☎ 776-6103; www.stjohncar rental.com)

### TAXI

Territorial law sets the island's taxi rates. They're listed in *St Thomas/St John This Week* magazine. From Cruz Bay it costs US$9 per person to Coral Bay, US$9 to Maho Bay and US$7 to Cinnamon Bay. Call the **St John Taxi Commission** (☎ 774-3130) for pickups.

The street in front of the Cruz Bay ferry dock swarms with cabs offering island tours. A two-hour circuit of the island costs US$50 per person for one or two passengers; it drops to US$25 per person when three or more take the tour.

## CRUZ BAY

Nicknamed 'Love City,' St John's main town indeed wafts a carefree, spring-break party vibe. Hippies, sea captains, American retirees and reggae worshippers hoist happy-hour drinks in equal measure, and everyone wears a silly grin at their great good fortune for being here. Cruz Bay is also the place to organize your hiking, snorkeling, kayaking and other island activities and to fuel up in the surprisingly good restaurant mix. Everything grooves within walking distance of the ferry docks.

## Orientation & Information

Ferries from St Thomas and the British Virgin Islands arrive at separate docks, though they are within steps of each other. Most businesses offer free island maps plus the biweekly *St John Sun Times* (with entertainment and restaurant bargain listings). Note that the 'visitor's connection' kiosks sprinkled around town are fronts for Westin time-share sales.

**Book & Bean** (☎ 799-2665; Southside Rd; ☷ 7am-4pm Mon-Fri, 8am-4pm Sat) In the Marketplace building, about a 15-minute walk northeast from the ferry dock. This is a good place to pick up *Trail Bandit* hiking maps.

**Connections** (☎ 776-6922; per 30min US$5; ☷ 8:30am-5:30pm Mon-Sat) Internet access. There's a sister outlet in Coral Bay (☎ 779-4994) by Skinny Legs restaurant.

**FirstBank** (☎ 776-6881) Branch with ATM near Woody's Seafood Saloon.

**Myrah Keating Smith Community Health Center** (☎ 693-8900; ☷ 8am-8pm Mon-Fri) About 2 miles east of Cruz Bay on Centerline Rd, this is the place to come for routine medical attention.

**Post office** (☎ 779-4227) Across the street from the British Virgin Islands ferry dock.

**US Customs & Immigration** ( ☎ 776-6741; ☽ 8am-noon & 1-5pm) Adjoins the British Virgin Islands ferry dock. If you arrive on a ferry or on a yacht from the British Virgin Islands, you must clear immigration here (typically a no-hassle process) before you head into town.

**Visitors center** ( ☎ 776-6450; ☽ 8am-5pm Mon-Fri) A small building next to the post office.

## Sights & Activities
### VIRGIN ISLANDS NATIONAL PARK

In the early 1950s, US millionaire Laurence Rockefeller discovered and fell in love with St John, which was nearly abandoned at the time. He purchased large tracts of the land, built the Caneel Bay resort, and then donated more than 5000 acres to the US government. The land became a national park in 1956, and over the years the government added a couple thousand more acres. Today Virgin Islands National Park covers two-thirds of the island, plus 5650 acres underwater.

It's a tremendous resource, offering miles of shoreline, pristine reefs and 20 hiking trails (see below). The **park visitors center** ( ☎ 776-6201; www.nps.gov/viis; ☽ 8am-4:30pm) sits on the dock across from the Mongoose Junction shopping arcade in Cruz Bay. It's an essential first stop to obtain free guides on hiking trails,

snorkeling spots, bird-watching lists and daily ranger-led activities.

For the record: more than 30 species of tropical birds nest in the park, including the banana quit, hummingbird and smooth-billed ani. Green iguanas, geckoes, hawksbill turtles, wild donkeys and an assortment of other feral animals roam the land. Largely regenerated after 18th-century logging, the island flora is a mix of introduced species and native plants, with lots of spiny cacti.

A great way to give back to the park is by volunteering for trail or beach **clean-ups** ( ☽ 8am-1pm Sat, Nov-Apr); meet at the maintenance parking lot (it's well marked) by the visitors center. Clean-ups also take place at Maho Bay and Cinnamon Bay beaches during the same timeframe on Thursdays.

### KAYAKING
Both these groups offer guided kayak tours with snorkeling time built in:

**Arawak Expeditions** ( ☎ 693-8312, 800-238-8687; www.arawakexp.com; half/full day US$50/90) Departs out of Cruz Bay; snorkel gear not included. Offers mountain biking tours (same prices), as well.

**Hidden Reef Eco-Tours** ( ☎ 877-529-2575; www.hiddenreefecotours.com; 3hr/5hr tours US$65/115) De-

---

**THESE TRAILS ARE MADE FOR WALKING**

St John's greatest gift to visitors (aside from the awesome snorkeling, feral donkeys, ecocamps and happy-hour booze) is its hiking trails. The national park maintains 20 paths, and any reasonably fit hiker can walk them safely without a local guide. The park visitors center provides trail details in the helpful free *Trail Guide for Safe Hiking* brochure. Uberenthusiasts should also buy the **Trail Bandit map** (www.trailbandit.org; US$4) that lists several additional footpaths; it's available at Book & Bean (p371), the Maho Bay Camps store (p376) or online.

If you prefer guided hikes, the National Park Service sponsors several free ones, including birding expeditions and shore hikes, but its best-known offering is the **Reef Bay Hike** ( ☎ 776-6201 reservations ext 238; US$21; ☽ 9:30am-3pm Mon & Thu year-round, plus Fri Dec-Apr). This begins at the Reef Bay trailhead, 4.75 miles from Cruz Bay on Centerline Rd. The hike is a 3-mile downhill trek through tropical forests, leading past petroglyphs and plantation ruins to a swimming beach at Reef Bay, where a boat runs you back to Cruz Bay (hence the fee). It's very popular, so try to reserve at least three days in advance.

These other favorite trails are each 2 to 3 miles round trip; all have identifying signs at the trailheads and small lots to park your car.

■ **Leinster Bay** Goes from the Annaberg sugar-mill ruins to fantastic snorkeling at Waterlemon Cay.

■ **Brown Bay** Breezy, butterfly-laden hike up and over a small ridge and past a conch-scattered beach.

■ **Ram's Head** Rocky, uphill slog to a worth-every-drop-of-sweat clifftop view.

■ **Lind Point** Departs from behind the visitors center, past the occasional donkey and banana quit, to secluded Honeymoon Beach.

---

### DIVING & SNORKELING ST JOHN

St John offers loads of snorkel hot spots accessible from shore. The park service publishes an oft-photocopied but useful brochure called *Where's the Best Snorkeling?* – pick it up at the park visitors center. Gold stars go to Leinster Bay/Waterlemon Cay (p376) and Salt Pond Bay (p376); see p375 for more locations.

The island also has cool dive sites, all of which are accessed by boat, including wreck dives on the *General Rogers* and RMS *Rhone*. A two-tank trip including gear costs US$95 (about US$150 to the *Rhone*). The following shops in Cruz Bay also offer dive certification, snorkel gear rental (US$7 to US$10 per day for a full set) and boat trips to the BVIs (about US$130 plus $25 in customs fees for a full day):

**Cruz Bay Watersports** ( ☎ 776-6234; www.divestjohn.com; Palm Plaza; ☾ 8am-6pm) Behind the Lumberyard.
**Low Key Watersports** ( ☎ 693-8999; www.divelowkey.com; Wharfside Village; ☾ 8am-6pm)

---

parts from Haulover Bay at the island's more remote east end; snorkel gear is included. Also offers night paddles.

### OTHER ACTIVITIES

The nonprofit group **Friends of the Virgin Islands National Park** ( ☎ 779-4940; www.friendsvinp.org) provides hiking, sailing and snorkel trips all over the island, as well as cooking, painting, jewelry-making and West African drumming workshops. Activities occur on various Wednesdays, Saturdays and Sundays; costs range from US$25 to $80.

### Festivals & Events

**8 Tuff Miles** (www.8tuffmiles.com) Popular road race from Cruz Bay to Coral Bay in late February.
**St John Blues Festival** ( ☎ 693-8120; www.stjohnbluesfestival.com) All-day music bash in Coral Bay on the third Saturday in March; tickets cost US$30.
**St John Carnival** ( ☎ 776-6450) The island's biggest celebration; surrounds Emancipation Day (July 3) and US Independence Day (July 4).

### Sleeping

St John's accommodations appeal to two groups: one group is upper-middle-class vacationers fond of villas and resorts, the other adventure travelers keen on camping and ecotourism (for which they must head to the North Shore). There's not much in the middle range. If you want to splash out and live the resort lifestyle, Gallows Point and Caneel Bay in particular do it well. Prices listed below are winter high-season rates; add 8% for tax.

**Samuel Cottages** ( ☎ 776-6643; www.samuelcottages.com; 4-person cottages US$125; ☒ ) These three peach-colored cottages are a stiff 10-minute walk uphill from the ferry dock, but you'll be hard-pressed to beat the value. They're sort of like state park cabins – nothing fancy,

but clean and spacious enough, with a fully equipped kitchen and deck for sitting and contemplating how much cash you're saving.

**Inn at Tamarind Court** ( ☎ 776-6378, 800-221-1637; www.tamarindcourt.com; s/d/q US$75/148/240; ☒ ) The rooms are small, thin-walled and lack frills such as private decks and water views, but Tamarind Inn does try hard with its friendly staff, bamboo-and-tiki decor and jumpin' courtyard bar-restaurant. A separate building holds six single rooms sharing two bathrooms.

**our pick St John Inn** ( ☎ 693-8688, 800-666-7688; www.stjohninn.com; r incl breakfast US$160-215; ☒ ☒ ) A step up in value (and steps away down a quiet side street) from Tamarind Inn, rooms here are decked out with tiled floors, handcrafted pine furniture and iron beds. Many also have water views or a kitchen. A homey atmosphere pervades, and guests grill fresh fish on the communal barbecue, laze on the sun deck or dip in the small pool.

**Gallows Point Resort** ( ☎ 776-6434, 800-323-7229; www.gallowspointresort.com; r US$435-575; ☒ ☒ ☒ ) It stands out for being small (only 15 suites), independently owned and walkable to Cruz Bay. Each suite has a full kitchen, a private deck and French doors that open onto water views. There's wi-fi access in the lobby.

**Caneel Bay** ( ☎ 776-6111, 888-767-3966; www.caneelbay.com; r from US$550; ☒ ☒ ☒ ) It's the resort that started it all, back in 1955. Located 2 miles north of Cruz Bay, Caneel Bay is where folks such as Angelina Jolie and Brad Pitt come when they need seven beaches, 11 tennis courts, five restaurants and all-round elegance. There are no phones or TVs in rooms.

Villa rentals can be reasonable, especially if you're accommodating more than two people. One-, two- and three-bedroom properties are all common. Most require a week-long stay in high season. One-bedroom villas could cost US$1500 to US$2700 per week.

**Carefree Get-Aways** ( ☎ 779-4070, 888-643-6002; www.carefreegetaways.com)

**Caribbean Villas** ( ☎ 776-6152, 800-338-0987; www .caribbeanvilla.com)

**Catered To** ( ☎ 776-6641, 800-424-6641; wwwcateredto.com)

**Coconut Coast Villas** ( ☎ 693-9100, 800-858-7989; www.coconutcoast.com)

## Eating & Drinking

OUR PICK **Hercules Pate Delight** ( ☎ 776-6352; pates US$3; ☺ 6am-2pm Mon-Fri, to 11am Sat) *Pates* can be overly greasy, but not the pillowy puffs of dough that Hercules fries. Stuffed with spiced chicken, beef, shrimp or salt fish, they're perfect for a morning or early afternoon snack. You'll find the wee joint behind Cool Breeze Jeep Rental, on the road leading toward the Lumberyard buildings.

**Mojo Café** ( ☎ 776-8399; Wharfside Village; mains US$7-14; ☺ breakfast, lunch & dinner) Mojo makes dishes that are all over the map. For breakfast and lunch it's American fare such as egg sandwiches, burgers and turkey clubs. Come evening, pork vindaloo, vegetarian dhal and other Indian food takes over. Eat at the three outdoor tables, or order as takeaway and walk a few steps to the beach for a picnic. Cash only.

**Woody's Seafood Saloon** ( ☎ 779-4625; mains US$8-17; ☺ lunch & dinner) St John's daily party starts here at 3pm, when the price on domestic beers drops to US$1. By 4pm the crowd in this tiny place has spilled over onto the sidewalk. Bartenders pass beers out a streetside window. While lots of folks just show up to cram in and whoop it up with fellow tanned bodies, you can actually get some reasonable pub food, such as grilled fish or corn-crusted scallops.

**Uncle Joe's BBQ** ( ☎ 693-8806; mains US$10-14; ☺ dinner) Locals and visitors go wild tearing into the barbecue chicken, ribs and corn on the cob at this open-air restaurant across from the post office. The chef grills the meats outside, perfuming the entire harbor-front with their tangy goodness. Cash only.

**Inn at Tamarind Court Restaurant** ( ☎ 776-6378; breakfast US$4-8, dinner mains US$10-14; ☺ breakfast & dinner, closed Sat eve) Each night brings a different themed menu to this jovial courtyard eatery. Monday is for Greek dishes, Tuesday is Mexican food, Wednesday is Thai fare, and Friday is for chowing prime rib. Fruit-filled pancakes, omelets and French toast fill breakfast plates.

**Morgan's Mango** ( ☎ 693-8141; Mongoose Junction; mains US$15-28; ☺ dinner) Take in a view of the harbor while dining on imaginative Caribbean recipes for dishes such as Haitian voodoo snapper or Cuban citrus chicken. The owners often bring in live acoustic acts (usually on Tuesday and Friday), making Morgan's a good choice for a fun or romantic night out.

**Rhumb Lines** ( ☎ 776-0303; Meada's Plaza; mains US$16-24; ☺ dinner, closed Tue) Tucked in a lush courtyard, this little restaurant has superb salads, sandwiches and fresh, healthy tropical cuisine served by happy, friendly hippies. At night, try selections from the 'pu pu' menu (US$4 to US$7 each), a mix of tapas-like treats. There's air-conditioned indoor seating, or outdoor seating under palms and umbrellas.

Self-caterers can head to **Starfish Market** ( ☎ 779-4949; Southside Rd; ☺ 7:30am-9pm), a full-service supermarket with good produce, a deli, and a wide selection of beer and wine. It's in the Marketplace building, about a 15-minute walk northeast from the ferry dock.

## NORTH SHORE

Life's a beach on the tranquil North Shore. A rental car is the easiest way to see the area via North Shore (Rte 20) and Centerline (Rte 10) Rds, but taxis also will drop you at the beaches for between US$5 and US$9 per person.

---

**TWIST MY ARM: THE SPOTS THE AUTHORS WANTED TO KEEP SECRET**

A mysterious bar with no phone, no address and no physical presence during certain hours of the day, **Joe's Rum Hut** (Wharfside Village; ☺ from 11am) is the Shangri-la of beachfront boozers. To find it, follow the 'Balcony Restaurant' signs through Cruz Bay's Wharfside Village shopping mall (Joe's sits on the floor below the eatery), and arrive after 11am, when a bartender materializes along with rum and a whopping bowl of limes. After that, it's all about sitting at the open-air counter, clinking the ice in your mojito (US$6) and watching porpoises glide through the bay out front.

## MONGOOSES, DONKEYS AND GOATS – OH MY!

Whether you are camping, hiking or driving on St John, it won't be long before you have a close encounter with the island's odd menagerie of feral animals. According to National Park Service estimates, 500 goats, 400 donkeys, 200 pigs and hundreds of cats roam the island, descendants of domestic animals abandoned to the jungle eons ago. White-tailed deer and mongooses are two other introduced species that multiplied in unexpected numbers.

Park rangers are most concerned with the goats and pigs, whose foraging wipes out underbrush and leaves hillsides prone to erosion. Many of the animals have grown adept at raiding garbage cans and food supplies in the camping areas, and the donkeys meandering on island roads pose a serious hazard to drivers.

Do not tempt these animals by offering them food or leaving food or garbage where they can get at it. And do not approach them for petting or taking a snapshot. While most have a live-and-let-live attitude and don't mind you stepping around them on the trails, they are all capable of aggression if provoked.

## Sights & Activities

### ANNABERG SUGAR MILL RUINS

Part of the national park, these ruins near Leinster Bay are the most intact sugar plantation ruins in the Virgin Islands. A 30-minute, self-directed walking tour leads you through the slave quarters, village, windmill, rum still and dungeon.

The schooner drawings on the dungeon wall may date back more than 100 years. Park experts offer **demonstrations** ( 10am-2pm Tue-Fri) in traditional island baking, gardening, weaving and crafting.

When you're finished milling around, hop on the **Leinster Bay Trail** that starts near the picnic area and ends at, yep, Leinster Bay (p376). It's 1.6 miles, round trip.

### BEACHES

Most beaches have rest rooms and changing facilities, and most are excellent for snorkeling. You can rent snorkeling gear at dive shops in Cruz Bay (p373), or at tourist-favorites Trunk and Cinnamon Bays. These sand patches to unfurl your towel upon are listed starting from Cruz Bay and moving eastward.

### Honeymoon Beach

Honeymoon is a mile hike from the park visitors center along the Lind Point Trail. It has no facilities, other than sea-grape trees to hang your clothes on, which perhaps accounts for the few visitors.

### Caneel Bay

This is the main beach in front of Caneel Bay resort. The resort has seven beaches, but this is the one it permits visitors to use. It's a lovely

place, with fair snorkeling off the east point. You must sign in as a visitor at the guardhouse when you enter the resort property.

### Hawksnest Bay

The bay here is dazzling to behold, a deep circular indentation between hills with a broken ring of sand on the fringe.

### Oppenheimer's Beach

On the eastern edge of Hawksnest Bay, the beach and house here belonged to Dr Robert Oppenheimer, one of the inventors of the atomic bomb. His daughter left the land to the children of St John.

### Jumbie Bay

Jumbie is the word for ghost in the Creole dialect, and this beach east of Oppenheimer's has a plethora of ghost stories. Look for the parking lot on the North Shore Rd that holds only three cars. From here, take the wooden stairs down to the sand.

### Trunk Bay

This long, gently arching beach is the most popular strand on the island and charges a US$4 fee. The beach has lifeguards, showers, toilets, picnic facilities, snorkel rental, a snack bar and taxi stand. No question, the sandy stretch is scenic, but it often gets packed. Everyone comes here to swim the underwater snorkeling trail, which truth be told, is pretty lame and murky.

### Cinnamon Bay

This exposed sweeping cove is home to the Cinnamon Bay Campground. The beach has

**US VIRGIN ISLANDS**

showers, toilets, a restaurant, grocery store and taxi stand. It also offers a full slate of activities through its **Watersports Center** ( 8:30-4:30pm), where you can rent snorkel gear (US$5 per day) or sailboats, windsurf boards and sea kayaks (each about US$20 per hour). Lessons including equipment cost US$60 per hour.

### Maho Bay

Maho's beach is the longest on St John. The water is shallow and less choppy than elsewhere, and it's a good bet you'll see green sea turtles in early morning or late afternoon. The bay fronts the island's premiere eco tent-resort, Maho Bay Camps.

### Leinster Bay

This bay adjoins the Annaberg mill ruins. Park in the plantation's lot and follow a dirt road/trail around Leinster Bay. Some of St John's best snorkeling is at the bay's east end, offshore at Waterlemon Cay, where turtles, spotted eagle rays, barracudas and nurse sharks swim. Be aware the current can be strong.

### Sleeping

Travelers unenthused by big swanky resorts will love the two ecofriendly options here. Bring the insect repellent.

**Cinnamon Bay Campground** ( 776-6330, 800-539-9998; www.cinnamonbay.com; campsites/equipped tents US$27/80, cottages US$110-140;  closed Sep) About 6 miles east of Cruz Bay on North Shore Rd (Rte 20), this campground-ecoresort sits along a mile-long crescent beach at the base of forested hills. It's really a campers' village with a general store, snack bar and restaurant, but with thick vegetation giving plenty of privacy. There are three accommodations options. You can use your own tent; stay in a 10ft x 14ft tent that sits on a solid wood platform and comes equipped with four cots, a lantern, ice chest, charcoal grill and gas stove; or stay in a cottage – a 15ft x 15ft concrete shelter with two screened sides, electric lights, grill, stove and ceiling fan. The best bets are using your own tent or the cottages; the equipped tents are a bit gloomy. Everyone uses the public toilet facilities and cold-water showers.

**Maho Bay Camps** ( 776-6226, 800-392-9004; www.maho.org; tents US$135, Harmony Studios US$215-240) Stanley Selengut's mega-popular, ecosensitive tent resort lies 8 miles east of Cruz Bay on North Shore Rd (Rte 20). The complex offers 114 'tents,' akin to fabric-lined cabins, which sit on wood platforms on a steep, forested hillside. Each unit has a sleeping area with twin beds, a propane stove, electrical outlets and an open-air terrace. The tents are so far off the ground, and the surrounding vegetation is so thick, it's like living in a tree house. To conserve water, guests use community low-flush toilets and pull-chain showers. The resort also recycles glass and other trash into crafts sold in its Arts Center; guests can take part in classes or watch free nightly glass-blowing demonstrations. For those seeking higher-grade amenities, the resort's adjoining Harmony Studios are condos with a private bathroom, kitchen and deck, plus solar-generated electricity, rainwater collection and roof wind scoops for cooling. Now for the sad news: Maho sits on leased land, and the lease runs out in 2011. Everyone is bracing for the land owners to sell out to big developers, and Maho will cease to be. Get here while you still can.

## CORAL BAY & AROUND

Coral Bay, St John's second town, is really just a handful of shops, restaurants and pubs clustered around the 1733 hilltop Emmaus Moravian Church. Two hundred years ago, it was the largest settlement on the island. Known then as 'Crawl' Bay, presumably because there were pens or 'crawls' for sea turtles here, the settlement owes its early good fortune to being the largest and best-protected harbor in the Virgin Islands. Today it serves as the gateway to the island's most remote beaches and coastal wilderness, ripe for hiking, horseback riding and ecocamping.

### Sights & Activities

Strap on your walking shoes for two essential hikes near Coral Bay. The first one is at **Salt Pond Bay**, a few miles from town down Rte 107 and a 10-minute walk from the road. The bay itself provides excellent snorkeling, though the water can get rough; keep an eye out for turtles and squids. At the beach's south end, the **Ram's Head Trail** takes off and rises to a windswept cliff jabbing out into the sea. The trek is a 2-mile round trip through rocky exposed terrain, so bring ample water and sun protection.

The second must-hike is the **Brown Bay Trail**, which starts a mile east of Coral Bay. The path runs for 3.2 miles, round trip, going over a small ridge and past a conch-scattered beach; sweet viewpoints and butterflies pop up en route.

Horseback riding enthusiasts can saddle up a trusty steed or donkey with **Carolina Corral** ( ☎ 693-5778; rides adult/child US$75/55; ☼ 10am & 3pm Mon-Sat) for a 1.5-hour beach, trail or sunset jaunt.

## Sleeping & Eating

our pick **Concordia Eco-Tents** ( ☎ 693-5855, 800-392-9004; www.maho.org; d US$155-185, apt US$150-225; ⌨ ) With the possible loss of his Maho Bay lease (see opposite), Stanley Selengut has pumped up his other ecocamp at Concordia. Each 'tent' has a private bathroom (unlike Maho), with composting toilet and solar-heated shower that, sigh, makes water temperature difficult to control sometimes. A kitchen (small refrigerator and two-burner propane stove) and sea view complete the package. The camp also offers studio apartments with slightly upgraded amenities, plus a café, activities center (for yoga and water sports), swimming pool and store for everyone to use. It's all strung together by boardwalks and steps up the steep hillside. About 2.5 miles south of Coral Bay, Concordia is quiet and remote. You'll likely want a rental car, though patient souls can access it by public bus.

**Vie's Snack Shack** ( ☎ 693-5033; mains US$7-12; ☼ 10am-5pm Tue-Sat) Vie Mahabir opened this plywood-sided restaurant next to her house in 1979, just after the government paved the road. She wanted to make a living while raising her 10 children. In the process, she perfected the art of garlic chicken with johnnycakes. Vie also will let you lounge (US$2.50 per day) or camp (US$25 per night) on her low-key beach. She's located east of town (on East End Rd) by Hansen Bay.

**Skinny Legs** ( ☎ 779-4982; mains US$8-11; ☼ lunch & dinner) Salty sailors, bikini-clad transients and East End snowbirds mix it up at this open-air grill just past the fire station. Overlooking a small boatyard, it's not about the view, but the jovial clientele and lively bar scene. Burgers win the most raves, so open wide for a cheeseburger, or try a grilled *mahimahi* (white-meat fish) sandwich.

**Miss Lucy's** ( ☎ 693-5244; mains US$16-25; ☼ lunch & dinner Tue-Sat, brunch Sun) Miss Lucy, the island's first female cab driver and one heck of a cook, passed away in 2007 at age 91. Her restaurants lives on, as famous for its Sunday jazz brunch and piña colada pancakes as for its weekday conch chowder, jumbo crab cakes and toasted goat-cheese salad – all served at water's edge under the sea-grape trees. Take Rte 107 to Friis Bay; it's en route to Concordia.

# ST CROIX

pop 53,200

St Croix (saint-croy) is the USVIs' big boy – it's more than twice the size of St Thomas – and it sports an exceptional topography spanning mountains, a spooky rainforest and a fertile coastal plain that, once upon a time, earned it the nickname 'Garden of the Antilles' for its sugarcane growing prowess.

The sugar plantations are colonial history, and today St Croix is notable for its scuba diving, rum distillery, hikes, marine sanctuary and, dare we say it, beer-drinking pigs.

St Croix is also distinguished by the fact that tourism is not its main income source. That honor goes to the Hovensa Oil refinery on the south shore. It's the world's fifth-largest facility, bringing in most of its oil from Venezuela. With so many locals working in 'regular' jobs, the vibe on St Croix is more suburban than bash-you-over-the-head idyllic – which actually makes for a refreshing, less-congested change of pace.

More than half of the island's residents are the descendants of former slaves; about 30% are second- or third-generation immigrants from Puerto Rico; and quite a few are young white Americans who come to run restaurants, inns and sports operations.

## Orientation

Geographically isolated St Croix drifts 40 miles south of the other Virgins. The island has two main towns: Christiansted, the largest, sits on the northeast shore. Frederiksted, its much sleepier counterpart, resides in the west end (the island's wet, mountainous and forested region). South of the mountains is the broad coastal plain that once hosted sugar plantations. Today it's a modern commercial zone where most of St Croix's population lives.

## Getting There & Away

### AIR

**Henry E Rohlsen Airport** (STX; ☎ 778-0589; www.viport .com/avifacilities.html) is on St Croix's southwest side and handles flights from the US, many connecting via San Juan, Puerto Rico or St Thomas. For airline details, see p387.

**Seaborne Airlines** ( ☎ 773-6442, 888-359-8687; www.seaborneairlines.com) flies seaplanes between St Thomas and St Croix – a sweet little ride (one way US$85, 25 minutes). They land in Christiansted's downtown harbor. For more information, see p388.

### BOAT
**VI Seatrans** ( ☎ 776-5494; www.goviseatrans.com) operates a passenger ferry from St Croix to St Thomas (one way US$50, 90 minutes) at 7:30am and 4:30pm Friday through Monday. Departures are from Gallows Bay, about a 0.75-mile walk east of downtown Christiansted.

## Getting Around
### BUS
**Vitran** ( ☎ 778-0898; fare US$1) buses travel along Centerline Rd between Christiansted and Frederiksted. The schedule is erratic; buses depart roughly every hour or two.

### CAR
Rentals cost about US$55 per day. Many companies, including the following, will pick you up at the airport or seaplane dock.
**Budget** ( ☎ 778-9636; www.budgetstcroix.com)
**Centerline Car Rentals** ( ☎ 778-0450, 888-288-8755; www.ccrvi.com)
**Olympic** ( ☎ 773-2208, 888-878-4227; www.olympicstcroix.com)

### TAXI
Taxis are unmetered, but rates are set by territorial law. Prices are listed in the readily available free tourist guide *St Croix This Week*. Taxis from the airport to Christiansted cost US$16 per person.

# CHRISTIANSTED
Christiansted evokes a melancholy whiff of the past. Cannon-covered Fort Christiansvaern rises up on the waterfront, and arcaded sidewalks connect several other colonial buildings. They abut Kings Wharf, the commercial landing where, for more than 250 years, ships landed with slaves and set off with sugar or molasses. Today the wharf is fronted by a boardwalk of restaurants, dive shops and bars. It all comes together as a well-provisioned base from which to explore the island.

## Orientation & Information
The main arteries are King St (eastbound) and Company St (westbound). Banks with ATMs cluster around Prince St.
**Governor Juan F Luis Hospital** ( ☎ 776-6311; 24hr) Next to the Sunny Isle Shopping Center on Centerline Rd, 2 miles west of Christiansted.
**Post office** ( ☎ 773-3586; cnr Company St & Market Sq)
**St Croix Landmarks Society** ( ☎ 772-0598; http://heritagetrails.stcroixlandmarks.org) Maps to ruins and cultural sites island-wide.
**Surf the Net** ( ☎ 692-7855; 1102 Strand St; per half hr US$5; 10am-5pm Mon-Sat, 10am-3pm Sun) Internet access.
**Visitors center** ( ☎ 773-1460; cnr Hospital & King Sts; 10am-5pm) It's located in the historic Scale House and operated by the National Park Service. The knowledgeable staff can provide information on island-wide attractions, plus town and island maps.

## Sights
Several painters, jewelry makers and photographers have galleries in town, with most on Company St near Queen Cross St. The **Art Thursday** (www.artthursday.com; admission free; 5-8pm, 3rd Thu of month) gallery hop takes place November through June.

### CHRISTIANSTED NATIONAL HISTORIC SITE
This **historic site** ( ☎ 773-1460; www.nps.gov/chri; 2100 Church St; admission US$3; 8am-5pm Mon-Fri, 9am-5pm Sat & Sun) includes several structures. The most impressive is **Fort Christiansvaern** (Christian's Defenses), a four-point citadel occupying the deep-yellow buildings on the town's east side, and the best-preserved Danish fort in the West Indies. Built between 1738 and 1749 out of Danish bricks (brought over as ships' ballast), the fort protected citizens from the onslaught of pirates, hurricanes and slave revolts, but its guns were never fired in an armed conflict. After 1878, the fort served as a prison and courthouse for the island. Cannons on the ramparts, an echoey claustrophobic dungeon and latrines with top-notch sea views await visitors who tour the site.

Other buildings nearby include the **Scale House**, where the Danish weighed hogsheads of sugar for export (the building now houses a visitors center). The **Custom's House**, recognizable by its sweeping 16-step stairway, served as the Danes' customs house for more than a century. Nearby, the three-story neoclassical **Danish West India and Guinea Company Warehouse** served as company headquarters; slaves were auctioned in its central courtyard. Next door, the 1753 **Steeple Building** served as Church of Lord God of the Sabaoth, the island's first house of worship.

### PROTESTANT CAY

This small triangular cay, located less than 200yd from Kings Wharf (a three-minute ferry ride, round trip US$3), is a sweet little oasis. It's the site of a mellow resort whose wide, sandy beach and bar-restaurant are open to the public. The **Beach Shack** ( ☎ 773-7060; www.cruzanwatersports.com; ☼ 9am-5pm) rents kayaks (US$15 per two hours) and snorkel gear (per day US$10). Some swimmers rave you can see just as much underwater life here as at Buck Island.

## Activities

Christiansted is chock-full of operators that book diving trips (see p380) and Buck Island tours (see p381).

For a wind-in-your-hair sailing experience, **World Ocean School** ( ☎ 626-7877; www.worldocean school.org; 2½hr tours adult/child US$45/30; ☼ 4:30pm Jan-May) provides daily trips aboard the sharp-looking, historic schooner *Roseway*. Added bonus: sailing with these folks supports their nonprofit group that teaches local students sailing and leadership skills. Departures are from Gallows Bay.

Hikers will love the guided ecowalks available. They depart from sites around the island; call or check the websites for schedules. Fees vary.

**St Croix Hiking Association** (www.stcroixhiking.org)
**St Croix Environmental Association** ( ☎ 773-1989; www.stxenvironmental.org) Offers bird-watching and snorkeling trips, too.
**Ay-Ay Eco-Hikes** ( ☎ 277-0410, 772-4079; eco@viaccess .net) Customized hikes.

## Tours

Several operators offer four-hour island tours (about US$45 per person) by van that go to the botanic garden (p384), rum factory (p383), Whim Plantation (p383), Frederiksted and Salt River. They depart from King St near Government House, and must be reserved in advance.

**Eagle Safari Tours** ( ☎ 778-3313; ☼ Mon-Sat)
**Rudy's Taxi Tours** ( ☎ 773-6803; ☼ Mon-Sat)
**Sweeney's Safari Tour** ( ☎ 773-6700, 800-524-2026; ☼ Mon-Fri)

## Festivals & Events

**St Patrick's Day** Cruzans go all out with a parade in Christiansted on March 17.
**St Croix Half-Ironman Triathlon** ( ☎ 773-4470; www .stcroixtriathlon.com) Participants strive for Ironman qualification in early May.
**Danish West Indies Emancipation Day** Cruzans celebrate on July 3 with a holiday from work, beach parties, family gatherings and plenty of fireworks over Christiansted's harbor.
**Cruzan Christmas Fiesta** ( ☎ 773-0495) From early December to early January, it's a month of pageants, parades and calypso competitions, putting a West Indies spin on the Christmas holidays.

## Sleeping

Tax is an additional 18%, and some places tack on an energy surcharge (about US$4). Prices listed below are winter high-season rates.

**King Christian Hotel** ( ☎ 773-6330, 800-524-2012; www.kingchristian.com; 59 Kings Wharf; r US$110-145; ☒ ☐ ☎ ) You can't miss this three-story, sand-colored building that looks like a Danish warehouse (which it was 200 years ago) right next to the National Park Service sites. The 39 rooms are typical midrange, flowery-bedspread types. They're fine, though you'll get a bigger bang for your buck at Hotel on the Cay. Offers wi-fi.

**our pick** **Hotel on the Cay** ( ☎ 773-2035, 800-524-2035; www.hotelonthecay.com; r from US$133; ☒ ☐ ☎ ) A truly cool place to stay, this hotel sits just offshore on its own little island called Protestant Cay (left), accessible by a three-minute ferry ride (free for guests). It's great value for the spacious rooms with full kitchenettes, cooking utensils and bright furnishings. The pièce de résistance: private balconies for taking in cool breezes, hearing waves lap the shore and watching pelicans dive-bomb for fish.

**Pink Fancy** ( ☎ 773-8460, 800-524-2045; www.pink fancy.com; 27 Prince St; r incl breakfast US$140-185; ☒ ☐ ☎ ) Sprawling through a historic 1780 Danish town house, this 13-room B&B was opened by a Ziegfeld Follies showgirl years ago. It retains a flamboyant, whimsical charm, its exterior painted sky blue with pink shutters, and its rooms outfitted with walnut floors, antiques and kitchenettes. It's on a quiet street away from the harbor, and wins serious praise from its repeat patrons. Offers wi-fi.

**Hotel Caravelle** ( ☎ 773-0687, 800-524-0410; www .hotelcaravelle.com; 44A Queen Cross St; r US$145-175; ☒ ☎ ) Located on the waterfront, this 43-room

**DIVING ST CROIX**

If you are a scuba enthusiast worth your sea salt, you'll be spending lots of time underwater in St Croix. It's a diver's mecca thanks to two unique features: one, it's surrounded by a massive barrier reef, so turtles, rays and other sea creatures are prevalent; and, two, a spectacular wall runs along the island's north shore, dropping at a 60-degree slope to a depth of more than 12,000ft. It gives a true look into 'the deep,' and there's nothing quite like it anywhere in the world.

The best dives on the north shore are at Cane Bay Drop-Off, North Star Wall and Salt River Canyon. The top west island dives are at the Butler Bay ship wrecks and Frederiksted Pier. While almost all dive operators offer boat dives, many of the most exciting dives, such as Cane Bay, involve beach entries with short swims to the reef.

The operators listed here go to the various sites and charge about US$65 for one-tank dives and about US$90 for two tanks (including equipment).

**Anchor Dive Center** ( ☎ 778-1522, 800-532-3483; www.anchordivestcroix.com; Columbus Cove) Specializes in dives in Salt River Canyon (where the shop is located).

**Cane Bay Dive Shop** ( ☎ 773-9913, 800-338-3843; www.canebayscuba.com) A friendly five-star PADI facility, across the highway from the beach and the Cane Bay Drop-Off, and with shops in both Christiansted and Frederiksted.

**Dive Experience** ( ☎ 773-3307, 800-235-9047; www.divexp.com; 1111 Strand St) This woman-owned shop has a strong environmental commitment and offers 'green' diving courses. The shop is in Christiansted.

**Scuba West** ( ☎ 772-3701, 800-352-0107; www.divescubawest.com; 12 Strand St) Specializes in west island dives, including awesome night dives on Frederiksted Pier (located across from the shop).

**St Croix Ultimate Bluewater Adventures** ( ☎ 773-5994, 887-567-1367; www.stcroixscuba.com; 14 Caravelle Arcade) Another ultra-professional company that dives all over the island; the shop is in Christiansted but the company will transport guests to Frederiksted.

property is similar in spirit to, though a bit fancier than, the King Christian Hotel. The more expensive rooms have harbor views. You can also get a harbor view by heading out to the pool and sundeck.

## Eating & Drinking

Note that the lower-priced places accept cash only.

**our pick** **Avocado Pit** ( ☎ 773-9843; 59 Kings Wharf; mains US$4-9; ⓥ breakfast & lunch) Young staff pour strong coffee and fruity smoothies at this wee café overlooking the fort and harbor. The granola-and-yogurt wins raves for breakfast, while the wraps (spicy tuna, tofu or avocado) make a delicious lunch or Buck Island picnic fare.

**Lalita** ( ☎ 719-4417; 54 King St; mains US$6-10; ⓥ breakfast & lunch) Health-food nuts and vegans: this is your place, serving everything from organic muesli to seaweed salad to hummus plates. Lalita's bulletin board is a good resource for yoga and other healing art classes; there's also wi-fi if you want to check your email.

**Singh's Fast Food** ( ☎ 773-7357; 238 King St; mains US$6-12; ⓥ lunch & dinner) When the roti craving strikes – and it will – Singh's will satiate with its multiple meat and tofu varieties. The

steamy, four-table joint also serves shrimp, conch, goat, turkey and tofu stews – all while island music ricochets off the pastel walls.

**Luncheria** ( ☎ 773-4247; 6 Company St; mains US$7-10; ⓥ lunch & dinner Mon-Sat) This fun Mexican cantina will quench your desire for margaritas and burritos, whether you order them to go or to eat in at the laid-back, shaded courtyard.

**Kim's Restaurant** ( ☎ 773-3377; 45 King St; mains US$9-12; ⓥ lunch & dinner) Come here for dynamite West Indian cooking and friendly conversation with cook and manager 'Big Kim.' The ambience is simple with peach-and-white tablecloths and a courtyard; the menu is written on a dry-erase board. Try the curried chicken or Creole-style conch, both served with rice and salad.

**Fort Christian Brew Pub** ( ☎ 713-9820; Kings Wharf at King's Alley; sandwiches US$8-13, dinner mains US$17-23; ⓥ lunch & dinner) Right on the boardwalk overlooking yachts bobbing in the sea, this open-air pub is primo for sampling the VI Brewing Company's small-batch suds. The New Orleans–style menu features jambalaya and spicy shrimp étouffée (a delicious tomato-based stew).

**Tutto Bene** ( ☎ 773-5229; 2006 Eastern Suburb; mains US$17-30; ⓥ dinner) There's no West Indian ambience and no ocean view, but that's not the

US VIRGIN ISLANDS

point at Tutto Bene. It stands apart by cooking traditional Italian food that will rock your world. Generous portions of fish, chicken and meat mains and creative pasta dishes are served in a sophisticated yet casual room. It's located 0.5 miles east of town.

## NORTH SHORE
Dramatic slopes, Chris Columbus' landing pad and hot dive sites await along the north shore.

About 4 miles west of Christiansted on Rte 80, the **Salt River Bay National Historic Park** is the only documented place where Christopher Columbus washed ashore on US soil. Don't expect bells and whistles; the site remains undeveloped beach. The 700 acres surrounding the Salt River estuary is an ecological reserve. The best way to see its mangroves and egrets is by kayak with **Caribbean Adventure Tours** ( ☎ 778-1522, 800-532-3483; www.stcroixkayak.com; 2½hr-tour US$45), located at the Salt River Marina on the bay's west side.

Sand seekers hit palm-fringed **Hibiscus Beach**, with good snorkeling and amenities, less than 2 miles west of Christiansted off Rte 75. **Cane Bay**, a long, thin strand along Rte 80 about 9 miles west of Christiansted, is also deservedly venerated. Cane Bay provides easy access to some of the island's best dives, and it's also the gateway into the rainforest's steep hills. The beach has several small hotels, restaurants, bars and the Cane Bay Dive Shop (opposite).

### Sleeping
The lodgings here are more casual than glamorous. The Cane Bay properties have onsite restaurants.

**our pick Inn at Salt River** ( ☎ 772-1684; www.arawakbaysaltriver.co.vi; 62 Salt River Rd; r incl breakfast US$140; 🅿 🖳 ) The pick of the local litter, this peachy B&B opened in 2007 and has 14 bright rooms, each with different color schemes and decor. For those without a vehicle, it's isolated from the beaches and eateries, but the owners make amends by providing daily transportation to Christiansted and Cane Bay. Offers wi-fi.

**Waves at Cane Bay** ( ☎ 778-1805, 800-545-0603; www.canebaystcroix.com; North Shore Rd; r US$140-155; 🅿 🖳 ) This small, tidy hotel has decent rooms (the owners continue a long, slow remodeling process). But it's really all about location: you can snorkel or dive right off the rocks out front.

**Cane Bay Reef Club** ( ☎ 778-2966, 800-253-8534; www.canebay.com; 114 North Shore Rd; r US$150-250; 🅿 🖳 ) This is good value because each of the nine rooms is like its own little villa overlooking the beach. The decor is dated but all suites include kitchens and private patios virtually hanging over the sea.

### Eating & Drinking
**Off the Wall** ( ☎ 778-4771; mains US$8-14; 🕙 lunch & dinner) After a day of diving at Cane Bay, climb out of the ocean and head to the beach's east end, where this open-air pub serves burgers, nachos and quesadillas to a happy crowd of drinkers.

**Lobster Reef Café** ( ☎ 719-9044; mains US$8-16; 🕙 lunch & dinner) For a pirate-meets-Gilligan's Island ambience, saunter over to Lobster Reef, where the namesake crustacean comes in fritter, salad, sandwich, bisque and grilled form. The café is 0.5 miles east of Cane Bay Beach.

## BUCK ISLAND REEF NATIONAL MONUMENT
For such small land mass – 1 mile long by 0.5 miles wide – Buck Island draws big crowds. It's not so much what's on top but what's underneath that fascinates: an 18,800-acre fish-frenzied coral reef system surrounding the island. The sea gardens and a marked underwater trail create first-rate **snorkeling** and shallow diving. Endangered hawksbill, leatherback and green sea turtles come ashore on the island's protected beaches. If you want to keep dry, a **hiking trail** circles the island's west end and leads to an impressive observation point.

Another reason to visit Buck Island is simply the trip itself. Visitors glide here aboard tour boats from Christiansted, 5 miles to the west. Most depart from Kings Wharf. Expect to pay US$50/85 (half/full day) per person, including snorkeling gear, with the following companies:

**Big Beard's Adventures** ( ☎ 773-4482; www.bigbeards.com; Queen Cross St by Kings Wharf) Trips are aboard catamaran sailboats.

**Caribbean Sea Adventures** ( ☎ 773-2628; www.caribbeanseaadventures.com; 59 Kings Wharf) Half-day trip is aboard a glass-bottom power boat; full-day trip is on a catamaran.

**Teroro II** ( ☎ 773-3161) A trimaran sailboat whose captain will entertain you completely; trips leave from Green Cay Marina, east of Christiansted.

## POINT UDALL & AROUND

Point Udall is the easternmost geographic point in the US territory. As you face into a 25-knot trade wind, the vista from the promontory high above the surf-strewn beaches is enough to make you hear symphonies. Others simply like the challenge of hiking the steep trails down the hillside to the isolated beaches on the south side of the point.

Some of St Croix's splashiest resorts take up the beachfront en route to Point Udall. **Divi Carina Bay Beach Resort** ( ☎ 773-9700, 877-773-9700; www.divicarina.com; 25 Estate Turner Hole, Grapetree Bay; r from US$245; 🅿 💻 🖥 ), on the southeast shore, draws visitors and locals alike. The former come to say at the 180 mod, wicker-furnished rooms. The latter come to win big at the island's only **casino** ( ☎ 773-1529).

## FREDERIKSTED

'Quiet' doesn't do Frederiksted justice. St Croix's second-banana town is utterly motionless, a patch of forsaken colonial buildings snoring beside a painted teal-blue sea. Once upon a time, cruise ships docked regularly at Frederiksted Pier, but high crime rates drove them away. Now they're starting to drift back (led by Disney, of all companies).

Other than the occasional boatload of visitors, it'll be you and that lizard sunning on the rock who will have this gritty outpost to yourselves. **Fort Frederik Beach** is the public strand just north of the old fort. When the prevailing trade winds blow, the beach remains as sheltered as a millpond; you can swim off it for excellent snorkeling around the pier. A couple of local dive shops (see p380) will facilitate your adventures.

With its out-of-the-mainstream, laissez-faire ambience, Frederiksted is the center for gay life on St Croix.

### Sleeping

**Frederiksted Hotel** ( ☎ 772-0500, 800-595-9519; www.frederikstedhotel.dk; 442 Strand St; r US$100-135; 🅿 💻 🖥 ) This Danish-owned, bright-blue hotel sits right smack downtown. Four floors are built around a courtyard and small pool, and many rooms have patios overlooking the pier. The 36 units each have tiled floors and standard hotel-style furnishings, plus a refrigerator.

**Sand Castle on the Beach** ( ☎ 772-1205, 800-524-2018; www.sandcastleonthebeach.com; 127 Estate Smithfield; r/ste incl breakfast from US$149/259; 🅿 🖥 ) Right on the beach about a mile south of Frederiksted, this establishment with 21 rooms is one of the few gay- and lesbian-oriented hotels in the USVIs. The motel-like rooms come with kitchenettes; most have sea views. There is also a video library and gas grills for cookouts, or you can have lunch or dinner at the oceanside restaurant aptly named the Beach Side Café.

### Eating

**Turtles** ( ☎ 772-3676; 37 Strand St; sandwiches US$7-9.50; 🕑 breakfast & lunch Mon-Sat) Chow your killer

---

### THE CRUX OF ST CROIX

Olasee Davis is an ecologist at the University of the Virgin Islands and a tour leader with **St Croix Hiking Association** (www.stcroixhiking.org). He's a lifelong Virgin Islander, and a resident of St Croix for more than 40 years.

**What's the biggest environmental issue facing St Croix today?**

Everything comes into the island, but it doesn't go back out. Abandoned cars are one of our biggest problems. They're left in the forest or bushes. We try to recycle them. Either we crush and ship the cars back to the US to be melted, or we make artificial reefs with them [after removing any harmful elements].

**What makes St Croix different from other islands?**

Our history and culture. We have historical structures all over the island, more probably than any other Caribbean island except Cuba. We have the buildings at Christiansted and Frederiksted, and more than 100 windmills. That's a lot for an 84-sq-mile area.

**What's your favorite place to hike?**

The north bay, at Annaly and Will Bay [by Hams Bluff] near Maroon Ridge. 'Maroons' were slaves who ran away from the plantations. They came here because the topography – the mountains and forest – made it difficult to for anyone to find them. It's no-man's-land. Some jumped off and killed themselves so as not to be recaptured. The virgin forest remains. It's an extremely historical and spiritual place.

sandwiches on homemade bread, or sip a fine cuppa coffee, at beachfront tables under sea-grape trees.

**Sunset Grill** ( ☎ 772-5855; sandwiches US$7-13, dinner mains US$17-33; ☺ lunch & dinner) Ahh, swing in beachfront hammocks while awaiting your fish and island dishes. Located 2 miles north of Frederiksted on Rte 63.

**Blue Moon** ( ☎ 772-2222; 17 Strand St; mains US$18-29; ☺ lunch Tue-Fri, dinner Tue-Sat, brunch Sun) Considered one of the best restaurants on the island, Blue Moon dishes up Caribbean, vegetarian and Cajun cuisine in a restored colonial warehouse. There's live jazz Wednesday and Friday nights.

**Le St Tropez** ( ☎ 772-3000; 227 King St; mains US$18-32; ☺ lunch Mon-Fri, dinner Mon-Sat) This *trés* authentic French bistro overflows with Mediterranean spirit and sophistication. Only 15 tables fill the intimate courtyard-terrace, which drips with the sound of Louis Armstrong and the scents of *coq au vin*. Good wines accompany it all.

## AROUND FREDERIKSTED

Many of the island's top sights surround Frederiksted. They cluster north of town in the rainforest, and south along Centerline Rd.

### Rainforest Area

In the island's wet, mountainous northwest pocket, a thick forest of tall mahogany, silk cotton and white cedar trees grow. Technically, as only about 40in of rain fall here per year, the **Caledonia Rainforest** is not a true 'rainforest.' No matter – it looks the part, with clouds, dripping trees and earthy aromas. Mahogany Rd (Rte 76) cuts through the spooky woods; it's twisty and pot-holed, so be careful.

Tucked into a steep hillside, about 20 minutes' drive from Frederiksted, is the unusual outdoor woodworking studio **St Croix Leap** ( ☎ 772-0421; Rte 76 Brooks Hill; ☺ 8:30am-5pm Mon-Fri, 10am-4pm Sat). Here, master sculptor 'Cheech' leads a band of apprentice woodworkers in transforming chunks of fallen mahogany.

The wild **Montpellier Domino Club** ( ☎ 772-9914) lies even deeper in the forest on Mahogany Rd. It's an open-air West Indian restaurant with live entertainment. But the big attraction is the famous beer-guzzling pigs: tourists line up to pay US$1 to watch pigs gnaw open cans of nonalcoholic brewskis and swill the contents. It's certainly not kosher (the animals live in confined pens), but you've never seen anything like it. The porkers used to drink the real thing until offspring were born suffering the symptoms of alcohol withdrawal.

**Paul & Jill's Equestrian Stables** ( ☎ 772-2880; www.paulandjills.com), 1.5 miles north of Frederiksted on Rte 63, offers trail rides that lead through hidden plantation ruins and the rainforest to hilltop vistas.

Hiking to **Hams Bluff** on the island's tiptop northwest corner unfurls views of sea-pounded cliffs; it's best to come with a guide (see p379).

Two ecologically minded lodgings have set up in the area. **Mt Victory Campground** ( ☎ 772-1651, 866-772-1651; www.mtvictorycamp.com; Rte 58; campsites/equipped tents/cottages US$30/85/95) is on a small working farm. The three perma-tents and two cottages are similar screened-in dwellings, each with a kitchen with cold-water sink, a propane stove and cooking utensils. There's no electricity, and guests share the solar-heated bathhouse. **Northside Valley** ( ☎ 772-0558, 877-772-0558; www.northsidevalley.com; 2 Estate Northside; villas per week US$800-1500) is a step up, offering five concrete-and-tile villas with private bathrooms and bamboo sheets, all washed using 'green' cleaning supplies. There is a one-week minimum stay. It's on the beach near Butler Bay.

### Centerline Road

Several sights lie south of Frederiksted on Centerline Rd (aka Rte 70).

#### ESTATE WHIM PLANTATION MUSEUM

Only a few of Whim Plantation's original 150 acres survive as this **museum** ( ☎ 772-0598; adult/child US$5/4; ☺ 10am-4pm Mon-Sat), but the grounds thoroughly evoke the colonial days when sugarcane ruled St Croix. Guided tours (adult/child US$10/4) leave every 30 minutes, or wander by the crumbling stone windmill and chimney on your own. Don't forget to ask for the Landmarks Society's map to other ruins around the island.

#### CRUZAN RUM DISTILLERY

To find out how does the islands' popular elixir gets made, stop by for a **distillery tour** ( ☎ 692-2280; www.cruzanrum.com; 3 Estate Diamond; adult/child US$4/1; ☺ 9:30-11:30am & 1-4pm Mon-Fri). The journey through gingerbread-smelling (from molasses and yeast), oak-barrel–stacked warehouses takes 20 minutes, after which you get to sip the good stuff. The factory is about 2 miles east of Whim Plantation.

US VIRGIN ISLANDS

**ST GEORGE VILLAGE BOTANICAL GARDEN**
Continuing east on Centerline Rd, you'll get to these **gardens** ( ☎ 692-2874; adult/child US$8/1; ☑ 9am-5pm). The 16-acre park built over a colonial sugar plantation does for the flora and fauna what Whim Plantation does for the grandeur of plantation days. More than 1500 native and exotic species grow on the grounds. Orchid-lovers, in particular, are in for a treat.

# DIRECTORY

## ACCOMMODATIONS

Staying in the USVIs can be downright expensive. However, hotels are at the mercy of the tourism traffic so, if you travel in the low or shoulder seasons, rates can drop as much as 40%. Many properties have three-night minimum stay requirements in the high season, December 15 through April 30. An 8% hotel tax plus a 10% service charge typically are added to bills.

If you're planning on staying a while, you might want to look into renting a condo or villa. Besides **Craigslist** (http://caribbean.craigslist.org) and the **VI Daily News** (www.virginislanddailynews.com), which both have listings throughout the USVIs, **McLaughlin Anderson Villas** ( ☎ 774-2790, 800-537-6246; www.mclaughlineanderson.com) rents on all the islands. For St Thomas– and St John–specific rentals, see p367 and p373, respectively.

## ACTIVITIES
### Diving & Snorkeling

Diving and snorkeling in the USVIs are superb, with warm water temperatures and incredible visibility. St Thomas (p369) and St John (p373) feature near-shore fringing reefs. St Croix sits atop its own narrow bank and divers can explore sheer walls encrusted with corals. Snorkelers can step in the water almost anywhere and find plenty of tropical fish, sea turtles, even nurse sharks. See p380 for more on St Croix diving.

### Fishing
The USVIs host several deep-sea fishing tournaments. Marlin is a spring/summer fish, sailfish and wahoo run in fall, and dorado show up in winter. Charters run out of American Yacht Harbor in Red Hook, St Thomas.

### Hiking
The most popular stomping grounds are in Virgin Islands National Park on St John (see p372). St Croix has guided ecohikes (p379).

### Sailing
Several companies sail the USVIs' turquoise seas, though it's not as big a deal here as in the British Virgin Islands. Still, day sails are popular from Red Hook (p370) on St Thomas, and to Buck Island (p381) from St Croix.

These companies offer multiday yacht charters from St Thomas:

**CYOA Yacht Charters** ( ☎ 777-9690, 800-944-2962; www.cyoacharters.com; Frenchtown Marina) Bareboat, ie do-it-yourself sailing.

**Island Yacht Charters** ( ☎ 775-6666, 800-524-2019; www.iyc.vi; American Yacht Harbor) Provides bareboat and crewed boats.

**Virgin Islands Charterboat League** ( ☎ 774-3944, 800-524-2061; www.vicl.org) Offers crewed boats.

---

### PRACTICALITIES

- **Newspapers & Magazines** The *VI Daily News* and *St Croix Avis* are the daily papers. *St Thomas/St John This Week* (www.stthomasthisweek.com) and *St Croix This Week* (www.stcroixthisweek.com) are invaluable resources providing local maps, entertainment listings, taxi rates and cruise-ship schedules. They're free and available at most businesses.

- **Radio & TV** The USVIs have two TV stations (channel 8 and 12) and several radio stations. WSTA-AM 1340 airs island music and talk.

- **Electricity** 110 volts; North American–style plugs have two (flat) or three (two flat, one round) pins.

- **Weights & Measures** Imperial system. Distances are in feet and miles; gasoline is measured in gallons.

- **Drugs** Pharmacies require prescriptions for common drugs such as antibiotics.

## Surfing & Windsurfing

In general, winter is the best surfing season, when swells roll in from the northeast and set up point breaks of 6ft and higher at places such as Hull Bay (p367). It's best to bring your own board, though you can rent equipment at Hull Bay and at Vessup Beach (p369).

The skimboarding community is starting to grow. Check St Thomas-based **Skim Caribbean** (www.skimprimary.com) for hot spots.

## BOOKS

Two recent books are *Musings of an Island Girl* by Henrita Barber, which collects essays she wrote as a *VI Daily News* columnist; and *Adrift on a Sea of Blue Light* by Peter Muilenburg, offering graceful tales of life at sea by a long-time St John boat captain.

Birders should check out *A Guide to the Birds of Puerto Rico & the Virgin Islands*, by Herbert Rafaela. Shell collectors should pick up *A Field Guide to Shells: Atlantic and Gulf Coasts and the West Indies* by R Tucker Abbott and Percy A Morris.

## BUSINESS HOURS

General USVIs business hours are listed here. Many places close on Sunday.

**Banks** 9am to 3pm Monday to Thursday, to 5pm Friday
**Bars & pubs** noon to midnight
**Government offices** 8am to 5pm Monday to Friday
**Post offices** 7:30am to 4:30pm Monday to Friday, 8:30am to noon Saturday
**Restaurants** breakfast 7am to 11am, brunch 10am-2pm, lunch 11am to 2pm, dinner 5pm to 9pm
**Shops** 9am to 5pm Monday to Saturday

## CHILDREN

The USVIs are a welcoming destination for children, with opportunities for swimming, hiking and sea creature touching at Coral World (p368). Many resorts have children's programs and babysitting services.

**Caribbean Nanny Care** ( 473-7500; www.caribbean nannyservices.com) offers babysitting services by trained, professional nannies. They will come to your hotel or take the kids off your hands for about US$30 per hour (minimum four hours). The group also rents out gear such as car seats, strollers and baby monitors.

## DANGERS & ANNOYANCES

St Thomas and St Croix both have reputations for crime, mostly robbery and petty theft. If you lock up your belongings and avoid walking alone at night, you should be fine.

Pesky mosquitoes bite throughout the islands, so slather on insect repellent.

## EMBASSIES & CONSULATES

With the exception of those listed here, there are no foreign embassies or consulates in the US Virgin Islands.

**Denmark** ( 776-0656; Scandinavian Center, Havensight Mall, Bldg 3; Charlotte Amalie, St Thomas)
**Sweden** ( 774-6845; 1340 Taarneberg; Charlotte Amalie, St Thomas)

## FESTIVALS & EVENTS

Larger events are listed here; see Festivals & Events sections for individual islands in this chapter for more.

**International Rolex Cup Regatta** ( 775-6320; www.rolexcupregatta.com) World-class racing boats gather at St Thomas for this three-day event in late March or earl April.

**St Thomas Carnival** ( 776-3112) Stemming from West African masquerading traditions, the St Thomas Carnival in late April is the second-largest carnival in the Caribbean after the one at Port-of-Spain, Trinidad.

**St John Carnival** ( 776-6450) A smaller version of the St Thomas Carnival, held in early July.

**Cruzan Christmas Fiesta** ( 773-0495) Puts a West Indies spin on the winter holidays (early December to early January), with pageants, parades and calypso competitions.

## GAY & LESBIAN TRAVELERS

Gays and lesbians have been some of the islands' most prominent entrepreneurs and politicians for decades. Sadly, however, the climate of 'don't ask, don't tell' still permeates. Of the three islands, St Croix is the most 'gay friendly,' with Frederiksted the center of gay life, but overall there aren't many structured outlets for meeting. One exception is Sand Castle on the Beach (p382), in Frederiksted.

## HOLIDAYS

Islanders celebrate US public holidays along with local holidays. Banks, schools and government offices are closed, and transportation, museums and other services are on shorter schedules.

**New Year's Day** January 1
**Three Kings Day** (Feast of the Epiphany) January 6
**Martin Luther King Jr's Birthday** Third Monday in January
**Presidents' Day** Third Monday in February
**Holy Thursday & Good Friday** Before Easter

**Easter & Easter Monday** Late March or early April
**Memorial Day** Last Monday in May
**Emancipation Day** July 3 – island slaves were freed on this date in 1873
**Independence Day** (Fourth of July) July 4
**Supplication Day** In July (date varies)
**Labor Day** First Monday in September
**Columbus Day** Second Monday in October
**Liberty Day** November 1
**Veterans' Day** November 11
**Thanksgiving Day** Fourth Thursday in November
**Christmas Day & Boxing Day** December 25 and 26

## INTERNET ACCESS

The US Virgin Islands' main towns have internet cafés, which you'll find listed under the chapter's Information sections. Rates are about US$3 to US$5 per half hour. A fair number of hotels also offer free wi-fi access for guests.

## INTERNET RESOURCES

**Entrée** (www.entreevi.com) Restaurant reviews throughout the USVIs.
**Gotostcroix.com** (www.gotostcroix.com) Useful trip-planning resource.
**St Croix This Week** (www.stcroixthisweek.com) Online version of the free magazine.
**United States Virgin Islands** (www.usvitourism.vi) USVIs Department of Tourism's official website.
**Virgin Islands This Week** (www.virginislandsthisweek.com) Online version of the ubiquitous weekly *St Thomas/St John This Week* magazine.
**Virgin Islands Travel** (www.usviguide.com) Accommodations, activity and transportation information separated by island.

## MAPS

Many businesses offer free fold-out maps of the various islands and their main towns. The widely available free tourist magazines *St Thomas/St John This Week* and *St Croix This Week* also have maps inside.

## MEDICAL SERVICES

You can receive medical care at facilities in Charlotte Amalie (p364), Cruz Bay (p371) and Christiansted (p378).

## MONEY

The US dollar is used throughout the USVIs. You'll find FirstBank, Scotiabank and Banco Popular in the main towns, with ATMs hooked into worldwide networks (Plus, Cirrus, Exchange etc).

## POST

The USVIs use the same postal system and mail rates as the United States. It costs US$0.42 to mail a 1oz letter within the country, US$0.72 to mail it to Canada or Mexico and US$0.94 for other international destinations.

## TELEPHONE

The USVIs' country code is ☎ 340, but you just dial the seven-digit local number on the islands. To call from North America, dial ☎ 1-340 + the local number. From elsewhere, dial your country's international dialing code + ☎ 340 + the local number. We've included only the seven-digit local number in USVIs listings in this chapter.

Pay phones are easy to find in commercial areas. Local calls cost US$0.35.

AT&T and Sprint provide the islands' cellular service. Phones that work in the US will work on the islands, often with no extra fee, but check with your provider. As in the US, it's very difficult to find SIM cards.

## TOURIST INFORMATION

The **USVI Department of Tourism** ( ☎ 800-372-8784; www.usvitourism.vi) posts loads of information on its website. It will also send you hard-copy materials. Or stop in at the visitors center on St Croix or St John.
**St Croix** ( ☎ 773-1460; ☉ 10am-5pm) In Christiansted's historic Scale House.
**St John** ( ☎ 776-6450; ☉ 8am-5pm Mon-Fri) In Cruz Bay, next to the post office.

## TRAVELERS WITH DISABILITIES

The Americans With Disabilities Act holds sway in the USVIs, so accessibility is decent. **Dial-A-Ride** (776-1277) helps with transportation needs on St Thomas. **Gimp on the Go** (www.gimponthego.com/dest5a.htm) reviews St John's accessibility. St John's Concordia Eco-Tents (p377) provide well-regarded accessible lodging.

## VISAS

Under the terms of the State Department's Visa Waiver Program, visitors from most

**EMERGENCY NUMBERS**

- **Ambulance** ☎ 911
- **Police** ☎ 911
- **Fire** ☎ 911

Western countries do not need a visa to enter the USVIs if they are staying less than 90 days. If you are staying longer, or if your home country does not qualify under the Visa Waiver Program (check www.united statesvisas.gov), you'll need to obtain a B-2 visa (US$131), which you can get at any US embassy.

## WOMEN TRAVELERS

It's safe for women to travel solo in the USVIs. Just use the same degree of caution you would in a big city at home: be aware of your surroundings and don't walk alone at night in unfamiliar areas.

## WORK

US citizens can work legally in the USVIs without any red tape, but it's difficult for travelers of other nationalities to get legal work here. Foreigners need a work visa, and securing one without a sponsor (meaning an employer) is nearly impossible. Contact your embassy or consulate for more information.

# TRANSPORTATION

## GETTING THERE & AWAY
### Entering the US Virgin Islands

Americans do not need a passports to visit the US Virgin Islands, but all other nationalities do. When departing the USVIs, Americans will be asked to show photo identification (such as a driver's license) and proof of US citizenship (such as a birth certificate). If traveling to any other Caribbean country (besides Puerto Rico, which, like the USVIs, is a US territory), Americans must have a valid passport in order to re-enter the US.

### Air

The USVIs have two airports.
**Cyril E King Airport** (STT; ☎ 774-5100; www.viport .com/avifacilities.html) St Thomas' modern facility (with two bare-bones restaurants, a shop and ATM), where most USVIs flights arrive and depart.
**Henry E Rohlsen Airport** (STX; ☎ 778-0589; www .viport.com/avifacilities.html) St Croix's small facility on the island's southwest side.

Almost all flights to the USVIs from outside the Caribbean either originate in or transit

through the US (including Puerto Rico) via these airlines:
**American Airlines** ( ☎ 800-433-7300; www.aa.com) Miami, New York, San Juan
**Continental Airlines** ( ☎ 800-523-3273; www.continen tal.com) Houston, Newark, San Juan
**Delta Airlines** ( ☎ 800-221-1212; www.delta.com) Atlanta, New York
**Northwest Airlines** ( ☎ 800-225-2525; www.nwa.com) Detroit, San Juan
**Spirit Airlines** ( ☎ 800-772-7117; www.spiritair.com) Fort Lauderdale
**United Airlines** ( ☎ 800-241-6522; www.united.com) Charlotte, Chicago
**US Airways** ( ☎ 800-428-4322; www.usairways.com) Charlotte

The following airlines fly to/from the USVIs from within the Caribbean:
**Air Sunshine** ( ☎ 888-879-8900, 800-327-8900; www .airsunshine.com) San Juan
**Cape Air** ( ☎ 800-352-0714; www.flycapeair.com) San Juan
**Liat** ( ☎ 774-2313; www.liatairline.com) Antigua
**Seaborne Airlines** ( ☎ 773-6442, 888-359-8687; www .seaborneairlines.com) St Thomas

### Sea
#### CRUISE SHIP

St Thomas is the most popular cruise ship destination in the Caribbean, with more than 1000 arrivals each year. These ships pull in to the West Indian Company dock in Havensight on the eastern edge of St Thomas Harbor, and to Crown Bay Marina to the west.

See p830 for more information.

#### FERRY
#### US Virgin Islands to British Virgin Islands

There are excellent ferry connections linking St Thomas and St John with Tortola, Virgin Gorda and Jost Van Dyke. *St Thomas/St John This Week* magazine prints the full timetables. You must have a valid passport to travel between the USVIs and British Virgin Islands.

Ferries travel several times daily from Charlotte Amalie (St Thomas) to Road Town (Tortola), often via West End (Tortola). Costs are similar (round trip US$49, 60 minutes); departures are from Charlotte Amalie's Marine Terminal.
**Native Son** ( ☎ 774-8685; www.nativesonbvi.com)
**Road Town Fast Ferry** ( ☎ 777-2800; www.roadtown fastferry.com)
**Smith's Ferry** ( ☎ 775-7292; www.smithsferry.com)

Ferries also travel from Red Hook (St Thomas) to the British Virgin Islands. **Inter-Island** ( ☎ 776-6597) goes to Jost Van Dyke on Friday, Saturday and Sunday (round trip US$50, 45 minutes); and to Virgin Gorda Thursday and Sunday (round trip US$60, 75 minutes). Native Son runs between Red Hook and Tortola (West End) four to five times daily (round trip US$45, 30 minutes). Inter-Island ferries also travel from Cruz Bay (St John) to West End (Tortola) three times daily (round trip US$45, 30 minutes).

### US Virgin Islands to Puerto Rico

**Transportation Services** ( ☎ 776-6282) used to operate a ferry twice a month from Charlotte Amalie's waterfront to Fajardo, Puerto Rico (round trip US$100, two hours). At press time, the service had been discontinued, but it may start up again.

### YACHT

Lots of yachts drift into the USVIs. Many pull into American Yacht Harbor in Red Hook, St Thomas. The bars and restaurants here are good places to enquire about hitching a ride as a crew member.

## GETTING AROUND
## Air

You have two choices for air travel within the USVIs:

**Cape Air** ( ☎ 800-352-0714; www.flycapeair.com) Flies between St Thomas' and St Croix's airports.

**Seaborne Airlines** ( ☎ 773-6442, 888-359-8687; www .seaborneairlines.com) Flies seaplanes between the downtown harbors of Charlotte Amalie, St Thomas and Christiansted, St Croix (one way US$85, 25 minutes). Flights depart almost every hour for the brilliant, convenient (no taxis needed!) ride. Be aware there's a baggage restriction of 30lb (16kg) and it costs US$1 per extra pound.

## Boat

The islands have frequent and inexpensive ferry services. Schedules are printed in the free *St Thomas/St John This Week* magazine; most businesses carry copies.

### ST THOMAS TO ST CROIX

**VI Seatrans** ( ☎ 776-5494; www.goviseatrans.com; round trip US$90; 90min) operates a year-round passenger ferry between St Thomas and St Croix. It sails Friday through Monday, twice each day. From St Thomas it departs from Charlotte Amalie's Marine Terminal. From St Croix

it leaves from the Gallows Bay terminal in Christiansted. Look for humpback whales during winter crossings.

### ST THOMAS TO ST JOHN

A ferry departs Red Hook for Cruz Bay (one way US$5, 20 minutes) at 6:30am and 7:30am, then hourly from 8am to midnight daily. It departs Cruz Bay hourly from 6am to 11pm daily.

The ferry service between Charlotte Amalie and Cruz Bay (one way US$10, 45 minutes) departs Charlotte Amalie at 9am, 11am, 1pm, 3pm, 4pm and 5:30pm daily, and Cruz Bay at 7:15am, 9:15am, 11:15am, 1:15pm, 2:15pm and 3:45pm daily. In Charlotte Amalie, catch the ferry at the waterfront, at the foot of Raadet's Gade.

**Boyson, Inc** ( ☎ 776-6294) runs car ferries between Red Hook and Enighed Pond beside Cruz Bay (round trip US$50, 20 minutes), with sailings almost every hour between 6am and 7pm.

## Bus

**Vitran** ( ☎ 774-5678) operates air-conditioned buses over the length of St Thomas, St John and St Croix. Fares are US$1 and buses run daily between 5:30am and 7:30pm (approximately one bus per hour).

## Car

Driving is the most convenient way to get around individual islands, but be prepared for unique driving conditions. First, driving is on the left-hand side of the road, and the steering column is on the left also. You'll see signs reminding you to 'keep your shoulder to the shoulder' and 'stay left!'. Island roads are narrow, steep, twisting and often pot-holed, and stray cows, goats and chickens constantly wander onto them.

Many of the major international car-rental companies operate in the US Virgin Islands, along with plenty of local firms. Most car-rental companies require that, if you rent a car, you must be at least 21, have a major credit card and a valid driver's license. Rental companies have desks at the St Thomas and St Croix airports.

High-season rates begin at about US$60 per day and can run as high as US$100, but you'll get a better price for a weekly rental. See the Getting Around section for each island in this chapter for car-rental agencies.

US VIRGIN ISLANDS

## Taxi

Territorial law requires that taxi drivers carry a government-set rate sheet, and those rates are published in the free *St Thomas/St John This Week* or *St Croix This Week*.

Many taxis are open-air pickup trucks with bench seats and awnings, able to carry 12 or so passengers. To hail one, stand by the side of the road and wave when the vehicle approaches.

# British Virgin Islands

What happens when steady trade winds meet an island-flecked channel with tame currents and hundreds of protected, salt-rimmed bays? Every mariner worth his sea salt sails there – which is how the British Virgin Islands (BVIs) became a sailing fantasyland. More than 40 islands bob in the group, welcoming visitors with an absurd amount of beach.

Tortola is the archipelago's father. It holds most of the population and commerce, and its demeanor is a little bit stern as a result. That doesn't mean it won't let its hair down at a full-moon party or out on the bay windsurfing. Virgin Gorda is the BVIs' beauty, beloved by movie stars, millionaires and yachties. Somehow she's maintained her innocence, with a clutch of exceptional national parks. Jost Van Dyke is the jovial island, where a man named Foxy is king and 'time flies when you ain't doin' shit,' as the T-shirts proclaim. Not-like-the-others Anegada floats in a remote reef; if you're looking to get away from it all, this atoll has a hammock waiting. Then there are the sprinkling of out islands – some uninhabited, some with just a beach bar, some with shipwrecks to dive on. You'll need your own boat to reach them, but since the BVIs are the world's charter-boat capital, you're in luck.

While the islands are British territories, there's little that's overtly British. The BVIs are quite close to, and intermingled with, the US Virgin Islands, though the BVIs are more virginal as far as development goes.

---

**FAST FACTS**

- **Area** 59 sq miles
- **Capital** Road Town, Tortola
- **Country code** ☎ 284
- **Departure tax** US$5 by sea (cruise ship passengers pay US$7); US$15 by air (plus US$5 security tax)
- **Famous for** Yacht charters, the Baths, Pusser's Rum, local resident Richard Branson
- **Language** English
- **Money** US dollar (US$); US$1 = €0.65 = UK£0.51
- **Official name** Virgin Islands, but it's referred to as 'British Virgin Islands' to distinguish it from the neighboring US Virgin Islands
- **People** British Virgin Islanders
- **Phrase** Limin' (pronounced 'lime-in'; means 'relaxing')
- **Population** 23,500
- **Visa** Unnecessary for citizens of most Western countries; see p415

# HIGHLIGHTS

- **Devil's Bay** (p405) Climb up, over and around sea boulders and grottoes to this sheltered sand crescent
- **White Bay** (p409) Drink at the jovial beach that birthed the rum-soaked Painkiller
- **Anegada** (p410) Leave the world behind on this remote island of hammocks and lobster dinners
- **RMS Rhone** (p398) Scuba dive on this famous shipwreck off Salt Island
- **Set Sail** (p416) Charter a boat and sail to out islands like Norman and Cooper

# ITINERARIES

- **One Day** Take one of the quick and frequent ferries to Virgin Gorda, splash around the Baths and Devil's Bay, grab a meal and drink before calling it a day.
- **One Week** Spend a day or two beaching in Tortola's Cane Garden Bay area, then ferry to Virgin Gorda to hike, snorkel and swim for a couple more. Spend two days slowing waaay down on either Jost or Anegada. Take a day-sail tour to the out islands.
- **Two Weeks** Island hop: hit the four main islands, plus nearby St Thomas and St John in the US Virgin Islands, by ferry. Or get adventurous and charter a boat to explore them all (including the out islands).
- **On a Budget** Yes, it can be done. Camp at Brewers Bay on Tortola, White Bay on Jost or Anegada Reef Hotel on Anegada. Buy low-cost take-away foods at Road Town Bakery on Tortola, Christine's Bakery on Jost and Dotsy's Bakery on Anegada. Spend your days on beaches (free) or at national parks (admission US$3). Use ferries for transportation.

## CLIMATE & WHEN TO GO

Reliably balmy with gentle trade winds, the BVIs' temperature averages 77°F (25°C) in winter (December through March) and 83°F (28°C) in summer (June through August). Though the islands get less than 50 inches of rain each year, count on brief tropical showers between July and November. Hurricane season peaks in August and September (mostly the latter).

The BVIs' high travel season is from December 15 to April 15. November, early December and May are good times to visit too, as hotel prices are lower and the cruise ships are fewer.

## HISTORY
### Columbus & the Pirates

On Christopher Columbus' second trip to the Caribbean in 1493, Caribs led him to an archipelago of pristine islands that he dubbed Santa Ursula y Las Once Mil Vírgenes (St Ursula and the 11,000 Virgins), in honor of a 4th-century princess raped and murdered, along with 11,000 maidens, in Cologne by marauding Huns.

By 1595, the famous English privateers Sir Francis Drake and Jack Hawkins were using the Virgin Islands as a staging ground for attacks on Spanish shipping. In the wake of Drake and Hawkins came French corsairs and Dutch freebooters. All knew that the Virgin Islands had some of the most secure and unattended harbors in the West Indies. Places like Sopers Hole (p399) at Tortola's West End and the Bight at Norman Island (p404) are legendary pirates' dens.

While the Danes settled on what is now the US Virgin Islands (USVIs), the English had a firm hold on today's BVIs. The middle island of St John remained disputed territory until 1717, when the Danish side claimed it for good. The Narrows between St John and Tortola has divided the eastern Virgins (BVIs) from the western Virgins (USVIs) for more than 250 years.

### Queen Elizabeth & the Offshore Companies

Following WWII, British citizens in the islands clamored for more independence. In 1949 BVIs citizens demonstrated for a representative government and got a so-called presidential legislature the next year. By 1967 the BVIs had become an independent colony of Britain, with its own political parties, a Legislative Council and an elected Premier (with elections every four years). Queen Elizabeth II also made her first royal visit to the BVIs in 1967, casting a glow of celebrity on the islands that they enjoy to this day. Royal family members still cruise through every few years.

In the mid-1980s the government had the shrewd idea of offering offshore registration to companies wishing to incorporate in the islands. Incorporation fees – along with tourism – now prop up the economy, with

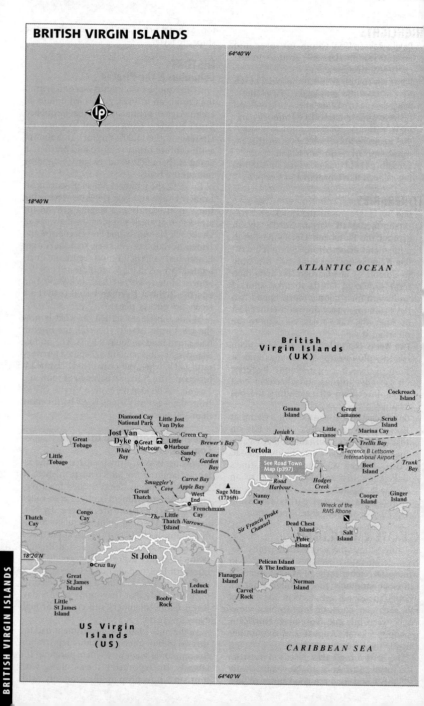

# BRITISH VIRGIN ISLANDS

64°40'W

18°40'N

ATLANTIC OCEAN

British
Virgin Islands
(UK)

Cockroach
Island

Great
Camanoe

Scrub
Island

Guana
Island

Little
Camanoe

Marina Cay

Diamond Cay
National Park

Little Jost
Van Dyke

Green Cay

Josiah's
Bay

Trellis Bay

Jost Van
Dyke

Great
Harbour

Little
Harbour

Brewer's Bay

Terrence B Lettsome
International Airport

White
Bay

Sandy
Cay

Cane
Garden
Bay

Tortola

Beef
Island

Trunk
Bay

Great
Tobago

See Road Town
Map (p397)

Little
Tobago

Carrot Bay
Apple Bay

Road
Harbour

Hodges
Creek

Smuggler's
Cove

West
End

Sage Mtn
(1716ft)

Cooper
Island

Ginger
Island

Great
Thatch

Frenchmans
Cay

Nanny
Cay

Wreck of the
RMS Rhone

Thatch
Cay

Congo
Cay

The
Little
Thatch
Island

Narrows

Sir Francis Drake
Channel

Dead Chest
Island

Salt
Island

St John

Peter
Island

18°20'N

Cruz Bay

Great
St James
Island

Leduck
Island

Flanagan
Island

Pelican Island
& The Indians

Norman
Island

Little
St James
Island

Booby
Rock

Carvel
Rock

US Virgin
Islands
(US)

CARIBBEAN SEA

64°40'W

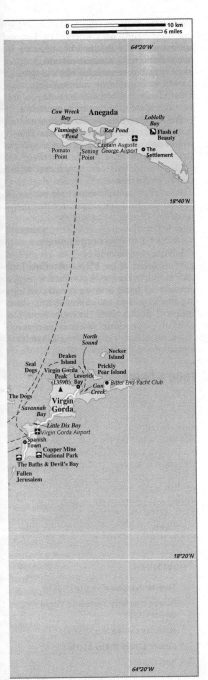

about 750,000 companies currently registered. Locals laughingly call their booming financial services industry 'legal money laundering,' and while that's not quite the case (although odd, one must admit, that of the 750,000 companies on the books, only 10,000 of them actually trade in the BVIs), it does create an unusual island economy infused with foreign accountants, trust lawyers and investment brokers.

## THE CULTURE

Despite their name, apart from little touches like Cadbury chocolate, the culture of the British Virgin Islands is West Indian to the core. The population is a mix of professional people working in financial services, folks working the tourist trade or raising livestock, and adventurers whose biochemistry is intricately tied to the seas. The official ethnic breakdown is 87% black, 7% white and the remainder mixed, East Indian or other.

The BVIs have one of the Caribbean's most stable economies. The per capita GDP is US$46,400 – higher than the UK, USA and Sweden, according to UN statistics. In general, most people live quite comfortably.

Some visitors complain the locals (particularly on Tortola) are unfriendly. The demeanor is not rude so much as reserved.

## ARTS

Fungi (*foon*-ghee, also an island food made of cornmeal and fish) is the local folk music. It uses homemade percussion like washboards, ribbed gourds and conch shells to accompany a singer. The full-moon festivals at Aragorn's Studio (p402) and Bomba's Shack (p401) are good places to hear it live.

Quite a few artists work on the islands. Aragorn's Studio hosts a local collective of potters, sculptors, coconut carvers and more; they sell their wares on site. Many local painters and artisans sell their colorful goods at Sunny Caribbee Spice Shop (p399) in Road Town.

The BVIs' most famous literary work was written by a Scotsman who never actually set foot in the region. Robert Louis Stevenson wrote *Treasure Island* (1883) after his seagoing uncle inspired him with tales of Norman Island (p404). Or so the story goes. Whatever the genesis, it's a rip-roaring pirate yarn about buried treasure and a one-legged, parrot-toting gent named Long John Silver.

# ENVIRONMENT
## The Land

The BVIs consist of more than 40 islands and cays. The group owes its existence to a series of volcanic eruptions that built up layers of lava and igneous rock, which created islands with three geographical zones: the coastal plain, coastal dry forests and the steep central mountains that dominate the island interiors. The one exception is easternmost Anegada, which is a flat coral island. Sage Mountain on Tortola is the highest point in the islands at 1716ft. Except where houses perch precariously on impossibly steep slopes, the mountains are dense subtropical forests. All of the timber is second- or third-growth; the islands were stripped for sugar, cotton and tobacco plantations in the colonial era. The BVIs have no rivers and very few freshwater streams.

Thousands of tropical plant varieties grow in the islands, and a short drive can transport a nature lover between entirely different ecosystems. Mangrove swamps, coconut groves and sea-grape trees dominate the coast, while mountain peaks support wet forest with mahogany, lignum vitae, palmetto and more than 30 varieties of wild orchid.

Islanders also grow and collect hundreds of different roots and herbs as ingredients for 'bush medicine.' Psychoactive mushrooms grow wild (and are consumed) on the islands, particularly on Tortola.

## Wildlife

Few land mammals are natives; most were accidentally or intentionally introduced. Virtually every island has a feral population of goats and burros, and some islands have wild pigs, horses, cats and dogs.

More than 200 species of bird inhabit the island, adding bright colors and a symphony of sound to the tropical environment. A few snake species (none of which are poisonous) slither around, along with a host of small and not-so-small lizards, including the 6ft-long rock iguanas of Anegada and the common green iguana found throughout the islands. Anoles and gecko lizards are ubiquitous, and numerous species of toad and frog populate the islands.

## Environmental Issues

Rapid urbanization, deforestation, soil erosion, mangrove destruction and a lack of freshwater keep environmentalists wringing their hands with worry. On Tortola, almost all of the flat land has been developed, and houses hang on mountain slopes like Christmas ornaments. High population growth and density have kept sewage treatment plants in a constant scramble to prevent the islands from soiling themselves.

Desalination plants make fresh water out of sea water and without them the islands would seriously lack water. When a storm strikes, islands lose power and diesel facilities shut down, forcing islanders to use rainwater cisterns.

Prior years of overfishing have put conch (a local shellfish) and lobster in a precarious situation. Currently, fishing for these creatures is not allowed from August 15 through November 1 so stocks can replenish.

Environmental concerns have resulted in the formation of the **BVI National Parks Trust** ( ☎ 494-3904; www.bvinationalparkstrust.org), which protects 15 parks and six islands, including the Dogs and Fallen Jerusalem, which are excellent dive sites. The entire southwest coast of Virgin Gorda is a collection of national parks that includes the giant boulder formations at the Baths.

# FOOD & DRINK

Soup and stew are staples. Generally, cast-iron pots are used for 'boilin' down' soups or stews, such as pepperpot – which combines oxtail, chicken, beef, pork and calf's foot with a hot pepper and *cassareep* (sauce made from cassava). *Tannia* (a root vegetable) soup is another traditional offering, as is *calabeza* (pumpkin) soup. Another popular dish is roti (*root-ee*), flatbread envelopes stuffed with curried meat, fish or poultry, often served with a tangy mango chutney.

Fungi (*foon-ghee*) is made from cornmeal and is usually served with fish and gravy.

---

**HOW MUCH?**

- **Two-tank scuba dive trip** US$110
- **Round-trip ferry Tortola to Virgin Gorda** US$25
- **Half-day sailing trip** US$80
- **Pusser's Rum 750ml bottle** US$10
- **Roti** US$11

*Daube* meat is a pot roast seasoned with vinegar, onion and native spices. Most dishes arrive with johnnycakes (fried bread).

Fish and shellfish are prevalent, and cooks will bake, grill, stew or boil whatever is the daily catch. Conch (pronounced conk) is often fried into crispy fritters. Fresh lobster is Anegada's claim to fame. As commercial fishing of conch and lobster is forbidden from August 15 through November 1 (see opposite), you're less likely to find them on menus during this period.

While tap water is usually safe, visitors with a sensitive stomach might want to stick to bottled water.

The BVIs are home to a popular cocktail called the Painkiller, a yummy mix of rum, orange juice, pineapple juice and a touch of coconut cream.

# TORTOLA

**pop 19,600**

Among Tortola's sharp peaks and bougainvillea-clad hillsides you'll find a mash-up of play places. Guesthouses and mountain villas mingle with beachside resorts. *Bon Appetite* cooks make island dishes next to elderly Mrs Scatliffe, who prepares them from her garden. You even get your choice of full-moon parties – artsy with Aragorn or mushroom-tea-fueled with Bomba.

About 80% of the BVIs' 23,500 citizens live and work on Tortola, so it's not surprising there's a lot of choice here. It's also the BVIs' governmental and commercial center, plus its air and ferry hub.

As for the name: in Spanish, *tortola* means 'turtledove,' which were the birds flying around with distinctive coos when Christopher Columbus came ashore. Most have since flown the coop (except on neighboring Guana Island).

## Orientation

At 21 sq miles in area, Tortola lies less than 2 miles east of the USVIs' St John, across a windswept and current-ripped channel called the Narrows. Tortola's long, thin, tall body stretches 14 miles from west to east but is rarely more than 2 miles wide. The altitude of Tortola's mountain spine creates steep slopes that come almost to the water's edge on the island's north and south shores. Scalloped bays ring the island; the deepest

serves as the harbor for the BVIs' largest town and capital, Road Town.

## Getting There & Away

### AIR

**Terrence B Lettsome Airport** (EIS; ☎ 494-3701) is on Beef Island, connected to Tortola by a bridge on the island's east side. Most international flights from North America and Europe connect through a hub (see p415).

### BOAT

There are two ports of entry for ferries: the main terminal is in Road Town, the other terminal is at West End on the island's, yes, western end. Ferries travel to St John (USVIs) and Jost Van Dyke from West End only. Ferries travel to Virgin Gorda and Anegada from Road Town only. Ferries travel to Charlotte Amalie on St Thomas (USVIs) from both Road Town and West End. For ferry costs and schedules within the BVIs, see p417). For sailings to/from the USVIs, see p416).

## Getting Around

Public transportation is nonexistent so people either rent cars or make use of the efficient taxis. Although everything looks close on the map, the ruggedness of Tortola's topography makes for slow travel.

### CAR

There are several local car-rental agencies on Tortola. High-season rates begin at about US$55 per day, and can run as high as US$90, but you'll get a better price for a weekly rental.

**Hertz** Airport ( ☎ 495-6600); Road Town ( ☎ 494-6228; www.hertzbvi.com)

**Itgo Car Rentals** ( ☎ 494-5150; Road Town) Good prices; located at Wickhams Cay 1.

**Jerry's Car Rental** ( ☎ 495-4111; www.info-res.com/jerry jeep; West End) A good option if you're coming in on a West End ferry. Jerry will pick you up at the dock.

### TAXI

Taxis are widely available; see p418 for further details.

The fare from Road Town to the West End, Cane Garden Bay and the airport is the same (one way US$21).

## ROAD TOWN

Let's be honest: the BVIs' capital is nothing special – no mega sights to see or scenery to drop your jaw. But there's nothing wrong with Road Town, either (unless it's the one or two cruise ships each day whose passengers quickly overwhelm the small area). It's a perfectly decent place to spend a day or night, and most visitors do exactly that when they charter their own boat or take the ferries to the outlying islands, including Virgin Gorda and the USVIs.

The town takes its name from the island's principal harbor, Road Bay, which has served as a 'roadstead' (staging area) for fleets of ships for centuries. It remains a convenient place to stock up on food, drinks and money before journeying onward.

Most of the town's pubs and restaurants are along Waterfront Dr. Main St, Road Town's primary shopping venue, is a nice retreat for anyone seeking shade and quiet. The narrow street winds along the western edge of town and has a collection of wooden and stone buildings dating back about 200 years.

## Information

Branches of Scotiabank, FirstBank and First Caribbean are all found on Wickhams Cay 1 in Road Town. All have ATMs.

**Bits 'n' Pieces** ( ☎ 494-5957; Wickhams Cay 1; per 30min US$5; ☼ 8am-5pm Mon-Fri, 9am-5pm Sat) Internet access: has four computer terminals and a printer.

**BVI Tourist Board** ( ☎ 494-3134, 800-835-8530; www .bvitourism.com; DeCastro St, Akara Bldg; ☼ 8:30am-4:30pm Mon-Fri) The main office provides a free map, which is sufficient for navigating roads.

**Peebles Hospital** ( ☎ 494-3497; Main St; ☼ 24hr) It has complete emergency services.

**Post office** ( ☎ 494-7423; Main St; ☼ 8:30am-4pm Mon-Fri, 9am-noon Sat)

**Serendipity Books** ( ☎ 494-5865; Main St; ☼ 8:30am-5:30pm Mon-Fri, 8:30am-3pm Sat) This bookshop has an upstairs café with internet access (per 30min US$5).

**Tourist office** ( ☎ 494-7260; ☼ 8:30am-4:30pm) This tiny office is at the ferry terminal.

## Dangers & Annoyances

Road Town has little street crime, but areas can become suddenly desolate after dark. Remain alert to your surroundings.

## Sights

The **JR O'Neal Botanic Gardens** ( ☎ 494-4557; www .bvinationalparkstrust.org; cnr Botanic Rd & Main St; admission US$3; ☼ 8am-4pm) is a four-acre national park and a pleasant refuge from Road Town's traffic, noise and heat. Benches are set amid in-

digenous and exotic tropical plants and there is also an orchid house, lily pond, small rainforest and cactus grove. The herb garden is rife with traditional bush medicine plants.

In the heart of Main St, the stark white-rubble walls of **HM Prison** date back to the 18th century. The fortress is still a working jail, and you can hear muffled voices and radio music from the cells at night. East of the prison, **St George's Episcopal (Anglican) Church** ( ☎ 494-3894; ☼ 10am-4pm Mon-Sat, 7am-4pm Sun) is another survivor of the 18th century. Inside is a copy of the 1834 Emancipation Proclamation that freed Britain's slaves in the West Indies. To the west of the prison, the 1924 **Methodist Church** is a fine example of a classic West Indian timber-framed construction.

Standing at the extreme south end of Main St, and looking like an imperial symbol, whitewashed 1880 **Government House** (admission US$3; ☼ 9am-2pm Mon-Sat) was once the British Governor's residence. Today it's a small museum with period furniture and historic artifacts.

## Activities

Boat charters are big, big business in the BVIs, and Road Town is where it all happens (primarily from the Moorings at Wickhams Cay 2). For more information on bareboat or crewed boat charters, see p416.

The following well-regarded day-sail operators run trips to Virgin Gorda, Jost Van Dyke, Anegada and Norman Island, among others; prices include snorkel gear.

**Patouche Charters** ( ☎ 248-494-6300; www.patouche .com; HR Penn Marina; half/full-day tours US$80/125) A 48ft catamaran.

**White Squall II** ( ☎ 494-2564; www.whitesquall2.com; Village Cay Marina, A Dock; full-day tours US$105) A traditional, 80ft schooner.

For diving and snorkeling hot spots, see the boxed text, p398.

**Last Stop Sports** ( ☎ 494-0564; www.laststopsports .com; Wickhams Cay 2, Mooring's Dock) Has great rates on kayak rentals (US$30/40 per single/double) and windsurfing equipment (from US$37 per day). It also rents surfboards, bikes and dive gear.

**We Be Divin'** ( ☎ 494-4320; www.webedivinbvi.com; Village Cay Marina; 1-/2-tank dive US$85/120) Look for the Aquaventure Scuba office, which works in conjunction with We Be Divin' here. Its boats run to all the major local dive sites.

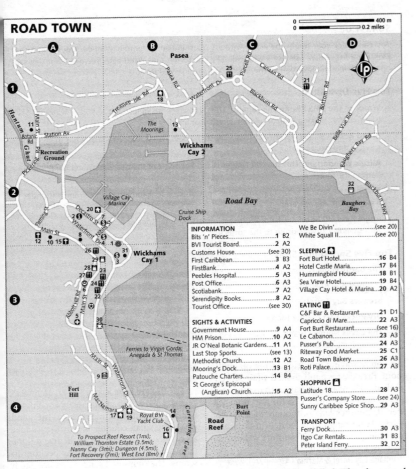

## ROAD TOWN

### INFORMATION
Bits 'n' Pieces.................................**1** B2
BVI Tourist Board...........................**2** A2
Customs House......................(see 30)
First Caribbean..............................**3** B3
FirstBank.......................................**4** A2
Peebles Hospital............................**5** A3
Post Office.....................................**6** A3
Scotiabank.....................................**7** A2
Serendipity Books..........................**8** A2
Tourist Office........................(see 30)

### SIGHTS & ACTIVITIES
Government House.........................**9** A4
HM Prison....................................**10** A2
JR O'Neal Botanic Gardens..........**11** A1
Last Stop Sports......................(see 13)
Methodist Church.........................**12** A2
Mooring's Dock...........................**13** B1
Patouche Charters........................**14** B4
St George's Episcopal
   (Anglican) Church.....................**15** A2

We Be Divin'........................(see 20)
White Squall II.....................(see 20)

### SLEEPING
Fort Burt Hotel...........................**16** B4
Hotel Castle Maria.......................**17** B4
Hummingbird House......................**18** B1
Sea View Hotel............................**19** B4
Village Cay Hotel & Marina..........**20** A2

### EATING
C&F Bar & Restaurant..................**21** D1
Capriccio di Mare........................**22** A3
Fort Burt Restaurant...............(see 16)
Le Cabanon..................................**23** A3
Pusser's Pub.................................**24** A3
Riteway Food Market...................**25** C1
Road Town Bakery........................**26** A3
Roti Palace.................................**27** A3

### SHOPPING
Latitude 18................................**28** A3
Pusser's Company Store.........(see 24)
Sunny Caribbee Spice Shop...**29** A3

### TRANSPORT
Ferry Dock...................................**30** A3
Itgo Car Rentals..........................**31** B3
Peter Island Ferry........................**32** D2

## Sleeping

**Sea View Hotel** ( ☎ 494-2483; seaviewhotel@surfbvi.com; cnr Waterfront Dr & MacNamara Rd; r/apt incl tax US$82/120; ✕ ☀ ) At the west end of town, this budget property has about 20 small rooms and efficiency apartments. It's nothing fancy (and despite the name, there's no view), but the motel-like rooms are clean and well kept. Unfortunately, the hotel fronts a busy road so noise can be a problem.

**Hotel Castle Maria** ( ☎ 494-2553; www.castlemaria .com; MacNamara Rd; s/d/q US$95/99/140; ✕ ▭ ☀ ) Located up the hill behind the Sea View Hotel, this 30-room property offers decent value in its harbor-view rooms, which have thick wood furnishings and private balconies. The non-view interior rooms tend to be dark, and all

rooms are somewhat faded. There's a good rooftop Thai restaurant that serves dinner.

**Fort Burt Hotel** ( ☎ 494-2587; www.bviguide.com/ fortburt; Waterfront Dr; r/ste from US$120/200; ✕ ▭ ☀ ) The hotel rises on the ruins of a 300-year-old Dutch fort that once guarded the harbor from a steep hillside. The 12 rooms have all amenities; most have sweeping sea views and some of the five suites even have private pools. Be ready to climb lots of steps – it'll help work off dinner at the gourmet restaurant on site.

**our pick Hummingbird House** ( ☎ 494-0039; www .hummingbirdbvi.com; Pasea; r incl breakfast US$135-160; ✕ ▭ ☀ ) This is a real B&B (the BVIs' only one), run by long-time UK transplant Yvonne. Tile floors, batik decor and thick towels fill the four breezy rooms; you'll feel

---

## SOAK IT UP

You can't stick your toe in the water without splashing an extraordinary underwater site in the BVIs. For a list of dive operators who will take you to the sites listed here, see p412. For day-sail operators who will take you to the snorkeling sites, see p396.

### Top Five Dive Sites

- **Wreck of the RMS Rhone** This famous 310ft shipwreck sits in just 30ft to 90ft of water off Salt Island (p404), making it an accessible wreck dive for all levels.

- **Blond Rock** A pinnacle between Dead Chest and Salt Islands, this coral ledge has many caves, crevices and deep holes.

- **Alice's Wonderland** This spot off Ginger Island has some of the best deepwater coral formations in the BVIs.

- **The Indians** Just off Norman Island, three cone-shaped rock formations rise from 36ft underwater to 30ft above water.

- **Angel Reef** Off Norman Island, this site is a crossroads for species from different habitats, with shallow canyons rising to the surface.

### Top Five Snorkeling Sites

- **The Baths** Virgin Gorda
- **Loblolly Bay** Anegada
- **Brewers Bay** Tortola
- **Dry Rocks East** Cooper Island
- **The Caves** Norman Island

---

like you're staying in a friend's big ol' guest room. Breakfast is a full cooked affair served poolside. There are surcharges to use the air-conditioner (per night US$20) and internet (per 30 minutes US$5), though wi-fi access is free. Hummingbird is located in the leafy Pasea neighborhood, a 25-minute walk from town, or US$4 cab ride.

**Village Cay Hotel & Marina** ( ☎ 494-2771; www.igy-villagecay.com; Wickhams Cay 1; r US$165-220; ✺ ▯ ▨ ) Located smack in the middle of Road Town overlooking the bay's yacht slips, Village Cay is a sweet place to rest your head, especially if you want to schmooze with fellow boaters. The 19 rooms and two condos have all the first-class amenities of a resort at a fraction of the price. There's also wi-fi. Everyone is onto the deal, so it books up fast. If nothing else, come for a drink at the pier-side bar-restaurant.

## Eating & Drinking

Tortolians love to eat out, and Road Town has restaurants to match every wallet. Pick up the free *Limin' Times* for entertainment listings. Self-caterers can stock up at **Riteway**

**Food Market** ( ☎ 494-2263; Pasea; ⏲ 7:30am-10pm Mon-Sat, to 9pm Sun).

**our pick Road Town Bakery** ( ☎ 494-0222; Main St; sandwiches US$5-8; ⏲ breakfast & lunch) New England Culinary Institute students bake the goods here. The small counter mostly serves takeaway, though you can eat at the five outdoor tables along with the chickens pecking for scraps. The soups and sandwiches are dandy, but it's the pumpkin spice muffins, brownies and fat slices of weep-worthy cake that will set you free.

**Capriccio di Mare** ( ☎ 494-5369; Waterfront Dr; mains US$9-14; ⏲ breakfast, lunch & dinner Mon-Sat) Set on the porch of a classic West Indian house across from the ferry dock, this Italian café draws both locals and travelers. Breakfast includes pastries and cappuccino. Lunch and dinner feature salads, pasta dishes and pizza, with plenty of wines to wash it all down.

**Roti Palace** ( ☎ 494-4196; Abbott Hill Rd; rotis US$9-16; ⏲ lunch & dinner) On a side street that leads up the hill off Main St, this cramped little restaurant serves some of the island's best roti at its open-air plastic tables. Fiery chutney sets off the chicken, beef, conch or vegetable fillings.

**Pusser's Pub** ( ☎ 494-3897; Waterfront Dr; mains JS$11-17; ☒ lunch & dinner) This English-style, nautical-themed pub gets lively with pizza, burger and sandwich eaters whooping it up at brass-ringed tables.

**C&F Bar & Restaurant** ( ☎ 494-4941; mains US$12-20; ☒ dinner Mon-Sat) For totally authentic West Indian cuisine, come to this neighborhood joint in Purcell Estate, east of Road Town. It's worth the trouble it takes to find (take a cab your first trip – about US$7 from the ferry dock). Tortolians show up in droves to consume barbecue seafood and curry dishes from chef Clarence Emmanuel.

**Le Cabanon** ( ☎ 494-8660; Waterfront Dr; mains US$20-30; ☒ dinner) Parisian Christopher Boisgirard concocts his bistro's escargot, foie gras and seafood dishes using provisions flown in from French St-Martin. The open-air terrace, carved from a classic West Indian house, becomes a happenin' scene at night.

**Fort Burt Restaurant** ( ☎ 494-2587; Waterfront Dr; mains US$20-35; ☒ breakfast, lunch & dinner) With a delightful view of the harbor, this upscale restaurant in the Fort Burt Hotel serves dishes (say, saltfish cakes or lobster with avocado salsa) created by students of the nearby New England Culinary Institute. It's a great place to come for romantic dinners.

## Shopping

Craft hawkers come out in droves around Wickhams Cay 1 when cruise ships sail into port, but the top shops are on Main St.

**Latitude 18** ( ☎ 494-7807; Main St) For those in need of flip-flops, sunglasses, Kipling bags or good-quality souvenir T-shirts, Latitude 18 stocks them all.

**Pusser's Company Store** ( ☎ 494-2467; Waterfront Dr) Adjoining Pusser's Pub, this shop sells logoed clothing and accessories, as well as bottles of Pusser's Rum – the blend served on Her Majesty's Royal Navy ships for 300 years.

**Sunny Caribbee Spice Shop** ( ☎ 494-2178; Main St) It's a favorite for its colorful array of island-made seasonings like 'rum peppers' and 'mango magic.' Spices are also packaged as hangover cures and bad-spirit repellents. The adjoining gallery sells paintings, pottery, jewelry and dolls by local craftspeople.

## AROUND ROAD TOWN

Just west of Road Town the road hugs the shoreline past a couple of historic sites and big resorts. The ruined walls and founda-

tions of the **William Thornton Estate** plantation great house lie unpreserved and unguarded just west of Nanny Cay. Thornton went on to design the US Capitol Building in Washington, DC.

Halfway between Road Town and West End, the **Dungeon** is a ruined fort built in 1794 by the Royal Engineers. It was dubbed the Dungeon because its underground cell holds remnants of what might be prisoners' graffiti.

Closer to the West End, **Fort Recovery** is the BVIs' oldest intact structure. Villas now surround the fort.

Just beyond Fort Burt, on the western border of Road Town, sits **Prospect Reef Resort** ( ☎ 494-3311, 800-356-8937; www.prospectreefbvi.com; r US$150-475; ☒ ☒ ), Tortola's largest resort. The 137 rooms come in several configurations, from garden studios (US$150) to two-bedroom villas (US$475). There are all the amenities you'd expect from a 44-acre seaside resort…except a beach. Prospect Reef compensates by running a regular glass-bottom ferry to Peter Island, 3 miles offshore. Tennis, fishing and yacht charters are at your doorstep, as is diving instruction with **Dive Tortola** ( ☎ 494-9200, 800-353-3419; www.divetortola.com; 1-/2-tank dive US$75/110).

A 'swim with the dolphins' program also operates on site, but remember: these are wild animals brought here forcibly, a practice that is widely condemned by environmental groups.

**Nanny Cay Resort & Marina** ( ☎ 494-4895; www .nannycay.com; s/d standard US$170/200, ste US$200-295; ☒ ☒ ), 3 miles west of Road Town, describes itself as 'an island unto itself,' and the description fits. The 42-room resort has two pools, two restaurants, a tennis court, marina, windsurfing school, dive shop, mountain bike center, boutiques and a minimarket – in short, it's a self-contained pleasure dome on a 25-acre islet. Rooms have kitchenettes, private balconies and wooden cathedral ceilings. **Island Surf & Sail** ( ☎ 494-0123; www.bviwatertoys .com; Nanny Cay) also offers windsurfing rentals and lessons for approximately US$100 per three-hour session.

## WEST END

The small settlement of West End has the main ferry terminal for vessels going to and from the USVIs (see p416) and Jost Van Dyke (see p408). **Sopers Hole** (www.sopershole.com), the former site of a 16th-century pirate's den, is a major anchorage, with a marina and shopping wharf that has some great restaurants and bars. Anyone needing transportation from here can call **West End Taxi Association** (☎ 495-4934).

**Jolly Roger Inn** ( ☎ 495-4559; www.jollyrogerbvi .com; mains US$9-20; ☯ breakfast, lunch & dinner) On the north side of Sopers Hole, next to the ferry dock, this popular restaurant and bar has a great waterfront location and the chefs serve up delicious grilled fish and pizzas. Locals and travelers flock to the Caribbean barbecue on Friday and Saturday nights. Five very basic rooms (shared/private bathroom US$70/112) sit above the restaurant.

**Pusser's Landing** ( ☎ 495-4554; mains US$18-27; ☯ lunch & dinner) This fun pub offers outdoor harborside seating and a Margaritaville ambience. The seafood-based dinners are a bit pricey for their quality. It's best to stick to snacks and booze (happy hour is from 5pm to 6:30pm).

## CANE GARDEN BAY AREA

A turquoise cove ringed by steep green hills, Cane Garden Bay is exactly the kind of place Jimmy Buffet would immortalize in song – which he did in 1978's 'Mañana.' The area's perfecto 1-mile beach and throngs of rum-serving bars and restaurants make it Tortola's most popular party zone.

Rid yourself of visions of a sprawling resort area, however; the sheer mountains dominate the landscape, so everything hugs the water along a small strip of road. South of Cane Garden Bay are a series of picturesque bays. Speckled amid clumps of shoreside holiday villas are small West Indian settlements. When you stay out here you're living among locals.

The north shore lies only a few miles as the crow flies from Road Town, but the winding, precipitous roads travel over the mountains, making it about a 25-minute drive.

### Sights & Activities

You can't miss the funky **North Shore Shell Museum** ( ☎ 495-4714; Carrot Bay; admission free), which also serves great meals in its restaurant. Just off the North Coast Rd at the west end of Cane Garden Bay, the **Callwood Rum Distillery** (tour US$1; ☯ 8:30am-6pm Mon-Sat) is the oldest continuously operated distillery in the Eastern Caribbean. The Callwood family has been producing Arundel rum here for generations, using copper vats and wooden aging casks. A small store sells the delicious local liquor.

### BEACHES

**Brewers Bay**, a palm-fringed bay on the north shore east of Cane Garden Bay, has excellent snorkeling and a tranquil scene – possibly because getting here involves either an expensive cab ride or a brake-smoking do-it-yourself drive down steep switchbacks. There are a couple of beach bars and a campground here.

**Cane Garden Bay** is probably on the postcard that drew you to the BVIs in the first place. The gently sloping crescent of sand hosts plenty of water-sports vendors and beachside bars. It's a popular yacht anchorage, and becomes a full-on madhouse when cruise ships arrive in Road Town and shuttle passengers over for the day.

**Apple Bay**, southwest of Cane Garden, is the 'surfing beach,' especially in late December to February when the consistent swells roll in. On many maps, Apple Bay includes Cappoons Bay, home of the infamous Bomba's Surfside Shack (see opposite).

**Long Bay** is an attractive 1-mile stretch of white-sand beach that spreads west of Apple Bay. **Smuggler's Cove**, at the island's southwestern tip, has good snorkeling.

### SAGE MOUNTAIN NATIONAL PARK

At 1716ft, Sage Mountain rises higher than any other peak in the Virgin Islands. Seven trails crisscross the 92-acre surrounding park. Pick up a trail map at the main entrance, about 0.3 miles from the car lot.

The park is not a rainforest in the true sense, because it receives less than 100 inches of rain per year, but the lush area possesses many rainforest characteristics. It's cool and damp, populated by bo-peep frogs and lizards. Hikers should keep an eye out for 20ft fern trees, mahogany trees, coco-plum shrubs and other flora that have not changed since the dinosaur days. You'll also see spectacular vistas of both the USVIs and BVIs. Allow two hours for your rambles.

### Festivals & Events

**BVI Music Festival** ( ☎ 495-3378; www.bvimusicfest.info) brings big-name acts like Percy Sledge and Wyclef Jean to wail at Cane Garden Bay in late May.

### Sleeping

You could feasibly stay at Cane Garden Bay without a car, but you'll need wheels to stay at any of the other lodgings.

---

## FULL MOONS, MUSHROOMS & A MAN NAMED BOMBA

**Bomba's Surfside Shack** ( ☎ 495-4148; Cappoons Bay) near Apple Bay has achieved mythic status in the Caribbean for reasons including bras, booze, full moons and trippy mushrooms.

The place truly is a shack, built from a mishmash of license plates, surfboards and graffiti-covered signposts espousing carnal wisdom such as 'Wood is Good!'. Bras and panties are woven throughout, along with snapshots of topless women. Very often, sitting smack in the middle of these photos and wearing a wide grin along with his trademark sunglasses, is Bomba.

Bomba started his bar-restaurant about 30 years ago to feed the surfers who still ride the waves curling out front. Today the shack is famous for its monthly full-moon parties, which feature an outdoor barbecue, live reggae and plenty of dancing and drinking. Bomba also serves free psychoactive mushroom tea (mushrooms grow wild on Tortola and are legal), and up to 500 people, both tourists and locals, show up for his bacchanals. Note to those who don't wish to end up topless in photos: mind your intake of tea and rum punch.

Even if you're not on-island during the full moon, the Bomba Shack is a sight to behold. It hosts live bands on Wednesday and Sunday evenings.

---

**Brewers Bay Campground** ( ☎ 494-3463; Brewers Bay; campsites/equipped tents US$20/40) Tortola's only commercial campground is around the bend from Cane Garden Bay, although it's a hell of a ride over zigzagging mountain roads. The sites sit under sea-grape trees and tall palms right on the beach. You can bring a tent or use the prepared sites (which include two cots, linens and a cook stove); the latter are a bit worn and gloomy, so you're better off with your own gear. Everyone shares the cold-water bathhouse and flush toilets. There's a beach bar for beer and other sustenance.

**Ole Works Inn** ( ☎ 495-4837; www.quitorymer.com; Cane Garden Bay; d with hill/beach view US$110/145; ☒ ☒ ) This bright yellow hotel can't be beat for ambience. Owner and reggae master Quito Rymer placed the 18 small rooms within the walls of a 320-year-old rum factory.

**Rhymer's Beach Hotel** ( ☎ 495-4639; Cane Garden Bay; d US$117; ☒ ) On the beach and right in the center of the action, Rhymer's was one of the area's first inns. The big pink concrete building with its restaurant and laundry shows serious signs of hard use, but the price and energy of the place make up for it. Rooms are mostly studios with kitchenette and patios.

**Sebastian's** ( ☎ 495-4212, 800-336-4870; www.sebastiansbvi.com; Little Apple Bay; r US$135-275; ☒ ) Well known for its friendly staff and its gorgeous stretch of beachfront, Sebastian's 26 rooms have teak furnishings, a sea view, a balcony and a refrigerator or kitchen. There's a good onsite restaurant if you're feeling too lazy to travel elsewhere.

**Heritage Inn** ( ☎ 494-5842; www.heritageinnbvi.com; Windy Hill; 1-/2-bedroom apt US$185/285; ☒ ☒ ) High on Windy Hill between Cane Garden Bay and Carrot Bay, this place has nine spacious apartments that seem to hang out in thin air. It also has a pool, sundeck, restaurant. Minimum stay three nights.

**Sugar Mill Hotel** ( ☎ 495-4355, 800-462-8834; www.sugarmillhotel.com; Apple Bay; studio/ste from US$325/340; ☒ ☒ ) In a league of its own for ambience, intimacy and customer service, this boutique hotel rises from the ruins of the Appleby Plantation that gave Apple Bay its name. Guests stay in the 16 studios and suites that hide on the steep hillside among mahogany trees, bougainvillea and palms. The property's centerpiece is the gourmet restaurant.

## Eating & Drinking

Many restaurants in this area turn into bars at night, offering live music, dancing or just solid boozing time.

**Palm's Delight** ( ☎ 495-4863; Carrot Bay; mains US$7-13; ☽ dinner) Located right on the water's edge, this family-style West Indian restaurant serves up great cheap eats and local ambience. Friday nights provide a lively scene, with families eating on the patio and a bar crowd watching cricket or baseball on the TV.

**North Shore Shell Museum** ( ☎ 495-4714; Carrot Bay; mains US$7-18; ☽ breakfast, lunch & dinner) This zany mix of fascinating museum and eatery, owned by Egberth Donovan, specializes in delicious big breakfasts and grilled fish dinners. The staff often lead the patrons in making fungi music by blowing and banging on conch shells. Call before coming, as hours can be erratic.

**Rhymer's** ( ☎ 495-4639; Cane Garden Bay; mains US$15-25; ☽ breakfast, lunch & dinner) Beachside Rhymer's (attached to the eponymous hotel) serves a great breakfast (about US$7), and the dinner menu includes fish and ribs. The bar draws beachgoers seeking refreshment.

**Quito's Gazebo** ( ☎ 495-4837; Cane Garden Bay; mains US$15-25; ☺ lunch & dinner, closed Mon) Another beachside draw, this bar-restaurant takes its name from its owner, Quito Rymer, whose band has toured with Ziggy Marley. You can dance up a storm to Quito's reggae rhythms, and hundreds pack the restaurant on weekends to do just that. Rotis and fresh salads make for popular light luncheons. At night grilled items such as snapper fill the menu.

**Mrs Scatliffe's Restaurant** ( ☎ 495-4556; Carrot Bay; mains US$25-32; ☺ dinner) Senior citizen Mrs Scatliffe serves West Indian dishes on her deck, using fruits and veggies she yanks straight from her garden. You must call for reservations before 5pm, since she'll be making the chicken-in-coconut or conch soup just for you. She's in the yellow building across from the primary school.

**our pick Sugar Mill Hotel** ( ☎ 495-4355; Apple Bay; mains US$25-36; ☺ breakfast, lunch & dinner) Foodies salivate over the mod Caribbean concoctions like poached lobster and eggplant Creole. Owners Jeff and Jinx Morgan, contributing writers for *Bon Appetite* magazine, oversee the constantly changing menu that's served in the restored boiling house of the plantation's rum distillery. Reservations are a must.

## EAST END

Tortola's eastern end is a mix of steep mountains, remote bays and thickly settled West Indian communities. **Beef Island**, the large isle off Tortola's eastern end, is home to the BVIs' only major airport, as well as an arts collective that ramps up during the full moon.

Local coppersmith Aragorn Dick-Read started **Aragorn's Studio** ( ☎ 495-1849; www.aragorns studio.com) under the sea-grape trees fronting **Trellis Bay**, a broad semicircular beach just east of the airport. The studio grew to include space for potters, coconut carvers and batik makers, all of whom you can see at work. He also hosts his own **full-moon party**, an artsy, family-friendly alternative to Bomba's bash (p401). Aragorn's event kicks off around 7pm with fungi music, stilt walkers and fire jugglers. At 9pm he sets his steel 'fireball sculptures' ablaze on the ocean.

The row of shops by Aragorn's also includes **Boardsailing BVI** ( ☎ 495-2447, 800-880-7873;

www.windsurfing.vi; Trellis Bay) for windsurfing rentals or lessons, a local produce market, a **cyber-café** (per 15min US$5) and the landing for Virgin Gorda's North Sound Express ferry (p417).

Beaches on the East End include **Josiah's Bay**, a dramatic windswept strand with a surfable point break in winter. There's a small beach bar here surrounded by acres of empty space. Several charming and inexpensive guesthouses lie inland on the valley slopes. **Lambert Bay**, to the east of Josiah's, offers a wide, palm-fringed beach.

### Sleeping

**Near-D-Beach Limin' Bar & Hostel** ( ☎ 443-7833; www .josiahsbaybvi.com; r/apt US$55/100) This no-frills guesthouse in Josiah's Bay caters mostly to surfers, since it's only a two-minute walk from the popular surfing beach. The three rooms each have a queen-size bed and simple furnishings; they all share gender-segregated, cold-water bathrooms and a game-filled common room. There's also a studio apartment with a private, hot-water bathroom and kitchenette.

**Serendipity House** ( ☎ 499-1999; www.serhouse .com; Josiah's Hill; r US$90-205; ☒ ☒ ) For tropical seclusion about half a mile from Josiah's Bay, this is one of the best values on Tortola, with special deals for longer stays. Canadians Carol and Bill Campbell welcome travelers with the invitation to 'spend a vacation, not a fortune.' There are four units, ranging from an apartment to a two-bedroom villa, all with full kitchens.

**Beef Island Guest House** ( ☎ 495-2303; www.beef islandguesthouse.com; r incl breakfast US$130) Located on Trellis Bay next to De Loose Mongoose restaurant, this place is a five-minute walk to the airport and therefore an excellent choice for anyone with a late arrival or early departure. Set on a thin beach among a grove of low coconut palms, the one-story guesthouse looks more like a contemporary West Indian home than an inn, but the four rooms have unexpected character. All rooms come with fans.

**Tamarind Club Hotel** ( ☎ 495-2477; www.tamarind club.com; r incl breakfast US$139-165; ☒ ☒ ) Just 100yd down the hill from Serendipity House near Josiah's Bay, the nine rooms at this red-roofed West Indian–style building surround a central garden and pool. The rooms have batik-print decor, but are a bit dark; each has a private veranda. The onsite restaurant serves good local dishes, and the swim-up bar is a fine touch.

# Eating

`our pick` **De Loose Mongoose** ( ☎ 495-2303; mains US$8-23; ⏾ breakfast, lunch & dinner, closed Mon) Next to the Beef Island Guest House, this windsurfer hangout is a great place to have breakfast, eat lunch or watch the sunset over dinner. Try the conch fritters, arguably the BVIs' best.

**Secret Garden** ( ☎ 495-1834; Josiah's Bay Plantation; mains US$12-22; ⏾ dinner, closed Tue) One of the most delightful places to eat on Tortola, Secret Garden sets its outdoor tables amid the distilling buildings of an old plantation (now an art gallery and boutique). The imaginative menu ranges from grilled swordfish Creole to coconut chicken or Bajan flying-fish pie. Reservations required.

**Fat Hog Bob's** ( ☎ 495-1010; Maya Cove; mains US$17-32; ⏾ breakfast, lunch & dinner) With a 100ft porch hugging the seaside, this fun-times rib house offers a huge and surprisingly creative menu, featuring items like baby-back ribs marinated in Guinness and crab-stuffed steak.

# VIRGIN GORDA

pop 3500

It's certainly a testament to Virgin Gorda's awesomeness that a billionaire such as Richard Branson – who could live anywhere in the world – chooses this little patch of earth. Of course, it should be noted he's not actually on Virgin Gorda, but has his very own personal island right offshore. But you get the point. And you should get to Virgin Gorda, an ideal blend of extraordinary sights, easy access, good restaurants and villas and, somehow, no rampant commercialism.

The giant granite rock formations of the Baths are the BVIs' biggest tourist attraction, and guess what? They live up to the hype, especially when combined with the hike up, over, around and through them to Devil's Bay. Trekkers can also summit Virgin Gorda Peak, relishing the cool breeze, and meander around wind-pounded Copper Mine National Park. Sea dogs can take ferries over to Bitter End Yacht Club and Saba Rock to drink with the yachties.

This is Virgin Gorda ('Fat Virgin' in Spanish) who, until the 1960s, sat quietly day-dreaming. Her population was only about 600 souls until Laurence Rockefeller constructed the Little Dix Bay resort, which brought jobs, roads and utilities. A few years later, the Virgin emerged from her slumber an undeniable beauty.

## Orientation

Virgin Gorda lies 8 miles east of Tortola. Its elongated, serpent shape makes it an easy place to navigate. The main highway, North Sound Rd, runs along the spine.

The prominent Virgin Gorda Peak, 1359ft high, dominates the northern half of the island. At its foot lies North Sound. The island's southern half is a rolling plain called 'the Valley.' Virgin Gorda's main settlement, Spanish Town, lies on the western shore of the Valley; the airport is 1 mile to the east.

## Getting There & Away

### AIR

**Air Sunshine** ( ☎ 495-8900, 800-327-8900; www.airsunshine.com) flies to Virgin Gorda Airport from San Juan and St Thomas. **Seaborne Airlines** ( ☎ 340-773-6442, 888-359-8687; www.seaborneairline.com) flies floatplanes to North Sound from St Thomas.

### BOAT

**Speedy's** ( ☎ 495-5240; www.speedysbvi.com) and **Smith's Ferry** ( ☎ 494-4454; www.smithsferry.com) run several times daily between Spanish Town and Road Town, Tortola (round trip US$25, 30 minutes). **North Sound Express** ( ☎ 495-2138) runs between Virgin Gorda's North Sound and Tortola's Beef Island; see p417 for details.

## Getting Around

### TO/FROM THE AIRPORT

**Virgin Gorda Airport** (VIJ; ☎ 495-5621) is on the Valley's east side. You can count on taxis waiting when flights arrive. Expect to pay about US$13 for a ride into Spanish Town; US$25 will get you to Gun Creek and the North Sound resorts.

### CAR

Virgin Gorda has several Jeep rental companies that will pick you up from the ferry and drop you off almost anywhere on the island. You'll pay US$55 to US$85 per day.
**L&S Jeep** ( ☎ 495-5297)
**Mahogany Car Rentals** ( ☎ 495-5469)
**Speedy's Car Rental** ( ☎ 495-5240)

### TAXI

Cab rates on Virgin Gorda are some of the highest in the Caribbean. The rate from the

## OUT ISLANDS

The BVIs 'out islands' (a Creole expression for remote or undeveloped cays) are a wonderful mix of uninhabited wildlife sanctuaries, luxurious hideaways for the rich and famous, and provisioning stops for sailors. Most are reachable only by charter or private boat. If you don't have your own vessel, hook up with a day-sail operator (p396).

### Guana Island

One mile off Tortola's northeast tip, this 850-acre island is the seventh-largest island in the BVIs. Guana takes its name from a rock formation called the 'Iguana Head' that juts out from a cliff at the island's northwest corner.

Today the island is a private nature reserve, home to flamingos, red-legged tortoises, seven sandy beaches and miles of hiking trails. Unfortunately, unless you're one of the 32 guests staying at the **Guana Island Club** ( ☎ 494-2354, 800-544-8262; www.guana.com; r/villas from US$1150-2150; ☒ closed Sep & Oct; ☒ ☐ ), you aren't allowed to visit. You can rent the entire island for US$26,500 a day.

### Norman Island

Since 1843, writers have alleged that treasure is buried on Norman Island, supposedly the prototype for Robert Louis Stevenson's book *Treasure Island*. It fits the bill: Norman is the BVIs' largest uninhabited land mass.

Two fantastic beach bars lure boaters. The **William Thornton** (Willie T; ☎ 494-0183) is a schooner converted into a restaurant-bar and moored in the bight. On the beach, **Pirate's Bight** ( ☎ 496-7827) is an open-air pavilion. Both have good food and the owners often bring in live West Indian bands or just crank Bob Marley and Jimmy Buffett over high-voltage sound systems.

Weekends are always a huge party scene; as one local puts it, 'Everyone just gets fucking mental.'

### Peter Island

This lofty L-shaped island, about 4 miles south of Tortola, is the BVIs' fifth-largest and home to the luxurious, all-inclusive **Peter Island Resort** ( ☎ 495-2000; 800-346-4451; www.peterisland.com; r from US$670; ☒ ☐ ☒ ). In the late '60s, Norwegian millionaire Peter Smedwig fell in love with the island and built a resort, which he operated until his death in the late 1970s.

Anyone with reservations (and a fat wallet) can come to the resort's **Tradewinds restaurant** ( ☎ 495-2000; mains US$25-55; ☒ breakfast, lunch & dinner). The Peter Island ferry (round trip US$20) sails from Road Town.

### Salt Island

This T-shaped island is a forlorn place. The salt making (which gave the island its name) still goes on here, but the RMS *Rhone* is the big attraction. The *Rhone* crashed against the rocks off Salt Island's southwest coast during a hurricane in 1867. Now a national park, the steamer's remains are extensive, making it one of the Caribbean's best wreck dives. See p56 for more on this dive.

### Cooper Island

Lying about 4 miles south of Tortola, Cooper Island is a moderately hilly cay and is virtually undeveloped except for the **Cooper Island Beach Club** ( ☎ 494-3721; www.cooper-island.com), whose restaurant makes it a popular anchorage for cruising yachts. Divers also swarm to the island's surrounding wrecks and sites.

### The Dogs

This clutch of six islands lies halfway between Tortola and Virgin Gorda. Protected by the BVI National Parks Trust, the Dogs are sanctuaries for birds and marine animals. The diving here is excellent.

### Necker Island

This private island belongs to Richard Branson, famous adventurer and scion of Virgin Atlantic Airways and Virgin Records. About 1 mile north of Virgin Gorda, Necker is one of the world's most luxurious retreats. If you've got US$40,000 you can rent it for the day (Branson not included).

BRITISH VIRGIN ISLANDS

North Sound resorts or Gun Creek to Spanish Town is US$25 for a 3-mile trip; from the ferry dock to the Baths is US$8 round trip. **Andy's Taxis** ( ☎ 495-5252, 495-5160) and **Mahogany Taxi Service** ( ☎ 495-5469) are the major providers.

## SPANISH TOWN & THE VALLEY

Spanish Town isn't a town so much as a long road with businesses strung along it. It's the commercial center of Virgin Gorda, and probably gets its name from a (severe) corruption of the English word 'penniston,' a blue woolen fabric used long ago for making slave clothing on the island, rather than from any Spanish connections. Islanders referred to their settlement as Penniston well into the 1850s.

The harbor dredged here in the 1960s is home to today's Yacht Harbour, the heart of Spanish Town. Overall the settlement is a sleepy place, but the mix of islanders, yachties and land travelers creates a festive vibe.

### Information

The mall fronting Yacht Harbour holds most of the town's services, including a couple of banks.

**BVI Tourist Board** ( ☎ 495-5181; Yacht Harbour mall; 🕑 9am-5pm Mon-Sat, 10am-2pm Sun)

**Chandlery Ship Store** (Yacht Harbour mall; per 10min US$5; 🕑 7am-5pm Mon-Fri, 8am-noon Sat & Sun) Has a couple of internet terminals.

**Nurse Iris O'Neal Clinic** ( ☎ 495-5337; 🕑 9am-4:30pm) On the ridge road in the Valley near the airport. There's a physician on staff, but for hospital services you must go to Tortola. Call ahead.

### Sights & Activities

#### THE BATHS

This collection of **giant boulders** (admission US$3), near the island's southwest corner, marks a national park and the BVIs' most popular tourist attraction. The rocks – volcanic lava leftovers from up to 70 million years ago, according to some estimates – form a series of grottoes that flood with sea water. The area makes for unique swimming and snorkeling; the latter is distinctive as many boulders also lurk under water.

The Baths would totally live up to its reputation for greatness if it wasn't overshadowed by adjacent **Devil's Bay** to the south, and the fantastically cool trail one must take to get there. Actually, there are two trails. The less exciting one takes off behind the taxis at the Baths' parking lot. But the trail you want

leaves from the Baths' beach and goes through the 'Caves.' During the 20-minute trek, you'll clamber over boulders, slosh through tidal pools, squeeze into impossibly narrow passages and bash your feet against rocks. Then you'll drop out onto a sugar-sand beach.

**Spring Bay** also abuts the Baths, but to the north. It has fine white sand (more than at the Baths), clear water and good snorkeling off the boulder enclosure called the Crawl.

While the Baths and environs stir the imagination, the places are often overrun with tourists. By 10am each morning fleets of yachts have moored off the coast, and visitors have been shuttled in from resorts and cruise ships. All you have to do, though, is wait until about 1pm, and you'll get a lot more elbow room.

The Baths' beach has a changing station, snack shack and snorkel gear rental (US$10). Taxis run constantly between the park and ferry dock (round trip US$8).

#### COPPER MINE NATIONAL PARK

You'll drive a heck of a winding road to reach this forlorn bluff at Virgin Gorda's southwest tip, but it's worth it to see the impressive stone ruins (including a chimney, cistern and mineshaft house) that comprise **Copper Mine National Park** (admission free; 🕑 sunrise-sunset). Cornish miners worked the area between 1838 and 1867 and extracted as much as 10,000 tons of copper, then abandoned the mine to the elements. A couple of trails meander through the ruins, and the hillside makes an excellent place for a picnic as the blue sea pounds below.

#### BEACHES

Beachcombers can wander for hours along Virgin Gorda's 14 beaches. The most beautiful ones are **Trunk Bay**, **Little Dix Bay** and – the best – **Savannah Bay**, which features more than 1 mile of white sand. No other beach provides such opportunities for long, solitary walks. Sunsets here can be fabulous.

#### DIVING

**Dive BVI** ( ☎ 495-5513, 800-848-7078; www.divebvi.com; 1-/2-tank dive US$80/105), at Yacht Harbour and Leverick Bay, has four fast boats that take you diving at any of the BVIs sites.

#### BOAT TRIPS

Two recommended day-sail operators depart from Yacht Harbour. Both companies supply lunch and beverages.

**Double 'D'** ( ☎ 495-6150; www.doubledbvi.com; half/
full-day trips US$55/95) A 50ft sloop.
**Spirit of Anegada** ( ☎ 499-0901; www.spiritofanegada
.com; half/full-day trips US$65/95) A 44ft schooner.

## Festivals & Events
Spanish Town around the yacht harbor fills
with *mocko jumbies* (costumed stilt walkers
representing spirits of the dead), fungi bands,
a food fair and parades for the **Virgin Gorda
Easter Festival** ( ☎ 495-5181), held Friday through
Sunday during the Christian holiday (usually
late March or April).

## Sleeping
**Ocean View Hotel** ( ☎ 495-5230; r US$85; ⚡ ) This
budget guesthouse, situated across the street
from Yacht Harbour and a 10-minute walk
from the ferry, has 12 units above the Wheel
House restaurant in a concrete-block building. Rooms are small with dingy blue furnishings, but they're clean and the grounds are
well maintained.

**Bayview Vacation Apartments** ( ☎ 495-5329; www
.bayviewbvi.com; apt US$110-145; ⚡ ) Each of these
apartments, behind Chez Bamboo restaurant,
has two bedrooms, a full kitchen, dining facilities and an airy living room. It's plain-Jane
ambience, with dowdy rattan furnishings,
but it can be a good deal, especially if you
have three or four people. There is a roof deck
for sunbathing.

**Fischer's Cove Beach Hotel** ( ☎ 495-5252; www
.fischerscove.com; r/cottage US$160/190) Surrounded by
gardens and located just a few steps from the
beach, Fischer's Cove has a collection of eight
triangular-shaped cottages and a main hotel
building with 12 dated studios. The cottages
have full kitchens, but no phones, TVs or
air-con; the hotel units do have phones and
TVs, and a few also have air-con. The popular
open-air restaurant overlooks the beach. It's
a 15-minute walk from ferry dock.

**our pick** **Guavaberry Spring Bay Homes** ( ☎ 495-
5227; www.guavaberrspringbay.com; cottages US$220) A
stone's throw from the Baths and plopped
amid similar hulking boulders, Guavaberry's
circular cottages come with one or two bedrooms, a kitchen, dining area and sun porch.
The setting amazes. Only some units have
air-conditioning, so ask for it when booking
if you need it.

**Little Dix Bay** ( ☎ 495-5555, 888-767-3966; www.little
dixbay.com; r from US$725; ⚡ 🖥 🍴 ) This is the re-
sort that rocketed Virgin Gorda to glory, and it

remains the island's swankiest, celebrity-filled
digs. An army of staff keep the grounds and 98
rooms perfectly coiffed, and it wafts an overall
South Seas vibe. Wi-fi costs US$20 per day.

## Eating & Drinking
**Mad Dog** ( ☎ 495-5830; mains US$7-12; ☯ breakfast, lunch
& dinner) Expatriates and tourists often gather at
this airy pavilion set among the rocks where
the road ends at the Baths. They can't resist
the piña coladas and sandwiches.

**Bath & Turtle** ( ☎ 495-5239; mains US$8-25; ☯ break-
fast, lunch & dinner) In a courtyard surrounded by
Yacht Harbour's mall, this casual pub cooks
up good pizza, quesadillas and seared ahi tuna
salad. At night it's a fun scene.

**Thelma's Hideout** ( ☎ 495-5646; mains US$12-22;
☯ breakfast, lunch & dinner) Find this West Indian
hangout on the side road leading to Little Dix
Bay resort. Seating is in an open-air courtyard,
and there is a stage where a band plays during
high season. Thelma will serve you breakfast,
but most travelers come here for her conch
stew. Make dinner reservations by 3pm.

**Rock Café** ( ☎ 495-5482; mains US$17-34; ☯ dinner)
Nestled among the boulders at the traffic circle
south of Spanish Town, this place has indoor
and outdoor dining, plus a popular terrace bar
that rocks with live music several nights per
week. The cuisine is mostly Italian, with pas-
tas, mahimahi, snapper and other fresh fish.

**our pick** **Mine Shaft Café** ( ☎ 495-5260; sandwiches
US$10-14, mains US$22-32; ☯ lunch & dinner) You can't
beat the location, high on a hill overlooking
the Atlantic on Copper Mine Rd. You can't
beat the food either, which includes burgers
(even the veggie variety), wraps and mains
like lobster in rum-lemon-cream sauce.
Owner Elton Sprauve throws a monthly full-
moon party, complete with live music, warm
breezes, cheap rum punch and grilled meats.
If you can't make that shindig, at least come
for a sunset cocktail.

**Chez Bamboo** ( ☎ 495-5752; small plates US$8-14,
mains US$22-40; ☯ dinner) Just north of Yacht
Harbour, this bistro (in a converted West
Indian home and yard) couldn't be in a better setting, amid candlelight and tropical
plants. The chefs specialize in French Creole
Caribbean cuisine; there's also a small plates
menu with saltfish croquettes and hummus.
Jazz, blues or calypso fills the air on weekend evenings. The only problem: the food is
overpriced. Still, the yacht owners pour in, so
reservations are a good idea.

The island's main grocery store, **Buck's Food Market** (☎ 495-5423; ☼ 7am-7pm), is located in Yacht Harbour's mall.

## NORTH SOUND & AROUND

Steep mountain slops rise up on Virgin Gorda's northern end. They reach their pinnacle at 1359ft Virgin Gorda Peak, part of protected **Gorda Peak National Park** (admission free; ☼ sunrise-sunset). Two well-marked trails lead to the summit off North Sound Rd, and make a sweet hike. It's easiest to start at the higher-up trailhead, from where it's a 30-minute, half-mile walk to the crest. You'll see Christmas orchids, bromeliads (pineapple family members), bo-peep frogs (named for their sound) and hummingbirds. The lookout tower at the top provides vistas of the entire archipelago. If you have time, return via the lower trail (about a 50-minute walk).

North of the park lies **North Sound**, the island's only other settlement, whose main job is to serve the big resorts and myriad yachts anchored in the surrounding bays. A mini-armada of ferries tootle back and forth from the Sound's **Gun Creek** to Bitter End Yacht Club (right) and Saba Rock Resort (right), both excellent for a happy hour drink and sea views at their bars, even if you're not staying there.

The strand of gently curving beach and vivid blue water at the Mango Bay Resort is called **Mahoe Bay**. **Mountain Trunk Bay**, **Nail Bay** and **Long Bay** lie north of Mahoe Bay and run nearly undisturbed for about 1 mile.

You can reach North Sound directly from Beef Island, Tortola, by ferry; see p417 for details.

It's all resorts over here, although Leverick Bay Resort also rents more than two dozen area villas through its **Virgin Gorda Rental Properties** (www.virgingordabvi.com).

**our pick** **Leverick Bay Resort** (☎ 495-7421, 800-848-7081, restaurant 495-7154; www.leverickbay.com; r US$149; ✷ 🖳 🕿 ) is great value. When you see the purple, green and turquoise buildings splashed up the hillside, you'll know you've arrived. The 14 rooms are dandy, each with two full beds, rattan furnishings, free wi-fi and a private balcony. Then there's the beach, marina, tennis court, dive shop, spa, market and internet café – oh, and the restaurant, which is open for breakfast, lunch and dinner (mains US$8 to $25) with nightly specials such as jumbo shrimp (Wednesday), crab (Thursday), pig roast and stilt dancers (Friday) and sushi (Saturday).

On a fleck of island just offshore from Bitter End Yacht Club, **Saba Rock Resort** (☎ 495-9966; www.sabarock.com; r incl breakfast US$175-550; ✷ ) is a warm and charismatic boutique resort with eight rooms, a restaurant and two bars. It's the most laid-back place to get your North Sound resort experience – the owners even make their own rum. Visitors can come over on a free ferry from Gun Creek (call the resort to arrange pick up) for a sip and to check out all the shipwreck booty on site, such as the cannon from the RMS *Rhone*.

**Mango Bay Resort** (☎ 495-5672; www.mangobayresort.com; villas US$245-450; ✷ 🕿 ), overlooking Mahoe Bay, is a compound of 12 Italian-style villas, from one-bedroom duplexes to four bedroom cottages, all nestled beside the beach.

**Bitter End Yacht Club & Resort** (☎ 494-2746, 800-872-2392; www.beyc.com; d incl meals US$860; ✷ 🕿 ), a sporty, all-inclusive resort at the east end of North Sound, has 85 villas adorned with batik bedspreads and teak floors. Some villas have hammocks, wrap-around verandahs and are open to the trade winds; others have air-con and decks; none have TVs. Rates include three meals a day and unlimited use of the resort's bountiful equipment for sailing, windsurfing, kayaking and much more.

The water-sports gear and Yacht Club bar are open to the paying public. Many people also come to the Clubhouse Grille for the monumental buffet (lunch US$22, dinner US$44.50). Whatever the pretense, you definitely should make the trip to Bitter End. A free ferry departs Gun Creek on the half hour.

# JOST VAN DYKE

**pop 200**

Jost (pronounced 'yoast') is a little island with a big personality. It may only take up 4 sq miles of teal-blue sea, but its good-time reputation has spread thousands of miles beyond. A lot of that is due to calypsonian and philosopher Foxy Callwood, the island's main man. But more on him later.

For over 400 years Jost has been an oasis for seafarers and adventurers. A Dutch pirate (the island's namesake) used the island as a base in the 17th century. In the 18th century it became a homestead for Quakers escaping religious tyranny in England. Quaker surnames, such as Lettsome and Callwood, survive among the islanders, mostly descendents of freed Quaker slaves.

In the late 1960s free-spirited boaters found Jost's unspoiled shores, and Foxy built a bar to greet them. The tide ebbed and flowed for a quarter century, and not much changed. Electricity arrived in 1991 and roads were cut a few years later.

Though locals now all have cell phones and websites, and Jost is no secret to yachters and glitterati (Jimmy Buffet and Keith Richards stop by), the island's green hills and blinding beaches remain untrammeled by development. As one local says, 'When Main Street is still a beach, you know life is good.' Hear, hear!

The island has no banks and relatively few accommodations. Many businesses shut down in September and October.

## Orientation

Jost floats about 4 miles northwest of Tortola. Ferries land at the pier on the west side of Great Harbour, the island's main settlement. It's about a 10-minute walk from the pier to the town center. The main road runs along Jost's south shore. If you follow it over the hill to the west for about 1 mile, you reach White Bay. Go east for about 2 miles to reach Little Harbour. Further northeast is Diamond Cay National Park and some secluded snorkeling sites.

## Getting There & Away

**New Horizon Ferry** ( ☎ 495-9278; www.jostvandykeferry .com; round trip US$20) sails five times daily between Tortola's West End and Jost's Great Harbour. On Friday, Saturday and Sunday, **Inter-Island** ( ☎ 776-6597; round trip US$50) makes the half-hour trip to Cruz Bay, St John (USVIs) and onward to Red Hook, St Thomas (USVIs). It leaves Jost at 9:15am and 3pm.

## Getting Around

**Paradise Jeep Rental** ( ☎ 495-9477; per day US$70) in Great Harbour can hook you up with a vehicle. You can call a **water taxi** ( ☎ 443-1488, 495-9969) if your destination involves the wet stuff.

## GREAT HARBOUR

In Jost's foremost settlement, Main St is a beach lined with hammocks and open air bar-restaurants, if that gives you a hint as to the vibe. Kick off your shoes, then join Foxy and friends to let the good times roll.

Other than hanging out, there's not much to do besides stop by **JVD Scuba** ( ☎ 495-0271; www.jostvandykescuba.com; 8am-6pm), which can set you up with ecotours, kayak rentals and dives.

The **customs office** ( ☎ 494-3450; 8:30am-3:30pm Mon-Fri, 9am-12:30pm Sat) is on Main St. The police station next door stocks a few brochures about local businesses.

If you want the true local lowdown, Foxy's your man. Stop by Foxy's Tamarind Bar or check out www.foxysbar.com.

Since most of Jost's businesses cater to crews from visiting yachts, almost all of the restaurants and bars stand-by on VHF radio channel 16 to take reservations and announce nightly events.

On the waterfront, just east of Foxy's, the gracious Ivy Chinnery Moses has four large studio apartments at the **Sea Crest Inn** ( ☎ 495-9024; seacrestinn@hotmail.com; apt US$145; ), each with a kitchenette and balcony.

**Christine's Bakery** ( ☎ 495-9281; mains US$5-12; breakfast & lunch) is the kind of out-island bakery you dream about. Christine has the settlement filled with the scent of banana bread, coconut and coffee by 8am; burgers and sandwiches are for lunch. She also rents out a couple of simple rooms above the bakery.

Rudy George runs **Rudy's Mariner's Rendezvous** ( ☎ 495-9282; mains US$17-32; lunch & dinner), a bar, restaurant and convenience store rolled into one. The oceanside restaurant serves delicious seafood; lobster and local fish are the specialties. Nearby, **Ali Baba's** ( ☎ 495-9280; mains US$22-35; breakfast, lunch & dinner) has a lazy, down-island atmosphere on its open-air patio. Patrons come for fresh fish and the Monday night pig roast (US$25).

**our pick** **Foxy's Tamarind Bar** ( ☎ 495-9258; www .foxysbar.com; mains US$22-35; lunch & dinner) is not to be missed. You probably heard about him long before you arrived: so who is this Foxy? Well, he's Foxy (Philiciano) Callwood, born on Jost in 1938, and he single handedly put the island on the map with this beach bar. Local bands play several nights a week (usually Thursday through Saturday) in season and draw a mix of islanders and party animals off the boats. The light fare is a mix of rotis (US$14) and burgers (about US$10), while the dinner mains are mostly meat and seafood. Foxy has his own microbrewery on site, so fresh tap beers accompany the food. For years Foxy sang his improvisational calypso at the

---

**SHIP AHOY**

No, it's not the booze playing tricks with your eyes. If you walk 'round back of Foxy's complex, you really do see a 32ft wooden sloop rising from the yard. It's the handiwork of the **JVD Preservation Society** (www.jvdps.org) or, more accurately, the local teenagers employed by the society to construct the *Endeavor II*.

It's part of a nonprofit project to provide Jost's kids with traditional boat-building skills and to keep them from straying into off-island temptations. The society pays the boys and girls for their efforts, they stay on the island and learn a time-honored trade, and in the process Jost preserves its culture.

'We're not building a boat,' says Kevin Gray, the long-time resident and ship captain who leads the project. 'The boat is building a community.'

The group has been hammering away since 2004; the *Endeavor* is scheduled for completion in late 2008. The kids will then learn to sail the sloop, as well as study local marine science and conservation.

Check **Sloop News** (www.sloopnews.org) for reports of their progress.

---

bar, but throat issues have curtailed the tunes for now.

## WHITE BAY

Jost's most attractive strand of beach hugs a barrier reef that shelters the bay from swells and waves, which makes for good swimming and anchoring. It's a primo place to stay, thanks to its multibudget lodging options and highly entertaining beach bars. It's a hilly, one-mile, bun-burning walk from Great Harbour.

**White Bay Campground** ( ☎ 495-9312, 495-9358; campsites/equipped tents/cabins US$20/40/65) is one of Virgin Islands' most popular stops for backpackers. Ivan, the owner, mixes it up by offering bare sites (the best of the bunch, right on the beach, where you can string your hammock between sea-grape trees), equipped tents (beds, linens) and cabins (add electricity to the beds and linens). Everyone shares the communal kitchen and cold-water bathhouse. The tents, cabins and facilities are very barebones, which may explain why Ivan recently added a couple of apartments with private bathrooms (from US$1000 per week). Ivan's Stress-Free Bar draws crowds for the cookouts and cold beer; it's a Jost institution.

**our pick** **Perfect Pineapple** ( ☎ 495-9401; www .perfectpineapple.com; villas from US$150; 🐾 ) has six great-value, white-with-purple-trim villas set on a steep hill back from the beach. Each unit has a full kitchen and private porch with ocean views. They're owned by Foxy's son Greg; the family also owns a restaurant down on the beach if you don't want to cook your own meals.

At **White Bay Villas** ( ☎ 410-571-6692, 800-778-8066; www.jostvandyke.com; villas from US$200) Bonnie rents out beachfront villas, some private and some with shared common areas. Rentals typically are for weekly stays, but you might snag a three- or five-night opening.

Right on the beach at White Bay's west end, **Sandcastle Hotel** ( ☎ 495-9888; www .sandcastle-bvi.com; d US$245-295) offers four cottages and two hotel rooms, all sans phone and TV (and only the hotel rooms have air-conditioning). The hotel holds the infamous Soggy Dollar Bar, which takes its name from the sailors swimming ashore to spend wet bills. It's also the bar that created the Painkiller, the BVIs' delicious-yet-lethal cocktail. The restaurant offers a four-course gourmet candlelit dinner for US$39 per person. Ruben Chinnery sings calypso on most Sunday afternoons, when lots of yachts stop by for lunch.

**One Love** ( ☎ 495-9829) Foxy's son Seddy owns this reggae-blasting beach bar. He'll wow you with his magic tricks, and certainly magic is how he gets the place to hold together – old buoys, life preservers and other beach junk form its 'walls.'

## LITTLE HARBOUR

This is Jost's quieter side, with just a few businesses. Little Harbour's east edge has a thin, steep strand of white sand perfect for sunbathing and swimming in water totally protected from wind and waves.

Swimmers can reach **Bubbly Pool**, a natural whirlpool formed by weird rock outcrops, via a goat trail from Foxy's Taboo.

Right on the water, **Sidney's Peace and Love** ( ☎ 495-9271; mains US$10-25; ☾ lunch & dinner) serves up West Indian specialties, along with burgers and barbecue. Live reggae bands play here most nights. Saturday night rocks with charter yacht crews. T-shirts left behind by visiting revelers decorate the rafters. A popular T-shirt for sale here proclaims 'Time flies when you ain't doin' shit.'

On the east side of the harbor, **Abe's by the Sea** ( ☎ 495-9329; mains US$10-30; ☾ breakfast, lunch & dinner) specializes in West Indian fish dishes. There's often live fungi music at night.

Foxy teams up with his daughter Justine at **Foxy's Taboo** ( ☎ 495-0218; mains $13-22; ☾ lunch & dinner) to serve easy, breezy dishes such as pizza and pepper-jack cheeseburgers for lunch, and more sophisticated fare (say lobster-stuffed tilapia) for dinner, all accompanied by Foxy's microbrews. Taboo sits in a scenic dockside shack by Diamond Cay.

# ANEGADA

**pop 200**

Anegada is a killer island. Literally. The island takes its name from the Spanish word for 'drowned' or 'flooded,' and that's what it did to more than 300 ships in the early years – it sunk 'em. The island is so low (28ft above sea level at its highest) that mariners couldn't see it to get their bearings until they were trapped in the surrounding coral maze known as Horseshoe Reef.

Today it's the salt ponds rife with flamingos, blooming cacti and giant rock iguanas that will slay you (figuratively, of course!). You can dive on many of the shipwrecks, or snorkel from ridiculously blue-watered beaches such as Loblolly Bay and Flash of Beauty.

The ferry takes only 1.5 hours to reach this easternmost Virgin, about 12 miles from Virgin Gorda, but you'll think you've landed on another planet. Its desert landscape looks that different, and its wee clutch of restaurants and guesthouses are that baked-in-the-sun mellow. It's a mysterious, magical and lonesome place to hang your hammock for a stretch.

The Anegada Reef Hotel, located near the dock, serves as the unofficial information center for the island. Anegada has no banks, so stock up before you get here.

## Orientation

Anegada is a coral atoll stretching about 12 miles from west to east and, at most, 3 miles from north to south. Because it's so pancake-flat, the island's horizon holds few visual landmarks except for odd clumps of casuarinas and coconut trees.

The main road starts at the airport in the island's center and swings by the Settlement, Anegada's only 'town' (a strong word for such a small place). From the Settlement, the road heads west to the yacht anchorage and ferry dock at Setting Point, then onward past several pristine beaches.

## Getting There & Away

**Smith's Ferry** ( ☎ 494-4454; www.smithsferry.com; round trip US$50) sails from Road Town, Tortola on Monday, Wednesday and Friday at 7am and 3:30pm; it departs Anegada at 8:30am and 5pm. The boat makes a quick stop at Spanish Town, Virgin Gorda, en route each way.

Otherwise, **Fly BVI** ( ☎ 495-1747, 866-819-3146; www.fly-bvi.com) offers charter flights from Tortola's airport from US$155 (round trip). Tiny Captain Auguste George Airport lies 1 mile northwest of the Settlement.

## Getting Around

Jeep rentals cost about US$75 per day at the Anegada Reef Hotel. Roads are unpaved sand for the most part.

**Tony's Taxi** ( ☎ 495-8037) waits for inbound ferries, and Tony will give you a three-hour island tour for about US$50. Shuttles (one way US$8) run to the beaches from the Anegada Reef Hotel.

## WEST END

If you take the ferry to Anegada, you'll arrive at Setting Point, by the Anegada Reef Hotel, which serves as the unofficial information center. **We Be Divin'** ( ☎ 494-4320, 541-0489; www.webedivinbvi.com) sits on the property's beachfront and can organize whatever activity your heart desires: shore dives (two tanks US$125), boat dives (two tanks US$150), snorkel gear rentals (per day US$20), kayak rentals (per day US$50) and ecotours (half day per person US$50). If you're interested in **fishing** or **cycling** enquire at the hotel's office, where they'll make arrangements.

The large salt pond at the west end of the island is home to a flock of flamingos, which were successfully reintroduced to the BVIs

---

**THE TIMES THEY ARE A-CHANGIN'**

Everard Faulkner, aged 75, is a retired builder who was born and raised on Anegada.

**What changes have you seen on Anegada over the years?**

We had 500 people here when I was a boy. Now there are about 200. I left, too. I went to St Thomas to work. When my father died in 1981, I came home to build his coffin. I decided to stay and build more. I built some of Neptune's Treasure and many of the other shops and hotels.

**How has the environment changed?**

We had more flamingos. People used to shoot them and eat them. Tastes like chicken, I hear. I've never eaten one. For a while we had no flamingos. So biologists brought in 18 from Bermuda. Now there are about 50 flamingos here on the salt pond. They eat shrimp, that's what makes them pink. Another thing: lobsters. They were just bait when I was a boy; we used them to catch fish. Now people pay a lot of money to eat lobsters.

**What makes Anegada different from other islands?**

The quiet. Nobody to trouble you. I get up in the morning and don't have to worry about a thing.

---

from 1987. The BVI National Parks Trust designated **Flamingo Pond** and its surrounding wetlands as a bird sanctuary; you can also see egrets, terns and ospreys nesting and feeding in the area.

Secluded **Cow Wreck Bay** stretches along the island's northwest end and offers good snorkeling in its shallow waters; kayaks are available, too.

The nine simple, color-washed rooms at **Neptune's Treasure** ( ☎ 495-9439; www.neptunestreasure.com; r from US$115; ✗ ) sit right on the sand and garner lots of loyalist patrons. The rooms surround a restaurant that's open for lunch and dinner, which has a meat-and-seafood menu (mains US$18 to US$30) similar to the island's other waterfront establishments, but with one difference: it's served in an air-conditioned dining room rather than the great outdoors.

Neptune's is a 15-minute walk west from the **Anegada Reef Hotel** ( ☎ 495-8002; www.anegadareef.com; r garden/ocean view from US$175/200; ✗ ▢ ). The island's first and largest hotel, this seaside lodge by the ferry dock has the feel of a classic out-island fishing camp. The property's 16 rooms and two-bedroom villas are nothing fancy, but the fishing dock, restaurant (mains US$8 to $30, open for breakfast, lunch and dinner) and beach bar here are Anegada's social epicenter. A lot of yachts pull up to join the party, while fish and lobster sizzle on the grill. For those on budgets: if you ask nicely, the owners will let you pitch a tent (US$20) in the garden.

ourpick **Anegada Seaside Villas** ( ☎ 495-9466; www.anegadavillas.com; villas US$200) has seven units, each with a fully equipped kitchen and big sea-view patio. People book a year in advance

in high season to stay in these one-bedroom, yolk-yellow concrete cottages. The onsite **Pomato Point Restaurant** ( ✗ lunch & dinner) has a cool 'museum' to explore (basically a side room that exhibits a bizarre mix of archeological relics and shipwreck items owner Wilfred Creque collected from local waters).

You want peace and quiet? It'll just be you and the wandering bovines who share the grounds at **Cow Wreck Villas** ( ☎ 495-8047, restaurant 495-9461; www.cowwreckbeach.com; villas US$250-300; ✗ ). Three sunny yellow-and-green cottages front the perfect, hammock-strewn beach. The open-air restaurant (mains US$10 to $25) features lobster, conch and shellfish cooked on the outdoor grill, and is open for lunch and dinner.

**Whistling Pines** ( ☎ 495-9521; mains US$20-40; ✗ lunch & dinner) is one of the island's newer bar-restaurants and offers the usual seafood suspects. Located on the beach between the Anegada Reef Hotel and Neptune's Treasure, Pines has good views of moored yachts out front plus an island rarity: a pool table.

**Potter's by the Sea** ( ☎ 495-9182; mains US$25-40; ✗ dinner) is the first place you stumble into when departing the ferry dock. Potter lived in Queens, New York and worked in the restaurant biz there for years, so he knows how to make customers feel at home while serving them ribs, fettuccine, curried shrimp and lobster. Graffiti and T-shirts cover the open-air walls; live bands play Monday and Tuesday.

## EAST END

The **Settlement**, Anegada's only town, lies on the East End. It's a picture of dead cars (you can get them on the island, but you can't get them off), laundry drying in the breeze and folks feeding goats and chickens. There are a couple of teensy shops where you can buy food and supplies.

The **Rock Iguana Nursery** ( ☎ 8am-4pm) sits behind the government administration building; just let yourself in. The Parks Trust started the facility because feral cats were eating the island's baby iguanas, endangering the rare species. So workers now bring the babes to the nursery's cages to grow safely. After two years, they're big enough to be released back into the wild, where they'll sprout to 6ft long.

Top beaches with thatched-umbrella shelters and bar-restaurants include **Loblolly Bay** on the northeast shore, about 2 miles from the Settlement. You can snorkel over a widespread area with spotted eagle rays and barracudas. At time of writing, a **kitesurfing facility** ( ☎ 549-2019) was set to open. Snorkeling at **Flash of Beauty**, just east of Loblolly, is through a more compact area but with bigger coral and lots of funny-looking fish.

Locals come to the small, tin-roofed **Dotsy's Bakery & Sandwich Shop** ( ☎ 495-9667; mains US$6-14; ✆ breakfast, lunch & dinner Mon-Sat) in the Settlement for her fresh-baked breads, breakfasts, fish-and-chips, burgers and pizzas.

After you finish snorkeling, climb up to shore to **Flash of Beauty Restaurant** ( ☎ 495-8014, 441-5815; mains US$9-18; ✆ lunch & dinner), where Monica and crew await with sandwiches, burgers, conch stew and, yep, lobster (it's usually lower-priced here, around US$40). She also makes a mean 'bushwhacker' – a milkshake-esque drink using seven liquors.

---

**LOBSTER LOWDOWN**

Cracking an Anegada lobster is a tourist rite of passage. Every restaurant serves the *mondo* crustaceans, usually grilled on the beach in a converted oil drum and spiced with the chef's secret seasonings. Because the critters are plucked fresh from the surrounding waters, you must call ahead by 4pm to place your order so each restaurant knows how many to stock. Most places charge US$50 to indulge. Note that lobster fishing is prohibited from August 15 through November 1 so stocks can replenish, thus they're not on menus (nor is conch) during that time.

---

Aubrey Levons' popular restaurant-bar **Big Bamboo** ( ☎ 495-2019; mains US$14-25; ✆ lunch & dinner) is on the beach at Loblolly Bay's west end and specializes in island recipes for lobster, fish and chicken.

# DIRECTORY

## ACCOMMODATIONS

One of the best things about the BVIs is the range of accommodations available, especially on Tortola, where you can find moderately priced guesthouses as well as swanky resorts. The **BVI Tourist Board** (www.bvitourism.com) provides lodging information on its website; it breaks out locally owned properties as 'Jewels' and has a special telephone number ( ☎ 866-468-6284) for more information. Some properties have three-night minimum stay requirements during the December 15 through April 15 peak season.

On every hotel bill, you'll see an added 7% government tax and often a service charge of 10% to 15% more.

## ACTIVITIES

Sailing is the BVIs' main claim to fame. For information on how to get on board, see the boxed text, p416.

### Diving & Snorkeling

The islands huddle to form a sheltered paradise of secluded coves, calm shores and crystal-clear water, which in turn provide outstanding underwater visibility, healthy coral and a wide variety of dive and snorkeling sites. Conservation is a big deal here, and there are lots of permanent mooring buoys. Safe, professional dive operators are plentiful and all go to the good spots, including the wreck of the RMS *Rhone*; see p398 for information on this and other top sites. Expect to pay about US$80 for a one-tank dive, US$110 for two tanks.

We recommend the following dive operators for their professionalism, friendliness and safety.

**Dive BVI** ( ☎ 495-5513, 800-848-7078; www.divebvi .com) Offices at Yacht Harbour and Leverick Bay, Virgin Gorda and at Marina Cay, Tortola.

**Dive Tortola** ( ☎ 494-9200, 800-353-3419; www.dive tortola.com) At Prospect Reef Marina, Tortola.

**Sail Caribbean** ( ☎ 495-1675; www.sailcaribbeandivers .com) At Hodges Creek Marina, Tortola.

**We Be Divin'** ( ☎ 494-4320; www.webedivinbvi.com)
Offices in Road Town, Tortola and Setting Point, Anegada.

## Surfing & Windsurfing
The BVIs offer ideal conditions for beginner and seasoned windsurfers. The water is warm and safe, the winds average a gentle 10 to 15 knots. Tortola's north coast serves surfers reliable swells from November to March, especially off Apple Bay and Josiah's Bay.

On Tortola, Island Surf & Sail (p399) and Boardsailing BVI (p402) offer windsurfing rentals and lessons for approximately US$100 per three-hour session. Last Stop Sports (p396) offers board rentals from US$37 per day.

## BOOKS
Birders should check out *A Guide to the Birds of Puerto Rico & the Virgin Islands* by Herbert Rafaela and *The Nature of the Islands: Plants & Animals of the Eastern Caribbean (A Chris Doyle Guide)* by Virginia Barlow. Shell collectors can use *A Field Guide to Shells: Atlantic and Gulf Coasts and the West Indies* by R Tucker Abbott and Percy A Morris.

Jinx and Jeff Morgan, owners of Tortola's Sugar Mill Hotel and highly acclaimed restaurant (see p402), fill their *Sugar Mill Caribbean Cookbook: Casual & Elegant Recipes Inspired by the Islands* with delicious recipes.

*The Cruising Guide to the Virgin Islands*, by Nancy and Simon Scott, is the essential guide for any sailor.

## BUSINESS HOURS
General BVI hours are below. Many places close on Sunday and many businesses shut down entirely in September and October.
**Banks** ⌚ 9am to 3pm Monday to Thursday, to 5pm Friday
**Bars & pubs** ⌚ noon to midnight
**Government offices** ⌚ 8:30am to 4:30pm Monday to Friday
**Post offices** ⌚ 8:30am to 4pm Monday to Friday, 9am to noon Saturday
**Restaurants** ⌚ breakfast 7am to 11am, lunch 11am to 2pm, dinner 5pm to 9pm
**Shops** ⌚ 9am to 5pm Monday to Saturday

## CHILDREN
The BVIs are an excellent destination for children. Many resorts have children's programs and babysitting services. Because this is such a big yachting and sailing destination, you'll see a lot of families around the marinas.

### PRACTICALITIES
- **Newspapers & Magazines** The three weekly newspapers are *Island Sun, BVI Beacon* and *StandPoint*. The free *Limin' Times* lists weekly entertainment.
- **Radio & TV** There are seven radio stations, including ZWAVE (97.3FM, reggae) and ZVCR (106.9FM, Caribbean). Puerto Rico's WOSO, at 1030AM, has international news, weather and hurricane coverage. For BVIs TV news, check Channel 5, the local-access channel.
- **Electricity** 110 volts; North American–style plugs have two (flat) or three (two flat, one round) pins.
- **Weights & Measures** Imperial system. Distances are in feet and miles; gasoline is measured in gallons.

On Virgin Gorda, **Tropical Nannies** ( ☎ 495-6493; www.tropicalnannies.com) provides babysitting services by trained, professional nannies. They'll come to your hotel or take the kids off your hands starting at US$15 per hour.

## DANGERS & ANNOYANCES
The BVIs have little street crime. Nevertheless, the usual rules of cautious conduct for travelers apply here. Drivers should be careful of wandering cattle, especially at night. Mosquitoes and sand fleas are an unfortunate part of life; you'll want good bug spray with you.

## EMBASSIES & CONSULATES
There are no foreign embassies or consulates in the BVIs. Head to the US Virgin Islands (p385) if you need consular assistance.

## FESTIVALS & EVENTS
As well as Tortola's monthly full-moon festivals at Bomba's Shack (p401) and Aragorn's Studio (p402), there are several big draws throughout the year.
**Virgin Gorda Easter Festival** ( ☎ 495-5181) Three-day celebration surrounding the Christian holiday in March or April; see p406.
**BVI Spring Regatta** ( ☎ 494-3286; www.bvispring regatta.org) The granddaddy of Tortola's myriad yacht races has become one of the Caribbean's biggest parties. It features seven days of small- and large-craft races in early April and provides a time-honored excuse to swill beer, sip

rum, listen to live music and party with sailors and crew from around the world.

**BVI Music Festival** ( ☎ 495-3378; www.bvimusicfest .info) Big-name acts wail at Cane Garden Bay, leading up to Foxy's regatta in late May; see p400.

**Foxy's Woodenboat Regatta** ( ☎ 495-9258) Foxy hosts several sailing events, but are none bigger than this regatta, held off Jost van Dyke over the US Memorial Day weekend in late May. Since 1974 the annual regatta has drawn in classic wooden yachts for four days of light racing and heavy partying.

**Highland Spring HIHO** ( ☎ 494-7963; www.go-hiho .com) Windsurfers converge on the BVIs in late June for the Hook-In-Hold-On races.

**BVI Emancipation Festival** ( ☎ 494-3134) Occurs over two weeks at the end of July and beginning of August. During this time, Tortola rocks from the West End to the East End, celebrating its African-Caribbean heritage.

Jost van Dyke also has garnered an international reputation as the place to be on New Year's Eve.

## GAY & LESBIAN TRAVELERS

While a fair number of islanders and travelers in the BVIs are gay, West Indian taboos on the lifestyle are slow to crumble. You are not likely to meet many 'out' gays or lesbians, nor are you likely to see public displays of affection among gay couples.

## HOLIDAYS

**New Year's Day** January 1
**Commonwealth Day** Second Monday in March
**Good Friday** Friday before Easter (in March or April)
**Easter Monday** April
**Whit Monday** May or June (date varies)
**Sovereign's Birthday** June (date varies)
**Territory Day** July 1
**BVI Festival Days** First Monday to first Wednesday in August
**St Ursula's Day** October 21
**Christmas Day** December 25
**Boxing Day** December 26

## INTERNET ACCESS

On Tortola and Virgin Gorda you'll find internet cafés near the main marinas; we've listed several places in the chapter's Information sections. Rates are about US$5 per half hour. Access is not common in hotels.

## INTERNET RESOURCES

**British Virgin Islands** (www.bvitourism.com) BVI Tourist Board's official website.

**BVI Beacon** (www.bvibeacon.com) The local newspaper's website, with news updates.

**BVI Welcome Magazine** (www.bviwelcome.com) Online version of the free tourist magazine that lists anchorages, beaches, diving sites and more.

**Foxy's** (www.foxysbar.com) The man, the legend, provides Jost info (dated but still useful).

**Limin' Times** (www.limin-times.com) When and where local bands are playing.

## MAPS

Pick up a free road map at the BVI Tourist Board (above). It covers all the islands and should suffice for driving trips.

## MEDICAL SERVICES

The BVIs' only hospital, **Peebles Hospital** ( ☎ 494-3497; Main St; ☯ 24hr), is in Road Town. The other islands have small, part-time clinics.

## MONEY

The US dollar is used throughout the BVIs. You'll find FirstBank, Scotiabank, First Caribbean and Banco Popular in Road Town, with ATMs hooked into worldwide networks (Plus, Cirrus, Exchange etc). Spanish Town has a couple of banks, but there's nothing on the other islands.

## POST

The BVIs have their own postal service. Tortola has five post offices, one at Road Town and small regional offices at Cane Garden Bay, Carrot Bay, East End and West End. Virgin Gorda has two. The other islands have none. Letters to the USA/Europe/ Australia cost US$0.50/0.60/0.75; postcards cost US$0.35/0.40/0.50.

## TELEPHONE

The BVIs country code is ☎ 284, but you just dial the seven-digit local number on the islands. To call from North America, dial ☎ 1 + 284 + the local number. From elsewhere, dial your country's international

---

**EMERGENCY NUMBERS**

- **Ambulance** ☎ 999, 911
- **Fire** ☎ 999, 911
- **Police** ☎ 999 or 911
- **Virgin Islands Search & Rescue** ☎ 767, VHF 16

dialing code then ☎ 284 + the local number. We've included only the seven-digit local number in BVIs listings in this chapter.

Many businesses also have toll-free numbers; these begin with ☎ 800, ☎ 888 or ☎ 877.

GSM phones work on the islands. SIM cards are available at local shops. They cost about US$20, which includes US$10 of air time (at roughly US$0.30 per minute calling time to the US). CCT Global and Digicel provide the local cellular service. Working pay phones are difficult to find.

Be prepared for whopping charges – the BVIs are one of the most expensive places in the world to call.

## TOURIST INFORMATION

Contact the **BVI Tourist Board** ( ☎ 800-835-8530; www.bvitourism.com or www.bvi.org.uk) pre-departure, or stop into one of its offices once you're on the islands.

**Tortola** ( ☎ 494-3134; DeCastro St, Akara Bldg; 8:30am-4:30pm Mon-Fri) In Road Town.

**Virgin Gorda** ( ☎ 495-5181; Yacht Harbour mall; 9am-5pm Mon-Sat, 10am-2pm Sun) In Spanish Town.

## TRAVELERS WITH DISABILITIES

The BVIs are not particularly accessible and do not have any specific services geared toward travelers with disabilities.

## VISAS

Visitors from most Western countries do not need a visa to enter the BVIs for 30 days or less. If your home country does not qualify for visa exemption (check www.bvi .org.uk/nationals_requiring_a_visa.asp. html), contact your nearest **British embassy** (www.ukvisas.gov.uk) or the **BVI Immigration Department** ( ☎ 494-3471).

## WOMEN TRAVELERS

It's safe for women to travel solo in the BVIs. Just use the same degree of caution you would in a big city at home: be aware of your surroundings, especially when walking alone at night.

## WORK

Only Belongers (naturalized citizens) can work without a permit in the BVIs. The government doesn't issue work permits easily, as it's keen to give jobs to locals.

---

> ### DEPARTURE TAX – AIR
>
> You must pay a US$20 departure tax to leave the BVIs by air. This is not included in the ticket price, and must be paid separately at the airport.

# TRANSPORTATION

## GETTING THERE & AWAY
### Entering the British Virgin Islands

Everyone needs a passport to enter the BVIs; some nationalities also need a visa (see left). Officials might ask to see a return ticket and proof of funds, though that's rare. It can take a half hour or so to clear customs. There's no reason why, other than it's just a slow-moving process. If you're arriving on a ferry from the USVIs, you'll clear through a **customs house** ( ☎ 494-3864; www.bviports.org) near the dock; there are customs houses in Road Town and West End on Tortola, and on Virgin Gorda and Jost Van Dyke.

### Air

The BVIs have three airports. **Terrence B International Lettsome Airport** (EIS; ☎ 494-3701) is the BVIs' main airport; it's a modern facility at Beef Island, off Tortola. **Virgin Gorda Airport** (VIJ; ☎ 495-5621) is a small facility with a restaurant, and Captain Auguste George Airport is a tiny facility on Anegada for charter flights.

There are no direct flights to the BVIs from the USA, Canada or Europe. Flights connect through hubs in the Caribbean, usually via Puerto Rico, St Thomas or Antigua. Some airlines flying to/from the BVIs:

**Air Sunshine** ( ☎ 495-8900, 888-879-8900; www.airsun shine.com) San Juan

**American Eagle** ( ☎ 495-2559, 800-433-7300; www.aa .com) San Juan

**Cape Air** ( ☎ 495-2100, 800-352-0714; www.flycapeair .com) San Juan

**LIAT** ( ☎ 340-774-2313; www.liatairline.com) Antigua

**Seaborne Airlines** ( ☎ 340-773-6442, 888-359-8687; www.seaborneairlines.com) St Thomas

**WinAir** ( ☎ 494-2347, 495-1298; www.fly-winair.com) St-Martin/Sint Maarten

### Sea
#### CRUISE SHIP

Cruise ships call at Road Town's harbor on Tortola. One or two ships typically arrive

## YACHT CHARTER BASICS

The BVIs provide it all: a year-round balmy climate, steady trade winds, little to worry about in the way of tides or currents, a protected thoroughfare in the 35-mile-long Sir Francis Drake Channel, and hundreds of anchorages, each within sight of one another. These factors make the islands one of the easiest places to sail, which explains why more than a third of all visitors come to do just that.

If you want to sail, there are three basic options: a sailing school; a bareboat charter (bare of crew but fully equipped) with or without a skipper; or a more luxurious crewed charter, complete with captain, cook and crew.

A typical week-long itinerary involves sampling the islands, while partially circumnavigating Tortola. The attraction of a sailing vacation is that you can sail or stay put as long as you want, look for quiet anchorages or head for the party spots and add on diving, hiking or shopping trips at will.

The cost of chartering a boat depends on the vessel's size and age and the time of year. It is a misconception that sailing is too expensive; once you do a little research you might be pleasantly surprised.

### Choosing a Company

Charter companies depend on their reputations. Ask for references and spend time talking with the company's representatives. Most companies sail out of the Moorings at Wickhams Cay 2 in Road Town.

For an up-to-date list of services, prices and equipment check the **Sail magazine website** (www.sailmag.com).

### Charters

**Catamaran Company** ( ☎ 494-6661, 800-262-0308; www.catamaranco.com)
**Horizon Yacht Charters** ( ☎ 494-8787, 877-494-8787; www.horizonyachtcharters.com)
**Moorings** ( ☎ 494-2331, 888-952-8420; www.moorings.com)
**Sunsail Yacht Charters** ( ☎ 495-4740, 888-350-3568; www.sunsail.com)
**Tortola Marine Management** ( ☎ 494-2751, 800-633-0155; www.sailtmm.com)

### Crewed Boats

People looking for a crewed-yacht vacation can contact the **BVI Charter Yacht Society** ( ☎ 494-6017; www.bvicrewedyachts.com), an overarching trade group for the industry. Crewed boats are also booked by brokers who know individual boats and their crews. The following is a list of reputable brokers.

**Catamaran Company** ( ☎ 494-6661, 800-262-0308; www.catamaranco.com)
**Ed Hamilton & Co** ( ☎ 800-621-7855; www.ed-hamilton.com)
**Sailing Vacations** ( ☎ 495-4740, 888-350-3568; www.sunsail.com)
**Sunsail Sailing Vacations** ( ☎ 800-327-2276; www.sunsail.com)

### Sailing Schools

**Bitter End Sailing School** ( ☎ 494-2745, 800-872-2392; www.beyc.com) The Bitter End Yacht Club (p407) on Virgin Gorda offers beginner to advanced courses.
**Offshore Sailing School** ( ☎ 800-221-4326; www.offshore-sailing.com) Has learn-to-cruise courses out of Road Town, Tortola.

each day during winter, and their passengers quickly overwhelm the small settlement. Many passengers flock via taxis to Cane Garden Bay beach, or else they hop on the ferry to Virgin Gorda to take a look at the Baths.

See p830 for more information on cruises and individual lines.

### FERRY

There are excellent ferry connections linking Tortola, Virgin Gorda and Jost Van Dyke with the USVIs' St Thomas and St John. You must have a valid passport to travel between the BVIs and USVIs.

**Smith's Ferry** ( ☎ 494-4454; www.smithsferry.com) and **Native Son** ( ☎ 495-4617; www.nativesonbvi.com) alternate departure times in traveling from Road Town to downtown Charlotte Amalie on St Thomas, first stopping at West End (round trip US$45, about 60 minutes). **Road Town Fast Ferry** ( ☎ 494-2323; www.roadtownfastferry .com) makes the trip to Charlotte Amalie direct (round trip US$49, 50 minutes).

Ferries travel from West End (Tortola) to Red Hook (St Thomas) four to five times daily (round trip US$45, 30 minutes) with **Native Son** ( ☎ 495-4617; www.nativesonbvi.com). Ferries also travel from West End to Cruz Bay (St John) three times daily (round trip US$45, 30 minutes) via **Inter-Island** ( ☎ 495-4166).

Inter-Island makes limited runs between Jost Van Dyke and Red Hook (St Thomas) via Cruz Bay (St John). Ferries sail the route twice daily on Friday, Saturday and Sunday (round trip US$50, 45 minutes). Inter-Island also operates between Virgin Gorda and Red Hook (St Thomas) via Cruz Bay (St John), with service once daily on Thursday and Sunday (round trip US$60, 75 minutes).

### YACHT
Lots of yachts drift into the BVIs. In Tortola they cluster in Road Town at the Moorings at Wickhams Cay 2; in Virgin Gorda they cluster at Yacht Harbour near Spanish Town; in Jost they cluster at Great Harbour; and in Anegada they're at Setting Point. Any of these places would be good for enquiring about hitching a ride as a crew member.

## GETTING AROUND
Ferries are the primary mode of transportation between islands and a great way to meet locals. None of the islands has public bus service.

### Air
To fly between islands you'll have to charter a plane. **Fly BVI** ( ☎ 495-1747, 866-819-3146; www.fly-bvi .com) is a well-regarded company that flies not only within the BVIs but to islands throughout the Caribbean.

### Boat
The islands have a frequent and inexpensive ferry service that's easy to navigate, despite

convoluted schedules. The full schedules are printed in most of the tourism guides, including the **BVI Welcome Guide** (www.bviwelcome.com), but the essentials are listed here.

See opposite for information on chartering a yacht.

### BEEF ISLAND TO NORTH SOUND
**North Sound Express** ( ☎ 495-2138) runs ferries from Trellis Bay on Beef Island (near Tortola's airport) to the north end of Virgin Gorda, stopping at the Valley (one way US$25, 20 minutes), Bitter End (one way US$35, 45 minutes) and Leverick Bay (one way US$20, 15 minutes). Reservations are required.

### ROAD TOWN TO ANEGADA
**Smith's Ferry** ( ☎ 494-4454; www.smithsferry.com; round trip US$50) sails from Road Town, Tortola on Monday, Wednesday and Friday at 7am and 3:30pm; it departs Anegada at 8:30am and 5pm. The boat makes a quick stop at Spanish Town, Virgin Gorda, each way.

### ROAD TOWN TO SPANISH TOWN
**Speedy's** ( ☎ 495-5240; www.speedysbvi.com) and **Smith's Ferry** ( ☎ 494-4454; www.smithsferry.com) run trips between Road Town, Tortola and Spanish Town, Virgin Gorda almost half-hourly (round trip US$25, 30 minutes).

### WEST END TO JOST VAN DYKE
**New Horizon Ferry** ( ☎ 495-9278; www.jostvandyke ferry.com; round trip US$20) sails five times daily between Tortola's West End and Jost's Great Harbour.

### Car
Driving is undoubtedly the most convenient way to get around individual islands, but be prepared for some crazy conditions. Steep, winding roads are often the same width as your car. Chickens and dogs dart in and out

of the roadway and, oh, did we mention the goats? Driving is on the left-hand side. Most cars come from the US, so the steering wheel is on the left-hand side of the vehicle.

Drivers often stop dead in the middle of the road. Watch for the flap: when drivers are about to do something (stop, turn etc), they flap their arm out the window. Be careful not to lose your keys; there are no locksmiths on the islands.

### RENTAL

There are several good local car-rental agencies on the islands. Often the vehicles are jeeps. High-season rates begin at about US$55 per day and can run as high as US$90, but you'll get a better price for a weekly rental. See each island's Getting Around section for local car-rental companies and their contact information.

## Taxi

Taxis are convenient and essential if you're not renting a car. Several are the open-air variety, with bench seats and awnings, able to carry up to 12 passengers; others are vans. Taxis do not have meters; fares are set rates (many of which are listed throughout this chapter).

**Beef Island Taxi Association** ( ☎ 495-1982)
**BVI Taxi Association** ( ☎ 494-3942)
**Waterfront Taxi Stand** ( ☎ 494-6362)
**West End Taxi Association** ( ☎ 495-4934)

# Anguilla

Something old, something new, something borrowed, something blue – wedding bells immediately come to mind, but what about Anguilla? As rabid consumerism devours many Caribbean hot spots, this little limestone bump in the sea has, thus far, maintained its charming menagerie of clapboard shacks (something old) while quietly weaving stunning vacation properties (something new) into the mix. Visitors will discover a melting pot of cultures (something borrowed) set along mind-blowing beaches (something very blue).

One of the most intriguing things about little Anguilla is that it's hard to decide whether or not the island is grossly underrated or if it actually garners more buzz than it deserves. Supporters cite the refreshing lack of development relative to neighboring islands (no casinos, nightclubs etc), and an earnest local vibe that remains very much intact. But on the other hand, extreme price hikes have turned the island into St-Barthélemy's stunt double for jetsetters.

While the debate will no doubt rage for years to come, most agree that the island's best feature (besides the oh-so-blue sea) is its malleability – Anguilla is a blank canvas, allowing visitors to design any vacation they please. Those seeking opulence and privacy can rent one of the many rambling villas, while those looking to dive headfirst into the gritty island culture will be sated with cold beer, reggae beats and nightly gatherings around smoky BBQs. And what's more satisfying than discovering a hidden local haunt which serves fresh lobster and big smiles for half the price of those big-name joints down the street?

## FAST FACTS

- **Area** 35 sq miles
- **Capital** The Valley
- **Country code** ☎ 264
- **Departure tax** US$20 airport & ferry terminal ($5 if returning the same day)
- **Famous for** Perfect beaches
- **Language** English
- **Money** Eastern Caribbean dollar (EC$); EC$1 = US$0.38 = €0.24 = UK£0.19
- **Official name** Anguilla
- **People** Anguillians
- **Phrase** Limin' (hanging out, preferably on a beach with a rum punch)
- **Population** 13,677
- **Visa** Not necessary for most nationalities; see p432

ANGUILLA

## HIGHLIGHTS

- **Beaches** (p430) Indulge in Anguilla's one true claim to fame – emerald waters and powder-soft sands ripped straight from the pages of your favorite travel magazine. Try the popular Shoal Bay East or the quieter windswept Junk's Hole
- **BBQ Tents** (p423) Devour succulent ribs with locals on their lunch break amid thick plumes of barbecue smoke
- **Live Music** (see boxed text, p424) Tap into Anguilla's nightly jam sessions at various hangouts around the island. The Dune Preserve draws in the big names, but don't forget to check out Sprocka's or the Pumphouse to hear some gifted local talent
- **Prickly Pear** (p428) Hop on a sailboat or catamaran and make your way over to this super-secluded mini-Anguilla, with its 360 degrees of flaxen sands and mellow turquoise waves
- **Private Villas** (p430) Rent a rambling beachside villa for the ultimate in privacy and pampering

## ITINERARIES

- **One Day** After arriving either at the airport or the ferry pier, rent a car and head to the Valley for an early lunch at one of the local BBQ tents. Continue east and spend the afternoon basking in the turquoise waters at Shoal Bay East, and then, depending on your mood, finish the day with a romantic dinner along Meads Bay, or hit the quaint bar scene in Sandy Ground.
- **Three Days** Grab a hotel room along Shoal Bay East or in the West End (penny-pinchers should try a place in the Valley) and spend your days worshipping the sun and evenings devoted to tracking down the nightly jam session – Sandy Ground's a good place to start.
- **One Week** Try out a villa rental rather than a hotel room for the utmost in privacy. Divide your time between doing absolutely nothing and taste-testing the flavorful local cuisine. Spend a sun-soaked day at Prickly Pear, and do a day trip to St-Martin/Sint Maarten to remind yourself why quiet Anguilla is tops for relaxation.

## CLIMATE & WHEN TO GO

The average annual temperature is 80.6°F (27°C), with the hottest weather occurring during the hurricane season from June to November. June, July and August, however, are known to be quite lovely as the intense humidity only kicks in around September, when hurricane season is at its peak. The average annual rainfall is 35in. The lightest rainfall is generally from February to April and the heaviest from October to December. Inflated high-season rates start around mid-December and go until mid-April. Many hotels shut down for the entire month of September and often October as well. Christmas or New Year's are crowded for obvious reasons, but surprisingly, February sees the most visitors.

## HISTORY

First settled by the Arawaks from South America over 3500 years ago, Anguilla was called 'Malliouhana,' which meant arrow-shaped sea serpent. The Arawaks settled the island for millennia, evidenced by many cave sites with petroglyphs and artifacts still visible today and studied by archaeologists.

Columbus sailed by in 1493, but didn't land on the island (probably because he didn't notice it since it's extremely flat compared to St-Martin/Sint Maarten next door). Britain sent a colony in 1650 to take advantage of soil that was hospitable to growing corn and tobacco. However, it wasn't hospitable to much else, and the plantation colonies that bloomed on nearby Caribbean islands, like St Kitts and Nevis, never defined Anguilla.

When the sugar plantations were abandoned due to a lack of viable soil and insufficient rain, small-scale industries, like sailing, fishing and private farming, began to crop up on the island. In 1834 Britain abolished slavery in its colonies, and many Anguillian ex-slaves took up positions as farmers, sailors and fishermen.

Soon after, Anguilla formed a federation with St Kitts and Nevis, which was disliked by most of the ex-slave population. Anguilla was allowed only one freeholder representative to the House of Assembly on St Kitts and was largely ignored, eventually culminating in the Anguilla Revolution in 1967. Anguilla Day marks May 30, 1967, the day Anguillians forced the Royal St Kitts Police off the island for good.

As a result of its revolt against St Kitts, Anguilla remains a British overseas territory. Under the Anguilla constitution, which came

# ANGUILLA

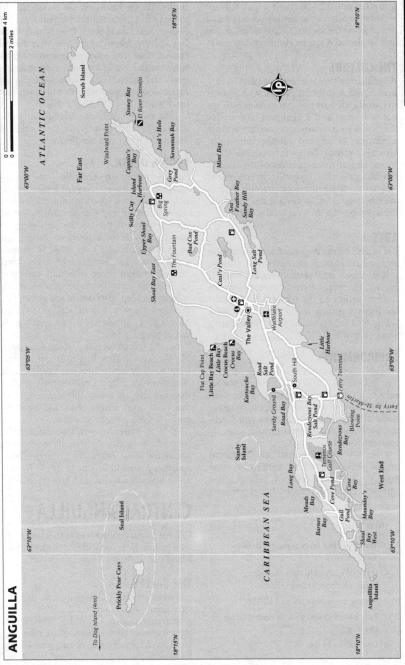

ATLANTIC OCEAN

Scrub Island

Far East

Stoney Bay
El Buen Consejo

Windward Point

Junk's Hole
Savannah Bay

Captain's Bay

Island Harbour

Mimi Bay

Scilly Cay

Upper Shoal Bay

Big Spring

Grey Pond

Sea Feather Bay

Sandy Hill Bay

The Fountain

Bud Cox Pond

Caul's Pond

Long Salt Pond

Shoal Bay East

Flat Cap Point

Little Bay Beach

Little Bay

Crocus Beach

Crocus Bay

Karrouche Bay

The Valley

Wallblake Airport

Little Harbour

Road Salt Pond

South Hill

Ferry Terminal

Ferry to St-Martin

Sandy Ground

Road Bay

Rendezvous Bay

Salt Pond

Blowing Point

Rendezvous Bay

Sandy Island

Long Bay

Temenos Golf Course

Cove Pond

Cove Bay

West End

Meads Bay

Barnes Bay

Gull Pond

Maunday's Bay

Shoal Bay West

CARIBBEAN SEA

Seal Island

Prickly Pear Cays

To Dog Island (4mi)

Anguillita Island

63°00'W
63°05'W
63°10'W

18°15'N
18°10'N

0       2 miles
0       4 km

into effect in 1982, one queen-appointed representative acts as the British governor and presides over the appointed Executive Council and an elected Anguilla House of Assembly.

## THE CULTURE

Anguillian culture is a blend of West Indian, British and African influences. As hockey is to Canada, sailboat racing is to Anguilla – the national sport and a vital part of everyday life. Races are a common occurrence and are a great way to hang out with the community. Upscale tourism drives the economy, and today, almost three-quarters of the island's inhabitants work in hospitality or commerce. Anguillians take pride in maintaining the balance between tourist development and the preservation of a thriving local society.

## ARTS

For a small island, Anguilla has an impressive arts and crafts scene that mostly focuses on inventive local artists rather than a rich textile history. There are currently about two-dozen resident artists on the island and 10 galleries displaying their work. A brochure for a self-guided tour is available from the tourist office (opposite).

## ENVIRONMENT

Anguilla lies 5 miles north of St-Martin/ Sint Maarten, an arid island shaped like an eel (its namesake). Almost 30 white-sand beaches have prompted countless imaginations to linger over whether one could subsist on a diet of coconuts to take an early retirement here.

Over 100 species of bird can be spotted on the island, including Antillean crested hummingbird, frigate, brown pelican, snow egret and black-necked stilt. Endangered sea

turtles, like the hawksbill, can be spotted offshore in five protected marine parks: Prickly Pear & Seal Island Reef, Dog Island, Little Bay, Sandy Island and Shoal Bay Island Harbor Reef. The most commonplace creatures on the island are the many roaming goats and sheep. Hint: if you see a slightly fuzzier-looking goat with its tail down, not up, it's actually a Caribbean sheep.

Like many Caribbean islands, Anguilla desalinates much of its water. Be mindful of letting the water run needlessly.

## FOOD & DRINK

Food is pricey on Anguilla – there's no escaping it. Almost everything sold on the island has been shipped in (much like every other island in the Caribbean); however, it's the hefty import tax that drives prices north. Anguilla does not have income tax, so each item brought on shore is charged a monstrous fee. Fortunately, many hotel and villa rooms come with fully equipped kitchens, so consider cooking some meals at home to keep costs down, and remember, groceries are priced in EC dollars, so don't have a heart attack when you spot a little can of soup for $6.

Lobster (common spiny lobster sans claws like the ones in New England) and crayfish (spotted spiny lobster) are two locally caught Anguillian specialties. Crayfish, while smaller than lobsters, are reasonably sized creatures that have sweet, tender meat, and are commonly served three to an order.

At local establishments, tap water usually comes from rooftop cisterns; however, most hotels run their rainwater through filters, and thus it should be fine to drink. Bottled water is readily available in grocery stores.

# CENTRAL ANGUILLA

Central Anguilla is devoted to function more than luxury. Here you will find the Valley (the island's capital) and Anguilla's airport.

## THE VALLEY

Although no part of Anguilla feels particularly urban, the Valley has the island's conglomeration of government buildings, which gives it a more conspicuous village vibe. The area was chosen as the colonial capital largely because of the abundance of arable soil; the

---

**HOW MUCH?**

- Taxi from the ferry terminal to the Valley US$16
- Daytrip to Prickly Pear including lunch and snorkeling US$80
- Smoky streetside BBQ ribs US$6
- Two beach chairs and an umbrella for the day US$10
- One gallon of gas US$5

island is mostly a limestone formation and thus there are only tiny pockets of viable land for farming. The main post office and most banks are located here, as are several large supermarkets.

## Information

**Anguilla Tourist Board** ( ☎ 497-2759, in USA 800-553-4939; www.anguilla-vacation.com; Coronation Ave, the Valley)

**Caribbean Commercial Bank** (CCB; ☎ 497-2571; www.ccb.ai)

**First Caribbean International Bank** ( ☎ 497-2301; www.firstcaribbeanbank.com)

**National Bank of Anguilla** (NBA; ☎ 497-2101; www.nba.ai)

**Post office** ( ☎ 497-2528; www.gov.ai/angstamp; ☒ 8am-3:30pm Mon-Thu, 8am-5pm Fri)

**Princess Alexandra Hospital** ( ☎ 497-2551)

**Public Library** ( ☎ 497-2441; the Valley; per 30min EC$5; ☒ 9am-5pm Mon-Fri, to noon Sat) Has internet access.

**Scotiabank Anguilla** ( ☎ 497-3333; bns.anguilla@scotiabank.com)

## Sights

Swing by the **National Trust of Anguilla** ( ☎ 497-5297; www.axanationaltrust.org; ☒ 8am-4pm Mon-Fri) and sign up for one of its heritage tours. There's not much in the way of preserved local history, but it's a good way to get under the skin of the island. It's best to book your tour 24 hours in advance and expect an 8am departure time.

The Valley's most interesting building is the **Wallblake House** ( ☎ 497-2944; ☒ tours 10am-2pm Mon, Wed & Fri). Built in 1787, it's the oldest structure on Anguilla and the only remaining plantation house on the island. Get a double dose of Caribbean history and check out the interior of the adjacent **St Gerard's church**, which has a unique design incorporating a decorative stone front, open-air side walls and a ceiling shaped like the hull of a ship.

## Sleeping

All accommodation in the Valley is located in the northwest part of town towards Crocus Bay. Prices here are reasonable compared to the rest of the island because of its inland location.

**Casa Nadine Guest House** ( ☎ 772-2517; www.casanadineguesthouse.com; r incl tax & service from US$45) At first glance Casa Nadine looks a tad derelict; the faded peach paint is falling off in chunks and mangy cats meow from the crevices in the eaves. But the rooms are sleepable and relatively clean, and no one dares to complain since it's the cheapest place on the island (by far). Room 5 is the 'swankiest' of the bunch (and we use term 'swanky' *very* loosely) featuring a large fridge, TV and views into the unkempt garden out back. The 10 other rooms are a mismash of amenities and quirks, like doorless bathrooms and windowless suites (which the owner explained were quite popular for those who want to sleep in). Though it may not be paradise, this little fixer-upper is a mere 10-minute walk from town and the beach.

**Lloyd's** ( ☎ 497-2351; www.lloyds.ai; s/d incl breakfast & tax US$99/135; ☒ ☐ ) Charming Lloyd's is hands down the best bang for your buck on Anguilla. This charming plantation-style B&B is slathered in bright yellows and accented by lime green clapboard shutters. Rooms are on the small side and have a palpable farmhouse quality, but that's all part of the charm. There are no ocean views, but the elevated terrain offers glimpses of the intriguing architectural jumble in the Valley. Offers wi-fi access.

**Crocus Bay Inn** ( ☎ 497-3298; www.crocusbayinn.com; ste US$145; ☒ ) Teeny tiny Crocus Bay Inn is a simple two-family bungalow across the street from the churning emerald waters of Crocus Bay. Behind the white-and-pink facade lies spacious apartment interiors outfitted with clean beige tiles and simple wooden cabinets throughout. The only downside is the noisy GE processing plant across the street beside the beach.

## Eating

**Hungry's** ( ☎ 235-8907; mains US$5-18; ☒ lunch & dinner Mon-Sat) Opposite the post office under a large almond tree, this popular operation serves up hearty island faves from a colorful truck covered in Caribbean stencil art. Irad and Papy, the owners/chefs, cater to long lines of working locals who stop through on their lunch break to grab a bowl of delectable conch soup (US$5) or unique lobster quesadillas (US$10).

**Ken's** (ribs US$6; ☒ lunch & dinner Fri & Sat) Every weekend, Ken's clan of spit-wielding cooks set up shop beside English Rose, near the corner of Carter Rey Blvd and Landsome Rd. Great puffs of smoke and steam billow out from underneath the large white tent as hungry customers gingerly smack their lips with anticipation. The juicy ribs are turned out by the

ANGUILLA

---

**TWIST MY ARM: THE SPOTS THE AUTHORS WANTED TO KEEP SECRET**

After 9pm on a Friday or Saturday **Fresh at Sprocka's** ( ☎ 497-0882; Airport Blvd; mains US$10-17; ☻ lunch & dinner) is the top spot to tap into Anguilla's chill local vibe. Known simply as 'Sprocka's,' this hidden gem near the airport dishes out cheap eats, but the main attraction is the hangout's namesake – Sprocka, the charismatic owner and homegrown musician. During the week he regales hotel guests at various resorts around the island, but on weekend evenings he retreats back to his bar and treats his faithful local following to an impressive array of musical selections.

---

dozen, and the do-it-yourself sauce bucket allows you drench your platter with an unlimited amount of sweet barbecue goodness. Grab a flaky johnnycake for an extra $0.50, and browse the collection of pirated DVDs to watch back at your villa while savoring your tasty meal.

**'Til Last Flight** ( ☎ 497-5169; Wallblake Airport; mains from US$8; ☻ breakfast & lunch) Who woulda thunk it – a restaurant at the airport that actually has delicious food for a reasonable price! Enjoy flavorful Anguillian favorites at this decidedly local haunt, and contemplate the bizarre phenomenon of going to the airport without taking a plane. Oh, and you guessed it, it's open 'til the last flight.

**English Rose** ( ☎ 497-5353; Carter Rey Blvd; lunch from US$8.95, dinner mains US$10-15; ☻ lunch & dinner Mon-Sat) Lunches are served cafeteria-style as locals line up to choose between savory goat stew, jerk chicken, and a selection of delectable side dishes like garlic pasta and creamy mashed potatoes. Make sure to get there on the early side – only one round of food is made for the day, and once its gone, they close until dinnertime. In the evenings, this casual spot retains its local vibe; small groups hunker down to watch the cricket match as the background thrums with island gossip and belly laughter. When in Rome…

**Koal Keel** ( ☎ 497-2930; Coronation Ave, Crocus Hill; mains $US24-30; ☻ dinner Mon-Sat) Housed in the original warden's quarters (one of the oldest structures on the island), the Valley's most romantic spot serves fusion Caribbean fare on crisp white tablecloths. You'll have to place your order 24 hours in advance for Koal Keel's specialty: 'rock oven chicken.' The in-house patisserie adds a certain French twist to the otherwise upscale West Indian atmosphere. Stop by on weekend evenings for some local live music.

If you're thinking about picking up groceries, the Valley has the largest selection at the lowest prices. All groceries are priced in EC dollars but US dollars are accepted everywhere. Try **JW Proctor** ( ☎ 497-2445; jw-proctors@anguillanet.com; The Quarter; ☻ 8am-8:30pm Mon-Fri, to 9:30pm Sat) or **Albert Lakes Marketplace** (Stoney Ground; ☻ 8am-8pm Mon-Fri, to 9pm Sat), which also has a great little hut in the parking lot called **Fat Cat** ( ☎ 497-2307; mains from $5; ☻ lunch & dinner), specializing in takeaway meals of various shapes and sizes. Call ahead for a picnic lunch prepared in a handy hamper. Fresh produce imported from St Lucia and Dominica is also available at the People's Market, a small green stall opposite the Anglican Church.

## SANDY GROUND

Although Sandy Ground isn't tops for ocean vistas, it's a worthy sleeping spot for those who only want to be a short stumble away from Anguilla's 'bar scene' (and we use that term loosely – true partiers should head one island over to Sint Maarten). The quaint cluster of bars and restaurants sits between the impossibly clear waters of Road Bay and a murky salt pond out back, which was commercially harvested until the 1970s, when it became economically unfeasible.

### Sights & Activities

As you come down the hill into Sandy Ground, check out **Pyrat Rums** ( ☎ 497-5003; www.patron spirits.com; ☻ 9am-5pm Mon-Sat). Nothing will wake you up in the morning quite like the sharp tang of locally made brew. Call ahead for a complimentary factory tour.

Friendly Dougie, the divemaster at **Special 'D' Diving** ( ☎ 235-8438; www.dougcarty.com; Sandy Ground), can practically call each fish, shark and turtle by name. And they'll come. He doesn't have an office so it's best to book ahead by phone or email. Boat tours are also on offer.

### Sleeping

Sandy Ground has a couple of options on the cheaper side of the spectrum; those searching for a true beach holiday should look elsewhere. There are several private villa options in the area as well, see p430 for information on rental agencies.

**Sea View Guest House** ( ☎ 497-2427; www.inns .ai/seaview; 1-/2-bedroom apt US$60/110) Across from the beach, both apartments are outfitted for a longer stay with full kitchens and maid service every other day. You'll be downstairs from a local Anguillian family who can help arrange diving and sightseeing adventures.

**Syd-An's Apartments & Villas** ( ☎ 497-3180; www .inns.ai/sydans; Sandy Ground; r from US$95; ✷ 💻 ) On Sandy Ground's main strip, across from the beach, Syd-An's has 10 pleasant apartments with separate bedrooms, full kitchens and cable TV situated around a convivial courtyard. Rooms with air-con cost a tad more.

**Ambia** ( ☎ 498-8686, in USA 203-699-8686; www.ambia -anguilla.com; r US$295, ste US$495; 💻 🐾 ) Perched on the side of a scrubby hill, Ambia's unassuming facade opens onto a large Zen space flanked by smooth wooden balusters and shade-bearing trees. The four rooms incorporate Asian stylistic elements (namely minimalism), and offer views of the distant moorings on Road Bay. There's wi-fi.

## Eating & Drinking

The undisputed top spot on Anguilla to get your drink on, Sandy Ground is chockablock with pub-style hangouts. On any given night of the week, at least one establishment offers up an enticing deal, whether it's live music, discount dinners, or two-for-one happy hours.

### SANDY GROUND ROAD

**Johnno's** ( ☎ 497-2728; meals US$7-14; ✷ noon-midnight, closed Mon) No shirt and no shoes will still get you service at this happening beach shack. Johnno's offers casual fare and tropical drinks to a blend of locals and travelers. Happy hour is from 5pm to 7pm, and there's live jazz on Sunday afternoons. Try the second location out on Prickly Pear island (see p428)

**Pumphouse** ( ☎ 497-5154, 497-5498; mains from US$13; ✷ dinner) At the far end of Sandy Ground, this former saltworks plant is now one of Anguilla's most chilled hot spots. The food is traditional pub grub with an international twist (like Korean quesadillas). Everyone gathers around on Thursday night for cheap drinks and live music. It offers wi-fi access.

**Ripples** ( ☎ 497-3380; mains US$15-25; ✷ lunch & dinner) The hip and happening spot for locals and travelers alike, Ripples serves staples like burgers and salads, but also Caribbean fusion dishes like Cajun fish with pineapple and lime salsa. It's open till midnight. Offers wi-fi.

**Roy's Bayside Grill** ( ☎ 497-2470; mains US$18-38; ✷ lunch & dinner) On the south end of Sandy Ground, Roy's feels a bit like a British pub along the beach. The conch chowder (US$10) is a must, but the pièce de résistance is the battered fish and chips (US$22). Stop by for Friday-night happy hour and take advantage of the discounted meal and drinks. It's a wi-fi hot spot.

**Elvis' Beach Bar** ( ☎ 461-0101, 772-0637; drinks from $3; ✷ until late) Affable Elvis, with his PhD in mixology, stirs up some serious island ale that'll make your lips pucker. His clique of loyal local patrons sits along log benches and barstools around the colorful bar – a beached wooden ship.

### SOUTH HILL

The following restaurants are located up the hill from Sandy Ground, along the main road connecting the Valley to the west end of the island.

**Geraud's** ( ☎ 497-5559; mains US$5-12; ✷ 5:30am-2pm Tue-Sat, 11am-2pm Sun) At the far west end of South Hill, just before entering the West End of the island, this quaint *boulangerie* bounces in the wee hours of the morning as the chefs hustle to bake the daily bread. By 2pm everything's been devoured including the tasty smoked-salmon sandwiches and quiche Lorraines.

**E's Oven** ( ☎ 498-8258; mains US$10-29; ✷ lunch & dinner, closed Tue) E's earns top marks across the board for great local food and competitive prices. Try the sweet potato lobster pancake (US$12), the chef's signature appetizer. Choosing the main course is a real nail-biter – should it be the Creole conch or grilled crayfish? Either way you can't go wrong.

**Tasty's** ( ☎ 497-2737; mains US$18-33; ✷ breakfast, lunch & dinner, closed Thu) A tad less expensive than the other island favorites of the same caliber, Tasty's offers creatively fused dishes, such as grilled tuna steak with orange Creole sauce or coconut-crusted fish fillet with spicy banana rum sauce. The bright teal and purple walls are smothered in shells and kitschy tropical paraphernalia.

ANGUILLA

---

**A ROYAL STAMP OF APPROVAL**

Allan Ruan is the self-proclaimed (and widely acknowledged) BBQ king, postmaster general and mayor of Prickly Pear.

**How has Anguilla changed in the last five years, and where do you see it heading in the future?**

In the last five years Anguilla has grown immensely – it's no longer being confused with Angola and Antigua! However, we can only hope that it does not get ahead of itself by growing too quickly. Anguilla is loved and revered because it's still quiet, and I sincerely hope it remains that way – it would be a shame if casinos started to emerge.

**What's the best advice for someone visiting Anguilla?**

According to my wife, Sue, the best advice would be to unpack half the things you were going to bring and be prepared to stay an extra week because chances are you will fall in love with the island and one week won't nearly be enough.

**What do you like to do on Anguilla to unwind?**

Days off are few and far between! But when Sue and I find time off, we love to sit and have a beer at Shoal Bay East by Uncle Ernies or Ku, and watch the sunset.

---

## BLOWING POINT

If you're coming to Anguilla by ferry, little Blowing Point will be the first community you encounter. Centered around the tiny pier, this little village consists of a small grocery, several parking lots full of rental cars and one quiet place to stay.

**El Rancho del Blues** (☎ 497-6164; Blowing Point) offers trail and beach rides on horseback.

A quick walk from the ferry pier, the seven apartment-style suites at the **Ferryboat Inn** (☎ 497-6613; www.ferryboatinn.ai; ste from US$200; ❄) offer stellar views of the jagged volcanic peaks of St-Martin/Sint Maarten nearby. The in-house restaurant with the same name spins delicious island cuisine.

# WESTERN ANGUILLA

As the island snakes in a westerly direction, lavish resorts unfurl along thick stretches of sand.

## MEADS BAY

Beautiful Meads Bay has a fat beach with thick dunelike sand. A row of resorts straddles the sea, although it feels significantly less crowded than Shoal Bay East. At the time of research, an enormous condo construction project was underway, which will undoubtedly change the face of this quiet, unpretentious cove.

### Activities

The Dutch-run **Anguillian Divers** (☎ 235-7742, 497-4750; www.anguilliandivers.com; Meads Bay) center operates on the west end of the island.

### Sleeping

**Sirena** (☎ 497-6827; www.sirenaresort.com; r from US$230; ❄ 💻 🏊) This is as good as it gets on Anguilla for less than US$300: two pools, a stylish on-site restaurant, up-to-date rooms, and a private spot on the sand with comfy beach chairs and umbrellas. Although you probably won't have a beach view from your room, Sirena's still a steal. During the summer months, prices drop around 50% depending on the type of room. Offers wi-fi access.

**Frangipani** (☎ 497-6442, in USA 866-780-5165; www.frangipaniresort.com; r US$350-475, ste $675-1800; ❄) This rambling Italian villa sits along a splendid stretch of perfect powdery sand punctuated by charming thatched umbrellas. Although decidedly Mediterranean in style, Frangipani incorporates a dash of Caribbean flair noticeable in the vibrant floral print bedspreads and hanging watercolors. Cheaper rooms face the gravel parking lot, while the large suites offer sweeping views of the sea and come with brand spankin' new kitchens. A small continental breakfast is included in the price.

**Carimar Beach Club** (☎ 497-6881, in USA 800-235-8667; www.carimar.com; 1-/2-bedroom ste from US$390/515; ❄) Each bougainvillea-draped Spanish-style apartment is equipped with a kitchen, living and dining rooms, and a balcony or patio. Ask the lovely staff about discounted low-season rates and special honeymoon packages.

**Malliouhana** (☎ 497-6111, in USA 800-835-0796; www .malliouhana.com; r from US$770; ❄ 💻 🏊) On a low cliff at the east end of Meads Bay, Malliouhana is one of the island's most fashionable luxury hotels. The rooms are gracefully appointed with Italian tile floors, marble baths, rattan furnishings, original artwork and large patios. Just strolling through the 25 acres of Mediterranean-style architecture and gardens will instill instant relaxation, and that's before you stroll to one of three adjacent beaches or get a massage at the top-notch spa. Offers wi-fi access.

## Eating

Almost every hotel along Meads Bay has a decent restaurant offering upscale fare and ocean views. There are also a couple of standout operations right along the smooth coral sand.

**B & D's** ( ☎ 497-6670; Long Bay; ribs US$7; ⏱ lunch & dinner, Fri & Sat) Just around the corner from the majestic Malliouhana, this tented BBQ shack gets rave reviews from locals and tourists alike; vacationing celebs have been known to stop through for some down-to-earth cookin'. Stock up on smoky barbecued perfection and don't forget to top off your ribs with the bread pudding and rum sauce. The hours tend to fluctuate – sometimes it's open on Thursday evenings and Sunday afternoons as well.

**Bananas By The Sea** ( ☎ 497-1208; lunch mains US$14-24, dinner mains US$28-39; ⏱ lunch & dinner Mon-Sat) This lovely option strikes the perfect balance between an upscale romantic atmosphere and chilled out sociable feel. You'll go bananas for the unobstructed ocean views and the wide selection of main courses, like the sesame-drenched tuna steak, the rack of lamb, and the inventive piña colada chicken. A charming linen tent on the sand can be arranged for a particularly romantic dinner.

## WEST END

Anguilla's rugged west end is largely the domain of wealthy vacationers who drop a thousand dollars per night on luxurious, butler-serviced suites. The pearly white sand at **Rendezvous Bay** beckons one to stroll its full 1.5-mile length. **Cove Bay** is next to Rendezvous Bay, within easy walking distance; **Seaside Stables** ( ☎ 235-3667; www.seaside-stables.com) is located here, offering horseback rides along the beach. Further along, **Shoal Bay West** isn't as stunning as its eastern namesake, but it's got fabulous snorkeling and a few nearby dive sites.

Stop by the ridiculous **Temenos Golf Club** ( ☎ 222-8200; www.temenosgolfclub.com; green fee $400), an 18-hole, 7100yd course designed by Greg Norman, to witness the fastest way in the world to drop a cool US$400 on a round of golf (we kid you not, that's $US22 per hole). The upside to playing at Temenos? You'll probably be the only one on the course.

## Sleeping

Most of Anguilla's celeb-seducing resorts are located along the milky sands of the island's secluded west end. All the options reviewed here (except Anguilla Great House) offer wi-fi.

**Paradise Cove Resort** ( ☎ 497-6603; www.paradise.ai; Cove Bay; ste US$280-625; 🍴 💻 ) A popular choice for those without a bottomless bank account, Paradise Cove is a comfy enclave featuring spacious rooms stocked with light Caribbean furnishings. The only downside is its inland location, although the ocean is only a 12-minute walk away.

**Anguilla Great House** ( ☎ 497-6061; in USA 800-583-9247; www.anguillagreathouse.com; Rendezvous Bay; ste US$290-340; 🍴 ) Although the name is a bit of a misnomer (it's more like the Anguilla Not-So-Great House), the rows of dated West Indian cottages offer ocean views at a smaller price tag than most of the other resorts on the island.

**CuisinArt** ( ☎ 498-2000, in USA 800-943-3210; www.cuisinartresort.com; Rendezvous Bay; ste from US$705; 🍴 💻 🏊 ) Although the name sounds more like a food processor than a top-notch resort, this expansive whitewashed paradise has so many perks and quirks that you'll probably never want to leave the grounds. Tag along on a detailed tour of the hotel's 18,000-sq-ft hydroponic greenhouse, which provides almost all of the fresh produce served in the on-site restaurants.

**Cap Juluca** ( ☎ 497-6666; in USA 888-858-5822; www.capjuluca.com; Maunday's Bay; r from US$825, ste from US$1670, villa from US$5245; 🍴 💻 🏊 ) One of Anguilla's sexiest resorts by far, Cap Juluca's long row of exclusive beachfront villas boasts idyllic views of the sea. If you're the type of traveler who likes to take home hotel mementos (soaps, slippers etc), you should consider bringing along an empty suitcase – each suite is loaded with designer fragrances, sandals, bathrobes. You name it, they have it.

**Covecastles** ( ☎ 497-6801, in USA 800-223-1108; www.covecastles.com; Shoal Bay West; villa from US$895; 🍴 💻 )

ANGUILLA

The curiously shaped villas at Covecastles look like the space-shuttle capsule that washes ashore during the opening credits of *I Dream of Jeanie*. While the exteriors are noticeably modern, the 20-year-old interiors are fairly sedate, sporting loads of sturdy wicker. The property was once owned by Chuck Norris, although fortunately (or unfortunately) only the dark mission-style terracotta tile harkens any flicker of a *Walker, Texas Ranger* theme.

### Eating

**Smokey's** ( ☎ 497-6582; Cove Bay; lunch from US$8, dinner from US$10; ☻ lunch & dinner Tue-Sun) Occupying a great spot right on the beach and open until the last person stumbles home, Smokey's offers a selection of local creations and typical American fare. Pizza and burgers are available for lunch, and dishes like curried goat are the mainstay of the dinner menu.

**Picante** ( ☎ 498-1616; mains US$10-18; ☻ dinner, closed Tue) A Caribbean taqueria? Why not. This unassuming roadside restaurant on the far west of the island's Albert Hughes Rd is a popular spot for a cheap nosh. A Californian couple runs the open-air, tin-roofed casual Mexican space, which seats about 30 on wood benches. Try the homebaked tortillas, enchiladas and fish tacos, and wash it all down with a salty margarita.

**Zurra** ( ☎ 222-8300; Temenos Golf Club, Rendezvous Bay; lunch US$12-30, dinner US$35-50; ☻ lunch & dinner) Owned and operated by the same folks who run Blanchard's restaurant on Meads Bay, this modern, whitewashed venue operates out of the opulent Temenos Golf Club. Gourmet dishes are served in a serene, Arabesque atmosphere dotted with vibrant Cubist-like paintings.

**Lucy's** ( ☎ 497-8875; Long Bay; mains from US$14; ☻ lunch & dinner, closed Wed) Specializing in

Anguilla home cookin', Lucy, the owner and chef, whips up scrumptious island faves like curried seafood, steaming stews and Creole goat.

### Entertainment

**Dune Preserve** ( ☎ 772-0637; www.dunepreserve.com; ☻ whenever) Imagine if a reggae star was given a huge pile of driftwood and old boats, and got to build his very own tree house on the beach. The result would be this, one of the grooviest places on the planet. Hometown star Bankie Banx has jammed and limed here for two-dozen years. Live music takes the stage on Wednesday, Friday and Saturday (plus Tuesday and Sunday during high season), and if you're lucky, you'll hear Bankie himself. Even if you aren't into the jammin' music scene, it's still worth stopping by for the delicious lunches created by Dale, the popular chef from Tasty's (p425). Try the Dune shine: fresh ginger, pineapple juice, white rum and bitters. Take the road past the Cuisinart resort (a dirt road) and make the first left turn down a seemingly impossible rocky road. This is also the home of the Moonsplash festival (p431).

# EASTERN ANGUILLA

The quiet eastern end of Anguilla features loads of rambling villas set along some of the island's most stunning beaches.

## SHOAL BAY EAST

Close your eyes and imagine the quintessential Caribbean stretch of white-sand beach. You've just pictured Shoal Bay East, a 2-mile-long beach with pristine sand, thoughtfully placed reefs ideal for snorkeling, glassy turquoise water and a remarkable lack of tourist development. Although during your visit, a few of the older hotels were being knocked down to make room for a gargantuan complex of million-dollar vacation villas…so come quick before the distinct Anguillian charm starts to vanish!

### Activities

**Shoal Bay Scuba** ( ☎ 497-4371, 235-1482; www.shoalbay scuba.com; Shoal Bay) is an ultraprofessional diving operation with high-quality equipment, good boats and a staff of well-trained divemasters. Matthew, the owner, has been living on Anguilla for 20 years and knows all the ins and outs of every dive spot around (and can offer some great dining tips postdive).

## Sleeping

**Elodia's** ( ☎ 467-3363; www.elodias.ai; r US$192, ste US$222-346; ✷ ) Little Elodia's occupies two cubes of apartment-style hotel rooms about 100yd from the beach along a clump of thick green grass. The suites could use a little sprucing up, but they get the job done, especially since there are sea views from every unit.

**Serenity Cottage** ( ☎ 497-3328; www.serenity.ai; incl service charge r US$275, ste US$385-495; ✷ 🖳 ) Sparkling after a fresh renovation, Serenity has charming suites that give Malliouhana a run for their money (and these rooms are half the price!).

**Kú** ( ☎ 497-2011, in USA 800-869-5827; www.kuanguilla.com; ste US$315-420; ✷ 💻 🖳 ) Kú's strongest suit is its prime slice of beachfront sand in the center of Shoal Bay East. The rooms are covered in coats of sterile white paint with nary a wall hanging in sight. It all feels a bit institutional and it doesn't help that the air-con is borderline cryogenic. However, the outside hangout spots foster an excellent social vibe, and there's a cool fountain at the entrance, which gushes with water while bursting with flames.

**Shoal Bay Villas** ( ☎ 497-2051; www.sbvillas.ai; r from US$370, ste US$385-555; ✷ 🖳 ) A splendid beachfront location, this place has 15 large, comfortable units with prim, tropical decor. All have ceiling fans, a kitchen, and a patio or balcony. Some rooms literally step onto the sandy stretch of perfection that will be your front yard. Baby-sitting available.

## Eating & Drinking

**Uncle Ernie's** ( ☎ 497-2542; mains US$6-10; ✷ breakfast, lunch & dinner) The cheapest place on Anguilla to buy a Coke (US$1), this bright green and purple shack teems with beachaholics loung-

ing on the wobbly plastic patio furniture while taking a break from the Caribbean sun. The food is far from tops, but hey, what do you really expect for US$6 on one of the most expensive islands in the world?

**Zara's** ( ☎ 497-3229; mains US$20-29; ✷ dinner) Located at the Allamanda Beach Club, Zara's serves up a hearty mix of seafood and 'rasta pasta' created by Shamash, the iconic local chef who gleefully sings his heart out while preparing your meal. Catch him in the winter months because during the summer he closes up and heads to the Hamptons to spread his Caribbean joie de vivre to cynical New Yorkers.

Sundays are a must along Shoal Bay East; hit **Elodia's** ( ☎ 497-1257) around sunset for its excellent live reggae band.

# FAR EAST

After Shoal Bay East, the quiet eastern seascape is a narrowing strip of breezy coves dotted by casbah-like villas and hidden eateries. **Island Harbour** is a working fishing village, not a resort area, and its beach is lined with brightly colored fishing boats rather than chaise longues. There are another half-dozen semisecluded beaches in the area, of which **Junk's Hole** is tops. This silent stretch of windswept sand gently forms a curving bay flanked by crooked palms – it's the perfect place to live out your castaway fantasies.

## Sights

Anguilla's only museum, the **Heritage Museum** ( ☎ 235-7440; adult/child US$5/3; ✷ 10am-5pm Mon-Sat), is set within a small bungalow and details the island's history through an impressive assortment of artifacts. Amble through the different rooms while experiencing a cleverly curated timeline of events from the settling of the ancient Arawaks to a recent visit from the queen.

## Sleeping

**Arawak Beach Inn** ( ☎ 497-4888; www.arawakbeach.com; Island Harbour; r from US$245; ✷ 🖳 ) Colorful Arawak Beach Inn sits on the far west side

**ANGUILLA**

of picturesque Island Harbour. Stacks of hexagon-shaped rooms stretch across the rock-strewn coast, and feature weathered wooden furnishings.

## Eating

**Smitty's** ( ☎ 497-4300; Island Harbour; meals US$12-25; ☺ lunch & dinner) The owner, Smitty, as he's known to his friends (and they are many), runs this casual beachside bar and restaurant offering fresh lobster and barbecue chicken and ribs as if he were having a barbecue party in his backyard.

**Palm Grove** ( ☎ 497-4224; Junk's Hole; lobster salad US$20; ☺ 11:30am-6:30pm) As you careen down the treacherous dirt road to Junk's Hole, you'll feel like you've made a wrong turn; fear not, a tasty lunch is soon in store. No doubt the only beachside shack ever featured in *Bon Appetit* magazine, Palm Grove magically churns out tasty seafood despite having no electrical power. Put your order in with chef–owner Nat – be it lobster or crayfish – and head down to the beach for the hour (or two) wait.

**Scilly Cay** ( ☎ 497-5123; mains US$25-40; ☺ noon-4pm, bar 11am-5pm, closed Mon & Sep-Oct & in rough weather) Pronounced 'silly key,' this unique lunchtime experience occupies a teeny atoll all to itself. Wave at the island and they'll send a boat over to the Island Harbour pier (behind Smitty's) to pick you up. Sunday afternoon's reggae band lures locals and tourists alike, and there's live music on Wednesday and Friday. Reputedly serves the best rum punch on the island.

**Hibernia Restaurant & Art Gallery** ( ☎ 497-4290; www.hiberniarestaurant.com; mains US$27-39; ☺ lunch Tue-Sun, dinner Tue-Sat winter, lunch Wed-Sat, dinner Wed-Sun summer) The owners of Hibernia travel to Asia every year during low season and bring back an assortment of exotic spices and flavors, which they incorporate into their ever-growing repertoire of fusion recipes. The adjacent art gallery features purchasable paintings and trinkets from their unusual journey. Hibernia is located about half a mile east of Island Harbour; follow the signs. Reservations advised.

# DIRECTORY

## ACCOMMODATIONS

Anguilla has a reputation as an expensive destination because…well, it is. You'll be hard-pressed to find any semblance of a lux-

ury vacation for under US$300. Most hotel rooms and villas around the island have kitchens or kitchenettes. Consider picking up some groceries in the Valley to reduce the costs of your vacation.

High-season rates usually run December 15 to April 15, but it's around Christmas and New Year's when prices rise astronomically. Most hotels charge significantly less in the low season.

Hotels charge a 10% government tax and 10% service charge.

One of Anguilla's many charms is its plethora of villas, available for every taste and budget. Prices range from around US$1000 per week for a studio during summer to US$35,000 per night for a seven-bedroom mansion at Christmas.

The following rental agencies can hook you up with a variety of properties fitting all different price ranges:

**Anguilla Luxury Collection** ( ☎ 497-6049; www .anguillaluxurycollection.com) Highly recommended.

**Island Dream Properties** ( ☎ 498-3200; www.island dreamproperties.com) Also highly recommended.

**Keene Enterprises** ( ☎ 497-2544; www.keenevillas.com)

**Kokoon Villas** ( ☎ 497-7888; www.kokoonvillas.com)

**Professional Realty Services** ( ☎ 497-3575; www .profgroup.com/provillas)

**Sunset Homes** ( ☎ 497-3666; www.sunsethomesonline .com)

Or make plans yourself by checking the website http://villas.ai. Part of the ever helpful www.news.ai website run by resident Bob Green, this website lists each villa and its direct reservation information.

Note: roosters don't pay heed to quiethour signs posted at hotels or villas, no matter the level of luxury. Bring earplugs.

## ACTIVITIES

### Beaches & Swimming

The pure white-sand beaches are high on most Anguillian visitors' lists as a must-see, must-relax destination. The most prized beaches are Shoal Bay East and Rendezvous Bay, although Junk's Hole and Kartouche Bay are tops for quiet sun worshipping.

### Diving & Snorkeling

Although it doesn't hold the allure of nearby dive havens, such as Sint Eustatius or Saba, Anguilla has clear water and good reef formations. In addition, a number of ships have been deliberately sunk to create new dive areas, bringing Anguilla's total to almost two-dozen diverse sites. Offshore islands popular for diving include Prickly Pear Cays (p428), which has caverns, ledges, barracudas and nurse sharks; several wrecks, including the 1772 natural sinking of the Spanish galleon *El Buen Consejo*, 109yd off Stoney Bay; and Sandy Island, which has soft corals and sea fans.

There are three diving operations on the island, located in Sandy Ground (p424), Meads Bay (p426) and Shoal Bay (p428).

Prickly Pear has excellent snorkeling conditions. Tour boats leave Sandy Ground for Prickly Pear at around 10am, returning around 4pm; the cost averages US$80, including lunch, drinks and snorkeling gear. Try **Chocolat** (☎ 497-3394) or if there's no answer check at Ripples restaurant (p425) in Sandy Ground. Shoal Bay East, Sandy Island and Little Bay are other popular snorkeling spots.

### Horseback Riding
There are operators offering horseback rides in Blowing Point (p426) and Cove Bay (p427).

### Golf
Anguilla's ultraflat terrain makes it one of the best islands in the Caribbean for golfing; unfortunately the green fees are laughably overpriced. Try the Temenos Golf Club (p427) if you want to pay US$400 a round.

## BUSINESS HOURS
In general, the government offices are all open from 8am to 3pm from Monday to Friday. Grocery stores are usually open from around 8am to 9pm on weekdays and Saturdays, with shortened hours on Sundays. The rest of the establishments on the island pretty much run according to island time, meaning that they open and close as they please. Breakfast hours are usually 7am to 10am, lunch falls around 11:30am to 2:30pm and dinner starts around 6pm and goes until 9pm. Food service after 9pm is limited to a couple of beach bars in Sandy Ground and a smattering of Chinese grub huts and BBQ stands.

## EMBASSIES & CONSULATES
There are no official embassies on the island. However, those seeking consular services can get in touch with the **Anguilla Tourist Board** ( ☎ 497-2759, in USA 800-553-4939; www .anguilla-vacation.com; Coronation Ave, the Valley), which has a list of local contacts that represent foreign nations.

## FESTIVALS & EVENTS
**Moonsplash** (www.dunepreserve.com) The hippest of Anguilla's festivals, Bankie Banx invites all his old reggae friends to the Dune Preserve (p428) in March for some late-night jamming. Guests have included Third World, the Wailers, and Toots and the Maytals.

**Anguilla Summer Festival** (www.festival.ai) Anguilla's carnival is its main festival, which starts on the weekend preceding August Monday and continues until the following weekend. Events include traditional boat racing, Carnival costumed parades, a beauty pageant, and calypso competitions with continuous music and dancing.

**Tranquility Jazz Festival** (early November; www .anguillajazz.org) This jazz festival attracts big names as well as talented local musicians, who play to an international audience of jazz aficionados in various hotels and other locations. The event culminates in a free beach jazz concert in Sandy Ground.

## HOLIDAYS
Anguilla has the following public holidays:
**New Year's Day** January 1
**Good Friday** Late March/early April
**Easter Monday** Late March/early April
**Whit Monday** Eighth Monday after Easter
**Anguilla Day** May 30
**Queen's Birthday** June 11
**August Monday** (Emancipation Day) First Monday in August
**August Thursday** First Thursday in August
**Constitution Day** August 6
**Separation Day** December 19
**Christmas Day** December 25
**Boxing Day** December 26

## INTERNET ACCESS

The **Public Library** ( ☎ 497-2441; the Valley; per 30min EC$5; ☑ 9am-5pm Mon-Fri, to noon Sat) in the Valley has internet access.

## INTERNET RESOURCES

**Anguilla News** (www.news.ai) A thoroughly researched website written by a local, but can be lacking in updates.
**Anguilla Tourist Board** (www.anguilla-vacation.com) The official tourism website for Anguilla is easy to navigate and lists all accommodations by type and price.

## MEDICAL SERVICES

The island's small **Princess Alexandra Hospital** ( ☎ 497-2551) is in the Valley.

## MONEY

There are four international banks on Anguilla; all are located in the Valley, and have ATMs dispensing US and EC dollars; see p423 for details.

A 15% service charge is added to most restaurant bills and no further tipping is necessary.

## POST

Anguilla's only **post office** ( ☎ 497-2528; www.gov .ai/angstamp; ☑ 8am-3:30pm Mon-Thu, 8am-5pm Fri) is in the Valley. Anguilla's zip code is AI 2640.

## TELEPHONE

Anguilla's area code is ☎ 264 and is followed by a seven-digit local number. If you are calling locally, simply dial the local number. To call the island from North America, dial ☎ 1-264 + the local number. From elsewhere, dial your country's international dialing code + 264 + the local number. We have included only the seven-digit local number in Anguilla listings in this chapter.

## TOURIST INFORMATION

**Anguilla Tourist Board** ( ☎ 497-2759, in USA 800-553-4939; www.anguilla-vacation.com; Coronation Ave, the Valley)

## TOURS

Taxi drivers provide two-hour tours of the island for US$50 for one or two people, US$8 for each additional person, although we highly recommend renting your own car, grabbing a map and exploring the island under your own steam. Even with the cost of gas it will be cheaper than hiring a guide.

**EMERGENCY NUMBERS**
- Ambulance ☎ 911
- Fire ☎ 911
- Police ☎ 911

## VISA

Citizens of many African, South American and former Soviet countries need to obtain visas.

# TRANSPORTATION

## GETTING THERE & AWAY
### Entering Anguilla

Visitors entering Anguilla must carry valid ID in the form of a passport and must declare the date on which they will be departing.

### Air

Anguilla's **Wallblake Airport** (AXA; ☎ 497-2514) accepts mostly smaller aircraft and will require a transfer before arriving from most international destinations (unless you are coming on your private jet).

The following airlines fly to and from Anguilla from within the Caribbean:
**American Eagle** ( ☎ 497-3131; www.aa.com) San Juan
**LIAT** ( ☎ 497-5002; www.liatairline.com) Antigua, St Thomas
**Transanguilla** ( ☎ 497-8690; www.transanguilla.com) Charters from Anguilla.
**Winair** ( ☎ 497-2748; www.fly-winair.com) St-Martin/ Sint Maarten and Antigua

Air France and KLM also run connecting flights through St-Martin/Sint Maarten; see p451 for details.

### Sea
#### FERRY

Ferries make the 25-minute run from Marigot Bay in St-Martin to Blowing Point in Anguilla an average of once every half-hour from 8am to 6:15pm. From Anguilla to St-Martin the ferries run from 7:30am to 7pm. As ferry companies change frequently, call the **dispatch center** ( ☎ 497-6070). The ferry terminal is 4 miles southwest of the Valley in the small village of Blowing Point.

The one-way fare per person is US$12 (US$15 on the last boat of the day) plus the US$20 departure tax when leaving. The fare for the passage is paid onboard the boat.

### YACHT
The main ports of entry are at Sandy Ground in Road Bay or Blowing Point. The **immigration and customs office** ( ☎ 497-2451; ⏰ 8:30am-noon & 1-4pm Sun-Fri, 1-4pm Sat) can be contacted on VHF channel 16.

## GETTING AROUND
There is no official public transportation on Anguilla. Visitors will either need to rent a car or rely on pricey taxi drivers. You may see bus-stop signs in various spots – there is a private company on the island that drives a shuttle around; however, there is no set schedule.

## Car
### DRIVER'S LICENSE
Visitors must buy a temporary Anguillian driver's license for US$20 cash, which is a small pink paper issued on the spot by the car-rental companies. Make sure each person driving has a valid license, as hefty fines are imposed on unlicensed drivers.

### RENTAL
Compact air-conditioned cars rent for about US$40 a day (usually US$5 cheaper in summer). Petrol prices are extremely high on the island: US$5 for 1 gallon of gas. Do not fill your tank up to the brim, especially if you staying on the island for less than a week. The island is very flat and there is rarely traffic – it takes quite a while to go through a tank of gas. If you're arriving by ferry, there are car-rental operations right at the pier. From the airport, most rental services are just a short ride away. It's best to book in advance during high season.

Try the following rental agencies:

**Apex/Avis** ( ☎ 497-2642; avisaxa@anguillanet.com; the Valley)

**Boo's Cars & Cycle Rentals** ( ☎ 497-2361; bass_car rental@hotmail.com; Rock Farm)

**Carib Rent A Car** ( ☎ 497-6020; caribcarrental@anguilla net.com; Meads Bay)

**Connor's Car Rental** ( ☎ 497-6433; mauricec@carib serve.net; South Hill)

**Island Car Rental** ( ☎ 497-2723; islandcar@anguilla net.com; Airport Rd)

**Triple K Car Rental** ( ☎ 497-2934; hertztriplek@anguilla .net; Airport Rd)

**Wendell Connor Car Rental** ( ☎ 497-6894, 235-6894; wendellconnor@caribcable.con; South Hill)

### ROAD RULES & CONDITIONS
Unlike the other islands in the region, on Anguilla, you drive on the left-hand side of the road. Steering wheels can be either on the left or right. The main roads around the island are well paved but the streets in the Valley are bumpy and riddled with potholes.

The island has six gas stations, all well marked on the tourist maps and our own Anguilla map (p421). Most close on Sundays.

## Taxi
Taxi fares have been standardized across the island. Taxis are readily available at the airport and ferry; there is a small taxi booth in both locations that can organize your transportation needs. From the airport, a taxi will cost US$8 into the Valley, US$12 to Sandy Ground and US$16 to Shoal Bay East. From the ferry, it's US$12 to Sandy Ground and US$16 to the Valley. Figure US$32 to cross the island and US$25 for an hour of service. Rates are for one to two people, with an additional person paying US$4, and service between 6pm and midnight costs an extra US$2 (service between midnight and 6am is an additional US$5). See opposite for taxi tours.

# St-Martin/ Sint Maarten

For hundreds of years the Caribbean was the colorful playground of wannabe imperialists who flexed their colonial muscles while transporting rum, slaves and gold between worlds. These faraway kingdoms would repeatedly conquer and retreat, radically changing the political geography with the spark of a cannon. After years of divvying up – and re-divvying up – these sand-strewn paradises like a game of Risk, only one of the 7000 islands in the entire Caribbean remained so dear to two separate empires that they decided to share it.

It's easy to understand why this stunning island – known as St-Martin to the French, and Sint Maarten to the Dutch – has captured the hearts of many. A mere glance reveals conical, coolie-hat-like peaks rising dramatically from the depths of the ocean, and gentle cerulean currents that tumble landward to kiss the bleach-blonde sands.

Today, the allure goes deeper than the island's natural gifts. The arbitrary division of land has given the scrubby island two very distinct personalities, like a set of Siamese twins. Although fundamentally one entity, both sides are engaged in an unconscious game of tug-of-war as they struggle to assert their individuality. At times they work as one, and in other instances they become a caricature of themselves by exaggerating the traits that makes them unique: the French cling to their European roots, as demonstrated by the food and local lingo, while the Netherlands Antilles side plays up their jammin' attitude by appealing to the hedonistic pleasures of visitors. But, although neither side likes to admit it, the whole really is greater than the sum of its parts.

## FAST FACTS

- **Area** St-Martin: 54 sq km; Sint Maarten: 34 sq km; Total: 88 sq km
- **Capital** St-Martin: Marigot; Sint Maarten: Philipsburg
- **Country code** St-Martin ( ☎ 590); Sint Maarten ( ☎ 599)
- **Departure tax** US$30; usually included in the price of your ticket
- **Famous for** Being the smallest area of land in the world divided into two nations
- **Language** St-Martin: French; Sint Maarten: Dutch; both sides: English, Creole, Papiamentu and Spanish
- **Money** St-Martin: euro (€); Sint Maarten: Netherlands Antillean guilder (ANG); US dollar (US$) is used on both sides; US$1 = ANG1.77 = €0.65 = UK£0.51
- **Official name** St-Martin/Sint Maarten
- **Population** St-Martin: 36,000; Sint Maarten: 40,000
- **Visa** Not necessary for visitors from North America or the EU; see p451

# HIGHLIGHTS

- **Beaches** (p448) Head to one of the 40-plus beaches on the island: sample Simpson Bay for the odd juxtaposition of cerulean waters underfoot and careening jumbo jets overhead; try Friar's Bay for a Rastafari safari; or go au naturel on Orient Beach
- **Grand Case** (p446) Gorge on sticky ribs at a beachside *lolo* shack or kick it up a notch and drop the big bling on a shmancy dinner that will transport your taste buds all the way to Paris
- **Day Tripping** (p449) Hop on a catamaran or sailboat and spend the day at sea visiting one of the island's scrubby satellites, such as Îlet Pinel, Tintamarre or even Prickly Pear out near Anguilla
- **Sunset Beach Bar** (p441) Visit this jammin' bar, a rite of passage for any visitor: drink a death-defying piña colada and don't forget to duck when the planes come in for landing at Juliana Airport
- **Oyster Pond** (p448) Stop at this remote harbor for a relaxed, pastoral atmosphere – it's half French, half Dutch, and all great

# ITINERARIES

- **One Day** One day on St-Martin/Sint Maarten is hardly enough time to even scrape the surface, but if you're arriving by cruise ship, or if you're simply day tripping from nearby Anguilla or St-Barthélemy, it's still worth swinging by to join the fray. Rent a car and make a beeline for Grand Case for an early lunch of sweet barbecue ribs at one of the Creole open-air *lolos*. Next, hit Orient Beach for some sand and sun, and before the day is done, a stop at the Dutch side's Sunset Beach Bar is a must – nurse a beer

as the jumbo jets make a dramatic (and noisy) landing right over your head.
- **Five Days** Oyster Pond is a great sleeping option for a short stay on the island as it straddles the French–Dutch border and maintains a chill island vibe. Spend half your time roaming around Orient Beach, Marigot and Grand Case on the French Side, then bop around Philipsburg and the casino-riddled area near the airport on the Dutch half. A rental car is a must.
- **Two Weeks** Scout out one of the myriad private villas on the island and spend your first week recharging your batteries along one of the quieter beaches like Friar's Bay, Baie Longue, or Le Galion. When you start feeling antsy, hit the fine dining in Grand Case, the lively bar scene at Maho Beach and, now that you've worked up the courage, wear your birthday suit to Orient Beach to get rid of those pesky tan lines.

## CLIMATE & WHEN TO GO

St-Martin/Sint Maarten averages an annual temperature of a perfect 26°C. July through October sees heat, humidity and, often, hurricanes; many establishments close entirely in September. The best times to visit St-Martin are November to early December and May to June.

## HISTORY

For a thousand years, St-Martin/Sint Maarten was sparsely populated by the Arawaks and later the fiercer Caribs. They named the island Sualouiga after the brackish salt ponds that made it difficult to settle.

Columbus sailed past on November 11, 1493, which happened to be the feast of St Martin of Tours, the island's namesake. The Dutch, however, were the first to take advantage of the land, a nice stopping-off point between Holland and their new colonies in Brazil and New Amsterdam (New York City). After a few abortive attempts by the Spanish to regain the island, now found to be brimming with lucrative salt deposits, the French and Dutch ended up fighting for control of it.

As the legend has it, the Dutch and the French decided to partition St-Martin/Sint Maarten from a march originating in Oyster Pond. The French walked northward, the Dutch south. While the French quenched their

---

### HOW MUCH?

- **Compact car rental per day** US$35
- **Juicy burger at Sunset Beach Bar** US$8
- **Catamaran daytrip to nearby islands** US$110
- **Bus from Grand Case to Marigot** US$4
- **Two beach chairs and an umbrella on Friar's Bay per day** US$22

ST-MARTIN/SINT MAARTEN

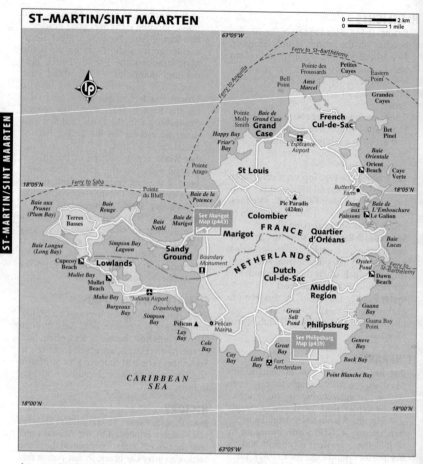

## ST–MARTIN/SINT MAARTEN

thirst with wine, the Dutch brought along dodgy gin. Halfway through, the Dutchmen stopped to sleep off the ill effects, effectively giving the French a greater piece of the pie.

St-Martin became a plantation island much like many of its neighbors. The end of slavery brought an end to the plantation boom and by 1930 the population stood at just 2000 hearty souls. Ironically, it was WWII that brought tourism to St-Martin/Sint Maarten. In 1943 the US Navy built large runways on the island to use as a base in the Caribbean. The French capitalized by using the runways to fly in tourists, by the 1950s bringing the population of St-Martin/Sint Maarten up to about 70,000 and making tourism the number one industry on both sides of the island.

Sint Maarten was a part of the Netherlands Antilles until 2005, when the five islands (Saba, Curaçao, Bonaire, Sint Eustatius and Dutch Sint Maarten) met on the Jesurun Referendum to decide the fate of the Netherlands Antilles. Sint Maarten, along with fellow populous island Curaçao, voted overwhelmingly to become an independent country within the Kingdom of the Netherlands. Now, a second referendum at the end of 2008 will change Sint Maarten's status once more as it distances itself even further from Dutch control. For more on the fate of the Netherlands Antilles, see p779.

## THE CULTURE

St-Martin/Sint Maarten's melting pot of ethnicities is like no other place in the Caribbean.

The island culture has its roots largely in African, French and Dutch influences, though scores of more recent immigrants – including many from the Dominican Republic, Haiti and China – have added their own elements to this multicultural society. Today, the island proudly claims that 80 different languages are spoken throughout, although French dominates St-Martin and English dominates Sint Maarten.

St-Martin/Sint Maarten has adapted to tourism better than any other island nearby. You'll rarely meet someone who was actually born on the island. As the smallest area of land in the world divided into two nations, each side functions symbiotically while attracting tourists in very different ways. The French side embraces its European roots and seeks to recreate a certain amount of 'Old World' atmosphere along the cobble sands. The Dutch side is a mixed bag of Caribbean clichés, but it all seems to work really well (for attracting tourists). Residents coexist with the constant hum of low-lying debauchery that accompanies the dozens of gentlemen's clubs, casinos and thriving discos. Some ignore it, some join in, but most simply accept that their beautiful island home plays host to one long adult spring break.

Topless sunbathing is customary on both sides of the island and nude sunbathing is sanctioned at Orient Beach.

## ENVIRONMENT
The west side of the island is more water than land, dominated by the expansive Simpson Bay Lagoon, which is one of the largest land-locked bodies of water in the Caribbean and has moorings for a large array of boats. The island's interior is hilly, with the highest point, Pic Paradis, rising 424m from the center of French St-Martin.

Herons, egrets, stilts, pelicans and laughing gulls are among the plentiful shorebirds in the island's brackish ponds. Frigatebirds can be spotted along the coast, and humming-birds and bananaquits in gardens. Lizards also are abundant.

## FOOD & DRINK
The food on St-Martin/Sint Maarten is worth the trip in itself – the French side draws from its close relationship with the motherland, and the Dutch side has a bevy of talented chefs lured to the island by high salaries and

gorgeous weather. Although the numbers of cheesy theme restaurants and fast-food joints can be overwhelming, especially on the Dutch side, the French side offers a plethora of traditional seafood *lolos* (barbecue shacks) and the gourmet capital of the Caribbean, Grand Case (p446).

Note that all restaurants on the Dutch side add tax and a 15% service charge to the bill; on the French side, tax is already included and tips are left up to your discretion.

French wine and Caribbean rum are not in short supply. All over the island you'll find guavaberry stores selling a black-face bottle of the island's signature liqueur.

# SINT MAARTEN
If you're arriving on the island from a far-flung destination, chances are you'll be landing on the Dutch side's Juliana International Airport (SXM) – one of the largest airports in the Caribbean and a transfer hub to many of the smaller islands orbiting nearby.

As the *Sint*illating side of the border, Holland's land claim gets continuously tweaked and tuned as it strives to be the ultimate holiday destination for adults. The construction laws are not particularly stringent, so the artificial landscape feels a bit garish in a Vegas-in-the-'80s kind of way. The capital of the Dutch side is Philipsburg, a gridiron town along a wide arcing bay that mostly functions as an outdoor shopping mall for cruise monkeys with cash to burn.

Those who are in the know used to say 'sleep on the Dutch side, eat on the French side', but this no longer holds true. In the last couple years, as the American dollar goes south, many excellent restaurants have opened their doors here, giving the more traditional French dining venues a run for their money. Similarly, many boutique businesses have moved to the Dutch side from the French side to regain their large American client base. And on the other side of the equation, accommodation in Sint Maarten is gradually turning into one big mess of timeshares, so have a look at the lodging choices on the French side – even though they are priced in euros, you can still snag an excellent deal.

This section starts at the far end of the Dutch, holding relative to the airport, and works its way back from Philipsburg along the winding cobbled coast, past Simpson Bay and on through Maho Bay, Mullet Bay and Cupecoy Beach before crossing over onto the French half. For information about Oyster Pond, which is split between both colonies, see p448.

## PHILIPSBURG

**pop 18,000**

Philipsburg, Dutch Sint Maarten's principal town, is centered on a long, narrow stretch of land that separates Great Salt Pond from Great Bay. There are some older buildings mixed among the new, but overall the town is far more commercial than quaint. Most of the action is along Frontstreet, the bayfront road, which is lined with boutiques, jewelry shops, restaurants, casinos and duty-free shops selling everything from Danish porcelain to Japanese cameras and electronics.

### Orientation

Four streets run east to west, and numerous narrow lanes (called *steegjes*) connect them north to south. Frontstreet has one-way traffic that moves in an easterly direction, and Backstreet has one-way traffic heading west. The north side of Philipsburg is sometimes referred to as Pondfill, as much of this area is reclaimed land. Parking is extremely limited as there are always twenty cars vying for a place to pull over, it's best to stop along the interior and walk up to Frontstreet.

### Information

Banks are plentiful along Frontstreet, and all deal in US dollars or Antillean guilders.

**Hospital** ( ☎ 543-1111) East of Philipsburg in the Cay Hill area.

**Post office** ( ☺ 7:30am-5pm Mon-Thu, to 4:30pm Fri) At the west end of E Camille Richardson St.

**Public library** ( ☎ 542-2970; Vogessteeg; internet access per 30min US$4; ☺ 9am-12:30pm Tue, Wed & Fri, 4-6:30pm Mon, Wed & Fri, 4-9pm Tue & Thu, 10am-1pm Sat)

**Sint Maarten Tourist Bureau** ( ☎ 542-2337; www.st-maarten.com; 33 WG Boncamper Rd; ☺ 8am-5pm Mon-Fri)

### Sights

The little **Sint Maarten Museum** ( ☎ 542-4917; Frontstreet 7; admission US$2; ☺ 10am-4pm Mon-Fri, to 2pm Sat) has displays on island history, including Arawak pottery shards, plantation-era

artifacts, period photos and a few items from HMS *Proselyte*, the frigate that sank off Fort Amsterdam in 1801. The little shop downstairs sells an assortment of Caribbean arts and crafts.

The largest zoo in the Caribbean, known as **Sint Maarten Park** ( ☎ 543-2030; admission US$5; ☺ 9:30am-6pm summer, to 5pm in winter) features over 80 different kinds of indigenous species. It's located at the northern edge of the Great Salt Pond.

### Activities

**Sint Maarten 12 Metre Challenge** ( ☎ 542-0045; www.12metre.com), at Bobby's Marina, has three-hour excursions on America's Cup racing yachts, which are large, fast and sleek. Its fleet includes *Stars & Stripes*, the very yacht Dennis Conner used in the 1987 challenge for the America's Cup in Australia. The trips cost US$70 per person.

### Sleeping

Philipsburg is largely the domain of cruise-ship folk who troll the boardwalk shops for tacky souvenirs, so if you're going to sleep on St-Martin/Sint Maarten you might want to look elsewhere for your ultimate slice of paradise. There are, however, a couple good reasons for building your nest within a stone's throw of the cruise docks. The area has recently received a much-needed facelift, so things sparkle a tad more than they used to; and the second draw is the fairly reasonable prices relative to the rest of the island. You can also save a bit of dough by not renting a car, since decent restaurants and bars are only a quick walk away.

**Joshua Rose Guest House** ( ☎ 542-4317; www.joshuaroseguesthouse.com; Backstreet 7; standard s/d/tr/q US$50/70/90/110; ☒ ) Nothing to write home about, but the small rooms are central and it has private baths, TV and refrigerator.

**Soualiga Guest House** ( ☎ 542-0077; soualigaguesthouse@hotmail.com; 29A Walter Nisbeth Rd; s/d US$55/65; ☒ ) On the backside of Philipsburg, away from the beach, this passable spot is hidden among a colorful mess of commercial businesses. Soualiga's best feature is its unbeatable price; rooms have TV and fridges.

**Seaview Beach Hotel** ( ☎ 542-2323; www.seaviewbeachhotel.com; Frontstreet; s US$79-99, d US$99-130, tr US$135-150, q US$145-160; ☒ ) Good prices, friendly service and a beachfront location

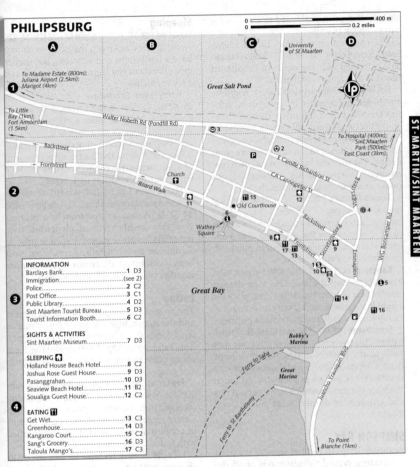

# PHILIPSBURG

ST-MARTIN/SINT MAARTEN

**INFORMATION**
| | |
|---|---|
| Barclays Bank | **1** D3 |
| Immigration | (see **2**) |
| Police | **2** C2 |
| Post Office | **3** C1 |
| Public Library | **4** D2 |
| Sint Maarten Tourist Bureau | **5** D3 |
| Tourist Information Booth | **6** C2 |

**SIGHTS & ACTIVITIES**
| | |
|---|---|
| Sint Maarten Museum | **7** D3 |

**SLEEPING** 🏠
| | |
|---|---|
| Holland House Beach Hotel | **8** C2 |
| Joshua Rose Guest House | **9** D3 |
| Pasanggrahan | **10** D3 |
| Seaview Beach Hotel | **11** B2 |
| Soualiga Guest House | **12** C2 |

**EATING** 🍽
| | |
|---|---|
| Get Wet | **13** C3 |
| Greenhouse | **14** D3 |
| Kangaroo Court | **15** C2 |
| Sang's Grocery | **16** D3 |
| Taloula Mango's | **17** C3 |

make this a good bet all round. Rooms aren't particularly inviting, but they're comfortable and come with refrigerators and cable TV. There's a predictably tacky casino on the 1st floor.

**Pasanggrahan** ( ☎ 542-3588, in the US ☎ 800-223-9815; www.pasanhotel.com; 19 Frontstreet; r from US$158; 🍽 ) The restaurant and lobby are in a former governor's residence, which feels like a Cuban plantation house, but most rooms are in less-distinguished side buildings. The standard rooms are simple and small with a shared seaside balcony. The deluxe rooms are larger and fancier, with private balconies and a view of Great Bay.

**Holland House Beach Hotel** ( ☎ 542-2572, in the US ☎ 800-223-9815; www.hollandhousehotel.com; d from US$200; 🍽 🖳 ) Has a central beachfront location in the heart of Philipsburg and 54 spacious rooms. Overall, they're Philipsburg's nicest, featuring hardwood floors, subtle trendy design details, balconies, cable TV, wi-fi, phones and, in most cases, a kitchenette. Top-floor suites have the best views.

## Eating & Drinking

If you have the time (and a car) head away from the waterfront area and explore the inland communities for cheap local eats. There's a great little shwarma joint up in Madame Estate – ask a local for directions to the bowling alley (there's only one) and you'll find a white-and-red truck-cum-kitchen parked across the street. The hard-to-miss **Heineken**

Book your stay online at lonelyplanet.com/hotels

**airplane** along the main road to Cole Bay is worth a peak as well.

The cheapest grocery store on the island, **Sang's Super Center** (☎ 542-3447; 3 Juancho Irausquin Blvd) is located near the outlet of Frontstreet towards the cruise ship marina.

**Get Wet** (Board Walk; mains from US$4; ✆ lunch & dinner) Owned and operated by a gang of canucks, this friendly yellow hut offers cheaper-than-cheap beer and hearty *poutine* – a traditional Canadian dish of French fries, chicken gravy and melted cheese (and in case you were wondering, Canada does indeed have its own repertoire of traditional dishes – although *poutine* pretty much starts and finishes the list.)

**Taloula Mango's** (☎ 542-1645; cnr Board Walk & St Rose Arcade; mains from US$7; ✆ lunch & dinner) A local favorite, this relaxed beachside joint is a great place to while away the afternoon over a few beers and some excellent American pub food. Live music on Friday nights.

**Kangaroo Court** (☎ 542-7557; 6 Hendrickstraat; mains from US$7; ✆ breakfast & lunch) This vine-draped cloister near the courthouse is a great place for a light bite. Choose from a tasty assortment of sandwiches, salads and homemade pastries.

**Greenhouse** (☎ 542-2941; mains US$10-28; ✆ lunch & dinner) This lively spot with a charismatic staff pulls in the punters during its happy hour from 4:30pm to 7pm, which has two-for-one drinks as well as half-price snacks. At lunch there are burgers, sandwiches, barbecued ribs and chicken; at dinner, meat and seafood dishes are served.

## SIMPSON BAY

Beautiful Simpson Bay has some of the most captivating crystal tidewater out of all the beaches on the island. At first glance it may seem surprising that the sleeping spots in the area are well priced compared to other parts of the island – then you'll hear the roaring jet engines of a plane getting ready to take off at Juliana Airport. Those who enjoy staying along Simpson Bay claim that they don't even realize that jumbo jets are careening through, although if you are sensitive to noise, this area is not for you.

### Activities

**Random Wind** (☎ 52-02-53; www.randomwind.com) runs a small sailboat out to some of the quieter bays around the island. Day trips run on Tuesdays through Fridays and cost US$95 per person.

### Sleeping

**Travel Inn** (☎ 545-3353; 15 Airport Rd; r US$119; ✆ ▯) Nothing fancy, but it gets the job done. Rooms have a few bumps and scratches, but they're generally clean and come with TV, a safe and a teeny balcony.

**Horny Toad Guesthouse** (☎ 545-4323, in the US ☎ 800-417-9361; www.thtgh.com; 2 Vlaun St; ste from US$198; ✆ ▯ ▯) Run by Betty, a lovely American woman with a tinge of the 'pahk the cah' Bostonian accent, this charming guesthouse right along the sea features a handful of apartment-style rooms sporting loads of wicker furniture. Offers wi-fi access.

**Mary's Boon** (☎ 545-7000, in the US ☎ 866-978-5899; www.marysboon.com; r from US$125, ste from US$250; ✆ ▯ ▯) A stone's throw from Juliana's runway, this freshly restored plantation-style inn offers beautiful rooms draped in upscale Caribbean design details. Expect four-post beds, coconut-made curios and charming wooden beams. There's wi-fi access.

### Eating

The row of restaurants between the airport and the drawbridge features a flashy mix of fried foods from burritos to juicy burgers. You can't go wrong if you're looking for a cheap place to coat your stomach with grub and grog.

**Top Carrot** (☎ 545-2281; Simpson Bay Yacht Club; mains US$5-10; ✆ breakfast & lunch Mon-Sat) A refreshing change from the usual greasy haunts, Top Carrot serves up scrumptious veggie options in a chilled out cushion-clad ambience stuffed with fashion magazines.

**Lal's** (☎ 557-9059; 126 Airport Rd; mains from US$10; ✆ dinner daily, lunch on weekends) Lost in the mess of car-rental lots by the airport, Lal's rarely beeps on the tourist radar, but locals come here time and time again for delicious Indian fare. Try the rich butter chicken.

**Tides** (☎ 545-7000; 117 Simpson Bay Rd; mains US$9-29; ✆ breakfast, lunch & dinner) Located along the sand at Mary's Boon, this breezy joint serves up a mean seafood salad with avocado (US$17).

**Stone** (☎ 526-2037; mains US$20-30; ✆ dinner) The Stone distinguishes itself from other restaurants on the island in two ways. First, everything is served on a steaming slab of granite. Not only is this a great gimmick, but it allows customers to cook their steaks for as long or as little as they want. Second, the enterprising owner and head chef is only 24 years old. Try the biltong soup – a South African mix of jerked beef and thick cheddar. Live classical guitar on Tuesdays.

## MAHO & MULLET BAY

If you have a few hours to kill before a connecting flight, make your way to Maho. The beautiful beach is situated at the end of the Juliana Airport runway, and perhaps the world's lone stretch of sand with a sign that reads: 'Low flying and departing aircraft blast can cause physical injury' (with the obligatory picture of a stick figure getting blown away).

If you aren't into waving at passengers as they land on the island, this flashy area of St-Martin/Sint Maarten offers countless casinos, clubs and restaurants.

### Activities

The island's golf course, the 18-hole **Mullet Bay Golf** ( ☎ 545-2801), has greens fees of around US$100, cart included. The old resort that winds its way throughout the course has been closed for around 15 years and desperately needs to be torn down – it is unsightly and quite distracting.

### Sleeping

Sleeping in the Maho area used to be much more popular than it is today. The hotels here could use a renovation and they rely heavily on tourists who book cheap package vacations. Construction has already started on myriad timeshares in the area – a fate that seems unavoidable for most of the Dutch side.

**Maho Beach Hotel** ( ☎ 545-2115, in the US ☎ 800-223-0757; www.mahobeach.com; r from US$200; 🞔 🖳 🖳 ) This 600-room bastion of mediocrity sits within waving distance of the Juliana Airport. The resort grounds include a casino, several restaurants, fitness center, indoor parking garage and a 1000-seat Vegas-style showroom. There's wi-fi access.

**Caravanserai Beach Resort** ( ☎ 545-4000, in the US ☎ 877-796-1002; www.caravanseraibeachresort.com; d from US$250, tr from US$300; 🞔 🖳 ) Our mothers always told us that when you have nothing nice to say, don't say anything.

### Eating & Drinking

**Bamboo Bernie's** ( ☎ 545-3622; sushi US$6-15; 🕑 lunch & dinner) Hidden just beyond Bliss, Bamboo Bernie's is a chic, tiki-torched hangout spot that specializes in Asian fusion cuisine. Try the 'sexy salmon' or ask about the secret Saavo sushi roll that isn't even marked on the menu.

Wednesday nights are the nights to come if you're looking for a more raucous affair.

**Bliss** ( ☎ 545-3996; breakfast/lunch/dinner around US$10/18/35; 🕑 practically 24hr) This experience is not for the faint of heart. The restaurant serves breakfast and Sunday brunch with main meals consisting of dishes like duck *confit* baguette and dorado filet with coconut carrot sauce. House music kicks up at about 11pm each night on the open-air dance floor, Tuesday is Martini Night, and Thursday to Saturday is DJ dancing to an international groove. Don't worry if all that dancing makes you get the munchies: the grill is open until 4am. It's a wi-fi hot spot.

**our pick** **Sunset Beach Bar** ( ☎ 545-3998; 2 Beacon Hill Rd; burgers US$8-10; 🕑 10am-11pm, sometimes to 1am) When you arrive at Sunset Beach Bar, grab a beer and check out the surfboard/chalkboard that lists the arrival times of the jumbo jets. As the minutes draw near, everyone rushes out onto the sand to get under the whooshing plane as it lands. Once you've mastered the landing, then try the take-offs. As the jets rev their engines, huge gusts of gale-force winds shoot across the beach, right beside the bar. Savvy daredevils wear snorkel masks so as to not inhale copious amounts of sand, others simply hold on to the chain-link fence for dear life while their personal effects are blown into the sea. Topless girls drink free and if you come on a Monday or Friday, there's a body artist that will paint you a bikini top. Hint: check in early at the airport, then hitch or catch a US$6 taxi to the bar. It's a wi-fi hot spot.

## CUPECOY BEACH

If you're looking for a beach that's quiet but not totally secluded, Cupecoy is a good choice. This pleasant white-sand beach is backed by low sandstone cliffs that eroded in such a way that they provide a run of small semiprivate coves. There's beach parking down an unmarked drive at the north side of the Ocean Club in Cupecoy.

# ST-MARTIN

While the Dutch side embraces every Caribbean cliché, the French half clings to its European roots and holds on for dear life. Noticeably devoid of casinos and skyscraping timeshares, the quieter French side is a charming mix of white sand beaches, cluttered town centers and stretches of bucolic mountainside.

As the euro continues to excel (and the American dollar declines), many businesses are having a hard time keeping up with their neighbors on the Dutch lands. Restaurants advertise one-for-one euro-to-dollar exchange rates on their meals, and hotels keep their prices as low as possible in order to compete with the big name resorts on the other side. Those in search of holiday hedonism should stick to Maho and Philipsburg, but if you're the type of traveler who is looking for a more subdued vacation you'll enjoy the slower-paced French side a great deal more.

This section starts where the Dutch coverage ends – in Marigot, the French side's capital, and the neighboring Terres Basses. Then we head across the island towards Grand Case, Orient Beach and down to Oyster Pond (which links back up to the beginning of the Dutch sub-chapter at Philipsburg).

## MARIGOT

**pop 12,500**

The capital of French St-Martin, Marigot is a bustling port town dominated by a stone fort high up on the hill. A distinctive European flavor is palpable here – there's a produce market, a gaggle of *boulangeries* (bakeries), and a few buildings with iron-wrought balconies and Belle Epoque lamp-posts.

### Orientation

Marigot has two ports: Port St-Louis and Port La Royale, each with a separate orbit of restaurants and businesses.

### Information

State-of-the-art bathrooms (US$1) are available in the West Indies Mall; they were designed by noted architect Philippe Starck.

**Bibliothèque Municipale** ( ☎ 87-85-87; Rue du Palais Justice; per 15/30min €1.50/3; ☽ 2-7pm Mon & Tue, 9am-7pm Wed, 11am-7pm Thu & Fri, 9am-1pm Sat)

**Change Point** ( ☽ 7:30am-7pm Mon-Sat) A forex bureau near the marina.

**Hospital of St-Martin** ( ☎ 52-25-25)

**Post office** ( ☎ 51-07-60; 25 Rue de La Liberté; ☽ 7am-5:30pm Mon-Fri, 7:30am-noon Sat)

**Tourist office** ( ☎ 87-57-21; www.st-martin.org; Port La Royale; ☽ 8:30am-1pm & 2:30-5:30pm Mon-Fri, 8am-noon Sat) Southwest of the marina.

### Sights

**Fort Louis** was constructed in 1767 by order of French King Louis XVI to protect Marigot from marauding British and Dutch pirates. It's been abandoned for centuries and contains only remnants from bygone eras, but the view alone is worth the 15-minute hike up (past the old hospital) to the ruins.

The **St-Martin Archaeological Museum** ( ☎ 29-22-84; ☽ 9am-4pm Mon-Fri, 9am-1pm Sat) covers everything from the Arawak period to island fashion in the 1930s, and features period photography, historical displays and artifacts from the pre-Colombian period.

### Sleeping

The hotels in the center of Marigot cater to island folk who live on smaller islands and need a place to crash while they do their bulk grocery shopping on St-Martin. Although they are priced in euros, these spots are still some of the cheapest places on the island.

**Centr'Hotel** ( ☎ 87-86-51; centrhotel.sxm@wanadoo.fr; rue du Général de Gaulle; s/d €45/55; ☒ ) This 21-room hotel has large, adequate rooms with TV, air-con, room safes, balconies and minibars.

**Le Cosy** ( ☎ 87-43-95; 8 rue du Général de Gaulle; s/d €58/88; ☒ ) Up a flight of stairs, little Le Cosy has 11 rooms set around a small open-air courtyard. The freshly painted rooms are quite large, although sparsely decorated. Reception is open only from 9am until noon.

**Hotel Le Patio** ( ☎ 29-12-32; hotel.lepatio@wanadoo.fr; rue de la République; s/d €69/89; ☒ ) Another hotel geared to utility rather than luxury. The rooms are clean and come with swatches of warm Caribbean color.

### Eating

For all your self-catering needs, there's **Match** ( ☽ 9am-8pm Mon-Sat, to 1pm Sun) on the north side of Marigot.

#### PORT LA ROYALE

Port La Royale Marina has a waterfront lined with restaurants offering everything from pizza and burgers to seafood and nouvelle cuisine. There's fierce competition, with some of the island's lowest menu prices and lots of chalkboard specials. The best bet is just to wander around and see what catches your fancy.

**La Croissanterie** (mains €5-13; ☽ lunch & dinner) Fantastically cheap. Go for the ham and cheese croissant sandwiches.

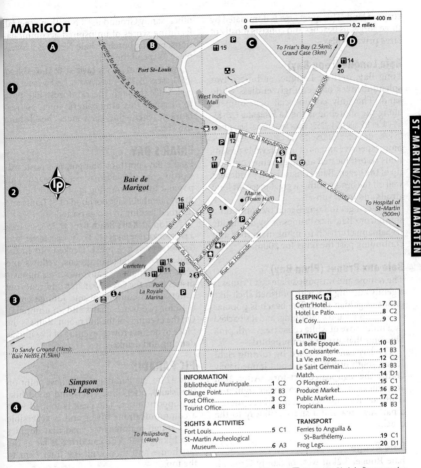

MARIGOT

**SLEEPING**
| | |
|---|---|
| Centr'Hotel | 7 C3 |
| Hotel Le Patio | 8 C2 |
| Le Cosy | 9 C3 |

**EATING**
| | |
|---|---|
| La Belle Epoque | 10 B3 |
| La Croissanterie | 11 B3 |
| La Vie en Rose | 12 C2 |
| Le Saint Germain | 13 B3 |
| Match | 14 D1 |
| O Plongeoir | 15 C1 |
| Produce Market | 16 B2 |
| Public Market | 17 C2 |
| Tropicana | 18 B3 |

**INFORMATION**
| | |
|---|---|
| Bibliothèque Municipale | 1 C2 |
| Change Point | 2 B3 |
| Post Office | 3 C2 |
| Tourist Office | 4 B3 |

**SIGHTS & ACTIVITIES**
| | |
|---|---|
| Fort Louis | 5 C1 |
| St–Martin Archeological Museum | 6 A3 |

**TRANSPORT**
| | |
|---|---|
| Ferries to Anguilla & St–Barthélemy | 19 C1 |
| Frog Legs | 20 D1 |

**Le Saint Germain** ( ☎ 87-92-87; mains €10; ☾ lunch & dinner) Enjoy savory and sweet crepes and a fantastic view of the marina.

**La Belle Epoque** ( ☎ 87-87-70; breakfast around €10, lunch & dinner around €14; ☾ 7:30am-11pm Mon-Sat, 5-11pm Sun) A charming harbourside spot with decorations plucked straight from a *vide grenier*.

**Tropicana** ( ☎ 87-79-07; mains €16-30; ☾ lunch & dinner) Great service and delicious food. Worth the splurge.

### PORT ST-LOUIS

**O Plongeoir** ( ☎ 87-94-71; mains €10-15; ☾ lunch & dinner) At the far end of Port St-Louis (north of the shopping mall), this open-air joint is a great place to sit back with a coffee and spy on Anguilla in the distance. Go for the tuna tartar (€15).

**La Vie en Rose** ( ☎ 87-54-42; Blvd de France; mains €15-20; ☾ lunch & dinner) One of the oldest eateries in Marigot, this fashionable French restaurant sits in a prime location near the harbor. Lunch is either on the patio or the casual 1st floor while dinner is served in the graceful upstairs dining room.

The **produce market** ( ☾ sunrise-2pm Sat) on Marigot's waterfront has tropical fruit such as passion fruit and bananas as well as local root vegetables.

## TERRES BASSES

Terres Basses (pronounced *tair boss*), also called the French Lowlands, is a verdant clump of lush, low-lying acreage connected to the larger part of the island by two thin strips of land. This quiet area is dominated by three gorgeous beaches and consists mostly of large private villas.

## Baie Longue (Long Bay)

Long Bay, or Baie Longue, embraces two splendid miles of seemingly endless white sand. The only commercial development along the shoreline is the **La Samanna** ( ☎ 87-64-00, in US 800-854-2252; www.lasamanna.com; r from US$995, ste from US$1825; 🐾 🖳 🚇 ), St-Martin's most expensive and most unbelievably pretentious resort, located at the extreme southern tip of the beach. Baie Longue is very wide and well off the beaten path – a great place for long strolls and quiet sunsets.

You can get to Long Beach by continuing south from Baie aux Prunes or by taking the La Samanna turn-off from the main road and continuing past the hotel for 800m.

## Baie aux Prunes (Plum Bay)

The remote and unspoiled Baie aux Prunes is a gently curving bay with polished shell-like grains of golden sand. The beach is popular for swimming and sunbathing, and it's backed by a little grove of white cedar trees with pink blossoms that attract hummingbirds.

The bay can be reached by turning right 1.3km south of Baie Rouge and immediately taking the signposted left fork. After 2km you will come to a junction; veer right and continue for another 300m, where there's a parking area and a short walkway to the beach.

## Baie Rouge

Baie Rouge, 3.2km west of Sandy Ground, is a long, beautiful sandy strand with good swimming, though if you have children be aware that the ocean floor drops off quickly to overhead depths. Although this golden-sand beach is just 150m from the main road, it retains an inviting natural setting. For the best snorkeling, swim to the right toward the rocky outcrop and arch. There are a few beach shacks renting snorkel gear or selling barbecued chicken, but this is a fairly secluded spot.

## SANDY GROUND & BAIE NETTLÉ

Sandy Ground is the long, narrow, curving strip of land that extends west from Marigot, with Baie Nettlé (Nettle Bay) on one side of the road and Simpson Bay Lagoon on the

other. Sandy Ground itself is nothing special, featuring scores of uninspired accommodations, but the beach at Baie Nettlé is a lovely place to spend the day.

For a tasty meal, try **Layla's** ( ☎ 51-00-93; lunch US$11, dinner US$20; 🕑 lunch winter, lunch & dinner summer); walk through the rainforest-like path to discover this atmospheric open-air restaurant, where chic Paris meets beach-bum fish shack.

## FRIAR'S BAY

Friar's Bay, north of Marigot, is a postcard-worthy cove with a broad sandy beach. This popular local swimming spot is just beyond the residential neighborhood of St Louis and the road leading in is signposted.

A stop at **Kali's Beach Bar** ( ☎ 72-62-05; www .kali-beach-bar.com; mains €10-15; 🕑 lunch winter, lunch & dinner summer) is a must. Decked out in the trademark Rastafarian greens, yellows and reds, this happenin' hangout serves up tasty dishes from the Creole kitchen and rents out water-sports equipment and lounge chairs (€16 for two beach chairs and an umbrella). On the evenings of the full moon, Kali's is the place to be for a rowdy evening of live music, dancing and drinks.

## PIC PARADIS

The 424m Pic Paradis, the highest point on the island, offers fine vistas and good hiking opportunities. The peak is topped with a communications tower and is accessible by a rough maintenance road that doubles as a hiking trail. You can drive as far as the last house and then walk the final 1km to the top.

A must for hikers and foodies, the **Loterie Farm** ( ☎ 87-86-16; rte Pic Paradis; mains €10-20; 🕑 closed Mon) on the way up to the peak, is an excellent place to spend the afternoon. The quiet plantation features a couple of hikes, a ropes course high up in the trees and a great restaurant that gets rave reviews by locals and tourists alike.

The road to Pic Paradis is 500m north of the 'L' in the road between Friar's Bay and Grand Case that splinters off to the inland community of Colombier. Take the road inland for 2km, turn left at the fork (signposted 'Sentier des Crêtes NE, Pic Paradis') and continue 500m further to the last house, where there's space to pull over and park (do not leave anything in your car; see p449).

### A TALE OF TWO ISLANDS

Corine Mazurier has lived all over the world, but has called St-Martin/Sint Maarten home for the last 20 years. She runs the popular Scoobidoo catamaran expeditions to several remote islands nearby (see below).

**What is the most palpable difference between the French side and the Dutch side?**
There's a slogan used by both tourist boards on the island: 'a little bit of European and a lot of Caribbean', and I really feel like that that sums up the difference between each half. The French part is probably the most 'French' (or European, even) out of any island in the Caribbean, while the Dutch part remains very Antillean.

**Is the French side really that much more expensive because of the euro?**
No. It's true that the strong euro (or rather, the weak dollar) is affecting the 'buying power' of the American tourists and thus the Dutch side may appear cheaper. However, there are hidden taxes, and 15% to 20% service charges added on to every bill, whereas the French businesses have no extra fees whatsoever (it is up to your discretion how much tip you want to leave). Ultimately everything on both sides has become more expensive in the last two years. We import *everything* onto the island and fuel prices are through the roof. That being said, I can assure you that Anguilla is way more expensive than either side of St-Martin, and they use US dollars!

**What does the future hold for this ever changing island?**
Well, St-Martin has two major industries: tourism and…tourism. The island is undoubtedly the most diverse out of any destination in the Caribbean. One can still find relatively secluded beaches, active beaches, casinos, excellent restaurants, high-class shopping, and local (Haitian and Dominican) arts and crafts. Everything is working really well because nothing is in excess. Major investors are forking over serious cash for a little piece of paradise, so real estate is booming. The biggest problem that I can see is that soon we will have an incurable traffic issue (there's already a serious problem), so the government needs to make sure that we do not overbuild. Fortunately, on the French side, strict government laws prohibit the construction of massive buildings, but on the Dutch side it's a whole different story. I think ultimately we rely too heavily on repeat vacationers and the island is getting a little lazy. St-Martin needs to shape up and clean up a little bit to show a better face and to attract newcomers, otherwise there will be trouble ahead.

## GRAND CASE

The small beachside town of Grand Case (pronounced *grond kaz*) has been dubbed the 'Gourmet Capital of the Caribbean.' The beachfront road is lined with an appealing range of places to eat, from local *lolos* to topnotch French restaurants. While dining is the premier attraction, there's also a decent beach and several cheap places to hang your hat.

### Activities

**Scoobidoo** ( ☎ 52-02-53; www.scoobidoo.com) offers excellent catamaran trips that go to Prickly Pear (p428) in Anguilla, Tintamarre or St-Barthélemy for around US$110 per person. It also offers sunset cruises and snorkeling trips (US$55 per person). Boats may also leave from Anse Marcel, depending on the trip.

### Sleeping

**Hotel Hevea** ( ☎ 87-56-85; hevea@outremer.com; 163 Blvd de Grand Case; s/d from €49/62; 🔀 ) The rooms at Hotel Hevea feel like Parisian studio apartments from the 1950s. A scruffy dog guards the calm inner courtyard, which features plenty of patio furniture and a barbecue.

**Chez Martine** ( ☎ 87-51-59; www.chezmartine.net; 140 Blvd de Grand Case; r from €75, ste €160; 🔀 💻 ) This spot has six basic-but-clean rooms with large windows and faux-Picasso murals. The breezy rooms on the second story get plenty of sunlight and have fleeting views of the beach.

**Grand Case Beach Club** ( ☎ 87-51-87, in the US ☎ 800-447-7462; www.grandcasebeachclub.com; ste from €S212; 🔀 💻 🐾 ) On the quiet northeast end of the beach, this gently sprawling place has 73 pleasant condo-like units with full kitchen and balcony. A great place to bring children, as those aged 12 and under stay free in all rooms other than the studios. Plus, there's an onsite pool, recreation room and tennis courts. Rates include continental breakfast at the well-regarded restaurant. There's also wi-fi access.

**Hotel L'Esplanade** ( ☎ 87-06-55, 866-596-8365; www.lesplanade.com; r from US$340; 🔀 💻 🐾 ) This romantic, impeccably run hillside hotel is a

ST-MARTIN/SINT MAARTEN

---

**TWIST MY ARM: THE SPOTS THE AUTHORS WANTED TO KEEP SECRET**

If you thought that Friar's Bay was a quaint little speck of sand, head to the northernmost point of the beach and you'll discover a dirt path that twists over a bumpy headland to the perfectly deserted **Happy Bay**. Equidistant from bustling Marigot and Grand Case, this surprisingly serene strip of powdery sand is completely bare (as are those who like to hang out here). The beach doesn't even get boat traffic because there isn't enough of a curvature in the bay to block the tidewater from dizzying swells.

---

quick hop from the hustle of Grand Case. The beautiful lofts and suites are sumptuous yet homey, and have fully equipped kitchen and private terrace, as well as wi-fi access, a pool and swim-up bar. It'll be tough to leave.

Check out l'Esplanade's equally charming sister property, **Le Petit Hotel** ( ☎ 29-09-65; www .lepetithotel.com; r from US$360; 🖲 ), on the other side of town.

### Eating

Each evening, a ritual of sorts takes place on Grand Case's beachfront road, with restaurants placing their menus and chalkboard specials out front, and would-be diners strolling along the strip until they find a place that strikes their fancy. Tuesday nights are when all the locals descend on the town.

**Calmos Cafe** ( ☎ 29-01-85; Blvd de Grand Case; mains €10-20; 🕐 lunch & dinner) Bury your feet in the sand while hanging out at this casual local fave. Come for a drink or for one of the overflowing dishes, either way Calmos is a great spot to escape the parade of fine-dining tourists.

**Le Pressoir** ( ☎ 87-76-62; 30 Blvd de Grand Case; mains €24-30; 🕐 dinner) Set in a beautiful bright yellow house with charming clapboard shutters – one of the last remaining traditional Creole houses – this fantastic restaurant gets loads of well-deserved praise for its warm atmosphere and scrumptious dishes. Prices are steep, but this is the place to splurge.

**Le Tastevin** ( ☎ 87-55-45; 86 Blvd de Grand Case; appetizers/mains around €15/25; 🕐 lunch & dinner) The full Parisian experience: excellent food served by slightly curt waiters. The white tablecloths gently flutter under your plate of mouthwatering pork tenderloin as the breezy ocean air swooshes through.

The big draw for penny-pinchers is the collection of **lolos** (meals under €14) between the main drag and ocean. These Creole barbecue shacks sit clustered around wooden picnic tables. There are six unique establishments (with oddly idiomatic names like Talk of the Town

or Sky's the Limit) comprising this steamy jungle of smoking grills – each one with its own specialty. Try succulent ribs or chicken legs, with a side of rice and peas.

### ANSE MARCEL

Beautiful Anse Marcel is first glimpsed from high up in the mountains as you gently descend into this hidden bay. This quiet port is the stomping ground for wealthier vacationers, as some of St-Martin/Sint Maarten's fancier properties are located here. One of the island's top hidden beaches, **Petites Cayes** is accessible via a small trail at the north end of Anse Marcel. Follow the path along the rugged headland – it's a bit of a walk, but definitely worth it.

**Scoobidoo** ( ☎ 52-02-53; www.scoobidoo.com) has catamaran trips (around US$110 per person), plus sunset cruises and snorkeling trips (US$55 per person). Boats also leave from Grand Case, depending on the trip.

Hidden behind iron gates, **Le Domaine** ( ☎ 52-35-35; www.hotel-le-domaine.com; r from €335; 🖲 🖳 🖭 ) is one St-Martin's most private hideaways. The stunning lobby opens up onto the perfectly manicured grounds set along the sea.

Up the hill, the **Marquis Hotel Resort & Spa** ( ☎ 29-42-30; www.hotel-marquis.com; Pigeon Pea Hill; r from €380; 🖲 🖳 🖭 ) is a stunning property featuring 17 brightly colored rooms with stunning views of the port down below. Both places have wi-fi access.

### FRENCH CUL-DE-SAC

French Cul-de-Sac is a small but spread-out seaside community just east of Anse Marcel and north of Orient Bay. This is the jumping-off point for the fun-filled Îlet Pinel – local fishers run boats back and forth all day to the islet's soft white sands.

The **Plantation Mont Vernon** ( ☎ 29-50-62; www .plantationmontvernon.com; admission free; 🕐 9am-5pm) is also located in the quiet headland. This restored plantation offers visitors a glimpse of the past (specifically gin and coffee in the 18th century) with recreated distilleries and mills set around a scenic garden. Lunch is available on Sundays.

## ORIENT BEACH (LA BAIE ORIENTALE)

Although this most perfect of beaches has become somewhat of a tourist settlement, it still retains a breezy Caribbean atmosphere. Snorkel-friendly reefs protect 5.5km of inviting white-sand beach. Restaurants, bars, water sports and an au naturel resort all call Orient Beach home.

### Sleeping

**L'Hoste Hotel** ( ☎ 87-42-08; www.hotehotel.com; Parc de La Baie Orientale; r from €230; ✄ ▯ ✎ ) Set slightly away from the sand, L'Hoste is the best bang for your buck near the booming Orient Beach. Rooms are cheered with bright colors and Caribbean knick-knacks.

**Club Orient Naturist Resort** ( ☎ 87-33-85; www .cluborient.com; 1 Baie Orientale; studios from €215, ste from €330; ✄ ▯ ✎ ) Walking around this ranch-style resort is like watching *Animal Planet* or the Discovery Channel: 'come see the elusive middle-aged male (with swinging beer belly in tow), as he plays boccie ball in the buff.' Club Orient offers a range of activities, all done in the nude – fine dining, water sports, sunbathing and sailing cruises. Six different levels of accommodations all feature fully equipped kitchens in semidetached cottages. And there's a completely stocked general store and car-rental agency available

### Eating & Drinking

The tiny village square just off of Orient Beach is one of the most charming spots on the entire island. Each restaurant offers overflowing patio seating that spills out the sides of each restaurant and onto the cobblestone roads. You'll find loads of beach bars on the sand as well.

**Kakao Beach** ( ☎ 87-43-26; mains €10; ✆ lunch & dinner) Gorge on ribs and cheeseburgers.

**Safari** ( ☎ 52-97-57; mains from €10; ✆ breakfast, lunch & dinner) European food served in an African safari theme. A great joint to grab a drink in the evening.

**Bikini** ( ☎ 87-43-25; mains €10-23; ✆ dinner) Colorful chairs plunked directed on the beach. A great place to grab a burger and escape the tropical sun.

**Thai Chi** ( ☎ 87-43-19; mains €15-25; ✆ dinner) Pan-Asian cuisine served up in a trendy atmosphere. Great sushi.

**La Chapelle** ( ☎ 52-38-90; mains €19-29; ✆ dinner) A cool spot set up in an actual church, the altar has been replaced with TVs stuck on the sports channel. Play some darts and try the delicious mussels.

**Kontiki** ( ☎ 87-43-27) Sunday night parties at this bar are not to be missed.

## LE GALION

Near the party on Orient Beach but with about one-tenth of the bustle, Le Galion is a quiet spot with plenty of shallow water and offshore reefs. A top stop for families, this sandy patch remains untouched by development as it is protected by the national marine reserve. Stop by **Tropical Wave** ( ☎ 87-37-25), the local water-sports outfitter, which will hook you up with windsurfing equipment or kayaks. **Bayside Riding Club** ( ☎ in St-Martin 87-36-64, in Sint Maarten 547-6822) is located along a bucolic stretch between Le Galion and Oyster Pond. The **OK Corral** ( ☎ 87-40-72), located at Baie Lucas, also has horseback rides.

Adults and children alike will walk away feeling like veritable butterfly-ologists after a visit to the **Butterfly Farm** ( ☎ 87-31-21; www.the butterflyfarm.com; adult/child US$15/10, admission valid for repeat visits; ✆ 9am-3:30pm), on a turn-off from the N7 in Quartier d'Orleans. Peer into cocooning chrysalises as butterflies flit above, adding to the magical wonderland feel. Guided tours cover biology, conservation and fun facts. Come early to see the butterflies at their most active.

Signposts between Orient Beach and Oyster Pond clearly point the way, although

---

**ÎLET PINEL**

This little islet, just 1km from French Cul-de-Sac is a great spot to spend a sun-soaked afternoon. Totally undeveloped (it's protected by the national forest system), Pinel is the domain of day-trippers, who are deposited on the island's calm west-facing beach, where there's good swimming, snorkeling (snorkel gear €10) and three drink-wielding restaurants.

It's easy to get to Pinel – simply go to the dock at the road's end in French Cul-de-Sac, where you can catch a small boat that departs roughly every 30 minutes. The five-minute ride costs US$6 round-trip and runs 10am to 4pm.

the road to the beach is ridiculously bumpy – the road feels almost impassible at times due to crater-sized divots.

## OYSTER POND

The Dutch–French border slices straight across Oyster Pond, which actually isn't a pond at all but a stunning sunken bay nestled between two jagged hills. Oyster Pond's biggest draw used to be **Dawn Beach**, on the Dutch side, however the recent completion of the clunky Westin hotel has transformed this charming scrap of sand into a bustling compound of roasting tourists. Most of the area's accommodations fall on the French side while the Dutch half features condos and vacation rentals.

**our pick** **Les Balcons d'Oyster Pond** ( ☎ 29-43-39; www.lesbalcons.com; 23 Av du Lagon; bungalow from €85; 🔀 🏊 ) is, without exaggeration, one of the best deals in the Caribbean. Sitting on the French side, this charming collection of villas gently spreads across a scrubby hill, and offers excellent views of the bay and quiet marina below. Although it's run like a hotel (by a lovely French couple), each cottage is privately owned and thus each one has a completely different decor – some have a Balinese-style darkwood theme, others are a cheery mix of Caribbean colors. Our favorite bungalow was number 20. Advanced bookings are imperative; we overheard people calling to make a reservation for their vacation in two years. Cash only. There's wi-fi access.

Just a few minutes' walk from the marina, **Columbus Hotel** ( ☎ 87-42-52; www.columbus-hotel.com; r incl continental breakfast from €$120) offers condo-type units featuring TVs, phone, kitchenette and a terrace or balcony. **Captain Oliver's** ( ☎ 87-40-26; www.captainolivers.com; s/d incl buffet breakfast from US$160/190; 🔀 🖳 🏊 ), a minicity at the marina, is perhaps the only hotel in the world where

you can be in two different countries at once. The rooms are technically on the French side, while the bar is actually Dutch. Rooms are fairly soulless but equipped with balconies, minibars, wi-fi access and spacious furnishings. The open-air restaurant features burgers with fries, seafood and steaks (from US$10 to US$25).

**Quai Ouest** ( ☎ 73-76-01; meals from US$8-16; 🕒 breakfast, lunch & dinner Mon-Sat), a small spot with no more than 10 tables, serves up mostly pizzas and a few meaty mains.

The big draw at the **Dinghy Dock Bar** ( ☎ 87-10-89; meals from US$8) is Happy Hour (5pm to 7pm) when customers get to mix their own drinks. Otherwise this snack bar with picnic tables on the marina dock serves up mediocre sandwiches, hot dogs and full meals, and has Foster's on tap for some strange reason.

# DIRECTORY

## ACCOMMODATIONS

There are plenty of places to hang your hat on the island, but it's best to book in advance, especially during high season. Despite the difference between the dollar and the euro, rooms on both sides come in at around the same price, even when factoring in the steep exchange rates. Most of the lodging on the Dutch side is turning into timeshares or large-scale resorts, while French properties tend to be much more quiet and quaint.

## ACTIVITIES
### Beaches & Swimming
The island has beautiful white-sand beaches that range from crowded resort strands to long, secluded sweeps. Most of the best and least-developed beaches are on the French side of the island.

---

**PRACTICALITIES**

- **Newspapers & Magazines** French side: *Saint-Martin's Week, Fax Info, Pelican;* Dutch side: *The Daily Herald, Today* (both in English); *Discover Saint Martin/Sint Maarten, Sint Maarten Events* and *Ti Gourmet.*
- **Radio & TV** For island music try Radio Calypso 102.1, or Radio 101.5 for reggae and dance music. Radio Transat is at 106.1FM. SXM-TV6 broadcasts from Phillipsburg in English.
- **Electricity** 220V, 60 cycles on the French side; 110V, 60 cycles on the Dutch side.
- **Weights & Measures** Metric.

The nudist Orient Beach is understandably crowded, even the clothing-optional section. Long Beach and Happy Beach are great for seclusion, which Baie Rouge and Îlet Pinel offers some decent snorkeling. All beaches are technically open to the public, although several resorts try to fake people out with privacy signage.

### Boat Trips
There are loads of operators taking tourists out into the blue. Safety standards are higher on the French side (which means noticeably less people on each boat), although the trips tend to cost a tad more.

Some recommended boat trips run from Simpson Bay (p440), Philipsburg (p438), Grand Case (p445) and Anse Marcel (p446).

### Diving & Snorkeling
The most popular dive spot is at Proselyte Reef, a few miles south of Philipsburg, where in 1802 the British frigate HMS *Proselyte* sank in 50ft (15m) of water.

In addition to the remains of the frigate, there are 10 dive sites in that popular area, including fascinating coral reefs with caverns.

See www.sint-maarten-info.com for a list of dive shops around the island. Serious divers should consider a day trip to Saba (p478).

### Golf
The island's golf course is at Mullet Bay (p441). True golf enthusiasts should head over to Anguilla; the island's flat terrain is much more conducive to the sport.

### Hiking
The island's most popular hike is up to Pic Paradis, St-Martin/Sint Maarten's highest point. Not only will this hike reward you with great views, but Pic Paradis also serves as a takeoff point for a few longer hikes that reach down to the coast.

For those who don't want to trek off on their own, guided hikes are offered by Sint Maarten's **Heritage Foundation** (☎ 542-4917), which is affiliated with the Sint Maarten Museum in Philipsburg.

### Horseback Riding
Horseback riding is available at Le Galion (p447) and the OK Corral (p447). The cost for a one-hour beach ride is typically US$40; a two-hour ride is between US$45 and US$60.

## BUSINESS HOURS
In general, restaurants are open from 7am to 10:30am for breakfast, 11:30am to 2:30pm for lunch, and 5pm to 11pm for dinner. French restaurants tend to open for dinner slightly later.

Banks tend to be open from 8am to 3pm on weekdays.

## CHILDREN
St-Martin/Sint Maarten is an especially good place to bring children. Many hotels offer discounts or free stays for children staying with their parents, and there are myriad activities scattered around the island that are perfect for the family from sailing daytrips to nature hikes.

## DANGERS & ANNOYANCES
All leased cars on the island have markings that show they are rentals, making them easy targets for petty thieves. Do not, and we repeat, do not leave anything whatsoever in your car when you leave it parked. Nothing. Not even your umbrella. Certain spots on the island are a bit more dangerous that others, like Pic Paradis, where every single car will be scoped out, no matter how dingy it looks. But it's not worth taking a chance anywhere or at anytime. Even if you don't mind that your umbrella was stolen, you might end up paying through the nose to repair your smashed-in window. Before taking your rental car off the lot, check the car doors – many have had the locks jimmied open at some point in their lives.

Oh but there's more. In the evenings, muggers have been known to follow cars home, and when the victim is driving through a particularly quiet patch of land, the assailants will purposefully bump the car to have a mini accident. After you pull over and get out of your car to check for damages, the thief will mug you and take off. In other instances petty criminals will follow victims all the way back to their hotel or villa and rob them as they walk from the car to their lodging. The best way to avoid these situations is to be mindful of who is behind and in front of you and if you feel like you are being followed, simply pull into a very public place, or continue driving past where you are staying until the driver goes in another direction. If you are bumped by another car, just continue driving. The highest concentrations of these crimes have occurred

ST-MARTIN/SINT MAARTEN

in the quiet area of Oyster Pond, which is largely the domain of wealthier tourists.

There's one more car-related scenario of note: as traffic becomes an ever increasing problem on the island, you make often find yourself waiting for long periods of time within moving an inch. Sometimes during bottleneck traffic, druggies and derelicts will start banging on the window of your 'parked' car begging (and sometimes threatening you) for money. Simply ignore them. This type of annoyance tends to happen around congested Marigot.

A good ole fashioned 'hold-up' is another petty crime that often makes the papers. In the last few years Grand Case has developed a bit of an edge and once in a while a robber will hold-up one of the posh restaurants, collect everyone's wallets and zoom out the door.

## EMBASSIES & CONSULATES

There are no embassies or consulates on St-Martin/Sint Maarten. St-Martin is represented in your home country by the embassy or consulate of France. Sint Maarten is represented by embassies and consulates of the Netherlands. After the referendum at the end of 2008, Sint Maarten's status as a Dutch colony will change, although consular decisions have not yet been solidified.

## FESTIVALS & EVENTS

**Carnival** (No, not the cruise line) On the French side, celebrations are held during the traditional five-day Mardi Gras period that ends on Ash Wednesday. It features the selection of a Carnival Queen, costume parades, dancing and music. On the Dutch side, which has the larger Carnival, activities usually begin the second week after Easter and last for two weeks, with steel-pan competitions, jump-ups, calypso concerts, beauty contests and costume parades. Events are centered at Carnival Village on the north side of Philipsburg.
**Heineken Regatta** (early March) This annual event bills itself as 'serious fun' and features competitions for racing yachts, large sailboats and small multihulls.

## HOLIDAYS

**New Year's Day** January 1
**Good Friday** Late March/early April
**Easter Sunday/Monday** Late March/early April
**Queen's Day** April 30; Dutch side
**Labor Day** May 1
**Government Holiday** The day after the last Carnival parade, about a month after Easter; Dutch side
**Ascension Thursday** 40th day after Easter
**Pentecost Monday** Eighth Monday after Easter; French side

**Bastille Day** July 14; French side
**Assumption Day** August 15; French side
**Sint Maarten Day** November 11
**Christmas Day** December 25
**Boxing Day** December 26; Dutch side

## INTERNET ACCESS

Wireless hot spots can be easily scouted throughout the island, including such places as the Sunset Beach Bar (p441) and Bliss (p441); even Juliana Airport has free (albeit temperamental) wireless access. Most hotels offer wi-fi services and many have computer terminals as well.

## INTERNET RESOURCES

**Saint Martin** (www.st-martin.org) The French side's official website.
**St-Maarten.com** (www.st-maarten.com) The official tourism website for the Dutch side.

## MEDICAL SERVICES

Medical services can be easily scouted in the capital towns of each side of the island: Marigot (p442) and Philipsburg (p438).

## MONEY

On the French side, everything is priced in euros (€), while on the Dutch side (despite the currency being the Netherlands Antillean guilder) items are always posted in US dollars. If you are paying with cash, it never hurts to ask the businesses on the euro-centric French side if they'll take one-for-one dollars to euros – often times you'll get a reluctant-yet-positive response.

ATMs blanket the island and transaction fees will cost substantially less than using the exchange bureaus. Note that American Express cards are rarely accepted on the island, especially on the French side.

## POST

For information on St-Martin's and Sint Maarten's post office facilities, please see p442 and p438, respectively.

## TELEPHONE

St-Martin's area code is ☎ 590 and Sint Maarten's is ☎ 599. Calls between the two sides are (annoyingly) treated as international calls. To call the Dutch side from the French side, dial ☎ 00-599 + the seven-digit number. To dial the French side from the Dutch side,

---

**EMERGENCY NUMBERS**

- **Fire** ☎ St-Martin 18, Sint Maarten 120
- **Police** ☎ St-Martin 87-88-33, Sint Maarten 542-2222

---

dial ☎ 00-590-590 + the six-digit number (that's the area code dialed twice).

To dial within the French telephone system, dial ☎ 0590 + the six-digit number. To dial within the Dutch telephone system, dial ☎ 0599 + the seven-digit number. We have included only the six- and seven-digit local numbers in the listings here. For French cell phones, the second 590 is replaced with 690.

## TOURIST INFORMATION
The main tourist offices are located in Marigot and Philipsburg; see p438 and p442, respectively.

## TRAVELERS WITH DISABILITIES
Although St-Martin is rugged and quite mountainous, the massive amount of tourist development has made it relatively hassle-free for disabled travelers to experience the island.

## VISAS
Visas are not necessary for North Americans, EU nationals and Australians. Some former Soviet states, Latin American countries and many African nationals will need visas, especially for the French side. Always remember that different visa situations apply for the neighboring islands, so read up on the red tape before planning a day trip.

## WOMEN TRAVELERS
An alcohol-fueled party environment is never the ideal place for a single female traveler, so extra caution should be exercised in these situations.

# TRANSPORTATION

## GETTING THERE & AWAY
### Entering the Island
Citizens of the EU need an official identity card or valid passport. Citizens of most other foreign countries need both a valid passport and a visa for France if entering the island on the French side.

A round-trip or onward ticket is officially required of Americans, Canadians and all non-EU citizens, regardless of whether one enters on the French or Dutch side.

People arriving by yacht can clear immigration at the **office** ( ☎ 542-2222) based in Philipsburg, Sint Maarten. The city-sized cruise ships all pull into Philipsburg as well.

## Air
There are two airports on the island: **Juliana Airport** (SXM; ☎ 545-2060; www.pjiae.com; Sint Maarten) and **L'Espérance Airport** ( ☎ 87-53-03; Grand Case, St-Martin). All international flights arrive at Juliana Airport and it is a major hub for carriers such as Winair, which flies on to Anguilla, St-Barthélemy, Saba, Sint Eustatius, Montserrat and other nearby islands. Prop planes head from L'Espérance to St-Barthélemy, Guadeloupe and Martinique.

Note that Juliana is either a crowded tedious experience, or a lovely, no-lines hop through – it's pretty much luck of the draw. Your best bet is to come early and hungry, check in and, if you end up with plenty of time, take a US$6 taxi to the Sunset Beach Bar (p441) for some memorable airport food.

The following airlines fly to/from the island:

**Air Canada** ( ☎ 888-247-2262; www.aircanada.com) Toronto
**Air France** ( ☎ 546-7602; www.airfrance.com) Paris
**American/American Eagle** ( ☎ 800-433-7300; www.aa.com) Miami, New York, San Juan, Santo Domingo
**Caribbean Airlines** ( ☎ 800-538-2942; www.bwee.com) Antigua, Barbados, Georgetown, Fort Lauderdale, Kingston, London, Manchester, Paramaribo, Port-of-Spain, Tobago
**Continental Airlines** ( ☎ 546-7671; www.continental.com) New York
**Delta** ( ☎ 546-7615; www.delta.com) Atlanta
**Insel** ( ☎ 546-7690; www.caribbeanjet.com) Aruba, Bonaire, Curaçao
**JetBlue** ( ☎ 546-7663; www.jetblue.com) New York
**KLM** ( ☎ 546-7695; www.klm.com) Amsterdam
**LIAT** ( ☎ in Sint Maarten 545-2403; www.liatairline.com) Anguilla, Antigua, Nevis, St Kitts, Tortola
**St Barths Commuter** ( ☎ 546-7698) St-Barthélemy
**Spirit** ( ☎ 546-7621; www.spiritair.com) Fort Lauderdale
**United** ( ☎ 800-538-2929; www.united.com) Chicago
**US Airways** ( ☎ 546-7683; www.usair.com) Charlotte, Philadelphia
**Winair** ( ☎ in Sint Maarten 545-2568; www.fly-winair.com) Anguilla, Nevis, Saba, St Kitts, St-Barthélemy, Sint Eustatius, Tortola, Santo Domingo

## Sea

### CRUISE SHIP

No less than 12 major companies land in Philipsburg and Marigot. Day-trippers head to duty-free shopping in the main towns or to beach excursions. Sometimes up to four ships a day are in port. For information on cruise ships, see p830.

### FERRY

Ferries depart from Marigot, Oyster Pond, Philipsburg and Simpson Bay for Anguilla, St-Barthélemy and Saba. Schedules and departure points are prone to change so call the **main ferry line** ( ☎ 87-53-03) in St-Martin for the most up-to-date information.

### St-Martin to Anguilla

Ferries make the 25-minute journey from Marigot Bay in St-Martin to Blowing Point in Anguilla an average of once every 30 minutes from 8am to 6:15pm (from 7:30am to 7pm from Anguilla to St-Martin).

The one-way fare is US$12 (US$15 on the last boat of the day). The fare for the passage is paid onboard the boat.

### St-Martin/Sint Maarten to St-Barthélemy

For information on reaching St-Barthélemy by ferry, see p467.

### Sint Maarten to Saba

See p480 for details about reaching Saba by ferry.

### YACHT

Yachts can clear immigration at Philipsburg and Marigot. There are marinas at Philipsburg, Marigot, Simpson Bay Lagoon, Oyster Pond and Anse Marcel.

## GETTING AROUND

Although the island is divided into two separate land claims, there are no official borders or border crossings (besides a couple of cheesy billboards welcoming drivers to each side of the island). Traffic moves as freely across both sides of the island as if it was one entity.

## Bicycle

**Frog Legs Cyclery** ( ☎ 87-05-11), next to the Match supermarket in Marigot, St-Martin, rents out mountain bikes from US$15 a day and organizes island cycling tours for US$20.

## Bus

Buses are by far the cheapest method of transportation, but remember that time is money. If you need to be somewhere fast, take a taxi or better yet rent a car. Buses do not have any set schedule and they come and go as they please until around 10:30pm. Buses charge US$2 for every town you pass through along your journey. Service mostly moves through Philipsburg, Mullet Bay, Simpson Bay, Marigot and Grand Case. When you need to get off, simply yell 'stop.'

In the capitals you have to stand at bus stops, which are called 'Bushalte' in Philipsburg. In rural areas you can flag down buses anywhere along the route. Buses have their final destination posted on the front shield, but most are bound for either Philipsburg or Marigot.

## Car & Motorcycle

### RENTAL

Car rental agencies are abundant on the island and are wiser choice than scooters. Motorbikes tend to get stolen and easily roughed up and, frankly, they aren't that much cheaper than a car. During low season, there's no need to book ahead, as you can simply arrive at Juliana Airport and bargain among the 10 or so booths for a price as low as US$25 per day. In high season, expect to pay around US$35 per day for the most compact car you can find. Weekly discount rates are usually on offer year-round.

Try **Banana Location** ( ☎ 0690-71-91-05; banana location@orange.fr) and you'll be guaranteed a clean, comfortable vehicle at a very reasonable price (€35). The affable owner delivers some of the top customer service on the island – he'll meet you at the airport to make sure you start your holiday off on the right foot.

The following companies have offices at Juliana Airport, Sint Maarten:
**Avis** ( ☎ 545-2316)
**Budget** ( ☎ 545-4030)
**Dollar** ( ☎ 545-3061)
**Hertz** ( ☎ 545-4440)
**Paradise Island** ( ☎ 545-2361)
**Sunshine** ( ☎ 545-2685)

### ROAD RULES

Driving is on the right side of the road on both sides of the island, and your home driver's license is valid. Road signs and car odometers are in kilometers.

The amount of traffic in Marigot, Grand Case and Philipsburg can shock visitors expecting a peaceful getaway. Traffic jams occur regularly. See p449 for important information about safety on the road.

## Hitchhiking

You'll see many locals with their thumbs out, but tourists shouldn't follow suit. Petty theft and violent crime is on the rise all over the island.

## Taxi

The government-regulated fares should be posted in each taxi. Rates increase in the evening or if there are more than three passengers. From Juliana Airport it's US$6 to Maho, US$15 to Marigot and US$22 to Grand Case. Taxi tours of the island last 1½ to three hours and cost US$20 to US$40 per person.

To hail a taxi, call ☎ 147 anytime day or night.

ST-MARTIN/SINT MAARTEN

# St-Barthélemy

The mere mention of St-Barthélemy conjures up fanciful dreams such as having cocktails with supermodels, sampling caviar with a four-digit price tag, or dropping some serious bling on a Dior bathing suit…for your miniature schnauzer. Does this stuff really happen in St-Barth? It sure does.

So how, you may ask, did St-Barth become *the* playground for the rich and famous? The question is answered simply by seeing the island. From afar, dozens of sky-scraping mountains dramatically rise to the heavens. As you get closer, these craggy peaks start to reveal their sexy beaches like a dirty secret. Then, when you arrive, the possibilities for decadence become obvious: perfectly positioned bays beg for shmancy restaurants and rolling hills yearn for rambling villas.

For the rest of us, St-Barth still has plenty to offer. Under its star-studded surface, the island has a quiet community of locals who can trace their ancestry back to rural Brittany or Normandy – and even the rugged coastal terrain dotted with lonely cottages feels bizarrely French. Rent a seaside villa with an ocean view and spend your days basking in the warm Caribbean sun. Escape in the evening to sample some savvy French-Creole fusion cuisine, or head to a vibrant local market for some floppy fish and legumes.

Whether you're after the glamorous life of the jet-setting glitterati, or simply a hushed bucolic village vibe, St-Barth can supply it. Just remember: while the two cultures of the island are almost diametrically opposed, they are ultimately united by their love of the Madonna (albeit different ones…).

## FAST FACTS

- **Area** 21 sq km
- **Capital** Gustavia
- **Country code** ☎ 590
- **Departure tax** €4.50
- **Famous for** Being the ridiculously expensive playground of the rich and famous
- **Language** French
- **Money** euro (€); €1 = US$1.56 = UK£0.79
- **Official name** Collectivité de Saint-Barthélemy
- **People** French
- **Phrase** I would like to thank the Academy…
- **Population** 7500
- **Visa** Not necessary for most nationalities; see p467

# HIGHLIGHTS

- **Beaches** (p464) Try Anse de Colombier in the far west for powdery white sand or head to Anse de Gouverneur in the east for a perfectly rugged stretch of beach – it's so hard to pick just one!
- **Gustavia** (p458) Strut your stuff while window-shopping and yacht-ogling in St-Barth's stunning fort-flanked capital
- **Fine Dining** (p457) Bust out the plastic – the island's legion of world-class chefs dedicate their careers to eliciting a visceral 'mmm!' from guests
- **Corossol** (p463) Step back in time to this charming village ripped straight from the tranquil western coast of France
- **Staying in Style** (p464) Set your Louis Vuitton luggage down at an opulent resort, such as the Guanahani, or slip away to a hidden beachside villa

# ITINERARIES

- **One Day** Take a puddle jumper or the ferry over from St-Martin/Sint Maarten and spend the day ogling giant yachts and shopping in Gustavia. For an early dinner try popular Le Select, or head to Public and eat at Maya's. Adventurous types with plenty of energy may consider grabbing a cab to the western lookout point at the end of Colombier and walking back to Gustavia.
- **Five Days** Get a room at the Guanahani in Grand Cul-de-Sac (if you've just won the lottery) or at Saline Gardens in Anse de Grande Saline and spend three blissful days by the beach. In the evenings try out some of the internationally acclaimed restaurants that pepper the island. On your last two days, undergo some retail therapy in Gustavia followed by a couple of hours roaming the quiet west coast, particularly around quaint Corossol.
- **Two Weeks** Snag one of the many private villas scattered around the island, and spend your first week at a different beach each day. Then get your adrenaline pumping with a sailing day trip and a scuba dive, plus some hiking in the east, and round out the week swiping your plastic at the boutiques in Gustavia.

# CLIMATE & WHEN TO GO

St-Barth has two seasons: the *caréme*, the dry season; and the *hivernage*, the hurricane season from July to November, when heavier rains are expected.

During Christmas the rates skyrocket from pricey to outrageously ridiculous, so this may be a time to avoid.

# HISTORY

Due to its inhospitable landscape and lack of freshwater, St-Barth never had a big Arawak or Carib presence.

When Christopher Columbus sighted the island on his second voyage in 1493, he named it after his older brother Bartholomeo. The first Europeans who attempted to settle the island, in 1648, were French colonists. They were soon killed by Caribs. Norman Huguenots gave it another try about 25 years later and prospered, not due to farming (which was near impossible) or fishing, but by setting up a way station for French pirates plundering Spanish galleons. You can still hear traces of the old Norman dialect in towns such as Flamands and Corossol.

In 1784, the French king Louis XVI gave St-Barth to the Swedish king Gustaf III in exchange for trading rights in Gôteburg. There are still many reminders of the Swedish rule – such as the name Gustavia, St-Barth's continuing duty-free status, and several buildings and forts – on the island. However, Sweden sold St-Barth back to France in 1878 after declining trade, disease and a destructive fire affected the island.

Throughout the 19th and early 20th centuries, St-Barth wasn't much more than a quaint French backwater, and life was tough for residents. Without the lush vegetation typical of the Caribbean, farming was difficult. Many former slaves emigrated to surrounding islands to find work, leaving St-Barth one of the only islands in the region without a substantial African population.

In the 1950s, tourists slowly started arriving at the tiny airport on small planes and private jets. The scrubby island suddenly found new natural resources: beaches, sunsets, quiet. Quick-thinking islanders created laws limiting mass tourism to guard their hard-earned lifestyle; as a result, you won't see casinos, high-rise hotels or fast-food chains, but you will pay for the atmosphere.

On December 7, 2003, an overwhelming 90% of the population of St-Barth voted to grant themselves more fiscal and political

# ST-BARTHÉLEMY

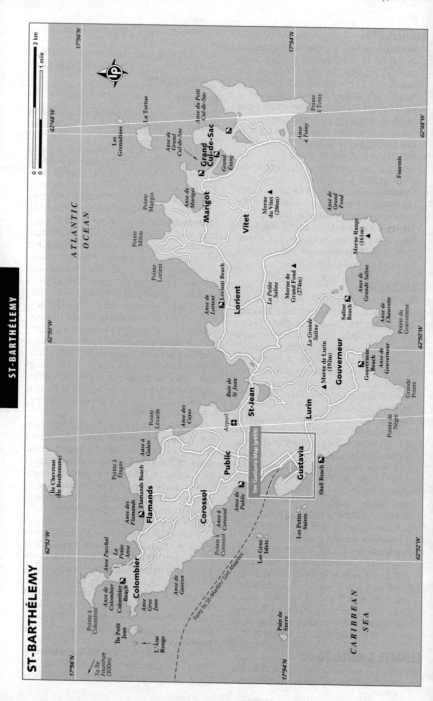

ST-BARTHÉLEMY

ATLANTIC OCEAN

CARIBBEAN SEA

La Tortue

Les Grenadines

Pointe à Toiny

Anse du Petit Cul-de-Sac

Anse à Toiny

Anse de Grand Cul-de-Sac

**Grand Cul-de-Sac**

Grand Étang

Fourmis

Pointe Mangin

Anse de Marigot

**Marigot**

**Vitet**

Morne du Vitet (286m)

Anse de Grand Fond

Pointe Milou

Morne Range (161m)

Pointe Lorient

Lorient Beach

**Lorient**

La Petite Saline

Morne de Grand Fond (274m)

Anse de Grande Saline

Anse de Lorient

La Grande Saline

Saline Beach

Anse de Chauvette

Pointe du Gouverneur

**Gouverneur**

Morne de Lurin (192m)

Gouverneur Beach

Anse de Gouverneur

Baie de St Jean

Pointe Lézarde

Anse des Cayes

**St-Jean**

Airport

**Lurin**

Grande Pointe

Pointe à Étages

Anse à Galets

Flamands Beach

**Flamands**

Anse des Flamands

**Public**

**Corossol**

Anse à Corossol

Anse de Public

See Gustavia Map (p459)

**Gustavia**

Shell Beach

Pointe de Nègre

Île Chevreau (Île Bonhomme)

Pointe à Corossol

Les Petits Saints

Anse Paschal

La Petite Anse

**Colombier**

Anse de Colombier

Colombier Beach

Les Gros Îslets

Ferry to St-Martin/Sint Maarten

Pain de Sucre

Pointe à Colombier

Île Petit Jean

Anse Gros Jean

Anse de Gascon

L'Âne Rouge

To Île Fourchue (300m)

2 km

1 mile

0
0

independence from France and Guadeloupe. As a member of Guadeloupe, St-Barth was part of an overseas *région* and *département*. After separation, the island became an 'overseas collectivity,' which meant that the island gained a municipal council rather than having a single islandwide mayor. Despite the separation, the island has remained part of the EU.

## THE CULTURE

Most residents of St-Barth fall into one of three categories: descendants of the pioneers from Normandy who have called St-Barth home for over 300 years; mainlanders setting up expensive shops and restaurants; or foreigners looking for a more relaxed lifestyle. As tourism blossomed, the first group of residents largely traded in their fishing careers for tourism-related jobs, so virtually everyone is working in hospitality of some sort.

The locals protect their slightly time-warped way of life while the glitzy Hollywood types strut around next door – many natives haven't seen their house key for years, and nor do they care whether Beyonce is being bootylicious at the next table – but neither group seems too bothered about the other's presence.

Despite the island's location, the general atmosphere is much more that of a quiet seaside province in France than a jammin' Caribbean colony.

## ARTS

For hundreds of years, St-Barth's residents were too busy toiling in near-impossible conditions to create much art, thus the traditional handicrafts were largely utilitarian. Head to Corossol, St-Barth's most 'local' area, you'll find hats and baskets woven by local women from the leaves of the lantana palms. These small woven concoctions sit at the front gates to many homes, and make a much more authentic souvenir that the €200 bathing suits on sale in Gustavia.

There are about 20 art galleries and spaces around the island devoted to exhibiting local paintings, photography and sculpture. For more information about visiting artists' studios, stop by the **Office Territorial du Tourisme** (☎ 27-87-27; Quai Général de Gaulle, Gustavia) for a detailed list of contact information. In recent years, as the island's luxury tourism continues

to boom, several lines of exclusive designer products (everything from jewelry to moisturizers) have become available.

## ENVIRONMENT

St-Barth's total land area is a mere 21 sq km, although its elongated shape and hilly terrain make it seem larger. The island lies 25km southeast of St-Martin/Sint Maarten.

St-Barth has numerous dry and rocky offshore islets. The largest, Île Fourchue, is a half-sunken volcanic crater whose large bay is a popular yacht anchorage, and a destination for divers and snorkelers.

St-Barth's arid climate sustains dryland flora, such as cacti and bougainvillea. Local reptiles include lizards, iguanas and harmless grass snakes. From April to August, sea turtles lay eggs along the beaches on the northwest side of the island. The islets off St-Barth support seabird colonies, including those of frigate birds.

In recent years St-Barth has taken environmental concerns very seriously and has committed to sustainable methods of energy production. The island utilizes a color-coded recycling system; be sure to toss glass in green containers and plastic in blue containers.

In 2001 St-Barth pioneered the first trash incinerator of its kind in the Caribbean. The incinerator is able to simultaneously burn trash, create energy and produce drinkable water, all with less pollution than older incinerators. It comes with a higher price tag, but islanders feel the result is worth it.

## FOOD & DRINK

An undisputed destination for foodies, St-Barth is the kind of place where every meal can be a work of art, and it's worth planning ahead to get the most for your money (because let's face it – this place ain't cheap!).

---

### HOW MUCH?

- Rental car per day €60
- Main course at a local restaurant €20
- Burger at Le Select €5
- A beach chair and an umbrella on St-Jean beach €30
- Relaxing on your towel at Anse de Gouverneur Free

---

ST-BARTHÉLEMY

Food is taken seriously here – many restaurants dish out meals made from recipes that have been kept secret for decades. A fusion of French and Creole tastes is common, giving each plate a certain St-Barth kick.

You'll find dozens of high-end restaurants on St-Barth, some attached to big-name hotels, others hidden on mountain peaks or tucked away in a residential neighborhood. Perhaps the best part of dining here is that each restaurant has a story to tell – a quirky history, a tale about the chef, or a tidbit of information relating to the eatery's founding.

# GUSTAVIA

**pop 1500**

About 50 years ago, Gustavia was a windswept fishing village; today this stunning port town is nothing short of majestic. Although relatively small when compared to other capitals in the Caribbean, Gustavia has plenty of places to 'see and be seen,' including myriad high-end boutiques, upmarket restaurants and a couple of historical sights.

## INFORMATION

Most places in Gustavia are open from Monday to Friday from 8am to noon, then from 2pm to 3:30pm.

Gustavia has wi-fi throughout town; to access it, buy a wi-fi card and email contact@saintbarth-telecom.com.

Public toilets are available behind the Office Territorial du Tourisme, and include showers for boaters.

**Banque des Antilles Française** ( ☎ 29-68-30) Has an ATM.

**Banque Nationale de Paris** (Rue Bord de Mer) Has an ATM.

**Bruyn Hospital** ( ☎ 27-60-35; Rue Jean-Bart) A small hospital.

**Change Caraïbes** (Rue du Général de Gaulle) Has an ATM.

**Doctor** ( ☎ 27-76-03) For after-hours medical attention.

**Funny Face Bookstore** ( ☎ 29-60-14; Carré d'Or) Stocks English-language books.

**Municipal Police** ( ☎ 27-66-66; Rue du Roi Oscar II)

**Office Territorial du Tourisme** ( ☎ 27-87-27; Quai Général de Gaulle; ☾ 9am-noon & 2-5pm Mon-Sat) Will help with accommodations, restaurant recommendations, island tours and activities. Has a map for a self-guided Gustavia walking tour.

**Pharmacie St Barth** ( ☎ 27-61-82; Rue de la République; ☾ 8am-7:30pm Mon-Fri, 8am-1pm & 3:30-7pm Sat & public holidays)

**Post office** ( ☎ 27-63-63; cnr Rue Jeanne d'Arc & Rue de Centenaire; ☾ 8am-3pm Mon, Tue, Thu & Fri, to noon Wed & Sat)

## SIGHTS

There aren't loads of sights on St-Barth, but it's worth stopping by the Office Territorial du Tourisme (left) to grab its small pamphlet, which offers a nuanced caption to some of the older structures in Gustavia, including the **Catholic church**, the **Swedish belfry**, the **Wall House** (La Pointe) and the **Anglican church**.

The site of old **Fort Gustave** has a couple of cannons and a slightly bottle-shaped lighthouse, but most people come here for the fine view of Gustavia and the harbor. A plaque points out local sights and landmarks. Across the harbor to the south is **Fort Oscar**, which is still used as a military installation, and from where you can see the islands of St Kitts and Sint Eustatius on a clear day.

At the **Musée Territorial** ( ☎ 29-71-55; admission €2; ☾ 8:30am-1pm & 2:30-5:30pm Mon, 8:30am-1pm & 2:30-5pm Tue, Thu & Fri, 8:30am-1pm Wed, 9am-1pm Sat) you can take a look at historical St-Barth, from the Carib settlements to the Swedish occupation, with old photos and traditional clothing.

After years of coaxing from his family, André Berry, the island's pack rat, finally opened a museum of oddities called **Le P'tit Collectionneur** ( ☎ 27-67-77; admission €2; ☾ 10am-noon & 4-6pm Mon-Sat). His collection features a diverse array of objects ranging from 18th-century British pipes to the island's first phonograph. In a roundabout way, these objects tell the story of St-Barth's colorful history.

## ACTIVITIES

A number of activities operators are located in Gustavia. Try the following places:

**Big Blue** ( ☎ 27-83-74) A dive center.

**Marine Service** ( ☎ 27-70-34; http://st-barths.com/marine.service; Quai du Yacht Club) A full-service center offering snorkeling and diving (tank dive €55, 10-dive package €480); shore and deep-sea fishing; and half- and full-day private and public boat charters. One popular boat trip is a half-day snorkeling trip aboard a catamaran.

**Ocean Must Marina** ( ☎ 27-62-25) Offers fishing trips.

**Totem Surf** ( ☎ 27-83-72) Rents surfing gear.

## SLEEPING

Accommodation in Gustavia is focused on the harbor rather than a powdery beach. The two cheapest places on the island are located here, as is one of the most expensive.

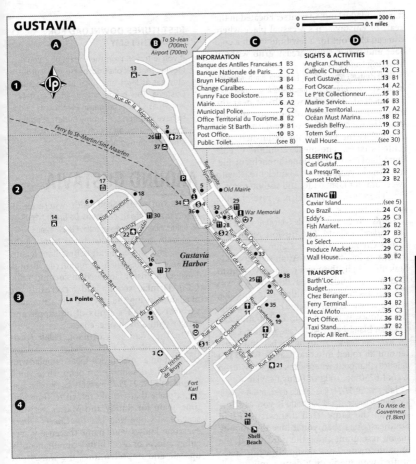

# GUSTAVIA

0 — 200 m
0 — 0.1 miles

To St-Jean (700m); Airport (700m)

Ferry to St-Martin/Sint Maarten

### INFORMATION
| | |
|---|---|
| Banque des Antilles Francaises..1 | B3 |
| Banque Nationale de Paris....2 | C2 |
| Bruyn Hospital.................3 | B4 |
| Change Caraïbes................4 | B2 |
| Funny Face Bookstore..........5 | B2 |
| Mairie..........................6 | A2 |
| Municipal Police...............7 | C2 |
| Office Territorial du Tourisme.8 | B2 |
| Pharmacie St Barth............9 | B1 |
| Post Office....................10 | B3 |
| Public Toilet...............(see 8) | |

### SIGHTS & ACTIVITIES
| | |
|---|---|
| Anglican Church.............11 | C3 |
| Catholic Church.............12 | C3 |
| Fort Gustave................13 | B1 |
| Fort Oscar..................14 | A2 |
| Le P'tit Collectionneur.....15 | B3 |
| Marine Service..............16 | B3 |
| Musée Territorial...........17 | A2 |
| Océan Must Marina...........18 | B2 |
| Swedish Belfry..............19 | C3 |
| Totem Surf..................20 | C3 |
| Wall House................(see 30) | |

### SLEEPING
| | |
|---|---|
| Carl Gustaf.................21 | C4 |
| La Presqu'île...............22 | B2 |
| Sunset Hotel................23 | B2 |

### EATING
| | |
|---|---|
| Caviar Island.............(see 5) | |
| Do Brazil..................24 | C4 |
| Eddy's......................25 | C3 |
| Fish Market.................26 | B2 |
| Jao.........................27 | B3 |
| Le Select...................28 | B2 |
| Produce Market.............29 | C2 |
| Wall House..................30 | B2 |

### TRANSPORT
| | |
|---|---|
| Barth'Loc...................31 | C2 |
| Budget......................32 | B2 |
| Chez Beranger...............33 | C3 |
| Ferry Terminal..............34 | B2 |
| Meca Moto...................35 | C3 |
| Port Office.................36 | B2 |
| Taxi Stand..................37 | B2 |
| Tropic All Rent.............38 | C3 |

Old Mairie

War Memorial

Gustavia Harbor

La Pointe

Fort Karl

Shell Beach

To Anse de Gouverneur (1.8km)

ST-BARTHÉLEMY

**La Presqu'île** ( ☎ 27-64-60; La Pointe; s/d €40/60; ) Popular with yachties, this hotel is not only a freakishly good deal for St-Barth, but is also reasonably comfortable and central. The rooms are small but clean, and the wraparound patio offers a beautiful spot to have breakfast and admire the Gustavia harbor.

**Sunset Hotel** ( ☎ 27-77-21; www.st-barths.com/sunset -hotel; Rue de la République; s €92-111, d €98-119, tr €126; ) The most central hotel in Gustavia, this is also clean, unpretentious and family run. The 10 rooms all have phones, TVs and refrigerators; the pricier ones also have a stunning view of the harbor and sunset, but get a bit of street noise. Rates also depend on the season. Book ahead – the owner proudly told us that all of his rooms were full every single night of 2007.

The **Carl Gustaf** ( ☎ 29-79-00; www.hotelcarlgustaf .com; Rue des Normands; ste from €1160) has 12 rooms perched high over the center of the port.

## EATING

There are loads of amazing restaurants in Gustavia and we highly encourage you to go out and sample any and all that don't appear in our list below – the following selection should just whet your appetite, so to speak.

**Le Select** ( ☎ 27-86-87; cnr Rue de la France & Rue du Général de Gaulle; burgers €5; 11am-2:45pm & 5:30-10:30pm Mon-Sat) When the bombshells were going off in *Casablanca* (the movie), everyone sought refuge at Rick's. Le Select is the equivalent in St-Barth – the bombshells being something much more figurative on this star-studded island, of course. Located in the heart of Gustavia, it's a casual place where you can chill out for a few hours with a cold beer and order some greasy grub without breaking the bank.

**Wall House** ( ☎ 27-69-43; La Pointe; lunch mains €9-26, dinner mains €14-29; ☺ lunch & dinner, closed lunch Sun) Located along the waterfront near the museum, with plenty of outdoor seating, Wall House has a view of the harbor that's as good as the view of the exquisitely presented dishes. The meals combine Creole ingredients with traditional French cuisine, resulting in recipes such as duck breast with sweet onion marmalade, and scallop carpaccio. The €9 daily special is a rare cheapie for St-Barth.

**Eddy's** ( ☎ 27-54-17; Rue du Centenaire; mains from €12; ☺ lunch & dinner) This fusion restaurant blends Creole, Caribbean, Cajun and French influences in a Southeast Asian setting (Eddy Stakelborough, the owner, actually went to Thailand to build the pavilion, which was then disassembled and shipped to this site, where it was reconstructed). Look for the teeny doorway across from Le Sapotillier.

**Caviar Island** ( ☎ 52-46-11; Carré d'Or; mains €16-48; ☺ 10am-1am Mon-Sat) A lounge, a bar and a restaurant all rolled into one, Caviar Island is a celebrity hangout where stars can easily drop a cool €750 on 100g of beluga caviar.

**Jao** ( ☎ 29-52-24; Rue Jeanne d'Arc; mains €21-38; ☺ lunch & dinner, closed Sun lunch) If you can forget that the same Thai dishes cost €1 in Southeast Asia then you'll love this moody fusion restaurant along the port. Pascal, the amiable owner, has designed a hip space stuffed with meditating deities and lipstick red pillows. The food is simply delicious.

If you've got your own kitchen, come to the **Fish Market** (Rue de la République; ☺ 6am-10pm) to pick up still-wriggling supplies. Local fishers bring in the catches of the day, including marlin, wahoo, dorado, tuna and langouste. Stop by the tiny **Produce Market** (Rue du Roi Oscar II) for your local fruits and vegetables.

## SHOPPING

Gustavia is a duty-free port and features the most exclusive labels in the world: Dior, Bulgari, Rolex etc. But there is also a slew of small, locally owned boutiques and labels, such as Made in Saint-Barth and Ligne Saint-Barth.

> **BEST ITUNES DOWNLOAD FOR ST-BARTHÉLEMY**
>
> If you're travelin' on the cheap, or if you're looking for a bit of atmosphere, you'll probably eat at least one meal at Le Select in Gustavia. This burger stand, affectionately known as Cheeseburger in Paradise, is said to have inspired the Jimmy Buffett song by the same name, although he claims that the joint was named after his song...

# AROUND GUSTAVIA

Check out pretty **Shell Beach**, where tennis star Yannick Noah co-owns **Do Brazil** ( ☎ 29-06-66; lunch sandwich €7-9, dinner mains €16-27, menu €29/42), a casually trendy sandwich bar fronting the beach. The dinner menu is Brazilian, featuring exotic tastes such as *moqueca* (shrimp, lobster and fish marinated in coconut milk; €32). Drinks, snacks and ice creams are available during the day. Go for a Brazilian *saravah* cocktail – a mix of pineapple and ginger with a dash of cachaça.

On the road to Corossol, **Public** (pronounced with a French accent) is a village centered on a small beach that's popular with locals and a desalinization plant. Here you'll find **Maya's** ( ☎ 27-75-73; mains €31-43; ☺ dinner Mon-Sat), a place that people return to time and time again for Randy and Maya's personal service; it's like that bar on *Cheers* where everyone knows your name (because you're either a local or a celebrity). Simultaneously upscale and unpretentious, the waterfront restaurant has a menu that changes everyday and can include tropical salads, fish dishes and Maya's world-famous coconut tart. It's worth nabbing a spot in advance.

# EASTERN ST-BARTHÉLEMY

East of Gustavia are dramatic sky-scraping mountains and isolated stretches of powder-soft sand. St-Barth's only airport is located here, as are most of the island's opulent hotels.

## ST-JEAN

Many hotels and restaurants line the main stretch of road in this tourist-heavy village, making parking difficult. Once you're off the road, the beach is delightful, the hotels comfortable and the dining eclectic, ranging from delis to tragically hip, techno-infused attitude factories.

## Information

St-Jean has a small branch post office, near the airport.

**American Express** ( ☎ 52-97-06; La Savane Commercial Center) Handles transactions in euros and dollars.

**Pharmacy** ( ☎ 27-66-61; La Savane Commercial Center).

## Activities

**Carib Waterplay** ( ☎ 27-71-22; caribwaterplay@wanadoo .fr) offers windsurfing lessons, as well as kayaking, surfing and snorkeling trips. It also rents kayaks.

**Hookipa Surf Shop** ( ☎ 27-71-31) rents surfing equipment.

## Sleeping

**Hotel Le Village St Jean** ( ☎ 27-61-39; www.villagestjean hotel.com; r €200, 1-bedroom cottage from €260, 2-bedroom cottage €620; 🅿 🖥 🐾 ) Comfort, charm and a yummy Italian restaurant: this place has it all. Patriarch André Charneau built the Village himself in 1968, and it has been lovingly run by his family ever since. Rooms vary from basic hotel rooms to deluxe cottages with kitchenettes and patios (the two-bedroom cottage has its own pool), ensuring good value on any budget – for St-Barth, that is. It's a five-minute walk uphill from the beach.

**Emeraude Plage** ( ☎ 27-64-78; www.emeraudeplage .com; Rue de St-Jean; r €350-855; 🅿 🖥 ) This gaggle of ghost white cottages, bungalows and studios is set in a sandy patch directly on the St-Jean beach. Tiled suites all have large bedrooms and come with a private terrace. Recent renovations include funky plasma-TV-cum-computer contraptions (there's also wi-fi), and minimalist whitewashed decor that looks a bit hospital-like from the wrong angle.

**Eden Rock** ( ☎ 29-79-89; www.edenrockhotel.com; cottage €615, ste €1095-1750; 🅿 🖥 🐾 ) St-Barth's first hotel stretches out and over a rocky promontory down to the white-coral St-Jean beach below. Each suite and cottage is luxuriously appointed with fine antiques, swashbuckling colors and an unbeatable view. Offers wi-fi access.

## Eating

**Kiki-é Mo** ( ☎ 27-90-65; Rue de St-Jean; light meals €6-15; 🕒 9am-7pm Mon-Sat) In the heart of St-Jean,

this full-service deli has delectable pizza, pasta and desserts, but the real draw is the scrumptious paninis.

**Sand Bar** ( ☎ 27-90-65; Eden Rock; mains €15-45; 🕒 lunch) If you're in the mood for a lunchtime splurge, look no further than Sand Bar, the elegant beach bar at the Eden Rock Hotel. The presentation of the food is artful and you'll be nibbling on your gourmet beach grub alongside an assortment of celebrities.

If you're preparing food at your villa or organizing a picnic, head to **Match** ( ☎ 27-68-16; 🕒 8am-1pm & 3-8pm Mon-Sat, 9am-1pm & 3-7pm Sun), located in the complex across from the airport. Packed with tropical fruit, and European and American food, it's also the best place to pick up reasonable French wines.

## GRAND CUL-DE-SAC

Beautiful Grand Cul-de-Sac yawns across a large horseshoelike bay, and has a sandy beach with good conditions for water sports. Fronting the open cove are several hotels and restaurants.

## Activities

There are a couple of activity outfitters in Grand Cul-de-Sac. **Ouanalao Dive** ( ☎ 0690-63-74-34) runs diving trips, while **Wind Wave Power** ( ☎ 27-82-57; St-Barths Beach Hotel) gives 1½-hour windsurfing lessons (about €60) and rents kayaks.

## Sleeping

**Les Ondines** ( ☎ 27-69-64; les.ondines@orange.fr; r €350-690; 🅿 ) You can practically touch the incoming tide from your apartment-style suite at this motel-like structure. When you start dropping €500-plus per night you should head to the Guanahani next door, but the cheaper rooms aren't bad, especially because they have a full kitchen and a living room, not to mention a prime spot on the sand.

**Le Sereno** ( ☎ 29-83-00; www.lesereno.com; ste/villa from €480/1130; 🅿 🖥 🐾 ) Le Sereno is back with a vengeance. After a bit of time off to get a much needed face-lift by Parisian designer Christian Liaigre, the property is now dedicated to relaxation and serenity through Zen-like decoration. Some would say that it's a bit too minimal (and thus not worth the price); others are awestruck at how the staff keeps the sheets so darn crisp and white. Offers wi-fi access.

**our pick Hotel Guanahani & Spa** ( ☎ 27-66-60; www.leguanahani.com; ste from €580; 🅿 🖥 🐾 )

**ST-BARTHÉLEMY**

'Guanahani' can only be uttered with an accompanying sigh of content and relaxation. The ultimate retreat and, with 70 rooms, the island's largest hotel, this stunning resort is a hidden village of brilliantly bright bungalows (with private plunge pools) flung across jungly grounds. Offers wi-fi.

### Eating

Across from the entrance to Le Sereno there's an open area with some picnic tables and a grill. At one time it was called Cocolobo, and since then it's changed hands a couple of times, but it's still worth checking out as there's usually somebody cooking up some cheap barbecue fare. If you get lost, ask someone for directions to 'where the old Gloriette used to be' and they'll almost definitely know the way.

## LORIENT

Lorient, the site of St-Barth's first French settlement (1648), is a small village fronted by a lovely white-sand beach. The town has a charming collection of old stone structures, including a small Caribbean-style convent and one of the island's three Catholic churches. Most of the island's small Portuguese population lives in the area – try the goat stew if you stop by one of the local haunts.

### Information

Lorient has a small **post office** ( 7-11am Mon-Fri, 8am-noon Sat).

### Sleeping

**Les Mouettes** ( ☎ 27-77-91; lesmouettes@domacces.com; cottage €140-199;  ) Les Mouettes' seven beachy bungalows sit in a row along Lorient's creamy flaxen sands. Prepare a relaxing dinner in your kitchenette and dine on your private terrace, then fall asleep to the sound of crashing waves gently wafting in through your slatted blue shutters.

**La Normandie** ( ☎ 27-61-66; normandiehotel@att.net; r from €158;  ) With a fresh coat of paint and a shopping spree at IKEA, this dance hall of yore has been transformed by its friendly new owners into a quaint stay. Tucked away in the interior of Lorient, it's a bit pricy for what you get – a small room and not a whole lot of sunlight – but this spick-and-span place is a comfortable choice when the seaside hotels in the same price bracket are already full. Offers wi-fi.

> **MONTBARS 'THE EXTERMINATOR'**
>
> In addition to having quite possibly the coolest name in history, Monsieur the Exterminator was a French-born pirate – and not a very nice one at that. He was present when his uncle was killed in a battle with Spanish conquistadores, and he spent the rest of his life exacting revenge (and borrowing a bit of plunder). Legend has it that Montbars buried treasure somewhere between Anse de Gouverneur and Anse de Grande Saline, but it has never been found. If you've been looking for a reason to borrow Grandpa's metal detector…

### Eating

**Maya's to Go** ( ☎ 29-83-70; Les Galeries du Commerce; dishes €5-20;  7am-7pm Tue-Sun) Maya's, the oh-so popular restaurant in Public, has a small *traiteur* (delicatessen) in St-Jean for those who don't have enough time to visit the legendary restaurant (read: those who can't afford it). If you're toying with the idea of doing a beach picnic à la gourmet, it's worth stopping in for some *petits creux* (snacks). There's wi-fi access here.

**Le Ti St Barth** ( ☎ 27-97-71; www.ksplaces.com; mains €25-68;  dinner) Like an evening in Baz Luhrmann's *Moulin Rouge*, Le Ti St Barth is a sumptuous jumble of dangling wrought-iron chandeliers and gushing velvet drapes. The menu features a mix of upscale barbecue options such as 'Zen tartare' (a tuna steak with guacamole), and in the late evening a local DJ swings by to give the place a li'l edge. It's located between Lorient and Marigot.

**K'Fé Massai** ( ☎ 29-76-78; set dinner €29-52;  dinner) With warm orange light emanating from pillars made from adobe and wicker, in the evening this restaurant-cum-lounge feels a bit like a hunting lodge at sunset. While the name and decor hint at an African theme, the cuisine is decidedly French. The €29 set dinner is a fantastic deal and features a choice of one starter, main course and dessert. Try the goat's-cheese salad and a main of mahimahi, then mix things up with a serving of *pain perdu* (French toast) with ice cream for dessert.

## VITET

Up the steep hill from Grand Cul-de-Sac is Vitet, where you'll find the oldest continuously operating restaurant on the island, **Hostellerie des Trois Forces** ( ☎ 27-61-25; www.3forces .net; r US$270-390). Called a 'holistic New Age inn' by owner Hubert Delamotte (a dead ringer for Salvador Dali, and the island's resident astrologer), this place has 12 rooms named after the signs of the zodiac; all have ocean views. The restaurant's famous menu, with its top-notch wine list, is a regularly rotating assortment of goodies including pesto frog legs, herbed chicken and St Tropez pie (brioche with a light orange-flower cream sauce). The restaurant is open for lunch and dinner. Astrological readings can be organized with Hubert if you know the exact time of your birth.

## ANSE DE GOUVERNEUR

This is a gorgeous, sandy beach lining a U-shaped bay that's embraced by high cliffs at both ends. It's one of the broadest and most secluded spots in the region, and it makes a splendid spot for sunbathing and picnics. The lack of visitors – even in high season – means that you'll often see sunbathers in their birthday suits. Join in and get rid of those tan lines!

Perched high on craggy **Morne de Lurin** (192m), just before the mountain tumbles into beautiful Gouverneur, sits **Santa Fe** ( ☎ 27-61-04; lunch mains €12-19, dinner mains €18-30; ☽ lunch & dinner). The owner (who was the former sommelier at ritzy Le Sapotillier in Gustavia), has designed a broad menu with a French-Creole twist, and while the food is fantastic throughout the day, it's best to come before sunset so you can appreciate the stunning oceanic views. Try the scallops daintily covered in flakey pastry (€23), and the molten chocolate cake with pear sorbet (€10).

## ANSE DE GRANDE SALINE

A long, lovely beach, broad and secluded, Anse de Grande Saline is named after the large salt pond nearby. The locals consider the beach to be one St-Barth's best, and it's a favorite spot for nudists and gay visitors. The nudists go right and the gay visitors go left, and if you're both, well, you can sunbathe in the middle.

**ourpick** **Salines Gardens** ( ☎ 41-94-29; www.salines garden.com; cottages €140-190) is the only accommodation in the area and is, without a doubt, the best deal on the island. Nestled slightly inland on the Grande Saline's parched terrain, five semidetached cottages

huddle around a small plunge pool shaded by thick stalks of bamboo. Each unit is styled with knickknacks and drapery from a far-flung destination: Essaouira, Pavones, Padang, Cap Ferret and Waikiki. The owner, Jean-Phillipe, with his gravelly French tones and chilled-out demeanor, creates a truly inviting and friendly ambience.

Bedecked with stone pillars and hidden behind thirsty desert shrubs, **Le Grain de Sel** ( ☎ 52-46-05; lunch mains €12-24, dinner mains €16-28; ☽ breakfast, lunch & dinner) is fantastic spot to savor traditional French and Creole meals before hitting the powdery sand for the day. The chef (who worked for many years at Maya's in Public) prepares a colorful assortment of palate pleasers such as crab-and-lentil salad (€16), conch fricassee (€25) and homemade lychee-mango ice cream (€8).

# WESTERN ST-BARTHÉLEMY

A quaint pastoral vibe is revealed as the cobbled roads curve west of Gustavia. Craggy, windswept cliffs and scrubby green hills with stone fences look like a postcard from the quiet coasts of western France.

## COROSSOL

This is one of the last remaining traditional villages on St-Barth. The villagers still speak in an old Norman dialect; the brown-sand beach is lined with blue and orange fishing boats, and stacks of lobster traps; and women still weave the leaves of the lantana palm into straw hats, baskets and place mats, which they line up on the walls in front of their homes to attract buyers.

This is where you'll find **Le Musée International du Coquillage** ( ☎ 27-62-97; admission €3; ☽ 9am-12:30pm & 3-5pm Tue-Sat), with over 9000 seashells on display. Owner Ingénu Magras started the museum half a century ago, many years after his father and he collected seashells during their fishing trips when he was in his teens.

**Carib Waterplay** ( ☎ 27-71-22; caribwaterplay@ wanadoo.fr) offers windsurfing lessons, as well as kayaking, surfing and snorkeling trips.

## FLAMANDS

A small village on the northwestern side of the island, Flamands retains a pleasant rural character. The village stretches along a curving bay whose long, broad white-sand beach and clear waters are very popular with beachgoers. There's easy beach access with streetside parking at the westernmost end of Anse de Flamands.

**Ranch des Flamands** ( ☎ 39-87-01; Merlette) offers 1½-hour horseback-riding excursions for beginner and experienced riders. Rides depart most days at 3:30pm and cost about €35 per person.

On the way down into Flamands, you'll pass a group of flagpoles marking the entrance to quiet **Auberge de Terre Neuve** ( ☎ 27-75-32; fax 27-78-99; gumbs.car.rental@wanadoo.fr; cottages €135-145; ⊠ ). Technically the front desk is located at the airport – the owners of this cluster of cottages also run Gumbs Car Rental, and a car rental from its lot is included in the lodging price. The cabins are painted in a pinkish color and the interiors have basic-but-comfy furniture set on sparkling white tiles. Balconies with barbecues abound, and the units higher up on the hill have scenic views.

As the snaking stone road starts to peter out at the far end of Flamands, little **Auberge de la Petite Anse** ( ☎ 27-83-09; apa@wanadoo.fr; cottages €120-180; ⊠ ) will emerge. Its clump of green-and-pink semidetached bungalows squat on a small ledge over the cerulean waters many feet below, and from behind the tattered drapes, guests can appreciate quiet vistas of rugged, rocky islands. The quirky shedlike reception area is strewn with curling paperbacks and thousands of brochures lauding the island's merits.

## ANSE DE COLOMBIER

Anse de Colombier is a beautiful secluded white-sand beach that's fronted by turquoise waters and backed by undulating hills. It's reached by boat or via a scenic 20-minute walk that begins at the end of the road in La Petite Anse, just beyond Flamands. The sandy bay is ideal for swimming, and there's fairly good snorkeling at the north side.

Perched high on the hill overlooking the sea, **Le P'tit Morne** ( ☎ 52-95-50; www.timorne.com; cottages from €139; ⊠ ⊠ ) offers dated, apartment-style cottages at a reasonable price. Each room is stocked with a kitchenette, TV and DVD player, and there's swimming pool for a dip.

# DIRECTORY

## ACCOMMODATIONS

St-Barth's largest hotel has a mere 70 rooms and the island's second biggest has barely half that number. The others are small, with usually less than a dozen rooms. This can be a wonderful thing – lots of intimacy, and unique design details – but it also means that during high season everything gets booked up fast. Virtually all hotels are priced in euros and there's a 5% tax surcharge added to your quoted rate.

There's no easy way to do St-Barth on the cheap, but with some advance planning you can scout out great deals on private villas, which are almost always a better choice than paying for a hotel room by the night.

## ACTIVITIES

St-Barth is so tiny that services from around the island can be organized at a moment's notice. Most activity-providers will come to your hotel or villa.

### Beaches & Swimming

With its numerous bays and coves, St-Barth boasts nearly two dozen beaches, which is quite impressive considering the island's miniscule size. Those looking for 'in-town' beaches will find that St-Jean, Flamands, Lorient and Shell Beach all have beautiful,

---

**PRACTICALITIES**

■ **Newspapers & Magazines** Newspapers include the *Weekly*, published in English on Friday from November to April, and *Today*. Tourist magazines include *St-Barth Magazine*, *Discover Saint Barthélemy*, *Tropical St Barth* and *Ti Gourmet*.

■ **Radio** For local radio, try Radio Transat on 100.3FM, and Radio Saint-Barth on 98.7FM.

■ **Electricity** The current used is 220V (50/60 cycles); standard Western Europe plugs are used. Many hotels offer American-style shaver adapters.

■ **Weights & Measures** The metric system and 24-hour clock are used here.

sandy strands. The most famous secluded beaches – Colombier, Grande Saline and Gouverneur – are as close to the picture-perfect Caribbean beach as possible, with long white expanses of sand and gently lapping warm waves.

## Boat Trips
Half-day trips cost about €65 per person, full-day trips €100 and sunset cruises €55. They usually include a meal or buffet, plus drinks and all snorkeling gear.

There are operators in Gustavia (p458), or try the following:

**Coté Mer** ( ☎ 0690-45-06-00; www.st-barths.com/cote-mer) Half- and full-day snorkeling trips, plus sunset cruises. Includes open bar, champagne and cold buffet.

**Splash** ( ☎ 0690-56-90-24; splash@stbarth.fr) Runs full-day snorkel trips with gourmet buffet to Île Fourchue.

## Diving & Snorkeling
If you dive on your own, you must pay a fee and register with the **St-Barth Natural Marine Reserve** ( ☎ 27-88-18). The **Mairie** (Town Hall; Gustavia; ⏲ 9am-noon & 2-3:30pm Mon-Fri) or any dive outfitter will be able to send you through the proper channels.

The most popular diving spots are off the islets surrounding St-Barth, which are rich in marine life and coral. Almost all of the dive sites and surrounding islands are managed by the marine reserve. There are dive centers in Gustavia (p458) and Grand Cul-de-Sac (p461), or try **Splash** ( ☎ 0690-56-90-24; splash@stbarth.fr).

Most of the dive centers can organize a snorkeling excursion, and many boat trips (see above) provide snorkeling gear.

## Fishing
Operators in Gustavia (p458) offer shore and deep-sea fishing, where catching tuna, wahoo or blue marlin is common. Renting a 21ft skippered motorboat for deep-sea fishing starts at about €400 for the day for four to seven people.

## Horseback Riding
Ranch de Flamands (opposite), near Flamands, runs horseback-riding trips.

## Kayaking
Tour operators in St-Jean (p461), Corossol (p463) and Grand Cul-de-Sac (p461) rent kayaks and organize trips.

---

### CONCIERGES
Tired of planning every last detail of your vacation? Why not hire someone else to do it? There are many concierge services on the island that can, for the right price, organize everything from your accommodations and flights down to babysitting and massages.

Try one of the following options:

**Caribbean Concierge** ( ☎ 27-72-39; www.thecaribbeanconcierge.com)

**Concierge** ( ☎ 49-43-55; eric@theconcierge.fr)

**Destination Management Services** ( ☎ 29-84-54; melanie.stbarths@wanadoo.fr)

**Premium IV** ( ☎ 29-00-07; www.premiumiv.com)

---

## Surfing
The main surfing spots are at Lorient, Anse des Cayes, St-Jean and Grand Cul-de-Sac. If you need to rent equipment, stop by St-Jean (p461) or Gustavia (p458), or try to finagle your way onto the property at one of the five-star hotels (although the prices are noticeably inflated.)

Daily prices run to €15 for a short board, €20 for a long board and €10 for a boogie board. Discounts can be arranged for longer rentals.

## Windsurfing
Grand Cul-de-Sac, the main windsurfing center, has a large protected bay that's ideal for beginners, and some nice wave action beyond the reef for advanced windsurfers. See p461 for outfitters.

There are also windsurfing outfitters located at St-Jean and Corossol; see p461 and p463 respectively.

## BOOKS
For an interesting and intelligent perspective on the island's local culture and cuisine, check out *Case et Cuisine*, written by two loyal tourists, David R Anderson and Dennis E Carlton, in cooperation with the head of the tourism board, Elyse Magras. The book explores the stories behind a variety of colorful dining options on the island, and often includes recipes. The dream-inducing photography lends additional flair to the text. The book can be purchased at several locations around the island; stop by La Normandie hotel (p462) in Lorient if you're having a hard time finding a copy.

ST-BARTHÉLEMY

## BUSINESS HOURS

Most businesses are open from 9am to 3:30pm, Monday to Friday, with a lunch break between about noon and 2pm. Shops tend to be open on Thursdays until late and, in high season, may stay open till 5pm on weekdays and may open on weekends. Many places shut on Wednesday afternoons; almost everything is closed on Sundays.

In general banks are open on weekdays from 8am to noon and from 2pm to 3:30pm. Post offices are generally open 8am to 11am from Monday to Saturday.

Restaurants serve breakfast from around 7am to 10am, lunch from 11:30am to 2:30pm and dinner from 7pm to 11pm.

## EMBASSIES & CONSULATES

Although the island is practically autonomous, consular services are still linked to France. A Swedish diplomatic figurehead is the only foreign representation on the island.

## FESTIVALS & EVENTS

A number of festivals are celebrated on St-Barth throughout the year. The **Office Territorial du Tourisme** ( ☎ 27-87-27; Quai Général de Gaulle) has a handy list of important events – it's definitely worth picking up as it's quite detailed.

**St-Barth Music Festival** Held in mid-January, this festival features two weeks of jazz, chamber music and dance performances.

**Carnival** Held for five days before Lent. Includes a pageant, costumes and street dancing, ending with the burning of a King Carnival figure at Shell Beach. Many businesses close during Carnival.

**St-Barth Film Festival** ( ☎ 29-74-70; www.stbarthff .org) The only festival of its kind, this showcases Caribbean talent in film and documentary. It's held in late April.

**Festival of St-Barth** August 24, the feast day of the island's patron saint, is celebrated with fireworks, a public ball, boat races and other competitions.

## GAY & LESBIAN TRAVELERS

The website www.gay.com points out, 'St-Barth is the most gay-popular spot on earth…without a gay bar,' and this pretty much sums up the nature of the island's gay tourism. Locals and other travelers are very laid-back and it's not uncommon to see gay couples holding hands at the beach or having a romantic dinner. But if you're looking for a bumpin' nightlife scene, you won't find it here.

## HOLIDAYS

St-Barth has the following public holidays:

**New Year's Day** January 1
**Easter Sunday** Late March/early April
**Easter Monday** Late March/early April
**Labor Day** May 1
**Ascension Thursday** Fortieth day after Easter
**Pentecost Monday** Seventh Monday after Easter
**Bastille Day** July 14
**Assumption Day** August 15
**All Saints Day (Toussaints)** November 1
**All Souls Day** November 2
**Armistice Day** November 11
**Christmas Day** December 25

## INTERNET ACCESS

Most hotels on the island offer some form of internet access, either via a computer terminal or via wi-fi; upscale venues offer both. There is wi-fi access throughout Gustavia; see p458 for details. Many restaurants around the island are starting to offer wi-fi connections as well. The tourism office in Gustavia has a list of wi-fi–friendly cafés.

## INTERNET RESOURCES

**St Barths Online** (www.st-barths.com) is the go-to place for anything you'd ever want to know about the island. It has links to accommodations and restaurants.

## MEDICAL SERVICES

There are medical facilities in Gustavia (p458) including a small hospital and eight local doctors. There are two pharmacies on the island, one in Gustavia (p458) and one in St-Jean (p461).

## MONEY

The currency used in St-Barth is the euro. US dollars are widely accepted, although you will not find the one-for-one dollar-to-euro trading that occurs on St-Martin/Sint Maarten.

There are six banks around the island, and an American Express office in St-Jean (p461). None of the ATMs on the island accept American Express.

## POST

The main post office is in Gustavia (p458), and there are two smaller branches – one in Lorient (p462) and the other near the airport in St-Jean.

# TELEPHONE

The telephone system has been a bit confusing since a changeover in 1996. The country code is ☎ 590, but to call St-Barth from abroad, you need to dial your country's international access code + St-Barth's country code *twice*, ie ☎ 590-590, + the local six-digit number.

Cell phones start with ☎ 0690; to call a cell phone from overseas, dial ☎ 590 + the number.

To call from within the French phone system, add '0' in front of the (single) country code, ie ☎ 0590 + the local number. We have included only the six-digit local number for St-Barth listings in this chapter.

Public telephones take all major credit cards and prices are listed. Prepaid phone cards are available for purchase throughout the island as well.

---

**EMERGENCY NUMBERS**

- Ambulance ☎ 16
- Fire ☎ 18
- Police ☎ 16
- Sea rescue ☎ 70-92-92

---

# TOURIST INFORMATION

The island's ultrahelpful tourism office, the Office Territorial du Tourisme, is located along the water in Gustavia (p458).

# VISAS

Citizens from the US, UK, Canada, Australia, Japan and New Zealand don't need visas. Citizens of several CIS, African and South American countries require visas valid for a French collectivity. Contact the **border police** (☎ 29-76-76) for more information.

# TRANSPORTATION

## GETTING THERE & AWAY
### Entering St-Barthélemy

Residents of EU countries need only a national identity card to enter St-Barth. Passports are needed for all other nationalities. See above for information on visas.

## Air

Located near the village of St-Jean, St-Barth's only airport, **Aéroport de St-Barthélemy** (SBH;

☎ 27-65-41), has the second-shortest runway in the world (the shortest is on Saba). Only teeny-tiny puddle jumpers can land on the island, ensuring the impossibility of mass tourism.

The following airlines fly to and from St-Barth:

**Air Antilles Express** ( ☎ 27-71-77; www.airantilles.com) Fort-de-Franc, Pointe-à-Pitre, St-Martin/Sint Maarten

**Air Caraïbes** ( ☎ 87-14-80; www.aircaraibes.com) Fort-de-France, Havana, Marie-Galante, Panama City, Paris, Pointe-à-Pitre, Port-au-Prince, Santo Domingo, St-Martin/Sint Maarten, San José, St Lucia

**St Barth Commuter** ( ☎ 27-54-54; www.stbarth commuter.com) St-Martin/Sint Maarten; charter flights throughout the Caribbean also available

**Winair** ( ☎ 27-61-01; www.fly-winair.com) Anguilla, Antigua, Barbuda, Montserrat, Nevis, St-Martin/Sint Maarten, St Kitts, Sint Eustatius, Tortola

Charter airlines are also available:
**Carib Aviation** ( ☎ in Antigua 268-462-3147)
**Inter Island Express** ( ☎ in Puerto Rico 253-1400)

## Sea
### FERRY

The ferry service between St-Barthélemy and St-Martin/Sint Maarten is often very choppy – it's a good idea to take motion-sickness pills beforehand. Your accommodation can usually reserve a seat for you on the boat for a minimal deposit; you simply pay the remaining part when you arrive at the pier for departure.

The main company is **Voyager** ( ☎ in St-Martin 87-10-68, in Sint Maarten 542-4096; www.voy12.com), which has two modern high-speed boats. One leaves Marigot, St-Martin, at 9am and 6:15pm for the 1½-hour journey; it departs Gustavia at 7:15am and 4:30pm. On Sunday and Wednesday, the boat leaves from Captain Oliver's Marina in Oyster Pond, St-Martin, and the ride is only 40 minutes. Fares are €58 one way, €67 for a same-day round-trip and €83 for a round-trip.

Also available is the high-speed catamaran, the **Edge** ( ☎ in Sint Maarten 544-2640), which makes the 45-minute trip to Gustavia daily from Pelican Marina on Simpson Bay, Sint Maarten, at 9am; it returns at 4pm. You need to check in 15 minutes in advance. A one-way trip costs US$45, a same-day round-trip is US$65, and a round-trip US$90. The US$15 departure tax is not included in the ticket price.

ST-BARTHÉLEMY

### YACHT

Those arriving by yacht can clear immigration at the **port office** ( ☎ 27-66-97), on the east side of Gustavia Harbor.

## GETTING AROUND

There is no bus system on St-Barth. Taxis are pricey, so strongly consider renting a car.

### Bicycle

Cycling around the island can be arduous, even for the healthiest individuals. The roads can be exceptionally steep.

### Car, Motorcycle & Scooter

#### DRIVER'S LICENSE

A driver's license from your home country is valid in St-Barth.

#### FUEL

There are only two gas stations – one in St-Jean and one in Lorient – on the island and both are closed on Sundays. During the week they are open during daylight hours (with the obligatory two-hour lunch break from noon until 2pm). If you're a desperate, there's an all-night gas pump at the airport, which only works with a credit card (although not usually with American plastic).

#### RENTAL

There are loads of car- and scooter-rental agencies throughout the island, with about a dozen concentrated in the airport terminal in St-Jean. The others mostly sit around Gustavia, although the cars are kept near the airport. In general, you will be discouraged from renting a scooter or motorcycle as the terrain is quite rugged and steep (and scooters aren't really that much cheaper than cars, especially as you won't spend that much on gas since the island is so tiny.) Prices between December and April hover around €60 for cars, while off-season prices drop to a less outrageous €35 to €40. Try the following options:

**Avis** ( ☎ 27-71-43; avis.sbca@wanadoo.fr) Located at the airport.

**Barth'Loc** ( ☎ 27-52-81) Located in Gustavia; also offers scooter rentals.

**Budget** ( ☎ 27-66-30; budgetsaintbarth@wanadoo.fr) Located at the airport and in Gustavia.

**Chez Beranger** ( ☎ 27-89-00; chezberanger@wanadoo .fr) Located in Gustavia; leases cars and scooters.

**Dufau** ( ☎ 27-54-83; nilsdufau@yahoo.com) Based in Public, mainly offers motorcycle rentals.

**Gumbs Rental** ( ☎ 27-75-32; gumbs.car.rental@wana doo.fr) Located at the airport. Is also the front desk for Anse de Terre Neuve.

**Meca Moto** ( ☎ 52-92-49; mecamoto3@wanadoo.fr) Located in Gustavia. Specializes in motorbikes.

**Soleil Caraibes** ( ☎ 27-67-18; soleil.caraibes@wanadoo .fr) Located at the airport; offers some of the best deals on the island.

**Tropic All Rent** ( ☎ 27-64-76; tropicall.rent@wanadoo .fr) Located in Gustavia; offers cars and motorbikes.

#### ROAD RULES

Driving is on the right-hand side, and the speed limit is 45km/h, unless otherwise posted. Some of the older roads are quite narrow so be mindful of other cars coming in the opposite direction.

### Hitchhiking

Hitchhiking is easy and relatively safe in St-Barth, although substantially more difficult the closer one gets to the far corners of the island. As always when hitchhiking, be cautious and obey your instincts.

### Taxi

Taxi prices go from pricey to outrageous. There are no set fares, so prices are all over the board. Generally prices increase by about 50% when it's dark out.

From Gustavia to the airport costs €10, while from Gustavia to Petit Cul-de-Sac it's around €25. From the airport it's €10 to St-Jean and around €12 to Lorient.

To book a taxi in Gustavia, call ☎ 27-66-31; at the airport, call ☎ 27-75-81. There's a taxi stand in Gustavia. You can also contact drivers directly – a list of drivers and their phone numbers is available at the Office Territorial de Tourisme (p458) in Gustavia.

# Saba

There once was a man and a woman who lived in a perfect garden. They were welcome in this idyllic thicket so long as they didn't eat the fruit of one particular tree. You probably know the rest of the story, but what you didn't know is that, although Adam and Eve ruined it for the rest of us, you can still have the chance to find your way back to Eden.

Paradise takes the form of a spiky volcano peak called Saba (pronounced *say*-bah) that pushes forth from the sea to pierce the lazy clouds above. It's hard to believe that this breathtaking retreat is but a 15-minute flight from garish casinos and condominiums, especially since the island's homogeneous white-green-brown architecture adds an extra sense of perfection to the naturally gifted enclave.

Just when you thought that nothing could be more beautiful than Saba's jagged volcanic landscape, a trip below the ocean's surface reveals a colorful kingdom of neon coral that teems with fat reef sharks, sea turtles and slippery fish. These dive sites rank amongst the top scuba spots in the world, and are fastidiously protected by the well-established national marine park.

While nearby islands have been snared by development conglomerates, Saba does its darndest to fly under the radar. Locals are steadfast in their efforts to preserve their close-to-nature lifestyle, which will undoubtedly prolong the island's status as the ultimate pristine getaway.

## FAST FACTS

- **Area** 13 sq km
- **Capital** The Bottom
- **Country code** ☎ 599
- **Departure tax** US$5 within the Netherlands Antilles; US$20 elsewhere
- **Famous for** Striking volcanic scenery, world-class diving
- **Language** Dutch is used in government; English is spoken in schools, homes and everywhere else
- **Money** Netherlands Antillean guilder (ANG); US dollars accepted everywhere; ANG1 = US$0.56 = €0.36 = UK£0.29
- **Official name** Saba
- **People** Sabans
- **Population** 1500
- **Visas** Not necessary for most residents of North America, the EU and Australia; see p480

## HIGHLIGHTS

- **Hiking** (p478) Explore the island's dramatic vertical peak and score killer views of the sea below
- **Diving** (p478) Hit the waves and explore stunning, submerged pinnacles that teem with nurse sharks and large colorful fish
- **Flying** (p473) Experience the thrill of landing on the world's smallest runway, and then hold your breath when you depart as your plane drives off the side of a cliff
- **Jo Bean Glass Art Studio** (p474) Head to this charming menagerie of colorful doodads and become a glass-blowing whiz under the tutelage of resident artist Jo Bean

## ITINERARIES

- **One Day** First, shed a tear that you only have a day to explore this incredible island. Then meet up with one of the dive boats for a two-tank half-day trip out to some of the finest reefs and submerged pinnacles in the Caribbean, if not the world. Break for a leisurely lunch amid chatty locals in Windwardside and, if you have enough energy, take a stab at the Sandy Cruz Trail in the late afternoon.
- **Three Days** Pick a hotel in Windwardside and spend your first day walking around the small town (be sure to stop by Jo Bean's glass studio to say hello), then head out into the bush for a rugged hike up to the top of Mt Scenery (887m), the highest point on the island. Spend the mornings of the following two days scuba diving with numerous reef sharks around sunken pinnacles; afternoons are best spent curled up with a good novel under the warm Caribbean sun. In the evenings taste-test the menus at spots around the island, including the Rainforest Restaurant at the Ecolodge Rendez-Vous.
- **One Week** Prearrange a package diving trip and spend the greater part of the week blowing bubbles with sharks, rays, barracuda and sea turtles. Take a day off and organize a guided hike through Saba's rugged forests. In the evenings hit up Windwardside's restaurants: Swinging Doors for steak Sundays, Tropics Cafe on Fridays for a burger and movie, and Brigadoon for sushi Saturdays. Then retreat to your cliffside cottage or colonial-style inn and click through your camera's postcard-worthy scenery shots, taken earlier in the day. After a week on Saba you'll know every local and all of their secrets.

## CLIMATE & WHEN TO GO

Saba's temperature averages 27°C (80°F) in July, but winter weather can dip down to 17°C (63°F) during the evening. With stately Mt Scenery covered in cloud forest, the island gets substantially more rain – 1m per year – and cloud cover than the rest of the Caribbean. Trade winds keep the island cool, especially at night, and blankets are a necessity even on some summer nights. Saba is the rare island in this region where a visit during July to September is actually pleasant, if there's not a hurricane. The dry season is December to July.

## HISTORY

Saba was intermittently inhabited by the Siboneys, Arawaks and Caribs before Columbus sailed past the island on his second voyage to the New World. Although English pirates and French adventurers briefly inhabited the island, it wasn't until 1640 that the Dutch set up a permanent settlement, the remains of which are still scattered around the island.

Saba changed hands a dozen times or so over the next 200 years, resulting in mostly Irish and English settlers, but Dutch ownership. Life on Saba for these pioneers was difficult at best. Many of the men made their living from the sea, leaving so many women on the island that it became known as 'The Island of Women.'

Because the steep topography of the island precluded large-scale plantations, colonial-era slavery was quite limited on Saba. Those colonists who did own slaves generally had only a few and often worked side by side with them in the fields, resulting in a more integrated society than on larger Dutch islands.

The close-knit community beat seemingly impossible conditions and thrived in this little outpost. Tourism found Saba when an airport was built in 1959, but it wasn't until 1970 that Saba got uninterrupted electricity.

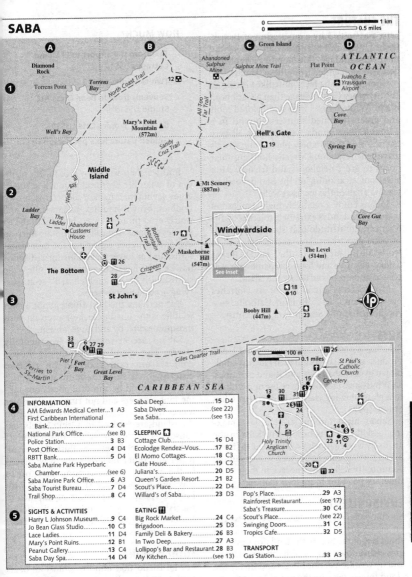

# SABA

**INFORMATION**
AM Edwards Medical Center...1 A3
First Caribbean International
Bank....................................2 C4
National Park Office.............(see 8)
Police Station.......................3 B3
Post Office...........................4 D4
RBTT Bank...........................5 D4
Saba Marine Park Hyperbaric
Chamber..........................(see 6)
Saba Marine Park Office.......6 A3
Saba Tourist Bureau..............7 D4
Trail Shop.............................8 C4

**SIGHTS & ACTIVITIES**
Harry L Johnson Museum......9 C4
Jo Bean Glass Studio...........10 C3
Lace Ladies.........................11 D4
Mary's Point Ruins..............12 B1
Peanut Gallery....................13 C4
Saba Day Spa.....................14 D4

Saba Deep..........................15 D4
Saba Divers....................(see 22)
Sea Saba.........................(see 13)

**SLEEPING**
Cottage Club......................16 D4
Ecolodge Rendez-Vous.......17 B2
El Momo Cottages..............18 C3
Gate House........................19 C2
Juliana's............................20 D5
Queen's Garden Resort.......21 B2
Scout's Place......................22 D4
Willard's of Saba................23 D3

**EATING**
Big Rock Market.................24 C4
Brigadoon..........................25 D3
Family Deli & Bakery...........26 B3
In Two Deep.......................27 A3
Lollipop's Bar and Restaurant.28 B3
My Kitchen....................(see 13)

Pop's Place........................29 A3
Rainforest Restaurant.........(see 17)
Saba's Treasure.................30 C4
Scout's Place.................(see 22)
Swinging Doors.................31 C4
Tropics Cafe......................32 D5

**TRANSPORT**
Gas Station........................33 A3

Saba was a part of the Netherlands Antilles until 2005, when the five islands (Saba, Curaçao, Bonaire, Sint Eustatius and Dutch Sint Maarten) met on the Jesurun Referendum to decide the fate of the Netherlands Antilles. Saba, along with Bonaire, voted overwhelmingly to become administered directly by the Netherlands. At the end of 2008, Saba was once again reshuffled when the Netherlands Antilles officially dissolved, with Curaçao and Sint Maarten gaining greater independence, while the governmental reins tightened on Saba, Sint Eustatius and Bonaire, bringing them closer to the Netherlands. For more on the fate of the Netherlands Antilles, see p779.

# THE CULTURE

Saba was settled by a smattering of British, Irish, Dutch and Scandinavian settlers and their African slaves. Most of the current residents are descended from these families.

Coming to Saba feels more like visiting an 18th-century Celtic village than a Caribbean island. White houses with clay-colored roofs and green-trimmed shutters abound in a *Truman Show* kinda way, but it's all very charming and extremely photogenic. Locals drive leisurely along streets, honking their horns to greet neighbors and friends. After a week of vacationing on the island, you'll be waving at all of the locals as well.

Sabans enjoy a relatively high standard of living. The island is extremely tolerant of differences, an attitude that started hundreds of years ago when slave and master had to work side by side to allow the island to thrive. Today, gay dive and tour companies are welcomed and even courted by the island.

Most Sabans attend one of six churches on the island: three Roman Catholic, two Anglican and one Seventh Day Adventist.

## ARTS

Saba has a small handicraft scene, and locals produce and sell beautiful items such as hand-blown glass, Saban lace and island paintings. In Windwardside you'll have the opportunity to a glass-blowing class at Jo Bean Art Glass Studio (p474).

Saba's most famous craft is lace making, a skill that was brought to Saba in the 1870s by a woman who'd been sent to live in a Venezuelan convent. Older women in the community still weave the lace in their spare time; see p474 for more information.

## ENVIRONMENT

Six completely separate temperate zones exist on Saba. Starting with steep cliffs that seem to shoot out of the ocean, the land progresses to grassy meadows, slopes with little vegetation, and up to hilltops, rainforests and finally the cloud forest covering the top of Mt Scenery.

For a place this small, there is an enormous amount of mammal, fish, bird and plant life on and surrounding the island, both native and introduced. Rare wild orchids peek out along the road or in the rainforest, and oleander and hibiscus flowers are endemic. The elephant ear plant has shade-bearing leaves as big as…well, elephant ears.

---

**HOW MUCH?**

- Taxi from the airport to El Momo Cottages US$12
- Two-tank dive US$80
- Souvenir from Jo Bean Glass Art Studio US$16
- Burger at Tropics Cafe US$10
- Guided nature hike per person US$15

---

Bird-watchers will enjoy spotting the plethora of avian life overhead as much as they'll enjoy saying their names: sooty terns, brown boobies, brown noddies, banana quits and pearly eyed thrashers are a handful of the 60 species of birds that call Saba home. Keep an eye out at higher elevations for hummingbirds, and at lower elevations for red-tailed hawks. Saba has its own unique reptile – the skittish little brown anoles lizard – seen scurrying around everywhere.

But perhaps the best thing about Saban wildlife is the obvious lack of a certain pest: mosquitoes are, by and large, absent.

Sabans are extremely environmentally aware. The island's water supply mostly comes from rain gathered on rooftop cisterns, or a small desalinization plant. Visitors should be mindful about not taking long showers and not running the water longer than absolutely necessary. Latrines on the island are referred to as 'ship toilets' because (gee, how can we put this daintily?) only natural refuse may be flushed away; all paper and other materials are to be placed in the garbage. In the continuous effort to stay 'green' locals are still grappling with how to reduce the amount of imports to the island (namely food). The Ecolodge Rendez-Vous (p475) is pioneering the creation of gardens.

## FOOD & DRINK

For an island that imports almost all of its food, Saba has a dizzying array of restaurant choices, from tiny bakery shacks to fine dining. You'll find a mix of interesting fruits growing on the island, including soursop and Saba lemon. Don't leave the island without trying homemade soursop ice cream, or grabbing a Saba lemon off of a drooping tree, scratching the peel, and taking a deep, satisfying whiff of the zest. Be sure to try one of the many homemade rums, which are often flavored with locally grown banana, mango, vanilla or 'Saba spice.' Many establishments – such as El Momo Cottages (p474) and Ecolodge Rendez-Vous (p475) – make and sell their own blends.

In Saba's continuous effort to 'go green,' there is a concerted attempt to reduce the amount of imported produce, and several establishments reap their crops straight from an onsite garden.

# SABA

Saba has four towns straddling the rugged cliffs between the teeny runaway and hidden seaport: Hell's Gate, Windwardside, St John's and the Bottom. The are all connected by one serpentine route known simply as 'the Road'.

## FLAT POINT

The aptly named Flat Point is precisely that: a flat point (Saba's only flat point, in fact), and the perfect place to plunk down an airport. The **Juancho E Yrausquin Airport** has the tiniest runway in the entire world, measuring a mere 400m, and by the time you figure out how to pronounce the airport's name, you'll have already landed on St-Martin/Sint Maarten. There's a small bar called Flight Deck inside the airport should you need a couple of frosty ones to ease your jitters before taking off; it's open one hour before and after each flight. Planes departing Saba don't actually lift off the ground; rather, the runway suddenly stops and the aircraft drives over a sheer cliff and glides away.

If you have a little time to kill before leaving, or after you arrive, leave your luggage in the waiting area ('theft' is barely word in Saba's lexicon) and quickly hike down to the **tide pools** beside the airport. You'll find dramatic waves crashing against the thick beads of volcanic rock.

## HELL'S GATE

If you are arriving by plane, Hell's Gate is the first 'town' you will pass through while making your way across the island. But back in the day, when visitors arrived by boat, Hell's Gate was the furthest settlement from the docks. The village earned its infernal name due to the fact that it was absolutely hellish to lug parcels

all the way here after they arrived by boat; it would often take an entire day for the residents of Hell's Gate to schlep their shipments across the volcano. Today, this teeny village is mostly residential, with one fine place to stay and eat, and a couple private cottages available for holiday rental (see www.sabatourism.com/cottages.html for more information about prices and bookings).

A quaint spot to rest your head, the **Gate House** ( ☎ 416-2416; www.sabagatehouse.com; s/d incl breakfast US$105/135, cottage US$155; 🖭 ) sits on a quiet stretch of land punctuated by orange and cashew trees. Warm Caribbean colors cheer the rooms, which also feature beautiful views of Saba's rugged cliffs and choppy sea. Fun French cuisine classes are on offer in the house kitchen and can be tailored to suit your cooking interests. Courses are US$120 and a maximum of six students are allowed to participate (so that's US$20 per person).

## WINDWARDSIDE

Although the Bottom is technically the capital of Saba, Windwardside is where most of the action takes place. One could say that Windwardside is to Sydney as the Bottom is to Canberra – on a much, much smaller scale, of course. Chances are, if you're sleeping on Saba, you'll be staying in this quaint hamlet of red roofs. The main area of town features all of the traveler necessities: banks, convenience stores, a post office, dive shops, a tourist office and many restaurants.

Booby Hill, a small subsection of Windwardside, sits just up the hill from the heart of town and is worth the short trek to check out the stellar views – particularly from Willard's of Saba Hotel – and snoop around a nifty little art studio.

### Information

**First Caribbean International Bank** ( ☎ 416-2216; 🕙 8:30am-3:30pm Mon-Fri) Does not have an ATM, although it offers a cash advance (in guilders or dollars) from your ATM card.

**Post office** ( 🕙 8am-noon & 1-5pm Mon-Fri, to noon Sat)

**RBTT Bank** ( ☎ 416-2454; 🕙 8:30am-3:30pm Mon-Fri) Has a 24-hour ATM.

**Saba Tourist Bureau** ( ☎ 416-2231; www.sabatourism .com; 🕙 8am-5pm Mon-Fri)

**Trail Shop** ( ☎ 416-2630; 🕙 10am-4pm Mon-Fri, 10am-2pm Sat & Sun) Located at the west end of Windwardside, this helpful outpost stocks a large selection of maps, books and souvenirs. It's a nonprofit organization set up by the Saba Conservation Foundation.

## Sights

Though light on sights, Windwardside has a couple of gems that are worth checking out when you're in the mood to take a break from reading your book on your balcony. If you are interested in traditional handicrafts, there is a small legion of older women on the island who spend their leisure hours creating Saban lace, which uses a special stitching technique that has been passed down for a couple of generations. These women, known locally at the **Lace Ladies**, gather at the Eugenius Centre, across the street from the RBTT bank, on Thursdays at 4pm for their weekly stitching bee and visitors are more than welcome to stop by.

Another local artist, Jo Bean, works out of her colorful studio up on Booby Hill. A visit to the **Jo Bean Glass Art Studio** ( ☎ 416-2490; www.jobeanglass.com; Booby Hill) is a must for every type of traveler. Discover how she works her magic during a half-day glass-blowing course (US$85), in which you'll be set up with a torch and an unlimited supply of thin glass shafts, which you melt down into swirling balls or cylinders. After you graduate the tutorial, you can start making beads of all shapes and sizes while incorporating gold foil and other quirky objects from around the shop. When the class is done, you'll proudly wear your creations home on a string of leather around your neck. The best part about the entire experience is hanging out with Jo Bean, a magnetic character who'll cheer you on as you fumble over your first beads, and dish out an inordinate amount of praise when you finally make a glass pearl that doesn't look a booger. If you don't have enough time to devote to a course, be sure to pick up a little glass frog, which sits on a rounded bead perfect for a necklace.

If you still have a craving for more local art, stop by Lambee's Place plaza, at the west end of Windwardside, and check out the **Peanut Gallery** ( ☎ 416-2509; ☷ 9am-5pm Mon-Sat), which features a color wash of local paintings, carvings and framed Saban lace.

In a gardenlike setting, the **Harry L Johnson Museum** (admission US$2; ☷ 10am-noon & 1-4pm Mon-Fri) sits just down the hill behind Scout's Place, surrounded by wildflowers, including black-eyed susans, the island's official flower. The small museum sits in a 160-year-old Saban home, which has the typical pearly

white façade, green-shuttered windows and earthy, clay-colored roof. The collection features a smattering of vintage black-and-white photographs, an 'authentic' Saban kitchen, an old piano and scores of antiques from Victorian times.

## Activities

All three diving outfits listed here have a good reputation for safety. Each offers several packages, as well as individual dives.

**Saba Deep** ( ☎ 416-3347; www.sabadeep.com; ☷ 9am-5pm Mon-Sat) Recently taken over by new owners. Boats depart from Fort Bay.

**Saba Divers** ( ☎ 416-2741; www.sabadivers.com; ☷ 9am-5pm Mon-Sat) Based at Scout's Place, this is a popular choice and has outgoing staff. The website has detailed listings of dive sites.

**Sea Saba** ( ☎ 416-2246; www.seasaba.com; ☷ 9am-5pm Mon-Sat) This pick of the litter gets our endorsement for its unwavering dedication to its clientele. In addition, it is passionate about marine education and keeping Saba a pristine place to visit.

After a long day of diving or hiking, relax with a massage, body scrub or foot treatment at the **Saba Day Spa** ( ☎ 416-3488; www.sabadayspa.com; 80-min massage US$100). The owner is a registered nurse and massage therapist, and spent many years working at the Ritz-Carlton spa on St Thomas.

## Sleeping

There are six places to stay in Windwardside, all of which have their own unique flavor, ranging from the charming-yet-rustic El Momo Cottages all the way up to the expensive Willard's of Saba, which commands sweeping views of the sea and one ridiculously hefty price tag. If you're looking for a bit more privacy, there are several holiday cottage rentals scattered throughout town, all of which have the archetypal Saban gingerbread architecture. Check out www.sabatourism.com/cottages/html for more information.

**El Momo Cottages** ( ☎ 416-2265; www.elmomo.com; s/d cottage with shared bathroom US$55/65, with private bathroom from US$75/85; ☐ ☐ ) The small clusters of cottages at El Momo are hidden along a steep, rugged hill smothered in juicy tropical foliage. You'll need a sherpa to haul your luggage up the myriad stone steps to your cabin. Seriously. After cursing under your breath and grabbing your chest to make sure you're not having a heart attack, you'll be rewarded with lovely views of the craggy island and churning sea. The highest cabin – the 'Cottage in the Sky' – is positively breathtaking and oozes rustic romantic charm. Solar-heated outdoor showers, hand built by the previous owners, ensure a clear, private view of the ocean while you suds up, but don't leave your organic soap in the bathroom – it will be devoured by mysterious forest critters during the night. This Robinson Crusoe–like resort has wi-fi and is 100% smoking free.

**Scout's Place** ( ☎ 416-2740; www.sabadivers.com; s/d incl breakfast from US$76/96; ▯ ) This lively 14-room hotel is owned by the same German couple who runs Saba Divers. There are three categories of rooms: the cheapest have refrigerator, cable TV, wi-fi and ceiling fan, while the spacious private cottages have grand four-poster beds and balconies with ocean views. Diving packages are also on offer.

**Ecolodge Rendez-Vous** ( ☎ 416-3348; www.ecolodge -saba.com; Crispeen Trail; cottages US$85-99; ▣ ) If staying deep in the forest at a place powered by solar panels sounds better than having a TV and phone in your room, then these green-conscious cabins might be the perfect place for you. Shower water is stored in bladderlike pouches and heated by the sun, so you won't have warm water in the morning, or on cloudy days, or…ever. However, the colorful cottages are covered in beautiful bright murals and all feature individual nature-related themes; there's also a lovely breeze and a sauna to keep you refreshed. One downside to staying at the ecolodge, though, is the lack of awesome ocean vistas available at most of the other accommodations. Dive packages can be arranged. If you decide that it's a tad to rustic for your taste, be sure to swing by the on-site Rainforest Restaurant for an organic/-asmic meal.

**Juliana's** ( ☎ 416-2269; www.julianas-hotel.com; s/d from US$100/125; ▨ ▯ ▣ ) Juliana's has a sociable vibe centered on the turquoise lap pool, which is also home to the resident giant inflatable swan. The comfortable rooms and prim, private cottages, all in the classic Saban gingerbread-house style, have colorful and airy decor. Each comes with a TV-DVD, wi-fi and terrace. Excellent dive package deals can be organized with friendly Sea Saba. Very gay friendly.

**Cottage Club** ( ☎ 416-2386; www.cottage-club.com; cottage US$118; ▨ ▣ ) This quaint collection of Saba-style cottages sits on a quiet, palm-fringed spot accented by welcoming swimming pool. Cottage Club is the only hotel in Windwardside without a restaurant, although all of the cottages have kitchens and the town's restaurants are only a short walk down the road.

**Willard's of Saba** ( ☎ 416-2498, 800-504-9861; www .willardsofsaba.com; Booby Hill; s US$300-600, d US$400-700; ▯ ▣ ) The highest hotel in the Kingdom of the Netherlands, Saba's most expensive sleeping spot offers heart-pounding views of the sea, 750m below. The seven rooms feel slightly dated, but guests lounge around the cozy hot tub and large heated lap pool. Willard's has the only tennis court in Windwardside, and you'll often find the locals using to court in the mornings before the sun gets too strong. Skip the fitness center; you'll get your daily dose of butt-robics just by climbing the dozens of stairs scattered around the property. Offers wi-fi.

## Eating & Drinking

Windwardside has the largest conglomeration of dining and drinking options on the island.

It's always best to book your dinner plans in advance: Saba's food shipments are sometimes limited and most restaurants only cook enough food each evening for guests with reservations; restaurants also sometimes close unexpectedly for the evening due to a variety of reasons. The hosts at each hotel are always happy to book your dining plans for you.

There's usually one restaurant each evening that offers a special dinner deal of some sort.

**Tropics Cafe** ( ☎ 416-2469; breakfast US$3-10, mains US$8-18; ☾ breakfast daily, lunch & dinner Tue-Sun) Edging Juliana's lap pool, Tropics has some great eats for very reasonable prices. Friday nights are busy, with a US$10 deal that gets you a delicious burger and drive-in-style movie projected onto a makeshift screen. If you chance upon a 'Caribbean night', you'll be rewarded with scrumptious lobster pasta worthy of the finest seafood restaurants in the Caribbean.

**Saba's Treasure** ( ☎ 416-2819; mains US$6-15; ☾ 10am-10pm Mon-Sat) The interior of this little cheapie feels like the hull of a wooden frigate. Choose from the assortment of dishes such as pan pizzas or sandwiches, and wash it down with a beer.

SABA

**CROCODILE JAMES**

He approaches slowly, raising one eyebrow and wielding a large machete-like knife – he's James Johnson, known as 'Crocodile James,' Saba's official trail ranger. Clad head to toe in khaki (which, according to legend, he only washes twice a year), he quickly plunks down his blade, warmly shakes your hand and whisks you away into the wilds of the island's jungle. A fifth-generation Saban, James knows the terrain oh-so intimately, and his unique tours are a quirky blend of history and biology – be ready for some off-trail trekking and prep your taste buds for sampling local vegetation.

The guided tours are US$60 for a maximum of four people (additional trekkers cost US$15 each), and last anywhere from one to four hours depending on your stamina (James could trek all the way through 'til tomorrow – it's in his Saban genes). Call ☎ 416-5428 to make arrangements.

**Scout's Place** ( ☎ 416-2205; lunch mains US$6-20, dinner mains US$9-24; ☺ breakfast, lunch & dinner) The food isn't anything to write home about, but Friday nights are not to be missed – locals pile in for an evening of karaoke (commonly called 'scary-oke'). Wolfgang, the owner, commandeers the microphone and belts out classics such as 'Splish Splash, I Was Takin' a Bath' with the utmost seriousness.

**Swinging Doors** ( ☎ 416-2506; mains US$10-20; ☺ 10am-9pm) Enter through the saloon-style swinging doors and grab a picnic table in the side courtyard for a tasty assortment of dishes that are one step above the usual pub grub. Tuesdays and Fridays feature cheap chicken and ribs, while Sundays are a must – the owner, Eddy, helms the grill and churns out juicy slabs of steak.

**My Kitchen** (Mijn Keuken; ☎ 416-2539; mains from US$11; ☺ lunch & dinner) Located near the Trail Shop, My Kitchen is a good place to stop after working up an appetite on a long hike. Sample a variety of Caribbean and European favorites.

**Rainforest Restaurant** ( ☎ 416-3348; www.ecolodge -saba.com; Ecolodge Rendez-Vous, Crispeen Trail; mains US$13-15; ☺ breakfast, lunch & dinner, closed dinner Mon) A soul-cleansing meal at the Rainforest Restaurant is a must. Virtually all of the food is homegrown, and the ever changing menu features an assortment of international dishes ranging from Asian curries to hearty English breakfasts. Try the tea made from herbs and spices that were plucked minutes earlier from the garden.

**Brigadoon** ( ☎ 416-2380; thebrig@unspoiledqueen.com; mains from US$15; ☺ 6:30pm-11pm, closed Tue) Those who visit the Brig are looking for a quality meal and aren't afraid to drop a couple of extra bucks on it. Chef Michael Chaamaa brings together an assortment of dishes from all over the world, ranging from fresh lobster to garlicky falafel. Thursday nights feature succulent prime ribs, and Saturday night sushi hour is a force to be reckoned with.

For a picnic lunch, hit Windwardside's largest grocery store, **Big Rock Market** ( ☎ 416-2280; ☺ 8am-7pm Mon-Sat), and browse the relatively impressive selection of international food and wine. There are a couple of stores on the street between Brigadoon and Big Rock Market that sell snacks and bulk items (not that you're looking for a pound of nutmeg…).

## MT SCENERY

The highest point on very-vertical Saba, Mt Scenery (887m) is officially the highest point in the entire Kingdom of the Netherlands. Views from the top are definitely worth the climb. The peak offers three distinct vistas: Windwardside, the Bottom and Hell's Gate. For detailed information about hiking to the top, see p478.

## ST JOHN'S

Little St John's, straddling a crooked cliff between Windwardside and the Bottom, was created when the locals could not decide where to build the island's school. Residents of each community squabbled over the matter for quite some time, and when no resolution was found, everyone compromised and constructed the school halfway between the villages. A simple cluster of gingerbread houses sits around the classroom buildings; besides that, there's one joint, **Lollipop's Bar and Restaurant** ( ☎ 416-3330; mains from US$10; ☺ lunch & dinner), where you can grab some chow on the way down to the Bottom. Hit the restaurant up for mouthwatering fish cakes and excellent ocean scenery, or stop by on a Sunday for the filling brunch. Thursday nights feature barbecued grub and reggae beats.

SABA

# THE BOTTOM

The Bottom is Saba's official capital, and houses the island's administrative and governmental buildings. The police station is located here (not that island has any crime); the large bell in the front yard was rung every hour on the hour until the 1990s.

Today, the Bottom is largely the domain of students studying at Saba Medical College, an accredited university offering the first 2½ years of medical education in a course that on par with those offered at US or Canadian medical schools. The 300 students give the island some much appreciated revenue and make up a whopping 20% of Saba's population. Snoop around the village for cheap eats as prices are slashed for the thrifty wannabe doctors.

**AM Edwards Medical Center** ( ☎ 416-3239) offers medical services, while the region's only hyperbaric facility, **Saba Marine Park Hyperbaric Chamber** ( ☎ 416-3288; ☼ 24hr), is on the right side of the road as you enter the Bottom from Windwardside.

It's worth stopping by the Bottom's **Catholic church** to check out what the locals refer to as 'Saba's Sistine Chapel.' Heleen Cornet, a respected local artist, spent two long years painting the church's altar with scenes that fuse images from the Saban jungle with biblical themes. Visit her website at www.heleencornet.com.

A 12-unit luxury resort set up a small hill overlooking the Bottom, the beautiful **Queen's Garden Resort** ( ☎ 416-3494; www.queensaba.com; deluxe/superior/royal ste US$225/300/375; ☐ ☎ ) is the choice retreat for royalty when it visits the island. Gorgeous views accompany rooms equipped with cable TV, wi-fi, a phone, four-poster beds and a separate living room. The pièce de résistance is the blue-tiled outdoor Jacuzzi in each suite. The hotel's restaurant (open for breakfast and lunch daily, and for dinner Wednesday to Monday) serves an elegant lineup of dishes – it's pricey, but worth the dough for a romantic soiree.

**Family Deli & Bakery** ( ☎ 416-3858; mains US$6-15; ☼ 8am-9pm Mon-Sat, 11am-4pm Sun) serves breakfast, lunch and dinner, plus light meals throughout the day, including cheese *pastechis* (deep-fried turnovers). Follow the smell of freshly baked bread.

## WELL'S BAY

As stunning as Saba is, the spike-shaped island doesn't have a beach to call its own. Well, there's Well's…sort of. After a large storm walloped the island in 1999, a small stretch of grainy sand began to appear and disappear with the tide. Commonly known amongst Sabans as 'Wandering Beach,' this cobbled stretch of beach-ish terrain is more of a tourist attraction than a place to recline with good book. If you plan to walk down to the 'beach' (locals often make the bunny ear quotation marks with their fingers when referring Well's Bay), make sure you arrange for someone to pick you up – climbing back up the steep-even-by-Saba-standards hill will be extremely arduous.

While you're visiting, check out **Diamond Rock**, a giant swirling pinnacle bursting skyward from below the waves just offshore. The torpedo-shaped mass is noticeably light in color, the result of years of guano bombardment by resident birds – don't let the locals trick you into thinking that they paint it white to warn watercraft not to crash into it.

A mere fifteen minutes' swim, at the northeast end of the bay, Torrens Point is a gathering spot for tropical fish (and snorkelers in the know).

## LADDER BAY

Before Fort Bay became Saba's official port, everything – from a Steinway piano to Queen Beatrix herself – was hauled up to the Bottom via the **Ladder**, a vertical staircase of over 800 steps. The area is now a moderately difficult trail that heads past an abandoned customs house and affords hikers beautiful views.

---

**MARY'S POINT RUINS**

A generation ago Saba was even more isolated than it is now. One village, Mary's Point, was a 45-minute walk from even the next village. In 1934 the Dutch government decided to move every single villager and house to an area behind Windwardside known as 'the Promised Land,' thus lessening the isolation of being so far from any other signs of civilization. You can see the ruins of Mary's Point while hiking on the Sandy Cruz Trail.

## FORT BAY

A mishmash of concrete structures, electrical parts and oil drums, Fort Bay is Saba's main port and probably the ugliest place on the entire island. Those arriving by ferry will pass through here first before being carted up the crag; divers will also pass through before heading out to sea.

The **Saba Marine Park office** (🕙 8am-noon & 1-5pm Mon-Fri, 8am-noon Sat) has a few brochures to give away, and sells marine-park-logo T-shirts and books on diving.

Although Pop is long gone, **Pop's Place** (☎ 416-3327; 🕙 11am-9pm Wed-Mon), on the waterfront, is a welcoming joint and the perfect place to stop after a dive. Go for one of the famous lobster sandwiches. Try **In Two Deep** (☎ 416-3438; 🕙 9am-3pm), next to Pop's, for great harbor views and a tasty surf-and-turf platter.

# DIRECTORY

## ACCOMMODATIONS

Most of Saba's accommodations are reasonably priced considering the limited number of options: when compared to the other islands in the Caribbean, sleeping on Saba is a steal. For a bit of rustic fun, try El Momo Cottages (p474), the cheapest place to crash on the island. If you want to go green, try a night at the Ecolodge Rendez-Vous (p475). The top-end resorts are conspicuously overpriced.

Check out www.sabatourism.com/cottages .html for a list of private vacation rentals. Most cottages are located in Windwardside or Hell's Gate.

The Saba Tourist Bureau (p480) offers help with booking accommodations.

Hotels often add a 5% government room tax; the 10% to 15% service charge is usually at the discretion of the visitor.

## ACTIVITIES
### Diving & Snorkeling

Although it seems hardly possible when you first approach Saba by air or ferry, this stunning volcanic island might even be more scenic below the ocean's surface. Divers and also adventurous snorkelers can find a bit of everything at 26 varied dive sites: steep wall dives just offshore, amazing submerged pinnacles, and varied marine life ranging from sharks to stingrays to turtles.

The Saba Marine Park has protected the area since 1987. It's the only self-supporting marine park in the world, maintained by a US$4 fee charged for each and every dive, a small price to pay for the pristine conditions. There is a hyperbaric chamber (p477), staffed by trained volunteers from the medical university and Saba Marine Park. There is no individual diving on Saba; all divers must register with the **Saba Marine Park office** (Fort Bay; 🕙 8am-noon & 1-5pm Mon-Fri, 8am-noon Sat) and go through a dive operator. See p56 for more on diving here.

For snorkelers, Well's Bay (p477) and the adjacent Torrens Point (p477) are popular spots, and there's even a marked underwater trail. Ladder Bay is also popular, but it's a good 30-minute hike down to the shore from the road and double that back up.

Dive operators are located in Windwardside; see p474 for details. Friendly **Dive Saba** (☎ in the US & Canada 800-883-7222; www.divesaba.com) offers fantastic deals on airfares, dive packages and hotels in Saba. It's based in the US, but can arrange trips for anyone.

### Hiking

Saba is a hiker's paradise. Many of the trails have been around for centuries, and were used by the earliest settlers to get from village to village.

When you're hiking, dress in layers, wear sturdy walking shoes and bring water. Some hikers might appreciate a walking stick. Stay on the trails as they traverse private land.

The island's premier hike is to the top of Mt Scenery, a three-part climb that ends at the highest point in the entire Kingdom of the Netherlands. The trail starts in the Bottom; the first part is called the Bottom Mountain Trail, while the second leg is the Crispeen Trail. The third and final part of the trail (which is the leg that most people do) starts behind the Trail Shop in Windwardside, and goes straight up and up until you reach the ethereal cloud forest. The best time to head out is about 9am or 10am, so you can reach the peak at around noon, the least cloudy part of the day, for a view that will make the pain in your calves well worth it.

The Sulphur Mine Track is a moderately strenuous hike past hot springs to an abandoned sulfur mine (exploration of the mine highly inadvisable). The relatively easy

---

**PRACTICALITIES**

- **Newspaper** *St Martin Herald* has one Saban correspondent.
- **Radio & TV** Voice of Saba is at 93.9FM and 1140AM. Radio Transat (broadcast from St-Martin/ Sint Maarten and playing reggae and dance tunes) is at 95.5FM. The island has cable TV.
- **Electricity** Electric current is 110V (60 cycles). North American plugs are used.
- **Weights & Measures** The metric system is used here.

---

Sandy Cruz Trail is the local favorite and leads past the deserted old village of Mary's Point (p477).

Before setting out on a hike, head to the Trail Shop (p473) for endless information and maps on Saba's hiking trails.

It's not illegal to hike on Saba without hiring 'Crocodile James' Johnson, but it might as well be. This fifth-generation Saban knows the island better than anyone else. For more information on James, check out page p476.

The only trail you shouldn't attempt without a guide is the North Coast Trail. All of the other trails are accessible to experienced hikers.

### Rock Climbing

Although it's still too early to pack your carabiner, Saba has a plethora of sheer rock faces that will making climbing enthusiasts drool. The **national park office** (Trail Shop, Windwardside) is in the process of tagging viable areas for single pitch climbs, so check in with them before your arrival to get the latest scoop on the project's status and completed paths.

## BUSINESS HOURS

Businesses on Saba are generally open 9am to 5pm Monday to Saturday. Restaurants serve breakfast from 7am to 10am, lunch from 11:30am to 2:30pm, and dinner from 6pm to 9pm; exceptions are noted in specific listings.

## COURSES

Local artist Jo Bean offers excellent half-day glass-blowing courses (US$85) at her charmingly cluttered studio in Windwardside. See p474 for detailed information.

Try your hand at gourmet French cooking in the kitchen at the Gate House in Hell's Gate. It's US$120 per class, with a maximum of six attendees, making it US$20 per head. See p473 for more information.

## DANGERS & ANNOYANCES

The only thing that could possibly be annoying is the steep topography of the island. Short walks are often arduous, but few complain since everyone returns from their holiday with a nice firm bottom.

## EMBASSIES & CONSULATES

There are no embassies on Saba.

## FESTIVALS & EVENTS

**Saba Summer Festival** The island's Carnival is a week-long event in late July that includes a Carnival queen contest, a calypso king competition, a costumed parade around the Bottom and a grand-finale fireworks display.

**Sea & Learn** (www.seaandlearn.org) In October the entire island becomes a learning center for naturalists, scientists and laypeople, who discover share the richness of Saban flora and fauna in a range of activities, from helping out on a shark research project to learning how to use tropical plants to make medicinal teas.

**Saba Days** Held in the first week in December, this features sporting events, steel bands, dance competitions, donkey races and barbecues.

## GAY & LESBIAN TRAVELERS

Although it's a complete coincidence that Saba's nickname is the 'Unspoiled Queen,' and the capital city is called the Bottom, Saba is one of the most gay-friendly spots in all of the Caribbean. It doesn't have the nightlife of St-Barthélemy, but it's a good spot for gays and lesbians looking for a relaxed outdoor vacation where appropriate displays of affection do not have to be limited the privacy their room.

## HOLIDAYS

**New Year's Day** January 1
**Good Friday** Friday before Easter
**Easter Sunday** Late March/early April
**Easter Monday** Late March/early April
**Queen's Day** April 30
**Labor Day** May 1
**Ascension Thursday** Fortieth day after Easter

SABA

**Christmas Day** December 25
**Boxing Day** December 26

## INTERNET ACCESS
Most of the hotels on Saba have computer terminals and wi-fi, including El Momo – although sitting in your rustic cabin in the jungle watching videos on YouTube can sometimes feel a little funny.

## INTERNET RESOURCES
**Saba Tourism** (www.sabatourism.com) is the official tourism website for Saba. It features excellent information about lodgings on the island, including private cottage rentals, plus information about ecotourism, wellness and special events.

## MAPS
The Trail Shop (p473) in Windwardside sells maps.

## MEDICAL SERVICES
Medical services are available in the Bottom (p477), including the region's only hyperbaric facility.

## MONEY
The official currency on Saba is the Netherlands Antillean guilder, also known as the florin. US dollars are accepted everywhere, though, and most prices at hotels and restaurants are listed in US dollars.

There are banks in Windwardside (p473).

## POST
There are no addresses or postal codes on Saba. Simply address correspondence to: Ms Johnson, Saba, Dutch West Indies.

There's a **post office** ( 8am-noon & 1-5pm Mon-Fri, 8am-noon Sat) in Windwardside.

## TELEPHONE
Saba's country code is ☎ 599 and is followed by a seven-digit local number. If you are calling locally, just dial the seven-digit number. To call the island from overseas, dial your country's international access code + ☎ 599 + the local number. We have included only the seven-digit local number in Saba listings in this chapter.

## TOURIST INFORMATION
Information can be found at the **Saba Tourist Bureau** ( ☎ 416-2231; www.sabatourism.com; 8am-5pm Mon-Fri).

## TRAVELERS WITH DISABILITIES
Wheelchair-bound travelers may have a difficult time on Saba as the island is extremely steep and riddled with thousands upon thousands of stairs.

## VISAS
Citizens of North America and most European countries do not need a visa to visit Saba. Other nationalities should check with the Dutch representation in their home country.

# TRANSPORTATION

## GETTING THERE & AWAY
### Entering Saba
Valid passports are required by all visitors.

### Air
Landing at Saba's **Juancho E Yrausquin Airport** (SAB; ☎ 416-2255; Flat Point) is the second-most thrilling activity undertaken on Saba. The first is taking off – the runway doesn't end with a comfy grassy meadow or even a fence, but at a sheer cliff. Don't worry, though: your pilot must pass a test every month to be able to fly into Saba.

Currently, the only airline flying into Saba is **Winair** ( ☎ 416-2255; www.fly-winair.com). It has five 15-minute flights a day to/from St-Martin/Sint Maarten, as well as a daily flight to/from Sint Eustatius.

### Sea
#### FERRY
There are two ferries that run visitors between Sint Maarten and Saba. The **Dawn II** ( ☎ 416-3671; info@sabactransport.com; adult/child one way US$35/18, round-trip US$60/30) travels on Tuesdays, Thursdays and Saturdays, leaving Saba at 6:30am and from Dock Maarten in Philipsburg at 5pm. The **Edge** ( ☎ 545-2640; adult/child one way US$45/23, round-trip US$65/33) leaves Pelican Marina in Simpson Bay at 9am Wednesday to Sunday,

---

**EMERGENCY NUMBERS**

- Ambulance ☎ 111
- Fire ☎ 111
- Police ☎ 111, 416-3237

SABA

arriving in Saba at about 10:30am. It departs Saba at 3:30pm, arriving at Pelican Marina at 5pm. It's worth double-checking the schedule as times may change.

## GETTING AROUND
There is no bus service on Saba. Most travelers hitchhike, walk or use taxis. Those who prefer walking should get well acquainted with the dirt trails, as they are significantly faster at getting you from point A to point B than following the road.

### Car & Motorcycle
Renting a vehicle on relaxing Saba will only give you grief. Lifelong residents won't even attempt some driveways (Willard's of Saba is especially notorious). The only two roads are narrow, steep and winding, with tight corners, and driving is difficult in just about every way. The island's sole **gas station** ( ☎ 416-3272; ☼ 8am-2:45pm Mon-Sat) is located in Fort Bay.

#### DRIVER'S LICENSE
A driver's license from your home country is valid in Saba.

#### RENTAL
OK, don't say we didn't warn you! **Caja's Car Rental** ( ☎ 416-2388; takijah77@hotmail.com; the Bottom) rents cars for about US$50 a day.

#### ROAD RULES
Driving is on the right-hand side of the road. Drivers tend to drive slowly as there are many sharp turns and two-way streets that only fit one car at a time.

### Hitchhiking
Hitchhiking is so common and necessary that it's virtually illegal *not* to pick up a hitchhiker. This is the most common method for tourists to get around, although you are highly encouraged to take a taxi to and from the airport so that the cabbies don't go out of business.

### Taxi
There is no central taxi dispatch number on Saba, but prices have been set in stone to prevent overcharging (although some drivers will still try to sneak a couple extra bucks out of you). There is an additional US$1 for transporting luggage. Your hotel or restaurant can arrange a cab; ask for Peddy.

SABA

# Sint Eustatius

Raise your hand if you've ever heard of Sint Eustatius. You haven't? Don't feel bad, intrepid traveler – how about Statia? (That's what the locals endearingly call this scrubby little island.) No? OK. How about this: which Caribbean island was once the busiest seaport in the world, but whose name most people don't even recognize today? Now we're on the right track…

Yes, it's true, this quiet speck on the map was the It spot during the 18th century, when valuable goods bounced between Europe, Africa and the New World. In fact, the naturally deep harbor was so sought after that the island changed hands 22 times before the Dutch permanently secured their claim.

Today, the island has shed all evidence of its former political importance and has garnered an avid cult following among scuba divers (Statia boasts some of the top sites in the Caribbean) and those who enjoy sun-kissed days full of blissful nothingness.

If Statia were to sign up for a Caribbean beauty pageant, it wouldn't take the crown, although it might have a running shot at being named Miss Congeniality. Unlike the other contestants, this honest island hasn't had any plastic surgery whatsoever – no grandiose landscaping, no condo development, and barely a hint of any urban planning. Oranjestad, the island's only town, is a charming collection of ramshackle structures, each one a quiet homage to a different era. Statia lets it all hang out.

## FAST FACTS

- **Area** 31 sq km
- **Capital** Oranjestad
- **Country code** ☎ 599
- **Departure tax** US$5.65 within Netherlands Antilles, US$12 elsewhere
- **Famous for** Seemingly infinite archaeological sites
- **Language** Dutch officially; English is spoken by everyone
- **Money** Netherlands Antillean guilder (ANG); US dollars accepted everywhere; ANG1 = US$0.56 = €0.36 = UK£0.29
- **Official name** Sint Eustatius
- **People** Statians
- **Phrase** Hi! (mandatory when passing anyone on the street)
- **Population** 2900
- **Visa** None needed for citizens of North America and most European countries; see p493

## HIGHLIGHTS

- **Diving** (p488) Cavort with reef sharks and sea turtles at one of Statia's many shallow shipwrecks
- **The Quill** (p486) Ascend this stunning volcano peak and wind your way down to the bottom of the interior crater, which drips like a rainforest and features impossibly huge trees
- **Archaeology** (p485) Uncover the island's remarkably rich history at one of the 600 documented archaeological digging sites – contact Secar to get involved
- **Oranjestad** (p485) Walk around the island's only town to find intriguing ruins in various states of disarray – many untouched for hundreds of years
- **Sint Eustatius Museum** (p486) Check out this fascinating collection of annotated artifacts, including the 2000-year-old skeleton in the basement

## ITINERARIES

- **Three Days** Spend your first two days blowing bubbles with rays and sea turtles at various dive sites including Charlie Brown, Barracuda Reef, Wreck City and Aquarium. Before leaving, spend your last morning hiking the Quill all the way down to the heart of the volcanic crater.
- **One Week** After following the three-day itinerary, spend another two days exploring additional scuba sites – try a night dive and explore the rougher Atlantic side of the island. Round out the week with an afternoon at the Sint Eustatius Museum, a hike in the Boven, a visit to teeny Zeelandia Beach and a laid-back walk through Oranjestad to see the city ruins, including Fort Oranje and the crumbling synagogue.
- **One Month** After checking all the sights off your to-do list, contact Secar and get in touch with your inner Indiana Jones by helping to unearth buried artifacts from the island's rich historical past. If nature's more your thing, sign up with Stenapa (Sint Eustatius National Parks Foundation) to volunteer at the Miriam C Schmidt Botanical Gardens.

## CLIMATE & WHEN TO GO

In January the average daily high temperature is 29°C (85°F), while the low averages 22°C (72°F). In July the average daily high is 32°C (90°F) and the average low hovers around 24°C (76°F).

The annual rainfall in Statia averages 114.5cm and is split between two distinct periods – the wet season and the dry season. Mid-January to June is the dry season while the remaining months corresponding with the hurricane seasons are obviously quite rainy. Relative humidity is in the low 70s from March to December and in the mid-70s in January and February.

Statia's relative lack of tourism means that prices stay the same most of the year. As a result, it's a good place to come December through April when nearby islands double their rates.

## HISTORY

Statia has been the Caribbean whipping boy for centuries. Caribs had already left Statia at the time Columbus came across the island, in 1493. Consequently, when the French arrived there was no indigenous population to be devastated by disease or enslavement. Then came the Dutch, who established the first permanent settlement here in 1636. Statia subsequently changed hands 22 times among the squabbling Dutch, French and British over the next couple of centuries.

Statia was a primary link between Europe and the Atlantic world for much of the later 18th century. As the English and French levied duty after duty on their islands, the Dutch made Statia a duty-free island in 1756. Subsequently, thousands of ships used Oranjestad as their main stopping point between Europe and the colonies in America, bringing arms and gunpowder to the rebellious colonists, among other things. At its heyday, Statia was home to no less than 10,000 full-time residents, both European

---

**HOW MUCH?**

- Taxi from the airport to Lower Town per person US$5
- One-tank dive US$45
- Curried shrimp with peas and rice at a local joint US$10
- Admission to the must-see Sint Eustatius Museum US$3
- Authentic Statian blue bead US$150

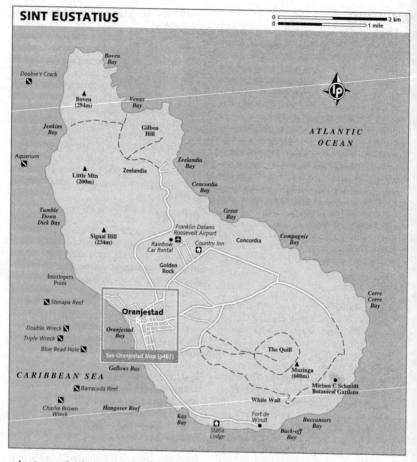

SINT EUSTATIUS

colonists and African slaves. The population rose to above 25,000 when taking into account the sailors that were in port for months at a time while their ships loaded and unloaded cargo.

On November 16, 1776, Statia's most infamous moment occurred. A member of the rebellious colonies' fledgling navy, the brigantine *Andrew Doria*, sailed into the harbor and fired a 13-gun salute signifying American independence. Statia responded with an 11-gun salute, cementing itself as the first foreign nation to recognize the new United States of America, and consequently the US and the Netherlands have the longest standing peaceful relationship between two nations in history. Plans are in the works to

have a replica of the ship created (see www.andrewdoria.org for more information).

Needless to say, Britain was none too pleased – although, contrary to popular belief, it wasn't the British navy's attack on Statia in 1781 that started the island's downhill spiral, which produced massive emigration and ultimately saw the demise of Statia's former glory as 'The Golden Rock.' It was actually the taxes imposed by the French in 1795 that eventually drove the merchants away to nearby islands such as St-Barthélemy (at the time a newly established Swedish colony) and St Thomas (designated a tax-free port by the Danish).

Statia had been part of the Netherlands Antilles, along with Bonaire, Curaçao, Saba and Sint Maarten since 1954. On Statia Day,

---

**VOLUNTEERING**

Statia has some amazing opportunities for educational volunteer trips. **Stenapa** ( ☎ 318-2884; www
.statiapark.org; Lower Town, Oranjestad) connects long- and short-term volunteers with opportunities
like tagging sea turtles on Zeelandia Beach, maintaining the Miriam C Schmidt Botanical Gardens,
staffing the office and cataloguing Statian flora. Contact Stenapa for more information.

For those looking to unleash their inner Indiana Jones, check out **Secar** (Sint Eustatius Center
for Archeological Research; ☎ 524-6770; www.secar.org; Oranjestad), the island's sanctioned organization
dedicated to unearthing and restoring relics from the past. For more information about Secar
see our interview with Grant (p489), the project's leading archaeologist.

---

November 16, 2004, the island adopted a new
flag, but in 2005 it voted to remain part of
the Netherlands Antilles. However, all four
other members voted to disband the island
nation group, effectually leaving Statia the
sole member of the Netherlands Antilles. In
December 2008 Statia will again have direct
ties to the Netherlands effectively ending the
half-century experiment in self-government.
For more on the fate of the Netherlands
Antilles, see p779.

## THE CULTURE
Most islanders are descendants of African
slaves brought over to work in the warehouses
in Lower Town and on the long-vanished
plantations. The culture is a mix of African
and Dutch heritages with many expats. A recent surge in immigrants has included an influx from the Dominican Republic, resulting
in a vibrant Latin addition to the local vibe.

## ENVIRONMENT
The Quill looms above the southern half
of the island. This extinct volcano, which
reaches 600m at Mazinga, the highest point
on the rim, is responsible for the high, conical appearance Statia has when viewed from
neighboring islands. Volcanologists maintain
the Quill is one of the most perfectly shaped
volcanoes in the world.

Cliffs drop straight to the sea along much
of the shoreline, resulting in precious few
beaches. At the north side of Statia there are
a few low mountains, while the island's central
plain contains the airport and Oranjestad.

Most of the northern end of the island is
dry with scrubby vegetation, although oleander, bougainvillea, hibiscus and flamboyant flowers add a splash of color here and
there. The greatest variety of flora is inside
the Quill, which collects enough cloud cover
for its central crater to harbor an evergreen
seasonal forest (which can feel at times like a
rainforest) with ferns, elephant ears, bromeliads, bananas, and tall kapok and silk cot-
tonwood trees that are many centuries old.
The island also has over two dozen varieties
of orchids, and new species are still being
found today.

There are 25 resident species of birds on
Statia, including white-tailed tropical birds
that nest on the cliffs along the beach north
of Lower Town, in Oranjestad. There are
also harmless racer snakes, iguanas, lizards
and tree frogs. Most other terrestrial animal
life is limited to goats, chickens, cows and
donkeys. The marine life offers additional
diversity with hundreds of fish species, extensive coral reefs, schools of cuttlefish and
large families of Caribbean spiny lobster.

## FOOD & DRINK
Tiny Statia has a remarkably diverse range of
interesting eating choices if you know where
to look. For local cuisine head to Golden
Rock, a 'suburb' (and we use that term very
loosely) of Oranjestad, for a smattering of
cheap local grub. The Fruit Tree in town
has an excellent assortment of tried-and-true
Statian cuisine. International eats are aplenty
as well – try Superburger for anything from
ice cream milkshakes to salt-fish sandwiches.
The Old Gin House is a good spot to grab a
drink, or try Ocean View Terrace for a lovely
view of the Caribbean Sea.

# SINT EUSTATIUS

Little Statia, as it's commonly known, has
but one town: Oranjestad. The rest of the
island is rugged, rural terrain. The island's
points of interest are located in town unless
otherwise noted.

## INFORMATION

The two main banks are First Caribbean National Bank and Windward Islands Bank (WIB). There's also an ATM on the corner of Fort Oranje Straat and Breedeweg.

The Old Gin House and Stenapa headquarters have internet access.

**Post office** ( ☎ 318-2207; Cottageweg; ☼ 7:30am-4pm Mon-Fri)

**Public library** (Oranjestad; internet access per hr US$5; ☼ noon-5pm Mon, 8am-5pm Tue-Fri) Offers internet facilities.

**Queen Beatrix Medical Centre** ( ☎ 318-2371; Oranjestad) Has quite a good reputation considering the island's remoteness and miniscule population. There are always two doctors on call 24 hours per day.

**Sint Eustatius Tourist Bureau** ( ☎ 318-2433; www .statiatourism.com; Fort Oranje)

## SIGHTS
### The Quill

Looming large over the rest of the island, the lone photogenic peak, known as the Quill (whose name is derived from the Dutch word *kwil*, meaning pit or hole), spikes high above the rolling terrain below. The once-active volcano now lies perfectly quiet and makes for a fantastic hiking day trip. Follow the markers deep down into the interior crater and witness a thriving rainforest-like environment stocked with dripping foliage and skyscraping trees that are several centuries old. See p489 for more information about hiking the Quill.

### Fort Oranje

Right in the center of town, **Fort Oranje** (admission free; ☼ 24hr) is one of the last remaining bastions of Statia's historic past, an intact fort complete with cannons, triple bastions and a cobblestone courtyard. The French erected the first rampart in 1629, but most of the fort was built after the Dutch took the island from the French in 1636. They added to the fort a number of times over the years.

The courtyard has a couple of memorials, including a plaque presented by US President Franklin Roosevelt to commemorate the fort's fateful 1776 salute of the American war vessel *Andrew Doria*. At the time, the British on neighboring Antigua didn't take too kindly to Statia being the first foreign power to officially recognize the new American nation. The British navy later sailed for Oranjestad and, led by Admiral George Rodney, mercilessly bombed it to high heaven, and then took possession of the island and all its wealth.

### Sint Eustatius Museum

Chock full o' history, this **museum** ( ☎ 318-2288; Oranjestad; adult/child US$3/1; ☼ 9am-5pm Mon-Fri, until noon Sat) gives meaning to the Statian tag line and license plate insignia, 'The Historic Gem.' Set up as an upper-class colonial-era house, the museum also houses a pre-Columbian collection of artifacts and information on slavery, nautical history and colonial relics. The entire venture has been funded by private donors, so it's a bit ramshackle; however, the exhibits are thoroughly informative. Head down to the basement and learn about the Saladoids, who came all the way from the Orinoco region in Venezuela to settle here. They had abandoned the island before the arrival of the Arawaks, but left behind several interesting burial grounds. The unearthed skeleton of a 60-year-old man sits on display and, if you look closely, you'll notice that his teeth are in remarkably perfect condition – a testament to the indigenous diet before sugar cane was introduced in the slave-trading days.

### Government Guesthouse

The Government Guesthouse is the handsome 18th-century stone-and-wood building opposite First Caribbean National Bank. It was thoroughly renovated in 1992 with funding from the EU and is now the government headquarters, with the offices of the lieutenant governor and commissioners on the ground floor and the courtroom on the upper floor. You'll see the lieutenant governor's Mercedes Benz parked out front – the nicest car on the island, by far.

---

**BEST BOOKS ABOUT SINT EUSTATIUS**

Those who most enjoy their visit to Statia have no qualms about copious amounts of down time – it's a great opportunity to snuggle up with a good read. Before arriving on the island consider swinging by the bookstore to check out *The Golden Rock*, by Ronald Hurst, and *The First Salute*, by two-time Pulitzer Prize winner Barbara Tuchman, both of which shed some light on the island's rich history.

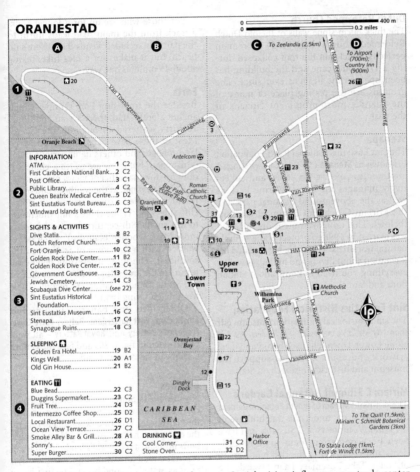

ORANJESTAD

| INFORMATION | |
|---|---|
| ATM | 1 C2 |
| First Caribbean National Bank | 2 C2 |
| Post Office | 3 C1 |
| Public Library | 4 C2 |
| Queen Beatrix Medical Centre | 5 D2 |
| Sint Eustatius Tourist Bureau | 6 C3 |
| Windward Islands Bank | 7 C2 |

| SIGHTS & ACTIVITIES | |
|---|---|
| Dive Statia | 8 B2 |
| Dutch Reformed Church | 9 C3 |
| Fort Oranje | 10 C2 |
| Golden Rock Dive Center | 11 B2 |
| Golden Rock Dive Center | 12 C4 |
| Government Guesthouse | 13 C2 |
| Jewish Cemetery | 14 C3 |
| Scubaqua Dive Center | (see 22) |
| Sint Eustatius Historical | |
| Foundation | 15 C4 |
| Sint Eustatius Museum | 16 C2 |
| Stenapa | 17 C4 |
| Synagogue Ruins | 18 C3 |

| SLEEPING | |
|---|---|
| Golden Era Hotel | 19 B2 |
| Kings Well | 20 A1 |
| Old Gin House | 21 B2 |

| EATING | |
|---|---|
| Blue Bead | 22 C3 |
| Duggins Supermarket | 23 C2 |
| Fruit Tree | 24 D3 |
| Intermezzo Coffee Shop | 25 D2 |
| Local Restaurant | 26 D1 |
| Ocean View Terrace | 27 C2 |
| Smoke Alley Bar & Grill | 28 A1 |
| Sonny's | 29 C2 |
| Super Burger | 30 C2 |

| DRINKING | |
|---|---|
| Cool Corner | 31 C2 |
| Stone Oven | 32 D2 |

The building, which once served as the Dutch naval commander's quarters, derived its name from the 1920s when it was used as a guesthouse.

## Synagogue Ruins

Those with a particular interest in Jewish history or old buildings can explore the roofless and slowly decaying yellow-brick walls of the Honen Dalim (which means 'She Who is Kind to the Poor'), an abandoned synagogue dating from 1739. It's 30m down the alleyway with Belle Époque lampposts, opposite the south side of the library in Oranjestad. It is the second-oldest synagogue in the western hemisphere and the *mikvah* (a cleansing bath for women) has been left intact.

Statia's rising influence as a trade center was accompanied by a large influx of Jewish merchants beginning in the early 1700s. These businessmen were of Sephardic descent and escaped to the Netherlands during the Spanish Inquisition. After the 1781 invasion, British troops stole much of the wealth from the Jewish merchants and by 1847 all of the Jews had been deported or left of their own will.

About 500m east of the synagogue ruins is a **Jewish cemetery** with gravestones dating from 1742 to 1843. It was here that clever Jews tried to avoid British plundering. Troops noticed an extremely large number of funerals for such a small community and, upon opening a casket, found valuables instead of bodies.

SINT EUSTATIUS

## Dutch Reformed Church

The thick 60cm stone walls of the old Dutch Reformed Church, built in 1755, remain perfectly intact, but the roof collapsed during a 1792 hurricane and the building has been open to the heavens ever since. The grounds are the resting place of many of the island's most prominent citizens of the past.

## Stenapa

The Sint Eustatius National Parks Foundation is known as **Stenapa** ( ☎ 318-2884; www.statiapark .org; Lower Town; ☽ 7am-5pm Mon-Fri) and collectively manages the Statia Marine Park as well as the aboveground national park and the Miriam C Schmidt Botanical Gardens (below). This nongovernment organization was started in 1998 to protect Statia's ample natural resources. The office has detailed information about diving and hiking, as well as everything you need to know about Statian flora and fauna.

## Sint Eustatius Historical Foundation

The small historical foundation museum **gift shop** ( ☎ 318-2856; Oranjestad; ☽ 9am-noon Mon-Sat) along Lower Town sells used books and local artwork and crafts. Proceeds support the museum and historical research on Statia.

## Miriam C Schmidt Botanical Gardens

The semiwild **Miriam C Schmidt Botanical Gardens** ( ☎ 318-2884) grow under the watchful eye of the Quill. Volunteers and Stenapa staff have been busy preparing them to show residents and visitors alike the rich biodiversity of Statia. Take Rosemary Laan towards the Quill and follow the dirt road that points to the Botanical Gardens. Take care, as it can be rough riding.

## Zeelandia

Zeelandia, about 3.2km northeast of Oranjestad, takes its name from Statia's first Dutch settlers, who were from Zeeland province in the Netherlands.

The dark-sand beach at Zeelandia Bay collects its fair share of flotsam and is not an ideal beach for swimming; the Atlantic side of the island is turbulent and there are dangerous currents and undertows. It is a reasonable strolling beach, however, and you can find private niches by walking south along the beach toward the cliffs.

For those who are up for a longer walk, a track from the main road leads north to the partially secluded Venus Bay. There's no beach, but it makes for a nice hike, taking about 45 minutes one way.

## Forts

Besides the imposing Fort Oranje, which anchors Oranjestad, there are an additional 18 forts scattered throughout the island. Most of these have been consumed by island foliage, and others lie in various states of disrepair, but a few are worth a glimpse if only for the magnificent views out to sea.

At **Fort de Windt**, at the southern end of the island, a couple of rusty cannons sit atop a cliff-side wall. While there's not much else to this small 18th-century fort (which looks more like a wooden platform), you'll be rewarded with a fine view of St Kitts to the southeast. The most interesting geological feature in the area is the white cliffs to the east of Fort de Windt, a landmark readily visible from neighboring islands.

Other forts and batteries include **Fort Amsterdam**, **Fort Rotterdam**, **Battery Corre Corre**, **Frederick's Battery** and **Royal Battery** – all were constructed in the 1780s and face the gentler Caribbean side of the island.

## Beaches

No one visits Statia for its beaches, which can't compare with those of other islands in the Caribbean. Volcanic Zeelandia Beach, on the east coast, has rough surf and undertows, butts up against the island's landfill, and is not recommended for swimming; nonetheless, it rates as Statia's second beach; the first being the strip of sand in front of Lower Town. From an archaeological perspective, this beach is absolutely fascinating because much of it was once reclaimed land (that has since been re-reclaimed by the sea) and the sturdy stone frameworks of old warehouses are visible beneath the emerald waters.

## ACTIVITIES
## Diving & Snorkeling

The waters off Sint Eustatius are blessed with stunning reefs and loads of attractions: reef dives, seahorses, colonial trading shipwrecks, giant octopuses, stingrays, barracudas, coral, lobster, tropical fish… The list could go on forever. Statia's diving is regarded as among the best in the Caribbean.

---

## VOLUNTEERS DIG SINT EUSTATIUS

R Grant Gilmore III is an American archaeologist who runs the Secar archaeological initiative. For additional information about Secar, see p485.

**What first brought you to Sint Eustatius?**

I first came to Statia on the invitation of Norman Barka, one of my archaeology professors at the College of William and Mary in Virginia, USA. Professor Barka had been working on the island since 1979. I first visited in 1997. I moved here permanently in 2004 to continue my research. I love the island dearly; in fact, my wife Joanna and I gave our daughter the middle name 'Eustatia' – an 18th-century variation of the island's moniker.

**What is Secar, and how does one get involved?**

First, most people haven't even heard of Sint Eustatius, and those who have probably don't know that there are over 600 documented archaeology sites scattered around the island. Secar provides an opportunity for people of diverse backgrounds to experience Statia's rich archaeology first hand. We are also dedicated to bridging the gap between the past and the future by protecting standing historic structures and archaeological sites on Statia and on other nearby islands. Secar volunteers are not only immersed in archaeology (they live at the archaeology lab), but they also are encouraged to engage in local social life as well. If you are interested in joining the team, email me at info@secar.org.

---

Part of what keeps it this way is the US$4 per day or US$20 per year pass fee paid to Stenapa (opposite) to help this foundation maintain the pristine conditions of the Statia Marine Park. There is also an additional US$1 per day harbor fee. Please take only photos and leave all historic objects and marine life alone (fines have been levied at the airport on divers found to have stashed more than just a blue bead or two).

For a deep dive, Doobie's Crack, a large cleft in a reef at the northwest side of the island, has black-tip sharks and schools of large fish. Try Blue Bead Hole if you're feeling particularly lucky and want to give bead hunting in an underwater sand dump a go. Adventurous types should do a night dive at Stenapa Reef to check out the creatures that hide during the day.

In the last 10 years, Statia has sunk several ships, creating some of the best wreck diving in the world. The *Charlie Brown* was sunk in 2003 and a map of its cavernous hull and quarters now hangs on the Stenapa wall so divers can plan their route beforehand. A dive to *Charlie Brown* is best done before 11am. Several colonial-era wrecks also exist under the waves, but most of them have deteriorated to the point where all that remains are the awesome rusty anchors. See p57 for more on Statia diving.

One-tank dives average US$45, two-tank dives US$75. Night dives, certification courses and multidive packages are also available. PADI Open Water courses will set you back US$375.

Statia has three diving operations:

**Dive Statia** ( ☎ 318-2435, in the US 866-614-3419; www.divestatia.com, www.mystatia.com; Oranjestad) The oldest dive center on the island. Friendly Rinda and Rudy run a solid operation.

**Golden Rock Dive Center** ( ☎ 318-2964, in the US 800-311-6658; www.goldenrockdive.com) Based at the Old Gin House, this scuba shop has been around for almost as long as Dive Statia. Michele and Glenn, the affable owners, make sure everything runs smoothly. There's a second location further down the coast where you suit up and do all the paperwork before departure.

**Scubaqua Dive Center** ( ☎ 318-2160; www.scubaqua .com; Oranjestad) A newer addition to the mix. Swiss- and Swedish-run.

## Hiking

The tourist office has a free hiking brochure with descriptions of 12 trails, and it can provide information on current trail conditions. Keep your eyes peeled for trail markers, which are usually small orange ribbons.

The most popular hike is to the Quill, Statia's extinct volcano. The Quill, and its surrounding slopes, was designated a national park in May 1998. The trail leading up the mountain begins at the end of Rosemary Laan in Oranjestad and it takes about 50 minutes to reach the edge of the crater. From there you can continue in either direction along the rim. The trail to the right (southeast) takes about 45 minutes and ends atop the 600m-high Mazinga, Statia's highest point. The shorter Panorama Track to the left offers great views and takes only about 15 minutes.

---

**BLUE BEAD FEVER**

When Peter Minuit purchased the island of Manhattan (the heart of present-day New York City) from its local inhabitants, he paid for the land with 60 Dutch guilders' worth of trinkets, including several alluring blue beads.

These glassy pentagonal balls were produced in Amsterdam and traded throughout all of the Dutch holdings around the world. According to legend, several hundred years ago a large wooden vessel that sank off the coast of Statia was carrying these precious beads by the barrelful. And even today a lonely little bead will, once in a while, wash ashore.

Although the price of the blue beads hasn't risen in value quite like the real estate of New York, these shimmering talismans are considered to be quite a find. They are the only historical artifacts that are allowed to leave the island and, after years of avid plundering, the chance of finding one is slim.

As you walk around Oranjestad, you'll notice that local expats regularly sport their found beads with pride while Zen-fully exclaiming 'you don't find the beads; the beads find you...'

---

A third option is the track leading down into the crater, where there's a thick rainforest-like jungle of tall trees, some with huge buttressed trunks. This steep track, which takes about an hour each way, can be very slippery, so sturdy shoes are essential.

Guided tours focusing on native flora and fauna can be organized through **Stenapa** ( ☎ 318-2884; www.statiapark.org; Lower Town, Oranjestad), which oversees the national park, or through **Sint Eustatius Tourist Bureau** ( ☎ 318-2433; www.statiatourism.com; Fort Oranje).

## SLEEPING

Take your pick from the five places to stay on wee Statia. Private house rentals (starting at US$100 per night) are also an option; contact Rinda at Dive Statia (p489) for more information.

**Country Inn** ( ☎ /fax 318-2484; countryinn@statiatourism.com; Concordia; s/d US$50/60; ✦ ) Within walking distance of the airport, Statia's lowest-priced lodging isn't fancy, but the six quaint rooms are clean and quiet. Breakfast is available for US$5 and Iris Pompier, the dedicated proprietor, will even cook you one of her fabulous lunches or dinners upon request. About a 20-minute walk or quick hitch from town. Credit cards are not accepted.

**Kings Well** ( ☎ /fax 318-2538; www.kingswellstatia.com; Van Tonningenweg, Oranjestad; s US$90-125, d US$110-140; ✦ ) Bursting with character from every vine-draped crevice, Kings Well is a colorful menagerie of horse-sized Great Danes, squawking pet macaws and swirls of hyper goldfish. The owners are some of the most down-to-earth folks you'll ever meet and tend to their B&B-style rooms with love and affec-

tion. Loads of wooden furnishings abound, and there's always a new project under way, like adding on an extra bedroom or creating new mosaic art.

**Statia Lodge** ( ☎ 318-1900, in France 33 6 9989 0403; www.statialodge.com; s/d/tr US$110/125/205; ✦ ✦ ) The newest digs on the island, beautiful Statia Lodge opened its doors two years ago and has been getting good reviews ever since. The 10 quiet wooden cabins are billed as 'ecolodges' and sit on a silent stretch of fenced-in land. A small beach bar and L-shaped pool are on the water's edge. The property is just beyond the limits of Oranjestad on the southern part of the island near Fort de Windt. Single and double rooms come with complimentary scooters; triple and family rooms come with a car.

**Old Gin House** ( ☎ 318-2319; www.oldginhouse.com; Bay Rd, Lower Town, Oranjestad; s US$135-300, d US$145-315; ✦ ▢ ✦ ) This beautiful, brick ginning station (no, not the booze – the cotton seeds) has been restored to its 17th-century glory, and makes for a romantic spot to relax and dine. Most of the hotel accommodations are situated in a two-story complex behind the original structure and feature strong air-conditioning, wi-fi access and satellite TV. The rooms have burgundy and black accents giving them a bit of a Moroccan feel, and bathrooms are slightly out of date, but the shower nozzles are new and provide excellent water pressure. Rates include continental breakfast. Rumor has it that the lodging will be getting a makeover soon – look out for rising prices.

**Golden Era Hotel** ( ☎ 318-2345, in the US 800-223-9815, in Canada 800-344-0023; goldenera@goldenrock.net;

Bay Rd, Lower Town, Oranjestad; d US$150; ❌ 🖥 🐾)
'Golden Era' probably refers to the last time
this place had a renovation – it really needs
a facelift. The property sits right along the
ocean and a few rooms have private balconies with unobstructed sea views. The
grounds are covered with yellow-bells and
oleander, and the pool bar practically forces
guests to lounge on a beach chair with a
mystery novel and a piña colada. All credit
cards accepted.

## EATING & DRINKING

Statia's no culinary capital relative to St-
Martin/Sint Maarten nearby, but there's a
wide enough assortment to keep the taste buds
curious every night of the week. There are
plenty of joints dishing out local recipes and,
bizarrely, seven Chinese restaurants serving
up cheap eats. All of the hotels on the island
serve lunch and dinner by request and are definitely worth a try (the Old Gin House dishes
out dinner to guests and others nightly).

**Intermezzo Coffee Shop** ( ☎ 318-2520; Heilligerweg,
Oranjestad; sandwiches from US$6; 🕑 breakfast & lunch,
closed Sat) Colorful Intermezzo is the best joint
to grab an espresso and a quick sandwich.
Stop in for pancakes on the first Sunday of
every month, and on the third Friday of each
month swing through for some live music and
complimentary hors d'oeuvres.

**Blue Bead** ( ☎ 318-2873; Bay Rd, Lower Town,
Oranjestad; lunch US$7-10, dinner US$12-20; 🕑 lunch & dinner) A breezy restaurant along Oranjestad Bay,
Blue Bead offers pleasant water-view dining
and reasonable prices. Try the special catch
of the day or go for a big pizza smothered
with veggies.

**Super Burger** ( ☎ 318-2412; Fort Oranje Straat,
Oranjestad; mains around US$8; 🕑 breakfast & lunch)
Skell, the owner, cooks up some (yeah, you
guessed it) super burgers, and there's a good
assortment of veggie dishes if you aren't in a
carnivorous kind of mood.

**Sonny's** ( ☎ 318-2929; Fort Oranje Straat, Oranjestad;
mains US$8-16; 🕑 lunch & dinner) This open-air,
lantern-filled joint doesn't win any culinary
prizes, but it's a great place to chill with
regulars over a bowl of cheap noodles. Free
delivery available.

**Fruit Tree** ( ☎ 318-2584; HM Queen Beatrix, Oranjestad;
mains US$10; 🕑 lunch) Friendly Fruit Tree has an
excellent assortment of home-cooked goodness. The fried fish cutlet and curried shrimp
get top marks. If you want to come for dinner

swing in during the day to let them know and
they'll stay open for you in the evening.

**Local Restaurant** ( ☎ 318-1513; Paramiraweg,
Oranjestad; mains US$10; 🕑 lunch & dinner) The name
pretty much says it all – this local spot on
Paramiraweg is run by the pots-and-pans-
wielding Mama, who dishes out hearty Statian
favorites such as stewed seafood.

**Ocean View Terrace** ( ☎ 318-2934; Fort Oranje Straat,
Oranjestad; mains US$11-18; 🕑 closed Sun) In the court-
yard next to the Government Guesthouse, this
place has a quiet open-air setting, and offers
stellar views and tasty seafood dishes. Stop by
for a li'l drunken karaoke on Friday nights.

**Smoke Alley Bar & Grill** ( ☎ 318-2002; Bay Rd, Lower
Town, Oranjestad; mains from US$12 🕑 lunch & dinner Mon-
Sat) Commanding an enviable location directly
over the ocean on the turn into Lower Town,
this open-air restaurant-cum-nightclub has
group bench seating, pulsing music at night
(with a DJ and dancing till late on Friday),
an eclectic crowd of medical students, locals
and foreigners…and mediocre food.

**Cool Corner** ( ☎ 318-2523; Paramiraweg, Oranjestad)
Also known as Chuckie's, after the affable
owner and chef, this hot spot at the top of
the Slave Path is *the* choice hangout for
the local expat crowd, especially on Friday
nights. Watch as Chuckie tends bar with an
impressive robotic efficiency while chatting
up the gaggle of usual patrons.

Spice things up with a stop at Stone Oven
in the late evening, and dance to soca and
salsa beats.

Hit **Duggins Supermarket** ( ☎ 318-2150; De
Windtweg, Oranjestad; 🕑 8am-8pm Mon-Fri, 6am-9pm Sat,
9am-1pm Sun) for all of your grocery needs. The
main supermarket on this duty-free island,
Duggins is packed with cheap European and
American brand names. You'll find loads of
Kittitians here, who boat over from next
door to stock up on cheap provisions.

# DIRECTORY

## ACCOMMODATIONS

The Sint Eustatius Tourist Bureau sanctions
five places to stay during your time on the
island. Three are located in Lower Town
near the water's edge, one sits out near the
airport and the fifth occupies a quiet patch
of land beyond Oranjestad in the district of
Whitewall (near Fort de Windt). Luxurious
pampering is not on the cards, although

---

**PRACTICALITIES**

■ **Newspapers & Magazines** Statia doesn't have its own newspaper but imports St Martin's *Daily Herald*.

■ **Radio & TV** Statia's sole radio station is at 92.3 FM. Cable TV comes mostly from the US but a few channels are from within the Caribbean.

■ **Electricity** 110V/60 cycles; North American–style sockets are common.

■ **Weights & Measures** Metric.

---

each hotel can adequately suit your sleeping needs. The general lack of tourism means that prices stagnate throughout the year. Plans for renovation of several properties mean that there may be an increase in tariffs over the next few years.

The government tax on hotels is 7% and restaurants affiliated with hotels charge 15% service fee in lieu of gratuities.

Camping is technically allowed on Statia, although the tourist office has never had a request in its history. If you're willing to pioneer through the bureaucracy, Zeelandia might be the best location to bunker down.

## ACTIVITIES

See p488 for information on activities.

## BUSINESS HOURS

Stores and offices are open during the week from 8am to 6pm while grocery stores usually open around 7:30pm and close at 7pm.

Restaurants usually serve breakfast between 7am and 10am, lunch starts around 11:30am and goes until 2:30pm, while dinner starts at 6pm and lasts until 10pm or later, depending on the establishment. Local joints tend to have more flexible hours.

The two most common religious groups on Statia are Seventh Day Adventists and Roman Catholics: on Saturday the Seventh Day Adventists' establishments are closed and on Sunday it's the Roman Catholics that close up shop.

## EMBASSIES & CONSULATES

There are no embassies on Statia.

## FESTIVALS & EVENTS

**Statia Carnival** With 10 days of revelry in late July, this is the island's biggest festival, culminating on a Monday. Music, jump-ups (including early-morning pajama ones), competitions and local food are the highlights.

**Statia Day** Fort Oranje is the site of ceremonies held on Statia Day, November 16, which commemorates the date in 1776 when Statia became the first foreign land to salute the US flag. On this date in 2004, Statia adopted a new flag.

**Golden Rock Regatta** Held in mid-November, this colorful sailing race is held between the nearby islands to commemorate Statia's importance during the American Revolution and the 11-gun salute that was fired from the island on November 16, 1776.

## HOLIDAYS

**New Year's Day** January 1
**Good Friday** Friday before Easter
**Easter Sunday/Monday** late March/early April
**Queen's Birthday** April 30
**Labor Day/Ascension Day** May 1
**Emancipation Day** July 1
**Antillean Day** October 21
**Statia Day** November 16
**Christmas Day** December 25
**Boxing Day** December 26

## MEDICAL SERVICES

See p486 for details.

## MONEY

The official currency is the Netherlands Antillean guilder (also called the florin), though US dollars are accepted everywhere.

## TELEPHONE

Statia's country code is ☎ 599. To call the island overseas, dial your country's international access code followed by ☎ 599 + the local number. We have included only the seven-digit local number in Statia listings in this chapter.

---

**EMERGENCY NUMBERS**

■ **Ambulance** ☎ 111
■ **Police** ☎ 111

---

## TOURIST INFORMATION

The **Sint Eustatius Tourist Bureau** ( ☎ 318-2433; www.statiatourism.com; Fort Oranje) has free island maps that show the roads and hiking trails. They are open during the week from 8am to noon, and 1pm to 5pm. Also check out the tiny tourism information desk at the airport, which is open when flights are landing. A new 63-page walking tour booklet has been assembled to give visitors a more in-depth perspective of the island, especially the ruins of Oranjestad.

## VISAS

Citizens of North America and most European countries do not need a visa to visit Statia. Other nationalities should check with the Dutch representation in their home country.

# TRANSPORTATION

## GETTING THERE & AWAY
### Entering Sint Eustatius

All visitors need a passport and onward or return ticket.

### Air

**Franklin Delano Roosevelt Airport** (EUX; ☎ 316-2887) is Statia's only airport. It's tiny and currently only accommodates the **Winair** ( ☎ 318-2303; www.fly-winair.com) puddle jumpers from St-Martin/Sint Maarten.

### Sea

There is currently no regular ferry service to Statia. Save for a few dive boats and the odd small ship, no cruise ships alight here. Virtually all tourist traffic arrives by airplane.

Yachts need to radio the Marine Park at VHF channel 16 or 17 as there are many protected spots around the island and there is only anchorage for about 10 yachts at a time.

## GETTING AROUND

Statia has no buses so renting a car is useful if you want to explore every nook and cranny of the island (which can easily be done in a day). If you're staying in Oranjestad, you won't need a car for most of your stay, but expect to do some serious walking, as the town is somewhat spread out. Hiking enthusiasts can easily access the trail up into the Quill from the center of Oranjestad by foot.

### Car & Motorcycle

Driving is on the right side of the road. Road conditions are spotty outside of Oranjestad and the road to the Miriam C Schmidt Botanical Gardens can be impassable after rain. Watch out for roaming goats, cows and chickens all over the island, even in town. Also keep an eye out for surprise one-way streets – they tend to appear out of nowhere and the locals can get very upset if you're heading the wrong way.

Little Statia has a ridiculous number of car rental agencies, including the following lot. Figure around US$35 per day, although deals are usually negotiable for weekly rates and such. Just remember, you get what you pay for.

**ARC Car & Jeep Rental** ( ☎ 318-2595; arcagency@megatropic.com) Rates between US$35 and US$45. All major credit cards accepted.

**Brown's Car Rental** ( ☎ 318-2266) Vans available for US$50. MasterCard accepted.

**Rainbow Car Rental** ( ☎ 318-2811; raintour@goldenrock.net; booth at airport) Rates from US$40.

**Reddy Car Rental** ( ☎ 524-2342) Rates from US$35 including tax and insurance.

### EXCESS BAGGAGE

Winair provides fun and friendly service over to Sint Eustatius; however, on virtually every flight over to the island, someone disembarks sans luggage even though they thought they saw it being loaded onto the plane. This is usually due to weight limits – frequently the captain realizes at the last minute that the plane has reached its full capacity and will hold back a couple suitcases for the next flight, when the passenger complement is perhaps not as large. If you are arriving or departing on the last flight out, you'll have to wait until the following day, or even longer, to retrieve your luggage.

It's a good idea to pack a small carry-on stocked with 48 hours' worth of essentials just in case you too become a statistic. Despite harsh airline restrictions on liquids, Winair keeps a slightly more relaxed attitude, so you can bring your insect repellant along.

## Hitchhiking

The usual safety precautions apply, but hitchhiking on Statia is considered to be very safe and easy, so it's perfectly fine to stick your thumb out at someone (and not in the Shakespearean kind of way).

## Taxi

The island's taxis congregate at the airport after flights arrive. If you're looking for a cab, ask a local to call one, or they'll just give you a lift. You can also try the dispatch line (☎ 318-2205) Figure US$5 per person per trip.

# St Kitts & Nevis

Near-perfect packages – that's how you might think of St Kitts and Nevis after a visit. The two-island nation combines beaches with the beauty of the mountains, plenty of activities to engage your body and some rich history to engage your mind. The legacies of the sugar industry have been recycled into pleasant plantation estates good for lunch or just a stay. And the local culture is almost a Caribbean cliché: mellow, friendly, familiar and with a pulsing soca beat.

But if the pair offer much that's similar, they also differ in the details. St Kitts is the larger and feels that way, from the hustle of intriguing Basseterre to the resort enclave of Frigate Bay. You could spend a few days exploring all of its beaches, with their cool bars, water activities and pure vacation vibe. Circling the main part of the island, there's plenty to see: the languid charms of the plantations and the astonishing bulk of Brimstone Fortress.

Nevis is a neater package. It has one volcanic mountain rather than a range and its one main road is a circle that takes you around the island in under two hours. There's a handful of beaches with the usual fun, and Charleston, the charming main town, can be walked end to end in 15 minutes. History here centers on the big names of Horatio Nelson and Alexander Hamilton. Nature walks take you into the verdant upper reaches of the peak.

Even if you just stay on one island, frequent ferry service means that you can easily enjoy both.

## FAST FACTS

- **Area** St Kitts: 68 sq miles; Nevis: 36 sq miles
- **Capital** St Kitts: Basseterre; Nevis: Charlestown
- **Country code** ☎ 869
- **Departure tax** St Kitts: US$22; Nevis: US$21
- **Famous for** Languid days, historic plantation inns
- **Language** English with a Creole or patois accent
- **Money** Eastern Caribbean dollar (EC$); EC$1 = US$0.38 = €0.24 = UK£0.19
- **Official name** Federation of St Christopher & Nevis
- **People** Kittitians, Nevisians
- **Phrase** Menono (I don't know); get dat do (get that done)
- **Population** 46,000 (35,000 on St Kitts; 11,000 on Nevis)
- **Visa** Not required for most nationalities; see p515

## HIGHLIGHTS

- **Brimstone Hill Fortress** (p505) Explore the only Unesco World Heritage site in the Leeward Islands
- **Plantation lunches** Take a long lunch at a plantation estate while touring either island, even if you don't stay at one
- **Basseterre** (p499) Explore the intriguing, shambolic and surprising vibrant capital of St Kitts
- **Frigate Bay Beach** (p502) Enjoy the mood – fun-filled by day, rum-fueled at night
- **Nevis hikes** (p511) Surmount the volcano, sample wild fruit, spot a monkey and more

## ITINERARIES

- **Two Days** On either island, spend your first day at the beach (Frigate Bay on St Kitts, Pinney's on Nevis) then spend your second day circling the island and exploring the capital.
- **Four Days** Do the two-day highlights for both islands.
- **One Week** Split your time between the two islands. Add in a lot more beach time as the extra days let you explore the sandy shores at will, looking for a favorite. Consider a night or two at a plantation inn.

## CLIMATE & WHEN TO GO

There's really no bad time to go to St Kitts and Nevis. The hot Caribbean summer contrasts with cool low-season deals at the resorts.

Winter days average a temperature of 81°F (27°C) while summers shoot up to a still respectable 86°F (30°C).

Annual rainfall averages 55in and is fairly consistent throughout the year. The driest months are February to June, and the hurricane (and rainy) season is July to November, although even during this period the weather can be gorgeous.

High-season rates start from around mid-December and go to mid-April. The best time to visit, price- and weather-wise, is November and early December.

## HISTORY

The island known today as St Kitts was called Liamuiga (Fertile Island) by the aggressive Carib people, who arrived about 1300 AD and chased out the peaceable agrarian bands who'd been in the area for hundreds of years. When Columbus sighted the island on his second voyage to the New World, in 1493, he named it St Christopher after his patron saint, later shortened to 'St Kitts.'

Columbus used the Spanish word for 'snow,' *nieves,* to name Nevis, presumably because the clouds shrouding its mountain reminded him of a snowcapped peak. Native Caribs knew the island as Oualie (Land of Beautiful Waters).

St Kitts and Nevis are the oldest British colonies in the Caribbean. Sir Thomas Warner founded a colony way back in 1623, only to be joined soon after by the French, a move the British only tolerated long enough to massacre the native Caribs. In one day, 2000 Caribs were slaughtered, causing blood to run for days at the site now known as Bloody Point.

A century and a half of Franco-British battles culminated locally in 1782, when a force of 8000 French troops laid siege to the important British stronghold at Brimstone Hill (p505) on St Kitts. Although they won this battle, they lost the war and the 1783 Treaty of Paris brought the island firmly under British control. During this era sugar plantations thrived on the islands.

Nevis had a colonial history similar to St Kitts. In 1628 Warner sent a party of about 100 colonists to establish a British settlement on the west coast of the island. Although the original settlement, near Cotton Ground, fell to an earthquake in 1680, Nevis eventually developed one of the most affluent plantation societies in the Eastern Caribbean. As on St Kitts, most of the island's wealth was built upon the labor of African slaves who toiled in the island's sugarcane fields.

By the late 18th century, Nevis, buoyed by the attraction of its thermal baths, had become a major retreat for Britain's rich and famous.

In 1816 the British linked St Kitts and Nevis with Anguilla and the Virgin Islands as a sin-

---

**HOW MUCH?**

- **Cold Carib beer** EC$5
- **Exotic fruits growing wild** Free
- **Two-tank dive** US$85
- **Visit to Alexander Hamilton's birthplace** US$5
- **Night in a historic plantation inn** US$200+

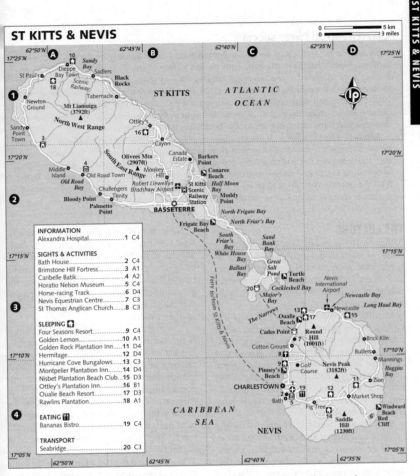

## ST KITTS & NEVIS

**INFORMATION**

| | |
|---|---|
| Alexandra Hospital | 1 C4 |

**SIGHTS & ACTIVITIES**

| | |
|---|---|
| Bath House | 2 C4 |
| Brimstone Hill Fortress | 3 A1 |
| Caribelle Batik | 4 A2 |
| Horatio Nelson Museum | 5 C4 |
| Horse-racing Track | 6 D4 |
| Nevis Equestrian Centre | 7 C3 |
| St Thomas Anglican Church | 8 C3 |

**SLEEPING**

| | |
|---|---|
| Four Seasons Resort | 9 C4 |
| Golden Lemon | 10 A1 |
| Golden Rock Plantation Inn | 11 D4 |
| Hermitage | 12 D4 |
| Hurricane Cove Bungalows | 13 C3 |
| Montpelier Plantation Inn | 14 D4 |
| Nisbet Plantation Beach Club | 15 D3 |
| Ottley's Plantation Inn | 16 B1 |
| Oualie Beach Resort | 17 D3 |
| Rawlins Plantation | 18 A1 |

**EATING**

| | |
|---|---|
| Bananas Bistro | 19 C4 |

**TRANSPORT**

| | |
|---|---|
| Seabridge | 20 C3 |

gle colony. In 1958 these islands became part of the West Indies Federation, a grand but ultimately unsuccessful attempt to combine all of Britain's Caribbean colonies as a united political entity. When the federation dissolved in 1962, the British opted to lump St Kitts, Nevis and Anguilla together as a new state. Anguilla, fearful of domination by larger St Kitts, revolted against the occupying Royal St Kitts Police Force in 1967 and returned to Britain as an overseas territory.

In 1983 St Kitts and Nevis became a single nation within the British Commonwealth, with the stipulation that wary Nevis could secede at any time. A period of corruption on St Kitts and pro-independence on Nevis in the 1990s almost brought an end to the federa-tion. Nevis – a major offshore tax haven – now has an economy stronger than that of its larger neighbor. This, coupled with the constant ir-ritation of having only three members in the 11-member governing assembly, may cause Nevis to hit the eject button soon.

St Kitts and Nevis is one of the 54 mem-bers of the Commonwealth and still retains a governor-general, appointed by the ruling monarch of Britain. The buck actually stops at the prime minister, who is the leader of the ruling political party, which at present is the center-left Labour Party. In its foreign relations, the region's smallest country has proven itself wily: by remaining one of the last nations to recognize Taiwan it has reaped benefits from the Taiwanese such as donated police cars.

**A BITTER END TO SWEET SUCCESS**

Sugar and slaves built St Kitts and Nevis. But the course of the industry on the islands diverged early on. French attacks in the early 18th century collapsed the sugar industry on Nevis and it never fully recovered. Many plantation families left and small plots of land were distributed to slaves freed at emancipation. On St Kitts, however, the plantations continued right up until 2005. In fact as you drive around the island, you will be struck by mile after mile of cane fields growing wild. Distribution to the masses, replacement by time-share condos, more golf courses – these are just some of the options for the land being debated now.

Although it had struggled for decades, time was finally called for the sugar industry on St Kitts by the EU, which moved to eliminate its huge subsidies and price supports. Its legacy is easily seen today. Besides the wild cane fields and abandoned mills that dot the land, there's the legacy of billions of British cavities and rotted teeth. St Kitts sugar was gobbled up in sweets as fast as it hit the English piers. On St Kitts, many of the former cane-field workers now work as security guards, protecting against those former workers who've yet to find jobs.

## THE CULTURE

Although the population is predominantly (90%) of African descent, culturally the islands draw upon a mix of European, African and West Indian traditions. Architecture is mainly British in style and cricket is the national sport.

St Kitts, more than Nevis, still feels like a place where people live and work, rather than just a tourist spot. Walk through a residential area on St Kitts on any given night and most residents will be out in the streets, listening to reggae or calypso blaring out of homes and chatting with friends. On weekend nights, many villages on Nevis have communal barbecues.

St Kitts and Nevis have an interesting mixture of leniency and propriety. You can get fined for using foul language in public, but you can drink while driving (note that doesn't mean you can drive drunk!), so keep an eye out on the road at night. Swimwear should be restricted to the beach and pool areas of resorts.

## ENVIRONMENT

Both islands have grassy coastal areas, a consequence of deforestation for sugar production. Forests tend to be vestiges of the large rainforests which once covered much of the islands, or they are second-growth.

Fairly narrow, darkish beaches are found around both islands but they are by no means ringed with sand. Away from developed areas, the climate allows a huge array of beautiful plants to thrive. Flowers such as plumeria, hibiscus and chains-of-love are common along roadsides and in garden landscaping.

Nevis is fairly circular and the entire island benefits from runoff from Nevis Peak. St Kitts' shape resembles a tadpole. The main body is irrigated by water from the mountain ranges. However, this is of little value to the geographically isolated, arid southeast peninsula which is covered with sparse, desertlike cacti and yucca.

The most popular wildlife on the islands is the skittish vervet monkey. Imported by French settlers from Africa, these monkeys can now be seen fairly regularly all over both islands. Even more ubiquitous is the mongoose, imported by plantation owners to curb rats from munching on their sugarcane (luckily for the nocturnal rats, mongooses hunt during the day, and rarely the twain did meet). Both islands provide plenty of avian life for bird-watchers.

Reefs around the two islands face the same threats as elsewhere in the region. On St Kitts, some of the best reefs ring the southeast peninsula. A new project is underway to limit the range of feral goats, whose overgrazing leads to increased runoff of reef-killing silt and organic matter.

## FOOD & DRINK

Excellent fresh fish is the norm on St Kitts and Nevis. From exotic shellfish to mild and succulent varieties of white fish, the denizens of the deep do their best to feed locals and visitors alike. Piquant stews are popular locally while many beachside joints serve simple preparations like grilled lobster to appreciative crowds.

Beef, chicken, goat and other meats are also common, especially in the simple eateries that can be found by wandering the side streets of Basseterre. Look for pepperpot, a rich stew with as many recipes as cooks. Excellent restaurants with creative menus can be found right across both islands. Of special note are the many plantation inns which serve romantic candle-lit dinners under the stars.

Tap water is safe to drink everywhere on the islands. Cane Spirit Rothschild, more commonly known as CSR, is a clear sugarcane spirit distilled on St Kitts. CSR is often served on the rocks with Ting, a popular grapefruit-flavored soft drink. Refreshing Ginseng Up and a crisp lager, Carib beer, are also bottled on St Kitts.

# ST KITTS

St Kitts definitely has a beat, and it's not just the one blasting from the many minibuses hauling folks hither and yon. Basseterre is a fascinating place to wander and it is still very much the commercial heart of the island. Locals bustle shop to shop making their purchases and there's only a bit of compromise offered for tourists and that's at the cruise-ship dock.

To the south on the arid peninsula, the island's best beaches have attracted both crowds of visitors and developers. The area around Frigate Bay is thick with condos and resorts. It's also thick with a lively band of beach joints on the west side, many of which rock on until well after midnight.

Around the main part of the island, abandoned sugar-cane fields climb hills dotted with plantation inns and sleepy villages. In the northwest, the country's one Unesco World Heritage site, Brimstone Hill Fortress National Park, preserves a vast 18th-century fort on a stunning hilltop setting.

That everything is slightly shambolic just keeps the island feeling more authentic.

## Getting There & Away
For details on transport options to St Kitts, see p515.

There are ferry services between St Kitts and Nevis; for further information, see p516.

## Getting Around
### BUS
Buses are privately owned minivans and are fairly new. But that doesn't mean they don't zip around the island at breakneck speeds. Decor is sedate but many have names such as 'Mr Strong.' In Basseterre, most leave from the bus stop on Bay Rd. Fares range from EC$2 to EC$6.

Bus service is fairly sporadic and there's no schedule, although buses are generally most plentiful in the early morning and late afternoon. The last bus is usually between 10pm and midnight. To avoid competition with tourist taxis, buses do not normally run to Frigate Bay (or points southeast).

### CAR & SCOOTER
Car-rental agencies:
**Avis** ( ☎ 465-6507, in the US 800-228-0668; Bay Rd, Basseterre)
**Caines Rent a Car** ( ☎ 465-2366; Princes St, Basseterre)
**TDC Auto Rentals** ( ☎ 465-2991; West Independence Sq, Basseterre) Affiliated with Thrifty.

For scooter hire, **Islandwide Scooter Rentals** ( ☎ 466-7841; midasscooter@caribsurf.com) will meet up with you wherever is convenient.

Basseterre has quite a few one-way streets, some of which are not clearly marked. Keep an eye out for road signs, and when in doubt, simply follow the rest of the traffic.

### TAXI
A taxi from the airport costs EC$20 to Basseterre, EC$35 to Frigate Bay, and EC$50 to St Paul's.

From the Circus (the main taxi stand in Basseterre), it costs EC$10 to anywhere within town, EC$20 to Frigate Bay and EC$85 to Brimstone Hill round-trip. Rates are 25% higher between 11pm and 6am. There's an EC$3 charge for each 15 minutes of waiting. To call a taxi, dial ☎ 465-4253.

## BASSETERRE
### pop 12,800
Keep your distance from the cruise-ship port and plunge into this heady mix of commerce and culture. Nothing in the capital has been overly gussied up, which means that surprises abound. Shops have names like 'Bold, Black & Beautiful.' Take time to pick out the surviving colonial buildings with their white porches; nod to folks lounging on their stoops, Carib in hand. If nothing else, you should buy a local a beer in thanks for not turning feral at the hordes of tubby tourists clogging the streets near the port.

## Information

Basseterre is a flop when it comes to buying books. Your best bet is the pot-boilers on offer at the Marriott Resort in Frigate Bay.

A number of international banks and ATMs can be found around the Circus.

**City Drug Store** ( ☎ 465-2156; Bank St; ☧ 8am-7pm Mon-Sat, to 11am Sun) Pharmacy; also sells magazines and newspapers.

**JNF General** ( ☎ 465-2551; ☧ 24hr) The main hospital on St Kitts is at the west end of Cayon St.

**NR Services** ( ☎ 466-5925; Bay Rd; ☧ 8am-7:30pm Mon-Sat, 11am-5pm Sun) Internet access (per minute EC$0.25), internet calling, public phones and phonecards.

**Philatelic Bureau** (Pelican Mall, Bay Rd) Colorful commemorative stamps are sold here, next door to the post office.

**Post office** ( ☎ 465-2521; Bay Rd; ☧ 8am-4pm Mon & Tue, to 3:30pm Wed-Fri) Next to Pelican Mall. Postcards to the US/Europe cost EC$0.80/1.20.

**St Kitts Tourism Authority** ( ☎ 465-4040; www.stkittstourism.kn; Pelican Mall, Bay Rd; ☧ 8am-5pm Mon-Fri) Small office that can answer questions.

## Sights

The focus of town is the **Circus**, a circular intersection surrounded by quaint buildings and storm-ravaged palms. In the center is a non-working fountain that continues the theme of tropically accented Georgian splendor.

One block east, **Independence Square** is a scruffy park surrounded by some real architectural gems like the battered old beauty on the northwest corner. Once called Pall Mall Sq, it was used in the 1790s for slave auctions. On the east side, **Immaculate Conception Cathedral** has an austere interior that belies the ornamented facade dating from 1928.

Wander the streets west to the imposing bulk of **St George's Anglican Church**, which dates from 1869 and is the fourth church built on this site. The French built the first one, called – you guessed it – Notre Dame, in 1670.

Head down to the water to the 1894 colonial **Treasury Building**. Its imposing form topped by a dome is a sign of the importance the British Empire placed on the plantations of St Kitts. Inside, the **National Museum** ( ☎ 465-5584; adult/child EC$5/free; ☧ 9am-5pm Mon-Fri, to 1pm Sat) has a gaggle of displays of widely varying quality on the 2nd floor. The historic displays do a good job of capturing some of the island's dramatic events. Just below, the gift shop has a few knick-knacks and some books.

Just beyond Cayon St, **Warner Park Stadium** ( ☎ 466-2007; office ☧ 8.30am-4.30pm Mon-Fri) shines after a massive refurbishment for the 2007 Cricket World Cup. Stop by to find out if any test matches are scheduled.

## Activities

**Pro-Divers** ( ☎ 466-3483; www.prodiversstkitts.com; Basseterre) offers single-tank boat dives without equipment for US$60, two-tank dives for US$85, night dives for US$80, a three-day Professional Association of Diving Instructors (PADI) certification course for US$400 and a half-day snorkeling trip for US$40. Equipment is available for rent. It's located at the Ocean Terrace Inn's Fisherman's Wharf.

**Kenneth's Dive Centre** ( ☎ 465-2670; kdcsk@yahoo.com; Bay Rd) is on the east side of Basseterre and offers similar services and rates.

## Sleeping

Most people will opt for something near the beaches but there's a certain energy to staying in town.

**Seaview Guest House** ( ☎ 466-5298; www.seaviewinnsk.com; Bay Rd; s/d from US$62/75; ☒ ) Conveniently located opposite the harborfront and the ferry terminal, the Seaview has 10 rooms that are simple and clean, with private bathrooms. While away your trip on the flower-covered veranda.

**Trinity Inn Apartments** ( ☎ 465-3226; www.trinityinnapartments.com; apt US$80; ☒ ) Four miles west of Basseterre, at Palmetto Point, is this two-story modern apartment block. The 10 one-bedroom units have kitchens and a timeless, basic decor.

**Palms Hotel** ( ☎ 465-0800; www.palmshotel.com; the Circus; ste US$85-180; ☒ ☐ ) Rooms in this rambling wooden colonial building overlooking the Circus are popular with business travelers. All 12 are large and won't challenge the blandest of expectations. The location is the best feature. Offers wi-fi.

**Ocean Terrace Inn** ( ☎ 465-2754, in the US 800-524-0512; www.oceanterraceinn.com; Wigley Ave; r US$165-325; ☒ ☐ ☒ ) Elegant and dignified, this 71-unit hotel sprawls over a hillside overlooking the harbor. It stops just short of being idiosyncratic (although the cannons on the roof qualify) and has a range of rooms and pools. Nos 30 to 43 are fronted by a broad lawn and are the most restful. Get a room near reception or the pool bar for the best wi-fi experience. There's not much else here

# BASSETERRE

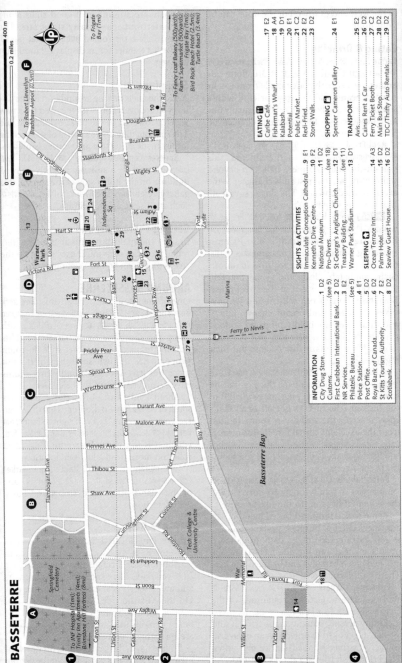

**0** _____ 400 m
**0** _____ 0.2 miles

To Frigate Bay (1mi)

To Robert Llewellyn Bradshaw Airport (0.5mi)

To Fancy Loaf Bakery (500yards); Ram's Supermarket (500yards); Frigate Bay (1mi); Bird Rock Beach Hotel (2.5mi); Turtle Beach (3.4mi)

To JNF Hospital (1mi); Trinity Inn Apartments (4mi); Brimstone Hill Fortress (8mi)

**INFORMATION**
| | |
|---|---|
| City Drug Store | 1 D2 |
| Customs | (see 5) |
| First Caribbean International Bank | 2 D2 |
| NR Services | 3 E2 |
| Philatelic Bureau | (see 5) |
| Police Station | 4 E1 |
| Post Office | 5 D2 |
| Royal Bank of Canada | 6 D2 |
| St Kitts Tourism Authority | 7 E2 |
| Scotiabank | 8 D2 |

**SIGHTS & ACTIVITIES**
| | |
|---|---|
| Immaculate Conception Cathedral | 9 E1 |
| Kenneth's Dive Centre | 10 F2 |
| National Museum | 11 D2 |
| Pro-Divers | (see 18) |
| St George's Anglican Church | 12 D1 |
| Treasury Building | (see 11) |
| Warner Park Stadium | 13 D1 |

**SLEEPING**
| | |
|---|---|
| Ocean Terrace Inn | 14 A3 |
| Palms Hotel | 15 D2 |
| Seaview Guest House | 16 D2 |

**EATING**
| | |
|---|---|
| Caribe Café | 17 E2 |
| Fisherman's Wharf | 18 A4 |
| Kalabash | 19 D1 |
| Potential | 20 E1 |
| Public Market | 21 C2 |
| Redi-Fried | 22 E2 |
| Stone Walls | 23 D2 |

**SHOPPING**
| | |
|---|---|
| Spencer Cameron Gallery | 24 E1 |

**TRANSPORT**
| | |
|---|---|
| Avis | 25 E2 |
| Caines Rent a Car | 26 D2 |
| Ferry Ticket Booth | 27 C2 |
| Main Bus Stop | 28 D2 |
| TDC/Thrifty Auto Rentals | 29 D2 |

at the west end of town but the hotel can fill your hours.

## Eating & Drinking

**Caribe Café** ( ☎ 465-5282; The Sands, Bay Rd; snacks EC$5; ☺ 8am-9pm) Climb up to this 3rd-floor café and enjoy a superb coffee made from locally roasted beans, use the wi-fi or chill with a sublime iced tea. Baked goods are equally fine and the views over the water may distract you from your laptop.

**Redi-Fried** ( ☎ 465-1301; Bay Rd; meals EC$11; ☺ 10am-midnight) Next to the cinema, this hole-in-the-wall is a mere half-step beyond stall-status, but that just adds character to the excellent fried chicken. The slogan says it all: 'We're ready when you're ready.'

**our pick** **Stone Walls** ( ☎ 465-5248; Princes St; meals US$11-50; ☺ breakfast, lunch & dinner Mon-Sat) Basseterre's best restaurant is also its most appealing. Surrounded by its namesake walls, the open-air dining area features luxurious chairs, white tablecloths and a small fountain that takes the spikes out of the street noise. Breakfasts range from saltfish and johnny-cakes to bagels and cream cheese. Lunch and dinner feature boldly prepared seafood and steaks. The bar provides just the right lubrication and many diners close out their night here.

**Kalabash** ( ☎ 466-2398; Cayon St; meals from EC$12; ☺ 8am-8pm Sun-Fri) Don't let the fascinating screed about what the pilgrims *really* did to the Indians (the turkeys got off easy) that's splayed across the wall divert your attention from the excellent casual fare in this narrow café. Salads, veggie curries, falafel sandwiches and luscious baked goods will have you shouting in the streets.

**Potential** ( ☎ 475-8373; Pond Rd; mains EC$15-50; ☺ 8am-8pm) A totally open-air corner café, the Potential lives up to the full promise of its name with a long and varied menu of salads, local curries, burgers, pasta and more. It gets extra credit for its daily blackboard of specials that can include local faves like crushed green bananas and breaded chicken. There's a full bar too.

**Fisherman's Wharf** ( ☎ 465-2754; meals US$20-30; ☺ dinner) The waterfront restaurant of the Ocean Terrace Inn is a fun place. Dinners, including freshly caught snapper fillet and lobster, are cooked to order over an open grill and accompanied by a self-service side buffet. The Friday fish fries are always jammed.

There are a number of good stalls along the waterfront selling tasty street fare. The green-walled, tin-roofed **public market** (Bay Rd) is worth a wander for its displays of local fruit and veg.

## Shopping

Avoid the malls lurking around Port Zante unless you are overcome with the need for a new watch. However, in the plaza behind the Old Treasury Building, there's a strip of stalls selling locally made crafts that are worth a browse.

**Spencer Cameron Gallery** ( ☎ 465-1617; 10 N Independence Sq) In a suitably brightly colored building on the north side of the square, this gallery celebrates the works of local artists such as Rosey Cameron Smith.

## Getting There & Around

Besides the main bus stop at the ferry terminal, you can stop minibuses going up the coasts on Cayon St and Wellington Rd.

## AROUND BASSETERRE

One of the island's better bargains, **Bird Rock Beach Hotel** ( ☎ 465-8914; www.birdrockbeach.com; Bird Rock; r from US$90; ✕ ▯ ▣ ), is 3 miles south along the shoreline from Basseterre. This well-maintained older motel-style 46-room property has its own small beach. It's not fancy but it is affordable and many rooms have ocean views from the balconies.

About 1 mile east of Basseterre, 0.5 miles south of where Bay Rd dead-ends into S Pelican Dr, your nose may lead you right to **Fancy Loaf Bakery** ( ☎ 465-5415; S Pelican Rd; ☺ 8am-5pm Mon-Sat), which sells top-notch bread, muffins, filled rolls and more from a low-end location.

Just north of Bay Rd, **Ram's Supermarket** ( ☎ 466-6065; S Pelican Dr; ☺ 8am-8pm) is one of the island's best food stores and has a wide selection.

## FRIGATE BAY

Frigate Bay, located 3 miles southeast of Basseterre, is an isthmus with the calm Caribbean-side Frigate Bay Beach on one (the west) side. Here you'll find the sun chairs and water-sports gear for rent during the day. On the Atlantic side, there are resorts and condos, although north of the Marriott the beach remains wild and uncrowded. Condos are sprouting everywhere.

Frigate Bay is the center for resort development on St Kitts and you know you're getting close by the blight of jewelry-store billboards lining the road. The area has several good restaurants but the real highlight is the dozens of beach bars lining the placid bayside sands. Many serve excellent food, others party all night.

Buses generally don't run to Frigate Bay, so if you don't have your own rental car you'll have to plan on doing some hefty walking or rely on taxis.

## Activities

For diving trips and equipment hire, try **Frigate Bay Divers** ( ☎ 466-8413; enquiry@frigatebay divers.com; Frigate Beach).

**Mr X's Watersports** ( ☎ 465-4995; www.mrxwater sports.com), near the Timothy Beach Resort, hires snorkel equipment for US$10 a day and also offers a snorkeling tour from US$25. It also rents Sunfish and Hobie Cat sailboats for US$20 to US$30 an hour, offers water skiing for US$15 a circuit, and provides a shuttle to South Friar's Bay for US$5 round-trip. Unlimited snorkeling, sailing, windsurfing, kayaking and boogie boarding for one day is available for US$60, or four days for US$150.

## Sleeping

The following places all offer wi-fi access.

**Frigate Bay Resort** ( ☎ 465-8935; www.frigatebay .com; r US$100-200; ❄ 🖳 🖭 ) Located on a knoll slightly above Frigate Bay Beach, this low-key place has 64 good-sized rooms and apartments wrapped around a sunny pool area. It's always worth spending the extra US$40 or so a night for the poolside view as the 'hillside' view can mean 'road' view. There's wi-fi at the bar.

**Timothy Beach Resort** ( ☎ 465-8597, in the US & Canada 800-288-7991; www.timothybeachresort.com; r US$120-250; ❄ 🖳 🖭 ) The best deal in Frigate Bay, this simple 60-unit low-rise hotel has rooms and apartments in several sizes which sleep up to six people. The cheapest rooms face the hill, most others have large balconies with sunset views. This is the closest place to the joys of Frigate Bay Beach.

**St Kitts Marriott Resort** ( ☎ 466-1200; www.mar riott.com; 858 Frigate Bay Rd; r from US$175; ❄ 🖳 🖭 ) Utterly out of scale from the rest of Frigate Bay, we hope nothing else comes along to dwarf it. This 513-room behemoth is the one major resort on the island and comes with every sort of activity and service. It also comes with plenty of opportunities to buy Marriott's time-share condos. Look for big discounts on the web.

**SeaLofts** ( ☎ 465-1075; www.sealofts.com; units US$200-360; ❄ 🖳 🖭 ) For two couples sharing, the two-bedroom two-level townhouse-style units here are good value. Each is a condo so decor can vary widely but all have balconies, cable TV, kitchens and wi-fi. The best have good views of the waves on the Atlantic Ocean. It's on the beach, and there are two tennis courts and a pool.

## Eating & Drinking
### BEACH BARS

The string of joints on the sand on Frigate Bay Beach should be a top destination no matter where you stay on St Kitts. Styles vary: at some your feet are in the sand and at others you're at a real table in an open-sided pavilion. At all the mood is just plain happy. Hours are as casual as the vibe – some close at 10pm, others at dawn.

**Mr X's Shiggidy Shack** ( ☎ 663-3983; meals from EC$32) Lanterns on battered picnic tables on the sand create the ambience at this very popular joint on the south end of the strip. Most opt for the tasty grilled lobster (EC$72). On many nights bands hook up to the generator and jam, on others, karaoke drives many to drink (more).

**Monkey Bar** ( ☎ 465-8050; meals from EC$40) The tables here are elevated above the sand and even feature tablecloths – that still doesn't mean anybody is wearing shoes. You can work up your own puns in relation to the signature drink, the Magnetic Monkey, although it does have appeal. Presiding over the cheery crowds chowing on grilled seafood and ribs is famed ex-boxer Roy Gumbs.

**Ziggy's** ( ☎ 662-3104; meals from EC$35) The party starts early at this jamming shack and goes late. Always a must-stop when bar-hopping across the sand.

### RESTAURANTS

The Atlantic side of the Frigate Bay development has several excellent restaurants. Although not the bacchanals of the bayside, they are wonderfully casual.

**PJ's Pizza Bar & Restaurant** ( ☎ 465-8373; mains from EC$30; 🕐 dinner Tue-Sun) Everything is fresh, from the pasta to the pizza, at this bistro run by two talented Canadians. The deceptively simple exterior gives little hint of the bold flavors within.

**Rock Lobster** ( ☎ 466-1092; mains US$15-40; 🕐 dinner Thu-Tue) Like the clam shells, you'll be clappin' for the Mediterranean-style seafood and tapas dishes at this relaxed open-sided patio and bar. Start with a plate of crispy calamari, follow up with the silky lobster bisque or maybe hold off for the namesake menu star. Just remember: watch out for that piranha!

## SOUTHEAST PENINSULA

St Kitts' southeast peninsula is a scrubby wild plain filled with expansive white-sand beaches, grassy hills, barren salt ponds and the occasional meandering cow. However, this is changing as condos begin to sprout along the beaches. Meanwhile, there still are some beaches that offer the kinds of idyllic escape that brought you to the Caribbean in the first place.

Heading south on the main road, which runs for 8 miles from Frigate Bay, you cross over a hill with good views back to Frigate Bay and hit the narrowest part of the isthmus. To the east, a dirt path takes you to the beach on **South Friar's Bay**, a calm bay with a refreshingly uncluttered beach and a couple of beach bars.

On the Atlantic side, the beach on **North Friar's Bay** is utterly wild, with stiff swells and not so much as a cold-beer vendor in sight. Park along the road and search out one of the narrow trails for access. There's good hiking throughout the area.

Further on, the road curves around the **Great Salt Pond**; watch the sides of the road for the island's greatest concentrations of green vervet monkeys. Look for the narrow track to the south (left) that leads to **Cockleshell Bay**, a gray-sand beach with a stunning view of Nevis.

Follow the signs down a dirt track for the **Reggae Beach Bar** ( ☎ 762-5050; Cockleshell Beach; meals from US$13; ❂ 10am-dusk), a sprawling beach bar that's a destination for day-tripping cruise-shippers. Burgers and conch fritters are big, as is the cocktail list. The staff are charmers, although they take a dim view of the conniving monkeys out to steal your lunch. There are free beach chairs, as well as snorkeling gear (US$10), kayaks (US$20) and more for rent.

At the west end of the beach, **Lion Rock Beach Bar** (meals US$15; ❂ 10am-dusk) is a low-key alternative. Feast on platters of fresh fish or ribs in between volleyball matches.

## AROUND NORTHERN ST KITTS

The green hills and abandoned cane fields spill down the mountains right to the shore

all around the main part of St Kitts. Circling the northern part of the island is a must, the only real decision you face is 'which way?' The entire circuit is about 35 miles and, with various stops and lunch at one of the plantation houses, can easily fill a day. Lunch may well be the deciding factor: if you get going early (say before 10am) start with the sight-heavy west coast, which will put you at the lunch spots on the far north and east coasts at about midday. Otherwise, with a late start, head first around the east, find some tasty food and then, well-sated, hit the sights in the west.

Rental car is the best way to make this trip. You can use minibuses but they stick to the main coast road and many of the places you want to visit are a hike inland. Without a car you can also take a tour (there are many) or hire a driver.

One interesting tour involves the **St Kitts Scenic Railway** ( ☎ 465-7263; www.stkittsscenicrailway .com; Bay Rd, Basseterre; adult/child from US$100/50), which follows the tracks of the old narrow-gauge sugar railway that circled the island. Sadly, the train only runs on 18 miles of the tracks along the east and north coasts. The other 12 miles is by bus, but this lets the attraction sell tickets in both directions.

Passengers ride in custom double-decker cars. You can sightsee from the open-sided upper deck or kick back with rum punch on the air-con lower deck. The tour takes three hours in total and schedules vary depending on when cruise ships are due. The station is a three-minute walk south of the airport.

### West Coast

About 4 miles west of Basseterre, look for **Bloody Point**, the site where more than 2000 native Caribs were massacred by joint British and French forces in 1626. Legend has it the place received its name because so much blood was spilled – it ran for three days straight.

After Bloody Point the road swings down to the seaside village of **Old Road Town**, the landing site of the first British settlers in 1623. On a narrow sliver between the road and the sea, **Sprat Net Bar & Grill** ( ☎ 465-6314; Old Road Bay; meals from EC$60; ❂ dinner Wed-Sun) is a popular place starting at sunset. A festive mix of visitors and locals chow down on succulent grilled lobster and ribs.

Just above Old Road Town, the 17th-century Romney Manor sugar estate has been turned into **Caribelle Batik** ( ☎ 465-6253;

⊗ 8:30am-4pm Mon-Fri), which has a small workshop where you can watch the colorful fabric being made (and buy some in the form of T-shirts etc). The grounds feature lush formal gardens.

The short drive to the batik shop is a history lesson in itself. Immediately past the nursery school on Wingfield Rd are several large black stones with **petroglyphs** left by Amerindians. The road then passes the ruins of a mill and goes through a vestige of rainforest before it reaches the old estate.

## Brimstone Hill Fortress National Park

Imposing **Brimstone Hill Fortress** ( ☎ 465-2609; foreign visitors adult/child US$8/4; ⊗ 9:30am-5:30pm) is the historical highlight of any visit to St Kitts and has been recognized by Unesco. Far larger than you'd think, this vast old military stronghold offers a personal glimpse into the violent and tumultuous past of the former Caribbean colonies.

The rambling 18th-century compound, which in its day was nicknamed the 'Gibraltar of the West Indies,' is one of the largest forts in the Caribbean. As a major British garrison, Brimstone Hill played a key role in battles with the French, who seized the fort in 1782 after the 1000 British soldiers inside were besieged for 30 days by 8000 French troops. The British regained it through the Treaty of Paris the following year and by the 1850s the fort was abandoned.

After a fire swept through Basseterre in 1867, some of the fort structures were partially dismantled and the stones used to rebuild the capital. In the 1960s major restoration was undertaken, and much of the fortress has been returned to its earlier grandeur. Queen Elizabeth II inaugurated the fort as a national park during her visit to St Kitts in October 1985. There is an excellent small museum as well as good displays scattered throughout the complex. The US$5 audioguide is worthwhile.

The main hilltop compound, the **Citadel**, is lined with 24 cannons and provides excellent views of Sint Eustatius and Sandy Point Town. Inside the Citadel's old barrack rooms are displays on colonial history that do a fine job of documenting life back in the day. In one hilarious cartoon, an enlisted man offers commentary on an officer who's just had a poop.

Also worthwhile is the short stroll above the cookhouse to the top of Monkey Hill, which provides excellent coastal views. A small theater next to the gift shop plays a brief video on the fort's history; a nearby canteen sells drinks and sandwiches.

Brimstone Hill, upon which the fortress stands, is an 800ft volcanic cone named for the odoriferous sulfur vents you will undoubtedly detect as you drive past the hill along the coastal road.

There's a good little café near the parking area. Winsome cats will appreciate any donation.

There is a 2-mile steep and winding uphill drive to the fort from the main coast road. Parking is near most of the important sights. If you want to use public transportation, minibuses from Basseterre to Sandy Point Town can drop you off where the access road meets the coast road. From there it's an energetic walk up to the fort.

## North Coast

As you continue from Brimstone Hill Fortress, you'll pass through **Newton Ground**, a long and bustling town strung along the main road. This part of the island is slated for tourism development and plans call for a golf course, condos, a strip mall or two and undoubtedly a Starbucks. The lowlands are covered with abandoned sugar-cane fields that run up the hills to **Mt Liamuiga**, the 3792ft volcano that dominates the island's interior.

Driving along the north coast, about 2 miles past Newton Ground, you encounter **St Paul's**, a former village of cane workers that retains its rural charm and has a couple of cute groceries for refreshments.

A half a mile east, look for signs that take you up through the cane fields on a 1-mile dirt road to **Rawlins Plantation** ( ☎ 465-6221; www.rawlins plantation.com; r from US$300; ⊠ ▢ ⊠ ), a former sugar estate that is among the most gracious of St Kitts' plantation inns. Accommodation is in comfortable cottages with wooden floors, four-poster beds and separate sitting rooms or verandas. Rates include breakfast and afternoon tea. This is an excellent stop for lunch on your tour of the island. There's a lavish and creative West Indian buffet (US$30) which you can enjoy from the tables on the broad veranda with views down to the coast and beyond to Sint Eustatius. At night, dinner (mains US$35 to US$50) features a creative menu of the expected seafood plus chicken and beef. Many of the seasonings are grown in the kitchen garden. The inn offers wi-fi.

Just west of the plantation, longtime local artist **Kate Spencer** ( ☎ 465-7740; www.katedesign .com; ☽ 11am-5pm) has a dream studio-gallery that enjoys fine views out to sea. Spencer's work embraces a variety of styles, and the results range from lush to stark. Prints of her evocative scenes of island life are a comparative bargain as are the postcards made from old island photos (EC$10).

The coast roads continues to the village of **Dieppe Bay**. The open Atlantic is east and the surf can often be spectacular. There are frequent thin strands of grey-sand beach.

Right in town, the **Golden Lemon** ( ☎ 465-7260; www.goldenlemon.com; r from US$200, villas from US$325; ☐ ☒ ) is a vision in yellow right down to the color of the walls and the hibiscus flowers. If you like the idea of staying at a historic property but want to be at the beach, this fits both bills. Each room in the 17th-century manor house is decorated differently. A long porch lined with proper, comfy wooden chairs looks across the small lawn to the surf. An adjoining villa has rooms and apartments that are modern and posh. The common areas have wi-fi. The restaurant in the manor house serves up tasty casual lunches (mains US$9 to US$20) that include salads, burgers, sandwiches and seafood. Dinner is more elaborate with a changing set four-course menu (US$35 to US$60). Reserve in advance for dinner.

### East Coast

Much of the east coast is thinly populated. Endless fields of sugar cane wave in the trade winds, never to decay a tooth again. The constant rustle of the leaves and the underlying roar of the surf are punctuated by the calls of songbirds. Signs reading 'Disasters… Swift, Sudden, Deadly. Let's get ready now!!!' add a sense of foreboding (we assume they mean hurricanes, but…).

At the south end of Sadlers, look for an old stone church down in the cane fields. There is a small melancholy cemetery; shortly beyond that a sign points to **Black Rocks**. A short drive down that side road ends at coastal cliffs and a view of some seaside lava rock formations. The cliffs are only a five-minute walk from the circle-island road.

Just north of Ottley's village, the coast road passes under a long stretch of beautiful mature plumeria trees. About a mile up a bumpy track above town, look for

**Ottley's Plantation Inn** ( ☎ 465-7234, in the US 800-772-3039; www.ottleys.com; r from US$300, cottages from US$500; ☒ ☐ ☒ ) A carefully manicured lawn fronts the 24 rooms scattered about in historic buildings and villas (some with plunge pools). 'Spot of croquet, old bean?' will seem appropriate in these gracious surrounds which include a high-end spa. Guests enjoy breakfast in the elegant open-air Royal Palm Restaurant, which makes a mean banana pancake. Lunch (US$12 to US$40) is popular with those touring the island. Choices include lobster wraps and excellent, inventive sandwiches. Dinner (three courses US$66) is a more formal affair with fine steaks and seafood.

Just below Ottley's village, you may notice what appears to be a high-security old sugar mill. Signs reveal that it is not the HQ of Dr No but rather a research facility doing experiments on the local monkeys. No wonder the simians favor the remote southeast peninsula.

# NEVIS

Nevis (nay-vis) is a smaller, neater version of St Kitts. It combines history, beauty and beaches in one tidy package; many – especially the locals – prefer it to its larger sibling. The only road of importance circles the island and you can make the circuit in a couple of hours. Stop to see the sights and have lunch at a plantation house and it can take all day.

There are good hikes in the hills and plenty of water sports at the beaches, which, like the rest of Nevis, are just large enough to suffice. Many people visit Nevis as part of a day trip but those in the know stay much longer. Sorting through the sights and activities, there's just enough to add spice to the day but not so much that important rest and relaxation are impeded. (Horatio Nelson fans, however, are likely to be so stimulated that they'll feel like they've died and been pickled in a barrel of brandy.)

The island's forested interior rises to scenic Nevis Peak, which is often cloaked in clouds. The coastal lowlands, where the larger villages are located, are much drier and support bougainvillea, hibiscus and other flowering bushes that attract numerous hummingbirds. It's a beautiful place.

## Getting There & Away

For details on transport options to Nevis, see p515.

There are ferry services between Nevis and St Kitts; for details, see p516.

## Getting Around

### BUS

Buses run south and east from Memorial Sq in Charlestown; there's also no problem catching a minibus north from here. Fare ranges from EC$1 to EC$5. The service almost circles the island except for a short stretch between Mannings and Zion.

### CAR & SCOOTER

Car-rental agencies:

**Nevis Car Rental** ( ☎ 469-9837; Newcastle).
**Parry's Car Rental** ( ☎ 469-5917; Charlestown).
**TDC Auto Rentals** ( ☎ 469-5690; tdcrentals@caribsurf .com; Bay Rd, Charlestown) Has an office across from the ferry dock; affiliated with Thrifty.

For scooter hire, **Forbes Scooter Rental** ( ☎ 469-2668) will meet up with you wherever is convenient.

### TAXI

Nevis taxi rates include the following: airport to Charlestown and Pinney's Beach hotels US$20, to Montpelier Plantation Inn US$32; from Charlestown to Four Seasons US$10, Oualie Beach Hotel US$15. Service between 10pm to 6am adds 50% extra. For taxis call ☎ 469-1483 or ☎ 469-5631 in Charlestown and ☎ 469-9790 in Newcastle or have your hotel arrange one.

## CHARLESTOWN

**pop 1800**

The ferry from St Kitts docks next to the center of Charlestown, Nevis' cute little capital, where all of the government and business structures coexist with tourist facilities and gingerbread Victorians. It's a fun spot for a stroll and is rarely overcrowded as large cruise ships bypass Nevis. Tourist tat is refreshingly limited.

The greater Charlestown area can be readily explored on foot – the museums and the Bath House are within walking distance. Just a 15-minute jaunt north of the center will put you on a lovely stretch of Pinney's Beach that's lined with coconut trees and invites languid strolls.

## Information

You will find banks north of the tourist office on Main St, including First Caribbean and Scotiabank.

**Alexandra Hospital** ( ☎ 469-5473; Government Rd)
**Chapter 1 Bookstore** ( ☎ 469-0607; Cotton Ginnery Mall) The nation's best bookstore has a small but inspired selection. Also magazines and newspapers.
**Downtown Cybercafé** ( ☎ 469-1999; Main St; internet per 15min US$5, long-distance calls to US or Europe per min EC$1; ☺ 8am-6pm Mon-Sat) Friendly house with laptop connections, CD burning, snacks and drinks.
**Nevis Tourist Office** ( ☎ 469-7550, in the US 866-55-NEVIS; www.nevisisland.com; ☺ 8am-4pm Mon-Fri, 9am-1pm Sat) A two-minute walk east of the pier in the old colonial-era treasury building. It's packed with staff and helpful brochures.
**Philatelic Bureau** ( ☺ 8am-4pm Mon-Fri) Commemorative stamps are sold here, near the public market.
**Post office** ( ☎ 469-5521; Main St; ☺ 8am-3:30pm Mon-Fri)

## Sights & Activities

Occupying a reconstructed Georgian-style building at the site where American statesman Alexander Hamilton was born in 1755, is the **Alexander Hamilton Museum** ( ☎ 469-5786; www.nevis -nhcs.org; Main St; adult/child US$5/2; ☺ 9am-4pm Mon-Fri, to noon Sat). The US founding father was born out of wedlock and there has always been debate about the identity of his father. His childhood (he moved to St Croix in 1765) was tumultuous: death, suicide and abandonment were all factors. Exhibits trace Hamilton's life. Shady grounds offer a lovely picnic or rest spot.

A couple of minutes' walk up Government Rd from the town center is a small and largely forgotten **Jewish cemetery**, which consists of a grassy field of horizontal gravestones. The oldest stone dates from 1679, and quite a few others date from the early 18th century, when an estimated 25% of the nonslave population on Nevis was Jewish. In addition, it's now believed that the site of the original synagogue, which may be the oldest in the Caribbean, has been identified. An ongoing excavation is about 75yd south of the cemetery; to get there, take the dirt path that begins opposite the cemetery's southwest corner and follow it to the **ruins** just beyond the government offices.

The **Horatio Nelson Museum** ( ☎ 469-0408; Building Hill Rd; adult/child US$5/2; ☺ 9am-4pm Mon-Fri, 10am-1pm Sat), about 100yd east of the old Bath House,

ST KITTS & NEVIS

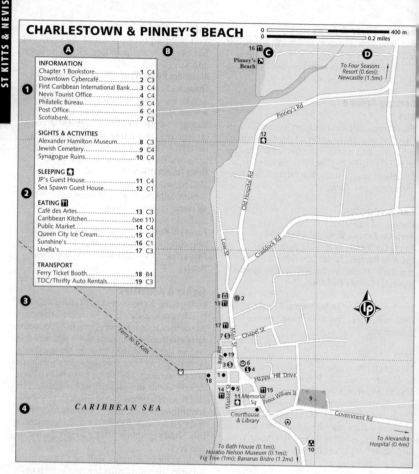

## CHARLESTOWN & PINNEY'S BEACH

0 — 400 m
0 — 0.2 miles

**INFORMATION**
Chapter 1 Bookstore..................1 C4
Downtown Cybercafé..................2 C3
First Caribbean International Bank.....3 C4
Nevis Tourist Office..................4 C4
Philatelic Bureau......................5 C4
Post Office............................6 C4
Scotiabank............................7 C3

**SIGHTS & ACTIVITIES**
Alexander Hamilton Museum..........8 C3
Jewish Cemetery......................9 C4
Synagogue Ruins.....................10 C4

**SLEEPING**
JP's Guest House......................11 C4
Sea Spawn Guest House..............12 C1

**EATING**
Café des Artes.......................13 C3
Caribbean Kitchen..................(see 11)
Public Market........................14 C4
Queen City Ice Cream................15 C4
Sunshine's...........................16 C1
Unella's..............................17 C3

**TRANSPORT**
Ferry Ticket Booth....................18 B4
TDC/Thrifty Auto Rentals............19 C3

Pinney's Beach

To Four Seasons
Resort (0.6mi);
Newcastle (1.5mi)

Pinney's Rd

Old Hospital Rd

Craddock Rd

Low St

Chapel St

Bay Rd

Ferry to St Kitts

*CARIBBEAN SEA*

Happy Hill Drive

Market St

Memorial Sq

Prince William St

Courthouse
& Library

Government Rd

To Bath House (0.1mi);
Horatio Nelson Museum (0.1mi);
Fig Tree (1mi); Bananas Bistro (1.2mi)

To Alexandra
Hospital (0.4mi)

contains memorabilia relating to Lord Nelson, whose fateful visit to the island in 1787 led to his unhappy marriage to Fanny Nisbet, the niece of the island's governor. Among the items on display is a plate from their wedding. It has a crack. Other exhibits relate to local history; there's an excellent selection of Nevis-related books for sale.

The **Bath House** was the first hotel built in the Caribbean, in 1778. Now restored, it is used for government offices. Its name comes from the mineral-laden springs just below. Popular with the spa set in colonial days, it's now a popular spot for locals to take a dip. Although spiffed up, the pools are still a bit rough and you may share your visit with a goat.

## Sleeping

Charlestown is home to the only budget options on Nevis.

**Sea Spawn Guest House** ( ☎ 469-5239; seaspawn@ yahoo.com; r US$50-65; ) Rooms here are simple, clean and less than 0.6 miles from both the town and Pinney's Beach. Rooms upstairs have cable TV and fridges and share a kitchen. Two budget rooms downstairs (EC$100) lack air-con and are 'aimed at older people.'

**JP's Guest House** ( ☎ 469-0319; jpwalters@caribsurf .com; r US$65) Two minutes from the ferry dock, this tidy place is on the 2nd floor of a commercial building. The 10 rooms have fans and fridges and look a bit like your sister's bedroom. The lounge has cable TV.

## Eating

**Queen City Ice Cream** ( ☎ 469-5989; Memorial Sq; cone EC$5; 🕑 11am-7pm) Choose from five or six flavors (coconut, yum!) that go down easy on a hot day.

**Caribbean Kitchen** ( ☎ 469-0572; dishes EC$10-30; 🕑 breakfast & lunch Mon-Sat) The name sums it up nicely: jerk chicken, steamed fish, fungi and more are offered. Other menu items are more prosaic: English breakfasts, burgers, sandwiches etc. This is a local lunchtime fave.

**our pick** **Café des Arts** ( ☎ 469-7098; meals EC$15-30; 🕑 breakfast & lunch Mon-Sat) Right next to the Hamilton museum, this quirky café serves local fare in a quiet garden courtyard shaded by banana trees. Pancakes, omelettes, many salads, paninis and more highlight the menu. Inside the old house there is a two-level gallery with local works.

**Bananas Bistro** ( ☎ 469-1891; mains from US$20; 🕑 dinner Mon-Sat) Perched a bit up the mountain on the ruins of the Hamilton Estate, Bananas is a state of mind not a fruit. Run by Gillian Smith, who also owns the delightful Café des Arts, this hand-built plantation-style house features a veranda that's the perfect place for both for smooth tropical drinks and ambitious Caribbean fusion cuisine. Think guava-barbecued shrimp and marinated tuna fillets. Expect to be happily surprised throughout the evening.

**Unella's** ( ☎ 469-5574; dishes EC$40-60; 🕑 8am-late) A 2nd-floor open-air restaurant, it has good views of the harbor and St Kitts. Dishes range from breakfasts to salads and sandwiches at lunch. At night the grilled seafood is the thing as are the potent drinks from the bar.

The **public market** (Market St; 🕑 7am-4:30pm Mon-Sat) is a great place to feel the fruit, low-hanging or otherwise. Huge bunches of bananas, rosemary, ginger, oranges are sold by local farmers.

## Getting Around

Charlestown is tiny so everything can be reached on foot. Buy tickets for the ferries at the booth located at the pedestrian area in front of the pier.

## PINNEY'S BEACH

Pinney's Beach is a decent stretch of tan sand that runs along the west coast within walking distance of Charlestown. The beach, which is backed almost its entire length by spiky coconut palms (many lost their tops during recent storms), has lovely views of St Kitts across the channel.

Some low-end beach bars coexist happily with a posh resort.

The 196 rooms at the luxury **Four Seasons Resort** ( ☎ 469-1111, in the US 800-332-3442; r from US$800) are discreetly set in low-rise buildings deeply spaced on the lush ground fronting the beach. The decor is a rich blend of muted tropical colors, and each room has a large patio. Amenities are many: three free-form pools, 10 tennis courts, a championship 18-hole golf course, full spa and several restaurants. Rates plummet to 50% in the low season.

Ten minutes' walk north of Charlestown on Pinney's Beach (and 30 seconds south of the Four Seasons) is **Sunshine's** ( ☎ 469-5817; meals US$14-30; 🕑 11am-late), a classic beach joint that's been getting people in a party mood for decades. It's home to the much-hyped Killer Bee, a loaded house punch whose effects are recorded in the hundreds of photos on the walls. The platters of grilled seafood are quite good.

The beach boozer for a new generation, the reggae shack/bar **Chevy's** ( 🕑 3pm-late) gets a good mix of locals and visitors who party 'til late just south of Sunshine's.

## OUALIE BEACH

Oualie Beach takes its name from an Indian word meaning 'beautiful waters', or so they say. It's a long, laid-back strip of gray sand fronted by waters that are indeed beautiful and are generally calm and good for swimming. There is a dive, water-sports and bike shop; you can rent beach chairs and enjoy the views of St Kitts.

Between here and Pinney's Beach, there are many low-rise condos cropping up. About midway, **St Thomas Anglican Church** stares serenely – and stolidly – out to sea. Goats keep the cemetery grounds trimmed.

**Windsurfing Nevis** ( ☎ 469-9682; windsurf@caribsurf .com; Oualie Beach) rents out bikes from US$25 per day. The owner, Winston Crooke, leads the island's mountain-biking team. It also rents out windsurfing boards from US$20 per hour and US$75 a day, and offers beginner lessons for US$55.

**Scuba Safaris** ( ☎ 469-9518; www.scubanevis.com; Oualie Beach) offers single-tank dives for US$65, two-tank dives for US$95, night dives for US$90 and also a half-day snorkeling trip for US$45.

---

**TWIST MY ARM: THE SPOTS THE AUTHORS WANTED TO KEEP SECRET**

On a quiet bit of Nevis coast just south of the airport, **Nisbet Plantation Beach Club** ( ☎ 469-9325; www.nisbetplantation.com; r from US$400; 🈳 💻 🐾 ) is an upscale beach resort on one of the island's nicest *and* least-visited beaches. Rooms have a plantation motif drawn from the site's history: it's the location of the old Nisbet plantation. The family here included Fanny Nisbet, who for little better and mostly worse, married Horatio Nelson on Nevis in 1787. The beachside café is a fine spot for a casual lunch (US$15) with views out to the stormy Atlantic.

---

Perched on a knoll at the north end of Oualie Beach, the accommodations at **Hurricane Cove Bungalows** ( ☎ 469-9462; www.hurricanecove.com; 1-/2-bedroom cottage from US$200/300; 🐾 ) are in 12 angular wooden cottages. Units have sublime views as well as kitchens, porches and ceiling fans. The view from the pool is captivating; snorkeling gear is free.

The family who runs **Oualie Beach Resort** ( ☎ 469-9735; www.oualiebeach.com; r from US$250; 🈳 💻 🐾 ) has been on Nevis for over 350 years. Rooms are scattered about the site in a several low-rise buildings. The architecture is humble but the units are comfortable and well equipped (including wi-fi). The many activities available make this a good spot for anyone who wants the beach as a holiday focus. (Anyone?)

## SOUTH NEVIS

The main circular road crosses the southern part of Nevis between cloud-shrouded Nevis Peak and Saddle Hill, passing through the districts of Fig Tree and Gingerland. This area was the center of Nevis' sugar industry in colonial days, and there are many crumbling sugar-mill stacks to evoke that era. A few of the former plantation estates have been converted into atmospheric inns. The entire area is lush and green; watch for mongooses darting across the road in search of rodents.

As the main road hits the east coast, the population thins out and the sloping, green flatlands – once sugar-cane plantations – run down to the turbulent Atlantic. It's desolate and dramatic. The road itself is much improved and smooth for most of its 22-mile route circling the island.

### Sights & Activities

The following sights are signposted along the main road.

#### ST JOHN'S ANGLICAN CHURCH

St John's, on the main road in the village of Fig Tree, is a stone church that dates from 1680. A copy of the church register, dated March 11, 1787, which records the marriage of Horatio Nelson and Fanny Nisbet, can be found in a glass case at the rear of the church. If you peek beneath the red carpet in the center aisle you'll find a continuous row of tombstones of island notables who died in the 1700s. Note that the Nelson marriage foundered in 1798 when Nelson met the notorious Lady Emma Hamilton.

#### BOTANICAL GARDENS OF NEVIS

Covering 8 acres of land only a few minutes' drive southwest of Montpelier Plantation Inn and just southeast of Charlestown, the **Botanical Gardens of Nevis** ( ☎ 469-3399; adult/child US$10/7; 🕘 9am-4:30pm Mon-Sat) displays an attractive array of tropical greenery, orchid and rose gardens, and a rainforest conservatory. Modern sculpture of varying taste accents the flora. On the grounds is the 1787 restaurant, see p512.

#### HORSE RACING

On the way to Windward Beach is the **horse-racing track**, the setting for a Nevisian pastime that takes place on various holidays during the year. The jockeys train throughout most of the year. Whether you're lucky enough to arrive during a race holiday (contact the tourist office in Charlestown for dates) or you just happen upon a training session at this makeshift track, the view of Windward Beach in the background is stunning.

To get there, turn south at the Gingerland post office in Market Shop and follow the signs.

#### WINDWARD BEACH

Windward Beach, also known as Indian Castle Beach, is the only easily accessible beach on the southern part of the island. Backed by beach morning glory and low scrubby trees, it has fine gray sand and fairly active surf. Unless it's a weekend, the odds are good that, with the exception of a few rummaging goats, you'll have the beach to yourself.

## NEVISIAN HERITAGE VILLAGE
This open-air **museum** (☎ 469-5521; Stoney Grove; adult/child US$3/1; ☼ 9am-3:30pm Mon-Sat), located 500m west of Zion, is a collection of cottages that gives visitors a view of the social evolution of Nevisian history dating back to Carib times. See a simple thatched Arawak shelter; try to lift a chattel house (simple wooden structures sugarcane workers would move from job to job – literally an early mobile home). It's not to be missed during Culturama (see p514) when residents engage in the old traditions.

## Sleeping & Eating
Three plantation estates offer elegant stays that are among the finest on the island. You can sample some of the vintage atmosphere at a casual lunch.

**Golden Rock Plantation Inn** (☎ 469-3346; www .golden-rock.com; r from US$200; 🖳 🏊) The funkiest choice among the plantation inns, the owner's great-great-great-great-grandfather built this lava-stone sugar plantation by hand in the 1810s. The seven rooms stress casual comfort over elegance and vary greatly in size and style. There's a spring-fed pool, tennis court and nature trails. Guests can use a shuttle to Charlestown and the beaches. Enjoy lunch (US$8 to US$22) on a cobblestone patio. Lobster salads and sandwiches are always crowd-pleasers. Dinner (from US$50) features a seasonal four-course meal and requires advance reservations.

**Montpelier Plantation Inn** (☎ 469-3462; www .montpeliernevis.com; r from US$290; 🖳 🏊) This 17th-century inn, just southeast of Charlestown, has hosted Horatio Nelson's doomed marriage to Fanny Nisbet in 1787 and much later, the doomed Princess Diana. Happily, the past is past and this beautiful estate evokes a relaxed contemporary elegance in addition to its long history. The luxuries are real but understated – you can select a book from the library, use the wi-fi and then loll

### HIKING BUCOLIC NEVIS
Many think Nevis has some of the best hiking in the Caribbean for its blend of nature and history. A Peace Corps volunteer on Nevis over 20 years ago, Jim Johnson fell in love with the island in more ways than one. He married his wife Nikki and stayed. Today he leads hikes through the highlands above the coast via **Top to Bottom** (☎ 469-9080; www.walknevis.com). There are over a dozen hikes, ranging from walks to estate ruins, monkey-spotting hikes in the jungle and the more strenuous hikes to the top of Nevis Peak. Each outing costs US$20, except for the challenging treks to Nevis Peak, which cost from US$30 to US$40. The fruit-spotting hike is a fave.

**For hiking what makes Nevis different from other nearby islands?**
The wide choice of trails and guides, from simple to extreme.

**Why is it a good place to hike?**
It still has much of its history in the form of hidden ruins as well as many nature areas for birds, butterflies and flowers.

**What's your favorite wild fruit and why?**
I like coconuts because of the taste and the challenge of opening them without a machete!

**And how do you do that?**
You put the coconut on a flat rock with the pointed end up and hit it at the right spot with a 10-pound stone; the husk should come off in one or two hits. Then poke a stick in and suck out the water. Hit the coconut right again and the meat comes loose from the shell. The tricky part is not hitting your foot with the stone as the coconut can bounce.

**What fruit surprises people?**
Most are surprised by tamarinds as they taste like very sour candy.

**What still surprises you as you hike Nevis?**
We often find new plants, bugs or birds even after doing the trails thousands of times. And I'm still surprised by how much has been lost or forgotten, but still exists in the form of hidden places up the mountain.

**Most amazing discovery in your years of walking that still makes you go 'wow'?**
I still find the bats (we have over eight species) amazing.

back for a snooze in the gazebo. Mealtimes, however, will perk you right up. Lunch (meals US$10 to US$20) is served on a shaded terrace and includes salads and sandwiches. Dinner (three courses from US$60) is a more elaborate affair featuring a changing menu of island produce, steak, duck and seafood. The wine list is extensive.

**Hermitage** ( ☎ 469-3477, in the US 800-682-4025; www.hermitagenevis.com; Gingerland; r from US$325; ▣ ▣ ) The solid-wood plantation house, which is over 260 years old and furnished with antiques, serves as a parlor and evening gathering spot. The various cottages and villas mirror the rustic construction. You can't help but feel transported to another era as you sit on your little porch (or swing in a hammock) taking in the views from the plantation's 800ft elevation. Lunch (US$10 to US$20) here is the usual casual affair with fresh fare like salads and sandwiches served on a lovely veranda. Dinner (four courses US$65) is more elaborate. The changing menus meld the Mediterranean with the Caribbean. Think molasses, rum, garlic, sun-dried tomatoes and more. The inn has wi-fi access.

**1787** ( ☎ 469-2875; Botanical Gardens of Nevis; mains US$10-20; ☽ lunch & dinner Thu-Tue) A good place for sundowners, 1787 (the name recalls the year of the ill-fated Nelson-Nisbet marriage, so don't pop the question here) has views from a broad veranda of the botanical garden and Nevis Peak. Lunches feature creative sandwiches like a grilled brie and prosciutto number, while dinner offers crowd-pleasing steaks and seafood.

# DIRECTORY

## ACCOMMODATIONS

Hotels on St Kitts and Nevis add a 7% government tax, a 2% island enhancement tax, and normally a 10% to 15% service charge onto room rates.

There are large resorts on each island, but most accommodations are still small-scale hotels, grand plantation inns, inexpensive guesthouses or condominiums. However, a resort building boom is underway in St Kitts.

Camping is technically allowed, but neither island is set up with facilities. Contact the tourist office on either island to inquire.

## ACTIVITIES

### Beaches & Swimming

The islands' beaches have a hard time competing with the stunning white stretches found on Anguilla and Antigua, but there are reasonable strands on St Kitts and a couple of attractive options on Nevis.

St Kitts' best beaches are on the south end of the island at Frigate Bay, Friar's Bay and in the sheltered bays of the southeast peninsula. Beaches along the main body of the island are thin strands of black and gray sands.

On Nevis, Pinney's Beach, which runs north from Charlestown, has a Robinson Crusoe look and feel. It's long and lovely, backed by coconut palms.

There's also a pleasant little beach at Oualie Bay.

### Boat Trips

There are no shortage of water-born fun boats aimed at the rum-guzzling, buffet-ravaging cruise-ship crowd. Most circle St Kitts or make a jaunt to Nevis. The following are somewhat less mob-minded and do allow you to enjoy a sail on the azure sea.

**Blue Water Safaris** ( ☎ 466-4933; www.bluewater safaris.com; St Kitts) Full-day catamaran cruises for US$75, with snorkeling, lunch on Pinney's Beach and an open bar thrown in. Sunset and moonlight cruises are US$40 per person, plus there are fishing charters.

**Leeward Island Charters** ( ☎ 465-7474; bookings@ spiritofstkitts.com; St Kitts) This class act offers a full day of snorkeling and lunch on the *Spirit of St Kitts* catamaran for US$80/40 for adults/children, as well as sunset cruises for US$45.

### Cycling

For information on cycle rentals on Nevis, see p509.

### Diving & Snorkeling

Most beaches popular with visitors will have some place for you to rent snorkeling gear, usually for about US$10.

#### NEVIS

Nevis' diving scene is a low-key affair, and features undisturbed coral reefs that are seldom visited by divers.

Two popular diving sites off Nevis are Monkey Shoals, a densely covered reef close to Oualie Beach, and Devil's Caves, on the western side of the island, with coral grottoes and underwater lava tubes in 40ft of water.

For diving and snorkeling trips and hire, see p509.

## ST KITTS

St Kitts has healthy, expansive reefs and varied marine life that includes rays, barracuda, garden eels, nurse sharks, sea turtles, sea fans, giant barrel sponges and black coral.

One popular dive spot is Sandy Point Bay, below Brimstone Hill, with an array of corals, sponges and reef fish as well as some coral-encrusted anchors from the colonial era. Among a handful of wreck dives is the 148ft freighter *River Taw*, which sank in 50ft of water in 1985 and now harbors corals and fish.

There are diving outfits at Basseterre (p500) and Frigate Bay (p503).

White House Bay, on the southeast peninsula of St Kitts, is a favorite place for snorkeling. All of the dive companies rent snorkel gear for around US$10 a day.

## Hiking

Both St Kitts and Nevis have an abundance of untouched native vegetation, a good selection of easy and tough treks, and great views from the mountainous interiors. Tracks on St Kitts and Nevis are not well defined, but there are moves to improve the tracks, and it's advisable to do any major trekking with a guide.

For hikes on Nevis, see the boxed text, p511.

**Greg's Safaris** ( ☎ 465-4121; www.gregsafaris.com) has a half-day hike into the rainforest of St Kitts for US$60. The guide moves at a measured pace, identifies flora and fauna, and stops to sample fruits along the way. Among three other hikes is a full-day tour of Mt Liamuiga volcano for US$90, including lunch.

## Horseback Riding

Nevis is the place for saddling up and exploring the verdant and sandy scenery. Rides typically start at around US$40 for one hour.

For riding on Nevis, try **Nevis Equestrian Centre** ( ☎ 469-8118; alitalk@caribcable.com; Cotton Ground), or head out to the beach, up to the mountain or both with **Hermitage** ( ☎ 469-3477; nevherm@caribsurf .com), which also offers carriage rides.

## Windsurfing

Oualie Bay, at the northwest side of Nevis, catches the trade winds and offers a sandy launch in shallow waters that's good for beginners. There are also opportunities for wave jumping and other advanced techniques. See p509 for rental and lesson information.

## Other Water Sports

For water skiing, sailing, kayaking and boogie boarding on St Kitts, see Mr X's Watersports (p503) at Frigate Bay.

For kayaking on Nevis, check with Windsurfing Nevis (p509) at Oualie Beach.

## BOOKS

*Creating the Better Hour: Lessons from William Wilberforce* by Chuck Stetson looks at the life of the important 18th-century British abolitionist who found his voice after he learned of the horrible conditions of the slaves on St Kitts.

*Out of Crowded Vagueness: A History of the Islands of St. Kitts, Nevis and Anguilla* by Brian Dyde is a recently published and highly readable history of the islands.

*Swords Ships and Sugar: A History of Nevis to 1900* by Vincent K Hubbard is an enthusiastic if rough-around-the-edges account of the island's past. It's widely sold on Nevis.

## BUSINESS HOURS

St Kitts and Nevis follow Caribbean conventions. Businesses are open 8am to 5pm Monday to Friday and often on Saturdays until about 2pm. Shops are open until 6pm or 7pm weekdays and until late Saturday afternoon. Touristy places will be open later

---

### PRACTICALITIES

■ **Newspapers & Magazines** Local newspapers include the weekly *Sun, Democrat* and *Observer* and the biweekly *Labour Spokesman*.

■ **Radio** For local radio try FM 90.3, 96.0 or 98.9 for reggae, soca, calypso or island music.

■ **Electricity** Most electric current is 220V, 60 cycles; many hotels supply electricity at 110V, and North American two-pin sockets are common.

■ **Weights & Measures** Imperial. Speed-limit signs are in miles, as are rental-car odometers.

and if not already open on Sunday, will do so if a cruise ship is in port.

Restaurants are good until 9 or 10pm (in general, breakfast is 7am to 10am, lunch noon to 2pm, and dinner 6pm to close); bars close somewhat later, especially on weekends. Nevis in particular is not an island for partying until dawn.

## CHILDREN

Reefs in resort areas protect the beaches making for gentle swimming conditions, while larger hotels often have programs for kids.

## DANGERS & ANNOYANCES

Common sense should prevail while walking around Basseterre at night. If the area looks dodgy, it is.

Driving at night on either island is a time for great caution: kids, dogs, goats and yes, enormous potholes, can appear out nowhere. And the law lets people swill beer while they fly over the lanes.

## EMBASSIES & CONSULATES

The **Honorary Council** ( ☎ 466-8888; Basseterre) for the UK is on St Kitts. For the main embassy representing the region, contact the UK embassy on Antigua (p536).

## FESTIVALS & EVENTS

**St Kitts Music Festival** (www.stkittsmusicfestival.net) This four-day festival in the last week in June brings together top-name calypso, soca, reggae, salsa, jazz and gospel performers from throughout the Caribbean.
**Culturama** Nevis has been celebrating this week-long event for over 30 years. Held in late July to early August, it features music, crafts, and beauty and talent pageants, culminating with a parade on Culturama Tuesday.
**Carnival** Running from December 24 to January 3, this is the biggest yearly event on St Kitts, with 10 days of calypso competitions, costumed street dances and steel-pan music. Many businesses are closed during this period.

## GAY & LESBIAN TRAVELERS

While there is no real gay scene on St Kitts and Nevis, there is no overt discrimination either.

## HOLIDAYS

Public holidays on St Kitts and Nevis include the following:

**New Year's Day** January 1
**Good Friday** Late March/early April
**Easter Monday** Late March/early April
**Labour Day** First Monday in May
**Whit Monday** Eighth Monday after Easter
**Emancipation Day** First Monday in August
**National Hero's Day** September 17
**Independence Day** September 19
**Christmas Day** December 25
**Boxing Day** December 26

## INTERNET ACCESS

Basseterre has internet cafés and most hotels offer wi-fi and computers in the lobby.

## MAPS

On St Kitts, the tourist office's *Road Map & Guide* will suffice for most visitors. On Nevis, the excellent *Journey Map* covers practically every crevice on the island and has a detailed road map of both the island and Charlestown. Both maps are available at most hotels, the tourist offices and many shops.

## MEDICAL SERVICES

Both islands have well-equipped hospitals. For St Kitts, see p500; for Nevis see p507.

## MONEY

The official currency is the Eastern Caribbean dollar, and although US dollars are accepted almost everywhere, ATMs don't dispense them. Instead, most large banks will issue dollars from a teller for a US$5 fee.

Hotels and restaurants add a 7% tax and usually a 10% service charge as well. When a restaurant doesn't add a service charge, a 10% tip is appropriate.

## POST

When mailing a letter to the islands, follow the addressee's name with the town and 'St Kitts, West Indies' or 'Nevis, West Indies.'

## TELEPHONE

The St Kitts and Nevis area code is ☎ 869. To call from North America, dial ☎ 1-869, followed by the seven-digit local number. From elsewhere, dial your country's international access code + ☎ 869 + the local phone number. We've included only the seven-digit local number in St Kitts and Nevis listings in this chapter. St Kitts numbers start with ☎ 465 or ☎ 466 and Nevis numbers with ☎ 469. Mobiles begin with ☎ 7.

---

**EMERGENCY NUMBERS**

■ **Ambulance** ☎ 911
■ **Police** ☎ 911

---

Phone calling cards are widely available. Local cell phones use the GSM system.

Avoid credit-card phones, as they charge a rapacious US$2 per minute or more locally, US$4 to other Caribbean islands or the US, and up to US$8 elsewhere.

For directory assistance, dial ☎ 411.

## TOURIST INFORMATION

**Nevis Tourist Office** ( ☎ 469-7550, in the US 866-556-3847; www.nevisnaturally.com; Main St; Charlestown; ☺ 8am-4pm Mon-Fri, 9am-1pm Sat) Highly useful.
**St Kitts Tourism Authority** ( ☎ 465-4040; www.stkitts tourism.kn; Pelican Mall, Bay Rd, Basseterre; ☺ 8am-5pm Mon-Fri) A small office.

## TRAVELERS WITH DISABILITIES

International resorts generally have good accommodations for people with disabilities. Otherwise much of the islands are something of a challenge. Fortunately most everything of interest can be reached directly by car. The must-see Brimstone Hill Fortress has both accessible and inaccessible areas.

## VISAS

Visas are not required by most nationalities for stays of less than six months.

## WOMEN TRAVELERS

Women won't find anything especially concerning about a visit to these islands as long as normal caution prevails.

# TRANSPORTATION

## GETTING THERE & AWAY
### Entering St Kitts & Nevis

Visitors from most countries need only a passport to enter St Kitts or Nevis (US citizens see the boxed text, p830), as well as a round-trip or onward ticket.

## Air

St Kitts has regional service plus nonstop flights to the US while Nevis has service that is mostly regional; to get here you'll need to change planes somewhere.

## NEVIS

**Nevis International Airport** (NEV; ☎ 469-9040), in Newcastle, is a small operation with an ATM.

The following airlines connect Nevis with these cities (some services are seasonal and only weekly):
**American Eagle** ( ☎ 800-433-7300; www.aa.com) San Juan
**LIAT** ( ☎ 469-9333; www.liat.com) Antigua
**Winair** ( ☎ 469-5302; www.fly-winair.com) Sint Maarten

## ST KITTS

St Kitts' modern international airport, **Robert Llewellyn Bradshaw Airport** (SKM; ☎ 465-8121), is located on the northern outskirts of Basseterre. The departure area is bright and airy but amenities are limited to a bare-bones snack bar. There is an ATM before security.

The following airlines connect St Kitts with these cities (some services are seasonal and only weekly):
**American/American Eagle** ( ☎ 800-433-7300; www.aa.com) Miami, New York-Kennedy, San Juan
**Delta** ( ☎ 800-221-1212) Atlanta
**LIAT** ( ☎ 465-8200; www.liat.com) Antigua, St Thomas, Sint Maarten
**US Airways** ( ☎ 800-622-1015; www.usairways.com) Charlotte, NC
**Winair** ( ☎ 465-2186; www.fly-winair.com) Sint Maarten

## Sea

Other than the ferries linking St Kitts and Nevis, there are no services to other islands.

### CRUISE SHIP

Scores of cruise ships on eastern Caribbean itineraries visit St Kitts, docking at Basseterre's deep-water harbor. It can be a good idea to email the tourist office when you know your travel dates to get the cruise schedule, as certain places such as the beaches in the south or the St Kitts Scenic Railway are mobbed. Nevis lacks a dock that can handle the enormous boats so visits are limited to passengers brought ashore by tender from small ships (usually under 300 passengers) anchored offshore or those on flying visits as part of excursions from St Kitts.

See p830 for information about cruise-ship travel throughout the Caribbean.

### YACHT

St Kitts and Nevis are right on the Eastern Caribbean yachting circuit, although their lack of natural harbors like those on Antigua

**ST KITTS & NEVIS**

keep the numbers of people mooring for any period of length low.

The two ports of entry are Basseterre and Charlestown. On both islands, customs is near the ferry dock and is open 8am to noon and 1pm to 4pm Monday to Friday. Boaters will need permits to visit other anchorages and a special pass to go between the two islands.

## GETTING AROUND
### Boat

Several passenger-only ferry companies provide service between Basseterre and Charlestown. The trip takes 35 to 45 minutes and is both a pleasant and scenic way to travel. Fares are set at adult/child EC$20/10 one way. In each port, be sure to pay the EC$1 port tax before you depart. Tickets are sold starting about 30 minutes before sailings. It's a good idea to arrive early as some boats sell out.

Each ferry company operates by its own schedule. Some are more reliable than others. It is a good idea to confirm schedules in advance, which you can do at the ports, tourist offices or by calling ☎ 466-4636. Between the various boats there's service roughly every two hours (much less frequently on Sundays). Boat quality varies: some lack open decks, forcing passengers into close proximity, which may or may not be a good thing when you hit swells.

Ferry boats include the following:
**Carib Breeze/Carib Surf** ( ☎ 466-6734; mmtscaribe@ hotmail.com) The most reliable service. Both boats are large, with enclosed cabins and large, sunny upper decks.
**Carib Queen** ( ☎ 664-9811) Two trips daily.
**Mark Twain** ( ☎ 469-0403) No open deck.
**Sea Hustler** ( ☎ 469-0403) No Sunday service; children under five free.

People with cars can use the new **Seabridge** ( ☎ 765-7053; www.seabridgeskn.com) car-ferry service. It links Major's Bay in the south of St Kitts with Cades Point on Nevis. It operates every two hours during daylight hours and trips take 45 minutes. The one-way fare is EC$75 for one car and a driver. Additional passengers cost EC$15. Round-trips cost EC$125. If you have a rental car on one island, this can be a good way to explore the other island on a day trip without having to rent another car.

You can also freelance your way across the 2 miles that separates the islands. At most of the southern beaches on St Kitts you're likely to find a fisherman willing to run you over to

Nevis or even St-Barthélemy or Sint Eustatius for very negotiable rates that start at US$30. The rides can be wet and wild.

### Bus

Buses on both islands can resemble minivan taxis, so check the front plate to be sure. An 'H' means private bus and a 'T' means taxi (an 'R' is a rental car and a 'P' or 'PA' is a resident's car).

### Car & Motorcycle
#### DRIVER'S LICENSE

Foreigners must purchase a visitor driver's license, which costs US$24 and is valid for 90 days. Most rental companies will issue you one when you fill out your contracts, and a license on one island is good for the other.

On St Kitts, you can also get a license at the **police station** (Pond Rd; ☯ 24hr) on the east side of Basseterre. It has a separate window designated for issuing visitor licenses.

#### RENTAL

Rental companies will usually meet you at the airport, ferry port or your hotel. Daily rates start at about US$40. You really won't need a 4WD for going anywhere – unless it's rainy season. Most of the major firms have local affiliates. Cars tend to be in good shape on St Kitts but apparently go to die on Nevis. Many on the latter are left-hand drive which can add to the challenge of left-side driving.

#### ROAD RULES

Drive on the left side of the road, often around goats, cows and pedestrians. Speed limits are posted in miles per hour, and are generally between 20mph and 40mph. Gas costs over EC$12 per gallon.

### Scooters

Scooters are good ways to get around either island. Distances are never far and there's always a good excuse to stop and explore a beach or historic ruin. Just watch out for the minibuses. Daily rates start at US$35 and there are discounts the longer you rent.

### Taxi

Taxis meet scheduled flights on both islands. See p499 and p507 for sample fares.

Taxi island tours on both islands cost around US$75. Those short on time can take a two-hour half-island tour for US$50.

# Antigua & Barbuda

On Antigua, life is a beach. It may seem like a cliché, but this improbably shaped splotch of land is ringed with beaches of the finest white sand, made all the more dramatic by the azure waters, which are so clear they'll bring a tear to your eye or a giggle to your holiday-hungry throat.

And if life on Antigua is a beach, its isolated neighbor Barbuda is a beach. The pair couldn't be any more different. While the first looks like something nasty under a microscope, the latter is just one smooth, sandy low-rise amidst the reef-filled waters. Birds, especially the huffing and puffing frigates, greatly outnumber people.

Back on Antigua, there are lots of people, many famous. Guitar-picker Eric Clapton, ragtrader Giorgio Armani, huckster scribe Ken Follett and taste-maker for the masses Oprah all have winter homes here. Some of the Caribbean's most exclusive resorts shelter in the myriad bays and inlets. But mere mortals thrive here as well. Visitors of every budget will find a beach they can – almost – call their own.

Meanwhile, the locals take the visiting mobs with a dash of grace that always has the backing of an English stiff upper lip should the situation get too dire. The island's British roots are on display in many ways, but especially when there's a good cricket test match on. Memories of the old empire, however, are far removed from the island's beat, which has some of the liveliest steel-drum music in the islands.

## FAST FACTS

- **Area** Antigua: 108 sq miles; Barbuda: 62 sq miles
- **Capital** Antigua: St John's; Barbuda: Codrington
- **Country code** ☎ 268
- **Departure tax** Antigua: US$20; Barbuda: none
- **Famous for** Antigua: cricket; Barbuda: frigate bird
- **Language** English
- **Money** Eastern Caribbean dollar (EC$); EC$1 = US$0.38 = €0.24 = UK£0.19
- **Official name** Antigua and Barbuda
- **People** Antiguans, Barbudans
- **Phrase** No big ting
- **Population** Antigua: 72,000; Barbuda: 1250
- **Visa** Not required for US, EU or Commonwealth visitors; see p538

## HIGHLIGHTS
- **Nelson's Dockyard** (p529) Visit the restored 18th-century British naval base; it makes for a fascinating excursion
- **Hawksbill Bay** (p527) Enjoy a string of four stunning beaches where you may just doff it all
- **Codrington Lagoon** (p533) Visit the Caribbean's largest rookery, home to thousands of frigate birds
- **Fig Tree Drive** (p528) Stop at a fruit stand under the dense canopy to sample an island treat: a black pineapple
- **St John's** (p523) Join the hubbub of a classic West Indian town and savor the flavors of the market

## ITINERARIES
- **Three or Four Days** Spend a day wandering St John's, taking in the museum, cathedral and market. Head south along the coast, sampling beaches, and then across Fig Tree Dr to Falmouth Harbour and Nelson's Dockyard. Spend the next day or two roaming the rugged east coast, Devil's Bridge, and the fabulous beaches at Half Moon and Nonsuch Bays. Consider a kayak nature trip.
- **One Week** Do everything above and then force yourself to spend another day searching out your favorite beach. After that, make a two-day trip to Barbuda to relax on isolated sandy shores and for some incredible bird-watching.

## CLIMATE & WHEN TO GO
There's really no bad time to go to Antigua and Barbuda. The heat of the Caribbean summer is matched by hot low-season deals at the resorts.

In January and February, the coolest months, the daily high temperature averages 81°F (27°C), while the nightly low tempera-

### HOW MUCH?
- **Rum punch on the beach** US$5
- **Round-trip between Antigua and Barbuda by air** US$200
- **Beachside double room** US$300
- **Short local bus ride** EC$1.50
- **Tasty rock lobster dinner** EC$80

ture averages 72°F (22°C). In July and August, the hottest months, the high averages 86°F (30°C) and the low 77°F (25°C).

Antigua is relatively dry, averaging about 45in of rain annually. The wettest months are September to November, when measurable precipitation occurs, on average, eight days each month. February to April is the driest period, with an average of three rainy days each month.

## HISTORY
### Early Times to the 17th Century
The first permanent residents in the area are thought to have been migrating Arawaks, who called today's Antigua 'Wadadli,' a name still commonly used today. They first established agricultural communities about 4000 years ago. Around AD 1200 the Arawaks were forced out by invading Caribs, who used the islands as bases for their forays in the region, but apparently didn't settle them.

Columbus sighted Antigua in 1493 and named it after a church in Seville, Spain. In 1632 the British colonized Antigua, establishing a settlement at Parham, on the east side of the island. The settlers started planting indigo and tobacco, but a glut in the supply of those crops soon drove down prices, leaving growers looking for something new.

In 1674 Sir Christopher Codrington arrived on Antigua and established the first sugar plantation, Betty's Hope. By the end of the century, a plantation economy had developed, huge numbers of slaves were imported, and the central valleys were deforested and planted with cane. To feed the slaves, Codrington leased the island of Barbuda from the British Crown and planted it with food crops.

### Nelson & Co
As Antigua prospered, the British built numerous fortifications around the island, turning it into one of their most secure bases in the Caribbean. Today's Nelson's Dockyard (see p529) was continually expanded and improved throughout the 18th century. Other forts included Fort James (see p525) near St John's.

The military couldn't secure the economy, however, and in the early 1800s the sugar market began to bottom out. With the abolition of slavery in 1834, the plantations went into a steady decline. Unlike on some other Caribbean islands, the land was not turned over to former slaves when the plantations went under, but was instead consolidated under the ownership of a few landowners. Consequently, the lot of most people only worsened. Many former slaves moved off the plantations and into shantytowns, while others crowded onto properties held by the church.

A military-related construction boom during WWII, and the development of a tourist industry during the postwar period, helped spur economic growth (although the shantytowns that remain along the outskirts of St John's are ample evidence that not everyone has benefited).

In 1967, after more than 300 years of colonial rule, Antigua achieved a measure of self-government as an Associated State of the UK. On November 1, 1981, it achieved full independence.

### Nest of Birds

Vere Cornwall (VC) Bird became the nation's first prime minister, and despite leading a government marred by political scandals, he held that position through four consecutive terms. He stepped down in 1994 to be succeeded by his son Lester.

Another son, Vere Bird Jr, received international attention in 1991 as the subject of a judicial inquiry that investigated his involvement in smuggling Israeli weapons to the Medellín drug cartel. As a consequence of the inquiry, Vere Bird Jr was pressured into resigning his cabinet post, but was allowed to keep his parliamentary position. A third son of VC Bird, Ivor, was convicted of cocaine smuggling in 1995.

Throughout the five-term family stranglehold on government, controversy continued to surround the Birds. In 1997, Prime Minister Lester Bird announced that a group of ecologically sensitive nearby islands (including Guiana Island) was being turned over to Malaysian developers to build a 1000-room hotel, an 18-hole golf course and a casino. This was met with widespread protest from environmentalists and remains mired in lawsuits. In 1999, VC Bird died, aged 89.

Finally, in March 2004, the Birds' reign of the 'aviary' (as Antigua had become known) ended. Their Antigua Labour Party (ALP) had held sway in government for a majority of the time following the first universal suffrage elections in 1951.

The United Progressive Party won a landslide victory and Baldwin Spencer became prime minister. In the years since, the government has struggled with the poverty found across much of the island. It has promoted tourism while at the same time edging politically closer to Cuba and Venezuela. It has also challenged the US ban on internet gambling sites and has had some success with the World Trade Organization. Many of these sites are based in Antigua.

## THE CULTURE

Away from the resorts, Antigua retains its traditional West Indian character, albeit with a strong British stamp. It's manifested in the gingerbread architecture found around the capital, the popularity of steel pan (steel band), calypso and reggae music, and in festivities, such as Carnival. English traditions also play an important role, as is evident in the national sport of cricket.

Many Barbudans originally come from or have spent time living on their sister island, Antigua, and favor the quieter pace of life on the more isolated Barbuda. In fact, many Barbudans working in tourism are happy with the trickle of tourists that the remote island attracts, and have been reluctant to court the kind of development Antigua has seen.

Approximately 90% of the 72,000 people who live on Antigua are of African descent. There are also small minority populations of British, Portuguese and Lebanese ancestry. The population of Barbuda is approximately 1250, with most of African descent.

Besides the Anglican Church, Antiguans belong to a host of religious denominations, which include Roman Catholic, Moravian, Methodist, Seventh Day Adventist, Lutheran and Jehovah's Witness. On Sundays, services at the more fundamentalist churches draw such crowds that roads are blocked and drivers pray for divine intervention.

## SPORTS

One of the best things Britain did for the West Indies was to introduce the local populace to cricket. It soon became the national passion of Antigua and is played everywhere – on beaches, in backyards or anywhere there's some flat, open ground. National and international games were long played at the fabled Antigua Recreation Ground in St John's.

However, important matches are now played at the new 20,000-seat Sir Vivian Richards Stadium, 4 miles east of St John's. It was built for the 2007 Cricket World Cup, but has caused controversy with such issues as cost over-runs.

Although the West Indies team has fallen from the dizzying heights of the 1970s and early '80s, the game is followed religiously, and the atmosphere at matches ripples with excitement. To see a match, ask around, as schedules change often, depending on the travel plans of various teams.

Viv Richards (King Viv or the 'Master-Blaster,' as he was known in his heyday), who hails from Antigua, is one of the most famous cricketers of the modern game. Known for his aggressive style of batting, he became captain of the West Indies team, and captained 27 wins in 50 tests between 1980 and 1991. These days, he does commentary for the BBC as well as some coaching.

Soccer and basketball are increasing in popularity, and national and club soccer games can produce much the same atmosphere as cricket.

## ARTS

Reggae and zouk (the latter means 'party,' and is a rhythmic music that originated in Martinique and Guadeloupe in the 1980s) are both popular on the island. You'll also hear calypso, a style of singing rooted in slave culture that was developed as a means of communication when slaves weren't allowed to speak, and soca, a rhythmic, more soulful style of calypso. By far the most popular musical style on Antigua is steel pan (also known as steel band or steel drum), the melodic percussion music that comes from tapping oil drums topped with specially made tin pans. Originally from Trinidad, the form has been adapted in Antigua, and has become an integral part of the annual Carnival and Christmas festivities.

Look for the band Burning Flames, a local legend that leads Carnival and is linked to the legendary soca master Arrow on nearby Montserrat.

## ENVIRONMENT
### The Land

Unlike its, at times, smoking neighbor to the southwest, Montserrat, Antigua is not dominated by a dramatic volcano. However, the southwest corner is volcanic in origin and quite hilly, rising to 1319ft at Boggy Peak, the island's highest point. The rest of the island, which is predominantly of limestone and coral formation, is given to a more gently undulating terrain of open plains and scrubland.

Antigua's land area is 108 sq miles. The island is vaguely rounded in shape, averaging about 11 miles across. The deeply indented coastline is cut by numerous coves and bays, many lined with white-sand beaches.

Barbuda, 25 miles north of Antigua, is nearly as flat as the surrounding ocean. A low-lying coral island, Barbuda's highest point is a mere 145ft above sea level. The west side of Barbuda encompasses the expansive Codrington Lagoon, which is bound by a long, undeveloped barrier beach of blindingly white sand.

### Wildlife

As a consequence of colonial-era deforestation for sugar production, most of Antigua's vegetation is dryland scrub. The island's marshes and salt ponds attract a fair number of stilts, egrets, ducks and pelicans, while hummingbirds are found in garden settings.

Guiana Island, off the northeast coast, has one of Antigua's largest remaining tracts of forest. It's the sole habitat for the tropical mockingbird, and supports the largest colony of nesting seabirds on Antigua. These include tropic birds, roseate terns, brown noddies and endangered whistling ducks. Unfortunately, Guiana Island and eight smaller adjacent islands are in the cross-hairs of resort developers and the battle to preserve them is ongoing. You can visit this still-magical area as part of kayak tours offered by Adventure Antigua; see p537 for details.

Barbuda's Codrington Lagoon has the largest frigate-bird colony in the Lesser Antilles. For more information on frigate birds, see p534.

## FOOD & DRINK

Antigua has a vast range of restaurants. Many are fairly renowned and standards are high. You can snack on savory local fare at simple places in St John's or splash out at a top-end resort with a top-name chef. Seafood is obviously the focus, and many people find the rock lobster, a hulking crustacean that has a succulent tail but no claws, actually affordable. (And you'll be forgiven if after a few rum punches you're humming a tune by the B-52s while digging in.)

Look for various Creole and other spicy accents to many dishes. Okra plays an unappreciated supporting role in many of the piquant pork and goat stews. Also, try one of the locally grown black pineapples, which are quite sweet, rather small and, despite the name, not at all black. On Barbuda, your choices are very limited and run closer to true local fare.

Cavalier and English Harbour are two locally made rums, and Antigua Brewery produces its own bog-standard lager under the Wadadli label.

# ANTIGUA

Unlike its smooth-edged neighbors, Antigua looks like something that went 'splat' on the pavement. But oh if everything that went splat were this good. Its myriad craggy inlets and corrugated coasts hug scores of perfect little beaches, while the sheltered bays have provided refuge for boats, from Admiral Nelson to pirates to sun-scorched yachties.

There's a distinct English accent to this classic Caribbean island with its narrow roads punctuated by candy-colored villages. You can explore most everything quickly, although the world-class sites of historic English Harbour will steal hours from your day. Take the time to savor the sand and sea: the former bright white, the latter beguiling blue.

## Getting There & Away

For information on getting to/from Antigua, see p538.

Antigua is connected to Barbuda by air and ferry; for details see p539.

## Getting Around
### BICYCLE
**Paradise Boat Sales** ( ☎ 460-7125; Jolly Harbour; www .paradiseboats.com) rents out mountain bikes from US$15 per day with discounts for longer periods.

**Bike Plus** ( ☎ 462-2453; Independence Dr, St John's) rents out a range of bikes from US$17.50 per day.

Some hotels also rent out bikes.

### BUS
Antigua's buses are privately owned and are predominantly minivans, although there are

a few midsize buses. Fares cost EC$1.50 to EC$5. Buses from St John's to Falmouth and English Harbour are plentiful, cost around EC$3 and take about 30 minutes. They start early and generally run until about 7pm. Rush hour is particularly bustling, with lots of buses between 4pm and 5pm. There are very few buses on Sunday.

The main bus station (West Bus Station) in St John's is opposite the public market. All destinations are allocated a number, and each bus displays a number that indicates where it's heading. Notices are posted about with destination numbers. Buses line up in a row and don't actually leave until they're full. So just find the bus you need, hop on, and hope it fills up and leaves before you melt.

Buses to the east side of the island leave from the East Bus Station, near the corner of Independence Ave and High St, and go to Piggots and Willikies. The numbering system doesn't apply here, so you'll need to ask around to find your bus.

There's no practical bus service to the airport, Dickenson Bay or other resort areas on the northern part of the island.

### CAR
There are more than a dozen car-rental agencies on Antigua including all the major brands. Most have representatives crammed into one tiny office at the airport. Agencies in the following list rent out cars for around US$50 a day, but can drop to as low as US$40 in the off-season. Many of the companies also offer basic 4WDs for the same rates, or for US$5 to US$10 more. Shop online before arriving, for the best deals.

All but the newest rental cars are generally quite beat, mostly because of the poor road conditions. Your best bet (though by no means a sure thing) for getting a roadworthy car is to book with one of the international agencies. Most car-rental agencies will deliver cars to your hotel free of charge.

Rental companies include the following:
**Avis** ( ☎ 462-2840; www.avis.com)
**Dollar** ( ☎ 462-0362; www.dollar.com)
**Hertz** ( ☎ 462-4114; www.hertz.com)
**Thrifty Rent-A-Car** ( ☎ 462-9532; www.thrifty.com)

Numerous gas stations are scattered around the island, including one just outside the airport terminal. Gas sells for around EC$10 per gallon.

ANTIGUA & BARBUDA

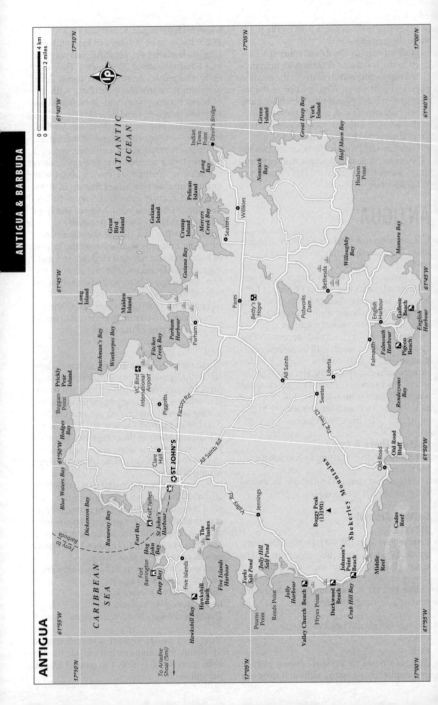

ANTIGUA

ANTIGUA & BARBUDA

## TAXI

Taxi fares are regulated by the government, but be sure to confirm the fare with the driver before riding away. Fares from the airport are US$12 to St John's, US$16 to Runaway or Dickenson Bays, US$24 to Jolly Harbour and US$31 to English Harbour. Fares are for up to four persons; a fifth person costs an additional 25%. Traveling around Antigua by taxi costs about US$90 per car for a half-day tour that takes in Nelson's Dockyard and Shirley Heights.

In St John's there's a taxi stand opposite the Public Market, and taxi drivers also hang around Heritage Quay.

Taxis are identifiable by number plates beginning with 'H.'

# ST JOHN'S

pop 36,000

Intriguingly shabby, St John's is worth a day's exploration. Good cafés, idiosyncratic shops, a grand cathedral, a cute little museum, a thriving market and more line the chaotic streets of the fairly compact center. There's a melange of buildings ranging from 19th-century survivors to modern-day horrors.

Almost half the island's residents live in and around St John's, which is busy during the day from Monday to Friday.

## Orientation

Most of the town's group-tourist activity is centered on two harbor-front complexes – the modern Heritage Quay, where cruise-ship passengers disembark, and Redcliffe Quay, where a cluster of period stone buildings and wooden huts have been transformed into gift shops, watch-purveyors and cafés. Popeshead St is the main route to the north and the island's main resort area.

## Information

### BOOKSTORES

**Best of Books** ( ☎ 562-3198; St Mary's St; ⏰ 9am-9pm Mon-Sat, 10am-3pm Sun) Good selection of international titles and newspapers, and a children's book section.

**Map Shop** ( ☎ 461-4749; St Mary's St) Old and new maps plus a small, funky book selection.

### EMERGENCY

**Police** (Newgate St) This is the main police station in town. The police headquarters ( ☎ 462-0125; American Rd) is on the eastern outskirts of St John's.

### INTERNET ACCESS

**Kangaroo Express** ( ☎ 562-3895; Redcliffe St; per hr US$12; ⏰ 8am-9pm Mon-Sat, 11am-7pm Sun) Surf, burn discs and print.

### MEDICAL SERVICES

**Holberton Hospital** ( ☎ 462-0251; Hospital Rd) Located just off Queen Elizabeth Hwy. (A new facility, Mt St John's Medical Centre, is set to open in 2008. It's the grand-looking structure on a knoll off Queen Elizabeth Hwy just east of St John's.)

**Old Nox Pharmacy** ( ☎ 562-4721; St Mary's St; ⏰ 8:30am-10pm) Small but useful selection of medicines.

### MONEY

ATMs are easily found throughout St John's.

**Royal Bank of Canada** (High St; ⏰ 8am-2pm Mon-Thu, 8am-noon & 2-4pm Fri)

### POST

**Post office** (Long St; ⏰ 8:15am-noon & 1-4pm Mon-Thu, 8:15am-noon & 1-5pm Fri)

### TELEPHONE

There is a row of pay phones along Temple St, south of St John's Anglican Cathedral.

**Cable & Wireless** (Thames St; ⏰ 8am-5pm Mon-Fri, 9am-noon Sat) Card phones can be found outside the building. Buy the cards inside.

### TOURIST INFORMATION

**Tourist office** ( ☎ 462-0480; www.antigua-barbuda.com; Ministry of Tourism, Queen Elizabeth Hwy; ⏰ 8am-4:30pm Mon-Thu, 8am-3pm Fri) Buried in a government building housing bureaucracies.

## Sights & Activities

### MUSEUM OF ANTIGUA & BARBUDA

This community-run **museum** ( ☎ 462-1469; cnr Market & Long Sts; adult/child EC$8/free; ⏰ 8:30am-4pm Mon-Fri, 10am-2pm Sat) occupies the old courthouse, a stone building that dates from 1750. It has a heart-warming collection of displays on island history that appears to have been assembled by an especially keen group of students.

It has a touchable section with stone pestles and conch-shell tools, and modest displays on natural history, the colonial era and the struggle for emancipation. The most popular exhibit is the well-worn bat of former West Indies' cricket team captain Vivian Richards. The section on shipwrecks includes a fair bit of philosophical discussion.

Ask for the brochure showing the town's historical buildings.

ANTIGUA & BARBUDA

ANTIGUA & BARBUDA

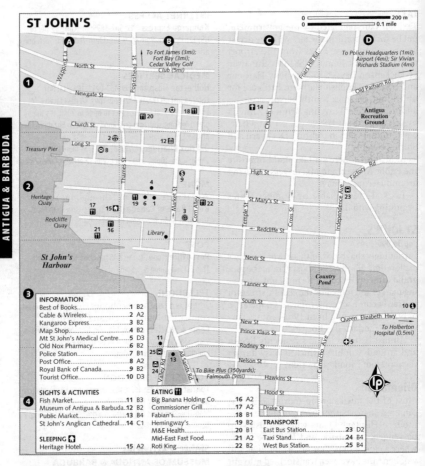

## ST JOHN'S

### INFORMATION
Best of Books.............................1 B2
Cable & Wireless.......................2 A2
Kangaroo Express.......................3 D3
Map Shop.................................4 B2
Mt St John's Medical Centre.....5 D3
Old Nox Pharmacy......................6 B2
Police Station............................7 B1
Post Office.................................8 A2
Royal Bank of Canada................9 B2
Tourist Office...........................10 D3

### SIGHTS & ACTIVITIES
Fish Market...............................11 B3
Museum of Antigua & Barbuda.12 B2
Public Market...........................13 B4
St John's Anglican Cathedral....14 C1

### SLEEPING
Heritage Hotel..........................15 A2

### EATING
Big Banana Holding Co............16 A2
Commissioner Grill...................17 A2
Fabian's...................................18 B1
Hemingway's............................19 B2
M&E Health.............................20 B1
Mid-East Fast Food..................21 A2
Roti King.................................22 B2

### TRANSPORT
East Bus Station.......................23 D2
Taxi Stand...............................24 B4
West Bus Station......................25 B4

## ST JOHN'S ANGLICAN CATHEDRAL

This twin-spired **cathedral** (btwn Newgate & Long Sts) is the town's dominant landmark and dominates the town as seen from the harbor. Conversely, its harbor views are sweeping. The original church dated back to 1681, but the current baroque-style stone structure was constructed in 1847, after a devastating earthquake.

The cathedral interior is unusual in that it's completely encased in pitch pine, creating a church-within-a-church effect that feels something like the inside of an old sailing ship. The interior can be viewed when the caretaker is around, which is usually until 5pm. The adjoining cemetery is a popular local picnic spot and de facto park.

## MARKETS

Even if you have no interest in self-catering, the large **Public Market** (Market St; 6am-6pm Mon-Sat) is a fine place for a stroll. Besides the iconic black pineapple and a plethora of fruits and vegetables, there are all manner of household and other items for sale. The bus station is just west and the entire area is a hive of activity during the day. Follow your nose to the **fish market** just north of the buses by the water.

## GOLF

**Cedar Valley Golf Club** ( 462-0161), a 10-minute drive north of St John's, has an 18-hole course with cart and club rentals.

## Festivals & Events

Antigua's renowned 10-day Carnival hits the streets of St John's from the end of July to early August; for more information, see p536.

## Sleeping

It's slim pickings for accommodations in St John's, but most visitors tend to favor beach resorts anyway.

**Heritage Hotel** ( ☎ 462-1247; www.heritagedowntown.com; Thames St; r EC$150-200; 🟰 🖵 ) Split over two buildings, this modern hotel is popular with business travelers. A waterfront annex has 19 rooms with kitchens while the main building (with shops on the ground floor) has 25 standard rooms. All have high-speed internet.

## Eating

Although there are good choices by the harbor, wander the streets for more authentic fare.

**Mid-East Fast Food** (Redcliffe St; mains EC$8-18; 🕑 10am-4pm Mon-Sat) While seated at picnic tables in the shade, cool off with a fresh smoothie and enjoy a falafel, sharwarma or hummus in pita.

**Fabian's** ( ☎ 562-4605; meals from EC$10-15; 🕑 lunch Mon-Sat) A big place by local standards, this locally popular restaurant has shady tables under trees on a side patio. Lunch plate specials are the thing; look for freshly caught fish or curried goat served with creamy fungi (the cornmeal porridge that's a regional staple).

**M&E Health** ( ☎ 562-4487; off Newgate St; mains EC$12; 🕑 breakfast & lunch) The decor is as simple as the healthy fare at this little café, which prominently features brown rice, soy milk and fish.

**Roti King** (St Mary's St; roti EC$13; 🕑 8:30am-midnight, closed Sun) An old wooden house is now home to some of the best cheap food in St John's. Enjoy fresh banana bread with a roti that comes with a variety of fresh and spicy fillings such as chicken, beef, veggies or conch.

**Hemingway's** (St Mary's St; meals EC$20-80; 🕑 breakfast, lunch & dinner Mon-Sat) Enjoy fine casual fare throughout the day at a table on the breezy 2nd-floor veranda at this popular restaurant and bar. Start the day with good banana pancakes and omelettes; later, choose from seafood, burgers and steaks. Service is cheery and the bar offers up a fine rum punch.

**Big Banana Holding Co** (Redcliffe St; pizza EC$22-50; 🕑 lunch & dinner Mon-Sat) This touristy warehouse-style pizzeria has shady seating outside and high ceilings inside. For a snack, snatch a slice.

**Commissioner Grill** (Redcliffe St; mains EC$30-85; 🕑 lunch & dinner Mon-Sat, dinner Sun) An upscale local crowd feasts on regional specialties like marinated conch salad and salt cod with fungi. The mood is laid-back, but there's a patina of class in this vintage wooden shop house.

## Shopping

Heritage and Redcliffe Quays are lined with souvenir, jewelry and duty-free stores aimed at folks just off the gangplanks. Wander the streets of the center to sample a variety of shops peddling everything from kitchen sundries to flamboyant shoes that would do any Carnival queen proud.

# FORT JAMES

Fort James, a small stronghold at the north side of St John's Harbour, was first built in 1675, but most of the present structure dates from 1739. It still has a few of its original 36 cannons, a powder magazine and a fair portion of its walls intact. The site reeks of atmosphere: it's moodily rundown and is rarely the scene of crowds.

Fort Bay, a narrow strip of sand backed by trees that stretches north from the fort, is popular with islanders.

**Russell's** ( ☎ 462-5479; mains EC$40-85; 🕑 lunch & dinner) A pearl within the shell of the fort, Russell's is housed in the reconstructed old officers' quarters. Enjoy drinks and views across the walls and harbor from the wide wooden verandas. Many come for sunset, but live jazz on Sunday nights really packs 'em in. The menu includes garlic shrimp, lobster and steaks.

# RUNAWAY BAY

Runaway Bay is a simple strip of sand just south of popular Dickenson Bay. It was battered by 1995's Hurricane Luis and has never fully recovered. The inland road and the salt marshes are still lined with rubble. Several of the modest beachfront hotels are in decline. On the plus side, the beach is recovering and is seldom crowded – or even trod.

# DICKENSON BAY

The middle market of Antigua's holiday-makers find fun and refuge at this long crescent of white sand on the northwest coast. The swimming is good and during the day there's no shortage of aquatic activities to lure punters off their loungers. At nightfall, as you enjoy a vivid sunset, classic beach bars serve rum punches by the bucketful.

The beach can get crowded, what with the vendors peddling junk, women hoping to braid hair and the hordes of funseekers from the massive Sandals resort that dominates the middle ground.

Still, the pervasive strains of clichéd reggae set the mood for a classic Caribbean beach vacation.

## Activities

**Tony's Water Sports** ( ☎ 462-6326) is typical of operators found on the larger beaches islandwide. It offers a range of boating activities, such as waterskiing (US$40), parasailing (US$60) and jet-skiing (US$50). Tony will take groups of up to four people deep-sea fishing (per half-day US$380) or snorkeling (per half-day US$20).

**Windsurf Antigua** ( ☎ 461-9463) rents boards (per hour US$25, per day US$70) and offers lessons (from US$55 for two hours). It also offers advice and deliver equipment islandwide.

## Sleeping

**our pick** **Siboney Beach Resort** ( ☎ 462-0806; www .siboneybeachclub.com; units US$170-325; ✕ 🖳 🏊 ) Set in its own little rainforest on the beach, Siboney has a variety of rooms and apartments in three-story blocks. It's not fancy, but it is awfully nice and cheery. Most units have small kitchenettes, nicely updated bathrooms, wi-fi, and patios or balconies. Friendly touches include free beach chairs.

**Dickenson Bay Cottages** ( ☎ 462-4940; www .dickensonbaycottages.com; 1-/2-bed apt from US$170/325; ✕ 🖳 🏊 ) A small, secluded complex of nicely furnished units ('cottages' is something of misnomer; don't expect a cute little hut at the end of a sandy path) in blocks set around a pool. The decor is vibrant. It's family friendly and a five-minute walk from the beach.

**Antigua Village** ( ☎ 462-2930; www.antiguavillage .com; studios from US$295; ✕ 🖳 🏊 ) This is a well-maintained beachside condominium complex, with 98 units spread around landscaped grounds. They're individually owned so the decor varies, but most are spacious with large balconies and fully equipped kitchens.

The price pecking order increases as you move from garden to pool to ocean views.

## Eating

**Chippy Antigua** ( ☎ 724-1166; beach road; mains EC$25-40; ✲ 4-9pm Wed & Fri) It doesn't look like much. In fact, it looks like what it is: a snack truck parked on gravel by the side of the road. But what snacks! Meals really. Superb fish and chips, scampi, homemade pies and more are on offer. There's a full bar and you can enjoy it all at plastic tables under the stars.

**Pari's Pizza** ( ☎ 462-1501; mains EC$30-80; ✲ lunch & dinner Tue-Sun) Besides the dish in the name of this houselike restaurant about five minutes up the hill from the beach, there are thick steaks and juicy ribs. It's almost opposite Dickenson Bay Cottages on the inland road. Take-out is available.

**Coconut Grove** ( ☎ 462-1538; mains EC$50-90; ✲ breakfast, lunch & dinner) Situated on the beach at Siboney Beach Resort, this Creole restaurant is always worth booking for its changing menu of seafood. The rock lobster is a winner, the rum punch deceitfully mellow and fresh-tasting (it kicks).

**our pick** **Papa Zouk** ( ☎ 464-6044; Hilda Davis Dr, Gambles Terrace; mains EC$50-100; ✲ dinner Mon-Sat) Modestly billing itself as a 'rum shop' is as accurate as calling it a 'snack bar.' This casual bistro turns out some of the most sophisticated seafood dishes on the island. The menu always reflects what's fresh and you can specify your preparation. Platters with Creole flavors are excellent for sharing. There are 200 kinds of rum behind the bar; the staff mix a mean P'tit Punch, an addictive concoction with marinated rum. Given the above and the inland location, take a cab.

## NORTH SHORE

The northern part of the island between Dickenson Bay and the airport has posh residential areas, a golf course, time-share condos and all-inclusive resorts. If you're not staying here, there's little reason to visit, although the best route between Dickenson Bay and the airport passes along the coast.

Off the coast on Long Island, **Jumby Bay** ( ☎ 462-6000; www.jumbybayresort.com; r from US$1250; ✕ 🖳 🏊 ) regularly wins plaudits as one of the best resorts in the Caribbean. The 51 rooms and villas all have water views from their perfect spot on the otherwise uninhabited island. Rates are for two people and include meals and drinks. Luxuries abound and the silky-smooth service includes niceties such as 24-hour room service and wi-fi. Access is by the resort's boat.

**Le Bistro** ( ☎ 462-3881; mains EC$80-140; Ⓨ dinner, closed Mon) is a little beacon amid the scrubland that not only draws the Hodges Bay swells, but gourmands from across the island. Chef-owner Patrick Gauducheau leads a talented team preparing elegant island fare such as linguini tossed with lobster. Presentations are exquisite, service immaculate. Book.

## FIVE ISLANDS

This peninsula west of St John's is linked to the island by a single road, which passes through the low-key village of Five Islands. The coast is a series of coves and beaches, dotted with numerous resorts.

**Deep Bay** is a pleasant little bay with a sandy beach and protected waters. The Royal Antiguan Hotel sits above the beach, and there's a fair amount of resort activity, but it's a good-sized strand and a nice swimming spot.

The coral-encrusted wreck of the **Andes** lies in the middle of Deep Bay with its mast poking up above the water. Approximately 100 years have passed since this bark caught fire and went down, complete with a load of pitch from Trinidad. The waters are shallow enough around the wreck to be snorkeled, but divers tend to bypass it because ooze still kicks up pretty easily from the bottom.

The remains of **Fort Barrington**, which once protected the southern entrance of St John's Harbour, are atop the promontory that juts out at the northern end of the bay. Although the fort was originally constructed in the mid-17th century, most of the present fortifications date from 1779. To hike up to the fort, simply begin walking north along the beach at Deep Bay; the trail takes about 10 minutes.

A salt pond separates Deep Bay from smaller Hog John Bay, where there's a beach, a couple of hotels and views of St John's.

Near the south end of the peninsula, located on Hawksbill Bay, the well-established **Hawksbill Beach Resort** ( ☎ 462-0301; www.hawksbill .com; r all inclusive from US$400; ❄ 🖳 🐆 ), situated on 37 acres, offers 111 rooms (all nonsmoking), cottages or apartments, and tends to attract more mature guests as well as Brits who appreciate the 'no shorts' rules at night. Rooms are airy, some with pitched ceilings and traditional decor.

Hawksbill Bay has a string of four lovely beaches; away from the eponymous resort, one section of Hawksbill Beach is reserved for nudists.

## JOLLY HARBOUR

Jolly Harbour is a busy marina and dockside condominium village on Antigua's west coast. Facilities include a pharmacy, internet place, boat rentals and charters, and a handful of restaurants and bars. There's also a dive shop, **Jolly Dive** ( ☎ 462-8305; www.jollydive.com; Jolly Harbour).

South of the marina development, the coast road parallels **Valley Church Beach**, a mostly undeveloped yet accessible strip of sand and palms where you can have a religious experience at the cute little beach bar.

**Jolly Harbour Golf Course** ( ☎ 480-6950) has an 18-hole course with cart and club rentals.

**Cocobay Resort** ( ☎ 562-2400; www.cocobayresort .com; all-inclusive per person from US$200; ❄ 🖳 🐆 ), a 49-unit development on a hillside south of Jolly Harbour, is a stylish retreat that eschews the usual resort paradigms. Creole garden cottages in pale Mediterranean colors have terracotta-tiled floors and earthy dark-wood furnishings. The picture-postcard infinity pool is only steps away from lovely Valley Church Beach.

A classic sailor's open-air bar, the **Deck** ( ☎ 462-6550; mains EC$25-50; Ⓨ lunch & dinner) crawls with seamen and wannabe pirates during cocktail hour. Actually, the boaters here are off yachts so it's not like you'll be shanghaied if you drop by – unless you want to be. Mop up the booze with good grub that includes fine burgers.

The Epicurean market sells sandwiches, liquor, groceries and British newspapers.

## JOLLY HARBOUR TO JOHNSON'S POINT BEACH

Heading south on the coastal road you'll pass one of Antigua's best beaches, **Darkwood Beach**, a wide swath of white sand and turquoise water that makes for a great swimming and snorkeling spot. There are some changing rooms, a few deck chairs, and a little beachside hut that serves tasty club sandwiches or barbecued fish during the day.

As you drive south look for a sign on a small house on the hill side of the road that

ANTIGUA & BARBUDA

reads 'The Nature of Things Museum.' Run by the feisty Winston Hazzard, inside you'll find over 250 types of sea shells and other flotsam. Admission costs US$2 and includes lectures on the environment, the behavior of tourists and many other topics. Hazzard offers fascinating 2½-hour nature walks up Boggy Peak (US$30) and will negotiate trips out onto the salt.

## FIG TREE DRIVE

After Johnson's Point Beach, the road passes pineapple patches, tall century plants, and pastures with grazing cattle and donkeys. High hills lie on the inland side of the road, topped by the 1319ft **Boggy Peak**, the island's highest point.

**Old Road**, a village with both a fair amount of poverty and two swank lodges, Curtain Bluff and Carlisle Bay, marks the start of Fig Tree Dr. From here, the terrain gets lusher as the road winds through patches of rainforest. The narrow 5-mile-long road is lined with bananas (called 'figs' in Antigua), coconut palms and big old mango trees. A recent paving makes it one of the better roads on the island and your biggest hazard will be driving too fast. Numerous roadside stands sell fruit, including baseball-sized black pineapples and fresh juices. Fig Tree Dr ends at the village of Swetes.

On the way to Falmouth Harbour you pass through the village of Liberta and by the **St Barnabus Anglican Chapel**, an attractive greenstone-and-brick church built in 1842.

## FALMOUTH HARBOUR

Large, protected and oh so picturesque, horseshoe-shaped Falmouth Harbour has two main centers of activity: the north side of the harbor, where the small village of Falmouth is located, and the more visitor-oriented east side of the harbor, which has most of the restaurants. The east side is within easy walking distance of Nelson's Dockyard.

Compared to the flash afloat, the marina is pretty low-key. There is wi-fi throughout and the bulletin boards are among the best for looking for passage or jobs afloat. **Lord Jim's Locker** ( ☎ 460-6910; Marina) has a good selection of books and maps.

### Sights

On the main road in Falmouth's center is **St Paul's Anglican Church**, Antigua's first church.

As one of the island's oldest buildings, dating from 1676, the church once doubled as Antigua's courthouse. You can get a sense of its history by poking around the overgrown churchyard, which has some interesting and quite readable colonial-era gravestones. Charles Pitt, the brother of the English prime minister William Pitt, was buried here in 1780.

### Sleeping & Eating

There are several restaurants, bars and cafés close to the marina at the east side of Falmouth Harbour.

**Zanzibar** ( ☎ 463-7838; www.zanzibarantigua.com; r US$40-85, cottage US$100-200; 💻 ) A great-value place near the marina, Zanzibar has six basic rooms that share bathrooms, and two very attractive cottages, one with a private beach and harbor views. Offers wi-fi access.

**Catamaran Hotel & Marina** ( ☎ 460-1036; www .catamaran-antigua.com; r US$150-210; 🍽 💻 ) On a little beach at the north side of Falmouth Harbour, this simple 16-room hotel is a good deal. The deluxe rooms on the 2nd floor have bathtubs and four-poster queen-size beds, and there are four ground-level units with kitchenettes.

**Last Lemming** ( ☎ 460-6910; meals EC$20-40; 🕑 10am-late) The kind of waterfront bar yachties dream of, this big, open place has a pool table, live music many nights, generous plates of hearty chow and stiff drinks. It's the perfect place to find out what's up afloat.

**Pasta Rite Ya** ( ☎ 764-2819; mains EC$20-50; 🕑 lunch & dinner) A simple but tasty waterfront Italian joint in an old house. Watch your mates swab the poop deck while you feast on big bowls of spaghetti with meatballs and other iconic treats.

**Abracadabra** ( ☎ 460-1732; mains EC$30-60; 🕑 5pm-late) It's magic! It's all things to all people: a 17th-century building where you can delight in seafood, a sand dance floor, a chilled out lounge area and more. Near the Nelson's Dockyard parking area. If you still have energy, stay for the open-air disco after 11pm.

## ENGLISH HARBOUR

English Harbour is the one must-see attraction on Antigua. It's the site of Nelson's Dockyard, a restored 18th-century British naval base named for English captain Lord Horatio Nelson, who spent the early years of his career here. Strolling the cobblestones it's not too hard to imagine you can hear the lashings of the whip and other old British naval traditions. Fortunately, no maggoty rolls are sold.

Two hilltop forts flank the entrance to the harbor, which is separated from Falmouth Harbour by a slender neck of land that, at its narrowest, is just a few hundred yards wide. The Nelson's Dockyard entrance is a five-minute walk from the Falmouth Harbour marina, so you can park once and visit both.

## Information

The following are all inside Nelson's Dockyard.

**Bank of Antigua** ( �») 9am-1pm Mon-Thu, 9am-noon & 2-4pm Fri, 9am-noon Sat) Just 100ft past the entrance; has an ATM.

**Post office** ( �») 9am-3pm Mon-Fri) At the entrance to Nelson's Dockyard.

## Sights & Activities

### NELSON'S DOCKYARD

This historic **dockyard** (www.nationalparksantigua .com; adult/12yr EC$13/free; �» 9am-5pm) is Antigua's most popular tourist sight, as well as the island's main port of entry for yachts. Try to ignore the frequent flocks of day trippers as you walk among the palm-flanked Georgian buildings. The dockyard, which dates from 1745, was abandoned in 1889 following a decline in Antigua's economic and strategic importance to the British Crown.

Restoration work began in the 1950s, and this former royal naval base now has a new life closely paralleling its old one – that of an active dockyard. And it's the only working Georgian marina in the western hemisphere. The handsome old brick-and-stone buildings have been converted into yachting and tourist-related facilities. The boat home and joiners' loft are nicely restored and it's easy to imagine a British frigate being prepared to sail out and blast a few French or pirate ships.

The dockyard is English Harbour's main center of activity. With all occupying old naval buildings there's a small market selling tourist tat, a handful of restaurants, inns and numerous boating facilities. There's also a dive shop, **Dockyard Divers** ( ☎ 460-1178; www .dockyard-divers.com; PO Box 184, Nelson's Dockyard). Take time to stop at the interpretive plaques that explain the history of the various buildings.

On entering, pick up the free map that shows the dockyard sights and businesses. A water taxi from the dockyard across the harbor to Galleon Beach costs US$10, round-trip.

The dockyard's small **museum** occupies a former officers' house and features a collection of nautical memorabilia. Displays in a room devoted to Lord Nelson examine the 'irritation, lust, piety and jealousy' he felt for the (married) Lady Emma Hamilton.

### FORT BERKLEY

A pleasant 10-minute stroll starting behind the Copper & Lumber Store Hotel leads to the site of this small fort, which overlooks the western entrance of English Harbour. Dating from 1704, it served as the harbor's first line of defense. You'll find intact walls, a powder magazine, a small guardhouse and a solitary cannon, the last of 25 cannons that once lined the fortress walls. There's also a fine harbor view at the top. Walk another 20 minutes up over the ridge and you reach secluded **Pigeon Point Beach**.

### SHIRLEY HEIGHTS

With its scattered 18th-century fort ruins and wonderful hilltop views, Shirley Heights is a fun place to explore. A bit over a mile up Shirley Heights Rd you'll reach **Dow's Hill Interpretation Centre** (admission EC$13, free with Nelson's Dockyard ticket; �» 9am-5pm), which features a viewpoint, and a missable audiovisual presentation on island history and culture.

For the best views and main concentration of ruins, continue past the museum; the road will fork after about 0.5 miles. The left fork leads shortly to **Blockhouse Hill**, where you'll find remains of the Officers' Quarters dating from 1787 and a clear view of sheltered Mamora Bay to the east.

The right fork leads to **Fort Shirley**, which has more ruins, including one that has been turned into a casual restaurant and bar. There's a sweeping view of English Harbour from the rear of the restaurant, while from the top of Signal Hill (487ft), just a minute's walk from the parking lot, you can see Montserrat 28 miles to the southwest and Guadeloupe 40 miles to the south. It's a perfect spot to watch the sun go down.

On Sundays, the fort hosts wildly popular barbecues that rock with steel drum bands and reggae. After dark, the dancing cranks up several notches.

ANTIGUA & BARBUDA

## Sleeping

All the accommodations reviewed here have wi-fi.

**Admiral's Inn** ( ☎ 460-1027; r US$100-180; 🄫 🖵 ) Built as a warehouse in 1788, the inn has 14 rooms with open-beam ceilings above the restaurant. The rooms vary in size and decor, and some are quite small. Room No 6 is larger and a good choice, while No 3 is a quiet corner room with a fine harbor view. Some rooms have air-con, none have tubs.

**Copper & Lumber Store Hotel** ( ☎ 460-1058; www .copperandlumberhotel.com; r US$195-325; 🖵 ) This beautifully restored hotel was built in the 1780s to store the copper and lumber needed for ship repairs. It now has 14 studios and suites, all with kitchens and ceiling fans, and some with antique furnishings. Rooms surround a lush courtyard and there's a good, vintage-feeling bar.

**Inn at English Harbour** ( ☎ 460-1014; www.theinn .ag; r from US$500; 🄫 🖵 🕭 ) With great views of the bay, this small beach resort on the southeast side of English Harbour looks like a cozy English lodge. Its 34 refined, airy rooms and suites have big balconies and baths, and are furnished with Thai-style teak beds. Activities include kayaking, cycling, tennis and sailing.

## Eating

**Dockyard Bakery** ( 🕭 breakfast & lunch Mon-Sat) Located behind the museum at Nelson's Dockyard, the baked goods here will draw you in like a sailor to rum. Sandwiches are best enjoyed under the 300-year-old sandbox tree out front.

**HQ** ( ☎ 562-2563; mains EC$50-100; 🕭 11am-late) Although the building dates from pre-acronym times, the name of this bar and restaurant describes its historic function. From the 2nd-floor tables on wide wooden verandas, diners can enjoy fine French fare while masts move like metronomes in the distance. On many nights there's live music.

**Admiral's Inn** (dinner mains EC$60-90; 🕭 breakfast, lunch & dinner) The changing chalkboard menu usually features salads, burgers and seafood at lunchtime, with more-elaborate dishes like lobster thermidor for dinner. The dining room reeks with history, and tables outside overlook the harbor.

## HALF MOON & NONSUCH BAYS

Half Moon Bay, on the southeastern side of the island, is an undeveloped crescent-shaped bay with yet another beautiful white-sand beach and turquoise waters.

Just north of Half Moon Bay at Nonsuch Bay, **Harmony Hall** ( ☎ 460-4120; www.harmonyhall antigua.com; s/d US$180/200; 🄫 🕭 ) is set amid the sturdy stone structures of an old sugar mill. Local art is sprinkled about the complex like sugar and you'll have plenty of solitude to enjoy it as the inn is quite remote. Regular boats take guests out to uninhabited Green Island. The candlelit open-air **restaurant** (mains EC$30-80; 🕭 dinner Fri & Sat) is known for its creative takes on Mediterranean fare.

## LONG BAY

On the east side of Antigua, Long Bay has clear-blue waters and a gorgeous white-sand beach that's reef-protected and good for snorkeling. Two exclusive resorts bookend the beach. Other than a few private homes and a couple of beach bars, there's little else in the neighborhood. If you have a car, this is a good place for a beachy day trip away from the hustle and bustle of Dickenson Bay.

### Devil's Bridge

A modest coastal sea arch, Devil's Bridge is at Indian Town Point, an area thought to be the site of an early Arawak settlement. To get here, turn east onto the paved road a third of a mile before the Long Bay Hotel turn-off. After a mile the road ends at a roundabout; from there the arch is a minute's walk to the east. Dramatic waves add excitement as they sometimes break over the rocks and erupt through blowholes.

On the east end of Long Bay, the 25-room, family-run **Long Bay Hotel** ( ☎ 463-2005; www .longbayhotel.com; r US$300-600; 🖵 ) has Creole-style rooms and cottages with wicker furnishings and sea views. It's almost all-inclusive: rates are for two people and include breakfast and dinner. Most activities are free; there's also wi-fi access. This is a good spot for a worry-free escape without the horrors of a huge package-tour resort.

## BETTY'S HOPE

Just southeast of the village of Pares, **Betty's Hope** ( ☎ 462-4930; admission US$2; 🕭 10am-4pm Tue-Sat) was the island's first sugar plantation, built by Christopher Codrington in 1674 and named in honor of his daughter Betty. Ruins of two old stone windmills, a still house (distillery) and a few other stone structures remain on the site, which is now under the jurisdiction of the Museum of Antigua & Barbuda. One of the mills has been painstakingly restored and returned to working condition. Although operated only on special occasions, the windmill sails remain up most of the year. Displays document Antigua's sugar industry.

# BARBUDA

Desert island. The mere phrase conjures up images of isolation, beaches, palm trees and the ephemeral concept of 'getting away from it all.' Barbuda may well be the model for the iconic desert isle.

A mere 25 miles north of Antigua, Barbuda remains one of the Eastern Caribbean's least-visited places. Other than its teeming frigate-bird colony and its beautiful beaches, most of which are best accessed by private boat, there's just not much here. And that's perhaps its greatest appeal.

The only village, Codrington, is home to most residents and is the site of the island's strip of an airport. Other than a small resort or two and a couple of guesthouses, there's not much here for tourists; locals and visitors in the know like it this way. In fact this very isolation has been the death of a couple of high-end resorts that had opened to much acclaim.

It's a tight-knit place, most of the 1250 islanders share half a dozen surnames and can trace their lineage to a small group of slaves brought to Barbuda by the Codrington brothers Christopher and John. They leased the island in 1685 from the British Crown and used it to grow food for Antigua's sugarcane workers. The family also quietly salvaged untold riches from ships that had run afoul of the surrounding reef.

During the 18th century, the Codrington family managed to keep their lease, which was negotiated at an annual rental payment of 'one fattened sheep,' for nearly two centuries. Their legacy remains well beyond the town's name – from the communal land-use policies that still govern Barbuda to the introduced goats, sheep and feral donkeys that range freely (to the detriment of the island flora).

Besides having the Caribbean's largest colony of frigate birds, Barbuda hosts tropical

ANTIGUA & BARBUDA

---

**GROWING UP BARBUDAN**

Asha Frank, 19, spent most of her life growing up on Barbuda. Like many people her age on small and thinly populated islands, she left – at age 15 – so she could have the kind of formal education impossible at home. Being a kid on a desert island would seem like a dream for many (especially those growing up someplace where a familiar parental refrain is: 'Have you shoveled the walk yet?'). Asha talks about growing up on tropical Barbuda.

**What's the best thing about growing up on Barbuda?**
The freedom. When I was a child there were no restrictions about where I played because it is such a safe place. I'd go fishing with friends or catch donkeys and ride them around the village. The young boys and girls are incredibly fit because they have so much exercise and good food.

**What's bad about being a kid there?**
There are not many bad things about Barbuda, although when you're a teenager it can be a bit boring and feel isolated. There are not many things for 16- to 20-year-olds to do other than the odd party and horse races. Hurricanes are a threat to the island, particularly during August and September and there are often long periods of drought. However, this only makes you appreciate things that are abundant elsewhere.

**What do you tell your friends in England about your home?**
Who wouldn't want to say they grew up in the Caribbean? Barbuda is different to all the other islands. Many people have never heard of it and often mistake it for Bermuda or Barbados. It has an untouched beauty; there are not many tourists. A lot of people come back in summer and it's almost like a reunion.

**You're now at university studying history and Caribbean studies. What's next?**
I live in London; it is a very impersonal place where you can easily be forgotten. In Barbuda it is like one big family and there are good manners and respect for everyone. I will definitely go back to live in the future because it is the only place I would call my true home.

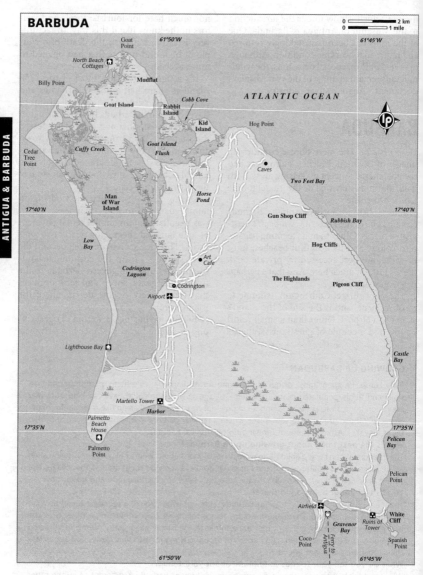

# BARBUDA

0 ——— 2 km
0 ——— 1 mile

*Goat Point*

*North Beach Cottages*

*Billy Point*

**Mudflat**

*Goat Island*

*Cobb Cove*

**Rabbit Island**

*Kid Island*

*Hog Point*

**ATLANTIC OCEAN**

61°50'W

61°45'W

*Cedar Tree Point*

*Cuffy Creek*

*Goat Island Flush*

*Caves*

*Two Feet Bay*

*Horse Pond*

**Man of War Island**

17°40'N

17°40'N

**Gun Shop Cliff**

*Rubbish Bay*

**Hog Cliffs**

*Low Bay*

*Codrington Lagoon*

*Art Cafe*

**The Highlands**

**Pigeon Cliff**

● Codrington

*Airport*

*Lighthouse Bay*

*Castle Bay*

*Martello Tower*

*Harbor*

**Palmetto Beach House**

17°35'N

17°35'N

*Pelican Bay*

*Palmetto Point*

*Pelican Point*

*Airfield*

*Gravenor Bay*

*Ruins of Tower*

**White Cliff**

*Coco Point*

*Ferry to Antigua*

*Spanish Point*

61°50'W

61°45'W

mockingbirds, warblers, pelicans, ibis, oyster-catchers, herons and numerous kinds of ducks. The island also has wild boar and white-tailed deer, both of which are legally hunted.

## Getting There & Away

Many people visit Barbuda as part of a day trip by air (the ferry schedules can be hell on day trips). Note that the early arrival and late departure give you *plenty* of time to see everything. Bring a book for those contemplative hours while you await your flight back to Antigua.

For information on getting to Barbuda from Antigua (there's no service from any other island) by air or scheduled ferry, see p539.

## Getting Around

Barbuda has no public transportation, but distances are too great and the dusty dirt roads too hot to make walking a practical means of exploring. Barbuda also has a reputation for tours that fail to materialize, drivers that don't show up at the airport or some other missing link. Confirm all reservations.

You should be able to arrange to hire someone to drive you around for about US$20 per hour – inquire at your lodgings. Some drivers may meet the morning plane. Among the several locals who will drive you, try the owner of the Green Door Tavern, **Byron Askie** ( ☎ 460-0164). He also rents out a car for US$50 per day. **Eric Burton** ( ☎ 460-0465) has a 32-seater bus for hire; both men will act as driver and tour guide, if needed. Other locals also organise tours; see p537 for details.

## CODRINGTON

The town of Codrington – a modest, low-key place – is on the inland side of Codrington Lagoon, a hefty 3.5 miles north of the nearest beach.

The town begins at the airport – simply walk north from there and you'll be in the center of it.

Codrington is home to Barbuda's post office, its bank and its police station, as well as to a government house that dates from 1743. In keeping with local norms, there are few signs and the concept of regular opening hours is elusive.

**Nedds Guest House** ( ☎ 460-0059, 724-7490; r US$50-135) is above a grocery store near the airport. Run by Mcarthur Nedd, it has four rooms with fans and private bath, and a communal kitchen. An enclosed yard crawls with over 100 turtles, which often seem to move to the beat of the gospel singers at the nearby Pentecostal church.

Located in a newish building, **Palm Tree Guest House** ( ☎ 784-4331, 779-1074; r US$65-130; ⚄ ) has seven rooms and is slightly away from the center of town. Rooms have satellite TV and those at the top end have kitchens.

You can't make a joke about what's behind the door at the **Green Door Tavern** ( ☎ 783-7243; ⚄ 7am–late) as it's almost always open. Local fare is on offer, including crowd-pleasers like lingfish, liver, tripe and on Saturdays, goat water. A popular drink is made from sea moss.

Artist Claire Frank creates her colorful works on silk at **Art Cafe** ( ☎ 460-0434), a studio-gallery-café. Hours are variable but it's always worth stopping by its typically rural setting to see who's about, whether it be human, donkey or goat. All the drivers know her. Here you'll find coffee and tea plus great conversation.

## CODRINGTON LAGOON

The expansive, brackish estuary of Codrington Lagoon, which runs along Barbuda's west coast, is an intriguing destination for bird-watchers. Up to 5000 frigate birds (p534) nest in the lagoon's scrubby mangroves – with as many as a dozen birds roosting on a single bush. Because of this density, the birds' nesting sites are all abuzz with squawking, and the sight of all those blood-red inflating throat pouches is mesmerizing.

The most popular time to visit the rookery is during the mating season, from September to April (December is peak time). While the male frigate birds line up in the bushes, arch their heads back and puff out their pouches with an air of machismo as part of the elaborate courtship rituals, the females take to the sky. When one spots a suitor that impresses her, she'll land and initiate a mating ritual. After mating, a nest is built from twigs that the male gathers. The female lays a single egg that both birds incubate in turn. It takes about seven weeks for the chick to hatch, and nearly six months for it to learn to fly and finally leave the nest.

And should you tire of frigates, there are about 170 other species of birds that call the lagoon home.

---

**WHEN YOU REALLY WANT TO GET AWAY...**

On a remote bit of sand in the far north of Barbuda, **North Beach Cottages** ( ☎ 726-6355; www.antiguanice.com/north_beach_cottages/index.html; d from US$400) has three simple but comfortable bungalows right on the beach. Aside from the odd squawk of a frigate bird, the crash of a coconut or the blissful sound of the surf, there's little to disturb you here. Run by locals, the cottages can only be reached by boat. Rates include all meals, of which lobster is a prominent feature. Drinks include fresh rum punch on tap – wahoo! There's a two-night minimum and you pay in advance.

ANTIGUA & BARBUDA

The nesting site is in the upper lagoon area known as Man of War Island and can be reached only by boat. A couple of boats can take visitors out to the rookery, but arrangements generally need to be made a day in advance. If you're staying on Barbuda, you can arrange it through your guesthouse – the cost is about US$60 per boat for up to four people, and the ride to the reserve takes about 40 minutes. For those visiting Barbuda for the day, there are day tours that include the rookery (see p537).

## WEST & SOUTH COASTS

The west coast of Barbuda is lined with magnificent white-sand **beaches** and turquoise waters. From Palmetto Point northward there's a beautiful pinkish strand that extends 11 miles, most of it lining the narrow barrier of land separating Codrington Lagoon from the ocean. Because of its isolation, however, the beach remains the domain of a few lone boaters and a shuttered boutique hotel. More-accessible beaches are found along the coast south of the harbor, with one of the finest sweeps along the stretch between two resorts.

The **harbor** has a customs office and a sand-loading operation – Barbuda's sands are used to bolster some of Antigua's resort beaches. To the northwest of the harbor is the 56ft-high **Martello Tower**, a former fortified lookout station that from a distance looks like an old sugar mill. About 0.5 miles north of Coco Point is a nice white-sand strand with near-shore coral formations that provide good snorkeling.

The pristine waters of **Gravenor Bay**, between Coco and Spanish Points, are a favored yacht anchorage with reef formations and excellent snorkeling. Near the center of the bay

is an old, deteriorating pier, while the ruins of a small **tower** lie about 0.5 miles away to the east.

Archaeologists believe that the uninhabited peninsula leading to **Spanish Point** was once the site of a major Arawak settlement. A dirt track connects both ends of the bay, and another leads northward from the east side of the salt pond.

**Lighthouse Bay** ( ☎ 866-875-1383; www.lighthouse bayresort.com; d from US$1150; 🗶 🖵 🖭 ) hopes to break the jinx that has bedeviled other upscale properties on Barbuda. Located on a thin bit of sand that divides the sea from Codrington Lagoon, the new nine-room, all-inclusive property has water views in all directions. It's a compact site and appeals to folks hoping to catch fish and/or pretty much do nothing. Offers wi-fi access.

## CAVES

To get under the skin of Barbuda, so to speak, explore some caves about five miles northeast of Codrington. Note that rain can flood out access. **Dark Cave** is an expansive underground cavern with pools of deep water, while another cave near Two Feet Bay contains the faded drawings of Arawaks.

# DIRECTORY

## ACCOMMODATIONS

Other than a couple of budget guesthouses in St John's and a handful scattered around the island, Antigua is mainly home to resort-type complexes, many of them offering all-inclusive packages. Some, such as Jumby Bay (see p526), are considered among the best in the Caribbean. There are a few good-value, moderate-range places around the island,

---

**FRIGATE BIRDS**

Frigate birds skim the water's surface for fish, but because their feathers lack the water-resistant oils common to other seabirds, they cannot dive into water. Also known as the man-of-war bird, the frigate bird has evolved into an aerial pirate that supplements its own fishing efforts by harassing other seabirds until they release their catch, which the frigate bird then swoops up in mid-flight.

While awkward on the ground, the frigate bird, with its distinctive forked tail and 6ft wingspan, is beautifully graceful in flight. It has the lightest weight-to-wingspan ratio of any bird and can soar at great heights for hours on end – making it possible for the bird to feed along the coast of distant islands and return home to roost at sunset without having landed anywhere other than its nesting site.

ANTIGUA & BARBUDA

---

## PRACTICALITIES

- **Newspapers & Magazines** The daily *Antigua Sun* and *Daily Observer* offer contrasting takes on local events.
- **Radio** Catch hourly news and weather on Gem radio, at 93.9FM, or the *Daily Observer's* radio station, 91.1FM.
- **Video Systems** NTSC is the standard video system.
- **Electricity** The current used mostly is 220V, but some places use 110V, 60 cycles; check first. North American two-pin sockets are common.
- **Weights & Measures** The imperial system is used here.

---

with prices from about US$100 for a double in summer and closer to US$150 in winter. Still, most of Antigua's accommodations easily charge double these prices.

If you plan on traveling in late summer, keep in mind that many of Antigua's hotels close for September, and some extend that a few weeks in either direction.

In addition to the rates given throughout this chapter, an 8.5% government tax and a 10% to 15% service charge are added to all accommodations bills. Check whether they are included in prices quoted when making reservations. Listed rates fall by almost half outside of peak season (December to April).

Barbuda has only a handful of places to stay.

## ACTIVITIES

See p537 for information on tours around the islands.

### Beaches & Swimming

Antigua's tourist office spouts that the island has 365 beaches, 'one for each day of the year.' While we dare you to fact-check that, the island certainly doesn't lack lovely strands. Most of Antigua's beaches have white or light golden sands with turquoise water – many are protected by coral reefs and all are officially public. You can find nice sandy stretches all around the island, and generally, wherever there's a resort, there's a beach. Prime beaches on the west coast include the adjacent Dickenson and Runaway beaches, Deep Bay and Hawksbill Beach to the west of St John's, and the less populated Darkwood Beach and Johnson's Point Beach to the south. On the east coast, Half Moon Bay and Long Bay are top contenders. Visitors based in the English Harbour area can make their way to Galleon Beach and the clear waters of se-

cluded Pigeon Beach. The far ends of some public beaches, including the north side of Dickenson, are favored by topless bathers, and nude bathing is practiced along a section of Hawksbill Beach.

### Diving

Antigua has some excellent diving, with coral canyons, wall drops and sea caves hosting a range of marine creatures, including turtles, sharks, barracuda and colorful reef fish. Popular diving sites include the 2-mile-long Cades Reef, whose clear, calm waters have an abundance of fish, and numerous soft and hard corals. Part of it is now protected as an underwater park. Ariadne Shoal offers reefs teeming with large fish, lobsters and nurse sharks. A fun spot for both divers and snorkelers is the wreck of the *Jettias,* a 310ft steamer that sank in 1917 and now provides a habitat for reef fish and coral. The deepest end of the wreck is in about 30ft of water, while the shallowest part comes up almost to the surface.

Barbuda has scores of shipwrecks along its surrounding reef. In fact the Codringtons gained their fortune through salvage rights. Many of the sites are seldom visited; organize the complex logistics through an Antigua dive shop.

The going rate is about US$60 for a one-tank dive, US$90 for a two-tank dive and US$90 for a night dive. Nondivers who want to view the underwater world but don't want to overly commit can opt for a half-day resort course that culminates with a reef dive (around US$110). Rates include the rental of tanks and weights, but you'll have to pay an extra US$10 to US$20 for a regulator, buoyancy compensating device (BCD), snorkel, mask and fins. Most resorts have a shop they are linked with but don't feel you have to use it. Dive shops will pick up and drop off across the island.

There are dive shops in Jolly Harbour (p527) and English Harbour (p529).

### Golf

There are golf courses at Jolly Harbour (p527) and near St John's (p524).

### Hiking

The historical society, which operates the Museum of Antigua & Barbuda (p523), sponsors a culturally or environmentally oriented hike once a month. Walks average about 90 minutes and typically visit old estates or interesting landscapes. These field trips are free, but donations are welcome. Check with the museum for details.

### Other Water Activities

Dickenson Bay has operators offering a range of boating activities (including waterskiing and parasailing), deep-sea fishing and windsurfing; see p526 for details.

## BOOKS

Antigua's best-known writer is Jamaica Kincaid, who has authored a number of novels and essays including *A Small Place* (1988), which gives a scathing account of the negative effects of tourism and government corruption on Antigua. Other works by Kincaid include the novel *Annie John*, which recounts growing up in Antigua, and *Mr Potter*, a beautiful tale about the meaning of family centered on one man who lives and dies on Antigua.

Harvard lecturer Robert Coram penned an incendiary investigation, *Caribbean Time Bomb* (1993), into corruption on Antigua and Vere Cornwall Bird's involvement with the US government.

## BUSINESS HOURS

Businesses are open 8am to 5pm Monday to Friday and often on Saturdays until about 2pm. Shops are open until 6pm or 7pm weekdays and until late Saturday afternoon. Touristy places will be open later and if not already open on Sunday will become so if a cruise ship is in port.

Restaurants are good until 9pm or 10pm, bars somewhat later. But this is not an island on which to party until dawn – unless you have your own boat.

## CHILDREN

Reefs protect the beaches making for gentle swimming conditions, while most of the many resorts have programs for kids.

## DANGERS & ANNOYANCES

Besides the usual regional cautions, note that St John's has some tough neighborhoods, which you'll easily sense before you've gone too far. In addition, stay alert in general when walking the streets, although street crime usually involves locals only.

## EMBASSIES & CONSULATES

**UK** ( ☎ 462-0008/9; britishc@candw.ag; Price Waterhouse Centre, 11 Old Parham Rd, St John's)

## FESTIVALS & EVENTS

**Antigua Sailing Week** (www.sailingweek.com) A major, week-long yachting event that begins on the last Sunday in April. It's the largest regatta in the Caribbean and generally attracts about 200 boats from a few dozen countries. In addition to a series of five boat races, there are rum parties and a formal ball, with most activities taking place at Nelson's Dockyard and Falmouth Harbour, where the majority of boats are anchored.

**Caribana Festival** Held in May, this is Barbuda's own Carnival, but it's by no means the grand affair of Antigua's Carnival.

**Carnival** Antigua's big annual festival is held from the end of July and culminates in a parade on the first Tuesday in August. Calypso music, steel bands, masqueraders, floats and 'jump-ups' (nighttime street parties) are all part of the celebrations.

## GAY & LESBIAN TRAVELERS

While there is no real gay scene on Antigua, there is no overt discrimination either.

## HOLIDAYS

Public holidays in Antigua and Barbuda:

**New Year's Day** January 1
**Good Friday** late March/early April
**Easter Monday** late March/early April
**Labour Day** first Monday in May
**Whit Monday** eighth Monday after Easter
**Carnival Monday & Tuesday** first Monday and Tuesday in August
**Antigua and Barbuda Independence Day** November 1
**VC Bird Day** December 9
**Christmas Day** December 25
**Boxing Day** December 26

# INTERNET ACCESS

St John's has internet cafés and most hotels offer wi-fi and computers in the lobby.

# INTERNET RESOURCES

An excellent resource for Barbuda is the community-run www.barbudaful.net.

# MEDICAL SERVICES

Antigua has good hospital facilities, see p523; Barbuda has quite basic service.

# MONEY

The currency of Antigua and Barbuda is the Eastern Caribbean dollar (EC$), and the official exchange rate is EC$2.72 to US$1.

US dollars are widely accepted. However, unless rates are posted in US dollars, as is the norm with accommodations, it usually works out better to use EC dollars.

Credit cards are widely accepted. Ask if there is a surcharge for using a credit card.

A 10% service charge is added to most restaurant bills, in which case no tipping is necessary.

# TELEPHONE

Antigua and Barbuda's area code is ☎ 268. To call from North America, dial ☎ 1-268, followed by the local number. From elsewhere, dial your country's international access code + ☎ 268 + the local phone number. We've included only the seven-digit local number in the listings in this chapter.

Phone calling cards are widely available. Local cell phones use the GSM system.

Avoid credit-card phones, as they charge a rapacious US$2 per minute or more locally, US$4 to other Caribbean islands or the US, and up to US$8 elsewhere.

For directory assistance, dial ☎ 411.

# TOURIST INFORMATION

The **Antigua & Barbuda Department of Tourism** (www.antigua-barbuda.org) operates a somewhat useful website. Information is also available from the tourist office in St John's (see p523). Otherwise, once you are on Antigua, you'll find the usual plethora of brochures. *Life in*

---

**EMERGENCY NUMBERS**

▪ **Ambulance** ☎ 462-0251
▪ **Police** ☎ 462-0125

---

*Antigua & Barbuda* is a weighty annual tome that will excite those whose idea of porn is lavish spreads of yachts and expensive watches.

# TOURS
## Antigua

Numerous companies offer tours of Antigua by land and sea, many timed for the convenience of cruise-ship passengers. The following are recommended for their ecological bent, which gets far beyond gift shops and beachy rum drinks.

**Adventure Antigua** ( ☎ 726 6355; www.adventureantigua.com) is run by Eli Fuller, a third-generation local. Many rave about his Eco-Tour (US$90) which takes in the still-unspoiled small islands of the north coast, including the aptly named Great Bird Island. The full day includes nature walks, snorkeling and a vast amount of insider info on the flora and fauna of the islands. A second tour, the Xtreme Circumnav (US$153), features a speedboat and is aimed at the Hummer set.

**Paddles** ( ☎ 463-1944; www.antiguapaddles.com; Seatons; adult/child US$55/45) gives a no-brainer hint of its tour type in its name. Guests explore the mangroves and shallows of the sparsely populated east coast via kayaks. The half-day trips include a motorboat shuttle, eco-explorations under your own paddle-power, snorkeling and the de rigueur time on a deserted beach.

## Barbuda

Besides the drivers listed previously (p533), several other locals will arrange outings on Barbuda. **George 'Prophet' Burton** ( ☎ 772-1209) has a minibus and offers a full-day tour with drinks and food for US$60 per person, a bargain. He can also make arrangements for divers who wish to explore the largely unexplored reefs.

Guesthouse-owner **Mcarthur Nedd** ( ☎ 724-7490) offers tours by van and boat. Another innkeeper, **Lynton Thomas** ( ☎ 773-9957) arranges day-long tours that meet flights for US$75 per person.

The helpful owner of the Art Café, **Claire Frank** ( ☎ 460-0434; ☼ 9am-5pm), can arrange tours, with advance notice.

# TRAVELERS WITH DISABILITIES

International resorts generally have good accommodations for people with disabilities. Otherwise, much of Antigua is something of a challenge. The must-see sights at English Harbour are set on wide, flat grounds, although individual buildings may be inaccessible.

## VISAS

Visas are not required by most nationalities for stays of less than six months.

## WOMEN TRAVELERS

Women won't find anything especially concerning about a visit to these islands.

## WORK

Short of turning something up in the yacht harbors – and you'll see plenty of posts on bulletin boards by sailors with *lots* of experience – there's little work here. Unemployment is high.

# TRANSPORTATION

## GETTING THERE & AWAY
### Entering Antigua & Barbuda

All visitors need a valid passport (US citizens see the boxed text, p830) and a round-trip or onward ticket, though immigration officials seem to be more interested in where you plan to stay. On arrival, you'll be given an immigration form to complete.

### Air

**VC Bird International Airport** (ANU; ☎ 462-0358) is about 5 miles from St John's center. It has an ATM, a **bureau de change** (☉ 7am-7pm Mon-Fri), a dozen car-rental companies and a post office. For those departing, it has a rudimentary café, a minute bookstore and paid wi-fi once you're past security.

Those arriving during peak afternoon hours should note that the immigration situation here is among the worst in the region. Waits of up to two hours are common and the staff are unlikely to present you with a warm welcome. Locals complain bitterly and all have horror stories such as the officer who rejects forms for having been filled out with the wrong shade of blue ink. The pernickety hassles can extend to your efforts to *leave* the island. Watch your shade of ink and handwriting skills!

The following airlines serve Antigua from these cities (some services are seasonal and only weekly):

**Air Canada** ( ☎ 800-744-2472; www.aircanada.com) Toronto
**American/American Eagle** ( ☎ 800-433-7300; www .aa.com) San Juan
**BMI** ( ☎ 800-788-0555; www.flybmi.com) Manchester
**British Airways** ( ☎ 800-247-9297; www.britishairways .com) London
**Carib Aviation** ( ☎ 481-2401/2/3; www.carib-aviation .com) Dominica, Guadeloupe, St Lucia
**Caribbean Airlines** (formerly BWIA; ☎ 800-744-2225; www.caribbean-airlines.com) Barbados, Kingston, Jamaica, Trinidad
**Continental** ( ☎ 800-231-0856; www.continetal.com) Newark
**Delta** ( ☎ 800-221-1212; www.delta.com) Atlanta
**LIAT** ( ☎ 462-0700; www.liat.com) Anguilla, Barbados, Dominica, San Juan, St Thomas, St Vincent, St-Marten/Sint Maarten, Trinidad
**US Airways** ( ☎ 800-622-1015; www.usairways.com) Charlotte, Philadelphia
**Virgin Atlantic** ( ☎ 800-744-7477; www.virgin-atlantic .com) London
**Winair** ( ☎ 462-2522; www.fly-winair.com) Montserrat, St-Marten/Sint Maarten

### Sea
#### CRUISE SHIP

Antigua is a major port of call for cruise ships. The island's cruise-ship terminal, at Heritage Quay in St John's Harbour, has a duty-free shopping center, and is within easy walking distance of St John's main sights. Cruise ships also anchor near Falmouth Harbor and taxi their passengers into the harbor for the day. See p830 for further details about cruise ship travel throughout the Caribbean.

#### FERRY

There is a sometime ferry service between Antigua and Montserrat. However, it is more off than on, much to the displeasure of locals who can't afford the high airfares. Check locally to see if it is running.

#### YACHT

Antigua's many fine, protected ports make it one of the major yachting centers of the Caribbean. A favorite place to clear customs is at Nelson's Dockyard in English Harbour. Other ports of entry are Falmouth Harbour, Jolly Harbour, St John's Harbour, and Crabbs Marina in Parham Harbour. If you're going on to Barbuda, ask for a cruising permit, which will allow you to visit that island without further formalities.

Antigua has many protected harbors and bays, and fine anchorages are found all around the island. Full-service marinas are at English Harbour, Falmouth Harbour, Jolly Harbour and Parham Harbour. Boaters can make reservations at many restaurants around Falmouth Harbour and English Harbour via VHF channel 68.

Barbuda's reefs, which extend several miles from shore, are thought to have claimed a good 200 ships since colonial times – a rather impressive number, considering that Barbuda has never been a major port. Some reefs remain poorly charted, and the challenge of navigating through them is one reason Barbuda remains well off the beaten path. If you're sailing to the island, bring everything you'll need in advance, because there are no yachting facilities on Barbuda.

## GETTING AROUND

See p537 for information on tours.

## Air

Unless you charter a plane or helicopter, your only option for getting to Barbuda by air is with **Carib Aviation** ( ☎ 481-2401/2/3; www .carib-aviation.com), which has 20-minute flights to/from Antigua to Barbuda most early mornings and late afternoons. Round-trip fares average US$200.

## Boat

The **Barbuda Express** ( ☎ 560-7989; www.antigua ferries.com; fare one-way/return EC$80/140) operates a rather quixotic service between St John's and Barbuda. On some days there are two round-trips, on others there is no service. The trip takes 90 minutes and is a civilized way to reach Barbuda, especially given the flight challenges (see above). However, there are reports that the ferry's posted schedule is not always followed so confirm everything one or more times in advance. This is especially important if you're hoping to use it for a day trip.

## Bicycle

Check with your hotel, many rent out a bike or two to guests.

## Bus

There is no public transport on Barbuda, but Antigua has a privately owned system of mini-vans and mid-sized buses. Fares cost from EC$1.50 to EC$5.

## Car & Motorcycle
### DRIVER'S LICENSE

When you arrive, you'll need to buy a local driving permit, available from car-rental agencies. It costs US$20 and is valid for three months.

### RENTAL

Antigua has numerous car-rental agencies, including all the major brands. On Barbuda, some locals rent out vehicles.

### ROAD CONDITIONS

Antigua's roads range from smooth to rough to deadly. You'll be cruising along when suddenly a hubcap-popping pothole appears. If you plan to get off the beaten track (especially in the east), it's best to hire a 4WD.

Be aware of goats darting across the road and of narrow roads in built-up areas, which can also be crowded with children after school finishes.

Finding your way around Antigua can prove difficult at times. The island is randomly dotted with green road signs pointing you in the right direction, but they peter out the further away you get from the main centers. Private signs pointing the way to restaurants, hotels and a few other tourist spots are far more frequent. Beyond that, locals are always happy to offer advice – at times an adventure in itself.

### ROAD RULES

Driving is on the left-hand side. The speed limit is generally 20mph in villages and 40mph in rural areas.

## Taxi

Taxis on Antigua have number plates beginning with 'H.' Fares are regulated by the government, but check the fare with the driver before riding away.

On Barbuda, you should be able to arrange to hire someone to drive you around.

ANTIGUA & BARBUDA

# Montserrat

Twenty years ago, Montserrat marketed itself as being 'The way the Caribbean used to be.' Little did anyone know that in a few short years the slogan would become horribly ironic for anyone who harkened back to a pre-Palaeozoic era when volcanic eruptions shaped the planet. A series of volcanic eruptions beginning in 1995 devastated the lower two-thirds of the island. By 1997, the capital and only significant town, leafy Plymouth, was an ash-covered wasteland.

Today almost 5000 people live in the northern one-third of the island that was unaffected by the volcano. Long the refuge of goats and a few herders, new settlements are rising over the steep brown hills. To the south, the rolling green hills that once inspired fanciful comparisons to Ireland (you know, the palms of Cork), are scarred by ash and lava flows.

It's all been quite a shock to this tight-knit island community. But more than 10 years after the calamity, life is moving forward. Visitors can see a new centre for the island taking shape around Little Bay. On drives down the coast to the exclusion zone, you can get a feel for the island's rich tropical life and take in jaw-dropping vistas of the destruction.

You can see everything on a day trip to Montserrat. Some, however, will relish the solitude and enjoy the chance to become a part of the island's rebirth. Just know that things which go bump in the night may be a boulder shot out of the mouth of the volcano.

## FAST FACTS

- **Area** 39 sq miles and expanding
- **Capital** Plymouth (abandoned after volcano)
- **Country code** ☎ 664
- **Departure tax** EC$55
- **Famous for** Massive volcanic eruption in 1995
- **Language** English
- **Money** Eastern Caribbean dollar (EC$); EC$1 = US$0.38 = €0.24 = UK£0.19
- **Official name** Montserrat
- **People** Montserratians
- **Phrase** Got some? (A Montserratian asking another if they have goat water, the local delicacy.)
- **Population** 4800
- **Visa** Not required for nationals of North America and most European countries; see p545

## ITINERARIES

**One Day** You can easily see the highlights during a day trip to the island. You basically drive down the east coast to Jack Boy Hill, then circle back to see what's a-building in Little Bay, Sweeny's, St John's etc, then you follow the west road down to the volcano observatory and check out the ruins of upscale expat neighborhoods and Plymouth.

## CLIMATE & WHEN TO GO

See Antigua (p518), which is visible from much of Montserrat, for details on the climate, which ranges from 77°F (25°C) in winter to 86°F (30°C) in summer. The only time that's potentially bad for a visit is during the hurricane season July to November, when storms may disrupt transport.

## HISTORY

Known to indigenous people as Alliougana, meaning 'Land of the Prickly Bush', the island lost this colorful moniker in 1493 when Columbus thought the craggy landscape reminded him of the jagged hills above the Monastery of Montserrat near Barcelona.

Irish Catholics were the first European settlers, arriving in the manner of Irish immigrants everywhere: in flight from English protestant persecution, this time from nearby St Kitts. After planting sugar cane across the island, the Irish in turn persecuted African slaves who were brought by the thousands to labor on plantations.

Although in flight from the English, the Irish didn't escape the government and Britain has ruled the island since 1632, except for brief periods in 1665, 1712 and 1782 when the locals allowed the French in as occupiers.

By the mid-1800s sugar production was in decline. The island stayed self-sufficient in food production, with limes and goats in the north being especially successful. So quiet were things that as recently as 1980s, a mere 30,000 annual tourists comprised 25% of the economy. In fact this was also largely why Montserrat preferred to stay a Crown Colony rather than being lumped in with one of the other independence-minded neighboring islands.

In 1989 Hurricane Hugo dealt the island a blow that required years of reconstruction. Things were mostly back together by 1995, when Montserrat's clichéd yet accurate status as a quiet paradise was forever changed. On July 18th the Soufrière Hills Volcano (now 3180ft; 969.3m) ended 400 years of volcanic dormancy.

The capital, Plymouth, was covered in ash and subsequently abandoned. Also lost were the airport and countless family farms and small villages. The 11,000 residents resettled in the north or emigrated to Britain, where they were extended full citizenship. Excited vulcanologists swarmed the island, declaring a Safe Zone, a Daylight Entry Zone and an Exclusion Zone (the area nearest the volcano).

Still, farmers continued to use their beloved lands, and on June 25, 1997, the volcano erupted again, requiring 50 helicopter airlifts and causing 19 deaths. Two months later, a superheated pyroclastic flow wiped out the remainder of Plymouth, and its historically significant architecture and character were lost forever.

Minor eruptions have continued since, with plumes of ash and the occasional burping of lava boulders not uncommon.

## THE CULTURE

The small population of Montserrat is tightly knit and drivers continually pause to chat with others.

More than 90% of the population is of African descent with a strong influence of Irish blood. Interestingly, the flag bears Montserrat's coat of arms which depicts a white woman clutching a harp and hugging a cross.

Irish heritage is much-revered; St Patrick's Day is the big blow-out of the year and the parties last for a week.

An increasing number of exiles are returning to the island as new houses are built. Many say that they never felt at home in Britain and miss their lives on the island. Still, the population remains at less than half its total pre-eruption and the economy is still trying to recover.

'Sports' means cricket, cricket, cricket. When the national team practices on the pitch near Little Bay, few cars pass without pausing for a critical look.

## ARTS

Despite its small size, Montserrat has played a critical role in Caribbean music. The soca musician Alphonsus Cassell made an enduring contribution to the beat of the region

MONTSERRAT

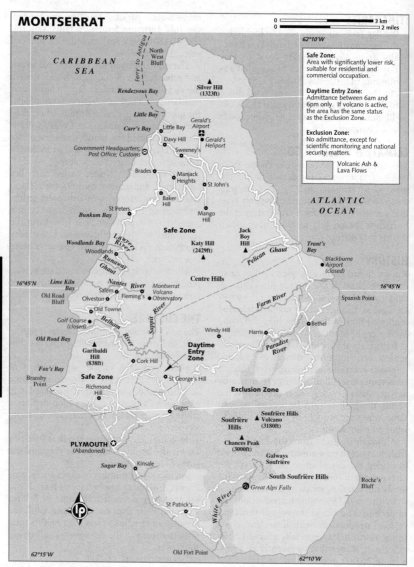

**MONTSERRAT**

0 — 3 km
0 — 2 miles

**Safe Zone:**
Area with significantly lower risk, suitable for residential and commercial occupation.

**Daytime Entry Zone:**
Admittance between 6am and 6pm only. If volcano is active, the area has the same status as the Exclusion Zone.

**Exclusion Zone:**
No admittance, except for scientific monitoring and national security matters.

Volcanic Ash & Lava Flows

CARIBBEAN SEA

62°15'W

North West Bluff

Ferry to Antigua

Silver Hill (1323ft)

Rendezvous Bay

Little Bay

Little Bay

Carr's Bay

Gerald's Airport

Davy Hill

Gerald's Heliport

Government Headquarters; Post Office; Customs

Sweeney's

Brades

Manjack Heights

St John's

Baker Hill

ATLANTIC OCEAN

St Peters

Bunkum Bay

Lawyers River

Mango Hill

Woodlands Bay

Safe Zone

Katy Hill (2429ft)

Jack Boy Hill

Trant's Bay

Woodlands

Runaway Ghaut

Pelican Ghaut

Blackburne Airport (closed)

16°45'N

Lime Kiln Bay

Nantes River

Salem

Montserrat Volcano Observatory

Centre Hills

Farm River

16°45'N

Old Road Bluff

Olveston

Fleming's

Old Towne

Spanish Point

Golf Course (closed)

Belham River

Sappit River

Old Road Bay

Garibaldi Hill (838ft)

Windy Hill

Harris

Bethel

Paradise River

Fox's Bay

Cork Hill

Daytime Entry Zone

Bransby Point

Safe Zone

St George's Hill

Richmond Hill

Exclusion Zone

Gages

PLYMOUTH (Abandoned)

Soufrière Hills

Soufrière Hills Volcano (3180ft)

Sugar Bay

Kinsale

Chances Peak (3000ft)

Galways Soufrière

South Soufrière Hills

Roche's Bluff

White River

Great Alps Falls

St Patrick's

Old Fort Point

62°15'W

62°10'W

62°10'W

(and the soundtracks of all-inclusive resorts) when under his stage name Arrow, he recorded 'Hot, Hot, Hot'. Since its release in 1982 it has sold over four million copies. He also has played a major role in local relief efforts and, when not on one of his many tours, lives in Sweeny's. Local musicians hoping to emulate Arrow can often be heard performing at the new cultural centre in Little Bay.

# ENVIRONMENT

Montserrat is a case study of how an island recovers from volcanic eruptions. More than 90 species of bird can still be found along with many small mammals, some rather sizable iguanas plus some huge frogs known locally as 'mountain chickens' which are both edible and taste like, well you know. Goats graze everywhere. The sides of the hills in the volcano are turning green once again with thick tropical vegetation, although floral progress is often impeded by ash emission.

Vegetation always had a tougher time in the more arid north, as it was the center of goat-herding. Efforts are now underway to plant trees amid the burgeoning housing estates.

## FOOD & DRINK

The local dish 'goat water' is far more loved than its dubious-sounding name would suggest. 'Got some?' is a frequent conversation starter and refers to the tangy, watery, clove-scented broth accented with floating goat meat.

# MONTSERRAT

As locals will tell you, the inhabited part of Montserrat is not the island's scenic highlight. Although, with its sharp cliffs, views far out to sea, crashing waves and local ennui,

there's a certain magnificent desolation about the place. The real sights here are the central volcano and accompanying devastation. Expect to hear some of those old film-strip narrator voices of doom in your head as you view 'the awesome force of nature', 'fury of the earth' etc.

Montserrat's few tourists come mostly for volcano-related day trips. Those who stay longer can expect quiet, with the laid-back locals offering a fair bit of rapport. Don't expect a long or even short list of must-do activities.

## INFORMATION

The small hillside village of Brades has ATMs, a bank, a few small shops, government offices, the post office and a pharmacy. Internet access is limited although there's wi-fi at the airport.

The **Montserrat Tourist Board** ( ☎ 491-2230; www .visitmontserrat.com; ⏰ 8am-4pm Mon-Fri) is in Brades. You can get maps and info here and from displays at the airport.

## SIGHTS & ACTIVITIES

About a 5km drive south along the east coast, the road turns into the hills and leads to a viewpoint at **Jack Boy Hill** from where you can see ash and mud flows to the south. The contrast of the view over flower-covered trees to the grey expanse that includes the remains of the old airport is stark.

**MONTSERRAT**

**FEELING HOT**

Born Alphonsus Celestine Edmund Cassell, Arrow is far and away Montserrat's most famous son. Even if you don't know his name, you know his music. 'Hot Hot Hot' is a standard across the Caribbean, beloved by locals and visitors alike. The vibrant soca mix was first recorded in 1982 and has been played worldwide since. It is a key song in Disney's *The Little Mermaid*.

**For many people Hot Hot Hot means vacation. How many times have you performed it?**
Hundreds and hundreds.

**What are you doing now?**
I'm semiretired. I turn down 90% of the gigs I'm offered although I will do a festival now and again. [This included the 2007 Cricket World Cup opening ceremonies.]

**Where's soca heading?**
Soca has always been such a pliable medium it's hard to really say, but it has done well fused with reggae – that trend, I think, is here to stay. The possibilities with hip-hop are endless.

**You live full time on Montserrat – what's the biggest challenge for the island?**
The biggest challenge for Montserrat now, and from the beginning of the crisis, is the brain drain. We have lost a lot of professionals, artisans and craftsmen. Now we see our children going away to study and we can only hope that most of them return. Montserrat needs its people.

**Will those who leave find better goat water elsewhere?**
Absolutely not!

Going south along the east coast, the road passes through of a vestige of the tropical forests. At **Runaway Ghaut** it's quite lush and a spring flows by the side of the road. From June to August the air is redolent with the smell of ripe mangoes.

The tourist office sells maps for rainforest hikes in the area, including the **Oriole Walkway**, which is named for the national bird.

Near Salem the land opens up and you have views of the wide Belham River Valley.

Looming over it all is **Soufrière Hills Volcano**, which isn't accessible. The **Montserrat Volcano Observatory** (MVO; ☎ 491-5647; www.mvo.ms; adult/child EC$10/free; ☼ 10am-3:15pm Thu) monitors the action of the volcano, as well as all volcanic activity in the Caribbean. There's an excellent film and good views, with vulcanologists anxious to explain that their field of study does not include the home of Mr Spock and lots of examples of stuff like 'breadcrust bombs' that are spat out of the earth during eruptions. Gas releases and minor tremors are ongoing.

Below the observatory, the road winds down to the ocean past small houses with lush fruit trees. Near the water past **Olde Town** is a duffer's and seaman's nightmare: the ash-covered remains of a golf course and a few pilings and desiccated palms that once were the marina.

If you have a driver or a 4WD vehicle, it's possible to cross the rock-strewn Belham River. On the south side is a surreal scene of abandoned luxury expat mansions. Here and there, owners are staying put, defiantly flying flags in the shadow of the volcano. An extremely rough road leads up **Garibaldi Hill** where you have views south over the Exclusion Zone to what's left of Plymouth. Once known for its tree-lined streets lined with colonial-era buildings and its grand cathedral, it's now an eerie distant ruin of structural shells half-buried in grey ash. The loss of Montserrat's commercial heart – if not its soul – is in stark evidence.

Back in the north, **Little Bay** is the focus of the 'new' Montserrat. There are ambitious plans for a new town centre just up the hill slightly from the beach (one hopes far above tsunami danger, given the island's past luck). Already finished is the Sir George Martin Auditorium, named for the former producer for the Beatles, who maintained a major recording studio on Montserrat until Hugo blew it away. A vibrant market is near-by.

Down by the little cove there's a small beach, a couple of rum shops and a pier.

Although much of the ocean surrounding the southern part of the island is still off-limits, what is left of Montserrat's **diving** is legendary. Best of all, it's been left in near-pristine condition because tourism is so limited. The **Green Monkey Dive Shop** (☎ 491-2628; www.dive montserrat.com; Little Bay) has dive packages that can include accommodations, and lessons. Full gear and one tank rent for US$35.

## SLEEPING & EATING

There is one hotel as well as several guesthouses, rentals and a hostel. The tourist office website lists everything available. Restaurants are few but there are simple cafés, rum shops and small grocers scattered about. The café at the airport is something of a community centre at flight times.

**Hot Rock Hostel** (☎ 491-9877; www.hotrockhostel .com; Salem; dm from US$25) In a rather isolated area just south of the volcano observatory, this small house is very clean and has a full kitchen and bunk beds.

**Montserrat Moments Inn** (☎ 491-7707; flogriff@ candw.ms; Manjack Heights; r US$55-100; ☒ ☐ ☒) Overlooking Brades and the coast, there are 12 rooms at this inn which incorporates parts of an old sugar mill. You can self-cater in the kitchen or arrange for meals.

**Erindell Villa** (☎ 491-3655; www.erindellvilla.com; Woodlands; r US$65; ☐ ☒) This is a good choice near the rainforest. Comfortable rooms come with ceiling fans, internet access and huge breakfasts. The owners are charmers and you can arrange for all meals here.

**Tropical Mansion Suites** (☎ 491-8767; www.tropical mansion.com; Sweeney's; r US$90-150; ☒ ☐ ☒) The island's one hotel is a good one. The 18 rooms are comfortable and popular with visitors on business. All have highspeed internet access and balconies.

# DIRECTORY

## ACCOMMODATIONS
See above for details on accommodation on the island.

## ACTIVITIES
See p543 for information on activities.

## BUSINESS HOURS
Businesses are open 8am to 5pm Monday to Friday and often on Saturdays until about

2pm. Shops are open until 6pm or 7pm weekdays and until late Saturday afternoon. Touristy places will be open later.

## DANGERS & ANNOYANCES

The volcano is a wild card, although recently it has been more quiet. Still it is always prudent to take precautions. Listen to what locals say regarding ash plumes and other events. Even when the mountain is calm, winds can kick up clouds of choking ash in areas nearby. And, obviously, respect restrictions of both the Daytime Entry Zone and the Exclusion Zone.

## MONEY

The currency of Montserrat is the Eastern Caribbean dollar (EC$), and the official exchange rate is EC$2.72 to US$1.

US dollars are widely accepted. However, unless rates are posted in US dollars, as is the norm with accommodations, it usually works out better to use EC dollars. There's little to buy using a credit card.

A 10% service charge is added to any dining bills you may manage to run up, in which case no further tipping is necessary.

## TELEPHONE

Montserrat's area code is ☎ 664. To call from North America, dial ☎ 1-664, followed by the seven-digit local number. From elsewhere, dial your country's international access code + ☎ 664 + the local phone number. We've included only the seven-digit local numbers in this chapter.

You can contact directory assistance on ☎ 411.

## TOURS

Several travel agencies on Antigua, including **Carib World Travel** ( ☎ 268-480-2999; www.carib-world .com), offer day trips to Montserrat for under US$200 per person.

---

**EMERGENCY NUMBERS**

- **Emergency** ☎ 999

---

## VISAS

Visas are not required by most nationalities for stays of less than three months.

# TRANSPORTATION

## GETTING THERE & AWAY

**Gerald's Airport** (MNI; ☎ 491-2533), named for its location, is in a small facility opened in 2005. The runway covers the top of the plateau and the sheer drops at either end add drama to any flight. The only service is provided by **Winair** ( ☎ 491-2362; www.fly-winair.com) which flies the 20-minute hop to Antigua several times daily. There are also daily flights to/from Sint Maarten, but most of these stop at Antigua. Fares can be as high as US$55 to US$100 each way. Flights often fill up and high winds can halt service for hours or days. Also note that the woeful immigration situation at VC Bird International Airport on Antigua means your wait to enter the country may be longer than your visit to Montserrat.

Ferry service to/from Antigua is an on-again, off-again affair. More often it is the latter, despite local pleas for this fare- and freight-friendly alternative to Winair.

## GETTING AROUND

Numerous locals will rent you their car for about US$50 per day, or you can hire a car and driver for US$20 per hour. This can be a delightful way to go as you'll learn much about Montserrat while you tour. **Reuben Furlonge** ( ☎ 492-2790) is a good choice and he makes a mean pot of goat water. The tourist office has lists of all local transport options.

---

**PRACTICALITIES**

- **Newspapers & Magazines** The *Montserrat Reporter* is an enthusiastic compendium of the week's events, as is its website, www.themontserratreporter.com.
- **Radio** Catch local news, tunes and eruption alerts on ZJB, 91.9FM.
- **Electricity** The current used mostly is 220V, but some places use 110V, 60 cycles; check first. You should find North American two-pin sockets.
- **Weights & Measures** The imperial system is used here.

# Guadeloupe

Guadeloupe mixes the best of France – a fully modern infrastructure and fantastic food – with a local culture that people here are proud of and want to share. Guadeloupe's two main islands look like the wings of a butterfly and are joined together by a mangrove swamp.

Grande-Terre, the eastern wing of the island, has a string of beach towns that offer visitors every variety of fun in the sun known to humankind. From surfing schools to beach bars to long stretches of beautiful sand where azure water laps at the toes of French mademoiselles, it's all here.

Basse-Terre, the western wing, is home to the national park, crowned by La Soufrière volcano. Hiking trails and a Jacques Cousteau underwater reserve offer adventure for those who want more go than slow in their holidays. But for the gourmets and sun worshippers there are still plenty of places to recharge while everyone else tires themselves out.

This isn't to say that both sides don't have something for everyone. It's one of the more developed islands in the Caribbean – those arriving at the thoroughly modern airport might be in for a shock if they were expecting a rural airstrip – but there are still plenty of rural patches between villages and you won't want for choice.

South of the butterfly-shaped 'mainland' of Guadeloupe are a number of small archipelagos that give a taste of Guadeloupe's yesteryear. Ranging from sheer chill on La Désirade to the barely discovered restaurants in Les Saintes, the smaller islands each have their own character and round out the long list of ingredients that make Guadeloupe.

GUADELOUPE

## FAST FACTS

- **Area** 1434 sq km
- **Capital** Basse-Terre
- **Country code** ☎ 590
- **Departure tax** None
- **Famous for** Its butterfly shape
- **Language** French, Creole
- **Money** euro (€); €1 = US$1.56 = UK£0.79
- **Official name** La Guadeloupe
- **People** Guadeloupeans
- **Phrase** Pas ni problem (No problem, no worries)
- **Population** 451,000
- **Visa** None required for residents of the US, UK, Canada, the EU, Australia and New Zealand; see p576

# HIGHLIGHTS

- **La Soufrière** (p564) Hike to the misty summit of the brooding volcano
- **Deshaies** (p562) Nourish your inner gourmet and encounter boaties from around the world
- **Ste-Anne** (p556) Soak up sun on the beautiful beach or the happening scene at a seaside café
- **Pigeon Island** (p565) Touch the underwater Jacques Cousteau statue at the reserve that bears his name
- **Terre-de-Haut** (p566) Walk across this tiny island, full of low-key sophistication

# ITINERARIES

- **Three Days** Spend a morning roaming Pointe-à-Pitre before heading west, stopping at Cascade aux Écrevisses or hiking to La Soufrière, then on to the west coast. Dive at the Réserve Cousteau, then wander east to Grande-Terre, following a clockwise route that takes in the Porte d'Enfer, Le Moule and some well-earned R&R at the beach in Ste-Anne.
- **One Week** Follow the plan for three days, then catch a boat to Terre-de-Haut, and walk to the fort, followed by a day or two exploring Marie-Galante. Head back to the mainland for an excursion to Pointe des Châteaux before a satisfying meal in St-François.

# CLIMATE & WHEN TO GO

It's no accident that December to May is when most people visit Guadeloupe; the weather is warm and dry at this time.

Pointe-à-Pitre's average daily high temperature in January is 28°C (82°F) while the low average is 19°C (66°F). In July the average daily high temperature is 31°C (88°F) while the low average is 23°C (73°F).

The annual rainfall in Pointe-à-Pitre is 180cm. February to April is the driest period, when measurable rain falls an average of seven days a month and the average humidity is around 77%. The wettest months are July to November, when rain falls about 14 days a month and the average humidity reaches 85%.

Because of its height, the Basse-Terre side is both cooler and rainier than Grande-Terre. Its highest point, La Soufrière, averages 990cm of rain per year. The trade winds, called *alizés*, often temper the climate.

# HISTORY

When sighted by Columbus on November 14, 1493, Guadeloupe was inhabited by Caribs, who called it Karukera (Island of Beautiful Waters). The Spanish made two attempts to settle Guadeloupe in the early 1500s but were repelled both times by fierce Carib resistance, and finally in 1604 they abandoned their claim to the island.

Three decades later, French colonists sponsored by the Compagnie des Îles d'Amérique, an association of French entrepreneurs, set sail to establish the first European settlement on Guadeloupe. On June 28, 1635, the party, led by Charles Liénard de l'Olive and Jean Duplessis d'Ossonville, landed on the southeastern shore of Basse-Terre and claimed Guadeloupe for France. They drove the Caribs off the island, planted crops and within a decade had built the first sugar mill. By the time France officially annexed the island in 1674, a slavery-based plantation system had been well established.

The English invaded Guadeloupe several times and occupied it from 1759 to 1763. During this time, they developed Pointe-à-Pitre into a major harbor, opened profitable English and North American markets to Guadeloupean sugar and allowed the planters to import cheap American lumber and food. Many French colonists actually grew wealthier under the British occupation, and the economy expanded rapidly. In 1763 British occupation ended with the signing of the Treaty of Paris, which relinquished French claims in Canada in exchange for the return of Guadeloupe.

Amid the chaos of the French Revolution, the British invaded Guadeloupe again in 1794. In response, the French sent a contingent of soldiers led by Victor Hugues, a black nationalist. Hugues freed and armed Guadeloupean slaves. On the day the British withdrew from

GUADELOUPE

---

## HOW MUCH?

- Taxi from the airport to Pointe-à-Pitre center €20
- One-tank diving trip €40
- Comfortable hotel double room €65
- Museum ticket €3.50
- Local fish meal €12

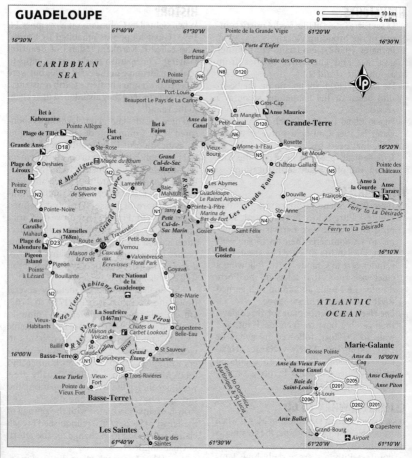

## GUADELOUPE

Guadeloupe, Hugues went on a rampage and killed 300 royalists, many of them plantation owners. It marked the start of a reign of terror. In all, Hugues was responsible for the deaths of more than 1000 colonists, and as a consequence of his attacks on US ships, the USA declared war on France.

In 1802 Napoléon Bonaparte, anxious to get the situation under control, sent General Antoine Richepance to Guadeloupe. Richepance put down the uprising, restored the pre-revolutionary government and reinstituted slavery.

Guadeloupe was the most prosperous island in the French West Indies, and the British continued to covet it, invading and occupying the island for most of the period between 1810

and 1816. The Treaty of Vienna restored the island to France, which has maintained sovereignty over it continuously since 1816.

Slavery was abolished in 1848, following a campaign led by French politician Victor Schoelcher (see p553). In the years that followed, planters brought laborers from Pondicherry, a French colony in India, to work in the cane fields. Since 1871 Guadeloupe has had representation in the French parliament, and since 1946 it has been an overseas department of France.

Guadeloupe's economy is heavily dependent upon subsidies from the French government and upon its economic ties with mainland France, which absorbs the majority of Guadeloupe's exports and provides 75% of its imports. Agriculture remains a cornerstone of the economy. The leading export crop is bananas, the bulk of which grow along the southern flanks of La Soufrière.

In August 2007 Hurricane Dean barreled through the Caribbean, destroying an estimated 80% of Guadeloupe's banana plantations with 160km/h winds that lifted the roofs right off buildings. Guadeloupe quickly recovered from the hurricane and concentrated on rebuilding its banana industry.

## THE CULTURE

Guadeloupean culture draws from a pool of French, African, East Indian and West Indian influences.

The mix is visible in the architecture, which ranges from French colonial buildings to traditional Creole homes; in the food, which merges influences from all the cultures into a unique Creole cuisine; and in the widely spoken local Creole language.

There's much emphasis on the French rules of politeness; *bonjour* and *au revoir* are almost always heard when entering or leaving an establishment, and older Guadeloupeans usually give a collective *bonjour* to everyone in general when entering a crowded restaurant or bar. To start a conversation or ask a question without a greeting is rude.

Guadeloupe is one place in the Caribbean where you're likely to see women wearing traditional Creole dress, especially at festivals and cultural events.

The total population of Guadeloupe is about 451,000, with 32% of the population aged under 20.

About three-quarters of the population is of mixed ethnicity, a combination of African, European and East Indian descent. There's also a sizable population of white islanders who trace their ancestry to the early French settlers, as well as a number of more recently arrived French from the mainland.

The predominant religion is Roman Catholicism. There are also Methodist, Seventh Day Adventist, Jehovah's Witness and Evangelical denominations, and a sizable Hindu community.

## ARTS

The island is fertile ground for the literary imagination, apparently. Guadeloupe's most renowned native son is St John Perse, the pseudonym of Alexis Léger, who was born in Guadeloupe in 1887. Perse won the Nobel Prize for literature in 1960 for the evocative imagery of his poetry. One of his many noted works is *Anabase* (1925), which was translated into English by TS Eliot.

The leading contemporary novelist in the French West Indies is Guadeloupe native Maryse Condé. Two of her best-selling novels have been translated into English. The epic *Tree of Life* centers on the life of a Guadeloupean family, their roots and the identity of Guadeloupean society itself. *Crossing the Mangrove* (1995) is a perfect beach read. Set in Rivière au Sel near the Rivière Salée, it unravels the life, and untimely death, of a controversial villager.

## ENVIRONMENT

Beaches line nearly every shore in Guadeloupe. Outside of the mountainous Parc National de la Guadeloupe, the interior is made for the most part of gently rolling fields of sugarcane. The beaches, hiking trails and picnic areas here are almost always completely litter-free.

The underwater life includes small sea horses, lobsters, lots of parrot fish, and crabs. Divers may occasionally spot a ray or barracuda, but for the most part the waters here support large schools of smaller fish.

Birds found on Guadeloupe include various members of the heron family, pelicans, hummingbirds and the endangered Guadeloupe wren. A common sighting is the bright yellow-bellied banana quit, a small nectar-feeding bird that's a frequent visitor at open-air restaurants, where it raids unattended sugar bowls.

You'll probably see drawings of raccoons on park brochures and in Guadeloupean advertising; it is the official symbol of Parc National de la Guadeloupe and its main habitat is in the forests of Basse-Terre.

Guadeloupe has mongooses aplenty, introduced long ago in a futile attempt to control rats in the sugarcane fields. Agoutis (short-haired, short-eared rabbitlike rodents that look a bit like guinea pigs) are found on La Désirade. There are iguanas on Les Saintes and La Désirade.

## FOOD & DRINK

Island cuisine is made up of a well-matched mix of both Creole and French cultures. Locals will equally enjoy a *pain au chocolat*

GUADELOUPE

---

**REPORTING FROM GUADELOUPE**

Hervé Pédurand, born in Guadeloupe, is the radio editor in chief of Guadeloupe Radio France Outre-Mer (RFO), the biggest and most influential news network on the island.

**What are your responsibilities at RFO?**

As the editor in chief of 17 journalists, I make sure that all the news in Guadeloupe gets covered on the radio. We work closely with Paris RFO. They report on all the important developments in France's overseas departments and use our stories – along with the RFO Caribbean network that includes Martinique and French Guiana – every day.

**For English-speakers, what do you think is the most common misunderstanding when it comes to Guadeloupe's relations with mainland France?**

Our situation intrigues Anglophones, especially our neighbors in the Caribbean. We're in the same region but we're not English or Spanish speakers, we're not independent and we call ourselves French! They don't understand this, even when they're still on good terms with their former governments. Also, sometimes we play the 'American' when we visit other Caribbean islands and tend to act superior, even if others don't take us as seriously as we take ourselves (we're always late for appointments, for example!).

**After seeing the rest of the island, I was really surprised that Pointe-à-Pitre was so dead at night. Why is that?**

After being a lively place for a long time, little by little Pointe-à-Pitre became a victim of a changing commercial landscape. The opening of big shopping centers just outside the city attracted shoppers who were tired of traffic jams and parking meters. The little shops that were downtown were forced to follow the shoppers outside the city. An urban renewal plan has just been approved by the state that will create a downtown business zone with tax breaks. We'll see soon how this works out.

---

(chocolate-filled croissant-like pastry) and *café crème* (espresso with steamed milk or cream) at 11am, followed by chicken *colombo* (curry) and ti-punch at lunchtime.

Guadeloupe is the second-largest consumer of fish per head worldwide so expect it on menus in many delicious guises. *Ouassous* (crayfish), *chatrou* (octopus) and more traditional fish such as *vivanneau* (red snapper) are generally served simply grilled, or marinated in aromatic Creole spices such as nutmeg, ginger, vanilla and fenugreek. *Lambi* (conch – the chewy meat of a large gastropod) is also prevalent, although overfishing has meant that conch is heading for the endangered species list and it's a good idea to avoid it.

Some typical Guadeloupean dishes include *accra* (a fried mixture of okra, black-eyed peas, pepper and salt), *crabes farci* (spicy stuffed land crabs), *colombo cabri* (curried goat), rice and beans, and breadfruit gratin. Another popular Creole dish is *blaff*, a seafood preparation poached in a spicy broth.

Markets are full of colorful exotic fruits and vegetables: small, sweet bananas and huge avocados, *christophines* (a common Caribbean vegetable shaped like a large pear), mangoes, pineapples and *maracudjas* (passion fruits).

For snacks, there are many *bokit* stands that serve a concoction that's a cross between a pita bread and panini. *Bokits* are filled with anything from ham to crab to grilled veggies. Another popular snack is sorbet coco, a coconut sorbet that's usually made on the spot in an old-fashioned ice-cream maker.

Tap water is safe to drink. There are lots of excellent local rums, and almost all distilleries have tasting rooms. Homemade flavored rums (that have fruit added) are also popular; in bars and restaurants you'll commonly see these in large glass jars behind the counter. Men, beware the *bois bandé*. It's an aphrodisiac; ask a trusted French-speaking friend for the literal translation.

A common restaurant drink (and the locals' beverage of choice) is ti-punch, where you're brought white rum, cane sugar and a fresh lime to mix to your own proportions. When serving ti-punch to friends, it's considered rude not to let guests pour their own dose. Locally brewed Corsaire beer goes well with Creole food and lazy days on the beach.

Good French wines are served at most restaurants, and can also be picked up (for reasonable prices) at supermarkets.

# GRANDE-TERRE

The southern coast of Grande-Terre, with its reef-protected waters, is Guadeloupe's main resort area. The eastern side of the island is largely open Atlantic, with crashing surf, and in comparison to the southern coast is barely touched by tourism. Northern Grande-Terre doesn't have much in the way of accommodations but it's probably the best place to spend a day driving around – sea cliffs on one side and swaying fields of sugarcane on the other. Pointe-à-Pitre, the island's biggest city, is in the southeastern corner of Grande-Terre.

## Getting There & Away

### AIR
For information on air travel to and from Grande-Terre, see p576.

### BOAT
For information on ferry travel to other Caribbean islands, see p577.

Ferries to Terre-de-Haut, Marie-Galante and La Désirade leave from Pointe-à-Pitre, Ste-Anne and St-François; see p577 for further information.

In Pointe-à-Pitre, all ferries leave from the Gare Maritime de Bergevin, 1km northwest of St-John Hotel.

### BUS
Buses to places in Basse-Terre leave from the northwest side of town near the Gare Maritime de Bergevin. It costs €3.70 to travel from Pointe-à-Pitre to the administrative capital of Basse-Terre, and €2.80 to Pointe-Noire (via Route de la Traversée).

## Getting Around

### TO/FROM THE AIRPORT
Taxis are easy to find at the airport; it costs about €20 into Pointe-à-Pitre center or you could rent a car on arrival. Thanks to the taxi union, there's no bus shuttle to town from the airport.

### BUS
Buses to Gosier, Ste-Anne and St-François leave from Rue Dubouchage at the east side of the harbor in Pointe-à-Pitre.

The bus from Pointe-à-Pitre to Gosier costs €1.30 (pay the driver) and takes about 15 minutes. If you're going to the Bas du Fort marina, you can take this bus and get off just past the university. Other fares from Pointe-à-Pitre are €1.90 to Ste-Anne and €2.40 to St-François.

### CAR
Car-rental information is covered on p578.

On weekdays, traffic in the center of Pointe-à-Pitre is congested and parking can be tight. There are parking meters (€1 per hour) along the east side of Place de la Victoire and on many of the side streets throughout the city.

### TAXI
You can call for a taxi by dialing ☎ 82-00-00 or ☎ 83-99-99 in the Pointe-à-Pitre area.

## POINTE-À-PITRE
pop 21,000

The main population center of Guadeloupe (more than 170,000 live in greater Pointe-à-Pitre) doesn't rank very high on an island must-see list – as a matter of fact, those who miss it haven't missed much. But as a hub of transportation and the location of a few decent museums, Pointe-à-Pitre can be a worthwhile stop for a day.

## History
In 1654 a merchant named Peter, a Dutch Jew who settled in Guadeloupe after being exiled from Brazil, began a fish market on an undeveloped harborside jut of land. The area

GUADELOUPE

---

**WHAT'S IN A NAME?**

At first glance, the names given to the twin islands that make up Guadeloupe proper are perplexing. The eastern island, which is smaller and flatter, is named Grande-Terre, which means 'big land,' while the larger, more mountainous western island is named Basse-Terre, meaning 'flat land.'

The names were not meant to describe the terrain, however, but the winds that blow over them. The trade winds, which come from the northeast, blow *grande* (big) over the flat plains of Grande-Terre but are stopped by the mountains to the west, ending up *basse* (flat) on Basse-Terre.

became known as Peter's Point and eventually grew into the settlement of Pointe-à-Pitre, located in the southwest of Grande-Terre.

Guadeloupe's largest municipality, Pointe-à-Pitre is a conglomerate of old and new and is largely commercial in appearance. There are a couple of small museums, but other than that the most interesting sight is the bustling harborside market.

## Orientation

From the outskirts, Pointe-à-Pitre looks pretty uninviting – a concrete jungle of high-rises and sprawling traffic. Venture into the center, though, and you'll find a much more attractive old town with peeling colonial architecture and palm-fringed streets.

The town hub is Place de la Victoire, an open space punctuated with tall royal palms that extends north a few blocks from the inner harbor. There are sidewalk cafés opposite its west side, a line of big old mango trees to the north and some older buildings along with the *sous-préfecture* (sub-prefecture) office at the park's east side.

While Pointe-à-Pitre is not a major tourist destination, visitors to Guadeloupe can expect to at least pass through the town, as it is the main port for ferries to Guadeloupe's outer islands and it also shelters the central bus terminal.

Central Pointe-à-Pitre is quite compact, and nothing is more than a five- or 10-minute stroll from Place de la Victoire.

## Information

### BOOKSTORES

**Boutique de la Presse** (Centre St-John Perse) Sells Institut Géographique National (IGN) maps of Guadeloupe.

**Espace St-John Perse** ( ☎ 82-93-26; 11 Rue de Nozières; ⏰ 8am-6pm Mon-Fri, to 1:30pm Sat) The largest and best-stocked bookstore in town has a small English-language section, and also sells computers and digital cameras.

**Le Presse Papier** (Place de la Victoire; ⏰ 8am-6pm Mon-Fri) Next to Délifrance, also sells the *International Herald Tribune* (€2) and a few English-language news magazines.

### EMERGENCY

**Police** ( ☎ 89-77-17)

### INTERNET ACCESS

**Cyber Ka** (Place de la Victoire; ⏰ 8am-6pm Mon-Fri, 7am-8pm Sat, per 30min €3) A lively place to check emails.

### MEDICAL SERVICES

**Centre Hospitalier Universitaire** (CHU; ☎ 89-10-10; Rte de Chauvel) The main hospital is north of the post office in a not-so-good area; take a cab at night.

### MONEY

**Banque Populaire** (Rue Achille René-Boisneuf; ⏰ 8am-noon & 2-4pm Mon-Fri)

**BDAF bank** (Sq de la Banque; ⏰ 7:45am-noon & 2-4pm Mon-Fri) Next to the tourist office.

**BNP bank** (Rue Achille René-Boisneuf; ⏰ 8am-noon & 2-4pm Mon-Fri)

**Change Caraïbe s** (21 Rue Frebault; ⏰ 8am-4:45pm Mon-Fri) A money exchange; it doesn't take coins.

### POST

**Post office** (Blvd Hanne; ⏰ 8am-6pm Mon-Fri, to noon Sat) A block north of the cathedral.

### TOURIST INFORMATION

**Tourist office** ( ☎ 82-09-30; www.lesilesdeguadeloupe .com; 5 Sq de la Banque; ⏰ 8am-5pm Mon-Fri, to noon Sat) Near Place de la Victoire; the friendly staff speaks good English.

## Dangers & Annoyances

Locals say that drug abuse – especially crack cocaine – is a problem here. The Place de la Victoire area has enough people until late at night to feel safe, but other parts of the city are downright spooky, and prostitutes and drug dealers are not uncommon sights.

The area around the Centre Hospitalier is especially dangerous and visitors should take a cab there at night if need be. Whereas the rest of the island is friendly, at times there's an aggressive mood here.

## Sights & Activities

### MUSÉE ST-JOHN PERSE

This three-level **municipal museum** (9 Rue de Nozières; adult/child €2.50/1.50; ⏰ 9am-5pm Mon-Fri, 8:30am-12:30pm Sat) occupies an attractive 19th-century colonial building. The museum is dedicated to the renowned poet and Nobel laureate Alexis Léger (1887–1975), better known as St John Perse. The house offers both a glimpse of a period Creole home and displays on Perse's life and work. Almost all of the exhibits are in French, but there are some newspaper illustrations and photographs from the city's past that make the admission price worth it.

GUADELOUPE

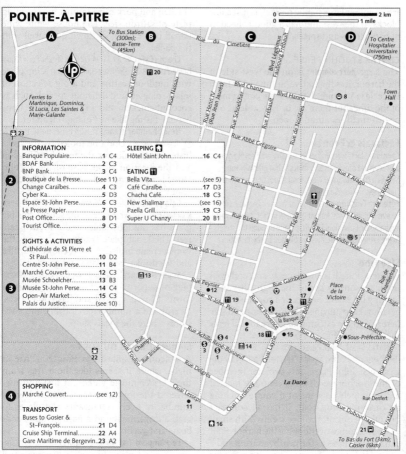

# POINTE-À-PITRE

0    2 km
0    1 mile

**INFORMATION**
Banque Populaire.............................1 C4
BDAF Bank.......................................2 C3
BNP Bank.........................................3 C4
Boutique de la Presse.............(see 11)
Change Caraïbes.............................4 C3
Cyber Ka..........................................5 D3
Espace St-John Perse.....................6 C3
Le Presse Papier.............................7 D3
Post Office.......................................8 D1
Tourist Office..................................9 C3

**SIGHTS & ACTIVITIES**
Cathédrale de St Pierre et
  St Paul........................................10 D2
Centre St-John Perse....................11 B4
Marché Couvert............................12 C3
Musée Schoelcher........................13 B3
Musée St-John Perse....................14 C4
Open-Air Market..........................15 C3
Palais du Justice......................(see 10)

**SLEEPING**
Hôtel Saint John...........................16 C4

**EATING**
Bella Vita...............................(see 5)
Café Caraïbe..................................17 D3
Chacha Café...................................18 C3
New Shalimar.......................(see 16)
Paella Grill.....................................19 C3
Super U Chanzy.............................20 B1

**SHOPPING**
Marché Couvert......................(see 12)

**TRANSPORT**
Buses to Gosier &
  St-François...................................21 D4
Cruise Ship Terminal....................22 A4
Gare Maritime de Bergevin..........23 A2

**GUADELOUPE**

## MUSÉE SCHOELCHER

Occupying an interesting period building, this **museum** ( ☎ 82-08-04; 24 Rue Peynier; admission €2; ⏰ 8:30am-12:30pm Mon-Sat, 2-5:30pm Mon & Tue, 2-6pm Thu & Fri) is dedicated to abolitionist Victor Schoelcher. The main exhibits in the museum are art pieces that belonged to Schoelcher, and artifacts relating to slavery. Some of the editorial cartoons on display show how much the French establishment hated Schoelcher for his abolitionist actions. Displays are in French, but there are brochures in English. Schoelcher's original reasoning behind the seemingly random art and sculpture displays was to give the people of Guadeloupe a chance to appreciate the fine arts.

## CATHÉDRALE DE ST PIERRE ET ST PAUL

Rather than the traditional arches, this weathered sand-colored church, nicknamed the 'Iron Cathedral,' is supported by iron girders intended to brace it against earthquakes and hurricanes. The church, which is a couple of minutes' walk northwest of Place de la Victoire, is worth a look, particularly on Sunday. Check out the Ali Tur–designed Art Deco **Palais du Justice** next door.

## PUBLIC MARKETS

There's a fun, colorful **open-air market** ( ⏰ 5am-2pm Mon-Sat) running along La Darse, the inner harbor. There are souvenir stalls on the little streets right next to the market, as well. The **Marché Couvert** (cnr Rues Peynier & Schoelcher; ⏰ 6am-

4pm), another large public market, is just a few blocks to the west and has a good collection of handicrafts and spices.

### CENTRE ST-JOHN PERSE

The large **port complex** is on the west side of the harbor, less than a five-minute walk from Place de la Victoire. Things seem closed most of the time, but there are usually at least one or two small restaurants open.

## Festivals & Events

**Carnival** Starts warming up in January with roving groups of steel-band musicians and dancers, but officially runs between the traditional week-long Mardi Gras period that ends on Ash Wednesday.

**Fête des Cuisinières** (Festival of Women Cooks) A colorful event held in early August. Women in Creole dress, carrying baskets of traditional foods, parade through the streets to the cathedral, where they are blessed by the bishop.

## Sleeping

Pointe-à-Pitre has few places to stay and even fewer reasons to spend the night. If you're looking for island culture or a cozy beachside getaway, keep moving. The only reason to stay here is if you're catching an international ferry the next morning.

**Hôtel Saint John Perse** ( ☎ 82-51-57; www.saint-john-perse.com; s/d incl breakfast €85/100; 🍴 🖳 ) In the Centre St-John Perse, this two-star member of the Anchorage chain is centrally located and extremely convenient if you're catching an early-morning boat. It has 44 compact but otherwise comfortable rooms with small shared balconies overlooking the harbor. Staff can arrange taxis to the nearby marina and a shuttle (€3) to the ferries. There is wi-fi, plus free luggage storage for guests who want to travel light to the outlying islands.

## Eating & Drinking

### DOWNTOWN

**Bella Vita** ( ☎ 89-00-54; Place de la Victoire; mains €6.50-14; 🍴 breakfast, lunch & dinner) The decor is very basic – it looks like it used to be a sub sandwich shop, in fact, but the people who work here are warm and welcoming. The pizzas are solid and range from tuna to the delicious *mafioso*. One of the best bets for a later evening meal.

**Paella Grill** ( ☎ 82-12-34; cnr Rues Frébault & St-John Perse; mains €7-10; 🍴 7am-4pm Mon-Sat) The signature paella at this indoor-outdoor eatery is quite the deal considering you get mussels, shrimp, chicken and pork mixed into a big steaming plate of saffron rice. The house white wine (small bottle €3) goes down quite well with the paella.

**Chacha Café** ( ☎ 89-61-94; cnr Rues St-John Perse & Quai Layrle; mains €8-14; 🍴 10am-3pm Mon-Sat) A hip place with outdoor seating and a big selection of salads, omelets and delicious specials such as coconut chicken, and a special *cythère* (ambarella, tasting like tart mango) fruit juice.

**New Shalimar** (Centre St-John Perse; mains from €8; 🍴 lunch & dinner) Don't be fooled by the lackluster outdoor dining, the food here is good and the location at the base of the St-John Hotel is a godsend for those sick of the city's seamy side.

**Café Caraïbe** (Place de la Victoire; mains €10-12; 🍴 lunch & dinner) On the west side of the square, this big place has outdoor tables and a French café feel. The kebab plate is quite tasty, as is the vanilla crème brûlée. A good choice of coffee and tea drinks, beer, wine and cocktails.

**Super U Chanzy** ( ☎ 90-83-77; Blvd Chanzy) is the biggest supermarket close to the center of town. It's well-stocked and has good prices. Nearby are a number of clothing and shoe stores where the locals shop.

### MARINA DE BAS DU FORT

A welcome respite from Pointe-à-Pitre at night, where it seems like the extras from the *Thriller* music video got lost and discovered the joys of crack cocaine. Here a number of lively restaurants and places to grab a drink surround a harbor full of sailboats and yachts.

**Le Pampam** ( ☎ 90-83-22; snacks €5-12; 🍴 8am-2am) A good place to grab a beverage and chill out, it has a range of nonalcoholic fruit drinks and shakes and a full page on the menu dedicated to specialty drinks. For an ostentatious aperitif, the *chouchou* (€20), made for two people, is a mix of rum, cointreau, passion and other fruit juices.

**La Fregates** (mains from €12; 🍴 11am-midnight) It's the restaurant here with the best balance between price and quality, and the crowds to prove it. After ordering the lobster dinner (€30) a server brings out the unlucky crustacean in a bucket, alive, and shows it like a bottle of wine.

## Shopping

The **Marché Couvert** (cnr Rues Peynier & Schoelcher; 🍴 6am-4pm) in Pointe-à-Pitre is a good place to buy island handicrafts, including straw dolls, straw hats and primitive African-style wood carvings. It's also a good spot to pick up locally grown coffee and a wide array of fragrant spices.

# GOSIER
## pop 26,000

Set 8km southeast of Pointe-à-Pitre, Gosier is really two towns: a cluster of high-rise hotels full of French families on one side and a growing Caribbean village next door.

It's the biggest tourist spot in Guadeloupe, and that's not necessarily a good thing. The hotels are packed one after the other and the lobbies can be madhouses in high season. But the series of scalloped coves gives almost every property a good beachside location.

The village center, about a 15-minute walk away from hotel central, feels a little run-down and lacks the fine beaches found in the main hotel area, but it is more local in character. It also has a small but swimmable beach and a good view across the water to l'Îlet du Gosier.

Many of Guadeloupe's most popular nightspots, attracting a young and fashionable French crowd until early morning, are clustered together on the outskirts of Gosier on the road to Pointe-à-Pitre.

## Information

**La Gazette** (Ave Général de Gaulle) Sells the IGN map of Guadeloupe and international newspapers.

**Post office** ( ☺ 8am-5pm Mon-Tue, Thu & Fri, 8am-noon Wed & Sat) In the Gosier village center.

## Sights

Just 600m off Gosier village is lovely **l'Îlet du Gosier**, a little undeveloped island surrounded by calm turquoise waters that have some nice snorkeling areas.

Motorboats (one way €4) shuttle beachgoers between Gosier and the island, departing from the little dock at the end of Rue Félix Éboué.

## Activities

Beach huts in front of the resort hotels rent out snorkeling gear for €12 a day, windsurfing equipment, Sunfish sailboats and larger Hobie Cat boats. Also available are fun boards, pedal boats and other water-activities gear.

## Sleeping
### BUDGET & MIDRANGE

**La Formule Économique** ( ☎ 84-54-91; www.laformule economique.com; 112-120 Lot Gisors, 97190 Gosier; d/studio from €45/54; ▧ ) Offering *hotellerie à la carte*, it calculates rates based on the amenities you select. The hotel's terrace bar and downstairs restaurant attract a younger clientele and some Paris Hilton look-alikes. Follow the signs in the village to find this place at the end of a dilapidated alley.

**Karaïbes Hotel** ( ☎ 84-51-51; www.karaibeshotel.com; 97190 Gosier; s/d €54/66; ▣ ) A two-star, brightly colored budget place in the main cluster of hotels, it has an ATM-like machine outside that takes a credit card and spits out keys for people with a reservation. Small but bright rooms and beach access make this the best bargain on the hotel strip. Offers wi-fi access.

**Canella Beach Residence** ( ☎ 90-44-00; www.canella beach.com; Pointe de la Verdure, 97190 Gosier; r from €81; ▧ ▨ ) Don't be put off by the surrounding ratty-looking marsh. Studios have rattan furniture, a queen or two twin beds, a little sitting area with sofa bed, TV, phone, a balcony and a kitchenette. Some studios on the ground level are wheelchair-accessible. There are also suites and duplex apartments. Rates include use of the pool, tennis courts, paddleboats and canoes.

### TOP END

The following are modern beachside resorts with standard top-notch amenities, including swimming pools, activity centers, restaurants and well-appointed rooms with balconies.

**La Créole Beach Hotel & Spa** ( ☎ 90-46-46; www .creolebeach.com; 97190 Gosier; r from €160; ▧ ▣ ▨ ) A snazzy 218-room complex, set in exotic gardens, right on the beach. Contemporary rooms have two double beds and French colonial–style furnishings. There are a number of water sports available. Although an attractive place, the big crowds in the public areas might be a damper on some vacations.

**Sofitel Auberge de la Vieille Tour** ( ☎ 84-23-23; www.sofitel.com; Montauban, 97190 Gosier; r from €190; ▨ ) This gorgeous 180-room inn incorporates an 18th-century windmill in the lobby, but most of the rooms are in more ordinary buildings. The friendliness of the staff, however, is underwhelming.

**Hotel Arawak** ( ☎ 84-24-24; www.hotelarawak.com; 97162 Pointe-à-Pitre; r from €205; ▧ ▨ ) An impressive airy lobby area belies the decent but unexceptional rooms. The mellow ambience and relative lack of big groups set this 200-room place apart from nearby hotels.

## Eating

The center of Gosier has a number of inexpensive eating options, and in the main beach hotel area, the Créole Village shopping center has half a dozen places to eat. Down the hill toward the beach is an Ecomax supermarket, and there's a daytime produce stand next to the post office.

**Le Bord du Mer** ( ☎ 84-25-23; mains €8-14; ☎ lunch & dinner) Right on the water in the center of the village, it has the broad choice of seafood one would expect of the location. If nothing else, it's a great place to soak up a coffee and the seaside view.

**Quatre Epice** ( ☎ 84-76-01; 25 Blvd Charles de Gaulle; mains €16-25; ☎ lunch & dinner) A brightly decorated old house converted into a restaurant with eclectic decorations throughout – including a lawn jockey and funky lamps. The food at this village restaurant is divine; start with *le tour d'île*, a sampler plate with stuffed crab curry, fish pâté, *accra* and *boudin* (blood sausage). The dessert and drinks menu lists no less than 11 aged rums (€5 to €7).

**Restaurant de l'Auberge** ( ☎ 84-23-23; Montauban, 97190 Gosier; dinner mains €18-30; ⏲ lunch & dinner) The Auberge de la Vieille Tour has Gosier's most upmarket fine-dining restaurant, serving traditional French and Creole cuisine.

## Drinking

Gosier is easily the most hopping nightlife spot on the island. Most of the fancy hotels have live music and poolside barbecues on a regular basis.

**La Route de la Bière** (Delirium Café; ☎ 88-17-94; 6 Rue Simon Radegonde; ⏲ 6pm-1am Tue-Sat) In the village near the Ecomax, this is the place to go if you like good times of the sudsy variety. There are 60 different beers here, nine of them on draft. It also has pizza, Friday-night karaoke, Saturday-night dancing and a pool table.

**Amazon** ( ☎ 42-74-21; 20 Blvd Charles de Gaulle; ⏲ 5-11pm Mon-Sat) A village bar that hosts salsa dancing on Tuesday nights, it also has the occasional concert. For those who want to make French friends, Anglophones are encouraged to come to the English conversation meetings organized by the club.

**La Cheyenne** (122 Ave de Montauban; ⏲ Fri & Sat) If bachelor- or beach-themed nights are your thing, you'll enjoy this massive disco, with big screens and thumping beats. It's just outside of town; look for the big wooden head of a Native American.

# STE-ANNE

### pop 20,000

The busy town of Ste-Anne sees a lot of tourists but the big resorts are well hidden and there's a good balance of amenities for tourists and authentic modern village life. It has a seaside promenade along the west side of town, a lively market and a fine white-sand beach stretching along the east side. The beach, which offers good swimming and is shaded by sea-grape trees, is particularly popular with islanders.

Ste-Anne is a good base for those who want to visit the islands of Les Saintes and, if flexible on time, Marie-Galante and La Désirade (in high season).

## Sights & Activities

In addition to the beach on the east side of town, another white-sand beach, **Caravelle Beach**, stretches along the east side of the Caravelle Peninsula, about 2km west of the town center. Its main tenant is Club Med, but the entire beach is public. There is a guarded gate to get to the beach, but anyone is free to walk right in. The unmarked road to Caravelle Beach is off N4, opposite Motel l'Accra Ste-Anne.

## Sleeping

### TOWN CENTER

**our pick** **Ti Village Creole** ( ☎ 85-45-68; www.tivillagecreole.fr; Dupré, 97180 Ste-Anne; studio/bungalow from €52/80; ❑ ❑ ❑ ) A little slice of paradise: you're a 10-minute walk from the hustle-bustle of central Ste-Anne in a tranquil hillside setting run by the well-traveled and informative Vincent. The modern bungalows all have big porches outside, and spacious living rooms and comfortable bedrooms within. Check out the ruins you can see from most balconies – it used to be an old windmill until a 2007 earthquake knocked most of it down. Offers wi-fi access.

**Auberge le Grand Large** ( ☎ 85-48-28; www.aubergelegrandlarge.com; Chemin de la Plage, 97180 Ste-Anne; r from €63; ❑ ❑ ) There are eight one-bedroom bungalows with kitchenettes and two deluxe bungalows with spacious kitchens and two bedrooms. The property completed a renovation in 2008, and the owner says that this grand dame of Ste-Anne hotels is 50 years young. Just a few steps from the beach and a row of restaurants and bars, the location is prime and rooms fill up far in advance. Offers wi-fi access.

**Hotel le Diwali** ( ☎ 85-39-70; www.lediwali.com; Plage de Ste-Anne; r from €220; 🅿 💻 ) This airy oasis at the end of Ste-Anne Beach is a class act with its colonial flair and generous use of dark wood and rattan. Guests can use the kayaks for free. The on-site restaurant is open to all and serves dinner every evening (mains €15 to €35) and sometimes serves lunch (mains €13 to €20), depending on demand.

**Au Verger de Ste-Anne** ( ☎ 88-27-56; www .guadeloupe-hebergement.com; 5 Lot Marguerite, 97180; 2-person cottage per week €450; 🅿 💻 ) Five blocks north of the beach in a very quiet section of town, this charming group of pastel-colored wooden chalets with garden decks and fully equipped kitchens is a good option.

### AROUND TOWN

**La Toubana** ( ☎ 88-25-78; www.toubana.com; 97180 Ste-Anne; r from €160; 🅿 🅿 ) About 2km west of central Ste-Anne, on a quiet coastal cliff overlooking the Caravelle Peninsula, this place doesn't look like much from the road but from the moment you step inside on wooden walkways that skirt small, almost Japanese-looking ponds, you know this is something special. The 32 rooms are all stylishly decorated and the on-site restaurant (meals from €18) has a cigar bar.

**our pick Casa Boubou** ( ☎ 85-10-13; www.casaboubou .fr; 2-person cottage per week €595; 🅿 💻 ) The 10 cottages here all have satellite TV, a DVD player that accepts memory cards, free wi-fi, a hammock and a BBQ grill. Guests enjoy free use of snorkeling equipment and three canoes just a few minutes (150m) away on Caravelle Beach. Book far in advance.

### Eating

Opposite Ste-Anne Beach is a row of simple open-air restaurants with tables in the sand and barbecue grills at the side.

**Kouleur Kreole** (Chemin de la Plage; salads €7-11, grills €11-19; 🕙 11am-10pm Tue-Sun) A popular spot that serves big tasty seafood grills or a variety of fresh salads; it also has a live band on Friday evenings. The food delivers. There's a small parking lot for clients.

**L'Americano** ( ☎ 88-38-99; mains €7-15; 🕙 6:30am-2am) Next to the market, this big, friendly

restaurant-bar shows football on large screens and serves great pizzas and savory crepes. Sweet-tooths might be happy to know that the restaurant makes its own chocolate. With dinner reservations, it has a free shuttle bus for area hotels; call for a pickup.

**Koté Mer Resto** (mains €7-18; 🕙 breakfast, lunch & dinner) Meaning 'Restaurant Near the Sea,' the name doesn't lie. A strong wave will tickle toes and a rogue wave may just drink your ti-punch. The menu spans the range from economical chicken or fish plates to the more expensive salad and lobster. At the height of lunch and dinner a two-man band often plays rock standards with an island sound.

### Shopping

**Village Artisanal** ( 🕙 8am-8pm) A bit west of the beach at the end of the promenade, it may look tacky at first glance but it's a good place to go for the bigger souvenirs (hammocks, sculptures) that are hard to find at the souvenir market in town.

**Géograines** ( ☎ 88-38-74; Durivage 97180) Just west of the Village Artisanal, this quirky place specializes in making things out of seeds – and it all looks good. It has seed wall hangings (from €30) and even a coffee table where black and white seeds are arranged to make a chess board set under glass (€600). The shop only uses Guadeloupean artisans and materials.

## ST-FRANÇOIS
### pop 10,000

St-François is a town with two distinct identities. The west side of town is a sleepy provincial backwater that's quite spread out, while the east side feels a lot like the small upscale marina that it is. The center of the action is the deep U-shaped harbor, which is lined with a handful of restaurants, hotels, car-rental offices, boutiques and marina facilities. Parts of it are pretty and others parts are torn up as there are plans for a massive renovation to make the area a huge pedestrian mall. Just north of the marina there's a golf course.

An undistinguished strand runs along the south side of the town center, but the best beaches in the area are just a 10-minute drive east of town in the direction of Pointe des Châteaux.

St-François is a major jumping-off point for trips to Guadeloupe's smaller islands; see p578 for details. The dock for boats to

La Désirade, Marie-Galante, and Terre-de-Haut on Les Saintes is at the south side of the marina, as is free parking.

## Information

**Banque Populaire** (☼ 7:45am-noon & 2-4:45pm Mon-Fri, 7:45am-12:30pm Sat) On the north side of the marina; has an exchange office.

**BNP bank** (☼ 8am-noon & 2-4pm Mon, Tue, Thu & Fri, 8am-noon Wed) Next to the post office, it has an ATM.

**Cyber Creation** (30min €3, printed page €0.20; ☼ 9:30am-1pm & 3:30-7pm Mon-Sat) An internet place where you can print boarding passes or just check emails. Located near the fishing port in the Galerie Comerciale, which also has snack shops, boutiques and a book store.

**L@robas Café** (per 15min/hr €1.90/6.50; ☼ 7am-2am Mon-Sat, 4pm-2am Sun) At the marina.

**Post office** (☼ 8am-1pm Mon-Sat) A block west of the harbor. Phone cards can be purchased at the Match supermarket.

**Tourist office** (☎ 88-48-74; www.ot-saintfrancois.com; Ave de l'Europe, 97118 St-François; ☼ 8am-noon Mon-Sat & 2-5pm most weekdays, to 12:30pm Wed)

## Activities

**Arawak Surf Action** (☎ 31-88-28; www.surfantilles.com; Base Nautique; ☼ 9am-noon & 2-5pm Mon-Sat) The place for surfing, windsurfing or stand-up paddle boarding.

**Tropicalys** (☎ 54-49-26; www.tropicalys.com; Plage du Bourg de Ste-Anne; 1-tank dive €34) At the marina, this small and friendly outfit takes divers to the nearby reef at 8am and 2pm every day.

St-François has Guadeloupe's only golf course, the 18-hole, par 71, **Golf Municipal de St François** (☎ 88-41-87), designed by Robert Trent Jones.

## Sleeping

Near the harbor and fishing port are a load of residences that advertise solely by small signs and a phone number; rooms are somewhere in the €50 per night range, depending on the length of stay.

**Nise & Hector** (☎ 88-40-19; Rue Paul Tilby; r from €40) Run by the kind folks at Jerco Chez Nise, these little apartments in the center of town don't have any sort of scenery to recommend them, but they are a good budget option.

**Le Golf Marine** (☎ 88-60-60; www.deshotelsetdesiles .com; Ave de L'Europe; s/d incl breakfast €80/95; ☒ ☒ ) Across from the 18-hole municipal golf course, not surprisingly the decor is very golf-centric. The 61 pleasant but unexciting rooms feature lots of white wicker and look

out either on the golf course or on the manicured garden paths behind the hotel. Be sure to check out the neat mosaics at the souvenir shop next door.

**our pick** **La Métisse** (☎ 88-70-00; www.im-caraibes .com/metisse; 66 Les Hauts de Saint François; r from €157; ☒ ☐ ☒ ☒ ) Tucked away in a complex of residential hotels above St-François, this pretty place sports a pool in the abstracted shape of Guadeloupe, an owner who used to be a pilot and bought the hotel after only a few hours on the island, and nine rooms named after the different ways to tie a Creole-style madras hat. It's relaxed and private – rooms that look out on the pool have a curtain on the front patio.

## Eating

**Café de la Marina** (mains €6-10; ☼ lunch & dinner) Tucked away in the southeast corner of the marina under the out-of-business Hotel Kayé La. The friendly proprietor serves calzones and pizzas in this fun place to hang out – it has one of the only pool tables in the city.

**Jerco Chez Nise** (☎ 88-40-19; Rue Paul-Tilby; meals €9-20; ☼ lunch Tue-Sun, dinner Tue-Sat) This tiny, recommended local favorite is a no-frills neighborhood restaurant behind the *mairie* (mayor's building). What it may lack in atmosphere with its strip lighting and tiled floor it more than makes up for with its delicious Creole cooking.

**Le Restaurant du Lagon** (☎ 88-75-44; mains €17-24; ☼ lunch & dinner Mon-Sat) At this jetty restaurant, south of the marina that shelters a big lagoon, the setting is ideal for a plate of freshly caught fish, and there's a gently buzzing ambience. Those who don't want to shell out for the fish can grab a ti-punch or juice (€3 to €5) and drink in the view.

On the southwest corner of the marina, there's a line of inexpensive harborside eateries that sell pastries, sandwiches, ice cream and grilled foods.

At the northwest side of the marina, west of Le Golf Marine, there's a large **Match supermarket** (☼ 8:30am-8pm Mon-Sat, to 1pm Sun); the **fruit and vegetable market** (Place du Marché) runs every day except Monday.

## POINTE DES CHÂTEAUX

Just a 20-minute drive from St-François is windswept Pointe des Châteaux, the eastern-most point of Grande-Terre. This dramatic coastal area has white-sand beaches, limestone cliffs and fine views of the jagged near-shore islets and the island of La Désirade.

Sometimes surfers set up on the small beach here to catch the rough, short-lived waves. A walk up a sandy path to the large cross takes about 10 minutes and is a good place to look back at Guadeloupe.

A snack stand sells coco sorbet (€2) and soft drinks here, and it makes it a point to ask people to properly throw away trash – as many visitors have apparently not done before.

## Sights

There are some more-protected white-sand beaches further to the northwest of Pointe des Châteaux. **Anse Tarare** is a popular nudist beach situated in a sheltered cove 2km west of the road's end. The dirt road north of the main road is marked by a sign reading 'Plage Tarare.'

A few minutes' drive to the west, a side road (follow the 'Chez Honoré' signs) leads about 1km north to **Anse à la Gourde**, a gorgeous sweep of white coral sands. The waters are good for swimming and snorkeling, but be careful of near-shore coral shelves.

For clothing-mandatory fun away from the beach, **La Maison de la Noix de Coco** ( ☎ 85-00-92; www.maison-de-la-noix-de-coco.com; admission free; ☼ 9am-6pm) is a souvenir shop dedicated to all things coconut. There's the usual kitschy Caribbean mementos here (see the Rastaman ashtray, fake hair and all) but many of the items, like polished coconut-husk lamps (from €70) are surprisingly classy. Visitors get a free sample of coconut milk on arrival.

## Sleeping & Eating

**Hostellerie des Châteaux** ( ☎ 85-54-08; www.hostellerie-des-chateaux.com, s/d incl breakfast €85/110; ☼ 🖳 🍴 ) Set on a spacious lawn inland from the road to Pointe des Châteaux, there are four bungalows and four rooms here, with daily housekeeping included with both types of accommodations. Michel, the owner, is a friendly guy and says that anyone is welcome to drop in at the on-site restaurant and bar (mains €16 to €30; open lunch and dinner Tuesday to Saturday, lunch Sun). Offers wi-fi access.

## LE MOULE

**pop 21,000**

The town of Le Moule served as an early French capital of Guadeloupe, and was an important Native American settlement in precolonial times. Consequently, major archaeological excavations have taken place in the area, and Guadeloupe's archaeological museum – under renovation at the time of writing – is on the outskirts of town. Unless you're a surfer or want a quiet base to explore the busier coastal towns or northern Grande-Terre, Le Moule is worth a visit but not a stay.

History buffs will enjoy the wide town square with a few historic buildings, including the town hall and a neoclassical Catholic church. Along the river are some discernible waterfront ruins from an old customs building and a fortress dating back to the original French settlement.

Baie du Moule, on the west side of town, is popular with kayakers and surfers, and has its own surf school. The world surf championships have taken place in Le Moule.

There's a rum distillery nearby, too.

## Information

**Cyber Box Call Shop** (44 Rue Duschassing; internet per hr €6; ☼ 8am-10pm) If staying in Le Moule, it might be worth becoming a member (€10) for reduced prices. International phone service averages €0.20 per minute.

**Tourist office** ( ☎ 23-89-03; www.ot-lemoule.com; Blvd Maritime Damencourt, 97160 Le Moule; ☼ 8:30am-noon & 2-5pm Mon-Fri, 8:30am-noon Sat) Lots of maps and free booklets (in French) on the area.

## Sights

The modern **Edgar Clerc Archeological Museum** (admission free; ☼ 9am-5pm Tue-Sun Sep-Mar, 10am-6pm Tue-Sun Apr-Aug), on a coastal cliff in the Rosette area, has Native American petroglyphs, pottery shards, tools made of shells and stone and an exhibition on local excavations. The museum is about 1km north on La Rosette road (D123), on the western outskirts of Le Moule. Museum staff say that the renovation has been going on for more than a year with no end in sight. The downside is that there are not too many exhibits open, and the ones that have stayed are all in French. On the upside, entry is now free.

For those who don't speak French but know how distilleries work, **Distillery Damoiseau** (www.damoiseau.com; admission free; ☼ self-guided tour 7am-2:30pm Mon-Sat, gift shop 8am-5:30pm Mon-Sat) is a nice chance to wander around at will. For those who don't know their fermentation from their distillation, the Musée du Rhum (p563) is a more educational option. The gift shop has a

GUADELOUPE

good selection of rums made on the premises and offers free tastings. To get to the distillery, look for the sign for Hotel Caraïbe after heading east out of town and take the first right. At the crossroads, take another right and look for the signs.

## Sleeping & Eating

The tourist office can provide a list of vacation rentals, including *gîtes* (small family-run facilities) and apartments in the area. There are a few small grocery stores in downtown Le Moule.

**Cottage Hotel** ( ☎ 23-78-38; www.cottage-residence .net; Rte de la Plage des Alizés; r per night/week €62/330; ⌘ ) The studios are the best bet with outdoor kitchens, a fridge and balconies that face the water. The beach here is not stellar, but close, and you definitely feel a bit out of the action, which can be a good thing.

**Le Spot** ( ☎ 85-66-02; Blvd Maritime Damencourt; mains €7; ⌘ lunch & dinner) Sporting a surf school, this is the place to hang out and watch the waves crash on the shore. It's a nice place to decipher the pamphlets from the tourism office next door and get a feel for what Le Moule has on tap.

# NORTHERN GRANDE-TERRE

A good place for a leisurely day of exploring, with plenty of sunbathing on quiet beaches included. The northern half of Grande-Terre is a rural area of grazing cattle and cane fields; the roads are gently winding but easy to drive.

From Le Moule, drive up past the archaeological museum in Rosette, then turn right on the D120 and follow that road north. As you get closer to Porte d'Enfer the route will be signposted.

## Anse Maurice

The first sight on the D120 coming from Le Moule, the nearly empty beach of Anse Maurice is accessed via a small road with concrete tracks and grazing goats. The water is clear and very shallow until you walk out a bit, partly why it's a favorite with families with small children. There's a bar-restaurant here if you want to take a break from the sun.

## Porte d'Enfer

After soaking up Anse Maurice go north on the D120 and follow the signs to Vigier. On your right, keep your eyes peeled for the Chez Coco restaurant; at the time of research this was the only way to find Port d'Enfer. The 'Port of Hell,' as it's called, is actually a long and narrow lagoon that could be mistaken for a river from the viewpoint further down the road. It's a great place to picnic, swim, or snorkel, but bring your own gear. The water crashing at the mouth of the lagoon would be the gates of hell for anyone foolish enough to venture beyond the calm waters.

## Pointe de la Grande Vigie

The island's northernmost point, Pointe de la Grande Vigie offers scenic views from its high sea cliffs. A rocky path – walkable in flip-flops but better in tennis shoes – makes a loop from the parking lot to the cliffs and has some fantastic views. Mind the cliffs – signs in French warn that there are sometimes rock slides and that people can fall off and die.

On a clear day you can see Antigua to the north and Montserrat to the northwest, both about 75km away.

## Anse Bertrand

Anse Bertrand, where the D120 starts to loop back south, has more of a rocky, crashing coast than a beach, but a few restaurants facing the local church and friendly locals make it worth a pit stop.

South of Anse Bertrand, near Port-Louis, is **Beauport Le Pays de La Canne** ( ☎ 22-44-70; www .lepaysdelacanne.com; adult/child €9/6; ⌘ 9am-5pm Mon-Sat), a shut-down sugarcane factory that's been turned into a learning center. Taking the 50-minute train ride through the old sugar plantation is worthwhile.

## Petit-Canal

South of Le Pays de La Canne, this is the place to go for a trip into the nearby mangroves.

**Clarisma Tours** ( ☎ 22-51-15; www.clarismatour.com; tours €15-50; ⌘ departures 9am & 4pm) offers a short sunset tour or a full-day outing with lunch and snorkeling included.

Petit-Canal was a major landing point for slaves kidnapped from Africa to work on the nearby sugar plantations. Near the church in the center of town are steps that lead to a stele that reads 'liberty.' The steps were built by slaves themselves and have the names of African tribes carved into them.

## South to Morne-à-l'Eau

Besides a **crab festival** every April, what brings tourists is the city-within-a-city at the cem-

**etery**, where N6 meets the N5. There's parking near the police station (*gendarmeries*) but be careful crossing the road. Terraced with raised vaults and tombs, many decorated in checkered black and white tiles, this is Guadeloupe's most elaborate burial ground. Locals are getting a little fed up with tour buses full of strangers gawking and taking photos of the resting places of relatives; a little courtesy and discretion is a good idea.

# BASSE-TERRE

Shortly after entering the island of Basse-Terre from Pointe-à-Pitre, you have a choice of three main routes: north along the coast, south along the coast, or across the interior along the Route de la Traversée, through the national park. Most of the destinations in Basse-Terre offer a nice balance between nature – including the national park and plentiful diving – and amenities for visitors.

## Getting There & Around

For information on buses from Grande-Terre and through the area, see p551.

Ferries run between Trois-Rivières and Terre-de-Haut in Les Saintes; for details see p578.

## ROUTE DE LA TRAVERSÉE

The road that heads across the center of the island, the Route de la Traversée (D23), slices through the Parc National de Guadeloupe, a 17,300-hectare forest reserve that occupies the interior of Basse-Terre. It's a lovely mountain drive that passes fern-covered hillsides, thick bamboo stands and enormous mahogany and gum trees. Other rainforest vegetation en route includes orchids, heliconia and ginger.

The road begins off the N1 about 15 minutes west of Pointe-à-Pitre and is well signposted. There are a few switchbacks, but driving is not tricky if you don't rush, and it's a good two-lane road all the way. Although the road could easily be driven in an hour, give yourself double that to stop and enjoy the scenery – more if you want to do any hiking or to break for lunch.

There are 200km of hiking trails here, and the many signs with pull-offs on the side of the road are the beginning of trails. Start before 3pm or so, as night falls quickly here.

The trails are well marked and the longer the hike, the better your chances of seeing very few people. Trails can be very muddy and rocky with lots of slippery tree roots; at least wear tennis shoes, if not hiking boots.

Don't miss the **Cascade aux Écrevisses**, an idyllic little jungle waterfall that drops into a broad pool. From the parking area the waterfall is just a three-minute walk on a semipaved trail. The roadside pull-off is clearly marked on the D23, 2km after you enter the park's eastern boundary. Try to go early; busloads of tourists arrive in the late afternoon. On the other side of the road from the parking lot is a trail to a picnic area with covered tables right near the river.

At **Maison de la Forêt**, 2km further west, there's a staffed **exhibit center** (www.guadeloupe-parcnational.com; 9:30am-4:30pm) with a few simple displays on the forest in French and pamphlets in English, including a basic map that shows the parking areas for trailheads and picnic areas. A map board and the beginning of an enjoyable 20-minute **loop trail** are at the back of the center. The trail crosses a bridge over the Bras David river and then proceeds through a jungle of *gommier* trees, tall ferns and squawking tropical birds. The **Bras David trail** (go left instead of right at the first fork) takes an hour, and is an enjoyable if muddy way to get deeper into the jungle.

## NORTHERN BASSE-TERRE

The northern half of Basse-Terre offers interesting contrasts. Starting from the west side of Route de la Traversée, most of the west coast is rocky and many of the drives snake along the tops of towering sea cliffs. There are a couple of attractive swimming beaches – Grande Anse is the most popular.

Once you reach the northern tip of the island the terrain becomes gentler and the vegetation dry and scrubby. Continuing down the east coast, the countryside turns into sugarcane fields and the towns become larger and more suburban as you approach Pointe-à-Pitre.

### Pointe-Noire

Pointe-Noire, between Plage de Malendure and Deshaies, is the epicenter of places that each specialize in one thing – chocolate, coffee etc. Most of these establishments are just north of the D23 (Route de la Traversée) on the N2, and signs abound for all of them.

GUADELOUPE

At **Maison Du Cacao** ( ☎ 98-25-23; adult/child €5/2.50; ☒ 9:30am-5pm Mon-Sat year-round & 9:30am-5pm Sun Dec-Feb), treat yourself to a cup of hot chocolate (€3) that's closer to the Mayan's sacrament of divinity than any powdered drink.

Set high on a hill off the D16, **Caféiere Beauséjour** ( ☎ 98-10-09; www.cafeierebeausejour .com; adult/child €7/3.50; ☒ 10am-5pm Tue-Sat) is an old colonial house and working plantation that tells the history of coffee (in French), explains the traditional processing of the bean, and lets people sample their product at tour's end. On the way down, beware of taking the wrong way. Some dead-end drives are so steep that it's a dicey proposition to turn a car around.

With an outdoor park to show off different species of trees and indoor exhibits showing all the different ways to work with wood, and products made out of wood, **Maison du Bois** ( ☎ 98-16-90; ilesauboisvivants@wanadoo .fr; adult/child €9/4.50; ☒ 9:30am-5pm Tue-Sat) is an arborphile's dream. It has an on-site seashell museum (extra €2) and restaurant.

Visitors must make reservations to get a guided tour of the private orchid garden **Le Parc aux Orchidées** ( ☎ 98-02-85; www.parcaux orchidees.com; adult/child €16/12; ☒ 10am-5pm Fri-Sun). The owners say that with more than 3000 orchids (400 species), this is the largest outdoor collection in the Caribbean.

## Deshaies
pop 4200

A nice harborside village surrounded by green hills, Deshaies (day-ey) is filled with plenty of eateries, ranging from tapas bars to small sandwich shops.

### INFORMATION

**Le Pélican Cyber Café** ( ☎ 28-44-27; per hr €5, all-day wi-fi €5; ☒ 8:30am-12:30pm & 4-7pm Mon-Fri) It also sells a variety of colorful hammocks and hanging chairs. For an internet café, it's an unusually lively place.

**Tropical Sub** ( ☎ 28-52-67; www.tropical-sub.com; dive €38; ☒ daily dives 9:30am & 2:30pm) On the main strip in Deshaies, it take divers and snorkelers to the Cousteau Reserve.

### SIGHTS & ACTIVITIES

Thanks to its sheltered bay, the village is a popular stop with yachters and sailors and has an international feeling. The local seafaring traditions have carried on into the tourist trade, with several dive shops and deep-sea fishing boats operating from the pier.

**Grande Anse**, 2km north of Deshaies, is a nice beach with no hotel development in sight. The waves break right near the shore and aren't terribly large, but are perfect for young body surfers who don't mind the sandy backwash that waves like this make. There are a number of beachside restaurants, some of which have their ocean views obstructed by the parking lot that's jam-packed during high season. **Les Hibiscus** ( ☎ 28-22-50; mains €6-13; ☒ lunch), however, is closest to the beach and has some of the best food and prices here.

### SLEEPING

**Fanelie** ( ☎ 28-45-48; www.fanelie.fr; Ferry Leroux; r from €45; ☒ ) On a small alley just a few hundred meters after Plage de Léroux, just south of Deshaies, the cottages here are immense, with big porches and individual BBQs. The decor is a bit old-fashioned and there's a baby crib in the bedroom; some may find it spooky. You can do laundry at reception for €4.50. Late risers, beware: roosters prowl the grounds and crow at the crack of dawn.

**Au Ti Sucrier** ( ☎ 28-91-29; www.autisucrier.com; Pointe Ferry; r from €100; ☒ ☒ ) Set 40m from Plage de Léroux, this place has 14 modern bungalows with outdoor kitchens and ocean views. The friendly owners have two big dogs, one of which is pure white and cuts quite the figure as he runs around the on-site aviary following the flight of the birds inside.

**Rayon Vert** ( ☎ 28-43-23; hotel.lerayonvert.free.fr; Pointe Ferry; r from €138; ☒ ☒ ) Highly recommended by travelers for the helpful staff, this place is named after the band of green that seafaring folk from around the world wait to see right at sunset. The 22 rooms all have a porch that opens up to sea views, a minibar and big bathrooms. It has one wheelchair-accessible room and an on-site restaurant.

**Domaine de la Pointe Batterie** ( ☎ 28-57-03; www.pointe-batterie.com; Chemin de la Batterie; studios/villas €125/275; ☒ ☒ ) A terraced property just outside of Deshaies, every luxurious room here has a sea view and the villas each have a small private pool. On-site spa services include flower baths (€45), chocolate wraps (€60) and a three-day regimen of sauna, massage and reflexology (€380).

### EATING & DRINKING

You'll find some of the best food around in the village and its hinterland.

**Barbuto** ( ☎ 89-87-28; www.barbutonyc.com; Blvd De Poissonniers; tapas plate €5-7, mains €13-21; ☑ 6pm-midnight Mon-Sat) This snazzy but warm tapas restaurant and bar is a good place to grab a drink and some snacks at the tables near the water. As well as tapas, the joint offers a mélange of French, Italian and Creole food. Barbuto also has another location in New York City.

**Le Coin des Pécheurs** ( ☎ 28-47-75; mains €14-34; ☑ lunch & dinner) An excellent little restaurant with vaguely nautical decor and a seaside terrace. At the northern entrance to the village on the main drag, this place serves Creole starters of *christophine farcie* (stuffed vegetable), and entrecôtes or grilled fish for mains.

**La Note Bleue** (mains €18; ☑ 9am-11pm Mon-Sat) At the south end of town, La Note Bleue has a big bar that's popular with the sailing set as well as landlubbers, and a French restaurant with indoor and outdoor seating.

**L'Amer** ( ☎ 28-50-43; mains €19-40; ☑ dinner Mon-Sat) Almost next door to Le Coin des Pécheurs, this chic, upmarket restaurant with a stylish blue and white interior and terrace is renowned for its salads and seafood such as delicious king prawns, flambéed in aged rum.

There's a Spar supermarket just south of town to stock up on food, snacks and drinks.

## Ste-Rose
pop 19,000

In days of yore, Ste-Rose was a major agricultural town. While sugar production has declined on Guadeloupe and a number of mills have closed, sugarcane is still an important crop on this northeastern tip of Basse-Terre, and there are a few rum-related tourist sights on the outskirts of town.

Visitors who follow the signs from the N2 to 'Bord de Mer' will find a row of restaurants, souvenir stalls, and places to take excursions to the nearby Îlet Caret, which one can see from the Bord de Mer. Reserve in advance.

**BleuBlancVert** ( ☎ 28-38-49; www.bleublancvert.com; adult/child €25/12) runs half-day trips to the island on a motorized raft. The trip includes a waterproof container, snorkeling gear and *planteurs* punch, a libation with rum, fruit juice and a little spice to make everything nice.

With a maximum of 12 people and snorkeling gear provided, the trip run by **Nico Excursions** ( ☎ 28-72-47; www.nicoexcursions.com; half-/full day €35/60) is also a good way to see the island.

Those who want to understand how the ambrosia called rum starts in the sugarcane fields and ends on their palates should really come to the **Musée du Rhum** (Rum Museum; ☎ 28-70-04; musee-du-rhum.fr; adult/child incl tasting €7/3.50; ☑ 9am-5pm Mon-Sat), which has thorough explanations in English. It's at the site of the Reimonenq Distillery, about 500m inland from the N2 in the village of Bellevue, just southeast of Ste-Rose. Exhibits include an old distillery, cane-extraction gears and a vapor machine dating from 1707. Check out the collection of butterflies, model boats (including Noah's Ark) and *coiffes* (madras head wraps).

Guadeloupeans say **Chez Franko** ( ☎ 28-86-51; Blvd St Charles, Bord de Mer; mains €13-20; ☑ lunch & dinner) is the best eating choice. The grilled fish is good, if a bit boney; the seafood stews are a better way to go if you don't want to work for your meal. Ring the cow bell at the counter if there's not a server in sight.

## SOUTH TO CAPESTERRE-BELLE-EAU

The N1, the road that runs along the east coast of Basse-Terre, travels through cattle pastures and sugarcane fields. For the most part it's pleasantly rural, but unless you're driving it may not be an area in which to spend much precious vacation time.

**Valombreuse Floral Park** ( ☎ 95-50-50; www.valombreuse.com; adult/child €5/2.50; ☑ 8am-6pm), nestled in the hills west of Petit-Bourg, is a pleasant 14-hectare botanical garden with lots of activities for kids. There's also a path to a waterfall that spills into a swimming hole. The road leading off the N1 to the park, 5km inland, is well signposted.

In the center of the village of **Ste-Marie**, a bust of Columbus and two huge anchors comprise a modest roadside monument honoring the explorer who landed on this shore in 1493.

The road is lined with flamboyant trees on the north side of **Capesterre-Belle-Eau**, a good-sized town that has a supermarket, some local eateries and a gas station.

## CHUTES DU CARBET

Unless it's overcast, the drive up to the Chutes du Carbet lookout gives a view of two magnificent waterfalls plunging down a sheer mountain face.

Starting from St Sauveur on the N1, the road runs 8.5km inland, making for a nice 15-minute drive up through a rainforest. It's a

GUADELOUPE

good hard-surfaced road all the way, although it's a bit narrow and twisting. Nearly 3km before the end of the road is a marked stop at the trailhead to **Grand Étang**, a placid lake circled by a loop trail. It's just a five-minute walk from the roadside parking area down to the edge of the lake, and it takes about an hour more to stroll the lake's perimeter. Due to the danger of bilharzia (schistosomiasis) infection, this is not a place for a swim.

The road ends at the Chutes du Carbet lookout. You can see the two highest waterfalls from the upper parking lot, where a signboard marks the trailhead to the base of the falls. The well-trodden walk to the second-highest waterfall (110m) takes 30 minutes; it's about a two-hour hike to the highest waterfall (115m). It's also possible to hike from the lookout to the summit of La Soufrière (see right), a hardy three-hour walk with some wonderfully varied scenery.

There are picnic facilities at the lookout, along with a few food stalls selling plate lunches of simple barbecue fare. This is a very popular spot for outings and can get quite crowded on weekends and holidays.

## TROIS-RIVIÈRES
### pop 9000
Most often visited as a jumping-off point to Les Saintes, this sleepy town has sharply curving streets, is surrounded by lush vegetation and has fine views of Les Saintes, just 10km offshore to the south.

For those who get seasick easily, Trois-Rivières has the shortest ferry ride and reputedly the calmest waters to Terre-de-Haut in Les Saintes. See p578 for details.

Don't miss the **Parc Archéologique des Roches Gravées** ( ☎ 92-91-88; admission €1.50; ☽ 9am-5pm), featuring rocks carved with petroglyphs of human, animal and abstract forms. Some of the rocks were found on the site; others were brought from around Basse-Terre. The visitor center at the entrance has informative displays and pamphlets on island history and there's an adventurous boulder-filled trail through the park. The park is on the road to the ferry dock 200m north of the waterfront.

There are a number of places to stay scattered in and around town and a few places to eat; very few stay open once the working day ends.

There are four rooms in the beautiful old house of **Le Paradis Vert** ( ☎ 92-61-61; paradis-vert@ wanadoo.fr; Le Petit Carbet, 97114 Trois-Rivières; r from €60),

which at one time was the center of a coffee and cocoa plantation. It's 1.6km north of the town center; look for the signs.

There are five slick, brightly colored bungalows at **Coco Zabrico** ( ☎ 92-83-50; cocoetzabrico .monsite.wanadoo.fr; Route de Gaigneron, 97114 Trois-Rivières; r from €70) outside of town. With a BBQ pit and a small play area for kids, it's a good base for the family.

The pizzas at **Pizzeria Total Végétal** (pizzas €7-15; ☽ lunch & dinner) are available in the evenings only and you should be prepared to wait – this build-your-own-pie place is very popular. During the day hungry visitors have a choice of a few simple dishes like couscous and chicken or beef stew and rice. Order at the counter.

Signs at the west side of the town center point the way from the N1 to the dock, 1km away, where the ferry leaves for Terre-de-Haut. La Roche Gravée restaurant, a few minutes' walk from the dock, provides parking for ferry passengers.

## LA SOUFRIÈRE
From Trois-Rivières there are a couple of ways to get to La Soufrière, the active 1467m volcano that looms above the southern half of the island.

The most direct route to La Soufrière is to follow the D8 northwest from Trois-Rivières, turn west on the N1 for a few kilometers and then follow the signs north to St-Claude. This is a nice jungle drive into the mountains; you'll cross some small streams and pass banana plantations before reaching the village of St-Claude, just south of the national-park boundaries. There's no food available in the park, but St-Claude has a few local restaurants and small grocers.

From St-Claude, signs point to La Soufrière, 6km to the northeast on the D11. The steep road up into the park has a few beep-as-you-go hairpin turns, and it narrows in places to almost one lane, but it's a good solid road all the way. If it's fogged in, proceed slowly, as visibility can drop to just a few meters.

The closed Maison du Volcan is the trailhead for a couple of hour-long walks, including one to Chute de Galleon, a scenic 40m waterfall on the Galion River.

There are a couple of viewpoints and picnic areas as the road continues up the mountain for the 15-minute drive to La Savane à Mulet, a parking area at an elevation of 1142m. From here, there's a clear view straight up La

Soufrière (when it's not covered in clouds or mist), and you can see and smell vapors rising from nearby fumaroles.

For an adventurous 1½-hour hike to La Soufrière's sulfurous, moonscapelike summit, a well-beaten trail starts at the end of the parking lot. It travels along a gravel bed and continues steeply up the mountain through a cover of low shrubs and thick ferns. In addition to a close-up view of the steaming volcano, the hike offers some fine vistas of the island. It's also possible to make a four-hour trek from La Savane à Mulet to the Chutes du Carbet lookout (p563).

The road continues further east another 1.75km, taking in a lookout and views of sulfur vents before it dead-ends at a relay station.

## BASSE-TERRE

**pop 13,000**

The rather grim administrative capital of Guadeloupe, Basse-Terre is somewhat active on weekdays during work hours, but almost deserted after dark and on weekends, with most shops and restaurants closed. The traffic getting in or out of the city moves at a snail's pace during daylight hours.

As an old colonial port town, there is some local character, but not much. The south side of town, along Blvd Gouverneur Général Félix Eboué, has a couple of rather imposing government buildings, including the Palais de Justice and the sprawling Conseil Général, the latter flanked by fountains. **Fort Louis Delgrès**, which dates from 1643, is on this side of town as well, as is the Rivière Sens Marina.

At the north side of town, opposite the commercial dock, is the old town square. It's bordered by the aging Hôtel de Ville (Town Hall), the tourist office, customs and some older two- and three-story buildings that are, overall, more run-down than quaint. There's an unadorned **cathedral** near the river, about five minutes' walk south of the square.

The bus station is on the shoreline at the western end of Blvd Gouverneur Général Félix Eboué. Opposite the north end of the station is the public market.

## PLAGE DE MALENDURE & PIGEON ISLAND

The road up the west coast from Basse-Terre (N2) follows the shoreline, passing fishing villages, small towns and a few black-sand beaches. The landscape gets drier as you continue north into the lee of the mountains. There's not much of interest for visitors until Plage de Malendure (Malendure Beach), a popular dark-sand beach that's the departure point for snorkeling and diving tours to nearby Pigeon Island (Îlet Pigeon).

### Activities

Jacques Cousteau brought Pigeon Island to international attention a few decades ago by declaring it to be one of the world's top dive sites. The waters surrounding the island are now protected as the **Réserve Cousteau**, an underwater park. There's an underwater statue of Mr Cousteau near the Jardins de Corail (Coral Gardens) dive site. Divers who touch the statue's head are supposed to have good luck, and good diving, for the rest of their underwater lives.

The majority of the dive sites around Pigeon Island are very scenic, with big schools of fish, coral walls and coral reefs that are shallow enough for good snorkeling. It's only a 10- to 15-minute boat ride to the dive sites, and almost all the shops have morning, noon and mid-afternoon outings.

There is a tourist information booth and a number of dive shops on Plage de Malendure; single-tank dives hover around €40. These shops are also the place to go to arrange snorkeling trips.

**Archipel Plongée** ( ☎ 98-93-93; www.archipel-plongee .fr; Pigeon; 🕑 9am-5:30pm) Some of the friendly dive masters here can make jokes in English, French, and can even make people laugh underwater.

**Centre National de Plongée** ( ☎ 98-16-23; www .cip-guadeloupe.com; Bouillante; 🕑 9am-5:30pm) Another respected dive shop on the beach.

**Les Heures Saines** ( ☎ 98-86-63; www.heures-saines .gp; Le Rocher de Malendure; 🕑 8:30am-5pm) This dive shop is hidden under the Le Rocher de Malendure restaurant. In addition to the standard dive offerings, it rents underwater cameras and offers Soufrière hikes, canyoning and can help arrange deep-sea fishing trips.

### Sleeping

In the center of the village of Pigeon, just south of Plage de Malendure, there are several private room-for-rent and *gîte* signs.

**ourpick Ti Gli Gli** ( ☎ 98-73-49; www.tigligli.com; Rue de Poirier; r from €50) At the very end of Rue de Poirier, this place provides fishing poles for the use of guests and an open-air grill to cook the catch. It also organizes hikes to La Soufrière and elsewhere. Even though the five bungalows are rustic and rely on natural ventilation, they have microwaves and toasters that run on solar power and have solar hot water. André Exartier, the owner, invites his musician friends to come by for music nights a few times per month and fires up the brick oven to make pizza. There's also a bird garden on the property. To get here, follow the signs that have a little bird wearing a scuba tank (André used to be a dive instructor).

**Le Jardin Tropical** ( ☎ 98-77-23; www.au-jardin-tropical.com; Rue de Poirier; r from €64; 🔡 💻 🗪 ) On steep street full of similar places, most with stellar views, Le Jardin Tropical stands out because of its friendly owners, a pool that feels nearly private and a little bar that opens up every night where the owner makes a wicked ti-punch. The bungalow rooms are sparkling clean, simply furnished but comfortable, and all have outdoor patios, kitchens and sea views. Offers wi-fi access.

## Eating

There are huts on Plage de Malendure selling cheap sandwiches and snacks, and a couple of simple open-air beachside restaurants with more substantial meals.

**Le Rocher de Malendure** ( ☎ 98-70-84; www.rocher-de-malendure.gp; Malendure, 97125 Bouillante; mains €16-40; 🕒 lunch & dinner) For something more upscale, this is the place to go. It has sushi plates and keeps its lobsters extra fresh in a small pool. The restaurant also rents simple studios from €61; a demi-pension (breakfast and dinner) per person is €30. The same folks run Le Jardin Tropical.

For supermarkets, you'll find a Leader Price and a Match on the southern outskirts of Plage de Malendure.

# TERRE-DE-HAUT

**pop 1800**

Lying 10km off Guadeloupe is Terre-de-Haut, the largest of the eight small islands that make up Les Saintes. Since the island was too hilly and dry for sugar plantations, slavery never took hold here. Consequently, the older islanders still trace their roots to the early seafaring Norman and Breton colonists and

many of the locals have light skin and blond or red hair.

Terre-de-Haut is unhurried and feels like a small slice of southern France transported to the Caribbean. Lots of English is spoken here thanks to a big international sailing scene, and it's definitely the most cosmopolitan of Guadeloupe's outlying islands.

Terre-de-Haut is only 5km long and about half as wide. Ferries dock right in the center of Bourg des Saintes, the island's only village. The airstrip is to the east, a 10-minute walk from the village center.

## Getting There & Away

This is the easiest island to visit in terms of choice. By sea you can get here from four cities on the southern coast of mainland Guadeloupe and by air from Pointe-à-Pitre.

### AIR

**Air Caraïbes** ( ☎ 82-47-00; www.aircaraibes.com) flies to Terre-de-Haut from Pointe-à-Pitre three or four times per week at 3:15pm, quickly turning around for the return trip at 3:40pm. The fare is roughly €142 return but check the company's website for special offers.

### BOAT

There are ferries between Terre-de-Haut and Pointe-à-Pitre, Ste-Anne and St-François (on Grande-Terre), and Trois-Rivières (on Basse-Terre); a ferry also runs between Terre-de-Haut and Terre-de-Bas. See p577 for details.

## Getting Around

If you just want to eat and make the steep walk to Fort Napoléon (more than a few seniors do it; youngsters have no excuse), there's no need to rent a motorbike.

### MINIBUS

Air-conditioned minibuses provide two-hour tours of the island for around €15 per person, if there are enough people. Drivers canvass arriving ferry passengers, or you can look for vans parked along the street between the pier and the town hall.

### MOTORCYCLE

Motorbikes are a great way to tour the island. Although roads are narrow, there are only a few dozen cars on Terre-de-Haut, so you won't encounter much traffic. With a motorbike you can zip up to the top of Le Chameau

See p577 for details.

GUADELOUPE

and Fort Napoléon, get out to the beaches and explore the island pretty thoroughly in a day. The motorbikes are capable of carrying two people, but because the roads are so windy, it's not advisable to carry a passenger unless you're an accomplished rider.

There are lots of rental locations on the main road leading south from the pier, but the ones that set up dockside seem as good as any. Try **Localizé** ( ☎ 99-51-99) or **Archipel Rent Services** ( ☎ 99-52-63) if you want to book in advance. If you arrive on a busy day, it's wise to grab a bike as soon as possible, as they sometimes sell out. Most charge €20 to €25 for day visitors and require a €200 deposit or an imprint of a major credit card. Motorbikes come with gas but not damage insurance, so if you get in an accident or spill the bike, the repairs will be charged to your credit card.

Motorbike riding is prohibited in the center of Bourg des Saintes and helmets are obligatory. You'll see people ignoring the law, but if you're not wearing a helmet and you run into police, you can expect to be stopped.

## BOURG DES SAINTES

Home to most of the island's residents, Bourg des Saintes is a picturesque village with a decidedly Norman accent. Its narrow streets are lined with whitewashed, red-roofed houses with shuttered windows and yards of flowering hibiscus.

At the end of the pier is a small courtyard with a gilded column commemorating the French Revolution; it's a bustling place at ferry times, quiet at others. Turn right and in a minute you'll be at the central town square, flanked by the *mairie* (town hall) and an old stone church.

It's a fun town in which to kick around. There are restaurants, ice-cream shops, scooter rentals, galleries and gift shops clustered along the main road, which is pedestrian-only during the day. Most shops close around 1pm; some reopen in the evening, but in the low season many places stay closed.

### Information

There are card phones at the pier. Most of the following points of interest are marked on blue and white signs in town. Hotels here usually don't have signs on the street.

**Crédit Agricole** ( ☎ 9am-2:30pm Tue, Thu & Fri) The island's sole bank. There's an ATM on Rue de la Grande Anse, next to the tourist office.

**Dr Ballabriga** ( ☎ 99-50-66) If you're sick, look for the blue-and-white house shaped like a boat (many people think it really is a boat) to your left as you enter the town. The doctor is in the house.

**L'Etage Cybercafé** (Upstairs Cybercafé; ☎ 81-53-57; per hr €5) It also sells memory cards and small computer accessories. On the main street near the pier.

**Post office** On the main road a few minutes' walk south of the town hall.

**Tourist office** ( ☎ 99-58-60; www.omtlessaintes.fr; 39 Rue de la Grande Anse; ☽ 8am-noon & 1:30-4:30pm Mon-Sat, 8am-2pm Sun) Its website has a useful English-language section.

### Activities

**Aquatic Park** is set behind the Ti Saintois restaurant and sandwich shop. The four swimming lanes in the harbor are a tad shorter than an Olympic-sized pool. Just show up and jump in.

**Pisquettes dive shop** ( ☎ 99-88-80 www.pisquettes .com) does morning and afternoon dives. **La Dive Bouteille** ( ☎ 49-80-91; www.dive-bouteille.com) offers certification courses, night dives, and kid-friendly dives in addition to the usual underwater outings.

### Sleeping

There are room-for-rent signs around the island. During high season the competition for rooms can be stiff so book ahead.

**Kanaoa** ( ☎ 99-51-36; www.hotelkanaoa.com; 97137 Les Saintes; s/d incl breakfast €90/115, bungalows from €120; ☒ ⍯ ) Outside the village in the direction of Fort Napoléon, this two-star hotel sits on the beach and has a private pier and restaurant. The hotel runs a shuttle bus around the island during daylight hours for guests to visit the main sights and beaches. In addition to the 19 hotel rooms, there are four duplex bungalows with kitchenettes.

**Auberge Les Petits Saints** ( ☎ 99-50-99; www .petitssaints.com; La Savane; studios €90-110, r €110-140; ☒ ⍯ ) This former mayor's residence is set in an opulent villa. Each room is decorated with objets d'art, well-chosen antiques, a big canopy bed and plenty of TLC. The decked swimming pool has fabulous views over the bay. There are two studios 100m away from the main building; they don't have the satellite TV and phones that the other rooms do. There's a small gym tucked behind the massive 200-year-old intricately carved wooden wall in the restaurant.

**LoBleu Hotel** ( ☎ 92-40-00; www.lobleuhotel.com; Fond de Curé, 97137 Les Saintes; s/d incl breakfast €91/93;

GUADELOUPE

# TERRE-DE-HAUT & TERRE-DE-BAS

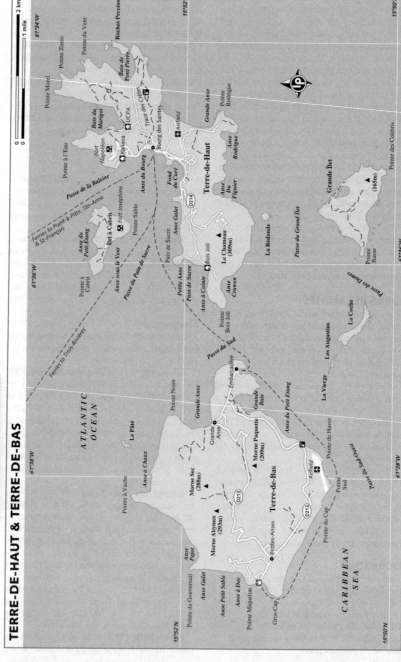

0        1 mile
0        2 km

**ATLANTIC OCEAN**

**CARIBBEAN SEA**

Pointe du Vent
Pointe Zozio
Roches Percées
Pointe Morel
Baie de Pont Pierre
Baie du Marigot
UCPA
Trace des Crêtes
Pointe à l'Eau
Fort Napoléon
Kanaoa
Bourg des Saintes
Airfield
Grande Anse
Pointe Rodrigue
Anse Rodrigue
**Terre-de-Haut**
Anse Du Figuier
Anse du Bourg
Fond du Curé
D214
Anse Galet
Pointe Sable
Fort Joséphine
Passe de la Baleine
Pointe à l'Eau
Anse du Petit Etang
Îlet à Cabrit
Anse sous le Vent
Pointe à Cabrit
Passe du Pain de Sucre
Pointe Noire
Pain de Sucre
Petite Anse
Anse à Cointe
Anse Craven
Pointe Bois Joli
Bois Joli
Le Chameau (309m)
La Redonde
Passe du Grand Îlet
**Grande Îlet** (165m)
Pointe des Colibris
Pointe Basse
Passe des Dames
La Coche
Les Augustins
La Vierge
Passe du Sud
Embarcadère
Grande Baie
Morne Paquette (209m)
Anse du Petit Etang
Pointe du Havre
Pointe Sud
Passe du Sud-Ouest
Airfield
**Terre-de-Bas**
D213
Grande Anse
Grande Anse
Morne Sec (288m)
Morne Abymes (293m)
Pointe Noire
Anse à Chaux
Pointe à Vache
Pointe du Gouvernail
Anse Pajot
Anse Galet
Anse Petit Sable
Anse à Dos
Pointe Miquelon
Gros-Cap
Petites-Anses
D213
Pointe du Cap

Ferries to Point-à-Pitre, Ste-Anne & St-François
Ferries to Trois-Rivières

15°52'N
15°50'N
61°38'W
61°36'W
61°34'W

😵 ) Right in the center of town, each of the 10 rooms in this stylish hotel is decorated in a different motif – Spanish, Asian, nautical. The ground-level restaurant (mains €12 to €17; open dinner) has a number of Lebanese dishes. With solar lamps that soak up the sun by day and glow at night, this is definitely the coolest place to be in the evenings.

## Eating
There are many casual restaurants around town that cater to day-trippers and offer a meal of the day in the €10 to €16 range.

**La Saladerie** ( ☎ 99-53-43; Anse Mirre; mains €10-17; 😋 lunch & dinner Wed-Sun) A popular spot hidden down some steps, it has a make-your-own salad menu and serves a number of fish dishes. It's a few minutes' walk north of the pier on the main road.

**Sole Mio** ( ☎ 99-56-46; http://solemio.monsite.wanadoo.fr; mains €10-18; 😋 lunch & dinner Mon-Sat) A restaurant and small art gallery overlooking the water, Sole Mio has nice views both inside and out. Try the *espadon* (swordfish) tartare and the traditional Santoise dessert *tourment d'amour* (love's torment), a cake-like concoction with melted chocolate in the middle, historically made by local women to provide solace while their sailor husbands were at sea.

**Auberge Les Petits Saints** ( ☎ 99-50-99; La Savane; mains €20-30; 😋 dinner Tue-Sun) The open-air terraced restaurant at this hotel specializes in fresh fish and seafood finely teamed with local produce.

## FORT NAPOLÉON
As destinations go, **Fort Napoléon** (adult/child €4/2; 😋 9:30am-12:30pm) is worth seeing for something to do while here. You can walk through on your own or join an informative 30-minute guided tour conducted in French. There's a cactus garden where iguanas often frolic, but the naval museum inside is only of interest to hard-core naval historians – the battle of Les Saintes is documented in exacting detail.

***

**TWIST MY ARM: THE SPOTS THE AUTHORS WANTED TO KEEP SECRET**

**Terre-de-Haut** in Les Saintes. Selfishly, I'd love to have it all to myself!

***

Built in the mid-19th century but never used in battle, the fort affords a fine hilltop view of Bourg des Saintes, and you can look across the channel to Fort Josephine, a small fortification on Îlet à Cabrit. On a clear day you can also see Marie-Galante and La Désirade.

Fort Napoléon is 1.6km north of the center of Bourg des Saintes; simply turn left as you come off the pier and follow the road uphill.

## BAIE DU MARIGOT
Baie du Marigot is a pleasant little bay with a calm protected beach about 1km north of Bourg des Saintes. It's fairly close to Fort Napoléon, so you could combine a visit to the two; after visiting the fort, turn left at the bottom of the winding fort road and bear left again a few minutes later as you near the bay.

## BAIE DE PONT PIERRE
The horseshoe-shaped Baie de Pont Pierre is a lovely reef-protected beach with light brown sand and a splendid setting; there are even tame goats that mosey onto the beach and lie down next to sunbathers. The beach is an easy 1.6km walk northeast of Bourg des Saintes.

## EAST-COAST BEACHES
The long, sandy **Grande Anse**, immediately east of the airport runway, has rough seas and water conditions, and swimming is not allowed. The north side of this windy beach is backed by clay cliffs.

South of Grande Anse and about 2km from town is **Anse Rodrigue**, a nice beach on a protected cove that usually has good swimming conditions.

## SOUTHWEST BEACHES
Two kilometers southwest of Bourg des Saintes is **Anse à Cointe**, a good beach for combining swimming and snorkeling. The snorkeling is best on the north side. You'll also find good snorkeling and a sandy beach at **Pain de Sucre** (Sugarloaf), the basalt peninsula that's about 700m to the north.

**Anse Crawen**, 500m south of Bois Joli, is a secluded, clothing-optional beach just a couple of minutes' walk down a dirt path that starts where the coastal road ends. It's a perfect spot for **nude snorkeling**; bring plenty of water and sunscreen.

GUADELOUPE

## LE CHAMEAU

A winding cement road leads to the summit of Le Chameau, which at 309m is the island's highest point.

To get to Le Chameau, turn south from the Bourg des Saintes pier and continue 1km on the coastal road. At Restaurant Plongée turn inland on the D214; 500m later, turn left on the cement road and follow it up 1.75km to where it ends at the tower.

From town it's a moderately difficult hour-long walk to the top. A more fun alternative is to ride a motorbike, which takes five minutes.

# TERRE-DE-BAS

### pop 1200

Lying just 1km to the west of Terre-de-Haut, Terre-de-Bas is the only other inhabited island in Les Saintes. A bit less craggy than Terre-de-Haut, Terre-de-Bas once had small sugar and coffee plantations and is populated largely by the descendants of African slaves. It's a quiet rural island, and tourism has yet to take root, but there is a regular ferry service between the islands, making it possible for visitors to poke around on a day excursion.

The main village, Petites-Anses, is on the west coast. It has hilly streets lined with trim houses, a small fishing harbor, and a quaint church with a graveyard of tombs decorated with conch shells and plastic flowers. Grande Anse, diagonally across the island on the east coast, is a small village with a little 17th-century church and a nice beach.

One-lane roads link the island's two villages; one of the roads cuts across the center of the island, passing between two peaks – Morne Abymes and Morne Paquette – and the other goes along the south coast. If you enjoy long country walks, it's possible to make a loop walk between the two villages (about 9km round-trip) by going out on one road and returning on the other. Otherwise, there's sometimes an inexpensive *jitney* (private minibus) that runs between the villages.

Petites-Anses has a good bakery and pastry shop, and both Petites-Anses and Grande Anse have a couple of reasonably priced local restaurants.

A ferry travels between Terre-de-Haut and Terre-de-Bas; see p578 for details.

# MARIE-GALANTE

### pop 16,300

Marie-Galante, 25km southeast of Guadeloupe proper, is the largest of Guadeloupe's outer islands. Compared with the archipelago's other islands, Marie-Galante is relatively flat, its dual limestone plateaus rising only 150m. It is roughly round in shape with a total land area of 158 sq km. Because of its shape, the island is often referred to as 'La Grande Galette,' which means 'the Big Crêpe.'

The island is rural in character; it's pretty much sugarcane, manioc fields and cows outside of Grand-Bourg, the surprisingly large main city. There are some lovely, uncrowded beaches and pleasant country scenery.

## Getting There & Away

### AIR

Air Caraïbes ( ☎ 82-47-00; www.aircaraibes.com) has three to four weekly flights to Marie-Galante from Pointe-à-Pitre (20 minutes) for €150, round-trip. The airport is midway between Grand-Bourg and Capesterre, 5km from either.

### BOAT

The interisland crossing to Marie-Galante can be a bit rough, so if you're not used to bouncy seas it's best to travel on a light stomach and sit in the middle of the boat. One saving grace is that the boats leaving from Pointe-à-Pitre are very big (and more stable) and quite comfortable. See p577 for details of ferry services.

## Getting Around

### BUS

During the day, except for Sunday, inexpensive minibuses make regular runs between the three villages.

### CAR & SCOOTER

There are car- and motorbike-rental places facing the ferry pier. Cars generally start at €25 per day and motorbikes at €15 to €20.

Be sure to inspect your vehicle closely as some of them, especially scooters, are haggard. The stiff competition has kept the quality and prices about equal, but **Auto Moto Location** ( ☎ 97-19-42; www.automoto-location.com) rents mountain bikes for €12 per day. **Hertz** ( ☎ 97-59-80; www.hertz.com; 3 Rue de La République) only rents out cars but is an international, Anglophone-friendly chain.

## MINIBUS

Minibus tour drivers are usually waiting for arriving ferry passengers at the ferry port. A four-hour guided tour that makes a nearly complete circle around the island costs between €12 and €15. Stops on the tour usually include a distillery, the Ste-Marie Hospital parking lot (best view on the island), a shop where people make manioc flour, and an abandoned slave plantation.

The buses will sometimes leave you on the beach in St-Louis for a few hours and pick you up in time to make the boat back to the mainland. Some of the tour guides don't speak much standard French, let alone English, so be sure to converse a bit to make sure they can explain everything clearly.

## GRAND-BOURG

Grand-Bourg is the commercial and administrative center of the island. The town was leveled by fire in 1901, and its architecture is a mix of early-20th-century buildings and more recent, drab concrete structures.

The ferry dock is at the center of town. The post office, customs office and town hall are all within a few blocks of the waterfront.

The **tourist office** ( ☎ 97-56-51; www.ot-marie galante.com; Rue du Fort) can provide you with information on local rental houses, *gîtes* and guesthouses. Its website has a comprehensive English-language section.

A pharmacy and a couple of banks with ATMs are on the square in front of the **Eglise Ste Marie**, which is worth a peek inside for its stained-glassed windows.

The **market** ( ☻ 7am-2pm), near the church, sells island trinkets and the usual assortment of flavored rums. There's a little snack shop, **Tizong La** (mains €6-11), open whenever the market is.

**Habitation Murat**, about 2km from Grand-Bourg on the north side of the road to Capesterre, is a partially restored 18th-century sugar estate built stone by stone by more than 300 slaves. Check out the walled garden in the back corner of the sprawling estate – there's a gate but it's hard to find.

Offering eight bungalows and an apartment, the gardened group of Creole-style homes at **Village de Canada** ( ☎ 97-86-11; www.village decanada.com; Section Canada, 97112 Grand Bourg; r from €70) is halfway between Grand-Bourg and St Louis. There are a few signs on the main road between the two cities that point the way.

Each of the three apartments at **L'Oasis** ( ☎ 97-59-55; oasis.mg@wanadoo.fr; Rue Sony Rupaire; r €70-90) has something special to recommend it – a small tropical garden, a Jacuzzi or a terrace. It's located in the city center, 1km from the beach; to find this friendly and clean place, head toward the Grand-Savane area and watch out for the signs.

**L'Ornata** ( ☎ 97-54-16; Place Félix Éboué; snacks from €5; ☻ breakfast, lunch & dinner) is a good place near the ferry port to kill some time. It's in a nice old Creole house and most of the tables are on the front porch.

Owned by a former soccer player, the pork chops at **Footy** ( ☎ 97-99-19; 97112 Grand Bourg; mains from €8; ☻ lunch & dinner) – notice all the giant black pigs on the island – are divine. It has live music in the club area in the back most Friday and Saturday nights. Make a right from the ferry dock on the main pier and head down the main road for a few minutes.

## ST-LOUIS

This fishing village is the island's main anchorage for yachters as well as a secondary port for ferries from Guadeloupe. There's a little market at the end of the dock, and a couple of restaurants and the post office are just east of that.

Although there are beaches along the outskirts of St-Louis, some of the island's most beautiful strands lie a few kilometers to the north. There's a great photo opportunity at the north tip of the island at Gueule Grande Grouffre, a dramatic stone maw that lets out into electric-blue waters.

**Village de Ménard** ( ☎ 97-09-45; www.villagede menard.com; Section Vieux Fort; bungalows from €70; ☒ ☒ ) is a small complex of 11 comfy bungalows on a cliff overlooking the bay. It's 2km from the beach in a quiet country setting. The poolside restaurant Océanite will prepare picnic baskets for day-trippers.

Just south of town, at the lovely beach Folle Anse, the three-star **La Hotel Cohoba** ( ☎ 97-50-50; www.deshotelsetdesiles.com; Folle Anse Cocoyer; r from €194; ☒ ☒ ) has 100 Creole-style bungalows in landscaped gardens. It's a family-friendly place that includes activities like beach volleyball and has a few interesting extras, like ox-cart rides and sailing, for a fee. On-site restaurant.

A beachside place with instruments inside for the live jazz nights and tables in the back that look out on the water, **Chez**

GUADELOUPE

---

**CANE JUICE**

Rum distilleries are among the island's main sights. The **Distillerie Poisson** ( ☎ 97-03-79; Habitation Edouard, Rameau, Grand-Bourg; tastings free; ☽ 7am-1pm Mon-Sat), midway between St-Louis and Grand-Bourg, bottles the island's best-known rum under the Père Labat label. **Distillerie Bielle** ( ☎ 97-93-62; Section Bielle, Grand-Bourg; tastings free), between Grand-Bourg and Capesterre, offers tours of its age-old distillery operation. Worth a visit for its historic setting, as well as its rum, is **Domaine de Bellevue** ( ☎ 97-26-50; Section Bellevue, Capesterre; tastings free; ☽ 9:30am-1pm).

All of the distilleries have gift shops.

---

**Henri** ( ☎ 97-04-57; www.chezhenri.net; mains from €11; ☽ lunch & dinner Mon-Sat) is the archetypal cool little Caribbean bar.

## CAPESTERRE

Capesterre, on the southeast coast, is a seaside town with a little fish market on the main road near **Feuillère beach**, one of the nicest strands on an island full of them. From the village you can explore sea cliffs and hiking trails to the north.

Another attractive beach, **Petite Anse**, is about 1km to the southwest.

**Le Soleil Levant** ( ☎ 97-31-55; www.im-caraibes.com/soleil-levant; d from €45; ☒ ☒ ) actually has three locations; the main building is perched above the center of Capesterre and the two smaller buildings are in town. The main structure has a nice big sundeck with great sea view, and a downstairs bar-restaurant where locals gather. **Résidence Marine** (r from €130), one of the in-town buildings, dedicates a floor to each of its three large apartments.

Set right on the sand on Petite Anse, the bungalows at **Le Touloulou** ( ☎ 97-32-63; www.letouloulou.com; r from €50 ☒ ☒ ) – some with and some without kitchenettes – all have spacious terraces for watching the waves roll in. It has an on-site **restaurant** (mains €16-28; ☽ lunch & dinner Tue-Sat) and a nightclub that opens up most weekend nights.

# LA DÉSIRADE

**pop 1700**

About 10km off Grande-Terre, La Désirade is the archipelago's least-developed and least-visited island. Even the nicest beaches are nearly deserted; for the ultimate do-nothing vacation it's a place that's hard to beat.

Looking somewhat like an overturned boat when viewed from Guadeloupe, La Désirade is only 11km long and 2km wide,

with a central plateau that rises 273m at its highest point, Grand Montagne.

The uninhabited north side of the island has a rocky coastline with rough open seas, while the south side has sandy beaches and reef-protected waters. There are no dive shops on the island or places to rent snorkeling equipment, so those who want to get below the surface of La Désirade should bring their own gear.

La Désirade's harbor and airport are on the southwest side of the island in **Beauséjour**, the main village. The island's town hall, post office and library are also in Beauséjour. There are smaller settlements at **Le Souffleur** and **Baie Mahault**.

In 1725 Guadeloupe established a leper colony on La Désirade, and for more than two centuries victims of the disease were forced to make a one-way trip to the island. The **leprosarium**, which was run by the Catholic Sisters of Charity, closed in the mid-1950s. Its remains, a chapel and a cemetery are just to the east of Baie Mahault.

La Désirade's main road runs along the southern coast and ends at an art deco–style **weather station** on the eastern tip of the island. Nearby is a **lighthouse**. The trip is worthwhile for the scenery, if nothing else. Gangs of goats that apparently don't see many cars wander the windswept fields here – it's an area of desolate beauty that feels a lot like Brittany in northern France.

## SLEEPING & EATING

**Oasis Hotel** ( ☎ 20-01-00; www.oasisladesirade.com; s/d €40/48, q studio €60; ☒ ) About 250m from the beach, this pleasant hotel is set in a white two-level Creole-style building. Nearby it has a brightly colored restaurant, Lagranlag (mains €8 to €15; open lunch and dinner Tuesday to Sunday), which specializes in gratins and seafood stews. Meal plans are available for an additional €12 to €22 per day.

GUADELOUPE

**ourpick Oualiri Beach Hotel** ( ☎ 20-20-08; www
.rendezvouskarukera.com; Beausejour 97127; s/d €74/80;
🅿 🖳 ) It has six hotel rooms and two bungalows set on a private beach. You'll find an
on-site restaurant (mains €14 to €20; open
breakfast, lunch and dinner) and a small playground in plain sight so the kiddies can wear
themselves out. There's a free 4pm snack time
for the kids and an outdoor shower for the
wee ones. It has music nights every few weeks,
and a brunch party every Sunday. Théodore
Compper, the owner, tells us he designed his
hotel to give adults a real vacation without
leaving the children at home.

**La Payotte** ( ☎ 20-01-29; mains from €8; ☺ breakfast,
lunch & dinner) Right on Grande Anse, it serves
a tasty variety of daytime dishes and has a
limited breakfast menu – but the coffee is
strong and the bread is fresh from the oven.
A two-minute walk away it has six rooms for
rent (double/quad €50/90) in a nice old house
shrouded by bougainvilleas.

**La Roulotte** ( ☎ 20-02-33; Plage du Souffler; mains from
€10; ☺ breakfast, lunch & dinner Mon-Sat) With plastic
tables in the sand, the food is good but not
great. What is great is the sign that asks diners
to order before swimming at the beach, and
the view of fishing boats bobbing with the
tiny waves. It has a patrons-only bathroom
near the outdoor wood stove that can come
in handy. It's 2.5km east of Beauséjour on
the main road.

## GETTING THERE & AWAY
There are ferries to St-François and Ste-Anne,
both on Grande-Terre; see p578 for details.

## GETTING AROUND
Scooter rentals are available at the ferry dock
for €10 to €20 a day. The coastal road is a lot
hillier than it appears from the boat, making
bicycling a sweaty workout. Most locals and
visitors prefer the scooters. Just be sure to
double-check your scooter – some of them
barely roll straight.

# DIRECTORY

## ACCOMMODATIONS
By Caribbean standards, nightly rates are
moderate, with budget-end hotels averaging
about €45, midrange €75 and upper-end about
€180. The prices listed are for high season
(December to May), when the majority of

people visit the island; prices can be up to 40%
lower during August and September, though
some hotels close in September.

Some of the best-value places to stay are
not hotels but comfortable family-run facilities known as *gîtes*. **Gîtes de France Guadeloupe**
( ☎ 82-09-30; www.gitesdefrance-guadeloupe.com; 97171
Pointe-à-Pitre) is an association of homeowners
who rent out private rooms and apartments.
This is how many French tourists can afford
to spend their long vacations here. There's
also **Gîtes de France** ( ☎ 73-74-74, in Paris 01-49-70-
75-75; www.gites-de-france.fr; 97209 Fort-de-France), with
a convenient website that has an English
option. Disabled travelers can search for
accessible accommodation.

There are nearly 8000 hotel rooms in
Guadeloupe, most in small to mid-size hotels. The bulk of the accommodations are
along the south coast of Grande-Terre, between Pointe-à-Pitre and St-François. Rooms
on the outlying islands of Les Saintes, Marie-
Galante and La Désirade are limited. By
Caribbean standards, rates are reasonable
and, as in France, taxes and service charges
are included in the quoted rate; many hotels
also include breakfast.

## ACTIVITIES
### Beaches & Swimming
White-sand beaches fringe Gosier, Ste-Anne
and St-François on Grande-Terre. At the
north side of the peninsula leading to Pointe
des Châteaux lie two remote beaches: Anse à
la Gourde, a gorgeous sweep of white coral
sands, and Anse Tarare, the adjacent nudist beach. While most of Grande-Terre's east
coast has rough surf, there is a swimmable
beach at Le Moule and a little protected cove
at Porte d'Enfer. On the west side of Grande-
Terre, Port-Louis is the most popular swimming spot, especially on weekends.

The beaches along Basse-Terre's rugged
northwest coast are wilder and less crowded,
with long, empty stretches of golden sands and
views of Montserrat smoldering in the distance. There are also a handful of black-sand
beaches along Basse-Terre's southern shore.

### Diving & Snorkeling
Guadeloupe's top diving site is the Réserve
Cousteau, at Pigeon Island off the west coast
of Basse-Terre. Spearfishing has long been
banned in this underwater reserve, and consequently the waters surrounding Pigeon Island,

**GUADELOUPE**

only 1km offshore, are teeming with colorful tropical fish, sponges, sea fans and coral.

There are numerous dive shops in Guadeloupe, especially in the Réserve Cousteau area (p565); the shops here drop snorkelers off in the very scenic shallower waters. Single-dive rates average €40, with discounts on multiple-dive packages.

## Golf

The only golf course on Guadeloupe is in St-François (see p558).

## Hiking

Guadeloupe has wonderful trails that take in waterfalls, primordial rainforest and botanical gardens. A number of them are simple 10- to 30-minute walks that can be enjoyed as part of a tour around the island.

Serious hikers will find many longer, more rigorous trails in the national park on Basse-Terre. The most popular are those leading to the volcanic summit of La Soufrière, the island's highest point, and to the base of Chutes du Carbet, the Eastern Caribbean's highest waterfalls. Both make for scenic half-day treks. Keep in mind that this is serious rainforest hiking, so be prepared for wet conditions and wear good hiking shoes.

The website of the **Guadeloupe Parc National** (www.guadeloupe-parcnational.com) has maps and hiking information.

## Surfing

Le Moule, Port-Louis and Anse Bertrand commonly have good surfing conditions from around October to May. In summer, Ste-Anne and St-François can have good wave action.

---

### PRACTICALITIES

- **Newspapers & Magazines** France-Antilles is the local daily newspaper.

- **Radio & TV** Tune into Radio France Outre-Mer (RFO) for public radio and TV.

- **Video systems** Use the Secam video system.

- **Electricity** The current used is 220V, 50 cycles; plugs use two circular prongs. Plug adapters are a good idea.

- **Weights & Measures** Guadeloupe uses the metric system and the 24-hour clock.

---

## Windsurfing

Windsurfing is quite popular on Guadeloupe. Much of the activity is near the resorts on the south side of Grande-Terre and on Terre-de-Haut. Windsurfing gear can be rented from beach huts for about €20 an hour.

**Union des Centres Sportifs de Plein Air** (UCPA; ☎ 88-64-80; www.ucpa.com; 97118 St-François) has week-long windsurfing/hotel packages in both St-François and Terre-de-Haut.

## BUSINESS HOURS

Most businesses are open Monday to Friday, 8am to noon, close for lunch, and then reopen from 2pm to 5pm. Banks follow a similar pattern, but usually don't reopen after lunch one day per week.

Unless otherwise noted, meal hours used in this chapter are as follows: breakfast 7am to 9am, lunch noon to 2pm, dinner 7pm to 9pm.

## CHILDREN

Because of all the French families that come here, there are a number of kid-friendly hotels and activities. Many hotels have activities just for kids and a special children's menu. Medical care and sanitation is of the same high quality as in mainland France.

## DANGERS & ANNOYANCES

Bilharzia (schistosomiasis) is found throughout Grande-Terre and in much of Basse-Terre, including Grand Étang lake. The main method of prevention is to avoid swimming or wading in fresh water.

There have been recent outbreaks of dengue fever, aka breakbone fever because of the joint and muscle pain it inflicts. It's potentially fatal. Health professionals advise using insect repellent containing DEET or Picaridin on exposed skin. Dengue outbreaks tend to occur wherever there's standing water – more frequent in cities than in the countryside.

Occasional islandwide strikes can grind tourism services to a screeching halt.

For the lowdown on the shady side of Pointe-à-Pitre, see p552.

## EMBASSIES & CONSULATES

Guadeloupe is represented in your home country by the embassy or consulate of France. There are no consulates or embassies on the island – you'll need to head to Dominica (p599) or Martinique (p624) – although there are a number of consular agents who may be able to help. These agents are listed under Practical Information on the website of the **Guadeloupe Islands Tourism Board** (www.lesilesdeguadeloupe.com).

## FESTIVALS & EVENTS

**Carnival** Celebrations are held during the traditional week-long Mardi Gras period that ends on Ash Wednesday. They feature costume parades, dancing, music and other festivities.

**Tour Cycliste de la Guadeloupe** A 10-day international cycling race held in early August.

**La Route du Rhum** A solo sailing competition that starts in northern France and ends in Pointe-à-Pitre. It takes place every four years in November; 2010 and 2014 are the next two.

## GAY & LESBIAN TRAVELERS

Guadeloupe usually earns OK marks from gay travel organizations. Homosexuality is legally protected under French law, but islander attitudes tend to be less tolerant. Gay couples usually do not publicly express affection or advertise their sexual orientation. Hoteliers don't seem to care who shares a bed.

## HOLIDAYS

Public holidays in Guadeloupe:

**New Year's Day** January 1
**Easter Sunday** Late March/early April
**Easter Monday** Late March/early April
**Labor Day** May 1
**Victory Day** May 8
**Ascension Thursday** 40th day after Easter
**Pentecost Monday** Eighth Monday after Easter
**Slavery Abolition Day** May 27
**Bastille Day** July 14
**Schoelcher Day** July 21
**Assumption Day** August 15
**All Saints Day** November 1
**Armistice Day** November 11
**Christmas Day** December 25

## INTERNET ACCESS

Most towns and villages have at least one internet café. In many places, the public library has one or two computers for free web access. Wi-fi at hotels is becoming more common.

## INTERNET RESOURCES

**Guadeloupe Radio France** (http://guadeloupe.rfo.fr in French) Video and radio reports on island news and culture.
**Guadeloupe Islands Tourism Board** (www.lesiles deguadeloupe.com) Has a good English-language section with a nice overview of everything on tap here.

## LANGUAGE

In the tourist towns near the capital (Gosier, Ste-Anne) and anyplace there's a large sailing community (Deshaies, St-François) a visitor can get by with just some basic French expressions. For exploration further afield a good command of basic French is very helpful. A phrase book is a great idea.

## MAPS

The best map of Guadeloupe is the Guadeloupe map published by the Institut Géographique National (IGN), sold at bookstores around the island for €9.70. There are free town maps in many of the highly visited destinations.

## MEDICAL SERVICES

Medical care is equivalent to mainland France: very good. The biggest hospital is the Centre Hospitalier in Pointe-à-Pitre, though there are smaller hospitals in almost every region. There are plenty of pharmacies everywhere; look for the green cross, often flashing in neon.

## MONEY

The euro is the island currency. Hotels, larger restaurants and car-rental agencies accept Visa, American Express and MasterCard.

Avoid changing money at hotel lobbies, where the rates are worse than at exchange offices or banks. Currency exchange offices, called *bureaux de change,* are scattered around Pointe-à-Pitre, and ATMs (called ABMs, *distributeurs de billets* or *distributeurs automatiques*) will usually give good rates.

## POST

There are post offices in all major towns. You can also buy postage stamps at some *tabacs* (tobacco shops), hotels and souvenir shops.

Mailing addresses given in this chapter should be followed by 'Guadeloupe, French West Indies.'

## TELEPHONE

The French West Indies country code is ☎ 590, but you just dial the six-digit local number in the islands. The area code for Guadeloupe is also ☎ 590, so to call from abroad dial your country's international access code plus ☎ 590-590 + the local six-digit number. To call from within the French phone system, omit the country code and add a '0': ☎ 0590 + the local number. We have

---

**EMERGENCY NUMBERS**

- Ambulance ☎ 18
- Fire ☎ 18
- Police ☎ 17

---

included only the six-digit local number for the Guadeloupe listings in this chapter. To dial a cell phone, call ☎ 0690 + the number.

### Cell Phones

Before leaving home, check with your home cell-phone service provider to see if they have a roaming agreement with one of the GSM networks in Guadeloupe – if it does, ask how much calls will cost; one network may be cheaper than others.

SIM cards (starting at €25) are available for unlocked cell phones and usually include some talk time before recharging. Digicel and Orange are the two main SIM card vendors.

### Phone Cards

Public phones in Guadeloupe accept French *télécartes* (phone cards) and, less often, coins. The cards cost €5, €10 or €15, depending on the calling time, and are sold at post offices and at shops marked *télécartes en vente ici*. For directory assistance, dial ☎ 12.

The cards that have users dial a toll-free number to place their calls are usually the best deal; they have to be activated on private phones but will then work fine on public phones.

## TOURIST INFORMATION

Many towns have at least a small tourism office where the staff is proficient in English. Pamphlets, mainly in French but with enough pictures and maps to get the gist, are available at airports and many hotels. Also check out the **Guadeloupe Islands Tourism Board** (www.lesilesdeguadeloupe.com).

## TRAVELERS WITH DISABILITIES

Stairs are a common difficulty for disabled travelers and many sidewalks have high curbs. Some hotels, however, have disabled-accessible rooms.

## VISAS

Citizens of the US, UK, Canada, Australia and New Zealand can stay for up to 90 days without a visa by showing a valid passport (US citizens see the boxed text, p830). EU citizens need an official identity card, passport or valid French *carte de séjour* (visitor card). Citizens of most other countries need a valid passport and a visa from a French consulate valid for admission to the Overseas French Department of Guadeloupe.

# TRANSPORTATION

## GETTING THERE & AWAY
### Entering Guadeloupe

You'll be required to fill out a simple immigration slip on arrival, outlining details of your stay and the purpose of your visit. All visitors officially require a return or onward ticket.

### Air

**Guadeloupe Le Raizet Airport** (PTP; Pole Caraïbes; ☎ 21-14-72) is north of Pointe-à-Pitre, 6km from the city center on N5. The terminal has a tourist information booth, car-rental booths, a couple of restaurants, ATMs and money-change bureaus. Immigration officers here are relatively fast and professional.

**Air Antilles Express** ( ☎ 21-14-47; www.airantilles.com) St-Barthélemy, St-Martin/Sint Maarten

**Air Canada** ( ☎ 21-12-77; www.aircanada.com) Montreal

**Air Caraïbes** ( ☎ 82-47-00; www.aircaraibes.com) Cayenne, Fort-de-France, Panama City, Paris, Santo Domingo, St-Barthélemy, St-Martin/Sint Maarten

**Air France** ( ☎ 82-61-61; www.airfrance.com) Cayenne, Fort-de-France, Miami, Paris

**American Airlines** (www.aa.com) San Juan

**Corsairfly** ( ☎ 21-12-11; www.corsairfly.com) Brest, Lyon, Nantes, Paris

**LIAT** ( ☎ 82-13-93; www.liat.com) Antigua

### Sea

Popular with yachties and sailors, there is mooring in Deshaies and St-François, and at the marina near Pointe-à-Pitre. Cruise ships regularly call on the island. There are a number of ferries to the outlying islands of Guadeloupe and other Caribbean destinations.

#### CRUISE SHIP

Cruise ships dock right in the city at Centre St-John Perse, Pointe-à-Pitre's old port complex, and at the spiffy new cruise ship terminal.

For more information on cruise lines servicing the region, see p830.

## FERRY

There are two companies providing regular ferry service between Guadeloupe, Martinique, Dominica and St Lucia. For information on services between Guadeloupe and its outlying islands, see the relevant sections in this chapter. All the ferries listed leave from the Gare Maritime de Bergevin in Pointe-à-Pitre.

**L'Express des Îles** ( ☎ harbor office 91-69-68, admin office 83-72-27; www.express-des-iles.com) operates large, modern catamarans between Guadeloupe, Martinique and Dominica. The boats have air-conditioned cabins with TV entertainment and a snack bar.

There are three weekly crossings to Fort-de-France, Martinique, from Pointe-à-Pitre (one way/round-trip €67/100). Ferries leave on Sunday, Wednesday and Friday, and the journey takes three hours.

Boats leave Pointe-à-Pitre for Roseau in Dominica, and Castries, St Lucia, on Friday, Wednesday and Sunday (one way/round-trip €67/100). It's nearly a seven-hour journey, usually with stops in Martinique and Dominica on the way.

Departure days and times for these services change frequently and often bear no relation to the printed schedule. The only way to be sure is to call L'Express des Îles or check with a local travel agent.

There are discounts of 50% for children aged two to 11, and 10% for passengers aged under 26, or aged 60 and older.

**Brudey Frères** ( ☎ 90-04-48; www.brudey-freres.fr) has a 350-passenger catamaran with a daily service between Pointe-à-Pitre and Fort-de-France (one way/round-trip €57/87). In season, there's an extra boat on Monday, Wednesday, Friday and Saturday.

It also has a regular service (every day in high season) between Guadeloupe and Dominica for €55/80 one way/round-trip and a once- or twice-a-week service to St Lucia (one way/round-trip €80/115).

Brudey offers discounts for youths and elders. Schedules change, so check current timetables.

### YACHT

Guadeloupe has three marinas:

**Marina de Bas du Fort** ( ☎ 90-84-85; www.caribbean-marinas.com/basdufort), between Pointe-à-Pitre and Gosier, has 700 berths, 55 of which are available for visiting boats.

**Marina de St-François** ( ☎ 88-47-28), in the center of St-François, has about 250 moorings, as well as fuel, water, ice and electricity.

**Marina de Rivière-Sens** ( ☎ 81-77-61), on the southern outskirts of the town of Basse-Terre, has 220 moorings, fuel, water and ice.

Customs and immigration offices are located in Pointe-à-Pitre, Basse-Terre and Deshaies.

The yacht charter companies **Antilles Sail** ( ☎ 90-16-81; www.antilles-sail.com) and **Dream Yacht Charter** ( ☎ 74-81-68; www.dreamyachtcharter.com) are based at Marina de Bas du Fort.

## GETTING AROUND

For travelers visiting more than one city, a car rental is almost a necessity. The main tourist spots on the southern coast of Grande-Terre are navigable without a car, but for the most part a vehicle comes in handy. Many hotels can arrange airport pickup and car rental.

### Air

**Air Caraïbes** ( ☎ 82-47-00; www.aircaraibes.com) has daily flights between Pointe-à-Pitre and Marie-Galante and Terre-de-Haut. See those island sections for details.

### Bicycle

Bicycles are an adventurous, somewhat strenuous way to see Terre-de-Haut and Marie-Galante. Rentals start at €10 per day.

### Boat

Ferries run between Grande-Terre and Terre-de-Haut, Marie-Galante and La Désirade. There are also ferries from Trois-Rivières on Basse-Terre to Terre-de-Haut.

#### POINTE-À-PITRE TO TERRE-DE-HAUT

A one-way trip takes about 50 minutes.

**Brudey Frères** ( ☎ 90-04-48; www.brudey-freres.fr) leaves Pointe-à-Pitre every day at 7:50am for Terre-de-Haut, departing Terre-de-Haut at 3:45pm (one way/round-trip €24/40).

**L'Express des Îles** ( ☎ 91-69-58; www.express-des-iles.com) leaves Pointe-à-Pitre for Terre-de-Haut at 8am Monday to Thursday, departing from Terre-de-Haut at 4:30pm (one way/round-trip €24/39).

#### POINTE-À-PITRE TO MARIE-GALANTE

A one-way trip takes about 40 minutes.

GUADELOUPE

**Brudey Frères** ( ☎ 90-04-48; www.brudey-freres .fr) leaves Pointe-à-Pitre for Marie-Galante every day of the week two to three times per day starting at 7:45am (one way/round-trip €24/39).

**L'Express des Îles** ( ☎ 91-69-58; www.express-des-iles .com) goes to Marie-Galante every day, three times per day, starting at 8:15am (one way/round-trip €24/40). On Sundays there's a 6:15pm departure from Grand Bourg – a nice way to spend a long day at the beach.

### ST-FRANÇOIS TO TERRE-DE-HAUT

From St-François, **Iguana** ( ☎ 22-26-31) ferries to Terre-de-Haut leave on Monday and Thursday at 7:30am and depart Terre-de-Haut at 3:30pm (one way/round-trip €20/30). In good weather, a one-way trip takes an hour and 10 minutes.

### ST-FRANÇOIS TO MARIE-GALANTE

The voyage takes 35 minutes each way.

**Colibri** ( ☎ 35-79-47; Port de Pêche) leaves St-François for Marie-Galante every day of the week two to three times per day starting at 7:45am (one way/round-trip €24/39).

From St-François, **Iguana** ( ☎ 22-26-31) has a ferry to St-Louis every day (in high season) starting at 7:30am and returning at 3:30pm (one way/round-trip €22/30).

### ST-FRANÇOIS TO LA DÉSIRADE

A one-way voyage takes 25 minutes.

**Colibri** ( ☎ 35-79-47; Port de Pêche) boats leave from St-François every day, twice per day, starting at 8am with the return trip at 3:30pm (one way/round-trip €16/22).

**Iguana** ( ☎ 22-26-31) has a ferry to La Désirade every day at 4:45pm with an additional 8am service on weekends (one way/round-trip €16/22).

### STE-ANNE TO TERRE-DE-HAUT

**Iguana** ( ☎ 22-26-31) leaves from Ste-Anne for Les Saintes every day at 7:30am, returning at 3:30pm (one way/round-trip €24/35). The trip takes about an hour.

### STE-ANNE TO MARIE-GALANTE

In high season **Iguana** ( ☎ 22-26-31) usually has one or two midweek round-trips from Ste-Anne (one way/round-trip €23/38). Check the handwritten sign in front of the ticket kiosk at the western end of the Village Artisanal in Ste-Anne for the week's schedule. The one-way crossing takes 30 minutes.

### STE-ANNE TO LA DÉSIRADE

In high season, **Iguana** ( ☎ 22-26-31) usually has weekend service from Ste-Anne (one way/round-trip €23/38). Check the handwritten sign in front of the ticket kiosk at the western end of the Village Artisanal in Ste-Anne for the week's schedule. The trip takes about 35 minutes one way.

### TERRE-DE-HAUT TO TERRE-DE-BAS

A Brudey Frères boat makes the 10-minute trip between Terre-de-Haut and Terre-de-Bas (€6 round-trip) four to six times daily, depending on the season, between 8am and 4pm.

### TROIS-RIVIÈRES TO TERRE-DE-HAUT

A one-way journey only takes 20 minutes.

**Brudey Frères** ( ☎ 90-04-48; www.brudey-freres .fr) leaves Trois-Rivières for Terre-de-Haut every day, twice per day, at 8:45am, departing Terre-de-Haut at 4:30pm (one way/round-trip €16/22).

**CTM Deher** ( ☎ 92-06-39; www.ctmdeher.com; Bord de Mer 97114, Trois-Rivières) heads to Terre-de-Haut from Trois-Rivières every day, twice per day, at 9am, departing at 4:30pm (one way/round-trip €14/21).

## Bus

Guadeloupe has a good public bus system that operates from about 5:30am to 6:30pm, with fairly frequent service on main routes. On Saturday afternoon service is much lighter, and there are almost no buses on Sunday.

Many bus routes start and end in Pointe-à-Pitre; see p551 for details.

Destinations are written on the buses. Bus stops have blue signs picturing a bus; in less developed areas you can wave buses down along their routes.

## Car

### DRIVER'S LICENSE

A driver's license from your home country is necessary to drive here.

### RENTAL

Several car-rental companies have offices at the airport and in major resort areas. Some agents will let you rent a car near your hotel and drop it off free of charge at the airport, which can save a hefty taxi fare.

Companies generally drop their rates the longer you keep the car, with the weekly rate working out to be about 15% cheaper, overall, than the daily rate. Nearly all companies use an unlimited-kilometers rate.

Rates for small cars are advertised from around €35 per day, although the rates offered on a walk-in basis and availability of cars can vary greatly with the season. It's a good idea to reserve ahead from December to May.

Car-rental companies:

**Avis** ( ☎ 21-13-49; www.avis.com)
**Budget** ( ☎ 21-13-49; www.budget.com)
**Europcar** ( ☎ 21-13-52; www.europcar.com)
**Hertz** ( ☎ 84-20-23; www.hertz.com)

### ROAD CONDITIONS

Roads are excellent by Caribbean standards and almost invariably hard-surfaced, although secondary and mountain roads are often narrow.

Around Pointe-à-Pitre there are multilane highways, with cars zipping along at 110km/h. Outside the Pointe-à-Pitre area, most highways have a single lane in each direction and an 80km/h speed limit.

### ROAD RULES

In Guadeloupe, drive on the right. Traffic regulations and road signs are of European standards. Exits and intersections are clearly marked, and speed limits are posted.

## Hitchhiking

Hitchhiking is fairly common on Guadeloupe, particularly when the bus drivers decide to go on strike. The proper stance is to hold out an open palm at a slightly downward angle. All the usual safety precautions apply.

## Taxi

Taxis are plentiful but expensive. There are taxi stands at the airport in Pointe-à-Pitre.

Fares are 40% higher from 9pm to 7am nightly, as well as all day on Sunday and holidays. You can call for a taxi by dialing ☎ 82-00-00 or ☎ 83-99-99 in the Pointe-à-Pitre area.

# Dominica

Whether you're into trekking high into the mountaintops or exploring the watery world below, Dominica is the place to go for those who prefer hiking boots over high heels and are content with a nightlife where the only music is the murmur of the jungle.

Dominica has surprisingly long drives for such a small island, so it's better to pick a spot or two and explore instead of bouncing around. If you can do it in the mountains (hiking, bird-watching, searching for hidden pools and waterfalls) or the water (diving, snorkeling, kayaking), you can do it in Dominica.

There are a few sandy beaches, but most require a little gumption to find and there are usually only a few lodging choices nearby, at most. There are no direct international flights and the island-hopping it takes to get here has kept the package tours at bay.

The locals are so friendly that it's almost fun to get lost just to have an excuse to approach people on their front porches. Whereas some of the bigger Caribbean cities are decidedly scary, in the capital city of Roseau the locals often stop visitors just to wish them a good visit.

Rasta culture is strong, and those offended by the sight of Rastafarians taking their sacrament might have to cover their eyes a time or two. Dominica is also the home to about 2200 Caribs, the only pre-Columbian population remaining in the eastern Caribbean.

## FAST FACTS

- **Area** 290 sq miles
- **Capital** Roseau
- **Country code** ☎ 767
- **Departure tax** EC$55 (US$20) for over 12 years
- **Famous for** Nature
- **Language** English, French patois
- **Money** Eastern Caribbean dollar (EC$);
  EC$1 = US$0.38 = €0.24 = UK£0.19
- **Official name** Commonwealth of Dominica
- **People** Dominicans
- **Phrase** irie (hello/goodbye/cool/good);
  check (understand)
- **Population** 72,400
- **Visa** Required for residents of former Eastern Bloc countries and citizens of China, India and Nigeria; see p600

DOMINICA

# HIGHLIGHTS

- **Canyoning** (p594) Don't just look at waterfalls, feel them wash over you in a canyon where no other visitors go
- **Morne Trois Pitons National Park** (p595) Inhale breathtaking mountain and atmospheric rainforest scenery in this Unesco World Heritage site
- **Portsmouth** (p590) Explore the Indian River or go on a sail-powered sunset wine and cheese cruise
- **Diving** (p598) Take the plunge and play in the bubbles of Champagne Beach, the star underwater attraction
- **Hiking** (p598) Step out on Dominica, from a leisurely walk to Emerald Pool to an unforgettable trek to Boiling Lake
- **Roseau** (p584) Wander around for shopping and eating deals and feel the friendliness of the locals warm up the modest capital city

# ITINERARIES

- **R&R** Consider chilling out for a few days at one of the luxurious properties in the Trafalgar Falls or Grand Bay areas to get on Caribbean time. After all, one of Dominica's hottest commodities is peace and quiet.
- **Turf and Surf Sampler Plate** Spend the first day in Roseau wandering between the markets and checking out the sights and arrange a tour to Boiling Lake for the next day. Hook up an afternoon snorkel or dive trip to Champagne Reef the next day, or just take it easy and enjoy the fresh fish in the fishing village of Scotts Head.

# CLIMATE & WHEN TO GO

A year-round tropical climate tempered by northeastern trade winds makes Dominica a good Caribbean destination for those who prefer a more moderate climate. Temperatures average between 75°F (24°C) and 86°F (30°C) year-round, with cooler temperatures in the mountains. There are short bursts of rainfall all year long. Most visitors come to Dominica between February and June, the island's driest months, when humidity is at a manageable average of 65%. April is the driest month with about 10 days of rainfall in Roseau, as opposed to the wettest month, August, when rainfall more than doubles. The rainy season lasts from July to late October, almost coinciding with the Caribbean's hurricane season (peaks in August and September). It can get cool in the mountains and a sweater is handy.

# HISTORY

Dominica was the last of the Caribbean islands to be colonized by Europeans due chiefly to the fierce resistance of the native Caribs. The Caribs, who settled here in the 14th century, called the island Waitikubuli, which means 'Tall is her Body.' Christopher Columbus, with less poetic flair, named the island after the day of the week on which he spotted it – a Sunday ('Doménica' in Italian) – on November 3, 1493.

Daunted by fierce resistance from the Caribs and discouraged by the absence of gold, the Spanish took little interest in Dominica. France laid claim to the island in 1635 and wrestled with the British over it through the 18th century.

In 1805 the French burned much of Roseau to the ground and since then the island remained firmly in the possession of the British, who established sugar plantations on Dominica's more accessible slopes.

In 1967 Dominica gained autonomy in internal affairs as a West Indies Associated State, and on November 3, 1978 (the 485th anniversary of Columbus' 'discovery'), Dominica became an independent republic within the Commonwealth.

The initial year of independence was a turbulent one. In June 1979 the island's first prime minister, Patrick John, was forced to resign after a series of corrupt schemes surfaced, including one clandestine land deal to transfer 15% of the island to US developers. In August 1979 Hurricane David, packing winds of 150mph, struck the island with devastating force. Forty-two people were killed and 75% of the islanders' homes were destroyed or severely damaged. To get a feeling of the hurricane's force, see the school bus at the Botanical Gardens in Roseau (p585).

In July 1980 Dame Eugenia Charles was elected prime minister, the first woman in the Caribbean to hold the office. Within a year of her inauguration she survived two unsuccessful coups and in October 1983, as chairperson of the Organization of East Caribbean States, endorsed the US invasion of Grenada.

**DOMINICA**

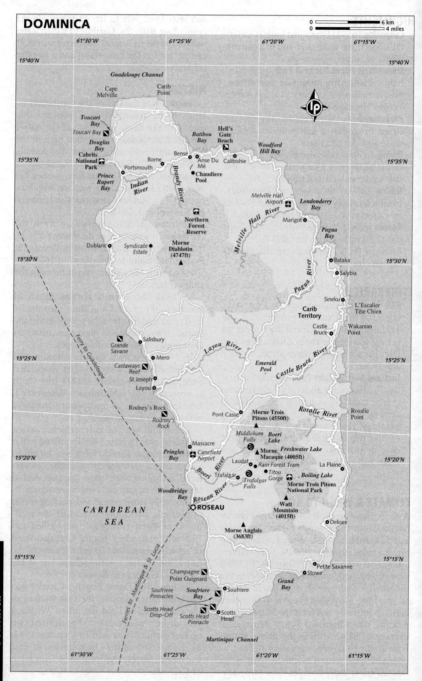

# DOMINICA

0 ——— 6 km
0 ——— 4 miles

Guadeloupe Channel

Cape Melville

Carib Point

Toucari Bay
Toucari Bay

Douglas Bay
Cabrits National Park

Portsmouth

Prince Rupert Bay

Indian River

Borne

Batibou Bay

Bense

Anse Du Mé

Chaudiere Pool

Hell's Gate Beach

Calibishie

Woodford Hill Bay

Melville Hall Airport

Londonderry Bay

Marigot

Pagua Bay

Northern Forest Reserve

Dublanc

Syndicate Estate

Morne Diablotin (4747ft)

Melville Hall River

Pagua River

Bataka

Salybia

Sineku

L'Escalier Tête Chien

Carib Territory

Castle Bruce

Wakaman Point

Grande Savane

Salisbury

Layou River

Mero

Castaways Reef

St Joseph

Layou

Rodney's Rock

Rodney's Rock

Pont Casse

Massacre

Pringles Bay

Canefield Airport

Woodbridge Bay

Roseau River

ROSEAU

CARIBBEAN SEA

Emerald Pool

Castle Bruce River

Morne Trois Pitons (4550ft)

Middleham Falls

Boeri Lake

Morne Macaque (4005ft)

Laudat

Rain Forest Tram

Trafalgar

Titou Gorge

Trafalgar Falls

Boeri River

Rosalie River

Rosalie Point

Freshwater Lake

La Plaine

Boiling Lake

Morne Trois Pitons National Park

Watt Mountain (4015ft)

Delices

Morne Anglais (3683ft)

Champagne Point Guignard

Soufriere Pinnacles

Soufriere Bay

Soufriere

Scotts Head Drop-Off

Scotts Head Pinnacle

Scotts Head

Petite Savanne

Stowe

Grand Bay

Martinique Channel

Ferry to Guadeloupe

Ferries to Martinique & St Lucia

Dominica's more recent political history has also been turbulent. After the sudden death of popular prime minister Roosevelt Douglas ('Rosie') in 2000, after only eight months in office, his successor – the radical Pierre Charles – also died on the job, four years later. In 2004 the then 31-year-old Roosevelt Skerrit stepped into the breach. A popular choice with young people, Skerrit comes from a Rastafarian farming family in the north of the island and is still leading the country today.

The Dominican and Chinese governments formalized relations in 2004 and the sparkling new Windsor Park sports (mostly cricket) stadium in Roseau is a gift from the Chinese that cost an estimated US$17 million. Skerrit broke off long-standing relations with Taiwan that same year, and said on the record that China will give Dominica US$122 million in aid.

In August 2007 Hurricane Dean beat up Dominica and the nearby islands – damage wasn't too heavy compared to Hurricane David, but there were at least two deaths.

In January 2008 Dominica joined the Bolivarian Alternative for the Americas, or ALBA – a regional trade group that includes Venezuela, Cuba, Bolivia and Nicaragua, designed to counterbalance American trade power. Plans for a Venezuelan oil refinery on Dominica are up on the air at the time of writing; after the refinery was announced, the tourism industry protested the plan, saying that it would ruin the island's image.

## THE CULTURE

Dominica draws on a mix of cultures: French place names feature as often as English; African language, foods and customs mingle with European traditions as part of the island's Creole culture; and the Caribs still carve dugouts (canoes), build houses on stilts and weave distinctive basketwork. Rastafarian and Black Pride influences are strong here.

Dominica's population is approximately 72,400; about a third lives in and around Roseau. While the majority of islanders are of African descent, about 2200 native Caribs also reside on Dominica, most of them on a 3700-acre reservation on the eastern side of the island.

With a 61% Roman Catholic population and religious observance commonplace, con-servative traditional values are strong. Family holds an important place in Dominican society, so much so that a government poster warning Dominicans of the dangers of transporting illegal drugs lists separation from family (followed by imprisonment and loss of life) as the number one deterrent to the crime.

Locals are worried about the proliferation of Chinese-owned businesses, and signs have been popping up around the country urging people to buy local.

Much ado has been made of the number of centenarians who live here – Ma Pampo is the most famous, dying at 128 years of age in 2003. The island does have a high percentage of centenarians but the hard evidence for some of the more extraordinary cases is murky. The average life expectancy at birth is now 75.1 years, making Dominica 78th in terms of life expectancy out of 222 countries.

## ARTS

Dominica's most celebrated author, Jean Rhys, was born in Roseau in 1890. Although she moved to England at age 16 and made only one brief return visit to Dominica, much of her work draws upon her childhood experiences in the West Indies. Rhys touches lightly upon her life in Dominica in *Voyage in the Dark* (1934) and in her autobiography, *Smile Please* (1979). Her most famous work, *Wide Sargasso Sea* (1966), a novel set mostly in Jamaica and an unmentioned Dominica, was made into a film in 1993.

## ENVIRONMENT

Dominica is an island of dramatic mountains that seem to come straight out of the sea, and what few beaches there are very lightly developed, at most. For the most part the nature here is untouched, save for the rusted cars that dot the roadsides like so many memorials to bad driving.

---

**HOW MUCH?**

- **Bottled water** EC$3
- **Kubuli beer** EC$4
- **Creole plate** EC$25
- **Tank of gas for 4WD** US$40
- **Accommodation outside Roseau** US$110

DOMINICA

## The Land

Mountainous throughout, Dominica is 29 miles long and 16 miles wide, and has a total land mass of 290 sq miles. It has the highest mountains in the Eastern Caribbean; the loftiest peak, Morne Diablotin, is 4747ft high. The mountains, which act as a magnet for rain, serve as a water source for the alleged 365 rivers that run down the lush green mountain valleys. En route to the coast, many of the rivers cascade over steep cliff faces, giving the island an abundance of waterfalls – 33% of the island's electricity is hydro-generated.

## Wildlife

Whales and dolphins roam the deep waters off Dominica's sheltered west coast. Sperm whales, which grow to a length of 70ft and have a blunt, square snout, are the whales most commonly sighted; the main season is October to March. Other resident toothed whales are the orca, pygmy sperm whale, pygmy killer whale, false killer whale and pilot whale. In winter, migrating humpback whales are occasionally spotted as well.

For near-shore divers, the marine life tends to be of the smaller variety – sea horses included – but there are spotted eagle rays, barracuda and sea turtles as well.

More than 160 bird species have been sighted on Dominica, giving it some of the most diverse birdlife in the Eastern Caribbean. Of these, 59 species nest on the island, including two endemic and endangered parrot species. The Sisserou parrot (*Amazona imperialis*), also called the imperial parrot, is Dominica's national bird. The Jaco parrot (*Amazona arausiaca*) is somewhat smaller and greener overall, with bright splashes of color.

The island used to have an abundance of large frogs, aka 'mountain chicken', but they've been a local delicacy for so long their numbers are dwindling. The island has small tree frogs, many lizards, 13 bat species, 55 butterfly species, boa constrictors that grow nearly 10ft in length and four other types of snake (none poisonous).

The most abundant tree on the island is the *gommier*, a huge gum tree that's traditionally been used to make dugouts.

## Environmental Issues

Cruise ships with a capacity for holding 3000 people dock here to refill water supplies and dump waste, which worries many environmentalists. People are also concerned about the impact of a planned Venezuelan oil refinery.

Despite objections by international environmental groups, Dominica allows whaling to take place in its waters.

## FOOD & DRINK

The food is simple here – 'chicken or fish?' is a question visitors soon get tired of – but the Creole-meets-Rasta cuisine leans on flavorful and fresh ingredients. The locals put hot sauce on almost everything, but it's in bottles so you can season to taste.

Vegetarians will have no trouble filling up on bean, rice and vegetable creations. Vegetable curries and *callaloo* soup are on most menus. *Callaloo* tastes a bit like spinach and on Dominica it's invariably a flavorful, creamy concoction.

There are lots of cheap takeaway places with 'snack' signs that sell salted and barbecued cod and tuna, and deep-fried bread cakes. Most bars frequented by locals also sell snacks.

The island grows a number of fruit, including bananas, coconuts, papayas, guavas, pineapples and mangoes, the latter so plentiful they litter the roadside in places.

Rivers flowing from the mountains provide Dominica with fresh water. Though tap water is generally safe, many travelers stick with bottled water.

Dominica brews its own beer under the Kubuli label; you'll see red-and-white signs all over the island with Kubuli's concise slogan – 'The Beer We Drink.' There's local rum that connoisseurs crave: Macoucherie. Don't be fooled by the plastic bottles or cheap-looking label, it's an undiscovered gem. 'Bush rums,' where locals soak various herbs, roots, and fruits in a bottle of rum, are on sale everywhere.

# DOMINICA

Once outside the capital city, visitors see that Dominica has its tiny villages and a few mountain enclaves, but for the most part, nature still rules the land.

## ROSEAU
pop 15,000

Roseau (rose-oh) is a colorful West Indian capital, its streets lined with old stone-and-wood buildings. For the budget-minded it's a good base because it offers the widest range of eating and accommodations. Dance hall and reggae music is blaring everywhere during the day while people zip around, but at night the city empties. The Chinese eateries popping up around Roseau might seem a bit odd, but more Chinese are setting up shop here and it's becoming more common to see Chinese signs on an otherwise classically Caribbean street. When crossing the street, look right.

## Orientation

Roseau is laid out in an easy to navigate grid system with many of the tourist facilities clustered around the cruise ship dock; the tourist office and Old Market are close by. Be aware that people use 'Dame Eugenia Charles Blvd' (the proper name of the street) and 'Bayfront' interchangeably in addresses.

## Information

**Chinese Medical Clinic** ( ☎ 448-4712; 86 King George St; consultation EC$40; ☽ 9am-6pm Mon-Fri) The place for acupressure massages and herbal remedies.

**Cyberland Internet Café** ( ☎ 440-2605; www.cyberland inc.com; cnr Cork & Great George Sts; 30-min access code valid for 24 hrs EC$3.50; ☽ 8am-10pm Mon-Fri, 10am-7pm Sat) Fast connections in air-conditioned comfort.

**Dominica Cable & Wireless** (Hanover St; ☽ 8am-7pm Mon-Fri) For phone card, fax and email services.

**First Caribbean Bank** (Old St)

**Lin's Laundry** (10 Castle St; load EC$12; ☽ 8am-6pm Mon-Fri, 8:30am-3:30pm Sat)

**New Charles Pharmacy** ( ☎ 448-3198; cnr Fields St & Cross Lane)

**Post office** (Dame Eugenia Charles Blvd; ☽ 8am-5pm Mon, to 4pm Tue-Fri) Check out the mural detailing the history of Dominica's postal service – Anthony Trollope came here in 1856 to set up the system, and policemen were the first mail carriers.

**Princess Margaret Hospital** ( ☎ 448-2231) In the Goodwill area on the north side of Roseau, off Federation Dr.

**Royal Bank of Canada** (Dame Eugenia Charles Blvd) Near the Old Market, this bank has an ATM that accepts credit and bank cards.

**Tourist office** ( ☎ 448-2045; www.discoverdominica.com; Roseau; ☽ 8am-5pm Mon, to 4pm Tue-Fri) Free maps and advice, located on the ground floor beneath the Dominica Museum.

## Sights

### BOTANIC GARDENS

The 40-acre **botanic gardens** (www.da-academy.org/dagardens.html; admission free) on the northeastern edge of Roseau's center is a sprawling place with big banyan trees and flowering tropical shrubs. Locals take leisurely strolls and picnics here. A must-see is the **Parrot Conservation and Research Centre**, an aviary housing Jaco and Sisserou parrots, the two parrot species found in Dominica's rainforests (see opposite).

After the aviary, the most worthwhile site here is the **monument** (of sorts) to Hurricane David. Near the forestry office you'll find a rusting school bus trapped under a huge African baobab tree. The bus was thankfully empty when the hurricane's 150mph winds ravaged the island in 1979.

Brochures describing the island's parks and trails are sold at the forestry office. The garden is the place to start for those who want to hike to the top of Morne Bruce (p587), which overlooks the park.

### OLD MARKET

The cobblestone plaza and small covered arcade of the Old Market has been the center of action in Roseau for the last 300 years. It's been the site of political meetings, farmers markets and, more ominously, executions and a slave market.

Nowadays it's a big souvenir stall where visitors buy bush rum, T-shirts, handicrafts and everything Rasta. To have time to chat with the local vendors, its best to avoid this market when the cruise ships dock.

### DOMINICA MUSEUM

This small but interesting **museum** (admission US$2; ☽ 9am-4pm Mon-Fri, to noon Sat) gives an overview of the history of Dominica and its people.

Besides pictures of a young Jean Rhys (p583), you'll find Native American artifacts, including stone axes and other tools, *adornos* (Arawak clay figurines) and a *gommier* dugout. Informative displays delve into Carib lifestyles, Creole culture and the slave trade. Old photos and drawings trace the history of Roseau from a swampy marsh to the island's biggest city.

### PUBLIC MARKET

Along the riverfront at the northwest end of Dame Eugenia Charles Blvd, you'll find the bustling **public market** ( ☽ 6am-6pm Mon, Wed & Fri, 6am-5pm Tue & Thu, 4am-6pm Sat). It's a good place to have a snack at one of the many cheap food stalls and is the place where locals get their produce and spices. A conch

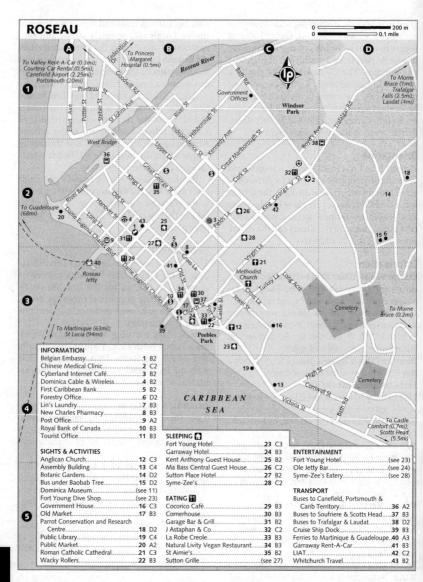

**ROSEAU**

## INFORMATION

| | |
|---|---|
| Belgian Embassy | 1 B2 |
| Chinese Medical Clinic | 2 C2 |
| Cyberland Internet Café | 3 B2 |
| Dominica Cable & Wireless | 4 B2 |
| First Caribbean Bank | 5 B2 |
| Forestry Office | 6 D2 |
| Lin's Laundry | 7 B3 |
| New Charles Pharmacy | 8 B3 |
| Post Office | 9 A2 |
| Royal Bank of Canada | 10 B3 |
| Tourist Office | 11 B3 |

## SIGHTS & ACTIVITIES

| | |
|---|---|
| Anglican Church | 12 C3 |
| Assembly Building | 13 C4 |
| Botanic Gardens | 14 D2 |
| Bus under Baobab Tree | 15 D2 |
| Dominica Museum | (see 11) |
| Fort Young Dive Shop | (see 23) |
| Government House | 16 C3 |
| Old Market | 17 B3 |
| Parrot Conservation and Research | |
| Centre | 18 D2 |
| Public Library | 19 C4 |
| Public Market | 20 A2 |
| Roman Catholic Cathedral | 21 C3 |
| Wacky Rollers | 22 B3 |

## SLEEPING

| | |
|---|---|
| Fort Young Hotel | 23 C3 |
| Garraway Hotel | 24 B3 |
| Kent Anthony Guest House | 25 B2 |
| Ma Bass Central Guest House | 26 C2 |
| Sutton Place Hotel | 27 B2 |
| Syme-Zee's | 28 C2 |

## EATING

| | |
|---|---|
| Cocorico Café | 29 B3 |
| Cornerhouse | 30 B3 |
| Garage Bar & Grill | 31 B2 |
| J Astaphan & Co | 32 C2 |
| La Robe Creole | 33 B3 |
| Natural Livity Vegan Restaurant | 34 B3 |
| St Aimie's | 35 B2 |
| Sutton Grille | (see 27) |

## ENTERTAINMENT

| | |
|---|---|
| Fort Young Hotel | (see 23) |
| Ole Jetty Bar | (see 24) |
| Syme-Zee's Eatery | (see 28) |

## TRANSPORT

| | |
|---|---|
| Buses to Canefield, Portsmouth & | |
| Carib Territory | 36 A2 |
| Buses to Soufriere & Scotts Head | 37 B3 |
| Buses to Trafalgar & Laudat | 38 D2 |
| Cruise Ship Dock | 39 B3 |
| Ferries to Martinique & Guadeloupe | 40 A3 |
| Garraway Rent-A-Car | 41 B3 |
| LIAT | 42 C2 |
| Whitchurch Travel | 43 B2 |

shell sounds every time a new batch of fresh fish arrives.

## CHURCHES

The **Roman Catholic Cathedral**, situated on Virgin Lane above the Methodist Church, is an old stone edifice where Gothic meets Caribbean. The upper windows are stained glass, but much like a typical Creole home, the lower windows are wooden shutters that open for natural ventilation. Architecture buffs should give it a look, but as attractions go it's only worth a quick pass from the street.

The **Anglican Church**, located opposite Peebles Park, is a gray stone-block church that was left with only its shell standing in 1979 after Hurricane David ripped off the original roof. The new roof is now made of tin.

### LIBRARY & AROUND

The **public library** (Victoria St) was built in 1905 with funding from US philanthropist Andrew Carnegie. The wrap around porch is a nice place to check out the sea views and there's a grassy area with a few stone benches to rest in the shade.

**Government House**, the white mansion with the expansive lawn, and the **Assembly Building** are both within about 100 yards of the public library.

### MORNE BRUCE

A rather exclusive hillside suburb that's northeast of Roseau. It has a couple of places to stay, but most people who venture up this way do so for the panoramic hilltop view of Roseau and its surrounds.

One way to get to the viewpoint, near the big cross that overlooks Roseau, is to drive up and park below the president's office. You can also hike to this point from the botanic gardens; the half-mile trail begins just east of the parrot aviary.

## Activities

The following dive shops are located in Rouseau:

**Anchorage Dive Center** ( ☎ 448-2638; www.ancho ragehotel.dm) At Anchorage Hotel in Castle Comfort, just south of Roseau. It also runs whale-watching trips.

**Dive Dominica** ( ☎ 448-2188; www.divedominica.com) At Castle Comfort Lodge; it's the island's oldest dive shop. Also runs whale-watching trips.

**Fort Young Dive Shop** ( ☎ 448-5000; www.fortyoung hotel.com/diving.cfm) At the Fort Young Hotel in central Roseau.

## Tours

**Wacky Rollers** ( ☎ 440-4386; www.wackyrollers.com; 8 Fort St; tours from US$60) offers jeep tours to Titou Gorge, as well as river tubing, kayak tours and zip-line outings.

## Festivals & Events

Roseau is packed solid for **Carnival**, and for the week of **Independence Day**; make hotel reservations in advance or you'll find yourself sleeping well out of town. For more information see p599.

## Sleeping

### TOWN CENTER

**Kent Anthony Guest House** ( ☎ 448-2730; 3 Great Marlborough St; s/d with shared bathroom US$30/35, s/d with private bathroom US$44/50) Humble yet clean, these nine rooms are about as cheap and central as it gets. The helpful proprietor, Austel (his sons are Kent and Anthony), can organize car tours. TVs with cable were on their way at the time of research.

**Syme-Zee's** (Syme-Zee's Eatery; symes_zee@hotmail .com; 34 King George V St; r US$40-60; ⊠ ) Above a popular restaurant-bar, this has 11 rooms, three of which have air-conditioning. Most of the rooms are set back from the main street, and it's surprisingly quiet given the midday hustle and bustle down below. There's a shared living room and laundry.

**Ma Bass Central Guest House** ( ☎ 448-2999; 44 Fields Lane; s/d US$55/60; ⊠ ) One of the best deals in Roseau. The friendly owner, Theresa Emanuel (better known as Ma Bass), earned her name from the medical students who stayed with her before she converted her home into a proper guesthouse. She keeps the place clean and goes out of her way to make guests feel at home. Groups should get the two back rooms that are next to each other and share a balcony – the perfect place to enjoy the night breeze.

**Sutton Place Hotel** ( ☎ 449-8700; www.sutton placehoteldominica.com; 25 Old St; s/d US$75/95, ste s/d US$105/135, all incl breakfast; ⊠ 💻 ) Roseau's answer to a boutique hotel, this place strikes a good balance between style and comfort. Many of the rooms have four-poster beds and the suites have a self-contained kitchen. The downstairs Cellar Bar was under renovation at the time of writing, but it's a real cellar and has a funky, intimate vibe that's not often experienced in this part of the world.

**Garraway Hotel** ( ☎ 449-8800; www.garrawayhotel .com; 1 Dame Eugenia Charles Blvd; r/ste from US$100/110; ⊠ 💻 ) Catering mainly to business travelers, the staff is friendly and professional and the rooms are nice enough, albeit a bit bland.

**Fort Young Hotel** ( ☎ 448-5000; www.fortyoung hotel.com; Victoria St; r US$90-115, ocean-front r US$110-175; ⊠ 💻 ⚓ ) The old cannons that decorate this 74-room hotel are a testament to its history as an 18th-century fort. Now, it's probably the swankiest option in town – the newer oceanfront rooms are the best, with stylish furnishings, dark wood floors, big baths and private outdoor patios. There are wheelchair-accessible rooms and a spa for chill-seekers. There's wi-fi access, and also a dive shop on the premises.

### CASTLE COMFORT

Those who are mainly interested in diving should consider the Castle Comfort area, about 1 mile south of Roseau.

**Sea World Guesthouse** ( ☎ 448-5068; r US$65; ✖ 🖳 ) This bright and simple guesthouse was undergoing construction of a new outdoor bar and grill at the time of research. There's no dive school, but there is an on-site restaurant and shared kitchen.

**Anchorage Hotel** ( ☎ 448-2638; www.anchorage hotel.dm; s/d US$66/85; ✖ 🖳 🖳 ) With an on-site restaurant, bar, dive school and whale-watching trips, this place has it all – including the skeleton of a giant sperm whale beside the pool. Rooms are simple but well appointed with cable TV, a fast internet hookup, and either a balcony or windows that open right over the water.

**Evergreen Hotel** ( ☎ 448-3288; r from US$110, lodge US$145; ✖ 🖳 🖳 ) Set on gardened grounds, the exterior feels more spacious than any other Castle Comfort hotel but the rooms in one of the two buildings (the three-storey one) are a bit small. The detached lodge (aka Honeymoon Hut) has a patio right above the water, and the rest of the rooms are set back on the grounds. There's no water access, but the hotels with dive schools are right next door.

**Castle Comfort Lodge** ( ☎ 448-2188; www.castle comfortdivelodge.com; 4-/7-night package US$700/958; ✖ 🖳 ) Renting its rooms as part of dive packages only, those who come for a scuba adventure will be in heaven. Dive packages include meals, two-tank boat dives every day, airport transfers and, at an additional cost, whale-watching. For those who prefer to go their own way, guests are welcome to grab a tank and jump off the pier whenever they see fit – fish-filled water is just a few fin strokes away.

## Eating

For those used to late dinners, be aware that even if a place normally serves dinner it's best to show up on the early side, unless otherwise noted.

**Natural Livity Vegan Restaurant** (naturallivity rastaurant@yahoo.com; 13 King George V St; mains EC$8-16; ✔ breakfast & lunch Mon-Thu & breakfast, lunch & dinner Fri) Lively up yourself for the Rastafarian proprietor, Dr J, who serves vegan goodness in the form of pizza, stews and tofu dishes while the reggae music booms in this open-air courtyard restaurant.

**Cornerhouse** ( ☎ 449-9000; 6 King George V St; mains EC$12-18; ✔ breakfast & lunch Mon-Fri) This 2nd-level restaurant is a good place to meet other travelers or just watch life go by on the street below. The breakfasts are solid and the Creole plates span the range of vegetarian to local fish. The homemade chili is good, too. Internet access is EC$3 per 15 minutes.

**St Aimie's** ( ☎ 440-4463; 35 Great George St; mains EC$12-24; ✔ breakfast, lunch & dinner Mon-Sat) Its motto is 'Just taste it!' and it's good advice. It doesn't look like much more than a shack, but the locals swear by this place and it serves dinner after most places have sold out of food. The fish and Creole dishes on the menu are standard fare, but the cook here works some special magic that takes the food above and beyond.

**Garage Bar & Grill** ( ☎ 448-5433; 15 Hanover St; mains EC$14-25; ✔ breakfast, lunch & dinner Tue-Sat) Set in an old stone house with open windows, this happening place feels more like an old castle than a garage – except for the bar stools that use old tires as a base. The food, especially the barbecue plates, is doubly good considering it looks more like a bar than a restaurant. Lots of local professionals wet their whistles after dark and it's often the last place to shut down in Roseau.

**Ocean Terrace Restaurant** (mains EC$15-70; ✔ breakfast, lunch & dinner) At the Anchorage Hotel, it may be out of Roseau, but those willing to make the short drive will be surprised by a second-level seaside casual dining room where the food tastes great. Its lunch menu is worthy for its sheer range of prices and dishes; and breakfast here is a pancake-lover's dream come true. At night it's more of a fine-dining experience.

**Cocorico Café** ( ☎ 449-8686; www.natureisle.com/ cocorico; cnr Dame Eugenia Charles Blvd & Kennedy Ave; mains US$9-16; ✔ breakfast & lunch Mon-Sat) Big open windows look out on the bay in this art gallery, duty-free shop and restaurant. It's quite popular with cruise-ship visitors, and the food from the French owners is something to crow about. Try the chicken in a coconut curry sauce, or one of the rum punches – some of the spiciest around. It's a wi-fi hot spot.

**La Robe Creole** ( ☎ 448-2896; www.larobecreole
.com; 3 Victoria St; mains EC$30-85; ☯ breakfast, lunch &
dinner) Serves top-notch Creole dishes and
seafood all day in a friendly environment
that you don't need to dress up for. The bar
has an extensive wine and spirits selection
and Erica's rum punch is quite the treat.
Anything seafood is highly recommended
and the daily specials are indeed special.

**Sutton Grille** (mains EC$50-120; ☯ breakfast, lunch &
dinner) At the Sutton Place Hotel, this courtyard
restaurant has a slightly Gothic, sumptuous
feel with its thick stone walls and wrought-
iron gates – be scared if a shadowy figure with
pointy teeth sits down. Fancy sandwiches or a
buffet lunch are available by day with a more
elaborate fish and steak menu later on.

The place to go for snacks, the fixings for
dinner or rum at local prices is the **J Astaphan
& Co** ( ☎ 448-3221; 65 King George V St; ☯ 8am-7pm
Mon-Sat) supermarket. Upstairs is a department
store with all the rain ponchos and extra socks
you'll ever need. The public market (p585) is
the place for fish, fruit and vegetables.

## Entertainment
Most entertainment is largely limited to a
sunset drink at one of the hotel bars.

**Fort Young Hotel** ( ☎ 448-5000; Victoria St) has a
happy hour from 6pm to 8pm and live steel-
pan music a bit later.

On Thursdays **Syme-Zee's Eatery** (38 King
George V St; ☯ 9pm-3am) has a live jazz jam session with talented local musicians.

The **Ole Jetty Bar** ( ☎ 449-8800; Garraway Hotel, 1
Dame Eugenia Charles Blvd; ☯ 5pm-11pm) has karaoke
nights on Friday. The bar is open until 11pm
or so on weekdays, later on weekends.

## Getting There & Away
### AIR
See p601 for information on flights to/from
Dominica.

### BOAT
For information on the ferry services be-
tween Roseau, Guadeloupe, Martinique and
St Lucia, see p601.

### BUS
The bus service is operated by private
minivans, recognizable by number plates
that begin with the letter 'H.' You can hail
a passing van from the street. There isn't a
bus station, but buses heading southward

(including to Castle Comfort, EC$1.50) tend
to congregate at the Old Market, while those
going north stop at West Bridge. Bus service
stops soon after the working day is over.

### CAR
For information on car-rental agencies in
Roseau, see p602.

## Getting Around
### TO/FROM THE AIRPORT
Avis and Budget car rentals are at Canefield
Airport, but other agencies will provide customers with free airport pick-up. Taxis are
readily available (five- to 10-minute journey set fare EC$25) from Canefield Airport.
Melville Hall has a wider selection of car-
rental companies and the hour-plus taxi ride
between Roseau is set at EC$50.

### TAXI
You can pick up a taxi on the street or call
**Dominica Taxi Association** ( ☎ 449-8553).

## LAYOU RIVER AREA
The Layou River, Dominica's longest, empties into the sea just south of Layou, at the
center of the west coast. It's a popular place for
freshwater swimming when it's not running
strong. North of the Layou River are the gray
pristine sands of Mero Beach.

## Sights
**Macoucherie Distillery** ( ☎ 449-6409; www.shillingford
estateltd.com; Macoucherie), makers of some of the
best rum in the Caribbean, is located between
the Layou River and Salisbury. This is a working distillery – visitors either can try their luck
by just stopping in or can call first. Be sure to
take the opportunity to stock up on potent
potables while you're here.

## Sleeping & Eating
**Tamarind Tree** ( ☎ 449-7395; www.tamarindtreedominica
.com; Salisbury; s/d incl breakfast from US$93/108;
☒ ▢ ☙ ) This cliffside property sets the
standard for ecofriendly Dominican hotels.
It posts its Green Globe certification online
and links to the report that shows exactly how
much water each guest uses on average, how
much trash the hoteliers recycle, etc. The hotel
faces the pool and has 12 comfortable rooms
that vary in amenities (some are fan-only). For
guests who want to dive, the owners here work
with the nearby Sunset Bay Club.

**DOMINICA**

**Sunset Bay Club** ( ☎ 446-6522; www.sunsetbayclub .com; s/d all-inclusive from US$144/238; 🖳 🏊 ) About 1 mile north of Salisbury, this beachside hotel is set on lush grounds where lizards scamper across the walkways. There's an on-site dive center, a small pool, a sauna, a nice open-air restaurant (mains EC$30 to EC$50; open lunch and dinner) and an on-site masseuse. It does beach clean-up and future-divemaster programs with the area's youth.

**Connie's Mero Beach Bar** (Mero Beach; snacks EC$4-10; 🕑 lunch & dinner) Those who go to Mero Beach can count on this place for snacks, drinks and friendly advice on local attractions. In the evening, Connie says she either closes early or keeps the barbecue fired up into the night, depending on how many people are around.

### Getting There & Away

There is a bus service from Roseau to Salisbury (EC$5.20, 45 minutes) or Portsmouth (EC$8.50, 1¼ hours).

## NORTHERN FOREST RESERVE

The Northern Forest Reserve is a huge area that encompasses 8800 hectares of land in the interior of the island, including 4747ft Morne Diablotin, the island's highest peak. The main habitat of Dominica's two endangered parrot species is in the eastern section of the reserve.

To get to the reserve, turn east on the signposted road that begins just north of the village of Dublanc, on the coast south of Portsmouth, and continue to Syndicate Estate, about 4.5 miles inland. There you'll find an easy mile-long loop trail (Syndicate Trail) to a parrot observatory platform, as well as the start of the trail leading up Morne Diablotin, a long and rugged hike that's best done with a guide – contact the **tourist office** ( ☎ 448-2045; www.discoverdominica.com; Roseau; 🕑 8am-5pm Mon, to 4pm Tue-Fri) in Roseau.

## PORTSMOUTH

Dominica's second-largest town sits on Prince Rupert Bay. The bay is a favorite with the sail boat set and there's an occasional mega-yacht lurking in the distance. Cabrits National Park, on the north side of town and Indian River, to the south, are the area's noteworthy attractions. Beside the two main sights, Portsmouth is a nice spot for whale-watching and dive excursions. The town center doesn't have much to offer other than some basic shopping, and

the place gets downright ominous at night. Ross University School of Medicine, just south of town, attracts a lot of international students, who add a cosmopolitan flavor.

### Information

**Computer Resource Center** (Bay Rd; per 30min EC$3; 🕑 9am-10pm) With fast internet connections, it also sells computer accessories on the expensive side.

**National Commercial Bank of Dominica** ( ☎ 445-5430) Just south of the town square parking lot (where you pick up the bus to Roseau).

**Police** (Bay Rd)

### Sights & Activities
#### DIVING & WHALE-WATCHING

**Cabrits Dive Center** ( ☎ 445-3010; www.cabritsdive .com; snorkeling trips US$15, dives from US$60) Chris, the friendly divemaster here, won't say if the diving on the north side of the island is better or not, but he does say there's a lot of variation – massive underwater boulders, gently sloping walls, some wrecks and, his favorite, the 'pole to pole' dive under a ship berth that's spawned its own ecosystem. In addition to the standard dive outings, Cabrits can help divers book accommodations and will pick up sailors who want to dive from their boats.

**Whaledive** ( ☎ 445-5131; www.whaledive.org; snorkeling trips US$20, whale-watching & dives from US$50) Founded by Dr Fitzroy Armour, known as 'the Jacques Cousteau of Dominica', these trips combine whale-watching and diving on a sail boat to cut down on noise and exhaust pollution for our underwater friends. Based at Picard Beach Eco-Cottages – which Armour owns along with a few other hotels on the island – Whaledive runs a daily sunset wine and cheese cruise.

#### INDIAN RIVER

Boat trips here wind up the shady river through tall swamp bloodwood trees, whose buttressed trunks rise out of the shallows, their roots stretching out laterally along the riverbanks. It can be a fascinating outing, taking you into an otherwise inaccessible habitat and offering a close-up view of the creatures that live at the water's edge.

Though almost everyone you meet in Portsmouth will offer to be your guide, you'll get a lot more from the trip if you go with one of the boaters who work with the Park Service; they can be found with the other rowers at the mouth of the river (see below). Or, if staying at a waterfront hotel, the front desk can call a guide to pick up groups at the pier for a small negotiable surcharge (per person US$2 to US$4).

The rowers, who set up shop along the coastal road at the river mouth, charge EC$35 per person for a tour that takes about 1½ hours, usually with a stop for drinks at the **Indian River Bush Bar** ( ☎ 445-3333; www.cobratours .dm; drinks US$3), run by the affable 'Cobra' (aka Andrew O'Brian). The dynamite rum punch is its signature drink, a mixture of fruits, herbs and 'local atmosphere' as Cobra puts it. Although it looks like it's only accessible via the river, locals can point you to a walking path that takes 10 minutes or so from town.

### CABRITS NATIONAL PARK

Located on a scenic peninsula 1.25 miles north of Portsmouth, **Cabrits National Park** (admission US$ 2.50; 🕑 8am-6pm) is the site of Fort Shirley, an impressive 18th-century British garrison. In addition to the peninsula, the park encompasses the surrounding coastal area, as well as the island's largest swamp. The Cabrits Peninsula, formed by two extinct volcanoes, separates Prince Rupert Bay from Douglas Bay. The coral reefs and waters of the latter are also part of the park, and good for snorkeling.

Cabrits is a fun place to explore. Some of the fort's stone ruins have been cleared and partially reconstructed, while others remain half-hidden in the jungle. The powder magazine to the right of the fort entrance has been turned into a small **museum** with restoration exhibits and a display of unearthed artifacts.

The fort is home to scores of hermit crabs, harmless snakes and ground lizards *(Ameiva fuscata)* that scurry about the ruins and along the hiking trails that lead up to the two volcanic peaks. The trail up the 560ft West Cabrit begins at the back side of Fort Shirley and the hike takes about 30 minutes. Most of the walk passes through a wooded area, but there's a panoramic view at the top.

### Sleeping

**Portsmouth Beach Hotel** ( ☎ 445-5142; www.avirtual dominica.com/pbh.htm; s/d US$50/60; 🏊 ) This hotel is situated on a lovely yellow-sand beach about 0.5 miles south of town. You'll find 80 rooms with kitchenettes here, although booking one

can be hard during the school year because most are rented out to medical students.

**Picard Beach Eco-Cottages** ( ☎ 445-5131; www .avirtualdominica.com/picard.htm; cottages from US$120; 🍴 💻 ) This place does a lot of neat things, such as using as little outdoor lighting as possible so as not to upset nesting turtles or stargazers; inviting guests to eat fresh fruit from the trees on property; and running sailboat-only whale-watching (opposite) and dive trips. But at the time of research, guests wouldn't know any of this unless they asked. Set no more than a few steps from the beach, the spacious cottages all have outdoor kitchens and porches that just beg for long days of lounging.

### Eating

**Purple Turtle Beach Club Bar & Restaurant** ( ☎ 445-5296; Michael Douglas Blvd; mains EC$10-20; 🕑 lunch & dinner) This Portsmouth institution is a favorite end-of-day drinking spot for locals and boaters alike.

**Big Papas Restaurant** ( ☎ 445-6444; bigpapas@ hotmail.com; Michael Douglas Blvd; mains EC$18-30; 🕑 lunch & dinner) In the heart of Portsmouth Lagoon north of the town center, this Jamaican food place is run by the friendly, and yes, big Aldrin Burnette with his wife Gloria. Try the super spicy jerk chicken or Indian curries with fish or chicken.

**Le Flambeau** (mains EC$25-40; 🕑 breakfast, lunch & dinner) Located at Picard Beach Eco-Cottages, this breezy beachside restaurant has a broad selection of Caribbean dishes and food from home. The burgers, although not quite a local specialty, are extremely good. It also has a nice choice of vegetarian plates and moderately priced fish and meat dinners.

**Blue Bay Restaurant** ( ☎ 445-4985; bluebayrestau rant@cwdom.dm; mains EC$35-60; 🕑 dinner) Word on the street is that this is the tastiest place in town. The French chef makes the usual array of fish and chicken dishes but the creamy seafood pasta is a must-try. Don't trust first impressions – follow the signs from the street and in a few steps the alley leads to this hip waterside eatery.

### Getting There & Away

From Roseau, bus service to Portsmouth (EC$8.50, one hour) leaves from the southeast side of the Roseau River near the public market. In Portsmouth, the town square, on Bay Rd, is the place to catch a minibus to other parts of the island. The road across from the square eventually leads to the airport – the drive takes about one hour.

## PORTSMOUTH TO PAGUA BAY

The route that cuts across the northern neck of the island from Portsmouth to the east coast is a stunning drive through mountainous jungle. Near the village of Bense, look out for signs for the hiking trail to **Chaudiere Pool**. It's a 45-minute hike each way, and the scenery and the deep swimming hole at the end are well worth it.

### Borne

Although Borne is useful navigation point more than a sight itself, it does have some places worth checking out.

The French-born Marie Frederick can turn something as simple as basil pasta into a feat of gourmet cooking at the **Indigo Art Gallery** ( ☎ 445-3486; www.indigo.wetpaint.com; Borne; mains US$20-50; ◷ lunch & dinner), which she runs with her husband Clem. This one-table tree house–like restaurant also sells Marie's art and some of Clem's handicrafts. There's a tree house cottage (room from EC$300) on site, but it's best to visit before booking. It's gorgeous but very rustic – there's no electricity and the outhouse can be hard to find in the dark. Bring a flashlight.

**Brandy Manor** ( ☎ 445-3619; Borne; r from US$65) is an oasis of order in the thick forest along Brandy River. There's one bungalow that stands alone and three simple rooms in the main house. There's no hot water except for solar shower bags. Guest can go swimming in the river and the owner can arrange rainforest horseback riding (US$45 to US$75). The restaurant and bar (mains EC$20 to EC$55; open breakfast, lunch and dinner) is by reservation only for non-guests.

### Calibishie

The first sizable town you will reach on the east coast, Calibishie is an attractive fishing village with a handful of friendly bars and restaurants, a craft store and a car-rental agency.

There are some good picnic beaches in the area. **Hell's Gate Beach**, half a mile west of town, looks out onto two striking rock columns protruding from the sea – the columns are collectively known as Devil's Rock. However, this beach is unsuitable for swimming. Further west is **Batibou Bay**, a scenic beach that's good for swimming and was featured in a certain pirate-movie trilogy starring Johnny Depp.

Calibishie makes a good pit stop for lunch or an overnight stay, particularly if you're catching a morning flight from nearby Melville Hall Airport.

The five self-contained apartments at **Dominica's Sea View Apartment** ( ☎ 445-8537; www.dominicasseaviewapartments.com; apt US$85-95; ◼ ) are on top of a hill overlooking Calibishie village – the view is stellar. All of the newly-constructed units have kitchens and dining rooms. A rental car to get food and mount the hill is highly recommended. Check in at Calibishie Lodges.

**Sea Cliff Cottages** ( ☎ 445-8998; www.dominica-cottages.com; cottages US$90-120, house per week US$720; ◼ ) are made up of three cottages and one fully-equipped house (2-week minimum in high season) are on a cliff that overlooks Hodges Beach. It's not the place to meet people or party, but for big groups on a budget or couples who want to 'connect,' it's a solid choice.

The scenic, extremely well-run **Calibishie Lodges** ( ☎ 445-8537; www.calibishie-lodges.com; apt US$105-160; ◼ ▯ ◼ ) has six apartments that sleep up to four people. The apartments have good-sized living areas, bright and modern furnishings, and come with balconies.

The excellent **Bamboo Restaurant** (mains EC$30-65; ◷ breakfast, lunch & dinner) here offers an inventive Creole menu, including dishes such as coconut crayfish and lobster with banana cake.

## CARIB TERRITORY

The 3700-acre Carib Territory, which begins around the village of Bataka and continues south for 7.5 miles, is home to most of Dominica's 2200 Caribs – properly known as Kalinago. It's a rural area with cultivated bananas, breadfruit trees and wild heliconia growing along the roadside. Many of the houses are traditional wooden structures on log stilts, but there are also simple cement

---

**TWIST MY ARM: THE PLACES THE AUTHORS WANTED TO KEEP SECRET**

The tree house cottage at Indigo Art Gallery (left) is a really special place. There's only one room, though, and it's definitely not for everyone.

DOMINICA

---

**FORWARD EVER, BACKWARD NEVER**

Clem Frederick, a man who works architectural miracles with stone and wood at Indigo Art Gallery (opposite) and other lodgings in the Borne area, isn't convinced that tourism is a good thing for Dominica. The deep-voiced, dreadlocked local shared his thoughts.

**I wanted to talk to you about the cool stuff here in Dominica.**

Well, what I suspect – when people are talking about 'cool stuff,' nobody really wants the cool stuff, you know.

**How do you mean?**

I mean, nobody wants cool stuff. You know why I say that? Because when a big man comes to nature island, his plan will never be to buy a mountain and just leave it like that. So, there's nothing cool concerning what people are speaking about.

**But, I'd like to think that there are some smart people who realize that keeping it like it is is going to bring more tourists.**

No, no. Nobody will be smart. They'll say 'forward ever, backward never.' They're just getting more foolish, because nobody really wants to live the local life, they're just talking about it.

**Well, how about places like this, or places in Roseau Valley? They're beautiful and they bring tourists, they bring money to the local economy, but they're set in nature.**

Yes, there are some, there will always be some. But some of the little places they are little because they just hope to be bigger. It's like if you go in the bush, and you see the Rasta man, and ask him if he likes the life, he'll say yes. But soon you'll see him again living in America (laughs). That's the way it is, man.

---

homes and, in the poorer areas, shanties made of corrugated tin and tar paper.

The main attraction here is **Kalinago Barana Aute** (Carib Cultural Village by the Sea; ☎ 445-7979; www .kalinagobaranaaute.com; Old Coast Rd, Crayfish River; site pass & tour EC$26; ☽ 9am-5pm) a traditional village showcasing a herbal medicine garden, canoe-building, arts and crafts.

The main east-coast road runs right through the Carib Territory. Along the road are several stands where you can stop and buy intricately woven Carib baskets and handicrafts.

## Sleeping & Eating

**Islet View Restaurant** (New Rd, Castle Bruce; mains EC$10-23; ☽ breakfast, lunch & dinner) The big outdoor porch overlooks Castle Bruce Beach and is a good place to take a break from a day at the beach or the long drive up the east coast. The thatched walls and big selection of hand-labeled bush rums behind the bar make the restaurant, with only one or two meals on the menu, look more like a friendly witch doctor's house than a roadside eatery.

**Gachette Cottages** ( ☎ 446-0700; www.gachette dominica.com; Castle Bruce; s/d US$60/70) The five free-standing cottages here all have kitchens and there's a river and fresh spring on the property. The friendly owner runs the Stewpot Restaurant (mains US$15 to US$40; open 11am to 10pm) right outside the hotel grounds. The cottages are inland from Castle Bruce Beach on the way to the Emerald Pool.

**Beau Rive Hotel** ( ☎ 445-8992; www.beaurive.com; s/d US$137/180; ▯ ▩ ) Set in tropical gardens over-looking Wakaman Point, this elegant hotel lies one mile north of Castle Bruce. It is run by Briton Mark Steele, who has made many small touches with the comfort of guests in mind – there are walking sticks and umbrel-las on either side of the front entrance and an all-white room decor shows that the place is truly spotless. The airy restaurant serves a set meat-free dinner (EC$83) as well as fish or chicken.

## Getting There & Away

Buses heading to Canefield (EC$2) and the Carib Territory (EC$9.50) leave from the southeast side of the Roseau River near the public market in Roseau.

## EMERALD POOL

The island's most accessible waterfall, Emerald Pool takes its name from its lush green setting and clear water. At the base of a gentle 40ft waterfall, the pool is deep enough for a dip but the water can be on the cool side.

The 0.3-mile path to get here winds through a rainforest of massive ferns and tall trees. On the way back there are two viewpoints – one is a panorama of the Atlantic Coast and the other is a great view of Morne Trois Pitons, Dominica's second-highest mountain. The path can get a bit slippery in places and sandals aren't advised, especially after rain.

Emerald Pool is generally serene except on cruise-ship days, when one packed minivan after another pulls up to the site – past 3pm is the best time to avoid the crowds.

The pool is on the road that runs between Canefield and Castle Bruce; it's an enjoyable winding drive with thick jungle vegetation, mountain views and lots of beep-as-you-go hairpin turns. It's about a 30-minute drive from Canefield and the trailhead is well-marked.

## TRAFALGAR FALLS

On the western edge of Morne Trois Pitons National Park, Trafalgar Falls are spectacular and accessible via a steep but smooth uphill walk. The 0.4-mile walk to the falls begins at Papillote Wilderness Retreat, about 1 mile east of the village of Trafalgar.

Start the walk at the bottom of the inn's driveway, where you'll find a cement track leading east. Follow the track until you reach a little snack bar; take the footpath that leads downhill from there and in a couple of minutes you'll reach a viewing platform with a clear view of the falls.

There are two separate waterfalls. Water from the upper falls crosses the Titou Gorge before plunging down the sheer 200ft rock face that fronts the viewing platform. At the base of the waterfall are hot sulfur springs. Look for yellow streaks on the rocks to find a good soaking spot.

The lower falls flow from the Trois Pitons River in the Boiling Lake area. This waterfall, gentler and broader than the upper falls, has a deep and wide pool at its base made for swimming.

Guys hang out at the start of the trail, touting as guides. Getting to the viewing platform is straightforward and doesn't require a guide, so if you plan to go only that far, save yourself the fee (roughly EC$20).

Going beyond the platform is trickier – crossing a river is the only way to get to the base of the falls. Depending on how sure-footed you are, a guide could be helpful in climbing down the boulders to the lower pool or clambering over to the hot springs.

Guide or not, be careful because the moss-covered rocks are as slippery as ice. This is a serious river, and during rainy spells it may be too high to cross. Flash floods from heavy rains in the mountains are a real danger – if you're in the river and the waters start to rise, get out immediately, preferably on the side closest to home.

Cocoa Cottages runs an awesome **canyoning trip** ( ☎ 448-0412; www.cocoacottages.com; US$150), a half-day of rappelling down waterfalls and floating in pools at the bottom of deep canyon walls. As Richard, the tour leader, puts it, 'A lot of people come to Dominica to look at waterfalls, but with canyoning you get to taste them, feel them, be in them.'

### Sleeping & Eating

**OUR PICK** **Papillote Wilderness Retreat** ( ☎ 448-2287; www.papillote.dm; s/d US$100/115, with breakfast & dinner per person extra US$40; 🖳 ) The American owner Anne Baptiste has planted the grounds with nearly 100 types of tropical flowers and trees. Actually, because of hurricanes, she says she's built this place twice in the course of her 30 years here. The rooms are spacious and, like the outside, feel luxurious with just a few simple touches – comfortable beds, stylish bathrooms, handmade quilts. Try to get a room near one of the three hot springs here. Papillote serves exemplary food, with lunchtime salads and hot Creole dishes (US$10 to US$15). Dinner (US$30) is by reservation and it's a delicious full-course meal. Anne usually dines in the evening here – be sure to say hi. The gift shop sells copies of Anne's *The Roseau Valley Guide* (US$3), a good book for travelers who base themselves in the area.

**Cocoa Cottages** ( ☎ 448-0412; www.cocoacottages .com; r from US$104, with breakfast & dinner per couple extra US$70) Run the by the affable Iris and Richard, who've created a very casual environment good for meeting interesting people from around the world at the communal dining tables at breakfast and dinner. The dinners are a bit pricey (US$30) considering that they're a serve-yourself family-style affair, but they are delicious. The living room has a drum kit, acoustic guitar, couches, books and games. Try to get the honeymoon suite – it's private and quiet.

### Getting There & Away

Buses go from Roseau to the village of Trafalgar (EC$2.75, 30 to 40 minutes); from there's it's no more than half a mile to either

---

**BEST ITUNES DOWNLOAD FOR DOMINICA**

Check out the *Dominica Tenement Yard* album. The group's leader, Trevy Felix of Boom Shaka fame, returned to his native Dominica and sought out roots reggae musicians who were living in the countryside. It's kind of like *The Buena Vista Social Club*, Dominica-style.

---

hotel. Taxis from Canefield Airport to either hotel cost EC$50.

To get to Trafalgar by car from Roseau, take King George V St north from the town center. After crossing a small bridge make an immediate left on what might feel like a small road and follow its serpentine twists and turns. Veer to the right at the first fork in the road (left will get you to the entrance of Morne Trois Pitons National Park) and look for the hotel signs.

## MORNE TROIS PITONS NATIONAL PARK

This national park and Unesco World Heritage site in the southern half of the island encompasses 17,000 acres of Dominica's mountainous volcanic interior.

Most of the park is primordial rainforest, varying from jungles thick with tall, pillarlike *gommier* trees to the stunted cloud-forest cover on the upper slopes of Morne Trois Pitons (4550ft), Dominica's second-highest mountain. The park has many of the island's top wilderness sites, including Boiling Lake, Boeri Lake, Freshwater Lake and Middleham Falls. Hikes to all four start at Laudat (elevation 1970ft), a small hamlet with fine mountain views.

See p593 for a description of Emerald Pool, located at the northernmost tip of the park.

All of the hikes below can be done as a (long) day trip from Roseau. Pretty much all hotels and guest houses can hook visitors up with a guide (per person US$40 to US$60), if one doesn't find you first.

## Sights & Activities

### HIKING

#### Boiling Lake

Dominica's pre-eminent trek, and one of the hardest, is the day-long hike to Boiling Lake, the world's second-largest actively boiling lake (the largest is in New Zealand). Geologists believe the 207ft-wide lake is a flooded fumarole – a crack in the earth that allows hot gases to vent from the molten lava below. The eerie-looking lake sits inside a deep basin, its grayish waters veiled in steam, its center emitting bubbly burps. The lake mysteriously

stops boiling every once in a while, but after some short breaks in 1998 and again in 2005, it's churning away just fine.

En route to the lake, the hike passes through the aptly named Valley of Desolation, a former rainforest destroyed by a volcanic eruption in 1880. The hike follows narrow ridges, snakes up and down mountains and runs along hot streams. Wear sturdy walking shoes and expect to get wet and muddy.

The strenuous 6-mile hike to the lake begins at Titou Gorge and requires a guide. Most of the guides stop on the way back at a 'secret' bathing hole.

### Middleham Falls

The trail to **Middleham Falls**, one of Dominica's highest waterfalls, takes you on an interesting rainforest walk. More than 60 species of tree, including the tall buttressed chataignier, form a leafy canopy that inhibits undergrowth and keeps the forest floor relatively clear.

There are usually guides available at the trailhead who charge about EC$60 to take you to the falls and the hike takes about 1¼ hours each way. If you don't use a guide, carry a compass or GPS unit and be careful not to stray off the main trail. It's all too easy to lose your bearings here.

### Other Trails

The walk to **Freshwater Lake**, Dominica's largest lake, is a straightforward hike that skirts the southern flank of Morne Macaque. As the 2.5-mile trail up to the lake is along a well-established 4WD track, this hike doesn't require a guide. It's a relatively gradual walk and takes about 2½ hours round-trip.

Hikers can continue another 1.25 miles from Freshwater Lake to **Boeri Lake**, a scenic 45-minute walk that passes mountain streams and hot and cold springs. The 130ft-deep Boeri Lake occupies a volcanic crater that's nestled between two of the park's highest mountains.

For a short walk and a dip there's the trail from Laudat to **Titou Gorge**, where a deep pool is warmed by a hot spring.

Hikers should also hire a guide to tackle **Morne Trois Pitons**, the park's tallest peak. It's a rough trail that cuts through patches of sharp saw grass and requires scrambling over steep rocks. The trail begins at Pont Casse, at the north side of the park, and takes about five hours round-trip.

### RAINFOREST TRAM

To get to the entrance of the **Rain Forest Tram Dominica** ( ☎ 448-8775; www.rfat.com; office cnr Old & King George V Sts, Roseau; US$55) head to Roxy's Mountain Lodge in the village of Laudat and look for the signs. The tram ride takes 45 minutes each direction. On the far side you can take a 20-minute guided tour that includes a walk across a dizzyingly high suspension bridge. For the price it's a bit underwhelming, but a decent introduction to what the rainforest has to offer. You can also buy tickets in Roseau.

### Sleeping & Eating

**Roxy's Mountain Lodge** ( ☎ 448-4845; s/d US$55/69) Based in the tiny village of Laudat, Roxy's is the place to stay for serious hikers. The rooms with kitchenettes were under renovation when we were at this friendly, family-run place. There's a TV room, a small bar and a restaurant with good-value lunchtime sandwiches – which staff can pack in a picnic basket for trekkers – and dinner meals.

### Getting There & Away

There's regular but limited bus service. Buses to Laudat (EC$4.75, 40 minutes) leave from the Roseau police station every other hour from 6:30am; buses return to Roseau from Laudat about 45 minutes later. Taxis from Roseau to Laudat cost EC$80.

To get to Laudat by car, take King George V St north from Roseau. After crossing the bridge over the Roseau River hang a left and continue up the Roseau Valley for 2.3 miles, at which point the road forks; take the left fork, marked 'Laudat.' The road is narrow and pot-holed, but it's passable. The trail to Middleham Falls begins on the left 2.5 miles up; the trail to Freshwater and Boeri Lakes begins opposite the shrine, half a mile further.

### GRAND BAY

The road that cuts across the southern tip of Dominica is one of the most pleasant and stress-free drives on the island. The wide (relatively speaking) and gently curving road skirts the base of Morne Anglais and crosses a few rivers before heading up along the east coast at Grand Bay.

**Zandoli Inn** ( ☎ 446-3161; www.zandoli.com; Roche Cassée, Stowe; s/d US$135/145; breakfast & set dinner plan per person US$45; 🖥 🐾 ) is a charming little place designed to induce a state of Zen, Caribbean-style. There aren't any TVs or radios and guests are asked to use headphones to listen to music. All five of the rooms have private balconies, sea views and solar hot-water showers. Walking paths on the hotel grounds have benches spaced throughout to take a rest on or just watch the little *zandoli* lizards (a sign of good luck) scamper by.

At **Jungle Bay Resort & Spa** ( ☎ 446-1789; www.junglebaydominica.com; Pointe Mulatre; r from US$175, full package s/d US$239/315; 🖥 🐾 ), a sprawling, rustic resort with 35 cottages, the owners made the laudable decision to blend the cottages into the jungle as much as possible. The 'Jungle Adventure Package' includes a daily massage, yoga classes, meals (sans alcoholic beverages) and carte blanche to drop in on any of the activities of the day, which range from rum-shop tours to snorkeling trips to Caribbean cooking classes. Travelers tell us the quality of the massages and food is variable, but the service is great and it's one of the most romantic getaways on the island. Another plus is that the management and staff here go out of their way to give back to the local community.

## SOUTH OF ROSEAU

The coastal road south of Roseau is a 30-minute drive that takes you through a couple of attractive seaside villages and ends at Scotts Head. There is a bus service from the Old Market in Roseau to Soufriere and Scotts Head (EC$3.50, 30 minutes).

### Soufriere
#### pop 950

Soufriere has a picturesque old stone **church** on the north side of the village. There are steaming sulfur springs in the hills above town, including one about a mile inland on the road that leads east from the village center.

**Nature Island Dive** ( ☎ 449-8181; www.natureislanddive.com), based in Soufriere, takes divers to many of the island's best dive spots just minutes away. It also rents out sea kayaks for US$55 per half-day; paddle around Soufriere Bay, or take an excursion up the coastline to snorkeling sites that can't be reached by land. If you want to stay on dry land, it rents out mountain bikes and leads half-day guided biking trips (per person US$65). You can explore old estate trails and the nearby sulfur springs; staff can recommend longer outings for serious bikers.

## Scotts Head

**pop 800**

On the southernmost tip of Dominica's west coast, Scotts Head is a picturesque fishing village and is the place to go for underwater exploration. It has a gem of a setting along the gently curving shoreline of Soufriere Bay, which is the rim of a sunken volcanic crater. The center of village activity in Scotts Head is the waterfront. It's a lively, welcoming scene, with frequent beach barbecues and dancing in the local bars.

Soufriere Bay is a designated nature reserve, and has some of the island's best dives (see p57 for details). Scotts Head Drop-Off is a shallow coral ledge that drops off abruptly more than 150ft, revealing a wall of huge tube sponges and soft corals. Just west of Scotts Head is the Pinnacle, which starts a few feet below the surface and drops down to a series of walls, arches and caves that are rife with stingrays, snappers, barracudas and parrotfish. Calmer waters more suitable for snorkelers and amateur divers can be found at another undersea mound, the Soufriere Pinnacle, which rises 160ft from the floor of the bay to within 5ft of the surface and offers a wide range of corals and fish.

**Champagne Reef** is where divers and snorkelers go to play in the volcanic bubbles that rise from the sea floor and make the shallow water look like a huge glass of champagne. **Irie Safari** ( ☎ 440-5085; iriesafari@cwdom.com; Pointe Michel) rents good snorkeling gear for around US$12

for the day; the dive center Nature Island Dive (opposite) is based in nearby Soufriere.

# DIRECTORY

## ACCOMMODATIONS

Dominica has only about 800 rooms available for visitors, mainly in small, locally run hotels and guesthouses along the west side of the island around Roseau and Morne Trois Pitons National Park, or near Portsmouth. Outside of Roseau, guesthouses and hotels are nearly identical in price and services. At many of the accommodations outside of bigger towns, off-property dining options are nonexistent – make sure you like the food and prices at your lodging's restaurant.

In 2006 Dominica introduced a value-added tax (VAT) of 10% for hotel rooms and 15% for most other items. Nearly all hotels and guest houses add the VAT and a minimum 10% service charge to bills.

See p815 for details on how accommodations price ranges are categorized in this book.

## ACTIVITIES

In response to the growing numbers of cruise-ship passengers, the government of Dominica has instituted user fees for all foreign visitors entering ecotourist sites. These include national parks and other protected areas.

The cost is US$2 per site, US$5 for a day pass or US$10 for a weekly pass, and the proceeds go to conservation efforts and maintenance of the park system. Passes are sold by car-rental agencies, tour operators, cruise-ship personnel and the forestry department, as well as at all of the major sites.

---

**HIDDEN GEMS**

Want more accommodation options? Try these spots.

**Rosalie Forest Eco Lodge** ( ☎ 616-1887; www.rosalieforest.com; Rosalie; dm US$22, r US$44/66) Jungle cabins, camping, village home stays and some real environmental cred on the east coast.

**Sister Sea Lodge** ( ☎ 445-5211; sangow@cwdom.dm; Picard Estate; s/d US$65/85) A little treasure at the end of leafy Lizard's Trail in Portsmouth.

**Crescent Moon Cabins** ( ☎ 449-3449; www.crescentmooncabins.com; Riviere la Croix; r US$156) People rave about this back-to-nature, remote place run by a Montessori teacher and professional chef.

**Silks** ( ☎ 445-8846; www.silks-hotel.com; Marigot; d US$200) A boutique hotel in a 17th-century-style mansion where 'worry' is a dirty word.

**DOMINICA**

## Beaches & Swimming

While Dominica doesn't have the sort of gorgeous strands that make it onto brochure covers, it's not without beaches. On the calmer and more popular west coast, they're predominantly gray-sand beaches.

The east coast has largely open seas with high surf and turbulent water conditions. There are a few pockets of golden sands just south of Calibishie that are sometimes calm enough for swimming and snorkeling, and there are a couple of roadside brown-sand beaches a bit further south.

## Cycling

Nature Island Dive in Soufriere (p596) rents mountain bikes and leads guided trips.

## Diving & Snorkeling

Dominica has superb diving. The island's rugged scenery continues under the water, where it forms sheer drop-offs, volcanic arches, pinnacles and caves.

Many of Dominica's top dive sites are in the Soufriere Bay area, a designated marine reserve (p597). Scotts Head Drop-Off, the Pinnacle and the Soufriere Pinnacle are favorite sites in the area. Also popular for snorkelers and beginners is Champagne Reef (p597), a subaquatic hot spring off Pointe Guignard, where crystal bubbles rise from underwater vents.

The north side of the island still has lots of unexplored territory. Popular sites north of Roseau include Castaways Reef, Grande Savane, Rodney's Rock, Toucari Bay and the wrecks of a barge and tugboat off Canefield.

There are dive shops in Rouseau (p587), Soufriere (p596), Scotts Head (p597), the Layou River area (p590) and Portsmouth (p590); see the appropriate section for listings. The going rate is about US$60 for a one-tank dive or a night dive and US$95 for a two-tank dive. Many dive centers offer beginners a resort course with an ocean dive for US$125. A number of the shops offer full PADI open water certification courses for around US$400.

In addition, most of the hotels with onsite dive outfits have one-week packages that include accommodations and multiple dives.

All the dive shops offer snorkeling tours or will take snorkelers out with divers. If you're tagging along with divers, make sure they're doing a shallow dive – staring down at a wreck 50ft under water isn't terribly interesting from the surface.

## Hiking

Dominica has some excellent hiking. Short walks lead to Emerald Pool (p593) and Trafalgar Falls (p594), two of the island's most visited sights. Cabrits National Park (p591) has a couple of short hikes. In the Northern Forest Reserve (p590), there's an easy hike through a parrot reserve and a rugged trail to the top of the island's highest mountain. The Morne Trois Pitons National Park (p595) offers serious treks into the wilderness, ranging from jaunts through verdant jungles to an all-day trek across a steaming volcanic valley that ends at a boiling lake.

The short hikes to the more popular destinations can generally be done on your own, but most wilderness treks require a guide who's familiar with the route.

Dominica's Forestry Division publishes brochures on many of the trails; each can be purchased for EC$1 or so at the forestry office in Roseau's botanical gardens (p585). There is a free Acrobat-format hiking guide on www.discoverdominica.com, the tourism office website.

## Kayaking

You can rent sea kayaks in Soufriere; see p596 for details.

---

### PRACTICALITIES

- **Newspapers** The *Chronicle* is the national newspaper.
- **Radio** Government-owned DBS radio station broadcasts on 88.1FM and 595AM.
- **Video Systems** NTSC is used on the island.
- **Electricity** 220/240V, 50 cycles. Outlets use a square three-prong plug; bring an adapter.
- **Weights & Measures** Dominica uses the imperial system.

## Whale-Watching

Operators in Portsmouth (p590) and Castle Comfort (p587) run whale-watching tours nearly every day (US$60) from October to August, but sightings are most common between November and March.

## BOOKS

*The Dominica Story – A History of the Island*, by Lennox Honychurch, the island's pre-eminent historian, is a must-read for those who really want to understand what makes Dominica what it is today. *In Search of Eden: Essays on Dominican History*, by Irving Andre and Gabriel Christian, provides a good introduction to Dominica's natural history.

## BUSINESS HOURS

Most businesses open from 8am to 4pm Monday to Friday with a lunch break from 1pm to 2pm. Banking hours are from 8am to 2pm Mondays to Thursdays, and 8am to 5pm on Fridays. On Saturdays, banks are closed but most shops open from 8am to 1pm.

## CHILDREN

For the most part, Dominica is a good place to travel with children. The medical care is good and the food is safe. Most adults have no problems with the tap water but young stomachs may be safer with bottled water, at least at first. Speaking of stomachs, being in the backseat on long drives on twisty mountain roads can be nauseating for the wee ones, and we'd suggest keeping the drives short.

## DANGERS & ANNOYANCES

The locals tend to drive much faster than tourists on the twisty, pot-holed roads and driving can be intense, though accidents are relatively rare.

Travelers have told us they've felt mildly taken advantage of with the confusing room tax and service charge situation. Some hotels include all taxes in their published rates, some include 10% VAT, while others include a 10% service charge and tack the VAT on afterwards. The best thing to do is ask before booking what the bill will look like with all taxes and service charges included.

## EMBASSIES & CONSULATES

**Belgium** ( ☎ 448-3012; 20 Hanover St, Roseau)
**China** ( ☎ 449-1385; dm.chineseembassy.org; Roseau)

**UK** ( ☎ 448-7655; c/o Courts Dominica Ltd, Castle Comfort)
**Venezuela** ( ☎ 448-3348; 20 Bath Rd, Roseau)

## FESTIVALS & EVENTS

**Carnival** Dominica's official celebrations are held on the two days prior to Ash Wednesday, but there are pre-Carnival events running from January. These include weekly competitions and parades: in the two weeks prior to Lent there are calypso competitions, a Carnival Queen contest, jump-ups and a costume parade.
**Independence Day/Reunion** The week leading up to Independence Day (November 3), or Creole Day, is packed with events. The vibrant celebration of local heritage includes parades, school kids in traditional outfits and special Creole menus. Live music is performed in restaurants, banks and grocery stores as well as on sidewalks all around Roseau. At major milestones (the 30th anniversary of independence is in 2008), Dominicans from all over the world return home.
**World Creole Music Festival** Music continues through the night at this music festival, usually held on the last weekend of October in Roseau. Big-name acts from the Caribbean rock on with African *soukous* (dance music), Louisiana zydeco and a wide variety of local bands and dance groups.

## GAY & LESBIAN TRAVELERS

It's a socially conservative country so some discretion is advised, but, hoteliers don't seem to care if two people of the same sex share a bed. Evangelical groups staged small protests in 2006 asking the government to ban gay cruise ships from stopping in Roseau, but the issue now seems to have gone away.

## HOLIDAYS

Public holidays on Dominica:
**New Year's Day** January 1
**Carnival Monday & Tuesday** Two days preceding Ash Wednesday
**Good Friday** Late March/early April
**Easter Monday** Late March/early April
**May Day** May 1
**Whit Monday** Eighth Monday after Easter
**August Monday** First Monday in August
**Independence Day/Creole Day** November 3
**Community Service Day** November 4
**Christmas Day** December 25
**Boxing Day** December 26

## INTERNET ACCESS

A few restaurants and hotels offer wi-fi, but hard-wired internet hookups are still much more prevalent. Internet cafés are only found

DOMINICA

in Roseau and Portsmouth, and usually charge EC$3 per half-hour.

## INTERNET RESOURCES

**Discover Dominica** (www.discoverdominica.com) Run by the government tourism bureau, it's a good site for information on what to see and do in Dominica, and where to stay.

**Dominica Academy of Arts & Sciences** (www.da-academy.org) Not easy to navigate but there's a load of information on Dominica's history and birdlife once you find it.

**Lennox Honychurch** (www.lennoxhonychurch.com) The place to go for Dominica history.

## MAPS

Free maps are available at most hotels and guesthouses, car-rental agencies and at the tourist office in Roseau.

## MEDICAL SERVICES

The Princess Margaret Hospital (with a hyperbaric chamber for decompression sickness) in Roseau, Marigot Hospital and the Portsmouth Hospital are the three main medical facilities. Intensive care units are available at Princess Margaret and Portsmouth hospitals. Several specialists and general practitioners operate private clinics.

## MONEY

Dominica uses the Eastern Caribbean dollar (EC$). At the time of writing, the bank exchange rate for US$1 was EC$2.68 for traveler's checks, EC$2.67 for cash. US dollars are widely accepted by shops, restaurants and taxi drivers, usually at an exchange rate of EC$2.60.

Most hotels, car-rental agencies, dive shops, tour operators and top-end restaurants accept MasterCard, Visa and, less often, American Express credit cards.

## POST

The main post office is in Roseau; there are small post offices in larger villages. The use of the word 'Commonwealth of Dominica' on mail is important to prevent mail being sent to the Dominican Republic by mistake.

## TELEPHONE

Dominica's country code is ☎ 767. To call from North America, dial ☎ 1-767 + the seven-digit local number. Elsewhere, dial your country's international access code, + ☎ 767 + the local number. Within Dominica you just need to dial the local number. We've included only the seven-digit local number in Dominica listings in this chapter.

For directory information dial ☎ 118; for international calls dial ☎ 0.

Dominica has coin and (more commonly) card phones. You can buy phone cards at telecommunications offices and convenience stores.

To see whether you can use your phone on the island's GSM networks, check with your cell service provider before you leave to see if it has a roaming agreement.

SIM cards for unlocked cell phones are available from Digicel at a number of convenience stores throughout Dominica. Rates are around EC$0.50 for outgoing calls. Incoming calls are free.

## TOURIST INFORMATION

There's a **tourist information booth** ( ☟ 6:15-11:30am & 2:15-6pm) at both airports and a **tourist office** ( ☎ 448-2045; www.discoverdominica.com; Roseau; ☟ 8am-5pm Mon, to 4pm Tue-Fri) in Roseau.

## TRAVELERS WITH DISABILITIES

Because of the mountainous landscape, most inland accommodations have steep stairs that might be hard to navigate. Some of the bigger hotels in Roseau, Castle Comfort and Portsmouth can make arrangements for disabled travelers.

## VISAS

Only citizens of former Eastern Bloc countries, China, India and Nigeria require visas.

## WOMEN TRAVELERS

Dominicans are for the most part courteous and respectful towards women. Of course, the rules of stranger danger and safety in numbers still apply.

---

**EMERGENCY NUMBERS**

- Ambulance ☎ 999
- Fire ☎ 999
- Police ☎ 999

## WORK

Foreigners who work here are often professionals who work for the government or own a hotel or restaurant. To legally work in Dominica you need a work permit from the **Ministry of Labour & Immigration** ( ☎ 448-2401; legalaffairs@cwdom.dm).

# TRANSPORTATION

## GETTING THERE & AWAY
### Entering Dominica

Most visitors to Dominica must have a valid passport; US citizens see the boxed text, p830. French nationals may visit for up to two weeks with an official Carte d'Indentité. A round-trip or onward ticket is – in principle – required of all visitors to the island.

### Air

There are no direct flights available from Europe or the US into Dominica, so overseas visitors must first get to a gateway island.

Dominica has two airports: **Canefield Airport** (DCF; ☎ 449-1990), just outside Roseau, and **Melville Hall Airport** (DOM; ☎ 445-7101; melvillehall airport@yahoo.com), on the secluded northeast side of the island. Both airports are lacking in facilities. Each has snack bar that may or may not be open. Immigration procedures tend to be slow.

On LIAT's printed schedule, the letters C and M after the departure time indicate which airport is being used. There's a **tourist information booth** ( ⌚ 6:15-11:30am & 2:15-6pm) at both airports, as well as a handful of car-rental firms.

The following airlines fly into and out of Dominica from within the Caribbean:
**American Eagle** ( ☎ 448-0628; www.aa.com) San Juan
**LIAT** ( ☎ 448-2421; www.liat.com; King George V St, Roseau) San Juan, Antigua, Barbados, St Lucia

### Sea

Roseau is a regular stop on the cruise ship circuit. There are ferries between Dominica and the nearby islands of St Lucia, Martinique and Guadeloupe. Portsmouth's Rupert Bay is the main sailboat and yacht mooring.

#### CRUISE SHIP

There are three cruise-ship docks in Dominica – one at Roseau, one just north of Roseau and one at Portsmouth – but the Roseau dock is far and away the most commonly used.

### FERRY

There are ferries to Guadeloupe, Martinique and St Lucia, all departing from Roseau.

**L'Express des Iles** ( ☎ 448-2181; www.express-des-iles .com; c/o Whitchurch Travel, Roseau) connects Dominica with both Pointe-à-Pitre in Guadeloupe (€67/100 one way/return, 2 hours, once daily Monday, Wednesday, Friday, Saturday and Sunday) and Fort-de-France in Martinique (€67/100 one way/return, 2 hours, once daily Monday, Wednesday, Friday, and Sunday) on modern catamarans. Both services do return trips on the same days. There's also a service to Castries in St Lucia (€67/100 one way/return, once daily Wednesday, Friday and Sunday).

These schedules change frequently; it's important to confirm departure times a couple of days in advance to avoid getting stranded on the island.

There are discounts of 50% for children aged under two; 10% for students and passengers under 12 years old; and 5% for passengers younger than 26 or older than 60.

**Brudey Frères** ( ☎ in Guadeloupe 590-590-90-04-48; www.brudey-freres.fr) in high season has a daily (except Friday) service at 9:30am between Dominica and Guadeloupe for €55/80 one way/round-trip.

The company has daily crossings, except Monday, to Fort de France, Martinique (one-way/round-trip €55/80).

Brudey also offers discounts for youths and elders. Schedules change, so check current timetables.

## GETTING AROUND
### Bus

There are buses between Roseau and Scotts Head, and between Roseau and Portsmouth, although the further north you go past Canefield the less frequent they become. Generally, they run from 6am to 6pm or a little later Monday to Friday, and until 2pm on Saturday. There aren't any services on Sunday. It's a cheap way to go, but is only advised for those with lots of time to spare.

### Car
#### DRIVER'S LICENSE

A local driver's license (US$12) is required, which can be picked up from immigration at either airport or at car-rental agencies any day of the week. Visiting drivers must be between the ages of 25 and 65, have a valid driver's license and at least two years of driving experience.

DOMINICA

**RENTAL**

**Avis** ( ☎ 448-2481) has daily rates beginning at US$48, while **Budget** ( ☎ 449-2080) has rates beginning around US$45. Both Avis and Budget car rentals are at Canefield Airport, but there are also car-rental agencies at Melville Hall Airport and elsewhere on the island. Those in Roseau include **Courtesy Car Rental** ( ☎ 448-7763; Goodwill Rd) and **Garraway Rent-A-Car** ( ☎ 448-2891). Also try **Valley Rent-A-Car** ( ☎ in Roseau 448-3233, in Portsmouth 445-5252).

Note that although most car rentals include unlimited mileage, a few local companies cap the number of free miles before a surcharge is added, so be sure to inquire in advance.

In addition to rental fees, most companies charge US$10 to US$15 a day for an optional collision damage waiver (CDW), though even with the CDW you may still be responsible for the first US$800 or so in damages. Some also charge around US$3 a day for additional drivers and an airport drop-off fee of US$20, even if that's where you picked up the car. A 15% VAT charge is also applied to the total bill.

A 4WD is recommended for exploring in the mountains – even some of the main roads at the higher altitudes are in bad condition. Most car-rental places offer 4WD vehicles starting at US$55 per day.

**ROAD CONDITIONS**

Road signs mark most towns and villages, and major intersections are clearly signposted. Very few roads have dividing lines and the first few days of driving it might feel like a head-on collision is always imminent.

Be careful of deep rain gutters that run along the side of many roads – a slip into one could easily bring any car to a grinding halt.

**ROAD RULES**

Dominicans drive on the left-hand side of the road. There are gas stations in larger towns around the island, including Canefield, Portsmouth and Marigot. The speed limit in Roseau and other towns is 20mph.

Honk the horn often around the blind curves. If causing a backup, the polite thing to do is pull over to the side of the road whenever it's safe to let traffic pass.

## Hitchhiking

Hitchhiking, alone or in a group, is always a risky proposition and is not advised. However, picking up hitchhikers, especially if there is only one of them and two or more of you, is a great way to meet locals and pick up good insider tips. Locals of either sex and of all ages hitchhike here.

# Martinique

Martinique is for (beach) lovers. And foodies. And divers. And hikers. And, especially, Francophiles. A marriage of Gallic culture and Caribbean customs, this overseas department of France is a sunnier, slightly less crowded version of the motherland.

People looking for the more sophisticated pleasures, whether they be the kind you put on your plate or the kind you put on a credit card, will be happy to know that good food and the latest fashions aren't optional here, but a mandatory fixture wherever visitors congregate.

Volcanic in origin, the island is crowned by the still-smoldering Mont Pelée, which wiped out Martinique's former capital of St-Pierre in 1902. There's plenty of hiking and nature-watching on the slopes of the volcano. And since this is often called the 'Isle of Flowers' there are botanical gardens tucked into the rugged landscape.

Long luscious beaches and loads of diving are the main attractions in the south. Fishing villages dot the coasts; most of them have managed to hang on their seafaring soul while offering plenty for visitors to see and do.

There's a lot going on here, but it all happens on Caribbean time. Except for the mountainous north, it's an exceptionally easy island to drive around. One can surf at Presqu'île de Caravelle in the morning and make it back to Fort-de-France in time (avoiding rush hour) to sample the city's budding nightlife.

## FAST FACTS

- **Area** 1080 sq km
- **Capital** Fort-de-France
- **Country code** ☎ 596
- **Departure tax** None
- **Famous for** Flowers, including hibiscus, frangipani and bougainvillea
- **Language** French, Creole
- **Money** euro (€); €1 = US$1.56 = UK£0.79
- **Official name** La Martinique
- **People** Martiniquans
- **Phrase** Un ti-punch s'il vous plait (One ti-punch, please); excusez-moi, savez-vous ou est…? (excuse me, do you know where… is?)
- **Population** 400,000
- **Visa** None required for residents of the US, UK, Canada, the EU, Australia and New Zealand; see p625

MARTINIQUE

## HIGHLIGHTS

■ **St-Pierre** (p613) See the devastation of Mont Pelée first-hand while the volcano broods in the distance

■ **Pointe du Bout** (p618) Take a sailboat tour in the redoubt of the sailing set – food and drink abound

■ **Les Salines** (p622) Stretch out on this beautiful long beach

■ **Ste-Luce** (p620) Drink and dive in this lively fishing village

■ **Presqu'île de Caravelle** (p616) Soak up the sun and sand by day, and gourmet flavors at night

## ITINERARIES

■ **Five Things You Really Should Try** Try to speak some French – even if you're reading straight from a phrasebook people will appreciate it. Go into a place where there are a lot of locals and order a ti-punch; on the other end of the spectrum, treat yourself to a great meal. You need to see Martinique from the water – on a ferry, sailboat or snorkeling trip – at least once. Finally, lie on the beach. Speedo-wearing grandpas abound here; beaches definitely aren't beauty contests.

■ **Village Life** Spend a day in a fishing village and get into the rhythm of an ancient way of life. Wake up before dawn and watch the fishermen preparing for the day, have a leisurely breakfast and then read on the beach while awaiting their return. Then, eat the day's catch for dinner!

## CLIMATE & WHEN TO GO

Martinique enjoys a year-round tropical climate though its busiest tourist period is during the dry season, from December to May, when temperatures average about 26°C (85°F). The rainy season begins in June and continues until the end of November, with heavy showers most days (September is the rainiest month and, along with August, is most prone to hurricanes). Martinique's average humidity is high, ranging from 80% in March and April to 87% in October and November. The mountainous northern interior is both cooler and rainier than the coast.

## HISTORY

When Christopher Columbus sighted Martinique, it was inhabited by Caribs, who called the island Madinina, which means 'Island of Flowers.' Three decades passed before the first party of French settlers, who were led by Pierre Belain d'Esnambuc, landed on the northwest side of the island. There they built a small fort and established a settlement that would become the capital city, St-Pierre. The next year, on October 31, 1636, King Louis XIII signed a decree authorizing the use of African slaves in the French West Indies.

The settlers quickly went about colonizing the land with the help of slave labor and by 1640 had extended their grip south to Fort-de-France, where they constructed a fort on the rise above the harbor. As forests were cleared to make room for sugar plantations, conflicts with the native Caribs escalated into warfare, and in 1660 those Caribs who had survived the fighting were finally forced off the island.

The British also took a keen interest in Martinique, invading and holding the island for most of the period from 1794 to 1815. The island prospered under British occupation; the planters simply sold their sugar in British markets rather than French markets. Perhaps more importantly, the occupation allowed Martinique to avoid the turmoil of the French Revolution. By the time the British returned the island to France in 1815, the Napoleonic Wars had ended and the French empire was again entering a period of stability.

Not long after the French administration was re-established on Martinique, the golden era of sugarcane began to wane, as glutted markets and the introduction of sugar beets on mainland France eroded prices. With their wealth diminished, the aristocratic plantation owners lost much of their political influence, and the abolitionist movement, led by Victor Schoelcher, gained momentum.

It was Schoelcher, the French cabinet minister responsible for overseas possessions, who convinced the provisional government to sign the 1848 Emancipation Proclamation, which brought an end to slavery in the French West Indies. Widely reviled by the white aristocracy of the time, Schoelcher is now regarded as one of Martinique's heroes.

On May 8, 1902, in the most devastating natural disaster in Caribbean history, the Mont Pelée volcano erupted violently, destroying the city of St-Pierre and claiming the lives of its 30,000 inhabitants. Shortly thereafter, the capital was moved permanently to Fort-de-France. St-Pierre, which had been regarded as the most cultured city in the

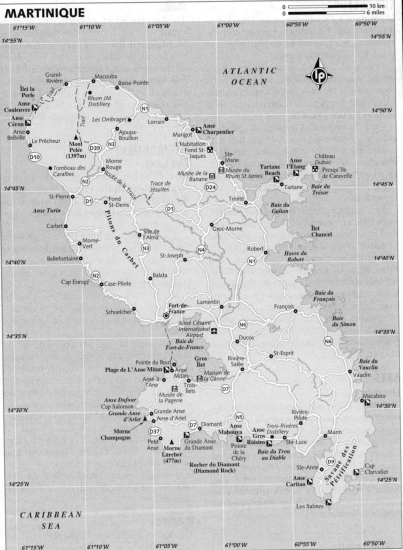

**MARTINIQUE**

French West Indies, was eventually rebuilt, but it has never been more than a shadow of its former self.

In 1946 Martinique became an Overseas Department of France, with a status similar to those of metropolitan departments. In 1974 it was further assimilated into the political fold as a Department of France.

In August 2007 Hurricane Dean pounded Martinique and entirely wiped out its banana crop. The hurricane caused damage estimated at $240 million, and also killed two people. Some of the hotels set on the island's plantations have shut their doors as a result and it's uncertain whether they'll reopen anytime soon.

MARTINIQUE

## THE CULTURE

Martinique's society combines French traditions with Caribbean Creole culture. Politeness is highly valued on Martinique, so brush up on your manners.

In general, always address people with the formal 'vous' rather than 'tu,' but know that if someone uses the more casual form of address first (which happens more often here than in France) it's fine to use tu.

Only the very nicest restaurants and clubs enforce a dress code; look for signs that read tenue correcte exigée (correct dress expected). Elsewhere, dress is casual but generally stylish; save beachwear for the beach. Topless bathing is common on the island, particularly at resort beaches.

Martinique's population is about 400,000, more than a quarter of whom live in the Fort-de-France area. The majority of residents are of mixed ethnic origin. The earliest settlers were from Normandy, Brittany, Paris and other parts of France; shortly afterward, African slaves were brought to the island. Later, smaller numbers of immigrants came from India, Syria and Lebanon. These days, Martinique is home to thousands of immigrants – some of them here illegally, from poorer Caribbean islands such as Dominica, St Lucia and Haiti.

## ARTS

### Literature

The Black Pride movement known as négritude emerged as a philosophical and literary movement in the 1930s largely through the writings of Martinique native Aimé Césaire, a poet who was eventually elected mayor of Fort-de-France. The movement advanced black social and cultural values and reestablished bonds with African traditions, which had been suppressed by French colonialism.

---

**HOW MUCH?**

- Taxi fare from the airport to Fort-de-France center €20

- One-tank diving trip €45

- Comfortable hotel double €80

- Sandwich €4

- Meal of fresh fish €12

---

### Music

The beguine, an Afro-French style of dance music with a bolero rhythm, originated in Martinique in the 1930s. A more contemporary French West Indies creation, zouk, draws on the beguine and other French-Caribbean folk forms. Retaining the electronic influences of its '80s origins, with its Carnival-like rhythm and hot dance beat, zouk has become as popular in Europe as it is in the French Caribbean.

## ENVIRONMENT
### The Land

At 1080 sq km, Martinique is the second-largest island in the French West Indies. Roughly 65km long and 20km wide, it has a terrain punctuated by hills, plateaus and mountains.

The highest point is the 1397m-high Mont Pelée, an active volcano at the northern end of the island. The center of the island is dominated by the Pitons du Carbet, a scenic mountain range reaching 1207m.

Martinique's irregular coastline is cut by deep bays and coves, while the mountainous rainforest in the interior feeds numerous rivers.

Martinique has lots of colorful flowering plants, with vegetation types varying with altitude and rainfall. Rainforests cover the slopes of the mountains in the northern interior, which are luxuriant with tree ferns, bamboo groves, climbing vines and hardwood trees like mahogany, rosewood, locust and gommier.

The drier southern part of the island has brushy savanna vegetation such as cacti, frangipani trees, balsam, logwood and acacia shrubs. Common landscape plantings include splashy bougainvillea, the ubiquitous red hibiscus and yellow-flowered allamanda trees.

### Wildlife

The underwater life tends to be of the smaller variety; lots of schools of small fish that swim by in a cloud of silver or red. There are a decent amount of lobsters hiking under rocks, and occasionally a ray will glide by.

Martinique has Anolis lizards, manicous (opossums), mongooses and venomous fer-de-lance snakes. The mongoose, which was introduced from India in the late 19th century, preys on eggs and has been responsible for the demise of many bird species. Some native birds, such as parrots, are no longer found on the island at all, while others have significantly declined in numbers. Endangered birds include the Martinique trembler, white-breasted trembler and white-breasted thrasher.

## FOOD & DRINK

Most restaurants serve either Creole or French food with an emphasis on local seafood. Red snapper, conch, crayfish and lobster are popular. The best value at many restaurants is the fixed-price menu, which is sometimes labeled *menu* – a three- or four-course meal that usually runs from €10 to €18, depending on the main course. Remember that this is France, so bring a good book or someone to talk to; it can take a couple of hours for all the courses to be served.

For more moderately priced meals there are a number of Italian restaurants and pizzerias on the island. Bakeries are good budget places to grab a quick meal, because most of them make sandwiches to go and some have a few café tables out front.

The island of Martinique grows much of its own produce, including some very sweet pineapples.

Water is safe to drink from the tap. In restaurants, if you ask for water you'll usually be served bottled water. There's no shame in asking for *une carafe d'eau* if you just want tap water.

The legal drinking age is 18. Lorraine is the tasty local beer, but island rums are far more popular. Martinique's de rigueur aperitif is ti-punch, a mixture of white rum, sugarcane juice and a squeeze of lime. Also popular is *planteur* punch, a mix of rum and fruit juice.

# FORT-DE-FRANCE

**pop 135,000**

Fort-de-France, the island capital, is the largest and most cosmopolitan city in the French West Indies. It's not exactly hopping at night, but there's a nice choice of hotels, eateries and places to grab a drink. Its harborfront setting with the Pitons du Carbet rising up beyond is a view best appreciated when approaching the city by ferry.

The narrow, busy streets here are lined with a mixture of ordinary offices, bargain-basement shops and crumbling early-20th-century buildings with wrought-iron balconies that wouldn't look out of place in New Orleans.

Give yourself a few hours to wander around and take in the handful of historic sites and museums the city has to offer. Most visitors tend to leave the capital by evening but those who do stay find that, even though one can take up the sights in a day, it's a nice city to spend some time in and it doesn't take long to get on friendly terms with the locals.

## ORIENTATION

La Savane, the city park, lines the eastern end of the harbor. Northwest of here you'll spot the spire of Cathédrale St-Louis, one of the city's most visible landmarks.

The main shopping street, Rue Victor Hugo, is lined with the boutiques that give shoppers a taste of Paris. It runs parallel to the waterfront.

The Pointe Simon area, on the southwestern edge of downtown, has emerged in recent years as the place to go for fun bars, clubs and restaurants.

### Maps

Institut Géographique National has a map of Martinique (€9.70), which is sold at the bookstore **Centrale Catholique** (57 Rue Blénac). The tourist office also has some city and country maps available, as do most hotels and car rental places.

## INFORMATION

### Bookstores

**Centrale Catholique** (57 Rue Blénac) Sells books in French about Martinique, and maps.

### Emergency

**Police** ( ☎ 17; Rue Victor Sévere)

### Internet Access

**Le Web Cyber Café** (4 Rue Blénac; per 15min €2; ☾ 11am-2am Mon-Fri, 6pm-2am Sat) A smoky but central 1st-floor bar.

### Medical Services

**Doctor hotline** ( ☎ 60-33-33) For after-hours service.
**Hôpital Pierre Zobda Quitman** ( ☎ 55-20-00) Located on the D13 on the northeast side of Fort-de-France near Lamentin.
**Pharmacie Glaudon** (cnr Rues de la Liberté & Antoine Siger)

## Money

Full-service banks can be found next door to Money Change Caraïbes on Rue Ernest Deproge and along Rue de la Liberté, opposite La Savane. Expect to pay a slightly higher commission at moneychangers due to later opening hours.

**Change Point** (Rue Victor Hugo; ⏲ 8am-5:30pm Mon-Fri, to 12:30pm Sat)

**Money Change Caraïbes** (4 Rue Ernest Deproge; ⏲ 7:30am-6pm Mon-Fri, 8am-12:30pm Sat)

## Post

**Main post office** (cnr Rues Antoine Siger & de la Liberté; ⏲ 7am-6pm Mon-Fri, to noon Sat) Head here to send faxes, buy phone cards and pick up poste restante mail.

## Telephone

Public card phones can be found at La Savane, opposite the post office and around the city.

## Tourist Information

**Tourist office** ( ☎ 60-27-73; www.tourismefdf.com; 76 Rue Lazare Carnot; ⏲ 8am-5pm Mon, Tue & Thu, to 12:30pm Wed & Fri) Has some useful brochures in English on activities and accommodations, and can arrange English-language walking or hiking tours (see p610). In peak season a tourist office kiosk is open on Rue Lamartine, near Cathédrale St-Louis.

## SIGHTS & ACTIVITIES
### Bibliothèque Schoelcher

Fort-de-France's most visible landmark, the **Bibliothèque Schoelcher** (Schoelcher Library; Rue de la Liberté; admission free; ⏲ 1-5:30pm Mon, 8:30am-5:30pm Tue-Thu, 8:30am-5pm Fri, 8:30am-noon Sat), is an elaborate, colorful building with a Byzantine dome. The work of architect Henri Pick, a contemporary of Gustave Eiffel, the library was built in Paris and displayed at the 1889 World Exposition. It was then dismantled, shipped in pieces to Fort-de-France and reassembled on this site. The ornate interior is interesting – the front section contains antique books, a series of changing exhibits on local architecture and history, and period furnishing, while the back is a functioning lending library.

### La Savane

Normally, this large central park sports grassy lawns, tall trees, clumps of bamboo, lots of benches and souvenir stalls, but it was undergoing a massive renovation at the time of writing. The plan is to turn the area into a cool, modern nexus of city life, including shopping and entertainment along a pedestrian-only mall.

Hopefully city planners will keep the **statue of Empress Josephine** holding a locket with a portrait of Napoleon. Years ago, the head was lopped off and red paint splashed over the body. The empress is not highly regarded by islanders, who believe she was directly responsible for convincing Napoleon to continue slavery in the French West Indies so that her family plantation in Trois-Îlets would not suffer.

### Fort St-Louis

Opposite the south side of La Savane is Fort St-Louis. The original fort, built in the Marshal Vauban style, dates from 1640, although most of the extensive fort that stands today is the result of subsequent additions. It is still an active military base and public tours were discontinued in September 2001, though there is some talk of restarting tours in the future.

### Cathédrale St-Louis

With its neo-Byzantine style and 57m steeple, the **Cathèdral St-Louis** (Rue Schoelcher) is one of the city's most distinguished landmarks. Built in 1895 by Henri Pick, a block northwest of La Savane, the church fronts a small square and is picturesquely framed by two royal palms. The spacious, elaborate interior is well worth a look.

### Musée Départemental d'Archéologie

For displays of Native American artifacts, including stone tools, ritual objects and pottery, head to this **archeological museum** (9 Rue de la Liberté; adult/child €3/1.50; ⏲ 1-5pm Mon, 8am-5pm Tue-Fri, 9am-noon Sat). It seems designed for children more than for adults. Dioramas of Carib villages are interesting for a minute or two but those who don't make it here aren't missing much – most signs are in French only.

### Palais de Justice

The Palais de Justice, a neoclassical courthouse built in 1906, is two blocks northeast of the cathedral and can only be viewed from the outside. The design resembles a French railroad station, as the plaque out front points out. The square fronting the courthouse has a statue of French abolitionist Victor Schoelcher.

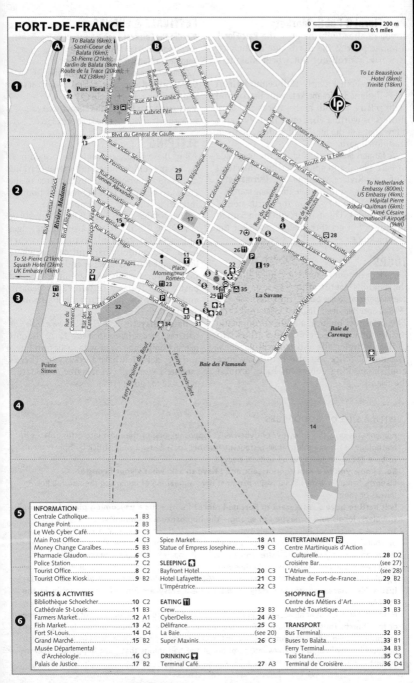

# FORT-DE-FRANCE

**INFORMATION**
Centrale Catholique...........................**1** B3
Change Point....................................**2** B3
Le Web Cyber Café............................**3** C3
Main Post Office...............................**4** C3
Money Change Caraïbes......................**5** B3
Pharmacie Glaudon............................**6** C3
Police Station...................................**7** C2
Tourist Office...................................**8** C2
Tourist Office Kiosk...........................**9** B2

**SIGHTS & ACTIVITIES**
Bibliothèque Schoelcher....................**10** C2
Cathédrale St-Louis..........................**11** B3
Farmers Market................................**12** A1
Fish Market.....................................**13** A2
Fort St-Louis...................................**14** D4
Grand Marché..................................**15** B2
Musée Départemental
  d'Archéologie................................**16** C3
Palais de Justice...............................**17** B2

Spice Market....................................**18** A1
Statue of Empress Josephine..............**19** C3

**SLEEPING**
Bayfront Hotel..................................**20** C3
Hotel Lafayette.................................**21** C3
L'Impératrice....................................**22** C3

**EATING**
Crew...............................................**23** B3
CyberDeliss......................................**24** A3
Délifrance........................................**25** C3
La Baie.........................................(see 20)
Super Maxinis...................................**26** C3

**DRINKING**
Terminal Café...................................**27** A3

**ENTERTAINMENT**
Centre Martiniquais d'Action
  Culturelle.....................................**28** D2
Croisiére Bar................................(see 27)
L'Atrium......................................(see 28)
Théatre de Fort-de-France..................**29** B2

**SHOPPING**
Centre des Métiers d'Art....................**30** B3
Marché Touristique...........................**31** B3

**TRANSPORT**
Bus Terminal....................................**32** B3
Buses to Balata................................**33** B1
Ferry Terminal.................................**34** B3
Taxi Stand.......................................**35** C3
Terminal de Croisière.........................**36** D4

## Parc Floral & Public Markets

If you're already in the area, the **Parc Floral**, a public park at the north side of the city, is worth a stroll but not worth making a special trip.

Fort-de-France's early-18th-century, Henri Pick–designed **spice market**, with its colorful stalls piled high with herbs, spices and local flowers, is worth a visit, even if only to grab a few snaps of the local stallholders, many in traditional garb.

A **farmers market** runs along the west side of Parc Floral and spills over into the street along the Rivière Madame. The **fish market** is a block to the south, while the **grand marché** – the best of the lot – is on the north side of Rue Isambert. The markets run from 5am to sundown, but get there before noon for the best pickings.

## TOURS

A variety of tours can be arranged through the island's **tourist office** ( ☎ 60-27-73; www.tourismefdf.com; 76 Rue Lazare Carnot; tours from €12; 🕙 8am-5pm Mon, Tue & Thu, to 12:30pm Wed & Fri). The offerings include a walk through the history of Fort-de-France and a bus trip to nearby waterfalls and tropical gardens. The tourist office can also help to arrange English-speaking guides for hikes around the island.

## FESTIVALS & EVENTS

**Mardi Gras Carnival** A spirited carnival during the five-day period leading up to Ash Wednesday.
**Semi-marathon** (www.sport-up.fr/semifortdefrance) A 22km marathon around the city in November.
**Guitar Festival** (www.cmac.asso.fr) A biennial festival held in December in even-numbered years.
**Martinique Jazz Festival** This biennial, week-long festival is held in December in odd-numbered years.

## SLEEPING

All of these hotels are centrally located near La Savane, unless noted otherwise. Parking can be near impossible, but this area of the city is so compact that the furthest point of interest is within a 10-minute walk.

**l'Impératrice** ( ☎ 63-06-82; 15 Rue de la Liberté; s/d from €60/80; 🔀 ) It's frayed around the edges but is still a good place to lay a weary head. The outdoor bar and café is where locals and tourists alike spend time watching the world go by over an anise-flavored pastis (€3). It has a certain ragged charm and all rooms have private bathrooms and phones.

**Hotel Lafayette** ( ☎ 73-80-50; www.lelafayettehotel.com; 5 Rue de la Liberté; r from €65; 🔀 🖳 ) Rooms here are simple and clean, with rustic furniture – and they definitely have a 1970s vibe. There's satellite TV and the wi-fi is free. Breakfast is available for guests (€7).

---

**WITH A SIDE OF GOOD VIBES**

François-Xavier is the co-owner of CyberDéliss (opposite), one of the most interesting places in Martinique. It's many things (bar, restaurant, internet spot), but we were struck by how it seems to be a gathering place for all sorts of people.

**So, I know you're a rum connoisseur and I have to ask: what's your favorite?**

Fleur de Canne St James. It's a white rum that does a great job of imparting the natural, flowery flavors of cane.

**Is it hard to have a restaurant in Fort-de-France? I notice it's a welcoming place for young travelers, locals and – maybe I'm wrong – the homosexual community.**

To have a restaurant here is a daily battle, and that's without taking into account that, on the one hand, the tourism market isn't really developed yet and, on the other, the rules for running a restaurant are very strict and restraining. But yes, our goal is to be a place of conviviality, a place where everyone can come 'live,' whether you're homosexual, young, a local, a professional.

**Speaking of the homosexual community in Martinique, what's the general mood? Besides just a few places, there definitely seems to be a scary amount of homophobia in the Caribbean.**

Homosexuality is not at all accepted in Martinique. It's barely tolerated because of the moralizing of the church. Thus, the majority of the population can't stand it. Homophobia is very real in Martinique, even from left-leaning politicians. You should read the web articles in *Têtu* [a French gay and lesbian magazine, www.tetu.com] about the bad things that have happened recently against homosexuals here.

**Le Beausèjour Hotel** ( ☎ 75-53-57; www.lebeause jour-hotel.com; 44 La Jambette; s/d €68/80; 🛜 ) Located a 10-minute drive east of the center of town. If being centrally located isn't so important, this is a great place to spend some time. The charming villa set in exotic gardens has its own restaurant and 12 rooms with TVs and private bathrooms. There are two disabled-access rooms.

**Bayfront Hotel** ( ☎ 55-55-55; bayfronthotel@yahoo .fr; 3 Rue de la Liberté; r from €85; 🛜 🖳 ) A new modern business hotel with all the mod cons one would expect. The 12 rooms here all have a Creole flair and some have nice water views.

# EATING & DRINKING

There are several cafés and restaurants opposite La Savane on Rue de la Liberté and in the Pointe Simon area.

Bakeries selling pastries and inexpensive sandwiches are scattered throughout the city. A few American fast-food chains have opened up – not the gourmet French experience but they're open at all hours in case of culinary emergency.

**Délifrance** ( ☎ 70-36-99; cnr Rues de la Liberté & Victor Hugo; sandwiches from €2.50; 😋 breakfast & lunch) This French chain serves standard but tasty enough sandwiches and quiche for lunch. The breakfast croissants are fresh from the oven. During lunch it's extremely busy with workers and cruise-ship visitors.

**Terminal Café** ( ☎ 63-03-48; 104 Rue Ernest Deproge; drinks €3-10; 😋 7pm-midnight) Has a big range of European (mainly Belgium and German) beers and a good selection of spirits and specialty drinks. The 'punch decouverte' is a sampler of rum punches in four flavors (€7), a good introduction to rum punches on the island.

**Super Maxinis** (cnr Rues de la Liberté & Perrinon; mains €4-9; 😋 breakfast & lunch) A cheerful, always busy café for decent daytime sandwiches salads or a midday ice cream.

**Crew** ( ☎ 74-04-14; 44 Rue Ernest Deproge; mains €10-19; 😋 breakfast, lunch & dinner Mon-Fri, lunch Sat) With full menus in English and French, this nautical-themed place looks like an old-fashioned harbor diner but the food is fine dining. The *salade du crew*, with foie gras on toast and roasted duck on a bed of lettuce, is scrumptious. A long list of French favorites and a rainbow of Creole standards are on offer here and there's a bar that's lively in the early evening.

**La Baie** ( ☎ 42-20-38; Rue de la Liberté; mains €10-22; 😋 lunch & dinner Mon-Fri, lunch Sat & Sun) This is a friendly place run by a native from Brittany. Try the *galettes* – savory crêpes made with buckwheat flour – the *forestièr* has ham, cream, mushrooms and tomatoes inside and comes with a salad. There's a good selection of white and aged rums, whiskies, wines and cognacs.

**CyberDéliss** ( ☎ 78-71-43; 113 rue Ernest Deproge; mains from €12; 😋 7am-10pm Mon-Sat) This full-fledged internet café (€5 per hour) is also a hip French restaurant that serves good, modern cuisine or inventive twists on Creole favorites. It's also a bar-café and the owners love to talk (in English) about and serve their favorite island rums.

# ENTERTAINMENT

Fort-de France's nightlife is fairly tame, but warms up surprisingly late in the evening in the Pointe Simon area.

## Cinemas

**Centre Martiniquais d'Action Culturelle** (CMAC; ☎ 70-79-39; www.cmac.asso.fr; 6 Rue Jacques Cazotte; adult/child €15/12) This cultural center runs an interesting program of indie films and documentaries.

## Theatre

Throughout the year CMAC (above) hosts theatrical shows in its state-of-the-art auditoriums.

**Théâtre de Fort-de-France** ( ☎ 59-43-29; Rue Victor Sévere; adult/child €15/9) Offers a program of traditional French drama, dance and mime for adults and children.

## Live Music

A handful of piano-bars offer live zouk, jazz and French music; you can pick up fliers at the tourist office or in hotel foyers, or check out the listings site **Martinique Scoop** (www.martini quescoop.com).

**L'Atrium** ( ☎ 70-79-39; www.atrium.mq; CMAC, 6 Rue Jacques Cazotte) Based at the CMAC, this relatively new cultural center hosts an impressive range of classical, jazz, opera and world-music concerts in its year-round program. Music, as they say, is the universal language.

**Croisière Bar** (cnr Rues Ernest Deproge & Isambert; 😋 lunch & dinner Mon-Sat) This spacious restaurant and bar has a live band in the evenings. It's easy enough to hear from street level what's playing at the top of the stairs.

## SHOPPING

The busy streets of downtown Fort-de-France are crammed with shops selling all manner of trinkets, clothing, jewelry and perfumes.

The main boutique area is along Rue Victor Hugo, particularly from Rue de la République to Rue de la Liberté.

There's an artisan market at **Centre des Métiers d'Art** (Rue Ernest Deproge) that has an okay selection of regional handicrafts for sale. Nearby is the **Marché Touristique** (Rue Ernest Deproge) a big indoor space packed with every type of souvenir, including madras dresses, T-shirts, wood carvings and beach towels adorned with Bob Marley's face.

## GETTING AROUND
### To/From the Airport

The Martinique Aimé Césaire International Airport is just a 15-minute drive from Fort-de-France. The traffic crawls during peak times (from 7am to 10am and 4pm to 7pm), so leave yourself an extra couple of hours if catching a flight. Taxis are readily available at the airport (about €20 to Fort-de-France). If you need to refuel a rental car, head for one of the 24-hour gas stations on the N5 near the airport.

Because of the taxi union, there's no direct bus service from the airport.

### Boat

There are boats from Fort-de-France to Trois-Îlets and Pointe du Bout; see p626 for details.

The ferries dock at the quay fronting the minibus parking lot. Be sure to verify you're on the right boat before it leaves as they are not clearly marked.

### Bus

The spiffy new 'Bus Mozaïk' company transports passengers around the city and to the suburbs in air-conditioned comfort. Fares start at €1.20, and there are well-marked bus stops around town. The main bus terminal is at Pointe Simon and buses to Balata leave from Parc Floral.

### Car

Parking in the city is not a problem on weekends and holidays, but is quite a challenge on weekdays. There's a parking lot along the north side of La Savane that's entered at the intersection of Ave des Caraïbes and Rue de la Liberté; it costs €1.50 per hour. Streetside parking is free in the evenings, on Sunday and on holidays.

### Taxi

There are often taxis prowling Rue Deproge looking for customers. There are also taxi stands at Terminal de Croisière and at Rue del la Liberte. Fares are metered (from La Savane to the spice market costs about €10).

# NORTHERN MARTINIQUE

Several roads head north from Fort-de-France. The most interesting sightseeing routes are the coastal road (N2) to St-Pierre and the Route de la Trace (N3), a truly scenic road that crosses the mountainous interior before hitting Morne Rouge and veering toward the northeast coast. The two routes can be combined to make a fine loop drive; if doing the whole loop, give yourself a full day.

## FORT-DE-FRANCE TO ST-PIERRE

The N2 north to St-Pierre passes along dry, scrubby terrain and goes through a line of small towns – a merging of modern suburbia and old fishing villages. If you were to drive without stopping, it would take about 45 minutes to make the 21km trip to St-Pierre from Fort-de-France.

It's worth swinging off the highway at **Case-Pilote** to take a peek at the old village center. There's good diving nearby; for more information, see p623. Turn west off the N2 at the Total gas station and you'll immediately come to a quaint stone church, one of Martinique's oldest. Just 75m south is a charming town square with a water fountain, a historic town hall, a tourist office and a moderately priced café.

Further north, the pretty town of **Carbet**, where Columbus briefly came ashore in 1502, fronts a long sandy beach and has a few tourist amenities, including a bunch of restaurants and a scenic garden.

**Anse Turin**, a long gray-sand beach that attracts a crowd on weekends, is along the highway 1.5km north of Carbet. Opposite the beach is the **Musée Paul Gauguin** ( ☎ 78-22-56; admission €4; ☼ 9am-5:30pm), marked by a few inconspicuous signs. More of an homage to the artist than a proper museum, it has Gauguin memorabilia, letters from the artist to his wife and reproductions of Gauguin's paintings – including *Bord de Mer I* and *l'Anse Turin – Avec les Raisiniers,* which were both painted on the nearby beach during Gauguin's five-month stay on Martinique in 1887.

Just north of the Gauguin museum is the driveway up to **Le Jardin des Papillons** (☎ 78-33-39; adult/child €4.60/2.30; ⏰ 9am-noon), where the scattered stone ruins of one of the island's earliest plantations have been enhanced with gardens and a butterfly farm. There's a restaurant on site and a small music museum called **Jardin Musical** (⏰ 1:30-4:30pm), where children can play on larger-than-life musical instruments in an old church. If lucky, visitors will see Bambouman, an accomplished musician who makes all of his own instruments out of bamboo and occasionally does shows and demonstrations here.

## ST-PIERRE
### pop 5000
St-Pierre is on the coast 7km south of Mont Pelée, the still-active volcano that destroyed the town in just 10 minutes at the beginning of the 20th century. This former capital of Martinique is an interesting town to wander in. There are numerous blackened ruins throughout St-Pierre, some of which are little more than foundations, while others are partially intact. Many of the surviving stone walls have been incorporated into the town's reconstruction. Even 'newer' buildings have a period character, with shuttered doors and wrought-iron balconies.

The center of town is long and narrow, with two parallel one-way streets running its length. All of the major sights have signs in French and English, and you can explore the area thoroughly in a few hours.

The central gathering spot is the waterfront town park, next to the covered market. A beach of soft dark gray sand fronts the town and extends to the south. There are sail boats and fishing boats in the harbor, and the sunsets here are postcard-perfect.

On the way out of town, notice the murals that commemorate the end of slavery.

## Sights & Activities
### MUSÉE VOLCANOLOGIQUE
This small but very interesting **museum** (Musée de Frank Perret; Rue Victor Hugo; admission €2.50; ⏰ 9am-

5pm), founded in 1932 by American adventurer and volcanologist Frank Perret, gives a glimpse of the devastating 1902 eruption of Mont Pelée. On display are items plucked from the rubble and historic photos of the town before and immediately after the eruption. The displays are in English and French. Maps of the city are handed out on request.

There's free parking adjacent to the museum, which occupies the site of an old hillside gun battery. The view from the old stone walls along the parking lot provides a good perspective of the harbor and city, and you can look straight down, to the left, on a line of ruins on the street below.

Just 1.5km north of town, the earth-science museum **Centre de Découverte des Sciences de la Terre** (☎ 52-82-42; www.cdst.org; adult/child €5/3; ⏰ 9am-4:30pm Tue-Sun) looks like a big white box set on top of some columns, and the parking lot is made entirely of grass. Inside is a permanent exhibit on Mont Pelée, in French, but there's a neat contraption that shows stereoscopic black-and-white period photos of the volcano's aftermath. Documentaries are screened all day long, but the one to watch is *Volcans des Antilles,* subtitled in English and shown at 10:30am, 1pm and 3:30pm, which recounts Pelée's tantrum and its dire consequences.

### RUINS
St-Pierre's most impressive ruins are those of the old 18th-century **theater**, just 100m north of the museum. While most of the theater was destroyed, enough remains to give a sense of the former grandeur of this building, which once seated 800 and hosted theater troupes from mainland France. A double set of stairs still leads up to the partial walls of the lower story.

On the northeast side of the theater you can go into the tiny, thick-walled **jail cell** that housed Cyparis, one of the town's only survivors (for more on the convict's amazing good fortune, see the boxed text, p614).

Another area rich in ruins is the **Quartier du Figuier**, along Rue Bouillé, directly below the volcanology museum. Two sets of steps, one just north of the theater and the other just south of the museum, connect Rue Victor Hugo with the bay-front Rue Bouillé.

### DIVING
**Tropicasub** (☎ 24-24-30; www.tropicasub.com; one-tank dive €45) offers a vast range of wreck dives (a

**MARTINIQUE**

---

### THE ERUPTION OF MONT PELÉE

At the end of the 19th century, St-Pierre – then the capital of Martinique – was a flourishing port city. It was so cosmopolitan that it was dubbed the 'Little Paris of the West Indies.' Mont Pelée, the island's highest mountain, provided a scenic backdrop to the city.

In the spring of 1902, sulfurous steam vents on Mont Pelée began emitting gases, and a crater lake started to fill with boiling water. Authorities dismissed it all as the normal cycle of the volcano, which had experienced harmless periods of activity in the past.

But on April 25 the volcano spewed a shower of ash onto St-Pierre. Some anxious residents sent their children to stay with relatives on other parts of the island. The governor of Martinique, hoping to allay fears, brought his family to St-Pierre.

At 8am on Sunday May 8, 1902, Mont Pelée exploded into a glowing burst of superheated gas and burning ash, with a force 40 times stronger than the later nuclear blast over Hiroshima. Between the suffocating gases and the fiery inferno, St-Pierre was laid to waste within minutes.

Of the city's 30,000 inhabitants, there were only three survivors. One of them, a prisoner named Cyparis, escaped with only minor burns – ironically, he owed his life to having been locked in a tomblike solitary-confinement cell at the local jail. Following the commutation of his prison sentence by the new governor, Cyparis joined the PT Barnum circus where he toured as a sideshow act.

Pelée continued to smolder for months, but by 1904, people began to resettle the town, building among the crumbled ruins.

---

number of ships sank in the 1902 eruption), canyon dives and trips to Îlet la Perle (right).

### Sleeping & Eating

**Les Maisonnettes du Volcan** ( ☎ 78-19-30; r.reynal@ maisonnettes.com; bungalow per week €520/630) These two bungalows, set 2km north of downtown St-Pierre in the middle of a wooded field, are made to sleep five people. This is a good place for people who want to spend time exploring the nearby volcano. Each bungalow has a washing machine, a TV and a kitchen.

**Chez-Marie Claire** ( ☎ 78-21-56; mains €10-15; ☼ breakfast & lunch Mon-Sat) This restaurant is set at the top of some steps inside the covered market. Diners can look down on the bustle below while eating Creole dishes such as stewed beef and freshwater crayfish. It's a friendly place, and the cook often comes by to make sure that guests enjoyed their meal.

**Le Guerin** ( ☎ 78-18-07; mains €13-17; ☼ lunch Mon-Sat) Also inside the covered market. There can be a wait during the lunch rush, but with some of the best *accra* (deep-fried balls of dough filled with fish or shrimp) on the island, the wait is worth it.

You will find an 8 à Huit grocery store in the center of town, a bakery south of the cathedral and a few small sandwich and pizza places scattered around.

## ST-PIERRE TO ANSE CÉRON

From St-Pierre, the N2 turns inland but the D10 continues north for 13km along the coast and makes a scenic side drive, ending in 20 minutes at a remote beach. The shoreline is rocky for much of the way and the landscape is lush, with roadside clumps of bamboo.

The limestone cliffs 4km north of St-Pierre, called **Tombeau des Caraïbes**, are said to be the place where the last Caribs jumped to their deaths rather than succumb to capture by the French.

The road ends at **Anse Céron**, a nice black-sand beach backed by the thick jungle rolling off the base of Mont Pelée. Anse Céron faces **Îlet la Perle**, a rounded offshore rock off the northwest coast. It's a popular dive site that's famous for its colorful, coral-covered walls, and it's a good place to see groupers, eels and lobsters when water conditions aren't too rough. The Anse Céron beach can get crowded, but it does have a shower, toilets, picnic tables and a snack shop.

A very steep one-lane route continues for 1.6km beyond the beach. This is the start of a six-hour, 20km **hike** around the undeveloped northern tip of the island to Grand-Rivière; see opposite for details.

## ROUTE DE LA TRACE

The Route de la Trace (N3) winds up into the mountains north from Fort-de-France. It's a beautiful drive through a lush rainforest of tall tree ferns, anthurium-covered hillsides and thick clumps of roadside bamboo. The road passes along the eastern flanks of the pointed volcanic mountain peaks of the Pitons du Carbet. Several well-marked hiking trails lead from the Route de la Trace into the rainforest and up to the peaks.

The road follows a route cut by the Jesuits in the 17th century; islanders like to say that the Jesuits' fondness for rum accounts for the twisting nature of the road.

Less than a 10-minute drive north of Fort-de-France you'll reach **Sacré-Coeur de Balata**, a scaled-down replica of the Sacré-Coeur Basilica in Paris. This domed church, in the Roman-Byzantine style, has a stunning hilltop setting – the Pitons du Carbet rise up as a backdrop and there's a view across Fort-de-France to Pointe du Bout below.

The **Jardin de Balata** ( ☎ 64-48-73; www.jardindebalata.fr; adult/child €6.20/2.30; ☺ 9am-5pm), on the west side of the road 10 minutes' drive north of the Balata church, is a mature botanical garden in a rainforest setting. If a visitor was only going to make one day trip, this should be it. This attractive garden takes about 30 to 45 minutes to stroll through and is a great place to photograph flowers and hummingbirds. There's also a path to a waterfall that spills into a bathing pool. It's common to see groups of vacationers splashing away; go on in, the water's fine.

After the garden, the N3 winds up into the mountains and reaches an elevation of 600m before dropping down to **Site de l'Alma**, where a river runs through a lush gorge. There are riverside picnic tables, trinket sellers and a couple of short trails into the rainforest.

Some 4km later, the N3 is intersected by the D1, which used to be a very scenic drive and the gateway to a popular hike, but at the time of research was closed. Locals give differing stories as to why (one amusing tale has a road worker accidentally bringing down the whole side of a mountain on the road).

Continuing north on the N3, the Route de la Trace passes banana plantations and flower nurseries before reaching a T-junction at **Morne Rouge**, which was partially destroyed by an eruption from Mont Pelée in August 1902, several months after the eruption that wiped out St-Pierre. At 450m, it has the highest elevation of any town on Martinique, and it enjoys some nice mountain scenery.

About 2km north of the T-junction, a road (D39) signposted to Aileron leads 3km up the slopes of Mont Pelée, from where there's a rugged trail (four hours round trip) up the volcano's south face to the summit.

## BASSE-POINTE & AROUND
As the N3 nears the Atlantic it meets the N1, which runs along the coast both north and south. The northern segment of the road edges the eastern slopes of Mont Pelée and passes through banana and pineapple plantations before reaching the uninspiring coastal town of Basse-Pointe, birthplace of *négritude* poet and early Black Power founder Aimé Césaire.

## GRAND-RIVIÉRE
### pop 840
From Basse-Pointe, there's an enjoyable 35-minute drive to Grand-Rivière along a winding, but good, paved road. En route you will go through the coastal village of Macouba (where there is the well-signed **Rhum JM distillery**), pass two trails leading up the northern flank of Mont Pelée, cross a couple of one-lane bridges and finally wind down into the town. Be sure to watch out for red lights and road signs, there are a few one-way-only stretches of rural road regulated by a traffic signal.

Grand-Rivière is an unspoiled fishing village scenically tucked beneath coastal cliffs at the northern tip of Martinique. Mont Pelée forms a rugged backdrop to the south, while there's a fine view of neighboring Dominica to the north. People for the most part are very warm, and the old men hanging out their windows seem to appreciate a friendly wave from visitors. Things seem to happen very slowly here at the end of world, so don't be in a hurry.

The road dead-ends at the sea where there's a fish market and rows of bright fishing boats lined up on a little black-sand beach. The waters on the west side of town are sometimes good for surfing. The **Syndicat d'Initiative** ( ☎ 55-72-74; www.grand-riviere.com) in the town center has local tourist information. Besides organizing hikes that range from 10km to 18km and take at least four hours, it also offers sea, canyoning and culinary excursions.

While there's no road around the tip of the island, there is a 20km **hiking** trail leading to Anse Couleuvre, on the northwest coast. The trailhead begins on the road opposite the quaint two-story *mairie* (town hall), just up from the beach. It's a moderately difficult walk so you might want to take one of the guided hikes organized by the Syndicat D'Initiative. Hikers arrive in Anse Couleuvre about five hours after leaving the town hall, and then return to Grand-Rivière by boat. The Syndicat D'Initiative is also a great source of information on the two trails that climb the north face of Mont Pelée, just outside the town.

The name of **Le Bout du Bout** (mains €5-10), a humble café, means 'the end of the end' and they're not lying because the N1 really does stop a few meters from here. It seems to be a rite of passage for French tourists to stop here for a Corsaire beer or one of the proprietor's fresh banana juices. If you drive past Le Bout du Bout, you'll have to back out, as the road just ends. Don't be too embarrassed; it happens a few times every hour.

On the outskirts of town near the river, people travel far and wide to **Yva Chez Vava** ( ☎ 55-72-72; meals €12-30; ☻ lunch) for large helpings of seafood and Antillaise specials, so it's best to book ahead.

On a side street just north of the Syndicat d'Initiative, the Creole restaurant **Chez Tante Arlette** ( ☎ 55-75-75; carinetantearlette@wanadoo.fr; 3 Rue Lucy de Fossarieu; mains €12-19; ☻ noon-9pm; ☒ ) is renowned for its seafood and lobster. There are three sleeping rooms upstairs (room including breakfast €60) and various packages are on offer starting at €75 per person – a weekend of hiking, romance or fine dining.

## BASSE-POINTE TO PRESQU'ÎLE DE CARAVELLE

The highway (N1) from Basse-Pointe to Lamentin runs along relatively tame terrain and is not one of the island's most interesting drives, although there are a few worthwhile sights. The communities along the way are largely modern towns that become increasingly more suburban as you continue south.

Some 2km from Ste-Marie lies **l'Habitation Fond St-Jacques** ( ☎ 69-10-12; admission €3; ☻ 9am-4pm), the site of an old Dominican monastery and sugar plantation dating from 1660. One of the early plantation managers, Father Jean-Baptiste Labat, created a type of boiler (the *père labat*) that modernized the distilling of rum. It's an impressive site and wandering the ruins feels like wandering the heart of an old European village. The site is 150m inland from the N1. Look for road signs to 'Fond St-Jacques.' Parking is on the street.

The **Musée du Rhum St James** ( ☎ 69-30-02; admission free, train tour €3; ☻ 9am-5pm Mon-Fri, to 1pm Sat & Sun), is set in a beautiful colonial home on the site of St James plantation's working distillery. Some of the signs are in English, and the numbered photos on the ground level are a nice overview of how sugar cane becomes rum. There's an occasional train tour of the distillery and the cane-laden estate, but it only runs if there are enough interested visitors, so the hours are sporadic. In the tasting room you can sample different rums; locals say this is the place to try some of the best rums Martinique has to offer. The plantation is on the D24, 200m west of the N1, on the southern outskirts of Ste-Marie.

The D24 road continues to twist in a general southwesterly direction to the **Musée de la Banane** ( ☎ 69-45-52; www.lemuseedelabanane.com; admission €7.50; ☻ 9am-5pm Mon-Sat, to 1pm Sun), dedicated to all things banana. Set on a terraced plantation, it's a pretty place but for what it is the entry fee seems steep. For those who go ape over the yellow fruit, it may be worth it – there's a banana cake and banana juice tasting at tour's end.

The N1 continues on south through cane fields and passes the Presqu'île de Caravelle.

## PRESQU'ÎLE DE CARAVELLE

A tour of the peninsula is well worth the time for the wild landscape and authentic fishing villages. A gently twisting road leads through lush scenery with spectacular views through sugarcane fields to the peninsula's main village, Tartane, and then on to Baie du Galion. On the north side of the peninsula are a couple of protected beaches – the long, sandy **Tartane beach** fronts the village and, one of the island's nicest, the gently shelving, palm-fringed beach of **Anse l'Étang**, which is a good, uncrowded place to surf.

Tartane beach, the larger of the two strands, has lots of fishing shacks, a fish market and colorful *gommier* boats; both places have plenty of beachside restaurants. There's an ATM across from the gas station in Tartane.

### Sights & Activities

Set on the tip of the peninsula is **Château Dubuc** (adult/child €3/1; ☻ 8am-6pm), the deteriorated ruins of a 17th-century estate. These sprawling grounds have some of the most extensive plantation ruins in Martinique and there's a very small museum. The master of the estate gained notoriety by using a lantern to lure ships into wrecking off the coast, and then gathering the loot. Several hiking trails start at the parking lot, including a 30-minute walk to the site of a historic lighthouse and stellar views.

Besides offering group or private surf lessons for people of all ages and experience levels on the nearby beach, **Ecole de Surf Bliss** ( ☎ 58-00-96; www.surfmartinique.com; btwn Anse l'Étang & Château Dubuc; private lesson per hr €40; ☺ 9am-5:30pm Fri-Wed) also rents surf and body boards. English is spoken.

## Sleeping

**Hotel Le Manguier** ( ☎ 58-48-95; www.hotellemanguier .com; r from €74; ✖ ) The hotel is perched high above the athletic grounds in the center of Tartane. The rooms are small and basic, with outdoor hot-plate kitchens, but they all have little balconies that face the Atlantic Ocean. A fresh coat of paint would make this place sparkle but, as is, its a good choice for those who prefer a stiff uphill walk from the village center over driving.

**Hotel Restaurant Caravelle** ( ☎ 58-07-32; www .hotel-la-caravelle-martinique.com; Route du Château Dubuc; r from €84; ✖ ) On the eastern outskirts of Tartane, this is a small, friendly hotel. Steps leading down to the fabulous Anse l'Étang were under construction when we visited. There is a hibiscus-covered, decked terrace with glorious views to the Atlantic. The simple studios all have colorful furnishings and well-equipped kitchenettes on a spacious front porch with great views.

**Residence Oceane Hotel** ( ☎ 58-73-73; www.residence oceane.com; Anse l'Etang, Route du Château Dubuc; r from €89); ✖ ) On the way to Château Dubuc, this hotel is a beauty with stunning ocean views. It's within walking distance of Ecole de Surf Bliss and the beach. Rooms are only cleaned every three days (daily cleaning €7).

## Eating

**Le Kalicoucou** (Route du Château Dubuc; pizza €8-15; ☺ lunch & dinner) On the eastern end of the main strip in Tartane, this is the place for pizza and beer – or, because of the French influence, wine. It also offers big salads (€8) and savory crepes (€4 to €7) as well as thin-crust, crispy pizzas that come with a kaleidoscope of toppings. Choose from delivery, take-away and eat-in options.

**Restaurant La Tartanaise** ( ☎ 58-54-87; Route du Château Dubuc; mains €11-17; ☺ breakfast, lunch & dinner Wed-Mon) Right on the seafront, the *accra* here has succulent little chunks of shrimp inside, and this is where many of the locals go for a ti-punch at day's end.

**La Table de Mamy Nounou** (lunch mains €12-24; ☺ lunch & dinner) Set in the Hotel Restaurant Caravelle, the fabulous restaurant features excellent seafood, grills and mouthwatering desserts. You order and take your appetizers in the lounge, and will be shown to your table when the meal is ready – you never feel like you're waiting. The duck cutlets and the steak in a Roquefort sauce are two dishes that are heartily recommended.

## TRINITÉ
pop 15,000

Trinité, 4.6km southwest of the village of Tartane, has some services that Presqu'île de Caravelle lacks. There's a few full-service banks and clothing stores along the main strip, and **Cyber Nésis** (35 Rue Victor Hugo; per hr €5; ☺ 9am-12:30pm & 2-7pm Mon-Fri, 9am-4pm Sat) is a decent internet café and computer store.

Between Trinité and the next town northwest, Ste-Marie, **Match Supermarket** ( ☎ 69-03-09; ☺ 8am-8pm Mon-Sat, 8am-noon Sun) is good for stocking up on groceries.

# SOUTHERN MARTINIQUE

Martinique's south has many of the island's best beaches and most of its hotels, and is definitely the center of gravity for tourism. The healthy competition between numerous hotels gives travelers more bang for their money. Sun worshippers should head straight to Ste-Anne's beaches – probably the best on the island – and those who want a central southern location should consider Ste-Luce, which is also a good spot for diving and has a few passable beaches.

The largest concentration of places to stay is in the greater Trois-Îlets area, which encompasses the uberresort of Pointe du Bout and the smaller, more authentic villages of Grande Anse and Anse d'Arlet. Other major resort areas are Diamant and Ste-Anne.

MARTINIQUE

The interior of the island's southern half is largely a mix of agricultural land and residential areas. Lamentin, the site of the international airport, is Martinique's second-largest city but, like other interior cities and towns, has little of interest to tourists.

# TROIS-ÎLETS
pop 3100

This small working town has a central square that's bordered by a little market, a quaint town hall and the church where Empress Josephine was baptized in 1763. Despite its proximity to the island's busiest resort area, the town has avoided developers' attention so far, though its charm has been tarnished by a constant flow of traffic through its main street.

A former sugar estate outside Trois-Îlets was the birthplace of the Empress Josephine. A picturesque stone building, formerly the family kitchen, has been turned into the **Musée de la Pagerie** ( ☎ 68-33-06; adult/child €5/1.50; 🕑 9am-5:30pm Tue-Fri, 9:30am-12:30pm Sat & Sun, closed Dec), containing the empress' childhood bed and other memorabilia. Multilingual tour guides relate anecdotal tidbits about Josephine's life, such as the doctoring of the marriage certificate to make the bride, Napoleon's elder by six years, appear to be the same age as her spouse. The road leading up to the museum, 3km west of Trois-Îlets on the D7, begins opposite the golf-course entrance. You can poke around in the photogenic ruins of the old mill opposite the museum for free.

The worthwhile **Maison de la Canne** (Sugarcane Museum; ☎ 68-32-04; adult/child aged 5-12 €3/0.75; 🕑 8:30am-5:30pm Tue-Sun) occupies the site of an old sugar refinery and distillery. Inside the main museum building are period photos and items such as the Code Noir (Black Code) outlining appropriate conduct between slaves and their owners. Displays are in French and English. The museum is on the D7, 3.5km east of Trois-Îlets' center.

There's a ferry between Fort-de-France and Trois-Îlets; see p626 for details.

# POINTE DU BOUT
pop 3000

Pointe du Bout, Martinique's most developed resort at the southern end of the Baie de Fort-de-France, is home to the island's most-frequented yachting marina and some of its largest resorts. The point is a Y-shaped peninsula, with the hotels fringing the coast

and the marina in the middle. All roads intersect south of the marina, and traffic can get congested.

The small public beach – Plage de l'Anse Mitan – which runs along the western side of the neck of the peninsula, is a good swimming beach and many people bring masks and fins. There's a swim park for the wee ones fenced by buoys.

The closer to the water, the more expensive the lodging is here. There are plenty of restaurants, upscale shops and bars, and it's a lively place at night.

## Information

Ferries to and from Fort-de-France (p626) leave from the west side of Pointe du Bout's marina, where a money-changing office, a laundry, the port bureau and marine supply shops are all clustered together. The marina also has a newsstand with some novels in English next to Hotel de la Pagerie. There are a number of car-rental firms near the hotel and a taxi stand next door. The Village Creole complex has souvenir shops, boutiques and a Crédit Agricole ATM.

There's an **Otitour** (L'Office du Tourisme des Trois Ilets; ☎ 68-47-63; www.trois-ilets.com; Rue Cha-Cha) tourism kiosk on Rue Cha-Cha, the street behind La Marine restaurant.

## Activities

**Coconasse** ( ☎ 98-82-28; www.coconasse.com; tours €75) is one of a few sailboat operators at the marina who give day tours that start around 11am and return after sunset. Snorkeling, a gourmet meal and plenty of rum punch are included. This is one of the most memorable and relaxing ways to see Martinique and the groups are always small.

**Espace Plongée** ( ☎ 66-01-79; www.espace-plongee -martinique.com; Pointe du Bout; 1-tank dive €47) offers morning and afternoon dives every day and, if enough people want to go, night dives. It's located right beside the water in the marina.

Although it's next to Hotel Carayou, **Windsurf Club Martinique** ( ☎ 66-19-06; www.wind surf-martinique.com; windsurfing per hr €20) is a separate business and anyone can visit the center (there's a guarded gate into the hotel). The wind howls here – a good thing.

## Sleeping

**Hotel de la Pagerie** ( ☎ 66-05-30; www.hotel-lapagerie .com; r incl breakfast from €99; 🍴 🛒 ) Tucked between a busy intersection and the inner harbor, this 94-bedroom hotel has straightforward rooms with floral decor – some have kitchenettes. There's an on-site restaurant and bar here too. It's an economical option compared to its neighbors.

**Hotel Carayou** ( ☎ 66-04-04; www.hotel-carayou.com; 97229 Trois-Îlets; s/d incl breakfast €270/290; ⊠ ⧉ ) The 200-room family-friendly Carayou sits on the peninsula that forms the northeast side of the marina. The modern rooms have faux-rustic furniture; they look like a studio rental, but without a fridge or kitchenette. On the hotel grounds is Windsurf Club Martinique, the only aquatic center in town. There are two restaurants and a small beach for guests.

**Sofitel Bakoua Martinique** ( ☎ 66-02-02; www.accor -hotels.com; 97229 Trois-Îlets; r from €430; ⊠ ⧉ ) The area's most exclusive resort has 138 rooms and suites that are comfortably furnished (the best 40 are on the beach) and guests have access to one of the area's best beaches and the hotel's water toys. It's a beautiful property inside and out.

## Eating

**Restaurant La Marine** ( ☎ 66-02-32; mains €12-19; ⊙ breakfast, lunch & dinner) The sailing set and land-lubbing tourists visit this open-air restaurant, fronting the marina, in equal measure. There are daily specials and a lobster lunch menu (€35), which includes an aperitif. If you happen to be here on a Wednesday try the daily special of *moules frites*: a big plate of mussels in a butter and garlic sauce with a side of French fries – here, they're just fries.

**La Grange** ( ☎ 66-01-66; mains €14-20; ⊙ 10am-11pm) The food, including fish tartar and grilled tuna, is good, but what's even better is the free wi-fi and quality cigars at this outdoor restaurant– indoor cigar bar. Cigars range from €5 to €15, and aficionados can get their Cuban cigar fix here. Wednesday is karaoke night, for those who dare, and Saturdays are for dancing.

**Le Ponton du Bakoua** ( ☎ 66-05-45; mains €18-30; ⊙ lunch & dinner Mon-Sat) Hard to find: head toward the Sofitel Bakoua Martinique and veer left on the little road that looks like a service alley; follow the road down to the sailboats bobbing in the breeze. The menu has the normal range of seafood favorites, albeit exceptionally flavorful, and it's one of the trendiest restaurants around. At night it is one of the most romantic spots on the island. Dinner reservations are a good idea.

# GRANDE ANSE
## pop 600

The pleasant little village of Grande Anse is located on Grande Anse d'Arlet Bay. It's set along a beachfront road that's lined with brightly painted fishing boats and a string of restaurants. The main street is pedestrian only; a nice change of pace that makes it that much more enjoyable to stroll along the long, narrow beach that's nice to look at but not so nice (because of fishing boats and no privacy) to tan on.

## Activities

**Plongée Passion** ( ☎ 68-71-78; 1-tank dive €45) On the beach right next to Ti Plage, it offers morning and afternoon outings every day. The operators decide which of the many numerous local dive spots to go to, depending on conditions and overall experience of the group. A very friendly, low-key crowd runs the place.

**Alpha Plongée** ( ☎ 48-30-34; www.alpha-plongee.com; 138 Rue Robert Deloy; 1-tank dive €45) It's on the main road tucked behind a private home; follow the signs. Runs morning and early afternoon dive trips.

## Sleeping & Eating

**Ti Plage** ( ☎ 29-59-89; mains €9-13; ⊙ lunch Tue-Sun) Next door to Localizé, this tastefully decorated little beachside restaurant with decked veranda is famous for its couscous royale special on Friday night. Otherwise, expect delicious smoked fish salad, duck confit or vegetarian *galettes*.

**Ti Sable** ( ☎ 68-62-44; mains €11-19; ⊙ lunch & dinner, closed Sep) A long-running favorite of many a traveler, this big beach hut with fairy lights is the place to be in the evening. The *chatrou* (octopus) in coconut milk is delicious. They also serve barbecued meats and exotic salads. Ti Sable hosts live music on weekends.

**Localizé** ( ☎ 68-64-78; www.localize.fr; studio per week from €469; ⧉ ) The 10 studios here are set in a sprawling, single-level Creole home that's right on the beach. It's a pleasant place to stay with a small library, wi-fi and a gardened exterior, and all of the rooms are decorated in exotic woods from around the world. Two of the studios can sleep four people with a main bedroom that's air-conditioned. Localizé also rents two fully equipped homes in the area (from €1300 per week).

MARTINIQUE

## ANSE D'ARLET
pop 3200

Anse d'Arlet is a typical pretty fishing village south of Grande Anse that makes the most of its gorgeous beachfront. There's an interesting 18th-century Roman Catholic church in its center (part of its roof was torn off in Hurricane Dean), a one-screen cinema and a handful of laid-back beach huts selling snacks at the northern end of the village.

There's a Crédit Mutuel with an ATM in the center of town and a small produce and fish market along the boardwalk.

**Chez Valy** (Valy & le Pecheur; ☎ 48-39-77; mains from €8, ☽ lunch & dinner) specializes in grilled seafood, and has an outdoor barbecue in the back where fresh, locally caught seafood is grilled. Chez Valy also has good salads, a great way to sample a wide variety of fruits of the sea.

The only accommodations right in the village, **Résidence Madinakay** ( ☎ 68-70-76; www .multimania.com/madinakay; 3 Allée des Arlesiens; r €58; ☒ ) is on the main street across from the beach. Run by the helpful Raymond de Laval, these simple, colorful studios all have kitchenettes and balconies. The indoor balconies have a window that looks out on a small bird garden full of twittering fine-feathered friends.

## DIAMANT
pop 3400

Diamant is a seaside town on the southern coast that's slightly more developed than its neighbors. The main road runs near, but not right on the beach. The gray sands of the strand here stretch for 2km beside town. But, because of a bad current and violent waves, be sure to ask at your hotel for a safe place to swim.

For visitors, the best things Diamant has to offer are some nice hotels and a row of pizzerias and snack places, an internet café and a few banks along the main drag. It's a good base to explore the western horn of the island – which, oddly enough, is shaped a little bit like France. The town also affords a nice view of Rocher du Diamant, a 176m-high volcanic islet that's a popular **dive site**, with interesting cave formations but tricky water conditions. To explore this underwater jewel, visit the dive operators at nearby Grande Anse (p619).

Just north of town on the D7 is the **Le Musée des Coquillages et de la Mer** ( ☎ 76-41-92; Hotel l'Ecrin Bleue; admission €5; ☽ 9am-6pm). Seeing hard-to-find shells found in Japan in the 1760s, or

off the coast of South Africa in the 1880s, is actually fun.

With 25 bungalows spread out across the spacious grounds, an unusually large hotel swimming pool and the Paillote Bleue Restaurant, **L'Anse Bleue** ( ☎ 76-21-91; www.hotel -anse-bleue.com; small/large bungalow €60/75; ☒ ) is a nice place to stay a spell. At the time of research, the bathrooms and kitchenettes in all the cottage were being renovated to give them more of a 'rustic luxury' look, characterized by well-crafted dark wood walls and classic cabin fixtures.

Just 1km west of town, lovely **Le Patio de l'Anse Bleue** ( ☎ 76-28-83; patio-anse-bleue@wanadoo.fr; r from €65; ☒ ☐ ) only has three high-ceilinged rooms, which are decorated with hand-painted furniture. Rooms all face onto a large open-air inner courtyard and Jacuzzi.

**our pick Diamant les Bains** ( ☎ 76-50-14; dia mantlesbains@wannadoo.fr; 97223 Diamant; r from €94; ☒ ☐ ☒ ) is run by the affable Marie-Yvonne Andrieu and her husband. One son is the chef at the on-site restaurant and the son, Jean-Marc, is an artist who did most of the hotel's paintings. The studios right on the beach (with fridge, but no cooking) are worth the extra money (€110). From the modest exterior that faces the main street one would never guess how spacious and pretty the hotel grounds are. Two bungalows have wheelchair access.

At the western end of the village, the always humming bar and café of **Planete Diamant** ( ☎ 76-49-82; mains €8-14; ☽ 11am-2am, closed Wed) has menus shaped like Saturn and salads named after bodies in our solar system. The heavenly salads include the Venus, with crab, salmon and shrimp, and the Mars, with grilled *lardon* (halfway between ham and bacon) and goat's cheese. The drink menu is impressive.

## STE-LUCE
pop 5800

Many of the tourists who come to this happening little fishing town are locals from other parts of the island. Ste-Luce has a number of bars and restaurants either right on the water or just a block or two away, and there are always a few tourists lounging around with a ti-punch in hand.

The hotels are far enough away from the N5 for you not to feel you're living on a freeway, but close enough to make this a great base to explore the southern half of the island. For divers there are two shops and numerous sites to choose from. The beaches – **Anse Mabouya**, 4km to the west of the center of town, and **Anses Gros Raisin**, which is really two beaches side by side 2km west of the city center – aren't worth a special trip, but for those staying in the area they provide a pleasant break and are rarely crowded.

There's a Crédit Mutuel bank with two ATMs on Rue Schoelcher. On the D7, where many of the hotels are located, is the 8 à Huit supermarket.

## Sights & Activities

Rum connoisseurs say it doesn't produce the best rum, but **Trois-Rivières Distillerie** ( ☎ 62-51-78; www.plantationtroisrivieres.com; Quartier Trois-Rivières; admission free, guided tour in French €2.50; ☒ 9am-5pm Mon-Fri, to 1pm Sat) is definitely one of the most-visited distilleries. The self-guided tour, with signs in English, starts near the parking lot; start at the first sign and follow the arrows. Many of the 'exhibits' are actually on-site souvenir and snack shops. The one notable souvenir shop is **Art & Nature** (www.artetnature-martinique .com), where the on-site artist makes paintings out of sand and earth from Martinique's 339 different natural colors and invites visitors to touch the paintings. The self-guided tour ends with a tasting at the rum boutique – it sells hard-to-find aged rums but if you want normal rums you'll find them cheaper at most supermarkets.

**Ste-Luce Plongée** ( ☎ 62-40-06; www.sainteluce plongee.fr; 15 Blvd Kennedy; 1-tank dive €44) does two daily dives to either nearby sites or further out at Rocher Diamant.

**Okeanos Club** ( ☎ 62-52-36; www.okeanos-club.com; 1-tank dive €45) offers two, sometimes three, daily dive outings. It's set in the Village Pierres & Vacances.

## Sleeping & Eating

Motorists should take the Trois Rivière exit on the eastbound N5 right before the Ste-Luce exit; the hotels listed here are in the rolling hills near the exit, and the town is 5km southeast of the exit on the D36 (make a left toward the sea).

**Le Verger de Ste-Luce** ( ☎ 62-20-72; d from €50; ☒ ☒ ☒ ) Bungalows surround a very small pool with sun chairs and there's a stand-alone Jacuzzi – and the friendly owner loves to speak English. The simple bungalows all have their own porch with a kitchenette and a good amount of greenery keeps the small place feel-ing private. Turn right after the Trois-Rivières exit and keep looking on the left – it's only 100m down the road.

**Hotel Le Panoramique** ( ☎ 62-31-32; r from €55; ☒ ☒ ) Just a little north of Le Verger de Ste-Luce on the same road. Five out of the 15 rooms have kitchenettes so be sure to specify. The rooms feel brand new and some have private balconies with panoramic views while other have small flatscreen TVs – and all have big beds, which one doesn't always find in Martinique. There's a bar and restaurant on the property, too.

**Hotel Corail Résidence** ( ☎ 62-11-01; www.karibea .com; d from €100; ☒ ☒ ) All of the 26 rooms have kitchenettes and little porches with an automatic screen that either shuts out the morning light or opens up to views of the sea down below. It's a 10-minute walk to Mabouya Beach. To get here, just trust the signs. The same company runs the nearby Karibea Resort.

**Casa Pepe** ( ☎ 62-30-99; 29 Rue Schoelcher; mains from €9; ☒ lunch & dinner Mon-Sat, lunch Sun) Decorated with bullfighting posters and a few huge murals of horses that aren't exactly tasteful, but interesting nonetheless, Casa Pepe has a number of Creole specialties but paella is what it does best. It might be wise to order the *paella géante* (giant, the only size available) to go, and eat half there and half at home.

**L'Epi Soleil** ( ☎ 62-36-12; 51 Blvd Kennedy; mains €9-13; ☒ breakfast, lunch & dinner) The mainstay of the street, the covered outdoor bar on the water-front across from the restaurant is a popular place that stays open into the night. The res-taurant serves sandwiches, salads and pizza.

## STE-ANNE
### pop 3300

The southernmost village on Martinique, Ste-Anne has an attractive seaside setting with its painted wooden houses and numer-ous trinket shops. Its most popular swim-ming beach is the long, lovely strand that stretches along the peninsula to Club Med, 800m north of the town center. Despite the number of visitors that flock to the town on weekends and during the winter season, Ste-Anne remains a casual, low-key place, with abundant near-shore reef formations that make for good snorkeling.

If the beach here is too crowded, Cap Chevalier is 6km east as the crow flies and beautiful Macabou is 12km northeast.

**MARTINIQUE**

There's a small **office of tourism** (www.sainte -anne.to) kiosk in the town center, near the pier, that has maps of the town and can help with car or hotel arrangements.

The dive shop **Plongée Caritan** ( ☎ 76-81-31; www.anse-caritan.com; Rte des Caraïbes) is located in the hotel Domaine de l'Anse Caritan.

## Sleeping

There are a number of gîtes scattered around the edge of the town's center.

**La Dunette** ( ☎ 76-73-90; www.ladunette.com; s/d incl breakfast €84/93; ⚡ ) In the center of town and overlooking the beach, this hotel has 13 rooms and a restaurant (mains €12 to €24, open 10am to 11pm) that has concerts on the weekends. The interior of the hotel looks a bit retro, but, rooms are spacious and clean. Get a room on the 2nd level for the best view.

**Domaine de l'Anse Caritan** ( ☎ 76-74-12; www .anse-caritan.com; Rte des Caraïbes; s/d from €161; ⚡ 🏊 ) This massive, modern, family-friendly hotel is at the end of a wooded lane just over 800m south of the village center. There are 96 contemporary rooms with kitchenettes. Rooms are a bit soulless but there's a sandy beach complete with inflatable aquatic playground, canoeing and dive center, so it's unlikely you'll be hanging out in the rooms.

## Eating

**Sn@ck Boubou** ( ☎ 76-28-46; 28 Rue Abbé Saffache; snacks €4-7; ☽ 8am-9pm) The salads and sandwiches are a good way to fill up cheap and it's open all day long. There's also good ice cream (per scoop €1.50), making it a nice place to cool off at the shaded sidewalk tables. Wi-fi is available at €3 per hour.

**Les Tamariniers** ( ☎ 76-75-62; 30 Rue Abbé Saffache; mains €10-22; ☽ lunch & dinner) The most up-market eatery in town. Try the Creole menu (€40), a three-course feast, including lobster grilled in aged rum.

**Poi et Virginie** ( ☎ 76-73-54; mains €12-24; ☽ lunch & dinner Thu-Mon, dinner Wed, closed Tue) This seaside spot has an inventive menu of Creole, French and Mexican cuisine. It's a popular place with a see-through floor on the porch with spot-lit fish swimming below – the ultimate in on-the-water dining.

## LES SALINES

Found at the undeveloped southern tip of the island, Les Salines is probably Martinique's finest beach. The gorgeous long stretch of golden sand attracts scantily clad French tourists and local families alike on weekends and holidays, but it's big enough to accommodate everyone without feeling crowded; it just might be necessary to pick a direction and keep walking along the beach until the crowds thin.

When we visited, the road that used to run along the beach was under construction, which meant that the parking lot was a big dirt field that got muddy and slippery after rain. While this situation continues, during peak times parking can be a messy hassle.

On a brighter note, this is one of the few beaches where camping is legal, but only during school holidays. Camp on the west side of the beach. Signs depicting tents guide the way.

Les Salines is about 5km south of Ste-Anne at the end of the D9. There are showers and food vans near the center of the beach, and about 500m further south you'll find snack shops selling reasonably priced sandwiches, burgers and chicken.

Les Salines gets its name from Étang des Salines, the large salt pond that backs it. Beware of poisonous manchineel trees (most are marked with red paint) on the beach, particularly at the southeast end; rainwater dripping off them can cause rashes and blistering. There's some good snorkeling at the west end of the beach.

# DIRECTORY

## ACCOMMODATIONS

There are 7800 rooms in more than 100 resorts, hotels and inns. Most of the island's hotels range from 12 to 40 rooms. By Caribbean standards, nightly rates are moderate, with budget hotels averaging about €60, midrange €85 and top end about €240. The prices listed are for high season (December to May), when the majority of people visit the island. Prices can be as much as 40% lower outside of peak times. Some hotels close in September.

Established campgrounds with facilities are virtually nonexistent on the island. Camping is allowed along the beach at Les Salines during the school holidays. For details on camping, call the **Office National des Forêts** ( ☎ 71 34 50; Fort-de-France).

**Gîtes de France** ( ☎ 73-74-74, in Paris 01-49-70-75-75; www.gites-de-france.fr; BP 1122, 97209 Fort-de-France)

---

**PRACTICALITIES**

■ **Newspapers** The daily *France-Antilles* newspaper centers on news from the French West Indies.

■ **Radio & TV** Tune into Radio France Outre-Mer (RFO) at 92MHz and 94.5MHz on FM or catch up on local TV on networks RFO 1 and RFO 2.

■ **Video Systems** The Secam video system is used on the island.

■ **Electricity** Voltage is 220V, 50 cycles, and plugs have two round prongs; a plug adapter will come in handy.

■ **Weights & Measures** Martinique uses the metric system for weights and measures, and the 24-hour clock.

---

offers rooms in private homes, with weekly rates beginning at around €280 for two people. The convenient website has an English option, and travelers with disabilities can search for accessible accommodation.

Taxes and service charges are included in the quoted rates. See p815 for details on how accommodations price ranges are categorized in this book.

## ACTIVITIES
### Beaches & Swimming

The sand on beaches on the southern half of the island is white or tan, while those on the northern half are gray or black. Many of Martinique's nicest beaches are scattered along the southwest coast from Grande Anse to Les Salines. Popular east-coast beaches include those at Cap Chevalier and Macabou to the south and the Presqu'île de Caravelle beaches (p616) of Anse l'Étang and Tartane. However, beaches along the northeast side of the island can have very dangerous water conditions and have been the site of a number of drownings.

### Diving & Snorkeling

St-Pierre has some of the island's top scuba-diving sites, with wrecks, coral reefs and plenty of marine life. More than a dozen ships that were anchored in the harbor when the 1902 volcanic eruption hit now lie on the sea bed.

Cap Enragé, northeast of Case-Pilote, has underwater caves harboring lots of sea life; to explore its underwater wonders, book a dive in St-Pierre (p613). Grande Anse (p619), with its calm waters and good coral, is a popular diving spot for beginners and a good area for snorkeling. Interesting diving but

trickier conditions are found at Rocher du Diamant (p620) and Îlet la Perle (p614).

You'll also find good snorkeling around Ste-Anne (p621) and along the coast from St-Pierre to Anse Céron (p614).

Expect to pay around €45 for a single dive. There are dive shops in Pointe du Bout (p618), Grande Anse (p619), Ste-Luce (p621) and St-Pierre (p613).

Most larger hotels rent out snorkeling gear and many provide it free to their guests. Some of the dive shops offer snorkeling trips, while others let snorkelers tag along with divers.

### Hiking

Martinique has many hiking trails. From Route de la Trace (p614), a number of signposted trails lead into the rainforest and up and around the Pitons du Carbet. Also popular is hiking around the ruins of Château Dubuc (p616) on the Presqu'île de Caravelle.

There are strenuous trails leading up both the northern and southern flanks of Mont Pelée. The shortest and steepest is up the southern flank, beginning in Morne Rouge (p615), and takes about four hours round-trip. The hike up the northern flank is 8km long and takes about 4½ hours one way; there are two trails, which begin just east of Grand-Rivière. Visit the Syndicat d'Initiative in Grand Rivière for detailed maps (p615).

*Syndicats d'initiative* organize hikes in various parts of the island, including one around the northern tip of the island between Grand-Rivière and Anse Couleuvre (p615), and the **Parc Naturel Régional** ( ☎ 64-42-59) leads other guided hikes several times a week.

Walk maps and advice (in French) can be found in the book *La Martinique à Pied*, available at many bookstores in Martinique, or write the regional hiking authority at cdrp.martinique@wanadoo.fr.

## BUSINESS HOURS

Most businesses are open Monday to Friday, 8am to noon, close for lunch, and then reopen from 2pm to 5pm. Banks follow a similar pattern, but usually don't reopen after lunch one day per week. Unless otherwise noted, breakfast is served from 7am to 9am, lunch noon to 2pm, and dinner 7pm to 9pm.

## CHILDREN

Children will be welcome on vacation in Martinique. Most restaurants will allow children to dine as long as they are accompanied by an adult. Practically all hotels will provide cots, and some hotels provide babysitting services. European brands of baby formula, foods and diapers can be bought at pharmacies.

## DANGERS & ANNOYANCES

The *fer-de-lance*, an aggressive pit viper, can be found on Martinique, particularly in overgrown and brushy fields. The snake's bite is highly toxic and sometimes fatal; it's essential for victims to get an antivenin injection as soon as possible. Hikers should be alert for the snakes and stick to established trails.

There is a risk of bilharzia (schistosomiasis) infection throughout the island; the main precaution is to avoid wading or swimming in fresh water.

Beware of manchineel trees on some beaches, particularly on the south coast, as rainwater dripping off them can cause skin rashes and blistering. They're usually marked with a band of red paint.

Occasional island-wide strikes can grind tourism services to a screeching halt.

After dark, it's not advisable to wander off the strip of restaurants and hotels along Rues de la Liberté and Ernest Deproge; mugging is the main concern.

## EMBASSIES & CONSULATES

**Germany** ( ☎ 50-38-39; Acajou, 97232 Le Lamentin)
**Netherlands** ( ☎ 73-31-61; 44/46 Ave Maurice Bishop, 97200 Fort-de-France)
**UK** ( ☎ 61-56-30; Route du Phare, 97200 Fort-de-France)

**US** ( ☎ 75-67-54; usconsulaireagencemartinique@wanadoo.fr; Hotel Valmeniere 615, Ave des Arawaks, 97200 Fort-de-France; ☺ 9am-noon)

## FESTIVALS & EVENTS

**Mardi Gras Carnival** Martinique has a spirited Carnival during the five-day period leading up to Ash Wednesday, though most of the action centers on Fort-de-France.
**St-Pierre** Commemorates the May 8, 1902 eruption of Mont Pelée with live jazz performances and a candlelight procession from the cathedral. On a smaller scale, every village in Martinique has festivities to celebrate its patron saint's day.
**Tour de la Martinique** Week-long bicycle race in mid-July.
**Tour des Yoles Rondes** Week-long race of traditional sailboats in early August.

## GAY & LESBIAN TRAVELERS

Fort-de-France has a little bit of a gay scene, but overall homophobia is prevalent (see p610).

## HOLIDAYS

**New Year's Day** January 1
**Good Friday** Late March/early April
**Easter Sunday** Late March/early April
**Easter Monday** Late March/early April
**Ascension Thursday** Fortieth day after Easter
**Pentecost Monday** Eighth Monday after Easter
**Labor Day** May 1
**Victory Day** May 8
**Slavery Abolition Day** May 22
**Bastille Day** July 14
**Schoelcher Day** July 21
**Assumption Day** August 15
**All Saints Day** November 1
**Fête des Morts** November 2
**Armistice Day** November 11
**Christmas Day** December 25

## INTERNET ACCESS

The chances of finding an internet café in a particular town on Martinique are 50%. In places that see a decent amount of tourists, restaurants and hotels increasingly offer wi-fi for free.

## INTERNET RESOURCES

**Martinique** (www.martinique.org) General information on the island, provided by the Martinique Promotion Bureau.
**Martinique Scoop** (www.martiniquescoop.com) Entertainment and nightlife information.

## LANGUAGE

French is the official language in Martinique, but islanders commonly speak Creole when chatting among themselves. English is spoken at larger hotels but is understood rather sporadically elsewhere so, if you don't have a fair command of French, a bilingual dictionary and phrasebook will prove quite useful.

## MAPS

Maps are available for free at all car-rental agencies and many hotels.

## MEDICAL SERVICES

Good medical care is available throughout the island, but not all doctors speak or understand English. There's a decompression chamber at the hospital in Fort-de-France.

## MONEY

The euro has been the island's currency since 2001. Hotels, larger restaurants and car-rental agencies accept Visa, MasterCard and, less commonly, American Express.

## POST

There are post offices in all major towns. You can also buy postage stamps at some *tabacs* (tobacco shops), hotels and souvenir shops.

Mailing addresses should be followed by 'Martinique, French West Indies.'

## TELEPHONE

The country code for Martinique is ☎ 596. We have included only the six-digit number for Martinique listings in this chapter.

To call from North America, dial ☎ 1-340 + the local number. When calling from within the French West Indies, dial ☎ 0596 + the local six-digit number. From elsewhere, dial your country's international access code, followed by the ☎ 596 area code *twice* in front of the six digits.

For directory assistance, dial ☎ 12.

For more information on phone cards and making long-distance calls, see p826.

---

**EMERGENCY NUMBERS**

- **Ambulance** ☎ 15
- **Fire** ☎ 18
- **Police** ☎ 17
- **Sea Rescue** ☎ 70-92-92

---

## Cell Phones

To see whether you can use your phone on the island's GSM networks, check with your cell service provider before you leave to see if it has a roaming agreement with any of the service operators here.

SIM cards (starting at €25) are available for unlocked cell phones and usually include some talk time before recharging. Digicel and Orange are the two main SIM card vendors.

## Phone Cards

Public phones in Martinique accept French *télécartes* (phone cards), not coins. The cards cost €5, €10 or €15, depending on the amount of calling time on them, and are sold at post offices and at shops with signs that say '*télécartes en vente ici.*'

## TOURIST INFORMATION

Many towns have at least a small tourism office where the staff will try to speak in English. Pamphlets, mainly in French but with enough pictures and maps to get the gist, are available at airports and many hotels. The **Martinique Promotion Bureau** (Comité Martiniquais du Tourisme; ☎ 61-61-77; www.martinique.org) is a good source of information on the island in English, French, Spanish and Portuguese.

## TRAVELERS WITH DISABILITIES

Some hotels have rooms that are accessible by travelers with disabilities. Sidewalk curbs are still a problem in most places.

## VISAS

Citizens of the US, UK, Canada, Australia and New Zealand can stay for up to 90 days without a visa by showing a valid passport (US citizens see the boxed text, p830). Citizens of the EU need an official identity card, valid passport or French *carte de séjour* (visitor permit).

# TRANSPORTATION

## GETTING THERE & AWAY
### Entering Martinique

A round-trip or onward ticket is officially required of visitors. This may be checked at customs upon arrival or, if you're coming from within the Caribbean, before you depart for Martinique.

## Air

**Martinique Aimé Césaire International Airport** (FDF;
☎ information line 42-18-77), formerly known as
Lamentin International Airport) has an information line. Immigration is courteous
and efficient at this large and modern airport, which has a number of ATMs, money
change bureaus and restaurants.

The following airlines service Martinique:

**Air Antilles Express** ( ☎ 42-16-71; www.airantilles.com)
Pointe-à-Pitre, St-Barthélemy, St-Martin/Sint Martin

**Air Caraïbes** ( ☎ 42-16-52; www.aircaraibes.com)
Castries, Paris, Panama City, Pointe-à-Pitre, Port-au-Prince,
St Lucia, St-Martin/Sint Maarten, San José, Santo Domingo

**Air France** ( ☎ 82-61-61; www.airfrance.com) Paris,
Pointe-à-Pitre

**American Airlines/American Eagle** (www.aa.com)
San Juan

**Corsairfly** ( ☎ 42-16-10; www.corsairfly.com) Brest,
Lyon, Paris

**LIAT** ( ☎ 42-16-11; www.liatairline.com) St Lucia

## Sea

Martinique is well visited by seafaring vessels. Cruise ships and interisland ferries call
on Martinique every day, and the island is
a favorite anchorage for private sailboats
and yachts.

### CRUISE SHIP

Cruise ships land at Pointe Simon in Fort-de-
France, at the western side of the harbor and
within easy walking distance of the city center
and main sights. The arrival facilities have
phones, rest rooms, a taxi stand and a tourist
information booth that opens on cruise-ship
days. See p830 for more on cruises.

### FERRY

Two companies provide regular boat service between Martinique and Guadeloupe,
Dominica and St Lucia. The ferries use
the **Terminal de Croisière** (sometimes called
Quai Ouest), 850m southeast of La Savane
in Fort-de-France.

**L'Express des Îles** ( ☎ 35-90-00; www.express-des-iles
.com) operates large, modern catamarans that
have air-conditioned cabins with TVs and
a snack bar. There are three weekly crossings from Fort-de-France to Pointe-à-Pitre,
Guadeloupe (one way/round trip €67/100,
three hours), on Sunday, Wednesday and
Friday. Boats leave Fort-de-France for
Roseau in Dominica every afternoon except

Wednesday (one way/round trip €67/100, 1½
hours) and for Castries in St Lucia every day
except Tuesday and Saturday (one way/round
trip €67/100, 80 minutes).

Departure days and times for these services change frequently and often bear no
relation to the printed schedule. The only
way to be sure is to call L'Express des Îles
or check with a local travel agent. There are
discounts of 50% for children aged under
two, 10% for students and passengers under
12 years old, and 5% for passengers younger
than 26 or older than 60.

**Brudey Frères** ( ☎ 70-08-50; www.brudey-freres.fr)
offers an express catamaran between Fort-
de-France and Pointe-à-Pitre (one way/
round trip €65/95) every day. In high season,
there's an additional crossing three to four
days per week. The company has crossings
between Fort-de-France and Dominica every
afternoon, with additional morning departures in high season (one way/round trip
€55/80). There's service between St Lucia
(one way/round trip €55/80) on Friday and
Sunday. Travel times are nearly identical to
L'Express des Îles.

Brudey also offers discounts for youths
and elders. Schedules change, so check current timetables.

### YACHT

The main port of entry is in Fort-de-France but
yachts may also clear at St-Pierre or Marin.

Yachting and sailing are very popular in
Martinique and numerous charter companies
operate on the island. **Sparkling Charter** ( ☎ 74-
66-39; www.sparkling-charter.com) and **Sunsail Antilles**
( ☎ 74-98-17; www.sunsail.com) are based at the
marina in Marin, as are a huge number of
other charter companies. **Star Voyage** ( ☎ 66-00-
72) is based at the Pointe du Bout marina.

## GETTING AROUND

If time is of essence, renting a car is the
most reliable form of transportation in
Martinique. Most hotels can arrange airport
pickup and car rental.

## Boat

A couple of regular *vedettes* (ferries) between
Martinique's main resort areas and Fort-de-
France provide a nice alternative to dealing
with heavy bus and car traffic – they also
allow you to avoid the hassles of city parking and are quicker to boot.

**Somatours Vedettes** ( ☎ 73-05-53) runs a ferry between Fort-de-France and Pointe du Bout. It's quite a pleasant way to cross and takes only 20 minutes. The boat runs daily from 6:30am to 5:15pm, every hour or so, and costs €3/6 one way/round trip.

**Vedettes Madinina** ( ☎ 63-06-46; www.vedettes madinia.com) runs a boat to Pointe du Bout daily from 6:20am to 6:30pm, every hour or so every day and costs €2.50/5 one way/round trip.

**Matinik Cruise Line** ( ☎ 76-73-45) runs a ferry about every 75 minutes between Fort-de-France and the town dock in the village of Trois-Îlets. The first boat departs Trois-Îlets at 6:10am and the last leaves Trois-Îlets for Fort-de-France at 5:45pm (€4/7 one way/ return, 15 minutes). There are no boats on Sunday. Supposedly there is a service to Ste-Anne (via Anse d'Arlet) but that couldn't be confirmed.

It's best to buy a one-way ticket only as sometimes your ride home might unexpectedly quit early that day.

There are also countless sailing tours and charters operating around the island. For the latest information, check with the local tourist office or at your hotel.

## Bus

Although there are some larger public buses, most buses are minivans, marked 'TC' (for *taxis collectifs*) on top. Destinations are marked on the vans, sometimes on the side doors and sometimes on a small sign stuck in the front window. Traveling by bus is best for shorter distances and for visitors with a lot of extra time in their itinerary.

Bus stops are marked *arrêt de bus* or have signs showing a picture of a bus. Fort-de-France's busy main terminal is at Pointe Simon, on the west side of the harbor. Buses from Fort-de-France to St-Pierre leave frequently Monday to Saturday, but less frequently on Sunday (€3.20, 45 minutes). Other bus fares from Fort-de-France are to Trois-Îlets (€2.40), Diamant (€5.70), Ste-Anne (€9.80) and Grand-Rivière (€5.70). For buses to the gardens of Balata, and Morne Rouge, head to the cemetery south of the Parc Floral in Fort-de-France; they leave about

every 30 minutes during the day, Monday to Saturday.

## Car
### DRIVER'S LICENSE
Your home driver's license is all that you will need to drive legally on Martinique's roads.

### RENTAL
There are numerous car-rental agencies at the airport and in Fort-de-France. You'll find the best rates on their websites, and local firms are generally cheaper than international agencies. Beware companies that list their address as 'Cruise Terminal' but are in fact near La Savane in the center of Fort-de-France.

An unlimited mileage rate is generally preferable to a lower rate that adds a charge per kilometer, particularly if you plan on touring the island.

You must be at least 21 years of age to rent a car, and some companies add a surcharge for drivers under the age of 25.

Car-rental companies at the airport:
**Avis** ( ☎ 42-11-00; www.avis.com)
**Budget** ( ☎ 42-04-04; www.budget-antilles.com)
**Carib Rentacar** ( ☎ 51-15-15; www.rentacar-caraibes .com/martinique/index.asp)
**Europcar** ( ☎ 42-42-42; www.europcar.mq)
**Hertz** ( ☎ 42-16-90; www.hertz.com)

### ROAD CONDITIONS
Roads are excellent by Caribbean standards, and there are multilane freeways (and rush-hour traffic) in the Fort-de-France area.

### ROAD RULES
In Martinique, drive on the right side of the road. Traffic regulations and road signs are the same as those in Europe, speed limits are posted, and exits and intersections are clearly marked.

## Taxi
The taxi fare from the airport is approximately €20 to Fort-de-France, €60 to Ste-Anne and €355 to Pointe du Bout or Anse Mitan. A 40% surcharge is added onto all fares between 8pm and 6am and all day on Sunday and holidays. To book a cab, call **24-hour taxi** ( ☎ 63-63-62, 63-10-10).

# St Lucia

Rising like an emerald tooth from the flat Caribbean Sea, St Lucia definitely grabs your attention. Glossed over as some sort of glam honeymoon spot, this mountainous island has much more to offer then just posh digs.

Who says the Caribbean is all about lying on the beach? If that's all you do in St Lucia you're missing out. The rainforest-choked interior is made for hiking; a canopy of green covers the island like a haze. Rolling hills grow to form volcanic mountains and reach to the sky. The iconic Pitons rise from the waves to the clouds like pyramids of volcanic stone.

This isn't some glammed-up, theme-park holiday spot – St Lucia has a pulse. Your senses are bombarded with the sights, smells and sounds of an island that's truly alive. Towns like Castries move and shake to the sound of car horns, the smell of rotis fresh from the oven and reggae blaring on the speaker.

Sure you can find a beach to sit on and a nice hotel right beside it. There is great scuba diving to be found under the waves and the sailing is top notch. But it's much more than that. If you're looking for a Caribbean destination that will let you get under the skin of West Indian life – St Lucia is the one.

## FAST FACTS

- **Area** 238 sq miles
- **Capital** Castries
- **Country code** ☎ 758
- **Departure tax** EC$68
- **Famous for** Jacquot parrot, the Pitons
- **Language** English, Creole
- **Money** Eastern Caribbean dollar (EC$); EC$1 = US$0.38 = €0.24 = UK£0.19
- **Official name** Saint Lucia
- **People** St Lucians
- **Phrase** Soon come back
- **Population** 170,000
- **Visa** Not required for US, EU or Commonwealth visitors; see p647

## HIGHLIGHTS

- **Soufrière** (p639) Tap into the local culture; enjoy the great diving and hiking too
- **Castries** (p632) Hit the buzzing market here, alive with locals, for some retail therapy
- **The Pitons** (p640) Climb these iconic towering peaks, or simply gaze at them over a cold beer
- **Marigot Bay** (p638) Explore this wineglass bay, with its small beach and beautiful surroundings
- **Rodney Bay** (p635) See what all the fuss is about then grab a meal on the beach and watch the sunset

## ITINERARIES

- **One Week** Basing yourself in Soufrière spend a day exploring the town and the surrounding beaches. Take a day or two to do some of the great hikes in the area – be sure to include a climb to the top of the Pitons in there. Travel north to the lively city of Castries. Spend a day exploring the area around Gros Islet and Rodney Bay before returning south to unwind for the day in the thermal pools in Soufrière.
- **All Go – All the Time** Who says you have to sit around on holiday? From a home base in Soufrière go for a scuba dive on the surrounding reef. Then head south for a day of kitesurfing on the south coast. Return to Soufrière and climb Petit Piton and take in the view. Saddle up and go for a mountain bike ride on the new purpose-built biking tracks at Anse Chastanet. Head north for a day of R&R on the beach at Rodney Bay before attacking the zip-lines found in the northern rainforests.

## CLIMATE & WHEN TO GO

As with most Caribbean destinations the winter season is the most popular time to visit St Lucia. The very un-winter weather brings the crowds and jacks up the prices, especially during the driest period from December to March. Winter weather is sublime with average high temperatures around 81°F (27°C). Summer is quiet and hot with the July temperatures averaging 85°F (29°C). Hurricane season falls between June and October – expect some more rain this time of year and maybe the odd storm.

## HISTORY

Archeological finds on the island indicate that St Lucia was settled by Arawaks between 1000 BC and 500 BC. Around AD 800 migrating Caribs conquered the Arawaks and established permanent settlements on the island.

St Lucia was outside the routes taken by Columbus during his four visits to the New World and was probably first sighted by Spanish explorers during the early 1500s. Caribs successfully fended off two British attempts at colonization in the 1600s only to be faced with French claims to the island a century down the road, when they established the island's first lasting European settlement, Soufrière, in 1746 and went about developing plantations. St Lucia's colonial history was marred by warfare, however, as the British still maintained their claim to the island.

In 1778 the British successfully invaded St Lucia, and established naval bases at Gros Islet and Pigeon Island, which they used as staging grounds for attacks on the French islands to the north. For the next few decades, possession of St Lucia seesawed between the British and the French. In 1814 the Treaty of Paris finally ceded the island to the British, ending 150 years of conflict during which St Lucia changed flags 14 times.

Culturally, the British were slow in replacing French customs, and it wasn't until 1842 that English nudged out French as St Lucia's official language. Other customs linger, and to this day the majority of people speak a French-based patois among themselves, attend Catholic services and live in villages with French names.

St Lucia gained internal autonomy in 1967 and then achieved full independence, as a member of the Commonwealth, on February 22, 1979. Politics have stabilized in recent times, with election results usually coming in the form of landslide victories for the opposing party. The downturn in the banana industry has meant that a diversification of industry is vital for economic prosperity – but, like everything in the Caribbean, change is slow.

## THE CULTURE

St Lucians are generally laid-back, friendly people influenced by a mix of their English, French, African and Caribbean origins. For instance, if you walk into the Catholic cathedral in Castries, you'll find a building of

ST LUCIA

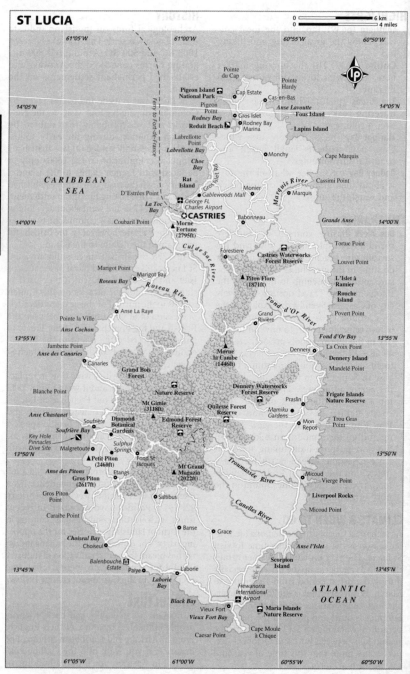

# ST LUCIA

| 0 | 6 km |
| 0 | 4 miles |

CARIBBEAN SEA

ATLANTIC OCEAN

Ferry to Fort-de-France

Pointe du Cap
Pointe Hardy
Pigeon Island National Park
Cap Estate
Cas-en-Bas
Pigeon Point
Anse Lavoutte
Fous Island
Rodney Bay
Gros Islet
Reduit Beach
Rodney Bay Marina
Lapins Island
Labrellotte Point
Labrellotte Bay
Monchy
Cape Marquis
Choc Bay
Rat Island
Cassimi Point
Gros Islet Rd
Monier
Marquis
D'Estrées Point
Gablewoods Mall
George FL Charles Airport
CASTRIES
Babonneau
Grande Anse
Coubaril Point
Morne Fortune (2795ft)
Cul de Sac River
Marquis River
Forestiere
Castries Waterworks Forest Reserve
Tortue Point
Louvet Point
Marigot Point
Marigot Bay
Roseau Bay
Roseau River
Piton Flore (1871ft)
L'Islet à Ramier
Rouche Island
Fond d'Or River
Anse La Raye
Grand Rivière
Povert Point
Pointe la Ville
Anse Cochon
Fond d'Or Bay
Jambette Point
Anse des Canaries
Morne la Combe (1446ft)
Dennery
La Croix Point
Dennery Island
Canaries
Mandelé Point
Blanche Point
Grand Bois Forest
Nature Reserve
Dennery Waterworks Forest Reserve
Praslin
Frigate Islands Nature Reserve
Anse Chastanet
Mt Gimie (3118ft)
Quilesse Forest Reserve
Mamiku Gardens
Trou Gras Point
Soufrière
Diamond Botanical Gardens
Edmond Forest Reserve
Mon Repos
Soufrière Bay
Key Hole Pinnacles Dive Site
Malgretoute
Sulphur Springs
Petit Piton (2461ft)
Fond St Jacques
Micoud
Vierge Point
Anse des Pitons
Gros Piton (2617ft)
Etangs
Mt Grand Magazin (2022ft)
Troumassee River
Liverpool Rocks
Gros Piton Point
Micoud Point
Caraibe Point
Saltibus
Canelles River
Banse
Grace
Anse l'Islet
Choiseul Bay
Choiseul
Balenbouche Estate
Laborie
Scorpion Island
Paiye
Laborie Bay
Black Bay
Hewanorra International Airport
Maria Islands Nature Reserve
Vieux Fort
Vieux Fort Bay
Cape Moule à Chique
Caesar Point

61°05'W   61°00'W   60°55'W   60°50'W

14°05'N
14°00'N
13°55'N
13°50'N
13°45'N

French design, an interior richly painted in bright African-inspired colors, portraits of a Black Madonna and child, and church services delivered in English. About 85% of St Lucians are Roman Catholics.

The population is about 165,000, one-third of whom live in Castries. Approximately 85% are of pure African ancestry. Another 10% are a mixture of African, British, French and East Indian ancestry, while about 4% are of pure East Indian or European descent.

The predominantly African heritage can be seen in the strong family ties that St Lucians hold and the survival of many traditional customs and superstitions. Obeah (Vodou) is still held in equal measures of respect and fear in places like Anse La Raye.

The local snakeman is visited by islanders for his medicinal powers; one such muscular remedy he uses involves massaging the thick fat of the boa constrictor on aching limbs.

There is an eclectic mix of cultural ideologies within St Lucia. Economic disparity has had a negative effect on the cultural identity of young people. Disenfranchised youth have turned to imported movements to find acceptance. There's the Rastafarian influence within the culture and an increasing alliance with urban American ghetto-thug-style culture.

As these groups have become more politicized police recrimination has increased and served to widen the gap of understanding. While there's a burgeoning drug culture, it is debatable whether this societal malaise is the chicken or the egg.

Though problems sound dire and are definitely on the rise, crime is still relatively low. Though many youth like to portray themselves as radical Rastas or ghetto thugs, they are more often then not harmless – slaves only to the fashion, not to the ideology.

## ARTS

In the art world, St Lucia's favorite son is writer Derek Walcott. The gifted poet and playwright won the Nobel Prize for literature in 1992. Strongly influenced by Tolstoy, Homer and Pushkin his writing is literate, intense and sweeping.

The musical sounds of the Caribbean are alive in St Lucia – calypso, reggae and dancehall all play an important role in the lives of locals. Though few artists are local, the grooves are a way of life and provide a soundtrack for everyone on the island.

> ### HOW MUCH?
>
> - **Taxi fare from Castries to Soufrière** EC$170
> - **Local bus fare from Castries to Soufrière** EC$8
> - **Comfortable hotel double room** US$110
> - **Bottle of Piton beer** EC$8
> - **Chicken roti** EC$15

## ENVIRONMENT
### The Land

The striking landmass of St Lucia is one of its defining features. At only 27 miles long the teardrop shaped island packs a variety of topography into its 238 sq miles. Standing nearly as tall as they are long, the rolling hills and towering peaks of the interior make this green island an apparition of altitude rising from the sea.

Banana plantations dominate every flat section of land, and some not so flat. The Caribbean cash-crop is a staple industry for St Lucia. Lush tropical jungle forms a rat's nest of gnarled rainforest, filling the interior of the island with thick bush.

In the north, the island flattens out a little and the beaches get a bit wider – allowing infrastructure to get a foothold. In the south, the land rises sharply and continues in folds of green hills that stretch right to the shoreline. It's in this portion of the island, near the town of Soufrière, that St Lucia's iconic landmarks are found. The twin peaks of the Pitons rise 2500ft from the sea and dominate the horizon. These extinct volcano cones have come to define St Lucia, pose for a thousand pictures and even adorn the national beer.

### Wildlife

St Lucia's vegetation ranges from dry and scrubby areas of cacti and hibiscus to lush jungly valleys with wild orchids, bromeliads, heliconia and lianas.

Under the British colonial administration, much of St Lucia's rainforest was targeted for timber harvesting. In many ways the independent St Lucian government has proved a far more effective environmental force, and while only about 10% of the island remains covered in rainforest, most of that has now

ST LUCIA

been set aside as nature reserve. The largest indigenous trees in the rainforest are the *gommier*, a towering gum tree, and the *chatagnier*, a huge buttress-trunked tree.

Fauna includes St Lucia parrots (see boxed text, p643), St Lucian orioles, purple-throated Carib hummingbirds, bats, lizards, iguanas, tree frogs, introduced mongooses, rabbitlike agouti and several snake species, including the fer-de-lance and the boa constrictor.

## FOOD & DRINK

There is a good mix of eating options in St Lucia. West Indian fare is popular, and grilled fish, beans and rice and rotis are standard practice. The French influence can still be felt with bakeries turning out fresh bead and other savory treats.

Restaurants of all ethnic descriptions can be found at hotels throughout the island, including Italian, French and European classics.

Piton, the local beer, is a refreshing lager that's brewed on the island. The light-colored brew is a nice drop on a hot day.

# CASTRIES

Walking along the crowded streets of Castries, one is bombarded with the kinetics of a city that is on the go. With the three-four rhythm of a throbbing calypso beat that permeates everywhere, the town has a pulse that ebbs and flows. Sights and smells overwhelm as slashes of color and wafts of fresh food snake through the crowded streets. The cultural soul of the city is the market area – it heaves and vibrates, with the locals scurrying to fetch their wares and sell their goods.

Busy, run-down streets – packed with pedestrians, cars, buses and taxis – form a grid of compact humanity. Sticky hot and minus any true aesthetics, the city's charm lives in the emotive response it evokes in the visitor.

## HISTORY

The city, which was founded by the French in the 18th century, was ravaged by fire three times between 1785 and 1812, and again in 1948. Consequently, most of the city's historic buildings have been lost.

An area that survived the last fire was Derek Walcott Sq, a quiet square surrounded by a handful of 19th-century wooden buildings that have gingerbread-trim balconies, an attractive Victorian-style library and the imposing Cathedral of the Immaculate Conception. Opposite the cathedral at the east side of the square is a lofty *saman* (monkey pod) tree that's estimated to be 400 years old.

The small city remains a friendly laid-back place with plenty of West Indian character.

## ORIENTATION

Castries, the island's commercial center and capital, is a bustling port city set on a large natural harbor. The liveliest part of the city is just southeast of the port, at Jeremie and Peynier Sts, the site of the colorful Castries Market.

## INFORMATION
### Bookstores
**Book Salon** (cnr Laborie & Jeremie Sts; ⌚ 8am-4pm Mon-Fri) A good selection of Caribbean titles, literary classics and the odd popular paperback thrown in.

### Cultural Centers
**Folk Research Centre** ( ☎ 453-1477; Mt Pleasant) Documents the island's folk history, language and dance.

### Emergency
**Fire, Medical & Police** ( ☎ 999)
**Police Headquarters** ( ☎ 452-3854/5; Bridge St)

### Internet Access
**ClickCom** ( ☎ 452-4444; 1st fl, La Place Carenage, Jeremie St; per 15min EC$2.50; ⌚ 8:30am-5pm) Good computers with a decent broadband internet connection.

### Medical Services
**Victoria Hospital** ( ☎ 452-2421; Hospital Rd) For medical emergencies.
**Williams Pharmacy** ( ☎ 452-2797; Bridge St)

### Money
Both of the following banks have ATMs that accept Plus and Cirrus cards.
**Bank of Nova Scotia** ( ☎ 456-2100; William Peter Blvd)
**Royal Bank of Canada** ( ☎ 456-9200; William Peter Blvd)

### Post
**General post office** (GPO; Bridge St; ⌚ 8:15am-4pm Mon-Fri)

### Telephone & Fax
There are plenty of card phones located around the city.
**Cable & Wireless** (Bridge St; ⌚ 7:30am-6:30pm Mon-Fri, 8am-12:30pm Sat) Here you can buy phone cards, get your cell phone sorted or make a cheaper long-distance call.

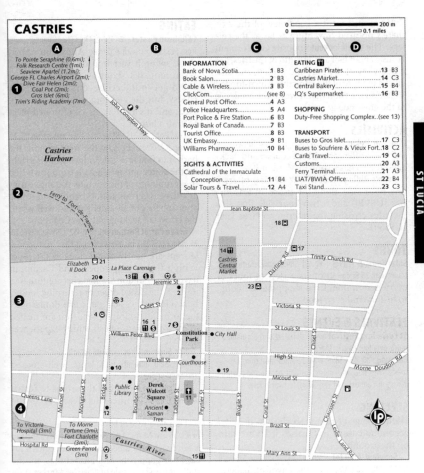

# CASTRIES

**INFORMATION**
Bank of Nova Scotia.................**1** B3
Book Salon.........................**2** B3
Cable & Wireless..................**3** B3
ClickCom..........................(see 8)
General Post Office...............**4** A3
Police Headquarters...............**5** A4
Port Police & Fire Station........**6** B3
Royal Bank of Canada..............**7** B3
Tourist Office....................**8** B3
UK Embassy........................**9** B1
Williams Pharmacy.................**10** B4

**SIGHTS & ACTIVITIES**
Cathedral of the Immaculate
  Conception......................**11** B4
Solar Tours & Travel..............**12** A4

**EATING**
Caribbean Pirates.................**13** B3
Castries Market...................**14** C3
Central Bakery....................**15** B4
JQ's Supermarket..................**16** B3

**SHOPPING**
Duty-Free Shopping Complex..(see 13)

**TRANSPORT**
Buses to Gros Islet...............**17** C3
Buses to Soufriere & Vieux Fort..**18** C2
Carib Travel......................**19** C4
Customs...........................**20** A3
Ferry Terminal....................**21** A3
LIAT/BWIA Office..................**22** B4
Taxi Stand........................**23** C3

**ST LUCIA**

## Tourist Information
**Tourist office** ( ☎ 452-4094; www.stlucia.org; La Place
Carenage, Jeremie St; 🕑 8am-12:30pm & 1:30-4pm Mon-
Fri, 9am-12:30pm Sat)

## SIGHTS
### Cathedral of the Immaculate Conception
The city's Catholic **cathedral** (Laborie St), built
in 1897, is a grand stone structure that has a
splendidly painted interior of trompe l'oeil
columns and colorfully detailed biblical
scenes. The island's patron saint, St Lucia,
is portrayed directly above the altar. The
church richly incorporates both Caribbean
and African influences, including images of a
Black Madonna and child, and the liberal use
of bright red, green and yellow tones.

## Morne Fortune
Sitting atop the 2795ft Morne Fortune, about 3
miles south of Castries center, is **Fort Charlotte**,
whose construction began under the French
and was continued by the British. Because
of its strategic hilltop vantage overlooking
Castries, the fort was a source of fierce fighting between the French and British in colonial
times. The fort buildings have been renovated
and given a new life as the Sir Arthur Lewis
Community College.

At the rear of the college, a small **obelisk** monument commemorates the 27th Inniskilling
Regiment's retaking of the hill from French
forces in 1796. Near the monument you'll also
find a couple of cannons and a fairly good view
of the coast north to Pigeon Point.

If you just want a good view of the city, there's no need to venture as far as the college. The **scenic lookout** opposite Government House, about half a mile south of Castries, has a fine view of the port and capital, and also gives a glimpse of the attractive crown-topped Victorian mansion that serves as the residence of the governor-general.

## ACTIVITIES

**Dive Fair Helen** ( ☎ 451-7716; www.divefairhelen.com; Vigie Marina) offers a variety of courses and packages. It also has a shop in Marigot Bay.

**Trim's Riding Academy** ( ☎ 450-8273) offers a one-hour ride along the beach in Cas-en-Bas (US$40) and a two-hour ride that also includes crossing the interior to Gros Islet (US$50).

## TOURS

**Solar Tours & Travel** ( ☎ 452-5898; www.solartoursand travel.com; 20 Bridge St) offers a slew of tours of every description, from shopping to hiking, to history and even food.

## FESTIVALS & EVENTS

**St Lucia Jazz Festival** (www.sluciajazz.org) Big-name music over four days in May.

**Carnival** ( ☎ 452-1859; www.luciancarnival.com) Castries' streets buzz with music, costume parade and calypso during this annual, and very lively, festival in July.

## SLEEPING

With a range of resorts so close to the city, accommodations in Castries itself are thin on the ground.

**Seaview Apartel** ( ☎ 452-4359; PO Box 527; s/d EC$189/216; 🗶 ) With all the flavor of diabetic chocolate, the Seaview is a means to an end for those desperate to be near the airport. Convenient for early flights, short stopovers and those wanting to be near downtown. The rooms are clean enough and there is air-conditioning.

**Green Parrot** ( ☎ 452-3399; s/d US$85/96; 🗶 ▢ 🗶 ) On Morne Fortune, 3 miles from town, this property sports tremendous harbor views. Situated on a hill overlooking town, the 40-year-old property is beginning to show its age. But amongst the slightly worn appearance lies a '60s charm that denotes a slight Austin Powers meets Fawlty Towers feel. There's wi-fi access, free shuttles into town and to the beach, and balconies attached to all the rooms.

## EATING

**Caribbean Pirates** ( ☎ 452-2543; La Place Carenage; mains from EC$15; 🕑 lunch & dinner) Ahoy you scurvy dogs, swing it yarr into this pirate-themed restaurant. It's about as authentic as one could get in the cruise-ship mall. Slightly cheesy, but the view out onto the harbor is great and it's a jovial, air-conditioned place to grab a burger.

**Coal Pot** ( ☎ 3452-5566; Vigie Cove; mains from US$20; 🕑 lunch & dinner) Follow the road around the harbor to find this little hidden gem. It's right on the water and far enough from town that the tranquility of the sea lulls you into a diner's dream. Fresh seafood and a charming atmosphere are all a delight and well worth the efforts of seeking out The Coal Pot.

**Green Parrot Restaurant** ( ☎ 452-3399; lunch EC$10-25, dinner EC$90) The views from this hilltop restaurant are nearly as delicious as the food. With a fusion of European and Caribbean flavors, the London-trained chef continues to impress the casual diner or returning foodie. Lunch is fairly casual but, come dinnertime, the formalities ramp up and you are treated to one of the more-posh dining experiences in town.

**JQ's Supermarket** (William Peter Blvd; 🕑 8am-5pm Mon-Fri, 8am-4pm Sat) is a large, well-stocked grocery store.

Follow the locals and the aroma to **Central Bakery** (Peynier St), where the bread is fresh and the pies are thick.

There is a row of bars, restaurants and bakeries along Mary Ann St, perfect for grabbing a sandwich and a beer and chatting with locals. For good rotis and local dishes, try the stalls at the south side of Castries Market. You can get drinking coconuts for EC$1 at the market and at the Darling Rd bus stands. If you're preparing the perfect picnic, you could pick up some fruit at the market.

## SHOPPING

On Jeremie St, on the west side of the market, you'll find vendors selling T-shirts, dolls, wood carvings, and other handicrafts and souvenirs.

Both **Pointe Seraphine**, on the north side of the harbor, and **La Place Carenage** (Jeremie St) have a **duty-free shopping complex** ( 🕑 9am-5pm) catering to cruise-ship passengers; there are a whole raft of shops selling liquor, jewelry, perfume and the usual duty-free items you'd expect. There are also some decent T-shirt vendors and other tourist-oriented gifts if that's what you're after.

If you want to see how the locals shop, or to stock up on the essentials (and not so essential), there is only one place to go – **Castries Central Market**. Sprawling in size and impossible to miss from the center of town you can get almost anything here from fruit and vegetables to souvenirs to household items.

## GETTING AROUND
### Getting To/From the Airport
Taxis are plentiful at George FL Charles Airport, which is very close to downtown. Agree on a fare before you depart. Rates from the airport are roughly: EC$20 to Derek Walcott Sq in central Castries; EC$40 to Reduit Beach; EC$50 to Rodney Bay Marina; and EC$80 to Marigot Bay.

There are no direct buses; the nearest bus stop is about 1 mile away, at the northern end of the airport runway.

### Taxi
You can hail a taxi on the street, ask your hotel to book one for you, or dial ☎ 452-1599. Always agree on a fare before you depart.

# NORTHERN ST LUCIA

The northern end of the island is a haven for resorts, tourists and history. The beaches are wide, the waves are benign, there are sights to see and the secret is out. You may end up having to share the sand up here but the trade-off is a much greater variety of accommodation, eateries and things to do.

## NORTH OF CASTRIES
Going north along Gros Islet Rd from Castries you are bombarded with hotel after hotel as the oceanside highway snakes its way to Rodney Bay. This portion of the island is overflowing with tourist infrastructure spanning most budgets. Most accommodations are either on the beach or a short walk to it from across the road.

Gablewoods Mall, just south of the Halcyon resort, has a supermarket, bank, pharmacy, bookstore and internet access.

The following accommodations are on Gros Islet Rd, 2 miles north of George FL Charles Airport. They all have restaurants too. For snacks, head to one of the many outlets at Gablewoods Mall.

Up the hill and away from the action, **Apartment Espoir** ( ☎ 452-8134; www.apartmentespoir.com; Castries; studios/d US$80/100) has 11 units, stunning views and a relaxed feel.

Recent renovations have improved **Villa Beach Cottages** ( ☎ 450-2884; www.villabeachcottages.com; Castries; cottages from US$200, under 12yr free; ❄ ⚼ ), a compact Choc Bay resort. Kitchenettes in each cottage are a plus, and the proximity to the sand is uberhandy. For those not fond of salt water there are two micro swimming pools on site to help you cool off. The honeymoon suite with its spiral staircase is a hit with romantics.

It's rare that an all-inclusive retains any sort of charm or intimacy, but **Sandals Halcyon** ( ☎ 452-3081; www.sandals.co.uk; PO Box 399, Castries; r from US$420; ❄ ⚏ ⚼ ), a foot soldier in the Sandals army, is a standout. The resort is large enough that you can escape the organized 'fun' and do your own thing. Rates include meals and a stack of activities, including scuba diving.

With a vast property and an emphasis on creating space amongst the guests, **East Winds Inn** ( ☎ 552-8212; www.eastwinds.com; Castries; s/d all-inclusive from US$600/800; ❄ ⚏ ⚼ ) really doesn't feel like the typical all-inclusive. The cottage-style rooms are nicely appointed. The staff who tend bar at the self-service pool bar and the resort's stretch of beach are among the best on the island. Offers wi-fi access.

## RODNEY BAY
Rodney Bay has a bit of a split personality. On one side there is the Rodney Bay Marina and then just down the way lies Reduit Beach. The marina is the stomping ground of sailors, the well heeled and the wannabes. The expansive floating parking lot sits adjacent to a series of shops, restaurants, banks and just about anything else a mariner might need.

The beach is home to a cluster of resorts that attract many a vacationer. The sandy shores of Reduit Beach are a big draw, though the sunburn per square footage of beach can get a bit much at times. The calm, turquoise waters are ideal for swimming and it's the sort of beach to which you go to be seen. The voluptuous volleyball players, taxi drivers hustling for fares and children breaking the sound barrier set a distinctive tone. Among the sea of people are several hotels,

ST LUCIA

enough restaurants to choose from and a few shops to liberate you from your savings. Rodney Bay is also home to a dive shop, **Frog's Diving** ( ☎ 450-8831; www.frogsdiving.com).

It's a pleasant 30-minute round-trip walk by road between the marina and the beach, and a small ferry crosses the lagoon between the two areas several times a day.

## Sleeping

**Bay Gardens** ( ☎ 452-8060; www.baygardenshotel.com; Rodney Bay; r from US$120; 🕸 🖳 🗟 ) This new kid on the block – you can still smell the paint – is a beautiful, spacious edition to the strip. Nice amenities and aesthetics too.

**Tuxedo Villas** ( ☎ 452-8553; www.tuxedovillas .com; ste from US$135; 🕸 🖳 🗟 ) Dwarfed by its neighbors, this unassuming hotel is a great basic option. All the rooms are equipped with kitchens and decorated in a style that screams color. The suites are large and well suited to those wanting to self cater, and the beach is just across the street.

**Ginger Lily Hotel** ( ☎ 458-0300; www.thegingerlily hotel.com; PO Box RB2528; r from US$185; 🕸 🖳 🗟 ) The exceptional staff at the Ginger Lily are up to the same high standard as this excellent hotel itself. Vaulted ceilings in the largish rooms lead to balconies complete with hammocks. Mango trees surrounding the property shower unsuspecting guests with fresh fruit. There's a tiny bar to have an evening tipple at, and an inviting pool to cool off in. A good location on the strip and a friendly feel complete the inviting picture.

**St Lucian By Rex Resort** ( ☎ 452-8351; www.rex resorts.com; PO Box 512, Castries; r from US$300; 🕸 🗟 ) If you're looking for a place abuzz with atmosphere and the energy of youth, this is a good bet. It consists of two interconnected hotels – one an all-inclusive, the other an à la carte option right next door. There are beach activities a go-go and a sprawling floor plan to get lost in. The rooms are awash with white-tiled, pastel walls and rattan furniture. There is a snaking faux-river pool, and the requisite swim-up bar and restaurant options.

## Eating

**Triangle** (meals from EC$10; 🕑 breakfast, lunch & dinner) If you're searching for a quick feed, Triangle is a great option. It's popular enough that the buffet has a relatively quick turn around so your lunch won't have been warming for that long, plus it's open until 2am.

**Lime** ( ☎ 452-7061; meals from EC$18; 🕑 lunch & dinner) Another local standout, this is a great spot to practice your Creole as you lounge by the picnic tables with the local crew. The buffet has the West Indian standards you'd expect and there are plenty of cold Pitons just waiting for you behind the bar.

**Edge** ( ☎ 450-3343; Harmony Suites; mains from EC$30; 🕑 dinner) With an eclectic mix of classic European dishes, Caribbean standards and sushi, the Edge does its best to please everyone. Nice views from the dining room help to wash down the tasty food.

**Razmataz** (mains from EC$32; 🕑 dinner) How two Nepali brothers ended up opening a restaurant in St Lucia is a mystery – but you'll be glad they did. The fantastic Indian curries pack in the crowds; the fusion of classic flavors and local ingredients is deservedly popular. Namaste, mon!

**Emeralds** ( ☎ 458-3300; mains from EC$40; 🕑 lunch & dinner) Sitting kitty-corner to the strip of hotels, Emeralds is a large, inviting place with enough seating for most of the island. Under the open-air dining area you can choose from an ample menu of mostly European favorites, with some Caribbean dishes thrown into the mix for good measure.

**Buzz Seafood & Grill** ( ☎ 458-0450; mains from EC$48; 🕑 dinner) Seafood is the order of the day at this 'buzzing' Rodney Bay eatery. It's a locals' favorite and is recommended for temporary locals too.

**Chic** ( ☎ 452-9999; Royal St Lucian; mains from EC$65; 🕑 dinner) It's a rare pleasure in St Lucia to actually eat inside, but this fine-dining standout is a joy for more than just that. The intimate dining room is the setting for fine seafood, game such as rabbit and delicately prepared beef and lamb. Outstanding food in a formal setting.

There are a couple of small stores selling groceries and spirits, and a well-stocked grocery store at the Rodney Bay Mall.

## Entertainment

**Late Lime** ( ☎ 452-7061; 🕑 11pm-1am) Above the Lime, this has music and dancing on Wednesday, Friday and Saturday nights.

**Triangle Pub** ( ☎ 452-0334) A no-nonsense booze hall that packs in the locals. There are karaoke nights, comedy nights and lots of debauchery in between.

**Spinnakers** ( ☎ 452-8491) Right on Reduit Beach, Spinnakers is a catch-all for locals, cruise shippers, and seemingly everybody else. Tables can be hard to come by, but the atmosphere is fun, rambunctious and very St Lucian.

In the early evening, don't be surprised if you're served two drinks for each one you order. Many local bars and restaurants are in competition to see who can put on the longest and most generous happy hour.

## GROS ISLET

Walking through the ramshackle fishing village that is Gros Islet, it's hard to fathom that the diamante-encrusted tourist trap of Rodney Bay is just up the road. This sleepy community is mercifully spared the trappings of tourism en masse. Brimming with character and full of interesting characters – Gros Islet is a great insight into the reality of St Lucia. The local community is a mix of fishers, Rastas, loafers and expats committed to a slower pace of life.

There are some interesting accommodation options here and some of the best authentic West Indian restaurants on the island. Rustic and so basic it's almost falling to bits, this town won't be the cat's meow for everyone. The contrast with its neighbors is astounding.

The village really heats up on Friday nights when the weekly jump-up gets going. Street stalls sell fresh fish, grilled chicken and other delights. The music plays at full volume and the dance moves flow more readily as the rum punch starts to take effect. It's a great party that will rage most of the night and is a classic St Lucian cultural adventure.

Most buses making the coastal drive north from Castries terminate in the center of Gros Islet.

### Sleeping

**Bay Guesthouse** ( ☎ 450-8956; www.bay-guesthouse.com; s/d US$30/35; ☐ ) Near the end of the beach it's hard to miss the safety orange building that is the Bay Guesthouse. This great property is run by a charming couple who have a great insight into the needs of the budget traveler. Cozy rooms and free wi-fi make it a great budget option. Everything you'd ever want for the very reasonable price, this could be the best budget place to stay on the island.

**Palm Haven** ( ☎ 456-8500; www.palmhavenhotel.com; s/d US$100/120) Splitting the difference and sitting half way between Rodney Bay and Gros Islet, Palm Haven is a nice compromise. On the opposite side of the road to the water, it features a decidedly un-resort-like flavor. This property is aimed at the Caribbean traveler so there are few frills, but the location is pleasant and the rates are affordable.

**Landings at St Lucia** ( ☎ 458-7300; www.thelandings stlucia.com; r from US$225; ☒ ☐ ☒ ) This sparkling new property on Gros Islet is a feast for the eyes. Luxurious and beautifully designed with the details in mind. The cathedral-like lobby leads to a channel, spilling into the sea. The rooms are freshly fitted out with four-poster beds, nice linen and exquisite views.

**East Winds Inn** ( ☎ 452-8212; www.eastwinds.com; r all-inclusive from US$600; ☒ ☒ ) All-inclusive resorts tend to capture their guests, insulating them from the reality of a destination. While true, this all-in resort is a good choice for those wanting to forgo exploration and deciding where you should eat for dinner. The green cottages dot the property and an attentive staff swarms around doing their bit. Rooms are pleasant and the return rate is a testament to its popularity.

### Eating & Drinking

**Somewhere Special** ( ☎ 450-8481; Gros Islet; mains from EC$6; ☽ breakfast, lunch & dinner) If you're looking for somewhere special to take your sweetie, this could be your best option in Gros Islet. This small restaurant serves yummy meals in its tiny dining room. They'll even do your laundry if you ask nicely.

**our pick Jambe Debois** (Pigeon Island, mains from EC$10; ☽ breakfast, lunch & dinner) Right in the heart of historic Pigeon Island National Park sits this little unassuming pub. It's a real find with the walls plastered with local art, a tiny book exchange out back and free wi-fi. The meals are hearty, tasty and served up under the thatched-roof patio. The views out onto the sea are top notch and on Sunday nights they have live jazz to soothe the soul.

**Sonia's Place** ( ☎ 450-0234; mains from EC$12; ☽ lunch & dinner) Sonia is a real charmer. Give her a call before you arrive and she'll make pretty much whatever you want for dinner. Her little shack of a restaurant isn't much to look at, but who cares, the food is brilliant.

**Yacht Haven** ( ☎ 458-7300; Landings at St Lucia; mains from US$35; ☽ lunch & dinner) Elegance on a deck – hard to believe, but this restaurant in the Landings development is a winner. Dark

ST LUCIA

hardwood decking, shade sails and views of the sea are all on display. The food is an up-scale mix of island favorites and imported delights. It's definitely a place to be seen, but the food is the best social pay-off.

**Village Gate** (Dauphin St) The heart and soul of the Friday jump-up is right here at the Village Gate. This is the place to grab a cold one with the locals, kick up your heels and let your hair down.

## PIGEON ISLAND NATIONAL PARK

Pigeon Island has a spicy history dating back to the 1550s, when St Lucia's first French settler, Jambe de Bois (Wooden Leg), used the island as a base for raiding passing Spanish ships. Two centuries later, British admiral George Rodney fortified Pigeon Island, using it to monitor the French fleet on Martinique. Rodney's fleet set sail from Pigeon Island in 1782 for his most decisive military engagement, the Battle of the Saintes.

With the end of hostilities between the two European rivals, the fort slipped into disuse in the 19th century, although the USA established a small signal station here during WWII.

In the 1970s a sandy causeway was constructed between Gros Islet and Pigeon Island, turning the island into a peninsula, and in 1979 Pigeon 'Island' was established as a national park.

It's a fun place to explore, with paths winding around the remains of **Fort Rodney**, whose partially intact stone buildings create a certain ghost-town effect. The grounds are well endowed with lofty trees, manicured lawns and fine coastal views. Near the gate is a kitchen dating from 1824 and further on is the main fortress. A vague path leads you around the coast of the 'island' – it's a great way to take it all in. The walk takes about 20 minutes.

At the top of Fort Rodney Hill, you'll find a small but well-preserved fortress, a few rusting cannons and a spectacular view. You can see south across Rodney Bay to the rolling hills dotting the coast, and north past Pointe du Cap to Martinique. For more views, continue north past the stone foundations of the ridge battery to the top of the 359ft **Signal Peak**, about a 20-minute walk.

**Pigeon Island** (admission EC$13; 9am-5pm, center closed Sun) is administered by the St Lucia National Trust. You find a pub and a restaurant selling sandwiches at moderate prices.

Most of the coastline around Pigeon Island is rocky, though there's a pleasant little sandy beach just east of the jetty.

It's about a 20-minute walk along the causeway from Gros Islet to Pigeon Point.

# SOUTHERN ST LUCIA

As the road heads south from Castries, it encounters the rising topography of the island – twisting and turning around hairpin corners and steep hills – and uncluttered ocean views. The jade-green jungle expands to the interior, and as the road nears Soufrière the Pitons emerge on the horizon and dominate the skyline.

Passing through the tiny fishing villages of Anse La Raye and Canaries, and the banana plantations that surround, the real St Lucia comes to the fore. Those keen for a full day on the road can make the scenic loop and circle the southern portion of the island via the coast road.

## MARIGOT BAY

Deep, sheltered Marigot Bay is a stunning example of natural architecture. Sheltered by towering palms and the surrounding hills the narrow inlet is said to have hidden the entire British fleet from its French pursuers. Yachts play the same trick these days – the bay is a popular place to drop anchor and hide away for a few nights. Even if you don't have a ship to hide – it's still a great place to get lost for the day.

The bay leapt to the attention of the world in 1967 when the Hollywood musical *Doctor Doolittle* was filmed in the bay. Residents, restaurateurs and hoteliers have been milking this ever since – but it's no surprise, the beautiful surrounds were made for the movies.

There is a small beach that juts out into the bay and is accessible by a small ferry that grinds a groove from one side of the bay to the other as it makes hundreds of trips per day (EC$5 round-trip).

**Dive Fair Helen** ( 451-7716; www.divefairhelen.com) is a well-run center that offers a variety of courses and packages; it also operates out of Vigie Marina (Castries).

A short ferry ride across the bay delivers you to **Marigot Beach Club** ( 451-4974; www.marigot diveresort.com; villas from US$175; ) . Though getting on in years, the pleasant outlook and

---

**BUS TA MOVE**

When it comes to cultural experiences on St Lucia, few can rival the simple act of taking the local bus. These pillars of public transport aren't hulking diesel beasts of civil infrastructure. No, they are more like a van that should have been sent to the wreckers a good decade ago.

They take car pooling to a whole new level, where five people would be comfortable, 10 would be cozy and 20 is what the driver wants. Squashed in like tinned fish on the way home from the cannery you more than get to know your neighbor. As added entertainment the thumping tunes provided by the driver gets the whole crowd into it – dancehall cranked up to 11 with 19 of your newest friends singing along.

And just to top it off the driver attacks the road with the ferocity of a rally-car driver on crack, power shifting into corners and cranking round blind hairpins like someone who's made peace with God. Not since Keanu Reeves said, 'Dude, there's a bomb on the bus' has public transport been this entertaining.

---

relaxed feel haven't faded a bit. Four-poster beds and kitchenettes come standard, and there is a small beach to kick back on. Offers wi-fi access.

The new kid on the Marigot Bay block, **Discovery** ( ☎ 458-5300; www.discoverystlucia.com; r from US$660; ✖ 🖳 💺 ) has upped the ante on the local luxury scale. It's popular with the super-yacht set, and fitted out with the posh fixtures and features you'd expect. The attention to detail is superb with wi-fi access, wooden in-lays, clean lines and wall-to-wall hardwood. It has an onsite spa and funky pool, and it offers yoga and tai-chi. Every room is a suite. Nice.

**Dolittle's Restaurant & Beach Bar** (Marigot Beach Club; mains from EC$25; ✆ lunch & dinner) is a classic Caribbean waterside eatery with plenty of fish and other relaxed fare on the menu; by night it raises its game a bit and gets a teaspoon more formal.

With a very *Sex in the City* vibe and a style best described as a penchant for illumination, **Pink Snail Bar** (Discovery; ✆ drinks from 6pm) is the place to be for a sunset cocktail or two. Pony up to the glowing pink bar and tuck into a nice glass of Bollinger.

## ANSE LA RAYE

Heading south along the coast from Marigot Bay, the winding road snakes its way through the tiny village of Anse La Raye. The smattering of colorful buildings is typical of every St Lucian fishing community, and the village itself gives a good insight into the daily lives of the locals. Things spice up on a Friday night when the sleepy village wakes up big time. 'Seafood Friday' has become one of the highlights for St Lucians from one end of the island to the other. Street stalls sell fish

of every variety that fit those magic criteria of being decadently delicious and amazingly affordable. The party gets a bit wild and goes most of the night. It will definitely be memorable, filled with food, refreshments and dance.

## SOUFRIÈRE

If one town were to be the heart and soul of St Lucia, it would have to be Soufrière. Where the resort communities elsewhere on the island glisten with the glow of affluence, this decidedly working class community is alight with a strength of spirit. The local people exude a warmth that is as endearing as it is impossible to fake. Though the buildings and infrastructure are not set in the 21st century, the character that the town has acquired is much greater than the sum of its parts.

The landscape surrounding the town is little short of breathtaking. The sky-scraping towers of rock known as the Pitons stand guard over the town. Jutting from the sea, covered in vegetation and ending in a summit that looks other worldly, these iconic St Lucian landmarks are the pride of Soufrière.

The French first settled here in 1746 and named the town Soufrière for the nearby sulfur springs that are still visited today. Though most visitors will only pass through or stop for the day, to really experience the place more time is needed. The accommodations fit every budget and the enveloping warmth of the community makes it nigh on impossible to leave.

### Information

**Soufrière tourist office** ( ☎ 459-7419; ✆ 8am-4pm Mon-Fri, 8am-noon Sat) On the waterfront.

## Sights & Activities

### ANSE CHASTANET

Anse Chastanet could be the quintessential St Lucian beach experience. Though only a mile or so from Soufrière, it feels like a lost tropical world. The tiny sheltered bay is protected by high cliffs and towering palms on the shore. The petite beach is great for a dip and the snorkeling just off shore is some of the best on the island.

You'll find a dive shop here (opposite) to take you deeper, a restaurant for refueling and a hotel if you just can't tear yourself away. It's a strenuous 35-minute walk from Soufrière, over the steep costal road. The views of the Pitons along the way make the effort worthwhile.

### SULPHUR SPRINGS

Looking like something off the surface of the moon the **Sulphur Springs** (admission EC$7; ☼ 9am-5pm) are saddled with the unfortunate tagline of being the world's only drive-in volcano. The reality is far from the garish description. There isn't a crater, or a cauldron of magma to check out – you'll have to be content with a bit of stinky, boiling muck. Bubbling mud is observed from platforms surrounded by vents releasing the oh-so-pleasant sulfur gas – scenting the air with a rotten-eggs aroma.

Be happy that the platform is there. A few years back, a tour guide ventured onto the soft earth and fell up to his waist in boiling mud. He was lucky to survive, and now has a great story to tell. Speaking of great stories, your entry fee includes a tour guide who has a fair bit to say – and they'll expect a tip for their trouble.

To get there from Soufrière, go south on the potholed Vieux Fort road, which winds uphill as it leaves town. About a five-minute drive out of Soufrière, take the downhill fork to the left at the Sulphur Springs sign, from where it's half a mile further to the park entrance.

### MORNE COUBARIL ESTATE

This **estate** ( ☎ 459-7340; adult/child EC$20/10; ☼ 9am-4:30pm), on the Vieux Fort road about half a mile north of Sulphur Springs, offers a great insight into the plantation world that dominated this country for so long. Before the days of tourism, and to this day to a lesser extent, this is how St Lucia paid its way in the world. You can wander through the working co-conut and cocoa plantation; check out the traditional buildings and the ruins of a sugar mill. There are horse-trekking options and the chance to learn about the local fauna.

### DIAMOND BOTANICAL GARDENS

The Diamond Estate's **botanical gardens, waterfall and mineral baths** (adult EC$16.50; ☼ 10am-5pm Mon-Sat, 10am-3pm Sun & holidays) are all at the same site.

Paths wind through the gardens, which are planted with tropical flowers and trees, including numerous heliconia and ginger specimens. At the back of the gardens a small waterfall drops down a rock face that is stained a rich orange from the warm mineral waters. The waterfall featured briefly in the movie *Superman II* as the site from where Superman plucked an orchid for Lois Lane.

The mineral baths date from 1784, when they were built atop hot springs so that the troops of King Louis XVI of France could take advantage of their therapeutic effects. The baths were largely destroyed during the French Revolution, but in recent times a few have been restored and are open to visitors.

The Diamond Estate is 1 mile east of the Soufrière town center, via Sir Arthur Lewis St, and the way is signposted.

### MALGRETOUT

Heading south from Soufrière along the dirt, coastal road you soon come upon the tranquil beach of Malgretout. It's a pleasant stretch of beach with some good snorkeling just off shore; there is even a little bar to wet your whistle after a dip.

A bit further on down the road is the picturesque **Pitons Waterfall** (EC$7.50). The grounds surrounding the falls are lush and alive with rainforest species. The falls themselves are great for a soak and are much less frequently visited compared to some of the other waterfalls in the area. To get to the falls from the beach, head up the paved road for about 200 yards and look out for the sign on the left.

### THE PITONS

These dueling peaks of stone aren't just nice to look at; you can climb them if the mood strikes. Though both will take the day to reach the summit, Petit Piton is steeper than its big brother Gros Piton and is a more strenuous climb. The track to the top of either spire is tricky to find and easy to lose. A guide is recommended, not only to show you the way,

---

**THE KIDS ARE ALRIGHT**

Delana Modeste is like an 18-year-old girl from almost anywhere. She has ambitions to see the world, to go to school in London or Paris. The difference is that in many people's eyes she's already found paradise just by being lucky enough to be born in St Lucia.

**So where do you live?**

I live here in Soufrière, I have my whole life. This is a great part of the island – it isn't too hot and busy like Castries. And it isn't overrun with tourists like Rodney Bay.

**What sort of people come to Soufrière?**

Mostly, it's independent travelers looking to get off the beaten track. People searching for a quiet place to stay. It's really peaceful here, it's just like when my grandma was young, not much has changed. There are more tourists now but things have remained much like they were when she was young.

**What are your favorite things to do around here?**

Well I love to go watch the rugby – but you have to go and hike the Pitons when you are here, and make sure you take in the little things like watching the local fishermen bringing in their catch or even just looking at the flowers. The longer you spend here, the more you see.

**What are some hidden places around here that are just amazing?**

I'm not going to tell you! You'll tell everyone and they won't be hidden anymore. People will just have to come here and discover them for themselves!

**Too right.**

---

but also to offer insight into the local flora and fauna

One recommended guide is **Jah-I** ( ☎ 787-5949; Gros Piton climb US$25, Petit Piton climb US$40), a friendly Rasta who's been guiding the peaks for 30 years and who offers discounts if you bring some friends.

### DIVING

**Action Adventure Divers** ( ☎ 459-5200) is a friendly crew running daily trips, while **Scuba St Lucia** ( ☎ 459-7000; www.ansechastanet.com; Anse Chastanet Resort) is a well-organized dive outfit, right on the beach at Anse Chastanet. Scuba St Lucia run PADI courses at all levels and are a friendly bunch; its rules are a bit antiquated, however, forcing certified divers to do a shore dive and demonstrate their skills before being allowed on the boats.

### CYCLING

**Bike St Lucia** ( ☎ 457-1400; www.bikestlucia.com; Anse Chastanet Resort; 2½hr for US$50), in Anse Chastanet, has miles of purpose-built, mountain-bike trails to test your single-track skills. The trails vary in degree of difficulty, from beginner to the advanced track designed by former world-champion Tinker Juarez.

## Sleeping

**Cascara** ( ☎ 457-1070; s/d/apt EC$40/50/60) Every now and then you get to meet a real character that

sticks in your memories long beyond crimson sunsets and soft sand beaches. Momma Chastante the owner of this quirky little establishment is just one of those people. Her warmth and charm more than make up for the fact that the rooms are about as basic as you can get. There are a few apartments with shared facilities and a couple of rooms with the bare bones of furnishings. The views down onto the harbor are great and the relaxed atmosphere permeates the whole place. On top of all this, it's so cheap you won't believe your eyes when you see the bill.

**Hummingbird Beach Resort** ( ☎ 459-7232; www .stlucia.co.uk; Soufrière; s/d from US$65/90; ✦ ◻ ◪ ) Perched only a few feet from the beach, this compact resort has a great feel. Tastefully decorated rooms, complete with four-poster beds surround the pool. The views of the Pitons from the balconies are fantastic and the attached restaurant is a winner too.

**Talk to me cool spot** ( ☎ 459-7437; West Coast Rd; r US$75) Up the hill and hidden away from view, you'd be hard pressed to stumble upon this spot. The rooms are basic and affordable if a little shabby. The hillside locale offers appealing views but makes for a somewhat cumbersome walk to town.

**Still Beach Resort** ( ☎ 459-7261; www.thestillresort .com; r from US$135; ✦ ) Tucked into the corner of Hummingbird Beach, it sports a huge, sunset-facing deck. The rooms are a bit average, but the price is right. It has an on-site dive shop and restaurant, and access to the sand.

**Mago Estate** ( ☎ 459-5880; www.magohotel.com; Soufrière; r from US$175; ❍ ☐ ☎ ) With more steps then a 5th-floor walk-up, Mago really is cut into the hill. The labyrinth of buildings fans out among the ferns, affording unobstructed views of Soufret and the Pitons. The rooms are pleasant enough, if only a little tired, but the balconies and hammocks more then make up for it. There is a great restaurant on-site and one of the best bars around – you'll find it tough to leave.

**Stonefield Estate** ( ☎ 459-7037; www.stonefield villas.com; PO Box 228, Soufrière; 1- to 3-bedroom villas from US$350; ❍ ☐ ☎ ) This laid-back, family-run property on a former estate is the island's ultimate in understated cool. The 11 hip villas feature sumptuous living areas in natural whitewashed stone and wood, stylishly simple rustic furniture, garden showers, and huge decks (some with private plunge pools) with double hammocks and glorious views over Petit Piton.

**Ladera** ( ☎ 459-7323; www.ladera.com; ste from US$600; ❍ ☐ ☎ ) Where some rooms come with a view, the views here come with a room. Everything you need for that dream holiday is at your beck and call at this spectacular resort. Rooms have their own pools that cut through the living area and form the outside edge of the living space. From your private aquatic sanctuary you can sip bubbly and watch the sun peek behind the Pitons through the unobstructed views of the open wall. Though prohibitively expensive for most travelers, for those with the means, the experience will be worth every dollar. Offers wi-fi access.

**ourpick Jade Mountain** ( ☎ 459-4000; www.jade mountainstlucia.com; PO Box 4000, Soufrière; r incl meals US$1600 to US$2050; ❍ ☎ ) If you're searching for the ultimate in luxury, privacy and rooms with a view in St Lucia – look no further. Jade Mountain is it. Sitting castle-like atop the hill overlooking the Pitons and the sea, this could very well be the best place to stay in the whole country. Each room comes complete with its own private infinity pool and the pinnacle of furnishings and fixtures. The Escher-like structure is an engineering marvel, complete with a rooftop bar with a view only rivaled by a helicopter. It is staunchly technology free, so no telephones, TVs or internet in the rooms – leave it all behind and embrace the pure decadent luxury.

## Eating

A handful of local restaurants offer good food at reasonable prices near the central square that borders Church, Sir Arthur Lewis and Bridge Sts.

**Camilla's** ( ☎ 459-5379; 7 Bridge St; mains EC$20-50; ❍ breakfast, lunch & dinner) Take your pick between the flouncy upstairs gourmet Creole restaurant with local specialties, such as goat stew and callaloo (root vegetable) soup, or the less-formal, café-cum-snack bar downstairs (open until 2am).

**Mago Estate** ( ☎ 459-5880; West Coast Hwy; mains US$22-27; ❍ breakfast, lunch & dinner) It's well worth the uphill journey to this wonderful eating establishment. The aesthetic look is like the cantina out of Star Wars, with an enormous boulder forming the uphill wall. Eclectic decorative decisions complete the interesting dining setting. The food is a French-influenced mixture of West Indian and European classics.

**Piti Piton and Treehouse** ( ☎ 459-7000; mains from EC$40; ❍ dinner) Though a little ways out from Soufrière, at the Anse Chastanet Resort, the journey is well worth the effort, as you are rewarded with one of the best meals in St Lucia. Many of the vegetables and herbs are grown to exacting standards, either on the property or by local farmers. The menu constantly changes with the season and the inspiration of the cooking team – safe to say, you're in good hands here.

**Hummingbird** (mains EC$40-120; ❍ breakfast, lunch & dinner) Mouth-watering local dishes are intermixed with old favorites to form a perfect culinary balance. The fish is prepared with style and flavor and served up with a great view. The service is a bit slow, but what's your hurry?

**Pirates Cove** (Bay St; mains EC$60-80; ☺ lunch & dinner) Right on the waterfront, you can watch the fishers arrive with their catch. Pasta and fish are the specialties with a catch-of-the-day platter that's great every day.

Located in the center of town, **Eroline's Foods** (Church St) is the local supermarket.

### Entertainment

Soufrière is a pretty quiet town as far as nightlife goes, but there is some fun to be found. Most hotels have a bar and a view so are prime real estate for a quiet cocktail. If it's a more lively night you seek, follow the music in town and you'll be sure to come across some trouble to get into.

**Ladera Resort** (☎ 459-7323; Soufrière) Even if you can't afford to spend the night at this spectacular resort, you can always pony up to the bar. Jaw-dropping views over the Pitons all washed down with the sweet taste of a rum punch and your main squeeze by your side.

Big Space bar is easy to find, as the downtown frontage is covered nearly completely by a sign for Piton beer. This is the bar to be on the weekends where the local crew gets on the lash and dances the night away.

## CHOISEUL

Choiseul, a little village south of Soufrière, has an active handicraft industry, and its roadside arts-and-crafts center is a good place to pick up locally made dolls, baskets, pottery and wood carvings.

Located between Choiseul and Paiye is **Balenbouche Estate** (☎ 455-1244; www.balenbouche .com; r US$110-180), the tranquil 18th-century estate home of the congenial Uta Lawaetz and her daughters. You can stay in the lov-ingly restored house furnished with simple, beautiful antiques, or in one of three hippy-ish garden cottages with mosaic-tiled baths. You really feel that you have stepped back in time here; complete the experience with a stroll round the grounds and truly atmospheric jungle-covered mill ruins.

## THE SOUTH & EAST COASTS

The road up the east coast from Vieux Fort is relatively straight and uneventful, passing through a few local villages and numerous banana plantations before turning inland at the town of Dennery and making a scenic, winding cut across the mountainous rainforest to Castries.

The guys at **Reef Kite & Surf** (☎ 454-3418; www .slucia.com/kitesurf; Vieux Fort) can sort you out with windsurfing and kitesurfing gear if you know what you're doing and lessons if you don't. This dedicated group of enthusiasts will have you praying for wind and trying to get air by the end of the day. Gear rentals are US$80 per day and a three-hour lesson costs US$125 (including gear).

**Maria Islands Nature Reserve** (☎ 454-5014; ☺ 9am-5pm Mon-Fri), east of Vieux Fort, is the only habitat of the *kouwes* snake, one of the world's rarest grass snakes, and the Maria Islands ground lizard. Because it's a sanctuary for terns, noddies and other seabirds, this two-island reserve is only accessible outside the summer nesting season.

**Mamiku Gardens** (☎ 455-3729; www.mamiku .com; ☺ 9am-5pm), between Mon Repos and Praslin, is a fascinating historic garden that has been left delightfully unmanicured. Wander among orchids, rock pools and aromatic plants, or visit the medicinal herb garden.

ST LUCIA

---

### ST LUCIA PARROT

The rainforest is home to the St Lucia parrot (*Amazona versicolor*), locally called the Jacquot, the island's colorful endemic parrot. Despite the Jacquot's status as the national bird and its appearance on everything from T-shirts to St Lucian passports, it has teetered on the brink of extinction, and occasionally made it onto island dinner tables in times past.

However, new environmental laws and a successful effort to educate islanders on the plight of the parrot seem to be working to save it. Fines for shooting or capturing parrots have been increased a hundredfold, while much of the parrots' habitat has been set aside for protection. So far, the protection measures have been a success; the 2000 parrot census found 800 birds, up from less than 100 in the mid-1970s. Most of the parrots nest in the Edmond and Quilesse Forest Reserves, east of Soufrière.

**Grande Anse**, 6 miles north of Dennery, is renowned for its nesting leatherback turtles. **Desbarra Turtle Watch Group** ( ☎ 284-2812), a local community group, organizes tours in season (March to August).

# DIRECTORY

## ACCOMMODATIONS

There is a real variety in accommodations on St Lucia. Good-value budget guesthouses and hotels are found in Soufrière and, to a lesser extent, to the north. Rodney Bay is dominated by larger-scale resorts where the amenities are inflated and the rates are in concert with that. The growth of all-inclusive resorts is changing the rooming landscape – more visitors are now spending all their time in their sequestered holiday cocoons, infrequently venturing out into the world.

Most hotels are near or on a beach and almost all of them have an on-site restaurant. Rates are often quoted in US dollars, but payment can be made in the equivalent EC dollars or with a major credit card.

See p815 for a guide to budget, midrange and top-end accommodation price ranges in this book.

## ACTIVITIES
### Adventure Activities

A new attraction has hit St Lucia. **Rain Forest Sky Rides** ( ☎ 458-5151; www.rfat.com) will give you a whole new perspective on the rainforest canopy. They have a rather sedate tramway (US$72) that escorts you through the canopy or a more adrenaline-filled option of a zip-line (US$85). The flying fox has 10 separate lines guaranteed to get you high with excitement.

### Beaches & Swimming

St Lucia has quite a few swimming options and all the beaches are open to the public. By Caribbean standards the beaches aren't spectacular. Most are either small, slightly dirty, overcrowded or a combination of all three.

The best of the lot can be found on the busier northwest side of the island. Gros Islet has a nice stretch of sand and the resort-dominated strip in Rodney Bay has a pleasant, albeit busy section of oceanfront.

The east side of the island is less protected and is subject to rougher seas and unpredict-able ocean currents – some beaches are closed to swimmers for this reason.

### Cycling

Bike St Lucia (p641) has miles of mountain-biking trails through the rainforest near Anse Chastanet.

### Diving & Snorkeling

If you think the above-ground scenery is spectacular in St Lucia, you should see it under the sea. The rugged, underwater landscape is pocketed with reefs and teeming with sea life.

Anse Chastanet, near Soufrière, has been designated a marine park. It boasts spectacular, near-shore reefs, with a wide variety of corals, sponges and reef fish; it's excellent for both diving and snorkeling.

There are a couple of wreck dives, including *Lesleen*, a 165ft freighter that was deliberately sunk in 1986 to create an artificial reef. It now sits upright in 65ft of water near Anse Cochon, another popular dive area. Anse Cochon is also a favored snorkeling stop on day sails to Soufrière.

There's good snorkeling and diving beneath Petit Piton and Gros Piton, the coastal mountains that loom to the south of Soufrière.

A popular dive just a bit further south is Keyhole Pinnacles, consisting of coral-encrusted underwater mounts that rise to within a few feet of the surface. For more information, see p55.

There are a number of dive shops on St Lucia, including in Castries (p634), Rodney Bay (p636), Marigot Bay (p638) and Soufrière (p641). Expect to pay US$40 to US$50 for a single dive.

### Hiking

Three main trails lead into the mountainous interior on public lands that are administered by the **Department of Forest & Lands** ( ☎ 450-2231).

The Barre de L'isle Trail is a good choice if you're on a budget, as you can get to the trailhead from Castries for EC$5 by hopping on a Vieux Fort bus (about 30 minutes). This lush rainforest hike, which is in the center of the island along the ridge that divides the eastern and western halves of St Lucia, leads to the top of the 1446ft Morne la Cambe. It provides some fine views along the way, and takes about three hours round-trip. The trailhead, which begins at the south side of the highway, is clearly marked. Monday to Friday,

Department of Forest & Lands personnel wait at the trailhead to collect the park fee and are available as guides.

As trailhead access for the other two forest-reserve hikes is inland from major roads and bus routes, these hikes are usually undertaken as part of an organized tour. The Des Cartiers Rainforest Trail at the Quilesse Forest Reserve begins 6 miles inland from Micoud and passes through the habitat of the rare St Lucia parrot. The Edmond Forest Reserve Trail begins about 7 miles east of Soufrière, crosses a rainforest of tall trees interlaced with orchids and bromeliads, and offers fine views of St Lucia's highest peak, the 3118ft Mt Gimie.

While the latter two forest-reserve hikes take only a few hours to walk, the travel time to either trailhead is about 90 minutes one way from Castries, so the hikes are full-day outings. The Department of Forest & Lands and the island's main tour agencies arrange outings several days a week.

A hike up either of the Pitons peaks takes about four hours round-trip, and shouldn't be done without an experienced guide (p640).

### Horseback Riding

Trim's Riding Academy (p634) offers horseback riding.

### Golf

The **St Lucia Golf & Country Club** (☎ 450-8523), on the northern tip of the island, has an 18-hole par-71 course and offers lessons (per half-hour around EC$105).

### Windsurfing & Kitesurfing

Head to Reef Kite & Surf (p643), on the windy south coast, for rental and lessons.

## BOOKS

Iconic St Lucian author Derek Walcott has a great body of work to choose from. His 1990 epic poem *Omeros*, published two years before he won the Nobel Prize for literature, is a shining example. The ambitious project, retelling Homer's *Odyssey* in the modern day Caribbean was praised for its panache, scope and success.

## BUSINESS HOURS

The following are common business hours in St Lucia; exceptions are noted in reviews.

**Banks** 8:30am to 3pm Monday to Thursday, 8:30am to 5pm Friday

**Bars** to midnight

**Businesses** 8:30am to 12:30pm and 1:30pm to 4:30pm Monday to Friday

**Government offices** 8:30am to 12:30pm and 1:30pm to 4:30pm Monday to Friday

**Restaurants** breakfast from 8:30am, lunch from noon, dinner 6:30pm to 9pm

**Shops** 8:30am to 12:30pm and 1:30pm to 4:30pm Monday to Friday, 8am to noon Saturday

## CHILDREN

Though not specifically a kid-oriented island, travel with children on St Lucia is fairly straightforward. The water is good for swimming and there are few big waves. One area of caution is on the roads – the drivers on St Lucia set a new standard for recklessness. Be sure to keep an eye on the little ones around the roadways.

## DANGERS & ANNOYANCES

Bilharzia (schistosomiasis) is endemic to St Lucia; the general precaution is to avoid wading or swimming in fresh water. See p841 for further details. Hikers should keep in mind that the poisonous fer-de-lance favors brushy undergrowth, so stick to well-trodden trails.

## EMBASSIES & CONSULATES

**Germany** (☎ 450-8050; Care Service Bldg, Massade Industrial Estate, Gros Islet)

**UK** (☎ 452-2484/5; NIS Waterfront Bldg, 2nd fl, PO Box 227, Castries)

---

### PRACTICALITIES

- **Newspapers & Magazines** *The Voice* is the island's main tri-weekly newspaper.
- **Radio** Tune into music, news and patois programs on Radio Caribbean International (101.1FM).
- **Video Systems** NTSC is the standard video system.
- **Electricity** The current used is 220V (50 cycles). The country uses three-pronged, square European-style plugs.
- **Weights & Measures** The imperial system is used here.

ST LUCIA

## FESTIVALS & EVENTS

**Atlantic Rally for Cruisers** (www.worldcruising.com; November-December) is a fun 'race' across the Atlantic starting off the coast of Spain and ending in St Lucia. Think of a car rally on the high seas that ends up in paradise.

## GAY & LESBIAN TRAVELERS

As with most destinations in the region, St Lucia isn't all that friendly to those with *alternative* lifestyles. Gay men should be especially aware that homosexuality is generally not accepted and travelers should exercise caution when in public. This outdated point of view sadly shows little sign of remission as homophobia is rampant and openly accepted.

## HOLIDAYS

**New Year's Day** January 1
**New Year's Holiday** January 2
**Independence Day** February 22
**Good Friday** Late March/early April
**Easter Monday** Late March/early April
**Labour Day** May 1
**Whit Monday** Eighth Monday after Easter
**Corpus Christi** Ninth Thursday after Easter
**Emancipation Day** August 3
**Thanksgiving Day** October 5
**National Day** December 13
**Christmas Day** December 25
**Boxing Day** December 26

Note that when some holidays fall on Sunday, they are celebrated on the following Monday.

## INTERNET ACCESS

Internet access is becoming more prevalent in all corners of the island. Larger hotels often have wireless connectivity for their guests and internet cafés can be found in most towns.

## INTERNET RESOURCES

**Government of St Lucia** (www.stlucia.gov.lc) Information about government matters.
**St Lucia Star** (www.stluciastar.com) A weekly online newspaper that offers a good insight into the country.

## MAPS

Basic maps are easily found at tourist information outlets and most hotels. Nautical charts can be found at marine supply shops and at bookstores in the larger towns.

## MEDICAL SERVICES

There is a hospital in Castries ( ☎ 453-7059) and in Vieux Fort ( ☎ 454-6041). There is also a clinic in Rodney Bay ( ☎ 452-7059).

## MONEY

The Eastern Caribbean dollar (EC$) is the island currency. US dollars are often accepted by taxi drivers and larger hotels – be sure when negotiating taxi fares and room rates that you are both talking about the same currency. Traveler's checks can be exchanged in banks and in larger hotels without issue.

Visa, American Express and MasterCard are widely accepted at hotels, car-rental agencies and high-end restaurants. You can get cash advances on your credit card through bank machines (provided your card has a security code or PIN). Also, bank cards that have either the Cirrus or the Plus symbol will usually work in bank machines. Royal Band and Scotia Bank readily accept foreign cards and are available in Castries and Rodney Bay.

An 8% tax and 10% service charge are added to the bill at all but the cheapest hotels and restaurants; there's no need for additional tipping.

## POST

Most towns and all cities have a central post office. Hours are usually 8:30am to 3pm Monday to Thursday, closing at 5pm on Friday.

## TELEPHONE

St Lucia's area code is ☎ 758. To call from North America, dial ☎ 1-758, followed by the seven-digit local number. From elsewhere, dial your country's international access code + ☎ 758 + the local number. We have included only the seven-digit local number for St Lucia listings in this chapter.

There are both card and coin phones around the island. Phone cards are sold at tourist-office booths, Cable & Wireless offices and many stores.

Cellular-phone users can use their phones in St Lucia. If you have a GSM phone that is unlocked you can purchase a new SIM card for it for EC$20 from **Cable & Wireless** (Castries; Bridge St; ☼ 7:30am-6:30pm Mon-Fri, 8am-12:30pm Sat). This gives you a local number to call from and is much cheaper in the long run compared to global roaming.

ST LUCIA

For more information on phone cards and making long-distance calls, see p826.

## TOURIST INFORMATION

There are tourist information booths in the arrivals hall of both of the island's airports. You will also find tourist information offices in all the larger towns.

**St Lucia Tourist Board** (www.stlucia.org) is the official site of the tourism board; it has great general information and is a good place to start.

## TOURS

The **St Lucia National Trust** ( ☎ 452-5005; www.slunatrust.org) can arrange tours to the island's coastal nature reserves: the Maria Island Nature Reserve, off the southeast coast, and the Frigate Islands Nature Reserve, off the east coast. Both are popular with bird-watchers.

## TRAVELERS WITH DISABILITIES

Most resorts have some facilities for disabled travelers, but it is best to enquire before heading out. Public buses are definitely not suitable for the disabled as the cramped minivans are a hassle for everyone to squeeze in and out of.

## VISAS

For all foreign visitors, stays of over 28 days generally require a visa.

## WOMEN TRAVELERS

St Lucia is generally a safe destination for women. Though normal precautions should be taken, the crime rate is relatively low.

## WORK

Travelers wishing to work in St Lucia will need to obtain a work permit before undertaking paid employment. For complete requirements have a look at www.stlucia.gov.lc.

# TRANSPORTATION

## GETTING THERE & AWAY
### Entering St Lucia

Most visitors must show a valid passport – French citizens can enter with a national identity card. Visitors to the island are required to fill in an immigration form on arrival detailing the length, purpose and location of their stay, plus any customs declarations they may have. An onward or round-trip ticket or proof of sufficient funds is officially required.

---

> **EMERGENCY NUMBERS**
>
> ■ **Ambulance & Fire** ☎ 911
> ■ **Police** ☎ 999

## Air

St Lucia has two airports: **Hewanorra International Airport** (UVF; ☎ 454-6355), in Vieux Fort at the remote southern tip of the island, and **George FL Charles Airport** (SLU; ☎ 452-1156), in Castries near the main tourist area.

Scheduled international flights land at Hewanorra, which has a longer runway, while flights from within the Caribbean and charters generally land at the more central George FL Charles Airport.

Both airports have tourist-information booths, taxi stands, phones, and booths for car-rental agencies. The tourist-information booths book rooms, sell phone cards and will exchange US cash into EC dollars at slightly disadvantaged rates. There is a EC$68 departure tax levied on all departing passengers.

Offices for the main airlines serving St Lucia are in central Castries.

The following airlines fly to/from St Lucia from within the Caribbean and beyond:

**Air Canada** ( ☎ 454-6038; www.aircanada.com) Montreal, Toronto

**Air Jamaica** ( ☎ 453-6611; www.airjamaica.com) Atlanta, Barbados, Boston, Chicago, Miami, Montego Bay, New York, Newark

**American Airlines** ( ☎ 4524-6777; www.aa.com) Chicago, Miami, New York

**British Airways** ( ☎ 452-3951; www.ba.com) London, Port of Spain

**Delta Airlines** ( ☎ 452-9683, www.delta.com) Atlanta

**LIAT** ( ☎ 452-3056, after hr 452-2348; www.liat.com) Barbados, St. Vincent, Trinidad, Dominica, Antigua

**Virgin Atlantic** ( ☎ 454-3610; www.virgin-atlantic.com) London, Manchester

## Sea
### CRUISE SHIP

Cruise ships dock in Castries. A number of berths, some on the east side of the harbor near the town center and others at Pointe Seraphine on the north side of the harbor, have a duty-free shopping complex.

### FERRY

The ferry service **L'Express des Îles** (www.express-des-iles.com) operates a daily 80-minute express catamaran between Castries and Fort-de-France on Martinique. It also has a service on Saturday and Sunday to Guadeloupe (six hours) and Dominica (four hours). Departure days and times change frequently; check in advance with any local travel agent. On St Lucia, tickets can be purchased from **Carib Travel** ( ☎ 452-2151; PO Box 102, Micoud St).

There is a crossing between St Lucia and Guadeloupe run by **Brudey Frères** ( ☎ 590-90-04-48; www.brudey-freres.fr), in Point-à-Pitre, Guadeloupe, once or twice a week (one way/return EC$80/115). Tickets can be purchased from local travel agencies.

For more information on these ferry boats, see p577.

### YACHT

Customs and immigration can be cleared at Rodney Bay, Castries, Marigot Bay or Vieux Fort. Most yachties pull in at Rodney Bay, where there is a full-service marina and a couple of marked customs slips opposite the customs office.

It's easy to clear customs and immigration at Marigot Bay, where you can anchor in the inner harbor and dinghy over to the customs office. Castries is a more congested scene, and yachts entering the harbor are required to go directly to the customs dock. If there's no room, you should head for the anchorage spot east of the customs buoy. At Vieux Fort, you can anchor off the big ship dock, where customs is located.

Popular anchorages include Reduit Beach, the area southeast of Pigeon Island, Rodney Bay Marina, Marigot Bay, Anse Chastanet, Anse Cochon and Soufrière Bay.

Yacht charters are available from **Sunsail** ( ☎ 452-8648) and **DSL Yachting** ( ☎ 452-8531), both at Rodney Bay Marina, and from the **Moorings** ( ☎ 451-4357), at Marigot Bay. For addresses and booking information, see p835.

## GETTING AROUND
### Bicycle

Bicycles are not really available for rent on St Lucia. The island's roads are very winding in places and the local drivers seem to relish taking blind corners with the ferocity of a Formula-1 driver. The roads are also peppered with hills and are devoid of any kind of shoulder. In other words, even if you could find a bicycle to ride, you probably wouldn't want to.

### Bus

Bus service is via privately owned minivans. They're a cheap way to get around, and the means by which most islanders get to town, school and work. St Lucia's main road forms a big loop around the island, and buses stop at all towns along the way. They're frequent between main towns (such as Castries to Gros Islet) and generally run until 10pm (later on Friday); however, there is no scheduled timetable. Very few buses run on Sunday.

If there's no bus stop nearby, you can wave buses down en route as long as there's space for the bus to pull over. Pay the fare directly to the driver. Buses leave their stops when they are full, so often catching a bus on the road is limited by the number of seats available. At times it's easier to backtrack to a larger town in order to find a bus that has a seat for you.

If you're trying to circle the island by public transportation, note that afternoon bus services between Soufrière and Castries are unreliable, so it's best to travel in a counterclockwise direction, catching a morning bus from Castries to Soufrière and returning via Vieux Fort (up the east coast) in the afternoon.

In Castries, buses going south to Soufrière and Vieux Fort or north to Gros Islet can be found east of the market on Darling Rd. Sample fares from Castries to Gros Islet (Route 1A) or Marigot Bay (Route 3C) are EC$2.50, to Vieux Fort (Route 2H) EC$7 and to Soufrière (Route 3D) EC$10.

Route numbers are displayed on the buses, but it's best to check with the driver, just in case. Buses are easily distinguishable from taxis as they have a green license plate, while taxis have a blue or red one.

### Car & Motorcycle
#### DRIVER'S LICENSE

Drivers on St Lucia must hold an International Driving Permit or purchase a local driving permit (EC$54), which is valid for three months.

#### RENTAL

Avis, Hertz and National, as well as smaller (and generally cheaper) local firms, operate out of both Hewanorra and George FL Charles airports, nearly all offering unlimited mileage.

The cheapest cars, those without air-conditioning, rent for about US$65 a day; you'll find the best rates on the internet. If you're planning an extensive tour of the island, it's advisable to hire a 4WD, as many of the roads are steep and smaller ones can become little more than potholed mudslides after a bout of rain.

Motorcycles and scooters are available from some rental-car companies. However, the hilly terrain, aggressive drivers and narrow roads make St Lucia suitable only for experienced riders.

## ROAD CONDITIONS
Roads vary greatly around the island, with some sections being newly surfaced and others deeply potholed. Make sure you have a workable jack and spare tire available. Many of the interior and southern roads are also very winding and narrow. Gas stations are distributed around the island.

## ROAD RULES
On St Lucia, drive on the left-hand side. Speed limits are generally 15mph (24km/h) in towns and 30mph (48km/h) on major roads.

ST LUCIA

# St Vincent & the Grenadines

Just the name St Vincent and the Grenadines evokes an emotive response with visions of exotic, idyllic island life. And the fantasy rings true. Imagine an island chain buried deep within the Caribbean Sea, uncluttered by tourist exploitation; white sand beaches on deserted islands, sky-blue water gently lapping the shore and barely a soul around.

Thirty-two islands dot the seascape, all vying to one-up each other in terms of tranquility. St Vincent is the largest in the group, home to the capital, Kingstown. This lively town is a throwback to colonial times with cobblestone streets and locals rushing about.

Once you get off the big island and into the Grenadines, everything changes. Gone is the traffic, the hustle and the pavement. All you're left with is a smattering of tiny islands waiting to be explored. Beaches stretch out before you, the pace of life slows to a crawl and the desire to go home vanishes.

You'll find unassuming budget hideaways, where you can escape from the world and (almost) live like a king on the income of a pauper. Or you can spend time on the island of Mustique where renting a house for the week will cost more than buying a luxury car.

These islands have enchanted sailors for centuries, and continue to do so. Whether you have your own vessel or are happy to hitch a ride, the island-hopping opportunities are irresistible. These islands were once the realm of real pirates but now they are the stomping grounds of the *Pirates of the Caribbean*. St Vincent and the Grenadines have jumped into the limelight thanks to Hollywood and they're not looking back.

## FAST FACTS

- **Area** 150 sq miles
- **Capital** Kingstown
- **Country code** ☎ 784
- **Departure tax** EC$40
- **Famous for** Deserted islands, yachting, *Pirates of the Caribbean* – and real pirates, too.
- **Language** English, French patois (increasingly rare)
- **Money** Eastern Caribbean dollar (EC$); EC$1 = US$0.38 = €0.24 = UK£0.19
- **Official name** St Vincent and the Grenadines
- **People** Vincentians (formal), Vincys (colloquial)
- **Phrase** Check it? (Do you follow me?)
- **Population** 118,000
- **Visa** No visa required; see p672

# HIGHLIGHTS

- **Tobago Cays** (p669) Visit the jewel of the Caribbean – these picture perfect islands are the essential SVG experience
- **Canouan** (p665) Check out the undeveloped half of this picturesque island, before it's too late
- **Kingstown** (p654) Hardwire yourself into the local scene, cruise the cobblestone streets of SVG's biggest city
- **Mustique** (p664) If you've got more dollars than sense, kick up your heels with rock stars and drop more coin than the GDP
- **Island-Hopping** (p661) Cruise the ocean, vagabond around the islands, find your own perfect beach or untouched bay and play pirate

# ITINERARIES

- **One Week** Spend a day or two in St Vincent, exploring the busy streets. Then head south and get ready to relax. Take the boat to Bequia and settle into the beach life. Go for a wander, if the mood takes you, and compare stretches of sand. Be sure to factor into your plans a day trip to the Tobago Cays aboard the *Friendship Rose*.
- **Island-Hopping Adventure** Start your journey in St Vincent and spend a few days on in the big island, then jump on a ferry and head to Bequia, where you'll be overwhelmed by the change of pace. After decompressing, loop back to St Vincent and catch the ferry south to Mustique, then onwards to Canouan, Mayreau, the Tobago Cays, Palm Island and finally to Union Island. Take as much time as you have – the slower the better.

# CLIMATE & WHEN TO GO

The climate varies between the islands, as the Grenadines to the south are slightly drier and marginally warmer than St Vincent. In St Vincent the dry season runs approximately from January to May. In July, the wettest month, rain falls for an average of 26 days, while in April, the driest month, it averages only six days. In January the average daily high temperature is 29°C (85°F), while the nightly low is 22°C (72°F). In July the average high is 30°C (86°F), while the nightly low is 24°C (76°F).

The high season (winter) runs from December to April/May. The wetter months can still be nice, and they keep the islands lush and green.

# HISTORY

St Vincent is not as remote as it appears and has actually been inhabited for some 7000 years. Originally it was sparsely populated by the hunter-gatherer Siboneys. Around 2000 years ago they were replaced by the Arawaks, who moved up from present-day Venezuela. The raiding Caribs eventually took over from the Arawaks, but held some of the islands for as little as 100 years before the arrival of the heavily armed Spanish. Fierce Carib resistance kept the Europeans out of St Vincent

---

**HOW MUCH?**

- Taxi from Kingstown to airport EC$25
- Ferry from St Vincent to Bequia EC$20
- Bottle of Hairoun beer EC$5
- Bed in a budget hotel US$30
- Villa for the week on Mustique US$40,000

---

long after most other Caribbean islands had fallen to the colonists. This was in part because many Caribs from other islands fled to St Vincent (Hairoun, as they called it) after their home islands were conquered – it was the Caribs' last stand. On the island, Caribs intermarried with Africans who had escaped from slavery, and the new mixed generation split along ethnic lines as Black Caribs and Yellow Caribs.

In 1783, after a century of competing claims between the British and French, the Treaty of Paris placed St Vincent under British control. Indigenous rebellions followed and British troops rounded up the 'insurgents,' forcibly repatriating around 5000 Black Caribs to Roatán island, Honduras. With the native opposition gone, the planters capitalized on the fertile volcanic soil and achieved the success that had eluded them. However, it didn't last long: two eruptions of La Soufrière, the abolition of slavery in 1834 and a few powerful hurricanes stood in the way of their colonial dreams. For the remainder of the British rule the economy stagnated; plantations were eventually broken up and land was redistributed to small-scale farmers.

In 1969, in association with the British, St Vincent became a self-governing state and on October 27, 1979 it was cobbled together with the Grenadines as an independent member of the Commonwealth. Tourism, for all its good and bad, has helped to reinvigorate the once flagging economy, although unemployment is still a major issue.

## THE CULTURE

Pigeonholing Vincy culture is a tough task. With 30 islands in the chain, the cultural variance is as vast as the ocean in which they sit. Locals tend to be conservative, quiet and a tough nut to crack for outsiders. Many view travelers as just another transient group and don't make much of an effort to open up. In St Vincent the residents are the product of a busier place so they tend to stick to themselves a bit more, creating a slightly cold exterior. However once you get onto the smaller islands the warmth freely shines through.

To a certain degree there is a feeling of detachment from the outside world. The isolation of the islands has created an interesting culture where there is a strong desire to emulate the images seen in the media. Hip-hop fashion has permeated the youth scene, with 50 Cent as likely to be heard on a car stereo as Bob Marley. American TV now dominates the airways and threatens to derail the cultural independence of St Vincent and the Grenadines (SVG).

The idea of conservation and environmentalism unfortunately isn't on the minds of many locals. There is rubbish on the land and the sight of someone casually tossing their KFC wrapper over the rail of an interisland ferry is sadly far too common.

Most locals find work in traditional industries such as fishing, microagriculture or laboring. Tourism also dominates the employment landscape with a growing number of Vincys moving up into management positions. The laid-back attitude of the locals can be perceived as lazy, uninterested or apathetic – but the reality is that behind the chilled exterior often sits an ambitious soul who wants a piece of the economic pie.

Christianity is the dominant faith on the islands, with several branches of the tree represented. The majority of islanders are Protestant, with Anglicans being the largest denomination. Other faiths include Methodist, Seventh Day Adventist, Jehovah's Witness, Baptist, Streams of Power and Baha'i. About 20% of Vincentians are Roman Catholic. Religion is taken seriously, with the Sabbath observed throughout, meaning that very little happens on Sunday – many restaurants and nearly all shops will be closed. You'll see Rastas around but few of them practice the religious elements associated with the faith, preferring to stick with music, weed and fashion as their expression of Rastafarianism.

## ARTS

Music is the cultural lifeblood of St Vincent. The infectious Caribbean rhythms permeate the air and are inescapable. Musical preference is divided along generational lines. Aging Rastas groove to the mellow jams of old-school reggae legends like Bob Marley and Pete Tosh. The younger generations are enchanted by the frenetic beats of modern dancehall and imported American hip-hop. This American influence is easily seen on the streets, with T-shirts displaying the rap star *de jour* being standard issue.

Miniature-boat building is a popular artistic endeavor and the craftsmanship on these miniature crafts is as exacting as for their grown-up cousins. Full-size construction of seaworthy vessels helped to put the boat-builders of St Vincent on the map. Their skills are widely known and respected throughout the region.

# ENVIRONMENT
## The Land
St Vincent is a high volcanic island, forming the northernmost point of the volcanic ridge that runs from Grenada in the south up through the Grenadine islands. It is markedly hilly and its rich volcanic soil is very productive – St Vincent is often called the 'garden of the Grenadines.' It has a rugged interior of tropical rainforest, and lowlands thick with coconut trees and banana estates. The valley region around Mesopotamia, northeast of Kingstown, has some of the best farmland and luxuriant landscapes.

The island of St Vincent makes up 133 sq miles of the nation's 150 sq miles. The other 17 sq miles are spread across 30 islands and cays, fewer than a dozen of which are populated. The largest of the islands are Bequia, Mustique, Canouan, Mayreau and Union Island. The larger Grenadine islands are hilly but relatively low-lying, and most have no source of freshwater other than rainfall. All have stunning white-sand beaches and abundant sea life.

## Wildlife
The crystal-clear waters surrounding St Vincent and the Grenadines are as abundant with sea life as any stretch of ocean on the globe. Plentiful reefs are a flurry of fish activity with turtles, moray eels, angelfish, barracuda, octopus, nurse sharks and countless other species calling the region home. Dolphins also frequent the area and are often seen surfing the bow waves of oceangoing vessels.

On land, the fauna become decidedly more sparse. The sun-drenched islands are home to

a few interesting species, like the St Vincent parrot, an endangered and strikingly beautiful bird that has multicolored plumage and is seen in the jungle interior of St Vincent. This rainforest also provides the home for *manicou* (opossum) and *agouti* (a rabbitlike rodent). *Agouti* roam freely on Young Island, where they are easy to spot.

## Environmental Issues
The concepts of climate change and environmental responsibility are slowly creeping into the collective mindsets of Vincentians. The government has started a program to try to curb damage done to the sea by overfishing and irresponsible boating practices. It's a great start, but getting locals to comply could be an uphill battle. A shocking amount of rubbish is crudely tossed into the sea and into ditches along the side of the road. Broken glass and the ever-present KFC wrappings are major features in gutters, ditches and roadways in Kingstown, especially.

As a visitor, lead by example: put your garbage in a bin and avoid taking shells, or damaging coral when you are snorkeling. Fresh water is also a major concern, with a combination of runoff, wells and desalination plants supplying the hydration for the islands. Demand outstrips supply when cruise ships roll up and refill their tanks and this continues to be a divisive issue for locals, depending on which side of the economic equation they sit.

## FOOD & DRINK
As far as West Indian food goes, SVG is one of the better destinations for enjoying its unique flavors. The fertile ground of St Vincent makes it a prime location for farming and the fruits and vegetables produced here are top quality and delicious. Likewise the sea provides a bounty of delights; lobster, shrimp, conch and fish are all popular and readily available.

Typical dishes include *callaloo* (a spinach-like vegetable) and savory pumpkin soup. Saltfish and rotis are common simple snacks and light meals. Rotis (curried vegetables, potatoes and meat wrapped in a flour tortilla) are a national passion and are on offer everywhere.

For the traveler there are countless eating options, with both traditional West Indian fare and European varieties freely available. Italian, French and even Mexican cuisine can be found on most islands – all have a seafood bent to them and do well fusing the local ingredients into their dishes.

Hairoun (pronounced 'high-rone') is the local beer. Brewed in Kingstown, the light lager is a tasty drop and very popular throughout the islands. On St Vincent, tap water comes from a reservoir and is generally safe to drink. On the outer islands water comes from rain collection, wells or desalination plants – so the quality can vary and the taste can be unpleasant at times. Bottled water is widely available and recommended.

# ST VINCENT

**pop 105,000**

St Vincent is the largest island and the hub that most travelers will pass through on their visit to SVG. Though not uninspiring, the allure of the Grenadines pulls most visitors away from here quickly.

The beaches are sadly on the average side and the frenetic pace of Kingstown tends to put off those in search of the quiet life. The lush green, rainforested interior has some pleasant hiking options. Vast banana plantations and other agricultural pursuits form the mainstay of farming in the region.

There are also opportunities to get an insight into traditional Vincy life as the towns and villages are unspoiled by tourism – unlike the resorts around the island that, for the most part, do their best to insulate guests from the realities of life on St Vincent, preferring to bathe them in rum punch and lull them to sleep with incessant steel-pan serenades.

## Getting There & Away

### AIR

The runway at ET Joshua Airport receives regular flights (with connections further afield) to/from Barbados, St Lucia, Grenada and Trinidad. See p673.

There are also intracountry flights to Bequia, Canouan, Mustique and Union Island. Ferries will take you to Barbados, through all of the Grenadines, where you can continue on to Grenada.

### BOAT

For details on the cargo or passenger mailboat ferries that ply the waters to Bequia and Union Island, see p673.

Fantasea Tours has day trips that head to Mustique, Bequia, Canouan, Mayreau and the Tobago Cays; see p657 for details.

## Getting Around

Buses are a good way to get around St Vincent, with fares ranging from EC$1 to ED$5, depending on the destination.

Cars can be rented from **Avis** ( ☎ 456-4389; ET Joshua Airport), while **Sailor's Cycle Centre** ( ☎ 457-1274; modernp@caribsurf.com; Upper Middle St), in Kingstown, rents road bikes and mountain bikes from EC$25 per day.

Taxis are available at the airport and at a couple of stands in central Kingstown. **Sam's Taxi Tours** ( ☎ 456-4338; sams-taxi-tours@caribsurf.com) offers day tours that take in the sights of either the west or east coast of St Vincent for around US$100 for up to two people.

# KINGSTOWN

**pop 30,000**

Rough cobblestone streets, arched stone doorways and covered walkways conjure up a forgotten era of colonial rule. The city of Kingstown heaves and swells with a pulsing local community that bustles through its narrow streets and alleyways. Hot, stagnant air envelops the town, amplifying the sounds of car horns, street hucksters and the music filtering through the crowd.

Though not a tourist destination in itself, for nearly all visitors to SVG Kingstown is the gateway to exploring the outer islands of the Grenadines. This popular hub is frequented by locals and travelers who use the bank, stock up on supplies and have a taste of town before heading out into the quiet of the surrounding islands.

There is more tourist infrastructure a few miles down the road from Kingstown in the towns of Villa and Indian Bay – this is where you will find the majority of the resorts on the island.

## Orientation

The city is hemmed in by the island's hilly topography, and the center consists of only about a dozen dense blocks. Ferries from the Grenadines arrive at the jetty just south of the city center.

### MAPS

You'll find basic maps of Kingstown in pamphlets and maps of the Grenadines

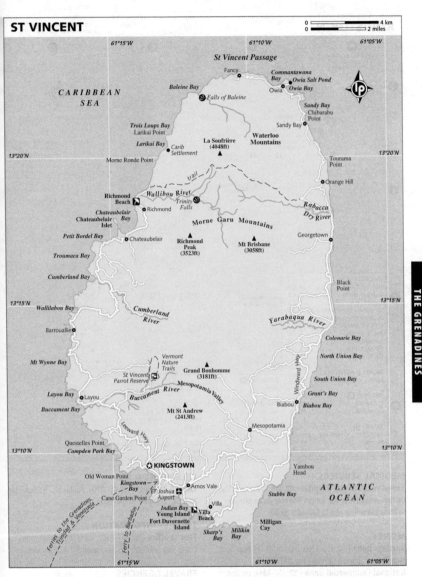

that are distributed through the **tourist office** (☎ 457-1502; www.svgtourism.com; Cruise Ship Terminal; ☺ 8am–noon & 1–4:15pm Mon-Fri) and various travel agencies and hotels.

## Information
### EMERGENCY
**Police station** (☎ 999; cnr Upper Bay & Hillsborough Sts)

### INTERNET ACCESS
**Ferry Terminal** (per hr US$2) A great way to kill some time while waiting for the ferry and also a good option if you're in this end of town. Good computers and a pretty fast connection.

**Office Essentials** (☎ 457-2235; oel@caribsurf.com; Bonadie Plaza, Upper Middle St, per hr EC$5.75) Provides internet access.

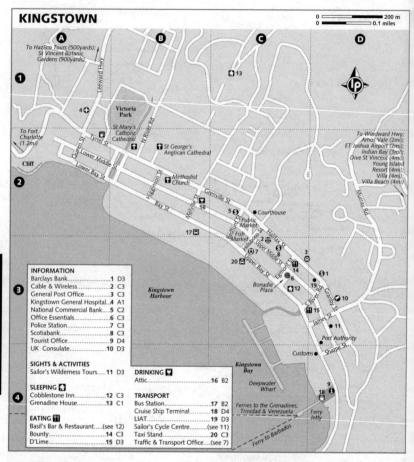

# KINGSTOWN

**INFORMATION**
| | |
|---|---|
| Barclays Bank | 1 D3 |
| Cable & Wireless | 2 C3 |
| General Post Office | 3 C3 |
| Kingstown General Hospital | 4 A1 |
| National Commercial Bank | 5 C2 |
| Office Essentials | 6 C3 |
| Police Station | 7 C3 |
| Scotiabank | 8 C3 |
| Tourist Office | 9 D4 |
| UK Consulate | 10 D3 |

**SIGHTS & ACTIVITIES**
| | |
|---|---|
| Sailor's Wilderness Tours | 11 D3 |

**SLEEPING**
| | |
|---|---|
| Cobblestone Inn | 12 C3 |
| Grenadine House | 13 C1 |

**EATING**
| | |
|---|---|
| Basil's Bar & Restaurant | (see 12) |
| Bounty | 14 C3 |
| D'Lime | 15 D3 |

**DRINKING**
| | |
|---|---|
| Attic | 16 B2 |

**TRANSPORT**
| | |
|---|---|
| Bus Station | 17 B2 |
| Cruise Ship Terminal | 18 D4 |
| LIAT | 19 D3 |
| Sailor's Cycle Centre | (see 11) |
| Taxi Stand | 20 C3 |
| Traffic & Transport Office | (see 7) |

## MEDICAL SERVICES
**Kingstown General Hospital** ( ☎ 456-1185; ✆ 24hr)
On the Leeward Hwy. For serious illness or decompression
sickness you will be sent to Barbados (p680).

## MONEY
**Barclays Bank** ( ☎ 456-1706; Halifax St; ✆ 8am-3pm
Mon-Thu, to 5pm Fri) Opposite the LIAT office.
**National Commercial Bank** ( ☎ 457-1844; cnr Bed-
ford & Grenville Sts; ✆ 8am-3pm Mon-Thu, to 5pm Fri)
**Scotiabank** ( ☎ 457-1601; Halifax St; ✆ 8am-2pm
Mon-Thu, to 5pm Fri)

## POST
**General post office** ( ☎ 456-1111; Halifax St;
✆ 8:30am-3pm Mon-Fri, to 11:30am Sat) Also offers
telephone service.

## TELEPHONE & FAX
**Cable & Wireless** ( ☎ 457-1901; Halifax St; ✆ 7am-7pm
Mon-Sat, 8-10am & 6-8pm Sun)

## TOURIST INFORMATION
**Tourist office** ( ☎ 457-1502; www.svgtourism.com;
Cruise Ship Terminal; ✆ 8am-noon & 1-4:15pm Mon-Fri)

## TRAVEL AGENCIES
**Fantasea Tours** ( ☎ 457-4477; www.fantaseatours.com;
Villa; ✆ 9am-5pm) A one-stop shop for all travel needs;
inbound, outbound and all around the islands.

# Sights & Activities
## FORT CHARLOTTE
Just north of the city and standing proudly
atop a 660ft ridge, **Fort Charlotte** ( ✆ daylight)

offers commanding views of both town and the Grenadines to the south.

Built in 1806 and named after King George III's wife, the fort was built to repel the French navy. In its heyday it was the home to 600 troops and 34 cannons. These days it's a fair bit quieter, but the walls and a few of the guns remain. It's a steep 30-minute walk from town or you can hop on a bus that will drop you off near the fort; then you only have to contend with the last 10 minutes uphill.

### ST VINCENT BOTANIC GARDENS

The oldest botanical gardens in the western hemisphere, the **St Vincent Botanic Gardens** (☎ 457-1003; Montrose; ✹ 6am-6pm) are lovingly tended and provide an oasis of calm that's only half a mile north from the frenzy of Kingstown. Originally established in 1762 to propagate spices and medicinal plants, the gardens now comprise a neatly landscaped 20-acre park with lots of flowering bushes and tall trees. There's a small **aviary** that is intermittently home to some of the island's remaining 500 endangered St Vincent parrots. Guided tours are available for US$2 per person.

### BEACHES

The beaches of St Vincent are sadly substandard, especially compared to the magnificent sandy examples found further south in the Grenadines. The best options on St Vincent are **Indian Bay Beach** and **Villa Beach**. Their proximity to local accommodations makes them a convenient place for a swim.

### DIVING & SNORKELING

**Dive St Vincent** (☎ 457-4714; www.divestvincent.com; Young Island dock, St Vincent) offers dive trips and instruction, as well as snorkeling trips.

Snorkeling can be OK a little way off Indian Bay Beach and Villa Beach.

## Tours

**Fantasea Tours** (☎ 457-4477; www.fantaseatours.com; Villa) Arranges sailing day tours from St Vincent to the Grenadine islands. One goes to Mustique and Bequia for US$70 per person, and another takes in Canouan, Mayreau and the Tobago Cays for US$90 per person.

**HazEco Tours** (☎ 457-8634; www.hazecotours.com; Gun Hill, Kingstown) Offers a range of tours with an emphasis on the outdoors. A half-day outing to the Vermont Nature Trails is US$30 per person, or a hiking trip to the summit of La Soufrière is US$100 for up to two people.

**Sailor's Wilderness Tours** (☎ 457-1274; www.sailor tours.com; Upper Middle St) One of the few operators offering mountain bike tours. Various cycling, hiking and cruising options are available.

## Festivals & Events

For more than 30 years **Vincy Mas** has been *the* big yearly event in St Vincent. This enormous carnival takes place at the end of June or in early July. The calypso and soca competitions culminate in a street party in Kingstown with steel bands, dancers and drinks. For more festivals and events, see p671.

## Sleeping

The majority of accommodations options are in the beachside communities of Indian Bay and Villa. There are a few places to stay in Kingstown itself, which is a good option if you need to catch an early flight or boat.

**Skyblue Apartments** (☎ 457-4394; skyblue@caribsurf .com; Indian Bay; s/d US$55/75; 🐾 🖳) Nestled in the suburban neighborhood of Indian Bay, this place has quirky extras aplenty, with turtles in the yard and a miniature golf course. Rooms are tidy and basic; all come equipped with kitchens. Offers wi-fi access.

**our pick Cobblestone Inn** (☎ 456-1937; www.thecob blestoneinn.com; Upper Bay St, Kingstown; d/tr US$65/75; 🐾 🖳) The Cobblestone Inn was built from the shell of an 1814 cobblestone warehouse and modernized into a fantastic urban hotel. Arched stone passageways connected with narrow stairs form a labyrinth that's as enticing as it is aesthetic. Rooms are nicely fitted out with Renaissance-style curtains and shiraz-colored hardwood. The stylish rooftop breakfast and lunch spot is the final cherry on top of this establishment that truly leaves no (cobble)stone unturned.

**Beachcombers Hotel** (☎ 458-4283; www.beach combershotel.com; Villa; s/d incl continental breakfast US$75/99; 🖳 🐾) This is a real find on the west side of Villa. Multicolored buildings dot the landscape in true Caribbean style. The basic rooms are perhaps a bit too basic, but the superior rooms really cut the mustard. Spacious grounds, a bar and a pool sweeten the deal.

**Fitness Quest Gym & Hotel** (☎ 457-5898; fitness quest@vincysurf.com; Villa; s/d US$84/108; 🐾 🖳) Some hotels have a gym, this gym has a hotel. Not nearly as grim as it sounds: the rooms have been soundproofed to keep the throbbing bass out and the facilities are quite good. Ocean views from the rooms, large kitchens and a decent living area make it a good option for longer stays. Free use of the gym too, so if you're looking to get ripped this could just be the place for you.

**Villa Lodge Hotel** ( ☎ 458-4641; www.villalodge.com; Indian Bay; s/d from US$110/130; ✖ ☐ ☎ ) Luscious landscaped grounds, large rooms and friendly staff make this a popular place for retuning guests. Just off the succulent sands of Indian Bay, each room is equipped with a balcony and some have sea views too. Offers wi-fi access.

**Grenadine House** ( ☎ 458-1800; www.grenadinehouse .com; Kingstown; s/d from US$200/233; ✖ ☐ ☎ ☎ ) High in the hills overlooking Kingstown, like a fortress of whitewashed luxury, Grenadine House is a step in a different direction compared to most properties on the island. Away from the beach and in the heart of suburbia, the views of town and of the Grenadines are fantastic. White linen with thread-counts to brag about, wicker headboards and fresh flowers complement the bedrooms. There are two bars on site and a double shot of restaurants too. The French Governor General, the original resident in the 1760s, would still approve.

**Young Island Resort** ( ☎ 458-4826; www.young island.com; Young Island; d incl meals US$535; ✖ ☎ ) It's only 200yds off shore, but the vaguely heart-shaped private Young Island is a whole world away. Swaying palms line the beach and shade the attractive villas that speckle the hillside. Abundant gardens of native plants assault the senses and the stilted bar sitting among the breakers teases your imagination. The villas are dead sexy, with plunge pools, killer views and everything you'd need to settle in for a good long stay.

## Eating & Drinking

**Bounty** ( ☎ 456-1776; Egmont St; meals from EC$10) Cruise upstairs to this cool little find. Rotis, mac and cheese, and other simple favorites populate the menu – good grub, unpretentious and tasty. There is a decent selection of souvenirs for sale here too and there are even nice views of town from the window side tables.

**X-Cape** (Villa; mains from EC$15) Head upstairs to take in the view and stay for a great local meal. The rotis are top shelf and the bamboo furniture, hardwood floors and drifting sea breeze all add up to make for a perfect island setting in Villa.

**French Veranda** ( ☎ 458-4972; Villa; mains from US$18) This outdoor bistro at the end of the road at Villa is a gastronomic delight. The menu drips with panache and is highlighted by delectable dishes such as curried conch and grilled farm fresh chicken – *bon appetite!*

**Basil's Bar & Restaurant** ( ☎ 457-2713; Upper Bay St; mains from EC$30; ✞ lunch & dinner) Downstairs in the Cobblestone Inn you'll find the door into the dungeonlike Basil's Bar & Restaurant. This upscale pub has a feel like you might have just stepped into a pirate movie, with darkened booths, filtered light and cobblestone walls. Both Caribbean classics and Western favorites populate the menu – it's a tasty option for lunch or dinner. It's popular with Kingstown professionals.

**our pick** **Lime** ( ☎ 458-4227; Villa; pub food from EC$25, mains from EC$40; ✞ breakfast, lunch & dinner) Classic travelers bar complete with '80s beer posters on the wall, signed undies and hand-drawn maps to secret islands. This Villa establishment does a great burger at lunchtime and the dinner menu is best described as eclectic, with the standards and a flair for the exotic including rabbit and pigeon up for grabs.

**Young Island Resort** (lunch US$20, dinner US$50; ✞ breakfast, lunch & dinner) There are few places that can boast that their specialty is bread, but here at Young Island the proof is in the pumpernickel. Every meal comes with a barge full of fresh breads to accompany the equally fresh seafood and other delights. Reservations are required for nonguests and be sure to drop by on a Saturday night when the steel band cranks up. If that's not your thing, be sure to avoid Saturday, as that's when the steel drum band cranks up.

**Attic** ( ☎ 457-2559; Melville St; cover EC$10-15; ✞ 5pm-late) A chilled 2nd-floor club in an old stone building, the Attic has live jazz a few nights a week and sometimes soca bands on Saturday.

**D'Lime** (Upper Bay St; ✞ 5pm-late) Looking for a cold beer on a hot day? Want to chat to some locals about Vincy life or a place to take a load off during the weekly jump-up? D'Lime's got you covered. Right on the main strip in the heart of town, this beer hall, rum shack and meeting place is a Kingstown classic.

## Shopping

Looking to get a cheap T-shirt, a mix CD of local reggae favorites or perhaps a dubious DVD of the latest Hollywood release? Look no further than Upper Middle Street. If nothing else, this lane of street stalls and tiny shops is a great spot to hang out with the locals in their element and find some real bargains.

## Getting There & Away

Kingstown is the transportation hub of SVG. If you arrive in St Vincent by boat, you will disembark in Kingstown; if you arrive by plane, you will land at ET Joshua Airport in the nearby suburb of Arnos Vale. There are numerous boats and airlines that service St Vincent (see p673).

The Cruise Ship Terminal at the south end of Kingstown Harbour receives international cruise ships and has tourist facilities, including information and shops.

The bus station is near the Little Tokyo Fish Market on Bay St, although buses can also be hailed along the road.

## Getting Around

There's an abundance of taxis and minivan buses to shuttle you around town, but it is easy to walk around Kingstown, which is surprisingly small. A taxi from the airport in Arnos Vale to Kingstown costs EC$25.

## WINDWARD HIGHWAY

The windward (east) coast of St Vincent is a mix of wave-lashed shoreline, quiet bays and small towns. Away from the tourism that dominates the southern coast of the island; this is a fine place to visit for those wanting to experience a more sedate version of St Vincent. The black-sand beaches meld into the banana plantations and the lush vegetation grows up into the hilly interior. Scruffy villages pop up from time to time, filled with down-to-earth locals and ramshackle buildings.

Buses from Kingstown to Georgetown are fairly regular (except on Sunday) and cost EC$6. Buses driving north from Georgetown are irregular, so get information from the Kingstown bus station before heading off.

As you head further north along the east coast, you really start to get off the beaten track. The jungle gets a bit thicker, the road a bit narrower, and towering **La Soufrière** volcano (4048ft) begins to dominate the skyline. Still active and slightly ominous, this striking feature is the hallmark of the northern end of St Vincent. About a mile north of Georgetown the road passes over an old lava flow from the 1902 eruption – a solemn reminder of the power of the volcano.

Heading yet further north the rough track turns inland and, amid the coconut palms and the banana plantations, the **hiking trail** to La Soufrière's crater begins. This 3.5-mile hike will take you up to the crater, where you can see the lake and, on a clear day, spectacular views of the island and the Grenadines.

Getting to the hike is a bit of mission in itself. The trailhead is 2 miles off the main road and bus access this far north is a bit sporadic. You can either arrange for a taxi, which will cost you over US$100 from Kingstown, or join a guided tour (see p657).

Continuing north you will hit **Sandy Bay**, a sizable village that has the island's largest concentration of Black Caribs. North of Sandy Bay is Owia Bay and the village of **Owia**, where you'll find the **Salt Pond**, tidal pools protected from the crashing Atlantic by a massive stone shield. This is a popular swimming hole with crystal-clear waters and a view of St Lucia to the north. There are thatched shelters, picnic tables and restrooms here.

## LEEWARD HIGHWAY

The Leeward Hwy runs north of Kingstown along St Vincent's west coast for 25 miles, ending at Richmond Beach. Offering some lovely scenery, the road climbs into the mountains as it leaves Kingstown, then winds through the hillside and back down to deeply cut coastal valleys that open to coconut plantations, fishing villages and bays lined with black-sand beaches.

About a 3-mile drive north of Kingstown is a sign along the Leeward Hwy, pointing east to the **Vermont Nature Trails**, 3.5 miles inland. Here you'll find the Parrot Lookout Trail, a 1.75-mile loop (two hours) that passes through the southwestern tip of the **St Vincent Parrot Reserve**.

The drive from Kingstown all the way to the gorgeous black-sand **Richmond Beach** takes about 1½ hours. There are weekday buses roughly every 15 minutes from Kingstown to Barrouallie (EC$4, 45 minutes). From there it is a 1-mile walk to Wallilabou Bay, and about four buses per day continue north to Richmond.

## Wallilabou Bay & Falls

The small village of Wallilabou has in recent times become one of the most recognizable places in all of SVG. *Pirates of the Caribbean*

---

**LIGHTS, CAMERA, PIRATES!**

Not since the days of Errol Flynn have the words *Pirates* and *Caribbean* been so firmly planted into the lexicon of the world cinema public. The *Pirates of the Caribbean* movie franchise has made eye patches, parrots on the shoulder and general skullduggery suddenly cool. You could argue that the world was ripe for a pirate adventure, but we're sure that having Johnny Depp and Keira Knightley prancing around the screen was a big factor.

Visitors to St Vincent and the Grenadines can get a bit closer to Captain Jack and his mates by visiting some of the locations that were used in the three films. The Tobago Cays were used extensively as were the seas off St Vincent and Bequia. A village set was built in Wallilabou on the west coast of St Vincent, where much of the first film was shot.

If you really want to get into the pirate spirit you can take a ride on the *Sacra Nouche* (p668). This vintage sailboat was used in the first film and now takes amateur pirates for a cruise among the Tobago Cays for the day. If you really want to go on a *Pirates* pilgrimage you should also check out locations in the Bahamas (see p84 and p99) and in Dominica (p592) – if ye dare! Yarrr!

---

filmed here, creating a full-scale seaside pirate village for scurvy dogs and old sea salts to call home. Many of the sets remain and it's a great spot for film buffs to get a behind-the-scenes look. Sadly the sets are starting to fall into disrepair – but efforts are under way to maintain them for the future.

**Wallilabou Falls** are near the inland side of the main road, about a mile north of Wallilabou Bay. Although only 13ft high, the falls are beautiful and drop into a waist-deep bathing pool.

**Wallilabou Anchorage** ( ☎ 458-7270; www.wallilabou.com; Wallilabou) runs the mooring facilities, and has a pleasant bayside restaurant and bar. Adjacent to the restaurant is its small hotel (rooms from US$50), with seafront accommodations.

### Falls of Baleine

The 60ft Falls of Baleine, at the isolated northwestern tip of the island, are accessible only by boat. These scenic falls, which cascade down a fern-draped rock face into a wide pool, are a few minutes' walk from the beach where the boats anchor.

Most tour operators charge around US$50 for the day tour and require at least three people to make the trip. **Sea Breeze Nature Tours** ( ☎ 458-4969) has both a 36ft sloop and a powerboat. It charges US$40 per person. The company also runs whale-watching trips.

# BEQUIA

**pop 5000**

Striking a balance between remoteness, accessibility, development and affordability – Bequia (beck-way) could very well be the most perfect island in the whole Grenadines chain. Stunning beaches dotting the shoreline, accommodations to fit most budgets and a slow pace of life all help to create an environment that is utterly unforgettable. There are fine restaurants to dine in, shops that retain their local integrity and enough golden sand and blue water to keep everybody chilled right out.

The northernmost island in the Grenadines group, Bequia is a snap to get to via daily ferry services and boasts a variety of small areas to explore. Though only 7 sq miles in size, this little island packs a punch with lots of hidden treasures to dig up. The main town of Port Elizabeth is a charming seaside place that is worth investing some time in. It is popular with the yachting set; the boats in the harbor originate from all over the globe and are a testament to the allure of the area.

### Getting There & Away
#### AIR

Bequia's airport is near Paget Farm, at the southwest end of the island, and is served by **Mustique Airways** ( ☎ 458-4380; www.mustique .com) and **SVG Air** ( ☎ 457-5124; www.svgair.com) – but flights are infrequent so most visitors take the ferry.

#### BOAT

The **Bequia Express** ( ☎ 458-3472; www.bequiaexpress .net) and **MV Admiral** ( ☎ 458-3348; www.admiralty -transport.com) ferries run between Bequia and St Vincent. See p673 for details. The docks are located in the center of Port Elizabeth. The ferries are generally punctual and serve basic food and drink, and the crossing takes only one hour. Tickets are sold upon entry; the fare is EC$15/25 one way/round trip.

Bequia is a popular port of call for sailors on an island-hopping journey. The **Bequia Customs and Immigration Office** ( ☎ 457-3044; 8:30am-6pm) is in Port Elizabeth opposite the ferry dock. Several shops in town cater to boats, where bulk supplies, ice and charts are easily found.

## Getting Around

As the island is small, many places are accessible on foot from Port Elizabeth. Everything else is a quick trip by bus, taxi or other motorized transportation.

### BUS

Port Elizabeth is full of 'dollar vans,' shared minibuses that will take you to most mainroad destinations on the island for EC$1 to EC$4 per trip. For route information, have a chat to the driver or drop into the tourist office in Port Elizabeth. It can sometimes get crowded, so isn't the best option if you're carrying luggage.

### CAR, MOTORCYCLE & BICYCLE

Opposite the waterfront in Port Elizabeth, **Handy Andy's** ( ☎ 458-3722) rents out mountain bikes (per day US$20), motor scooters (US$25), Honda 250cc motorcycles (US$55) and Jeep Wranglers (US$75). Vehicles can also be rented from **Sunset Rentals and Island Tours** ( ☎ 458-3782; Port Elizabeth).

### TAXI

Taxis on Bequia are great fun; the open-air pickup trucks have bench seating in the back and wind-generated air-conditioning. The fees are set and should be agreed upon prior to departure. The drivers are friendly and can act as good tour guides (EC$65 per hour) if you're keen to see the island.

From Port Elizabeth it costs EC$20 to Lower Bay or Friendship Bay, and EC$30 to the airport. Taxis meet flights at the airport and there is a glut of them near the docks in Port Elizabeth.

## PORT ELIZABETH
### pop 2500

The charming little town of Port Elizabeth is little more than a line of shops rimming the beach of Admiralty Bay. Restaurants, grocery stores and shops line the strip, weaving an interesting fabric that's a joy to walk among.

The harbor is often packed with yachts and the streets are busy with visitors and locals going about their days. But remember, we're talking 'busy' by Grenadine standards, so in the grand scheme it remains a sleepy seaside town.

### Orientation

A narrow sidewalk along the shoreline at the south side of Port Elizabeth – known as the Belmont Walkway – provides the main access to many of the town's restaurants and accommodations. For those arriving by sea, one of the first ports of call will be the **Bequia Customs and Immigration Office** ( ☎ 457-3044; 8:30am-6pm).

ST VINCENT & THE GRENADINES

### ISLAND-HOPPING

The chain of islands that make up St Vincent and the Grenadines is so perfect for a seafaring adventure, it's as if some all-powerful mariner conjured them for their own pleasure. Just because you don't own a yacht, or for that matter don't know a yard-arm from a jib sail, doesn't mean that you can't cruise these islands by sea. There are several ways to get around, from crewing on yachts or hopping on scheduled ferries to hitching rides on water taxis or even stowing away on the mail boat. All are easily sorted once you're on the ground and are reliable ways to get from one island to another.

Besides being a great way to get under the skin of these islands, traveling by sea is also the green way to go. Just think of the good earth karma you get from every gallon of jet fuel you *don't* burn.

With a bit of flexibility you can easily piece together a trip starting in St Vincent and ending in Grenada (or the reverse) while hitting most of the islands along the way. It's a great adventure, and a throwback to the traveling of old – tossing your pack onto a rickety old boat as it casts off and heads into the open sea to a new port among these sun-kissed islands.

## Information
### BOOKSTORES
**Bequia Bookshop** ( ☎ 458-3905; Front St; ⏱ 8:30am-5pm Mon-Fri, 9am-1pm Sat) The best bookstore in the Grenadines stocks everything from charts and survey maps to yachting books, flora and fauna guides, and West Indian, North American and European literature.

### INTERNET ACCESS
**Digicel** (per hr EC$18; ⏱ 8am-9pm Mon-Fri, 9am-9pm Sat & Sun) This Caribbean cell-phone provider has a herd of computers out back, all with fast connections and comfy chairs.
**Maria's Cafe** (wi-fi per hr EC$18) Just down the road from the main marina, and upstairs. Sit on the balcony, grab a drink and check your email via a wi-fi connection.

### MONEY
The following banks have a 24-hour ATM:
**National Commercial Bank** ( ☎ 458-3700; Front St; ⏱ 8am-1pm Mon-Thu, 8am-1pm & 3-5pm Fri)
**RBTT** ( ☎ 458-3845; Front St; ⏱ 8am-2pm Mon-Thu, to 5pm Friday)

### POST
**Port Elizabeth post office** ( ☎ 458-3350; ⏱ 9am-noon & 1-3pm Mon-Fri, 9-11:30am Sat) Opposite the ferry dock on Front St.

### TELEPHONE
Coin and card phones are located in front of the post office on Front St.

### TOURIST INFORMATION
**Bequia Tourism Association** ( ☎ 458-3286; www .bequiatourism.com; ⏱ 9am-noon & 1:30-4pm Mon-Fri, 9am-noon Sat) Located in the small building on the ferry dock, it's staffed by helpful locals and is a great starting point for your stay.

## Dangers & Annoyances
Beware of manchineel trees around Lower Bay Beach as they can cause a rash. Also be careful walking on the roads as they are narrow, devoid of footpaths and the drivers always seem to be in a hurry.

## Sights & Activities
### BEACHES
There are a few nice beaches in the close vicinity to Port Elizabeth. The best is the divine **Princess Margaret Beach**. Located just around the corner from Port Elizabeth, it is one of the loveliest stretches of sand on the island. To get there requires a slightly contrived journey, traveling on the main road south and turning down the narrow road to the beach.

**Friendship Bay** on the southeast corner of the island is another great place to spend the day. It's a strenuous yet short walk over the spine of the island to get there, or a short taxi or bus ride.

### BOAT TRIPS
There are a few options for tours through the Grenadines by boat. Some are infrequent and all have flexible and variable schedules. Drop into the tourist office and have a look at the notice board to see which boats are going where and when.

**Friendship Rose** ( ☎ 495-0886; www.friendshiprose .com; day trips adult/child US$125/62) is an 80ft vintage schooner that is a beautiful example of boat building – even to a steadfast landlubber. This former mail boat now runs tours throughout the Grenadines to various islands on a relaxed schedule. There are day trips to Mustique, Canouan, Young Island and to the Tobago Cays. You can also charter the boat and have your own private seafaring adventure.

### DIVING
You don't have to go far for great diving on Bequia – there are some top sites just on the edge of Admiralty Bay. There are two excellent dive shops in Port Elizabeth that visit dive sites around the island; both offer similar services at comparable prices.
**Bequia Dive Adventures** ( ☎ 458-3826; www.bequia diveadventures.com; Belmont) Charges US$40 per dive if you prepay on the internet.
**Dive Bequia** ( ☎ 458-3504; www.dive-bequia.com; Belmont) Charges US$60 per dive.

## Sleeping
**Julie's Guesthouse** ( ☎ 458-3304; julies2007@hotmail .com; Front St; s/d from EC$33/50; ✉ 🖥 ) It may not look like much from the outside, but after you wind your way back through the laneway and up the steps, all efforts are rewarded. Pleasant, basic and clean rooms are on offer at a great price. The central location isn't the best if you are there to lounge on the sand – but you are definitely in the heart of the action.

**L'Auberge des Grenadines** ( ☎ 458-3201; www .caribrestaurant.com; s/d US$40/60; 🖥 ) Tucked up into one of the nicer restaurants in town is this delightful little place to stay. There are only three rooms, so you have to get in quick. Nothing fancy here but there's great food only steps away, the ocean only a few steps further, and great staff to take care of you.

**Frangipani Hotel** ( ☎ 458-3255; www.frangipanibequia.com; Belmont Walkway; s US$60-175, d US$70-200) Reputations precede Frangipani, known throughout the island as one of the premier places to stay – the buzz hits the nail right on the head. This converted house has 15 rooms and a good location on the beach. The 2nd floor of the wooden-shingled house has pleasantly simple rooms. Out back are the modern garden units, with stone walls and harbor-view sundecks. The restaurant and bar are popular in the evening.

**Gingerbread Hotel** ( ☎ 458-3800; www.gingerbreadhotel.com; Belmont Walkway; ste from US$160) Like a set piece from a production of Hansel and Gretel, Gingerbread looks exactly as you'd expect, with ornate eaves nailed to a steep roof. Spotless rooms, some with four-post beds, sit behind swaying palms and a grassy verge only a stone's skip from the baby-blue sea.

**our pick** **Firefly** ( ☎ 458-3414; www.fireflybequia.com/; r from US$600; ⚙ 🍴 ) Up and over the hill, and only five minutes by car, you are transported into a whole new world of tranquil luxury. Modeled after its sister property on Mustique, which shares its name, this new addition to the scene more than ups the standards of decadence. There are but a handful of rooms, tastefully decorated with a minimalist flare, accented with muslin-draped bedposts, snow-white furnishings and views worthy of royalty. Innovative and delicious extras, like iPod-included sound systems and a bottle of vino to help you settle in, just prove that management knows a thing or two about doing all the little things right.

## Eating & Drinking

**our pick** **Green Boley** ( ☎ 457-3625; Belmont Walkway; boneless chicken roti EC$8, fish burger EC$10) Just look for the fluorescent-green bamboo shack on the beach, filled with locals sipping cold beer and eating hearty West Indian fare. The chalkboard menu doesn't swim far from the standards but they're done well – tasty favorites like fish burgers won't break the bank and will leave you smiling.

**Gingerbread Restaurant** ( ☎ 458-3800; lunch EC$12-25, dinner from EC$35; ⏰ 8am-9:30pm) Up the steps at the Gingerbread Hotel, this 2nd-floor eatery is a spacious, vaulted-ceiling dining room with a view. Lunch brings on sandwiches and casual fare, while dinner classes it up a notch, with seafood the main go.

**Frangipani Restaurant & Bar** ( ☎ 458-3255; Belmont Walkway; lunch EC$12-30, dinner from EC$35; ⏰ 7:30am-9pm) This popular seaside bar-restaurant offers sandwiches, burgers, salads, omelets and fresh fish dishes until 5pm, and then seafood and West Indian fare is served at dinner. There's live music on Thursday and occasionally on other nights.

**Porthole** (Belmont Walkway; mains from EC$15; ⏰ breakfast, lunch & dinner) Not far from town, Porthole along the walkway. You won't find many tourists with sunburn in here; locals, lifers and those in the know frequent it for the yummy local grub. Rotis for lunch topped off with cricket on the telly, all served up in a setting best described someplace between ramshackle and falling to bits.

**Tommy Cantina** (mains from EC$20; ⏰ lunch & dinner) Don't let the steady stream of tourist traffic deter you. Tommy Cantina has good-value, freshly prepared Mexican standards plus a great viewpoint for the nightly sunset. There's a healthy list of cocktails to get the party going and one of the best burritos east of Baja.

**Mac's Pizzeria** ( ☎ 458-3474; Belmont Walkway; pizzas from EC$40; ⏰ 11am-10pm) Mac's packs in the crowds. Its fearsome reputation is known far and wide – and it delivers the best pizza around. A few steps from the beach, sit on a deck crammed with tables and overflowing with happy diners swapping slices and telling lies.

## Shopping

The artistic community in Bequia is formidable and luckily there is a great selection of shops in which to purchase their wares. Model boats, paintings, prints and crafts are available and of good quality. The market is a good spot to get T-shirts and other tourist-oriented paraphernalia.

**Garden Boutique** ( ☎ 458-3892) Ever wanted to own a boat? Well, here's your chance – and this one you can actually afford (*and* it will fit in your luggage). Beautifully crafted model boats, prints, batik and other locally made specialties are all found here.

**Noah's Arcade** (Belmont Walkway) Watercolors, prints and locally made stuff all of a good standard and under the same roof.

**Bequia Market** ( ⏰ vegetable market 7am-6pm Mon-Sat, to 4pm Sun) It's hard to miss the local market, just off the water, near the centre of town. In classic Caribbean style it has a bit of everything for everyone: fresh fish caught daily, fruit off the vine and a staggering selection of T-shirts and other tourist crap that you'll be embarrassed to wear once you get home. Rest assured you are supporting the local economy no matter what you purchase.

## LOWER BAY
**pop 500**

The tiny beachside community of Lower Bay is a charming oasis of Caribbean calm. The stunningly clear waters of Admiralty Bay spread out in front like a turquoise fan, while the golden beach meets the sea and unites into that synergy of surf and sand you've been looking for. There's not much to do here – it's quiet by comparison to Port Elizabeth (not that Port Elizabeth ever gets going beyond a gentle purr) – but it has a few places to stay, a couple to eat and enough square footage of sand to keep the beach bunnies happy. From the bus stop on the main road it's a 10-minute walk down to the beach, along the steep paved road.

The location of **Keegan's** ( ☎ 458-3530; keegans bequia@yahoo.com; Lower Bay; d US$50-60, d incl breakfast & dinner US$80-90; ❄ ) is hard to beat – right off the sand. The hotel has character and a restaurant that belts out karaoke on a Saturday night. On the downside, the rooms are older than most of the guests and the standards of cleanliness could use some work – but the location is tops.

With an unforgettable name, **Can't Remember the Name** (dinner from EC$60; ❄ 6pm-late) is an airy beach bar that serves up fresh fish for lunch and dinner. There's an inviting bar to dock up to any time of day, great meals, occasional live music and a cool atmosphere.

## FRIENDSHIP BAY

If all the hustle and bustle of the rest of Bequia is getting you down, head over to Friendship Bay where things are even quieter. Located on the southeast coast of the island, this small settlement is about 1.5 miles from Port Elizabeth.

Just up the road from the beach is **Friendship Garden Apartments** ( ☎ 458-3349; www.friendshipgarden apt.com; d per week US$560), a no-nonsense, affordable place to stay. The apartments are simple and well laid out with everything a family needs for a vacation without the extras that start to amp up the price.

Right next door to the Friendship Garden and a nearly identical property, **Island Inn Apartments** ( ☎ 458-3706; www.islandinnsvg.com; d per week from US$500) is also a great family option with apartments that feature full kitchens. The rooms are clean and it's a short stroll to the beach.

**Friendship Bay Resort** ( ☎ 458-3222; www.friend shipbay.vc; ste US$250-700), a sprawling Swedish-run resort, has just undergone extensive renovations and has a fresh new look. The distinctly European feel has the ambience of a ski lodge looking over the sea. The 24 rooms are often booked by families over from the old country to enjoy some Caribbean sunshine.

Don't worry, you won't need the repellant at **Moskito** ( ☎ 458-3222; Friendship Bay Resort; mains from EC$70; ❄ 11am-10pm). This great restaurant and bar has a feel that can only be described as lived-in: darkened wood, hemp rope and a sea view. The bar has swings rather than stools and the frequent lobster specials are as good as they sound.

# MUSTIQUE
**pop 3000**

What can you say about Mustique other than 'Wow!'? First take an island that is nearly unfathomably beautiful, stunning beaches and everything else you expect to find in paradise, then add to the mix accommodations that defy description or affordability. With prices that exclude all but the super-rich, film stars and burnt-out musicians, this island is the exclusive playground of the uberaffluent. The private island is run by the Mustique Company who assures that this paradise is only visited by the well heeled.

For those lucky enough to have inherited a small fortune, starred in a Hollywood blockbuster or fronted a band like the Rolling Stones, luxury awaits. There are 70 private villas and houses on the island that will accommodate you in the height of luxury. The beaches are sublime and the small island, only 5 miles in length, has everything one could ever want in a private Caribbean hideaway. Though out of reach for almost everybody, it's a must-do if your idea of a holiday is not seeing change out of 50 grand.

## SLEEPING & EATING

**Firefly Mustique** ( ☎ 488-8414; www.mustiquefirefly.com; r incl meals & transportation US$850-1050; ❄ 💻 🍸 ) Set on a steep cliffside overlooking Britannia Bay, each of its four supremely well-appointed rooms has a private bathroom, ocean view and unique styling. Although it is pricey (but relatively cheap by Mustique standards), Firefly is not stuffy and is a popular hangout in the evenings. It's a first-rate option for a honeymoon. Offers wi-fi access.

**Mustique Company** ( ☎ 448-8000, in USA 212-758-8800, in UK 0162-858-3517; www.mustique-island.com; villas per week US$8500-45,000) when you get the urge to spend more money on a vacation than the GDP of SVG, this is the place to do it. Nothing is short of perfection and every need is catered for. Each villa comes with its own staff of servants, housekeepers and cooks. (Stays must be for a minimum of seven nights.) But if that all sounds just a bit too ghetto, you can upgrade to one of the company's premium estates that will set you back up to US$150,000 per week. Why buy a Ferrari when you can rent a really nice house in the Caribbean for a week?

**Basil's Bar & Restaurant** ( ☎ 488-8350; www .basilsbar.com; dinner from EC$70; ☺ 9am-late) Famous Basil's is a delightful open-air thatch-and-bamboo restaurant that extends out into Britannia Bay, and is the place to eat, drink and meet up with others in Mustique. The bar hosts the Mustique Blues Festival in late January each year.

## GETTING THERE & AWAY

Mustique's airport is served by **Mustique Airways** ( ☎ 458-4380; www.mustique.com), **SVG Air** ( ☎ 457-5124; www.svgair.com) and private jet. For more details, see p673. Britannia Bay is Mustique's port of entry and the only suitable anchorage for visiting yachts; immigration and customs can be cleared at the airport. It is also possible to hop on one of the tour ships from Bequia (see p657) to get to the other Grenadines.

# CANOUAN

**pop 1250**

Canouan (cahn-oo-ahn) is an interesting place, both historically and aesthetically. This stunningly beautiful hook-shaped island has some of the quietest, cleanest and most supremely aesthetic beaches in the entire Grenadines chain, and some of the most secluded hideaways too. In contrast it is also home to one of the biggest developments in the region and is on the cusp of irreversible development that threatens to change this paradise forever.

In the mid-1990s, the development that has since transformed the island started on the northern end of Canouan. The Raffles Resort, which now occupies nearly half the landmass, is the prototypical ultraposh hideaway. Complete with a Donald Trump–operated casino, this resort has privatized beaches and sequestered most of the tourists.

Reaction is mixed: with the rest of the island a virtual ghost town and high-flying tourists rarely venturing beyond the gates of their hotel, the economic benefits are few and far between for the average local. The flip side is that the independent traveler can enjoy an authentic town, beaches that are deserted and a local community that is warm and welcoming. But with airport expansion, the construction of a huge marina and further development on the horizon, the question is, for how long?

## ACTIVITIES

Diving can be arranged with **Dive Canouan** ( ☎ 458-8044; www.tamarind.us) through Tamarind Beach Hotel & Yacht Club.

## SLEEPING

**our pick** **Ocean View Inn** ( ☎ 482-0477; www.oceanview -can.com; Charlestown Bay; s/d from US$105/125; ☒ ) There

---

**TWIST MY ARM: THE SPOTS THE AUTHORS WANTED TO KEEP SECRET**

Part of coming to St Vincent and the Grenadines is finding that perfect beach where you really feel like you've been stranded in paradise. The problem is that so many of these perfect spots have been spoiled with hotels, developments and private houses. But don't despair, there are a few slices of unadulterated perfection to be found out there. On Canouan, if you're willing to take a bit of a hike and get off the beaten track, you can get to that deserted beach with the ultrablue water. **Twin Bay**, on the east side of the island just south of the big development, is a hidden morsel of tranquility. Ask a local for directions, pack a lunch and get lost in paradise for the day.

---

**THE PRICE OF PROGRESS**

Zuri Reid calls the luscious island of Canouan home. This young and ambitious hotel manager has big plans. He dreams of opening his own hotel one day, a place that respects the local community and can live in cooperation with the villagers on the island.

**So what do you think are the real highlights of this area?**

Well, people really have to experience island hopping, they have to go and see the Tobago Cays. While they are here in Canouan, people should take the time to visit in the local community. It's not a very big or busy place but the people are really heart-warming.

**What do you think about all the development that is happening in Canouan?**

Some of it is good, and some of it is a little too extreme. For instance, at the moment they are concentrating their development on one side of the island and removing a lot of the nature in the process. There should be an emphasis on keeping things green and letting people experience the natural beauty of the island. Sometimes it feels like the development is out of control. The big development happened so rapidly that everyone is doing their own thing and it isn't organized or planned.

**So does the island feel busier with a resort taking up nearly half the land?**

No, not really. The people who come and stay in the big resort just stay behind the big locked gates and never bother to come and see the village or see the other parts of the island.

**It can't be all bad?**

There are some good things; they provide a lot of jobs for local people. And the water that they make in their desalination plant can be bought by locals during the dry season.

**What about the impact on the environment?**

Well, there are more people coming to the island now so there is more garbage. But it's not just tourists, people from St Vincent leave their garbage on the ground, construction projects leave pallets and other bits of waste – it has to go somewhere, and we don't have the space for it here. If everyone worked together this whole island could be green, but at the moment no one is working together so we have a long way to go. There is a push to change things though: the Sustainable Grenadines Project has just started to try and help hotels and businesses to become greener – which I think is a great step.

---

are few options for the budget traveler on Canouan – luckily this place not only fits the budget but also exceeds expectations. Rooms don't necessarily inspire long-term lounging, but the included breakfast, proximity to the beach and laid-back vibe are worth every penny. On top of all that, the staff rock!

**Tamarind Beach Hotel & Yacht Club** ( ☎ 458-8044; www.tamarindbeachhotel.com; s/d US$280/325) Giant thatched-roof buildings stand guard over the beach and invite you in for pure relaxation. Elegant rooms accented with white walls and chocolate-colored hardwood entice the visitor and make it hard to return to the daily grind. The beach is right out front and is a fine selection of sand. Two restaurants on site, a dive center and water sports are all thrown in too.

## EATING

**Majella's on the Beach** ( ☎ 482-0269; Grand Bay; meals from EC$34; ☽ lunch & dinner) Flatbread pizzas, fresh fish from the grill, quesadillas and more are all served up beachside, just a stumble away from the main wharf. With tables aplenty and a great vantage point to take in what little action there is, you can't go wrong.

**Hill Top Restaurant & Bar** ( ☎ 458-8264; meals from EC$40) This well-known restaurant is located – not surprisingly – on a hill, overlooking Grand Bay. It serves West Indian seafood and other dishes, including tasty vegetarian options, and has a good variety of wines.

**Pirate Cove** ( ☎ 458-8044; Tamarind Beach Hotel; meals from EC$40; ☽ lunch & dinner) Shiver me timbers, the food is a good find here, with Western standards and a mean pizza that's in competition with Majella's for the best on the island. The location overlooking the sea, and the great variety of grub makes this a popular spot for the salty sea dog in all of us, with casual dining beside the bar and bandstand.

## GETTING THERE & AWAY

The airport is served by Mustique Airways, SVG Air and American Eagle. For international flight links to Canouan and interisland air travel, see p673. Ferries from St Vincent connect Canouan with the other Grenadine islands (see p673).

# MAYREAU

## pop 500

The compact palm-covered island of Mayreau sits just west of the Tobago Cays. With only a handful of roads, no airport and a small smattering of locals, Mayreau is the paradigm for chilled. The small village that sits beside Saline Bay is the sole habitation, rising up the hill to give commanding views of the sea.

Over the ridge and down to the other side you are confronted with the sublime Saltwhistle Bay. Picture perfect and the star of countless racks of postcards, this white-sand beach defies description. The thin strip of sand leads to a point where the ocean laps on both sides, sometimes only a few feet away. The azure water is a mecca for boaters – yachts drop anchor in the bay and bob along with the swaying palms.

The island is wonderfully quiet, until the cruise ships arrive to vomit passengers onto the land for a short excursion. Clad in socks, sandals and sunburn, they traipse around for a few hours. Luckily the invaders are soon to leave and you are left with the island the way it's supposed to be – nice and quiet.

## SLEEPING

There are only two hotels on the island, but it is also possible to rent a room or a house, sometimes for a better nightly rate. Ask around at restaurants such as Robert Righteous & De Youths.

**Dennis' Hideaway** ( ☎ 458-8594; www.dennis-hide away.com; d US$65) Stuck among the scattered plot of houses that make up 'town' is the no-nonsense Dennis' Hideaway. It's a great budget option – actually it's the only budget option on the island, and luckily it's worth staying in. Standard rooms and a restaurant are there, but the beach isn't – that's a 10-minute walk away.

**Saltwhistle Bay Club** ( ☎ 458-8444; www.saltwhistle bay.com; d incl breakfast & dinner US$480) Set on a stunning stretch of sand on a sheltered bay, rimmed with swaying palms and azure water just begging to be splashed in. The 16 guests can dine beneath thatched shelters on the beach. Rooms are tasteful and inviting, and nearly as alluring as the setting. The atmos-

phere is idyllic, the feel is cathartic and the setting is like something out of a tropical lucid dream.

## EATING

**Combination Café** (fish sandwich EC$18; 🖳 ) A casual two-story spot right on the edge of town, this bar-restaurant has friendly management and an excellent selection of fish dishes and sandwiches. It's a good place to meet and converse with locals, and it also has internet access (per hour EC$20). The views from the upstairs bar are not impeded by electrical wires like most outlooks from town.

**Island Paradise** (barbecue US$45) Up the hill from town, the local uberrelaxed mentality continues here. While it has the best view of any of the local eateries, the decor is the sparsest and the food is the most basic. Having said that, it's a great authentic place to grab a meal and dig into some West Indian classics such as roti, seafood and sandwiches.

**Robert Righteous & De Youths** ( ☎ 458-8203; lunch EC$35-50, dinner EC$45-65) This place is overflowing with Rasta flavor and enough Bob photos to make you think you're in a college dorm room. It's hard to tell how authentic the Rastafarianism theme is, with a good selection of carnivorous items on the menu – but no matter, the food is tasty and the vibe is, as you'd expect, chilled out. Go for the lobster.

## GETTING THERE & AWAY

For information on ferries connecting Mayreau with the other Grenadine islands, see p673. When leaving Mayreau, talk with the management at Dennis' Hideaway, who can check the variable boat schedule for you.

The **Captain Yannis** ( ☎ 458-8513; yannis@carib surf.com; Yacht Club, Union Island) catamaran tours from Union Island can drop passengers off at Mayreau and pick them up the following day for the usual cost of its day tour (US$80). For details, see p668.

# UNION ISLAND

## pop 3000

Union Island is one of those places that tends to polarize visitors. Some find charm in the scrubby streets and eclectic alleyways. Some just see the transient nature of the town of

Clifton, the dirt and the concrete. It's not for everyone but there are some highlights in this anchor of the Grenadines chain.

As the island is just across the channel from Carriacou (Grenada), most visitors to Union are on the way to someplace else. The gateway to the Tobago Cays and the logical place to gather supplies for a Grenadines sailing mission, the small town of **Clifton** is alive with Argonauts getting ready to hit the high seas.

The energetic little town has some nice places to eat and just down the coast some decent beaches can be discovered, too. The quiet fishing village of **Ashton** is nice alternative to the frenetic pace of Clifton.

## INFORMATION

**Internet Café** ( ☎ 485-8258; youngbuffalo@yahoo.com; Clifton; per hr EC$10; ☯ 8am-4:30pm Mon-Fri, to noon Sun)

**National Commercial Bank** ( ☯ 8am-1pm Mon-Thu, 8am-1pm & 3-5pm Fri) Towards the airport. Has a 24-hour ATM.

**Union Island Tourist Bureau** ( ☎ 458-8350; ☯ 9am-noon & 1-4pm) On the main road in Clifton.

## ACTIVITIES

The three 60ft sailboats owned by **Captain Yannis** ( ☎ 458-8513; Yacht Club; yannis@caribsurf.com) – the catamarans *Cyclone*, *Typhoon* and *Tornado* – account for most of the daytime sailing business from Union Island. The cruise (US$80) includes a stop on Palm Island, a few hours in the Tobago Cays for lunch and snorkeling, and an hour on Mayreau before returning to Union in the late afternoon. There's a good buffet lunch, and an open bar of rum punch and beer. The boats leave Clifton around 9am, but schedules are flexible.

Sure you've seen *Pirates of the Caribbean*, but have you actually sailed on one of the boats from the iconic trilogy? Well, here's your chance. The **Sacra Nouche** ( ☎ 458-8418; US$80) was used in the filming of the first flick and now offers daily trips out to the Tobago Cays so you can go play Captain Jack for the day and see some pretty stunning scenery at the same time.

The owner of **Grenadines Dive** ( ☎ 458-8138; www.grenadinesdive.com; Clifton), Glenroy, will pick you up on Petit St Vincent, Palm Island or Mayreau. This is your best choice for diving in the Tobago Cays or surrounding islets.

## SLEEPING & EATING

**Clifton Beach Hotel** ( ☎ 458-8235; Clifton; s/d from US$31/50; ☒ ) You'll be hard pressed to actually find the beach and even if you do it isn't the main attraction. There always seems to be rooms available as the hotel is easily twice as big as it needs to be. The CBH is getting a bit old and tired – it's well in need of a tart-up. Rooms are at times windowless, always basic, small, hot and cheap. The central location and the dirt-cheap tariff save the day here.

**Anchorage Yacht Club Hotel** ( ☎ 458-8221; d from US$110; ☒ ) This is at the far end of the beach and near the airport – well, actually everything is near the airport on this tiny island. Popular with visiting sailors, midmarket holiday makers and those willing to spend a few extra dollars for a roof over their heads, the rooms are nice but not spectacular. There is an enormous restaurant and bar out front that is a popular place with guests and visitors too.

**L'Aquarium** (Clifton; lunch/dinner from EC$38) Don't let the reasonable prices deter you. The food in this French and Italian fusion restaurant is top flight, both in preparation and presentation. L'Aquarium is perched on the waterfront where yachties gather to watch their homes bob in the swell and landlubbers come to salivate over the food. The atmosphere is class, with white linen, extra forks and an aquarium the size of a family home dominating one wall of the establishment.

**Captain Gourmet** ( ☎ 458-8918; Clifton; pain au chocolat EC$5) Get your pinky up in the air and sip an espresso at this café-cum-yacht-provision shop. The distinctive French flavor permeates and divine decadence is for sale throughout. There is free wi-fi for those dining in, so grab a *pain au chocolat* and get wired.

**Blue Pelican Bar** (Clifton) It's worth the effort to find the Blue Pelican. Wander down the road away from the harbor and search for the narrow passageway lined with art galleries, minibars and hardware counters. Then climb the 51 steps to the tiny bar overlooking the sea. Everything is painted blue and it's barely big enough for the captain and his first mate – but it's great; once you find it you won't want to leave.

## GETTING THERE & AWAY
### Air

SVG Air, LIAT and Mustique Airways have flights to Union Island. For further details, see p673.

## Boat

### MAIL BOAT

For details on the MV *Barracuda,* which connects Union Island with St Vincent's other main islands, see p673. For details of boat services between Union Island and Carriacou, see p673.

### YACHT

Midway between the airport and central Clifton, **Anchorage Bay Yacht Club** ( ☎ 458-8221) has stern-to berths for 15 boats, ice, water, fuel, showers and laundry facilities. Other popular anchorages are at Chatham Bay, on Union Island's west coast, and the west sides of Frigate Island and Palm Island.

## GETTING AROUND

Union is pretty small and even the most sedate won't have trouble exploring on foot. The airport is an easy 200yd walk from Clifton and Ashton is a 1.5-mile walk from town. There are a few taxis and buses around; alternatively you can also easily hitch a ride from a friendly local.

# OTHER ISLANDS

If you really want to get off the beaten track, be sure to explore the smaller islands in the SVG group. What these islands lack in infrastructure and accommodation options, they more than make up for in delightful obscurity.

## TOBAGO CAYS

Ask anyone who's been to SVG what their highlight is and you're bound to hear all about the Tobago Cays. These five small islands ringed with coral reefs are just the sort of thing you've imagined the Caribbean comprises.

Free of any sort of development, the islands sit firmly in a national park and are only accessible via boat on a day trip from one of the Grenadines. And what a day trip it can be – the snorkeling is world class and the white-sand beaches look like a strip of blinding snow.

These islands really are the pride of the country and there has been a serious push to protect them – mooring buoys and an increased awareness of human impact are helping, but on a busy day it's plain to see that the risk of these jewels being loved to death is a real worry. Be sure you visit with a reputable operator, take your rubbish home and do your part to preserve these natural wonders. For information on day trips to the cays, see p657, p662 and opposite.

## PALM ISLAND

Once called Prune Island, the now more attractively titled Palm Island is just a 10-minute boat ride southeast of Clifton, Union Island. It's a small, whale-shaped isle dominated by a private resort. **Casuarina Beach** has long been a popular anchorage with yachters, and is a stopover on many day tours between Union Island and the Tobago Cays.

The very plush **Palm Island Beach Club** ( ☎ 458-8824; www.palmislandresorts.com; s/d/tr from US$715/815/1015; ✖ 🖳 🛋 ) is a delightful place to hole-up for a week. The palatial grounds are spotted with palms (obviously) and dotted with villas. The rooms are well fitted out, with an emphasis on luxury living and a penchant for sea views. The large pool is a nice place for mixing with your fellow guests and the iguanas that frequent the grounds stick around to keep you company. A convivial beachside bar and restaurant welcomes day-trippers.

## PETIT ST VINCENT

It's not called petit for nothing – this island is the southernmost and smallest in the Grenadines chain. Sequestered and exclusive, PSV has a formidable reputation as one of the best private islands in the world. That reputation isn't unwarranted – the beaches are just as spectacular as its neighbors' and having the place (almost) to yourself makes the price seem a bit more affordable.

The **Petit St Vincent Resort** ( ☎ 954-963-7401; www.psvresort.com; r US$755-960; 🖳 ) is the only accommodations option on the island – thankfully it's divine. The cottages are designed with luxury and privacy in mind. There are spacious sun decks only feet from the ocean and living spaces that bristle with fine stonework and whitewashed luxury. There are two staff members per bungalow, ensuring that your every wish is fulfilled. When you want to call on *your* staff, simply raise the flag out front and they'll be right there. The prices are all-inclusive and there is little to do on the island so this is a great option for those wanting to really get away from it all.

ST VINCENT & THE GRENADINES

# DIRECTORY

## ACCOMMODATIONS

There are a wide range of accommodations options throughout SVG. Some places are decidedly casual where the rates are low and the atmosphere supremely chilled. Other places you will have to remortgage the house to spend the week and are expected to dress accordingly. Having said that, there are beds to be found to suit most budgets and the scale of operations is generally quite small. Hotels and resorts are for the most part quite personal, with only a few rooms for the relaxed staff to look after.

Rates usually spike during the busy high season (winter, December to April/May) so those looking to save some money should consider visiting outside this short peak period. The rates listed in this chapter do not include 10% VAT that is added to all hotel rooms, or the 10% service charge that is frequently tacked on to bills – be sure to clarify exactly what price you are being quoted. Prices are in either EC$ or US$, depending on the hotel.

There are no campgrounds on SVG, and camping is not encouraged.

## ACTIVITIES

### Beaches & Swimming

The beaches in SVG are one of the main reasons to come to this hidden-away corner of the Caribbean. Some of the very best stretches of sand in the world can be found around here. Most are quiet, free of big waves and offer good swimming and snorkeling. The beaches on St Vincent are a bit of a letdown, but the shores of the Grenadines are the real find.

### Boat Trips

See p657, and p668 for information on boat trips through the Grenadines.

### Diving & Snorkeling

The warm clear waters of SVG draw divers from around the globe. They come to swim with a stunning array of sea life, from reef-hopping angelfish and grass-munching sea turtles to ocean predators like nurse sharks. The reefs are pristine with forests of soft and hard coral colored with every hue of the rainbow. Wrecks, rays and the odd whale just add to the appeal. Spearfishing is prohibited.

Visibility is often unlimited and the warm water makes for comfortable diving. Great sites can be found at the very recreational depth of 60ft to 80ft and currents are minimal.

The going rates are around US$60 for a single dive, US$100 for a two-tank dive and US$75 for a night dive. A 'resort course' for beginners that includes a couple of hours of instruction and a shallow dive is available for around US$70. Dive prices come down considerably for larger packages.

Many dive shops also offer complete certification courses. Bequia Dive Adventures (p662), one of the best-regarded shops on the islands, charges US$420, and offers the industry-standard Professional Association of Diving Instructors (PADI) accreditation.

There are also dive shops in Kingstown (p657), on Union Island (p668) and on Canouan (p665).

Most dive shops run snorkeling trips in parallel with their dive excursions. You

---

**PRACTICALITIES**

▪ **Newspapers & Magazines** There are two local weekly newspapers: the *Vincentian* and the *News*. *Cross Country* comes out midweek and the *Herald* is a daily paper that covers international news. You can buy international news magazines at the airport. The *Caribbean Compass* is an excellent monthly paper that covers marine news and travel issues. Two useful (and free) tourist magazines are *Ins and Outs* and the smaller *Life in St Vincent and the Grenadines*.

▪ **Radio & TV** The one local AM radio station, NBCSVG, broadcasts at 705kHz. Three stations broadcast on the FM band: NICE FM 6.3, HITZ FM107.3 and WE FM99.9. St Vincent has one broadcast TV station, SVGBC, on channel 9, and two local cable TV broadcasters. Additionally, most hotels pick up US cable.

▪ **Electricity** The electric current is 220V to 240V (50 cycles). British-style three-pin plugs are used.

▪ **Weights & Measures** Imperial system.

can also hire a water taxi to shuttle you to good snorkeling spots, although unless you are a very strong swimmer this is not recommended as the floating taxis have no safety precautions.

## Hiking

There are few developed hiking trails in SVG. Of note are the Vermont Nature Trails (p659) and the La Soufrière volcano trail (p659), both on St Vincent.

## Water Sports

The trade winds that sway the palms are an advantage for sailors of craft big and small. Most resorts have small sailboats (Hobie Cats and Sunfish) for guests to borrow or rent. Windsurfing and, to a lesser extent, kitesurfing are available in some resort locations. Kayaks are often available for those nonwindy days and snorkeling equipment is usually on offer too.

## BUSINESS HOURS

Shops are generally open from 8am to 5pm Monday to Saturday and closed on Sundays. Restaurants that serve breakfast as well as lunch and dinner open at 8am and close at about 9pm – or when the last customer is finished.

## CHILDREN

While there are few accommodations or restaurants in SVG that go out of their way to cater to families with children, some of the more tranquil islands are great for relaxed family time. Most resorts allow children, but you should always check ahead.

## DANGERS & ANNOYANCES

Manchineel trees are poisonous so be sure not to eat their applelike fruit or shelter under them during a rainstorm – the sap causes blisters on the skin and is quite painful.

## EMBASSIES & CONSULATES

Only the **UK** ( ☎ 457-1701; Granby St, PO Box 132, Kingstown) has representation in SVG. For the US and other countries, see the consulate in Barbados, p697.

## FESTIVALS & EVENTS

The carnival, called Vincy Mas (supposedly short for St Vincent Masquerade, although there are a few competing theories), is the main cultural event of the year.

**Blessing of the Whaleboats** Held on the last Sunday in January, on Bequia.

**National Heroes' Day** March 14.

**Easter Regatta (Bequia)** Around Easter, this is SVG's main sailing event.

**Easterval (Union Island)** Around Easter, a three-day music and costume festival.

**May Day** Held on May 1.

**Canouan Regatta** Five days of sailing and events in May.

**Vincy Mas** This carnival lasts for 12 days in late June or early July.

**Nine Mornings Festival** Carolers and steel bands take to the streets, with parties every day from December 16 through Christmas.

## GAY & LESBIAN TRAVELERS

Like most Caribbean nations, the view of gay and lesbian travelers is backward and outdated to say the least. You won't find any gay-friendly events, resorts or cruises here. Gay and lesbian travelers should be cautious with public affection but should otherwise be fine.

## HOLIDAYS

**New Year's Day** January 1

**St Vincent & the Grenadines Day** January 22

**Good Friday** Late March/early April

**Easter Monday** Late March/early April

**Labour Day** First Monday in May

**Whit Monday** Eighth Monday after Easter

**Caricom Day** Second Monday in July

**Carnival Tuesday** Usually second Tuesday in mid-July

**Emancipation Day** First Monday in August

**Independence Day** October 27

**Christmas Day** December 25

**Boxing Day** December 26

## INTERNET ACCESS

Internet access is widely available on all the larger islands in SVG. Wi-fi access has become increasingly abundant too, so those toting a laptop will be able to connect easily to the net. Most towns will have some version of an internet café and the majority of hotels have some form of access.

## INTERNET RESOURCES

Some of the better sites for info on SVG:

**Bequia Tourism Association** (www.bequiatourism.com) The official site of the Bequia Tourism Association, this is your best place to learn more about Bequia and to search for accommodations.

**Gov.vc** (www.gov.vc) The official SVG government site.

**Ins & Outs** (www.insandoutssvg.com) A nicely presented online magazine all about SVG.

**St Vincent & the Grenadines** (www.svgtourism.com) This official site is a good place to start for basic information.

**St Vincent & the Grenadines Diving** (www.scubasvg .com) The perfect starting point for divers wanting to plan a SVG dive holiday.

**Searchlight** (www.searchlight.vc) A good online SVG newspaper highlighting what's going on.

## MAPS

Tourist maps are easily obtained from the tourist information sites and hotels. Nautical charts can be found in bookstores and marine supply shops.

## MEDICAL SERVICES

There are six public and three private hospitals throughout the islands and several clinics located throughout the country. Each island has some form of medical facility and the standard of care is reasonably high.

## MONEY

The Eastern Caribbean dollar (EC$ or XCD) is the local currency. Major credit cards are accepted at most hotels, car-rental agencies, dive shops and some of the larger restaurants. All of the major islands, except for Mayreau, have a bank and 24-hour ATMs (which usually accept international cards).

There is 15% VAT that is added onto most retail items; this will already be included in the price. Most hotel rates have 10% VAT and 10% service charge added on top of them.

## POST

Post offices can be found on all of the islands. See individual sections for locations and hours.

## TELEPHONE

St Vincent phone numbers have seven digits. When calling from North America, dial

---

☎ 1-784 followed by the local number. From elsewhere, dial your country's international access code, followed by ☎ 784 and the local number. We have included only the seven-digit local number in SVG listings in this chapter.

Both coin and card phones can be found on the major islands. Phonecards can be purchased at Cable & Wireless offices or from vendors near the phones. It costs EC$0.25 to make a local call. For more information on card phones and making international calls, see p826.

Cell phones are widely used in St Vincent and the Grenadines, and it is possible to use your own phone on these networks. You can either set your phone for global roaming before leaving home or get a local SIM card for it once you get to SVG. Provided that your phone is unlocked, this new card allows for cheaper local dialing. They can be purchased for around US$10 from the Cable & Wireless office.

## TOURIST INFORMATION

The main office of the **Department of Tourism St Vincent & the Grenadines** ( ☎ 457-1502; www .svgtourism.com; Cruise Ship Terminal, Kingstown) is on St Vincent. In addition, there's a tourist information desk at St Vincent's ET Joshua Airport, and branch tourist offices in Bequia and Union Island.

## TRAVELERS WITH DISABILITIES

Travelers with disabilities, especially those in wheelchairs will have difficulty traveling throughout SVG. There are rarely sidewalks, pathways are often sand and ferries and other seagoing transport are not designed with special needs in mind.

## VISAS

Visas are not required unless you want to work in the islands.

## WOMEN TRAVELERS

Women traveling in SVG needn't expect any hassles unique to this country. There are the usual annoyance of extra attention from the local men and the constant queries about taxi hire and bus pick-up but generally it's a pretty safe place to be. Drunken European sailors at the popular yachting ports can be annoying, but they too are mostly harmless.

---

---

**EMERGENCY NUMBERS**

- Ambulance ☎ 999
- Coast Guard ☎ 999
- Fire ☎ 999
- Police ☎ 999

# TRANSPORTATION

## GETTING THERE & AWAY
### Entering the Islands
All visitors should carry a valid passport with them. A round-trip or onward ticket is officially required.

Passengers arriving on Union Island from Carriacou must pay EC$10 to Customs for entry. Passengers departing Carriacou pay EC$1 to Immigration. Arrivals are expected to register at the island's customs office, located at the ferry dock.

### Air
There are no direct flights to SVG from outside the Caribbean, as the runway is too small to land jet aircraft. International passengers first fly into a neighboring island and then switch to a prop plane for the final leg of their journey. Bequia, Mustique, Canouan and Union Island all have small airports, and Palm Island has a small private airfield.

The main point of entry for most travelers is **ET Joshua Airport** (SVD; ☎ 458-4011) in Kingstown, St Vincent. The majority of international flights connect through here, where many travelers switch to oceangoing travel. The airport itself is small and offers little for the traveler other than a small information kiosk in the arrivals hall. There is a EC$40 departure tax payable by all departing passengers.

The following airlines fly to and from SVG from within the Caribbean and also offer interisland flights in the Grenadines:

**American Eagle** ( ☎ 800-433-7300; www.aa.com)
From Canouan to St Lucia and San Juan
**LIAT** ( ☎ 457-1821; www.liat.com; Halifax St, Kingstown)
From St Vincent to Grenada, Trinidad, Barbados, St Lucia, Antigua and Puerto Rico
**Mustique Airways** ( ☎ 458-4380; www.mustique.com)
Connecting St Vincent, Bequia, Mustique, Canouan, Union and Barbados
**SVG Air** ( ☎ 457-5124; www.svgair.com) Private air charters and scheduled flights to St Vincent, Bequia, Canouan, Mustique, Union Island, Palm Island, Petit St Vincent, Carriacou, Grenada, Martinique, Dominica, St Lucia and Barbados

### Sea
The *MV Jasper* is a boat service that runs between Union Island and Carriacou, Grenada, (EC$20, one hour). It departs Union

every Monday and Thursday at 7:30am for Carriacou, returning at 12:30pm on the same days.

You could also try hopping on one of the various commercial ships that haul goods back and forth between Union Island and Carriacou or Petit Martinique, Grenada, or pay a water taxi (EC$100 to EC$150) for the bumpy 40-minute ride.

## GETTING AROUND
### Air
See left for information about flights within St Vincent and the Grenadines.

### Bicycle
Bikes are hard to come by; perhaps it's because of the hilly topography, crazy drivers and compact nature of the islands. On St Vincent there is at least one place to get your gears on (p654), and you can also hire bikes on Bequia (p661).

### Boat
Fares from St Vincent are EC$15 to Bequia, EC$20 to Canouan, EC$25 to Mayreau and EC$30 to Union Island. The schedule is a bit flexible; it's always a good idea to check around the port for updates on the progress of a boat.

The **Bequia Express** ( ☎ 458-3472; www.bequia express.net) and the **MV Admiral** ( ☎ 458-3348; www .admiralty-transport.com) ferries run between Bequia and St Vincent. Between the two companies there are numerous daily sailings on near identical boats. Boats leave Bequia at 6:30am, 8:30am, 9:30am, 2pm, 4:30pm and 5pm Monday to Friday; at 6:30am, 9:30am, 4:30pm and 5pm Saturday; and at 7:30am, 4.30pm and 5pm Sunday. Departures from St Vincent are at 8am, 10am, 11:30am, 1pm, 4pm, 4:30pm, 6pm and 7pm Monday to Friday; 8:30am, 9am, 12pm, 12:30pm, 6pm and 7pm Saturday; and 8:30am, 9am, 6pm and 7pm Sunday.

The mail boat MV *Barracuda* carries passengers and cargo five times weekly between St Vincent, Bequia, Canouan, Mayreau and Union Island. According to the published timetable, on Monday and Thursday it leaves St Vincent at 11am, Bequia at 1pm, Canouan at 3pm and Mayreau at 4:30pm, and arrives finally at Union Island at 5pm. On Tuesday and Friday it leaves Union Island at 6:30am, Mayreau at 7:30am, Canouan at 8:45am and Bequia at 11am, and arrives in St Vincent at noon. On Saturday the boat skips Bequia, leaving St Vincent at 11am, Canouan at 3:30pm and Mayreau at 4:30pm, arriving at Union Island at 5pm, and then departing Union at 6:30pm, finally arriving back in St Vincent at 11:30pm. However, all of these times are very approximate; it's best to arrive on time and be patient – there is no way the mail boat is going to be punctual.

The MV *Gem Star* leaves Kingstown on Tuesday and Friday at 12pm, stops in Canouan and arrives in Union Island when it feels like it. On Wednesday and Saturday it does the reverse route, departing Union Island at 8:30am.

See p657, p662 and p668 for information on boat tours through the Grenadines.

## Bus

Buses are a good way to get around St Vincent; you can catch a bus on Bequia and on Union Island, but these islands are so small that buses are usually redundant.

The buses themselves are little more than minivans that are often jammed to a capacity not seen in the outside world. You can expect to get to know at least 20 fellow commuters as you are jammed, packed and squeezed into every available space in the bus. There's a conductor on board who handles the cash and assigns the seats. When you get to your stop, either tap on the roof or try to get the attention of the conductor over the thumping music and they'll stop for you just about anywhere.

## Car

### RENTAL

Rentals typically cost from US$50 a day for a car and from US$65 for a 4WD. Seventy-five free miles are commonly allowed, and a fee of EC$1 is charged for each additional mile driven. Note that collision-damage insurance is not a common concept, and if you get into an accident you're likely to be liable for damages.

There are car-rental agencies on St Vincent (p654) and Bequia (p661), but most of the Grenadine islands have no car rentals at all. On some islands there are no roads.

### ROAD RULES

Driving is on the left-hand side. To drive within SVG you must purchase a local license (EC$40). In Kingstown, licenses can be obtained at the **Traffic & Transport office** ( 24hr), inside the police station.

## Taxi

Taxis are abundant on most islands and affordable for shorter trips. Agree on a fare before departure.

# Barbados

Half a million people can't be wrong. That's the number of visitors Barbados attracts annually, and it doesn't take long before you see why they come by the planeload: the coasts are ringed by the kinds of azure-water and white-sand visions that fuel the fantasies of Brits, Americans and Canadians stuck shivering away in some snowy winter clime.

Many Caribbean islands have beaches, but where Barbados differs is what lies behind the surf and sand. No matter your budget or style, you can find a place to stay that suits you, whether cheap, funky, restful or posh. All the comforts of home are close at hand if you want them as Barbados is one of the most developed islands in the region. The literacy rate approaches 98% and the capital Bridgetown and its surrounds are booming.

Away from the go-go west and south coasts, however, is where you'll find what makes the island special. Rather than clinging to the slopes of a steep volcanic centre, Barbados has a rolling terrain of limestone hills. Amid this lush scenery are fascinating survivors of the colonial past. Vast plantation homes show the wealth of these settlers and face up to the brutality of the slave trade. Museums document this engrossing history while several botanic gardens exploit the beauty possible from the perfect growing conditions.

The wild Atlantic-battered east coast is a legend with surfers; those looking for action will find wind-surfing, hiking, diving and more. Barbados is a great package, and despite its popularity, you'll have no trouble making it your own. Away from the glitz, it's still a place of classic calypso rhythms, an island-time vibe and world-famous rums.

## FAST FACTS

- **Area** 432 sq km
- **Capital** Bridgetown
- **Country code** ☎ 246
- **Departure tax** B$25 for stays over 24 hours
- **Famous for** Beaches, rum, flying-fish sandwiches
- **Language** English
- **Money** Barbados dollar (B$ or BBD); B$1 = US$0.50 = €0.32 = UK£0.25
- **Official name** Barbados
- **People** Barbadian (formal), Bajan (slang)
- **Phrase** Goodie (in response to most questions, eg 'how was your weekend?')
- **Population** 282,000
- **Visa** Not required for US, EU or Commonwealth visitors; see p698

BARBADOS

## HIGHLIGHTS

- **White-Sand Beaches** (p694) Unwind on the blissful beaches fringing the island such as Enterprise Beach
- **Bajan Sports** (p678) Join the raucous crowds at a cricket match, one of the island's sporting passions
- **Tropical Gardens** (p692) Enjoy the lush beauty of the island's rich floral wonders, such as the Andromeda Botanic Gardens.
- **Flying-Fish Sandwiches** (p679) Sample Barbados' most popular dish: cheap, tasty and always fresh
- **Plantation Houses** (p691) Experience the beautiful present and ugly past at grand homes such as St Nicholas Abbey

## ITINERARIES

- **Four Days** Depending on your budget, stay on the mid-priced south coast or the fancier west coast, go diving or snorkeling and spend an afternoon in Bridgetown.
- **One Week** As above but spend a couple of days exploring the interior and the East Coast.
- **Wandering Barbados** Get lost! Head into the hills of Central Barbados and take roads at random. It's green, beautiful and full of sights and surprises. Plus you're on an island, so you can't get lost for long.

## CLIMATE & WHEN TO GO

The climate in Barbados tends to be nice year-round: in January, the average daily high temperature is 28°C (83°F), while the low average is 21°C (70°F). In July, the average daily high is 30°C (86°F), while the average low is 23°C (74°F). February to May are the driest months (April averages only seven days of rain), while July is the wettest month with some 18 days of rain.

---

### HOW MUCH?

- **Taxi from the airport to Bridgetown** B$46
- **Flying fish sandwich** B$10
- **One night in a moderate double on/near the beach** US$120
- **Fee to use any beach** Free

---

The tourist high season runs from mid-December through mid-April. June through October is the hurricane season: September and October are the most humid months and have the highest hurricane risk – although many years see none.

Like the rest of the region, the temperate season is also high season, so expect prices to peak December to April. Other times Barbados is wetter and hotter but also much cheaper.

## HISTORY

The original inhabitants of Barbados were Arawaks, who were driven off the island around AD 1200 by Caribs from South America. The Caribs, in turn, abandoned (or fled) Barbados close to the arrival of the first Europeans. The Portuguese visited the island in 1536, but Barbados was uninhabited by the time Captain John Powell claimed it for England in 1625. Two years later, a group of settlers established the island's first European settlement, Jamestown, in present-day Holetown. Within a few years, the colonists had cleared much of the forest, planting tobacco and cotton fields. In the 1640s they switched to sugarcane. The new sugar plantations were labor intensive, and the landowners began to import large numbers of African slaves. These large sugar plantations – some of the first in the Caribbean – proved immensely profitable, and gave rise to a wealthy colonial class. A visit to a plantation estate, like the one at St Nicholas Abbey (p691), will give some idea of the money involved.

The sugar industry boomed during the next century, and continued to prosper after the abolition of slavery in 1834. As the planters owned all of the best land, there was little choice for the freed slaves other than to stay on at the canefields for a pittance.

Social tensions flared during the 1930s, and Barbados' black majority gradually gained more access to the political process. The economy was diversified through the international tourism boom and gave more islanders the opportunity for economic success and self-determination. England granted Barbados internal self-government in 1961 and it became an independent nation on November 30, 1966, with Errol Barrow as its first prime minister. While not flawless, Barbados has remained a stable democracy.

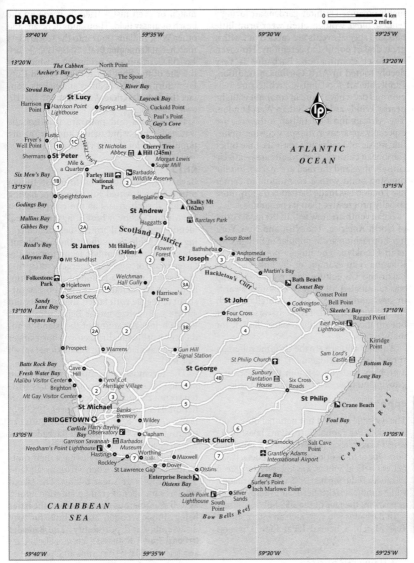

BARBADOS

Owen Arthur and the Barbados Labour Party were in power from 1993 to 2008. In a campaign that saw 'change' as the popular theme, David Thompson and the left-leaning Democratic Labour Party won the election (see boxed text, p679). Unlike other Caribbean islands, Barbados maintains its sugar industry; although the majority of the economy is now based on tourism and offshore banking. Condos are building as fast as the concrete dries.

## THE CULTURE

Bajan culture displays some trappings of English life: cricket, polo and horse racing are popular pastimes, business is performed in a highly organized fashion, gardens are lovingly tended, older women often wear prim little hats and special events are carried out with a great deal of pomp and ceremony. However, on closer examination, Barbados is very deeply rooted in Afro-Caribbean tradition. Family life, art, food, music, architecture, religion and dress have more in common with the nearby Windward Islands than West London. The African and East Indian influences are especially apparent in the spicy cuisine, rhythmic music and pulsating festivals. Like other Caribbean cultures, Barbadians are relatively conservative and the men are macho, but the ongoing bond with a cosmopolitan center like London has made Barbados slightly more socially progressive than its neighbors.

Bajan youth are now within the media orbit of North America. The NBA and New York hip-hop fashion are as popular in Bridgetown as in Brooklyn. The hugely popular singer Rihanna is an example of the links between Bajan and US culture. Her reggae-style rap was nominated for slew of Grammy awards in 2007 and she won for 'Umbrella,' which she performed with Jay-Z. It was number one on the charts in the US and the UK for many weeks.

Another similarity to the US is the suburban sprawl around Bridgetown. Traffic is often a problem and you can join the masses at a growing number of air-conditioned malls.

## SPORTS

The national sport, if not national obsession, is cricket. Per capita, Barbadians boast more world-class cricket players than any other nation. One of the world's top all-rounders, Bajan native Garfield Sobers, was knighted by Queen Elizabeth II during her 1975 visit to Barbados, while another cricket hero, Sir Frank Worrell, appears on the face of the B$5 bill.

In Barbados you can catch an international Test Match, a heated local First Division

---

**A HAIRY ENCOUNTER**

The explorer Pedro Albizu Campos stopped on Barbados in 1536 en route to Brazil. He had no interest is settling the island, but it was he who named the island Los Barbados (Bearded Ones) – presumably after the island's fig trees (Ficus citrifolia), whose long, hanging aerial roots resemble beards.

---

match or even just a friendly game on the beach or grassy field. Thousands of Bajans and other West Indians pour into the world-class matches at **Kensington Oval** ( ☎ 436-1397; ✆ 9am-4pm), in Garrison near Bridgetown, which was the site of the final in the 2007 World Cup. For information, schedules and tickets, contact the **Barbados Cricket Association** ( ☎ 436-1397; www.bcacricket.org).

Horse races and polo are traditionally watched, while windsurfing and surfing are popular with locals and visitors alike.

## ARTS

Barbadian contributions to West Indian music are renowned in the region, having produced such greats as the calypso artist the Mighty Gabby, whose songs on cultural identity and political protest speak for emerging black pride throughout the Caribbean. These days, Bajan music leans toward the faster beats of soca (an energetic offspring of calypso), *rapso* (a fusion of soca and hip-hop) and dancehall (a contemporary offshoot of reggae with faster, digital beats and an MC). Hugely popular Bajan soca artist Rupee brings the sound of the island to audiences worldwide. Bridgetown-born singer Rihanna has made a huge international splash (see left).

The foremost contemporary Barbadian novelist is George Lamming, who has written six novels and several collections of short fiction. His most acclaimed novel, 1953's *In the Castle of My Skin*, portrays what it was like to grow up black in a colonial Barbados that was struggling toward independence.

Island architectural styles have their roots in the colonial era, when virtually all land belonged to large sugar estates. The island still has a number of grand plantation homes as well as numerous chattel houses, the latter being simple wooden homes built for easy disassembly and portability. The **Barbados National Trust** ( ☎ 436-9033; http://trust.funbarbados .com; house visit B$15; ✆ Wed) runs an Open House program offering visits to some of the island's grander private homes. In addition, many houses, especially those in the central highlands, have regular opening hours.

## ENVIRONMENT
### The Land
Barbados lies 160km east of the Windward Islands. It is somewhat pear-shaped, measur-

---

**BARBADOS HAS AN ELECTION**

The January 2008 national elections in Barbados were a moving example of how democracy can function when everybody plays by the rules. Although it had been in power for 15 years, the Barbados Labour Party and their long-time leader Owen Arthur lost 20 to 10 in terms of seats. Despite having ruled all aspects of Bajan life for 15 years, Arthur and the BLP were gracious in defeat and congratulated the victorious Democratic Labour Party and the new prime minister, David Thompson. There were no riots, claims of malfeasance or any other high jinks to spoil an orderly transition. On election day itself, Bajans in their Sunday best went to the polls, which were free of politicking. Many of the polls were in historic sites and extremely polite monitors explained to tourists that things were closed due to the election. The entire process can best be described as civilized. Barbados should be proud.

---

ing 34km from north to south and 22km at its widest. The island is composed largely of coral accumulations built on sedimentary rocks. Water permeates the soft coral cap, creating underground streams, springs and limestone caverns. Most of the island's terrain is relatively flat, rising to low, gentle hills in the interior. However, the northeastern part of the island, known as the Scotland District, rises to a relatively lofty 340m at Barbados' highest point, Mt Hillaby. The west coast has white-sand beaches and calm turquoise waters, while the east side of the island has turbulent Atlantic waters and a coastline punctuated by cliffs. Coral reefs surround most of the island and contribute to the fine white sands on the western and southern beaches.

The Andromeda Botanic Gardens (see p692), in a gorgeous setting above Bathsheba, have a huge range of beautifully displayed local flora.

### Wildlife

The majority of Barbados' indigenous wildlife was overwhelmed by agriculture and competition with introduced species. Found only on Barbados is the harmless and elusive grass snake. The island also shelters a species of small, nonpoisonous, blind snake; plus whistling frogs, lizards, red-footed tortoises and eight species of bat.

Hawksbill turtles regularly come ashore to lay their eggs, as does the occasional leatherback turtle. As elsewhere, the turtles face numerous threats from pollution and human interference. The **Barbados Sea Turtle Project** ( ☎ 230-0142; www.barbadosseaturtles.org) is working to restore habitat and populations.

Most if not all mammals found in the wild on Barbados have been introduced. They include wild green monkeys, mongooses, European hares, mice and rats.

More than 180 species of bird have been sighted on Barbados. Most of them are migrating shorebirds and waders that breed in North America and stop over in Barbados en route to winter feeding grounds in South America. Only 28 species nest on Barbados; these include wood doves, blackbirds, bananaquits, guinea fowl, cattle egrets, herons, finches and three kinds of hummingbird.

### Environmental Issues

The forests that once covered Barbados were long ago felled by the British planters. One of the knock-on effects is that the country now has a problem with soil erosion. This loose dirt, along with pollution from ships and illegally dumped solid wastes, threatens to contaminate the aquifers that supply the island's drinking water.

## FOOD & DRINK

Bajan food is similar to other West Indian cuisines, in that it has African and East Indian influences, but it also has unique ingredients and variations. Make sure to try the ubiquitous and iconic flying fish, which is served fried in delicious sandwiches all over the country. It's a mild white fish that is great sautéed or deep-fried.

Some of the local dishes include *conkies* (a mixture of cornmeal, coconut, pumpkin, sweet potato, raisins and spices, steamed in a plantain leaf), *cou-cou* (a creamy cornmeal and okra mash), *cutters* (meat or fish sandwiches in a salt bread roll), *jug-jug* (a mixture of Guinea cornmeal, green peas and salted meat), roti (a curry filling rolled inside flat bread), pumpkin fritters and pudding and *souse* (a dish made out of pickled pig's head and belly, spices and a few vegetables). Surprise your taste buds with the fiery 'Hill's Hot Balls', which aren't a creation of *South Park's* Chef but rather spicy cheese puffs. Sooth your palette with one of the many varieties of local bananas that are green even when ripe (look for them in markets).

In touristed areas, you'll find every kind of cuisine you desire (and some you may not) from fast food to inventive, creative fare from chefs with international reps. Seafood in all its forms is most popular as is Italian, Asian...you name it.

Those who have been stuck with instant coffee in the Windward Islands will welcome a good range of real coffees in Barbados. Tap water is safe to drink; it comes from underground reservoirs that are naturally filtered. For those who prefer something a little harder, Barbadian rum is considered some of the finest in the Caribbean, with Mount Gay being the best-known label. The island beer, Banks, is refreshing after a day in the hot sun.

Tours of rum factories are a very popular visitor activity. Among the more notable are those run by Malibu Beach and Mount Gay on the north side of Bridgetown (see p682).

# BRIDGETOWN

**pop 97,000**

Barbados' bustling capital, Bridgetown, is also the island's only city and is situated on its only natural harbor. Its many sights and old colonial buildings can easily occupy a day of wandering. Head along the side streets of the main drags to discover residential neighborhoods scattered with rum shops and chattel houses.

Many enjoy taking a respite from their day at one of the cafés or snack stands along the south banks of the Constitution River. There is good shopping, especially along Broad St and on pedestrian-only Swan St, which buzzes with the rhythms of local culture.

## ORIENTATION

Bridgetown sits on attractive Carlisle Bay on the southwest corner of Barbados. The city is developed around an inlet from the bay known as the Careenage, and connects directly to most highways across the island. There's a nice beach and a several bars along Bay Street south of the center. The entire area is in St Michael Parish.

# INFORMATION
## Bookstores

**Cave Shepherd** ( ☎ 431-2121; Broad St) This department store has a wide selection of Caribbean and international literature plus the UK's *Sunday Times*.

**Cloister Bookstore** ( ☎ 426-2662; Hincks St) Carries local and international literature and best-sellers.

## Internet Access

**Connect** ( ☎ 228-8648; Shop 9, 27 Broad St; per 10min B$3; ☒ 9am-5pm Mon-Fri, 9:30am-4pm Sat) Upstairs in the Galleria Mall behind Nelson's Arms (enter from Lancaster Lane). Laptop connections and cheap calls.

**Gig@bytes** ( ☎ 435-6893; ☒ 7am-7pm Mon-Sat, noon-6pm Sun) near Fairchild St and Swing Bridge; has drinks and snacks, plus wi-fi.

## Libraries

**National Library** ( ☎ 426-3981; Coleridge St; ☒ 9am-5pm Mon-Sat) To check out books here you'll pay a refundable deposit of B$20. The deposit is valid also at Holetown, Speightstown and Oistins branches.

## Medical Services

**Collins Pharmacy** ( ☎ 426-4515; 28 Broad St) Prescriptions, sundries, shoe and watch repair.

**Queen Elizabeth Hospital** ( ☎ 436-6450; Martindale's Rd; ☒ 24hr)

## Money

Banks are generally open 8am to 3pm Monday to Thursday and 8am to 5pm Friday, and most have 24-hour ATM access.

**Barbados National Bank** ( ☎ 431-5700; Broad St) At the west end. There's a branch on Fairchild St.

**Scotiabank** ( ☎ 426-7000; Broad St) At the west end. There's also a branch on Fairchild St.

## Post

**Post office** (Cheapside; ☒ 7:30am-5pm Mon-Fri)

## Tourist Information

**Barbados Tourism Authority** ( ☎ 427-2623; www .barbados.org; Harbour Rd; ☒ 8:15am-4:30pm Mon-Fri) Answers questions, offers brochures; a branch office at the cruise-ship terminal opens when ships are in port.

## Travel Agencies

**Going Places Travel** ( ☎ 431-2400; ground fl, Speedbird House, Independence Sq) Branch of regional agency.

## SIGHTS & ACTIVITIES
### Central Bridgetown

All of the following sites can be reached on foot.

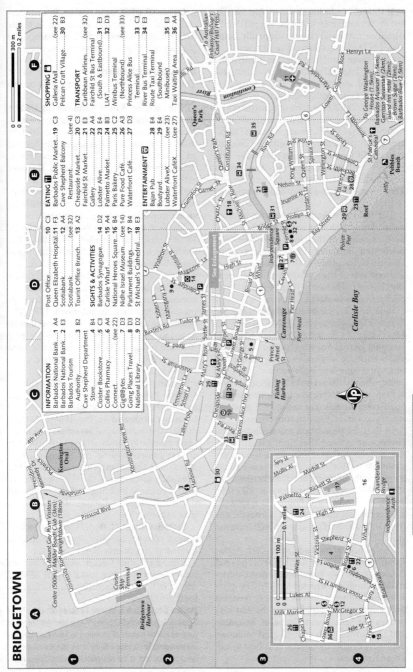

**St Michael's Cathedral** (St Michael's Row; admission free; 9am-4pm Sun-Fri, to 1pm Sat) is the island's Anglican cathedral. It was originally completed in 1665 to accommodate 3000 worshipers, but came tumbling down in a hurricane a century later. The scaled-down, but still substantial, structure (it's also a hurricane shelter…) that stands today dates from 1789 and seats 1600. At the time of construction it was said to have the widest arched ceiling of its type in the world. Among the island notables tightly packed into the adjacent churchyard are Sir Grantley Adams (Barbados' first premier and the head of the West Indies Federation from 1958 to 1962) and his son Tom (prime minister of Barbados from 1976 to 1985).

The triangular **National Heroes Square** (formerly known as Trafalgar Sq) marks the bustling center of the city. The square once celebrated Battle of Trafalgar hero Lord Horatio Nelson (whose statue still stands on the west side of the square), but was eventually changed to honor 10 Bajan heroes – from cricket heroes to slave leaders.

Built in 1833, the small **Barbados Synagogue** (Synagogue Lane; admission free; 10am-4pm Mon-Fri), between James St and Magazine Lane, near National Heroes Sq, was abandoned in 1929 and beautifully restored in 1986. The island's first synagogue was built on this site in the 1600s, when Barbados had a Jewish population of more than 800. Over the following years the population dwindled to one in 1929 owing to emigration and Christian conversion.

In 1931 the population rebounded when a large group arrived after fleeing discrimination in Poland. The community now numbers about 100 and their entire history is well documented in the beautiful new **Nidhe Israel Museum** ( ☎ 436-6869; Synagogue Lane; adult/child: B$25/12.50; 9am-4pm Mon-Sat). It is housed in a restored 1750 synagogue that is just across from the one from 1833 above. It's massively built from cut coral blocks that glow in the sun.

The **parliament buildings** ( ☎ 427-2019; tours 10am & 2pm Mon-Fri) on the north side of National Heroes Sq are two stone-block, neo-Gothic-style buildings constructed in 1871. The west-side building with the clock tower contains public offices; the building on the east side houses the Senate and House of Assembly and is adorned with stained-glass windows depicting British monarchs. It is best to call ahead for tours.

**Carlisle Wharf** (Hincks St) is a small commercial building. The real attraction is at the back where benches overlook the harbor and plaques chart the local maritime heritage.

## Around Bridgetown

The following sites are within a mile or two of Bridgetown's center.

The excellent **Barbados Museum** ( ☎ 427-0201; Garrison; adult/child B$11.50/5.75; 9am-5pm Mon-Sat, 2-6pm Sun) is housed in an early-19th-century military prison. It has engaging displays on all aspects of the island's history, beginning with its early indigenous residents. The most extensive collections cover the colonial era, with exhibits on slavery, emancipation, military history and plantation-house furniture, all accompanied by insightful narratives.

Just west, the **George Washington House** ( ☎ 228-5461; Bush Hill, Garrison; adult/child B$20/5; 9am-4:30pm Mon-Fri) can truly claim that the great man slept here. After decades of research and debate, it was finally shown that this 18th-century estate had been the home of the future US president and his brother Lawrence (see opposite) during their fateful stay in 1751. The beautifully restored home shows what it must have looked like during their stay. A large museum brings 1750s Barbados to life. Lush gardens include a herb patch and café.

About 2km south of central Bridgetown, spreading inland from the south side of Carlisle Bay, is the **Garrison area**, the home base of the British Windward and Leeward Islands Command in the 1800s. A focal point is the oval-shaped **Savannah**, which was once parade grounds and is now used for cricket games, jogging and Saturday horse races. Standing along the west side of the Savannah are some of the Garrison's more ornate colonial buildings, where you'll find the world's largest collection of 17th-century iron cannons.

**Barbados Blue** ( ☎ 434-5764; www.divebarbadosblue.com; Hilton Hotel, Needham's Point) dive shop is located at Needham's Point.

Rum has longed been a critical part of local life and you can make it part of your life as well at two facilities run by famous local distilleries:

**Malibu Beach Club & Visitor Centre** ( ☎ 425-9393; Brighton Beach; tours B$20; 9-4pm Mon-Fri) Coconut-flavored Malibu is more of an export to Americans barely old enough to drink than a Bajan drink, but the company has a popular tour at the beachfront distillery. Spend time in a beach chair after the tour/samples. About 3km north of the center.

**Mount Gay Rum Visitors Centre** ( ☎ 425-8757; www.mountgay.com; Spring Garden Hwy; tours B$14; ⏰ 9am-3:30pm Mon-Fri) The aged rums here are some of Barbados' best – the visitors centre is about a kilometer north of Bridgetown Harbour. Other tour options include transport and food, from B$60.

## SLEEPING

Few visitors stay in Bridgetown and there are few accommodations available. Aquatic Gap, just south of town, is the first spot with any hotels to speak of; however, it is recommended that you head the few minutes further to Hastings, Rockley, Worthing, St Lawrence Gap or beyond for a more relaxed beach atmosphere.

**Island Inn Hotel** ( ☎ 436-6393; www.islandinnbarbados.com; Aquatic Gap; r from US$160; 🅿 🖳 🅿 ) This 23-room hotel is partially built in a restored 1804 garrison building that was originally a military rum store. It is near the beach off Bat St, close to town and has all-inclusive rate options. It's a relaxed option – just don't look at the hideous nearby Hilton or you'll turn into a pillar of salt.

## EATING

**Paris Bakery** ( ☎ 436-0504; Cheapside; snacks from B$3; ⏰ breakfast & lunch Mon-Fri) Enjoy take-out banana bread, coconut bread and other treats at this delectable little bakery.

**Balcony Restaurant** ( ☎ 227-2121; Broad St; lunch B$10; ⏰ lunch Mon-Sat) The in-house restaurant at the landmark Cave Shepherd Department Store has a small daily buffet of island favorites like curries and salads. Ask a local where they go for lunch and they point here. The fresh juices are excellent.

**Pure Food Café** ( ☎ 436-4537; Chapel St; lunch from B$10; ⏰ lunch Mon-Sat) Unadorned, like your

arteries after a meal here. Enjoy excellent fresh fruit juices and wholesome fare like the popular split pea soup.

**Gallery** ( ☎ 435-7053; Galleria Mall, 27 Broad St; meals B$15-25; ⏰ breakfast & lunch Mon-Sat) You can literally look down upon the gem-seeking tourist hordes from the popular balcony at this pub. English breakfasts morph to burgers and airborne Pisces sandwiches at lunch.

**Waterfront Café** ( ☎ 427-0093; Careenage; meals from B$25; ⏰ lunch & dinner) Always packed, especially at the breezy tables on the river. Lunches include a fine version of a flying fish sandwich; dinners are more elaborate and have Mediterranean color and flair. There's live music ranging from steel pan to jazz.

**Lobster Alive** ( ☎ 435-0305; Bay St; meals from B$40; ⏰ lunch & dinner) The name is only true until you order. Lobster bisque and grilled lobster are just some of the choices on the crustacean-heavy menu at this ramshackle joint on the beach. On many nights there's smooth jazz.

**Brown Sugar** ( ☎ 426-7684; lunch buffet B$40, dinner B$45-80; ⏰ lunch Sun-Fri, dinner daily) The much-loved Brown Sugar, next to the Island Inn Hotel at Aquatic Gap, is a lush paradise inside and out. The excellent West Indian buffet is popular; dinner is off a menu that includes shrimp Creole, lobster, flying fish and much more. The Bajan bread pudding is a rummy delight. Book at dinner.

Even if you're not intending to buy, the **Cheapside Market** (Cheapside) is a fascinating place to browse local produce in a grand old market hall recently restored by the thoughtful Chinese government. It has some nice snack stands on the second floor. Southwest across Princess Alice Hwy, the Public Market has all things briny fresh from the boats.

**Palmetto Market** (Swan St), at the east end, is another good place for fresh produce and snacks. But for a meal or a cheery drink with amiable and voluble locals, **Fairchild St**

**BARBADOS**

---

**GEORGE WASHINGTON SLEPT HERE**

In 1751, at age 19 – some 38 years before he would become the first US president – George Washington visited Barbados as a companion to his half-brother Lawrence, who suffered from tuberculosis. It was hoped that the tropical climate would prove therapeutic.

The two rented a house in the Garrison area south of Bridgetown and stayed on the island for six weeks. The newly restored George Washington House (opposite) gives fascinating look at the trip and the time. As it was, Lawrence never recovered and died the next year.

The legacy of another American founding father, Alexander Hamilton, can be found on Nevis (see p507).

Market (Fairchild St) has snacks stands, cafés and rum shops in a long row along the river. The markets are usually open 7am to late afternoon Monday to Saturday.

## DRINKING

While visitors are welcome in Bridgetown's many rum shops, these watering holes don't cater to foreigners. Along Baxters Rd, just north of the center, you'll find a concentration of these bars, where alcohol flows and fish is fried up until late at night. Although women will not be turned away, be warned that rum shops are a macho haunt.

**Bajan Pub** ( ☎ 436-1664; Bay St; ☷ 5pm-late) For an accessible rum shop-style experience, check out this old place which is one of several on the stretch. Note how old cannons are now used as posts.

**Boatyard** ( ☎ 436-2622; Bay St; ☷ 11am-2am) An over-amped beach bar that pushes the sex-on the-beach angle hard, the boatyard gets visitors by the busload who come for the daytime drinking contests and beach activities. During sunset there is a three-hour all-you-can-drink deal (US$25). Late night it's a club with DJs and live music (cover varies).

## ENTERTAINMENT
### Sports

Cricket matches are played throughout the year at the **Kensington Oval** ( ☎ 436-1397; ☷ 9am-4pm) in Garrison near Bridgetown, which was the site of the final in the 2007 World Cup. The **Barbados Cricket Association** ( ☎ 436-1397; www .bcacricket.org) is the source of all things cricket.

Horse races are held at the Garrison Savannah on Saturday afternoons throughout the year, except April and September. **Barbados Turf Club** ( ☎ 426-3980; www.barbadosturfclub.com) offers seats in the grandstand starting at B$20, but for no charge you can also watch the races from benches under the trees around the outside of the track – you can also place a bet at booths on the south or west side.

### Live Music

The Waterfront Café (p683) has live music every night but Sunday; Lobster Alive (p683) has jazz many nights.

## SHOPPING

**Pelican Craft Village** ( ☎ 426-0765; Princess Alice Hwy) This ever-evolving complex of galleries and workshops, between downtown and the cruise-ship terminal, features the works of many local artists. The Barbados Arts Council has a shop here with the works of more than 30 of its members usually on show.

The island's grand old department store, **Cave Shepherd** ( ☎ 227-2121; Broad St), has a well-priced rum and quality souvenir section.

## GETTING THERE & AWAY

As most people stay along the southern coast they will arrive and depart in minibuses from the **Route Taxi Terminal** (Nursery Rd) along the river. A little closer in toward the center of town is the **River Bus Terminal** (Nursery Rd), which sends minibuses along central and eastern routes.

Public buses going south and east leave from the **Fairchild St Bus Terminal** (Bridge St), north of Fairchild. Public buses and minibuses going north up the west coast leave from the **Princess Alice Terminal** (Princess Alice Hwy), at the west end.

## GETTING AROUND

Bridgetown is easily covered on foot, although taxis can be flagged on the street if necessary, or hailed from the waiting area.

# SOUTH COAST

The south coast is the island's tourism epicenter, with most of the budget-to-midrange accommodations along its fine white-sand beaches. This virtually uninterrupted stretch of development runs from the outskirts of Bridgetown all the way to the airport.

Hastings, Rockley and Worthing are part of one long commercial strip. St Lawrence Gap and Dover Beach is a surprisingly appealing area off the main road. East of Oistins, development begins to thin. Starting with Silver Sands the coast is fairly sedate (except for the surf and wind). All are linked by the main road along the coast, which, while designated Hwy 7, is never called that. The entire area is in Christ Church Parish.

## Getting There & Away

Frequent No 11 minibuses from the route-taxi terminal in Bridgetown run along Main Rd (Hwy 7) on the southern coast and link the south coast villages. Private taxis are relatively easy to find in the main tourist areas.

# HASTINGS & ROCKLEY
**pop 22,000**

Just a 15-minute bus ride from Bridgetown are the first major tourist areas of Hastings and Rockley. They are home to a lot of midrange hotels and some attractive, popular beaches, the largest being Accra Beach. Commercialism rules and the streetscape is a Babel of signs. The center of activity is Rockley Beach, a roadside white-sand public beach with shade trees, snack kiosks and clothing vendors. About halfway between Bridgetown and Rockley is Hastings Rock, a nice spot to enjoy views of the ocean. On weekends, community groups set up flea markets and hold activities around the gazebo in the small park above the water.

## Information

There are plenty of banks and ATMs along the main road. Most have 24-hour ATMs.

**Net Shack** ( ☎ 228-5841; Hastings Plaza; per hr B$12; ✆ 9am-10pm Mon-Sat, 10am-9pm Sun) Surfing, laptop connections, printers & DVD rentals.

## Sleeping

**Tree Haven Beach Apartments** ( ☎ 435-6673; kentolaya@caribsurf.com; Main Rd, Rockley; apt from US$75; ❄ ) This affordable, laid-back option has three OK units just across the road from the beach and right near Bubba's bar. This is one of the cheapest options here; try for the second-floor unit.

**Coconut Court Beach Resort** ( ☎ 427-1655; www .coconut-court.com; Main Rd, Hastings; r from US$160; ❄ 🖳 🛎 ) Coconut Court is a five-story beachfront 125-room hotel filled with package tourists – good for families. In the right light, the institutional green paint can take on a turquoise hue from the azure waters right out front. Look for deals on the internet.

## Eating & Drinking

**Mojo** ( ☎ 435-9008; Main Rd, Rockley; meals under B$20; ✆ 11am-late) A big old house by the side of the road, Mojo has a wide veranda plus all sorts of nooks inside for nuzzling your companion or listening to the excellent music. Monday is open-mike night and some of the island's best acoustic players drop by. Food ranges from burgers to bar snacks.

**Opa!** ( ☎ 435-1234; Hastings; mains from B$40; ✆ lunch & dinner) There's Greek favorites right on the water here, and the sea breezes will put you in mind of some other lovely islands half a planet

away. Groups enjoy frittering the night away between waves of small-plate treats. A gelato stand next door awaits your indulgence.

**Champers** ( ☎ 435-6644; Rockley; meals from B$60; ✆ lunch & dinner Mon-Sat) This long-time favorite has a dreamy new location off the main road right on the water. There's barely an obstruction between you and the view. Elegant meals are served on cream-colored tablecloths and include the usual range of grilled seafoods plus fresh pastas. Brits will understand the name means 'Champagne' – drink some at the lower level lounge.

# WORTHING
**pop 8000**

Worthing sits between the developed tourist areas of Hastings and Rockley and St Lawrence Gap. It's a good base if you're on a tight budget but still want to be near all the action. It has relatively inexpensive places at which to eat and a handful of lower-priced guesthouses that are either on the beach or a short walk away. The creatively named Sandy Beach, which fronts Worthing, is a nice strip of white powder. Several budget places are stashed away on the small nearby streets. It's a nice little scene. St Lawrence Gap is nearby, but the walk at night on the narrow, busy road can be perilous.

## Information

The **Big B Supermarket** ( ☎ 430-1366; Worthing; ✆ 8am-6:30 Mon-Thu, 8am-7:30pm Fri & Sat, 9am-2pm Sun) literally offers one-stop shopping. It has a deli, bank, ATM, pharmacy and a good bookstore. It's just north of the main road at the central intersection.

## Sights

Just east of Worthing, the **Graeme Hall Nature Sanctuary** ( ☎ 435-9727; www.graemehall.com; Main Rd; adult/child B$25/12.50; ✆ 8am-6pm) provides a wonderful respite from the developments. Lush gardens are spread over 14 hectares, which front the vastly larger mangroves and swamp. Boardwalks, trails and displays detail the many species of bird living in one of the island's last wild places.

## Sleeping

**House Cleverdale** ( ☎ 428-3172, 428-1035; karibik@sun beach.net; 3rd Ave; r from US$28; 🖳 ) Set back just a bit from the beach and away from the main road, this large wooden home is a popular budget

**BARBADOS**

spot. The three rooms and two apartments have mosquito nets, fans and wi-fi. Bathrooms and a large kitchen are shared. The owner has other cheap places nearby.

**Maraval Guest House** ( ☎ 435-7437; 3rd Ave; r from US$35) Down the street from Cleverdale, Maraval has attractive, simple rooms with shared bath and in-room sinks. There's access to a well-equipped kitchen and a pleasant living room with TV and stereo. This friendly and comfortable place is good for longer stays.

**Southern Heights Holiday Accommodation** ( ☎ 435-8354; http://southernheightsbarbados.com; Worthing; 🖳 ) There are 12 one-bedroom apartments in this custom-built complex that is a 15-minute walk from Sandy Beach. Go up the road that passes the Big B Supermarket and look for the sign to the right. Units have kitchens and cable TV.

## Eating

Worthing has some good inexpensive dining choices and a few garish midrange themed restaurants. For a nice dinner you are better off heading down the road to St Lawrence Gap.

**Carib Beach Bar & Restaurant** ( ☎ 435-8540; 2nd Ave; lunch B$12-16, dinner B$24; ✾ restaurant lunch & dinner) This open-air eatery right on Sandy Beach is the hub of local holiday life. Seafood and burgers are the main items on the menu, enjoy 'em at picnic tables on the sand while you watch waves break on the reef offshore. The bar boogies long after the kitchen closes.

**CaféBLUE** ( ☎ 435-7699; Main Rd; meals from B$11; ✾ breakfast, lunch & dinner Mon-Sat) This popular way-casual café has made-to-order sandwiches and rotis, good tea and coffee drinks (including iced versions of both), fruit smoothies, salads and baked goods.

## ST LAWRENCE GAP & DOVER BEACH
**pop 25,000**

The town of St Lawrence is almost lost along the busy main road. Instead the real action lies along a mile-long road that runs close to the beach. Lined with hotels, bars, restaurants and shops, this street is actually more pleasurable than it sounds. It's not commercialized to the point of being gross and it's mostly free of traffic, allowing night-time strolling.

The west end is known as St Lawrence Gap; the east end carries the Dover Beach moniker.

The latter has a nice, broad ribbon of white-sand beach that attracts swimmers, bodysurfers and windsurfers.

## Information

The street has several internet places, ATMs, convenience stores and small groceries.

## Sleeping

**Rio Guest House** ( ☎ 428-1546; www.rioguesthouse.net; St Lawrence Gap; s from US$40, d from US$55; 🖳 🖳 ) This backpacker special has nine unpretentious fan-cooled rooms. Singles share a bathroom and some rooms have air-con. It's in a tranquil location, off the main drag but about one minute from the beach and nightlife.

**Dover Woods Guest House** ( ☎ 420-6599; www.sandy groundbarbados.com; Dover Beach; s/d from US$55/65) Huge trees keep this large house shaded and cool. Located on estate-sized grounds at the east end of the strip, it has four large rooms which share a kitchen TV lounge and covered patio.

**Sandy Ground** ( ☎ 420-2720; www.barbados.org/rest/davids/gallery.htm; St Lawrence Gap; s/d from US$90/130; 🖳 ) This modern, two-story block has 10 rooms that are both tidy and nicely equipped with fridges and cable TV. It's just across from the Rio Guest House.

**Little Bay Hotel** ( ☎ 435-7246; www.littlebayhotel barbados.com; St Lawrence Gap; r from $130; 🖳 🖳 ) Right at the entrance to the Gap off the main road, the Little Bay is also right on the water. Opt for a room with a balcony for the full seashore effect. The rooms aren't large but are good-value for the price. There's wi-fi, but not all rooms pick it up.

**Southern Palms Beach Club** ( ☎ 428-7171; www.southernpalms.com; St Lawrence Gap; r from US$250; 🖳 🖳 🖳 ) A traditional, older beach resort that is stays in the pink – literally. Most of the various three-story blocks are decked out in a cheery pink tone. Interiors are closer to motel standard but the balconies and patios are large. Off at one end there are bungalows (from US$400) that look like something out of Hollywood. Offers wi-fi.

## Eating & Drinking

One of the pleasures of the Gap is wandering the street at night comparing the many restaurants. Your hunger will be spurred on by the many street vendors who set up at night selling juicy burgers, grilled chicken and the ubiquitous macaroni pie. Bars range from humble to vaguely swank. Blues and show tunes at many of them keep the chatter mellow until past midnight.

**our pick** **Café Lanoara** ( ☎ 236-4334; Dover Beach; ☯ noon-11pm) Really a collection of outdoor furniture served from a small stall, this completely open-air bar is run by Abdul, a true gentleman and a scholar. Lots of local professionals gather at the candle-lit tables and discuss the day's events while jazzy strains play in the background.

**Bean & Bagel** ( ☎ 420-4606; Dover Beach; meals from B$20; ☯ breakfast & lunch) As the name implies, this is the place for fresh bagels. American-style breakfasts are also the thing – enjoy a scrumptious, sumptuous omelette on the large shaded deck. Lunch brings salads and sandwiches. There's wi-fi here.

**McBride's Pub & Cookhouse** ( ☎ 435-6352; St Lawrence Gap; meals B$30; ☯ dinner, bar until 2am or later) Fuel up with classic deep-fried bar chow to the strains of sports on TV. Later, enjoy a changing line-up of live music that mixes salsa, techno, karaoke and reggae. If you want a read on the crowd, note how often the theme is 'greatest hits of the '70s and '80s'.

**Pisces** ( ☎ 435-6564; St Lawrence Gap; meals from B$70; ☯ dinner) This large restaurant stretches right along the waterfront; waves lap against the foundations below. The view at sunset followed by the twinkling lights of the coast and fishing boats is captivating. Little candles illuminate fine seafood dishes (as you'd expect from the name). The wine list favors the US, France and Australia. Its always busy – come at 9pm for a relaxing time after the rush.

**David's Place** ( ☎ 435-9755; St Lawrence Gap; meals B$85; ☯ dinner Tue-Sun) One of the most romantic choices in the Gap, you first encounter a proper bar as you enter. Further in the lights dim and you're at tables overlooking the bay, which laps gently below. Waiters glide about with seafood and steak dishes that feature accents of Creole and curry.

## Entertainment

Several popular venues in the Gap jam with live bands and DJs. Most have a cover charge, sometimes up to B$30 and sometimes partially redeemable for drinks. Several of the bars have live music one or more nights, or like McBride's (above), have live music most nights.

Consider starting off in St Lawrence Gap and then heading to the wild pleasures of the Boatyard in Bridgetown (see p684) or nearby Oistins (below) on weekend nights for a wilder and more Bajan experience.

**Reggae Lounge** ( ☎ 435-6462; St Lawrence Gap; cover varies; ☯ 9pm-late) The Reggae Lounge not only plays classic reggae, but dancehall, hip-hop and more. Although the cover charge can hit B$30 everything's gonna be all right, especially on Mondays when the cover includes unlimited drinks.

## OISTINS

pop 16,000

This decidedly local yet modern town a few miles east of St Lawrence is best known as the center of the island's fishing industry. Oistins' heart is the large, bustling seaside fish market, which on Friday and Saturday hosts the island's best party, with soca, reggae, pop and country music, vendors selling barbecued fish and plenty of rum drinking. It's roughly 80% locals, 20% tourists and makes a fun scene, whether you're out for partying or just getting a solid local meal at a fair price. The height of the action is between 10pm and 2am. Also look for **Lexie's** ( ☎ 428-1405; Oistins Beach; ☯ 24hr), a never-closes beach bar that spins, of all things, ballroom music.

Immediately east of Oistins, **Enterprise Beach** is a long and shady public beach with full facilities. Right behind the sand, **Little Arches Hotel** ( ☎ 420-4689; www.littlearches .com; Enterprise; r from US$250; ☒ ☐ ☒ ) is one of the most characterful choices on the South Coast. Once a Mediterranean-style mansion, the hotel now has 10 rooms in a variety of shapes and sizes, some with private whirlpools. Privacy is at a maximum and there are lots of arty touches throughout. It's on the quiet beach access road. Offers wi-fi.

## SILVER SANDS

pop 11,000

At the southernmost tip of the island, between Oistins and the airport, is the breezy Silver Sands area. Although you'll need to avoid some characterless large resorts there are good small choices popular with kitesurfers and windsurfers. In January and February, everything fills up for the Windsurfing Championship. Most of the No 11 route taxis continue to Silver Sands from Oistins.

**BARBADOS**

**deAction Beach Shop** (☎ 826-7087; www.irieman-talma.com/actionstore.htm; Silver Sands) is run by local board-legend Brian Talma; board rentals average US$200 per week; windsurfing and kitesurfing lessons begin at US$40 per hour.

**Zed's Surfing Adventures** (☎ 428-7873; www.barbadossurf.com; Surfer's Point) runs beginners' surf classes (US$80), as well as surf tours around the island. It's affiliated with Surfer's Point Guest House.

In addition to the following listings, there are a number of private places in the Silver Sands area that can be rented by the week. Many windsurfers stay a night or two in a hotel and then, through word of mouth, find a shared house or apartment nearby. The appeal of Surfer's Point at the east end speaks for itself.

Set on a rocky shore and near the beach, family-run **Round Rock Apartments** (☎ 428-7500; www.barbados.org/apt/a40.htm; Silver Sands; r from US$95) has seven large self-catering units in a well-maintained older building. A pleasant ocean-view restaurant serves a full breakfast and meals through the day (from B$12).

**ourpick** **Peach and Quiet Hotel** (☎ 428-5682; www.peachandquiet.com; Inch Marlow; r from US$120) is ripe for your booking (fruity name aside). The 22 airy rooms come with sea-view patios set around a secluded pool. There's an oceanside bar and a restaurant. The owner, Adrian Loveridge, leads excellent walks across the island.

The HQ of Zed's Surfing Adventures, **Surfer's Point Guest House** (☎ 428-7873; www.barbadossurf.com; Surfer's Point; apt US$100-180; ❄ 💻) is on a little point amid a very good break. The seven units here come in various sizes; some have balconies with views, all have kitchens and wi-fi. There's a small protected pool out front for kids.

# SOUTHEAST COAST

St Philip, the diamond-shaped parish east of the airport, is sparsely populated, with a scattering of small villages. Along the coast are a couple of resort hotels and fine beaches.

## Getting There & Away

Minibus 11 continues into the southeast of Barbados after heading east from Oistins.

## CRANE BEACH

Crane Beach, situated 7km northeast of the airport, is a hidden beach cove backed by cliffs and fronted by aqua blue waters. It is generally regarded as one of the best beaches on the island. An adventurous trail over rocks along the water accesses the beach from the end of a small road about 700m east of the Crane Beach Hotel. Parking is bad but the sands are simply wonderful. Bring a picnic and make a day of it.

You would never guess that the **Crane Beach Hotel** (☎ 423-6220; www.thecrane.com; r from US$210; ❄ 💻 🏊) was once a small inn in an old mansion. Those roots can still be found in the lovely restaurants that overlook the beach and ocean (L'Azure, for example, has upscale Caribbean fare, with lunch and dinner from US$20; book in advance). Elsewhere hundreds of condos and resort facilities have appeared. If you like the kind of place that has an entire shop devoted to items bearing its logo, you'll love this sprawling, swank Shangri-La. Offers wi-fi.

# WEST COAST

Barbados' west coast has lovely tranquil beaches that are largely hidden by the majority of the island's luxury hotels and condos. In colonial times, the area was a popular holiday retreat for the upper crust of British society. These days, the villas that haven't been converted to resorts are owned by wealthy and famous people from all over the world. Although all the beaches are all public, the near constant development means that you only get a few coastal glimpses.

Hwy 1, the two-laner that runs north from Bridgetown to Speightstown, is bordered much of the way by a close mix of tourist facilities and residential areas.

## Getting There & Away

Minibuses along the west coast depart from near the general post office on Cheapside in Bridgetown and follow Hwy 1.

## PAYNES BAY

Fringed by a fine stretch of white sand, gently curving Paynes Bay, in St James, is perhaps the west coast's most popular spot for swimming and snorkeling. Beach access walkways are clearly marked by roadside signs. The main public beach site at the southern end of the bay has picnic tables, rest rooms and a laid-back Friday-night fish fry. Follow your nose to the public fish market at the north end of the strand.

**Angler Apartments** ( ☎ 432-0817; www.anglerapartments.com; Clarke's Rd 1, Derricks; r from US$120; ✷ ) is an unpretentious place with 13 older, basic apartments. Studios in an adjacent old plantation house are similar but smaller. There's a little patio bar. It's at the south end of Paynes Bay, off a road east of the main road. Right on the beach at Paynes Bay, everything at **Tamarind Cove Hotel** ( ☎ 432-1332; www.tamarindcovehotel.com; Paynes Bay; r from US$350; ✷ ▣ ▣ ) is discreet about this understated luxury resort. The 110 rooms are decked out in a restful palette of beachy pastels. All have balconies or patios and views of either one of the three pools or the ocean. The beach is right out front, a new spa inside.

**Crocodile's Den** ( ☎ 432-7625; Paynes Bay; ☽ 4pm-3am) is a good option for an evening fish *cutter* to accompany a cold Banks and a game of pool. There's frequently a live band, sometimes with salsa music. Other good options where locals and visitors mix are nearby.

# HOLETOWN
**pop 32,000**

The first English settlers to Barbados landed at Holetown in 1627. An obelisk **monument** along the main road in the town center commemorates the event – although the date on the monument, which reads 'July 1605,' is clearly on island time.

Despite being the oldest town on the island, Holetown is a rather bustling place. There's a cute little nightlife area squeezed into a wedge between the main road and the beach. Shopping areas include the West Coast Mall, right across from the beach. It has an internet stand, ATM, pharmacy and a branch of **Cave Shepherd** ( ☎ 419-3110; ☽ 8:30am-6pm Mon-Fri, 8am-4pm Sat, 9am-2pm Sun) which includes a good book department.

## Sights & Activities

At the north end of Holetown, **Barbados Marine Reserve** ( ☎ 425-1200; Folkstone) has its headquarters on a nice shady public beach at Folkstone. The **visitor centre** (admission B$5; ☽ 9:30am-5pm Mon-Fri, 10am-6pm Sat & Sun) includes a small museum with displays on the reserve, which extends for a few miles north and south. You can rent

snorkeling gear (from B$10) and there are lockers. From here you can walk along the water to Holetown.

The dive shop **Hightide Watersports** ( ☎ 432-0931; www.divehightide.com; Coral Reef Club) is located at the Coral Reef Club.

## Sleeping & Eating

The Holetown area can be a black hole for those on a budget. Many of the island's poshest resorts, such as the Fairmont Glitter Bay (the former home of the Cunard family), occupy vast swaths of beach while charging the moon.

**Coral Reef Club** ( ☎ 422-2372; www.coralreefbarbados.com; Holetown; r from US$450; ✷ ▣ ▣ ) This family-owned 88-room luxury hotel has 12 acres of gorgeous landscaped grounds surrounding an elegant gingerbread fantasy of a main building. Unlike some other top-end places around Holetown, this place oozes with character. You may actually find yourself needing to be convinced to leave the grounds. Offers wi-fi.

**Surfside Beach Bar** ( ☎ 432-2105; lunch from B$10, dinner from B$25; ☽ 9am-late) A typical beach bar with picnic tables set on wood platforms that are one storm away from qualifying as driftwood. Cheap drinks, burgers, grilled flying fish are on offer. There's steel-pan music and barbecue Sunday nights.

**Ragamuffins** ( ☎ 432-1295; 1st St; mains from B$45; ☽ dinner) One of several delightful little nightspots in this enclave, Raggamuffins is in a 60-year-old chattel house painted a stylish olive and turquoise. Dishes are all Caribbean with some added attitude: the blackened fish with aioli is pure joy. On Sunday there's a drag show.

## NORTH OF HOLETOWN

**Mt Standfast** is home to hawksbill turtles that feed on sea grasses just off its shore. Most snorkeling tours make a stop here to offer fish to the turtles and to allow customers to swim among them. Without a tour, you can rent snorkeling gear at the beach and get advice for your own freelance turtle viewing. **Dive Barbados** ( ☎ 422-3133; www.divebarbados.net) is a well-known dive shop located at Mt Standfast.

**Mullins Beach** is a popular family-friendly beach along Hwy 1 between Holetown and Speightstown. The waters are usually calm and good for swimming and snorkeling. Parking is good all along this postcard-perfect crescent.

BARBADOS

## SPEIGHTSTOWN

**pop 45,000**

Easily the most evocative small town on Barbados, Speightstown combines old colonial charms with a vibe that has more rough edges than the endlessly upscale precincts to the south. The town is a good place for a wander, soaking it up and chatting with its characters. Since the main road was moved east, traffic is modest, so take time to look up at the battered old wooden facades, many with overhanging galleries. During the sugarcane boom, Speightstown was a thriving port and the main shipping line ran directly from here to Bristol, England.

There are ATMs, pharmacies and other shops. **Jordan's Supermarket** ( ☎ 422-2191; Queen St; 8am-8pm) has sundries, supplies and goods for picnics and expeditions along the coast or up into the hills to the east.

The **Reefers & Wreckers** ( ☎ 422-5450; www.scuba diving.bb) dive shop is located here.

Among the many shops, **Livia's Hat Shop** ( ☎ 245-4312; Queen St) has the best selection of chapeaus on the island. Prices average B$30 and Livia decorates many herself – think restrained Carmen Miranda.

A radiant vision in white stucco, **Arlington House** ( ☎ 422-4064; Queen St; adult/child B$25/12.50; 9am-5pm Mon-Sat) is an 18th-century colonial house that now houses an engaging museum run by the National Trust.

If you are interested in staying on here for a longer period of time, apartment and house rentals can be arranged for reasonable rates (from around US$40 per night) through the amiable Clement 'Junior' Armstrong, who manages the Fisherman's Pub (below). **Sunset Sands Apartments** ( ☎ 438-1096; www.sunsetsands .com; Sand St; ste from US$110; ) Just north of the town center across from the beach, the Sunset Sands has four attractive suites in a building with solid colonial charm. The upstairs apartments have stunning ocean views and there's a secluded garden.

**Eat's Bar** ( ☎ 422-3462; cnr Mango Ln & Queen St; meals from B$7; breakfast, lunch & dinner) is a simple stand in a little house that serves up chicken – fried, stewed or in a curry – rotis, steamed fish and other flavorful local dishes.

**our pick Fisherman's Pub** ( ☎ 422-2703; Queen St; meals B$12; 11am-late Mon-Sat, 6pm-late Sun), on the waterfront next to a pint-sized beach, is a local institution that serves up fish from the boats floating off the back deck. Like a seal with a new ball, it's always lively and unpredictable. On Wednesdays, there is steel-pan music. As the evening wears on, the scene gets more Bajan. Try the national dish of *cou-cou* and flying fish here.

Look for a mango-colored wood building tucked down a little alley: **Mango's by the Sea** ( ☎ 422-0704; Queen St; mains B$50-90; dinner Sun-Fri). Overlooking the water, the interior mixes elegant (white tablecloths, candles, local art) with the casual (thatched decor). Dinners comprise the usual shellfish and steaks with nightly specials. The herb and garlic shrimp are an explosion of local flavors.

## SHERMANS

Just past the road that turns inland to St Lucy, Shermans is a narrow enclave of fine holiday homes and lovely local places; most seem to be competing to grow the most flowers. The narrow road runs through the tiny fishing village of **Fustic**, which has a couple of good rum shops.

The boutique hotel **Little Good Harbour** ( ☎ 439-3000; www.littlegoodharbourbarbados.com; Shermans; villas from US$300; ) has 21 one- to three-bedroom villas in a little compound near the water. The decor combines wicker with linens in units that open completely to the outside and flowering trees.

The **Fish Pot Restaurant** (mains B$30-70; lunch & dinner) is in an 18th-century sugar warehouse that once was connected to a wharf. The service is smart, the dishes were swimming out front not that long ago and the wine list is long.

# CENTRAL BARBADOS

Several important roads cross the rolling hills of the island's interior. There's a wealth of historical and natural sights here and you can spends days winding around small roads far from the hustle crowds of the west and south coasts. What follows are three main routes that take in major attractions and which can be combined in various ways to produce some delightful circle tours of the Barbados.

## Getting There & Away

Having your own transport will give you total freedom on the routes that follow. However you can also cover most of them by public bus, as all follow major routes. There will be some walking to access sites off the main road. One real hike, but a beautiful 6.5km one, is necessary to access the St Nicholas Abbey and Cherry Tree Hill off Hwy 2.

## SPEIGHTSTOWN TO BATHSHEBA

The road going into the hills east of Speightstown steadily climbs through historic sugarcane fields. The ruins of mills dot the landscape. Including the jaunt to St Nicholas Abbey, this route covers about 26km.

Eventually after about six miles you'll come to a fork in the road – if you continue on Hwy 2 to the east, you'll encounter **Farley Hill National Park** ( ☎ 422-3555; Hwy 2; per car B$3.50; ☺ 8:30am-4:30pm), which has 7 hectares of lovely gardens surrounding the ruins of an old estate. Barbadians love this park for its views to the Atlantic and picnic here in droves on Sundays. It's also one of the venues for the Barbados Jazz Festival (see p697).

**Barbados Wildlife Reserve** ( ☎ 422-8826; adult/child under 12 B$23/11.50; ☺ 10am-4pm) is a walk-through zoo opposite Farley Hill, with short paths that meander through a mahogany forest. The main attraction here is a colony of green monkeys. From September to January, the monkeys go marauding across the countryside in search of food and monkey business. If they're out when you're there, you'll get a ticket so you can come back again. Note that if the monkeys seem on good behavior, it's because the reserve is run by the Barbados Primate Research Centre, whose activities are just what the name implies.

Just above the reserve, good trails lead to the 19th-century **Grenade Hall Signal Station**, which has been restored. It was used by British troops for communications using flags and semaphores and was part of the chain that included one at Gun Hill (p692).

Back at the fork in the road, if you turn to the left (north) you are on one of the best little scenic drives on Barbados. The narrow road winds under a cathedral of huge trees arching overhead to **St Nicholas Abbey** ( ☎ 422-8725; admission B$25; ☺ 10am-3:30pm Sun-Fri), a Jacobean-style mansion that is one of the oldest plantation houses in the Caribbean and must-see stop on any island itinerary. Owner and local architect Larry Warren has undertaken a massive improvement program. The grounds are now simply gorgeous, with guinea fowl wandering among the flowers.

The interior recreates the mansion's 17th-century look, right down to the furniture. An old steam engine has been restored and the plantation is again bottling its own rum and molasses; you can taste some and enjoy a snack at the serene café.

About 700m southeast of the abbey, the road passes **Cherry Tree Hill**, which has grand views right across the Atlantic coast. From here the road heads downhill through fields of sugarcane that seem to envelop the car.

Look for **Morgan Lewis Sugar Mill** ( ☎ 422-9213; adult/child B$10/5; ☺ 8am-4pm Mon-Fri), 2km southeast of Cherry Tree Hill, which claims to be the largest intact sugar windmill surviving in the Caribbean. The interior has a simple display of historic photos, a few artifacts of the plantation era and the original gears, shaft and grinding wheel.

The road continues on a sinuous path downhill until it rejoins Hwy 2. Heading towards the coast, you pass through the little town of Belleplaine where you veer east to the road to Bathsheba. Running along the rugged coast through low sand dunes, this is one of the prettiest roads on Barbados. Look for **Barclays Park**, which has picnic tables under the trees, immaculate bathrooms and constantly roiling waves pounding the seemingly endless beach. Many who try to swim here wash ashore in South Africa.

The coast road continues another 5km south to Bathsheba.

## BRIDGETOWN TO BELLEPLAINE

This route takes you past sites that show the beauty of the myriad plants that thrive on Barbados. It also goes near Harrison's Cave, a subterranean attraction that has been closed while new whiz-bang gewgaws are added. The road, Hwy 2, runs for about 16km to Belleplaine.

**Tyrol Cot Heritage Village** ( ☎ 424-2074; Codrington Hill; adult/child B$11.50/5.75; ☺ 9am-5pm Mon-Fri) is a somewhat contrived 1920s Bajan village centered on the former home of Sir Grantley Adams, first premier of Barbados. The site, on Hwy 2 just north of Bridgetown, is complete with chattel houses where artists work on their crafts.

About 8km northeast of the Everton Weeks Roundabout on the bypass, look for a road crossing Hwy 2. Just west, **Welchman Hall Gully** ( ☎ 438-6671; Hwy 2, Welchman Hall; adult/child B$15/7; ☺ 9am-5pm) is a thickly wooded

BARBADOS

ravine with a walking track that leads you through nearly 200 species of plant, including spices like nutmeg. Such gullies were too difficult for growing crops and as a result preserve some of the tropical forests that once covered the island.

Just east of Hwy 2, **Flower Forest of Barbados** (☎ 433-8152; Hwy 2; adult/child B$14/7; ⌚ 9am-5pm) is another natural sight. The 20-hectare botanic garden is on the site of a former sugar estate which has many stately mature citrus and breadfruit trees. Paths meander among examples of almost every plant growing on the island. Who knew there were this many kinds of flower?

Hwy 2 curves down through more sugarcane before reaching Belleplaine. Here you have a decision: turn west for the beauty of St Nicholas Abbey (p691) or turn east for the wild beauty of the Atlantic coast (p691).

## BRIDGETOWN TO BATHSHEBA

Hwy 3 is a lovely road that goes up and over the middle of Barbados, on a 16km route that links the west and east coasts. Along the way there are some historic sights and some bucolic scenery.

Driving Hwy 3, 3km east of the Clyde Wolcott Roundabout on the bypass, look for signs for **Gun Hill** (☎ 429-1358; Fusilier Rd; adult/child B$10/5; ⌚ 9am-5pm Mon-Sat) on a small road turning south. There's a couple of twists and turns as you travel 1.5km to this 1818 hilltop signal tower with its impressive views of the surrounding valleys and the southwest coast. The island was once connected by six such signal towers that used flags and lanterns to relay messages. The official function of the towers was to keep watch for approaching enemy ships, but they also signaled colonial authorities in the event of a slave revolt.

About 8km after the Gun Hill turn on Hwy 3, you'll see squat little **St Joseph's Church** on the left. Turn on the road that goes south to the right and after only 250m you'll see the unrestored 1819 **Cotton Tower**, another of the signal towers. From here it is a short drive downhill on Hwy 3 to Bathsheba.

# EASTERN BARBADOS

The wild Atlantic waters of the east coast are far removed from the rest of the island. The population is small, the coast craggy and the waves incessant. It's a place of beautiful windblown vistas and a real haven for surfers. For sights along the coast road north of Bathsheba, see p691.

> **DETOUR**
>
> Hwy 3B runs northeast of Gun Hill through some small verdant valleys and plains. It's worthwhile to literally lose yourself here amid the pretty farms punctuated by the odd colonial-era building. Turn north on one of the many small roads any time you want to rejoin Hwy 3.

## BATHSHEBA

**pop 5100**

Bathsheba is the main destination on the east coast although there's no real 'there' here as things are scattered along about 1 mile of sandy, wave-tossed shore and in the hills immediately behind. This is prime surfing country. It's also good for long beach walks as you contemplate feeling you've reached the end of the world. At the south end of Bathsheba's beach, reefs afford enough protection for limited swimming. Note the iconic 'Mushroom Rock', one of several rocks carved into shapes that will cause mycologists to swoon.

At night, it's very quiet here. For excitement there are the lyrical croaks of whistling frogs and the flash of fireflies.

### Sights & Activities

#### ANDROMEDA BOTANIC GARDENS

At the top of the southern entrance to Bathsheba, the splendid **Andromeda Botanic Gardens** (☎ 433-9261; andromeda.cavehill.uwi.edu; Hwy 3; adult/child B$17.50/9; ⌚ 9am-5pm, last admission 4:30pm) cover 2.5 hectares and have a wide collection of introduced tropical plants, including orchids, ferns, water lilies, bougainvillea, cacti and palms. Self-guided walks of various lengths enjoy the floral beauty and splendid views.

#### SURFING

The world-famous reef break known as **Soup Bowl** is right off the beach in northern Bathsheba. It is one of the best waves in the Caribbean islands. Don't underestimate the break just because the region is not known for powerful surf – Soup Bowl gets big.

Moreover, the reef is shallow and covered in parts by spiny sea urchins. This is not a spot for beginners. Soup Bowl hosts the world's top surfers in international surf competitions in November when the Atlantic is at its strongest. Overall, the best months are August to March. You can rent boards (per day US$40) and get info at Smokey's Soup Bowl Cafe (right).

## Sleeping & Eating

Accommodation is limited in Bathsheba and that's good. Who wants crowds? Note that until it is renovated, we can't recommend the Edgewater Inn despite its prime location.

**Atlantis Hotel** ( ☎ 433-9445; www.atlantisbarbados .com; Tent Bay, Bathsheba; s/d incl breakfast from US$85/110) One cove south of Bathsheba, Atlantis was the original hotel in the area. It has 10 simple rooms in a solid old wooden building facing the sea. Breakfast is included and you can arrange for other meals, which you can enjoy on the patio. Fabled Bajan author George Lamming is often in residence.

ourpick **Sea-U! Guest House** ( ☎ 433-9450; www .seaubarbados.com; Tent Bay, Bathsheba; r incl breakfast from US$140; 🖳 ) The pick of Bathsheba lodging, the Sea-U has a mannered main house with an addictive porch looking out to sea from the hillside location. Cottages and a restaurant pavilion round out the verdant site. The seven units have kitchen facilities,

wi-fi and a nonclichéd island motif. There's no TV, kids under eight or smoking. Dinner is served Monday to Saturday.

**Smokey's Soup Bowl Cafe** ( ☎ 254-1018; meals from B$10; 🕙 10am-late) The eponymous Smokey enjoys million-dollar views from his simple joint across from the famous surf break. When not surfing, he cooks up local foods and raps with folks over drinks late into the night.

**Roundhouse Restaurant** ( ☎ 433-9678; meals from B$40; 🕙 breakfast, lunch & dinner) This popular touristy restaurant has customers throughout the day who sit around, sip cocktails and savor the views south over Soup Bowl. You can enjoy banana bread with your breakfast, sandwiches and salads at lunch, and specials such as breadfruit soup at dinner.

## Getting There & Away

A taxi can be negotiated for about B$60 from Bridgetown or the south coast, or catch one of the regular buses from Bridgetown that travel Hwys 2 and 3. The trip takes about 45 minutes.

# BATHSHEBA SOUTH TO CHRIST CHURCH PARISH

Few people take the time to follow the coast south of Bathsheba. They should. Look for signs on the roads, which stays well up the hillside, for **Martin's Bay**, a little notch in the

---

### A SPOONFUL OF A SOUP BOWL SURFER

Ken Mayers is a lifelong resident of Bathsheba and one of the area's best surfers. He's been surfing for 30 years, teaches the sport to others and is on the Barbados national surf team.

**Your father surfed?**

In the late 1940s the he would cut down trees and use those to go belly boarding. In the 1950s tourists – hippies really – started hanging out here in Bathsheba. They would go down to the cow fields in the morning looking for mushrooms. They brought board surfing along with them and the local guys like my dad picked it up.

**What makes Bathsheba's Soup Bowl a good place for surfing?**

It's a strong right-handed break which has three takeoff points that can be surfed point to point if you are fast and can read the wave.

**When should people surf here?**

For good surfers, it's September to November when it is the hurricane season and the start of cold fronts. Kelly Slater calls it a 9+ on a scale of 10. For beginners March to May is best.

**And why?**

Besides the great surfing, you can interact with local guys. They're all pretty friendly and good about helping you figure the place out. Plus for visitors it's a good place to enjoy the local culture.

**What do students worry about?**

Will the board hit me? Is the wave to big? What's under the water? I tell them, trust me in my field.

coast that features a sliver of a beach and a sweet little rum shop. Like elsewhere, this isn't swimming country, but the ceaseless surf is captivating. After about two more miles look for another steep road, this one leading down to **Bath Beach**. It's about 1.5km and has a long beach of golden sand. Unlike other parts of this coast, a reef makes swimming possible. Oodles of picnic tables are empty on weekdays, but are crowded with laughing families on weekends.

The road continues south before turning inland through canefields. Look for an iconic Anglican pile of rocks, **St Philip Church**. Here you turn south, following signs to **Sunbury Plantation House** ( ☎ 423-6270; www.barbadosgreat house.com; tours adult/child B$15/7.50; ⏰ 10am-4:30pm). Built in the mid-17th century, it was painstakingly restored after a fire in 1995. The house has 60cm-thick walls made from local coral blocks and ballast stones, the latter coming from the ships that set sail from England to pick up Barbadian sugar. The interior retains its plantation-era ambience and is furnished in antiques. The grounds serve as mere backdrops to the busloads of tourists who come for the lunch buffets (B$37.50).

Continuing south from the plantation house, you reach the busy village of Six Cross Roads, where your route options live up to the promise of the name. You can head southeast to Crane Beach, southwest to Oistins or west to Bridgetown.

# DIRECTORY

## ACCOMMODATIONS
You can find some place to stay at every price point on Barbados, although there are quite a few more places at the top end than at the budget end.

The west coast, or tellingly the 'Platinum Coast', is home to most of the posh resorts and boutique hotels plus rental apartments and a smattering of more affordable places. The south coast aims for the masses and there are many places to stay, ranging from simple guesthouses to beachfront hotels. Your money will go further in the south; the west is where you go if money is no concern. Throughout the rest of the island you'll find a number of interesting places, including cool and funky places in and around Bathsheba.

In high season (December to April), expect to spend at least US$100 per night for a nice midrange double on, or more likely near, a beach. But shop around online as there are deals to be had.

The tourism authority maintains a list of families that rent out bedrooms in their homes, from about US$25 per person per night. Camping is generally not allowed.

Most hotels add a 7.5% government tax plus a 10% service charge, and many have a minimum stay. As elsewhere in the Caribbean, rates decline by as much as 40% outside of high season.

## ACTIVITIES
### Beaches & Swimming
Some of the island's prettiest beaches and calmest waters are along the west coast. Top spots include Paynes Bay and Mullins Bay – lovely white-sand beaches that are easily accessible.

The southwest side of the island also has some fine beaches, including Sandy Beach in Worthing, Rockley Beach, Dover Beach and Enterprise Beach. On the southeast side is Crane Beach, a scenic stretch of pink-tinged

---

**PRACTICALITIES**

■ **Newspapers & Magazines** Barbados has two daily newspapers, the *Barbados Advocate* and the *Nation*. The UK's *Daily Mail* is sold in touristy areas for those who need a dose of Middle England.

■ **Radio & TV** The government-owned TV station CBC broadcasts on Channel 8. Local radio is on FM 92.9 and 98.1 or AM 790 and 900; there's soca music on FM 95.3; and gospel on FM 102.1.

■ **Electricity** The current used is 110V, 50Hz, with a flat two-pronged plug; many hotels have 240V converter outlets in the bathrooms.

■ **Weights & Measures** Barbados uses the metric system; however, many islanders still give directions in feet and miles and sell produce by the pound.

---

**BEST BAJAN BEACHES**

■ **Crane Beach** (p688) This isolated beach with brilliant white sands is a tranquil paradise.

■ **Bath Beach** (opposite) On weekdays this long ribbon of sand is all but empty *and* you can go swimming.

■ **Paynes Bay Beach** (p688) North of Bridgetown, this calm, sandy bay is a family favorite.

■ **Enterprise Beach** (p687) Just east of Oistins, this lovely beach has fine facilities.

■ **Bathsheba Beach** (p692) This rugged coastline is gorgeous to walk and hairy to surf.

---

sand that's popular with bodysurfers but rough for swimming.

Around Bridgetown, the locally popular Pebbles Beach on Carlisle Bay and the area around the Malibu rum distillery are appealing.

The east coast has dangerous water conditions, including shallow reefs and strong currents, and only the most confident swimmers and surfers should take to the waters. Most of the Bathsheba area is best enjoyed from shore.

## Boat Trips

Day cruises are a popular way to explore the island. Many of the larger boats are floating parties, while the smaller operations tend to be more tranquil. For those who want the scuba experience without getting wet, there are submarine cruises.

**Atlantis** ( ☎ 436-8929; www.atlantisadventures.com) Operating in most of the Caribbean's major destinations, the *Atlantis* is a 28-seat submarine lined with portholes. Departs from Bridgetown and tours the coral reef off the island's west coast for US$100.

**El Tigre** ( ☎ 417-7245; www.eltigrecruises.com) Offers a three-hour cruises with snorkeling from B$120.

**Harbour Master** ( ☎ 430-0900; www.tallshipscruises .com) Four-deck party vessel with a water slide attached. Voyages average US$80 and include lunch and water activities. Also offers pirate-themed party cruises. Arrrrr!

## Diving & Snorkeling

The west coast of Barbados has reef dives with soft corals, gorgonians and colorful sponges. There are also about a dozen shipwrecks. The largest and most popular, the 111m freighter *Stavronikita*, sits upright off the central west coast in 42m of water, with the rigging reaching to within 6m of the surface. In Bridgetown's Carlisle Bay, the coral-encrusted tug *Berwyn* lies in only 7m of water and makes for good snorkeling as well as diving.

One-tank dives with gear average B$110, and two-tank dives B$180. For beginners, most dive companies offer a brief resort course and a shallow dive for B$120 to B$160. Many also offer full PADI certification courses for B$700 to B$900. Rates often include free transportation from your hotel; many dive shops can arrange cheap accommodation for their clients.

Some better-known Barbadian dive shops are found near Bridgetown (p682), Mt Standfast (p689), Speightstown (p690) and Holetown (p689).

Snorkeling sets can be rented for about B$20 per day at beach water-sports huts, dive shops and some hotels and restaurants. Snorkeling tours are common; many dive shops offer good ones. The Barbados Marine Reserve (p689) has good snorkeling and you can rent gear there. Carlisle Bay is also popular and the beach bars will rent gear.

For indepth information on local diving, get a copy of *Barbados Dive Guide* by Miller Publishing (www.barbadosbooks.com).

## Golf

The well-heeled of Barbados support several golf courses. The oldest public course is the **Barbados Golf Club** ( ☎ 428-8463; www.barbadosgolfclub .com; Durants) where greens fees begin at US$120, although top-end hotels often offer discounts to guests. It was redesigned in 2000 by Ron Kirby and is 6km long.

## Hiking

The **Barbados National Trust** ( ☎ 436-9033; http://trust .funbarbados.com) leads guided hikes in the countryside. Hike leaders share insights into local history, geology and wildlife. Locations vary, but all hikes end where they start, cover about 8km and are run on Sundays at 6am and 3:30pm. There is no fee. Route information can be found in the free tourist publications and is also available by calling the trust.

**BARBADOS**

Adrian Loveridge at the Peach and Quiet Hotel (p688) near Silver Sands, leads nature hikes during the high season.

A nice hike to do on your own is along the old railroad bed that runs along the east coast from Belleplaine to Martin's Bay. The whole walk is about 20km, but it can be broken into shorter stretches.

### Horseback Riding

**Wilcox Riding Stables** ( ☎ 428-3610) near the airport offers one-hour rides. The trails are in Long Beach on the southeast coast, and cost around B$100, including hotel pickup.

### Surfing

Barbados has some surprisingly good waves for the Caribbean. The biggest swells hit the east coast, with prime surfing at the Soup Bowl (p692), off Bathsheba, and another spot called Duppies, up the coast. South Point and Rockley Beach on the south coast are sometimes good as is Brandon's, which is next to the Hilton Hotel at Needham's Point.

There are local guys renting out boards on the beach at most of the popular surf spots. Prices are negotiable depending on the quality of the board, but even the nicest board should never be over B$15 to B$20 per hour.

There are two good surf schools of note: Zed's Surfing Adventures, based at Silver Sands (p688); and **Surf Barbados** ( ☎ 256-3906; www.surf-barbados.com), which transports clients to various spots depending on conditions. Surf Barbados' beginners class costs US$75 for two hours.

### Windsurfing & Kitesurfing

Barbados has good windsurfing and kitesurfing, with the best winds from December to June. Silver Sands, at the southern tip of the island, has excellent conditions for advanced boarders, while Maxwell, just to the west, is better for intermediates. Most beginners also take lessons in Silver Sands, where there is also board rental available (p688).

## BOOKS

The most common type of book on Barbados is the coffee-table photograph book. *Barbados: Portrait of an Island,* by Dick Scoones, is one of the better choices should you need extra weight in your baggage.

Numerous books cover Barbadian history and sights. *The History of Barbados* by Robert H Schomburg examines mice breeding in 1950s Rhodesia…well no, it's a thorough study of the island's past. *To Hell or Barbados: The Ethnic Cleansing of Ireland* by Sean O'Callaghan traces the scores of Irish sent by Cromwell to work as slaves on sugar plantations.

*Treasures of Barbados* by Henry Fraser, president of the Barbados National Trust, surveys island architecture.

Books on Barbadian political figures include *Tom Adams: A Biography* and *Grantley Adams and the Social Revolution,* both by local historian FA Hoyos.

Those interested in the natural features of Barbados may enjoy *Geology of Barbados,* by Hans Machel, or *A Naturalist's Year in Barbados,* by Maurice Bateman Hutt.

*The Barbadian Rum Shop: The Other Watering Hole,* by Peter Laurie, is an overview of the history of the rum shop and the role that it has played in Barbadian life. A variety of Bajan cookbooks can also be found at most bookstores.

## BUSINESS HOURS

Most banks are open from 8am to 3pm Monday to Thursday, and until 5pm on Friday. A few branches are also open Saturday morning. Most stores are open at least from 8am to 5pm Monday to Friday and until noon Saturday. Larger supermarkets and shops aimed at visitors stay open until at least 8pm.

## CHILDREN

Barbados is generally a family-friendly destination. A number of resorts have organized children's activities or in-house daycare/baby-sitting.

Most beaches are safe for children to play on and many of the south- and west-coast beaches are calm enough for younger swimmers. The east-coast surf is too powerful for novice swimmers of any age.

## DANGERS & ANNOYANCES

Crime, including assaults on tourists, is not unknown on Barbados. Most crimes, however, are simple tourist scams – normal precautions should suffice.

Beware of pickpockets in Bridgetown – keep your valuables secure around the bustling center on Swan and Broad Sts. There are some slick hustlers who hang out at the entrance to St Lawrence Gap and also around south coast nightlife venues. Steer clear unless you want to invest in someone's habit.

Sidewalks are narrow or nonexistent and roads are curvy, so use caution even while walking along quiet streets.

Portuguese man-of-war jellyfish are occasionally encountered in Barbadian waters (although they are large, slow and usually easy to spot), and poisonous manchineel trees grow along some beaches.

Truth be told, the greatest risk is a bad sunburn.

## EMBASSIES & CONSULATES

**Australia** ( ☎ 435-2834; www.embassy.gov.au/bb.html; Bishop's Court Hill, St Michael)

**Canada** ( ☎ 429-3550; www.dfait-maeci.gc.ca/barbados; Bishop's Court Hill, St Michael)

**Cuba** ( ☎ 435-2769; embacubalcg@sunbeach.net; Palm View, Erdiston Dr, St Michael)

**France** ( ☎ 435-6847; Bulkeley Great House, Bulkeley, St George)

**Germany** ( ☎ 427-1876; Dayrell's Rd, Pleasant Hall, Christ Church)

**UK** ( ☎ 430-7800; www.britishhighcommission.gov.uk/Barbados; Lower Collymore Rock, St Michael)

**USA** ( ☎ 436-4950; http://barbados.usembassy.gov; Wildey Business Park, Wildey, St Michael)

## FESTIVALS & EVENTS

Barbados has visitor-friendly events through the year. Some of the larger ones:

**Jazz Festival** (January; www.barbadosjazzfestival.com) Celebrates Barbadians' historic love of jazz with major performers from the US, UK and Caribbean.

**Holetown Festival** (February) This festival celebrates the February 17, 1627 – the arrival of the first English settlers on Barbados. Holetown's week-long festivities include street fairs, a music festival at the historic parish church and a road race.

**Oistins Fish Festival** (Easter weekend) Commemorates the signing of the Charter of Barbados and celebrates the skills of local fishermen. It's a seaside festivity with events focusing on boat races, fish-filleting competitions, local foods, crafts and dancing.

**Congaline Carnival** (late April) This is a big street party with music and arts. The focus of the event is an all-day band parade and conga line that winds its way from Bridgetown to St Lawrence Gap.

**Crop-Over Festival** (mid-July) The island's top event. It originated in colonial times as a celebration to mark the end of the sugarcane harvest. Festivities stretch over a three-week period beginning in mid-July with spirited

calypso competitions, fairs and other activities. The festival culminates with a Carnival-like costume parade and fireworks on Kadooment Day, a national holiday, in August.

**National Independence Festival of Creative Arts** (November) Features talent contests in dance, drama, singing and the like. Performances by the finalists are held on Independence Day (November 30).

There is also a handful of international sporting events in Barbados, including the International Windsurfing Championships in February; the Reef Surfing Championship in November; and the early December 10km marathon, Run Barbados.

## GAY & LESBIAN TRAVELERS

Barbados is a conservative and religious place that is generally opposed to homosexuality. That said, there are a few openly homosexual Bajan couples (although they still tend to be discreet) and even the rare transvestite.

Homosexual visitors to Barbados will need to be judicious outside of international resorts and especially in smaller, more traditional towns.

## HOLIDAYS

Public holidays in Barbados:

**New Year's Day** January 1
**Errol Barrow Day** January 21
**Good Friday** late March/early April
**Easter Monday** late March/early April
**Heroes' Day** April 28
**Labour Day** May 1
**Whit Monday** Eighth Monday after Easter
**Emancipation Day** August 1
**Kadooment Day** First Monday in August
**UN Day** First Monday in October
**Independence Day** November 30
**Christmas Day** December 25
**Boxing Day** December 26

## INTERNET ACCESS

There are internet places in Bridgetown, most of the tourist centers and larger towns. Wi-fi is increasingly common at hotels and many have a computer guests can use.

## INTERNET RESOURCES

**Barbados Hotel & Tourism Association** (www.bhta.org) The Barbados Hotel and Tourism Association is a great resource for accommodation needs.

**Barbados National Trust** (http://trust.funbarbados.com) The Barbados National Trust website has links to the many historic sites around the island.

BARBADOS

**Barbados.org** (www.barbados.org) Omnibus website with lots of travel-related links.

**Fun Barbados** (www.funbarbados.com) General travel information site with links to offers and hotels.

**National News** (www.nationnews.com) *National News* is Barbados' daily newspaper.

**Visit Barbados** (www.visitbarbados.org) Official site of the Barbados Tourism Authority; more flash than substance.

**Yellow Pages** (www.yellowpages-caribbean.com) Follow the links to a searchable version of the Barbados *Yellow Pages*.

## MEDICAL SERVICES

Barbados has a high standard of health-care. Your accommodation can direct you to local doctors, all of whom speak excellent English. The country's main hospital is in Bridgetown (p680).

## MONEY

You'll certainly want some Barbados dollars on hand, but larger payments can be made in US dollars, frequently with a major credit card. Hotels and guesthouses quote rates in US dollars (as do many dive shops and some restaurants), although you can use either US or Barbadian currency to settle the account.

The common street exchange rate is B$2 to US$1 for traveler's checks or cash, although true rates can fluctuate a couple of cents either way.

ATMs and banks are easy to find in larger towns and major tourist areas. Cash is dispensed in Barbados dollars.

## TELEPHONE

The area code for Barbados is ☎ 246. To call from North America, dial ☎ 1-246 + the local seven-digit number. From elsewhere, dial your country's international access code + ☎ 246 + the local number. We have included only the seven-digit local number for Barbados listings in this chapter.

View your room phone (or a pay phone in tourist areas) with the same skepticism you would a person with a knife in a dark alley. The more it is emblazoned with 'Call Home' come-ons, the more likely you'll end up paying US$3 or more per minute for your call. Buy phone cards from vendors or use internet call centers where the rate averages US$0.50 per minute.

If you have a GSM mobile phone you can purchase a SIM card for local service for B$50, which includes B$25 in calling credit. Rates within Barbados start at B$0.10 per minute;

to the UK and US from B$0.80 per minute. The two carriers are Bmobile from Cable & Wireless (www.bmobile.com.bb) and Digicel (www.digicelbarbados.com). Both has shops across the island.

## TOURIST INFORMATION

The free annual, *Ins & Outs of Barbados*, is encyclopedic, filled with watch ads and so large that your holiday will be over if you drop it on your toe.

**Barbados Hotel & Tourism Association** ( ☎ 426-5041, 429-2845; www.bhta.org; 4th Ave, Belleville, St Michael; ☯ 8am-5pm Mon-Sat)

**Barbados Tourism Authority** (www.visitbarbados.org); Bridgetown ( ☎ 427-2623; Harbour Rd; ☯ 8:15am-4:30pm Mon-Fri); Grantley Adams International Airport ( ☎ 428-5570; ☯ 8am-10pm or until the last flight arrives); Cruise ship terminal ( ☎ 426-1718; ☯ when ships are in port)

## TOURS

Most tour companies offer a variety of half- and full-day options that either provide an overview with stops at key sites or emphasize special interests such as nature and gardens. There are a huge range of choices, as you'll see from the brochure racks. Most, however, follow very set routes and you may well feel part of a herd. The various 4WD options are for those with Hummer-envy.

One delightful option is run by the **Barbados Transport Board** ( ☎ 436-6820; www.transportboard.com; adult/child B$15/10; ☯ tours 2-7pm Sun). These delightful tours of the island are popular with locals and the itinerary varies each week. Buses depart from Independence Sq, Bridgetown.

The going rate for custom tours by taxi drivers is B$50 an hour, but you can usually negotiate with individual drivers to work out your own deal. Hotels usually have drivers they work with.

See p695 for information on boat trips.

## TRAVELERS WITH DISABILITIES

International resorts generally have good accommodations for people with disabilities. Otherwise much of Barbados is something of a challenge.

## VISAS

Visas are not required for stays of up to six months for citizens of the US, Canada, Australia, Japan and the EU. Other should confirm their status.

## WORK
Foreigners will find it difficult to get a job without sponsorship.

## WOMEN TRAVELERS
Women won't find anything especially concerning about a visit to Barbados.

# TRANSPORTATION

## GETTING THERE & AWAY
### Entering Barbados
Nearly all visitors will enter the country through Grantley Adams International Airport or Bridgetown's cruise-ship terminal. All foreigners entering Barbados should be in possession of a valid passport and a return or onward ticket. Cruise-ship passengers who stay less than 24 hours are not required to carry a valid passport.

## Air
**Grantley Adams International Airport** (BGI; ☎ 418-4242; www.gaiainc.bb) is on the island's southeast corner, about 16km from Bridgetown. It is the largest airport in the Eastern Caribbean and the major point of entry for the region.

The **Barbados Tourism Authority** ( ☎ 428-5570; 🕑 8am-10pm or until the last flight arrives) booth can help you book a room and is a good place to pick up tourist brochures. There are a number of ATMs in the departures area of the airport (we'd put them near arrivals ourselves…) as well as the **Barbados National Bank** ( 🕑 8am-3pm Mon-Fri) which exchanges money.

Once through security, departing passengers will find numerous shops, including a good bookstore and a food court.

Unless noted otherwise, airlines have offices only at the airport. The following connect Barbados with these cities (some services are seasonal and only weekly):

**Air Canada** ( ☎ 428-5077; www.aircanada.com) Montreal, Toronto
**American/American Eagle** ( ☎ 800-744-0006; www.aa.com) Miami, New York, San Juan
**BMI** ( ☎ 800-788-0555; www.flybmi.com) Manchester
**British Airways** ( ☎ 436-6413; www.britishairways.com) London
**Caribbean Airlines** (formerly BWIA; ☎ 800-744-2225; www.caribbean-airlines.com; Fairchild St, Bridgetown; 🕑 8am-4pm Mon-Fri) Kingston, Trinidad
**Delta** ( ☎ 800-221-1212; www.delta.com) Atlanta

---

### EMERGENCY NUMBERS

- **Ambulance** ☎ 511
- **Coast Guard Defense Force** ☎ emergencies 427-8819, nonemergencies 436-6185
- **Fire** ☎ 311
- **Police** ☎ 211

---

**LIAT** ( ☎ 428-0986; www.liat.com; Fairchild St, Bridgetown; 🕑 8am-5pm Mon-Fri, to noon Sat) Antigua, Dominica, Grenada, St Lucia, St Vincent, Tobago, Trinidad
**US Airways** ( ☎ 800-622-1015; www.usairways.com) Charlotte, Philadelphia
**Virgin Atlantic** ( ☎ 228-4886; www.virgin-atlantic.com; Parravicino Office Complex, Hastings; 🕑 8am-5pm Mon-Fri, to noon Sat) London
**XL** (www.xl.com) London

## Sea
### CRUISE SHIP
About 450,000 cruise-ship passengers arrive in Barbados each year as part of eastern Caribbean itineraries. Ships dock at Bridgetown Harbour, about 1km west of the city center. The port has the usual duty-free shops and a branch office of the **Barbados Tourism Authority** ( ☎ 426-1718; 🕑 when ships are in port).

See p830 for details about cruise ship travel throughout the Caribbean.

### YACHT
Because of Barbados' easterly position and challenging sailing conditions, it is well off the main track for most sailors.

## GETTING AROUND
### To/From the Airport
If you're traveling light, it's possible to walk out of the airport to the road and wait for a passing bus. Look for buses marked 'Sam Lord's Castle' (or just 'Castle') if you're going east, 'Bridgetown' if you're going to the south coast. For the west coast, occasional buses run to Speightstown, bypassing the capital; alternatively, take a bus to Bridgetown, where you'll have to change to the west-coast terminal.

Make sure the bus driver knows your destination.

Taxis are plentiful, the 'official' prices (subject to negotiation) from the airport to the island's main destinations include: Bathsheba

BARBADOS

B$73, Bridgetown Harbour B$46, Holetown B$58, Prospect B$53 and Speightstown B$73. Many hotels offer pick-up services for only somewhat more.

## Bicycle

Barbados is predominantly flat and is good for riding. Most shops require a credit card or B$100 deposit for rentals. Your hotel can hook you up with a rental, there are also usually bikes available at the cruise ship port.

## Bus

It's possible to get to virtually any place on the island by public bus. There are three kinds of bus: government-operated public buses, which are blue with a yellow stripe; privately operated minibuses, which are intermediate-size buses painted yellow with a blue stripe; and route taxis, which are white, individually owned minivans that have 'ZR' on their license plates. All three types of bus charge the same fare: B$1.50 to any place on the island. You should have exact change when you board the government bus, but minibuses and route taxis will make change.

Most buses transit through Bridgetown, although a few north–south buses bypass the city. Buses to the southeast part of the island generally transit through Oistins.

Bus stops around the island are marked with red-and-white signs printed with the direction in which the bus is heading ('To City' or 'Out of City'). Buses usually have their destinations posted on or above the front windshield.

Buses along the main routes, such as Bridgetown to Oistins or Speightstown, are frequent, running from dawn to around midnight. You can get complete schedule information on any route from the **Transport Board** ( ☎ 436-6820; www.transportboard.com).

## Car & Motorcycle
### RENTAL

Barbados doesn't have any car-rental agents affiliated with major international rental chains. There are, instead, scores of independent car-rental companies, some so small that they are based out of private homes.

Despite the number of companies, prices don't seem to vary much. The going rate for a small car is about B$150 a day including unlimited mileage and insurance. Most companies rent out strange, small convertible buggies called 'mokes,' which are usually cheapest (they look like the odd car in *Fantasy Island*). Rental cars are marked with an 'H' on the license plate.

While most car-rental companies don't have booths at the airport, most will deliver your car there or to your hotel. Note that among the small agencies, some aren't especially professional and complaints are common.

Some of the larger, more established companies include:

**Courtesy Rent-A-Car** ( ☎ 431-4160; www.courtesy rentacar.com)
**Direct Rentals** ( ☎ 420-6372; www.barbadoscars.com)
**Stoutes Car Rental** ( ☎ 416-4456; www.stoutescar.com)
**Top Class Car Rentals** ( ☎ 228-7368; www.topclass rentals.com)

### ROAD CONDITIONS

Highways are not very well marked, although landmarks are clearly labeled, as are some roundabouts (traffic circles) and major intersections. The most consistent highway markings are often the low yellow cement posts at the side of the road; they show the highway number and below that the number of kilometers from Bridgetown.

All primary and main secondary roads are paved, although some are a bit narrow. There are plenty of gas stations around the island except on the east coast. Some stations in the Bridgetown area are open 24 hours.

Expect rush-hour traffic on the roads around booming Bridgetown.

### ROAD RULES

In Barbados, you drive on the left. At intersections and narrow passages, drivers may flash their lights to indicate that you should proceed. Temporary driving permits are required; they cost B$10 and can be obtained through your car-rental agency.

## Taxi

Taxis have a 'Z' on the license plate and usually a 'taxi' sign on the roof. They're easy to find and often wait at the side of the road in popular tourist areas.

Although fares are fixed by the government, taxis are not metered and you will have to haggle for a fair price. The rate per kilometer is about B$2 and the flat hourly rate B$50. 'Official' fares from Bridgetown include: Bathsheba (B$58), Oistins (B$31) and Speightstown (B$46).

# Grenada

Isn't that the place that the US invaded in the '80s? Didn't it get munched by a hurricane a few years ago? Grenada is used to bad press. But like a fighter on the ropes, it's come out swinging and has reinvented itself as the next big thing.

The one big island and two small ones plonked in the sea in the southeast corner of the Caribbean are undiscovered and rarely visited. For the smallest independent country in the western hemisphere, this place has a lot to offer.

Grenada Island is elliptically shaped and alive with a rainforested interior. Underrated beaches line the coast and sublime scuba diving is on offer just below the surface. St George's, the largest town, has one of the most picturesque waterfronts in all of the Caribbean. Stone buildings, forts from a forgotten time and houses of all colors meld into a hilly buffet of urban aesthetics. Friendly, welcoming locals go about their lives and are happy to include you in the process.

Carriacou is a step back in time. With a cadence a notch or two slower then Grenada Island, this petite isle is a relaxed affair where endearing locals and an eclectic village life is added to sublime scenery. And if that sounds too busy, head over to Petit Martinique where even less happens – and the locals like it that way.

Yes, Grenada did get invaded by Uncle Sam, but that's old news. And yes, a hurricane obliterated much of the island in 2004, but they've rebuilt. Life moves on, and so has Grenada.

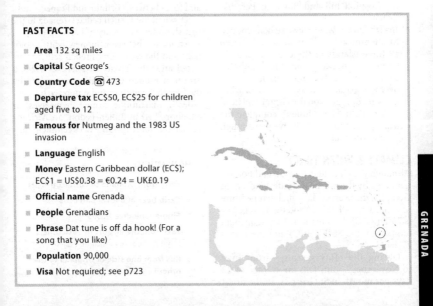

## FAST FACTS

- **Area** 132 sq miles
- **Capital** St George's
- **Country Code** ☎ 473
- **Departure tax** EC$50, EC$25 for children aged five to 12
- **Famous for** Nutmeg and the 1983 US invasion
- **Language** English
- **Money** Eastern Caribbean dollar (EC$); EC$1 = US$0.38 = €0.24 = UK£0.19
- **Official name** Grenada
- **People** Grenadians
- **Phrase** Dat tune is off da hook! (For a song that you like)
- **Population** 90,000
- **Visa** Not required; see p723

GRENADA

## HIGHLIGHTS

- **Carriacou** (p716) Grenada's little sister has all the aesthetics of the big island – beautiful beaches, quiet streets and friendly locals
- **St George's** (p707) With a waterfront that's second to none, this buzzing city is one of the liveliest in the region
- **Windward** (p718) Watch the local boat-builders knock together a seaworthy vessel before your eyes
- **Petit Martinique** (p719) See how many laps you can do walking around this microparadise
- **Morne Rouge Bay** (p712) Make the effort to get out to this beach, where the sand is soft and the water is super blue – it's one of Grenada's best

## ITINERARIES

- **Three Days** Spend your time on the island of Grenada. Sample the beach at Grand Anse then compare it to Morne Rouge Bay the next day. Head into St George's for the day, check out the churches and forts, and wander through the eclectic streets.
- **One Week** After completing the three-day itinerary, cruise over to Carriacou and settle into a few days of exploration. Be sure to head over to Windward, up to the hospital hill and down to Paradise Beach.
- **The Trifecta** Go where few are bold enough to attempt and split your time between all three islands in the country. Start in Grenada, checking out the highlights from the three-day itinerary, then cruise over to Carriacou to see how the beaches measure up. Jump on the *Osprey* and head over to Petit Martinique to complete the triple play. Ten days will give you enough time to do it all.

## CLIMATE & WHEN TO GO

Although the climate is tropical and hot, it's tempered by the northeast trade winds. In St George's, the average daily high temperature in January is 84°F (29°C) and the average low is 75°F (24°C). In July the average daily high temperature is 86°F (30°C) and the low is 77°F (25°C).

During the rainy season – from June to November – rain falls an average of 22 days per month in St George's. In the driest months, January to April, there's measurable rainfall for 12 days a month; this is the best time to visit. Hurricane season runs from June to November.

## HISTORY
### Colonial Competition

In 1498 Christopher Columbus became the first European to sight the island of Grenada, during his third voyage to the New World. It wasn't until 1609, however, that English tobacco planters attempted to settle on the island and, within a year, most were killed by Caribs. Some 40 years later, the French 'purchased' the island from the Caribs for a few hatchets, some glass beads and two bottles of brandy. Not all Caribs were pleased with the land deal and skirmishes continued until French troops chased the last of them to Sauteurs Bay at the northern end of the island. Rather than submitting to the colonists, the remaining Caribs – men, women and children – jumped to their deaths off the rugged coastal cliffs.

French planters established crops that provided indigo, tobacco, coffee, cocoa and sugar, and imported thousands of African slaves to tend to the fields. Grenada remained under French control until 1762, when Britain first recaptured the island. Over the next two decades, colonial control of the land shifted back and forth between Britain and France – until 1783, when the French ceded Grenada to the British under the Treaty of Paris.

Animosity between the new British colonists and the remaining French settlers persisted after the Treaty of Paris. In 1795, a group of French Catholics, encouraged by the French Revolution and supported by comrades in Martinique, armed themselves for rebellion. Led by Julien Fedon, an African-French planter from Grenada's central moun-

---

**HOW MUCH?**

- **Ferry from Grenada to Carriacou** EC$80
- **Carib beer at a local pub** EC$5
- **Single tank dive** US$55
- **Taxi from the airport to St George's** Daytime EC$30, nighttime EC$40
- **Bus from one side of Grenada to the other** EC$6

tains, they attacked the British at Grenville. They captured the British governor and executed him along with other hostages. Fedon's guerrillas, who controlled much of the island for more than a year, were finally overcome by the British navy. Fedon was never captured. It's likely he escaped to Martinique, or drowned attempting to get there, though some islanders believe he lived out his days hiding in Grenada's mountainous jungles.

In 1877 Grenada became a crown colony, and in 1967 it converted to an associated state within the British Commonwealth. Grenada, Carriacou and Petit Martinique adopted a constitution in 1973 and gained collective independence on February 7, 1974.

## Independence

One-time trade unionist Eric Gairy rose to prominence after organizing a successful labor strike in 1950, and was a leading voice in both the independence and labor movements. Gairy established ties with the British government and monarchy and was groomed to become the island's first prime minister when Britain relinquished some of its Caribbean colonies. After independence Gairy's Grenada United Labour Party (GULP) swept to power.

Gairy made early political missteps, such as using his first opportunity to speak in front of the UN to plead for more research into UFOs and the Bermuda Triangle. There were rumors of corruption, of ties with the notorious General Augusto Pinochet of Chile and of the use of a group of thugs (called the Mongoose Gang) to intimidate and eliminate adversaries. Power went to Gairy's head and this former labor leader was soon referring to his political opposition as 'sweaty men in the streets.'

## Revolutions, Coups & Invasions

Before dawn on March 13, 1979, while Gairy was overseas, a band of armed rebels supported by the opposition New Jewel Movement (NJM) party led a bloodless coup. Maurice Bishop, a young, charismatic, London-trained lawyer and head of the NJM, became prime minister of the new People's Revolutionary Government (PRG) regime.

As the head of a Communist movement in the backyard of the US, Bishop tried to walk a very fine line. He had ties with Cuba and the USSR, but attempted to preserve private enterprise in Grenada. A schism developed between Bishop and hardliners in the govern-

ment who felt that he was incompetent and was stonewalling the advance of true communism. The ministers voted that Bishop should share power with the hardline mastermind (and Bishop's childhood friend) Bernard Coard. Bishop refused and was placed under house arrest. While Coard had the support of the majority of the government and the military, Bishop had support of the vast majority of the public.

On October 19, 1983, thousands of supporters spontaneously freed Bishop from house arrest and marched with him and other sympathetic government ministers to Fort George. The army was unmoved by the display and Bishop, his pregnant girlfriend (Minister of Education Jacqueline Creft) and several of his followers were taken prisoner and executed by a firing squad in the courtyard. To this day, it is unclear if the order came directly from Coard – although most believe that it did.

Six days later, 12,000 US marines, along with a few soldiers from half a dozen Caribbean countries, were on Grenadian shores. Seventy Cubans, 42 Americans and 170 Grenadians were killed in the fighting. Most of the US forces withdrew in December 1983, although a joint Caribbean force and 300 US support troops remained on the island for two more years. The US sunk millions of dollars into establishing a new court system to try Coard and 16 of his closest collaborators.

Fourteen people, including Coard and his wife, were sentenced to death for the

GRENADA

murder of Bishop. Although the death sentences were commuted to life in prison in 1991, the most recent appeal for full clemency and release from prison was rejected in February 2005.

## The New Era

After the US invasion (or intervention), elections were reinstituted in December 1985, and Herbert Blaize, with his New National Party, won handily. Many PRG members reinvented themselves politically and found jobs in the new administration. From 1989 to 1995, different political parties jockeyed for control and a few short-term leaders came and went, but all within the democratic process.

In 1995 Dr Keith Mitchell became prime minister and has steadily held the position until the time of this book's printing. Although Mitchell had success building the tourism economy, his term has been plagued by accusations of corruption and financial misdealing. He has also been criticized for a weak initial response to the devastation of 2004's Hurricane Ivan.

## THE CULTURE

Grenadian culture is an eclectic mix of British, French, African and East and West Indian influences. A growing number of expatriates from Canada, the UK and, to a lesser extent, the United States are making Grenada home.

Almost 60% of all Grenadians are Roman Catholic. There are also Anglicans, Seventh Day Adventists, Methodists, Christian Scientists, Presbyterians, Scots Kirk, Baptists, Baha'i and an increasing number of Jehovah's Witnesses. Because of the pervasive influence of Christian ideals, Sunday is a pretty quiet day around the islands – you can expect most things to be closed.

The largely religious population makes for a fairly conservative culture – at least at a surface level. Once you scratch beneath the squeaky-clean veneer, you can see a population that enjoys having a few drinks and kicking up its heels.

As one local put it, 'It isn't little old Grenada anymore.' Education is on the rise and the population is quite learned. The political awareness of the general populace is high – probably because of their brush with political infamy in the '80s. Likewise, the impact of Hurricane Ivan in 2004 was a sobering experience for islanders – forcing the nation culturally to grow up.

The people themselves are friendly and welcoming. They are proud of their tiny nation and take care of it – there is less rubbish in the ditches and a sense of civic responsibility is palpable.

The sport of cricket is followed with near fanaticism in Grenada. In 2007, the cricket world cup was staged in part here and the mighty West Indies side is a national treasure.

## ARTS

Like much of the Caribbean, reggae dominates the airwaves. Steel bands can be heard playing live gigs most nights – though they mostly play for rum-punch-sloshed tourists. Dancehall is the flavor for the younger generation and is heard mostly at maximum volume filtering from speeding buses, nightclub dance floors and the best kitchens on the island.

## ENVIRONMENT
### The Land

Grenada Island, Carriacou and Petit Martinique comprise a total land area of 133 sq miles. Grenada Island, at 121 sq miles, measures 12 miles wide by 21 miles long. The island is volcanic, though part of the northern end is coral limestone. Grenada's rainy interior is rugged, thickly forested and dissected by valleys and streams. The island rises to 2757ft at Mt St Catherine, an extinct volcano in the northern interior. Grenada's indented southern coastline has jutting peninsulas, deep bays and small nearshore islands, making it a favorite haunt for yachters.

Carriacou, at just under 5 sq miles, is the largest of the Grenadine islands that lie between Grenada and St Vincent. Most of the others are uninhabited pinnacles or sandbars in the ocean.

### Wildlife

The wildlife in Grenada can be divided into two very distinct categories – those that live on land and creatures that call the ocean home. The variance in altitude on Grenada Island makes for a wide range of distinct ecosystems. The lush rainforests that cover the hilly interior are home to an interesting menagerie of wild creatures. Mona Monkeys introduced from Africa a century ago are curious and social and often drop in for a visit.

**A PHOENIX RISES**

On September 7, 2004, Hurricane Ivan made landfall on the island of Grenada. Unaccustomed to hurricanes, it had been nearly 50 years since the last major storm lashed the island. The perception of Grenada being below the hurricane belt was shattered all in one tragic night. Ivan struck with force, leaving behind a wave of destruction that saw 90% of buildings damaged or destroyed. The economy was ruined, towns were decimated and staple crops like nutmeg and cocoa were obliterated.

The following months and years were a dark chapter for this small Caribbean nation. Massive support came from its island neighbors helping rebuild what was destroyed. Crops were re-sewn and hotels rebuilt. But within that period of rebirth, instead of simply rebuilding what was once there, opportunity was found.

Hotels, schools, churches and restaurants have all been built bigger and better. New buildings have incorporated sustainable practices and larger floor plans. Structures that were long overdue to be upgraded were leveled and the new buildings are a massive improvement to what was once there.

As this book goes to print, the final touches of the big rebuild will be finishing up. There is a whole host of new and upgraded facilities for the traveler to experience. The reconstruction is almost complete and, for the first time in a long time, Grenada, new and improved, is open for business!

Armadillo, opossum and mongoose also call the island home.

Birds, both migratory and resident, nest in the tall trees and soar on the thermal updrafts. Tiny hummingbirds search for nectar while pelican, brown booby, osprey hawk, endangered hook-billed kite and hooded tanager fly further afield.

In the ocean, sea turtles cruise the grassy shoals and hunt for food and come ashore to nest and lay their eggs. These endangered grandfathers of the sea are sometimes slaughtered for their shells – be sure to avoid buying anything made from turtle shell and preserve these beautiful animals.

A whole range of reef fish populate the surrounding waters. Snorkelers and divers have the pleasure of swimming amongst barracuda, butterfly fish and the odd nurse shark.

## FOOD & DRINK

Eating in Grenada is an eclectic pleasure – the native West Indian fare is tasty, and a good number of restaurants cater to foreign tastes, with Italian, Mexican and French food readily available.

The oddly named oil down is the national dish and consists of vegetables and meat boiled down and reduced into a thick stew – coconut milk is added to give it a distinctive flavor. Other West Indian favorites are regularly on offer. Callaloo (a dish that resembles boiled spinach), beans and rice and fresh fish are mealtime regulars. *Lambi*, as it is known in Grenada, or conch, as it is called elsewhere in the Caribbean, can also be found on menus; however, travelers should keep in mind that the overfishing of *lambi* is a big issue, and the sustainability of this seafood is in doubt. Think before you eat and consider alternatives. Budget eateries and lunch counters will always have rotis on offer. They consist of curried vegetables, potatoes and meat rolled up into a tortilla – delicious and cheap.

Tap water is generally safe to drink on Grenada, and bottled water is readily available if you'd prefer.

Carib, the local beer, is a refreshing, lightly colored brew and is the perfect addition to a hot day. Following the Caribbean tradition, rum is the national spirit. Rum punch flows like water from many a drinking hall, where you can sip the potent cocktails and wonder just how much punch there actually is in the mix.

Grenada is known as the spice island and supplies a staggering percentage of the world's nutmeg. The lively spice is a national treasure and even features on the country's flag. The spice plantations are big money earners and the prospect of buying cheap spices isn't lost on most visitors. Spice vendors are at nearly every corner hawking gift baskets filled with the local flavors.

GRENADA

# GRENADA ISLAND

**pop 90,000**

The island of Grenada is an almond-shaped, beach-rimmed gem of a place with 75 miles of coastline surrounding a lush interior filled with tropical rainforest. Most of the tourist infrastructure is on the southwest corner of the island, which – conveniently – is where you'll also find the airport and some of the nicest beaches.

## Getting There & Away

For information on getting to and from the island, see p723 and p724.

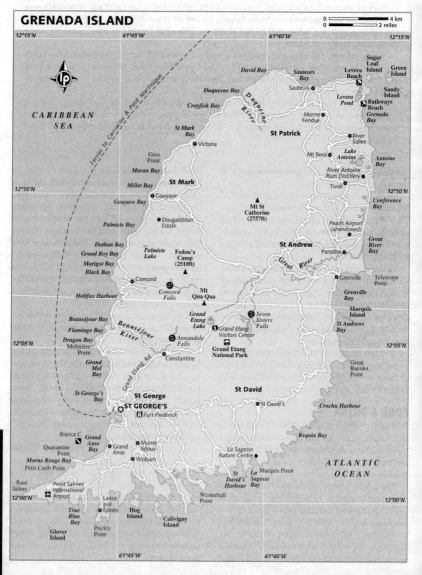

**GRENADA ISLAND**

## Getting Around

### BUS

Buses are a great way to get around the island; they are inexpensive and fun. These privately run minivans run a series of routes crisscrossing the island.

Although larger destinations are posted on the front of the bus, you may need to ask the conductor or driver which bus is best to get to smaller places outside town. There are stops along all the major routes, and you can flag down a bus pretty much anywhere.

The central terminal in St George's is the place to find more information and to catch a bus to anywhere. Fares in the greater St George's area and to Grande Anse are EC$1.50. From St George's, fares are EC$3 to La Sagesse, EC$3.50 to Gouyave or Grand Etang, and EC$5 to Grenville or Sauteurs. Depending on passengers, it takes about 45 minutes from St George's to Grenville and 1½ hours to Sauteurs.

Buses run frequently all day from around 7am. They start getting hard to catch after 6pm, so head home early enough so as not to get stuck. A few buses run on Sunday, though they are much more infrequent.

### CAR

Grenada Island has numerous rental agencies. Local ones can offer you a better deal on prices, but the international chains have better insurance deals. Cars cost from around US$45 a day; 4WDs US$80. Optional Collision Damage Waiver (CDW) insurance, which limits your liability in the event of an accident, starts at an additional US$12 per day.

Grenadian agencies:

**Dollar** ( ☎ 444-4786; Point Salines International Airport)

**Gap Rentals** ( ☎ 438-4098) They'll pick you up from the airport or hotel.

**Indigo Car Rentals** ( ☎ 439-3300; www.indigocarsgrenada.com) Offers free coolers for the car.

**Sanvics 4x4** ( ☎ 444-4753; www.sanvics.com) Specializes in jeeps.

### TAXI

Taxi fares are supposedly regulated by the government, although sometimes you have to negotiate a bit. From the airport to Grand Anse or Lance aux Épines costs EC$25; to St George's EC$30. From central St George's it costs EC$8 to other parts of the city, EC$25 to Grand Anse or Morne Rouge and EC$35 to Lance aux Épines.

Elsewhere, taxis charge EC$4 per mile up to 10 miles and EC$3 per mile after that. The waiting charge is EC$15 per hour. Taxis can be hired for a flat EC$40-per-hour rate for sightseeing. An EC$10 surcharge is added to fares between 6pm and 6am.

## ST GEORGE'S

pop 30,500

The harbor of St George's is like something out of an old watercolor painting of a forgotten seaside village. Colonial buildings are mixed with bright Caribbean stalwarts. Churches are made of stone, and a towering fort overlooks the town. European in feel and distinctly Caribbean in its look, the inner harbor is one of the most aesthetic in the region.

Stroll along the narrow, steep streets looking in the pleasant shops and smelling the fresh seafood wafting from the dockside restaurants. Traffic negotiates the hilly laneways as the mish-mash of jumbled streets form a labyrinth of stone throughways.

### Orientation

The focal point of town is the harborside road called the Carenage. Along the waterfront you'll find a few shops and restaurants. To get to the city center one must walk up and over the hill on Young or Lucas Sts, or cut through the narrow Sendel Tunnel on Monckton St (be sure to walk along the west side of the tunnel, where cars make room for walkers).

Further south from the Carenage, the road sweeps around an inlet called the Lagoon, on its way to the resorts at Grand Anse.

### Information

#### BOOKSTORES

**Sea Change Bookshop** ( ☎ 440-3402; the Carenage) A good selection of popular titles, local authors and pulp.

#### INTERNET ACCESS

There is a free wireless hot spot in the Port Louis Marina.

**Compu-Data** ( ☎ 443-0505; St John's St; per hr EC$6; ☽ 8am-7pm) Best price in town.

#### MEDICAL SERVICES

**St George's General Hospital** ( ☎ 440-2051; Fort George Point) The island's main medical facility.

#### MONEY

**RBTT** ( ☎ 440-3521; cnr Cross & Halifax Sts; ☽ 8am-3pm Mon-Thu, 8am-5pm Fri) Has a 24-hour ATM.

GRENADA

**Scotiabank** ( ☎ 440-3274; Halifax St; ☷ 8am-3pm Mon-Thu, to 5pm Fri) Has a 24-hour ATM.

### POST
**Main post office** ( ☎ 440-2526; Lagoon Rd; ☷ 8am-3:30pm Mon-Fri)

### TELEPHONE & FAX
**Cable & Wireless** ( ☎ 440-1000; www.candw.gd; the Carenage; ☷ 7:30am-6pm Mon-Fri, 7:30am-1pm Sat, 10am-noon Sun)

### TOURIST INFORMATION
**Grenada Tourist Board** ( ☎ 440-6637; www.grenada grenadines.com; ☷ 8am-4pm Mon-Fri) At the southern end of the Carenage.

### TRAVEL AGENCIES
**Astral Travel** ( ☎ 440-5127; the Carenage; ☷ 8am-5pm Mon-Fri, to noon Sat) Astral's a switched-on travel agency with info and affiliation to all the relevant airlines and travel services.

## Sights
### GRENADA NATIONAL MUSEUM
This **museum** (cnr Young & Monckton Sts; adult/child EC$5/2.50; ☷ 9am-4:30pm Mon-Fri) is in need of some love, but there is some decent information on the history of Grenada, colonial times and the US invasion.

### FORTRESSES
**Fort George** (Church St; admission free; ☷ 6am-5pm), Grenada's oldest fort, was established by the French in 1705 and is the centerpiece of the St George's skyline. The police now use the interior for their headquarters but the public is allowed to wander amongst the stone structure and climb to the top of the walls to see the cannons and get easily the best view in town. Well worth the steep uphill walk.

**Fort Frederick** (admission US$1; ☷ 8am-4pm), constructed by the French in 1779, was soon used – paradoxically – by the British to defend against the French. It now provides a striking panoramic view that includes Quarantine Point, Point Salines and Grover Island. You'll find it atop Richmond Hill, 1.25 miles east of St George's.

### CHURCHES
The picturesque, 19th-century churches of downtown St George's were once highlights of the skyline. In 2004 Hurricane Ivan changed all that. While these three magnificent structures still remain, all suffered heavy damage and lost their roofs. At the time of writing these churches were lagging behind in the rebuilding efforts; they're all in the early stages of being repaired and rebuilt.

Erected in 1825, **St George's Anglican Church** (Church St) features a four-sided clock tower that serves as the town timepiece. The roof is gone now and the brilliant white interior is open to the sky, but the clock remains.

The **Catholic Cathedral** (Church St) sits at the top of the hill and has a great vantage onto the town. Ivan all but gutted this landmark and at present efforts are underway to restore this cathedral to its former glory.

**St Andrew's Presbyterian Church** (Church St), immediately north of Fort George, fared worst of all in the hurricane. There isn't much left of the interior, and the shell of the place of worship is all that still sits intact – but once again, efforts to rebuild are happening.

## Activities
Try **Green's Bike Shop** ( ☎ 435-1089; Tyrell St; rental per day EC$40; ☷ 8am-4:30pm Mon-Fri, to 2pm Sat) for bike rental.

## Sleeping
**Lazy Lagoon** ( ☎ 443-5209; lazylagoon@caribsurf.com; Lagoon Rd; s/d US$42/59) Funky, cool and comfortable describes this budget hideaway. Tucked in amongst the outskirts of St George's, several colorful cottages dot the hill across from the marina. The rooms are bright and basic with a bed, bathroom and not much more. The bar is a fun place to be with a host of local regulars, travelers and a festive atmosphere. Recent renovations have upped the rooming capacity and ballooned the bar, all while retaining the intimate feel.

**Tropicana Inn** ( ☎ 440-1586; tropicana@caribsurf .com; Lagoon Rd; s/d/t US$75/100/120; ☒ ) Right on the main road, between town and the marina sits the Tropicana. The rooms are not overly large but are clean and have good amenities for the price. The road can be a bit noisy, but the balconies on the upper floors offer good views and the restaurant serves good local cuisine.

## Eating
**Melissans** ( ☎ 449-1314; the Carenage; mains from EC$8; ☷ lunch & dinner) Vegetarians delight at this meat-free eatery. Pizzas, sandwiches and mixed plates all come recommended at this

GRENADA

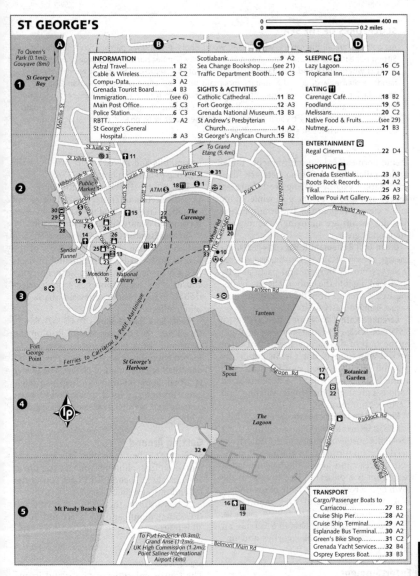

# ST GEORGE'S

0 ——————— 400 m
0 ——————— 0.2 miles

**INFORMATION**
Astral Travel...........................1 B2
Cable & Wireless...................2 C2
Compu-Data..........................3 A2
Grenada Tourist Board.......4 B3
Immigration.......................(see 6)
Main Post Office..................5 C3
Police Station.......................6 C3
RBTT......................................7 A2
St George's General
  Hospital............................8 A3

Scotiabank...........................9 A2
Sea Change Bookshop......(see 21)
Traffic Department Booth....10 C3

**SIGHTS & ACTIVITIES**
Catholic Cathedral............11 B2
Fort George.......................12 A3
Grenada National Museum..13 B3
St Andrew's Presbyterian
  Church............................14 A2
St George's Anglican Church..15 B2

**SLEEPING**
Lazy Lagoon.......................16 C5
Tropicana Inn......................17 D4

**EATING**
Carenage Café....................18 B2
Foodland............................19 C5
Melissans.............................20 C2
Native Food & Fruits........(see 29)
Nutmeg.............................21 B3

**ENTERTAINMENT**
Regal Cinema.....................22 D4

**SHOPPING**
Grenada Essentials..............23 A3
Roots Rock Records............24 A2
Tikal...................................25 A3
Yellow Poui Art Gallery......26 B2

**TRANSPORT**
Cargo/Passenger Boats to
  Carriacou..........................27 B2
Cruise Ship Pier..................28 A2
Cruise Ship Terminal...........29 A2
Esplanade Bus Terminal......30 A2
Green's Bike Shop...............31 C2
Grenada Yacht Services.......32 B4
Osprey Express Boat...........33 B3

low-maintenance shop. Tofu comes intertwined with the local classics making for a delightful and healthy fusion of West Indian flavors.

**Native Food & Fruits** (Esplanade Mall; soup EC$10) This spot is located in the very nonlocal Esplanade Mall, but come lunchtime the counter is lined wide and deep with hungry Grenadians. They come from all over town for the pumpkin and pig's tail soup and the fresh juices. The soup is great for the adventurous and the juices are tops in everyone's book.

**Victory Bar & Grill** ( ☎ 435-7263; Port Louis Marina; mains from EC$16; ⏱ lunch & dinner) Located at the yacht club, its unsurprisingly nautical

GRENADA

---

**SCULPTURES OF THE SEA**

Art galleries are all the same – white walls, wood floors, pretentious patrons. Well not this one. Sitting beneath the surface of the sea, in Molinière Bay (2 miles north of St George's) on the west coast is where you'll find this gallery. Life-size sculptures depicting a circle of women clasping hands, a man at a desk and a solitary mountain biker are amongst the collection. The artist, Jason Taylor, has created a garden of art that is a platform for sea life. As the pieces age, coral will grow on them, creatures will make there homes around them and they will become a part of the sea. To see the art you'll have to get in the water with one of the local scuba-diving companies – trust me, it's worth the effort.

---

theme permeates the establishment. Tables under sailcloth and fishing nets are filled with happy yachties eating fresh burgers, kebabs and lobster off the grill while taking in the view of the harbor. The atmosphere is fun, the parrots are annoyingly friendly and the food is great.

**Ocean Grill Restaurant & Bar** ( ☎ 440-9747; the Carenage; mains from EC$25; ☼ breakfast, lunch & dinner) It serves mostly burgers and pasta at jetty level, looking into the harbor. The shady dining area is a refuge from the midday sun for a casual lunch of tasty food.

**Carenage Café** ( ☎ 440-8701; the Carenage; roti EC$15, pizza EC$35; ☼ breakfast, lunch & dinner) Right in the hub of the harbor action and often packed with tourists, don't let its popularity put you off. It's a good spot for a roti and a fine helping of shade. The decently sized patio is a great spot for people-watching and Carib consumption.

**Nutmeg** ( ☎ 440-2539; the Carenage; rotis EC$7; mains from EC$38; ☼ lunch & dinner) Those wanting to get above the hustle and bustle of the waterfront need look no further then Nutmeg. Popular with tourists and locals, the balcony-laden restaurant is a pleasant place to take in the town over a roti or a nice plate of seafood.

A well-stocked and well-maintained grocery store, **Foodland** ( ☎ 440-1991; Lagoon Rd; ☼ 7.30am-8pm Mon-Thu, to 10pm Fri & Sat) has an ample selection of local favorites and imported goodies.

## Entertainment

**Regal Cinema** ( ☎ 440-2403; Paddock Rd; tickets EC$10) For a quiet evening, check out the (mainly Hollywood) films at this small theatre.

## Shopping

**Yellow Poui Art Gallery** ( ☎ 440-3001; Young St) This stunning commercial gallery features work from over 80 local artists. Beautiful water-

colors, oils and mixed media line the walls and beg to be taken home.

**Tikal** ( ☎ 440-2310; Young St) With a large and varied selection of crafts, prints, fabrics and ceramics, Tikal is a good one-stop shop when it comes to quality Grenadian-made gifts.

**Grenada Essentials** ( ☎ 435-5958; Monckton St) Shop with a guilt-free conscience – 100% of the profits go towards environmental projects like sea turtle protection and other worthy causes. This small shop has a good selection of locally produced jewelry, batik and other collectables.

**Roots Rock Record Shop** ( ☎ 440-8423; Gore St; CDs EC$25-30; ☼ 7:30am-6pm Mon-Fri) Roll up the steps and check out this great, small, local record shop. Little surprise that reggae and dancehall are the tunes of choice. The owner is a real character who can help you navigate through the local music you've been hearing and help you take some of it home with you.

## Getting Around

St George's is best (and most efficiently) explored on foot, although you can flag down any bus along Lagoon Rd to get you to the far end of town (EC$2.50).

A taxi to/from the airport costs EC$40 (EC$50 at night) and takes around 20 or 30 minutes.

## GRAND ANSE
pop 22,000

The tourist epicenter on the island is undoubtedly Grand Anse Beach. The flowing strip of beach is one of the best on the island and is justifiably popular. You can see why the decision was made back in the day that this was the place to plant some hotels. It's an odd sort of town, with no real center to speak of; it's best described as a strip of hotels along the beach. Most budgets are accommodated for somewhere along the strip, with an emphasis on midrange and higher-end accommodations and eateries.

## Information

Several banks and ATMs are spread out along the road through town. At the Spiceland Mall there is a grocery story, food court and a few shops.

## Activities

**Aquanauts Grenada** ( ☎ 444-1126; www.aquanauts grenada.com) offers all the usual dive shop services, from boats to gear to training. Open-water courses cost US$460. There's also a branch at True Blue Bay.

## Sleeping

**Grenada Grand Beach Resort** ( ☎ 444-4371; www .grenadagrand.com; r from US$140; ❄ ⬛ ⬚ ) Don't let the big exterior put you off; this enormous complex actually has a fairly intimate feel. The rooms are nothing to write home about, but the facilities are impressive. The 300ft-long, river-like pool is a big hit with kids, and the swim-up bar is a hit with the older kids. The staff are friendly and there seems to be every amenity you'd need onsite. There are often good deals to be had, as the number of rooms is huge.

**Flamboyant Hotel** ( ☎ 444-4247; www.flamboyant .com; r US$145-550; ❄ ⬛ ⬚ ) Up on the hill adjacent to Grand Anse Beach, the Flamboyant Hotel is a sprawling property that spans both sides of the road. There are great views of the sea and the rooms are pleasant if a bit uninspiring. After indulging in a complimentary kayak rental or snorkel there's a lively restaurant and bar onsite to keep you fueled up

**Coyaba Beach Resort** ( ☎ 444-4129; www.coyaba .com; s/d US$270/330; ❄ ⬛ ⬚ ) Coyaba saw the silver lining in getting a good kicking from Hurricane Ivan in 2004. They've rebuilt and improved upon their good foundation, adding rooms and improving facilities. Set upon a great stretch of beach and priding itself on exceptional service the nice rooms nearly justify the price.

**Mount Cinnamon** ( ☎ 439-0000; www.mountcinna mongrenada.com; ste from US$500; ❄ ⬛ ⬚ ) Newly reinvented and hot off the press, Mount Cinnamon is a feast to the eyes. With a color palate best described as carib-technicolor the wildly energetic decor is confronting and fun. Safety orange refrigerators, hot-pink shag

carpet and purple walls all accent the beautifully appointed suites. It's choc-a-bloc with modern amenities, including wi-fi access, and some of the best views around. A steep uphill trek from the beach is the only downside to this exceptional property.

## Eating

The town of Grand Anse is a bit of misnomer as it is more of a strip of hotels along the beach then a town. A whole host of eating options can be found along the strip, if you know where to look. Most hotels have restaurants and happily accept non-guests dropping in for a meal. If you're craving a quick bite, there is decent budget eating at the Spiceland Mall.

**Southside Restaurant and Bar** ( ☎ 444-1975; roti EC$9; ⏲ 8am-8pm) Also known as D Green Grocer, this small West Indian takeout place, on the main road by the roundabout, is recognizable by the large Carlsberg beer logos on the roof and front. It has one of the better boneless chicken rotis of any fast-food shop on the island.

**La Boulangerie** (mains from EC$20; ⏲ lunch & dinner) Italian food sold under a French name mixed in with Caribbean flavors. Gorgeous pizzas and pastas that will bring you back for seconds – all popular with ex-pats, travelers and the odd local.

**Carib Sushi** ( ☎ 439-5640; mains from EC$20; ⏲ lunch & dinner Mon-Sat) Local seafood is rolled into the mix at this casual sushi bar. Mix and mingle on the outdoor picnic tables before diving into tempura, sushi, sashimi and noodles.

**Sapphire** ( ☎ 439-3900; mains from EC$45; ⏲ breakfast, lunch & dinner) A mix of French and Caribbean flavors is at work here. The twinkling lights of the outdoor dining area foster a romantic setting for an evening meal. Diners relaxing to the sounds of the sea and the fading light of day are treated to well-presented dishes that are gluttonously satisfying.

The biggest grocery store on the island, **Real Value Supermarket** (Spiceland Mall; ⏲ 8am-9pm Mon-Thu, 8am-10pm Fri & Sat, 10am-7pm Sun) has everything you'd ever need to self-cater. Grab a snack, a cold drink or an ice cream on a hot day.

## Entertainment

**Owl** ( ☎ 444-4247; Flamboyant Hotel) There's cricket on the TV, a sea breeze filtering in and a pool table to keep you busy. The Owl staff keep the party going into the wee hours with drink specials and other debaucherous means. It's

GRENADA

a popular hangout for a whole range of local folks. The cocktail list has more pages than the phone book, and the bar stools are hard to leave behind.

## MORNE ROUGE BAY
### pop 12,000

Though just down the way from Grande Anse beach the succulent sands of Morne Rouge Bay are in a wholly different league. This far superior stretch of beach is a shining example of the snow-white sand and crystal-clear blue water that the Caribbean is known for. Mercifully quiet and pristine, there are only a handful of buildings housing a couple of hotels and restaurants.

### Sleeping & Eating
**Gem Holiday Beach Resort** ( ☎ 444-4224; www.gembeachreort.com; s/d US$103/126; 🅿 🖵 ) Just up from the beach, this place is a real gem. Nothing too fancy, but all the basics you'd need. Tidy, friendly and a great budget option on one of the best beaches on the island.

**our pick** **Laluna** ( ☎ 439-0001; www.laluna.com; cottages from US$730; 🖵 🏊 ) There's a simple elegance to these 16 Balinese-inspired cottages. Beautiful appointments and a penchant for the luxurious await the traveler lucky enough to have the means to enjoy such a well-heeled establishment. A secluded beach and a delightfully delicious restaurant are provided to keep you occupied. The property is secluded and slightly hard to find – just like paradise should be.

**Sur La Mer Restaurant** ( ☎ 444-2288; mains from EC$30; 🕑 breakfast, lunch & dinner) No need to stray too far from the sand, this beachside restaurant will sort you out with a simple lunch or dinner. West Indian fare with a flare for seafood and an enticing bar with views of the lapping waves.

### Entertainment
**Fantasia 2001** ( ☎ 444-2288; 🕑 10pm-late Wed-Sat) Has a dance floor that resembles a roller rink or maybe a bull-fighting ring – depending on your perspective. Fun, safe and lively this is definitely the spot to groove with the locals and mix with other travelers into the wee hours.

## POINT SALINES & TRUE BLUE BAY
### pop 16,000

The area around Point Salines is dominated by Grenadian anomalies – the airport and St George's Medical School. The school, which is populated by young Americans, is a sprawling and pleasant campus. Ronald Reagan cited the risk to the safety of students at this American-run facility as a justification of the 1983 invasion of Grenada. It feels like you could be on a campus anywhere in the States – perhaps that's the point.

True Blue Bay is a relaxed corner of the island with some nice high-end hotels, some good eateries and the yacht moorings.

**Aquanauts Grenada** ( ☎ 444-1126; www.aquanauts grenada.com; True Blue Bay Resort) is the dive-shop juggernaut on the island. It has it all, from the boats to the gear to an army of staff. Open-water courses cost US$460. There's also a branch at Grande Anse.

Hurricane Ivan gave **True Blue Bay Resort & Marina** ( ☎ 433-8783; www.truebluebay.com; True Blue Bay; r US$210-515; ❄ 🖵 🏊 ) a good kicking, but it's come back with a vengeance, rebuilding to a new standard. Like a carpet of children's jellybeans lining the hill, its multicolored huts pop off the green grass. Apartment units feature full kitchens and an adobe decorative scheme that is quite striking. The family-owned resort is an island favorite. Offers wi-fi access.

The best feature of **Point Salines Hotel** ( ☎ 444-4123; www.pointsalineshotel.com Point Salines; s/d US$110/120; 🖵 🏊 ) is its proximity to the airport. The five-minute drive makes it appealing for those early-morning flights, but there are much better options around for an extended stay. The rooms are clean, small and overpriced, and there's wi-fi access.

Popular with expat students from the nearby medical school, **Bananas Restaurant & Bar** ( ☎ 439-4369; www.bananasgrenada.com; True Blue Rd; mains from EC$30; 🕑 9am-late) is a good place to come and check out the doctors of tomorrow getting smashed and playing doctor with each other. The dance club out back is fun and the massive open-air patio is a good place to mingle. The food is a bit overpriced, but the drinks are cold and the atmosphere is hot.

Right around the corner from the med school, **Mocha Jumby** ( ☎ 439-2227; True Blue Rd; mains from EC$18; 🕑 breakfast, lunch & dinner) is a popular café for lunch. The tasty burgers and pizza bring the students in and the free wi-fi and subarctic air-con keeps 'em there.

## LANCE AUX ÉPINES
### pop 9100

Lance aux Épines (lance-a-peen) is the peninsula that forms the southernmost point of Grenada. It's home to some of the nicer beaches on the island and some of the more-upmarket establishments. The marina is a pleasant place to explore, with members of the sailing set frequenting it and spicing up the atmosphere.

## Information

There's a customs and immigration office at the full marina of **Spice Island Marine Services** ( ☎ 444-4257; www.spiceislandmarine.com; Prickly Bay).

## Activities

If you're here for scuba, **ScubaTech** ( ☎ 439-4346; www.scubatech-grenada.com; Calabash Hotel) is well organized and delivers good wreck dives.

## Sleeping

**Lance aux Épines Cottages** ( ☎ 444-4565; www.laecottages.com; r US$154-335; ⊠ ▯ ) You can't argue with the location. It's right on the beach, so your biggest worry is tracking sand into your cottage. Beautiful views are augmented by attractive rooms that come complete with kitchens and large living areas. Well set-up for families, the games room is a big hit with the kiddies.

**Calabash Hotel** ( ☎ 444-4334, www.calabashhotel.com; r from US$570; ⊠ ▯ ▣ ) This is easily the nicest place to bed down for the night in the Lance aux Épines area. The beautifully manicured grounds sit hand in hand with a standard of service that is second to none. With little touches, like having breakfast delivered to your room, and the ambience of swaying palms on the beach, the setting is ripe for relaxation. Offers wi-fi access.

## Eating

**Red Crab** ( ☎ 444-4424; mains from EC$22; ☽ 11am-2pm & 6-11pm Mon-Sat) The roadside patio isn't the most aesthetic place to dine on the island, but the outstanding food more then makes up for it. There's a great selection of seafood that's a good catch for those on a budget, and the service is impeccable too.

**Prickly Bay Marina Pizzeria** ( ☎ 439-5265; pizza from EC$28 ☽ lunch & dinner) Pizzas that are world famous in Grenada are baked, sliced and munched dockside. Picnic tables, a pool table and a cozy seaside bar all add up to a very chilled mix of food and fun.

## LA SAGESSE NATURE CENTRE

Sitting along a coconut-tree-lined bay with protected swimming and a network of hiking trails, **La Sagesse Nature Centre** ( ☎ 444-6458; lsnature@caribsurf.com; tours US$32) occupies the former estate of the late Lord Brownlow, a cousin of Queen Elizabeth II. His beachside estate house, built in 1968, has been turned into a small inn.

La Sagesse is about a 25-minute drive from St George's on the Eastern Main Rd. The entrance is opposite an old abandoned rum distillery. Buses bound for the province of St David can also drop you here (EC$3.50).

The **manor house** ( ☎ 444-6458; www.lasagesse .com; manor r US$195), at La Sagesse Nature Centre, features lots of character and history and has 12 airy rooms with double beds. There is also a modern building with five additional rooms and three suites. The beachside **restaurant** ( ☽ breakfast, lunch & dinner) has fish sandwiches and burgers for EC$20.

## GRAND ETANG ROAD

The forested area that you encounter along Grand Etang Rd is the antithesis of the sand and surf on the coast. The mountainous center of the island is often awash with misty clouds, and looks like a lost primordial world. The hills are a tangle of rainforest brimming with life – including monkeys that often get a bit too friendly. A series of hiking trails snake through the wilderness sanctuary providing access for the ambitious into the fertile forest.

To get to the area, take River Rd or Sans Souci Rd out of St George's, and when you reach the Mt Gay traffic circle, take the road north. Alternatively, take bus 9 (EC$5) from the main bus station in town and enjoy the views as the van winds its way along the twisting road.

## Annandale Falls

An idyllic waterfall with a 30ft drop, Annandale Falls is surrounded by a grotto of lush vegetation. There's a pool beneath the falls where you can take a refreshing swim. Unfortunately, it can get packed with tourists when cruise ships are in port.

In the village of Constantine, located 3.5 miles northeast of St George's, turn left on the road that leads downhill immediately past the yellow Methodist church. After three-quarters of a mile you'll reach the **Annandale Falls visitors center** (admission free; ☽ 8am-4pm Mon-Fri). The falls are just a two-minute walk from the center.

**THE SILVER LINING**

'I think Hurricane Ivan was the best thing that ever happened to this island.' Not the statement you'd expect to hear from someone whose own hotel was nearly destroyed by the storm and whose grandmother's house was obliterated. But Grenada isn't a straightforward place, and Nigel Fleming isn't a straightforward sort of guy.

Nigel was born in Grenada, educated in Canada and returned to the island nine years ago to open a hotel. He runs the Lazy Lagoon Hotel (p708) in St George's. You can usually find him behind the bar, entertaining the regulars and locals alike.

**Why do you describe it as the 'best thing' to happen to Grenada? Ivan did so much damage, and destroyed so many people's livelihoods.**

It was cleansing for the island. It was devastating, but it took away a lot of shit and allowed people to use insurance and outside investment to improve the infrastructure of the island. People are more aware now of how vulnerable we are – people make it count now.

**It must have been like going through a war?**

Very much so. It was like a scene out of a war, devastation everywhere; it shook people up. Luckily there weren't a lot of deaths attributed to the hurricane. One thing that really changed was how people look at life. In Grenada people don't usually show emotion in public, but after the hurricane I saw couples walking down the street holding hands – it was such a big change.

**So is it better or worse then before?**

Much better. Things have been rebuilt bigger and better; there is more business opportunity. People got off their asses and fixed things and got on with life.

**What about environmental issues like sustainability? Are people thinking about climate change in Grenada?**

People here don't have a clue; it's not even on the radar. We have no recycling; all the plastic juice bottles just go straight into the landfill. Sometimes the government talks about making changes, but there is no action. They need to start to restrict the import of plastic bottles. All of our beer and soda comes in glass bottles – which get washed and re-used, but the plastic just goes straight to the landfill. There just isn't an awareness of these issues – not like overseas.

**What is the impact of having the American Medical School on the island?**

It's good for the economy; they put a lot of money into the pockets of locals. They rent houses and buy groceries, but they don't really mix with the local people. They just stick to themselves; they can't be bothered to explore the island. But the ones that do get a lot more out of their education – I can't imagine not wanting to explore this place.

## Grand Etang National Park

Two and a half miles northeast of Constantine, after the road winds steeply up to an elevation of 1900ft, a roadside sign welcomes visitors to **Grand Etang National Park** (admission US$2).

Half a mile past the road sign, the visitor center sits to the side of the road overlooking Grand Etang Lake – a crater lake that forms the centerpiece of the park. The **Grand Etang visitors center** ( ☎ 440-6160; ❧ 8:30am-4pm Mon-Fri, Sat & Sun if cruise ships are in) has a few displays explaining the local foliage, fauna and history. Outside the center there are a series of independent booths hawking souvenirs, spices and cold drinks.

The following are some of the hiking trails in the park:

**Concord Falls** Serious hikers branch off shortly before the end of the Mt Qua Qua Trail to pick up this five-hour trek (one

way from the visitors center) to Concord Falls. From the falls, you can walk another 1.5 miles to the village of Concord on the west coast and take a bus back to St George's.

**Fedon's Camp** A long, arduous hike that leads deep into the forested interior, to the site where Julien Fedon, a rebel French plantation owner, hid out after his 1795 rebellion (see p702).

**Grand Etang Shoreline** This 1½-hour loop walk around Grand Etang Lake is gentle, but it can get muddy and doesn't offer the same sort of views as the higher trails.

**Morne La Baye** This easy walk starts behind the visitors center and takes in a few viewpoints, passing native vegetation along the way.

**Mt Qua Qua** This is a moderately difficult three-hour round-trip hike that leads to the top of a ridge, offering some of the best views of the interior forest.

**Seven Sisters Falls** The hike to this series of seven waterfalls in the rainforest east of the Grand Etang Rd is considered the best hike in Grenada. The main track starts from the tin shed used by the banana association, 1.25 miles north of the visitors center on the right side of the Grand Etang Rd. The hike takes only about two hours round-trip; a small fee is sometimes charged.

# GRENVILLE
**pop 15,600**

For travelers who want to get beyond the gloss and prefabricated tourism of areas such as Grand Anse, all they need to do is take a trip to the other side of the island. Grenville is a bustling little town that sees little tourist traffic. The agricultural hub of the East Coast, this seaside community is a good insight into the daily lives of the average Grenadian. Two miles north of town is the old airport that used to serve as the main landing strip for the island. It's disused and derelict now, but you can take a look at a couple of rusting planes that are relics of the American invasion.

Grenville is fairly easy to get to by bus 9 (EC$6, about 40 minutes) from St George's, along scenic Grand Etang Rd.

## Eating

**our pick** **Melting Pot** ( lunch & dinner) Upstairs overlooking the waterfront and a traditional favorite, you're sure to meet up with the local crew here. Windies stalwarts like callaloo, beans and rice, and stewed fish are all made by the local ladies and served up deli style. Great food for an even better price.

**Good Food** (Convent Hill; meals EC$7-12) The name, although not the most imaginative, really does sum it up. Good Food is a wonderful choice for trying local cuisine – chicken, beef or fish – and is a top spot to sample the Grenadian national dish, oil down. Which, for the uninitiated, is vegetables boiled down to a stew, with coconut milk added to give it a distinctive flavor. Chase your food down with one of the delicious fresh fruit juices.

**Bains** ( lunch & dinner; plates EC$10) Follow the winding steps up to the roof and into the tiny dining room where the elevated platform dishes out commanding views of town. Pull up a chair and dig into a mixed plate of chicken, veggies and all the fixings for EC$10. Drink up the views and kick back island style.

## Shopping

Be sure to stop in at the **Culture Joint** ( 415-8838; St. Andrews) in the small village of St Andrews, just outside Grandville. PJ, the resident artist, works in his small shop, mak-

ing arts and crafts out of local materials. Cups and mugs, baskets and lampshades are all carved or woven from bamboo. There are some nice pieces all at good prices. PJ is also a great guy to talk to and get the scoop on the local scene.

# NORTH OF GRENVILLE

The **River Antoine Rum Distillery** ( 442-7109; tours EC$5; 8am-4pm Mon-Fri) has produced rum since 1785 and claims to have the oldest working water mill in the Caribbean. It is south of Lake Antoine and most easily accessed from Tivoli (bus EC$5, 1½ to two hours).

**Lake Antoine**, a crater lake in an extinct volcano, is a mile south of River Sallee. This shallow crater lake is host to a large variety of wildlife. The lake's perimeter trail makes for a beautiful walk, and it's excellent for bird-watchers.

# BATHWAYS BEACH & AROUND

From River Sallee, a road leads to Bathways Beach, a stretch of coral sands. At the north end, a rock shelf parallels the shoreline, creating a very long, 30ft-wide sheltered pool that's great for swimming.

**Sandy Island** is one of three small islands that sit off the coast of Bathways Beach. It is uninhabited and home to crystal-clear waters. There's also a beautiful beach on the leeward side that offers fine swimming and snorkeling. It's possible to arrange for a boat to take you from Sauteurs to Sandy Island; make inquiries with the fishermen on Sauteurs beach. Expect to pay about EC$150 per boat, round-trip.

# LEVERA BEACH

Backed by eroding sea cliffs, Levera Beach is a wild, beautiful sweep of sand. Just offshore is the high, pointed Sugar Loaf Island (also called Levera Island), while the Grenadine islands dot the horizon to the north. The beach, the mangrove swamp and the nearby pond have been incorporated into Grenada's national-park system and are an important waterfowl habitat and sea-turtle nesting site.

The road north from Bathways Beach to Levera Beach is usually passable in a vehicle, but it can be rough, so most visitors end up hiking. The walk from Bathways Beach takes about 30 minutes. Stick to the road, as sea cliffs and rough surf make it impossible to walk along the coast between the two beaches.

## SAUTEURS
pop 15,000

On the northern tip of the island, the town of Sauteurs is home to some fascinating local history. The literal English translation of Sauteurs is 'Jumpers'. This strange name stems from 1651 when the town was the scene of a rather grim incident. The local Carib families, in an effort to escape the advancing French army, elected to throw themselves off the 130ft-high cliffs that line the coast. Today, the cliffs are referred to as Caribs' Leap and the town itself is a fine example of local life – well off the tourist trail.

## VICTORIA
pop 2640

The cliffside west coast road is an interesting journey – views of the sea are interspersed with the occasional falling rock. The cliffs above the road can play havoc with the road surface. Victoria is one of the larger towns on the coast. It has a few locally oriented amenities, including a nutmeg-processing plant. Buses to St George's cost EC$3.50.

## GOUYAVE
pop 14,700

Gouyave, between Victoria and Concord, is a supremely attractive fishing village with a warm small-town feel. It is well worth spending an afternoon or longer here, just walking around, relaxing, having a drink and taking in the ambience.

On the town's main road is a large **nutmeg-processing station** (admission US$1; 8am-4pm Mon-Fri). A worker will take visitors on a tour through fragrant vats of curing nuts and various sorting operations for the admission fee, plus a small tip. Just south of the bridge, on the south side of Gouyave, a road leads inland 0.5 miles along the river to the **Dougaldston Estate**, where cocoa and spices are processed.

## CONCORD FALLS

There are a couple of scenic waterfalls along the Concord River. The lowest, a picturesque 100ft cascade, can be viewed by driving to the end of Concord Mountain Rd, a side road leading 1.5 miles inland from the village of Concord. These falls are on private property and the owner charges US$1 to visit them.

The half-mile trail to the upper falls begins at the end of the road. There have been some muggings in this area in the past, so it is recommended that you don't hike alone, and leave your valuables at your hotel.

# CARRIACOU
pop 9000

The fact that most people don't realize that there are in fact *three* islands in the nation of Grenada is a fitting introduction to Carriacou (carry-a-cou). Like its minor island sibling, this humble isle is oft forgotten.

Where the island of Grenada can feel touristy and busy, you'll struggle to ever feel that way here. You won't find cruise ships, big resorts or tacky souvenir shops. This is West Indian life the way it was 50 years ago – quiet, laid back and relaxed. This beautiful little island is thankfully off the radar of most travelers, leaving its green hills and white beaches ripe for discovery.

The island itself is joy to experience with some tremendous hiking to be found and some hidden beaches that are destined to make your all time best of list.

## Getting There & Away
### AIR

To check on flights between Grenada Island and Carriacou, contact **SVG Air** ( ☎ 444-3549; www.svgair.com).

### BOAT

See p724 for details of transport to/from Carriacou by boat.

## Getting Around
### TO/FROM THE AIRPORT

It is best to get to and from the airport by taxi. A ride from the airport to Hillsborough is EC$15, while a trip to Tyrrel Bay or Bogles is EC$20.

### BUS

Buses (privately owned minivans) charge EC$2.50 to go anywhere on the island, or EC$1 if the distance is less than a mile. The two main routes run from Hillsborough – one south to Tyrrel Bay, the other north to Windward. Minibuses start at around 7am and stop at around sunset.

GRENADA

## CAR

There are a few places to rent vehicles on Carriacou, with rates typically around US$50 per day. **Quality Jeep Rental** ( ☎ 443-8307; joseph_grenada@yahoo.com; rental per day US$40), in L'Esterre, southwest of the airport, has good prices. There is a gas station on Patterson St in Hillsborough.

### TAXI

Some minibuses double as taxis, and usually you can count on a couple of them swinging by the airport when a flight comes in or by the pier when the boat arrives.

You can hire a taxi for a 2½-hour island tour, costing EC$150 for up to five people, or you can tour just the northern half, which takes half as long and costs EC$75.

# HILLSBOROUGH

### pop 5000

The gentle pace of Carriacou is reflected in the sedate nature of its largest town, Hillsborough. With only a couple of streets loosely packed with uninspired architecture, there is little to actually see or do here. Having said that, the quiet streets and welcoming nature of the local population leave an endearing impression, despite the fact there is little to be done other then hang out.

The town is centered around the lively pier area where most of the action takes place. The beach adjacent is nothing spectacular, but is a pleasant place to kick back.

## Information

**Ade's Dream Guest House** ( ☎ 443-7317; adesdea@ caribsurf.com; Main St; per hr EC$10) Reasonably fast internet connection, friendly folks and a nice spot.

**Cable & Wireless** ( ☎ 443-7000; Patterson St; ⏰ 7:30am-6pm Mon-Fri, to 1pm Sat) Free wi-fi if you have your own computer and are happy to pull up a chair in the waiting area.

**National Commercial Bank** ( ☎ 443-7289; Main St) Has a 24-hour ATM.

**Post office** ( ☎ 443-6014; Main St; ⏰ 8am-3pm Mon-Fri) Located at the pier.

**Princess Royal Hospital** ( ☎ 443-7400) In Belair, outside of Hillsborough.

**Tourist office** ( ☎ 443-7948; Main St; ⏰ 8am-noon & 1-4pm Mon-Fri) Located across from the pier.

## Sights

The small, community-run **Carriacou Museum** ( ☎ 443-8288; Patterson St; admission EC$5; ⏰ 9:30am-3:45pm Mon-Fri) has an interesting collection of Native American artifacts, a display about African heritage and paintings by local artists. There is also an collection of colonial-era objects, including an old urinal.

## Activities

The first and still the best shop on Carriacou, **Carriacou Silver Diving** ( ☎ 443-7882; www.scubamax .com) has two-tank dives for US$85.

## Sleeping

**John's Unique Resort** ( ☎ 443-8345; johnresort@grena dines.net; Main St; r from US$25; 🛠 ) Situated just on the outskirts of town heading towards Bogles, you'd be hard-pressed to name what is truly unique about John's – but it is, nonetheless, a winner. Turtles in the front yard greet you as you arrive. The rooms are large and clean and have sunny balconies. A restaurant onsite can put together a great plate of local food for a good price and the staff are friendly and helpful.

**Grand View Hotel** ( ☎ 443-8659; www.carriacougrand view.com; s/d US$60/70; 🛠 🖳 🖳 ) Just down the road and up the hill from town, Grand View more then lives up to its name. Towering over the harbor and the surrounding hills, this property is a hidden gem. Some rooms are a bit petite, with double beds so close you could mistake them for a super-duper-king size. Every room has a balcony to take in the vista, there is a pool to cool off and the rooms catch the sea breeze, making it a cool and pleasant place to bivouac during your Carriacou stay.

**Hotel Laurena** ( ☎ 443-8759; s/d US$75/85, 🛠 🖳 ) One of the larger accommodation options on the island, Laurena has spacious rooms with a good selection of amenities. Catering to families, rooms have fridges and balconies. The staff are friendly and some rooms have Jacuzzi tubs to soak your troubles away. Offers wi-fi access.

**Ade's Dream Guest House** ( ☎ 443-7317; www.ades dream.com; Main St; r from EC$85; 🛠 🖳 ) Popular with inter-island travelers, those on a budget and people wanting to be right amongst the action, Ade's is in the dead center of town, above a bustling grocery/hardware/liquor/everything-else store. There are basic rooms with shared facilities and self-contained units with kitchens – all are clean and well maintained. It's a popular spot often booked

GRENADA

to the hilt when the rest of the island is a ghost town.

## Eating

**Eat of the Town** (plates EC$18 ⊙ lunch & dinner) Decorated with torn linoleum, drab decor and plastic tables, Eat of the Town is the classic Caribbean dive. Don't judge this book by the cover – the food is awesome. Mountainous plates of fish, rice and all the trimmings for an unbeatable price. Pull up a folding chair and dig in!

**ourpick Green Roof Inn** ( ☎ 443-6399; www.green roofinn.com; mains from EC$55; ⊙ dinner) Half a mile up the road from Hillsborough, this is the place to be for dinner. Be sure to reserve a spot as the tiny dining area fills fast. The ever-changing menu will be sure to feature fresh fish, steak and lobster if you're lucky. Great views are served with every meal and the small bar will keep you well hydrated. It also has six rooms if you want to stay the night. And you should – the tasteful decor and comfortable style are as inviting as the meals.

## NORTH OF HILLSBOROUGH

The northern part of Carriacou is a delightful place to visit, with some wonderfully unique towns and stunning scenery. The central road cuts across the spine of the island making the journey as pleasant as the destination.

You can easily catch a bus or taxi to complete the journey, but as a hike this is a fantastic, if a little grueling afternoon out. From Hillsborough head north, taking Belair Rd, about a third of a mile north of Silver Beach Resort, and follow it uphill for half a mile, then bear right on the side road that leads to the hospital. The **hospital** sits atop the hill and has a magnificent view of the bay and offshore islands.

Continuing north from the hospital, the road traverses the crest of **Belvedere Hill**, providing sweeping views of the east coast and the islands of Petit St Vincent and Petit Martinique. There are also the remains of an **old stone sugar mill** just before the Belvedere Crossroads.

From here, the route northeast (called the High Rd) leads down to **Windward**, a charming small village with a shop, school and little else. It is, however, the home of boat building on the island. If you're lucky the lads will be out building a seafaring craft in the traditional way – the same way they've done it for a century.

The road from Windward leads another mile to **Petit Carenage Bay**, at Carriacou's northeastern tip. There's a good beach, and views of the northern Grenadines from here.

The cottages at **Bayaleau Point Cottages** ( ☎ 443-7984; www.carriacoucottages.com; Windward; US$85-US$115; ☐ ) are a breath of fresh, tropical air. There are blue, green, red and yellow varieties to choose from – all set up to perfection, with all the basic amenities you need for a relaxed holiday. The balconies, hammocks and home touches make it hard to want to leave. Wheelchair access is also available.

Reservation for Mr Frodo Baggins? **Round House** ( ☎ 443-7841; Bogles; dinner from EC$55) is, you guessed it, a round house, that perhaps was designed with Middle-earth in mind. It's run by Grenada's Chef of the Year, so the food – European dishes infused with Caribbean classics all served up fresh – more then meets your expectations. Everything a growing Hobbit needs.

## SOUTH OF HILLSBOROUGH

The small village of **L'Esterre**, just southwest of the airport, is a quiet little place with precious little going on. The biggest reason to venture to this portion of the island is to visit the aptly named **Paradise Beach**. This nice stretch of sand is the closest beach to Hillsborough and has some eclectic eating, sleeping and shopping options just off the sand.

## Sleeping & Eating

**Paradise Inn** ( ☎ 443-8406; Paradise Beach; s/d from US$30/45) Charming sandside living, right on Paradise Beach. Eight simple rooms look onto a grassy courtyard and are only steps from the sea. There's a great little restaurant and bar, tucked under a tree even closer to the waves, that serves up a good meal.

**ourpick Cow Foot** (Belview South; mains from EC$10; ⊙ lunch & dinner) Sometimes the best restaurants have the worst names. A uniquely local establishment near the microtown of Belview South, just off the South Coast. Nothing flash here, just tables, chairs and hands down the best roti on the island. The owner is a real character who makes it a memorable dining experience, not just for the delicious food.

**Hard Wood Bar & Snacket** (Paradise Beach; dinner from EC$25; ⊙ breakfast, lunch & dinner) Near the center of Paradise Beach this green, yellow and red shack dishes out cold beers and fresh

GRENADA

---

### TWIST MY ARM: THE PLACES THE AUTHORS WANTED TO KEEP SECRET

A beach is a beach isn't it? No, afraid not. There is more to a good beach than just sand and water. Every beach aficionado knows that there's something intangible about a great stretch of sand that makes it more valuable than the sum of its parts.

**Anse La Roche**, on Carriacou, is most definitely something special. This idyllic stretch of the softest sand you may ever get the pleasure of sinking your toes into is a hidden prize for those willing to make the effort to seek it out. Protected by dense bush and cliffs on its flanks, this secluded beauty – rarely visited, except by the adventurous, those in the know and the sea turtles that nest amongst the sand – will be a private paradise.

The treasure trail goes a little like this. From the town of Bogles take a left at the (white) sign for the High North Park. Follow that road, which quickly turns to dirt, for 20 minutes on foot. Look for a red-painted rock on the left-hand side of the road and follow the rough path through the forest for 15 minutes. All going right, you should be spat out onto a beach that you'll be bragging about for years.

---

fish meals oozing with local flavor. A serene, quintessentially Caribbean setting: sand, sea and suds. Locals, lifers, ex-pats and the odd traveler pony up to the bar and settle in for a cold one on a hot day.

### Shopping

**Fidel Productions** ( ☎ 404-8866; Paradise Beach; ⊙ 9am-5pm Mon-Sat) This charming little shop built into an old disused shipping container, is a creative cave of artistic niceties featuring locally made T-shirts original artworks, jewelry, ceramics and some great photographs. All are for sale. Everything appears to be well made and is reasonably priced.

### TYRREL BAY & THE NEARSHORE ISLANDS

**Tyrrel Bay** (population 750) is a deep, protected bay with a sandy (although somewhat dirty) beach. It is a popular anchorage for visiting yachters and hosts a number of regattas throughout the year. Since the opening of a commercial dock in Tyrrel Bay in 2005, it is receiving more boat traffic. There are a few sleeping and eating options in town. Buses run with some frequency to Hillsborough (EC$2, 15 minutes).

**Sandy Island**, off the west side of Hillsborough Bay, is a favorite daytime destination for snorkelers and sailors. It's a tiny postcard-perfect reef island of glistening sands surrounded by turquoise waters. Snorkelers take to the shallow waters fronting Sandy Island, while the deeper waters on the far side are popular for diving. Water taxis (EC$50 to EC$75 return) run from Tyrrel Bay (20 minutes) or Hillsborough (15 minutes). Be clear about when you want to be picked up. As the island takes only a couple of minutes to walk around, a whole afternoon can tick by very slowly.

**White Island** makes for a nice day trip. It has a good, sandy beach and a pristine reef for snorkeling. White Island is about one mile off the southern tip of Carriacou. Water taxis run from Tyrrel Bay (about EC$75 return, 30 minutes).

# PETIT MARTINIQUE

**pop 1000**

They don't call it Petit for nothing – this little island is a scant one mile in diameter. Small, charismatic and infrequently visited, Petit Martinique is an ideal spot to get away from everything.

With a steep volcanic core rising a stout 740ft at its center, there is little room on the island for much else. The solitary road runs up the west coast, but it is rarely used – locals prefer to walk, nothing is very far and what's the hurry? The population subsists on the fruits of the sea. Fishermen and mariners earn their crust from the ocean.

With barely a thousand inhabitants, most of whom are related to each other, this is a place to find peace, quiet – and precious little else.

### SLEEPING & EATING

**Melodies Guest House** ( ☎ 443-9052; www.spiceisle.com/melodies; r US$30-50) Melodies has simple rooms, some with balconies facing the impossibly blue ocean. It is worth the couple of extra dollars for an ocean-view room. The

GRENADA

downstairs restaurant and bar serves good local food and stiff cocktails – sometimes followed by a round of drunken karaoke.

**Palm Beach Guest House** ( ☎ 443-9103; www .petitemartinique.com/palmbeachguesthouse; s/d EC$100/160) Connected to the Palm Beach Restaurant this basic guesthouse has two simple rooms. The frills are few, but the location is great and the atmosphere is endearing. It's a short 10-minute walk to the beach, and the apartments overlook the bay, providing wonderful views.

## GETTING THERE & AWAY

The *Osprey* catamaran ferries passengers between Grenada, Carriacou and Petit Martinique daily (see the schedule on p725).

A water taxi can take you from Carriacou to Petit Martinique. They are cheaper from Windward (EC$120, about one hour) than from Hillsborough.

# DIRECTORY

## ACCOMMODATIONS

The beaches are the main tourist draw to Grenada, so it's no wonder they are where you will find most of the accommodations. St George's is a lively town with much going on – perhaps too much going on, as it's a bit hectic for most overnight tastes.

Down the road in Grand Anse and further on in Lance aux Épines is where you'll find the majority of the beds. These beachside communities have all the amenities a traveler might need, although the towns themselves are a bit soulless, so be sure to dip your toes into the cultural ocean of St George's.

Carriacou and Petit Martinique are small enough that the places to stay are mixed right in with the local population. There's no doubt you'll get to mix with the locals here – they'll be your neighbors.

Camping is allowed in Grand Etang National Park, but there are no established facilities and the park is in one of the rainiest parts of the island. Arrangements can be made through the park **visitors center** ( ☎ 440-6160; 🕑 8:30am-4pm Mon-Fri, Sat & Sun if cruise ships are in). There is a modest camping fee.

## ACTIVITIES

See p723 for tours of Grenada, and p724 for information on chartering a yacht.

### Beaches & Swimming

Grenada is a beach lover's dream, with a plethora of sparkling sand to sink your toes into. On Grenada itself Grand Anse is an obvious highlight and the star of many a postcard. Morne Rouge Bay, just over the peninsula from Grand Anse, is another standout with the same style of sand and water but with much fewer people.

The islands of Carriacou and Petit Martinique are chockabloc with world-class stretches of ocean just begging to be leapt into. The swimming on all of these beaches is top notch, with light surf, few currents and soft sandy bottoms.

### Cycling

The hilly terrain is a turn-off for some cyclists and great fun for others. If you're keen, you can rent bikes in St George (p708).

### Diving & Snorkeling

The waters around Grenada have extensive reefs and a wide variety of corals, fish, turtles and other marine life. One popular dive is the wreck of the *Bianca C* ocean liner, off Grenada's southwest coast. Strong currents

---

### PRACTICALITIES

■ **Newspapers & Magazines** The weekly *Grenada Today* and *Grenadian Voice* are the island's two main weekly papers. International newspapers, including *USA Today,* can be found in large grocery stores. The tourist office issues *Discover Grenada,* a glossy magazine with general information on Grenada, Carriacou and Petit Martinique.

■ **Radio & TV** Grenada has three local TV stations and four radio stations. Most larger hotels also have satellite or cable TV, which pick up major US network broadcasts.

■ **Electricity** The electrical current is 220V, 50 cycles. British-style three-pin plugs are used.

■ **Weights & Measures** Grenada uses the imperial system.

GRENADA

and a depth of more than 100ft make it strictly for experienced divers only.

Molinière Point (see Sculptures of the Sea, p710), north of St George's, has some of the best snorkeling around Grenada, though land access is difficult. Most dive shops will take snorkelers along with divers to check out spots like Molinière Point.

Grenada has a number of other good snorkeling spots. They include Sandy Island (p715), off the northeast coast of Grenada Island, and, off the coast of Carriacou, White Island (p719) and (another) Sandy Island (p719).

As always it's best to dive with a company that knows what they are doing; there are good dive shops in Grande Anse (p711), True Blue Bay (p712), Lance Aux Épines (p713) and Hillsborough (p717). Dives cost around US$55 per dive.

## Hiking

Grenada's most popular hiking area is the Grand Etang rainforest, where trails wind through a forest of mahogany and ferns, leading to a crater lake, waterfalls and mountain ridges. For details on specific trails, see p714.

## BOOKS

There are few bookstores around the islands. Books can be found for loan or trade in some guesthouses, and many Grenadians are willing to share books from their homes.

A good book about geology, flora and fauna is *A Natural History of the Island of Grenada*, by John R Groome, a past president of the Grenada National Trust. *The Mermaid Wakes: Paintings of a Caribbean Isle* is a hardcover book featuring paintings by Carriacou artist Canute Calliste; the text, by Lora Berg, is about island life.

*Grenada 1983*, by Lee Russell, and *Urgent Fury: The Battle for Grenada*, by Mark Adkin, are detailed accounts of the events that surrounded US President Ronald Reagan's invasion of Grenada in 1983. While both books are rather pro-US, they shouldn't be dismissed as propaganda – they do show some of the complexities from both sides. *Revolution in Reverse*, by James Ferguson, presents a critical account of Grenada's development since the US invasion.

Lorna McDaniel's *The Big Drum Ritual of Carriacou: Praisesongs for Rememory of Flight* explores the Big Drum rituals, as practised in Carriacou, that call ancestors as part of an Afro-Caribbean religious experience. Performed since the early 1700s, it is the only ceremony of its type that has survived in the Caribbean.

*Grenada: A History of its People*, written by University of the West Indies senior lecturer Beverley Steele, follows the history of the island people from the early days of Arawak settlement to the present.

## BUSINESS HOURS

In general, businesses are open from Monday to Saturday from 9am to 5pm. Restaurants that are open for breakfast open at 8am, lunch is served from noon and dinner from 6pm. Closing time is often more a matter of when the last diners finish, but generally 10pm is a safe bet. Pubs and bars will stay open until 2am on the weekend. Few businesses or restaurants open on a Sunday. The exception is when they are located in a hotel, in which case they are usually open seven days a week.

## CHILDREN

While Grenada is not specifically a family destination, it has many areas where children can have some free range, such as Carriacou, Lance aux Épines and Morne Rouge. Keep your eye on the little ones around the roads in St George's as the traffic can be on the wild side, and also in some of the forts as the walls are tall and are without railings or barriers.

## DANGERS & ANNOYANCES

St George's is a busy little city, but for the most part is very safe. Regular precautions are recommended such as being careful at night and not being a target for opportunistic thieves. You will be asked time and time again on the beach if you want to buy jewelry, T-shirts and spices. Most of these peddlers are harmless and a simple 'No, thank you' sends them on their way.

## EMBASSIES & CONSULATES

**UK** ( ☎ 440-3536; 14 Church St, St George's)
**USA** ( ☎ 444-1173; Lance aux Épines)

## FESTIVALS & EVENTS

The **Grenada Board of Tourism** (www.grenadagrena dines.com) can provide all details on yearly festivals and events.

GRENADA

**Port Louis Sailing Festival** (January) This major sailing event features races, parties and races to parties.
**Carriacou Carnival** (usually early February)
**Grenada Triathlon** (May) Swim, bike and run your way to a good time. Teams and individuals compete for fun and prizes.
**Grenada Carnival** (second weekend in August) The big annual event. The celebration is spirited and includes calypso and steel-pan competitions, costumed revelers, pageants and a big, grand-finale jump-up on Tuesday.

## GAY & LESBIAN TRAVELERS

Attitudes to same-sex couples in Grenada (and the Caribbean generally) are not modern or tolerant. Gay and lesbian couples should be discreet in public to avoid hassles.

## HOLIDAYS

**New Year's Day** January 1
**Independence Day** February 7
**Good Friday** Late March/early April
**Easter Monday** Late March/early April
**Labour Day** May 1
**Whit Monday** Eighth Monday after Easter
**Corpus Christi** Ninth Thursday after Easter
**Emancipation Days** First Monday & Tuesday in August
**Thanksgiving Day** October 25
**Christmas Day** December 25
**Boxing Day** December 26

## INTERNET ACCESS

St George's has a growing number of internet cafés. Some hotels provide internet access and there are a few cafés on Carriacou. Rates runs from EC$6 to EC$12 per hour. Increasingly, wireless internet-access points are popping up around Grenada; many marinas' hotels and restaurants offer free wi-fi.

## INTERNET RESOURCES

**Grenada Explorer** (www.grenadaexplorer.com) This is an online tourist guide with a gluttony of helpful info.
**Grenada Hotel & Tourism Association** (www.grena dahotelsinfo.com) The Grenada Hotel & Tourism Association maintains this site from which you can book accommodations online.
**Grenada Tourism Information** (www.grenadagrena dines.com) This is the official site of the Grenada Board of Tourism, and features links to masses of excellent information.
**Grenada Visitor Forum** (www.grenadavisitorforum.com) This user-generated site is a good venue to converse with other travelers.

**Jason de Caires Taylor** (www.underwatersculpture.com) Have a look at the incredible underwater gallery off the west coast – without even getting wet.

## MAPS

Tourist maps are available from the tourism information centers and most hotels. More-detailed road maps are available at car-rental agencies and bookstores. Navel charts are available at the ports, bookstores and bulk-supply stores.

## MEDICAL SERVICES

There is a hospital in St George's and on the hill above Hillsborough on Carriacou. The emergency number for an ambulance is ☎ 911.

## MONEY

The official currency is the Eastern Caribbean dollar (EC$ or XCD). A growing number of 24-hour ATMs all over Grenada dispense Eastern Caribbean dollars. Most hotels, shops and restaurants will accept US dollars, but you'll get a better exchange rate by changing to Eastern Caribbean dollars at a bank and using local currency. Major credit cards are accepted by most hotels, top-end restaurants, dive shops and car-rental agencies. Be clear about whether prices are being quoted in Eastern Caribbean or US dollars, particularly with taxi drivers.

An 8% tax and 10% service charge is added to many hotel and restaurant bills. If no service charge is added at restaurants, a 10% tip is generally expected. Prices quoted in this chapter do not include the 18% tax and charge.

## POST

Grenada's main post office is in St George's, and there are smaller post offices in many villages and on Carriacou. Mail service is pretty slow and packages are expensive. Postcards to anywhere are reasonable, though.

## TELEPHONE

Grenada's area code is ☎ 473. When calling from within Grenada, you only need to dial the seven-digit local phone number. When calling from North America, dial ☎ 1-473 + the local number. From elsewhere, dial your country's international access code + ☎ 473 + the local number. We have included only the seven-digit local number for Grenada listings in this chapter.

Grenada has coin-operated and card phones. Coin phones take 25-cent coins (either EC or US) or EC$1 coins. Card phones accept the same Caribbean phone card used on other Eastern Caribbean islands; cards are sold at the airport and numerous shops. Americans can also use their US-based calling card or credit card to make long-distance calls – but it's best to check the rate before talking for too long.

## TOURIST INFORMATION

The **Grenada Board of Tourism** (www.grenadagrena dines.com; Grenada Island ☎ 440-2279; the Carenage, St George's; Carriacou ☎ 443-7948; Main St, Hillsborough) has offices on Grenada Island and Carriacou. There's also a tourist office booth at Point Salines International Airport, just before immigration, where you can pick up tourist brochures; the staff can also help you book a room.

## TOURS

The following tours are for Grenada Island; for information on taxi tours of Carriacou, see p717.

**Adventure Jeep Tours** ( ☎ 444-5337; www.adventure grenada.com) This reputable operator has full-day tours that take in all of the major sights.

**Henry's Safari Tours** ( ☎ 444-5313) Various treks into the interior are offered by this company, which specializes in hiking tours. Lunch and drinks are included. Try the five-hour tour that includes a hike to the Seven Sisters Falls.

**Kennedy Tours** ( ☎ 444-1074; www.kennedytours.com) Prides itself on having the best guides on the island. They run tours of every description and are flexible and friendly.

**Mandoo Tours** ( ☎ 440-1428; www.grenadatours .com) Offers full- and half-day tours of the island and can be tailored for historical or photographic interests. It has quality vehicles with air-conditioning.

**Spice Kayaking & Eco Tours** ( ☎ 439-4942; www.spice kayaking.com) Go for a paddle amongst the beaches, mangroves and bays. The tours will have you on the water for half the day, or from dawn till dusk if you prefer.

## VISAS

Visas are not required for Americans, Canadians, visitors from Commonwealth countries and most other countries. A passport is required, however, along with an onward ticket. Upon entry you will be issued a 30-day tourist visa that prohibits work. Visitors are allowed to stay for up to three months.

---

> ### EMERGENCY NUMBERS
>
> - **Ambulance** ☎ 911
> - **Fire** ☎ 911
> - **Police** ☎ 911

## WOMEN TRAVELERS

It's unusual for local women to travel alone at night, and as such, female travelers are likely to attract attention. However, taking care if you're out after dark is prudent for both sexes. Otherwise, women needn't expect too many hassles.

## WORK

Those wishing to work in Grenada need to obtain a work permit from the Ministry of Labour in St George's.

# TRANSPORTATION

## GETTING THERE & AWAY
### Entering Grenada

All visitors should present a valid passport and an onward ticket, or sufficient funds to support your stay.

### Air

**Point Salines International Airport** (GND; ☎ 444-4101, 444-4555; fax 444-4838) has car-rental offices, an ATM, wi-fi, pay phones and a restaurant. A tourist office booth is in the arrivals section before you reach immigration.

The following airlines fly to/from Grenada from within the Caribbean and further afield:

**Air Jamaica** ( ☎ 439 2093; www.airjamaica.com) New York

**American Eagle** ( ☎ 444-2222; www.aa.com) San Juan

**British Airways** ( ☎ 444-1221; www.ba.com) London

**LIAT** ( ☎ 440-5428; www.liatairline.com) Trinidad, Tobago, Barbados, St Vincent

**Virgin Atlantic** ( ☎ 439 7470; www.virgin-atlantic.com) London

Carriacou's Lauriston airport is a modest affair with a single ticket counter for all flights. **Prime Travel** ( ☎ 443-7362) has a desk at the airport and can help with ticket sales, car rentals and other travel essentials.

**SVG Air** ( ☎ 444-3549; www.svgair.com) has private air charters and scheduled flights to

GRENADA

724 TRANSPORTATION •• Getting Around

Grenada, St Vincent, Bequia, Canouan, Mustique, Union Island, Palm Island, Petit St Vincent, Martinique, Dominica, St Lucia and Barbados.

Sometimes, if all flights are fully booked, it is possible to organize a group and split the cost of a charter flight to/from Carriacou – contact Prime Travel for details.

## Sea

### CRUISE SHIP

Grenada is a port of call for numerous cruise ships. They dock at the purpose-built pier just north of the harbor in St George's, Grenada Island. For more information on cruises, see p830.

### FERRY

The **MV Jasper** is a boat service that runs between Carriacou and Union Island (EC$20, one hour) in St Vincent & the Grenadines. It departs from Union Island every Monday and Thursday at 7:30am for Carriacou. It returns at 12:30pm on the same days. For information on entry requirements, see p673.

You could also try hopping on one of the various commercial ships that haul goods back and forth between Union Island and Carriacou or Petit Martinique, Grenada, or pay a water taxi (EC$100 to EC$150) for the bumpy 40-minute ride.

### WATER TAXI

If the ferry schedule doesn't work into your plans or the thought of a bumpy, open-ocean crossing in a motorboat appeals, there is the water taxi option. It will cost you about US$75 for the 40-minute journey from Carriacou to Union island. Ask around at the waterfront for a suitable driver and be sure to trust your instincts when it comes to evaluating someone's seafaring skills.

### YACHT

Immigration (open 8am to 3:45pm Monday to Friday) can be cleared on Grenada Island at **Spice Island Marine Services** ( ☎ 444-4342) on Prickly Bay, or at **Grenada Yacht Services** ( ☎ 440-2508) in St George's. Most yachts anchor in St George's in the nearby lagoon. If for some reason you decide not to clear immigration at one of the marinas, you can get all of the necessary stamps at the police station in St George's.

On Carriacou, clearance can be made in Hillsborough.

Whether you're a salty sea dog or a life-jacket-toting land-lover **Horizon Yacht Charters** ( ☎ 439-1000; www.horizonyachtcharters.com; True Blue Bay Marina) will set you up with the boating holiday you're looking for. Seeing Grenada by sea really is the way to go and this crew can help you do it. You can arrange to have a crewed yacht, where all you have to do is sit back and enjoy the ride. Or you can get your hands dirty, swing it yarrr and hit the high seas as captain of your own private pirate ship.

**Moorings** ( ☎ 444-4439; www.moorings.com) bases its yacht-charter operation at Secret Harbour, and **Sea Breeze Yacht Charters** ( ☎ 444-4924) is at Spice Island Marine Services in Lance aux Épines.

The most frequented anchorages are along the southwest side of Grenada, including Prickly Bay, Mt Hartman Bay, Hog Island and True Blue Bay.

## GETTING AROUND
### Air

**SVG Air** ( ☎ 444-3549; www.svgair.com) has flights between Grenada Island and Carriacou.

### Boat

When it comes to seafaring travel in Grenada there are two schools of thought. You can either hitch a ride on a cargo ship that will be slow, not really fixed to any sort of schedule and cheap. Or you can hop onto The *Osprey* a high-speed catamaran that will leave right on time, be fast enough to blow you cap off and be relatively expensive. Both will get you where you want to go. It's just a decision about whether you are a 'snack bar and air-conditioning' sort of traveler or a 'sit on your luggage' one.

### CARGO/PASSENGER BOATS

Island hopping on cargo boats is an interesting and adventurous way to travel around the Caribbean. Predicting any sort of a schedule is near impossible, but that's half the fun. Boats change all the time, and time and date of departure are often more dependent on the cargo than the wishes of passengers. The best way to go about it is to head down to the dock and ask around and see what you can put together. On Grenada Island it's best to go to the large boats on the north side of the Carenage in St George's. On Carriacou they can be found at Hillsborough's town pier or sometimes in Tyrrel Bay. The fare on the larger boats is about EC$20 one way; buy your ticket on board.

## CATAMARAN
**Osprey** ( ☎ 440-8126; www.ospreylines.com) is the fastest and most reliable way to move amongst the islands of Grenada. The 144-seat motorized catamaran connects Grenada's three populated islands in less than two hours (per person one way/round-trip Grenada to Carriacou EC$80/160, Carriacou to Petit Martinique EC$30/60). Reservations are rarely required, except on holidays. Tickets are either purchased on board or from the office prior to departure. In St George's the *Osprey* departs from the east side of the Carenage.

The *Osprey* schedule:
**Carriacou to Grenada Island** Departs 6am and 3:30pm Monday to Saturday, and 3:30pm Sunday.
**Carriacou to Petit Martinique** Departs 10:30am Monday to Saturday, 7pm Monday to Thursday, 9.30am Sunday.
**Grenada Island to Carriacou and Petit Martinique** Departs 9am and 5:30pm Monday to Friday, 9am Saturday, and 8am and 5:30pm Sunday.
**Petit Martinique to Carriacou and Grenada Island** Departs 5:30am Tuesday to Friday, 3pm daily.

## YACHT
See opposite for information on charters.

## Bus
There are buses on both Grenada Island and Carriacou, and they are a great way to experience the local community. There'll be shoppers, school kids and commuters crammed into the van. The oftenoverflowing

seats rock back and forth to the tunes as the driver maniacally toots their horn at friends and potential passengers.

## Car & Motorcycle
### DRIVER'S LICENSE
To drive a vehicle you need to purchase a Grenadian driving license (US$12). You can get it from most car-rental companies, police stations or the **Traffic Department booth** ( ☎ 440-2267) at the fire station on the east side of the Carenage in St George's. Grenada's larger towns, including Grenville, Sauteurs and Victoria, have gas stations.

### RENTAL
There are many rental agencies on Grenada Island, and a few on Carriacou; see p707 and p717 for details.

### ROAD RULES
Driving is technically on the left-hand side of the road, but you can expect buses in particular to be going full bore wherever the hell they want to. The roads are very narrow and curvy and local drivers attack them with great speed. For safety, slow down when approaching blind curves and use your horn liberally. There are few road signs on the island, so a road map and a measure of caution are useful when driving.

## Taxi
You'll find taxis on Grenada Island; see p707 for sample fares. Some minibuses on Carriacou double as taxis (see p717 ).

# Trinidad & Tobago

It's Carnival in Port of Spain. Soca music throbs in the streets, and a woman furrows her brow, shaking and gyrating as the beads on her bikini seem close to flying off. She is Trinidad and Tobago. An East Indian couple serves pungent curried doubles at lightning speed on the street corner, fishermen plunk their catch on splintering docks as the new morning spreads over an azure ocean, an oil-industry businessman walks from crumbling streets into a modern air-conditioned building where he navigates the global economy for his nation, and a crazy-haired steel-pan player lays into an oil drum reaching a seventh-level of ecstasy – they are all Trinidad and Tobago.

National pride, a sordid history of slavery and indenture, and the love of music and limin' unite the myriad colors, ethnicities and cultures that make up the dual-island nation of Trinidad and Tobago. Dive in. Feel the rhythm of the islands and the people who love to see you dance. All the while, experience beaches so mesmerizing you'll forget your name, first-class diving through coral wonderlands, a Carnival to end all Carnivals, and luxuriant rainforests prime for bird-watching, hiking, and cycling.

But don't expect anyone to hold your hand. The oil and gas industry leaves tourism low down on the priority list. Upscale resorts and hotels are out there, and more so on Tobago, but generally you jump in the mix and accept the services that facilitate a sun-drenched ball, whether it be peaceful, sand-filled, rollicking, or all of the above.

## FAST FACTS

- **Area** 5128 sq km
- **Capital** Port of Spain, Trinidad
- **Country code** ☎ 868
- **Departure tax** TT$100
- **Famous for** Carnival, calypso, soca, steel-pan music
- **Language** English, Hindi, Creole, Spanish
- **Money** Trinidad and Tobago dollar (TT$); TT$10 = US$1.60 = €1.03 = UK£0.29
- **Official name** Republic of Trinidad and Tobago, West Indies
- **Phrase** You limin' tonight? (Are you hanging out tonight?)
- **People** Trinidadian or Tobagonian (formal); Trini, Bago'mon or Trinbagonian (colloquial)
- **Population** 1.3 million
- **Visa** Not necessary for US, UK, Canadian and most EU citizens; others see p773

## HIGHLIGHTS

- **Port of Spain's Carnival** (p738) Wine and grine in Trinidad's bustling big city, which grooves to a permanent beat during the world's hottest Carnival
- **Bird-Watching** (p747) Spot hundreds of Trinidad's bird species at Asa Wright Nature Centre, or the scarlet ibis at Caroni Bird Sanctuary and sea birds galore on Little Tobago
- **Diving** (p758) Explore underwater canyons and shallow coral gardens in Tobago's crystal-clear waters
- **Northern Range** (p747) Hike or cycle in Trinidad's coastal mountain range, which boasts waterfalls, wildlife and ruggedly gorgeous coastline
- **Music** (p744) Savor the islands' music – whether it's soca, calypso, steel pan, or parang, it is inextricably woven into this culture that sings on the sidewalk

## ITINERARIES

- **Limin'** On Friday night, hit the St James nightlife in Port of Spain, then dance at Zen. On Saturday eat shark and bake on Maracas Bay and chill out on the beach till the DJ comes out at night. Take the ferry to Tobago on Sunday and stay in Buccoo, just in time for Sunday School. Hole up for the rest of the week in a guesthouse in Charlotteville, eating yummy local food, drinking Carib and taking in the rays on Pirate's Bay.
- **Outdoor Adventure** Mountain bike around rainforest-enveloped military relics in Chaguaramas, Trinidad. See the Nariva Swamp by kayak. Base in Grande Rivière for day hiking, turtle-watching and surfing. Cycle Toco to Matelot. In Brasso Seco, begin your two- to three-day coastal rainforest backpack to Blanchisseuse. In Tobago, explore the Forest Reserve. On Pigeon Point, learn to windsurf. Mountain bike to Highland Falls. Then, in Charlottesville, spend several days trmping in the 'bush' and sea kayaking.

## CLIMATE & WHEN TO GO

Because of Trinidad's southerly location, temperatures are equable year-round. Its average daily temperature is 27°C (80°F). For temperatures in Port of Spain, see the climate chart on p821. Average humidity hovers around 75%.

The only real seasons in Trinidad and Tobago are the rainy season (June to November) and the dry season (December to May). The high season is January to March, with a noticeable peak in February when Carnival draws hordes of visitors and the cost of hotel rooms skyrockets. Booking ahead is essential at this time.

Accommodations are cheaper and crowds almost nonexistent in the shoulder seasons – October to December and April to June – though you should do a little dance to ingratiate the rain lords.

Sitting outside the hurricane belt, the islands generally don't experience the severe storms like northerly islands.

## HISTORY
### Early History

Caribs and Arawaks lived alone on Trinidad until 1498, when Columbus arrived and christened the island La Isla de la Trinidad, for the Holy Trinity.

The Spanish who followed in Columbus' wake enslaved many of Trinidad's Native American inhabitants, stealing them to toil in the new South American colonies. Gold-hungry Spain gave only scant attention to Trinidad's land, which lacked precious minerals. Finally in 1592, the Spanish established their first settlement, San Josef, just east of present-day Port of Spain. Over the next two centuries the Spanish and French imported slaves from West Africa to cultivate tobacco and cacao plantations.

British forces took the island from the Spanish in 1797. With the abolishment of slavery in 1834, slaves abandoned plantations; this prompted the British to import thousands of indentured workers, mostly from India, to work in the cane fields and service the colony. The indentured labor system remained in place for over 100 years.

Tobago's early history is a separate story. Also sighted by Columbus and claimed by Spain, Tobago wasn't colonized until 1628, when Charles I of England decided to charter the island to the Earl of Pembroke. In response, a handful of nations took an immediate interest in colonizing Tobago.

During the 17th century Tobago changed hands numerous times as the English, French, Dutch and even Courlanders (present-day Latvians) wrestled for control. In 1704 it was declared a neutral territory, which left room for pirates to use the island as a base for raiding ships in the Caribbean. The British established a colonial administration in 1763, and within two decades slave labor established the island's sugar, cotton and indigo plantations.

Tobago's plantation economy wilted after the abolition of slavery but sugar and rum production continued until 1884, when the London firm that controlled finances for the island's plantations went bankrupt. Plantation owners quickly sold or abandoned their land, leaving the economy in a shambles.

## A Free Colony

In 1889 Tobago joined Trinidad as a British Crown Colony. Even though Trinidad and Tobago's demand for greater autonomy grew and anticolonial sentiment ripened, the British didn't pay attention until 1956, when the People's National Movement (PNM), led by Oxford-educated Dr Eric Williams, took measures to institute self-government. The country became a republic of the Commonwealth in 1976.

### HOW MUCH?

- **Maxi taxi** TT$3 to TT$5
- **Diving certification** US$375
- **Beach-chair rental** TT$20
- **Bottle of Carib** TT$9
- **Roti** TT$12 to TT$20

Frustration with the leftover colonial structure led to the 'Black Power' movement, which created a political crisis and an army mutiny, but ultimately strengthened national identity. Bankrupt and without prospects, the country's luck changed in 1970 with the discovery of oil, which brought instant wealth and prosperity. During the 1980s, when oil prices plummeted, a recession hit and political unrest ensued. Accusations of corruption and complaints from an underrepresented East Indian community led to the PNM's defeat in 1986 by the National Alliance for Reconstruction (NAR).

Corruption blossomed in a judicial system congested with drugs-related trials (the country is a stopover in the South American drug trade). In July 1990, members of a minority Muslim group attempted a coup, stormed parliament, and took 45 hostages, including Prime Minister ANR Robinson. Though the coup failed, it undermined the government, and the PNM returned to power.

Vast petroleum and natural gas reserves discovered in the late 1990s helped stabilize the economy. In 1995 Basdeo Panday of the United National Congress (UNC) beat the PNM's Patrick Manning in a controversial election, seating the first prime minister of Indian descent. A stalemated political process led Manning again to win the 2002 and 2007 elections for prime minister. The prime minister is the head of government, while the president (George Maxwell Richards) is the head of state.

Today, political parties are largely divided along ethnic lines, with the PNM being the predominant party of Afro-Trinidadians and the UNC representing the East Indian community. Local government is divided into three municipalities, eight counties and the island of Tobago. Tobago has its own legislative assembly and since 1987 has exercised an internal self-government to protect its interests.

## THE CULTURE

Trinidadians and Tobagonians love to party and take every opportunity to shamelessly sing, dance and lime (hang out) whenever the whim hits. Official and unofficial celebrations are plentiful with lots of great food and rum. Most revolve around calypso (a popular Caribbean music developed from slave songs), its offspring soca (faster and very danceable) or steel pan (music produced on oil drums), great food, and large amounts of rum. Like other Caribbean destinations, the pace is slow. Though their energy is bountiful, Trinis see rushing and stress as entirely unnecessary. Residents laugh easily and often, taking time to visit with one another and discuss everything from politics to the lyrics of the new soca tune dominating the airwaves.

Prime Minister Patrick Manning's plan to reach 'developed country' status by the year 2020 is an ambitious agenda, calling for dramatic reform of everything from education and employment to health care and poverty-reduction. Vision 2020's mission statement says:

> By the year 2020, Trinidad and Tobago will be a united, resilient, productive, innovative and prosperous nation with a disciplined, caring, fun-loving society comprising healthy, happy and well-educated people…

It's a tall order. Over the past decade, Trinidad and Tobago has grown steadily every year, thanks especially to foreign investment and the oil and gas industry. But Vision 2020 demands more than economic growth and requires a total shift in mindset. It sounds idyllic in the prime minister's speeches, and many locals support the plan. However, others think it's an overzealous program that will entice foreign investment but ultimately deepen economic disparity. As politicians shake hands with CEOs over cocktails and garlic shrimp, 21% of Trinbagonians remain in poverty. Manning was re-elected in 2007, yet many people are unsatisfied with the progress of the administration, especially local environmentalists who have seen little change accompanying the prolific promises.

While business in the energy sector is booming, Trinidad and Tobago's government grapples with standard of living. Twenty-one percent of folks live in poverty, and many people live without easy access to potable water, adequate housing or quality health care. Working with the UN Development Programme (UNDP), the government aims to halve poverty by 2015. There are government programs in place that pay the unemployed to do half-days of manual labor. You'll see young people loafing about in reflective gear doing 'road work.' Some say this 'easy money' isn't helping the real problem and is even making it worse by keeping people slouched against government funding.

The average home in Trinidad and Tobago is a friendly place where stew is a-simmer and vibrant conversation fills the air. Traditional roles still dominate. Women cook, clean and take care of the kids. The inequality between women and men remains depressingly Stone Age. While women generally receive a higher level of education and fill about half the professional and management jobs, they earn about 50% less than men in equitable roles. In 2002, for example, professional women earned an average annual income of about US$5500, while men at the same professional level earned US$12,400.

Many men think it's natural for a man to 'stray' from a committed relationship, but they'd think it an unforgivable sin if a woman were to do the same. Things are slowly changing, however, as sassy Trinbagonian women gain more vital roles in government and demand better standards of treatment.

Of the country's 1.3 million inhabitants, just 54,000 live on Tobago. Trinidad has one of the most ethnically diverse populations in the Caribbean, a legacy of its checkered colonial history. The majority is of East Indian (40.3%) and African (39.5%) descent. The remaining 20% of islanders are of mixed ancestry, but there are also notable minorities of European, Chinese, Syrian and Lebanese people. In addition, a community of a few hundred native Caribs lives in the Arima area.

Roughly a third of all islanders are Roman Catholic. Another 25% are Hindu, 11% are Anglican, 13% are other Protestant denominations and 6% are Muslim. Traditional African beliefs also remain strong in some areas, as does Rastafarianism.

## SPORTS
### Cricket
Introduced by the British in the 19th century, cricket isn't just a sport in Trinidad and Tobago, it's a cultural obsession. It's a necessity, like oxygen or rum. International cricket star Brian Lara – the 'Prince of Port of Spain' – hails from Trinidad and his popularity ranks up there with Jesus. When the West Indies team sweeps in for a test match, everything grinds to a halt as people stick to their TVs to capture the action.

The main venue is the Queen's Park Oval, home to the **Queen's Park Cricket Club** ( ☎ 622-4325; www.qpcc.com; 94 Tragarete Rd), a few blocks west of the Queen's Park Savannah in Port of Spain. The Oval, originally built in 1896, is the site of both regional and international matches and is one of eight Caribbean venues that hosted the 2007 ICC Cricket World Cup, holding 25,000 spectators and having the northern hills as a spectacular backdrop. Call the cricket club for ticket information.

## Soccer

Referred to as football in this British-influenced country, soccer is second only to cricket in the minds of spectators who cheer endlessly for the national team, the **Soca Warriors** (www.socawarriors.net). The team plays at the **Arima Municipal Stadium** ( ☎ 667-3508) in Arima and **Ato Boldon Stadium** ( ☎ 623-0304), a 30-minute drive south of Port of Spain in Couva. For information, contact **Trinidad & Tobago Football Federation** ( ☎ 623-7312; www.ttffonline.com/cms).

## Cycling

Velodromes in Queen's Oval Port of Spain, Arima, and Skinner Park in San Fernando host cycling meets and sponsor road races. Tobago hosts two major cycling events: the Tobago Cycling Classic and the Beacon Cycling Series. For information on cycling events contact the **Trinidad & Tobago Cycling Federation** ( ☎ 624-0384). Also see the boxed texts, p749 and p764.

## ARTS
## Literature

Trinidad boasts a number of acclaimed writers, among them Samuel Selvon, Michael Antony, Earl Lovelace and CLR James. St Lucian native Derek Walcott, the 1992 Nobel Prize winner in literature, has lived on Trinidad for much of his adult life.

Trinidad's foremost literary figure is Vidiadhar Surajprasad (VS) Naipaul. Both praised for his artistic merit and harshly criticized for his unflattering portrayal of postcolonial societies, he has been coolly received in his native Trinidad, a country he has not inhabited for many years. VS' *A House for Mr Biswas* creates a vivid portrait of East Indian life on Trinidad. *Fireflies* and *Beyond the Dragon's Mouth* by Shiva Naipaul, VS Naipaul's younger brother, also adeptly depict Indian family life on Trinidad.

## Music

Stop for a moment on the streets of Trinidad and Tobago and listen. You'll likely hear the fast beat of soca playing on a maxi-taxi radio, or kids drumming on metal garbage cans, or a woman singing while walking home. Often festive, sometimes political or melancholy, music digs down deep to the core truth and emotion of island life.

Although Carnival happens in February, there's always plenty of great live music, especially in the months leading up to Carnival. Every day, music brings people together, regardless of age or race. In bars and outdoor venues, it's common to see young kids, teenagers and grandparents partying together.

### CALYPSO

A medium for political and social satire, calypso hearkens back to the days when slaves – unable to chat when working – would sing in patois, sharing gossip and news while mocking their colonial masters. Mighty Sparrow, long acknowledged the king of calypso, has voiced popular concerns and social consciousness since the 1950s. Another famous calypsonian, David Rudder, helped revive the musical form in the mid-1980s by adding experimental rhythms, unearthing both the cultural importance and flexibility of calypso. Lord Kitchener (1922–2000) was an incredibly popular nationally and internationally famous calypsonian.

### SOCA

The energetic offspring of calypso, soca was born in the 1970s, and uses the same basic beat but speeds things up, creating danceable rhythms with risqué lyrics, pointed social commentary and verbal wordplay. Soca dominates the nightclub scene and rules the airwaves.

### STEEL PAN (STEEL BAND)

Rhythm and percussion are the beating heart behind Carnival. Traditionally, percussionists banged together bamboo cut in various lengths, or simply drummed on whatever they could – the road, sides of buildings, their knees. When African drums were banned during WWII, drummers turned to biscuit tins, then oil drums discarded by US troops. Today, drums come in a variety of sizes, each producing a unique note. Heard together, they become a cascading waterfall of sound. During Carnival, some bands are transported on flatbed trucks along the parade route. All bands aim to win Panorama, the national competition that runs throughout Carnival season.

### PARANG
Heard mostly at Christmas time, parang originated in Venezuela. Lyrics are sung in Spanish and accompanied by guitars and maracas. At first heard only in rural areas inhabited by Hispanic Trinis, parang has evolved into a nationwide phenomenon. At Christmastime, groups of parang carolers wander through neighborhoods, and appreciative audiences serve them food and booze.

### CHUTNEY
This up-tempo, rhythmic music is accompanied by the *dholak* (Northern India folk drum) and the *dhantal* (a metal rod played with a metal striker). Chutney songs celebrate social situations – everything from women witnessing a birth to men partying at a bar. It's a fusion of classical Hindu music with more contemporary sounds.

## ENVIRONMENT
### The Land
Geographically, boot-shaped Trinidad was once part of the South American mainland. Over time a channel developed, separating Trinidad from present-day Venezuela. The connection to South America is noticeable in Trinidad's Northern Range, a continuation of the Andes, and in its abundant oil and gas reserves, concentrated in southwestern Trinidad.

The Northern Range spreads east to west, forming a scenic backdrop to Port of Spain. The rest of the island is given to plains, undulating hills and mangrove swamps. Trinidad's numerous rivers include the 50km Ortoire River, and the 40km Caroni River dumping into the Caroni Swamp.

Tobago, 19km northeast of Trinidad, has a central mountain range that reaches almost 610m at its highest point. Deep, fertile valleys run from the ridge down toward the coast, which is niched with bays and beaches.

### Wildlife
Because of its proximity to the South American continent, Trinidad and Tobago has the widest variety of plant and wildlife in the Caribbean: 430 species of bird, 600 species of butterfly, 70 kinds of reptiles and 100 types of mammals, including red howler monkeys, anteaters, agouti and armadillos.

Plant life is equally diverse, with more than 700 orchid species and 1600 other types of flowering plants. Both islands have luxuriant rainforests, and Trinidad also features elfin forests, savannas and both freshwater and brackish mangrove swamps.

### Environmental Issues
Water pollution is a huge environmental concern on Trinidad and Tobago. Agricultural chemicals, industrial waste and raw sewage seep into groundwater and eventually the ocean. Reef damage is due mostly to pollution, as well as overuse.

Tourism strains the water supply, especially in Tobago, where resorts are plentiful and the freshwater supply limited. Be sure to conserve water. On Tobago, a resort filled with people taking extra-long showers can truly affect the freshwater supply.

Unsustainable development is rampant in this eco-destination. Deforestation and soil erosion are direct results. Sand erosion is a special concern on the northeast coast of Trinidad, where leatherback turtles lay eggs.

In Tobago, the health department 'fogs' mosquitoes with Malathion, which has serious negative impacts on other insects, snails, worms, crustaceans, fish, birds, toads and frogs, and reduces soil fertility. Get out of town for a while if they start to fog.

**Environmental Management Authority** ( ☎ 628-8042; www.ema.co.tt) is charged with monitoring environmental issues but, as in other developing countries, the pressure of 'progress' trumps preservation. **Environment Tobago** (www.sccoft.de/et) is an informative source about issues facing the island.

## FOOD & DRINK
Trinidad and Tobago's food is a lovely fusion of Indian, Creole, Chinese and African. East Indian–influenced roti (curried meat or vegetables rolled up in flatbread) and buss up shut (like roti but the 'bust up shirt' is the flatbread used to scoop up the goodies) are hallmark lunches. 'Doubles,' a similar fast food, is curried chickpeas wrapped in mini-flatbreads. Another popular fast food is 'shark and bake,' a slab of fresh grilled or fried shark served in deep-fried bread – Maracas Bay is famous for it. Curried meats

and seafood are common, as is pelau (rice mixed with peas, meat and coconut). Coo coo and callaloo (okra-speckled polenta and coconut-infused greens) are sumptuous staples. Fried ripe plantains are a sinful favorite.

You'll find Creole and Chinese restaurants everywhere, and in the cities and bigger hotels you'll find more extensive international fare. East Indian and Seventh Day Adventists populations make vegetarian options prevalent. Soy milk is in most grocery stores.

A favorite of locals is KFC, with more locations per capita than anywhere in the world.

Tap water is safe to drink, when not drinking the Caribbean's premium beer, Carib, which hails from Trinidad. Another local beer, Stag, is promoted as 'a man's beer' for the slightly higher alcohol level.

The islands produce various rums. Though most touted are Royal Oak and Black Label, Puncheon is very popular and will knock you on your butt. Locally produced Hard Wine has a naughty infusion of herbs known to enhance virility. A variety of sweetened fresh-fruit juices are popular, such as sugar-cane and citrus juices, as well as a drink called *mauby* (made from the bark of the rhamnaceous tree, sweetened with sugar and spices) and milkshakes made with sea moss.

# TRINIDAD

Put the tourists of Trinidad in a room and you'll have an awkward party: on one side will be wallflower bird-watchers tangled in camera and binocular straps and on the other, the side with the bar, you'll have the party-hound Carnival fans turning up the music and tying their ties around their foreheads.

However, here's the secret: there's much more to Trinidad unseen through binoculars or beer goggles. Of course, the swamps and forests are a bird-watcher's dream, and Port of Spain's Carnival will blow your mind. Yet Trinidad is also laden with verdant hiking and biking trails that wind you to gushing waterfalls and deserted bays. The rural, untouristed northeast coast harbors rugged beaches of shocking beauty and a true taste of Trini life. In the southwest, you can particularly see how East Indian culture has fused with the other ethnicities of this island. Earthy curry fills the air and flamboyant temples come out of nowhere.

Trinidad tends to treat tourists in a blasé manner, sometimes like swatting a fly away and sometimes with an annoyed gesticulation to come closer, come closer. After all, the booming oil and gas industry is the real bread and butter. And maybe to you that's a boon. Genuine adventure, unfluffed by a traditional tourist industry, awaits you in Trinidad if you choose to accept.

## Orientation

Virtually the shape of a molar tooth sitting on its side, Trinidad is surrounded by four bodies of water – the Caribbean (north), Atlantic Ocean (east), Gulf of Paria (west) and the Columbus Channel (south) – making each coast a little different. Port of Spain, the country's bustling capital, sits along a wide bay on the Gulf, and most of the country's better-known attractions are within an hour's drive of the city. Driving, you could get from one side of the country to the other in less than three hours, maybe less if you're a pro at bumpy, winding roads.

West of the capital, a peninsula pointing toward Venezuela leads to Chaguaramas, one of the Caribbean's chief yachting centers. North of Port of Spain, the Saddle Rd becomes the North Coast Rd leading to popular north-coast beaches. East of Port of Spain is Piarco International Airport, and the key northern towns of Arima and Sangre Grande. Along the desolate east coast lie endless palm-fringed beaches. To the northeast is the remote Northern Range and the turtle-nesting areas of Grande Rivière and Matura. To the south of Port of Spain are Chaguanas – the heart of East Indian Trinidad – and San Fernando – the industrial center of the country.

## Getting There & Away
### AIR
Trinidad's only airport, **Piarco International Airport** (POS; ☎ 669-4868), is 25km east of Port of Spain. There's a tourist office, car-rental booths, ATMs and eateries near the ticketing area. There's also luggage storage (TT$15 per piece of luggage per day). A currency exchange office inside the terminal is open 6am to 10pm. For details of flights to and from Trinidad, see p774 and p774.

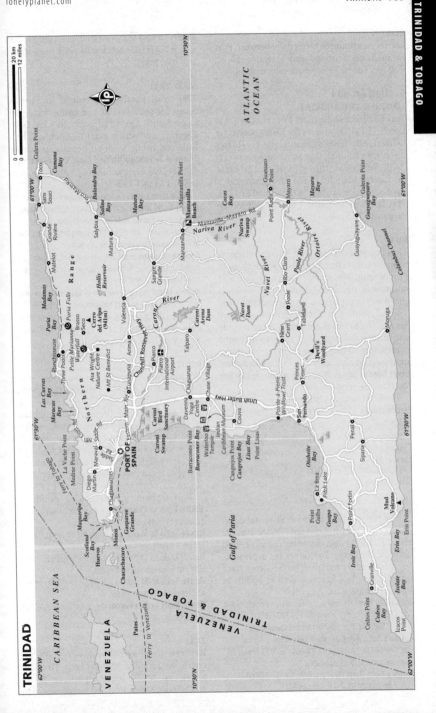

# TRINIDAD

20 km
12 miles

0
0

ATLANTIC
OCEAN

CARIBBEAN SEA

VENEZUELA

VENEZUELA

TRINIDAD & TOBAGO

Ferry to Tobago
Ferry to Venezuela

Patos

Galera Point
Toco
Cumana Bay
Sans Souci
Grande Riviere
Matelot
Madamas Bay
Paria Bay
Blanchisseuse
Three Pools
Las Cuevas
Maracas Bay
La Vache Point
Medine Point
Diego Martin
Maraval
Saddle Rd
Eastern Main Rd
PORT OF SPAIN
Chaguaramas
Scotland Bay
Maqueripe Bay
Huevos
Monos
Gasparee Grande
Chacachacare

Northern Range

Balandra Bay
Toco Main Rd
Saline Bay
Salybia
Matura Bay
Matura
Hollis Reservoir
Paria Falls
Petite Marianne Waterfall
Brasso Seco
Cerro del Aripo (941m)
Arima
Asa Wright Nature Centre
Mt St Benedict
Tunapuna
Piarco
Piarco International Airport
St Joseph
Churchill Roosevelt Hwy
Valencia
Caroni River
Sangre Grande
Nariva River
Manzanilla
Manzanilla-Mayaro Rd
Nariva Swamp
Cocos Bay
Manzanilla Beach
Manzanilla Point
Matura Bay

Guanaro Point
Mayaro Bay
Galeota Point
Mayaro
Point Radix
Río Claro
Poole River
Poole
Guayaguayare Bay
Guayaguayare
Columbus Channel

Navet River
Navet Dam
Ortoire River
Caroni Arena Dam
Talparo
Daverne
Yoga Centre
Chaguanas
Chase Village
Indian Caribbean Museum
Waterloo Temple
Couva
Barrancones Point
Barrancones Bay
Cangrejos Point
Cangrejos Bay
Lisas Bay
Point Lisas

Caroni Bird Sanctuary
Caroni Swamp

Gulf of Paria

New Grant
Princes Town
Pointe-à-Pierre Wildfowl Trust
San Fernando
Devil's Woodyard
Tableland
Moruga

Penal
Siparia
Mud Volcano
Erin Point
Erin Bay
Icacos Point

Otaheite Bay
Oropouche Bay
Point Fortin
Point Galba
Guapo Bay
La Brea
Pitch Lake

Irois Bay
Cedros Point
Cedros Bay
Granville
Isolate Bay

Uriah Butler Hwy

## BOAT

Ferries run multiple times daily between Port of Spain on Trinidad and Scarborough on Tobago. See p775 for more information.

## Getting Around
### TO/FROM THE AIRPORT

Taxi fare from the airport to Port of Spain is US$25 (TT$150), and it's the easiest way to get to town. Alternatively, during the day (better if you aren't alone), take an Arouca route taxi (to the left outside the terminal) and get off at the Eastern Main Rd (TT$4); from here, catch a red-striped maxi-taxi to the capital (TT$5). Taxi fare to Maraval is TT$180, and to San Fernando TT$250.

## BUS

Most buses traveling around Trinidad originate from the City Gate terminal on South Quay in Port of Spain. Bus service tends to be slow and notoriously unreliable. However, buses are a cheap way to get around if you're not in a rush. The red, white and black Express Commuter Service (ECS) buses are faster, more reliable and air-conditioned. They are geared toward commuters, so they run most frequently in the morning and afternoon. Check the **information/ticket booth** ( ☎ 623-7872; www.ptsc.co.tt; ⏰ 8am-8pm Mon-Fri) at the terminal for schedules.

Buses from City Gate terminal:

| Destination | Fare | Duration |
|---|---|---|
| Blanchisseuse | TT$8 | 2hr |
| Chaguanas | TT$4 | 1 hr |
| Chaguaramas | TT$2 | 1hr |
| Maracas Bay | TT$4 | 1hr |
| San Fernando | TT$6 | 1½hr |
| Sangre Grande | TT$6 | 1hr |

## CAR

A number of small, reliable car-rental companies operate on Trinidad. Prices average about TT$300 a day, including insurance and unlimited mileage. Discounts are usually offered for weekly rentals. The following have offices in Port of Spain, as well as booths at Piarco International Airport:

**Econo-Car Rentals** (www.trinidad.net/econocar; Airport ( ☎ 669-2342); Port of Spain ( ☎ 622-8074; 191-193 Western Main Rd) Has reliable cars and cheap rates.

**Kalloo's Auto Rentals** (www.kalloos.com; Airport ( ☎ 669-5673); Port of Spain ( ☎ 669-4868; 31 French St) Also runs a taxi service (opposite).

**Singh's Auto Rentals** Airport ( ☎ 669-5417); Port of Spain ( ☎ 623-0150; 7-9 Wrightson Rd)

**Thrifty** ( ☎ 669-0602; www.thrifty.com) Doesn't have an office in Port of Spain, but can make pickup arrangements beyond the airport.

## MAXI-TAXI

The main maxi-taxi terminal in Port of Spain for southbound and eastbound buses is on South Quay, adjacent to City Gate. Figuring out which maxi to catch can be a little confusing, so don't hesitate to call the **Trinidad & Tobago Unified Maxi Taxi Association** ( ☎ 624-3505). Depending on distance, maxis cost TT$2 to TT$5.

The maxi-taxi color-coding system:

**Green-band maxis** Serve areas south of Port of Spain, including Chaguanas and San Fernando (from San Fernando, maxi-taxis connecting to outlying areas have black or brown stripes), leaving from City Gate.

**Red-band maxis** Serve areas east of Port of Spain, including Laventille, Arima and Sangre Grande, leaving from South Quay, near City Gate.

**Yellow-band maxis** Serve Port of Spain's western and northern suburbs. Maxis to Chaguaramas via St James leave from the corner of South Quay and St Vincent St; maxis traveling to Blanchisseuse via Maraval leave from the corner of Prince and George Sts.

## ROUTE TAXI

Within Port of Spain, the route taxi is the predominant mode of public transportation. Outside the city center, route taxis can be hailed along the route. Official taxis have an 'H' ('hired') on their license plate. Occasionally, drivers of private vehicles (with 'P' on the license plate) also offer route-taxi service, though it's best to be familiar with the driver or know they're legit before hopping in. Route taxis cost between TT$2 to TT$5.

Port of Spain route taxi pickup points:

**Route Taxis to Chaguanas** Corner South Quay and Charlotte St (east side).

**Route Taxis to Maraval** (circling the Savannah) On the corner of Oxford and Charlotte Sts.

**Route Taxis to St Ann's** (circling the Savannah) Corner Hart and Frederick Sts (south side).

**Route Taxis to St James** (via Tragarete Rd) Corner Hart and Frederick Sts (north side).

**Route Taxis to San Fernando** Corner South Quay and St Vincent St.

## TAXI

Between 10pm and 6am there's a 50% surcharge on Trinidad's regular taxis. To call for a taxi, dial ☎ 669-1689 (airport), or ☎ 625-3032 (Independence Sq taxi stand), one of the

> ### QUICK REFERENCE: ESSENTIAL TNT TERMS
>
> **chip** – to rhythmically shuffle following soca trucks during Carnival
>
> **doubles** – two pieces of flatbread folded over curried garbanzo beans (channa); hot dogs are to NYC street food as doubles are to TnT
>
> **grine** – to wine in close proximity and in synch with someone else
>
> **jump up** – to dance enthusiastically
>
> **la blash** – a good time on the beach
>
> **lash out** – to party hard
>
> **lime** – to hang out, party or be unproductive
>
> **no problem** – commonly used phrase that could be the country motto
>
> **roti** – large soft flatbread wrapping a curried meat or vegetable middle
>
> **wine** – to roll your hips to the beat of soca

numerous stands in Independence Sq in Port of Spain. There's also a useful taxi stand near Queen's Park Savannah.

**Kalloo's Taxi Service** ( ☎ 622-9073; 31 French St; ⌚ 24hr) has an office less than a block north of Ariapita Ave and is convenient after an evening of limin'. It also offers guides-for-hire services that will take you anywhere on the island (TT$900 per day) and car rentals (from TT$300 per day).

You can arrange island tours with individual taxi drivers. For an all-day tour, drivers will generally ask about TT$400 to TT$700.

## PORT OF SPAIN
**pop 50,500**

'Leave as fast as possible,' many will advise about Port of Spain. One can understand why. This frantic metropolitan hub is bursting at the seams. The oil and gas business is booming and skyscrapers are being flung up everywhere. Materials and labor are being imported. As could be surmised, the traffic is horrendous, and public transportation is nonsensical improvisation. With all this going on, tourist infrastructure remains on the sidelines waving a wilting flag.

That being said, Port of Spain can grow on you. Its hot concrete streets and buildings simmer a melting pot of cultures like Indian, African, Chinese and Venezuelan. It's loud. People can be cheerful and crass, giving all sorts of attitude but afterwards quickly warming up to you. They unexpectedly break into song.

The downtown bustles with street vendors flanking the modern buildings and mall arcades. Ariapita Ave is hip, like a kiss on each cheek. St James is happening, like a low five. Laventille flips you the bird.

During Carnival season, it would be hard not to fall in love with this gritty mess of a city. Fetes rock all corners, steel-pan music fills the air around panyards, mas camps (see boxed text, p738) are hard at work on their costumes, and come Carnival Saturday through Carnival Tuesday, this city will school you on the most comprehensive partying in the world.

### Orientation

Port of Spain lies about 25km northwest of Piarco International Airport. Downtown is an area about 140 square blocks between Park St on the north side, Wrightson Rd to the west, St Ann's River to the east and the Gulf of Paria to the south. The 'center' of town is along Independence Sq, not really a square but two one-way streets running along a narrow pedestrian strip. Here you can pick up a route taxi and find travel agents, banks and cheap food. The south end of Frederick St is the central shopping area.

North of downtown, Queen's Park Savannah pulsates with cricket matches and cultural events, circumnavigated by the 3.7km Circular Rd. The northern neighborhoods of St Ann's, Cascade and Maraval are more relaxed. West of downtown, the lively areas of Woodbrook (where you'll find Ariapita Ave, which is famous for its restaurants) and St James, which has the most animated nightlife. East of downtown and St Ann's River is the Central Market. Further east are the poorer neighborhoods of Laventille (the birthplace of pan music) and Barataria.

### Information
#### BOOKSTORES
**Metropolitan Book Suppliers** ( ☎ 623-3462; 13 Frederick St; ⌚ 9am-5:30pm Mon-Thu, 8:30am-5:30pm

# PORT OF SPAIN

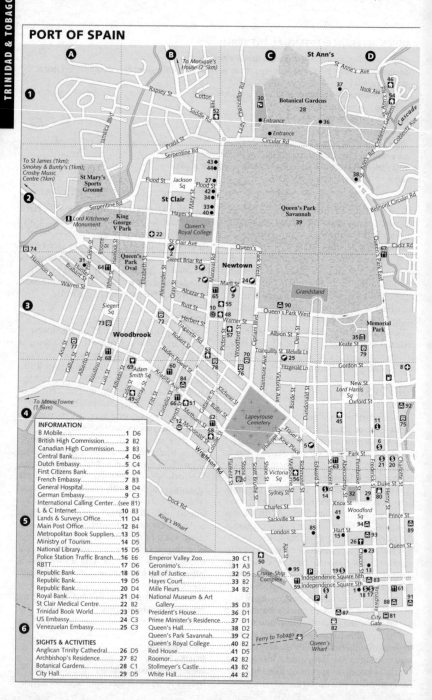

INFORMATION
B Mobile..................................1 D6
British High Commission..........2 B2
Canadian High Commission....3 B3
Central Bank...........................4 D6
Dutch Embassy.......................5 C4
First Citizens Bank..................6 D4
French Embassy.......................7 B3
General Hospital.....................8 D4
German Embassy.....................9 C3
International Calling Center...(see 81)
L & C Internet........................10 B3
Lands & Surveys Office..........11 D4
Main Post Office.....................12 B4
Metropolitan Book Suppliers...13 D5
Ministry of Tourism................14 D5
National Library......................15 D5
Police Station Traffic Branch...16 E6
RBTT......................................17 D6
Republic Bank........................18 D6
Republic Bank........................19 D5
Republic Bank........................20 D4
Royal Bank.............................21 D4
St Clair Medical Centre...........22 B2
Trinidad Book World...............23 D5
US Embassy............................24 C3
Venezuelan Embassy...............25 C3

SIGHTS & ACTIVITIES
Anglican Trinity Cathedral......26 D5
Archbishop's Residence...........27 B2
Botanical Gardens...................28 C1
City Hall.................................29 D5

Emperor Valley Zoo................30 C1
Geronimo's.............................31 A3
Hall of Justice.........................32 D5
Hayes Court............................33 B2
Mille Fleurs.............................34 B2
National Museum & Art
 Gallery.................................35 D3
President's House....................36 D1
Prime Minister's Residence.....37 D1
Queen's Hall...........................38 D2
Queen's Park Savannah...........39 C2
Queen's Royal College............40 B2
Red House..............................41 D5
Roomor..................................42 B2
Stollmeyer's Castle..................43 B2
White Hall..............................44 B2

**SLEEPING** 🛏️
| | |
|---|---|
| Abercromby Inn | 45 D4 |
| Alicia's House | 46 D1 |
| Coblentz Inn | 47 E1 |
| Forty Winks Inn | 48 C3 |
| Gingerbread House | 49 B4 |
| Hyatt Regency | 50 C5 |
| Inn a Citi | 51 B4 |
| Kapok Hotel | 52 B1 |
| La Calypso | 53 B3 |
| L'Orchidée | 54 D1 |
| Par-May-La's Inn | 55 C3 |
| Pearl's Guest House | 56 C5 |
| Sundeck Suites | 57 C3 |
| Tourist Villa | 58 B4 |

**EATING** 🍴
| | |
|---|---|
| Apsara | (see 67) |
| Battimamzelle | (see 47) |
| Breakfast Shed | 59 C6 |
| Garibaldi | 60 B4 |
| Hosein's Roti Shop | 61 D6 |
| Lagniappé | 62 B4 |
| Mother Nature's | 63 D4 |
| Pataraj | 64 A3 |
| Rituals | 65 B3 |
| Sweet Lime | 66 B4 |
| Tamnak Thai | 67 D2 |
| Tiki Village | (see 52) |
| Veni Mangé | 68 A3 |

**DRINKING** 🍷
| | |
|---|---|
| Crow Bar | 69 B4 |

**ENTERTAINMENT** 📺
| | |
|---|---|
| Fifty One Degrees | 70 C3 |
| Island People | 71 C5 |
| Legacy | 72 B3 |
| Mac Farlane | 73 A3 |
| Phase II Pan Grove | 74 A2 |
| Renegades | 75 D4 |
| Silver Stars | 76 C4 |
| Trini Revellers | 77 A3 |
| Woodbrook Playboyz | 78 B4 |
| Zen | 79 D3 |

**SHOPPING** 🛍️
| | |
|---|---|
| Cleve's One Stop Music Shop | 80 D5 |

**TRANSPORT**
| | |
|---|---|
| City Gate | 81 D6 |
| Ferries to Tobago | 82 D6 |
| Independence Taxi Stand | 83 D6 |
| Kalloo's Auto Rentals | (see 84) |
| Kalloo's Taxi Service | 84 B4 |
| LIAT | 85 C5 |
| Maxi Taxi Terminal (Eastbound) | 86 E6 |
| Maxi taxis to Chaguaramas | 87 D6 |
| Maxi taxis to Laventill, Arima & Sangre Grande | 88 D6 |
| Maxi taxis to Maraval, Maracas & Blanchisseuse | 89 D5 |
| Queen's Park Savannah Taxi Stand | 90 C3 |
| Route Taxis to Chaguanas | 91 D6 |
| Route Taxis to Maraval | 92 D4 |
| Route Taxis to St Ann's | 93 D5 |
| Route Taxis to St James | 94 D5 |
| Route Taxis to San Fernando | (see 87) |
| Singh's Auto Rentals | 95 D5 |

Fri, 9am-1pm Sat) Upstairs in the Colsort Mall, with a great selection of Caribbeana.

**Trinidad Book World** ( ☎ 623-4316; cnr Queen & Chacon Sts; ⏰ 8:30am-4:30pm Mon-Thu, 8:30am-5:30pm Fri, 8am-1pm Sat) Good general bookstore opposite the cathedral also selling maps and local literature.

### INTERNET ACCESS

**International Calling Center** (City Gate, South Quay; per hr TT$10; ⏰ 6am-11pm) You'll find many centers like this downtown along Independence Sq.

**L and C Internet Services** ( ☎ 622-6467; 26 Maraval Rd; per hr TT$10; ⏰ 7am-7pm Mon-Fri, 10am-5pm Sat & Sun)

### LAUNDRY

Public laundries are scarce, but many hotels and guesthouses have facilities or can arrange for it to be done.

### LIBRARIES

**National Library** ( ☎ 623-6962; www.nalis.gov.tt; cnr Hart & Abercromby Sts; ⏰ 8am-6pm Mon-Fri, 8:30am-noon Sat)

### MEDICAL SERVICES

**General Hospital** ( ☎ 623-2951; 56-57 Charlotte St) A large full-service hospital.

**St Clair Medical Centre** ( ☎ 628-1451; www.medcorp limited.com; 18 Elizabeth St) A private hospital preferred by expatriates. There are also smaller hospitals in the towns of Arima, San Fernando and Mt Hope, the latter near Tunapuna.

### MONEY

The major banks – Central Bank, RBTT, Republic Bank, Royal Bank and First Citizens Bank – all have branches on Park St east of Frederick St and on Independence Sq. Most are open 8am to 2pm Monday to Thursday, and 8am to 1pm and 3pm to 5pm Friday, and have 24-hour ATMs.

### POST

**Main post office** ( ☎ 669-5361; Wrightson Rd; ⏰ 8am-4pm Mon-Fri) TT Post has outlets all over town.

### TELEPHONE

**International Calling Center** (City Gate, South Quay; ⏰ 6am-11pm) This center has private calling booths for making international calls (TT$1 per minute to the USA, Canada, UK and Europe).

**b Mobile** ( ☎ 824-8788; www.bmobile.co.tt; cnr Chacon & Independence Sq South; ⏰ 8:30am-4:30pm Mon-Fri, Sat 8am-1pm) For TT$125 you can buy a cell phone and use prepaid phone-card inserts (TT$.50 to TT$1.00 per minute within Trinidad and Tobago and TT$1 to TT$1.25 per minute to the US).

### TOURIST INFORMATION

**Tourism Development Company** (TDC; ☎ 675-7034; www.gotrinidadandtobago.com) Has a helpful outlet at Piarco International Airport ( ☎ 669-5196; ☯ 8am-4:30pm).

**Ministry of Tourism** ( ☎ 624-1403; www.tourism.gov.tt; cnr Duke & St Vincent Sts; ☯ 8am-4:30pm Mon-Fri) Provides useful information and brochures.

## Dangers & Annoyances

Port of Spain has a reputation for high crime and, although some of it is hype, some of it is valid. Robberies, kidnappings and murders are increasingly common due to drug-related violence. Traveling solo at night is not a good idea especially if you're female and especially around Nelson St, the harbor and east of downtown. The Laventille neighborhood has been riddled with violent crime as of late. Also, be cautious when walking from your hotel, especially at night.

Since crime around Carnival has been increasing, the police have done a good job cracking down. If you use common sense, your Carnival can be safe.

Beware of parking downtown. The street signs can be confusing and police often tow cars. You're better off using a public parking

---

## CARNIVAL – BETTER GET READY

Several ideas float around about the birth of Carnival. Some say it's a spin-off of ancient Greece's Bacchus celebrations; others suggest Carnival was used by African slaves as a means of mimicking colonial authority while paying homage to African mythology and music. The majority of celebrants say Carnival (meaning 'farewell to the flesh') marks the approach of Lent, the ultimate indulgence before the upcoming sober disciplines.

Whatever the origin, Trinidad hosts the big daddy of Caribbean carnivals, and anyone can participate.

### PRE-CARNIVAL HIGHLIGHTS

- Pre-Carnival fetes, or parties, happen all month long and can take many different forms, held in a backyard or a club venue.
- Panorama, a steel-pan competition for the national title of best band, begins the Saturday two weeks before Carnival and culminates in the final competition on the Saturday before Carnival.
- Calypso Monarch semifinals, when the calypso stars of the year battle it out for the title of number one, take place the Saturday before Carnival.
- National Single Pan Bands final, International Soca Monarch finals, and Carnival King and Queen semifinals are on Carnival Friday.
- Kiddie Mas, which is painfully cute, takes place the Carnival Saturday and possibly on Sunday as well.
- Dimanche Gras has a fantastic show at Queen's Park Savannah with the crowning of Carnival King and Queen and Calypso Monarch finals.

### MAS CAMPS

Mas (masquerade) camp headquarters are workshops where respected designers create intricate and lavish Carnival costumes. Trinis save the whole year to buy the costume which costs between TT$1500 and TT$3500 and ensures two days of all-inclusive drink-filled parading and dancing. Foreigners can buy their costumes online, and they go quick so get one sooner than later.

If you would like to visit a mas camp or join a mas band (the collective group of masqueraders) for Carnival, here are some good choices:

**Mac Farlane** ( ☎ 628-4168; www.macfarlanecarnival.net; 49 Rosalino St) This medium sized band enacts the traditional concept of Carnival by focusing on costume creativity and sets a precedent of theatrics and metaphorical presentation.

**Trini Revelers** ( ☎ 354-5911; www.trinirevellersmas.com; 35 Gallus Street) Strikes a nice balance between skimpy glam and traditional costumes; see p740 for an interview with a researcher for the Trini Revelers.

lot (TT$35 per day). You bail out your car at the police station on South Quay.

## Sights
### QUEEN'S PARK SAVANNAH
'The Savannah' was once part of a sugar plantation and is now a public park. Appreciative residents play soccer and cricket and fly kites in the park's expansive grassy field. It's a great place to walk or simply hang out and people-watch, especially in the crowded early evening when the scorching heat subsides. Many people jog here despite the thick traffic zooming around the perimeter. You'll find fresh coconut juice and snow cones being sold and many benches on which to enjoy them. Concerts and

Carnival events take place on the **grandstand** at the south side of the park. The 3.7km road circling the park has one-way traffic, and locals call it the world's largest roundabout.

### MAGNIFICENT SEVEN
Along the west side of the Queen's Park Savannah are the Magnificent Seven, a line of seven eccentric and ornate colonial buildings constructed in the early 20th century. From south to north, they are the Germanic Renaissance **Queen's Royal College** (a boys' high school); **Hayes Court** (the Anglican bishop's residence); **Mille Fleurs** (headquarters for the Law Association); **Roomor** (a private residence); the Catholic **Archbishop's Residence**; stately **White Hall**

**Island People** ( ☎ 625-1386; www.islandpeoplemas.com; 11 Stone St) This and the next camp would be described as 'bead and bikini bands' and are highly popular.
**Legacy** ( ☎ 622-7466; www.legacycarnival.com; 88 Robert St)

### CARNIVAL MONDAY
#### Playing J'ouvert
Mud Mas. Dirty Mas. Revelers have permission to indulge in their most hedonistic, crazy, ecstatic inclinations as they welcome in Carnival. At around 4am, partiers file into the streets and chip, jump up, wine and grine, slather themselves and others in mud, paint, glitter and/or chocolate, and basically go mad while following trucks blasting soca and selling alcohol. There's nothing official about J'ouvert, so get the scoop about different bands and locations on arrival. Playing is cheap or free. Remember to keep your street smarts and stay with your group.

#### Playing Mas
Tens of thousands parade and dance in the street throughout the day and into the night, accompanied by soca trucks with DJs and steel bands. Playing mas on Monday is more informal than on Tuesday because players just wear band T-shirts, so it isn't as glittery and majestic as the Tuesday mas, but it can be arguably more of a party. Different sections can mix, and the tone is markedly more casual yet uproarious.

### CARNIVAL TUESDAY
#### Playing Mas
Pretty Mas. This is the moment the entire country has prepared for. People put aside their identity for the day and enter into a world of fantasy and revelry as they flaunt the artistic genius and sumptuous displays of Trinidad's mas camp designers to the beat of booming soca.

#### Last Lap
At midnight, Carnival culminates in a last lap around the Savannah – one last chance to go insane, dance and enjoy festival spirit before resigning to Lent or just getting back to the daily grind.

### WEDNESDAY
People traditionally go to the beach, most notably Maracas Bay, Manzanilla and Mayaro on the east coast, for one final post-Carnival lime. If you want to go Tobago's beaches, book the ferry or flight way in advance.

Locations, times, and prices of events change yearly. Information on the upcoming Carnival is available from the **National Carnival Commission of Trinidad & Tobago** ( ☎ 627-1350; www.ncctt.org).

(the prime minister's office); and **Stollmeyer's Castle**, built to resemble a Scottish castle, complete with turrets. Unfortunately, these buildings are not open to the public, but it's worth passing by for a look.

### EMPEROR VALLEY ZOO

Just north of Queen's Park Savannah is the 2.5-hectare **Emperor Valley Zoo** ( ☎ 628-9177; adult/child TT$4/2; ⏰ 9:30am-5:30pm), which opened in 1947. Though small, the zoo has an interesting collection of more than 220 animals, including many indigenous creatures like red howler monkeys, scarlet ibis, agoutis and various snakes. Several cats such as ocelots prowl around in cages, and you can get very close to a skinny and hot-looking Siberian lion.

East of the zoo is the entrance to the **Botanical Gardens** (admission free; ⏰ 6am-6:30pm), which date from 1818 and have grand trees and attractive strolling paths, plus pavilions containing orchids and anthuriums. The **President's House** (closed to the public), a mansion originally built as the governor's residence in 1875, is adjacent to the gardens, as is the **prime minister's residence** (closed to the public).

### NATIONAL MUSEUM & ART GALLERY

Housed in a classic colonial building, the **museum** ( ☎ 623-5941; museum@tstt.net.tt; cnr Frederick & Keate Sts; admission free; ⏰ 10am-6pm Tue-Sat, 2-6pm Sun) contains interesting historical exhibits on Native American settlers, African slaves and indentured Indians. There are also geological displays, and explanations of colonial agriculture and the technology behind oil exploration. One room devoted to Carnival has a nice exhibit on the evolution of steel-pan instruments and a photo gallery of calypso greats. There's also a room full of costumes. On the top floor the art exhibits are intriguing and express the vibe of Trinidad and Tobago.

### INDEPENDENCE SQUARE

The hustle and bustle of downtown culminates along Independence Sq, two parallel streets that flank a promenade featuring benches, chess tables and food kiosks. On the west end of the promenade tower the Central Bank buildings, and the east end is marked by the commanding 1836 Roman Catholic Cathedral.

South of the promenade is imposing City Gate, a huge Victorian building that was

---

#### BEHIND THE CARNIVAL SCENE

Enrico Rajah is a researcher for the Trini Revelers Mas Camp (p738).

**What role does Carnival play in Trinidad and Tobago's culture?**

When the French came in 1863 they brought the Masquerade Ball. Their slaves watched on, adopted it, satirized it, and infused their own creativity. Now known as Carnival, it's still an outlet for people to express themselves in a way they never would in the day to day. For the two days of Carnival, people assume another character and live a fantasy. Problems are thrown aside, and come Wednesday, we are ready to face everything again.

**How has Carnival evolved? There seems to be controversy over the 'beads and bikinis' bands.**

Well, it's always been lewd and vulgar. In the early 1900s it was called the Jammette Carnival, the Prostitute Carnival. In the more traditional Carnival, the costumes' main function is of artistic and cultural expression. Recently, costumes have gotten smaller and smaller, as well as showier…beads and bikinis. Some say it's a deterioration of tradition, yet it's what the people want, especially the younger generation. Therefore, 'beads and bikinis' bands are in fact expressing popular culture. Trini Revelers tries to strike a balance between the flashier outfits and traditional costuming.

**How do you go about creating costumes for your chosen theme?**

A huge part of our band is education. For instance, in 2008's Que Viva México theme, the cultures and traditions of Mexico were researched intensely so we could extract the most intriguing aspects of their culture and portray them accurately. And of course add our personal beautifying touch of Carnival. But we educate our players about the theme and significance of the costumes.

**What makes Carnival here stand out from other famous Carnivals in the World?**

It's the best in the world. And what makes it so unique is that anyone can play mas and participate, whereas in other places like Brazil and New Orleans, people are mainly spectators. Everyone jumps up here.

formerly the city's train station. Today it's a transportation hub, the terminus for all buses and maxi-taxis. West of City Gate is King's Wharf, the landing point for anyone arriving by boat. It's also where you catch the ferry to Tobago. Nearby is the Cruise Ship Complex, with overpriced souvenir stalls pandering to tourists exhaled by giant ships.

## WOODFORD SQUARE

Sometimes referred to as the University of Woodford Sq because of its occasional use by soapbox speakers and gospel preachers, this public park marks the symbolic center of downtown. Dr Eric Williams, Trinidad and Tobago's first prime minister, lectured to the masses here about the importance of sovereignty, which later led to the country's independence from Britain. Woodford Sq remains a 'speakers corner' where people can express opinions. Upcoming discussion topics are posted on a chalkboard on the southeast corner of the square.

Surrounding the park are some interesting edifices, including **Red House**, the imposing red Renaissance-style parliament building constructed in 1906; and the contemporary steel-and-concrete **Hall of Justice** and **City Hall**. Opposite the square's southwest corner is the National Library (p737).

The majestic, Gothic-designed **Anglican Trinity Cathedral** at the south side of Woodford Sq dates from 1818. Its impressive ceiling is supported by an elaborate system of mahogany beams, a design modeled on London's Westminster Hall. Stained-glass windows open to the breeze, and there's a marble monument to Sir Ralph Woodford, the British governor responsible for the church's construction.

## QUEEN'S HALL

Right off Queen's Park Savannah sits this mural-festooned **theatre** ( ☎ 624-1284; www.queens halltt.com; 1-3 St Ann's Rd; ☯ 8am-4pm Mon-Fri plus show times). It was built in the 1950s, when there was a palpable need to have a proper concert hall for the extremely talented musical and theatrical artists of Trinidad. Call for show information.

## Sleeping

Visitors to Port of Spain are generally here for cricket, Carnival, bird-watching or business. The average hotel guest isn't here to chill out on vacation (Tobago's beaches lure those tourists), so many hotels offer efficient if slightly uninspired lodgings. Most places offer Carnival packages that are a set number of days and can be over twice the regular room price.

Rates listed below are high-season rates around the Carnival season, but other times places tend to slash their prices. Beware that sometimes hotels don't include a 10% service charge and 15% VAT in advertised prices.

### BUDGET

**Pearl's Guest House** ( ☎ 625-2158; 3-4 Victoria St; r US$20) Bare-bones, cheap and centrally located, this most basic accommodation has a shared bathroom and kitchen. Its communal balcony is pleasant.

**Abercromby Inn** ( ☎ 623-5259; www.abercromby inn.com; 101 Abercromby St; basic s/d US$27/41/52, deluxe s/d/tr US$67/79/96; ☒ ☐ ) It provides basic accommodation, straight up. There are proper guest services, the rooms are clean, and it boasts a great location in the heart of Port of Spain. There's a deck and communal sitting room.

**Inn a Citi** ( ☎ 625-5911; www.innacitiplace.com; 37 Ariapita Ave; s/d with shared bathroom $40/55, with private bathroom $45/60; ☒ ) Occupying a 2nd floor above businesses, this hotel has a homestay kind of feel and good guest services: laundry, kitchen facilities and cell-phone rentals.

**La Calypso** ( ☎ 622-4077; lacalypso@tstt.net.tt; 46 French St; r with shared bathroom US$41, with private bathroom US$65; ☒ ) In the heart of Woodbrook's entertainment zone, this ultrasecure, nonlinear structure has 18 basic, clean rooms in its crooks and crevices, some with Carnival-view balconies.

**our pick Par-May-La's Inn** ( ☎ 628-2008; www.par maylas.com; 53 Picton St; s/d incl breakfast US$48/64; ☒ ) In walking distance from Queen's Park Oval, the Savannah and Woodbrook is this secure and airy hotel adorned with a pleasant balcony and communal spaces conducive to conversation. Rooms are well cared for, the staff is professional and the price includes a continental breakfast, making it excellent value in Port of Spain.

**Tourist Villa** ( ☎ 627-5423; touristvilla@fiberline.tt; 7 Methuen St; s/d/tr US$55/65/75; ☒ ☐ ) This well-worn place on a quiet street has lots of balconies and a small pool. The rooms are unexceptional but acceptable.

**Sundeck Suites** ( ☎ 622-9560; www.sundecktrini dad.com; 42-44 Picton St; s/d/tr apt US$60/75/95; ☒ ) A block away from Par-May-La's Inn, and owned by the same management, Sundeck offers no-frills suites, each with equipped kitchens and a small deck. Guests can enjoy mountain views from atop its broad 130-sq-meter rooftop deck.

### MIDRANGE & TOP END

**Monique's Guesthouse** ( ☎ 628-3334; www.moniques trinidad.com; 114-116 Saddle Rd; s/d/tr US$65/70/80, with kitchen US$70/75/85; 🞬 🖳 ) In Maraval, 3km north of Queen's Park Savannah, Monique's has 10 pleasant rooms. Its hillside annex has 10 large studios with cooking facilities and balconies from which you can sometimes spot parrots in the treetops. Friendly owners, Michael and Monica Charbonne, organize nature tours for guests.

**Gingerbread House** ( ☎ 625-6841; www.trinidadgin gerbreadhouse.com; 8 Carlos St; s/d incl breakfast US$65/95; 🞬 🖳 ⚐ ) In this renovated 1920s home you feel much like a house guest, staying in one of three high-ceiling rooms which are spacious and pleasantly decorated. There are a number of comfortable communal areas and the back deck has a creatively tiled mini-pool. Breakfast is included.

**Alicia's House** ( ☎ 623-2802; www.aliciashousetrinidad .com; 7 Coblentz Gardens; s/d from US$75/83; 🞬 🖳 ⚐ ) You feel as though you're staying in a Trini's home at this bustling guesthouse whose kitsch is almost comforting. Just north of Queen's Park Savannah, it has simple rooms, some with shared bathroom. Meals are served in its restaurant.

**Forty Winks Inn** ( ☎ 622-0484; www.fortywinks.com; 24 Warner St; s/d incl breakfast US$94/109; 🞬 🖳 ⚐ ) Nicely located in Woodbrook, this vibrantly decorated house has five cheerful rooms and an intimate atmosphere. There is a patio on top, lush with plants, where you can enjoy the sunset.

**L'Orchidée** ( ☎ 621-0618; www.trinidadhosthomes .com; 3 Coblentz Gardens; s/d/ste incl breakfast $100/150/200;

---

### EARLY FLIGHT?

The two species of hotels near the airport, dilapidated and expensive, creates a lose-lose situation. Of the latter species, **Piarco International Hotel** ( ☎ 669-3030; piaricohotel@mailcity.com; 8-10 Golden Grove Rd; s/d US$170/190; 🞬 ⚐ ) has clean, well-kept, unexceptional facilities with free airport transfers.

---

🞬 🖳 ) It's a cozy 12-bedroom inn that is tastefully done with pleasing color accents in the tile work and art on the walls. There's an adorable breakfast space. In the garden you'll find the inn's namesake growing. Offers wi-fi.

**our pick Coblentz Inn** ( ☎ 624-0541; www.coblentzinn .com; 44 Coblentz Ave; s/d incl breakfast US$105/108; 🞬 🖳 ) Somewhere between a European boutique hotel and B&B, the 16-room Coblentz Inn is a peaceful haven that feels far away from city chaos even though it's relatively close to the Savannah. The immaculate rooms are uniquely themed and decorated, and the sitting areas exude comfort with their sumptuous furniture, garden terrace and a reading library. With continental breakfast offered in the adjoining Battimamzelle restaurant (opposite), the Coblentz offers excellent value. Offers wi-fi.

**Kapok Hotel** ( ☎ 622-5765; www.kapokhotel.com; 16-18 Cotton Hill; s/d from US$165/181; 🞬 🖳 ⚐ ) Not just a business hotel, the Kapok boasts an authentic Caribbean vibe. It's located toward the south end of Saddle Rd, throwing distance from Queen's Park Savannah. The rooms are decked out with rattan furnishings and high-speed internet. There's an outdoor pool, self-service launderette and two restaurants, including the popular Polynesian-themed Tiki Village (opposite).

**Hyatt Regency** ( ☎ 623-2222; www.trinidad.hyatt.com; 1 Wrightson Rd; r from US$300; 🞬 🖳 ⚐ ) Spanking new and taking up a fat piece of ocean real estate next to the Ferry Terminal is this luxury hotel with prices as high as its skyscraper building. It is arguably one of the most upscale hotels in the country with its army of staff presenting any amenities one could imagine.

## Eating

Pickup trucks selling coconut water (TT$6) can be found around Queen's Park Savannah, and you can find places to grab a bite around Independence Sq. Local food suppliers shut down around 3pm. Dinner is only offered in more formal restaurants or international chains. However, St James neighborhood is your best bet for street food at night.

### BUDGET

**Hosein's Roti Shop** ( ☎ 627-2357; cnr Independence Sq South & Henry St; mains TT$15-25; ⏲ lunch & dinner) On the south side of town, this is a hugely popular carryout for mini-rotis and dhal *puri* (a type of roti stuffed with split peas).

**Pataraj** (cnr Tragarete & White St; roti TT$15-25; 10:30am-4, closed Sun) Right before entering St James, you'll find this eatery that serves some of the most mouth-watering roti in the city.

**Mother Nature's** ( ☎ 627-6986; cnr Park & St Vincent Sts; TT$15-40; 5am-4pm Mon-Sat) Whole wheat roti? Yes, it exists here as well as dairy-free deserts (including a showcase of ice creams) and vegetarian dishes sieved from the local repertoire.

**Rituals** ( ☎ 622-1382; cnr Marli St & Maraval Rd; sandwich TT$30; 6:30am-7pm) This coffee shop serves smoothies, coffee drinks (TT$15 to TT$20), paninis, bakery goods and bagel sandwiches. If you squint, you might think you're in Starbucks. Trinidad's business class comes here to tap the wi-fi and take refuge from the heat in the blasting air-conditioning.

**Breakfast Shed** (Wrightson Rd; mains TT$40; breakfast & lunch) Right on the water, Trini women sell homemade food from stalls around the perimeter of an open-air, picnic-benched eating area. You can grab a fresh cane juice or sea moss shake at Mr Juice's stall. The large servings of Trinidadian fare include fish, dasheen (a type of taro), plantains, rice and other local savories.

## MIDRANGE

**Sweet Lime** ( ☎ 624-9983; cnr Ariapita Ave & French St; mains TT$50-190; lunch & dinner) This restaurant-bar has an open-air kitchen, plant-laden outdoor seating, and a pool room and dance floor in the back. The set-menu lunch is economical, local and heaping. The expensive dinner menu includes salads, grilled meats and fish, and vegetarian options. It's a wi-fi hot spot, sometimes.

**Lagniappe** ( ☎ 622-9764; 13A Ariapita Ave; mains TT$70-100; 7am-5:30pm Tue-Fri, 9am-4pm Sat, 9am-2pm Sun) On Ariapita Avenue, this European bakery nestles into a cozy café space with a patio. It serves luscious salads, gourmet sandwiches, finely prepared local dishes, and has a lovely brunch on the weekends. The coffee drinks will lull you with their richness.

**Tiki Village** ( ☎ 622-5765; 16-18 Cotton Hill; mains TT$70-140; ) The Kapok Hotel's Tiki Village has great views of the Savannah and downtown, an Asian-themed ambience, and a menu stocked with Chinese favorites that are infused with Polynesian and Trini flavors. It's very vegetarian friendly and has a lunch buffet served Monday to Friday.

**Veni Mangé** ( ☎ 624-4597; 67A Ariapita Ave; mains TT$90-150; 11am-3pm Mon-Sun, dinner from 7pm Wed & Fri) West Indian flavor, art, foliage and enthusiasm infuse this vibrant restaurant. Serving Caribbean cuisine with classic French influences, it's considered one of the best spots for lunch (it's only open for dinner two days a week). Try the beef dumplings or the grilled fresh fish with tropical chutney. There are also veggie options.

### TOP END

**Tamnak Thai** ( ☎ 625-0647; 13 Queen's Park East; mains TT$70-300; 11am-3pm & 6-11pm Mon-Fri, dinner only Sat & Sun) The outside patio has lovely tropical wood tables and a lily-pad pond while the inside is quiet and cool. Dishes include lemongrass-infused soups; seafood salad; vegetable, lamb and shrimp curries; and spicy tofu with vegetables.

**Apsara** ( ☎ 623-7659; 13 Queen's Park East; mains TT$90-250; lunch & dinner Mon-Sat) Specializing in North Indian cuisine, Apsara is named after the dancers of the court of Indra, who, it's said, could move freely between heaven and earth. Favorites like tandoori, curry and biryani dishes will melt in your mouth. Vegetarians have many options here. Apsara shares a building with Tamnak Thai.

**Garibaldi** ( ☎ 772-2942; 32 Fitt Street; mains TT$125-250; dinner Mon-Sat) Although there are other good Italian restaurants in town, this one proves to be most authentic, serving delectable homemade pastas as well as lovely meat and fish mains. The decor is elegant with black-and-white pictures adorning the walls and simple table settings.

**Battimamzelle** ( ☎ 621-0541; 44 Coblentz Ave; breakfast & lunch TT$175, mains TT$200; breakfast, lunch & dinner Mon-Sat) Brainchild of chef Khalid Mohammed, Battimamzelle (the local word for butterfly) appeals to more than just your salivary glands. A feast for the eyes, the vibrant decor mimics the colors of tropical birds, with yellow, green and red walls and colorful local art throughout. Nestled in the fabulous Coblentz Inn, the small restaurant boasts a creative menu featuring meats, seafood or whatever delicious, beautiful meal the chef wants to create.

## Drinking

The name of the **Crow Bar** ( ☎ 627-8449; cnr Ariapita Ave & Carlos St; occasional cover charge TT$50) is never far from a Trini's lips when discussing popular

---

**PANYARDS**

Panyards are little more than vacant lots where steel bands store their instruments for much of the year. Come Carnival season, panyards become lively rehearsal spaces, pulsating with energy and magnificent sound. Here, you can witness one of the most important and sacred parts of Trinidad's urban landscape. You feel the music, and you begin to understand it, relate to it and love it. Band members span gender and age; you could see an eight-year-old girl drumming alongside her great-grandfather.

Steel bands start gearing up for Carnival as early as late September, sometimes rehearsing and performing throughout the year. The best way to find out about practice and performance schedules is by asking around. You can also contact **Pan TrinBago** ( ☎ 623-4486; www.pantrinbago.co.tt).

Some popular panyards that welcome visitors:

**Phase II Pan Groove** ( ☎ 627-0909; Hamilton St)

**Renegades** ( ☎ 624-3348; 138 Charlotte St)

**Silver Stars** ( ☎ 633-4733; 56 Tragarete Rd)

**Woodbrook Playboyz** ( ☎ 628-0320; 27 Tragarete Rd)

---

places to go have a drink. Right on trendy Ariapita, the open-air bar has a nice sound system and serves them cold.

The suburb of St James, just west of central Port of Spain, becomes a hub of activity almost any evening. Rub shoulders with politicians, cricket stars or just about anyone at **Smokey & Bunty's** (97 Western Main Rd), a hole-in-the-wall watering hole and the center of St James action. A myriad of busy bars surround it if you want to hop around.

## Entertainment

Port of Spain's nightlife is especially happening Thursday through Saturday, but the St James neighborhood is known to always be rocking and the place find a proper lime when all else fails. Many times bars have live music or DJ's. Cover charges vary and can get up to TT$100.

If you'd like someone to accompany you on your first night on the town, contact Gunda Harewood for an **evening entertainment tour** ( ☎ 625-2410, 756-9677; gunda@wow.net). An evening out might include visits to a couple of panyards, a local live band and guidance in choosing the best street snacks. About three hours of fun and transportation costs US$45 per person.

### NIGHTCLUBS

**Zen** ( ☎ 625-9936; www.zen.tt; Keat St; ☼ 10pm-late Wed, Fri, Sat; cover TT$60-100) Just behind the museum, this three-tier club is replete with slick modern decor and Buddha statues. Buddha probably wouldn't patronize this hot spot, with its VIP Champagne room, make-out

nooks and myriad dance floors, but you might want to shake it all night here to soca, hip-hop and other popular beats. A dress code is in effect.

**Fifty One Degrees** ( ☎ 627-0051; www.51degrees.com; 51 Cipriani Blvd; weekend cover charge TT$100; ☼ 7pm-very late Tue-Sat) Not just a dance club, this Port of Spain nightlife waypoint has piano bar, comedy and live bands.

### CINEMAS

**MovieTowne** ( ☎ 627-8277; www.movietowne.com; Audrey Jeffers Hwy, Invaders Bay; tickets adult/child TT$45/35; ☒ ) Besides 10 wide-screen movie theaters, there's also a shopping mall, restaurants, and video arcades that collaborate to mirror megaplexes in any given American suburb. It's west of the center.

## Shopping

The central area of Port of Spain, especially around Independence Sq, Queen St and Frederick St, is filled with malls and arcades selling everything from spices to fabric by the yard. Music is the best souvenir to shop for in Port of Spain. Street vendors sell pirated recordings, or get originals at **Crosby's Music Centre** ( ☎ 622-7622; 54 Western Main Rd) in St James opposite Smokey & Bunty's, or at **Cleve's One Stop Music Shop** ( ☎ 624-0827; 58 Frederick St), in a small shopping center downtown. You can also pick up CDs at the airport.

## AROUND PORT OF SPAIN
### Chaguaramas

A 30-minute drive from the capital, Chaguaramas (sha-guah-*ra*-mas) was the site of a major US military installation during WWII, and it was just in the 1990s when the land was fully handed back over to Trini possession. Now the harbor has a slew of marine facilities and is the hot spot for traveling sailors and yachties because it sits safely out of the hurricane belt and has comparatively inexpensive marina and dry-docking facilities.

There is a handful of internet cafes in town. **2M International Calling Centre** (106 Western Main Rd; per hr $TT12) is a good one that has bulletins for people trying to hitch yachts to Venezuela or other islands while offering their services as crew members. Car-rental places also sprinkle the town.

Port of Spain's growing cycling community flock to Chaguaramas' 6000-hectare designated national park in order to train and recreate throughout its rainforest and bamboo forests. On old military grounds enveloped by bamboo forest, a local group of **mountain bike** enthusiasts have made 15km to 20km of single-track among towering stalks and roller-coaster riverbeds. A guide that knows the mountain-biking trails in and out is local Courtney Rooks (who rents suspension mountain bikes) of Paria Springs Tours (p749).

Furthermore, the town of Chaguaramas is the launching point for tours to a chain of five offshore islands, locally known as 'Down the Islands.' You can rent kayaks at the **Kayak Centre** ( ☎ 723-3348; per hr TT$35). Boating tours, as well as hiking, swimming, and historical tours, can be arranged by appointment with the **Chaguaramas Development Authority** ( ☎ 868-634-4227; www.chagdev.com). Popular tours include the boat trip out to **Gasparee Grande** (TT$125, three hours), at the south side of Chaguaramas Bay, where you can swim in tidal pools and visit caves that drip with stalactites.

The most distant island, 360-hectare **Chacachacare**, was once a leper colony; camping is permitted on the now-deserted isle, replete with beaches and stunning cliff views of Venezuela. **Scotland Bay**, on the western edge, has a pleasant beach that's accessible only by boat. Arrange independent boat trips with boatmen at the Island Property Owners' jetty, on the west side of Chaguaramas. Expect to pay at least TT$195 per person for Gasparee Grande or Scotland Bay. For fishing charters around the area contact **Classic Sport Fishing Charters** ( ☎ 680-1357; per day US$750).

While you're there, you might want to check out the interesting **Chaguaramas Military History & Aerospace Museum** ( ☎ 634-4391; adult/child TT$20/10; ☾ 9am-5pm), which depicts Trinidad and Tobago's complex military history.

## SLEEPING
**Bight** ( ☎ 634-4427; www.peakeyachts.com; 5 Western Main Rd; r US$55; ☒ ) Simple, tidy rooms overlooking the bay make the Bight good value for the price. Its restaurant (mains from TT$75; open breakfast, lunch and dinner) has terrace dining where people drink colorful cocktails. Inside there's a pool table, darts and big-screen TVs.

**Coral Cove Hotel** ( ☎ 634-2040; Western Main Rd; r US$90; ☒ ) This is another little hotel near the water that is unremarkable but clean and near a handful of restaurants.

**CrewsInn Hotel & Yachting Center** ( ☎ 634-4384; www.crewsinn.com; Point Gourde; s/d US$177/194; ☒ ☐ ☒ ) As the highest-end option in town, its bright rooms all have patios and complete amenities, though are arguably overpriced. This hotel-and-marina complex houses the open-air upscale Lighthouse Restaurant (mains from TT$100; open breakfast, lunch and dinner), the main draw of which is the covered deck overlooking the marina.

## EATING & DRINKING
Most of the marinas have somewhere to munch seafood and sip a Carib. The clubs here are only rented out for events so the limin' is low-key.

**Roti** (Power Boats, Western Main Rd; rotis from TT$18; ☾ 11am-1pm) There's a nameless blue roti hut tucked in a corner of the Power Boats Marina that serves terribly famous roti and buss up shut. The hut serves food until it runs out, so get there sooner than later.

**Café Feeloh** ( ☎ 634-2436; Coral Cove Marina; set lunch TT$40; ☾ breakfast, lunch & dinner) This eatery has a French feel with smoking allowed, crepes served, and a wall lined with French novels. However, the set lunch is local fare. Dinner is by reservation only.

**Sails** ( ☎ 634-4426; Power Boats Marina; draft beer TT$8; ☾ 11am-12am) This popular hangout has seating on the water, pool tables inside and steel pan on Sundays. You can get bar and grill food here as well as shepherd's pie and some local food such as callaloo soup.

**Lure** ( ☎ 634-2783; sweetwatermarina@tstt.net.tt; Sweet Water Marina; ☾ dinner) Yachtie-recommended and touted as the best eats in Chagaramas, this high-end harborside restaurant is a great place to run away from Port of Spain for a nice dinner out. It has a variety of seafood, meat, and pasta dishes, and the Paella Marina for two (TT$285) surely won't disappoint. The open-air bar on top hosts karaoke on Fridays.

## Mt St Benedict

A Benedictine **monastery** sits on 240 hectares on a hillside north of Tunapuna, 13km east of Port of Spain. Though not a major sight in itself, the monastery attracts people who want to stay or eat at its secluded guesthouse, birdwatch or walk in the rainforest. Today, the monastery is home to just 20 aging monks.

The thickly wooded hills behind the monastery provide hiking opportunities and possible glimpses of hawks, owls and numerous colorful forest birds, and maybe a monkey. A favorite **hike** is to the fire tower, which offers good views and birding. It takes about half an hour one way from the guesthouse.

**Pax Guest House** ( ☎ 662-4084; www.paxguesthouse .com; s/d incl breakfast US$55/92, dinner extra US$10; ﹇ ) is a restored colonial house and the oldest guesthouse in the West Indies. Pax welcomes visitors from all over the world who come to do research, write poetry or study wildlife. Hosts Gerard and Oda welcome visitors as though they're family, and bend over backwards to arrange day trips, transportation and bird-watching hikes. As a birding expert, Gerard has excellent guide contacts. A peaceful retreat, the guesthouse's 18 rooms feature teak floorboards, washbasins and fine views, but no TVs or telephones. Some rooms have simple twin beds, others antique four-poster queen-size beds; some have private bathrooms. Unless you have a car, it's inconvenient to get around, so rates include a full breakfast; the healthy multicourse dinner (US$10) is local, delicious fare.

Nonguests can come for dinner or a delightful afternoon tea with scones or Trinidadian sweet bread (dessert cakes or rolls). Reservations are essential for meals but not necessary for tea (served from 3:30pm to 6pm).

To arrive at Mt St Benedict from Port of Spain, take the Eastern Main Rd then St John's Rd 3.3km north. For public transport, take a maxi to Tunapuna and get off at St Johns Rd where you will usually get a maxi up to Pax within an hour before 5pm. Leaving Pax, maxis start around 6am.

## Asa Wright Nature Centre

A former cocoa and coffee plantation transformed into an 80-hectare nature reserve, the **Asa Wright Nature Centre** ( ☎ 667-4655; www .asawright.org; adult/child TT$60/36) blows the minds of bird-watchers and makes a worthwhile trip, even if you can't tell a parrot from a parakeet. The center has won a number of ecotourism awards, lauded as one of the 'world's ultimate outposts.' It constantly seeks to buy land for the land trust.

Located amid the rainforest of the Northern Range, the center has attracted naturalists from around the world since its founding in 1967. The property has a lodge catering to birding tour groups, a research station for biologists and a series of hiking trails. Day visitors can only view the center on a guided tour (10:30am and 1:30pm); reservations should be made at least 24 hours in advance.

Bird species found here include blue-crowned motmots, chestnut woodpeckers, channel-billed toucans, blue-headed parrots, 14 species of hummingbird and numerous raptors. The sanctuary is home to the elusive nocturnal guacharo (oilbird). To protect the oilbirds, tours are limited. Guests staying at the center's lodge can view them for free (nonguests TT$150).

The **lodge** ( ☎ 667-4655, in the USA 800-426-7781; s/d summer US$125/155, winter US$180/225; ﹇ ) has some rooms in the weathered main house and others in nearby cottages; all are quite simple with private bathrooms. Rates are high but include three ample meals a day, afternoon tea, and rum punch each evening. During high season there is a minimum of a three-day stay that includes an oilbird cave tour. Guests are also offered excursions to other natural areas in Trinidad for an extra cost. Airport transfers can be arranged for US$50 per person, round-trip. Nonguests can eat at the lodge, but reservations must be made 48 hours in advance, except for lunch.

The Centre is about a 1½-hour drive from Port of Spain. At Arima, 26km from Port of Spain, head north on Blanchisseuse Rd, turning left into the center after the 7½-mile marker sign. A taxi to Asa from Port of Spain that would take you there and back (essentially an all-day affair) costs about TT$400 to TT$600; one-way is TT$100. For public

## WORD ON THE BIRD

Trinidad and Tobago is excluded from many Caribbean birding books because of the sheer magnitude of additional species here – about 430 in total. Torn from Venezuela, these islands share mainland diversity in their swamps, rainforests, ocean islets, lowland forests, and savannahs. Thus, birders love to indulge their hobby in a top-notch locale while enjoying a gorgeous island.

### HIGHLIGHT BIRDING SPOTS
### Trinidad

- Asa Wright Nature Centre
- Caroni Bird Sanctuary
- Pointe-à-Pierre Wildfowl Trust
- Mt St Benedict
- Brasso Seco

### Tobago

- Little Tobago
- St Giles Island
- Grafton Caledonia Wildlife Sanctuary
- Tobago Forest Reserve

### ACCOMODATIONS

In Trinidad and Tobago, there are a number of lovely hotels and guesthouses situated at prime birding sites that cater to bird-watchers. These quiet and peaceful retreats connect you with savvy guides, and you can practically bird-watch from your room. On Mt St Benedict in Trinidad, Pax Guest House (opposite) is a birder's haven. On Tobago, there are some great choices: Cuffie River Nature Retreat (p763), Adventure Eco-Villas (p763) and Arnos Vale Hotel (p763).

### BOOK RECOMMENDATIONS

*A Guide to the Birds of Trinidad and Tobago* by Richard Ffrench has good descriptions but limited plates. Detailed plates can be found in *A Guide to the Birds of Venezuela* by Rodolphe Meyer de Schauensee and William H Phelps Jr. In addition to James Bond's well-regarded *Field Guide to Birds of the West Indies*, there's *The Trinidad and Tobago Field Naturalists Club Trail Guide*, describing hiking trails on the islands, complete with sketch maps.

transportation, take a maxi to Arima and catch another maxi going up Blanchisseuse Rd; they are most frequent during going-to-work and getting-off-work hours.

## NORTH COAST

Following Saddle Rd north from Port of Spain, the road becomes the North Coast Rd, climbing over the mountains of the Northern Range through a forest of tall trees, ferns and bamboo while hugging the Caribbean coastline. Just east of Maracas Bay, you'll come across quieter and less commercial **Las Cuevas Bay**, a beautiful U-shaped bay; there's surfing at its west end and calmer conditions at its center. Finally, you'll hit the settlement of Blanchisseuse before the road passes a small suspension bridge and narrows into impassability.

Maxi-taxis and route taxis travel to Maracas Bay, but transport to Blanchisseuse is far less frequent.

### Maracas Bay

Just 40 minutes' drive from Port of Spain, Maracas Bay has Trinidad's most popular beach. The wide, white-sand beach, thick with palm trees contrasting against the backdrop of verdant mountains, remains an irresistible lure for both locals and travelers.

In summer the water is mostly flat, but at other times the bay serves up good waves for bodysurfing. There's a lifeguard, changing rooms (TT$1, open 10am to 6pm), showers, picnic shelters and huts selling cold Caribs and infamous shark and bake. You can also rent beach chairs, hammocks and umbrellas. On weekends the beach gets pretty crowded

## AMERINDIAN LEGACY

In Arima, there remains a small community of Amerindian descent who still follow some traditional customs. Arima has the **Amerindian Museum** (Cleaver Woods; admission free; ☒ 8am-4pm) displaying artifacts, and local shaman **Cristo Adonis** ( ☎ 395-0999; www.kacike.org) will show you around or take you on an educational hike where you learn about the medicinal plants and spirituality of the Amerindians.

and a DJ will be most likely spinning. During the week it can feel almost deserted. On Mondays the locals tend to get together and play music.

Right on the bay, **Maracas Bay Hotel** ( ☎ 669-1914; www.maracasbay.com; Maracas Bay; r US$70; ☒ ▢ ▣ ) is the only hotel in Maracas and is accordingly overpriced. Its rooms are simple, a bit musty, face the ocean, and have balconies. Its restaurant (mains TT$60 to TT$150) is under a giant pagoda and has both bar food and seafood and meat dishes. To grab a beer and lime with the locals, head to **Arnold's on the Bay** (beer TT$10), a small, open-air dive bar on the western side of the bay.

## Blanchisseuse

pop 800

The road narrows east of Maracas Bay ending up at the tiny village of Blanchisseuse (*blon-she-suhze*), where beautiful craggy coastline dotted with weekend homes can seem romantic or harsh, depending on your mood. The three beaches aren't the best for swimming, especially in the fall and winter, but the surfing can be okay.

Laundry inspired the town's name. Village women who washed their clothes in the nearby Marianne River were called 'washerwomen' and this was translated to *blanchisseuse*, the French word for 'launderer,' during the French occupation.

Blanchisseuse makes a great base for hiking, especially to **Paria Falls**. The trailhead starts just past the suspension bridge that spans the Marianne River, just before the end of the North Coast Rd. About two hours each way, the hike winds through the forest, over the Jordan River to the spectacular waterfalls, where you're greeted with a clear, refreshing bathing pool. Keep on going for 20 minutes

and you'll hit **Paria Bay**, a picturesque, deserted beach. Continuing east will lead you on a scenic coastal hike that dumps you out in Matelot. From Blanchisseuse to Matlot is around 32km. Backpacking is possible and having a guide is suggested because parts of the trail aren't well marked and in the past there have been warnings of assaults on foreigners. **Eric Blackman** ( ☎ 669-3995) can arrange a guide or short kayaking trips to the Three Pools, three luscious pools found less than a mile up the Marianne River. There are trails flanking the river if you want to meander up there yourself.

If hiking is not your thing, you can go to Blanchisseuse Fishing Port and hire a fisherman to take you (from TT$250) to and from Paria Bay or **Madamas Bay**, which will most likely be deserted.

Hotels in Blanchisseuse don't have such a stringent service-industry standard, but you can hear or see the ocean from most. Ask around for guesthouses for a more intimate Trini experience.

Casual and comfortable, **Almond Brook** ( ☎ 758-0481; trellxtc@hotmail.com; Lamp Post 16, Paria Main Rd; r incl breakfast TT$250) has three pleasant, clean rooms. The appealing communal deck outside the rooms looks to the ocean. There's a large shared kitchen and meals can be arranged (TT$40 per person).

A professional, well-run place owned by boisterous, welcoming German Gottfried Franz, **Laguna Mar** ( ☎ 669-2963; www.lagunamar.com; 65½-mile marker, Paria Main Rd; r TT$400; ☒ ) comprises three buildings on the hillside at the end of the road, plus a four-bedroom cottage. Try to snag a room in the far building, which has a righteous common room with shared kitchen and deck.

A marvelous French woman, Ginnette Holder, and her Trini husband take care of three comfortable, endearing cottages at **Second Spring** ( ☎ 669-3909; secondspring@trinidad.net; Lamp Post 191, Paria Main Rd; studio/cottage US$60/100). They can arrange meals; count yourself lucky if Ginnette cooks for you.

**Los Cocos** (meals TT$90), a small, cozy place near the end of the road and under the same ownership as Laguna Mar, can do meals such as fresh curry fish or chicken platters if set up with a bit of notice.

If you are planning to stay in Blanchisseuse for a while, shop for provisions before coming, as the nearest grocery store is in Maraval. Booths here will sell you basics.

## BRASSO SECO

This friendly village (pop 350) in the middle of lush rainforest can no longer thrive on an illustrious agriculture economy and therefore its Tourism Action Committee has begun a small ecotourism initiative. If you want fantastic hiking or bird-watching in the rainforest, but don't need frilly accommodations and are interested in experiencing rural Trinidad, this is the place for you.

There are some great day hikes of varying lengths to waterfalls: Double River Waterfalls, Madamas Falls and Sobo Falls. The 13km trek to Paria Bay from Brasso Seco is one of the most gorgeous in Trinidad, passing the famous Paria Falls. Also, you can arrange to scramble up Cerro del Aripo, the tallest mountain in Trinidad (941m).

You can make the hike to Paria Bay into a fine coastal backpacking trip with camping on beautiful bays by continuing all the way to Matelot to the east. There's basic beachside shelter and facilities at **Tacaribe** ( ☎ 330-7546; campsite TT$100), 11 miles from Brasso Seco, that you could use overnight before ending up at Matelot.

Guides can be arranged through the **Tourist Action Committee** ( ☎ 669-6218; www.brassosecoparia .com; day hike per group TT$300, multiday hike per person

---

### CYCLING TRINIDAD

The traffic, crazy drivers and narrow roads are out of hand near cities. However, if you love cycling and have an adventurous streak, there are some spectacular rides for you in the more remote areas and back roads. Plus, mountain biking is a great way to experience the natural glory of the island.

#### 'Best of' Road Rides

- Toco to Matelot Out-and-Back (about 48km) – Absolutely stunning coastal scenery with lots of hills and very little traffic (the road ends in Matelot). Eating post-ride at Mrs Bravo's Sea Sands Camp (p753) in Toco is highly recommended.
- Blanchiseusse Rd (39km) – Once you're out of Arima, any part of this road is gorgeous: it heads straight through the heart of the Northern Range passing through rainforest and by small farms. Asa Wright Nature Centre is great for lunch, with the turnoff to Petite Marianne Waterfall halfway back down to Blanchisseuse. There are big ascents and descents.
- Chaguaramas – There are some beautiful, flat roads with little traffic in Chaguaramas' national park.

Also try the ride from Maracas Bay to Blanchiseusse and Cora River

While riding, beware of dogs (they usually are all bark, but are disconcerting), narrow roads, blind corners, honking (not malicious, usually jovial, but disconcerting) and opportunists (go with a guide or in a group, especially if you're female).

#### Mountain Biking

Nature guide Courtney Rooks of Paria Springs Tours (see following) knows mountain biking in Trinidad. He may have even made the trail. Chaguaramas and Brasso Seco have beautiful rides. Courtney has suspension rentals.

#### Guides & Rentals

**Anton Roberts** ( ☎ 763-2013) He's a cycling guide who will show you Trinidad's road rides.

**Geronimo's** ( ☎ 622-2453; 15 Pole Carew St) A reliable bike shop in Port of Spain that rents good bikes and sells quality merchandise.

**Paria Springs Tours** ( ☎ 622-8826; www.pariasprings.com; tours per person US$75-100) The company to go to for mountain biking.

**Pathmaster** ( ☎ 374-7847; www.thepathmaster.com) Andy Whitwell's guides provide reliable, professional service and rentals, as well as the highest prices.

per day TT$300). **Carl Fitzjames** ( ☎ 718-8605) is one of the few guides in the country who will lead multiday camping treks in the rainforest.

Rosa is famous for being a whiz in the Caribbean kitchen, and staying in **Rosa's** ( ☎ 664-6753; r incl 2 meals TT$300) back bedroom is a yummy and authentic experience of rural Trinidad. Or stay at the **Pachenco's** ( ☎ 669-6139; person incl 2 meals TT$250) house (by the church) with three bedrooms and a sitting area. It's basic and does the trick. You eat Ms P's home-made meals next door.

# WEST COAST
## Caroni Bird Sanctuary
Caroni Bird Sanctuary is the roosting site for thousands of scarlet ibis, the national bird of Trinidad and Tobago. At sunset the birds fly in to roost in the swamp's mangroves, giving the trees the appearance of being abloom with brilliant scarlet blossoms. Even if you're not an avid bird-watcher, the sight of the ibis flying over the swamp, glowing almost fluorescent red in the final rays of the evening sun, is not to be missed.

Long, flat-bottomed motorboats, holding up to 30 passengers, pass slowly through the swamp's channels. To avoid disturbing the birds, the boats keep a fair distance from the roosting sites, so bring along a pair of binoculars. Expect to also see herons and egrets, predominant among the swamp's 150 bird species. Note that during the summer months very few ibis are sighted, but the trip is still worthwhile.

The main companies offering tours of the swamp are **David Ramsahai** ( ☎ 663-4767), **Nanan's Bird Sanctuary Tours** ( ☎ 645-1305; nantour@tstt.net .tt) and **Sean Madoo Tours** ( ☎ 663-0458). All the companies offer 2½-hour tours, starting at 4pm daily, for US$10 per person. Reservations for the tours are recommended, but if you just show up you'll probably be able to find space on one of the boats. If your main interest is photography, the light is more favorable in the morning. Morning tours, which leave at 4:30am, can be arranged through David Ramsahai.

The sanctuary is off the Uriah Butler Hwy, 14km south of Port of Spain; the turnoff is marked. If you don't have your own vehicle, Nanan's Bird Sanctuary Tours provide transport from Port of Spain for an extra US$35 per person. Many guesthouses and hotels in Port of Spain also arrange trips.

## Carapichaima
The Carapichaima area is between Chaguanas and Couva and is easily accessed from the north by the Uriah Butler Hwy. This region is the heart of Trinidad's East Indian population. Their forbears mostly came to Trinidad as indentured servants between 1845 and 1917 to compensate for the labor loss when slavery was abolished, and they now own most of south-central Trinidad. Roti eateries are all over and Hindi temples are hard to miss.

### CHAGUANAS
Chaguanas (sha-*gwon*-as) comes alive during the annual festivals of Phagwa and Divali (see p771), which celebrate Hindu traditions. Along the main road south of Chaguanas, potters make the touted **Chaguanas pottery**, including *deya* (tiny earthenware lamps) and other ceramic items using traditional methods.

### WATERLOO TEMPLE
This tranquil, almost surreal Hindu **temple** (donation suggested; ☺ 8am-3pm Tue, Thu & Sat, 9-11am Sun) sits at the end of a causeway jutting 90m off the central west coast. Its formal name is Siewdass Sadhu Shiv Mandir, after its creator. Grateful for his safe return from India through the WWI-embattled waters of the Pacific, Sadhu committed himself to building a temple. Construction began in 1947 on state-owned land. When the state demolished his efforts, Sadhu began building out in the sea, carrying each foundation stone on his bicycle to the water's edge. When he died in 1970, his work was still incomplete. In 1994 the Hindu community completed the temple. It is accessed through the Waterloo Bay Recreation Park. The site is a common place for Hindis to throw their loved ones' ashes to sea. Visitors are welcome, with no admission charge.

To get to Waterloo, travel south from Port of Spain on the Uriah Butler Hwy to Chaguanas, then 58.5km on the Southern Main Rd to St Mary's. Turn west on the Waterloo Rd until you reach the temple. Alternatively, take a maxi-taxi to Chaguanas (TT$6), then another to St Mary's (TT$2), from where you can get a route taxi (TT$3) to the temple.

### INDIAN CARIBBEAN MUSEUM
Just inland from Waterloo Temple, this very interesting **museum** (admission free; ☺ 10am-5pm

Wed-Sun) is dedicated to the East Indian history and experience in Trinidad. For being just one large room, it does a comprehensive job presenting Trinidad's East Indian roots. Some gorgeous antique sitars and drums are displayed as well as photographs and informational displays about early East Indian settlers. Other highlights include local art, traditional Hindi clothing, a display of a traditional East Indian Trini kitchen (replete with a *chulha,* the earthen stove where roti is made), and crazy pictures of Brits with their East Indian indentured servants.

### DAVENNA YOGA CENTRE

Just look for the giant, towering monkey-god statue. Bereft of yoga and meditation classes, the impressively garish Davenna Yoga Centre is not so much a Hindu spiritual center as an intended tourist site. The only Southern Indian–style temple in the western hemisphere, it's an incredible sight to behold in the middle of a small Trinidadian town. Take the Chase Village exit from the highway and a kilometer down the road you'll see the turnoff for Orange Field Rd; the Davenna Yoga Centre is a couple of kilometers down.

## Pointe-à-Pierre Wildfowl Trust

This is a special place. Despite being in the midst of the island's sprawling oil refinery a few miles north of San Fernando, **Pointe-à-Pierre Wildfowl Trust** ( ☎ 658-4200, ext 2512; adult/child/teen TT$10/3/6; ☯ 8am-5pm Mon-Fri, 10am-5pm Sat & Sun), a wetland sanctuary, has an abundance of birdlife in a highly concentrated 26 hectares. There are about 90 bird species, both wild and in cages, including endangered waterfowl, colorful songbirds, ibis, herons and other wading birds. In a 20-minute stroll around the grounds, you can easily spot a few dozen species.

A nonprofit organization, the trust is an environmental education center that rehabilitates and breeds endangered species. The birds are released into the wild, where they bolster natural populations. The visitors center has small exhibits and a gift shop.

Reservations should be made a day in advance, so the refinery guards know you're coming. Several entrances lead into the surrounding PetroTrin Oil Refinery, and gate access to the sanctuary occasionally changes, so get directions when you make reservations.

## San Fernando
pop 75,300

Trinidad's second-largest city, San Fernando is also the center of the island's gas and oil industries. Anyone looking for real cultural immersion will enjoy San Fernando, as few tourists come through the town. Most of the action happens at shops and stands around Harris Promenade or you can find great views on San Fernando Hill.

As the transportation hub for the region, maxi-taxis and route taxis run regularly to Port of Spain and other outlying areas. Most of the town's hotels cater to visiting oil and gas types who are in town on business.

This 40-room, family-owned **Tradewinds Hotel** ( ☎ 652-9463; www.tradewindshotel.net; 36-38 London St; s/d US$109/120, ste s/d US$153/164, all incl breakfast; ✖ ▣ ▨ ) offers reasonable value. It has an outdoor pool, bar, restaurant, spa and gym. Room configurations range from a small standard room to the deluxe suite with kitchen and Jacuzzi.

The hotel's **Treehouse Restaurant** (dinner mains US$110-300; ☯ 5am-midnight) serves up good breakfasts, sandwiches, seafood and meat dishes. Views from the patio are spectacular.

## Pitch Lake

Some 22km southwest of San Fernando near the town of La Brea is **Pitch Lake** ( ☎ 651-1232; tours TT$30; ☯ 9am-5pm). Once thought of as a punishment of the gods by the Amerindians, this bubbling lake of pitch is perhaps Trinidad's greatest oddity. Bird-watchers will find it of interest as well for the species it attracts. This 40-hectare expanse of asphalt is 90m deep at its center, where hot bitumen is continuously replenished from a subterranean fault. The lake, one of only three asphalt lakes in the world, has the single largest supply of natural bitumen, and as much as 300 tons are extracted daily. The surface of Pitch Lake looks like a clay tennis court covered with wrinkled elephant-like skin. During the rainy season, people sit in its warm sulfurous pools. On the tour, the guide sagely takes you across via the solid parts. High heels are not recommended. Call ahead to book a tour or you can just show up.

## EAST COAST

Trinidad's east coast is wild and rural. The mix of lonely beaches with rough Atlantic waters, mangrove swamps and coconut plantations creates dramatic scenery. It's deserted most of the year, except for holidays, especially post-Carnival when people flood in for beachside relaxation.

Few hotels operate on the east coast. Sometimes people will come down for a weekend beach lime, but places are mainly patronized the week after Carnival. Rates listed here are for the high season (January to May) and drop dramatically in the low season.

Long, wide and windswept, **Manzanilla Beach**, the main beach, has caramel-colored sand, palm trees and white-beach morning glory. The strong winds and tempestuous waters make swimming a challenge, but the post-Carnival crowd comes in droves to play in the surf and sun. A public beach facility at the northern end has changing rooms, snacks and lifeguards.

The immaculate 16-room family-run **Hotel Carries on the Bay** ( ☎ 668-5711; r US$385; ⋈ ) sits on the main road as you approach Manzanilla Beach. Just steps from the beach, its bright, spacious rooms are some of the best maintained in the area. The restaurant here serves three meals (TT$25 to TT$45) a day.

Right on the north end of Manzanilla Beach, **D' Coconut Cove** ( ☎ 691-5939; 33-36 Calypso Rd; s/d US$925/1125, upstairs room add TT$400; ⋈ ⋈ ) is a cheerful all-inclusive hotel (except alcohol) that has 12 spacious, uniquely decorated rooms with private decks overlooking the beach. The indoor-outdoor restaurant serves breakfast, lunch and dinner.

The Manzanilla–Mayaro Rd, along the east coast, is narrow but traffic is light. Cows and water buffalo roam freely, coconut palms and orange heliconia line the roadside and you can easily spot vultures, egrets and herons along the way.

The road continues south, skirting the freshwater **Nariva Swamp**, an international Ramsar-protected site with more than 6000 hectares of wetlands of 'international im-portance.' A few tour guides offer boat trips through the swamp but tours must be arranged ahead of time. Winston Nanan of **Nanan's Bird Sanctuary Tours** ( ☎ 645-1305; nantour@ tstt.net.tt; tours per person US$100, minimum 2 people) has day-long trips including lunch and transportation from Port of Spain. **Paria Springs** ( ☎ 622-8826; www.pariasprings.com; per person US$95) offers kayaking tours of the swamp coupled with expert birding guides and is one of the best ways to experience the swamp. **Caribbean Discovery Tours** ( ☎ 624-7281; www.caribbeandiscovery tours.com) also offers kayak tours.

After crossing the Ortoire River, Trinidad's longest, you'll encounter a couple of small settlements with simple wooden houses on stilts before reaching the small beach town of **Mayaro**, where a sign points west to San Fernando, 56km away. Mayaro has a smattering of accommodation options. Eats can be found in town or on Church St. There is a small, minimally maintained beach facility. At the festive **Mayaro Entertainment Center** ( ☎ 310-0806; 37 Radix Village), which is an open-air restaurant 1km away from the beach, you will find live music on the weekends, traditional food and a small connected hotel with basic rooms (room TT$350). **Moondrop Beach Resort** ( ☎ 678-4915; cnr Church & Gould St; apt TT$500; ⋈ ) also rents a couple of self-sufficient beachside apartments.

Several houses further south are available for rent to primarily local families, who bring their own bedding, food and cleaning supplies. If you're traveling with friends, these can be quite a good deal for a peaceful stay. **BBS Beach Resort** ( ☎ 678-4310; apt TT$450) has four four-bedroom apartments with full kitchens.

## NORTHEAST COAST

'When you out, you out. When you in, you in,' is what they say about this remote area. Tourism, for the most part, hasn't caught

---

**EFFICIENCY DEFICIENCY: NO PROBLEM, MON**

One of the most magical things about Trinidad and Tobago is the warm, laid-back attitude of the people. Somehow, the vibe infuses your soul and you can relax in a way incomprehensible at home.

There's a price, however. A restaurant might close because staff is limin'. The bus might decide to charter itself for a family beach trip. Your taxi driver could be late because he was waiting for doubles. Service-industry folk prioritize animated cell-phone chats. No problem.

Sometimes you want to tell them where to put their relax. Yet, this is the way of things. Try to go with the flow, appreciate it for what it is, and you'll be less stressed.

onto the rugged coastline beauty with waterfalls, hiking trails, swimming holes and rivers nearby. Not to mention San Souci, one of its beaches, is one of the best places to surf on the island, with lesser places in Grand Rivière and Matura Bay. This region is also the epicenter of leatherback turtle conservation on the island. Accommodations aren't abundant but you can find some nice places to hang your hat.

Inaccessible from Blanchisseuse, this quiet region is bounded by Matelot in the north and Matura in the southeast. The area is accessed via Arima or Sangre Grande (known as Sandy Grandy), where the Eastern Main Rd forks and the Toco Main Rd extends northeast along the coast. Getting here is easiest by far with your own vehicle, but it's possible to arrive via public transportation through the Sangre Grande hub.

## Toco

Sleepy to the point of catatonic, this little village is near some deserted, picturesque beaches and has some modest guesthouses, none with signs. A highlight is the **Sea Sands Camp** ( ☎ 670-8356; Paria Main Rd; per person incl all meals TT$90) run by local herbalist Mrs Bravo. Her hostel-like guesthouse by the ocean has several rooms filled with bunk beds with foam mattresses. The accommodations are clean, but extremely basic. The treasure here is the homey, good-humored atmosphere that provides you with the experience of real Trinidad. If bunk beds aren't your thing, you can still call ahead and arrange a mostly organic meal of some of the best local food and juices on the island. Mrs. Bravo sells homemade Noni wine, local remedy teas that she harvests herself, and the acclaimed sea moss. Local surf spot **San Souci** is a short drive (or nice bike ride; see p749) away.

A lighthouse here marks **Galera Point**, which offers fantastic views of the dramatic coastline, and nearby is a tiny cultural **museum** located in the school and open weekdays.

## Grande Rivière

pop 350

This tiny coastal village now has a number of small nature-oriented resorts that cater to foreign bird-watchers, sea-turtle fans, and general lovers of the outdoors. Though some sections of beach are surfable in winter, other parts are gentler.

Based in a tiny office here is **Grand Rivière Nature Tour Guide Association** ( ☎ 469-7288; 117 Hosang St), a local group dedicated to protecting the turtles. It offers night-time turtle tours (TT$65) on the beach and provides the required permit during the turtle season (March to August). The tours explain this ancient, endangered species and educate about the importance of conservation. The association also offer bird-watching excursions and hiking tours (US$20 to US$50) to waterfalls, swimming holes and seldom visited natural wonders in the area.

You can ask locals about guesthouses, but the majority of official tourist accommodations here are higher-end. There's no significant place to buy groceries, so hotels provide meals from their restaurants.

The five bungalows dappling **Acajou** ( ☎ 670-3771; www.acajoutrinidad.com; 209 Paria Main Rd; bungalow US$110) are beside the mouth of a river flowing into the ocean. The decor is simple and fresh with rich wood and bright white linens and cushions. French doors open to hammocked patios that look towards the ocean. No air-conditioning, TV or phones makes this a fantastic retreat.

The adorable, well-done rooms at **Le Grande Almandier** ( ☎ 670-1013; www.legrandealmandier.com; 2 Hosang St; s/d/ste TT$538/675/1000; 🖳 🞨 ) have quaint balconies overlooking the sea, and their laid-back café has rooftop seating. Of Grand Rivière's beachside accommodations, this is the best value.

Local art and murals adorn the beachside **Mt Plaisir Estate Hotel** ( ☎ 670-8381; www.mtplaisir .com; Grande Rivière; r incl breakfast TT$633, ste TT$945). Its rooms feature teak floors and handcrafted furnishings. It offers airport shuttles (TT$630, one way). The restaurant (mains TT$90 to TT$150) serves fresh seafood, organic fruits and vegetables and homemade bread.

## Matura & Around

The most developed **turtle conservation** effort underway in Trinidad is run by **Nature Seekers** ( ☎ 727-3933; www.natureseekers.org) in Matura, which runs educational programs and turtle tours (TT$90) in Matura Bay. **Earthwatch** (www.earthwatch.org) supports Nature Seekers' effort by contracting it for volunteer programs. Independent volunteering can happen when Earthwatch isn't there, but tours run the whole turtle season (March–August).

Volunteers stay in Nature Seekers' basic **guest house** (dm/r TT$250/350, incl meals TT$375/475).

The only other official accommodation nearby is in Salybia (Sally Bay). **Salybia Nature Resort & Spa** ( ☎ 668-5959; www.salybiaresort .com; Mile 13.75, Toco Main Rd, Salybia; r TT$1125-TT$2175; 🔀 🖳 🔲 ) frequently hosts conferences, and the rooms are overpriced, some of them showing their years. Check the must-factor before deciding. The grounds are replete with lush tropical landscaping, a pool, waterfall and a tumultuous beach.

Right across from the resort is a sign for the **Rio Seco Waterfall Trail** in Matura National Park, which leads to a swimming hole and a waterfall. It's a 45-minute hike from the trailhead.

# TOBAGO

While Trinidad booms with industry and parties all night, tiny Tobago (just 42km across) slouches in a deck chair with a Caribe in hand watching its crystalline waters shimmer in the sun. Though Tobago is proud of its rainforests, fantastic dive sites, stunning aquamarine bays and nature reserves, it's OK with not being mentioned in a Beach Boys song. It accepts its tourists without vigor, but rather with languor, and allows them to choose between plush oceanside hotels or tiny guesthouses in villages where you walk straight to the open-air bar with sandy bare feet, and laugh with the locals drinking rum.

When Hurricane Flora ripped by in 1963, she basically blew away the agro-based plantation economy. The government then turned its rebuilding efforts to tourism. Though there's enough infrastructure to make navigating Tobago easy, it's not over-run…yet. Don't dally in visiting because times are changing. Sleepy Tobago is increasingly being woken by a jostling tourism industry that loves it for its great value, beauty and genuinely friendly culture.

## Orientation

Most of the white-sand beaches and tourist development are centered on the southwestern side of Tobago, starting at Crown Point and running along a string of bays up to Arnos Vale. The lowlands that predominate in the southwest extend to Tobago's only large town, Scarborough. The coast beyond is dotted with small fishing villages and the interior is ruggedly mountainous, with thick rainforest. Divers and snorkelers, and those seeking mellow days visit the easternmost villages of Speyside and Charlotteville. The nearby uninhabited islets of Little Tobago, Goat Island and St Giles Island are nature reserves abundant in both bird and marine life.

## Getting There & Away

### AIR
Most people get to Tobago by taking the 20-minute flight from Trinidad (see p774), although a couple of airlines now offer direct flights from Europe. The Crown Point International Airport, like Tobago, is small, relaxed and rarely rushed.

### BOAT
A slower, less expensive alternative to flying to Tobago is to take the ferry from Port of Spain, Trinidad, to Scarborough, Tobago (see p775).

## Getting Around
Getting around any of Tobago's small towns is easy on foot. Buses and route taxis aren't as readily available as they are on Trinidad, but there's enough to get you from point A to point B.

### BICYCLE
There are rental places on the island, and biking is a fine way to navigate around the towns, and sometimes town to town, on Tobago.

### BUS
There is a regular bus service from Scarborough to Crown Point, Plymouth (via Buccoo and Mt Irvine) and most villages on the island. The Scarborough bus terminal is a short walk from the ferry terminal off Milford Rd on Sangster Hill Rd. Buses to/from Crown Point (TT$2) and Plymouth (TT$2) run frequently from dawn to 8pm. Service decreases at night and on weekends.

Other departures from Scarborough are: Charlotteville via Speyside (TT$8, 1½ hours, seven departures from 5am to 6pm), Parlatuvier via Castara (TT$6, 45 minutes, departures at 6am, 2:30pm, 4pm and 6pm) and Roxborough (TT$5, 30 minutes, six departures from 6:30am to 4pm).

# TOBAGO

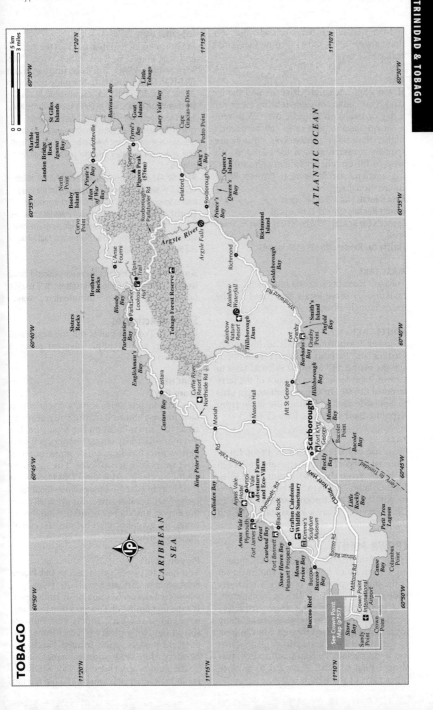

Note that buses aren't reliable and you don't always know if they'll come (see boxed text, p752).

### CAR
If you want a leisurely drive around the island, you could consider renting a car for a day or two. You must be over 25 to rent a car on Tobago, and rates can be slightly higher than on Trinidad. Gas stations are sparsely scattered around the island, so it's wise to fill up when you can. The following agencies are at or near Crown Point International Airport:

**Auto Rentals** ( ☎ 639-0644; airport)
**Baird's Rentals** ( ☎ 639-2528; airport)
**Spence's Car Rental** ( ☎ 639-7611; Store Bay Rd, Crown Point)
**Thrifty Car Rental** ( ☎ 639-8507; airport)

### MAXI-TAXI
Tobago's maxi-taxis have a blue band. These taxis mostly serve locals and travel can be excruciatingly slow.

### ROUTE TAXI
In lower Scarborough, taxis to Plymouth, Castara, and Parlatuvier depart from opposite the market (TT$5 to TT$8), and taxis to Crown Point leave from in front of the ferry terminal (TT$6). In upper Scarborough, taxis to Speyside and Charlotteville leave from Republic Bank by James Park (TT$12).

### TAXI
Taxis are available at Crown Point International Airport and charge about TT$25 to hotels around Crown Point, TT$30 to Pigeon Point, TT$50 to Scarborough, TT$60 to Mt Irvine or Buccoo and TT$260 to Charlotteville. There's a taxi stand at Club Pigeon Point.

## CROWN POINT
Home of the island's airport, quickly sprawling Crown Point on Tobago's southwest tip is the tourist epicenter, offering a relatively wide range of accommodations, restaurants, and some nightlife. The area's attractive beaches and extensive services make many tourists stay put. Even though you can look to the fringes for a good roti, anyone wanting to appreciate Tobago's cultural charms should plan to push eastward to explore other parts of the island.

## Information
In Crown Point, Republic Bank, at the airport, and RBTT, next to the Clothes Wash Café, have 24-hour ATMs. You'll also find banks and ATMs in Scarborough. In Speyside there's no ATM. Charlotteville has an unreliable one.
**Clothes Wash Café** ( ☎ 639-0007; Airport Rd; ☷ 8am-9pm) Check your email (per hr TT$20) during the spin cycle at this internet café-slash-laundry. You can use the coin-operated washers and dryers (about TT$30 each load) here, or drop it off and they'll do it for you for around twice as much.
**RCS** ( ☎ 631-8597; Spence Plaza, Milford Rd; per 30min TT$10; ☷ 9am-6pm Mon-Fri, to 2pm Sat) On the 2nd floor in Spence Plaza, you'll find flat-screen computers.
**Tourist office** ( ☎ 639-0509; Crown Point International Airport; ☷ 8am-10pm) The staff provide comprehensive information and can help you book a room or find hiking and bird-watching tour guides.

Anyone needing medical services should head to the **Scarborough General Hospital** ( ☎ 639-2551; Calder Hall Rd; ☷ 24hr), a 15-minute drive away.

## Sights & Activities
In Crown Point, it's all about the beach and the water, and a couple of great beaches deliver.

### BEACHES
#### Store Bay
You'll find white sands and good year-round swimming at Store Bay, the body of water close to Crown Point on the west side. It's a center of activity where vendors sell souvenirs and hawkers push glass-bottom boat tours of Buccoo Reef. The facilities include a clean rest room (TT$1). Several food huts here serve up delicious local food (see p760). It's just a five-minute walk from the airport and there's no admission fee. At times, the glass-bottom boat pushers can be overly persistent.

#### Pigeon Point
You have to pay to get access to **Club Pigeon Point** (admission TT$18, weekly pass TT$75; ☷ 9am-7pm), whose facilities are harmoniously landscaped. It's the fine dining of Tobago's beaches, with bars and snack bars, toilets and showers spread out along plenty of beachfront. The postcard-perfect, palm-fringed beach has powdery white sands and clear aqua water.

The wind here is a huge draw for windsurfers and kitesurfers who weave and flip around

# CROWN POINT

0                400 m
0          0.2 miles

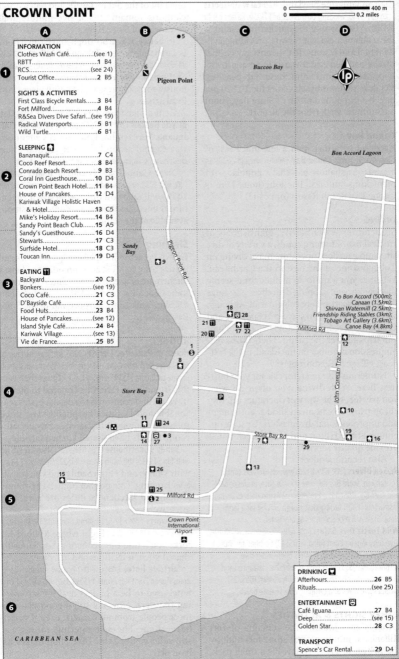

**INFORMATION**
Clothes Wash Café..................(see 1)
RBTT..........................................**1** B4
RCS........................................(see 24)
Tourist Office...........................**2** B5

**SIGHTS & ACTIVITIES**
First Class Bicycle Rentals......**3** B4
Fort Milford.............................**4** B4
R&Sea Divers Dive Safari....(see 19)
Radical Watersports.................**5** B1
Wild Turtle...............................**6** B1

**SLEEPING** 🏠
Bananaquit...............................**7** C4
Coco Reef Resort.....................**8** B4
Conrado Beach Resort.............**9** B3
Coral Inn Guesthouse.............**10** D4
Crown Point Beach Hotel.....**11** B4
House of Pancakes.................**12** D4
Kariwak Village Holistic Haven
 & Hotel.................................**13** C5
Mike's Holiday Resort............**14** B4
Sandy Point Beach Club........**15** A5
Sandy's Guesthouse................**16** D4
Stewarts...................................**17** C3
Surfside Hotel..........................**18** C3
Toucan Inn..............................**19** D4

**EATING** 🍴
Backyard...................................**20** C3
Bonkers..................................(see 19)
Coco Café................................**21** C3
D'Bayside Café........................**22** C3
Food Huts................................**23** B4
House of Pancakes................(see 12)
Island Style Café.....................**24** B4
Kariwak Village......................(see 13)
Vie de France..........................**25** B5

**DRINKING** 🍷
Afterhours...............................**26** B5
Rituals...................................(see 25)

**ENTERTAINMENT** 🎭
Café Iguana.............................**27** B4
Deep.......................................(see 15)
Golden Star.............................**28** C3

**TRANSPORT**
Spence's Car Rental................**29** D4

*Buccoo Bay*

*Pigeon Point*

*Bon Accord Lagoon*

*Sandy Bay*

*Store Bay*

To Bon Accord (500m);
Canaan (1.5km);
Shirvan Watermill (2.5km);
Friendship Riding Stables (3km);
Tobago Art Gallery (3.6km);
Canoe Bay (4.8km)

*Crown Point International Airport*

*CARIBBEAN SEA*

Pigeon Point Rd

Milford Rd

John Gorman Trace

Store Bay Rd

Milford Rd

their aquamarine playland. **Radical Watersports** ( ☎ 631-5150; windsurf boards per hr TT$250, kayaks per hr TT$100; 🕑 9am-5pm), at the northernmost end, is the center of these wind sports, providing quality rental and lessons. It also rents kayaks that can be paddled east towards the mangrove-y 'No Man's Land' and deserted beaches. Vendors rent out beach chairs for TT$20 per day. It's just 1.5km north of Store Bay, about a 15-minute walk from the airport.

### Canoe Bay

Accessed by a dirt road a few miles east of Crown Point, **Canoe Bay** (adult/child TT$15/10) is a gorgeous shallow bay that's popular with picnicking families. The lone hotel here is Canoe Bay Beach Resort (opposite).

### DIVING

Stupendous water clarity, giant shoals of tropical fish, stunning corals, a variety of dive sites and excellent operators make diving on Tobago some of the best in the Caribbean. Whether you want to do mellow coral-seeing dives or current-zipping drift dives past huge turtles and sharks, Tobago's got it all. Although serious divers tend to stay up at Speyside and Charlotteville, dive operators in Crown Point run trips all over the island. There is one recompression chamber on the island, in the east-coast village of Roxborough.

Numerous dive operators vie for your business here. With diving, you often get what you pay for, so be wary of operators offering cheap trips – it can mean shoddy equipment and unprofessional divemasters. Upscale operators at the Hilton and Coco Beach hotels provide quality service.

Also recommended:

**R&Sea Divers** ( ☎ 639-8120; www.rseadivers.com; Toucan Inn, Store Bay Rd; dive US$40) Safe, professional and friendly, R&Sea is a Professional Association of Diving Instructors (PADI) facility that's been around for a long time. Staff will pick up divers at any hotel.

**Wild Turtle Dive Safari** ( ☎ 639-6558; www.wildturtle dive.com; Pigeon Point Rd; dive US$40) Certified by PADI and diver recommended, it offers open-water dive certification (US$375) as well as refresher, advanced and divemaster classes. The overnight Dive Safari (US$325) includes five dives and camping on a remote beach.

### OTHER SIGHTS & ACTIVITIES

Other sights include the remains of **Fort Milford**, a crumbling coral-stone fort built by the British in 1777. Today, it's a small park,

but a bit of the old fort walls and half a dozen cannons remain. It's a five-minute walk southwest of Store Bay.

In between Scarborough and Crown Point is Lowlands, where **Tobago Art Gallery** ( ☎ 639-0457; artgal2@hotmail.com: Hibiscus Drive, Lowlands; 🕑 10am-5pm Mon-Fri) is located. The studio houses some impressive, beautiful pieces from local artists.

Rent a bike from James Percy of **First Class Bicycle Rentals** ( ☎ 494-2547; per day TT$60) by Café Iguana. He even has tandems. It's a fantastic way to tool around the area. Rental prices decrease when renting for multiple days.

Near Canoe bay, **Friendship Riding Stables** ( ☎ 620-9788; www.friendshipridingstables.com; 90min ride TT$250) will take you on an equestrian adventure. Sometimes there are volunteer positions available at the stable.

## Sleeping

Crown Point has inexpensive guesthouses and luxury resorts. Most accommodations have a kitchenette or access to one. Unless otherwise indicated, all accommodations are less than a 1.5km walk to the airport and to the Store Bay beach.

### BUDGET

**House of Pancakes** ( ☎ 639-9866; kittycat@tstt.net.tt; cnr Milford Rd & John Gorman Trace; dm TT$95, r with shared/private bathroom TT$195/265; 🔀 💻 ) Over the years this friendly operation has catered to budget travelers and continues to keep its prices reasonable and facilities hospitable. The three rooms are simple, with shared or private bathroom. Guests have shared kitchen facilities.

**Sandy's Guesthouse** ( ☎ 639-9221; Store Bay Rd; s/d with fan TT$135/180, with air-con TT$270/360; 🔀 ) Stay with Valerie and Hugh Sandy and you stay in a welcoming Tobagonian home. The rooms and shared kitchen facilities are scrubbed attentively.

**Stewarts** ( ☎ 639-8319; Airport Rd; s/d TT$150/170, d with air-con TT$320; 🔀 ) Right where Milford Rd forks you'll find this economical option with shared kitchen facilities and balconies.

**Surfside Hotel** ( ☎ 639-0614; www.surfsidetobago .com; Pigeon Point Rd; r from TT$250-350; 🔀 💻 ) This hotel used to be a budget deal for scrounging travelers. Now it's still a good place to meet people from all corners, even if prices have risen. The self-catering rooms are still solid value. Extra Dive Shop makes its base here.

**Coral Inn Guesthouse** ( ☎ 639-0967; John Gorman Trace; s/d US$40/60; ❄ ⬚ ) This clean guesthouse quietly set back from Store Bay Rd has self-contained apartments with two bedrooms each. The friendly owner, Veda Gopaul, lives upstairs. Rates are negotiable for longer stays.

**Scarborough House** ( ☎ 730-1764; www.scarborough housejs.com; 24 Dillon St, Bon Accord; s/d US$40/60; ❄ ⬚ ) Joyce Scarborough provides you with an intimate experience in her columned home. The downstairs contains a variety of self-contained apartments, and there's a cute pool in the back. Name your breakfast, American or local (US$7), and Joyce will whip it up. It's in Bon Accord, east of the center.

**Mike's Holiday Resort** ( ☎ 639-8050; Store Bay Rd; apt TT$300; ❄ ) Centrally located in the heart of Crown Point, Mike's has 12 clean, modern apartments with large kitchens that are updated and cheerful. In a town of skyrocketing prices, this is a deal.

**Bananaquit** ( ☎ 639-9733; www.bananaquit.com; Store Bay Rd; studio/loft US$60/65) The arrangement of these spacious 14 apartments around the courtyard garden creates a community feel. The lofts upstairs can sleep up to six people. Guests can use the pool at neighboring Store Bay Resort. It's a five-minute walk to Store Bay beach.

**Canoe Bay Beach Resort** ( ☎ 685-4785; www.canoe baytt.com; Canoe Bay; s/d TT$400/460; ❄ ⬚ ) Set on 17.6 hectares in Canoe Bay, this resort is a quiet, low-key place featuring 18 apartment-style villas, a bar, restaurant and several huts along the beach.

### MIDRANGE & TOP END

**Conrado Beach Resort** ( ☎ 639-0145; www.holiday intobago.com/conradobeachresort.html; Pigeon Point Rd; s US$90-110 d US$100-115; ❄ ⬚ ) A short walk from Pigeon Point, this no-frills beach resort proves to be good beachside hotel value. Sand and surf are at stumbling distance. The rooms are clean, many with ocean-view balconies. There is a restaurant and bar on-site.

**Crown Point Beach Hotel** ( ☎ 639-8781; www .crownpointbeachhotel.com; d studio US$90, cabana US$100, 1-bedroom apt US$130; ❄ ⬚ ) Somewhat clinging to yesteryear, this hotel enjoys a good beachfront location next to Fort Milford. All rooms have kitchenettes and views of the ocean. There's also a pleasant pool, tennis courts and a restaurant.

**Toucan Inn** ( ☎ 639-7173; www.toucan-inn.com; Store Bay Rd; r US$100-120; ❄ ⬚ ) This 20-room hotel creates an intimate, relaxing atmosphere with four circular duplex cabins arranged around a pool and a section of rooms wrapping around a lush garden. The simple rooms have teak furnishings and comfortable beds. Also on the grounds is the Bonkers bar-restaurant. It's a 10-minute walk to Store Bay.

**Sandy Point Beach Club** ( ☎ 639-0820; www.sandy pointbeachclub.com; Sandy Point; apt US$100-250; ❄ ⬚ ) A good-value option for families or bigger groups, this resort mostly rents its comfortable, well-attended apartments for week-long stays. The apartments range in size from studios to four-bedroom units that sleep 10. Shuttles to other beaches run daily.

**Summerland Suites** ( ☎ 631-5053; www.summer landsuites.info; Roberts Street, Bon Accord; 1-bedroom apt/2-bedroom apt TT$540/660; ❄ ⬚ ) Set in a quiet Bon Accord neighborhood, these new self-contained suites are slickly laid along a long skinny pool. The apartments are meticulous with updated, tasteful furnishings.

**Kariwak Village Holistic Haven & Hotel** ( ☎ 639-8442; www.kariwak.co.tt; r from US$150; ❄ ⬚ ) Off Store Bay Rd, just a two-minute walk from the airport, Kariwak nestles in lush landscaping. The duplex cabanas line paths that wind through tropical gardens. It's both rustic and refreshing. There's an organic herb garden, two pools (one with waterfall), and free yoga and tai chi classes. The Kariwak Village restaurant serves some of Tobago's freshest, tastiest food.

**Coco Reef Resort** ( ☎ 639-8572; www.cocoreef.com; r low/high season from US$310/460; ❄ ⬚ ⬚ ) Coco Reef pays elegant homage to luxurious colonial architecture, but a real highlight is the gorgeous Cuban art that lavishes the entire facility. Rooms overlook pretty Coconut Bay, and guests enjoy top-tier amenities and excellent service. The resort is just next to the Store Bay parking lot off Milford Rd. Offers wi-fi.

## Eating

**D'Bayside Cafe** ( ☎ 708-4406; Spence Plaza, Milford Rd; roti TT$15-20; ⏱ 7am-10pm Mon-Sat) Tucked a bit off of Milford Rd, this local haunt has tasty rotis and fresh juice. The interior has air-con and outside there are umbrella tables.

**Vie de France** ( ☎ 631-8088; mains TT$20-50; ⏱ 6:30am-8pm) Don't let the name fool you. This is the closest thing to an American diner that you'll find in Tobago, replete with greasy spoon faves. Just across from the airport, it's a great place for a preflight bite. Plus, the coffee shop Rituals is attached for your caffeine fix.

**Island Style Cafe** ( ☎ 708-4406; Spence Plaza, Milford Rd; roti TT$25-30; ☺ 7am-10pm Mon-Sat) Locals stop by here for breakfast bake that you can load with interesting goodies, to grab a roti, or for barbecue dinner. It's cheap, local and yummy.

**House of Pancakes** ( ☎ 639-9866; cnr Milford Rd & John Gorman Trace; mains TT$35-80; ☺ breakfast) Lauded as the best breakfast in town, there are flapjacks, fresh juices and smoothies, and omelets served until noon on a pleasant wooden deck.

**Backyard** ( ☎ 639-7264; Milford Rd; mains TT$35-80; ☺ noon-7pm Mon-Fri) It's a treat to visit this colorful roadside café that brings a European spin to local ingredients. The dishes are light and flavorful and the juices – like papaya guava (TT$18) – are lovely. It's vegetarian friendly.

**Bonkers** ( ☎ 639-7173; Toucan Inn, Store Bay Rd; breakfast & lunch mains TT$40-70, dinner mains TT$70-200; ☺ breakfast, lunch & dinner) This veranda restaurant and bar serves tasty breakfasts, sandwiches, salads, and fish and chips. On Mondays and Wednesdays there's live steel pan or African drumming at 7pm.

**Coco Café** ( ☎ 639-0996; Old Store Bay Rd; mains TT$50-150; ☺ dinner) Candlelit and breezy, the wistful ambience, complimented by friendly staff, leads you to a lovely experience. You won't go wrong choosing from its cocktail or seafood menus.

**our pick** **Kariwak Village** ( ☎ 639-8442; Kariwak Village Hotel; breakfast TT$70, dinner from TT$120; ☺ breakfast, lunch & dinner) Beneath the thatched roofs and coral stone walls of this open-air restaurant, the Kariwak chefs create masterpieces of Caribbean and Creole cuisine using fresh ingredients including organic herbs and vegetables from the garden. Breakfast includes a healthy bowl of fresh fruit, eggs, fish, homemade granola and homemade toast. At lunch and dinner, you can do no wrong with the specials, usually featuring grilled fish and seafood. There are vegetarian options, too.

**Shirvan Watermill** ( ☎ 639-0000; mains TT$75-180; ☺ dinner from 6:30pm, closed Mon) On Shirvan Rd between Crown Point and Buccoo Bay, this longtime popular restaurant sits under a coral-columned gazebo beside the mill of a former sugar estate. It has lovely outdoor dining and some of the island's best food, such as delicate soups and salads, meats, chicken Creole and lobster.

The best place to each lunch is at the row of food huts opposite the beach at Store Bay. Several huts run by local women offer delicious heaping local dishes like rotis, shark and bake, crab and dumplin', and simple plate lunches for TT$20 to TT$50. **Sylvia's** ( ☺ 7am-4ish) has delicious oil down (breadfruit sautéed in a curry sauce) amongst other scrumptious local dishes. Also, across from the airport starting around 10am (ending when all is sold) a lady sells doubles for TT$2.50 a pop out of the back of a car and is known throughout the island.

There are several minimarts on Store Bay Rd but for big grocery shops head east of Crown Point to **Pennysaver's** (Milford Rd), near Canaan. Also, in Bon Accord, tiny **E and F Health Foods** ( ☎ 639-3992; 7 Alfred Crescent, Bon Accord; ☺ 9am-4pm Mon-Fri) sells whole wheat bakery items and freshly ground peanut butter.

## Drinking
**Afterhours** ( ☎ 639-8397; ☺ 10am-late) Karen Quashie runs this reliable bar-restaurant that serves food and drinks when most of quiet little Tobago is head to pillow.

## Entertainment
**Café Iguana** ( ☎ 631-8205; www.iguanatobago.com; cnr Store Bay & Milford Rds; ☺ 6-10pm Thu-Tue) This stylish, casual hangout serves up good cocktails and live jazz-inspired tunes. The menu offers good local cuisine, but most folks come for the Friday and Saturday night jazz music.

**Golden Star** ( ☎ 639-0873; cnr Milford & Pigeon Point Rds; occasional cover charge TT$30) Like a rice staple in Crown Point's entertainment menu, it may not be the saucy exotic main, but it satiates you. This locally popular club features live steel bands, Afterwork Lime with DJs, and, occasionally, local bands.

**Deep** (Sandy Point Beach Club, Sandy Point; cover charge TT$40; ☺ 10pm-late Thu-Sat) DJs spin soca, salsa and merengue at this dance destination.

**Shade** ( ☎ 639-9651; Bon Accord; ☺ 6pm-late) Locals, foreigners, tourists all flock to Shade for a proper party lime. It's probably the hippest place on the island to wine and grine.

## BUCCOO
If you stay in Buccoo, people in other parts of Tobago will raise their eyebrows and possibly say, 'Ah, going local.' The narrow tan-sand beach of Buccoo Bay doesn't compete with the generous white sands of Store Bay,

and its amenities aren't as refined, but tiny Buccoo offers a taste of true local flavor: friendly folks who define laid-back, breathtaking sunsets over the bay, and the infamous Sunday School party every week.

## Festivals & Events

**Sunday School** Lacking any religious affiliation, 'Sunday School' is the sly title for a weekly street party held in Buccoo every Sunday night. Until around 10pm, partygoers are mostly tourists enjoying rum drinks and music, plus local food at TT$100 per head. Later in the night, folks from Buccoo and all over the island come to 'take a wine' or just hang out. Steel pan starts at about 9pm, and later on, DJs spin everything from reggae to soca, and dance parties usually evolve.

**Easter Weekend** One of the largest events in Tobago happens over the Easter weekend, when everyone flocks to Buccoo for a series of open-air parties, massive feasts and – the highlight of it all – goat races. Taken very seriously, goat racing draws more bets than a Las Vegas casino. The competing goats get pampered like beauty contestants and the eventual champion is forever revered. The partying stretches throughout the weekend and the big races happen on Tuesday. Also look out for the live crab races, certainly less high-profile but equally bizarre.

## Sleeping

**Miller's Guesthouse** ( ☎ 660-8371; www.millers-guesthouse.tripod.com; 14 Miller St; dm TT$90; r TT$130-150; ☒ ) The hostel digs here are perfect for a budget traveler and attached is a popular bar for an afternoon beer.

**Rusty's** ( ☎ 639-9461; Miller St; apt TT$200; ☒ ) Not scrupulously clean, but the price can't be beat for fully equipped oceanside apartments that share a patio looking over the bay.

**Seaside Garden Guesthouse** ( ☎ 639-0682; www.tobago-guesthouse.com; Buccoo Bay Rd; r US$35-50, apt US$90; ☒ ) One of the nicest small guesthouses in Tobago and stumbling distance from Sunday School, the Seaside Garden Guesthouse has rooms and apartments that are meticulously cared for. A tastefully decorated sitting room with a bay window enhances the serenity of the place while the communal kitchen is equipped to create a gourmet masterpiece.

## Eating & Drinking

**Shakey's** ( ☎ 302-8088; Buccoo Main Rd; shakes TT$9, mains TT$25) Everyone loves wild-eyed Shakey, who serves up homemade ice cream, fat sea-moss-and-peanut-butter shakes and fresh local food.

**ourpick La Tartaruga** ( ☎ 639-0940; www.latartaruga.com; Buccoo Bay Main Rd; mains TT$75-225; ☽ dinner, closed Sun) It's surprising to find this authentic fine Italian restaurant with scrumptious homemade pastas and delectable wine (it has the second-largest Italian wine cellar in the Caribbean) tucked away in tiny Buccoo. But it's a treat indeed. The ambience melds lively Caribbean colors and art with a candlelit patio fit for a romantic Italian café.

**Captain's Sand Bar** (Buccoo Bay Main Rd; ☽ afternoon-late) It's the most jovial, laid-back dive in Buccoo. You can drink a cold one, chat with locals, and listen to the latest soca booming from the sound system. It also has internet

---

### BUCCOO REEF

Stretching offshore between Pigeon Point and Buccoo Bay, the extensive Buccoo Reef was designated as a marine park in 1973 and a Ramsar Site in 2006. The fringing reef boasts five reef flats separated by deep channels. The sheer array of flora and fauna – dazzling sponges, hard corals and tropical fish – makes marine biologists giddy.

Glass-bottom boat reef tours are an accessible way to explore Tobago's incredible treasure. Tours leave from Store Bay, Pigeon Point and the village of Buccoo. Most operators charge US$15 to US$20 per person for a two-hour trip. The boats pass over the reef (much of which is just a meter or two beneath the surface), stop for snorkeling and end with a swim in the **Nylon Pool**, a calm, shallow area with a sandy bottom and clear turquoise waters. **Johnson & Sons** ( ☎ 639-8519; tours TT$90) runs a good 2½-hour tour, leaving from Buccoo at low tide when snorkeling is best.

Despite efforts of conservation groups like the **Buccoo Reef Trust** (www.buccooreeftrust.org), Buccoo Reef has unfortunately been battered by too much use and not enough protection. In addition to anchor damage, reef walking and overfishing, polluted runoff from sewage, construction and agricultural activities floods the water and smothers the reef.

Do your part and never walk on or touch coral and avoid products made from coral or marine species (like turtle-shell jewelry).

access (TT$20 per hour). A mas camp is based here during the Carnival season.

## LEEWARD ROAD

The stretch of coastline from Mt Irvine Bay to Plymouth has exclusive resorts hugging their own bays; elegant villas; and a golf course. Like a sloppy adolescent propping its feet on the table in a fancy living room, Black Rock's tiny Pleasant Prospect is right in the middle. It's a teeny surfer haunt: a cluster of cheap unofficial accommodation, eateries and a few good places to lime.

### Sights & Activities

A roadside public recreation facility at **Mt Irvine Beach**, 200m north of Mt Irvine Bay Hotel, has sheltered picnic tables and changing rooms, plus a good beachside restaurant (see Surfer's Restaurant & Bar, opposite), roti shacks and a decent craft shop. Surfers migrate here from December to March. You can rent sit-on-top kayaks and surf boards on the beach. Also, Frankie Tours and Rentals (p773) is based in the parking area.

On a rocky hill at the north side of Stone Haven Bay is **Fort Bennett**, about 500m west of a marked turn-off on the main road. The British built the fort in 1778 to defend against US enemy ships. Little remains of it other than a couple of cannons, but there's a good view of the coast.

Turn right off the main road by Mt Irving Golf Course and you'll see signs leading you to **Kimme's Sculpture Museum** ( ☎ 639-0257; Bethel; admission TT$20; ☺ 10am-2pm Sun or by appointment). German eccentric Luise Kimme sells and displays fantastic, 2m to 3m wood-and-metal Caribbean-themed sculptures from her whacked-out mansion.

**Grafton Caledonia Wildlife Sanctuary** ( ☺ 8am-4pm) is right by Grafton Beach Resort – fol-

---

> #### YOGA, ANYONE?
>
> Some upscale hotels on Tobago offer yoga classes free to guests, but outsiders can join for around TT$50. Call for scheduling. Here are some options:
>
> ▪ Le Grand Courlan Resort & Spa (right)
>
> ▪ Kariwak Village Holistic Haven & Hotel (p759)
>
> ▪ Blue Haven Hotel (p766)

---

low signs inland, and it's a short walk to the sanctuary. After Hurricane Flora in 1963, Brit Eleanor Alefounder converted her 36 hectares into a bird sanctuary. There are some short hiking trails, and the bird-watching is touted as some of the best on the island. The birds come out of the rafters at the 4pm feeding time. Her family rents out the simple yet spacious **estate house** (www.graftonhouse-tobago.com) on the property.

### Sleeping

Resorts and rental villas dominate on this stretch of coastline, but Pleasant Prospect has a handful of unofficial guesthouses.

**Two Seasons** ( ☎ 729-9329; Pleasant Prospect; r US$15-25) Right above the Fish Pot restaurant, this basic four-room apartment has a shared balcony, living room and bathroom. It's pretty darn clean for housing a jovial, limin', surfer crowd. Your experience here will be interactive.

**Seahorse Inn** ( ☎ 639-0686; www.seahorseinn tobago.com; Stone Haven Bay; r incl breakfast summer/winter US$175/135; ✸ ) A nice contrast to the big resorts, this lovely guesthouse, just below the Grafton Beach Resort, is a low-key establishment with four spacious rooms with teak floors and broad balconies facing Stone Haven Bay.

**Villas at Stonehaven** ( ☎ 639-0361; www.stonehaven villas.com; US$400-950) is one of several companies that rent out villas. This could be a good choice for families or groups who plan on staying longer than a few days.

An exclusive, all-inclusive resort, **Le Grand Courland Resort & Spa** ( ☎ 639-9667, in the USA 800-655-1214; www.legrandcourland-resort.com; Stone Haven Bay, Black Rock; r US$318-402; ✸ 🖳 🖭 ) overlooks Stone Haven Bay. Rates include high-class amenities, drinks and all meals. Under the same ownership is **Grafton Beach Resort** ( ☎ 639-0191, in the USA 800- 223-6510; www.grafton-resort.com; Stone Haven Bay; d garden view/ocean view US$185/195; ✸ 🖳 🖭 ), a cheaper all-inclusive across the street.

### Eating & Drinking

Pleasant Prospect has a cluster of local bars, eateries, and even a Rituals coffee shop. Each hotel mostly has its own restaurant.

**Joanne's Fingerlickin' Tasty Food** (Pleasant Prospect; TT$25-35; ☺ lunch) A food booth that has delightful local fare, fresh juices and homemade baked goods.

**Fish Pot** ( ☎ 635-1728; Pleasant Prospect; mains TT$30-80; ☺ lunch Mon-Sat, dinner Wed-Fri) Very reasonable and recommended around the island, this laid-back restaurant specializes in seafood and is equipped with an open-air patio. There's music on Friday nights.

**Surfer's Restaurant & Bar** (☎ 639-8407; Mt Irvine Beach; mains TT$60-150) This casual spot serves up delicious fish stew, fish and bake, and sandwiches.

**Seahorse Inn Restaurant & Bar** (Seahorse Inn, Stone Haven Bay; mains TT$70-200; ☾ lunch & dinner) Sitting alfresco amid a tropical setting overlooking the water, with the sound of waves crashing below, this special restaurant specializes in gourmet Creole cuisine.

In Pleasant Prospect, the Oceanview Bar is an unpretentious bar nooked into a cliff overlooking the ocean. It's a great place to snag a beer after a day of sand and surf. It has barbecue Fridays as well. Right across the road, Moon Over Water also is a good place to hang with folks.

## ARNOS VALE ROAD

You could just call it the Rodeo Dr of bird-watching. There are a smattering of nature reserves as well as lovely higher-end accommodations which cater to nature lovers and bird-watchers.

Quietly plush and decadently verdant, **Arnos Vale Hotel** (☎ 639-2881; www.arnosvalehotel .com; Arnos Vale Rd; r from US$215; ☒) is frequented by nature lovers wanting retreat and premium bird-watching. The lovely veranda restaurant is known for its afternoon tea (TT$60). The rooms are fresh feeling, with tranquil balconies. Amenities include a pool, bar, gym, pleasant strip of beach, massage services, airport transfers, car rentals and tour arrangements.

**Adventure Farm and Nature Reserve** (☎ 639-2839; call to arrange visit) is a 5-hectare working organic estate that has retained about a hectare of wild area, which is home to a wealth of bird species and is revered for its hummingbirds. You can also come to learn about tropical agriculture practices, buy organic fruit, or take some short hikes around the estate.

**our pick** **Adventure Eco-Villas** (☎ 639-2839; www.adventure-ecovillas.com; Arnos Vale Rd, Adventure; s/d/ste $100/150/200; ☒) is run by owner Ean Mackey who cares for the two lovely on-site cottages which have updated kitchens, hardwood floors, tons of windows that open into the forest, a huge bath tub, and a spacious

deck. You feel a part of the environment as if you were camping, but you're actually in a styled-out cottage.

Follow signs off Arnos Vale Rd down a rough road for 20 minutes to the charming, secluded **Cuffie River Nature Retreat** (☎ 660-0505; www.cuffieriver.com; Runnemede; r from US$150, for full board add per person US$60) at the edge of the rainforest. Utterly designed for bird-watching fanatics, it has a highly trained birding guide on hand to lead hikes around the area. The spacious, comfortable rooms equipped with balconies are flooded with natural light. There is also an ecofriendly swimming pool and a number of fresh-water springs nearby. Full board (of tasty food, much of it harvested locally) is offered. Alternatively, you could enquire about the two self-catering apartments.

## PLYMOUTH

Though the largest town on the west coast, Plymouth is home to just a few thousand inhabitants and isn't a major destination. At the end of Shelbourne St is the **Mystery Tombstone** of Betty Stiven, who died in 1783, presumably during childbirth. Her tombstone (that seems to fascinate people) reads cryptically, 'She was a mother without knowing it, and a wife without letting her husband know it, except by her kind indulgences to him.'

Plymouth was the first British capital of Tobago, and it was here that the British built **Fort James** in 1811, the remains of which stand 200m west of the tombstone. Affording extraordinary views of Great Courland Bay, this small hilltop fortification remains largely intact.

Coming back from Fort James, turn right after the bus stop and continue 150m to the **Great Courland Bay Monument**, an odd concrete creation honoring the early Courlander colonists who settled the area in the 17th century.

## CASTARA & AROUND

About an hour's drive from Plymouth, Castara is a fishing village that has become popular with tourists not wanting the inundated Crown Point scene. People love the wide, sandy beach, relaxed atmosphere and picturesque setting. However, the village is on the cusp of feeling overcrowded itself during high season. Snorkeling is good in the calm inlet to the right of the main beach. **King David**

**Tours** ( ☎ 660-7906; www.kingdavidtobago.com) is based here, providing hiking and boating tours.

North of Castara, the road winds past a stretch of coast that's punctuated by pretty beaches and villages, unhurried places with kids playing cricket on the road. At **Englishman's Bay**, a superb undeveloped beach shaded by stands of bamboo and coconut palms draws snorkelers to its gentle waters – a coral reef lies 20m offshore. Eula's Restaurant, serving overpriced roti and fat plates of local fare, caters to the handful of visitors. Rustic latrines are provided.

## Sleeping

If you ask around, you'll find unofficial guesthouses that accommodate Castara's tourist overflow.

**Riverside Cottage** ( ☎ 764-8715; r US$35-50) Set off the main road, this guesthouse is run by a local family and the handful of clean rooms could capture the flavor of a bona fide Tobagonian house. The rooms share a kitchen.

**Naturalist Beach Resort** ( ☎ 639-5901; www.naturalist-tobago.com; d apt US$45; 🌊 ) This cheerful, family-run place is at beach level, and its cozy (but well-used) apartments include kitchens, fans and air-con, and are all different; some have water views, others don't. The newer 'Blue Marlin Suite' (US$120) enjoys a primo beachfront spot. The resort has an internet café and restaurant. Airport transfers can be arranged.

**Alibaba's Beach Apartments** ( ☎ 686-7957; www.alibaba-tours.com; Depot Rd; r US$75; 🌊 ) This well-run bunch of apartments have magnificent beach-facing balconies, kitchens, and comfortable rooms with bamboo and seashell

details. Alibaba's Tours is conveniently run out of the hotel and will take you on boat, jeep, rainforest or island tours for US$70 to US$100 per person.

**Sandcastles** ( ☎ 635-0933; www.sandcastlestobago.com; r incl breakfast US$75-125; 🌊 ) This friendly place set on a cliff 10 minutes' walk from the beach has two self-contained apartments with dramatic views. Owners Adam and Rea are welcoming and helpful.

## Eating & Drinking

**Almond Tree** ( ☎ 638-3595; mains TT$35-75; 🕑 lunch & dinner) This beachfront, open-air eatery has heaping plates of local food.

**Boat House** ( ☎ 660-7354; mains from TT$60; 🕑 breakfast, lunch & dinner) Between the colorful decor, bamboo detailing and beachside ambience, this restaurant achieves a festive atmosphere. The seafood dishes are accompanied by fresh vegetable side dishes and salad. On Wednesdays it has an extensive menu and Steel Pan.

**Margarite's** (mains from TT$65; 🕑 lunch & dinner) This cute eatery right off the main road serves up local specialties. The menu changes regularly.

**D Lime** ( ☎ 733-6983; beer TT$8) Just off the beach, this small open-air bar sometimes has music and always has a cold one.

## PARLATUVIER

Just west of Bloody Bay is Parlatuvier, a tiny fishing village on a striking circular bay. A smattering of guesthouses and rooms for rent are popping up because people are drawn to its seclusion and bright waters. It's still low key, but won't stay this way for

---

### CYCLING TOBAGO

Tobago has less traffic than Trinidad, especially on the remote eastern part of the island. Small Tobago has some nice roads, usually hilly, that bring you through amazing landscapes: Roxborough–Parlatuvier Rd, which passes straight through the forest reserve; Arnos Vale Rd to Mason Hall; Buccoo to Charlotteville along the northern coast. If cycle touring is your shtick, it's possible to circumnavigate the island.

For mountain biking, a guide is suggested. Contact **Mountain Biking Tobago** ( ☎ 681-5695; www.mountainbikingtobago.com; PO Box 1065, Bon Accord; per person US$40). Owner Sean de Freitas is a straight-shooting guide who provides solid rentals and cycling equipment. He'll show you the mountain biking that Tobago has to offer. The Highland Falls ride is particularly awesome, ending up at a splendid swimming hole and waterfall. He also guides road rides.

Besides renting from Mountain Biking Tobago, beater bikes are rented near the Crown Point area, or you can rent a bike in Trinidad and bring it over on the ferry, or BYO. You'll be limited with skinny tires due to road conditions. Beware of blind corners, narrow roads and dogs.

**TOBAGO FOREST RESERVE**

The paved Roxborough–Parlatuvier Rd crosses the island from Roxborough to Bloody Bay, curving through the rainforest. The 30-minute drive through completely undeveloped jungle passes pretty valleys and mountain views, making it the best drive on the island.

The road passes through the Tobago Forest Reserve, which was established in 1765 – this makes it the oldest forest reserve in the Caribbean. A number of trailheads lead off the main road into the rainforest where there's excellent bird-watching.

Three-quarters of the way from Roxborough, the **Gilpin Trail** branches northeast to Bloody Bay, a 5km walk through the rainforest. Authorized guides at the trailhead charge US$20 per person to take you down to a waterfall, or US$50 for a two-hour hike through the forest to the Main Ridge lookout hut, a bit further down the road. Rubber boots, walking sticks and rain gear are provided for managing the muddy trails. The lookout hut affords scenic views of Bloody Bay and the offshore Sisters Rocks. On a clear day you can see Grenada 120km away. Reputable guides include Castara-based David Williams of **King David Tours** ( ☎ 660-7906; www .kingdavidtobago.com).

long and might soon go the way of Castara, its tourist-filled neighbor.

If you're up for **waterfalls hikes**, there are several from Parlatuvier. Walk up the river across from the Riverside Restaurant for a rocky 45 minutes till you hit the waterfall. For a shorter, easier hike, walk up the rough road lining the river across from Jetty Rd to check out waterfalls and beautiful dipping pools.

Further on east, at Bloody Bay, you can catch the Roxborough–Parlatuvier Rd through the Tobago Forest Reserve (see the boxed text, above).

You can stay at **Toni's Guesthouse** ( ☎ 635-0040; apt TT$200-250) whose four spacious, clean apartments look over the bay. There's also self-contained apartments at **Parlatuvier Tourist Resort** ( ☎ 639-5639; r TT$150; ⊠ ), above Chance's grocery store. The only restaurant in town is **Riverside Restaurant** ( ☎ 639-4935; mains TT$75-110; ☽ lunch & dinner), which caters to tourists driving through and serves local fish and chicken plates.

## SCARBOROUGH
**pop 16,800**

Located 15 minutes' drive east of Crown Point, Scarborough is the island's only city, a crowded port with bustling one-way streets and congested traffic. Tobagonians come here to bank, pay bills or send packages. There are some good places to grab a bite and a neat public market, but most people will want to push onward. If you arrive late or leave early, there's fine accommodation.

### Information

There are branches of Republic Bank and Scotiabank just east of the docks, both equipped with ATMs. There's another ATM right outside the ferry terminal. There are no reliable ATMs in eastern Tobago.

**MG Photo Studios** ( ☎ 639-3457; Scarborough Mall; per 30min TT$10; ☽ 8:30am-6pm Mon-Fri, to 2pm Sat; ⊠ ) Across the ferry terminal, in the Scarborough Mall; it has internet access.

**Post office** (Post Office St; ☽ 7:30am-6pm Mon-Fri, 9am-1pm Sat) There's a TT Post postal outlet in the ferry terminal too.

**Scarborough General Hospital** ( ☎ 639-2551; Calder Hall Rd; ☽ 24hr) On route to Fort King George, it handles most emergencies and medical issues on Tobago.

**Tobago House of Assembly Tourism Branch** ( ☎ 639-4333; Mount Mary Rd; ☽ 8am-4pm Mon-Fri) The main office is on Mount Mary Rd, past the esplanade west of the cruise-ship complex. There's also an office at the ferry terminal.

### Sights & Activities

The **Botanical Gardens** (admission free; ☽ dawn-dusk) occupies the 7 hectares of a former sugar estate. It's a pretty place, with a variety of flowering trees and shrubs, including flamboyants, African tulips and orchids (in an orchid house).

Immediately beyond the hospital, **Fort King George** (admission free; ☽ daylight hr) sits on a hill at the end of Fort St. Built by the British between 1777 and 1779, it's the only substantial colonial fortification remaining in Tobago and is worth a visit for its history and magnificent coastal view. Benches under enormous trees allow you to gape at the harbor and observe exotic birds darting about. Cannons line the fort's stone walls.

The officers' quarters now contains the small but worthy **Tobago Museum** (☎ 639-3970; tobmuseum@tstt.net.tt; admission TT$10; � 9am-4:30pm Mon-Fri), which displays a healthy collection of Amerindian artifacts, maps from the 1600s, military relics, a small geology exhibit and a very interesting collection of watercolor paintings by Sir William Young that depict Tobago from 1807 to 1815.

## Sleeping

Those arriving on the evening ferry will find a couple of cheap guesthouses a short distance from the waterfront.

**Sandy's Bed & Breakfast** (☎ 639-2737; www.tobagobluecrab.com; cnr Robinson & Main Sts; r US$60; ☒) Behind the Blue Crab Restaurant, amicable owners Ken and Alison Sardinha rent out three rooms in their home. The rooms are pleasantly simple with pine floors, nice furniture and views overlooking Rockly Bay.

**Hope Cottage** (☎ 639-2179; hcghtobago@hotmail.com; Calder Hall Rd; r per person with shared bathroom TT$100, s/d with private bathroom TT$150/250; ☒) A solid budget option, Hope Cottage is found near Fort King George, a half-hour walk uphill from the dock (taxi TT$15 to TT$20). Within this former home of 19th-century governor James Henry Keens (acting governor from 1856 to 1857 and buried in the backyard), guests have access to a big kitchen, TV room, dining room, backyard and front porch.

**Blue Haven Hotel** (☎ 660-7400; www.bluehaven hotel.com; Bacolet Bay; low/high season d US$185/238, ste US$275/355; ☒ ☐ ☒) Robinson Crusoe supposedly was stranded at this beach, but today it's home to the Blue Haven, a romantic, tastefully done resort hotel. Amenities here include a beachside pool, tennis courts, wi-fi and spa services, and each room has an oceanfront balcony.

There are a few reasonably priced accommodation options perched on a hillside overlooking the bay along the Windward Rd to Bacolet Bay. **Sea View Guesthouse** (☎ 639-5613; s/d TT$180/240) is an economical option looking over the ocean with self-contained apartments. **Della Mira Guesthouse** (☎ 639-2531; s/d TT$220/270; ☒ ☒) has friendly staff that run a clean hotel with a little ocean-view restaurant. Some rooms have sea-view balconies and are good value.

## Eating & Drinking

**Patsy's Doubles** (double TT$2.50; � from 4pm most days) Found in the parking lot just east of the ferry terminal, Patsy is known throughout the island for her lovely bundles of garbanzo and flatbread goodness.

**Lal's Roti** (☎ 639-3606; Dutch Fort; roti TT$10-18; � 8am-5pm Mon-Sat) Locals say the tasty rotis here are the best in town, and there's an open-air space to munch on your hot curried feast.

**Ma King's Dinette** (Wilson Rd; mains TT$35-65; � 10am-5pm Mon-Sat) Opposite the market, this popular eatery offers all sorts of local specialties, like cassava and fried fish. Plus, it has fresh-squeezed juices and a soy dish option.

**Ciao Café and Pizzeria** (☎ 639-3001; Burnett St; from TT$40; � lunch-late Mon-Sat, lunch only Sun) Both locals and foreigners come to lime at this adorable café, side by side with an authentic Italian pizzeria. You'll find the best homemade gelato (TT$11 to TT$17) in Trinidad and Tobago here.

**Shore Things** (☎ 635-1072; Old Milford Rd, Lambeau; mains TT$50-120; � 10am-6pm Mon-Sat) Even though it's a couple kilometers west of the city, this is one of the most pleasant oceanside cafes on the island, serving crepes, fresh juices and salads. It also sells local art and tasteful souvenirs.

**Blue Crab Restaurant** (☎ 639-2737; www.tobago bluecrab.com; cnr Main & Robinson Sts; lunch TT$55, dinner mains TT$85-165; � lunch Mon-Fri) A family-run restaurant with pleasant alfresco seating and good West Indian food. You'll have a choice of fresh juice and main dishes such as Creole chicken, flying fish or garlic shrimp. There is dinner by reservation on Monday and Friday.

**Barcode** (☎ 635-2633; www.barcodetobago.com; cover varies; � 7pm-close) A popular nightspot with a wide variety of rums and a dress code. It also has pick-up service.

# WINDWARD ROAD

Just east of Scarborough is the more rural part of the island. It is less appealing to tourists because the beaches have darker sand and tend to be rough. The Windward Rd, which connects Scarborough with Speyside, winds past scattered villages, jungly valleys and white-capped ocean. You'll see signs for a lonely guesthouse or two. Exploring this part of the island, beyond just passing through, would require your own vehicle or bike. The further east you go, the more ruggedly beautiful the scenery becomes. Although much of the road is narrow and curvy with a handful of blind corners, it's drivable in a standard vehicle and bikable if you're gutsy and fit. If you were to drive straight through from Scarborough to Speyside, it would take about 1½ hours.

Five miles east of Scarborough is Granby Point, a jut of land separating Barbados Bay from Pinfold Bay. In 1764 the British established a temporary capital on the east side of Barbados Bay and built **Fort Granby** at the tip of the point. Little remains other than a solitary soldier's gravestone, but day-trippers will find a couple of hilltop picnic tables, a gorgeous ocean view and a brown-sand beach with changing rooms.

Past Goodwood, you'll see signs for **Rainbow Nature Resort** ( ☎ 660-4755; www.mckennas-rainbow .com; Lure Estate, Goldsborough; tour TT$50). The signs will lead you down a rough dirt road past a big organic farm for 15 minutes by car. The resort charges a bit much for the small, darkish rooms (US$70 to US$120), but it offers two-hour tours to waterfalls, around the organic farm, and through the forest. **Rainbow Waterfall** is a 25-minute hike from here, and the **Two Rivers Waterfall** is a 90-minute hike down a rough dirt road.

The triple-tiered, well-touristed **Argyle Falls** (admission TT$40; ⏱ 7am-5:30pm) are just west of Roxborough; the entrance is 600m north of the Windward Rd. This has become very popular (it's a cruise-ship excursion), so go early to skip crowds. On top of admission, you pay one of the heckling guides US$10 to lead you on the 20-minute hike up to the falls. Guides swarm the entrance; official guides wear khaki uniforms and carry ID. At 54m, this is Tobago's highest waterfall, cascading down four distinct levels, and each level has its own pool of spring water. **Roxborough** has a gas station and a few stores where you can pick up snacks.

## SPEYSIDE

The small fishing village of Speyside fronts Tyrrel's Bay, and attracts divers and birders. It's the jumping-off point for excursions to uninhabited offshore islands, including Little Tobago, a bird sanctuary 2km offshore, and St Giles Island. Protected waters, high visibility, abundant coral and diverse marine life make for choice diving. Nondivers can take glass-bottom boat/snorkel tours. Speyside funnels visitors into high-end, diver-oriented hotels much more than its neighbor Charlotteville, where mixing with the locals is more of a

possibility. There's a public beach with facilities at the south end of the bay. There are no ATMs in town.

### Sights & Activities

Also known as Bird of Paradise Island, **Little Tobago** was the site of a cotton plantation during the late 1800s. In 1909 Englishman Sir William Ingram imported 50 greater birds of paradise from the Aru Islands, off New Guinea, and established a sanctuary to protect the endangered bird. In 1963 Hurricane Flora devastated the habitat and decimated the flock.

Now managed by the government, Little Tobago remains an important seabird sanctuary and will prove to be decadent for birdwatchers. Red-billed tropic birds, magnificent frigate birds, brown boobies, Audubon's shearwaters, laughing gulls and sooty terns are some of the species found here. For those who want to hike, the hilly, arid island, which averages just 1.5km in width, has a couple of short trails with captivating views.

Several operators run glass-bottom boat tours. The trip to Little Tobago, a 15-minute crossing, includes bird-watching on Little Tobago and snorkeling on Angel Reef. Masks and fins are provided. **Frank's** ( ☎ 660-5438; Batteaux Bay; tours US$20; ⏱ 10am & 2pm), based at Blue Waters Inn, and **Top Ranking Tours** ( ☎ 660-4904; tours US$20), departing from the beach near Jemma's restaurant, are recommended.

The diving at Little Tobago is some of the region's best. For details, see p56.

### Sleeping

**Top Ranking Hill View Guest House** ( ☎ 660-4904; www.caribinfo.com/toprank; s/d US$45/75; ⌘ ) Reached via a series of steps from Top Hill St, about a 10-minute walk from the beach, this guesthouse is a quiet retreat that has clean, nicely furnished rooms with one or two double beds. Wraparound balconies provide excellent views of both the ocean and rainforest. Top Ranking also runs boat tours and has a minimart (at the bottom of the steps).

**Speyside Inn** ( ☎ 660-6642; www.speysideinn.com; 189-193 Windward Rd; s/d US$85/130; ⌘ ⌘ ) Quite lovely, this butter yellow hotel houses bright balcony rooms looking over the ocean, and cottages nestled out back in the jungly landscaping. Extra Divers shop makes its home here.

**Manta Lodge** ( ☎ 660-5268, in the USA 800-544-7631; www.mantalodge.com; s/d with ceiling fan US$95/115, with air-con US$115/135, all incl breakfast; 🍴 ⚍ ) Catering to divers, this is a modern plantation-style house fronting the beach. Its airy rooms have wicker furniture and ocean-view balconies. The ground-level bar-restaurant opens onto the small pool. The hotel is also home to the reliable Tobago Dive Experience dive shop.

**Blue Waters Inn** ( ☎ 660-2583; www.bluewatersinn .com; Batteaux Bay; r from US$200; 🍴 ⚍ ) The most upscale place to stay and geared to divers, Blue Waters sits on pretty Batteaux Bay, just 1km from the main road. The rooms all have patios and great views. Guests get use of tennis courts, beach chairs and kayaks. There's also a restaurant, bar, spa services and Aquamarine Dive, a full-service PADI dive center.

## Eating

Choices are slim in Speyside, but the following are good.

**Veryln's Roti Shop** (roti TT$15; 🕑 lunch) Coming into town from the west, there's a bright yellow shack right before the beach facilities where Veryln sells her delicious roti and homemade baked goods.

**Redman's** (mains TT$50; 🕑 lunch & dinner, closed Sun) A raised-deck affair, this local hangout is cheaper and less refined than Jemma's and Birdwatchers.

**Birdwatchers Restaurant & Bar** ( ☎ 660-5438; mains TT$70; 🕑 lunch & dinner) Kick back on the candlelit deck and enjoy fresh seafood and cold beers at this friendly place. The menu changes with the catch of the day.

**Jemma's** ( ☎ 660-4066; mains from TT$80; 🕑 breakfast, lunch & dinner Sun-Thu, breakfast & lunch Fri) Nestled in a tree-house setting and blessed by sea breezes, Jemma's boasts excellent atmosphere and food. The cuisine features fresh local food, including fish, chicken and shrimp dishes, and prices are on the higher end. It doesn't serve booze but you are welcome to bring your own.

## CHARLOTTEVILLE

There are about four winding kilometers over the mountains from Speyside to Charlotteville, a delightful little fishing village nestled in aquamarine Man of War Bay. This secluded countryside town accepts the trickle of off-the-beaten-track tourists with mostly jovial spirits and occasionally apathy. Less hoity-toity than Speyside, the tourist services are still good. A couple of internet cafés line the main drag and a semifunctional ATM is be-

side the police station. Tickets for an unreliable bus to Scarborough can be bought at the gas station (TT$8). A maxi taxi (TT$12) might come before, so you can wait till you see the bus, then join the rushing crowd to buy your ticket.

## Sights & Activities

A palm-studded brown-sand beach good for swimming edges **Man of War Bay**, the large, horseshoe-shaped harbor that fronts the village. When it's calm, there's excellent snorkeling and fantastic beach limin' at **Pirate's Bay**, 800m across the point at the north side of Charlotteville, and good snorkeling around **Booby Island**, just southwest of the village.

An excellent way to see the bay and arrive at snorkeling sights is via kayak. **Tobago Seakayak** ( ☎ 320-0885; www.seakayaktobago.com; 17 Charlotteville Estates; 3hr kayak/snorkel tour per person US$40, rental per hr US$15) has a nice fleet of sea kayaks and accompanying equipment. Kayak fishing trips can also be arranged. **Workshop Sea Tours** ( ☎ 660-6281; www.workshopseatours.net; Bay St), based right in town, also offers fishing charters (US$250), snorkel (per person US$40) and offshore island tours, and bird-watching excursions. The office has laundry and internet services.

Scuba divers should contact **Charlotteville Adventure Dive Centre** ( ☎ 660-6176; www.banana -boat-tobago.com; 6 Mac's Lane, Banana Boat, Campbelton; dive US$40). Located in Banana Boat, this full-service PADI-certified dive center rents out full gear and offers a variety of dive trips and certification. Packages include quaint, colorful, clean accommodations.

If you are up for some exploring on dry land, take a walk to the site of the old **Fort Campbelton**, on the west side of the bay, which offers a good coastal view; or take a more substantial hike up **Flagstaff Hill**, a popular spot to picnic and watch the birds circling St Giles' Island. Also, you can bag the tallest peak in Tobago, **Pigeon Peak** (576m), from Charlotteville. Peter Trotman, manager of Tobago Seakayak, knows the area well and will guide hiking and bird-watching trips. Many of these trails and old roads are patronized by recreational bikers, though there is no bicycle rental in town.

## Sleeping

Besides the following listings, there are several small, unofficial guesthouses in Charlotteville.

**Charlotte Villas** (www.charlottevilla.com; US$55-130) In the south part of town, these three fully equipped, high-ceiling apartments are spacious, simple and relaxing with tons of natural light flooding in.

**Cholson Chalets** ( ☎ 639-8553; 74 Bay St; studio US$40, 2-bedroom apt with kitchen US$60, per extra person US$12; ✦ ) Cholson Chalets is a clean, well-run place just steps from the ocean. The fresh green-and-white beach house exterior complements the fishing-town vibe. It has nine units of varying size equipped with kitchens.

**Man-O-War Bay Cottages** ( ☎ 660-4327; www.man-o-warbaycottages.com; Charlotteville Main Rd; 1-/4-bedroom cottage US$60/155; ⬛ ) Plotted in a little botanical garden, with lots of tropical trees, ferns and flowering plants, these 10 simple cottages with kitchens and screened, louvered windows are open to breezes and sounds of the surf. Naturalist Pat Turpin owns the cottages; you'll find them beachside, about five minutes' walk south of the village.

**Top River Pearl** ( ☎ 660-6011; www.topriver.de; 32-34 Spring St; r from US$70, apt from US$105-160; ✦ ) Although it's not on the beach, this guesthouse, just 180m up Spring St from the waterfront, is a treat with its laid-back coffee bar and expansive bay views. With furnishings built from local teak, mahogany trimmings, and red-tiled floors, each of the four immaculate apartments has a balcony with ocean views, plus minikitchen.

### Eating & Drinking

**Banana Boat Beachfront Bar** ( ☎ 660-6176; 6 Mac's Lane; mains from TT$45; ⊙ lunch & dinner) This is a chilled-out place to kick back with fellow divers and travelers. The kitchen riffs on local fare: coconut curried shrimp with veggies (TT85), crab claws (TT$45), and salads topped with feta made from local goat's milk. You can also rent rooms here (single/double US$35/55).

**Gail's** ( ☎ 660-4316; mains from TT$50; ⊙ 7pm-close, closed Sun) Located at the northern end of the waterfront, Gail's serves up freshly caught fish with fantastic local side dishes. Many of the ingredients come straight from Gail's garden.

**Sharon's & Pheb's** ( ☎ 660-5717; Bay St; mains TT$60-80; ⊙ lunch & dinner) Doing amazing things with fresh fish, beef, chicken and vegetables, most of which grow nearby, chef Sharon cooks up truly fantastic local cuisine. Don't miss out on barbecue Wednesdays. There's indoor or outdoor seating.

**Top River Pearl Cappuccino Cafe** ( ☎ 660-6011; 32-34 Spring St; cappuccino TT$20; ⊙ 8:30am-6:30pm Mon-Sat) Within a guesthouse, this breezy outdoor café provides proper cappuccino and espresso. Plus it whips up breakfast, pasta dishes, and milkshakes blended with fresh fruit.

A handful of family-run restaurants in Charlotteville offer good, economical food. Most are open for lunch and dinner, except during the rainy season, when hours become more sporadic. Jane's Quality Kitchen provides seating in the shade of an almond tree with excellent views of the bay and local limin'. G's Tasty Kitchen, an open-air eatery by the waterfront, serves a mean roti (TT$15), plus fish and chicken plates (TT$40). At the beach facility, there are restrooms and the Charlotteville Beach Bar & Restaurant, which dishes up all the local favorites as well as cocktails; it also has DJs on the weekend.

There are a couple of minimarts in town. Along the waterfront are small huts selling rotis, baked goods, and fresh produce.

# DIRECTORY

## ACCOMMODATIONS

Both islands have good-value guesthouses and small hotels. Airport tourist offices can help you book a room, but finding a room on Trinidad and Tobago is seldom a problem, except during Carnival season when reservations should be made far in advance (FYI: rates increase dramatically).

Trinidad and Tobago is less expensive than many places in the Caribbean, so budget options abound (from US$20 night), especially in the low or shoulder seasons (roughly April to early December) when hotels dramatically drop rates.

Each year, the **TDC** ( ☎ 675-7034; www.gotrinidadandtobago.com) publishes a small *Accommodation Guide* and it also features updated listings of B&Bs, guesthouses and hotels on its website. On Tobago, try the helpful **Tobago Bed & Breakfast Association** ( ☎ 639-3926; 1-3 Crooks River), if you can get hold of them.

A 10% hotel room tax, 10% service charge, *plus* the government's 15% value-added tax (VAT) can add 35% more to your bill. Most advertised accommodations rates include the tax and service charge, but not always.

# ACTIVITIES

See p773 for tour operators.

## Bird-Watching

See p747 for information on Trinidad and Tobago's fantastic bird-watching.

## Cycling

Trinidad and Tobago have some wonderful cycling opportunities; see p749 and p764, respectively, for details.

## Diving & Snorkeling

Tobago is most definitely a diving destination. You won't break the bank, and you'll see top-notch coral outcrops, marine life and underwater landscapes. An enclave of operators are located in Crown Point (p758), but they take divers to sights all over the island. The other big concentration of dive shops is in Speyside (p767), where the posh hotels sport their own shops. Both Speyside and lower-key Charlotteville (p767) are closest to the best dive sites near Little Tobago (p767).

## Fishing

Tour companies in Tobago (p773) take people on popular rum-and-fish boat trips, and have more serious sport-fishing expeditions as well. On Trinidad you'll find a number of fishing charters in the yachtie haven of Chaguaramas (p745).

## Hiking

Trinidad and Tobago are endowed with some fantastic hiking opportunities. In Trinidad, Brasso Seco (p749) has a local cooperative that has knowledgeable hiking guides. In Grand Rivière (p753) there is also a locally based organization that provides guides that show you some off-the-beaten track walks, plus there are some spectacular trails near Blanchisseuse (p748).

Tobago has its fantastic forest reserve (p765), snaked with trails, in the middle of the island, and there are also opportunities for hiking on the east side near Charlotteville (p768). There are some shorter strolls in Grafton Caledonia Wildlife Sanctuary (p762), through the Adventure Farm and Nature Reserve (p763), near Rainbow Nature Resort (p767), and on Little Tobago (p767).

## Kayaking

On Trinidad you can rent kayaks in Chaguaramas (p745). Arranging a kayaking tour through local operators to go to Nariva Swamp (p752) is the best way to see wildlife. You can also arrange tours to various other locations on the island.

On Tobago you can hire kayaks and a guide in Charlotteville (p768) and tootle around to white-sand beaches. You can also rent kayaks at Mt Irvine Bay (p762), plus the more upscale hotels often have kayaks for their guests.

## Surfing

Although Trinidad and Tobago are not renowned spots for surfing, you can still find surfers having good days in winter at Sans Souci Beach, near Toco, on Trinidad, and at Mt Irvine Bay (p762) on Tobago. You'll have to ask the surfers at Mt Irvine to find out other secret spots around the island.

## Windsurfing & Kitesurfing

On Tobago, Pigeon Point (p756) is *the* place, and it's given a hearty thumbs up by the windsurfing community.

---

### PRACTICALITIES

- **Newspapers & Magazines** There are three daily newspapers: the *Trinidad Express, Newsday* and the *Trinidad Guardian. Discover Trinidad & Tobago* is a helpful tourist magazine found at tourist offices and many hotels.

- **Radio & TV** There are two local TV stations: the Information Channel (channels 4 and 16) carries CNN newscasts, and the state-owned TTT (channels 2, 9, 13 and 14) shows a variety of programs. About 15 independent radio stations blast the airwaves.

- **Electricity** The electric current is 115/230V, 60hz. US-style plugs are used.

- **Weights & Measures** Trinidad and Tobago uses the metric system. Highway signs and car odometers are in kilometers, but some road markers still measure miles.

## BOOKS

For details on Carnival and the music associated with it, grab a copy of Peter Mason's *Bacchanal* or Peter van Koningsbruggen's *Trinidad Carnival: Quest for a National Identity*. And for those interested in food, *Callaloo, Calypso & Carnival: the Cuisine of Trinidad & Tobago*, by Dave deWitt and Mary Jane Wilan, has recipes and tidbits on the country's exotic flavors. *Sweet Hands: Island Cooking from Trinidad and Tobago* by Ramin Ganeshram is a worthwhile cookbook. For bird-watching guides, see p747. For Trinidad and Tobago literature, see p730.

## BUSINESS HOURS

**Bars** ☷ noon to midnight
**Banks** ☷ 8am to 2pm Monday to Thursday, 8am to noon and 3pm to 5pm Friday.
**Offices** ☷ 8am to 4pm Monday to Friday.
**Post offices** ☷ 8am to 3pm Monday to Friday
**Restaurants** ☷ 11am to 10pm; nontourist restaurants close at 3pm
**Shops** ☷ 8am to 4pm Monday to Wednesday, to 6pm Thursday and Friday, to noon Saturday; however, most malls are open later and all day Saturday.
**Tourist offices** ☷ 8am to 4pm Monday to Friday, and 9am to noon on Saturday

## CHILDREN

Kids of all ages flock with their parents to Tobago's beaches, and most facilities are family oriented. In Trinidad, the tourism is less family oriented, but higher-end hotels usually accommodate children. During Carnival, Kiddie Mas is a sight not to miss, whatever age.

## DANGERS & ANNOYANCES

Tobagonians warn of rampant lawlessness in Trinidad, and Trinidadians say crime is increasing in Tobago. While such claims substantiate a real crime increase, they tend to exaggerate the dangers of travel on the islands. At night, avoid walking alone at night, especially around dark, desolate areas and particularly in Port of Spain. Theft can be a problem, especially in touristy parts of Tobago, so keep an eye on your valuables.

The perceived (often real) disparity between 'rich' travelers and 'poor' locals is sometimes too much to bear. Paranoia is unnecessary, but you should be aware of your belongings, and avoid carrying large sums of cash. When you go to the beach, even the more remote ones, don't bring anything of value.

Some travelers find the aggressive selling tactics of souvenir hawkers or boat-ride sellers annoying. Just be firm but polite and you'll usually be left alone. Women may also feel frustrated by the overt attention of men, but – again – be firm but polite. While flirting will invite more hassle, a friendly, formal greeting can be disarming. Whether you're male or female, a 'good morning' is the first step to befriending a local.

Trinidad and Tobago gets its share of no-see-ums (tiny fleas that munch on your skin), especially in the afternoon and early evening. Mosquitoes in the rainforest can also be a bother. A good, strong bug spray will make you a much happier person.

If you've traveled around other Caribbean islands you may have encountered a lax attitude toward drugs. Beware – smoking pot in Trinidad and Tobago is a serious offense and getting caught can quickly ruin your holiday.

AIDS and HIV is an increasingly dire problem in the Caribbean, and Trinidad and Tobago is not excluded, especially Tobago. UNAIDS reported that 27,000 people were infected in 2006. If you do choose to have sexual relations, always use a condom. For the most current information, check out www.unaids.org. The national AIDS hotline is ☎ 625-2437.

## EMBASSIES & CONSULATES

All of the following are located in Port of Spain:
**Canada** ( ☎ 622-6232; Maple Bldg, 3-3A Sweet Briar Rd)
**France** ( ☎ 622-7446; Tatil Bldg, 11 Maraval Rd)
**Germany** ( ☎ 628-1630; 7-9 Marli St)
**Netherlands** ( ☎ 625-1201; Life of Barbados Bldg, 69-71 Edward St)
**UK** ( ☎ 622-2748; 19 St Clair Ave)
**USA** ( ☎ 622-6371; 15 Queen's Park West)
**Venezuela** ( ☎ 627-9821; 16 Victoria Ave)

## FESTIVALS & EVENTS

Trinidadians and Tobagonians love to celebrate life, and this is reflected in the many events held throughout the year. Trinidad's main annual event is Carnival (see the boxed text, p738), which formally begins two days before Ash Wednesday, in early February.

Several East Indian festivals, primarily in Trinidad, the dates of which vary with the lunar calendar, draw large crowds.
**Phagwa** A Hindu festival celebrating spring and harvest, with lots of dancing, and singing of Hindi folk songs. It

all culminates when participants are sprayed with *abeer*, a lavender-colored water. The main events take place in Chaguanas, on Trinidad, in March.

**Hosay** This three-night Muslim celebration in March/April commemorates the martyrdom of the prophet's grandsons. Key events include the parading of brightly decorated replicas of the martyrs' tomb, and the Moon Dance, in which a dancing duo cavorts through the streets to tassa drums rhythms.

**Easter Weekend** The entire village of Buccoo, on Tobago, celebrates Easter, featuring goat and crab races.

**Pan Ramajay** A competition of small steel bands, held in May.

**Tobago Heritage Festival** Tobago celebrates traditional culture, food and lifestyle in this two-week outpouring of creativity in July. Each village has its own celebration.

**Emancipation Day** This public holiday on August 1 celebrates the abolishment of slavery in 1834 with cultural events and a power-boat race from Trinidad to Tobago.

**Caribbean Latin Jazz Festival** Held in September.

**World Steel Band Festival** Held in October.

**National Pan Chutney Competition** In November.

**Divali** The Hindu festival of lights, held in November. Elaborate towers are constructed of thousands of *deya* (tiny earthenware lamps). Festivities take place in and around Chaguanas, on Trinidad.

**National Parang Competition** Held in December.

## GAY & LESBIAN TRAVELERS

Though not as bad as some other Caribbean islands, Trinidad and Tobago still is pretty closed to the idea of same-sex relationships. Due to the macho nature of the men, they feel especially threatened and can be derogatory towards homosexuality in order to hide their insecurity. There are enclaves of places, such as the more touristy spots or upper-echelon spots in metropolitan areas, where being out and expressing affection is OK. Just be wary that there may be negative repercussions in the wrong places.

## HOLIDAYS

Carnival Monday and Tuesday, and some religious festival days, are unofficial holidays, with banks and most businesses closed.

**New Year's Day** January 1
**Good Friday** Late March/early April
**Easter Monday** Late March/early April
**Spiritual Baptist/Shouter Liberation Day** March 30
**Indian Arrival Day** May 30
**Corpus Christi** Ninth Thursday after Easter
**Labour Day** June 19
**Emancipation Day** August 1
**Independence Day** August 31

**Republic Day** September 24
**Christmas Day** December 25
**Boxing Day** December 26
**Eid Ul Fitr** (Muslim New Year) Late December/January

## INTERNET ACCESS

Internet service is widely available in bigger cities and in most smaller towns as well. The rate is about TT$10 per half hour. Some hotels will have access for guests. Wireless is slow to become prevalent but is coming around.

## INTERNET RESOURCES

**Go Trinidad and Tobago** (www.gotrinidadandtobago .com) TDC's website, with good information on hotels, transportation and current events.

**Ins and Outs** (www.insandoutstt.com) Good information on restaurants, bars and entertainment.

**myTobago** (www.mytobago.info) Has tourism information plus a forum for visitors and locals to exchange ideas and information.

**Trinidad and Tobago Guide** (www.trinidad-guide.info) Not as flashy as other sites, but provides good practical travel information.

## MAPS

The tourist office distributes free, reasonably good maps of both Trinidad and Tobago. Detailed topographical maps (TT$23 each) can be found in Port of Spain at the **Lands & Surveys office** (Frederick St) and at **Trinidad Book World** ( ☎ 623-4316; cnr Queen & Chacon Sts; ☒ 8:30am-4:30pm Mon-Thu, 8:30am-5:30pm Fri, 8am-1pm Sat).

## MONEY

The official currency is the Trinidad and Tobago dollar (TT$). Banks will exchange a number of foreign currencies, but you'll generally get better rates for US dollars or euros. In this book, we quote rates as they are given in Trinidad and Tobago, whether it be in TT$ or US$. Tipping is not expected, but when done, conveys you are really satisfied.

## POST

Postcards to any country are TT$3.25; letters (20g) cost TT$2.50 to send to other Caribbean countries, TT$3.75 to the USA, Canada, the UK or Europe, and TT$4.50 to Australia, or anywhere else in the world.

## TELEPHONE

The country's area code is ☎ 868. When calling from North America, dial ☎ 1-868 +

the local number. From elsewhere dial your country's international access code + ☎ 868 + the local number. Within the country, just dial the seven-digit local number (as we have listed in this chapter).

Public phones are numerous but many nonfunctional. Your best bet is to purchase a Telecommunications Services of Trinidad and Tobago (TSTT) phone card, use calling centers, or if you're needing to make calls frequently, it's easiest and cheap to get a cell phone.

## TOURIST INFORMATION

**Tourism Development Company** (TDC; ☎ 675-7034; www.gotrinidadandtobago.com) Has an office at Piarco International Airport.

**Tobago House of Assembly Tourism Branch** ( ☎ 639-4333; Mount Mary Rd; ⏲ 8am-4pm Mon-Fri) There's also a branch at the ferry terminal.

## TOURS

See also individual towns and locations for more tour operators. For a list of approved tour guides: www.gotrinidadandtobago .com.

### Tobago

**David Rooks Nature Tours** ( ☎ 756-8594; www.rooks tobago.com) Operated by perhaps the most renowned naturalist in the country. David Rooks, former president of the Trinidad & Tobago Field Naturalist Club ( ☎ 624-8017; www.wow.net/ttfnc), lives in Charlotteville and leads three-hour bird-watching trips on the island (US$85 per person).

**Frankie Tours and Rentals** ( ☎ 631-0369; www .frankietours-tobago.com; Mount Irvine Beach facilities; tours per person US$15-75) Offers turtle, bird-watching and rainforest tours as well as glass-bottom snorkel tours around the island, 24-hour taxi service, and car rentals.

**Grand Slam Charters** ( ☎ 683-1958; Crown Point) provides offshore fishing charters (US$300 to US$500 for up to four people) or a righteous lime on his snorkel tour charters which include drinks, a barbecue and sound system. Additionally inshore fly-fishing trips (US$170 for one to two people) are offered to conquer the elusive bonefish.

**Mountain Biking Tobago** ( ☎ 681-5695; www.moun tainbikingtobago.com; per person US$40). Owner Sean de Frei-tas is a straight-shooting guide who provides solid rentals and cycling equipment. He'll show you the mountain biking that Tobago has to offer.

**Tobago Tours** ( ☎ 631-2246; www.tobagotour.com; Pigeon Point; from US$50 per person) Will take you to snorkeling sites all over the island, hiking, bird-watching, and can arrange fish-and-rum boat tours.

### Trinidad

On Trinidad, these companies are recommended for island-wide tours and adventure activities:

**Island Experiences** ( ☎ 625-2410, 756-9677; gunda@ wow.net) Highly recommended. Gunda Harewood offers 'ecocultural tours' (TT$75 to TT95 per person) throughout the island. Tours aim to show the country's underbelly and to impart local knowledge and lore. Gunda also does the excellent evening entertainment tour through Port of Spain (p744).

**Caribbean Discovery Tours** ( ☎ 624-7281; www.carib beandiscoverytours.com) A big, professional company offering island and city tours, hiking, kayaking and bird-watching.

**Paria Springs** ( ☎ 622-8826; www.pariasprings.com) Run by a local mountain biker and wildlife expert, tours include bird-watching, cycling, hiking and kayaking.

**Pathmaster** ( ☎ 374-7847; www.thepathmaster.com) This efficient and professional upscale operator offers adventure activities.

**PTSC Know Your Country Tours** ( ☎ 624-9839) Started as a way for locals to learn more about their country, the Public Transport Service runs weekend-only minibus tours of Trinidad that cost TT$30 to TT$80.

## TRAVELERS WITH DISABILITIES

Seeing as tourist infrastructure is already wobbly here, Trinidad and Tobago does not stand out as a destination that has extensive facilities for travelers with disabilities. However, the higher-end hotels and resorts should be able to accommodate.

## VISAS

Visas are not necessary for citizens of the US, Canada, the UK or most European countries for stays of less than three months.

Visas are required by citizens of Australia, New Zealand, South Africa and India, and some other Commonwealth countries (including Nigeria, Papua New Guinea, Sri Lanka, Tanzania and Uganda). In most countries, visas are obtained through the British embassy, or you can pay TT$400 to TT$2000 upon arrival. For more, contact **Trinidad and Tobago Immigration** ( ☎ 669-5895; www.immigration.gov.tt).

## WOMEN TRAVELERS

A woman traveling alone, especially on Trinidad, is about as common as snow. Men will stare, make kissy noises, hiss, or offer to be anything from your protector to your sex slave. Says one Trini woman, 'Trini men feel compelled to let women know they are noticed and appreciated.' While the constant attention can wear on your nerves, most men are harmless. Your best bet is to smile politely, or ignore it altogether and move on.

# TRANSPORTATION

## GETTING THERE & AWAY
### Entering Trinidad & Tobago

Provided that you have a valid passport (US citizens see the boxed text, p830), coming and going from Trinidad and Tobago is easy. When you arrive, you'll fill out an Immigration Arrival Card. Customs officials require that you fill out the line that asks you where you are staying; if you don't know where you're staying, list any local hotel.

A TT$100 departure tax must be paid upon departure, payable in TT or US dollars (about US$16). For the ferry to Venezuela, it's TT$75. At the Trinidad airport, the fee can be paid via a special ATM machine. Keep your receipt, or you'll have to pay it again at security.

### Air

Airports in both Trinidad and Tobago handle international air traffic, but the bulk of international flights arrive and depart from Trinidad.

#### AIRPORTS

**Crown Point International Airport** (TAB; ☎ 639-8547; www.tntairports.com) Located in Crown Point, 11km southwest of Scarborough, on Tobago.

**Piarco International Airport** (POS; ☎ 669-8047; www.piarcoairport.com) Located 25km east of Port of Spain, on Trinidad.

#### AIRLINES

Airlines flying to Trinidad:

**Air Canada** ( ☎ 1-800-247-2262; www.aircanada.com) Toronto

**American Airlines/American Eagle** ( ☎ 1-800-233-5436; www.aa.com) Miami, San Juan

**Caribbean Airlines** ( ☎ 625-8246; www.caribbean-airlines.com) Antigua, Barbados Caracas, Fort Lauderdale, New York, Toronto

**Continental** ( ☎ 1-800-523-3273; www.continental.com) Houston

**Delta** ( ☎ 1-800-21-1212; www.delta.com) New York

**LIAT** ( ☎ 625-9451; www.liatairline.com) Anguilla, Antigua, Barbados, Curaçao, Dominica, Grenada, Guadeloupe, Martinique, Nevis, St Kitts, St Vincent, San Juan, Santo Domingo, St-Martin/Sint Maarten, St Croix, St Lucia, St Thomas, Tortola

Airlines flying to Tobago:

**British Airways** ( ☎ 0844-494-0-787; www.britishairways.com) London

**LIAT** ( ☎ 625-9451; www.liatairline.com) Antigua, Barbados, Grenada, St-Martin/Sint Maartin, St Kitts, St Lucia, St Vincent, Tortola

**Virgin Atlantic** ( ☎ 454-3610; www.virgin-atlantic.com) London

### Sea
#### CRUISE SHIP

Cruise ships dock on the south side of Port of Spain. The large cruise-ship complex contains a customs hall, souvenir and clothing shops, car-rental agencies, taxis and a couple of local eateries. There's a smaller cruise-ship facility in central Scarborough on Tobago. See p830 for more information on cruises.

#### FERRY

A ship leaves for Guiria, Venezuela, at 9am on Wednesdays (arrives at 7am) from **Pier One** ( ☎ 634-4472) in Chaguaramas. It takes 3½ hours, costs TT$404 and there's a TT$75 departure tax.

#### YACHT

Out of the hurricane path, Trinidad and Tobago is safe haven for yachters. Trinidad's Chaguaramas Bay has the primary mooring and marina facilities as well as an immigration and customs office for yachters. Tobago is an upwind jaunt, but sometimes yachts moor at Charlottesville or Scarborough. TDC publishes an online **Boater's Directory** (www.boatersenterprise.com), with an array of information for yacht travelers, or try the **Trinidad and Tobago Sailing Association** ( ☎ 634-4210).

## GETTING AROUND
### Air

Flying between Trinidad and Tobago is an easy 20-minute flight costing TT$300 per person each way. The checked baggage weight allowance is 20kg. While it's wise to book in advance, it is often possible to buy tickets at the airport on the day of departure. **Caribbean Airlines** ( ☎ 625-8246; www .caribbean-airlines.com) has a monopoly on these interisland flights.

## Boat
While the trip between Queen's Wharf in Port of Spain (Trinidad) and the main ferry dock in Scarborough (Tobago) was formerly a five-hour boat ride, the government has now leased 'Fast Ferries' that make the interisland journey in a mere 2½ hours; the journey costs TT$50 one way. It's a cheaper, comfortable way to travel, except if you are prone to seasickness. There is a bar, cafeteria and deck, and movies are played in the air-conditioned interior.

Usually there are two to four departures daily from both islands, in the morning and afternoon. Around the Carnival season, it's best to buy your tickets as far as possible in advance. The office doesn't answer phones on weekends, but you can go down and buy tickets day of. For availability call the **Port Authority** ( ☎ Trinidad 625-3055, Tobago 639-2181; www .patnt.com). Schedules are online.

## Bus
Buses on both islands provide a substantial means of transportation for locals. Many people take buses to and from work in neighboring towns, and children depend on buses to get to and from school. Buses offer travelers an inexpensive way to get around, especially on longer cross-island trips, but beware that buses are slow and unreliable. For shorter distances, travelers are better off taking maxi-taxis or route taxis. Check the bus information for Trinidad (p734) and Tobago (p754).

## Car
### RENTAL
Driving yourself can be a great way of getting around the islands. Car rentals start at about TT$300, and include insurance and unlimited mileage. See p734 (Trinidad) and p756 (Tobago) for more information.

### ROAD RULES
Cars drive on the left, and the car's steering column is on the right (as in the UK). Your

home driver's license is valid for stays of up to three months.

Twisting, narrow roads and fast, horn-happy drivers can make driving on the islands an adventure; in Port of Spain, traffic, complicated roads and poor signage can make driving a white-knuckle experience. Your best bet is to study a map before you get in the car, take a deep breath and practice Zen-like patience. You will get the hang of it, and you'll find driving much easier if you simply relax a little and follow the flow. Be aware that fellow road users will stop suddenly to drop off a friend, say 'Hi' to a neighbor or pick up a cold Carib. Sometimes they'll simply stop, while other times they'll wave an arm up and down to signal they are about to do something.

The ignored speed limit on highways is 80km/h, and 50km/h to 55km/h on city streets. Gas is about TT$2.75 a liter for regular and it will cost TT$120 to fill a tank.

## Hitchhiking
Hitching a ride is very common with islanders, especially with children, who hitch to and from school, and with workers trying to get home at night. However, hitching is not a safe mode of transportation for foreign visitors, especially women (your want of a ride will be misconstrued for a want of other things).

## Maxi-Taxi
Maxi-taxis are 12- to 25-passenger minibuses that travel along a fixed route within a specific zone. They're color-coded by route and frequently reflect the personality of the driver – you may hop on a bus blazoned with 'Jah Mon' and booming with Rasta music, or catch a ride on a bus dedicated to Jesus. Regardless, maxis run 24 hours, are very cheap and are heavily used by the locals; catching one can be a great cultural experience. Rides cost TT$2 to TT$12, depending on how far you go. You can flag a maxi at any point along its route, or hop on at the appropriate taxi stand. Keep in mind that, due to their frequent stops, maxi-taxis will take a long time to get from A to B.

On Trinidad, many maxi-taxis operate out of the maxi-taxi terminal adjacent to City Gate. For information on Trinidad's maxi-taxi color-coding system, see p734. On Tobago, all maxis have a blue band.

For information about maxi-taxi routes, contact **Trinidad & Tobago Unified Maxi Taxi Association** ( ☎ 624-3505).

## Route Taxi

These taxis are shared cars that travel along a prescribed route and can drop you anywhere along the way. They look like regular cars, except that their license plates start with an 'H' (for 'hire'). See p734 (Trinidad) and p756 (Tobago) for island-specific info.

## Taxi

Regular taxis, locally called 'tourist taxis,' are readily available at the airports on both islands, the cruise-ship complex on Trinidad and hotels. These vehicles are unmetered but follow rates established by the government; hotel desks and the airport tourist office have a list of fares. Make sure to establish the rate before riding off. For island-specific taxi information, see p734 (Trinidad) and p756 (Tobago).

# Aruba, Bonaire & Curaçao

Slaves, Dutch traders, Indians, pirates and more have all contributed to the rich and unique stew that is the ABCs: Aruba, Bonaire and Curaçao. Close to Venezuela and South America, these small islands are far away in every other sense. Although they have long been on the trade routes, they are not like the islands of the Eastern Caribbean either, as they have a heavy Spanish influence on top of the Dutch and African.

And just as you start generalizing about all three you have to stop, as they are really quite different. Aruba is the kid who opens the door for others – in this case hundreds of thousands of tourists a year who find winter refuge on its fine beaches. Bonaire is the kid who blows off school. Ringed by some of the most fabulous reefs on the planet, it concentrates on its natural pleasures. Meanwhile, Curaçao is busy working hard to play hard. It mixes commerce with Unesco-recognized old Willemstad and a coast of hidden beaches.

These differences, plus others like wealth and population size, have brought the ABCs to where they are today: three very separate places going in their own directions. Once unified as the Netherlands Antilles, these three islands in the Lesser Antilles are now busy growing up and finding their own identities. You may wish to get acquainted with all three.

## FAST FACTS

- **Area** Aruba: 181 sq km; Bonaire: 285 sq km; Curaçao: 471 sq km
- **Capital** Aruba: Oranjestad; Bonaire: Kralendijk; Curaçao: Willemstad
- **Country code** Aruba: ☎ 297; Bonaire: ☎ 599; Curaçao: ☎ 599-9
- **Departure tax** Aruba: included in ticket; Bonaire: international US$20, interisland US$6; Curaçao: international US$22, interisland US$7
- **Famous for** Aruba: beaches; Bonaire: diving; Curaçao: city and rural charm
- **Language** Dutch, Spanish, English, Papiamento
- **Money** Aruba: Aruban florin (Afl); Bonaire & Curaçao: Netherlands Antillean guilder (NAf or ANG); US$1 = Afl1.79 = NAf1.78 = €0.65 = UK£0.51
- **Official Names** Aruba; Bonaire; Curaçao
- **People** Arubans; Bonairians; Curaçaoans
- **Phrase** Bon bini (Welcome!)
- **Population** Aruba: 104,000; Bonaire: 14,500; Curaçao: 138,000
- **Visa** Most nationalities do not need a visa for a 90-day stay on each of the islands; see p812

## HIGHLIGHTS

- **Bonaire's Reefs** (p799) Enjoy Unesco-recognized natural beauty from your hotel's back dock
- **Arashi Beach** (p791) Savor the least-touristed of Aruba's many fine white beaches
- **Willemstad** (p802) Immerse yourself in Unesco-recognized Dutch colonial heritage, with the grit of a busy port town
- **Curaçao's Beaches** (p809) Explore hidden beaches on the jagged west coast, all linked by a road through lush lands
- **Nighttime Kralendijk** (p797) Sample the wonderful little restaurants and bars of Bonaire's village of a capital

## ITINERARIES

- **Three Days** Pick one of the ABCs and stay there, as this is the minimum time required to enjoy any of the three islands.
- **One Week** Either have a very relaxing time on one island or try two, depending on your taste.
- **Beaches and Diving** Decide you're going to find your favorite beach and dive spot on each island and then compare and pick your best of all three. Take as long you can; two weeks would be a start but a month is really the minimum. Lucky you!

## CLIMATE & WHEN TO GO

Average temperature for the ABCs year-round is a perfect 28°C (82°F). High noon is a bit warmer and at night it can get breezy, but mostly you'll be fine in shorts and T-shirt. The islands are fairly dry, averaging a little over 1in (2.5cm) of rain per month. Much of this falls from September to early December. The islands usually miss the Caribbean hurricane season, although

---

**HOW MUCH?**

- **Tanks of air for a week of diving on Bonaire** US$200
- **Aruba beach access** Free
- **Tour of Curaçao's harbor** US$20
- **Cold beer** US$2 to US$3
- **Night at beach resort** US$100 to US$300

---

a couple passed to the north in 2007 and dumped a lot of water.

As always, when you go depends on how cold you are. If you just have to warm up December to April, then you can join the crowds during high season. Otherwise, the islands are more accessible and rates much cheaper other times of the year. The high season for cruise ships runs October to April. Outside of these times the port towns can be almost sleepy.

## HISTORY

For information on Aruba's, Bonaire's and Curaçao's history, see p780, p792 and p799, respectively.

## THE CULTURE

If Aruba, Bonaire and Curaçao were named, say, Moe, Larry and Curley and their initials were MLC, it might be easier for outsiders not to link them so closely. For despite their proximity geographically and alphabetically, the cultures of the three islands have many differences, mainly due to their history after colonization.

Bonaire was populated with a few thousand African slaves who worked the salt flats. After slavery ended, their descendents lived quiet lives farming and raising animals, largely ignored by the world. Not until the explosion of postwar tourism and scuba diving did the island open itself to the outside. The result is a large island with a small population of African-Caribbeans rooted in traditional ways, yet welcoming of the opportunity brought by travelers from around the world.

Curaçao was also populated by African slaves, but its superb port drove its economy after slavery ended and the cultural roots today are a mix of African-Caribbean, Latin American and European. Willemstad is at times relaxed, frenetic and buttoned-down. The population is growing and there's money to be made. Out in the country – increasingly the home of commuters – traditional ways of life are fading.

Aruba had neither resources to exploit nor any geographic advantage, so it was large ignored during the colonial era. Here the indigenous population survived and were later joined by immigrants from Latin America looking for work in the refinery and Dutch people who were simply looking for sun. It feels new and it largely is, with wealth coming

---

### DAG NETHERLANDS ANTILLES

In Dutch 'dag' means goodbye and that's what's happening to the Netherlands Antilles. Really nothing more than grab-bag of Dutch holdings in the Caribbean, it never was an entity that had popular appeal. Islanders always saw themselves as residents of their island first.

The Netherlands Antilles was always destined for a break-up and laws were written to allow this. Aruba flew the coop first, in 1986, and never looked back. It is an independent country within the Netherlands, which effectively means it's autonomous but saves a lot of money on operating embassies, having a military and the like. The other five island-nations within the NA began holding votes and talks about their future in 2005. By 2008 it was clear: the NA was being disbanded. Curaçao and Sint Maarten are going the route of Aruba. Bonaire, Saba and Sint Eustatius are going much closer to the Netherlands and will effectively be municipalities of Holland and nice warm, beautiful ones at that.

---

from the one million visitors who arrive each year. Still there is a bit of island culture to be found and locals love a good gossip session fueled by rum.

Because of these differences, the ABCs have never been close. Politically they were linked within the Netherlands Antilles, but with the dissolution of that political entity (above) they are more separated than ever.

## ARTS

The main form of art on the ABCs is music. Here it takes on a vibrant mix of European, African and new forms. No style is sacred and improvisation is the rule. At times you'll hear Creole, blues, jazz, rock, pop, rap and more. Some songs combine all of these elements and more. Making music is popular and many people on the islands play in small groups with friends and relatives. No social gathering of any significance is complete without some live music.

The best architecture on the islands is the Caribbean-colored old Dutch colonial styles, with their thick walls defending against the heat. An excellent place to see this architecture in its purest form is at the restored Hotel Kura Hulanda (p805) in Willemstad, Curaçao.

Modern buildings tend to be utilitarian. The only flair in architecture you'll find is in buildings such as resorts for tourists, although here the styles can range from the derivative of traditional styles to modern styles with no roots or context in the ABCs.

## ENVIRONMENT
### Wildlife

The ABCs are primarily arid, with cactuses and other hardy plants that can make do with the minimal rainfall each year. Reptiles –

especially huge iguanas – are the main creatures native to the land. However, each island has mangroves in some parts and these attract more birds than the islands do tourists. Some of the species are quite spectacular, from Bonaire's flamingos to the brightly colored parrots found everywhere.

In the water is where the ABCs are truly rich in life. Coral reefs grow in profusion along the lee coasts of all three islands, especially Bonaire. Hundreds of species of fish and dozens of corals thrive in the clear, warm waters. Sharks, dolphins and rays are among the larger creatures swimming about.

### Environmental Issues

All three of the ABCs suffer from an ongoing shortage of fresh water, which mostly comes from desalinization plants. The reef concerns common throughout the region are germane here as well. See p48 for details.

Aruba's most visible environmental woe is the puffing stacks of the oil refinery at the south end of the island, although smog also comes from world's second-largest desalinization plant, south of the airport, which roars away 24/7. Locals have pressed for growth controls that balance the island's healthy economy with its limited water and other resources. This has slowed but by no means stopped the development of hotels and condos on the long strip to the north. At busy times, roads through Oranjestad are jammed. The waters around Aruba are for the most part quite clean; diving and swimming are good. Many hotels feature tropical birds, such as parrots, in small cages where guests pointedly ignore the 'Don't Touch' signs. These sociable birds are not meant to be cooped up.

Bonaire has few major environmental concerns. Protections of the marine park are strict and any environmental damage from the salt ponds is limited mostly to the ponds themselves. Green initiatives include a plan to finally put all that wind to use producing electricity, a new program to discourage plastic bag use, and the replacement of septic tanks with sewers.

One only has to glimpse the *Mad Max*–like array of blazing pipes and belching stacks to know that the number one environmental issue on Curaçao is air and water pollution from the Venezuelan-run oil refinery and other industry built on the inner harbor (Schottegat) of Willemstad. Given the importance of these installations to the local economy, efforts to control their negative effects are modest at best. The growing traffic problem and exhaust-spewing diesels means that getting stuck in a traffic jam is both a possibility and very unpleasant.

## FOOD & DRINK

Because of the arid conditions, food in the ABCs has always been hearty. Thick stews made with meats such as goat and chicken, and vegetables such as okra and squash, have been predominant. Spices were used to give things variety. The Dutch brought a love of cheese, but dishes made with this have mostly always been a special treat.

Even today most fruits and vegetables are imported. Seafood, however, is common and good, especially shellfish. While a huge array of foods is available in places geared toward visitors, locals have been quick to forsake goat stew and an appetite for fast food has exploded. Traditional food includes the much-loved *funchi* (fungi elsewhere in the region), which is based on corn meal, *cabrito* (goat), curries and fish.

Dutch and American brands dominate the ABC beer market. However Aruba's Balashi can be found throughout the island where it is popular because it is *not* Dutch or American, but rather local. You will at times see it on Bonaire and Curaçao as well. It is a typically light pilsner-style lager.

# ARUBA

When you see a Nathan's hot dog vendor on the beach and groups of men going orgasmic when the New York Giants make a three-yard gain, you could be forgiven for thinking you're in New York, albeit a much warmer version. Indeed it is Americans from the east coast fleeing winter that make Aruba the most touristed of the ABCs.

And that's not really surprising given that it has miles of the best beaches, plenty of package resorts and a compact and cute main town, Oranjestad, which is ideally suited for the two-hour strolls favored by day-tripping cruise-ship passengers. It's all about sun, fun and spending money (lots of money – it's an expensive island).

But venture away from the resorts and you'll find that Aruba offers more. At the island's extreme ends are rugged, windswept vistas and uncrowded beaches. Arikok National Wildlife Park is an alien landscape of cactuses, twisted *divi-divi* trees and abandoned gold mines.

Mostly, however, Aruba is a place to do as little as possible. It wears its hospitality on its sleeve and in the national anthem, which includes the unlyrical line 'The greatness of our people is their great cordiality.'

## History

Humans are first thought to have lived on Aruba some 4000 years ago. Spain claimed the island in 1499, but its inhospitable arid landscape provoked little colonial enthusiasm and the native Arawaks were largely left alone. The Dutch took claim in 1636 and, except for a British interlude in the early 19th century, have maintained control since.

Prosperity came to the island in the form of the huge oil refinery built to refine Venezuelan crude oil in the 1920s. This large complex occupies the southeastern end of Aruba and dominates the blue-collar town of San Nicolas. Jobs at the plant contributed to the development of a local middle class. Automation meant workers had to look elsewhere, and the island has successfully transferred its economy from dependence on refining oil to relaxing tourists.

The three islands of the ABCs have never been chums, and Aruba was able to leverage its affluence to break away from the rest of the Netherlands Antilles and become an autonomous entity within the Netherlands in 1986. Talk of achieving full independence has not become anything more than that: talk.

Aruba made an unwanted media splash in the US starting in 2005 when an Atlanta teenager disappeared while on holiday. The resulting controversy has left deep scars on the island (see p784).

## Orientation

Smallest of the ABCs in landmass, Aruba is not quite 30km long and 9km wide. Life is centered on Oranjestad. Almost all the hotels and resorts stretch north from here along Eagle and Palm Beaches. The far north is classically barren and windswept, and is dominated by the California Lighthouse. In the south of the island there are various industries interspersed with some good beaches. Inland you'll find the homes of ordinary Arubans scattered throughout the low rolling brown hills known in Papiamento as *cunucu* (country). The east features the wilds of Arikok National Wildlife Park, and much rugged and inaccessible shoreline.

Driving the length of the island when there is little traffic takes about 40 minutes. Road signs – especially street signs – and building numbers are scarce.

## Getting There & Away

Flights to Aruba land at **Reina Beatrix International Airport** (AUA; ☎ 297-582-4800; www.airportaruba.com); for information, see p813. Airlines flying between the ABC islands change frequently; see p814.

## Getting Around

If you just want to stay at your hotel with only a few forays into Oranjestad and perhaps a hotel-arranged tour, then you won't need a car. Taxis and local buses will get the job done; however, buses don't travel to the more extreme parts of the island to the north, east or south, or into Arikok National Wildlife Park. For freedom to explore Aruba, a car – at least for a couple of days – is essential.

### BUS

The **main bus depot** (Lloyd G Smith Blvd) is right in the center of Oranjestad. **Arubus** (☎ 297-588-0616) buses 10, 10A and 10B serve the hotel areas from Oranjestad. Buses run every 15 to 30 minutes from 6am to 11:30pm and cost US$1.30 one way. Buses 1 and 8 link Oranjestad to the airport every 30 to 60 minutes.

Buses do not go to the rugged parts of the island to the north, east or south, or into Arikok National Wildlife Park.

### CAR

You'll know the tourists not only by the V-registrations of their rental cars but also by their actual use of turn signals. All the major car-rental companies have offices at the airport. It's worth comparing prices with local outfits, including the following:

**Economy Car Rental** (☎ 297-583-0200; www.economyaruba.com)

**Optima Rent-A-Car** (☎ 297-582-4828; www.optimarentacar.com).

### TAXI

Taxis are easy to come by at hotels and resorts. Fares are set for fixed distances. From the airport to the High-Rise Resorts costs US$25, for example. Extra passengers cost US$2 and you can charter a taxi for touring for US$45 per hour.

## ORANJESTAD & THE NORTH

Oranjestad (pop 27,000) is a large island town that combines a mix of local commerce with the breathless pursuit of visitor business. It's an interesting place to wander around, if for no other reason than the glimpse of daily Aruban life it provides. But when the cruise ships are in port, it is best to stay well clear as everything is jammed.

At other times, there's an appealing mix of old and new structures intermingled with scads of shops, bars and restaurants. At night when the boats have reabsorbed their passengers the town is quiet.

Almost all of Aruba's hotels and resorts are northwest of town. This area has wide roads, lush landscaping and excellent beaches. It's really a world unto itself, similar to beachside developments found the world over.

### Orientation

It's hard to get anywhere on Aruba without passing along Lloyd G Smith Blvd, Oranjestad's main street and the central island artery linking the tourist resorts of the north with the airport to the south. Little in Oranjestad is more than a 10-minute walk from the Yacht Basin in the town center.

Large tourist developments begin less than 3km north of Oranjestad's center. Both conveniently and accurately, the hotels and condos along Eagle Beach are known as the Low-Rise Resorts. A rapidly developing area stretching

ARUBA, BONAIRE &
CURAÇAO

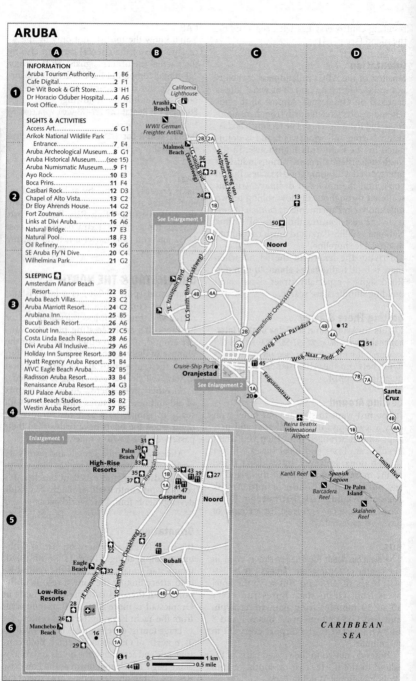

# ARUBA

**INFORMATION**
Aruba Tourism Authority..........1 B6
Cafe Digital............................2 F1
De Wit Book & Gift Store..........3 H1
Dr Horacio Oduber Hospital.....4 A6
Post Office............................5 E1

**SIGHTS & ACTIVITIES**
Access Art.............................6 G1
Arikok National Wildlife Park
  Entrance.............................7 E4
Aruba Archeological Museum..8 G1
Aruba Historical Museum......(see 15)
Aruba Numismatic Museum....9 F1
Ayo Rock..............................10 E3
Boca Prins............................11 F4
Casibari Rock........................12 D3
Chapel of Alto Vista...............13 C2
Dr Eloy Ahrends House...........14 G2
Fort Zoutman........................15 G2
Links at Divi Aruba.................16 A6
Natural Bridge.......................17 E3
Natural Pool..........................18 F3
Oil Refinery...........................19 G6
SE Aruba Fly'N Dive................20 C4
Wilhelmina Park.....................21 G2

**SLEEPING**
Amsterdam Manor Beach
  Resort...............................22 B5
Aruba Beach Villas.................23 C2
Aruba Marriott Resort.............24 C2
Arubiana Inn.........................25 B5
Bucuti Beach Resort...............26 A6
Coconut Inn..........................27 C5
Costa Linda Beach Resort.......28 A6
Divi Aruba All Inclusive...........29 A6
Holiday Inn Sunspree Resort...30 B4
Hyatt Regency Aruba Resort....31 B4
MVC Eagle Beach Aruba..........32 B5
Radisson Aruba Resort............33 B4
Renaissance Aruba Resort.......34 G3
RIU Palace Aruba...................35 B5
Sunset Beach Studios.............36 B2
Westin Aruba Resort...............37 B5

California
Lighthouse

Arashi
Beach

WWII German
Freighter Antilla

Malmok
Beach

Verhadeweg van Westpuntstraat Noord

36
23

24

13

50

**Noord**

Kamingtingh Omeststraat

Weg Naar Paradera

12

51

Weg Naar Piedr Plat

7B  7A

**Santa
Cruz**

See Enlargement 1

JE Irausquin Blvd

LG Smith Blvd (Sasakiweg)

4B

4A

2B

2A

**Cruise-Ship Port**
**Oranjestad**
See Enlargement 2

45

Fergusonstraat

1A

20

Reina Beatrix
International
Airport

1B

1A

4B

4A

LG Smith Blvd

Kantil Reef

**Spanish
Lagoon**

Barcadera
Reef

**De Palm
Island**

Skalahein
Reef

---

**Enlargement 1**

31
Palm  30
Beach  33

**High-Rise
Resorts**

35
37

1B
1A

**Gasparitu**

53  43
39
41  47

27

**Noord**

JE Irausquin Blvd

25

48

**Bubali**

Eagle
Beach  32
22

LG Smith Blvd (Sasakiweg)

**Low-Rise
Resorts**

28

4
26

**Manchebo
Beach**

29

16

4B  4A

1B

1A

1

44

*CARIBBEAN
SEA*

0 ————————— 1 km
0 ————————— 0.5 mile

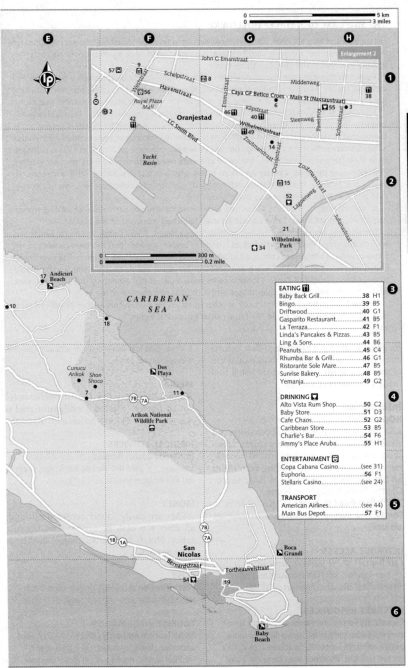

**EATING**
Baby Back Grill............................**38** H1
Bingo..........................................**39** B5
Driftwood...................................**40** G1
Gasparito Restaurant..................**41** B5
La Terraza...................................**42** F1
Linda's Pancakes & Pizzas.........**43** B5
Ling & Sons................................**44** B6
Peanuts......................................**45** C4
Rhumba Bar & Grill....................**46** G1
Ristorante Sole Mare..................**47** B5
Sunrise Bakery............................**48** B5
Yemanja.....................................**49** G2

**DRINKING**
Alto Vista Rum Shop...................**50** C2
Baby Store..................................**51** D3
Cafe Chaos.................................**52** G2
Caribbean Store..........................**53** B5
Charlie's Bar...............................**54** F6
Jimmy's Place Aruba...................**55** H1

**ENTERTAINMENT**
Copa Cabana Casino.............(see 31)
Euphoria.....................................**56** F1
Stellaris Casino.....................(see 24)

**TRANSPORT**
American Airlines..................(see 44)
Main Bus Depot..........................**57** F1

## THE SAD CASE OF NATALEE HOLLOWAY

On the night of May 30, 2005, an 18-year-old American teenager, Natalee Holloway, disappeared while on school fun trip to Aruba. That she has never been seen again is about the only fact anyone involved in the case can agree upon.

Fueled by nonstop coverage on American cable TV stations, the disappearance became a sensation in the US, Aruba and in the Netherlands. Many claimed that Holloway had been drinking heavily and had ended up in the company of Joran van der Sloot and two brothers that night.

Hundreds of volunteers searched the island for any trace but nothing was found. Meanwhile suspicion pointed to the three local men. And that's where it stayed for the next several years. During that time, they were jailed at different times for questioning but prosecutors were unable to build a case sufficient for bringing charges. Meanwhile coverage on American TV was constant. With their fairly small audiences, the cable channels need sensational events to draw viewers. With Holloway they had a pretty American blond who was lost in a foreign land, a surefire ratings – and profits – builder. (Cynics will note that women who disappear who are not young, cute and American are ignored by these shows.)

In the meantime, Holloway's relatives were accusing Aruban authorities of incompetence, corruption and collusion. Some Americans even launched a boycott of the island.

For Arubans, who pride themselves on their 'happy island,' it was simply too much. Anger and resentment grew. Meanwhile the lack of a body or evidence meant that the cops couldn't move forward, even as allegations continued to swirl around the original three suspects. The case finally began unraveling in late 2007 when van der Sloot proved a) unable to stay silent, and b) unable to resist the spotlight of Dutch TV. Soon tapes were made of him admitting that Holloway died while she was with him and that he got others to help him dispose of the body.

Exactly how Holloway died was still another question for prosecutors as they pondered their next move in a case that could live longer than its original victim.

for about 1.5km leads to the High-Rise Resorts along Palm Beach. This area – about 6km north of the Yacht Basin – is also where you'll find many restaurants and shops.

## Information

### BOOKSTORES

Like the rest of the ABCs, bookstores on Aruba are more like stationery stores. Hotel shops usually have selections limited to hackneyed potboilers; if your reading aspirations go beyond the turgid prose of Patterson or Clancy, bring books from home.

**De Wit Bookshop** ( ☎ 297-582-1273; Caya GF Betico Croes 94; ⏰ 8:30am-5pm Mon-Sat) Bestsellers, magazines and Barbie.

### INTERNET ACCESS

**Café Digital** ( ☎ 297-588-5459; Warfstraat; per hr US$6; ⏰ 9am-7pm Mon-Sat, 11am-6pm Sun) Cheap international phone calls, across from Port of Call Mall.

### INTERNET RESOURCES

**Community Forum** (www.aruba.com/forum/) Almost every imaginable question and issue is discussed on the tourism authority's community forum area. Looking for a gay bar? Look here. Wondering about the cost of a taxi?

Ask here. Want to know the best new restaurant? The posts with opinions will pour in.

### MEDIA

Among the many free tourist publications, *Aruba Tips for Travelers* is a delightful read as it is written by a local who has a lot of insight.

### MEDICAL SERVICES

**Dr Horacio Oduber Hospital** ( ☎ 297-587-4300; Sasakiweg; ⏰ 24hr) Near the Low-Rise Resorts, a large and well-equipped hospital.

### MONEY

ATMs are easily found across the island; all offer you cash in Aruban and US currency. Hotels and banks change money at average rates.

### POST

**Post office** (Port of Call Mall; ⏰ 8am-noon, 1-4pm Mon-Fri) Near the cruise-ship port; small.

### TOURIST INFORMATION

**Aruba Tourism Authority** ( ☎ 297-582-3777; www .aruba.com; Lloyd G Smith Blvd; ⏰ 7:30am-noon & 1-4:30pm Mon-Fri) Helpful staff can answer questions.

Part of a trio buildings that comprise the Aruban tourism-industrial complex.

## Sights

Oranjestad is good for walking. It lacks any real must-see sight; rather, it's best to just stroll and enjoy the scores of small Dutch colonial buildings painted in a profusion of colors. All of the following sights are easily visited on foot.

**Fort Zoutman** (Oranjestraat) is not much to look at, but what's left dates from the 18th century. Best-preserved is the **Willem III Tower**, built to warn of approaching pirates. Fortunately, at that time Aruba was seen as having little in the booty department and pirates typically gave the island a pass.

In the base of the tower is the **Aruba Historical Museum** ( ☎ 297-582-6099; Fort Zoutman 4). See how a mélange of cultures (African, European, Caribbean and indigenous) have combined to create the island's unique character but not just yet: the museum was closed in 2008 for reconfiguration.

Nearby, note **Dr Eloy Ahrends House** (Oranjestraat), an elegant, thick-walled 1922 house, which is now part of the city-council complex. At night it's lit up like an emerald. Across Lloyd G Smith Blvd by the Yacht Basin, **Wilhelmina Park** is a shady refuge replete with lush tropical gardens.

Housed in a restored old merchant's house, **Access Art** ( ☎ 297-588-7837; Caya GF Betico Croes; ⏰ 10am-8pm Mon-Sat) displays a wide range of works by artists from Aruba and the region. Look for the ethereal works by Johannes van Boekhoudt. A veranda has breezy views of shoppers from the 2nd-floor location.

The **Aruba Numismatic Museum** ( ☎ 297-582-8831; Zuidstraat 7; admission US$5; ⏰ 9am-4pm Mon-Fri, 9am-noon Sat) doesn't just have displays of Aruba's unusual currency past and present (at one time a coin shortage forced locals to cut up coins like pies), but it also has thousands of items used as money worldwide from the 3rd century BC to the present.

Stone tools found on Aruba dating from 4000 BC will be the dowager stars of the **Aruba Archeological Museum** ( ☎ 297-582-8979; Shelpstraat) once it opens in new quarters that are actually old: some grand colonial buildings from 1929 are being restored and will be the home of the museum and its fascinating collection.

## Activities

Much as people think they want to spend days on end by the beach or pool, the reality is that they soon get bored. Scores of companies on Aruba offer pricey diversions such as 4WD tours, ATV tours and numerous other acronym-related tours for people who left their Viagra at home. The activities that really do the island proud involve wind and water.

Most activities companies will provide transport to/from wherever you are staying.

### DIVING & SNORKELING

While it is not quite Bonaire, Aruba has some world-class diving around its shores. One of the most popular spots is the wreck of the large WWII German freighter *Antilla*, which is close to shore and at times is visible above the surface. It lies between Arashi and Malmok Beaches.

Visibility is often upwards of 30m, which makes for excellent fish-spotting and photography. Reefs are plentiful with many right off **De Palm Island**, the barrier island off the southwest coast. **Kantil Reef** here has a steep drop-off, and it's easy to spot perky parrotfish, bitchy barracudas and spiny lobsters. Other noted nearby reefs include **Skalahein** and **Barcadera**.

Costs for diving and snorkeling are competitive. Daily snorkeling gear rental is about US$20, two-tank dives with all equipment about US$75 and week-long PADI open-water courses about US$400.

Most hotels have a close relationship with at least one dive operator. And many dive shops can set you up with cheap accommodation. Recommended dive shops include the following:

**Mermaid Sport Divers** ( ☎ 297-587-4103; www.scubadivers-aruba.com)

**Native Divers Aruba** ( ☎ 297-586-4763; www.nativedivers.com)

**Roberto's** ( ☎ 297-993-2850; Holiday Inn Beach, High-Rise Resort area) Custom snorkeling trips, rates US$125 for two, US$175 for four.

**SE Aruba Fly'N Dive** ( ☎ 297-588-1150; www.searuba.com)

### GOLF

The **Links at Divi Aruba** ( ☎ 297-586-1357; JE Irausquin Blvd; greens fee US$80) is a nine-hole addition to the Divi resort empire in the Low-Rise Resorts area. Fees include the use of a cart. Club rental is another US$25.

### HORSEBACK RIDING

**Rancho del Campo** ( ☎ 297-585-0290; www.ranchodel campo.com) is one of the better outfits for touring Aruba by horse. It offers rides to the Natural Pool and the Natural Bridge on the rugged northeast coast. Tours cost from US$60. Certainly riding a fertilizer-producing critter to these attractions is better than tearing across the landscape in a 4WD – as many operators promote.

### KAYAKING

**Aruba Kayak Adventure** ( ☎ 297-582-5520; www .arubakayak.com; tours from US$72) takes novices and pros alike out on a fascinating circuit of the mangroves and shoreline near Spanish Lagoon on the south coast. Although you're unlikely to encounter one now, this once was a pirate's hangout. What's a pirate's favorite island? Arrrrrrrrr-ruba.

### SPAS

Day spas are popular on Aruba. Many of the resorts feature world-class services, including **Mandara Spa** ( ☎ 297-520-6750; www.mandaraspa .com; Aruba Marriott Resort, Lloyd G Smith Blvd 101) and **Intermezzo Day Spa** ( ☎ 297-586-0613; www.arubaspa .com; Westin Aruba Resort, JE Irausquin Blvd 77), which has several locations, including the Westin Aruba Resort.

### WINDSURFING & KITESURFING

It always seems to be blowing on Aruba. That, coupled with the usually flat water on the west side of the island makes Aruba a premier place for windsurfing and kitesurfing.

**Aruba Active Vacations** ( ☎ 297-741-2991; www .aruba-active-vacations.com) is the island's main windsurfing operator. It's based to the right on the beach at Fishermen's Huts, a prime bit of windsurfing water south of Malmok Beach. Rentals start at US$55 per day and a variety of lessons are available. It also does kitesurfing for similar rates.

## Tours

Scores of companies offer day trips on sailboats and yachts. Many are pegged to the sunset. Other outfits organize pub crawls aboard colorfully decorated school buses replete with horns blaring what might be 'Babba-loo!!!'

**De Palm Tours** ( ☎ 297-582-4400; www.depalm.com) has a near lock on mainstream organized tours. Its heavily promoted tours crisscross

the island taking vacationers on a dizzying variety of trips. Tour prices start at US$39 for a sightseeing tour.

Popular with kids and kidlike adults, the **Atlantis Submarine** ( ☎ 297-588-6881; www.atlantis adventures.com; adult/child US$100/50) is the Aruba edition of the attraction found at islands throughout the Caribbean and Hawaii. In an hour-long tour, you submerge over 30m and, as one of the New Jersey–minted passengers might say, 'go swimming with the fishes.'

## Festivals & Events

Every Tuesday night, the **Bon Bini Festival** (admission US$3; ☒ 6:30-8:30pm) is staged at Fort Zoutman by a local tourism association. The event attracts some top folkloric talent from around the island, and local foods and handicrafts are sold.

As elsewhere in the region, **Carnival** is a huge, feathered-boa deal. The climax is the Grand Parade that closes down Oranjestad the Sunday before Ash Wednesday. It's so big that the next day is a national holiday so Aruba can sleep it off.

## Sleeping

Accommodations on Aruba are ideally suited to the sort of mass-market tourism the island targets. The two main clusters of resorts – the descriptively named Low-Rise Resorts and High-Rise Resorts – are all fairly large three- and four-star properties. This is not the island for little boutique inns or posh five-star resorts. In fact the area between the two clusters is rapidly filling in with what could give it the name 'Time-Share Land'.

For the beachside resorts, trawl through online booking services; no one pays rack rates, although 20% tax and service charges are common. Although the major chains dominate, you can find interesting, locally owned places at a reasonable price.

### BUDGET

Lower-priced places to stay tend to be inland away from the beaches, although the drive or walk can be fairly short. Most have a certain utilitarian charm and are good choices for divers or others planning all-day activities where the joys of a beach-front hotel would be unappreciated.

**Coconut Inn** ( ☎ 297-586-6288, 866-978-4952; www .coconutinn.com; Noord 31; r US$65-100; ☒ ☐ ☒ ) Near the collection of restaurants in Noord on a small road north of Noord Ave, the Coconut has a few of the eponymous trees in its simple grounds. The 40 rooms are motel-room basic but the pool is a large rectangle of aqua joy.

## MIDRANGE

The bulk of Aruba's accommodations are midrange in price. Condo-type units can be the best value, as they come with fully equipped kitchens.

**Arubiana Inn** ( ☎ 297-587-7700; www.arubianainn .com; Bubali 74; r US$85-100; 🅿 🛎 ) About a 15-minute walk east from Eagle Beach and near some food outlets, this 18-room small hotel is popular with Europeans on budget packages. The rooms have a dash of style and services include free coolers for taking cold drinks to the beach. Offers wi-fi access.

**MVC Eagle Beach Aruba** ( ☎ 297-587-0110; www .mvceaglebeach.com; JE Irausquin Blvd 240; r from US$100; 🅿 🖵 🛎 ) Thank Dutch taxpayers for this amazing deal right across from Eagle Beach. Owned by the Dutch Navy, it's a basic two-story block with 16 rooms facing a small pool. Although beefy seaman-types abound, it's open to the masses, who enjoy the best deal in Aruba for the location. Don't expect any frills, but it does have a convivial bar-restaurant where you can debate the finer points of the Battle of Jutland.

**our pick** **Sunset Beach Studios** ( ☎ 297-586-3940, 800-813-6540; www.aruba-sunsetblvds.com; Lloyd G Smith Blvd 486; r US$90-130; 🅿 🖵 🛎 ) Right across the coast road from rocky Malmok Beach, this 10-room property has a carefree funky charm. Units in front can take in the sunset, while those in back view the pool. All have kitchenettes. Some of the island's best windsurfing is right out front. Offers wi-fi access.

**Aruba Beach Villas** ( ☎ 297-586-1072, 800-320-9998; www.arubabeachvillas.com; Lloyd G Smith Blvd 462; r $120-250; 🅿 🖵 🛎 ) Nicely located across the coast road from breezy Malmok Beach, the 31 units here are bright and have kitchenettes. Those facing the beach have large patios with sun chairs. Guests, who include many windsurfers, have free use of snorkeling and windsurfing gear, plus kayaks. The high-rise beach area is a five-minute walk south. Offers wi-fi access.

## TOP END

The difference between a midrange resort and top end one on Aruba may be the deal you get online.

**Renaissance Aruba Resort** ( ☎ 297-583-6000; www .renaissancearuba.com; Lloyd G Smith Blvd 82, Oranjestad; r US$175-450; 🅿 🖵 🛎 ) The Renaissance Aruba Resort is in Oranjestad and splits its 560 rooms between a large complex with a casino and shopping mall in the heart of town, and a lush tropical complex out by the water. The two are linked by little shuttle boats that leave from a watery atrium in the city complex and both are linked by boat to a third facility: a small island offshore with a beach. The comfortable rooms span the gamut, but be sure to avoid the gloomy ones overlooking the indoor atrium. The resort offers wi-fi access.

**Amsterdam Manor Beach Resort** ( ☎ 297-587-1492; www.amsterdammanor.com; JE Irausquin Blvd 252; r from US$200; 🅿 🖵 🛎 ) At the north end of blindingly white Eagle Beach, this 72-unit family-run resort mimics a Dutch village. Rooms and buildings come in a variety of shapes and sizes; all have kitchenettes. Some have sizable balconies or terraces with views.

**Bucuti Beach Resort** ( ☎ 297-583-1100; www.bucuti .com; Lloyd G Smith Blvd 55B; r US$200-300; 🅿 🖵 🛎 ) One of the classiest choices among the Manchebo Beach low-rises, the 63-room Bucuti has a vaguely Spanish feel. Guest rooms are large, with kitchenettes and deep balconies, many with ocean views. The Tara wing is quite luxurious. There is a café in a concrete pirate ship. (What do you get if you cross a pirate with zucchini? A squashbuckler.) Children are discouraged. Offers wi-fi access.

**Divi Aruba All Inclusive** ( ☎ 297-525-5200; www .diviaruba.com; JE Irausquin Blvd 45; all-inclusive r US$275-500; 🅿 🖵 🛎 ) The 203-room Divi Aruba is an older property with mature palm trees that give it a relaxed Polynesian feel. There is a large section of units in one-story blocks euphemistically called *casitas* that have a retro concrete-block charm. Rates are all-inclusive and the food is in the 'piles o' chow' category, but the beach here is good and sweeps down to a companion property, the Divi Tamarijn.

**Costa Linda Beach Resort** ( ☎ 297-583-8000; www .costalinda-aruba.com; JE Irausquin Blvd 59; apt US$250-500; 🅿 🖵 🛎 ) There's nothing overly exciting about the five-story Costa Linda, an older time-share property (dig those '70s graphics baby!). But it has a fine position on Manchebo Beach and the one-, two- and three-unit apartments are large, with good-sized balconies and full kitchens. Offers wi-fi access.

The High-Rise Resort area is the top-end holiday ghetto of Aruba. Almost all the hotels are affiliated with major chains. The properties pack in thousands of guests who compete for pool loungers, elbow each other like seals on Palm Beach and seek comfort in US$15 rum punches. It's not an area that will appeal to many independent travelers but you may find an incredible deal online (quite common really) or your dowager aunt may demand the entire family have a group holiday.

These are the major properties; all offer wi-fi access.

**Aruba Marriott Resort** ( ☎ 297-586-9000; www.marriottaruba.com; Lloyd G Smith Blvd 101; r US$200-450; 🅿 🖳 🛋 ) Over 400 rooms with good balconies but seems to function as a venue for sales of Marriott timeshares.

**Holiday Inn Sunspree Resort** ( ☎ 297-586-3600; www.aruba.sunspreeresorts.com; JE Irausquin Blvd 230; r from $250; 🅿 🖳 🛋 ) Older, huge, 630 rooms, not recommended.

**Hyatt Regency Aruba Resort** ( ☎ 297-586-1234; www.aruba.hyatt.com; JE Irausquin Blvd 85; r US$200-550; 🅿 🖳 🛋 ) Has an elegant Moorish motif, but the beach is crowded as are the tropical birds displayed in small cages; 360 rooms.

**Radisson Aruba Resort** ( ☎ 297-586-6555; www.radisson.com/aruba; JE Irausquin Blvd 81; r from US$300; 🅿 🖳 🛋 ) Possibly the nicest of the bunch. Extensive, lush grounds; 359 rooms.

**RIU Palace Aruba** ( ☎ 297-586-1941; JE Irausquin Blvd 230; d from US$500; 🅿 🖳 🛋 ) Feels and looks huge, with 450 rooms. All-inclusive, unlimited booze policy may not be compatible with afternoon bingo sessions broadcast loudly in the pool area.

**Westin Aruba Resort** ( ☎ 297-586-4466; www.westin.com; JE Irausquin Blvd 77; r US$200-450; 🅿 🖳 🛋 ) A cramped site and at its roots a 1970s property with 480 rooms. Also has tropical birds in cages.

## Eating

Aruba has the best line-up of restaurants on the ABCs. There are plenty of over-priced joints, franchises (Hooters!) and fast food outlets near the resorts but a short walk or drive inland in Noord you'll find a nice range of locally owned places. Oranjestad also has some fine choices.

### BUDGET

Snack trucks are an island institution. Look for these spotless trucks in the parking lots near the Yacht Basin serving up a range of ultra-fresh food from sunset well into the wee hours. Locals debate who sells the best conch sandwich and you may want to conduct your own research. Other tasty options include ribs and anything with curry. Most everything is under Afl10.

**Ling & Sons** ( ☎ 297-583-2370; Schotlandstraat 41; ⏰ 8am-8pm Mon-Sat, 8am-1pm Sun) All those kitchenettes demand a good supermarket and this is it. It has a large deli, a salad bar and more.

**Sunrise Bakery** ( ☎ 297-587-9200; Bubali 72; snacks Afl4; ⏰ 8am-5pm) This aromatic bakery with sweet and savory treats is near budget hotels and close to other popularly priced takeaways, cafés and groceries.

**Linda's Pancakes & Pizzas** ( ☎ 297-586-3378; Palm Beach 6D, Noord; meals Afl7-12; ⏰ lunch & dinner Tue-Sun) Near several other places to eat, the nice covered terrace here is a good spot for breakfast pancakes, burgers or, as you'll guess from the name, good homemade pizza.

**Peanuts** ( ☎ 297-583-4343; Caya GF Betico Croes, Oranjestad; mains Afl8-18; ⏰ breakfast, lunch & dinner Wed-Mon; 🛋 ) Come out of your shell at this cute upscale café aimed at locals. The name refers to the iconic local sauce, which is served with a variety of grilled meats. Other good options include spicy soups, seafood salads and fall-off-the-bone ribs.

**Baby Back Grill** ( ☎ 297-563-3880; Caya GF Betico Croes, Oranjestad; meals from Afl12; ⏰ lunch & dinner) This is like a snack truck, but it doesn't go anywhere and there are shady picnic tables. This completely open-air restaurant grills up tender ribs through the day for appreciative masses.

### MIDRANGE

**Rhumba Bar & Grill** ( ☎ 297-588-7900; Havenstraat 4, Oranjestad; mains US$8-25; ⏰ lunch & dinner Mon-Sat) This open-air restaurant has a good outdoor café vibe. Settle into one of the wicker chairs and watch the day-trippers stampede when someone yells 'cheap watches!' Salads, sandwiches and seafood are featured.

**Bingo** ( ☎ 297-586-2818; Palm Beach 6D, Noord; meals Afl12-28; ⏰ dinner; 🛋 ) Near Linda's, this popular Dutch-run café is both a genial bar and a good place for a casual meal. Enjoy bar fare like burgers at tables inside and out or opt for more ambitious specials like ham with melon or garlic *gambas* (shrimp). The bar stays open until 2am.

**La Terraza** ( ☎ 297-583-6046; Marina Mall, Oranjestad; meals US$10-15; ⏰ lunch & dinner Mon-Sat; 🛋 ) Enjoy the views over the yacht basin from this large 2nd-floor café. Dine outside on the terrace or inside in the air-con. Enjoy well-presented casual fare such as salads, sandwiches, pasta and grilled seafood. It's popular with families.

**Ristorante Sole Mare** ( ☎ 297-586-0077; Palm Beach 23, Noord; mains US$15-30; ☺ dinner; ☒ ) It's hard to resist the appealing facade on this family-run Italian classic. Once inside you won't resist the food either. Classic pasta dishes like *spaghetti alle vongole* are joined by excellent garlicky seafood creations. The wine list is short but has key words like Chianti.

### TOP END

**Gasparito Restaurant** ( ☎ 297-586-7044; Gasparito 3, Noord; mains US$17-30; ☺ dinner; ☒ ) Gasparito has fine Aruban dining inside a classic old country house or outside on the candlelit patio. Old family recipes prepared here include *keshi yena*, a meat-filled cheese wonder, and shrimp marinated in brandy and coconut milk. A vegetarian platter is the menu sleeper: plantains and more in a Creole sauce.

**Driftwood** ( ☎ 297-583-2515; Klipstraat 12, Oranjestad; mains US$18-32; ☺ dinner Wed-Mon; ☒ ) Toss back a couple too many of the serious cocktails at this 1960s supper club and you'll expect Dean Martin to walk in. Owned by a local fisherman, the changing menu reflects what he and his pals have caught. Grilled lobster is simple and simply terrific.

**Yemanja** ( ☎ 297-588-4711; Wilhelminastraat 2, Oranjestad; mains from US$24; ☺ dinner; ☒ ) Two colonial buildings behind the Aruba Parliament have been transformed into the island's most stylish eatery. Cobalt blue glassware provides accents to the sleek and airy dining areas. Most items on the menu are grilled over wood. Try the seared tuna, the marinated rock lobster or the tenderloin.

## Drinking

With resorts hogging so much of the waterfront, Aruba lacks the kind of bamboo beach shacks peddling rum punches that are basic to so many a Caribbean island. Instead, opt for a local spot where you can make friends and let the evening drift away. Bingo (opposite) is a popular place for a drink. Rum shops (p790) are another amiable option.

**Cafe Chaos** ( ☎ 297-588-5547; Lloyd G Smith Blvd 60, Oranjestad; ☺ 7pm-2am Sun-Fri, 7pm-4am Sat) Crooners warble from the jukebox at this smallish place popular with local professionals. On many nights there's live acoustic, jazz or blues.

**Jimmy's Place Aruba** ( ☎ 297-582-2550; Kruisweg 15; ☺ 4pm-2am Sun-Thu, 4pm-4am Fri & Sat) A friendly and low-key bar popular with gay and lesbian visitors. Watch for live music and themed dance parties; climaxes after 2am.

## Entertainment
### CASINOS

Almost every high-rise resort has a casino, many of which are quite small. Slot machines are by far the most common game, and facilities at even the flashiest places are not comparable to anything in Las Vegas. Slots are typically open 10am to 4am, tables 6pm to 4am.

**Stellaris Casino** ( ☎ 297-586-9000; Aruba Marriott Resort, Lloyd G Smith Blvd 101) One of the largest casinos, always busy and a bit flashy.

**Copa Cabana Casino** ( ☎ 297-586-1234; Hyatt Regency Aruba Resort; JE Irausquin Blvd 85) Glitzy; cover bands offer cover while you lose your shirt.

### NIGHTCLUBS

Aruba is not the place to come if you want the latest in techno or even something that's simply late.

**Euphoria** ( ☎ 297-588-9450; Royal Plaza Mall, Oranjestad; ☺ 9pm-4am) On the top floor of the small mall, Euphoria dazzles with light shows. Most nights it's a mixture of reggae, house and hip-hop.

## Shopping

Numerous shopping malls cluster around Lloyd G Smith Blvd and the cruise-ship port. Most international luxury brands are amply represented. Bargaining is not encouraged. For a local experience, stroll Caya GF Betico Croes, Oranjestad's main shopping street.

## NORTHEAST COAST

Near Arashi Beach is a road leading to the **California Lighthouse**, on the island's northern tip. This tall sentinel is named for an old shipwreck named *California*, which is *not* the ship of the same name that stood by ineffectually while the *Titanic* sank (despite much local lore to the contrary). The views over the flat land extend in all directions, and when it's especially clear you can see all the way to Oranjestad. The surf is always pounding and dunes extend far inland.

On the opposite side of Aruba from the high-rises, **Chapel of Alto Vista** is a remote 1950s

ARUBA, BONAIRE & CURAÇAO

church built on the site of one dating to 1750. The road to salvation here is lined with signs bearing prayers, starting in temptation at the Alto Vista Rum Shop, east of Noord. Look for the *divi* tree right out of central casting; it looks like a question mark caught in a hurricane.

Further south along the northeast coast are two popular natural attractions. **Natural Bridge** is one of several on Aruba, but this one comes with a decent (and well-signed!) road and a gift shop. Wave action hollowed out a limestone cave on the sea cliffs that later collapsed, leaving the 'bridge.' Mobs descend when cruise ships are in port, but other times it's a moody and windswept spot.

A detour back inland takes you to the **Natural Pool**, a depression behind a limestone ridge that often fills with sea water thanks to wave action. Given the rough swimming conditions on the east coast of Aruba, this is a good spot for a dip. Again, your enjoyment may depend on the number of day-trippers with the same goal. The road out here passes by **Ayo Rock**, a smooth-sided geologic wonder popular with rock climbers. It also has some ancient drawings. And take time to stop at the **Donkey Sanctuary** ( ☎ 297-584-1063; donations appreciated; ⏰ usually daylight hr, call) where you can make an ass out of yourself petting these winsome critters. Originally brought to Aruba by the Spaniards, many donkeys now live in the wild where they fall prey to speeding tour buses. Injured ones are brought here to recuperate.

For postcard shots, you should also visit **Casibari Rock**, about 1.5km west of Ayo Rock.

Steps lead to the top where there are good views across the island.

## ARIKOK NATIONAL WILDLIFE PARK

Arikok National Wildlife Park comprises 20% of the island. It's arid and rugged, and can easily occupy a full day of exploring. The **park entrance hut** (admission free; ⏰ office 7am-5pm, park 24hr) has useful maps and other information. To get here, follow the marked roads east from the busy *cunucu* town of Santa Cruz (a place locals say still feels the most like the Aruba where they grew up – ignoring the KFC).

Two gardens inside the park entrance are worth visiting. **Cunucu Arikok** and **Shon Shoco** have short trails with signs and labels describing the many native plants. More than 70% of the types of plant here are used in traditional medicine. The land is mostly pretty scruffy and there are remnants of old gold mines built long ago by Europeans and slaves.

The principal road is about 11km long and links the west entrance near Santa Cruz with the southern one near San Nicholas, allowing a circular tour. Although slow going, it's doable in your budget rental car. A 4WD vehicle will let you enjoy tracks off the main circuit that include sand dunes, rocky coves, caves and remote hiking trails. Watch out for the many iguanas as you drive and stop once and a while and listen for the bray of wild donkeys.

Numerous hiking trails lead across the hilly terrain. Bring water and ask for recommendations at the entrance hut. Look for the park's three main types of tree: the

---

### RUM SHOPS

Throughout Aruba's hinterlands you will see rum shops. These island institutions are part bar, part café and part social center. Here's where you'll meet anyone from taxi drivers to accountants. Although there are dozens and they come in all sizes, it's not hard to identify them as they invariably are plastered with Balashi, Amstel and/or Heineken signs. The rum itself is often locally produced and may drive you to drink – beer.

The rules are simple: you stand, drink rum – or beer – have a snack and unburden yourself to whoever is nearby. On Friday after work, crowds spill out into the streets. A good place to sample this culture is **Baby Store** ( ☎ 297-585-0839; ⏰ 6:30am-8:30pm), which is on the main road 2 miles (3km) north of Santa Cruz near the Piedra Plat Church. Beers cost Afl3 and a *frekedel* (a Dutch-derived meatball made with plantain) is Afl2.

An especially accessible rum shop, **Caribbean Store** ( ☎ 586-5544; Palm Beach; ⏰ 8am-11pm), can be found in Noord, east of the resorts; it has stand-up tables in a dirt parking lot and a cheery bar inside. Another popular stop for locals and visitors alike is the **Alto Vista Rum Shop** ( ⏰ 11am-7pm) near the Chapel of Alto Vista. San Nicholas is also good for rum shops; you'll see them on most corners.

## ARUBA'S BEACHES

Aruba has the best beaches of the ABCs; most are along the south and west coasts. Here are some you won't want to miss, going counterclockwise from the north.

- **Arashi Beach** Near the island's northwest tip, this is a favorite with locals and popular with families. There is good body surfing, some shade and just a few rocks right offshore.
- **Malmok Beach** Shallow waters extending far out from shore make this a popular spot for windsurfers. Not the best place for simple sunbathing as it's rather rocky.
- **Palm Beach** Classic white-sand beauty, but only for those who enjoy the company of lots of people as it fronts the array of High-Rise Resorts.
- **Eagle Beach** Fronting a stretch of the Low-Rise Resorts just northwest of Oranjestad, Eagle is a long stretch of white sand. The best all-around choice for everyone, from singles to couples to families with kids.
- **Manchebo Beach** Just south of Eagle, this large beach reaches out to a point. Popular with topless sunbathers (an activity frowned on elsewhere).
- **Baby Beach** Nice curve of sand in the uncrowded south. The waters are calm. Nearby Coco's Beach is almost as nice, except for the view of the refinery.
- **Boca Grandi** Reached by a rough road, this small cove is often deserted but for a few windsurfers. As is typical of windward beaches, conditions here are often hazardous, albeit dramatic.
- **Andicuri Beach** A hidden gem on the isolated east coast, this black-pebble beach is often the scene of photo shoots. Near the Natural Bridge, the beach is reached by a road that demands 4WD. Swimming can be treacherous, and the winds make reading a challenge.

iconic and bizarrely twisted *divi-divi*; the *kwihi*, with its tasty sweet-sour long yellow beans; and the *hubada*, which has sharp, tough thorns. Spiky aloe plants abound – see how many of the 70 varieties of cactus you can identify.

Near the coast you will see a small creek, which is the only natural supply of water on Aruba. It flows into a mangrove by the ocean. Here you can also see vast **sand dunes**. At **Boca Prins** on the coast there is a dramatic and dangerous beach in a narrow cove that forms explosive surf. Nearby, your table stays crumb-free at **Boca Prins Cafe** ( ☎ 297-584-5455; meals US$8-16; ⏲ 10am-6pm) as it is totally open to the constant winds.

For safer swimming, a rough road leads north to **Dos Playa**, which as the name implies is two beaches. Otherwise, from Boca Prins you can head south along the wave-tossed coast and end up in San Nicolas.

### SAN NICOLAS

A small town near the island's ill-placed **oil refinery**, San Nicolas preserves Aruba's former rough-and-ready character long since banished from Oranjestad. Prostitution is legal here and a string of windowless bars in the 'Red Zone' open at night. It's all tightly regulated and the streets are pretty safe.

**Charlie's Bar** ( ☎ 297-584-5086; Zeppenfeldstraat 56; meals US$6-20; ⏲ 11am-late) is the big draw here. Started in 1941, it is still run by the same family and is a community institution. The walls are lined with a hodgepodge of stuff collected over the decades: everything from beach flotsam to local sports trophies to artwork by customers. The food combines local dishes with plenty of fresh seafood.

South of San Nicolas and the oil refinery are dramatic vistas and cliffs.

# BONAIRE

Bonaire's worldwide appeal to divers is its amazing reef-lined coast, all of which is a national park. But while no diving (or snorkeling) initiate will be disappointed, Bonaire also has much to offer above the surface, including world-class windsurfing. Although the beaches are mostly slivers of rocky sand, several take on a pink hue from ground coral washed ashore. Also in the pink are the flamingos found throughout the salt flats and mangroves of the south.

Bonaire has a real community feel: your innkeeper may be your divemaster by day or your waiter at a friend's restaurant at night.

Much of the infrastructure on the island supports diving: where else can you find a hotel with a drive-through air-tank refilling station? However, there are some good restaurants, and the main town of Kralendijk has a modest but enjoyable nightlife. If you're not a diver – or an avid reader – you may not find much to fill a week on Bonaire, but a few days will pass delightfully. And just in case you forget why most people come, check out the license plate of the car in front of you, it says: 'Diver's Paradise.'

## History

The Arawaks lived on Bonaire for thousands of years before Spain laid claim in 1499. A mere 20 years later there were none left as the Spanish sent all the natives to work in mines elsewhere in the empire. The only reminder that the Arawaks once lived on Bonaire are a few inscriptions in remote caves. No one knows what they mean.

The depopulated Bonaire stayed pretty quiet until 1634, when the Dutch took control. Soon the Dutch looked to the flat land in the south and saw a future in salt production. Thousands of slaves were imported to work in horrific conditions. You can see a few surviving huts at the south end of the island (p798). When slavery was abolished in the 19th century, the salt factories closed. The population, a mix of ex-slaves, Dutch and people from South America, lived pretty simple lives until after WWII, when the reopening of the salt ponds (this time with machines doing the hard work) coupled with the postwar booms in tourism and diving gave a real boost to the economy.

Meanwhile relations with Curaçao, capital of the Netherlands Antilles, slowly turned frosty. Locals felt ignored by their wealthier neighbor and lobbied for change. In 2008 Bonaire returned to direct Dutch rule as a rather far-flung municipality within the Netherlands. See p779 for details on the dissolution of the Netherlands Antilles.

## Orientation

Bonaire is the second largest of the ABCs at 285 sq km. The main town of Kralendijk is just north of the airport. Major roads loop north midway up the island to Rincon and south past Lac Bay, the southern tip and the salt pans. Rough secondary roads circle the far north and Washington-Slagbaai National Park, and reach parts of the remote east coast. You can drive the main roads in half a day.

Almost all hotels and other businesses are in or near Kralendijk.

## Getting There & Away

Bonaire's **Flamingo Airport** (BON; ☎ 599-717-5600) is immediately south of Kralendijk. For information on flights from the rest of the world, see p813.

Airlines flying between the ABC islands change frequently; see p814.

## Getting Around

There is no public bus service on Bonaire. However, dive operators will haul you wherever you need to go. You can see all of the island in one or two days of driving, so you might consider renting a car for just that period. Many places to stay offer packages with a car thrown in cheap.

Most international car-rental firms are at the airport. The main local operator is **AB Carrental** ( ☎ 599-717-8980; www.abcarrental.com).

There are a couple of gas stations in Kralendijk, including **Gas Ekspres** ( ☮ 599-717-7171; Kaya Tribon; ☮ 7am-10pm).

Taxis from the airport to hotels in Kralendijk cost US$8 to US$18 depending on which end of town you're going to. A taxi to any place on the island costs no more than US$25.

## KRALENDIJK
### pop 3100

Bonaire's capital and main town has a long seafront that's good for strolling day or night. The smattering of low-rise colonial-era buildings in mustard and pastels add charm. The small but delightful selection of restaurants, cafés and bars mean that fun is never far. Shops are limited but you can get all the essentials – including pricy baubles.

## Orientation

Located one block back from the waterfront, Kaya Grandi is the main commercial street.

Hotels can be found south of the cruise-ship port on Julio A Abraham Blvd, as well as north past the sea inlet on Kaya Gobernador N Debrot.

## Information
### BOOKSTORES
Bring reading material from home, as it's easier to spot a manta ray off the reef than it is to find a decent book.

**Addo's Bookstore** ( ☎ 599-717-6618; Kaya Grandi 36; 🕑 9am-1pm, 3-6pm Tue-Fri, 9am-5pm Sat) A welcome addition! Bestsellers, regional fiction, guidebooks and maps.

### EMERGENCY
**Scuba Diving Emergencies** ( ☎ 599-717-8187)

### INTERNET ACCESS
Most hotels have internet access points.

**Bonaire Access** ( ☎ 599-717-6040; Harbourside Shopping Centre, Kaya Grandi 31; per 15min US$4; 🕑 10am-6pm) Wi-fi password US$10 per day.

**Chat 'n' Browse** ( ☎ 599-717-2281; Kaya Gobernador N Debrot 79; per hr US$8; 🕑 7:30am-7pm Mon-Fri, 7:30am-6pm Sat & Sun) Top choice. Stocks phonecards, Cuban cigars, ice cream and more. Wi-fi password US$5 per day.

### INTERNET RESOURCES
**Bonaire Insider** (www.bonaireinsider.com) A compendium of news, info and lively comments.
**Bonaire Talk** (www.bonairetalk.com) This newsgroup and bulletin covers Bonaire issues and information.
**InfoBonaire** (www.infobonaire.com) Lots of highly useful island info.

### MEDIA
The *Bonaire Reporter* (www.bonairereporter .com) is a free newspaper that actually covers controversial issues on the island. *Bonaire Affair* and *Bonaire Nights* are both good tourist freebies.

### MEDICAL SERVICES
**St Franciscus Hospital** ( ☎ 599-717-8900; Kaya Soeur Bartola 2; 🕑 24hr)

### MONEY
Prices are given in local currency more often on Bonaire than Aruba, but US dollars are just as welcome. ATMs are common in Kralendijk.

### POST
**Post office** ( ☎ 599-717-8508; Kaya Simon Bolivar 11; 🕑 7:30am-noon & 1:30-4pm Mon-Fri)

### TOURIST INFORMATION
**Bonaire Tourist Office** ( ☎ 599-717-8322; www.tour ismbonaire.com; Kaya Grandi 2; 🕑 9am-5pm Mon-Fri) Answers questions and has a good selection of brochures.

## Sights
Follow the cannons south along the waterfront to **Fort Oranje**, a small bastion built in the 1700s by the Dutch and modified often through the years. It's now the courthouse.

The small one-room **museum** (admission free; 🕑 8am-noon & 1:30-4:30pm Mon-Fri) has a good display of vintage photos among other displays. Behind an unmarked door to the left of the museum are the cleanest public toilets in town.

Slightly out from the town center, the **Bonaire Museum** ( ☎ 599-717-8868; Kaya J Ree 7; adult/child NAf2/1; 🕑 8am-noon & 2-5pm Mon-Fri) is in an 1885 house filled with folklore displays. Look for the detailed paintings of local mythology by Winifred Dania.

**JanArt Gallery** ( ☎ 599-717-5246; Kaya Gloria 7, Antriol; 🕑 10am-5pm Tue-Thu & Sat, 5-7pm Fri) is a bright blue-and-yellow house brimming with local art. Just off Kaya Papa Cornes.

## Activities
### CYCLING
Roads to the south end of the island with its windswept flat expanses and Lac Bay are ideal for cycling.

**Cycle Bonaire** ( ☎ 599-717-2229; Kaya Gobernador N Debrot 77; 🕑 8:30am-4:30pm) Rents high-end bikes from US$15 per day, organizes guided excursions.

**De Freewielen** ( ☎ 599-717-8545; Kaya Grandi 61; 🕑 8:30am-5:30pm Mon-Fri, 8:30am-1:30pm Sat) is run by a Dutch cyclist, with rentals per day from US$14.

### DIVING & SNORKELING
For details of the Bonaire Marine Park, see the boxed text, p799.

### KAYAKING & WINDSURFING
For details on kayaking and windsurfing on Lac Bay, see p798.

## Tours
**Karel's** ( ☎ 599-790-8330) Runs daily boats (US$14 per person; four trips per day) to Turtle Beach on Klein Bonaire. It also has a pirate-themed sunset cruise (US$40), with an open bar guaranteed to keel-haul your liver.
**Outdoor Bonaire** ( ☎ 599-791-6272; www.outdoor bonaire.com) Leads active tours that include rock climbing, kayaking, caving and more; tours from US$40.

ARUBA, BONAIRE &
CURAÇAO

# BONAIRE

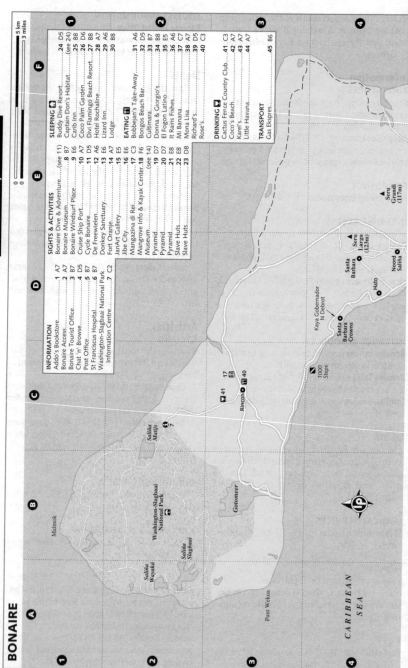

**INFORMATION**
| Addo's Bookstore | 1 A7 |
| Bonaire Access | 2 A7 |
| Bonaire Tourist Office | 3 B7 |
| Chat 'n' Browse | 4 D5 |
| Post Office | 5 B7 |
| St Franciscus Hospital | 6 B7 |
| Washington-Slagbaai National Park Information Centre | 7 C2 |

**SIGHTS & ACTIVITIES**
| Bonaire Dive & Adventure | (see 11) |
| Bonaire Museum | 8 B7 |
| Bonaire Windsurf Place | 9 E6 |
| Cruise Ship Port | 10 A7 |
| Cycle Bonaire | 11 D5 |
| De Freewieler | 12 A6 |
| Donkey Sanctuary | 13 E6 |
| Fort Oranje | 14 A7 |
| JanArt Gallery | 15 E5 |
| Jibe City | 16 E6 |
| Mangazina di Rei | 17 C3 |
| Mangrove Info & Kayak Center | 18 F6 |
| Museum | (see 14) |
| Pyramid | 19 D7 |
| Pyramid | 20 D7 |
| Pyramid | 21 E8 |
| Slave Huts | 22 E8 |
| Slave Huts | 23 D8 |

**SLEEPING**
| Buddy Dive Resort | 24 D5 |
| Captain Don's Habitat | (see 24) |
| Carib Inn | 25 B8 |
| Coco Palm Garden | 26 D6 |
| Divi Flamingo Beach Resort | 27 B8 |
| Hotel Rochaline | 28 A7 |
| Lizard Inn | 29 A6 |
| Lodge | 30 B8 |

**EATING**
| Bobbejan's Take-Away | 31 A6 |
| Bongos Beach Bar | 32 D5 |
| Cultimara | 33 B7 |
| Donna & Giorgio's | 34 B8 |
| El Fogon Latino | 35 E5 |
| It Rains Fishes | 36 A6 |
| Mi Banana | 37 C7 |
| Mona Lisa | 38 A7 |
| Richard's | 39 D5 |
| Rose's | 40 C3 |

**DRINKING**
| Cactus Fence Country Club | 41 C3 |
| Coco's Beach | 42 A7 |
| Karel's | 43 A7 |
| Little Havana | 44 A7 |

**TRANSPORT**
| Gas Ekspres | 45 B6 |

5 km
3 miles

CARIBBEAN
SEA

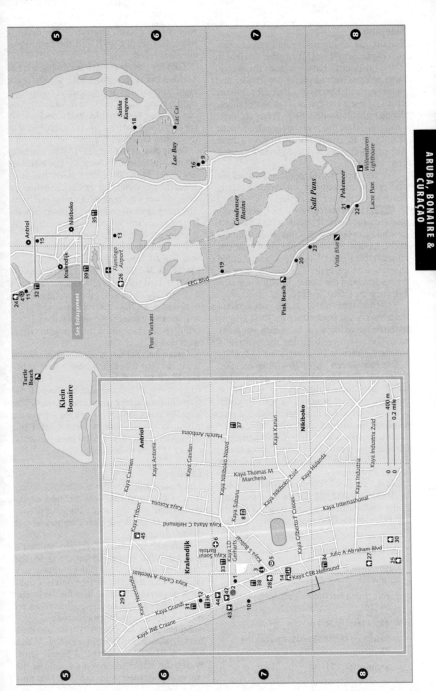

## Sleeping

Bonaire has an interesting and varied selection of places to stay. Unlike other Caribbean islands it doesn't have much in the way of large resorts; instead places are smaller and more personal. Divers are catered for at many places; at some you can enjoy excellent shore-diving right off the back deck. Prices are lower on average than much of the region, and wide variations in rooms mean that you have numerous choices at most places to match your budget.

See the tourist information websites for oodles of apartment and condo rentals. Many are being built near the airport.

**our pick** **Lizard Inn** ( ☎ 599-717-6877; www.lizardinn bonaire.com; Kaya America 14; s/d from US$56/62; ✦ ▯ ) A new budget place five minutes' walk from the shore; has a nice little compound of basic but comfortable rooms. Nothing is fancy but the showers are superb, the TVs satellite, the mattresses firm and the owner, Khalito Gomaa, a helpful gem. Offers wi-fi access.

**Hotel Rochaline** ( ☎ 599-717-8286; www.hotelrocha linebonaire.com; Kaya Grandi; r US$60-70; ✦ ▯ ) Right in the center of town, the hotel runs a popular café. The rooms are basic but the location is excellent. Offers wi-fi access.

**Coco Palm Garden** ( ☎ 599-717-2108; www.cocopalm garden.com; office: Kaya van Eps 9; r & apt US$70-110; ✦ ▯ ▣ ) Coco Palm rents a variety of rooms and apartments in various brightly painted houses in a little neighborhood just south of the airport. Bed sizes vary, as do amenities like sofas, patios, kitchens etc (although you can always count on a hammock). The office has a pool and wi-fi, and is near all the units.

**Lodge** ( ☎ 599-717-5410; www.thelodgebonaire.com; Kaya Inglatera 12; r US$75; ✦ ▯ ) Balinese teak furniture and statues lend an exotic air to this otherwise simple B&B near the centre. Twelve rooms face a small courtyard. The decor is basic, but there's wi-fi and the bathrooms are nicely tiled.

**Carib Inn** ( ☎ 599-717-8819; www.caribinn.com; Julio A Abraham Blvd; r & apt US$100-160; ✦ ▯ ) There are eight simple units here in a small compound right on the water; most have kitchens. You can get your tanks refilled and a dock allows for easy dive-boat pick-up. It's a short walk to the center. Offers wi-fi access.

**Buddy Dive Resort** ( ☎ 599-717-5080; www.buddy dive.com; Kaya Gobernador N Debrot 85; r from US$120, apt from US$190; ✦ ▯ ▣ ) Divers never had it so good: the reef is right off the deck and there's a drive-through air-tank refill station out front. The more than 70 rooms and apartments are large and in two- and three-story blocks. All apartments have kitchens and views.

**Divi Flamingo Beach Resort** ( ☎ 599-717-8285; www.diviresorts.com; Julio A Abraham Blvd 40; r US$120-200; ✦ ▯ ▣ ) This hodgepodge of a resort has standard rooms in all shapes and sizes – some in largish blocks, others hutlike. Coats of bright paint have given it a tropical motif and the two pools are newly refreshed. It has full dive facilities and a small casino. Offers wi-fi access.

**Captain Don's Habitat** ( ☎ 599-717-8290; www.habitat bonaire.com; Kaya Gobernador N Debrot; r & apt US$160-300; ✦ ▯ ▣ ) Belying that logo of a pirate flag bearing a skull impaled by a sword, the Captain runs a very comfortable resort. The large 85 units are set on spacious grounds. Air tanks are available 24 hours a day. (And the resort is a leader in local environmental causes.) Offers wi-fi access.

## Eating

The Kralendijk area has a splendid collection of places to eat. You can find everything from simple places with scrumptious local fare to beachside barbecues to fine (yet casual) dining.

**Bobbejan's Take-Away** (Kaya Albert Engelhardt 2; meals from NAf20; ☻ dinner Fri-Sun) Don't let the name fool you; there are tables here out back under a nice tree. But getting one is a challenge as *everybody* comes here for the super-tender ribs and the velvety peanut sauce on the Indonesian plate of chicken satay.

**Bongos Beach Bar** ( ☎ 599-717-7238; Eden Beach Resort, Kaya Gobernador N Debrot; meals US$8-20; ☻ lunch & dinner) Classic stereotypical beach joint. Watch the sunset while you get sand in the cracks of your toes; tables in a shady hut plus

---

**VISITORS AS ATMS**

Government fees for visitors to Bonaire add up quickly:

- Park diving fee: US$25 (nondiving US$10)
- Room tax: US$5.50 per day
- Departure tax: US$32 (US$8 within the ABCs)
- Security tax: US$1.40

out on the beach. Burgers and casual fare through the day. On Friday nights there's a popular barbecue.

**Mi Banana** (Kaya Nikiboko Noord; meals NAf10; ☏ lunch Tue-Sun, dinner Tue-Thu) A local fave, this simple place in Antriol serves a huge range of plate specials including spicy fish, goat and pork-chop numbers. Good for take-away as well.

**ourpick El Fogon Latino** ( ☏ 599-717-2677; Kaya Nikiboko Zuid; meals NAf10-20; ☏ lunch & dinner Wed-Mon) Direct from Colombia, this little café has tables on a porch or in its breezy dining room. The light and crispy fried Dorado filet is superb, as are the many other meaty plate meals. Skip the potatoes for the succulent fried plantains. It's on the road to Lac Bay.

**Donna & Giorgio's** ( ☏ 599-717-3799; Kaya CEB Hellmund 25; mains NAf20-40; ☏ dinner Thu-Tue) This inviting open-air restaurant is on a quiet corner across from the water. The classic Italian menu has many treats: an *antipasti misto* for the indecisive, a *pasta gamberoni* for those wanting garlicky shrimp, and eggplant parmigiana for those wanting sensual comfort. Book.

**Mona Lisa** ( ☏ 599-717-8718; Kaya Grandi 15; mains NAf30-40; ☏ dinner Mon-Sat) This local institution is a tropical version of a traditional Dutch brown café. Choose from excellent food displayed on a changing blackboard menu. Specials include a Dutch cheese salad and soup made with local fish. All the seafood is excellent. Book.

**It Rains Fishes** ( ☏ 599-717-8780; Kaya JNE Craane; mains NAf30-40; ☏ dinner Mon-Sat) Enjoy creative seafood fare at this stylish open-air bistro across from the shore. Everything is spot-on, right down to the pepper grinders on the tables. Service is jolly and must-have dishes include the garlic *gambas* and the fish special.

**Richard's** ( ☏ 599-717-5263; Julio A Abraham Blvd 60; mains NAf30-40; ☏ dinner Tue-Sun) The mood of casual elegance at the open-air tables on the water is set by the white tablecloths accented by blue napkins. There's nothing between you and the ocean but the dock where the daily fresh fish specials are delivered. Reserve.

The best supermarket is **Cultimara** ( ☏ 599-717-8278; Kaya LD Gerharts 13; ☏ 7:30am-7pm Mon-Sat, 8am-2pm Sun), with a decent but hardly upscale selection.

## Drinking

Bongos Beach Bar (opposite) is good for a sunset drink. Kralendijk does not party late – there are fish to spot at dawn.

**Little Havana** ( ☏ 599-701-0717; Kaya Bonaire 4; ☏ 5pm-2:30am) A classic atmospheric bar in a historic whitewashed building. Walk through the open doors and you pass back many decades in time. Sit at the rich wooden bar and enjoy a fine Cuban cigar while album covers featuring jazz greats stare down from the walls. The tunes lean towards classic rock.

**Coco's Beach** ( ☏ 599-717-8434; Kaya Bonaire; ☏ 11am-midnight) Lots of tropical plants and tables covered in local fabrics set the mood at this fun outdoor bar on the waterfront. On Saturday a steel band plays at 7pm.

**Karel's** ( ☏ 599-790-8330; Waterfront; ☏ 10am-2am) Two bars set on a concrete pier over the water. Many drink specials include free rum punch at 5pm Tuesday.

## NORTH OF KRALENDIJK

The road north along the coast is like a roller-coaster, but in good shape. There are great vistas of the rocky seashore and frequent pullouts for the marked dive sites. About 5km north of Kralendijk the road becomes one way, north, so you are committed at this point. After another 5km you reach a T-junction. To the right is the direct road Rincon. Turn left (west), following the coast until the road turns sharply inland. Good views of the large inland lake, Gotomeer, are off on the left. Flamingos stalk about in search of bugs. The road passes through some lush growth and ends in Rincon.

Bonaire's second town, **Rincon** is rather sleepy and that may simply be because it's old. Over 500 years ago Spaniards established a settlement here a) because it was fertile and b) because it was hidden from passing pirates. Most of the residents are descended from slaves, who worked the farms and made the long trek to the salt flats in the south. Homes have a classic Caribbean look and are painted in myriad pastel shades.

The town has a popular **market** ( ☏ 8am-2pm Sat) with a oodles of the area's produce. Almost any day of the week you can pause at **Rose's** ( ☏ 599-562-6364; meals from NAf10; ☏ lunch Thu-Tue), a local institution run by Rose herself. A genial mix of folks enjoy plate lunches of local fare (fish stew, goat, fried chicken etc) at tables scattered under trees. You can get a beer here pretty much during any daylight hour.

About 1.5km on the road to the coast, look for **Mangazina di Rei** ( ☏ 599-786-2101; www.mangazinadirei.org; adult/child US$10/free; ☏ 8am-5pm Mon-Fri), the second-oldest stone building on Bonaire. It has been restored and includes exhibits about its use as a storehouse for provisions that were doled out to slaves. Tours are fascinating and include a glass of tasty sorghum juice.

## Washington-Slagbaai National Park

Covering the northwest portion of the island and comprising almost 20% of the land, Washington-Slagbaai National Park is a great place to explore. Roads are rough and all but impassable after a rain, but it's well worth the effort. The terrain is mostly tropical desert, and there is a proliferation of cactuses and birds. Look for flamingos in the lowlands and parrots perched on shrubs. Large bright green iguanas are just one of the many reptile species you might find. You'll also see lingering evidence of the aloe plantation and goat ranch that used to be here – don't run over any wild descendents of the latter.

There is an excellent **information center** ( ☎ 599-717-8444; www.stinapa.org; adult/child US$10/5; ☺ 8am-5pm, last entry at 2:45pm) and museum at the entrance; the latter has an excellent history section on the island. From here you can take one of two drives: a five-hour, 33km route or a three-hour, 24km route. Regular cars are discouraged but not banned. There are picnic, dive and swimming stops along the way.

Two hikes are best done well before the heat of noon: the 90-minute Lagadishi loop, which takes you past ancient stone walls, a blowhole and the rugged coast; and the two-hour Kasikunda climbing trail, which takes you up a challenging path to the top of a hill for sweeping views.

The park entrance is at the end of a good 4km concrete road from Rincon. Along the way you'll pass the **Cactus Fence Country Club** ( ☎ 599-568-9613; ☺ from 11am Sun), which – true to its name – is surrounded by one of the living cactus fences common on Bonaire. There's no golf here, but there is good music, a barbecue and a friendly crowd.

## EAST OF KRALENDIJK

The road from Kralendijk to Lac Bay is a highlight. Off the main road, a branch goes around the north side of the water. At first you drive through groves of cactus so thick that it's like driving through someone's crew cut. Close to the water there are dense mangroves and flocks of flamingos. It's a popular ride for cyclists.

Along this road, the **Mangrove Info & Kayak Center** ( ☎ 599-790-5353; www.mangrovecenter.com; ☺ Mon-Sat) is right on the mangroves and offers kayak tours (from US$25). It has displays with information about the protected Lac Bay mangroves, which are part of the marine park. About 5.5km from the turn-off the road ends at Lac Cai, a sandy point with a small beach, a snack stand, and mountains of huge pearly white and pink conch shells.

**Lac Bay** itself is one of the world's premier windsurfing destinations. The wind-swept shallows are good year-round for beginners; peak conditions are November to July and pros descend in May and June.

At the end of the main road on the south side, locally owned **Bonaire Windsurf Place** ( ☎ 599-717-2288; www.bonairewindsurfplace.com; ☺ 10am-6pm) rents equipment (from US$40) and gives lessons (from US$45). It has a glassed-in café and a good veranda for watching the action on the water.

Next door, **Jibe City** ( ☎ 599-717-5233; www.jibecity.com; ☺ 10am-6pm) has similar rates and a café open to the breeze.

South of Lac Bay, a good road follows the flat windward coast, which has pounding surf along a desolate coast. You'll see nary another human.

## SOUTH OF KRALENDIJK

The south end of Bonaire is flat and arid, and you can see for many miles in all directions. Multihued salt pans where ocean water evaporates to produce salt dominate the landscape. Metal windmills are used to transfer water out of the ponds. As evaporation progresses, the water takes on a vibrant pink color from tiny sea organisms. The color complements the flamingos, which live in a sanctuary and feed in the ponds.

Along the coast you will see the legacy of a vile chapter in Bonaire's past: tiny restored **slave huts**. Living conditions in these miniscule shelters are hard to imagine now, but they were home to hundreds of slaves, who worked in the salt ponds through the 19th century. The three different-colored 10m **pyramids** along the coast are another legacy of the Dutch colonial era. Colored flags matching one of the pyramids were flown to tell ships where they should drop anchor to load salt.

ARUBA, BONAIRE & CURAÇAO

### DIVING IN BONAIRE

Bonaire's dive sites are strung along the west side of the island. The closeness of the reefs and the clarity of the waters make for unparalleled access for divers. You can reach more than half of the identified dive sites from shore (or your hotel!). The range of fish species is amazing, and diving goes on around the clock.

For all of its fame as a diving location, Bonaire doesn't slouch in the organization department. The Unesco World Heritage **Bonaire Marine Park** ( ☎ 599-717-8444; www.bmp.org) covers the entire coast of the island to a depth of 200ft (60m). There are almost 90 identified dive sites and they are numbered using a system adopted by all the dive operators on the island. Most maps show the sites and as you are driving along coastal roads you'll see painted yellow rocks identifying the sites. See the Diving & Snorkeling chapter for information on diving off Klein Bonaire, p56. It's the vast arid mass just west of Kralendijk.

Conservation is taken seriously. All divers must purchase a tag from any dive operator with the proceeds going to infrastructure maintenance. Tags good for one year coast US$25, a day-pass aimed at visitors off cruise ships costs US$10. Snorkelers and those using the parks on land pay a US$10 fee to get a tag good for the year. Divers new to Bonaire must receive an orientation from a dive operator. It goes without saying: don't touch or collect anything.

The park website is an excellent resource. Additionally, the widely distributed and free *Bonaire Dive Guide* has basic descriptions and a map of all the sites. One of the most famous is **1000 Steps** on the west coast. It's named not for the 72 steps from the road down to the water but the way the climb feels when you return. Myriad coral here supports turtles, eels and many other fish.

A good guide to Bonaire's waters is *New Guide to the Bonaire Marine Park* by Tom van't Hof.

Every place to stay has a relationship with a dive operator or conversely – like Captain Don's Habitat – is a dive operator with a place to stay. Most offer myriad packages.

**Bonaire Dive & Adventure** ( ☎ 599-717-2229; www.bonairedive and adventure.com; Kaya Gobernador N Debrot 77; ☯ 8:30am-4:30pm) is a well-regarded free-standing dive operation. It has a full range of rental equipment. Unlimited tanks of air or nitrox for six days cost US$120.

With so many sites accessible from land, snorkelers also find Bonaire a very rewarding destination. Most diver operators have snorkeling options. Additionally **Sea Cow Charters** ( ☎ 599-785-7727) offers good-value tours by day and night (from US$30).

Just north of the slave huts, **Pink Beach** is a long sliver of sand that takes its color from pink coral washed ashore. It's pretty rough and you'll want a thick pad for sunbathing, but the swimming (not to mention the diving and snorkeling) is good. The beach is even better to the south at the **Vista Blue** dive spot.

On the south side of the airport runway, 2.5km east of the coast road, the nonprofit **Donkey Sanctuary** ( ☎ 599-9560-7607; adult/child US$6/3; ☯ 10am-4pm) is home to offspring of donkeys left to wander the island when slave-era salt production ceased. About 400 are still wild, others live here after they get sick, injured or, as the staff say, just get lonely.

# CURAÇAO

Curaçao balances the real with the surreal. The real is a bustling island with a traffic-bedeviled capital, Willemstad. The surreal is all the reasons that make it an appealing place.

It has a rich history dating back to the 16th century and central Willemstad boasts fascinating old buildings and excellent museums. Remnants of plantations dot the countryside and some are now parks. The west coast has oodles of beautiful little beaches, many good for diving.

Back on the real side, Curaçao has a lot of economic activity beyond tourism, which means that Willemstad, apart from its historical core, has factories, many humdrum neighborhoods and at times bad traffic. Catering to visitors is not the primary aim.

All this makes Curaçao the most balanced of the ABCs; urban pleasures vie with natural wonders for your attention.

## History

Like Aruba and Bonaire, Curaçao was home to the Arawaks until the Spanish laid claim

# CURAÇAO

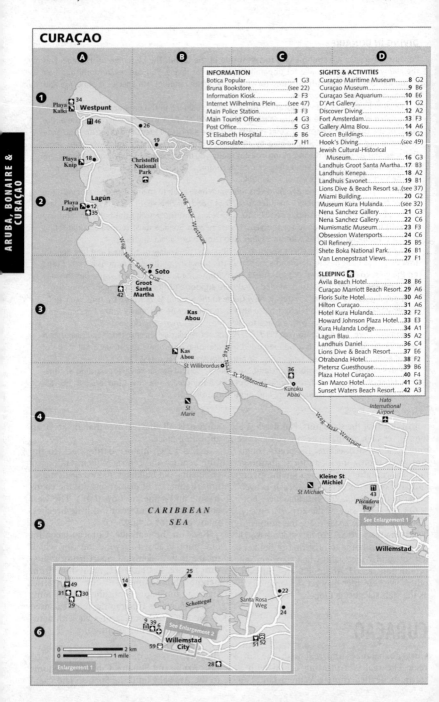

**INFORMATION**

| | |
|---|---|
| Botica Popular | **1** G3 |
| Bruna Bookstore | (see 22) |
| Information Kiosk | **2** F3 |
| Internet Wilhelmina Plein | (see 47) |
| Main Police Station | **3** F3 |
| Main Tourist Office | **4** G3 |
| Post Office | **5** G3 |
| St Elisabeth Hospital | **6** B6 |
| US Consulate | **7** H1 |

**SIGHTS & ACTIVITIES**

| | |
|---|---|
| Curaçao Maritime Museum | **8** G2 |
| Curaçao Museum | **9** B6 |
| Curaçao Sea Aquarium | **10** E6 |
| D'Art Gallery | **11** G2 |
| Discover Diving | **12** A2 |
| Fort Amsterdam | **13** F3 |
| Gallery Alma Blou | **14** A6 |
| Green Buildings | **15** G2 |
| Hook's Diving | (see 49) |
| Jewish Cultural-Historical Museum | **16** G3 |
| Landhuis Groot Santa Martha | **17** B3 |
| Landhuis Kenepa | **18** A2 |
| Landhuis Savonet | **19** B1 |
| Lions Dive & Beach Resort sa | (see 37) |
| Miami Building | **20** G2 |
| Museum Kura Hulanda | (see 32) |
| Nena Sanchez Gallery | **21** G3 |
| Nena Sanchez Gallery | **22** C6 |
| Numismatic Museum | **23** F3 |
| Obsession Watersports | **24** C6 |
| Oil Refinery | **25** B5 |
| Shete Boka National Park | **26** B1 |
| Van Lennepstraat Views | **27** F1 |

**SLEEPING**

| | |
|---|---|
| Avila Beach Hotel | **28** B6 |
| Curaçao Marriott Beach Resort | **29** A6 |
| Floris Suite Hotel | **30** A6 |
| Hilton Curaçao | **31** A6 |
| Hotel Kura Hulanda | **32** F2 |
| Howard Johnson Plaza Hotel | **33** E3 |
| Kura Hulanda Lodge | **34** A1 |
| Lagun Blau | **35** A2 |
| Landhuis Daniel | **36** C4 |
| Lions Dive & Beach Resort | **37** E6 |
| Otrabanda Hotel | **38** F2 |
| Pietersz Guesthouse | **39** B6 |
| Plaza Hotel Curaçao | **40** F4 |
| San Marco Hotel | **41** G3 |
| Sunset Waters Beach Resort | **42** A3 |

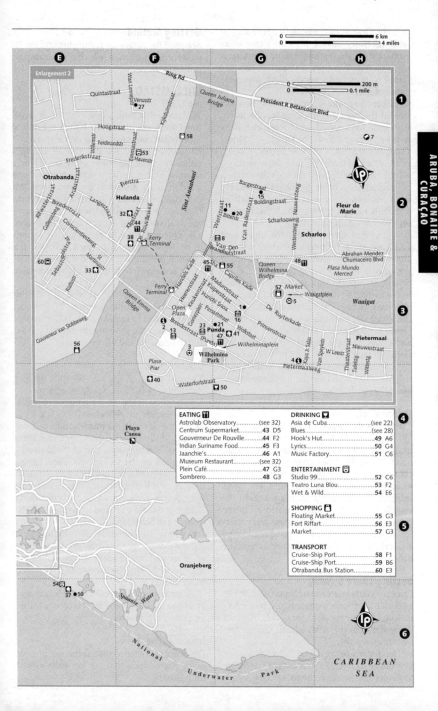

ARUBA, BONAIRE & CURAÇAO

**EATING** 🍴
Astrolab Observatory.............(see 32)
Centrum Supermarket.............**43** D5
Gouverneur De Rouville.........**44** F2
Indian Suriname Food............**45** F3
Jaanchie's.................................**46** A1
Museum Restaurant...............(see 32)
Plein Café................................**47** G3
Sombrero................................**48** G3

**DRINKING** 🍷
Asia de Cuba........................(see 22)
Blues.....................................(see 28)
Hook's Hut...............................**49** A6
Lyrics.......................................**50** G4
Music Factory.........................**51** C6

**ENTERTAINMENT** 🎭
Studio 99.................................**52** C6
Teatro Luna Blou.....................**53** F2
Wet & Wild...............................**54** E6

**SHOPPING** 🛍
Floating Market.......................**55** G3
Fort Riffart..............................**56** E3
Market.....................................**57** G3

**TRANSPORT**
Cruise-Ship Port.....................**58** F1
Cruise-Ship Port.....................**59** B6
Otrabanda Bus Station...........**60** E3

in 1499. Origins of the island's name are lost with one story linking it to the name of an Arawak tribe, while another more improbably says that it derives from the Spanish *curación* (cure) in honor of several sailors who were cured of illness on the island.

Either way, the arrival of the Spanish proved the opposite of a cure for the locals, who were soon carted off to work elsewhere in the empire or killed. The Dutch West India Company arrived in 1634, and so did slavery, commerce and trade. Half the slaves destined for the Caribbean passed through the markets of Curaçao. Many of the plantation houses have been restored and can be visited, including Landhuis Kenepa (p809), which has displays on Curaçao's African heritage.

The end of slavery and colonialism sent Curaçao into a 19th-century economic decline. Subsistence aloe and orange farming provided a meager living for most. Oil refineries to process Venezuelan oil were built in the early 20th century and this fuelled the economy. Relative affluence and Dutch political stability have made Curaçao a regional center for commerce and banking. Tourism and a growing expat population provide additional income. Curaçao is on its way to being an independent entity within the Netherlands, just like its rich and envied neighbor Aruba. See p779 for details.

### Orientation

Curaçao is the largest of the ABCs at 471 sq km. Willemstad is home to almost two-thirds of the population and surrounds Schottegat, one of the world's finest deep-water ports. The coast on both sides of Willemstad is where most of the large resorts are found. The lower third of the island is arid, rugged and little visited. Half of the island is northwest of the capital. It's pretty, at times verdant and perfect for diving on the lee side. A good road loops around the area. At the northwest tip is the little town of Westpunt.

### Getting There & Away

Curaçao's **Hato International Airport** (CUR; ☎ 599-9-839-3201; www.curacao-airport.com) receives international flights; see p813 for details. Airlines flying between the ABC islands change frequently; see p814.

The departure tax is US$32 which may or may not be included in your airfare. For flights to Aruba and Bonaire, the fee is US$8.

### Getting Around

See p807 for details on getting around the island from Willemstad, which is the transport hub of Curaçao.

## WILLEMSTAD

pop 72,000

Willemstad is both a big city and a small town. Residents live in the hills surrounding Schottegat, and much of the city is sprawling and rather mundane. But this all changes radically in the old town. Here the island's colonial Dutch heritage sets a genteel tone amid markets, museums and even a nascent café culture. Wandering the Unesco World Heritage–recognized old town and absorbing its rhythms can occupy a couple of days. The Queen Emma Bridge regularly swings open to let huge ships pass through the channel, a sight in itself, and these interruptions 'force' you to take one of the enjoyable water ferries.

Once the capital of the dissolving Netherlands Antilles, central Willemstad seems content to remake itself as the favored destination for a growing number of cruiseship passengers and visitors.

### Orientation

The old town of Curaçao is split by Sint Annabaai, which is really a channel to Schottegat. On the west side is Otrobanda, an old workers' neighborhood, which still has shops popular with the masses and a mixture of beautifully restored buildings and areas rough around the edges. East of the channel – and linked by the swinging Queen Emma Bridge – is Punda, the old commercial center of town, and home to stores, offices and markets. North across the Queen Wilhelmina Bridge is the old port and warehouse neighborhood of Scharloo.

Arching over all is the 56m-high Queen Juliana Bridge, which allows even the largest ships to pass underneath. (If more bridges are needed, the Netherlands will need more queens.)

A multilane ring road circles Schottegat and links the busy suburbs. It is often a traffic and smog nightmare.

### Information

On Sundays when cruise ships are in port many places open that are normally closed for business.

## BOOKSTORES

Bring books you really want to read from home. Finding good titles on Curaçao can be hit or miss.

**Bruna Bookstore** ( ☎ 599-9-738-8394; Zuikertuin Mall, off Santa Rosa Weg) Excellent selection of books and magazines at the new upscale mall near Asia de Cuba bar.

## EMERGENCY

**Main police station** ( ☎ 911; Wilhelminaplein, Punda; ☻ 24hr)

**Tourist emergency line** ( ☎ 599-9-465-3333)

## INTERNET ACCESS

**Internet Wilhelmina Plein** ( ☎ 599-9-461-9609; Wilhelminaplein 25, Punda; per hr US$2; ☻ 8am-7pm Mon-Fri, 10am-6pm Sat) Laptop connections, cheap calls, web cams and more.

## INTERNET RESOURCES

**Curaçao** (www.curacao.com) Curaçao Tourism Board's website has good community forums.

**Gay Curaçao** (www.gaycuracao.com) A good source for gay and lesbian information.

## MEDICAL SERVICES

**Botica Popular** ( ☎ 599-9-461-2376; Columbusstraat 15, Punda; ☻ 8am-8pm) Full-service pharmacy.

**St Elisabeth Hospital** ( ☎ 599-9-462-5100; www .stelisabethhospital.com; Breedestraat 193, Otrobanda; ☻ 24hr) Large and well equipped.

## MONEY

ATMs are common and give a choice of local or US currency. US dollars are accepted everywhere, and banks will change money during usual hours. There's also a **foreign-exchange desk** ( ☻ 8am-7pm Mon-Sat, 8am-4pm Sun) in the departure hall of the airport.

## POST

**Post office** (Waaigatplein 1, Punda; ☻ 7:30am-5pm Mon-Fri) Buy stamps at this faded monolith for international postcards/letters (NAf1.55/2.85).

## TOURIST INFORMATION

**Information kiosk** ( ☻ 8am-4:30pm Mon-Sat, open Sun when cruise ship is in port) This kiosk by the Queen Emma Bridge on the Punda side has a wealth of information and is everything the unhelpful main tourist office ( ☎ 599-9-434-8200; Pietermaai 19) is not.

## Dangers & Annoyances

Curaçao's urban mix includes some real poverty. Although street crime is not a huge problem, it is important to exercise the sort of caution you may have forgotten on Aruba or Bonaire.

In some of the deeper recesses of Otrobanda, drug-related crime is an everyday problem.

## Sights

To fully explore Willemstad you'll need at least a very full day, but probably two.

### PUNDA

The much modified **Fort Amsterdam** is now home to government and official offices. Inside the large courtyard you can soak up the rich colors of the Dutch colonial architecture dating from the 1760s. Parts of the old battlements weave through the complex, and there is a small **museum** in the church that has been under renovation for some time.

Since 1651 the oldest continuously operating Jewish congregation in the western hemisphere is the Mikvé Israel Emanuel Synagogue, which houses the **Jewish Cultural-Historical Museum** ( ☎ 599-9-461-1633; Hanchi Snoa 29; admission US$5; ☻ 9-11:45am & 2:30-4:45pm Mon-Fri). Items from the long history of the congregation are displayed; the building dates to 1732.

The **markets** (p807) are always fascinating and a good place to see the dwindling amount of commerce in Punda aimed at locals rather than tourists.

One of Punda's sedate pleasures is sitting on the wall along the Sint Annabaai channel and watching huge ships pass while the Queen Emma Bridge shuttles back and forth to make way and pedestrians risk it all in daring leaps.

For details on using the Queen Emma Bridge and ferry service across Sint Annabaai, see p807.

The **Numismatic Museum** ( ☎ 599-9-434-5500; Kaya Prince; admission NAf3.50; ☻ 10am-4pm Tue-Fri) has stamps from around the world (dare we say it lest the curators go, well, postal, the 1693 building – Punda's oldest – is more interesting).

### OTROBANDA

One of the best museums in the Caribbean, **Museum Kura Hulanda** ( ☎ 599-9-434-7765; Klipstraat 9; adult/child NAf15/9; ☻ 10am-5pm) is part of the sensational hotel of the same name and is inside 19th-century slave quarters. The brutal history of slavery in the Caribbean is documented here in superb and extensive exhibits. Look for the unflinching account by John

Gabriel Stedman of slavery in 1700s Suriname. On Wednesday evenings at 7:30pm, reenactors bring this sordid period to life in a living history show (adult/child NAf 15/7.50). At all times the museum has guides ready to answer questions and give context.

Follow Wan Lennepstraat uphill into a safe and historic neighborhood for great **views** of the city and harbor.

About half a mile (800m) north in a residential neighborhood, the **Curaçao Museum** (☎ 599-9-462-3873; Van Leeuwenhoekstraat; adult/child US$3/1.75; 8:30am-4:30pm Mon-Fri, 10am-4pm Sun) is housed in an 1853 hospital for yellow-fever victims. Inside the beautiful verandas is lots of historical stuff, sort of like you'd find in a huge attic.

### SCHARLOO

The **Curaçao Maritime Museum** (☎ 599-9-465-2327; www.curacaomaritime.com; Van Brandhofstraat 7; adult/child NAf10/6; 9am-4pm Tue-Sat) is the other superb museum in Willemstad. Engaging displays trace the island's history detailing how the Dutch West India Company kicked Spain's butt to gain control of the ABCs through to the commercial boom of the 20th century, when the port was where commerce from the US, Europe, the Caribbean and Latin America met. Well worth the 90-minute time investment are the museum's **harbor tours** (adult/child NAf20/12.50; 2pm Wed & Sun) which take in the industrial specter of Schottegat.

The docks in the neighborhood are mostly closed, but wander around and you'll see many building restorations in progress, including the art deco **Miami Building** (Bitterstraat 3-9). At night a counter across the street serves beer to cheery locals. Another amazing colonial survivor is the rambling **green building** on the south side of Bargestraat just east of Van Raderstraat. Note the arched veranda with a profusion of neoclassical details. Throughout Scharloo, old mansions are being saved from a unique form of rot caused when the salt trapped in the original coral building blocks escapes and literally dissolves the structure.

### GALLERIES

Willemstad has a thriving art scene.

**D'Art Gallery** (☎ 599-9-462-8680; Werfstraat 6, Scharloo; 9am-5pm) is in Scharloo behind the restored mansion, Villa Maria, and specializes in contemporary styles.

The **Nena Sanchez Gallery** (☎ 599-9-461-2882; Windsraat 15, Punda; 10am-6pm Mon-Sat) displays the vibrant and colorful works of the longtime local artist. There is a **second location** (☎ 599-9-738-2377; Bloempot Shopping Center) near the upscale Zuikertuin Mall off Santa Rosa Weg.

Located about 3km northwest of Otrobanda, **Gallery Alma Blou** (☎ 599-9-462-8896; Frater Radulphusweg 4; 9am-12:30pm & 2-5:30pm Mon-Sat) has the largest collection of works by local artists. It's housed in the restored Landhuis Habaai, a Dutch plantation house from the 17th century.

## Tours

Several local historians offer tours of the Unesco World Heritage–listed old town. They cost US$10 to US$20 per person and booking is essential.

**Old City Tours** (☎ 599-9-461-3554) Architect Anko van der Woude focuses on the buildings of Otrobanda during a weekly walk (NAf11; 5:15pm Thu).

**Otrobanda Tours** (☎ 599-9-767-3798) Jopi Hart leads walks through the historic working-class neighborhood. They take place at 5:15pm on Wednesday.

**Talk of the Town Tour** (☎ 599-9-747-4349) Custom walks of Punda led by Eveline van Arkel (by appointment).

**Tour Guide Curaçao** (☎ 599-9-526-8930) Michael Brouwer leads walks around the old town and elsewhere on the island.

## Sleeping

With the very notable exceptions of Avila Beach Hotel and Hotel Kura Hulanda, accommodations in Willemstad place function over form (when they function…). Note that some beachfront properties are a mile or two from Punda.

### BUDGET & MIDRANGE

Curaçao could use more decent budget accommodations.

**Pietersz Guesthouse** (☎ 599-9-462-5222/9510; www.pietersz.com; Roodeweg 1, Otrobanda; r US$40-75; ) One of the largest food wholesalers to Curaçao and Bonaire has, rather incongruously, two historic guesthouses near each other in a serene part of Otrobanda. Both have been restored and the rooms are both comfortable and large. The decor is basic but there are kitchenettes and some are good for families as they sleep four. The center is just 400m east of the guesthouse.

## DIVING & SNORKELING IN CURAÇAO

Curaçao's reefs are home to almost 60 species of coral, much of it the hard variety. That coupled with the 98ft (30m) visibility and the warm water make the island very popular with divers, especially locals. The main areas for diving are from Westpunt south to St Marie; central Curaçao up and down the coast from St Michael; and the south, beginning at the Curaçao Sea Aquarium. The latter coast and reefs have been protected as part of the **National Underwater Park**. There are hundreds of species of fish, including reef octopus, trumpetfish, bridled burrfish and yellow goatfish.

Most resorts have relationships with dive operations. Among the better-known operators are Discover Diving (p809), Lions Dive & Beach Resort (p808) and **Hook's Diving** ( ☎ 599-9-461-0515; www.hooksdiving.com; Hook's Hut, Piscadera Bay).

ARUBA, BONAIRE & CURAÇAO

**Otrobanda Hotel** ( ☎ 599-9-462-7400; www.otrobandahotel.com; cnr Breedestraat & De Rouvilleweg, Otrobanda; r US$80-100; ✱ ⬜ ☒ ) Despite the premier position on the water, this 45-room hotel could use a bit of lodging Viagra (although it is six stories…). Still if you can get a good deal, the uninspired rooms and so-so pool area (but with great views!) will seem inconsequential. Rooms do have high-speed internet.

**San Marco Hotel** ( ☎ 599-9-461-2988; www.sanmarcocuracao.com; Columbusstraat, Punda; r US$90-120; ✱ ⬜ ) This six-story pile shouldn't be your first choice but it's a useful option simply because it often has rooms available (which are clean). But if you make a reservation, get as many confirmations as possible, as the front desk can be shambolic. The included breakfast is not appetizing. Offers wi-fi access.

**Howard Johnson Plaza Hotel** ( ☎ 599-9-462-7800; www.howardjohnson.com; Bionplein, Otrobanda; r from US$105; ✱ ⬜ ☒ ) The American motel classic has a brightly colored 50-unit, four-story hotel overlooking the channel in Otrobanda. Rooms have that king-size-bed vibe and include high-speed internet, fridges and more.

**ourpick Avila Beach Hotel** ( ☎ 599-9-461-4377; www.avilahotel.com; Penstraat 130; r US$110-400; ✱ ⬜ ☒ ) Ever expanding, the Avila Beach combines rooms in the 18th-century home of a Dutch governor with new wings of increasingly luxurious accommodation. The grounds are elegant and the beach is a fine crescent of sand. Not all the 156 rooms receive wi-fi. There is a small museum (adult/child NAf5/3; open 10am to noon Tuesday, Wednesday, Friday and Sunday) in the hotel, dedicated to revolutionary Simón Bolívar, who stayed here plotting his assault on the Spanish.

**Plaza Hotel Curaçao** ( ☎ 599-9-461-2500; www.plazahotelcuracao.com; Plasa Pier, Punda; r US$120-200; ✱ ⬜ ☒ ) Recent renovations have helped this prominent hotel at the entrance to Sint Annabaai, but it still has some rough edges. Most of the average rooms in the 14-story tower lack balconies, but the views of ship traffic from the mezzanine-level pool are superb. Part of the hotel is built into old battlements and the pool bar is a fine place for sunset views of cruise ships leaving port.

### TOP END

A new upscale Renaissance Resort (a Marriott brand) should be open at the Fort Riffart cruise ship port by 2009.

**Hilton Curaçao** ( ☎ 599-9-462-5000; www.hiltoncaribbean.com; John F Kennedy Blvd, Piscadera Bay; r US$180-300; ✱ ⬜ ☒ ) The address is fitting, as Kennedy was president about the time this 1960s veteran was envisioned. It has vast grounds that include the 17th-century remains of Fort Piscadera and two rather old-fashioned pools. Depending on your room choice, from your large balcony your room will either view Piscadera Bay or power-plant smokestacks. Which to choose? Offers wi-fi access.

**Curaçao Marriott Beach Resort** ( ☎ 599-9-736-8800; www.marriott.com; John F Kennedy Blvd, Piscadera Bay; r US$200-300; ✱ ⬜ ☒ ) With its own beach on Piscadera Bay, this 247-room resort has a lush tropical feel. Rooms have decent-sized balconies, and most have views of the large pool and ocean. Offers wi-fi access.

**Hotel Kura Hulanda** ( ☎ 599-9-434-7700; www.kurahulanda.com; Langestraat 8, Otrobanda; r US$220-500; ✱ ⬜ ☒ ) One of the Caribbean's finest hotels is also a sight in itself. Architect Jacob Gelt Dekker took a run-down workers neighborhood in Otrobanda and created an amazing hotel that is really a village of restaurants, cafés and rooms. (Many a shot in tourist brochures showing 'Curaçao' was taken here.) The 80 rooms, with their hand-carved mahogany furniture and old-time luxuries, may make you feel like a plantation pasha. Offers wi-fi access.

**Floris Suite Hotel** ( ☎ 599-9-462-6111; www.floris suitehotel.com; John F Kennedy Blvd, Piscadera Bay; ste US$250-350; ✷ ⬛ ⬛ ) The Floris' striking and minimalist design makes up for it not being right on the beach. The 71 rooms – more like suites – are large and look out onto lush grounds with Piscadera Bay beyond; all have high-speed internet (there's wi-fi in the lobby). If you subscribe to *Wallpaper*, you will feel right at home.

## Eating

The cafés on the Wilhelminaplein are delightful places to while away an hour. Keep your eyes open for humble backstreet eateries serving good traditional fare. But keep your wallet closed for most of the touristy places lining the Punda side of Sint Annabaai and the Waterfront Terrace in the old walls south of the Plaza Hotel.

**Centrum Supermarket** ( ☎ 599-9-869-6222; cnr Weg Naar Westpunt & Weg Naar Bullenbaai; ✷ 8am-7:30pm Mon-Sat, 8am-1pm Sun) A popular large supermarket with a bakery and a deli.

**Sombrero** (Westersteeg, Scharloo; snacks under NAf6; ✷ 7am-11pm) Ask the name of this unsigned stand and people will point at the shape of the roof. But a sign isn't needed to find the long list of simple local street fare on offer. Sit on a plastic chair on the sidewalk, enjoy the passing parade and delight in empanadas, sandwiches and beer.

**Indian Suriname Food** ( ☎ 599-9-528-3398; Maanstraat 3, Punda; meals from NAf8; ✷ lunch & dinner Mon-Sat) One of a few simple little places hidden in Willemstad's narrow back streets, this one has four tables and serves excellent fresh rotis with myriad fillings.

**our pick Plein Cafe** ( ☎ 599-9-461-9666; Wilhelmina-plein 19-23, Punda; meals from NAf8; ✷ 7:30am-11pm) This Dutch café and its neighboring twin are so authentic that if it were 30°F (–1°C) and raining, you'd think you were in Amsterdam. Waiters scamper among the outdoor tables with trays of drinks and dishes of simple food like sandwiches (try the *frikandel*, a meaty Dutch classic). Often busy with locals in the evening. It's a wi-fi hot spot.

**Museum Restaurant** ( ☎ 599-9-434-7700; Hotel Kura Hulanda, Langestraat 8, Otrobanda; mains US$12-25; ✷ lunch & dinner) One of several excellent restaurants in the Kura Hulanda, you can dine under a canopy of lush tropical trees here. The menu is eclectic – from salads to sandwiches to pasta – with regional touches, like Cuban banana cream soup.

**Gouverneur De Rouville** ( ☎ 599-9-462-5999; De Rouvilleweg 9, Otrobanda; mains US$15-25; ✷ lunch & dinner, bar until 1am) Excellent Caribbean food is served in this restored colonial building in Otrobanda. Try the *karni stuba*, a piquant beef stew. Enjoy wide views of Punda and the waterfront from the tables on the shady veranda. There's also a secluded courtyard and a fine bar.

**Astrolab Observatory** ( ☎ 599-9-434-7700; Hotel Kura Hulanda, Langestraat 8, Otrobanda; mains US$23-40; ✷ dinner Tue-Sat; ✷ ) The top restaurant in the Kura Hulanda is set amid little fountains and gardens that will have you thinking of *A Midsummer Night's Dream*. The food changes daily, reflecting both what's in season and the whim of the chef, who creates a fusion of French and Caribbean cuisines.

## Drinking

Yes, you can drink curaçao here, but note that the namesake booze of the island is now a generic term for liquor flavored with bitter oranges. For obscure reasons the concoction is often dyed blue. While duty-free shops burst with stuff from numerous distillers, locals prefer rot-gut rum and beer – in that order.

The Plein Cafe (left) is an atmospheric choice for a drink.

**Blues** ( ☎ 599-9-461-4377; Avila Beach Hotel, Penstraat 130; ✷ 5pm-midnight Tue-Sun) On a pier over the water, this swanky bar is the coolest venue in town. It has live jazz Thursday and Saturday and happy hours nightly plus a good tapas menu.

**Asia de Cuba** ( ☎ 599-9-747-9009; Zuikertuin Mall; ✷ 5pm-late) Set in an open-air building at an upscale mall off Santa Rosa Weg, this hip and stylish venue morphs between being a gregarious spot for drinks and snacks with friends early in the evening to a dance venue later on. DJs and live bands play cutting-edge dance tracks.

**Lyrics** (Waterfortstraat, Punda; ✷ 10pm-3am Thu-Sat) A popular gay bar built right into the touristy arches of the old waterfront walls, Lyrics is popular with locals and visitors. Look for the rainbow flag right out front.

**Music Factory** ( ☎ 599-9-461-0631; Salina 131; ✷ 8pm-2am Mon-Wed, 8pm-3am Thu, 8pm-4am Fri & Sat) This cheery bar is a good place near several clubs to hook up with locals and find out what the latest clubs are. Finance your holiday with the NAf100 prize for karaoke singing on Wednesday nights. It is about 3km east of Punda.

**Hook's Hut** ( ☎ 599-9-462-6575; Piscadera Bay; ❤ to 1am) This beach café on calm Piscadera Bay appeals to visitors and expats. Lounge at tables on the sand while enjoying sandwiches and seafood (mains US$8 to US$20; lunch and dinner) to the beat of a steel band. Several humble and nameless joints in nearby fishermen's huts cater to beach-going, beer-drinking locals.

## Entertainment
### NIGHTCLUBS
Willemstad has several clubs catering to the local passion for music and dancing. Places come and go, check out the free weekly *K-Pasa,* which lists entertainment around the island. The beach-party place Wet & Wild (p808) lives up to its name on weekend nights.

**Studio 99** ( ☎ 599-9-465-5555; Lindberghweg; cover varies; ❤ 9pm-1am Tue-Thu, 10pm-4am Fri & Sat) Near a couple of other clubs and the Music Factory bar, this huge and popular place has karaoke and DJs during the week and local bands on weekends. It is located about 3km east of Punda.

### THEATER
**Teatro Luna Blou** ( ☎ 599-9-462-2209; www.lunablou .org; Havenstraat 2-4) Offers a varying schedule of offbeat films, dance and live theater. There's a shady open-air café before performances.

## Shopping
Real shops favored by locals are fleeing Punda for strip malls in the suburbs, leaving a lot of watch and gem vendors in their wake. Still you can find some interesting items by wandering the back streets and waterfront.

**Floating Market** (Sha Capriles Kade) A colorful place to see piles of papayas, melons, tomatoes and much more. The vendors sail their boats the 70km from Venezuela every morning.

**Market** (Waaigatplein; ❤ 7am-2pm Mon-Sat) Near the Floating Market, this large UFO-shaped market sells cheap household goods, snacks and more. An extremely nice man will fix your shoes for NAf1.

Heavily hyped, **Fort Riffart** is a shadow of its former solid self. The walls have been punched out for gift shops aimed at the hordes plowing through from the nearby cruise-ship port.

## Getting There & Around
Watching the long Queen Emma Bridge move ponderously aside for passage of a huge ship is one of the simple pleasures of Willemstad. There's always someone literally leaping onto the end as it swings away from Punda. If the bridge is open, look for flags by the pilot's cabin: orange means it has been open less than 30 minutes, blue means it has been open longer and *may* soon close. When the bridge is open, two old free public ferries nearby cruise into action. The four-minute ride on these is a treat in itself.

### BUS
The bus network is designed to transport the local commuter, but a couple of routes are useful for visitors: No 4B links the airport to Otrobanda (20 minutes, departs hourly) and No 9A follows the coastal road to Westpunt (one hour, every two hours). The **bus stations** ( ☎ Punda 599-9-465-0201, Otrobanda 599-9-462-8359) are near the post office in Punda and near the base of Arubastraat in Otrobanda. Fares are NAf1.25 to NAf1.75 depending on distance; buses run from about 7am to 9pm. Note that trying to cover the island north of Willemstad by bus will be an all-day affair, with a lot of patient waiting by the side of the road.

### CAR
One of the greatest challenges to getting around Willemstad (and the rest of Curaçao) is the lack of road signs. Where they do exist, the sun is fading them into oblivion. Fortunately, locals are happy to help.

Because attractions are so spread out across Curaçao, you may choose to rent a car. All the major international car-rental agencies have counters at the airport.

### TAXI
Plans call for the installation of meters in taxis, meanwhile fares are fixed. From the airport to most hotels and Willemstad costs US$12 to US$20. Taxis hang around hotels, otherwise order one from **central dispatch** ( ☎ 599-9-869-0747).

ARUBA, BONAIRE & CURAÇAO

## SOUTH OF WILLEMSTAD

Residential neighborhoods make up much of the land immediately south of the center of Willemstad and there is long beach parallel to the coast road. Spaanse Water, a large enclosed bay to rival Schottegat, is becoming an upscale residential area as people are drawn by its beaches and sheltered waters. There's little further south to the tip of Curaçao except arid scrub.

### Sights

Following the coast south from Punda for a little over 4km you get to the **Curaçao Sea Aquarium** ( ☎ 599-9-461-6666; www.curacao -sea-aquarium.com; Bapor Kibra; adult/child US$15/7.50; ⏱ 8:30am-5:30pm). On a man-made island, this heavily hyped attraction anchors an entire development that includes hotels, bars and artificial beaches.

The Seaquarium, as it's known, is home to over 600 marine species including sea lions, sting rays and sharks. Visitors can swim in pools with the inmates (snorkeling US$34, diving US$54). More controversial is the play-with-the-dolphins attraction in which visitors for a fee can get in the water with mammals (US$80 to US$160). The hype encourages one to kiss and hug the dolphins. There's no word on the dolphins' views on this.

### Sleeping

Condos are proliferating like sharks to chum. **Royal Resorts** ( ☎ 599-9-465-6699; www.royalresorts .com) represents many of these time-share properties and villas. Rates for multiroom units begin at about US$300 a night.

**Lions Dive & Beach Resort** ( ☎ 599-9-434-8888; www .lionsdive.com; Bapor Kibra; r US$160-200; ⏱ 🖥 🚐 ) No more just a beach dive for weary divers, Lions Dive is now a full-service resort with very comfortable rooms in three-story buildings right on the beach. And divers will still find the eponymous dive shop here.

### Eating & Drinking

Lions Dive & Beach Resort has a couple of sedate restaurants.

**Wet & Wild** ( ☎ 599-9-562-0400; Bapor Kibra; meals US$6-20; ⏱ 9am-late) By day this ribbon of white sand is a family-friendly beach café and bar with a full range of activities (adult/child NAf6/3; not charged if you just eat and drink). By night the name takes on new and at times literal meanings as it transforms into a beach club and disco. Music is provided by DJs and the in-house radio station (Dolphin Radio 97.3FM). The action gets frenetic after midnight from Thursdays onwards when the shadowy recesses of the beach provide no end of lurid cover.

## NORTH OF WILLEMSTAD

Looping around the northern part of Curaçao from Willemstad is central to any visitor's itinerary. Parks, villages and beaches all await discovery. You can do the loop in a day but spend time on any of the fine beaches and you'll need two. (Nonstop, the drive would take a little over two hours.)

Buses travel along both coasts to/from Willemstad and Westpunt about once every two hours.

### West Coast

There are scores of often beautiful beaches hidden in coves along the west coast.

About 6km north from Otrobanda, **Kleine St Michiel** is a traditional fishing village on a tiny bay. The small ruins of a 17th-century Dutch fort are on the cliffs above the water. There are a few beachfront cafés and bars. On weekends there is usually a live band playing a heady mix of Curaçaoan Creole. The place gets jammed.

To head to the north end of the island via the northwest coast, take the main road, Weg Naar Westpunt (literally, 'road to Westpunt'), 8km from Willemstad to Kunuku Abao, where you turn left or west onto the Weg Naar St Willibrordus. For 18km you drive through some of the most lush countryside in the ABCs. At some points huge trees form canopies over the road.

Shortly after the turn west, the road runs past old farms with thatched roofs and salt flats with pink flamingos. The village of St Willibrordus is dominated by an old church.

About 4km past the village, look for signs to the beautiful beach **Kas Abou**. It's another 4km down a narrow toll road (NAf10 to NAf12.50 per car), but the reward is worth it, with turquoise waters, good snorkeling and an excellent café-bar.

Passing through the hamlet of Groot Santa Martha, there are a couple of stores where you can stop for a cold drink. **Landhuis Groot Santa Martha** ( ☎ 599-9-864-2969; admission NAf5; ⏱ 8am-

---

### CURAÇAO'S BEACHES

The west coast of Curaçao north of Willemstad is a serrated edge of little coves, many hiding beautiful white-sand beaches. Beaches like **Kleine St Michiel**, **Kas Abou**, **Playa Lagún**, **Playa Knip** and **Playa Kalki** are lapped by azure waters and have rental loungers, snorkeling gear and cafés. But for real joy, look for beaches less-trammeled. There are dozens in and around the ones above. If you see a little road heading towards the water, take it and you may be rewarded.

Closer to Willemstad, two private beach clubs, **Hook's Hut** (p807) and **Wet & Wild** (opposite) offer myriad activities, bars, restaurants and often raucous fun well into the night (or morning).

---

4pm Mon-Fri) is one of the best preserved of the dozens of Dutch colonial houses that dot the islands. A sugarcane plantation was started here in the 17th century to supply the rum and molasses trade. The main house dates from 1700 and is part of a large complex of relics from the era. Recent restorations have worked wonders, and the complex is now a vocational school for mentally and physically challenged people. Some produce beautiful handicrafts which are for sale.

A 3km side road from Groot Santa Martha twists through the hills to the coast and the **Sunset Waters Beach Resort** ( ☎ 599-9-864-1233; www.sunsetwaters.com; all-inclusive per person US$150-220; 🛏 🖳 🏊 ). This secluded low-key resort is built on the side of a hill above the beach. The well-maintained rooms are comfortable and many have balconies. The lobby has wi-fi. Watch for herds of goats.

At Lagún the road nears the coast and the first of many fabulous beaches. **Playa Lagún** is a narrow and secluded beach situated on a picture-perfect narrow cove sided with sheer rock faces. There's shade and a snack bar. Just back from the sand, **Discover Diving** ( ☎ 599-9-864-1652; www.discoverdiving.nl) rents diving and snorkeling equipment (US$9), leads tours and gives lessons. Its introductory dive for novices is a bargain at US$60.

On the south cliffs overlooking the cove, **Lagun Blau** ( ☎ 599-9-864-0557; www.lagunblau.nl; apt from US$95; 🛏 🖳 🏊 ) is a new 12-unit compound built around a pool. These good-sized, sun-drenched bungalows are a good deal for families and divers. Offers wi-fi access.

About 2km on from Lagún is **Landhuis Kenepa**, the main house of another 17th-century plantation. The hilltop site is stunning, but the real importance here is that this was where a slave rebellion started in 1795. Several dozen torched their miserable huts and joined up with hundreds of others who were refusing to work. Eventually the plan-

tation owners regained control and killed the leaders, but the event set in motion protests that continued for decades. A museum here, the **Museo Tula** ( ☎ 599-9-888-6396; adult/child US$3.50/1; 🕙 9am-4:30pm Tue-Sun), tells this story and explores the African roots of Curaçao.

Down the hill from the plantation, **Playa Knip** is really two beaches. Groot Knip is the size of a football field, while Klein Knip is, well, small. Both have brilliant white sand, shady shelters, azure waters, places to rent snorkeling gear and snack bars. Avoid weekends when half the island shows up for a dip.

In the small village of Westpunt, **Playa Kalki** has parking, lockers and kayak rental. On the main road you'll have a tough time missing **Jaanchie's** ( ☎ 599-9-864-0126; mains US$6-15; 🕙 noon-8pm), a local institution where you can sample a full menu of island delicacies, like okra soup and goat stew. Some of the meats are rather exotic but fear not: it all tastes like chicken. Don't worry about choosing, the waitresses will sort you out.

Willemstad's superb Hotel Kura Hulanda has opened a beach resort here, the **Kura Hulanda Lodge** ( ☎ 599-9-839-3600; www.kurahulanda.com; Westpunt; r from US$200; 🛏 🖳 🏊 ). The grounds are a tropical garden, there's a private white-sand beach and the common areas are in thatched huts around a pool. The 74 units are in a more substantial villas and come with various view and size options. There is a dive shop onsite. Offers wi-fi access.

From here the road turns east and heads south along the northeast coast.

### East Coast

The windward side of the island is rugged and little developed. To take this route from Willemstad, stay on Weg Naar Westpunt past the junction at Kunuku Abao as you head north.

---

**SURFING THE WIND & WAVES**

The best place for surfing – by wind or wave – is an isolated beach, **Playa Canoa**, on the east coast, about 8 miles by an at times rugged road from Willemstad. The wind and wave conditions are good through much of the year and you'll find both good breaks and flatter areas for windsurfing.

Get information and rent gear at **Obsession Watersports** ( ☎ 599-9-736-5659; Schottegatweg Oost; ♡ 9am-6pm Mon-Sat). Rates for surfboards and windsurfboards start at US$30 per day.

---

Just beyond the turn look east for the orchid- and bougainvillea-lined entrance to **Landhuis Daniel** ( ☎ 599-9-864-8400; www.landhuis daniel.com; r US$35-65; ✘ ▯ ▮ ), a rambling lodge and restaurant run by a Dutch family. The eight rooms are basic (some are fan only), but the pool and gardens have country charm, and there's wi-fi access. The restaurant (mains US$8 to US$20; open breakfast, lunch and dinner) draws many for its changing menu of local, Creole and French dishes prepared with ingredients from the organic garden. Kids love all 25 types of pancake on offer.

About 25km north of Willemstad lies **Christoffel National Park** ( ☎ 599-9-864-0363; admission US$10; ♡ 7:30am-4pm Mon-Sat, 6am-3pm Sun), an 1800-hectare preserve formed from three old plantations. The main house for one of the plantations, **Landhuis Savonet**, is at the entrance to the park. It was built in 1662 by a director of the Dutch West India Company.

The park has two driving routes over 32km of dirt roads, and sights include cactuses, orchids, iguanas, deer, wave-battered limestone cliffs and caves with ancient drawings. At the entrance is an excellent museum and a café. You can also make arrangements to tour the park by horse. Call ☎ 599-9-697-8709 for details.

Just north, **Shete Boka National Park** ( ☎ 599-9-864-0444; admission NAf3; ♡ 9am-5pm) is a geologic and oceanic festival. Trails lead from a parking area right off the coast road to natural limestone bridges on the shore, sea turtle sanctuaries, a big blowhole and isolated little beaches in narrow coves. Boka Tabla, a cave in the cliffs facing the water is the most popular – and closest – walk.

The road after the park follows the windswept northeast coast to Westpunt.

# DIRECTORY

## ACCOMMODATIONS

All three islands have beach resorts, with Aruba having by far the most. Bonaire has lots of small inns geared toward divers. Curaçao has the most varied range of places to stay, with some interesting non-beach choices in Willemstad. Camping is uncommon. High-season prices usually run mid-December to mid-April. Rates – and crowds – fall by a third or more during other times.

Hotel taxes and fees are as follows: Aruba, 6% tax plus 10% to 15% service charge; Bonaire, US$6.50 per person plus 10% to 15% service charge; and Curaçao, 7% room tax plus 12% service charge.

## ACTIVITIES

Diving is the number one activity on the ABCs, with the azure waters and pristine reefs of Bonaire being a destination of dreams for many (p799). It is also popular on Curaçao (p805) and Aruba (p785). Snorkeling is also ideal, and the waters around the islands never get below a comfy 70°F (21°C).

Swimming is popular. Although the best beaches are on Aruba (p791), you can find good ones on Bonaire (p799) and some very nice hidden ones on Curaçao (p809).

Bonaire is big with windsurfers, who find near ideal conditions on Lac Bay (p798). On Aruba, go to Malmok Beach (p786) and on Curaçao, make your way to the remote Playa Canoa on the north coast (left).

Away from the water, activities are less common. Besides the thrills of resort pursuits as diverse as tennis and shuffleboard, there is golf on Aruba. All three islands have extensive national parks that make for good exploring, but the arid terrain gets hot and at noon you will understand what it means to be a lizard. Hiking in these areas is best done early and late in the day when you can also enjoy sunrises and sunsets respectively.

## BUSINESS HOURS

Most banks are open from 8am to 4pm Monday to Friday. Most stores are open at least from 8am to 6pm Monday to Friday and until 2pm Saturday. Larger supermarkets and shops aimed at visitors stay open until at least 8pm.

## CHILDREN

The ABCs are good destinations for families. Almost all resorts have activities for kids – some quite extensive. In addition, the famous reefs protect the beaches from really nasty surf, although the windward sides of the islands can get rough. However, note that unlike Aruba, Bonaire and Curaçao are not overstocked with sights specifically aimed at kids, like amusement parks or themed attractions.

## DANGERS & ANNOYANCES

Cable TV chatter aside (see p784), Aruba is a safe for tourists as is Bonaire. Curaçao is generally safe although a few rough areas in Willemstad bear caution (p803). On all three, take the usual precautions regarding dark alleys and leaving valuables lying around or in parked cars.

## EMBASSIES & CONSULATES

Visa-free travel to the ABCs means that most people will not need diplomatic assistance prior to traveling. For official dealings with the islands, other nations go through the Netherlands. There are no embassies or consulates on the ABCs.

## FESTIVALS & EVENTS

**Carnival** (January or February) This is a big deal on the islands, especially Curaçao where a packed schedule of fun begins right after New Year's Day. Aruba's parades are an explosion of sound and color.

**Simadan** (Early April) Bonaire's harvest festival is usually held in the small town of Rincon, and celebrates traditional dance and food.

**Séu Parade** Curaçao's 'Feast of the Harvest' features parades replete with lots of folk music and dancing on Easter Monday. People in rural areas go a little nuts.

**Aruba Music Festival** (October) Aruba's annual two-day international concert attracts international and local talent.

## GAY & LESBIAN TRAVELERS

The ABCs are tolerant of homosexuality, and gays and lesbians should expect little trouble. Curaçao even has a prominent gay bar.

## HOLIDAYS

The ABCs observe the following holidays:

**New Year's Day** January 1
**Good Friday** Friday before Easter
**Easter Monday** Monday after Easter
**Queen's Birthday** April 30
**Labour Day** May 1
**Ascension Day** Sixth Thursday after Easter
**Christmas Day** December 25
**Boxing Day** December 26

In addition to the above, each island has its own holidays. Note that some of these could change as the Netherlands Antilles is dissolved.

**Aruba** GF (Betico) Croes Day (January 25); Carnival Monday (Monday before Ash Wednesday); National Day (March 18)

**Bonaire** Carnival Rest Day (usually in January); Bonaire Day (September 6); Antillean Day (October 21)

**Curaçao** Carnival Monday (Monday before Ash Wednesday); Flag Day (July 2); Antillean Day (October 21)

---

### PRACTICALITIES

- **Newspapers & Magazines** Each of the islands has English-language newspapers aimed at tourists that combine oodles of local PR with dollops of international news. Newspapers from the US are surprisingly hard to find. International magazines are available.

- **Radio & TV** Most hotels have at least a few satellite TV channels in English. The islands have numerous FM and AM radio stations. On Aruba, 89.9FM features the cheery boosterisms of the Dick Miller Show between 7pm and 8pm.

- **Video Systems** NTSC, the standard used in North America.

- **Electricity** 110AC to 130AC (50 to 60 cycles), North American two-pin sockets are used.

- **Weights & Measures** Metric system.

ARUBA, BONAIRE & CURAÇAO

## INTERNET ACCESS

There are internet places across the ABCs. Wi-fi is increasingly common at hotels and many also have a computer guests can use.

## LANGUAGE

If you only speak English, you won't have a problem on the ABCs. Some locals may have limited English skills, but the sheer numbers of English-speaking visitors coupled with the fact that locals often speak a polyglot of languages, including English, means that you will always be able to sort things out.

## MEDICAL SERVICES

There are modern hospitals on all three islands. For Aruba see p784, for Bonaire see p793 and for Curaçao, see p803.

## MONEY

You can pay for just about everything in US dollars on the ABCs. Sometimes you will get change back in US currency, other times you will receive it in Aruba florins (Afl) or Netherlands Antillean guilders (NAf or ANG) on Bonaire and Curaçao. Both currencies are divided into units of 100. Some of the coins are quite charming such as the square Aruban 50-cent piece. Most ATMs on Aruba and Curaçao let you withdraw currency in US dollars.

## TELEPHONE

The area code for Aruba is ☎ 297, for Bonaire and Curaçao it is 599. To call from North America and elsewhere, dial your country's international access code (011 in North America) + ☎ 297 or 599 + the local number. On Curaçao, a 9 has been added in front of all the seven-digit numbers. When dialing within an island, omit the area code.

Telephone service on the ABCs is reliable. All the usual warnings about pirates posing as phones in hotel rooms apply on the ABCs. Your international dial-home services may or may not work, which means you will probably have to pay extortionate hotel rates. Worse are scores of private pay phones that have signs touting 'Phone Home!' for those feeling guilty about leaving their kids, dog or parents' money at home. Few disclose rates, which cost US$3 or more per minute.

To call home, use phonecards bought in convenience stores – which clearly trumpet their low rates – or call from internet places, which always have cheap rates.

If you have a GSM mobile phone, you can purchase a SIM card for local service for US$20, which includes US$6 of calling credit. Local rates start at US$0.10 per minute; to the UK and US from US$0.33 per minute. The two carriers on Aruba are **Setar** (www.www.setar.aw) and **Digicel** (www.digicelgroup.com), which also serves Bonaire and Curaçao. Cell phone shops are common.

## TOURIST INFORMATION

**Aruba Tourism Authority** (www.aruba.com) A well-funded entity, with a comprehensive and useful website. See p784 for the office in Oranjestad.
**Curaçao Tourism Board** (www.curacao.com) Offers a mixed bag of services. For the equally mixed quality of personal assistance, see the tourist office in Willemstad (p803).
**Tourism Bonaire** (www.tourismbonaire.com) Does a good job of promoting the island and answering questions. See p793 for the office in Kralendijk.

## TRAVELERS WITH DISABILITIES

The many international resorts on Aruba are all generally accessible as are the ones on Bonaire and Curaçao. All three of the islands are fairly flat and stairs are uncommon so they don't pose an impossible challenge even if there are few local accessibility regulations.

## VISAS

Travelers from most countries can visit the ABCs without a visa for up to 90 days.

## WOMEN TRAVELERS

Women should take their usual precautions on a visit to the ABCs.

## WORK

Foreigners will find it difficult to get a job without sponsorship.

# TRANSPORTATION

## GETTING THERE & AWAY
### Entering Aruba, Bonaire & Curaçao

All visitors need a passport and a return or onward ticket to enter the islands; US citizens see the boxed text, p830.

## Air

Aruba is the main entry point for the ABCs, with extensive service from North America and the Caribbean. However Bonaire and Curaçao are gaining nonstop flights from North America; all three have nonstop service from Europe.

### ARUBA

Aruba's **Reina Beatrix International Airport** (AUA; ☎ 297-582-4800; www.airportaruba.com) is a busy, modern airport.

Passengers flying to the US absolutely must take heed of their airline's warning to check in three hours before flight time. Actually four hours might be better because all US-bound passengers clear customs and immigration *before* they leave Aruba. Most flights back to the US leave during a small timeslot in the afternoon and the US-staffed immigration facilities are not up to the task. If possible, try to avoid going home on a weekend when things are the worst. Once ensconced in the terminal, there are bookstores, places for internet access and fast food places just like the ones at home.

The following airlines serve Aruba from these cities (some services are seasonal):
**Air Canada** ( ☎ 800-247-2262; www.aircanada.com) Toronto
**American/American Eagle** ( ☎ 297-582-2700; www.aa.com; Ling & Sons Super Center, Schotlandstraat 41, Aruba) Boston, Miami, New York, San Juan
**Avianca** ( ☎ 297-582-5484; www.avianca.com) Bogota, Colombia
**Continental** ( ☎ 800-1507; www.continental.com) Houston, Newark, New York
**Delta** ( ☎ 800-1515) Atlanta, New York
**JetBlue** ( ☎ 297-588-5388; www.jetblue.com) New York
**KLM** ( ☎ 297-582-3546; www.klm.com) Amsterdam
**Tiara Air** ( ☎ 297-588-4272; www.tiara-air.com) Punto Fijo
**United** ( ☎ 297-582-9592; www.united.com) Chicago, Washington
**US Airways** ( ☎ 800-1580; www.usairways.com) Boston, Charlotte, Philadelphia
**Venezolana** (http://ravsa.com.ve) Caracas

### BONAIRE

Bonaire's **Flamingo Airport** (BON; ☎ 599-717-5600) is indeed painted pink and should be named for John Waters. It is immediately south of Kralendijk. See p796 for departure tax info.

The following airlines serve Bonaire from these cities (some services are seasonal):
**American Eagle** ( ☎ 599-717-3598; www.aa.com) San Juan
**Continental** ( ☎ 599-717-7474; www.continental.com) Houston, Newark
**Delta** ( ☎ 599-717-7474) Atlanta
**KLM** ( ☎ 599-717-7474; www.klm.com) Amsterdam

### CURAÇAO

Curaçao's **Hato International Airport** (CUR; ☎ 599-9839-3201; www.curacao-airport.com) has a decent level of services and amenities for passengers after security. There are ATMs in the departure area. The departure tax is US$32, which may or may not be included in your airfare. For flights to Aruba and Bonaire, the fee is US$8.

The following airlines serve Curaçao from these cities (some services are seasonal):
**Air Jamaica** ( ☎ 876-922-3460; www.airjamaica.com) Kingston, Montego Bay
**American** ( ☎ 599-9-736-7799; www.aa.com) Miami
**Avianca** ( ☎ 599-9-839-1182; www.avianca.com) Bogota
**Continental** ( ☎ 800-231-0856; www.continental.com) Newark
**Delta** ( ☎ 800-221-1212) Atlanta
**KLM** ( ☎ 599-9-736-1422; www.klm.com) Amsterdam
**LIAT** ( ☎ 888-844-5428; www.liat.com) Trinidad

## Sea
### CRUISE SHIPS

The ABCs are part of cruise-ship itineraries that cover the Caribbean.

Cruise ships flock to Aruba; it's not unusual to have more than 10,000 passengers descend on the island in a single day. Curaçao has similar aims with new facilities under construction in Willemstad. Bonaire's relationship with cruise ships is more complex. The port can't handle many but the money is welcome. Many locals take a dim view, going so far as to blame cruise ships for spoiling Christmas in 2007 (visiting boats prevented freight barges from using the port in December, which meant that some items in stores ran out).

### YACHTS

The ABCs are off the typical yachting routes and receive few boats.

ARUBA, BONAIRE & CURAÇAO

## GETTING AROUND

The only way to get between the ABCs is by air. On the islands, many travelers opt for a rental car for all or part of their visit. Public transportation outside of the core of Aruba and Curaçao is limited, although taxis are common.

### Air

Although there is no other option, interisland service in the ABCs has a checkered past. The routes are busy, but have not proved profitable for airlines. Operators come and go with such frequency that you should double-check that an airline truly exists before trying to make a booking. Fares typically depend on when you book them and average US$80 to US$150 one way between islands.

The following airlines provide air service between the ABCs.

**DAE** (Dutch Antilles Express; ☎ 599 717 0808; www.flydae .com) The largest airline with service between all three islands.

**Insel Air** ( ☎ 599 9737 0444; www.fly-inselair.com) Flies from Curaçao to Aruba and Bonaire but not between the two nonstop.

**Tiara Air** ( ☎ 297-588-4272; www.tiara-air.com) A small carrier.

### Bicycle

Although there are no bike lanes on the ABCs, many people enjoy riding along the many flat roads on each of the islands, especially Bonaire. You can rent bikes at many resorts and bike shops.

### Bus

Aruba (p781) and Curaçao (p807) both have limited networks of local buses.

### Car & Motorcycle

Major car-rental companies can be found at each of the ABC airports. In addition, there are numerous reliable local firms that offer competitive rates. For details on car rental agencies for Aruba, see p781, for Bonaire, see p792 and for Curaçao, see p807.

Main roads are generally in pretty good condition; however, roads in national parks and other remote spots can be quite rough.

Consider renting a 4WD or other vehicle with high ground clearance if you want to go exploring. Driving is on the right-hand side, seat belts are required and motorcyclists must use helmets. Gasoline is easily found.

Road signs are sporadic. Outside of well-marked resort areas, you will soon discover just how friendly the locals are as you stop often for directions.

### Taxi

Taxis are available on all the islands; see p781, p792 and p807 for Aruba, Bonaire and Curaçao, respectively.

# Caribbean Islands Directory

## CONTENTS

| | |
|---|---|
| Accommodations | 815 |
| Activities | 817 |
| Books | 819 |
| Business Hours | 819 |
| Children | 819 |
| Climate Charts | 821 |
| Customs | 821 |
| Dangers & Annoyances | 821 |
| Embassies & Consulates | 822 |
| Festivals & Events | 822 |
| Gay & Lesbian Travelers | 822 |
| Holidays | 823 |
| Insurance | 823 |
| Internet Access | 823 |
| Legal Matters | 824 |
| Maps | 824 |
| Money | 824 |
| Photography & Video | 825 |
| Post | 826 |
| Solo Travelers | 826 |
| Telephone | 826 |
| Time | 827 |
| Tourist Information | 827 |
| Travelers with Disabilities | 827 |
| Visas | 828 |
| Women Travelers | 828 |
| Work | 828 |

This chapter gives you a broad overview on all things practical in the Caribbean islands. This book covers hundreds of islands, so the information given here is based on collective generalizations to give you a sense of the region as a whole and to help you plan your trip. Start your search here (subjects are listed alphabetically) then turn to the Directory sections in individual chapters for more specific details.

## ACCOMMODATIONS

A wide range of accommodations awaits travelers in the Caribbean, from inexpensive guesthouses and good-value efficiency apartments – which have refrigerators and partial kitchens – to elaborate villas and luxury beachside resorts. The bulk of our listings fall somewhere in between.

In this book the phrase 'in summer' refers to the low season (mid-April to December) and 'in winter' to the high season (December to mid-April). Throughout the book we've listed high-season rates unless otherwise noted. Keep in mind that hotel rates can be up to 30% cheaper in the low season and in most places they'll fluctuate with tourist traffic.

The price structure we have followed applies to most of the islands. However, not all islands have rooms in all price categories – many have no budget accommodations at all, while other islands are less expensive across the board. The individual chapters outline any deviations but, in general, 'budget' means US$75 or less, 'midrange' means US$76 to US$200 and 'top end' means US$201 and up.

Some hotels close for a month or so in late summer, usually around September. If business doesn't look promising, some of the smaller hotels and guesthouses might even close down June to September.

'Private bath' in this book means the room has its own toilet and shower – it does not necessarily mean that it has a bathtub and in most cases it will not. If having a TV or telephone is important to you, check, although satellite/cable TV is pretty common.

### Camping

Camping is limited in the Caribbean and on some islands freelance camping is either illegal or discouraged – usually to protect nature or because of crime. This is certainly not the rule everywhere, however, and it's best to check with the local tourist office for rules and regulations.

There are a number of camping possibilities throughout the US Virgin Islands and on Puerto Rico.

### Guesthouses

The closest thing the Caribbean has to hostels, guesthouses are usually great value. Often in the middle of a town or village and rarely alongside a beach, they offer good opportunities for cultural immersion. Rooms usually have a bed and private bath and some have communal kitchens and living

---

**PRACTICALITIES**

- **Newspapers** Most Caribbean islands have their own newspapers and these are well worth reading to gain insight into local politics and culture. International newspapers, such as the *International Herald Tribune* and *USA Today*, are available on only a few islands. International glossy magazines are more common.

- **Radio & TV** Most islands have their own radio stations, which are a great way to tune in to the latest calypso, reggae, soca and steel-pan music. Local TV stations offer mostly soap operas. The prevalence of satellite TVs means that CNN, BBC World, HBO and others are common.

- **Video Systems** The local system is NTSC, but videotapes are sold in various formats.

- **Electricity** The electric current varies in the islands. On many the current is 110V, 60 cycles (as in the US), but others have 220V, 50 cycles (as in Europe). Adapters are widely available at shops and hotels. Check the Practicalities boxes in the individual chapters.

- **Weights & Measures** Some Caribbean countries use the metric system, while others use the imperial system and a few use a confusing combo of both; check the individual chapters. Each chapter uses the system of measurement followed in that country..

---

rooms. In some areas you can arrange private homestays, where you stay in the home of a local family. These are most readily available in Cuba, where they are known as casas particulares.

## Hotels

Looking at the Caribbean as a whole, you'll see that hotel rooms can range from flea-ridden hovels to massive 1000-room resorts, to glorious villas hovering over the sea. Prices run the gamut as well. Look a little closer and you realize that on the islands themselves the hotel options seem in short supply. On one island, for example, there will be a lot of budget accommodations but few 'nicer' hotels; elsewhere, you'll see dozens of top-end resorts but not a budget hotel in sight. If you're trying to plan a trip, it's a good idea to read through the Accommodations listings in each chapter to find out the range of hotels available on each island.

The **Caribbean Hotel Association** (www.caribbean hotels.com) has helpful links that connect to the individual islands' hotel associations.

### ALL-INCLUSIVE RESORTS

Born in Jamaica and now prevalent across the Caribbean, all-inclusive resorts allow you to pay a set price and then nothing more once you set foot inside the resort. You usually get a wristband that allows you free access to the hotel or resort's restaurants, bars and watersports equipment. Many properties have jumped onto the 'all-inclusive' bandwagon, but don't necessarily supply the goods. Be sure to find out exactly what 'all-inclusive' includes, the variety and quality of food available, whether or not all drinks are included and if there are any hidden charges. At some places the food is produced by the ton for mass consumption: think all-you-can-eat chicken McNuggets.

### Rental Accommodations

If you're traveling with your family or a large group, you might want to look into renting a villa. Villas are great because you have room to stretch out, do your own cooking and enjoy plenty of privacy. Rentals cost anywhere from US$600 per week for a basic villa with bedrooms, kitchen and living space, to US$15,000 per night for a beachside estate with staff. For even more, you can rent an island. Agencies on the individual islands rent properties; the following rent villas throughout the region:

**At Home Abroad** ( ☎ in the USA 212-421-9165; www .athomeabroadinc.com)

**Caribbean Way** ( ☎ in the USA 514-393-3003, 877-953-7400; www.caribbeanway.com)

---

**BOOK YOUR STAY ONLINE**

For more accommodation reviews and recommendations by Lonely Planet authors, check out the online booking service at www.lonelyplanet.com/hotels. You'll find the true, insider lowdown on the best places to stay. Reviews are thorough and independent. Best of all, you can book online.

**Heart of the Caribbean** ( ☎ in the USA 262-783-5303, 800-231-5303; www.hotcarib.com)
**Island Hideaways** ( ☎ in the USA 703-378-7840, 800-832-2302; www.islandhideaways.com)
**Owners Syndicate** ( ☎ in the UK 020-7401-1088; www.ownerssyndicate.com)
**West Indies Management Company** (Wimco; www.wimcovillas.com)

## ACTIVITIES

For anyone tired of lazing around (imagine that!), the islands have plenty to offer and, with water everywhere, it's no wonder that aquatic sports dominate the activity roster for most vacationers.

### Cycling

Cycling and moutain biking are becoming popular in the Caribbean islands as the bike culture takes hold. Hotels often rent bikes and there are shops that both rent and repair bikes on most of the major islands. Note that road conditions can often be a bit dubious, with narrow, rough conditions posing challenges.

### Diving & Snorkeling

Undoubtedly graced with several of the world's best diving spots, the Caribbean offers plenty of underwater fun for everyone, from first-time snorkelers and novice divers to salt-crusted pros. Check out the Diving & Snorkeling chapter (p52) for more information.

### Fishing

Ask Hemingway – there's good deep-sea fishing in the Caribbean, with marlin, tuna, wahoo and barracuda among the prime catches. Charter fishing-boat rentals are available on most islands. Expect a half-day of fishing for four to six people to run to about US$400. Charter boats are usually individually owned and consequently the list of available skippers tends to fluctuate; local tourist offices and activity desks can provide the latest information.

### Golf

The Caribbean has some of the world's most beautiful and challenging golf courses, where both major and local tournaments are held throughout the year. Green fees vary greatly, from around US$30 at smaller courses to US$150 and more, plus caddy and cart, at the renowned courses. Most places offer club rentals, but serious golfers tend to bring their own. Some of the best golf courses are found on Jamaica, Nevis, Barbados, and in the Bahamas, Dominican Republic and the Cayman Islands.

While it's lovely to swing away at your favorite course, be aware that the building of golf courses often comes at a huge environmental cost, including habitat destruction and massive water waste. But just as kiddies expect a water-slide with their pool, many adults expect a golf course with their holiday.

---

**AUTHOR FAVORITES**

Here's some of the favorite accommodation options the authors of this book found during their research:

- St-Martin is very expensive. Les Balcons d'Oyster Pond (p448) is the standout hotel of the century – the nicest property I saw on the island. (Brandon Presser, St-Martin/Sint Maarten)

- St Joseph's Home for Boys Guest House (p268), Port-au-Prince. I reckon this is probably the best budget place I have stayed on any trip in any country. More like a home than a hostel, it's a 'family' of ex-street boys and you're welcomed into the family too. Communal meals, lovely building. (Paul Clammer, Haiti)

- Momma Chastante, the owner of quirky Cascara (p641) in St Lucia, is one of those characters you never forget. On top of all this it's so cheap; you won't believe your eyes when you see the bill. (Scott Kennedy, St Lucia)

- Tiamo Resort (p102); I love its sustainable-tourism philosophy. (Amy C Balfour, the Bahamas)

- Paraíso Caño Hondo (p317) is one of the more special places to stay anywhere in the Dominican Republic, even though a stay here couldn't be further from the typical beach resort experience. (Michael Grosberg, Dominican Republic)

---

**HIKING PRECAUTIONS**

Some rainforest hiking trails take you into steep, narrow valleys with gullies that require stream crossings. The capital rule here is that if the water begins to rise it is not safe to cross, as a flash flood may be imminent. Instead, head for higher ground and wait it out.

On island hikes, long pants will protect your legs from sharp saw grass on overgrown sections of trails. Sturdy footwear with good traction is advisable on most hikes. Mosquitoes can get downright aggressive, so be sure to have good bug repellant with you.

Most experienced hikers know what to bring, but here's a quick reminder:

- a flashlight (island trails are not a good place to be caught unprepared in the dark)
- lots of fresh drinking water
- a snack
- a trail map or a compass
- rain gear (especially on long hikes)
- strong bug repellant with plenty of DEET

---

## Hiking

Verdant peaks rise high above dramatic valleys, volcanoes simmer and waterfalls rumble in the distance. Rainforests resonate to a chorus of birdsong and reveal more green than you've ever imagined. Most people come to the Caribbean for the beaches, but many islands draw hikers seeking rugged terrain and stunning mountain vistas.

If you're looking to get your legs moving on mountain trails, you'll want to head to the higher, rainforested islands. On lofty Dominica you can hike to a variety of waterfalls, take an easy rainforest loop trail through a parrot sanctuary or hire a guide for an arduous trek. Or explore smoldering volcanoes on Guadeloupe and Martinique. St Lucia's trails lead to the world-famous Pitons and trekfilled national parks surround the Dominican Republic's impressive Pico Duarte. The Parc National la Visite offers excellent hiking on Haiti. In the US Virgin Islands the forested island of St John is mostly protected parkland, filled with hiking trails that lead to sand-swept beaches. The small but steep island of Saba has some good easy-access hiking, including a lightly trodden network of footpaths that once connected Saba's villages, before the introduction of paved roads and cars just a few decades ago. Jamaica, Grenada, Bonaire and Nevis also have good hiking trails.

On many of the smaller low-lying islands there are few, if any, established trails, but, as cars are also scarce, the dirt roads that connect villages can make for good walking. On several islands, especially in the Bahamas, and Turks and Caicos, the only hiking you'll do is walking along a sandy beach. For more detailed information on hiking see the individual island chapters.

## Horseback Riding

Horseback riding can be a fun way to explore a place. On many islands outfitters offer guided rides along mountain trails and quiet valleys, or trips along remote beaches. A few combine both in a single outing. Specific information on horseback riding can be found in the individual island chapters.

## Sailing

The Caribbean is a first-rate sailing destination and boats and rum-sipping, saltyskinned sailors are everywhere. On many public beaches and at resorts, water-sports huts rent out Hobie Cats or other small sailboats for near-shore exploring. Many sailboat charter companies run day excursions to other islands and offer party trips aboard tall ships or sunset cruises on catamarans (usually complete with champagne or rum cocktails). Boat rentals abound for experienced sailors and there are plenty of crewed charters for those just finding their sea legs.

Due to island proximity, calmer waters and plenty of protected bays, Antigua, the US Virgin Islands and British Virgin Islands offer some of the best sailing and charter opportunities in the Caribbean. For information on renting your own bareboat sailboat or chartering a crewed yacht, check out p835.

---

**ISLAND TIME**

It's important to remember that this is the Caribbean and life moves at a slow, loosely regimented pace. You'll often see signs in front of shops, bars and restaurants that say 'open all day, every day' and this can mean several things; the place could truly be open all day every day of the week, but don't count on it. If business is slow, a restaurant, shop or attraction might simply close. If a bar is hopping and the owner's having fun, it could stay open until the wee hours of morning. If the rainy season is lasting too long, a hotel or restaurant might simply close for a month. If a shop owner has a hangover, doctor's appointment or date, or simply needs a day off – hey mon, store's closed. In other words, be aware that hard and fast rules about opening times are hard to come by. The only consistent rule is that Sundays are sacred and 'open every day' generally translates to 'open every day except Sunday.'

Once you get in sync with local rhythms you'll see the concept of 'island time' as a blessing, not a curse.

---

## Surfing

Except for Barbados, which is further out into the open Atlantic, the islands of the Eastern Caribbean aren't really great for surfing. Once you head north and west, however, you can find particularly surfable swells on Puerto Rico's west coast; Jamaica's north and east coasts; the north coasts of the US Virgin Islands and British Virgin Islands; and the north and south coasts of the Dominican Republic. Even Curaçao has a nascent scene.

In late summer swells made by tropical storms off the African coast begin to race toward Barbados, creating the Caribbean's highest waves and finest surfing conditions. The most reliable time for catching good, high, surfable waves is September to November. Bathsheba, on Barbados' east coast, is the center of activity. See p693 for an interview with a local surfing expert.

Surfing is also possible at times in Guadeloupe, Trinidad and Tobago, and St-Martin/Sint Maarten.

## Windsurfing

Favorable winds and good water conditions throughout the area have boosted the popularity of windsurfing, or sailboarding, in recent years. Public beach facilities rent out equipment and offer lessons to first-timers, and some resorts offer the use of windsurfing gear free to guests. Aruba and Bonaire have regular championships. St Thomas in the US Virgin Islands is another good spot.

## BOOKS

A discussion of any pertinent books from or about each destination is included in its Directory section.

## BUSINESS HOURS

Business hours vary from island to island, but there are a few general rules. On most islands, business offices are open 8am or 9am to 4pm or 5pm weekdays. Most tourist information centers are open 8am to 4pm weekdays and 9am to noon on Saturday.

Shops are open 9am to 5pm Monday to Saturday (malls stay open later). Post offices are generally open 8am to 3pm weekdays; and banking hours are normally 8am to 3pm Monday to Thursday, or 8am to 5pm on Friday.

Restaurants are usually open from 11am to 10pm daily, though many also serve breakfast and open earlier. In general, think 7am to 10am for breakfast, noon to 2pm for lunch and 6pm to 10pm for dinner.

Bars are often open from noon to midnight, although in some party zones, bars stay open until the last person leaves.

Throughout the Caribbean, Sundays can be very quiet, with only businesses aimed at tourists open. In many towns everything is closed on Sunday unless there's a cruise ship in port.

Specific business hours for each island are listed in the individual chapter directories; exceptions to the hours listed in the chapter directories are noted in reviews.

## CHILDREN

Children in the Caribbean are encouraged to talk, sing, dance, think, dream and play. They are integrated into all parts of society: you see them at concerts, restaurants, churches and parties. Most families can't afford baby-sitters, so parents bring their kids everywhere. As a result children are a vibrant part of the cultural fabric and if you travel with children you'll find this embracing attitude extends to your kids too.

Children often seem more independent in the islands. You'll notice that kids playing in the streets are rarely supervised. By culture and imperative, children are taught to look

---

### KIDS IN THE CARIBBEAN  *Carolyn B Heller*

'Boat, go fast! Boat, go fast!'

My two-year-old daughter is shrieking excitedly as the water taxi zips us across the bay from Tortola to Virgin Gorda. Her twin sister is more apprehensive about this boat journey, but soon she, too, is squealing with delight. Our first Caribbean adventure with our kids is off to a good start.

Taking the kids on their first-ever boat ride. Digging on a sandy beach. Wandering rainforest trails. Meeting local children. It's simple adventures like these that make the Caribbean such a great region for travel with kids.

#### Where to Stay

Resorts offer scores of kid-friendly amenities, but our family's favorite Caribbean stays have been at alternative lodgings where we felt more like part of the community. At a family-run gîte in Guadeloupe, the owner's young son taught our daughters to play 'cache cache' – the game they knew as 'hide and seek.' In Grenada we rented an apartment from a grandmotherly lady who offered advice on everything from where to eat to navigating the local bus system and she introduced our girls to her neighbors – twins the same age. Our hosts at a Marie-Galante B&B shared their supper of breadfruit and pigs' tails and (after we tucked the kids into bed upstairs) swapped stories over freshly-made ti-punch.

Before booking any lodging, ask for details to assess its child-friendliness. Do they welcome kids or accept them grudgingly? Is there a kitchen or at least a refrigerator, so you can shop at local markets and avoid the expense of always eating out? Are there safe places where kids can play? Even if the beach is nearby, is it across a heavily-trafficked street?

#### What to Bring

Pack light! Kids can live in T-shirts, shorts and a bathing suit, but bring long-sleeved shirts and lightweight long pants to protect them from mosquitoes and the sun. A quick-drying shirt they can swim in will help guard against sunburn, too. Bring sandals they can wear in the water, as well as comfortable sneakers or walking shoes. Zip-top plastic bags are handy for holding everything from snacks to wet swimsuits.

Don't expect to find high-quality car seats – if you're going to be driving, bring your own. We found it easier to carry toddlers in a backpack than to navigate a stroller down sand-covered lanes.

#### Keeping Safe

To help kids acclimate to the Caribbean heat, take it easy at first and make sure they drink plenty of water. For sun protection, children should wear sunscreen and lightweight clothing, including a hat, whenever they're outside. In the evening be sure kids cover up to keep mosquitoes at bay. Bring insect repellent formulated for children and whatever medication you normally use to treat insect bites.

#### What to Do

Many activities that adults enjoy – swimming, hiking, going to the market, joining in local festivals – are fun for kids, too. Try to meet local children and sample new foods. Just adapt your adventures to your kids' ages and abilities. When a hike to the Baths on Virgin Gorda proved too challenging for our toddlers, we discovered a cave-like 'room' in a shallow pool nearby where the kids could splash and play.

Remember to allow plenty of rest time, too. After all, even when you're having an exciting 'Boat, go fast' day, you're still on vacation.

out for each other. The concept of 'it takes a village to raise a child' is alive and well in the Caribbean; there's an unspoken cultural understanding that adults look out for kids, whether they are family or not.

For complete details about traveling with children in the Caribbean, see opposite.

## CLIMATE CHARTS

For more information on the climate of the Caribbean islands, see individual chapters.

## CUSTOMS

All the Caribbean islands allow a reasonable amount of personal items to be brought in duty free, as well as an allowance of liquor and tobacco. Determining what you can take home depends on where you're vacationing and your country of origin. Check with your country's customs agency for clarification.

Spear guns are prohibited in the waters around many islands, so divers interested in spear fishing should make advance inquiries. Most islands prohibit unregistered firearms; travelers arriving by boat who have guns on board should declare them on entry. Some islands are free of rabies and have strict rules on the importation of animals; this is mainly of interest to sailors, who might not be allowed to bring their pets onto land.

## DANGERS & ANNOYANCES

One of the most common hazards in the Caribbean are the roads. Although your beater rental can perish in a killer pothole, you may perish from the maniacal driving of others. Roads are often narrow, which doesn't slow others down in the slightest. And pedestrians may be at just as much risk as they have nowhere to walk away from traffic. All you can do is please your mom by being careful.

### Crime

In terms of individual safety and crime, the situation is quite varied in the Caribbean. It's hard to imagine more tranquil areas than Saba and Statia, where most people don't even have locks on their doors, whereas walking the streets of Port of Spain (Trinidad) or Fort-de-France (Martinique) after dark can certainly be a risky venture, especially for women (see p828 for more information specific to female travelers).

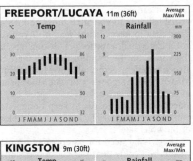

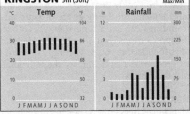

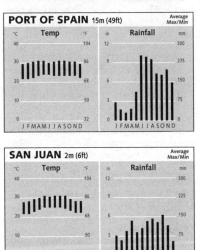

In most areas there is a huge disparity between the income of locals and the (real or perceived) wealth of visitors. If you venture beyond the borders of your resort or tourist area, you may observe populations devastated by poverty, a lack of medical supplies and no clean water in places like Jamaica and Haiti. Add to this drug production and trafficking and you can see why crime is a problem in some areas.

Theft can occur, so it's best to keep your valuables close to you at all times and it's a good idea to never flaunt wealth. If you've got a car, you'll want to lock belongings in the trunk, but be mindful that car theft is also a problem (especially St-Martin/Sint Maarten where goods and cars disappear in seconds). Many resorts and hotels have gated security or guards to keep nonguests out. Still, where possible, lock your valuables in the hotel safe.

There is no need for paranoia and most visitors will enjoy their Caribbean trip without incident, but being aware of your surroundings can go a long way. Of course, the precautions you should take depend on which island you're visiting. For a better grasp of the situation, see the individual island chapters.

## Manchineel Trees

Manchineel trees grow on beaches throughout the Caribbean. The fruit of the manchineel, which looks like a small green apple, is poisonous. The milky sap given off by the fruit and leaves can cause severe skin blisters, similar to the reaction caused by poison oak. If the sap gets in your eyes, it can result in temporary blindness. Never take shelter under the trees during a rainstorm, as the sap can be washed off the tree and onto anyone sitting below.

Manchineel trees can grow as high as 40ft (12m) with branches that spread widely. The leaves are green, shiny and elliptical in shape. On some of the more visited beaches, trees will be marked with warning signs or bands of red paint. Manchineel is called *mancenillier* on the French islands and *anjenelle* on Trinidad & Tobago.

## Pesky Creatures

Although some people groove to the music of nature, others do not. Squawking roosters and croaking frogs often begin their chorus in the predawn hours, so light sleepers may want to bring along earplugs. You can expect to find mosquitoes and sandflies throughout the region, both of which can be quite voracious. In addition, a few of the islands have chiggers, no-see-ums and centipedes.

Bring along strong insect repellant that is at least 25% DEET. Kinder, gentler solutions seem to only discourage the kinder, gentler bugs, leaving your skin open to the most voracious predators.

## EMBASSIES & CONSULATES

It's important to realize what your own embassy – the embassy of the country of which you are a citizen – can and can't do to help you if you get into trouble. Generally speaking, it won't be much help in emergencies if the trouble you're in is remotely your own fault. Remember that you are bound by the laws of the country you are visiting. Your embassy will not be sympathetic if you end up in jail after committing a crime locally, even if such actions are legal in your own country.

In genuine emergencies you might get some assistance, but only if other channels have been exhausted. For example, if you need to get home urgently, a free ticket is exceedingly unlikely – the embassy would expect you to have insurance. If you have all your money and documents stolen, it might assist with getting a new passport, but a loan for onward travel is out of the question.

Not all Caribbean nations have diplomatic representation. See the individual chapter directories for a list of foreign embassies in each region and island representation abroad.

## FESTIVALS & EVENTS

Specific information on festivals and special events, which vary throughout the region, is found in the Directory sections of the individual island chapters. Carnival is a huge party throughout the Caribbean. See opposite for some of our favorite festivals.

## GAY & LESBIAN TRAVELERS

Parts of the Caribbean are not particularly gay-friendly destinations and on many of the islands an element of overt homophobia and machismo is prevalent. See the Directory sections of the individual chapters for details.

The situation for gay men and lesbians is a low-profile one and public hand-holding, kissing and other outward signs of affection are not commonplace. Still, there are several niches for gay travelers. Particularly friendly islands include Cuba, Dominican Republic, Puerto Rico and the US Virgin Islands. The tolerant Dutch attitude makes Aruba, Bonaire, Curaçao and Sint Maarten friendly to gay travelers and the French influence on St-Martin, Guadeloupe and Martinique makes them reasonably tolerant. Saba is a gay-friendly little island, although there's not a lot happening, but neighboring St-Barthélemy offers a welcome attitude and nightlife aplenty.

---

### FAVORITE FESTIVALS & EVENTS

No matter what Caribbean island you land on, you'll quickly discover one thing: everybody loves to party! No matter what time of year, come rain or shine, you'll find plenty of live music, dancing in the streets and countless reasons to celebrate. Here are a few of our favorites:

- **Carnival, Port of Spain** (p738) Trinidad spends all year gearing up for its legendary street party, with steel-pan bands, blasting soca and calypso music and outrageous costumes.
- **Junkanoo** (p73) The Bahamas national festival takes over Nassau, starting in the twilight hours on Boxing Day (December 26). It's a frenzied party with marching 'shacks,' colorful costumes and music.
- **Carnaval, Santiago de Cuba** (p185) Cuba's oldest, biggest and wildest celebration is held in the last week of July.
- **Fiesta de Santiago Apostal** (p353) Puerto Ricans celebrate their mixed African and European ancestry during the last five days of July by donning colorful *vejigante* masks (colorful papier-mâché masks depicting often scary characters from African and European mythology) and parading through the streets of Aldea Loíza.
- **Crop-Over Festival** (p697) Barbados' big three-week festival marks the end of the sugarcane harvest. Festivities start in mid-July with calypso competitions and end with a big parade.
- **Carnival, Antigua** (p536) Antigua's annual carnival takes place at the end of July and culminates in a grand parade, with plenty of music and mayhem to get you in the festive mood.
- **Reggae Sumfest** (p242) Die-hard Rastafarians and Marley followers come from all over the world to jam with the masses at Jamaica's top reggae festival, held every July in Montego Bay.

---

Jamaica unfortunately is a special case in terms of harassment (and worse) of gay people. Violent crimes happen and the police generally do nothing. The country should be considered unsafe for gay and lesbian people.

Outward affection on most of the former British islands is also not recommended. The comments here are general and each region of each island is different. For a better idea on the gay climate of each island, turn to the chapter directories. See also p833 for information on gay and lesbian cruises.

Good websites with information on gay and lesbian travel to the Caribbean as well as links to tour operators:

- gaytravel.com
- gaytravel.co.uk
- www.outtraveler.com
- www.outandabout.com

## HOLIDAYS

A useful list of public holidays, which vary throughout the region, is found in the Directory sections of the individual island chapters.

## INSURANCE

Travel insurance covering theft, loss and medical problems is a wise idea. At the very least it will bring you piece of mind and at best it could save you thousands of dollars. Before opting for a policy think about the coverage you require. There are a wide variety of policies and you'll want one to suit your itinerary. Check the fine print as some policies exclude 'dangerous activities' such as diving which would be a major problem for many Caribbean travelers. Check to see whether you have coverage through your credit-card company and find out about any penalties involved if you need to cancel flights or rebook hotels. Finally, as with all travel documents, make a couple of extra copies – one to leave at home and one to pack in your bag.

## INTERNET ACCESS

Internet access is generally easy throughout the Caribbean. Only on more remote islands or in cheaper homestays or guesthouses will you be unlikely to find at least a computer you can use for internet access. For those who carry their own laptop, iPhone or other wi-fi-enabled device there's good news: wi-fi is becoming common, especially at midrange and top-end hotels on the more visited islands. Even if a place doesn't have wi-fi in every room it often has it in the lobby or pool area.

(Some have it in bars so you can get liquored up and send intemperate emails.) Note that some resorts may charge as much US$15 per day for internet access.

Internet access shops and cafés are common anywhere tourists gather or in large towns. Locals are online as much as you are. Libraries are also good sources. When in doubt, just ask.

## LEGAL MATTERS

Due to the widespread stereotype that everyone in the Caribbean is a pot-smoking Rasta, some visitors take a casual attitude about sampling island drugs. When in Rome, er Kingston, right? Well, be forewarned that drug-trafficking is a serious problem throughout the Caribbean and most officials have little to no tolerance of visitors who come in and assume it's OK to partake. Penalties vary throughout the islands, but getting caught smoking or possessing marijuana (or any illegal drug for that matter) can send you to jail in a hurry.

While it's not strictly enforced, the legal drinking age is mostly 18 on the islands with the odd exception (Antigua: 16). And you wonder why the Caribbean has become the spring-break destination of choice for college students? In many places you must be at least 25 years to rent a car.

## MAPS

Island tourist offices typically provide free tourist maps that will suffice for most visitor needs. Travelers who intend to explore an island thoroughly, however, may want something more detailed.

**Blue Water Books & Charts** ( ☎ 800-942-2583; www .bluewaterweb.com) A Florida-based company and one of the world's best resources for nautical charts, electronic charts and books.

**IGN** ( ☎ in Paris 01-43-98-80-00; www.ign.fr) A Paris-based map seller with maps of the French West Indies.

**International Travel Maps & Books** ( ☎ 604-879-3621; www.itmb.com) A Vancouver-based company that publishes maps for both popular and obscure destinations.

**Map Link** ( ☎ 805-692-6777, 800-962-1394; www.map link.com) A California-based distributor that sells maps from hundreds of different publishers.

**Stanfords** ( ☎ 020-7836 1321; www.stanfords.co.uk) A UK-based map specialty store, with outlets in London, Manchester and Bristol, which sells British Ordnance Surveys, maps and nautical charts.

## MONEY

There are 13 official currencies in the Caribbean, which can make things a bit confusing if you're jumping back and forth between islands. Fortunately, the US dollar (US$) is accepted on virtually all of the islands (Cuba being the obvious exception). Many places quote prices and car rentals in US dollars. Banks can usually exchange British pounds (UK£), euros (€) and Canadian dollars (C$), which are not commonly accepted anywhere. On islands like Aruba and Anguilla, ATMs give you the option of withdrawing cash in US currency. Note that the euro has replaced the US dollar as the tourist currency of choice on

### EXCHANGE RATES

| Local Currency | US$1 | C$1 | €1 | UK£1 |
| --- | --- | --- | --- | --- |
| Aruban florin (Afl) | 1.79 | 1.79 | 2.78 | 3.53 |
| Bahamian dollar (BS$) | 1.00 | 1.01 | 1.56 | 1.97 |
| Barbadian dollar (B$) | 1.99 | 2.00 | 3.10 | 3.94 |
| Cayman Islands dollar (CI$) | 0.82 | 0.82 | 1.27 | 1.62 |
| Cuban convertible peso (CUC$) | 0.95 | 0.96 | 1.48 | 1.88 |
| Dominican Republic peso (RD$) | 33.80 | 33.98 | 52.58 | 66.74 |
| Eastern Caribbean dollar (EC$) | 2.65 | 2.66 | 4.12 | 5.23 |
| Euro (€) | 0.64 | 0.65 | 1.00 | 1.27 |
| Haitian gourde (HTG) | 38.13 | 38.33 | 59.31 | 75.26 |
| Jamaican dollar (J$) | 71.12 | 71.48 | 110.63 | 140.35 |
| Netherlands Antillean guilder (ANG) | 1.77 | 1.78 | 2.76 | 3.50 |
| Trinidad & Tobago dollar (TT$) | 6.25 | 6.28 | 9.73 | 12.34 |
| US dollar (US$) | 1.00 | 1.01 | 1.56 | 1.97 |

For current exchange rates see www.xe.com.

French-influenced islands like Guadeloupe, Martinique and St-Barthélemy.

Countries whose official currency is the US dollar include Turks and Caicos, Puerto Rico, US Virgin Islands and British Virgin Islands. Countries with their own dollars include the Bahamas (BS$), Cayman Islands (CI$), Barbados (B$), Jamaica (J$), and Trinidad and Tobago (TT$). Cuba has the Cuban Convertible Peso (CUC$) and the Dominican Republic uses Dominican Pesos (RD$). Haiti uses the gourde (HTG), though US dollars are widely used.

The Eastern Caribbean dollar (EC$) is the official currency of Anguilla, Antigua and Barbuda, Dominica, Grenada, Montserrat, St Kitts and Nevis, St Lucia, and St Vincent and the Grenadines.

The soon-to-be former Netherlands Antilles islands of Saba, Sint Eustatius, Sint Maarten, Bonaire and Curaçao still use the Netherlands Antillean guilder (written 'NAf', ANG or 'Fls', and also known as the 'guilder'); and Aruba uses the Aruba florin (Afl). The French West Indies islands of St-Martin, Guadeloupe, Martinique and St-Barthélemy use the euro.

## ATMs & Credit Cards

ATMs are found on most islands throughout the region. Major credit cards are widely accepted, most commonly Visa and MasterCard. American Express may only work at resorts, high end resorts and pricey gem and watch stores. Note that on some islands, hotels may add a surcharge for credit-card payments, so you might want to inquire in advance.

## Cash

As the US dollar is accepted almost everywhere, it's handy to carry some for when you first arrive. Many airports have banks or currency exchange booths where you can pick up local cash, so it's not necessary to have local currency before you arrive. Generally, it's best to carry smaller denominations to pay for taxis, street snacks or tips.

## Tipping

The tipping situation varies. On some islands it's automatically added to your restaurant bill as a service charge (typically 10-15%), while on other islands you're expected to add a tip of about 15% to the bill.

## Traveler's Checks

Traveler's checks in US dollars are accepted but becoming rather uncommon as people switch to using ATMs for their cash needs.

# PHOTOGRAPHY & VIDEO

The Caribbean islands create the perfect backdrop for any photographer's dream shots. Succulent sunsets give color a whole new meaning; tropical flowers burst with pink and orange and yellow; green peaks sit at impossible angles; turquoise water seems to dance along the white-sand beaches; your family and friends have tans and sun-kissed hair; the local people wear colorful clothing and eat marvelously strange delights. Incredible photos are just a click away.

## Film & Equipment

For those using film, basic print rolls can be found but check expiration dates; you are best off bringing it from home. If you shoot slide film, either bring what you need or leave your camera at home.

Travelers with digital cameras will want to bring along enough memory capacity to last the trip. Although at most internet places where tourists go you can download your photos to the internet and make friends jealous worldwide in nearly real time, saving you the need to carry lots of memory cards.

Only try to buy camera gear if you lose something critical. Prices are high and selection is low.

## Photographing People

It's common courtesy to ask permission before taking photos of people. Occasionally those who have their pictures taken without permission will become quite upset and may demand money. In some places, kids have realized the income potential in this and will offer to pose for you and then expect payment. As a general rule, adults are much more reluctant to have their pictures taken unless there's been some social interaction.

## Technical Tips

Beware that the high air temperatures in the tropics, coupled with high humidity, greatly accelerate the deterioration of film; store exposed film in a dark, cool place. Don't leave your film or digital camera in direct sunshine any longer than necessary. Bring along extra Ziploc bags for storing your camera in when you're at the beach or on a boat trip.

Remember that sand and water are intense reflectors and in bright light they'll often leave foreground subjects shadowy. You can try attaching a polarizing filter, but the most effective technique is to take photos in the gentler light of early morning and late afternoon.

## POST

Postal systems vary greatly in the Caribbean. Specific information on island post offices is given in the individual island directories.

## SOLO TRAVELERS

Though traditionally a destination for lovers, honeymooners, families and groups, the Caribbean is a terrific place to travel alone. Solo travelers find that they can mosey up to any beach bar and find a cold Carib and good conversation. Single sojourners will also get closer to the local population. Whether out of necessity or curiosity, you're more apt to chat with a local fisherman or make friends with a taxi driver when you're going it alone. Many hotels, however, assume double occupancy and charge rates per room. Women traveling alone will want to be careful and aware that they'll get lots of extra attention (see p828).

## TELEPHONE

Overall, the telephone systems work relatively well throughout the Caribbean. You can make both local and long-distance calls from virtually all public phones; most use phone cards that often have very good rates. Coin phones are rare.

Avoid the credit-card phones found in airports, hotels and rather strategically outside some tourist bars, as they charge a steep US$2 per minute for local calls, US$4 to other Caribbean islands or the US and as much as US$8 per minute to elsewhere. Many bear monikers like 'Global Phone' or 'Phone Home'. View the phone in your hotel room with the same suspicion you'd have of a person with a knife in a dark alley: rates can be extortionate.

Internet calling is popular. Use your own laptop if you find a wi-fi or a high speed connection that will allow Skype or iChat to work. Or use the internet phones at an internet place – international rates are usually under US$0.50 per minute.

### Cell Phones

The use of cell phones is quite widespread throughout the Caribbean and most islands have their own network. You'll be able to use your cell on most islands if it is a GSM phone but be prepared to pay extortionate roaming fees. Check rates and whether your phone will work before you go.

One good alternative if you will be on an island for more than two weeks is to buy a SIM card for your GSM phone locally. This gives you local rates which are often quite cheap calling anywhere in the world. Digicel (www.digicel.com), for one, operates on many islands and will sell a SIM card for US$20 that includes US$6 of calling credit.

### Phone Cards

If you're going to be doing much calling in the Caribbean, you'd be wise to purchase a public phone card, as these are widely used throughout the Caribbean.

Phone cards, the size of a credit card, are either inserted into the phone or have a private code that you dial before each call. Each card has an original value and the cost of each call is deducted automatically as you talk. You discard it when the initial value of the card runs out.

It's a good idea to buy cards in smaller denominations, as the per-unit cost is virtually the same on all cards and you won't get a refund for unused minutes. Each island has its own system, shared only by other islands with the same national affiliation. If you're island hopping, the card you buy in St Thomas will work on the other US Virgin Islands, but it won't, for example, work on St-Barthélemy.

### Phone Codes

For Caribbean Island country codes, see inside the front cover as well as the Fast Facts box at the beginning of each individual island's chapter.

In this book we have included only the local number in the listings in each regional chapter, unless the country code needs to be dialed for local calls or for inter-island calls, in which case we have included the country code in the listings.

Check the Telephone section of the Directory in destination chapters to find out how to dial to and from that country.

## TIME

The Bahamas, Turks and Caicos, Jamaica, the Cayman Islands, Cuba, Haiti and the Dominican Republic are on Eastern Standard Time (EST), five hours behind Greenwich Mean Time (GMT). All the other islands are on Atlantic Standard Time (AST), four hours behind GMT. Only the Bahamas, and Turks and Caicos observe Daylight Savings Time. To check the time in relation to your city of origin, check www.timeanddate.com.

## TOURIST INFORMATION

Tourism makes the world go round in most of the Caribbean. As a result, travel information is often available by the kilo. Most islands have a tourist information center in the main town and several have satellite offices at the airport.

But not all national tourism bureaus are created equal. Some seem to be the dumping ground for the unemployable uncles of the ruling party in power; others are smart, sharp operations that do much to make it easier for people to visit and enjoy the island (what a concept!). A few real heroes include Anguilla, Nevis and St-Barthélemy.

See the Directory section in the individual island chapters for contact details of national tourism offices and other useful information sources.

## TRAVELERS WITH DISABILITIES

Unfortunately, travel in the Caribbean is not particularly easy for those with physical disabilities. Overall there is little or no consciousness of the need for easier access onto planes, buses or rental vehicles. One exception is Puerto Rico, where good compliance with the Americans with Disabilities Act means many sights and hotels have wheelchair accessibility.

Visitors with special needs should inquire directly to prospective hotels for information on their facilities. The larger, more modern resorts are most likely to have the greatest accessibility, with elevators, wider doorways and wheelchair-accessible baths.

---

### VOLUNTEER OPPORTUNITIES IN THE CARIBBEAN

Many programs in the Caribbean have a large element of holiday fun mixed in with good intentions. 'Volunteer' programs (you often pay hefty fees for the honor) include ones with themes like 'learn to dive while saving the reef'. If only it was that easy. The following organizations have programs whose actual value to the places 'served' varies greatly. Generally the greater the time commitment, the greater opportunity you'll have to actually do something useful.

**Caribbean Volunteer Expeditions** (www.cvexp.org) A US-based organization that sends volunteers to work on archaeology projects, artifact restoration and environmental preservation projects throughout the Caribbean. Fees typically cost about US$800 per week, including accommodations, food and land transportation, but not airfare.

**Earthwatch** (www.earthwatch.org) As it says on the homepage, 'Leonardo DiCaprio and Earthwatch want *you* to be a hero for the planet.' Projects include hanging out in rainforests in Puerto Rico and swimming with tropical fish in US Virgin Islands. Rates for two-week courses range from US$700 to US$4000, including meals, accommodations and airfare.

**Global Volunteers** (www.globalvolunteers.org) Longtime organizer of volunteer projects. Many last up to 24 weeks or more. In Jamaica, a program rehabilitates houses in the Blue Mountains. Fees for a two-week stint are US$2000.

**Greenforce Conservation Expeditions** (www.greenforce.org) A UK-based organization that specializes in wildlife conservation expeditions for gap-year and university students who work with scientists to study the Andros reef system in the Bahamas. Cost is around £2300 for 10 weeks.

**Habitat for Humanity** (www.habitat.org) An international nonprofit, ecumenical Christian housing organization where volunteers build simple, affordable housing for people in need. Costs vary, depending on the size and scope of the project.

**Healing Hands for Haiti** (www.healinghandsforhaiti.org) A foundation dedicated to bringing rehabilitation medicine to Haiti. You don't need a medical background to join a 10-day medical mission, which costs about US$1500, not including airfare.

While land travel may present some obstacles, cruises are often a good option for travelers with disabilities in the Caribbean. Many cruise lines can coordinate shore-based excursions in wheelchair-accessible tour buses.

Travelers with disabilities might want to get in touch with national support organizations in their home country. These groups commonly have general information and tips on travel and are able to supply a list of travel agents specializing in tours for the visitors with special needs. Here are some resources:

**Access-Able Travel Source** ( ☎ 303-232-2979; www .access-able.com) A US-based organization with an excellent website that has links to international disability sites, travel newsletters, guidebooks, travel tips and information on cruise operators.

**Radar** (www.radar.org.uk) A UK-based advocacy organization providing general information on overseas travel.

**Society for Accessible Travel and Hospitality** ( ☎ 212-447-7284; www.sath.org) This advocacy group and resource has much information on travel for travelers with disabilities.

## VISAS

Passport and visa requirements vary from island to island; specific information is given in the individual island directories. There are revised passport regulations for US citizens traveling from the Caribbean; see p830.

## WOMEN TRAVELERS

Although the situation varies between islands, machismo is alive and well, and women need to take precautions. Men can get aggressive, especially with women traveling alone. On many islands they have few qualms about catcalling, hissing, whistling, sucking their teeth or making kissy sounds to get your attention. While much of this is simply annoying, it can make women feel unsafe and vulnerable.

Like it or not, you'll feel so much safer traveling with a male companion. For women who love traveling alone, just be sensible and careful. Avoid walking alone after dark, heading off into the wilderness on your own, hitching or picking up male hitchhikers. Generally try to avoid any situation where you're isolated and vulnerable. Don't wear skimpy clothing when you're not on the beach – it will just garner you a lot of unwanted attention. Also note that 'harmless flirtation' at home can be misconstrued as a serious come-on in the Caribbean.

It's also worth singling out Cuba as being a good place for solo women travelers. See the Directory sections of the island chapters for specific details.

## WORK

The Caribbean has high unemployment rates and low wages, as well as strict immigration policies aimed at preventing foreign visitors from taking up work.

Generally the best bet for working is to crew with a boat or yacht. As boat-hands aren't usually working on any one island in particular, the work situation is more flexible and it's easier to avoid hassles with immigration. Marinas are a good place to look for jobs on yachts; check the bulletin-board notices, strike up conversations with skippers or ask around at the nearest bar. Marinas in Miami and Fort Lauderdale are considered good places to find crew jobs as people sailing their boats down for the season stop here looking for crew.

You can also look for jobs with a crew placement agency like Florida-based www .crewfinders.com or UK-based www.crew seekers.co.uk. Note, however, that many other people will have the same idea.

# Caribbean Islands Transportation

## CONTENTS

| | |
|---|---|
| **Getting There & Away** | **829** |
| Entry Requirements | 829 |
| Air | 829 |
| Sea | 830 |
| **Getting Around** | **833** |
| Air | 833 |
| Bicycle | 834 |
| Boat | 834 |
| Bus | 835 |
| Car & Motorcycle | 836 |
| Hitchhiking | 836 |

# GETTING THERE & AWAY

This chapter gives a broad overview about the many options for travel to the Caribbean and ways you might get around once you are there. See the Transportation sections in the relevant destination chapters for details specific to each island.

Flights and tours can be booked online at www.lonelyplanet.com/travel_services.

## ENTRY REQUIREMENTS

Generally your passport is all that's required to enter most Caribbean islands (the exception is always Cuba). Fill out your entry form in black ink (some places such as Antigua are notoriously fussy) and have in mind the name of a hotel in case you are asked where you plan to stay, even if you plan to sort it out later.

---

**THINGS CHANGE...**

The information in this chapter is particularly vulnerable to change. Check directly with the airline or a travel agent to make sure you understand how a fare (and ticket you may buy) works and be aware of the security requirements for international travel. Shop carefully. The details given in this chapter should be regarded as pointers and are not a substitute for your own careful, up-to-date research.

---

Only occasionally will you be asked to show an onward air ticket or prove sufficient funds and then only if you look like a bum. On islands that ask for your length of stay, always pad the figure substantially so as to avoid having to extend the length of your stay, should the sun-kissed beaches and azure waters keep you there longer than you had planned.

Visa and document requirements vary throughout the Caribbean. For specific information, turn to the Directory sections at the end of each regional chapter.

## AIR
### Airports & Airlines

It doesn't matter which island you fly into, touching down on Caribbean land is always a thrilling experience. Some islands, like Saba, Montserrat or Sint Eustatius, have tiny runways, where small regional planes miraculously land on airstrips that don't look much longer than Band-Aids. When you fly into the Bahamas you feel like you're surely going to land in the ocean. Other islands, like Dominica, look like vague colonial outposts, surrounded by cane fields, dusty roads or mountains. Conversely, there's airports like those in Barbados, Aruba and Sint Maarten which are as big and modern as anywhere in the world.

Most major airlines in North America fly direct to the more popular islands in the Caribbean. In fact such service is so widespread that even places as tiny as Bonaire have nonstop service to major US cities. Generally however, getting to the Caribbean from US cities without hub airports will involve changing planes somewhere. American Airlines has major hubs for its extensive Caribbean service in Miami and San Juan, Puerto Rico.

You can reach the Caribbean nonstop from Europe. Proving that old colonial ties linger, airlines from the UK serve former British colonies like Barbados and Antigua; French airlines serve the French-speaking

## US TRAVEL LAW

As part of the Western Hemisphere Travel Initiative, which aims to tighten US border controls, the US has announced that, effective June 1, 2009, all US citizens traveling to the Caribbean will need a passport to re-enter the US if traveling by air. If traveling by sea (eg on a cruise ship), you will need a passport or a passport card to re-enter the US. The latter is essentially a wallet-sized US passport that is only good for land and sea travel between the US and Canada, Mexico and the Caribbean.

The law does not affect the US state territories of Puerto Rico and the US Virgin Islands, which will continue to be allow established forms of identification like valid drivers' licenses.

islands; and Dutch carriers fly to Aruba, Bonaire and Curaçao. There are no direct flights to the Caribbean from Australia, New Zealand or Asia – travelers fly via Europe or the US.

Also note that service to the Caribbean is seasonal. An island that has, say, weekly nonstop flights from Chicago in January may have none at all in June.

Each destination chapter in this book lists all the airlines flying to each island and the cities they serve.

### CHARTERS

Charter flights from the US, Canada, UK and Europe offer another option for getting to the islands. Fares are often cheaper than on regularly scheduled commercial airlines, but you usually have to depart and return on specific flights and you'll probably have no flexibility to extend your stay. Such flights also often come as part of packages that include stays in resorts.

Browse the sites below and check with a travel agent as they are usually the frontline sales force for these travel companies and their many competitors.

**Apple Vacations** (www.applevacations.com) From the US.
**Air Transat** (www.airtransat.ca) From Canada.
**Funjet Vacations** (www.funjet.com) From the US.
**XL UK** (www.xl.com) From the UK.

### Tickets

The cost of plane tickets to the Caribbean varies widely, with the peak winter season (December to April) having the highest prices (but also the most flights). Try some of the following websites to compare schedules and prices. Take careful note of itineraries. One airline may offer a route that requires you to change planes twice while another has nonstop service. Is it really worth saving US$50 to spend eight more hours in traveling and

run all the risks that come with trying to make connections?

- www.cheaptickets.com
- www.expedia.com
- www.farecast.com
- www.kayak.com
- www.orbitz.com
- www.sta.com
- www.travelocity.com

The above sites will search a myriad of possible connections across dozens of airlines. Try at least three and once you have an idea of which airlines have the best fares and service for the route you want, go to their websites as often there are bargains only available from an airline's website.

## SEA
### Cruises

More than two million cruise-ship passengers sail the Caribbean annually, making it the world's largest cruise-ship destination. While the ships get bigger (new ships carry over 5000 passengers) the amenities also grow, and today your ship can have everything from climbing walls and an in-line skating rink to nightclubs and waterfalls. Most ships hit four or five ports of call, sometimes spending a night, other times only a few hours.

The typical cruise-ship holiday is the ultimate package tour. Other than the effort involved in selecting a cruise, it requires minimal planning – just pay and show up – and for many people this is a large part of the appeal.

For the most part, the smaller, 'nontraditional' ships put greater emphasis on the local aspects of their cruises, both in terms of the time spent on land and the degree of interaction with islanders and their environment. While the majority of mainstream cruises take in fine scenery along the way, the time on the islands is generally quite limited, and the opportunities to experience a sense of island life are more restricted.

Because travel in the Caribbean can be expensive and because cruises cover rooms, meals, entertainment and transportation in one all-inclusive price, cruises can also be comparatively economical.

But it is also important to understand the effects that cruises have on the Caribbean. Many port towns have been transformed into one big shopping area for gems and watches – all at supposedly cheap prices. Local culture is turned into sort of a generic 'happy islander' cliché. Then there are the social consequences of having 5000 people or more suddenly descend upon a port: daily life is effectively smothered. The cruise lines also wield immense political power. While independent travelers to an island may be barraged with taxes and fees that go for improving local lives (and at times lining politicians' wallets), cruise-ship passengers generally pay less. Islands that try to impose higher port fees to cover the costs of the cruise ships find mysteriously that less boats are scheduled to turn up.

Environmental concerns are also well-documented. One need only see the black smoke belching forth from a cruise ship's smokestack as it leaves port to understand that these boats aren't green. Dumping waste at sea is a problem that has been documented countless times.

Good sources for getting a well-rounded picture of the industry include:

**Bluewater Network** (www.bluewaternetwork.org) An international environmental group that monitors cruise ship pollution.

**Cruise Critic** (www.cruisecritic.com) An in-depth site for people who like to cruise. The message boards are excellent, with detailed critical opinions and information on ships, islands and more.

**Cruise Junkie** (www.cruisejunkie.com) An excellent site that provides a well-rounded view of the industry, including safety and environmental issues.

**Flying Wheels Travel** (www.flyingwheelstravel.com) Specializes in disabled-accessible Caribbean cruises.

**US Centers for Disease Control** (www.cdc.gov) Follow the travel links to the well-regarded sanitation ratings for ships calling in US ports.

## COST

The cost of a cruise can vary widely, depending on the season and vacancies. While it will save you money to book early, keep in mind that cruise lines want to sail full, so many will offer excellent last-minute discounts, sometimes up to 50% off the full fare.

You'll pay less for a smaller room, but beware that the really cheap rooms are often claustrophobic and poorly located (be sure to

---

### CLIMATE CHANGE & TRAVEL

Climate change is a serious threat to the ecosystems that humans rely upon, and air travel is the fastest-growing contributor to the problem. Lonely Planet regards travel, overall, as a global benefit, but believes we all have a responsibility to limit our personal impact on global warming.

#### Flying & Climate Change

Pretty much every form of motor travel generates $CO_2$ (the main cause of human-induced climate change) but planes are far and away the worst offenders, not just because of the sheer distances they allow us to travel, but because they release greenhouse gases high into the atmosphere. The statistics are frightening: two people taking a return flight between Europe and the US will contribute as much to climate change as an average household's gas and electricity consumption over a whole year.

#### Carbon Offset Schemes

Climatecare.org and other websites use 'carbon calculators' that allow jetsetters to offset the greenhouse gases they are responsible for with contributions to energy-saving projects and other climate-friendly initiatives in the developing world – including projects in India, Honduras, Kazakhstan and Uganda.

Lonely Planet, together with Rough Guides and other concerned partners in the travel industry, supports the carbon offset scheme run by climatecare.org. Lonely Planet offsets all of its staff and author travel.

For more information check out our website: lonelyplanet.com.

---

### INDEPENDENT TRAVEL BY CRUISE SHIP?

It may seem a contradiction in terms, but you can be an independent traveler on a cruise ship. If you view the boats as floating hotel rooms that simply transport you each night to a new island, than you are halfway there. The key is what you do in port.

Excursions sold by the cruise lines tend to focus on either cattle-like tours of the island that leave you mooing by the end of the well-trodden trail or focus on generic activities or experiences that have no real context to the island. Instead, be your own tour director. Freelance guides and drivers are available in every port. So too are rental cars and – if you have enough time – ports are often close to bus terminals which allow you to travel the island with locals for next to nothing. Basically your only constraint on doing and seeing the things outlined in this book is time. One imaginative couple rented snorkeling gear when their boat docked in Bonaire. They then got a taxi to a point a few miles up the coast and spent the afternoon snorkeling their way back to the port viewing the island's legendary shoreline reefs.

Another important consideration about independent travel by cruise ship is the opportunity it provides to put money into local economies. By charting your own course on land and purposely patronizing local businesses, you have a much greater direct impact with your money than if it is funneled through large operators.

Unfortunately cruise companies refuse any request for one-way trips, point-to-point travel or stop-offs during voyages. They don't want the hassle.

---

ask before booking). Some cruise lines provide free or discounted airfares to and from the port of embarkation (or will provide a rebate if you make your own transportation arrangements), while others do not.

Meals, which are typically frequent and abundant, are included in the cruise price. Alcoholic drinks are usually not included and are an important profit-center for the lines. A new trend that many cruise companies are enthusiastically promoting involves extra-cost dining venues that give passengers the opportunity to spend money for meals in more exclusive restaurants. Note that tipping is usually expected and can add 20% or more to your shipboard account. Many lines have gotten around the discretionary nature of tips (which are the primary wages for the crew) by automatically putting them on your bill.

A myriad of guided land tours and activities are offered at each port of call, each generally costing US$35 to US$100 or more. These tours are also a major profit centre for the cruise lines so there is great sales pressure before and during your trip.

Most cruises end up costing US$200 to US$400 per person, per day, including airfare from a major US gateway city.

Port charges and government taxes typically add on another US$150 per cruise. Be sure to check the fine print about deposits, cancellation and refund policies, and travel insurance.

### BOOKING A CRUISE

Most cities have travel agents that specialize in cruises. Read weekend newspaper travel sections and check the Yellow Pages.

The internet is an excellent place to make arrangements. Large travel-booking sites like Expedia, Orbitz and Travelocity have oodles of options. The cruise line's own sites will offer deals or upgrades not found elsewhere. Then there are specialist websites for cruising. Some have spectacular deals as lines dump trips at the last moment that otherwise would go unsold.

Recommended sites include the following:
**Cruise411** ( ☎ 800-553-7090; www.cruise411.com)
**Cruise.com** ( ☎ 888-333-3116; www.cruise.com)
**Cruise Outlet** ( ☎ 800-775-1884; www.thecruiseoutlet.com)
**Cruise Web** ( ☎ 800-377-9383; www.cruiseweb.com)
**Vacations To Go** ( ☎ 800-419-5104; www.vacationstogo.com) Especially good last-minute deals.

### TRADITIONAL CRUISES

The following cruise lines sail large vessels on numerous itineraries to many Caribbean islands. Note that through their various brands, Carnival and Royal Caribbean control 90% of the market in the Caribbean.
**Carnival Cruise Lines** ( ☎ 800-227-6482; www.carnival.com) The largest cruise line in the world. Its enormous boats offer cruising to the masses on myriad Caribbean itineraries.
**Celebrity Cruises** ( ☎ 800-437-3111; www.celebritycruises.com) An important brand of Royal Caribbean, it

has huge boats that offer a more upscale experience than Carnival and RCI. It is a major Caribbean player.

**Costa Cruises** ( ☎ 800-462-6782; www.costacruises.com) Owned by Carnival, Costa is aimed at European travelers, which means bigger spas, smaller cabins and better coffee. Boats are huge, and are based on those sailing for its parent company.

**Cunard Line** ( ☎ 800-728-6273; www.cunard.com) Owned by Carnival, Cunard Line operates the huge *Queen Mary II* and *Queen Victoria*. The focus is on 'classic luxury' and the boats have limited Caribbean sailings.

**Disney Cruise Line** ( ☎ 888-325-2500; www.disney cruise.com) Disney's ships are like floating theme parks, with features like movie theaters, children's programs and large staterooms that appeal to families. Disney sails from Florida through the Bahamas.

**Holland America** ( ☎ 800-577-1728; www.hollandame rica.com) Owned by Carnival. Holland America offers a traditional cruising experience to generally older passengers. It has limited sailings in the Caribbean during the Alaska winter (its summer market).

**Norwegian Cruise Line** (NCL; ☎ 800-327-7030; www .ncl.com) Offers 'freestyle cruising' on large cruise ships which means that dress codes are relaxed and dining options more flexible than other lines.

**Princess Cruises** ( ☎ 800-568-3262; www.princess.com) Owned by Carnival, Princess has huge boats that ply the Caribbean and offer a slightly older crowd a huge range of activities and even classes while aboard.

**Regent Seven Seas Cruises** ( ☎ 877-505-5370; www .rssc.com) Smaller ships (maximum 700 passengers) focus on luxury cabins and excellent food.

**Royal Caribbean International** (RCI; ☎ 800-398-9819; www.royalcaribbean.com) The arch-rival to Carnival has a huge fleet of mega-ships (some carry over 5600 people) that is aimed right at the middle of the market. It has itineraries everywhere in the Caribbean all the time.

### NONTRADITIONAL CRUISES

**Sea Cloud Cruises** ( ☎ 888-732-2568; www.seacloud .com) The fleet includes a four-masted, 360ft-long (110m) ship dating to 1931 and a modern sibling. On both, sails are set by hand. This German-American company operates luxury cruises in the Eastern Caribbean.

**Star Clippers** ( ☎ 800-442-0551; www.starclippers.com) These modern four-masted clipper ships have tall-ship designs and carry 180 passengers. Itineraries take in smaller islands of the Eastern Caribbean.

**Windjammer Barefoot Cruises** ( ☎ 800-327-2601; www.windjammer.com) Boats are all true-sailing vessels and the passengers – like the crew – tend to be young. Good choices for the budget and active-minded, the boats get into parts not visited by larger vessels.

**Windstar Cruises** ( ☎ 800-258-7245; www.windstar cruises.com) These luxury four-mast, 440ft (134m) boats have high-tech, computer-operated sails and carry under 400 passengers. Note that the sails aren't the main means of propulsion most of the time. Trips travel throughout the Windward and Leeward Islands.

### GAY & LESBIAN CRUISES

The following US-based companies organize gay-friendly cruises on major cruise lines to the Eastern Caribbean:

**Gay Cruise Vacations** ( ☎ 888-367-9398; www.gay cruisevacations.com) These popular all-gay vacations on giant cruise ships travel throughout the Caribbean on mostly seven-day trips.

**RSVP Vacations** ( ☎ 800-328-7787; www.rsvpvacations .com) Good for active travelers, RSVP has trips on both large cruise ships and smaller yachts.

## Ferry

Once a week, a passenger ferry travels between Chaguaramas, Trinidad, and Guiria, Venezuela, offering an alternative for people traveling to/from South America. See p774 for details.

# GETTING AROUND

## AIR
### Airlines in the Caribbean

Regional airlines, from large to small, travel around the Caribbean. A certain level of patience and understanding is required when you island-hop. Schedules can change at a moment's notice or there may be delays without explanation. For the number of flights that happen daily in the Caribbean, there are very few accidents, so your best bet is to relax and enjoy the ride.

Regional planes are sometimes like old buses, seemingly stopping at every possible corner to pick up passengers. You'll sometimes get stuck on what you could call the 'LIAT shuffle' – where your plane touches down and takes off again from several different airports. For example, if you're flying from St Thomas to Trinidad, you might stop in Antigua, St Lucia and St Vincent before making it to Trinidad. This can easily turn a short flight into half a day. Again, it's best just to enjoy the ride.

There are myriad airlines operating within the Caribbean. You'll find full details in the individual chapters for each island. However there are some large carriers with dozens of connections, which will give you ideas for itinerary building:

---

**THREE FLYING RECOMMENDATIONS**

The authors of this book learned from experience three things you should remember:

- Try not to arrive on a regional flight in the afternoon when most of the North American and European flights arrive, swamping immigration and customs. We flew from Montserrat to Antigua: the flights was 15 minutes, the wait in immigration lines was 2½ hours.

- Keep anything essential you might need for a few days with you. Luggage often somehow misses your flight – even if you see it waiting next to the plane as you board. It may take days – if ever – to catch up with you.

- Check in early. Bring a book and snack and hang out. We saw people with confirmed seats repeatedly bumped after flights checked in full and their alternative was days later. Two hours is not bad if you're prepared for the wait. In many airports, you could check in early and then go do someplace else like the incredibly fun beach bars near the Sint Maarten airport.

---

**Air Jamaica** ( ☎ 800-523-5585; www.airjamaica.com) Provides links across the region from its hubs in Kingston and Montego Bay.

**American Airlines/American Eagle** ( ☎ 800-433-7300; www.aa.com) Provides a huge network of service from its hubs in Miami and San Puerto Rico.

**Caribbean Airlines** ( ☎ 800-744-2225; www.caribbean-airlines.com) Links to major islands from its hubs in Barbados and Trinidad.

**LIAT** ( ☎ 268-480-5601; www.liat.com) The major local carrier of the Eastern Caribbean, you're bound to fly it. Locals love to zing it with phrases like Leaves Island Any Time but it is pretty reliable. Based in Antigua, it flies medium-sized prop planes and serves almost every island with an airport.

## Air Passes

Air passes are a thing of the past in the Caribbean, at least for now. But with advance planning you can get fares that offer similar savings.

# BICYCLE

The popularity of cycling in the Caribbean depends on where you go. Several islands are prohibitively hilly, with narrow roads that make cycling difficult. On others, such as Cuba, cycling is a great way to get around. Many of the islands have bicycles for rent; for details see the island chapters. Bike shops are becoming more common. Most ferries will let you bring bikes on board at no extra charge; regional airlines will likely charge you a hefty fee, so it's best to check ahead if you're going to island-hop with your bike.

# BOAT
## Ferry

For a place surrounded by water, the Caribbean islands don't have as many ferries as you'd think. However, regional ferries travel between several island groups. These can be a nice change of pace after cramped airplanes, smelly buses and dodgy rental cars.

An extensive and inexpensive ferry network connects the US Virgin Islands and British Virgin Islands. Other ferry services that are available include Anguilla and St-Martin/Sint Maarten; St-Martin/Sint Maarten, Saba and St-Barthélemy; St Kitts and Nevis; St Vincent and Bequia; Grenada and Carriacou; and Trinidad and Tobago. Ferries also run between Guadeloupe, Martinique and the outlying islands of Terre-de-Haut, Marie-Galante and La Désirade. Popular and successful fast catamaran ferries connect the islands of Guadeloupe, Dominica, Martinique and St Lucia. Catamarans also sail between St-Martin/Sint Maarten and St-Barthélemy for day trips. In the Bahamas, a high-speed ferry links Nassau to outlying islands.

Details on regional ferry service are in the relevant individual island chapters.

## Yacht

The Caribbean is one of the world's prime yachting locales, offering diversity, warm weather and fine scenery. The many small islands grouped closely together are not only fun to explore but also form a barrier, providing relatively calm sailing waters.

The major yachting bases are in the British Virgin Islands, St-Martin/Sint Maarten, Antigua, Guadeloupe, Martinique, St Lucia, St Vincent and Grenada.

It's easiest to sail down-island, from north to south, as on the reverse trip boats must beat back into the wind. Because of this, several yacht-charter companies only allow sailors to take the boats in one direction, arranging for their own crews to bring the boats back to home base later.

Information on ports and marinas can be found in the individual island chapters.

For information on signing on to crew on a boat or a yacht to reach the Caribbean or to get around once there, see p828.

### YACHT CHARTERS
You can choose from two basic types of yacht charter: bareboat (sail it yourself) and crewed (you relax, someone else sails). Some yacht-charter companies offer everything from live-aboard sailing courses to full luxury living.

With a bareboat charter you rent just the boat. You are the captain and you sail where you want, when you want. You must be an experienced sailor to charter the boat. Bareboat yachts generally come stocked with linen, kitchen supplies, fuel, water, a dinghy, an outboard, charts, cruising guides, a cellular phone and other gear. Provisioning (stocking the boat with food) is not included, although sometimes it is provided for an additional fee.

With a crewed charter the yacht comes with a captain, crew, cook and provisions. You don't have to know how to sail, or anything else about boats. You can either make your own detailed itinerary or provide a vague idea of the kind of places you'd like to visit and let the captain decide where to anchor.

Costs vary greatly. The more established companies generally charge more than small, little-known operators, and large ritzy yachts of course cost more than smaller, less luxurious boats. For more details on yacht charters, see the boxed text, p416.

The following charter companies offer both bareboat and crewed yacht charters in the Caribbean:

**Catamaran Company** ( ☎ 800-262-0308; www.catamarans.com)
**Horizon Yacht Charters** ( ☎ 877-494-8787; www.horizonyachtcharters.com)
**Moorings** ( ☎ 888-952-8420; www.moorings.com)
**Sunsail** ( ☎ 888-350-3568; www.sunsail.com)
**TMM Yacht Charters** ( ☎ 800-633-0155; www.sailtmm.com)

### CHARTER BROKERS
For those who don't want to be bothered shopping around, charter-yacht brokers can help. Brokers work on commission, like travel agents, with no charge to the customer – you tell them your budget and requirements and they help make a match.

A few of the better-known charter-yacht brokers are:

**Ed Hamilton & Co** ( ☎ 800-621-7855; www.ed-hamilton.com)
**Lynn Jachney Charters** ( ☎ 800-223-2050; www.lynnjachneycharters.com)
**Nicholson Yacht Charters** ( ☎ 800-662-6066; www.yachtvacations.com)

## BUS
Inexpensive bus service is available on most islands, although the word 'bus' has different meanings in different places. Some islands have full-size buses, while on others a 'bus' is simply a pickup truck with wooden benches in the back. Whatever the vehicle, buses are a good environmental choice compared to rental cars and they are excellent ways to meet locals. People are generally quite

### WHICH SIDE?
What side of the road to drive on depends on the island, and this can prove particularly confusing if you're island-hopping and renting cars on each island. Adding to the confusion, some cars have steering columns on the opposite side of the car. As a rule, drivers stick to the following:

#### Left Side of the Road (Like the UK)
Anguilla, Antigua & Barbuda, Bahamas, Barbados, British Virgin Islands, Cayman Islands, Dominica, Grenada, Jamaica, St Kitts and Nevis, St Lucia, St Vincent, Trinidad and Tobago, Turks and Caicos, US Virgin Islands.

#### Right Side of the Road (Like the US)
Aruba, Bonaire, Cuba, Curaçao, Dominican Republic, Guadeloupe, Haiti, Martinique, Puerto Rico, Saba, St-Barthélemy, Sint Eustatius, St-Martin/Sint Maarten.

friendly and happy to talk to you about their island. Buses are also often the best way to hear the most popular local music tracks, often at an amazingly loud volume.

Buses are often the primary means of commuting to work or school and thus are most frequent in the early mornings and from mid- to late afternoon. There's generally a good bus service on Saturday mornings, but Sunday service is often nonexistent.

Buses can get crowded. As more and more people get on, children move onto their parents' laps, kids share seats, people squeeze together and everyone generally accepts the cramped conditions with good humor. Whenever someone gets off the back of a crowded minivan, it takes on the element of a human Rubik's Cube, with seats folding up and everyone shuffling; on some buses there's actually a conductor to direct the seating.

## CAR & MOTORCYCLE

Driving in the Caribbean islands can rock your world, rattle your brains and fray your nerves. At first. Soon, you'll get used to the chickens, goats, stray dogs and cows wandering the roadways. You'll get the hang of swerving like a maniac, of slowing for no reason, of using your horn to communicate everything from 'Hey, I'm turning right!' to 'Hey, you're cute!' to 'Hey, [expletive] you!'

It often seems like the only time island residents rush is when they get in their cars. For no apparent reason, many islanders like to haul ass through traffic, roar around twisting roads and use highways to test just how fast their cars will go. Truly, you will get used to all this.

### Driver's License

You'll need your driver's license in order to rent a car. On most of the former British islands, you'll also need to purchase a local driver's license (US$12 to US$20) when you rent a car, but you can do that simply by showing your home license and dishing out the appropriate fee.

## Rental

Car rentals are available on nearly all of the islands, with a few exceptions (usually because they lack roads). On most islands there are affiliates of the international chains, but local rental agencies may have better rates. Or they may simply be more hassle. Always understand what rental insurance coverage your credit card or personal auto insurance provide – if any. Purchasing insurance from the rental company can add over US$10 a day to your bill and you may already be covered.

During the busy winter high season, some islands simply run out of rental cars, so it's a good idea to book one in advance, especially if you want an economy car. On many islands you need to be 25 years old to rent a car. Cars may be in good shape or they may be beaters, cast-offs from another land sent to die an island death. Check the Transportation section of each chapter for specific details.

## HITCHHIKING

Hitchhiking is an essential mode of travel on most islands, though the practice among foreign visitors isn't as common.

If you want to hitch a ride, stand by the side of the road and put your hand out. Be aware that this is also how locals flag taxis and since many private cars look like taxis, this can be confusing (note that most taxis have the letter 'H' – for Hire – on their front license plate). Foreign women traveling alone should not hitchhike – your want for a ride could be misconstrued as a want for something else. Men traveling alone should also be cautious. Though most drivers will happily give you a ride, others might see you as a target, especially if you're carrying around expensive luggage or camera equipment.

If you're driving a rental car, giving locals a lift can be a great form of cultural interaction and much appreciated by those trudging along the side of the road while – comparatively – rich foreigners whiz past. Again, be cautious and obey your instincts.

# Health David Goldberg MD

## CONTENTS

**Before You Go** 837
Insurance 837
Recommended Vaccinations 837
Medical Checklist 837
Internet Resources 837
Further Reading 838
**In Transit** 838
Deep Vein Thrombosis (DVT) 838
Jet Lag & Motion Sickness 838
**In The Caribbean Islands** 839
Availability & Cost of Health Care 839
Infectious Diseases 839
Traveler's Diarrhea 842
Environmental Hazards 842
Traveling with Children 843

Prevention is the key to remaining healthy while abroad. Travelers who receive the recommended vaccinations and follow common-sense precautions usually come away with nothing more than a little diarrhea.

From a medical point of view, the Caribbean is generally safe as long as you're reasonably careful about what you eat and drink. The most common travel-related diseases, such as dysentery and hepatitis, are acquired by consumption of contaminated food and water. Mosquito-borne illnesses aren't a significant concern on most of the islands, except during outbreaks of dengue fever.

# BEFORE YOU GO

Bring medications in their original containers, clearly labeled. A signed, dated letter from your physician describing all medical conditions and medications, including generic names, is also a good idea. If carrying syringes or needles, be sure to have a physician's letter documenting their medical necessity.

## INSURANCE

If your health insurance does not cover you for medical expenses while abroad, consider supplemental insurance; travel agents and the internet are good places to start looking. Find out in advance if your insurance plan will make payments directly to providers or reimburse you later for overseas health expenditures.

## RECOMMENDED VACCINATIONS

Since most vaccines don't produce immunity until at least two weeks after they're given, visit a physician four to eight weeks before departure. Ask your doctor for an International Certificate of Vaccination, which will list all the vaccinations you've received. This is mandatory for countries that require proof of yellow-fever vaccination upon entry, but it's a good idea to carry it wherever you travel. See p838 for recommended vaccinations.

## MEDICAL CHECKLIST

Recommended items for a personal medical kit:
- acetaminophen/paracetamol (eg Tylenol) or aspirin
- adhesive or paper tape
- antibacterial ointment (eg Bactroban) for cuts and abrasions
- antibiotics
- antidiarrheal drugs (eg loperamide)
- antihistamines (for hay fever and allergic reactions)
- anti-inflammatory drugs (eg ibuprofen)
- bandages, gauze and gauze rolls
- DEET-containing insect repellent for the skin
- iodine tablets (for water purification)
- oral-rehydration salts
- permethrin-containing insect spray for clothing, tents and bed nets
- pocketknife
- scissors, safety pins and tweezers
- steroid cream or cortisone (for allergic rashes)
- sunblock
- syringes and sterile needles
- thermometer

## INTERNET RESOURCES

There is a wealth of online travel-health advice. A good place to start is lonelyplanet.com. The **World Health Organization** (www.who.int/ith/) publishes a superb book called *International Travel & Health,* which is revised

### REQUIRED & RECOMMENDED VACCINATIONS

| Vaccine | Recommended for | Dosage | Side effects |
|---|---|---|---|
| chickenpox | travelers who've never had chickenpox | 2 doses, 1 month apart | fever; mild case of chickenpox |
| hepatitis A | all travelers | 1 dose before trip; booster 6-12 months later; | soreness at injection site; headaches; body aches |
| hepatitis B | long-term travelers in close contact with local population | 3 doses over 6 months | soreness at injection site; low-grade fever |
| measles | travelers born after 1956 who've only had 1 measles vaccination | 1 dose | fever; rash; joint pains; allergic reactions |
| rabies | travelers who may have contact with animals and may not have access to medical care | 3 doses over 3-4 weeks | soreness at injection site; headaches; body aches |
| tetanus-diphtheria | all travelers who haven't had a booster within 10 years | 1 dose lasts 10 years | soreness at injection site |
| typhoid | all travelers to Haiti, and for extended stays in rural areas on other islands | 4 capsules by mouth, 1 taken every other day | abdominal pain; nausea; rash |
| yellow fever | travelers to rural areas in Trinidad & Tobago | 1 dose lasts 10 years | headaches; body aches; severe reactions rare |

annually and is available on its website at no cost. Another website of general interest is **MD Travel Health** (www.mdtravelhealth.com), which provides complete travel-health recommendations for every country, updated daily, at no cost.

It's usually a good idea to consult your government's travel-health website before departure, if one is available:

**Australia** (www.smartraveller.gov.au)
**Canada** (www.hc-sc.gc.ca/english)
**UK** (www.doh.gov.uk)
**USA** (www.cdc.gov)

## FURTHER READING

If you're traveling with children, Lonely Planet's *Travel with Children*, by Cathy Lanigan, is useful. *ABC of Healthy Travel*, by E Walker et al, and *Medicine for the Outdoors*, by Paul S Auerbach, are other valuable resources.

# IN TRANSIT

## DEEP VEIN THROMBOSIS (DVT)

Blood clots may form in the legs during plane flights, chiefly because of prolonged immobility. Note that the longer the flight, the greater the risk. Though most blood clots are reabsorbed uneventfully, some may break off and travel through the blood vessels to the lungs, where they could cause life-threatening complications.

The chief symptom of DVT is swelling or pain in the foot, ankle or calf, usually but not always on just one side. When a blood clot travels to the lungs, it may cause chest pain and difficulty in breathing. Travelers with any of these symptoms should immediately seek medical attention.

To prevent the development of DVT on long flights, you should walk about the cabin, perform isometric compressions of the leg muscles (ie contract the leg muscles while sitting), drink plenty of fluids, and avoid alcohol and tobacco.

## JET LAG & MOTION SICKNESS

Jet lag is common when crossing more than five time zones, and is characterized by insomnia, fatigue, malaise or nausea. To avoid jet lag, try drinking plenty of (nonalcoholic) fluids and eating light meals. Upon arrival, get exposure to natural sunlight and readjust your schedule (for meals, sleep etc) as soon as possible.

Antihistamines such as dimenhydrinate (Dramamine) and meclizine (Antivert, Bonine) are usually the first choice for treating motion sickness. Their main side effect is drowsiness. A herbal alternative is ginger, which works like a charm for some people.

# IN THE CARIBBEAN ISLANDS

## AVAILABILITY & COST OF HEALTH CARE

Acceptable health care is available in most major cities throughout the Caribbean, but may be hard to locate in rural areas. In general, the quality of health care will not be comparable to that in your home country. To find a good local doctor, your best bet is to ask the management of the hotel where you are staying or contact your local embassy. In many countries, the US embassy posts a list of English-speaking physicians on its website.

Many doctors and hospitals expect payment in cash, regardless of whether you have travel-health insurance. If you develop a life-threatening medical problem, you'll probably want to be evacuated to a country with state-of-the-art medical care. Since this may cost tens of thousands of dollars, be sure you have insurance to cover this before you depart (see p837).

Many pharmacies are well supplied, but important medications may not be consistently available. Be sure to bring along adequate supplies of all prescription drugs.

## INFECTIOUS DISEASES

### Bancroftian Filariasis

Otherwise known as elephantiasis, bancroftian filariasis occurs in Haiti, the Dominican Republic and some other islands. The disease is carried from person to person by mosquitoes. In severe cases, filariasis may cause enlargement of the entire leg or arm, as well as the genitals and breasts. Most cases occur in longtime residents, but travelers should be aware of the risks and should follow insect protection measures, as outlined on p842.

### Dengue Fever

Dengue fever is a viral infection common throughout the Caribbean. Dengue is transmitted by Aedes mosquitoes, which bite mostly during the daytime and are usually found close to human habitations, often indoors. They breed primarily in artificial water containers, such as jars, barrels, cans, cisterns, metal drums, plastic containers and discarded tires. As a result, dengue is especially common in densely populated, urban environments.

Dengue usually causes flulike symptoms, including fever, muscle aches, joint pains, headaches, nausea and vomiting, often followed by a rash. The body aches may be quite uncomfortable, but most cases resolve uneventfully in a few days. Severe cases usually occur in children under age 15 who are experiencing their second dengue infection.

There is no treatment for dengue fever except to take analgesics such as acetaminophen or paracetamol (Tylenol) and drink plenty of fluids. Severe cases may require hospitalization for intravenous fluids and supportive care.

There is no vaccine. The cornerstone of prevention is protection against insect bites; see p842.

### Fascioliasis

This is a parasitic infection that is typically acquired by eating contaminated watercress grown in sheep-raising areas, especially in Cuba. Early symptoms of fascioliasis include fever, nausea, vomiting and painful enlargement of the liver.

### Hepatitis A

Hepatitis A is the second-most common travel-related infection (after traveler's diarrhea). The illness occurs throughout the world, but the incidence is higher in developing nations. It occurs throughout the Caribbean, particularly in the northern islands.

Hepatitis A is a viral infection of the liver that is usually acquired by ingestion of contaminated water, food or ice, though it may also be acquired by direct contact with infected persons. Symptoms may include fever, malaise, jaundice, nausea, vomiting and abdominal pain. Most cases resolve without complications, though hepatitis A occasionally causes severe liver damage. There is no treatment.

The vaccine for hepatitis A is extremely safe and highly effective. If you get a booster six to 12 months later, it lasts for at least 10 years. You should get it before you go to any developing nation. Because the safety of hepatitis A vaccine has not been established for pregnant women or children under the age of two, they should instead be given a gammaglobulin injection.

### Hepatitis B

Like hepatitis A, hepatitis B is a liver infection that occurs worldwide but is more common

HEALTH

in developing nations. The disease is usually acquired by sexual contact or by exposure to infected blood, generally through blood transfusions or contaminated needles. In the Caribbean the risk is greatest in Haiti and the Dominican Republic. The vaccine is recommended only for long-term travelers (on the road more than six months) who expect to live in rural areas or have close physical contact with locals. Additionally, the vaccine is recommended for anyone who anticipates sexual contact with the local inhabitants or a possible need for medical, dental or other treatments (especially if transfusions or injections are involved) while abroad.

Hepatitis B vaccine is safe and highly effective. However, a total of three injections are necessary to establish full immunity. Several countries added hepatitis B vaccine to the list of routine childhood immunizations in the 1980s, so many young adults are already protected.

## HIV/AIDS

HIV/AIDS has been reported in all Caribbean countries. More than 2% of all adults in the Caribbean carry HIV, which makes it the second-worst-affected region in the world, after sub-Saharan Africa. The highest prevalence is reported in the Bahamas, Haiti, and Trinidad and Tobago. In the Caribbean most cases are related to heterosexual contacts, especially with sex workers. The exception is Puerto Rico, where the most common cause of infection is intravenous drug use. Be sure to use condoms for all sexual encounters. If you think you might visit a piercing or tattoo parlor, or if you have a medical condition that might require an injection, bring along your own sterile needles.

## Leishmaniasis

Reported in the eastern part of the Dominican Republic, leishmaniasis is transmitted by sand flies, which are about one-third of the size of mosquitoes. The most common form of the disease is manifested in skin ulcers on exposed parts of the body, developing over weeks or months. Leishmaniasis may be particularly severe in those with HIV.

There is no vaccine. To protect yourself from sandflies, follow the same precautions as for mosquitoes (see p842), except that netting must be a finer mesh: at least 18 holes to the linear inch (or seven holes to the linear centimeter).

## Malaria

In the Caribbean malaria occurs only in Haiti, and in certain parts of the Dominican Republic such as Bávaro and Punta Cana. For those areas, the first-choice malaria pill is chloroquine, taken once weekly in a dosage of 500mg, starting one to two weeks before arrival, continuing through the trip and for four weeks after departure. Chloroquine is safe, inexpensive and highly effective. Side effects are typically mild and may include nausea, abdominal discomfort, headache, dizziness, blurred vision or itching. Severe reactions are uncommon.

Protecting yourself against mosquito bites (see p842) is just as important as taking malaria pills, since pills are never 100% effective.

If you think you may not have access to medical care while traveling, you should bring along additional pills for emergency self-treatment, which you should undergo if you can't reach a doctor and you develop symptoms that suggest malaria, such as high-spiking fevers. One option is to take four tablets of Malarone once daily for three days. If you self-treat for malaria, it may also be appropriate to start a broad-spectrum antibiotic to cover typhoid fever and other bacterial infections. The drug of choice is usually a quinolone antibiotic such as ciprofloxacin (Cipro) or levofloxacin (Levaquin). If you start self-medication, you should try to see a doctor at the earliest possible opportunity.

If you end up with a fever after returning home, see a physician, as malaria symptoms may not occur for months.

## Rabies

Rabies is a viral infection of the brain and spinal cord that is almost always fatal. The rabies virus is carried in the saliva of infected animals and is typically transmitted through an animal bite, though contamination of any break in the skin with infected saliva may result in rabies. Animal rabies occurs on several of the Caribbean islands, particularly in the small Indian mongoose.

Rabies vaccine is safe, but a full series requires three injections and is quite expensive. Most travelers don't need rabies vaccine, but those at high risk for rabies, such as animal handlers and spelunkers, should certainly get the vaccine. In addition, those at lower risk for animal bites should consider asking for the vaccine if they are traveling to remote areas and might not have access to appropriate medical care if needed. The treatment for a possibly rabid bite consists of rabies vaccine with rabies-immune globulin. It's effective, but must be given promptly.

All animal bites and scratches must be promptly and thoroughly cleansed with large amounts of soap and water, and local health authorities should be contacted to determine whether or not further treatment is necessary.

## Schistosomiasis

A parasitic infection that is carried by snails and acquired by exposure of skin to contaminated freshwater, schistosomiasis has been reported in parts of the Dominican Republic, Guadeloupe, Martinique, Puerto Rico, Antigua and Barbuda, Montserrat and St Lucia. To find out whether or not schistosomiasis is present in the areas you'll be visiting, go to the World Health Organization's **Global Schistosomiasis Atlas** (www.who.int/wormcontrol/documents/maps/country/en/).

Early symptoms may include fever, loss of appetite, weight loss, abdominal pain, weakness, headaches, joint and muscle pains, diarrhea, nausea and a cough, but most infections are asymptomatic at first. Long-term complications may include kidney failure, enlargement of the liver and spleen, engorgement of the esophageal blood vessels and accumulation of fluid in the abdominal cavity. Occasionally, eggs may be deposited in the brain or spinal cord, leading to seizures or paralysis.

When traveling in areas where schistosomiasis occurs, you should avoid swimming, wading, bathing or washing in bodies of freshwater, including lakes, ponds, streams and rivers. Toweling yourself dry after exposure to contaminated water may reduce your chance of getting infected, but does not eliminate it. Saltwater and chlorinated pools carry no risk of schistosomiasis.

## Typhoid

Typhoid is uncommon on most of the Caribbean islands, except Haiti, which has reported a number of typhoid outbreaks.

Typhoid fever is caused by ingestion of food or water contaminated by a species of salmonella known as *Salmonella typhi*. Fever occurs in virtually all cases. Other symptoms may include headache, malaise, muscle aches, dizziness, loss of appetite, nausea and abdominal pain, diarrhea or constipation. Possible complications include intestinal perforation, intestinal bleeding, confusion, delirium and (rarely) coma.

Typhoid vaccine is recommended for all travelers to Haiti, and for travelers to the other islands who expect to stay in rural areas for an extended period or who may consume potentially contaminated food or water. Typhoid vaccine is usually given orally, but is also available as an injection. Neither vaccine is approved for use in children under the age of two. If you get typhoid fever, the drug of choice is usually a quinolone antibiotic such as ciprofloxacin (Cipro) or levofloxacin (Levaquin), which many travelers carry for treatment of traveler's diarrhea.

## Yellow Fever

Yellow fever occurs among animals on Trinidad and Tobago, but has not been reported among humans there in recent years. However, the yellow-fever vaccine is strongly recommended for travelers going outside urban areas in Trinidad and Tobago.

There's no yellow fever on the other Caribbean islands, but the following require proof of yellow-fever vaccination if you're arriving from a yellow-fever-infected country in Africa or the Americas: Aruba, Anguilla, Antigua and Barbuda, the Bahamas, Barbados, Bonaire, Curaçao, Dominica, Grenada, Guadeloupe, Haiti, Jamaica, Montserrat, Saba, St Kitts and Nevis, St Lucia, St Vincent and the Grenadines, Sint Eustatius, Sint Maarten, Trinidad and Tobago.

Yellow-fever vaccine is given only in approved yellow-fever vaccination centers, which provide validated International Certificates of Vaccination (yellow booklets). The vaccine should be given at least 10 days before any potential exposure to yellow fever and remains effective for approximately 10 years. Reactions to the vaccine are generally mild, and may include headaches, muscle aches, low-grade fevers or discomfort at the injection site. Severe, life-threatening reactions have been experienced but are extremely rare. In general, the risk of becoming ill from the vaccine is far less than the risk of becoming ill from yellow fever, and you're strongly encouraged to get the vaccine.

HEALTH

The yellow-fever vaccine is not recommended for pregnant women or children less than nine months old. These travelers, if arriving from a country with yellow fever, should obtain a waiver letter, preferably written on letterhead stationary and bearing the stamp used by official immunization centers to validate the International Certificate of Vaccination.

## TRAVELER'S DIARRHEA

To prevent diarrhea, avoid tap water unless it has been boiled, filtered or chemically disinfected (with iodine tablets); eat fresh fruits or vegetables only if cooked or peeled; be wary of dairy products that might contain unpasteurized milk; and be highly selective when eating food from street vendors.

If you develop diarrhea, be sure to drink plenty of fluid, preferably an oral rehydration solution containing lots of salt and sugar. A few loose stools don't require treatment, but if you start having more than four or five stools a day, you should start taking an antibiotic (usually a quinolone drug) and an antidiarrheal agent (such as loperamide). If diarrhea is bloody, persists for more than 72 hours or is accompanied by fever, shaking chills or severe abdominal pain, you should seek medical attention.

## ENVIRONMENTAL HAZARDS
### Bites & Stings

Do not attempt to pet, handle or feed any animal, with the exception of domestic animals known to be free of any infectious disease. Most injuries from animals are directly related to a person's attempt to touch or feed the animal.

Any bite or scratch by a mammal, including bats, should be promptly and thoroughly cleansed with large amounts of soap and water, then an antiseptic such as iodine or alcohol should be applied. The local health authorities should be contacted immediately regarding possible postexposure rabies treatment, whether or not you've been immunized against rabies. It may also be advisable to start an antibiotic, since wounds caused by animal bites and scratches frequently become infected. One of the newer quinolones, such as levofloxacin (Levaquin), which many travelers carry in case of diarrhea, would be an appropriate choice.

### MOSQUITO BITES

To prevent mosquito bites, wear long sleeves, long pants, a hat and closed-in shoes. Bring along a good insect repellent, preferably one containing DEET, and apply to exposed skin and clothing, but not to eyes, mouth, cuts, wounds or irritated skin. In general, adults and children over 12 should use preparations containing 25% to 35% DEET, which usually lasts about six hours. Children between two and 12 years of age should use preparations containing no more than 10% DEET, applied sparingly, which will usually last about three hours. Products containing lower concentrations of DEET are as effective, but for shorter periods of time. Neurological toxicity has been reported from DEET, especially in children, but appears to be extremely uncommon and generally related to overuse. Compounds containing DEET should not be used on children under the age of two.

Insect repellents containing certain botanical products, including eucalyptus oil and soybean oil, are effective but last only 1½ to two hours. Repellents containing DEET are preferable for areas where there is a high risk of malaria or yellow fever. Products based on citronella are not effective.

For additional protection you can apply permethrin to clothing, shoes, tents and bed nets. Permethrin treatments are safe and remain effective for at least two weeks, even when items are laundered. Permethrin should not be applied directly to skin.

Don't sleep with the window open unless there is a screen. If sleeping outdoors or in accommodations that allow entry of mosquitoes, use a bed net, preferably treated with permethrin, with edges tucked in under the mattress. The mesh size should be less than 0.06in (1.5mm). If the sleeping area is not otherwise protected, use a mosquito coil, which will fill the room with insecticide through the night. Wristbands impregnated with repellent are not effective.

### SEA STINGERS

Spiny sea urchins and coelenterates (coral and jellyfish) are a hazard in some areas. If stung by a coelenterate, apply diluted vinegar or baking soda. Remove tentacles carefully, but not with bare hands. If stung by a stinging fish, such as a stingray, immerse the limb in water at about 115°F (45°C).

### SNAKEBITES

Snakes are a hazard on some of the Caribbean islands. The fer-de-lance, which is the most lethal, has been spotted on Martinique and St Lucia. It generally doesn't attack without provocation, but may bite humans who accidentally come too close as it lies camouflaged on the forest floor. The fer-de-lance is usually 5ft to 6ft long, but may reach up to 9ft. Its coloration is gray or brown, with light stripes, dark diamond markings and a yellow throat.

The bushmaster, which is the world's largest pit viper, may be found on Trinidad. Like other pit vipers, the bushmaster has a heat-sensing pit between the eye and nostril on each side of its head, which it uses to detect the presence of warm-blooded prey.

Coral snakes, which are retiring and tend not to bite humans, are reported in Trinidad as well as other islands.

If a venomous snakebite occurs, place the victim at rest, keep the bitten area immobilized and move the victim immediately to the nearest medical centre. Avoid tourniquets, which are no longer recommended.

## Heatstroke

To protect yourself from excessive sun exposure, stay out of the midday sun, wear sunglasses and a wide-brimmed sun hat, and apply sunblock with SPF15 or higher. Sunblock should be generously applied to all exposed parts of the body about 30 minutes before sun exposure, and reapplied after swimming or vigorous activity. Travelers should also drink plenty of fluids and avoid strenuous exercise when the temperature is high.

## Water

Tap water is safe to drink on some of the islands, but not on others. Unless you're certain that the local water is not contaminated, you shouldn't drink it.

Vigorous boiling for one minute is the most effective means of water purification. At altitudes greater than 6500ft, boil for three minutes.

Another option is disinfecting water with iodine pills. Instructions are usually enclosed and should be carefully followed. Or you can add 2% tincture of iodine to 4½ cups of water (five drops to clear water, 10 drops to cloudy water) and let it stand for 30 minutes. If the water is cold, longer times may be required. The taste of iodinated water may be improved by adding vitamin C (ascorbic acid). Iodinated water should not be consumed for more than a few weeks. Pregnant women, those with a history of thyroid disease and those allergic to iodine should not drink iodinated water.

A good number of water filters are on the market. Those with smaller pores (reverse osmosis filters) provide the broadest protection, but they are relatively large and are readily plugged by debris. Those with somewhat larger pores (microstrainer filters) are ineffective against viruses, although they remove other organisms. Manufacturers' instructions must be carefully followed.

## TRAVELING WITH CHILDREN

In general, it's safe to take children to the Caribbean. However, because some of the vaccines listed in this chapter are not approved for use in children, you should be particularly careful to avoid giving kids tap water or any questionable foods or beverages. Make sure children are up to date on all routine immunizations. It's sometimes appropriate to give children some of their vaccines a little early before visiting a developing nation. You should discuss this with your pediatrician.

HEALTH

# Language

## CONTENTS

| | |
|---|---|
| Who Speaks What Where? | 844 |
| Phrasebooks & Dictionaries | 847 |
| **French** | **847** |
| Accommodations | 847 |
| Conversation & Essentials | 847 |
| Directions | 847 |
| Health | 848 |
| Language Difficulties | 848 |
| Emergencies | 848 |
| Numbers | 848 |
| Shopping & Services | 848 |
| Time & Dates | 849 |
| Transportation | 849 |
| **Spanish** | **849** |
| Accommodations | 849 |
| Emergencies | 850 |
| Conversation & Essentials | 850 |
| Directions | 850 |
| Health | 850 |
| Language Difficulties | 851 |
| Numbers | 851 |
| Shopping & Services | 851 |
| Time & Dates | 851 |
| Transportation | 852 |

The rich and colorful language environment of the greater Caribbean is testament to the diverse array of people that have come to call its many shores home. From a colonial past that saw the annihilation of virtually all traces of indigenous culture (and language) there is the legacy of Dutch, English, French, Portuguese and Spanish. Stir in a blend of elements from a veritable Babylon of other tongues and you begin to understand why almost every part of every island has its own peculiar linguistic offering.

Outside the predominant colonial languages, perhaps the most notable influences can be traced back to the slaves brought to the islands from West Africa to be exploited by the colonial masters. European tongues, creoles, patois (*pa*-twa), local accents and pidgins all go into the melting pot to create a linguistic symphony as rich and diverse as the region's enchanting musical offerings.

## WHO SPEAKS WHAT WHERE?
### Bahamas
English is the official language of the Bahamas and it is used in all facets of daily life. It's spoken by everyone but a handful of Haitian immigrants, who speak their own creole.

'True-true' Bahamanians, mostly black, usually speak both Bahamian Standard English (BSE) and their own distinct island patois, a musical Caribbean dialect with its own rhythm and cadence. Though there are variances among the islands, and between blacks and whites, all sectors of Bahamian society understand patois, the language of the street. Even educated Bahamians, who tend to speak in a lilting Queen's or Oxford English, will sometimes lapse into patois at unguarded moments.

### Cuba
Spanish is the official language of Cuba. Away from the hotels and tourist centers, few people speak English and then only very poorly. Despite this, many Cubans have some knowledge of English, since it's taught in primary school from grade six.

Cuban Spanish is rich, varied and astoundingly distinct. Slang and *dichos* (sayings) so dominate daily conversation that even native Spanish speakers sometimes get lost in the mix. Borrowing words from African languages, bastardizing English terms (Spanglish), and adopting language from movies, marketing and sports, Spanish in Cuba is constantly evolving, with newly invented words surfacing all the time.

### Eastern Caribbean
English is the main language spoken on all the islands except the French West Indies (Guadeloupe, Martinique, St-Barthélemy and French St-Martin), where French is the primary language.

English speakers can travel throughout the Eastern Caribbean without problems, and the difficulty of getting around the French West Indies for people who don't speak French is generally exaggerated. Although many people outside the hotel and tourism industry don't speak English, as

### A LITTLE HAITIAN CREOLE

Here are a few basics to get you started in the predominant lingo of Haiti.

| | |
|---|---|
| **Good day.** | Bonjou. (before noon) |
| **Good evening.** | Bonswa. (after 11am) |
| **See you later.** | Na wè pita. |
| **Yes.** | Wi. |
| **No.** | Non. |
| **Please** | Silvouple. |
| **Thank you.** | Mèsi anpil. |
| **Sorry/Excuse me.** | Pàdon |
| **How are you?** | Ki jan ou ye? |
| **Not bad.** | M pal pi mal. |
| **I'm going OK.** | M-ap kenbe. |
| **What's your name?** | Ki jan ou rele? |
| **My name is ...** | M rele ... |
| **May I take your photograph?** | Eske m ka fè foto ou? |
| **Do you speak English?** | Eske ou ka pale angle? |
| **I don't understand.** | M pa konprann. |
| **I'm looking for ...** | M'ap chache ... |
| **Where does the bus leave from?** | Kote taptap pati? |
| **I'd like to change money.** | Mwen ta vle chanje lajan. |
| **How much is it?** | Konbyen? |
| **I'm lost.** | M pèdi. |
| | |
| **Where is/are ... ?** | Kote ... ? |
| the toilets | twalèt yo |
| the hospital | lopital la |

long as you have a phrasebook and a reasonable English-French dictionary – and a measure of patience and a sense of humor – you should be able to get by.

Dutch is spoken on the islands of Saba, Sint Eustatius and Dutch Sint Maarten. While it remains the official language of government and is taught in schools, for most practical purposes it is a secondary language after English. See the boxed text (p846) for some basic Dutch words and phrases.

On many Eastern Caribbean islands the local language is Creole, a complex patois of French, English, and West African languages with remnants of Carib, the language of the indigenous people of the same name who once thrived in the region. In addition, Hindi is spoken among family members on islands with sizable Indian populations, most notably on Trinidad.

## Dominican Republic & Haiti

Spanish is Dominican Republic's official language and the language of everday communication. Some English and German is also spoken within the tourist business.

Any traveler who doesn't already speak some Spanish and is intending to do some independent travel in the Dominican Republic outside Santo Domingo or Puerto Plata is well advised to learn a little Spanish and carry a Spanish-English dictionary. See p849 for some useful Spanish words and phrases.

While for many years French has been considered the official language of Haiti, only 15% of the population can speak it, mainly the educated elite. The majority of the population speaks only Haitian Creole, and beyond the major centres it's the only sure means of communication. Language in Haitian society deepens the already massive divisions between social classes, as the government and the judicial system operate in French, and most schools also teach in French, further disadvantaging those who only speak Creole. Since the 1980s there has been a movement among reformists toward the increased use of Creole in civil society. Politicians have begun to make more speeches in Creole, musicians sing in it, more radio stations broadcast in it and there is now a weekly Creole-language paper, *Libète* (Liberty).

The vocabulary of Creole is predominantly French, peppered with a little English and Spanish, but the structure is considered to be closer to that of West African languages. It is worth learning a few phrases to use in smaller restaurants and for greetings (see the boxed text above for some basic words and phrases).

The number of English-speaking Haitians is on the rise, and in the larger cities, a combination of English and pidgin French will generally get you from A to B and enable you to order a beer when you get there.

## Jamaica

Officially, English is the spoken language. In reality, Jamaica is a bilingual country, and English is far more widely understood than spoken. The unofficial lingo, the main spoken language of poor Jamaicans, is called patois, a musical dialect with a staccato rhythm and cadence, laced with salty

LANGUAGE

## A FEW DUTCH WORDS & PHRASES

While it isn't necessary to speak Dutch to survive on the islands of Saba, Sint Eustatius and Dutch Sint Maarten, these Dutch basics might help you make some new friends in the East Caribbean. In the pronunciation guides, the 'backwards e' (ə) is a neutral vowel sound, like the 'a' in 'ago'; **kh** is like a raspy hiss produced in the throat.

**Hello.**
  *Dag/Hallo.*              dakh/ha-*loa*
**Goodbye.**
  *Dag.*                    dakh
**Yes.**
  *Ja.*                     yaa
**No.**
  *Nee.*                    nay
**Please.**
  *Alstublieft.* (pol)      als-tu-*bleeft*
  *Alsjeblieft.* (inf)      a-shə-*bleeft*
**Thanks.**
  *Bedankt.* (pol or inf)   bə-*dangt*
**That's fine/You're welcome.**
  *Graag gedaan.*           khraakh khə-*daan*
**Excuse me.**
  *Pardon.*                 par-*don*
  *Excuseer mij.*           eks-ku-*zayr* may
**I'm sorry.**
  *Sorry/Excuses.*          so-ree/eks-*ku*-zəs
**How are you?**
  *Hoe gaat het met*        hoo khaat hət met u/yow
  *u/jou?* (pol/inf)
**I'm fine, thanks.**
  *Goed, bedankt.*          khoot, bə-*dangt*
**What's your name?**
  *Hoe heet u?* (pol)       hoo hayt u
  *Hoe heet je?* (inf)      hoo hayt yə
**My name is ...**
  *Ik heet ...*             ik hayt ...

idioms, and wonderfully and wittily compressed proverbs.

Patois evolved from Creole English and a twisted alchemy of the mother tongue peppered with African, Portuguese, and Spanish terms and, in this century, Rastafarian slang.

Patois is deepest in rural areas, where many people don't know much standard English. Although it's mostly the lingua franca (linking language) of the poor, all sectors of Jamaica understand patois, and even polite, educated Jamaicans lapse into

patois at unguarded moments. Most Jamaicans will vary the degree of their patois according to whom they're speaking.

## Puerto Rico

Every Puerto Rican learns to speak Standard Modern Spanish in school, and this is the language you'll hear from hotel and restaurant staff if you address them in Spanish. However, many seasoned Spanish speakers find themselves a little off balance when they first hear Spanish in Puerto Rico. The Spanish you hear on the streets is Antillian Spanish or, as it's known locally, Boricua (the language of Borinquen). For a number of reasons, an ear accustomed to Castillian, Mexican or South American dialects of Spanish can take a little time to get used to the rhythm and sound of spoken Boricua.

Travelers hoping to submerge themselves in the island's rich culture need to have some command of basic Spanish, as well as some sense of the distinctions between Puerto Rican and other kinds of Spanish. However, even if you speak Spanish well, you can expect Puerto Ricans, proud of their hard-earned English skills, to address you in English. One of the great rewards for many travelers to Puerto Rico is remaining long enough at a destination to hear the locals address them in Spanish.

## Turks & Caicos

The official language of Turks and Caicos is English. The local islanders' distinct dialect bears much resemblance to the dialect of the Bahamas. The Haitians speak their own French-based creole patois, which foreigners may find difficult to follow. However, rarely is it as incomprehensible as it can be in Jamaica, for example.

## Virgin Islands

English is the main language spoken throughout the Virgin Islands, although you'll hear quite a bit of Spanish if you visit St Croix (see p849 for Spanish words and phrases). For the most part, islanders speak Standard English, but color it with an accent that is lyrical and euphonious. This distinctive accent derives from the traditional dialect of the islands, the so-called Creole, Calypso or West Indian, which blends West African grammar and speech patterns with colonial English, Danish, French and Dutch. Creole varies significantly from island to island, each displaying its own particular brand of local slang. It is easy to understand when spoken slowly, but sometimes islanders use their language as code when they speak to each other quickly and sprinkle in a strong dose of slang; *Doan worry. Dem jus' limin' and fowl bus'ness no cockroacy.* (Don't worry. They are just relaxing, and it's best to mind your own business.)

## PHRASEBOOKS & DICTIONARIES

An excellent resource to facilitate your hopping around the French-speaking islands is Lonely Planet's *French Phrasebook*. It's lightweight and compact, and it'll provide you with all the basics you need to get around and make new friends. There are also a number of good French-English/ English-French pocket dictionaries, such as those published by Langenscheidt, Larousse and Oxford Hachette.

On the Spanish-speaking islands, Lonely Planet's *Latin-American Spanish Phrasebook* is the perfect companion. Another recommended resource is the compact and surprisingly comprehensive University of Chicago *Spanish-English, English-Spanish Dictionary*.

# FRENCH

The French used in the Caribbean reflects hundreds of years of intermingling with English as well as West African languages. In addition to borrowing words freely from these other tongues, it's flatter in intonation, with less of the traditional French lilting cadence. Also, speakers of Creole pay less attention to gender; anything or anyone can be *il*. Nevertheless, in the following phrases both masculine and feminine forms have been indicated where necessary. The masculine form comes first and is separated from the feminine by a slash.

## ACCOMMODATIONS

| I'm looking for a ... | Je cherche ... | zher shersh ... |
|---|---|---|
| campground | un camping | un kom·peeng |
| guesthouse | une pension (de famille) | ewn pon·syon (der fa·mee·ler) |
| hotel | un hôtel | un o·tel |
| youth hostel | une auberge de jeunesse | ewn o·berzh der zher·nes |

### Do you have any rooms available?
*Est-ce que vous avez des chambres libres?*
e·sker voo·za·vay day shom·brer lee·brer
### May I see it?
*Est-ce que je peux voir la chambre?*
es·ker zher per vwa la shom·brer

| I'd like ... | Je voudrais ... | zher voo·dray ... |
|---|---|---|
| a single room | une chambre à un lit | ewn shom·brer a un lee |
| a double-bed room | une chambre avec un grand lit | ewn shom·brer a·vek un gron lee |
| a twin room with two beds | une chambre avec des lits jumeaux | ewn shom·brer a·vek day lee zhew·mo |

| How much is it ...? | Quel est le prix ...? | kel e ler pree ... |
|---|---|---|
| per night | par nuit | par nwee |
| per person | par personne | par per·son |

## CONVERSATION & ESSENTIALS

| Hello. | Bonjour. | bon·zhoor |
|---|---|---|
| Goodbye. | Au revoir. | o·rer·vwa |
| Yes. | Oui. | wee |
| No. | Non. | no |
| Please. | S'il vous plaît. | seel voo play |
| Thank you. | Merci. | mair·see |
| You're welcome. | Je vous en prie. | zher voo·zon pree |
| | De rien. (inf) | der ree·en |
| Excuse me. | Excuse-moi. | ek·skew·zay·mwa |
| I'm sorry. | Pardon. | par·don |

### What's your name?
*Comment vous appelez-vous?* (pol)
ko·mon voo·za·pay·lay voo
*Comment tu t'appelles?* (inf)
ko·mon tew ta·pel
### My name is ...
*Je m'appelle ...*
zher ma·pel ...
### Where are you from?
*De quel pays êtes-vous?* der kel pay·ee et·voo
*De quel pays es-tu?* (inf) der kel pay·ee e·tew
### I'm from ...
*Je viens de ...*
zher vyen der ...
### I like ...
*J'aime ...*
zhem ...
### I don't like ...
*Je n'aime pas ...*
zher nem pa ...

## DIRECTIONS
### Where is ...?
*Où est ...?*
oo e ...
### Go straight ahead.
*Continuez tout droit.*
kon·teen·way too drwa

## SIGNS

| Entrée | Entrance |
|--------|----------|
| Sortie | Exit |
| Ouvert | Open |
| Fermé | Closed |
| Interdit | Prohibited |
| Toilettes/WC | Toilets |
| Hommes | Men |
| Femmes | Women |

**Turn left.**
*Tournez à gauche.*    toor·nay a gosh
**Turn right.**
*Tournez à droite.*    toor·nay a drwat
**at the corner**
*au coin*    o kwun
**at the traffic lights**
*aux feux*    o fer
**far (from)**
*loin (de)*    lwun (der)
**near (to)**
*près (de)*    pray (der)

## HEALTH

| **I'm ill.** | *Je suis malade.* | zher swee ma·lad |
| **It hurts here.** | *J'ai une douleur ici.* | zhay ewn doo·ler ee·see |
| | | |
| **I'm ...** | *Je suis ...* | zher swee ... |
| **asthmatic** | *asthmatique* | (z)as·ma·teek |
| **diabetic** | *diabétique* | dee·a·bay·teek |
| **epileptic** | *épileptique* | (z)ay·pee·lep·teek |
| | | |
| **I'm allergic to ...** | *Je suis allergique ...* | zher swee za·lair·zheek ... |
| **antibiotics** | *aux antibiotiques* | o zon·tee·byo·teek |
| **nuts** | *aux noix* | o nwa |
| **peanuts** | *aux cacahuètes* | o ka·ka·wet |
| **penicillin** | *à la pénicilline* | a la pay·nee·see·leen |
| | | |
| **diarrhea** | *la diarrhée* | la dya·ray |
| **nausea** | *la nausée* | la no·zay |

## LANGUAGE DIFFICULTIES

**Do you speak (English)?**
*Parlez-vous (anglais)?*    par·lay·voo (zong·lay)
**Does anyone here speak English?**
*Y a-t-il quelqu'un qui parle anglais?*    ya·teel kel·kung kee par long·glay
**I understand.**
*Je comprends.*    zher kom·pron
**I don't understand.**
*Je ne comprends pas.*    zher ner kom·pron pa

## EMERGENCIES

**Help!**
*Au secours!*    o skoor
**There's been an accident!**
*Il y a eu un accident!*    eel ya ew un ak·see·don
**I'm lost.**
*Je me suis égaré/e. (m/f)*    zhe me swee·zay·ga·ray
**Leave me alone!**
*Fichez-moi la paix!*    fee·shay·mwa la pay

| **Call ...!** | *Appelez ...!* | a·play ... |
| **a doctor** | *un médecin* | un mayd·sun |
| **the police** | *la police* | la po·lees |

## NUMBERS

| 0 | zero | zay·ro |
|---|------|--------|
| 1 | un | un |
| 2 | deux | der |
| 3 | trois | trwa |
| 4 | quatre | ka·trer |
| 5 | cinq | sungk |
| 6 | six | sees |
| 7 | sept | set |
| 8 | huit | weet |
| 9 | neuf | nerf |
| 10 | dix | dees |
| 11 | onze | onz |
| 12 | douze | dooz |
| 13 | treize | trez |
| 14 | quatorze | ka·torz |
| 15 | quinze | kunz |
| 16 | seize | sez |
| 17 | dix-sept | dee·set |
| 18 | dix-huit | dee·zweet |
| 19 | dix-neuf | deez·nerf |
| 20 | vingt | vung |
| 21 | vingt et un | vung tay un |
| 22 | vingt-deux | vung·der |
| 30 | trente | tront |
| 40 | quarante | ka·ront |
| 50 | cinquante | sung·kont |
| 60 | soixante | swa·sont |
| 70 | soixante-dix | swa·son·dees |
| 80 | quatre-vingts | ka·trer·vung |
| 90 | quatre-vingt-dix | ka·trer·vung·dees |
| 100 | cent | son |
| 1000 | mille | meel |

## SHOPPING & SERVICES

**I'd like to buy ...**
*Je voudrais acheter ...*    zher voo·dray ash·tay ...
**How much is it?**
*C'est combien?*    say kom·byun

**Can I pay by ...?**
*Est-ce que je peux payer avec ...?*
es·ker zher per pay·yay a·vek ...

| | | |
|---|---|---|
| **credit card** | | |
| *ma carte de crédit* | ma kart der kray·dee | |
| **traveler's checks** | | |
| *des chèques de voyage* | day shek der vwa·yazh | |

| more | *plus* | plew |
|---|---|---|
| less | *moins* | mwa |
| smaller | *plus petit* | plew per·tee |
| bigger | *plus grand* | plew gron |

**I'm looking for ...** *Je cherche ...* zhe shersh ...

| a bank | *une banque* | ewn bonk |
|---|---|---|
| the hospital | *l'hôpital* | lo·pee·tal |
| the market | *le marché* | ler mar·shay |
| the police | *la police* | la po·lees |
| the post office | *le bureau de poste* | ler bew·ro der post |
| a public phone | *une cabine téléphonique* | ewn ka·been tay·lay·fo·neek |
| a public toilet | *les toilettes* | lay twa·let |
| the telephone centre | *la centrale téléphonique* | la son·tral tay·lay·fo·neek |

## TIME & DATES

| What time is it? | *Quelle heure est-il?* | kel er e til |
|---|---|---|
| It's (8) o'clock. | *Il est (huit) heures.* | il e (weet) er |
| It's half past ... | *Il est (...) heures et demie.* | il e (...) er e day·mee |
| today | *aujourd'hui* | o·zhoor·dwee |
| tomorrow | *demain* | der·mun |
| yesterday | *hier* | yair |

| Monday | *lundi* | lun·dee |
|---|---|---|
| Tuesday | *mardi* | mar·dee |
| Wednesday | *mercredi* | mair·krer·dee |
| Thursday | *jeudi* | zher·dee |
| Friday | *vendredi* | von·drer·dee |
| Saturday | *samedi* | sam·dee |
| Sunday | *dimanche* | dee·monsh |

| January | *janvier* | zhon·vyay |
|---|---|---|
| February | *février* | fayv·ryay |
| March | *mars* | mars |
| April | *avril* | a·vreel |
| May | *mai* | may |
| June | *juin* | zhwun |
| July | *juillet* | zhwee·yay |
| August | *août* | oot |
| September | *septembre* | sep·tom·brer |
| October | *octobre* | ok·to·brer |
| November | *novembre* | no·vom·brer |
| December | *décembre* | day·som·brer |

## TRANSPORTATION
### Public Transportation

| What time does ... leave/arrive? | *À quelle heure part/arrive ...?* | a kel er par/a·reev ... |
|---|---|---|
| boat | *le bateau* | ler ba·to |
| bus | *le bus* | ler bews |
| plane | *l'avion* | la·vyon |
| train | *le train* | ler trun |

| I'd like a ... ticket. | *Je voudrais un billet ...* | zher voo·dray un bee·yay ... |
|---|---|---|
| one-way | *simple* | sum·pler |
| round trip | *aller et retour* | a·lay ay rer·toor |

| I want to go to ... | *Je voudrais aller à ...* | zher voo·dray a·lay a ... |
|---|---|---|

| ticket office | *le guichet* | ler gee·shay |
|---|---|---|
| timetable | *l'horaire* | lo·rair |

### Private Transportation

**I'd like to hire ...**
*Je voudrais louer ...*    zher voo·dray loo·way ...

| a car | | |
|---|---|---|
| *une voiture* | ewn vwa·tewr | |
| a bicycle | | |
| *un vélo* | un vay·lo | |

**Is this the road to ...?**
*C'est la route pour ...?*    say la root poor ...

**Where's a gas/petrol station?**
*Où est-ce qu'il y a une station-service?*    oo es·keel ya ewn sta·syon·ser·vees

**Please fill it up.**
*Le plein, s'il vous plaît.*    ler plun seel voo play

**I'd like ... liters.**
*Je voudrais ... litres.*    zher voo·dray ... lee·trer

# SPANISH

In Spanish, nouns are either masculine or feminine, and there are rules to help determine gender (with exceptions, of course!). Where both masculine and feminine forms are included in this language guide, they are separated by a slash, with the masculine form first, eg *perdido/a* (lost).

## ACCOMMODATIONS

**I'm looking for ...**
*Estoy buscando ...*    e·stoy boos·kan·do ...

**Where is ...?**
*¿Dónde hay ...?*    don·de ai ...

| a guesthouse | *una pensión* | oo·na pen·syon |
|---|---|---|

## EMERGENCIES

| Help! | ¡Socorro! | so·ko·ro |
| Go away! | ¡Déjeme! | de·khe·me |
| | | |
| Call ...! | ¡Llame a ...! | ya·me a |
| an ambulance | una ambulancia | oo·na am·boo·lan·sya |
| a doctor | un médico | oon me·dee·ko |
| the police | la policía | la po·lee·see·a |

**It's an emergency.**
 Es una emergencia.  es oo·na e·mer·khen·sya
**Could you help me, please?**
 ¿Me puede ayudar,  me pwe·de a·yoo·dar
 por favor?  por fa·vor
**I'm lost.**
 Estoy perdido/a. (m/f)  es·toy per·dee·do/a

| a hotel | un hotel | oon o·tel |
| a youth hostel | un albergue | oon al·ber·ge |
| | juvenil | khoo·ve·neel |

**Are there any rooms available?**
 ¿Hay habitaciones libres?
 ay a·bee·ta·syon·es lee·bres
**May I see the room?**
 ¿Puedo ver la habitación?
 pwe·do ver la a·bee·ta·syon

| I'd like a ... | Quisiera una | kee·sye·ra oo·na |
| room. | habitación ... | a·bee·ta·syon ... |
| single | individual | een·dee·bee·dwal |
| double | doble | do·ble |
| twin | con dos camas | kon dos ka·mas |

| How much is it | ¿Cuánto cuesta | kwan·to kwes·ta |
| per ...? | por ...? | por ... |
| night | noche | no·che |
| person | persona | per·so·na |

## CONVERSATION & ESSENTIALS

| Hello. | Hola. | o·la |
| | Saludos. | sa·loo·dos |
| Good morning. | Buenos días. | bwe·nos dee·as |
| Good afternoon. | Buenas tardes. | bwe·nas tar·des |
| Good evening/ | Buenas noches. | bwe·nas no·ches |
| night. | | |
| Bye. | Hasta luego. | as·ta lwe·go |
| Yes. | Sí. | see |
| No. | No. | no |
| Please. | Por favor. | por fa·vor |
| Thank you. | Gracias. | gra·syas |
| Many thanks. | Muchas gracias. | moo·chas gra·syas |
| You're welcome. | De nada. | de na·da |

| Pardon me. | Perdón. | per·don |
| Excuse me. | Permiso. | per·mee·so |

(used when asking permission)
| Forgive me. | Disculpe. | dees·kool·pe |

(used when apologizing)

**How are you?**
 ¿Cómo está usted? (pol)  ko·mo es·ta oos·ted
 ¿Cómo estás? (inf)  ko·mo es·tas
**What's your name?**
 ¿Cómo se llama? (pol)  ko·mo se ya·ma
 ¿Cómo te llamas? (inf)  ko·mo te ya·mas
**My name is ...**
 Me llamo ...  me ya·mo ...
**Where are you from?**
 ¿De dónde es? (pol)  de don·de es
 ¿De dónde eres? (inf)  de don·de e·res
**I'm from ...**
 Soy de ...  soy de ...

## DIRECTIONS

**How do I get to ...?**
 ¿Cómo puedo llegar  ko·mo pwe·do ye·gar
 a ...?  a ...
**Is it far?**
 ¿Está lejos?  es·ta le·khos
**Go straight ahead.**
 Siga derecho.  see·ga de·re·cho
**Turn left.**
 Voltée a la izquierda.  vol·te·e a la ees·kyer·da
**Turn right.**
 Voltée a la derecha.  vol·te·e a la de·re·cha
**Can you show me (on the map)?**
 ¿Me lo podría indicar  me lo po·dree·a een·dee·kar
 (en el mapa)?  (en el ma·pa)

| **SIGNS** | |
| Entrada | Entrance |
| Salida | Exit |
| Información | Information |
| Abierto | Open |
| Cerrado | Closed |
| Prohibido | Prohibited |
| Servicios/Baños | Toilets |
| Hombres/Varones | Men |
| Mujeres/Damas | Women |

## HEALTH

**I'm sick.**
 Estoy enfermo/a.  es·toy en·fer·mo/a
**Where's the hospital?**
 ¿Dónde está el hospital?  don·de es·ta el os·pee·tal
**I'm allergic**  Soy alérgico/a  soy a·ler·khee·ko/a

| to ... | a ... | a ... |
|---|---|---|
| **antibiotics** | los antibióticos | los an-tee-byo-tee-kos |
| **nuts** | las fruta secas | las froo-tas se-kas |
| **penicillin** | la penicilina | la pe-nee-see-lee-na |

| **I'm ...** | Soy ... | soy ... |
|---|---|---|
| **asthmatic** | asmático/a | as-ma-tee-ko/a |
| **diabetic** | diabético/a | dee-ya-be-tee-ko/a |
| **epileptic** | epiléptico/a | e-pee-lep-tee-ko/a |

| **I have ...** | Tengo ... | ten-go ... |
|---|---|---|
| **diarrhea** | diarrea | dya-re-a |
| **nausea** | náusea | now-se-a |

## LANGUAGE DIFFICULTIES

**Do you speak (English)?**
¿Habla (inglés)?    a-bla (een-gles)
**Does anyone here speak English?**
¿Hay alguien que hable    ai al-gyen ke a-ble
inglés?    een-gles
**I (don't) understand.**
(No) Entiendo.    (no) en-tyen-do
**What does ... mean?**
¿Qué quiere decir ...?    ke kye-re de-seer ...

## NUMBERS

| 0 | cero | ce-ro |
|---|---|---|
| 1 | uno/a (m/f) | oo-no/a |
| 2 | dos | dos |
| 3 | tres | tres |
| 4 | cuatro | kwa-tro |
| 5 | cinco | seen-ko |
| 6 | seis | seys |
| 7 | siete | sye-te |
| 8 | ocho | o-cho |
| 9 | nueve | nwe-ve |
| 10 | diez | dyes |
| 11 | once | on-se |
| 12 | doce | do-se |
| 13 | trece | tre-se |
| 14 | catorce | ka-tor-se |
| 15 | quince | keen-se |
| 16 | dieciséis | dye-see-seys |
| 17 | diecisiete | dye-see-sye-te |
| 18 | dieciocho | dye-see-o-cho |
| 19 | diecinueve | dye-see-nwe-ve |
| 20 | veinte | vayn-te |
| 21 | veintiuno | vayn-tee-oo-no |
| 30 | treinta | trayn-ta |
| 31 | treinta y uno | trayn-tai oo-no |
| 40 | cuarenta | kwa-ren-ta |
| 50 | cincuenta | seen-kwen-ta |
| 60 | sesenta | se-sen-ta |
| 70 | setenta | se-ten-ta |
| 80 | ochenta | o-chen-ta |
| 90 | noventa | no-ven-ta |
| 100 | cien | syen |
| 200 | doscientos | do-syen-tos |
| 1000 | mil | meel |

## SHOPPING & SERVICES

**I'd like to buy ...**
Quisiera comprar ...    kee-sye-ra kom-prar ...
**How much is it?**
¿Cuánto cuesta?    kwan-to kwes-ta
**What time does it open/close?**
¿A qué hora abre/cierra?    a ke o-ra a-bre/sye-ra

**Do you accept ...?**
¿Aceptan ...?    a-sep-tan ...
**credit cards**
tarjetas de crédito    tar-khe-tas de kre-dee-to
**traveler's checks**
cheques de viajero    che-kes de vya-khe-ro

| **I'm looking for ...** | Estoy buscando ... | es-toy boos-kan-do ... |
|---|---|---|
| **the ATM** | el cajero automático | el ka-khe-ro ow-to-ma-tee-ko |
| **the bank** | el banco | el ban-ko |
| **the exchange office** | la casa de cambio | la ka-sa de kam-byo |
| **the market** | el mercado | el mer-ka-do |
| **the pharmacy** | la farmacia | la far-ma-sya |
| **the post office** | los correos | los ko-re-os |
| **the telephone centre** | el centro telefónico | el sen-tro te-le-fo-nee-ko |
| **the tourist office** | la oficina de turismo | la o-fee-see-na de too-rees-mo |

## TIME & DATES

| **When?** | ¿Cuándo? | kwan-do |
|---|---|---|
| **What time is it?** | ¿Qué hora es? | ke o-ra es |
| **It's (one) o'clock.** | Es la (una). | es la (oo-na) |
| **It's (seven) o'clock.** | Son las (siete). | son las (sye-te) |
| **half past (two)** | (dos) y media | (dos) ee me-dya |
| **today** | hoy | oy |
| **tonight** | esta noche | es-ta no-che |
| **tomorrow** | mañana | ma-nya-na |
| **yesterday** | ayer | a-yer |
| **Monday** | lunes | loo-nes |
| **Tuesday** | martes | mar-tes |
| **Wednesday** | miércoles | myer-ko-les |
| **Thursday** | jueves | khwe-ves |
| **Friday** | viernes | vyer-nes |

| | | |
|---|---|---|
| **Saturday** | *sábado* | *sa*·ba·do |
| **Sunday** | *domingo* | do·*meen*·go |
| | | |
| **January** | *enero* | e·*ne*·ro |
| **February** | *febrero* | fe·*bre*·ro |
| **March** | *marzo* | *mar*·so |
| **April** | *abril* | a·*breel* |
| **May** | *mayo* | *ma*·yo |
| **June** | *junio* | *khoo*·nyo |
| **July** | *julio* | *khoo*·lyo |
| **August** | *agosto* | a·*gos*·to |
| **September** | *septiembre* | sep·*tyem*·bre |
| **October** | *octubre* | ok·*too*·bre |
| **November** | *noviembre* | no·*vyem*·bre |
| **December** | *diciembre* | dee·*syem*·bre |

## TRANSPORTATION
### Public Transportion

| | | |
|---|---|---|
| **What time does** | *¿A qué hora ...* | a ke o·ra ... |
| **... leave/arrive?** | *sale/llega?* | *sa*·le/*ye*·ga |
| **the boat/ship** | *el barco* | el *bar*·ko |
| **the bus** | *el autobus* | el ow·to·*boos* |
| **the plane** | *el avión* | el a·*vyon* |
| **a ticket to ...** | *un boleto a ...* | bo·*le*·to a ... |

| | | |
|---|---|---|
| **one way** | *ida* | *ee*·da |
| **return** | *ida y vuelta* | *ee*·da ee *vwel*·ta |
| **bus station** | *la estación de* | la es·ta·*syon* de |
| | *autobuses* | ow·to·*boo*·ses |
| **ticket office** | *la boletería* | la bo·le·te·*ree*·a |

## Private Transportation

**I'd like to hire ...**

| | |
|---|---|
| *Quisiera alquilar ...* | kee·*sye*·ra al·kee·*lar* ... |
| **a bicycle** | |
| *una bicicleta* | *oo*·na bee·see·*kle*·ta |
| **a car** | |
| *un auto/un coche* | oon *ow*·to/oon *ko*·che |

**Is this the road to ...?**

| | |
|---|---|
| *¿Se va a ... por esta* | se va a ... por *es*·ta |
| *carretera?* | ka·re·*te*·ra |

**Where's a gas/petrol station?**

| | |
|---|---|
| *¿Dónde hay una bomba?* | *don*·de ai *oo*·na *bom*·ba |

**Please fill it up.**

| | |
|---|---|
| *Lleno, por favor.* | *ye*·no por fa·*vor* |

**I'd like ... liters.**

| | |
|---|---|
| *Quiero ... litros.* | *kye*·ro ... *lee*·tros |

# Glossary

**accra** – fried mixture of okra, black-eyed peas, pepper and salt

**agouti** – short-haired rabbitlike rodent resembling a guinea pig with long legs; it has a fondness for sugarcane

**Arawak** – linguistically related tribes that inhabited most of the Caribbean islands and northern South America

**bake** – sandwich made with fried bread and usually filled with fish

**bareboat** – sail-it-yourself charter yacht usually rented by the week or longer

**beguine** – Afro-French dance music with a bolero rhythm that originated in Martinique in the 1930s; also spelled 'biguine'

**bomba** – musical form and dance inspired by African rhythms and characterized by call-and-response dialogues between musicians and interpreted by dancers; often considered a unit with *plena*, as in *bomba y plena*

**breadfruit** – large, round, green fruit; a Caribbean staple that's comparable to potatoes in its carbohydrate content and is prepared in much the same way

**bush tea** – tea made from the islands' leaves, roots and herbs; each tea cures a specific illness, such as gas, menstrual pain, colds or insomnia

**cabrito** – goat meat

**callaloo** – spinachlike green, originally from Africa; also spelled 'kallaloo'

**calypso** – popular Caribbean music developed from slave songs; lyrics reflect political opinions, social views and commentary on current events

**Carnaval** – see *Carnival*

**Carnival** – major Caribbean festival; originated as a pre-Lenten festivity but is now observed at various times throughout the year on different islands; also called *Carnaval*

**casa particular** – private house in Cuba that lets out rooms to foreigners

**cassareep** – molasses-like sauce made from *cassava*, water, sugar and spices

**cassava** – a root used since precolonial times as a staple of island diets, whether steamed, baked or grated into a flour for bread; also called 'yucca' or 'manioc'

**cay** – small island; comes from an Arawak word

**cayo** – coral key (Spanish)

**chattel house** – type of simple wooden dwelling placed upon cement or stone blocks so it can be easily moved; often erected on rented land

**chutney** – up-tempo, rhythmic music used in celebrations of various social situations in Trinidad's Indian communities

**colombo** – spicy, East Indian–influenced dish that resembles curry

**conch** – large gastropod that, due to overfishing, is headed for the endangered-species list; its chewy meat is often prepared in a spicy *Creole*-style sauce; also called *lambi*

**conkies** – mixture of cornmeal, coconut, pumpkin, sweet potatoes, raisins and spice, steamed in a plantain leaf

**cou-cou** – creamy cornmeal and okra mash, commonly served with saltfish

**Creole** – people: person of mixed Black and European ancestry; language: local pidgin that's predominantly a combination of French and African; food: cuisine characterized by spicy, full-flavored sauces and heavy use of green peppers and onions

**dancehall** – contemporary off-shoot of reggae with faster, digital beats and an MC

**dasheen** – type of taro; the leaves are known as *callaloo*, while the starchy tuberous root is boiled and eaten like a potato

**daube meat** – pot roast seasoned with vinegar, native seasonings, onion, garlic, tomato, thyme, parsley and celery

**dolphin** – a marine mammal; also a common type of white-meat fish (sometimes called *mahimahi*); the two are not related, and 'dolphin' on any menu always refers to the fish

**duppy** – ghost or spirit; also called *jumbie*

**flying fish** – gray-meat fish named for its ability to skim above the water, particularly plentiful in Barbados

**fungi** – semihard cornmeal pudding similar to Italian polenta that's added to soups and used as a side dish; also a Creole name for the music made by local *scratch bands*; 'funchi' on Aruba, Bonaire and Curaçao

**gade** – street (Danish)

**gîte** – small family-run accommodations (French)

**goat water** – spicy goat-meat stew often flavored with cloves and rum

**gommier** – large native gum tree found in Caribbean rainforests

**green flash** – Caribbean phenomenon where you can see a green flash as the sun sets into the ocean

**guagua** – local bus; *gua-gua* in Dominican Republic

**houngan** – Vodou priest

**I-tal** – natural style of vegetarian cooking practiced by Rastafarians

**irie** – alright, groovy; used to indicate that all is well

**jambalaya** – a Creole dish usually consisting of rice cooked with ham, chicken or shellfish, spices, tomatoes, onions and peppers

**jintero/a** – tout or prostitute; literally 'jockey'

**johnnycake** – corn-flour griddle cake

**jug-jug** – mixture of Guinea cornmeal, green peas and salted meat

**jumbie** – see *duppy*

**jump-up** – nighttime street party that usually involves dancing and plenty of rum drinking

**lambi** – see *conch*

**limin'** – hanging out, relaxing, chilling; from the Creole verb 'to lime'

**mahimahi** – see *dolphin*

**mairie** – town hall (French)

**manchineel** – tree whose poisonous fruit sap can cause a severe skin rash; common on Caribbean beaches; called *mancenillier* on the French islands, and *anjenelle* on Trinidad and Tobago

**manicou** – opossum

**mas camp** – workshop where artists create *Carnival* costumes; short for 'masquerade camp'

**mauby** – bittersweet drink made from the bark of the rhamnaceous tree, sweetened with sugar and spices

**mento** – folk calypso music

**mocko jumbies** – costumed stilt walkers representing spirits of the dead; seen at *Carnival*

**mojito** – cocktail made from rum, mint, sugar, seltzer and fresh lime juice

**mountain chicken** – legs of the crapaud, a type of frog found in Dominica

**native seasoning** – homemade mixture of salt, hot pepper, cloves, garlic, mace, nutmeg, celery and parsley

**négritude** – Black Pride philosophical and political movement that emerged in Martinique in the 1930s

**obeah** – system of ancestral worship related to Vodou and rooted in West African religions

**oil down** – mix of *breadfruit*, pork, *callaloo* and coconut milk; national dish of Grenada

**out islands** – islands or cays that lie across the water from the main islands of an island group

**Painkiller** – popular alcoholic drink made with two parts rum, one part orange juice, four parts pineapple juice, one part coconut cream and a sprinkle of nutmeg and cinnamon

**paladar** – privately owned restaurant in Cuba serving reliable, inexpensive meals

**panyards** – place where *steel pan* is practiced in the months leading up to *Carnival*

**parang** – type of music sung in Spanish and accompanied by guitars and maracas; originated in Venezuela

**pate** – fried pastry of *cassava* or *plantain* dough stuffed with spiced goat, pork, chicken, *conch*, lobster or fish

**pepperpot** – spicy stew made with various meats, accompanied by peppers and *cassareep*

**plantain** – starchy fruit of the banana family; usually fried or grilled like a vegetable

**playa** – beach (Spanish)

**plena** – form of traditional Puerto Rican dance and song that unfolds to distinctly African rhythms beat out with maracas, tambourines and other traditional percussion instruments; often associated with *bomba*

**público** – collective taxis; *publique* in Haiti

**quelbe** – blend of jigs, quadrilles, military fife and African drum music

**rapso** – a fusion of *soca* and hip-hop

**reggaeton** – mixture of hip-hop, reggae and *dancehall*

**roti** – curry (often potatoes and chicken) rolled inside flat bread

**rumba** – Afro-Cuban dance form that originated among plantation slaves during the 19th century; during the 1920s and '30s, the term 'rumba' was adopted in North America and Europe for a ballroom dance in 4/4 time; in Cuba today, 'to rumba' means 'to party'

**salsa** – Cuban music based on *son*

**Santería** – Afro-Caribbean religion representing the syncretism of Catholic and African beliefs

**snowbird** – North American, usually retired, who comes to the Caribbean for its warm winters

**soca** – energetic offspring of *calypso*; it uses danceable rhythms and risqué lyrics to convey pointed social commentary

**son** – Cuba's basic form of popular music; it jelled from African and Spanish elements in the late 19th century

**souse** – dish made out of pickled pig's head and belly, spices and a few vegetables; commonly served with a pig-blood sausage called 'pudding'

**steel pan** – instrument made from oil drums or the music it produces; also called 'steel drum' or 'steel band'

**Taíno** – settled, *Arawak*-speaking tribe that inhabited much of the Caribbean prior to the Spanish conquest; the word itself means 'We the Good People'

**taptap** – local Haitian bus

**timba** – contemporary *salsa*

**Vodou** – religion practiced in Haiti that is a synthesis of West African animist spirit religions and residual rituals of the *Taino*

**zouk** – popular French West Indies music that draws from the *beguine*, cadence and other French Caribbean folk forms

# The Authors

## RYAN VER BERKMOES
### Coordinating Author, St Kitts & Nevis, Antigua & Barbuda, Montserrat, Barbados, Aruba, Bonaire & Curaçao

Ryan grew up in a beach town and always feels at home with a little sand lodged between his toes. He's written about beaches worldwide but still can never get over the stunningly turquoise Caribbean and its often blindingly white beaches. Yes it's a cliché, but it can also be breathtaking. Ryan also wrote the Destination Caribbean Islands, Getting Started, Itineraries, Snapshots, Caribbean Islands Directory and Caribbean Islands Transportation chapters.

## AMY C BALFOUR
### The Bahamas

Hooked on the Caribbean since winning a Bahamas trip in law school, Amy's always ready to return to the islands. Following that big win, fortunes dropped and she became a deskbound attorney, living her life in six-minute billable increments. Hearing the call of Hollywood, she ditched stability to try her hand at screenwriting and, after toiling as a document reviewer in downtown LA, she took a writer's assistant gig with *Law & Order*. Amy recently jumped from TV into full-time freelance writing; she's the author of Lonely Planet's *Los Angeles Encounter*, and has written for the *Los Angeles Times*, *Women's Health*, *Every Day with Rachael Ray*, *Backpacker*, *Redbook* and *Travelers' Tales*.

## PAUL CLAMMER
### Haiti

Molecular biologist, tour leader and now a travel writer, Paul has a penchant for heading to places many people head away from – on this trip he added Haiti to his previous work for Lonely Planet in Afghanistan and Nigeria. Getting behind the headlines, he's happy to report they're never as bad as the papers would have us believe – something a tour of Port-au-Prince's nightlife happily bore out. He'd like to think that Haiti first came to his attention from reading Graham Greene's *The Comedians*, but secretly wonders if childhood viewings of *Live and Let Die* didn't also play their part. He's already planning his trip to Carnival.

---

**LONELY PLANET AUTHORS**

Why is our travel information the best in the world? It's simple: our authors are passionate, dedicated travellers. They don't take freebies in exchange for positive coverage so you can be sure the advice you're given is impartial. They travel widely to all the popular spots, and off the beaten track. They don't research using just the internet or phone. They discover new places not included in any other guidebook. They personally visit thousands of hotels, restaurants, palaces, trails, galleries, temples and more. They speak with dozens of locals every day to make sure you get the kind of insider knowledge only a local could tell you. They take pride in getting all the details right, and in telling it how it is. Think you can do it? Find out how at **lonelyplanet.com**.

THE AUTHORS

### MICHAEL GROSBERG
**Dominican Republic**

Michael was raised in the Washington, DC, area, studied philosophy in Michigan and Israel, and then worked in business on a small island in the Northern Marianas. After a long trip through Asia and then across the US, he left to work as a journalist in South Africa. Michael's interest in Latin America began in earnest while pursuing work in literature in New York City, and his Spanish-language skills were improved by long and short trips in the region, including to Panama, Mexico, Ecuador, Puerto Rico and, of course, the Dominican Republic. More recently he has taught literature and writing in several NYC colleges, and headed around the world on other Lonely Planet assignments.

### SCOTT KENNEDY
**Turks & Caicos, St Lucia,
St Vincent & the Grenadines, Grenada**

Scott Kennedy grew up in the very untropical mountains of western Canada – perhaps that's why he's always been drawn to warm places. A divemaster, mojito connoisseur and sometime surfer, Scott has had sand in his surf trunks on beaches from Aitutaki to Zanzibar. In 2000 Scott moved to the Cayman Islands and spent six months falling in love with the Caribbean; he's had a long-distance love affair with the region ever since. He now lives in Queenstown, New Zealand, where he longs for snow white beaches and the green flash. Visit Scott's website at www.adventureskope.com.

### RICHARD KOSS
**Jamaica**

Ever since he first saw *The Harder They Come*, Richard dreamed of becoming a 'rude boy.' And although life as a Jamaican gangster lost its appeal over time, his infatuation with the island and all things Jamaican grew. A collector of vintage reggae, a rum aficionado and an ardent lover of jerk (some might call him a jerk-lover), he leapt at the opportunity to cover Jamaica when Lonely Planet came knocking. A native New Yorker, Richard has also worked on Lonely Planet's *New England* and *Jamaica* guides.

### JOSH KRIST
**Guadeloupe, Dominica, Martinique**

Josh Krist's first trip to the Caribbean was as a helper on a sailboat that traveled from Martinique to Grenada, with many stops along the way. As a diver he's explored reefs around the world but the Caribbean is still the best. He's lived in France and is marrying into a French family, so he can make bad jokes in French while not offending anyone; he also likes the good life, eating fine food and being in the warm sun. In short, he's getting ready for a full-time life of luxury in the Caribbean, but his destiny is thwarted every Wednesday and Saturday night at 7pm when the lottery numbers refuse to cooperate.

## TOM MASTERS
**Cuba, Cayman Islands**

Tom first experienced exhilarating Cuba at the end of 1999, when he traveled around the island with friends and saw in the new millennium in Havana. He's since been back to dive in various places around the Caribbean, and has a particular love of the Isla de la Juventud and Little Cayman. When not diving in the waters of the Caribbean, Tom works as a freelance writer in London. More of his work can be seen at www.mastersmafia.com.

## JENS PORUP

Jens is a playwright, novelist, essayist and guidebook author who lives in Cali, Colombia. He doesn't believe in taking holidays (it's better to live the life you want every day), but his curiosity got the better of him when Lonely Planet offered to send him to the Dominican Republic. He still doesn't believe in holidays, but if he did, he'd head to the southwest, his favorite part of the country. His website is at www.jensporup.com. Jens contributed to the Dominican Republic chapter.

## BRANDON PRESSER
**Anguilla, St-Martin/Sint Maarten, St-Barthélemy, Saba, Sint Eustatius**

After diving off the coasts of six continents, and working at a marine-life conservation center on the Caribbean's front door, Brandon was primed to take on the grueling task of hunting for hidden beaches on Anguilla and St-Barth. It wasn't all fun and games of course – he also devoted some serious time to testing ti-punch recipes on St-Martin/Sint Maarten. Brandon has written several other guides for Lonely Planet, including the recent *Thailand's Islands & Beaches*. When he's not on the road, this nomadic Canadian returns to his motherland to show off his tan and practice the fine art of couch surfing.

## BRENDAN SAINSBURY
**Puerto Rico**

Brendan is a Brit from the London area who is now based in Vancouver, Canada. His previous Lonely Planet work has included getting robbed in Cuba, getting lost in Angola and running 150 miles across the Moroccan desert to write a 600-word blog about the Marathon des Sables.

## ELLEE THALHEIMER
**Trinidad & Tobago**

The Caribbean continues to entice Ellee back to its warm shores and complex cultures. She has traveled, lived, worked and cycled throughout the region: she learned merengue in sweaty clubs in the Dominican Republic, used a machete on an ecotourism project on the Caribbean coast of Costa Rica, learned to scuba dive on Cay Caulker and got heat exhaustion cycling in Cuba. In Trinidad and Tobago, she grined on a sidewalk during the Carnival and was OK with that. She is a freelance writer, yoga instructor and bicycle guide based in Portland, Oregon.

## KARLA ZIMMERMAN
**US Virgin Islands, British Virgin Islands**

During her island travels, Karla hiked by feral donkeys on St John, ate an embarrassing number of *pates* on St Thomas, got splashed by beer-guzzling pigs on St Croix, bashed through the Baths on Virgin Gorda and relaxed into a stupor on Jost. She lives in Chicago with her husband, Eric, and writes travel features for newspapers, books, magazines and radio. She has authored or coauthored several of Lonely Planet's North American titles.

## CONTRIBUTING AUTHORS

**Nate Cavalieri** explored the south coast of Puerto Rico entirely on bicycle, recovering from the blisteringly hot afternoon rides with icy Medallas. When not traveling, he lives in Sacramento, California, where he is a writer and musician. Nate contributed to the Puerto Rico chapter.

**David Goldberg MD** completed his training in internal medicine and infectious diseases at Columbia-Presbyterian Medical Center in New York City, where he has also served as voluntary faculty. At present, he is an infectious-diseases specialist in Scarsdale, New York, and the editor-in-chief of the website MDTravelHealth.com. David wrote the Health chapter.

**Carolyn B Heller** first traveled to the Caribbean with her twin daughters when the girls were toddlers, and they've since snorkeled in Puerto Rico, learned to cook salt cod and plantains in Grenada, cheered for the French soccer team on Marie-Galante, and hiked through the rainforest in Guadeloupe. A freelance travel and food writer who's contributed to several Lonely Planet guidebooks, Carolyn has also written for a variety of publications, including the *Boston Globe*, *Los Angeles Times*, *FamilyFun* magazine, and *Travelers' Tales Paris*. She lives with her family in Vancouver, British Columbia. Carolyn wrote the Kids in the Caribbean box.

**Debra Miller-Landau** was a water baby from the get-go, growing up dipping her toes in the Pacific Ocean along the British Columbia coast. In California, she worked as a senior editor for Lonely Planet's Scuba Diving & Snorkeling series, where she read about so many Caribbean destinations that she finally had to get to the bottom of it (literally). To date, she's logged hundreds of underwater hours and an equal amount of time chatting with locals over a cold Carib. Deb wrote the Diving & Snorkeling chapter.

# Behind the Scenes

## THIS BOOK

This 5th edition of *Caribbean Islands* was written by
Ryan Ver Berkmoes, Amy C Balfour, Paul Clammer,
Michael Grosberg, Scott Kennedy, Richard Koss,
Josh Krist, Tom Masters, Jens Porup, Brandon
Presser, Brendan Sainsbury, Ellee Thalheimer and
Karla Zimmerman. The 4th edition of *Caribbean
Islands* was written by Debra Miller, Gary Chandler,
Conner Gorry, Thomas Kohnstamm, Alex Leviton,
Oda O'Carroll, Ginger Adams Otis, Liza Prado,
Michael Read and Ryan Ver Berkmoes. Kevin An-
glin coordinated the 3rd edition (known as *Eastern
Caribbean*), and Ned Friary and Glenda Bendure
coordinated the 2nd and 1st editions.

This guidebook was commissioned in Lonely
Planet's Oakland office, and produced by the
following:

**Commissioning Editors** Jay Cooke, Marina Kosmatos,
Lucy Monie
**Coordinating Editors** Susan Paterson, Laura Stansfeld,
Louisa Syme
**Coordinating Cartographer** Owen Eszeki
**Coordinating Layout Designer** Jim Hsu
**Managing Editor** Imogen Bannister
**Managing Cartographer** Alison Lyall
**Managing Layout Designer** Celia Wood
**Assisting Editors** David Andrew, Janice Bird, Chris
Girdler, Charlotte Orr, Tom Smallman, Simon Williamson

**Assisting Cartographers** Alissa Baker, Barbara Benson,
Marion Byass, Tony Fankhauser, Karen Grant, Tadhgh
Knaggs, Lyndell Stringer
**Assisting Layout Designer** Margie Jung
**Cover Designer** Pepi Bluck
**Project Manager** Craig Kilburn
**Language Content Coordinator** Quentin Frayne

**Thanks to** Heather Dickson, Tamara D'Mello, Brice
Gosnell, Errol Hunt, Lisa Knights, Adam McCrow, Wayne
Murphy, Malcolm O'Brien

## THANKS
### RYAN VER BERKMOES

Huge thanks go to the amazing team of authors
who worked on this book. The talent, dedication
and humor shown was some of the best in over
10 years with Lonely Planet. Thanks go to the
in-house team that included Lucy Monie at the
start, and then Marina Kosmatos, who picked up
the project in beachy California and took it home
to beachy Australia. Lots of people were essential to my time in the islands being a success.
Thanks go to Khalito Gomaa and Danilo Christian
on Bonaire; the magnificent Genevieve De Palm
and Helianthe Janssen Steenberg on Curaçao; the
hot and amazing Arrow on Montserrat; the simply
wonderful Angelique France on Nevis; and the

### THE LONELY PLANET STORY

Fresh from an epic journey across Europe, Asia and Australia in 1972, Tony and Maureen Wheeler
sat at their kitchen table stapling together notes. The first Lonely Planet guidebook, *Across Asia
on the Cheap,* was born.

Travelers snapped up the guides. Inspired by their success, the Wheelers began publishing
books to Southeast Asia, India and beyond. Demand was prodigious, and the Wheelers expanded
the business rapidly to keep up. Over the years, Lonely Planet extended its coverage to every
country and into the virtual world via lonelyplanet.com and the Thorn Tree message board.

As Lonely Planet became a globally loved brand, Tony and Maureen received several offers for
the company. But it wasn't until 2007 that they found a partner whom they trusted to remain true
to the company's principles of traveling widely, treading lightly and giving sustainably. In October
of that year, BBC Worldwide acquired a 75% share in the company, pledging to uphold Lonely
Planet's commitment to independent travel, trustworthy advice and editorial independence.

Today, Lonely Planet has offices in Melbourne, London and Oakland, with over 500 staff members and 300 authors. Tony and Maureen are still actively involved with Lonely Planet. They're
traveling more often than ever, and they're devoting their spare time to charitable projects. And
the company is still driven by the philosophy of *Across Asia on the Cheap*: 'All you've got to do
is decide to go and the hardest part is over. So go!'

delightful Tony Johnson on Antigua. At home it's Erin Corrigan and Annah – one is beautiful in a bikini, the other looks better in her cat box.

## AMY C BALFOUR

Thanks to Anne and Keene, Kenny Broad, and Sarah Wise for the pretrip scoop. Extra warm thanks to TJ and Erin Baggett for welcoming me Christmas Day, not to mention carting me around with Julie and Emily's assistance. Nancy and Michael, Brian, and Friends of the Environment, your Abaco insights were great. A special shout out to wonderful Penny Turtle – wish I could share more stories! Thanks to Peter and Betty for their Exuma assistance, and to the Small Hope staff and guests for their hospitality. Thanks Lucy, Marina, Ryan and Alison for guiding me through my first multicountry adventure.

## PAUL CLAMMER

*Krik? Krak!* Thanks above all goes to Jacqueline Labrom for her generosity of time and friendship in Port-au-Prince. Extra thanks also to Céline Chauvel, Jean Cyril Pressoir, Michael Geilenfeld, Leah Gordon and Richard Morse (the latter two proving that the Oloffson bar still remains the best place for serendipitous encounters). Cheers to André Eugene and the rest of the Grand Rue artists, along with Maurice Etienne in Milot, Mary at Radio Ibo, Toni Monnin in Pétionville and Christian Barriere in Port Salut. At Lonely Planet, big cheers as usual for Ryan VB. And thanks to Jo for holding the fort at home.

## MICHAEL GROSBERG

Special thanks to my fellow author Paul Clammer for his patience and cooperation; the same for Erin Corrigan and to author Jens Porup. To Rafael Antonio, my personal guide to DR culture. To Kim Bedall for sharing her knowledge of humpback whales. To Joseph who helped me with the police after my car was stolen. To Paul and Kate Hayes in Las Galeras; to Emily Maguire for her advice on Dominican literature and Juan Herrera for his tips on Santo Domingo. And most importantly to Rebecca Tessler: we will both always remember this trip.

## SCOTT KENNEDY

Thanks to my fellow authors, our fearless leader RVB, the dynamic editing duo of Marina Kosmatos and Lucy Monie, and the cartography skills of Alison Lyall. On the islands I was showered with help from too many people to mention – here are some of the all stars: Porter Williams, Delana Modeste, Zuri Reid, Nigel Fleming, Mark McLean, Melanie Clifton-Harvey, PJ Jones, Smitty, Ned Myopus, Adrian Nankivell and Neal Hitch and family. And a big thanks to

all of the hoteliers, restaurateurs and fellow travelers who helped me along the way, and most of all to my wife Sophie – for everything.

## RICHARD KOSS

Thanks to all the gracious people I met in Jamaica for their insights into that wonderful island. Thanks to Marina Kosmatos at Lonely Planet and coordinating author Ryan Ver Berkmoes for their infinite patience and wisdom, and to Gary Campbell and Anja Mutić for their company on the south coast leg of my trip. Finally, thanks to Latrell for not chewing up the furniture while I was away.

## JOSH KRIST

Thanks to Hélène Goupil, wife-to-be, navigator extraordinaire, and attuned to every accent mark in the French language; Alex Robinson, awesome friend, travel companion and photographer; Petch Somsakul, who brought warm Thai vibes to the Caribbean; Edine and Gros Pa; Lisa Berman and Dan Keeler, partners in crime; Andreas and Bianca Schnubel; Rosemary and Jacob Whitt; William, Jesse, Kerri and Miriam Krist; David Burgin; Jeff Ficker, David Proffitt and Joe Vazquez; Didier Bruneel and Mayte Saras; Jacqui Cerullo; Regis, Joëlle, and Elodie Goupil; Isabelle Motamedi; and all the locals who took the time to chat with me.

## TOM MASTERS

Thanks to James Bridle for braving non-veggie-friendly Cuba and for an unforgettable Christmas in Remedios! Thanks to the crews at Casa Abel in Havana, the wonderful Ángel at Hostal Florida Center in Santa Clara, the whole family at La Paloma in Remedios, and at El Mirador in Santiago de Cuba. In the Caymans many thanks to Eldemire's Guest House, Brac Reef on Cayman Brac and to the South Cross Club on Little Cayman. Also many thanks to Jonathon and Toby for their company in Santiago on New Year's Eve. Thanks to Lucy Monie and Marina Kosmatos at Lonely Planet, and to Ryan Ver Berkmoes for holding the project together!

## BRANDON PRESSER

Thanks to everyone I met while island-hopping, especially Yves and Joelle Michallet, Corine Mazurier, Tsara Lawrence, Lynn Costerano, Paul Cizek, Dale and Bob Oakes, Mickael Jurado, the gang at Secar, Beth Mears, Michele Faires, and the Diamonds International folks on Anguilla. *Merci à tous!* At Lonely Planet, thanks to the savvy production staff, especially Marina Kostmatos, and Lucy Monie. A hug to Alex Leviton, and props to Ryan Ver Berkmoes, coordinator extraordinaire.

## SEND US YOUR FEEDBACK

We love to hear from travelers – your comments keep us on our toes and help make our books better. Our well-traveled team reads every word on what you loved or loathed about this book. Although we cannot reply individually to postal submissions, we always guarantee that your feedback goes straight to the appropriate authors. Each person who sends us information is thanked in the next edition – and the most useful submissions are rewarded with a free book.

To send us your updates – and find out about Lonely Planet events, newsletters and travel news – visit our award-winning website: **www.lonelyplanet.com/contact**.

We may edit, reproduce and incorporate your comments in products such as guidebooks, websites and digital products, so let us know if you don't want your comments reproduced or your name acknowledged. For a copy of our privacy policy visit www.lonelyplanet.com/privacy.

And last but not least, a shout out to 17 Benefit St, and hugs to Elena for peanut-butter-and-jammin' with me Carib-style.

### BRENDAN SAINSBURY

Thanks to Marina for writing the script, Ryan for reining it in, Maria Antonia for the gorgeous apartment, Shannon for the two-wheeled tour of Vieques, Liz for her iron nerves on the Ruta Panorámica, Emilio for his enthusiastic *recorrido* of El Yunque and Kieran for – well – just being Kieran.

### ELLEE THALHEIMER

On these lovely islands, so many warm people pointed their fingers in the right direction for me. It would have been much less fun researching without you and the bike, Princess. A huge thanks to Gerard, who was so amusing and helpful. Courtney, your family and country are beautiful; thanks for showing me. Thanks to *bello* Gabrielle and Andria, Suzanne, Jap, and Anne Marie. Sylvie, your oranges are divine. Sula, you'd be my best friend. To Laura (for helping me realize), Diane Wilson, Sandra Bao and Poopie. At Lonely Planet, my gratitude goes to Marina, Ryan, and Lucy.

### KARLA ZIMMERMAN

Thanks to the following people for sharing their knowledge: Olasee Davis, Everard Faulkner, Ley Ordenes, Kevin Gray, Susan Keilitz, Lisa Beran, Kelly Smith and the folks from the Zimmerman Agency (BVI) and M Booth & Associates (USVI). Thanks to Ryan Ver Berkmoes, Marina Kosmatos, Lucy Monie and the coauthor brigade for patience and idea slinging. Thanks most of all to Eric Markowitz, the world's best partner-for-life.

## OUR READERS

Many thanks to the travelers who wrote to us: Stuart Allbaugh, Sola Bankole, Chris Brady, Petra Bridgemohan, Mikkel Brink-Pedersen, Nancy Burke, Susan Carels, Maggie Corrigan, Sian Crosweller, Hans Curvers, Dianne Denton, John Dipaolo, Francois Duclos, Gavin Dunbar, Robert Dutilh, Martina Ehrbar, Jean-Romain Falconnet, Heidi Frith, Krishna Gagné, Michael Ganz, Geoffrey Giles, Katie Gordon, Melissa Grella, Sam Handbury-Madin, Dianne Heede, Mieke Hermans, Kacie Hill, Richard Hopkins, Karl Ike, Carolyn Johnson, Jp Jp, Michaela Karger, Stanley J Kaster, Marie Kelly, Allan Kirch, Ogata Kuniko, Alona Lisitsa, Chris Lynch, Karen Maher, Jenny McDermott, John McEnroe, Elizabeth Minter, Ian Missenden, Bruno Moncorge, Michael Muenter, Sharmaine Nelson, Veronica Newton, Michael O'Dwyer, John Oconnell, Trygve Olfarnes, Jonas Orveus, Bethany Palmer, Stephane Panchout, Allen Pearl, Scott Petersen, John Pinzl, Bob Platel, Markus Schocker, Reto Schwab, Laetitia Sernaglia, Martin Shankeman, Nancy Shneiderman, Kathi Siegert, Michael Simone, Benjamin Singer, Siegfried Stapf, Jennifer Talbot, Rachel Toaff-Rosenstein, John Valiulis, Essa van Leighton, Martha van Genderen, Meghan Ward, Tony Wheeler, Steve Willard, John Williams, Kay Wilson, Mary Wimmer, Lesley Yeung, Ombretta Zanetti, Manuele Zunelli

## ACKNOWLEDGMENTS

Many thanks to the following for the use of their content:

Globe on title page ©Mountain High Maps 1993 Digital Wisdom, Inc.

Internal photographs p7 by Greg Johnston / Lonely Planet Images; p8 by Donald Nausbaum / Alamy; p9 (left) by Greg Johnston / Lonely Planet Images; p9 (right) by Helder Filipe / Alamy; p10 by Mark Webster / Lonely Planet Images; p11 (left) by Danita Delimont / Alamy; p11 (right) by Lee Foster / Lonely Planet Images; p12 by Christopher Baker / Lonely Planet Images; p13 by Robert Harding Picture Library Ltd / Alamy; p14 by Allan Montaine / Lonely Planet Images; p15 (left) by Richard Cummins / Lonely Planet Images; p15 (right) by Richard I'Anson / Lonely Planet Images; p16 by Eric Wheater / Lonely Planet Images.

All images are the copyright of the photographers unless indicated. Many of the images in this guide are available for licensing from Lonely Planet Images: www.lonelyplanetimages.com.

# Index

## A

Abacos 87-92
accommodations 815-17, see
    also individual countries
Accra Beach 685
activities 10-11, 31, 817-19, 10, 11
    see also individual activities
Adventure Farm & Nature Reserve 763
AIDS 840
air travel
    to/from the Caribbean islands
        829-30
    within the Caribbean islands 833-4
amber 294
Amerindian people 748
Andicuri Beach 791
Andros 100-2
Andros Town 100-2
Anegada 410-12, **392-3**
Anguilla 419-33, **421**, 14
    accommodations 430
    arts 422
    business hours 431
    climate 420
    culture 422
    embassies 431
    environment 422
    food 422
    history 420-2
    internet resources 432
    money 432
    music 429, 431
    travel to/from 432-3
    travel within 433
    visas 432
animals 48-9, see also birds, turtles
    dolphins 30, 48-9, 124
Annaberg Sugar Mill Ruins 375
Annandale Falls 713
Anse à Cointe 569
Anse à la Gourde 559
Anse Bertrand 560
Anse Céron 614
Anse Chastanet 640
Anse Crawen 569
Anse d'Arlet 620
Anse de Colombier 464
Anse de Gouverneur 463
Anse de Grande Saline 463
Anse La Raye 639

Anse La Roche 719
Anse l'Étang 616
Anse Mabouya 621
Anse Marcel 446
Anse Maurice 560
Anse Rodrigue 569
Anse Tarare 559
Anse Turin 612
Anses Gros Raisin 621
Antigua & Barbuda 517-39, **522**, **532**
    accommodations 534-5
    arts 520
    books 536
    business hours 536
    climate 518
    culture 519
    embassies 536
    environment 520
    food 520-1
    history 518-19
    internet resources 537
    language 812
    money 537
    music 520
    safe travel 536
    sports 519-20
    travel to/from 538-9
    travel within 539
    visas 538
Antigua 521-31, **522**
Apple Bay 400
Appleton Rum Estate 252
aquariums & zoos
    Ardastra Gardens & Zoo 70
    Atlantis Aquariums 76
    Barbados Wildlife Reserve 691
    Butterfly Farm (Grand Cayman)
        198-9
    Butterfly Farm (St Thomas) 366
    Butterfly Farm (St-Martin) 447
    Coral World 368-9
    Curaçao Sea Aquarium 808
    Donkey Sanctuary (Aruba) 790
    Donkey Sanctuary (Bonaire) 799
    Emperor Valley Zoo 740
    Rock Iguana Nursery 412
    Sint Maarten Park 438
    turtle farm 204
Arashi Beach 791
Arawak people 41

architecture 360
area codes 826-7
Arecibo Observatory 342
Argyle Falls 767
Arikok National Wildlife Park 790-1
Arnos Vale Rd 763
art galleries, see galleries
Arthur's Town 102
arts 45, see also books, individual
    countries, music
    painting 45, 265, 361
Aruba 780-91, **782-3**
Aruba, Bonaire & Curaçao 777-814,
    **782-3**, **794-5**, **800-1**
    accommodations 810
    arts 779
    books 799
    business hours 810-11
    climate 778
    culture 778-9
    embassies 811
    environment 779
    food 780
    history 779, 780-1, 784, 792,
        799-802
    internet resources 784, 793, 803
    language 812
    money 812
    music 779, 811
    safe travel 803, 811
    travel to/from 813
    travel within 814
    visas 812
Asa Wright Nature Centre 746-7
Ashton 668-9
ATMs 825
Aux Cayes 271-2
Ayo Rock 790

## B

Baby Beach 791
Bacardi Rum Factory 342
Bahamas, the 59-110, **62-3**, 15
    accommodations 102
    arts 61
    business hours 103
    climate 60
    culture 61
    embassies 104
    environment 61-3

Bahamas, the *continued*
food 63-4
history 60-1
internet resources 104
language 844
money 104
music 61
safe travel 67, 103-4
travel to/from 106-8
travel within 108-10
visas 106
Bahía Mosquito 344
Baie aux Prunes 444
Baie de Pont Pierre 569
Baie du Marigot 569
Baie du Moule 559
Baie Longue 444
Baie Mahault 572
Baie Nettlé 444
Baie Rouge 444
Balneario Escambrón 332
Bambara 129
bancroftian filariasis 839
Baracoa 180-3
Barbados 675-700, **677**, 15
accommodations 694
arts 678
books 696
business hours 696
climate 676
culture 677-8
embassies 697
environment 678-9
food 679-80
history 676-7
internet resources 697-8
money 698
music 678
safe travel 696-7
travel to/from 699
travel within 699-700
visas 698
Barbados Marine Reserve 689
Barbados Wildlife Reserve 691
Barbuda 531-4, **532**
Barclays Park 691
Barkers National Park 204
baseball 43, 44, 282, 293-4
Basse-Pointe 615
Basse-Terre 561-6, **548**
Basseterre 499-502, **501**

Basse-Terre town 565
Bassins Bleu 271
Bath Beach 694
Baths, the 405
Bathsheba 692-3
Bathways Beach 715
Batibou Bay 592
Battery Corre Corre 488
Bávaro 296-300, **298**
Bayahibe 317
beaches 31
Anguilla 426, 427, 428, 429, 430, 14
Antigua & Barbuda 525, 527, 530, 534, 535
Aruba, Bonaire & Curaçao 791, 798, 808, 809
Bahamas, the 70, 80-2, 86, 87, 89, 93, 95, 97, 15
Barbados 685, 686-7, 688-9, 691, 692, 694-5
British Virgin Islands 400, 402, 405, 407, 409, 412
Cayman Islands 196-204, 206
Cuba 159, 161, 168, 170, 181
Dominica 589, 592, 598
Dominican Republic 297, 301, 303-4, 310, 311
Grenada 710-13, 715-16, 718-19, 720
Guadeloupe 555, 556, 558-9, 560, 562, 569, 570, 571, 572, 573
Haiti 271, 272, 273
Jamaica 233-4, 235, 242, 247, 250-1
Martinique 612, 614, 616, 618, 620-1, 622, 623
Puerto Rico 332-3, 343, 344, 346, 382
Saba 477
St Kitts & Nevis 502, 504, 506, 509, 512
St Lucia 638, 635-6, 640, 644
St Vincent & the Grenadines 657, 659, 662, 664, 665, 667, 669, 670
St-Barthélemy 460-5
St-Martin/Sint Maarten 440, 441, 444, 445, 446, 447, 448-9
Sint Eustatius 488
Trinidad & Tobago 745, 747-8, 752, 753, 756-8, 760-1, 762, 763, 764, 767, 768
Turks & Caicos 116, 121, 127-8, 129, 130
US Virgin Islands 367, 369, 375-6, 379, 382

beaches, nudist
Antigua & Barbuda 527, 535
Guadeloupe 559, 569
St-Barthélemy 463
St-Martin/Sint Maarten 447
Beauséjour 572
Beef Island 402
Bellfield Landing Pond 128
Belvedere Hill 718
Bequia 660-4
Betty's Hope 530-1
bicycle travel, *see* cycling
bilharzia (schistosomiasis) 574, 624, 645, 841
Billy's Bay 250-1
birds 49, 533-4, 643
bird-watching
Antigua & Barbuda 533-4
Aruba, Bonaire & Curaçao 798
Bahamas, the 83
books 385, 413, 747
British Virgin Islands 410-11, 413
Cayman Islands 194-5, 207, 209, 211
Dominica 590
Grenada 715
Haiti 270, 274
Jamaica 242, 246, 250, 251
Puerto Rico 350
Saba 472
St Lucia 647
St Vincent & the Grenadines 659
Trinidad & Tobago 746, 747, 749, 750, 751, 752, 753, 762, 763, 765, 767, 768, 773
Turks & Caicos 116, 123, 128
US Virgin Islands 372, 385
Black River 250
Black River Great Morass 250
Black Rocks 506
Blanchisseuse 748-9
Bloody Bay 765
Bloody Bay Marine Park 55, 194, 209
Bloody Point 504
Blowing Point 426
Blue Beach 344
Blue Lagoon 234
Blue Mountains, the 231
Blue Mountains-John Crow National Park 231
Bluff, the 207
boat travel, *see also* boat trips, yachting
itineraries 33

to/from the Caribbean islands 830-4
within the Caribbean islands 834-5
boat trips 818, *see also* boat travel, yachting
 Aruba, Bonaire & Curaçao 786, 793
 Bahamas, the 70-2, 89, 98
 Barbados 695
 British Virgin Islands 396, 405-6
 Cuba 183
 Dominica 590-1
 Dominican Republic 298
 Guadeloupe 560, 563
 Jamaica 242, 251
 Martinique 618
 Puerto Rico 344, 346, 352
 St Kitts & Nevis 512
 St Vincent & the Grenadines 657, 660, 661, 662, 668
 St-Barthélemy 458, 465
 St-Martin/Sint Maarten 438, 440, 445, 449
 Trinidad & Tobago 745, 752, 761, 763-4, 767, 773
 Turks & Caicos 124
 US Virgin Islands 370, 379, 381, 384
Boca del Diablo 304
Boca Grandi 791
Boca Prins 791
Bodden Town 205
Boeri Lake 595
Bogue Lagoon 242
Boiling Lake 595
Bonaire 791-9, **794-5**
Bonaire Marine Park 55, 56, 799
Bond, James 48, 90, 98, 342
bonefishing, *see* fishing
Booby Cay 247
Booby Island 768
Booby Pond Nature Reserve 209
books, *see also individual countries*
 biographies 32
 bird-watching 385, 413, 747
 diving 52, 799
 fiction 32
 food 49
 health 838
 history 32, 41, 42
 language 847
 religion 45
Borne 592
Bosque Estatal de Guánica 350
Boston Bay 234
Bottom, the 477

Bourg des Saintes 567-9
Bozo Beach 311
Brades 543
Brasso Seco 749-50
Brewers Bay 367, 400
Bridgetown 680-4, **681**
Brimstone Hill Fortress National Park 505, 9
British Virgin Islands 390-418, **392-3**
 accommodations 412
 arts 393
 books 413
 business hours 413
 climate 391
 culture 393
 environment 394
 food 394-5, 412
 history 391-3
 internet resources 414
 language 846-7
 money 414
 music 393, 400
 safe travel 396, 413
 travel to/from 415-17
 travel within 417-18
 visas 415
Buccoo 760-2
Buccoo Reef 761
Buck Island Reef National Monument 381
bus travel 835-6
business hours 819, *see also individual countries*

# C

Cabarete 310-13
Cabbage Beach 76-7
Cabrits National Park 591
Caicos Islands 120-30, **112**
Calabash Bay 250-1
Caledonia Rainforest 383
Calibishie 592
California Lighthouse 789
Callwood Rum Distillery 400
calypso music 46, 730
Cane Garden Bay 400-2
Caneel Bay 375
Canoe Bay 758
canoeing, *see* kayaking
Canouan 665-7
canyoning 594
Cap Chevalier 621
Capesterre 572
Capesterre-Belle-Eau 563
Cap-Haïtien 272-3

Captain Bill's Blue Hole 101
car travel 835, 836
Carapichaima 750-1
Caravelle Beach 556
Carbet 612
Carib people 41
Carib Territory 592-3
Carnival 45, 185
 Antigua & Barbuda 536, 823
 Aruba, Bonaire & Curaçao 786, 811
 Cayman Islands 212
 Cuba 823
 Dominica 599
 Dominican Republic 290, 319-20
 Grenada 722
 Guadeloupe 554, 575
 Haiti 261, 275
 Jamaica 225, 236, 254
 Martinique 610, 624
 Puerto Rico 353
 St Kitts & Nevis 514
 St Lucia 634
 St-Barthélemy 466
 St-Martin/Sint Maarten 450
 Sint Eustatius 492
 Trinidad & Tobago 738-9, 740, 744, 823
 US Virgin Islands 385
Caroni Bird Sanctuary 750
Carrefour Badyo 270
Carriacou 716-19
Cascada El Limón 301, 306, 9
Cascade aux Écrevisses 561
Case-Pilote 612
cash 825
Casibari Rock 790
Castara 763-4
Castillo de San Pedro del Morro 175
Castries 632-5, **633**
Castro, Fidel 138-9, 174
Casuarina Beach 669
Cat Island 102
cathedrals, *see* churches
caves
 Barbuda 534
 Gran Caverna de Santo Tomás 161
 Parque de las Cavernas del Río Camuy 342
Cayman Brac 206-8
Cayman Islands 192-214, **198-9, 208-9**
 accommodations 210-11
 arts 194
 business hours 211
 climate 193

Cayman Islands *continued*
  culture 194
  embassies 212
  environment 194-5
  food 195
  history 193-4
  money 212
  travel to/from 213
  travel within 213-14
  visas 213
Cayo Blanco 170
Cayo Jutías 161
Cayo Levantado 301
Cayo Santa María 168
cell phones 826
Chacachacare 745
Chaguanas 750
Chaguaramas 744-6
Chalk Sound National Park 121
Chapel of Alto Vista 789
Charlestown 507-9, **508**
Charlotte Amalie 363-8
Charlotteville 768-9
Chaudiere Pool 592
Cherry Tree Hill 691
children, travel with 819-21
  Antigua & Barbuda 536
  Aruba, Bonaire & Curaçao 811
  Bahamas, the 103
  Barbados 696
  British Virgin Islands 413
  Cayman Islands 197, 211
  Cuba 149, 184
  Dominica 599
  Dominican Republic 290, 319
  Grenada 721
  Guadeloupe 574
  health 843
  Jamaica 254
  Martinique 624
  Puerto Rico 333, 352
  St Kitts & Nevis 514
  St Lucia 645
  St Vincent & the Grenadines 671
  St-Martin/Sint Maarten 449
  Trinidad & Tobago 771
  US Virgin Islands 385
Choiseul 643
Christiansted 378-81
Christmas Rebellion 244
Christoffel National Park 810

**000** Map pages
000 Photograph pages

churches, *see also* convents & monasteries, synagogues
  Anglican Trinity Cathedral 741
  Catedral de San Cristóbal de la Habana 144
  Catedral Primada de América 288
  Cathedral of the Immaculate Conception 633
  Chapel of Alto Vista 789
  Iglesia de San José 331
  St James Parish Church 242
  St Michael's Cathedral 682
  St Paul's Anglican Church 528
  Ste Trinité Episcopalian Cathedral 267-8
Chutes du Carbet 563-4
cigars
  Bahamas, the 69, 75
  Cuba 145, 166, 174
  Dominican Republic 294
Cinnamon Bay 375-6
Citadelle, the 273-4
Clifton 668-9
climate 27-8, 821, *see also* hurricanes, *individual countries*
climate change 831
Club Med Beach 95
Coakley Town 100-2
Cockburn Town 115-19, **117**
cockfighting 282-3, 294
Cockleshell Bay 504
Coco Point 534
Codrington 533
Codrington Lagoon 533-4
coffee 51
  Guadeloupe 562
  Haiti 266
  Jamaica 225
  Puerto Rico 338, 353
Coki Bay 369
Columbus, Christopher 41
Columbus Landfall National Park 116
Como Hill 102
Concord Falls 716
Constanza 297
consulates 822, *see also individual countries*
convents & monasteries
  Convento de la Orden de los Predicadores 288
  l'Habitation Fond St-Jacques 616
  Monasterio de San Francisco 289
  Mt St Benedict 746
Cooper Island 404
Copper Mine National Park 405

Coral Bay 376-7
Cormier Plage 273
Corossol 463
costs 28-9
Côte des Arcadins 270
Cottage Pond 128
Cove Bay 427-8
Cow Wreck Bay 411
Coward, Sir Noël 239
Crane Beach 688
credit cards 825
Creole 845
cricket 43-4
  Antigua & Barbuda 519-20
  Barbados 678, 684
  Grenada 704
  Jamaica 229
  St Kitts & Nevis 500
  Trinidad & Tobago 729-30
crime 821-2
Croix des Bouquets 270
Crown Point 756-60, **757**
cruises 830-3
Cruz Bay 371-4
Cruzan Rum Distillery 383
Cuba 135-91, **137**
  accommodations 183
  arts 45, 140
  books 184
  business hours 184
  climate 136
  culture 139-40
  embassies 185
  environment 140
  food 140-1
  history 136-9
  language 844
  money 186
  music 140, 155-6, 12
  safe travel 184-5
  travel restrictions 189
  travel to/from 188, 189
  travel within 188-91
  visas 187-8
Cueva del Aguas 181
Culebra 346-7
culture 43, *see also individual countries*
Cupecoy Beach 441
Curaçao 799-810, **800-1**
customs regulations 821
cycling 817, 834
  Aruba, Bonaire & Curaçao 793
  British Virgin Islands 410
  Dominica 597, 598
  Dominican Republic 312, 316, 318

Grenada 708, 720
Jamaica 247
Puerto Rico 333, 350
St Kitts & Nevis 509
St Lucia 641
St Vincent & the Grenadines 657
Trinidad & Tobago 730, 745, 749, 758, 764, 768, 773
Cyvadier Plage 271

# D
Damajagua 313
dancehall music 46, 220
Darkwood Beach 527
Davenna Yoga Centre 751
Dawn Beach 448
Deep Bay 527
Deep Vein Thrombosis 838
Dellis Cay 123
dengue fever 839
Deshaies 562-3
Devil's Bay 405
Devil's Bridge 530
Diamant 620
Diamond Botanical Gardens 640
diarrhea 842
Dick Hill Creek 128
Dickenson Bay 525-6
Dieppe Bay 506
digital photography 825-6
disabilities, travelers with 827-8
    Antigua & Barbuda 537-8
    Aruba, Bonaire & Curaçao 812
    Bahamas, the 105
    Barbados 698
    British Virgin Islands 415
    Dominica 600
    Guadeloupe 576
    Martinique 625
    Puerto Rico 354
    St Kitts & Nevis 515
    St Lucia 647
    St-Martin/Sint Maarten 451
    Trinidad & Tobago 773
    Turks & Caicos 133
    US Virgin Islands 386
Distillerie Bielle 572
Distillerie Poisson 572
diving & snorkeling 52-8, 817
    Anguilla 424, 427, 428-9, 430-1
    Antigua & Barbuda 527, 529, 530, 535-6
    Aruba, Bonaire & Curaçao 55, 56, 785, 798, 799, 809, 810

Bahamas, the 70, 83, 86, 87, 89, 91, 92, 93, 98, 101, 102-3
Barbados 682, 688-9, 690, 695
books 52, 799
British Virgin Islands 56, 396, 398, 399, 400, 404, 405, 408, 410, 411, 412-13
Cayman Islands 55, 199-200, 206, 207, 209, 211
courses 52-3
Cuba 160, 164, 170, 183
Dominica 57, 587, 590, 591, 596-7, 598
Dominican Republic 298, 304, 307, 310, 312, 318
emergencies 477, 793
Grenada 710, 711, 712, 713, 715, 717, 719, 720-1
Guadeloupe 555, 559, 560, 563, 565, 567, 569, 572, 573-4
Haiti 274
internet resources 54
Jamaica 236, 242, 247, 252-3
Martinique 613-14, 618, 619, 620, 621, 622, 623
Montserrat 544
Puerto Rico 333, 344, 346, 350-1, 352
responsible diving 54-5
Saba 55, 56-7, 474, 477, 478, 10
St Kitts & Nevis 500, 503, 509, 512-13
St Lucia 55-6, 634, 638, 640, 641, 644
St Vincent & the Grenadines 58, 657, 662, 665, 668, 669, 670-1
St-Barthélemy 458, 461, 463, 464, 465
St-Martin/Sint Maarten 447, 449
Sint Eustatius 55, 57, 488-9
Trinidad & Tobago 56, 758, 761, 763, 764, 767, 768, 770, 773
Turks & Caicos 57, 116, 119, 123, 124, 130-1
US Virgin Islands 369, 372-3, 375, 376, 379, 380, 381, 384
Doctor's Cave Beach 242
Dogs, the 404
dolphins 30, 48-9, 124
Domaine de Bellevue 572
Dominica 580-602, **582**
    accommodations 597
    arts 583
    books 583, 599
    business hours 599

climate 581
culture 583
embassies 599
environment 583-4
food 584
history 581-3
internet resources 600
money 600
music 595, 599
safe travel 599
travel to/from 601
travel within 601-2
visas 600
Dominican Republic 278-323, **280**, 9
    accommodations 318
    arts 283
    books 283, 319
    border crossings 321
    business hours 319
    climate 279
    culture 282
    embassies 319
    environment 283-4
    food 284
    history 307
    language 845
    money 320
    music 283, 290, 312
    safe travel 285, 319
    travel to/from 321-2
    travel within 322-3
    visas 320
Dos Playa 791
Dover Beach 686-7
drinks 51, see also coffee, rum
driver's licenses 836
driving, see car travel
drugs 254, 771, 824
Dungeon 399
Dunn's River Falls 235
Dutch language 846

# E
Eagle Beach 791
East Bay Islands National Park 128
East Caicos 130
East End (Anegada) 411-12
East End (Grand Cayman) 205
East End (St Thomas) 368-70
East End (Tortola) 402-3
El Mogote 316
El Yunque (Cuba) 181
El Yunque (Puerto Rico) 343
Elbow Cay 90-1
electricity 816

elephantiasis 839
Eleuthera 92-6
embassies 822, *see also individual countries*
Emerald Pool 593-4
emergencies, *see inside front cover*
English Harbour 528-30
Englishman's Bay 764
Enterprise Beach 687
environment 46-9, *see also individual countries*
environmental issues 26, 48, 49, *see also* responsible travel
    Aruba, Bonaire & Curaçao 779-80
    Bahamas, the 63
    Barbados 679
    British Virgin Islands 394
    Dominica 584
    Dominican Republic 283-4
    Grenada 705
    Haiti 266
    St Vincent & the Grenadines 653, 666
    Trinidad & Tobago 731, 761
    US Virgin Islands 362, 375
Estate Whim Plantation 383
events, *see* festivals
exchange rates 824, *see also inside front cover*
Exuma Cays 98
Exuma Cays Land & Sea Park 98
Exumas 96-100

**F**
Fairy Hill 234
Falls of Baleine 660
Falmouth 246
Falmouth Harbour 528
Farley Hill National Park 691
fascioliasis 839
Ferry 97
ferry travel 833, 834
festivals 822, 823, *see also* Carnival, music festivals, regattas
    Anguilla Summer Festival 431
    Annual Music & Cultural Festival 131
    BVI Emancipation Festival 414
    Crop-Over Festival 697, 823
    Cruzan Christmas Fiesta 379, 385
    Easter Weekend 761

    Fiesta de Santiago Apostal 353, 823
    Independence Day 599
    Jamaica Coffee Festival 225
    Junkanoo 73, 823
    Las Parrandas 168
    Nine Mornings Festival 671
    Pirates Week 212
    Saba Summer Festival 479
    Sunday School 761
    Vincy Mas 657
    Virgin Gorda Easter Festival 406, 413
Feuillère 572
Fig Tree 510
Fig Tree Dr 528
Firefly 238-9
fishing 817
    Bahamas, the 72, 83, 89, 98, 103
    British Virgin Islands 410
    Cayman Islands 200-1, 207, 209, 211, 212
    Dominican Republic 298
    Jamaica 232, 242, 247, 253
    Puerto Rico 333, 344
    St-Barthélemy 458, 465
    Trinidad & Tobago 745, 768, 770, 773
    Turks & Caicos 118, 124
    US Virgin Islands 384
Five Islands 527
Flagstaff Hill 768
Flamands 463-4
Flamingo Pond (Anegada) 410-11
Flamingo Pond (North Caicos) 128
Flash of Beauty 412
Flat Point 473
Flower Forest of Barbados 692
food 49-51, 412, *see also individual countries*
football 730
Fort Bay (Antigua) 525
Fort Bay (Saba) 478
Fort Frederik Beach 382
Fort George Cay 123
Fort George Land & Sea National Park 123
Fort-de-France 607-12, **609**
forts
    Brimstone Hill Fortress 505, 9
    Castillo de la Real Fuerza 144
    Castillo de San Pedro del Morro 175
    Fort Amsterdam (Curaçao) 803
    Fort Amsterdam (Sint Eustatius) 488
    Fort Barrington 527

    Fort Bennett 762
    Fort Campbelton 768
    Fort Charles 230-1
    Fort Charlotte 656-7
    Fort Christiansvaern 378
    Fort de Windt 488
    Fort Frederick 708
    Fort George 708
    Fort Granby 767
    Fort James 525
    Fort King George 765-6
    Fort Napoléon 569
    Fort Oranje 486
    Fort Recovery 399
    Fort Rodney 638
    Fort Rotterdam 488
    Fort Shirley 591
    Fortaleza Ozama 288
    Frederick's Battery 488
    Fuerte San Cristóbal 331
    Fuerte San Felipe del Morro 331
    Parque Histórico Militar Morro-Cabaña 159
Frederiksted 382-3
Freeport 79-86, **81**, **82**
French language 847-9
French Cay 123
French Cul-de-Sac 446-7
Frenchman's Bay 250-1
Frenchman's Cove 233-4
Frenchman's Creek 121
Fresh Creek 100-2
Freshwater Lake 595
Friar's Bay 444
Friendship Bay 662, 664
Frigate Bay 502-4
full-moon parties 401, 402, 444
Fustic 690

**G**
galleries
    Access Art 785
    Anguilla 422
    Centro Wilfredo Lam 144
    Grand Rue artists 268
    Kate Spencer 506
    Molinière Bay 710
    Museo de Arte de Puerto Rico 332
    Museo del Arte de Ponce 348
    Museo Nacional de Bellas Artes 148
    Museum of Haitian Art 267
    National Gallery 223
    National Museum & Art Gallery 740

St-Barthélemy 457
Tobago Art Gallery 758
Willemstad 804
Garcia Beach 344
gardens & parks
Andromeda Botanic Gardens 692
Barclays Park 691
Botanical Gardens of Nevis 510
Diamond Botanical Gardens 640
Flower Forest of Barbados 692
Graeme Hall Nature Sanctuary 685
Jardín Botánico Nacional 289
Jardin de Balata 615
JR O'Neal Botanic Gardens 396
Le Parc aux Orchidées 562
Mamiku Gardens 643
Miriam C Schmidt Botanical
  Gardens 488
Queen Elizabeth II Botanic Park 205
St George Village Botanical Garden
  384
St Vincent Botanic Gardens 657
Shaw Park Gardens 236
Valombreuse Floral Park 563
Wreck of the Ten Sails Park 205
Garibaldi Hill 544
Gasparee Grande 745
gay & lesbian travelers 822-3
Antigua & Barbuda 536
Aruba, Bonaire & Curaçao 811
Bahamas, the 104
Barbados 697
British Virgin Islands 414
Cayman Islands 195, 212
Cuba 185-6
Dominica 599
Grenada 722
Guadeloupe 575
Jamaica 255
Martinique 610, 624
Puerto Rico 340, 353
Saba 479
safe travel 823
St Kitts & Nevis 514
St Lucia 646
St Vincent & the Grenadines 671
St-Barthélemy 463, 466
Turks & Caicos 131-2
US Virgin Islands 385
geography 46-8
George Town 196-204, **198-9**
Gold Rock Beach 86
golf 817
Anguilla 427, 431
Antigua & Barbuda 524, 527

Aruba, Bonaire & Curaçao 785
Barbados 695
Cayman Islands 201
Dominican Republic 297, 318-19
Guadeloupe 558
Jamaica 225, 232, 236, 242,
  247, 253
St Lucia 645
St-Martin/Sint Maarten 441, 449
Gorda Peak National Park 407
Gosier 555-6
Gouyave 716
government 24-6
Governor's Harbour 96
Grace Bay Beach 121
Graeme Hall Nature Sanctuary 685
Grafton Caledonia Wildlife
  Sanctuary 762
Gran Caverna de Santo Tomás 161
Grand Anse 710-12
Grand Bahama 77-87, **78**
Grand Bay 596
Grand Case 445-6
Grand Cayman 196-206, **198-9**
Grand Cul-de-Sac 461-2
Grand Étang 564
Grand Etang National Park 714-15
Grand Etang Rd 713-15
Grand Turk 115-19
Grand-Bourg 571
Grande Anse (Grande-Terre) 562
Grande Anse (Martinique) 619
Grande Anse (St Lucia) 644
Grande Anse (Terre-de-Bas) 570
Grande Anse (Terre-de-Haut) 569
Grande Rivière 753
Grande-Terre 551-61, **548**
Grand-Rivière 615-16
Gravenor Bay 534
Great Guana Cay 92
Great Harbour 408-9
Great Morass 250
Great Pedro Bay 250-1
Great Salt Pond 504
Green Turtle Cay 91-2
Greenwood Great House 245-6
Gregory Town 95-6
Grenada 701-25, **703**, **706**
  accommodations 720
  arts 704
  books 721
  business hours 721
  climate 702
  culture 704
  embassies 721

environment 704-5
food 705
history 702-4, 705
internet resources 722
money 722
music 704
safe travel 721
travel to/from 723-5
travel within 724-5
visas 723
Grenada Island 706-16, **706**
Grenade Hall Signal Station 691
Grenville 715
Groot Knip 809
Groot Santa Martha 808-9
Gros Islet 637-8
Gros Piton 640-1
Guadeloupe 546-79, **548**, **568**
  accommodations 573
  arts 549
  books 549
  business hours 574
  climate 547
  culture 549
  embassies 574-5
  environment 549
  food 549-50
  history 547-9
  internet resources 575
  money 575
  language 575
  safe travel 552, 574
  travel to/from 576-7
  travel within 577-9
  visas 576
Guana Island 404
Guevara, Ernesto 'Che' 138, 159, 165
Guiana Island 520
Gun Creek 407
Gun Hill 692
Gustavia 458-60, **459**

## H
Habitation Murat 571
Hagley Gap 231
Haiti 260-77, **262**
  accommodations 274
  arts 45, 265
  books 274
  business hours 274
  climate 261
  culture 264-5
  embassies 275
  environment 265-6
  food 266

Haiti *continued*
history 261-4
internet resources 276
language 276, 845
money 276
music 265, 269
safe travel 266-7, 275
travel to/from 277
travel within 277, 16
visas 276
Half Moon Bay 530
Hams Bluff 383
Happy Bay 446
Harbour Island 93-5, 15
Hastings 685
Havana 141-58, **142-3**, **146-7**
accommodations 149-53
attractions 144-9
drinking 155
entertainment 155-7
food 153-4
travel to/from 157-8, 159
travel within 158
Hawksbill Bay 527
Hawksbill Cay 98
Hawksbill Creek 87
Hawksnest Bay 375
health 837-43
heatstroke 843
Hell 204
Hell's Gate 473
Hell's Gate Beach 592
hepatitis A 839
hepatitis B 839-40
hiking 818
Antigua & Barbuda 536
Aruba, Bonaire & Curaçao 790-1, 798, 810
Barbados 691, 692, 695-6
British Virgin Islands 400, 405, 407
Cayman Islands 205, 207, 211
Cuba 161, 163-4, 170, 181, 183
Dominica 590, 591, 592, 595-6, 598
Dominican Republic 314-16, 318
Grenada 713, 714-16, 721, 723
Guadeloupe 561, 564, 565, 570, 574
Haiti 270, 272, 274
Jamaica 220, 231, 233
Martinique 614, 615-16, 623-4

Montserrat 544
Puerto Rico 343, 350, 352
Saba 476, 477, 478-9
safety 818
St Kitts & Nevis 511, 513
St Lucia 640-1, 644-5
St Vincent & the Grenadines 659, 671
St-Martin/Sint Maarten 444, 449
Sint Eustatius 489-90
Trinidad & Tobago 746, 748, 749-50, 753, 762, 763-4, 765, 767, 768, 770, 773
Turks & Caicos 129-30
US Virgin Islands 372, 375, 376-7, 379, 381, 382, 383, 384
Hillsborough 717-18
historic buildings & sites, *see also* forts, plantations
Bibliothèque Schoelcher 608
Capitolio Nacional 145
Casa Blanca 329
Christiansted National Historic Site 378-9
Citadelle, the 273-4
Cuartel Moncada 174-5
Devon House 223-5
Elbow Cay Lighthouse 90
Faro a Colón 289
George Washington House 682
Gran Teatro de La Habana 148
Greenwood Great House 245-6
Habana Vieja 144-5, **142-3**
La Fortaleza 331-2
Mangazina di Rei 797-8
Morgan Lewis Sugar Mill 691
Nelson's Dockyard 529
Palacio de los Capitanes Generales 144
Parc Archéologique des Roches Gravées 564
Parque de Bombas 348
Pedro St James 205
Rose Hall Great House 245
Sans Souci 273-4
slave huts 798
Zona Colonial 285-9, **286-7**
history 32, 41-3, *see also individual countries*
hitchhiking 836
HIV/AIDS 840
Hog John Bay 527
Holetown 689
holidays 823
Honeymoon Beach (St John) 375

Honeymoon Beach (Water Island) 369
horse racing 510, 684
horseback riding 818
Anguilla 426, 427
Aruba, Bonaire & Curaçao 786, 810
Bahamas, the 83
Barbados 696
Cayman Islands 201
Cuba 170
Dominican Republic 297, 304, 306
Haiti 271
Jamaica 236
St Kitts & Nevis 513
St Lucia 634
St-Barthélemy 464
St-Martin/Sint Maarten 447, 449
Trinidad & Tobago 758
Turks & Caicos 118
US Virgin Islands 377, 383
Horsestable 127-8
Hull Bay 367
hurricanes
damage caused by 26, 48, 49
Hurricane Ivan 705, 714
hurricane season 27
internet resources 32
hyperbaric chambers 477

**I**
Île-à-Vache 272
Îlet Caret 563
Îlet Pigeon 565
Îlet Pinel 447
immigration 828, 829, 830
Indian Bay Beach 657-8
Indian Castle Beach 510-11
Indian River 590-1
Indian Town Point 530
insurance 823, 837
internet access 823-4
internet resources, *see also individual countries*
accommodations 816
diving 54
health 837-8
hurricanes 32
media 32
pirates 32
sports 44
transporation 830, 831
travel 32
Isla Culebrita 346
Isla de la Juventud 160
Isla Desecheo 350-1
Isla Saona 297, 298

INDEX

Island Harbour 429-30
Island Village Beach 235
itineraries 30, 33-40

## J

Jack Boy Hill 543
Jacmel 270-1
Jamaica 215-59, **217**
  accommodations 252
  arts 219-20
  books 219-20
  business hours 253-4
  climate 216
  culture 218-19
  embassies 254
  environment 220-1
  films 219
  food 221
  history 216-18, 244
  internet resources 255
  language 255, 845-6
  money 256
  music 220, 235, 242, 247, 255
  safe travel 223, 235, 239, 254
  travel to/from 256-7
  travel within 257-9
  visas 256
Jarabacoa 314-18
Jardin de Balata 615
Jérémie 272
jet lag 838
Jolly Harbour 527
Josiah's Bay 402
Jost van Dyke 407-10, **392-3**
JR O'Neal Botanic Gardens 396
Jumbie Bay 375
Junk's Hole 429-30

## K

Kalinago Barana Aute 593
Kartouche Bay 430
Kas Abou 808, 809
kayaking
  Antigua & Barbuda 537
  Aruba, Bonaire & Curaçao 786, 798
  Bahamas, the 83, 93, 98, 103-10
  Dominica 596-7
  Grenada 723
  Puerto Rico 333, 344, 346
  St-Barthélemy 461, 463, 465
  Trinidad & Tobago 745, 748, 752, 758, 768, 770, 773
  Turks & Caicos 118
  US Virgin Islands 369-70, 372-3
Kenscoff 270

Kingston 221-30, **224-5**, **226-7**
Kingstown 654-9, **656**
Kite Beach 311
kitesurfing
  Aruba, Bonaire & Curaçao 786
  Bahamas, the 93, 98, 103
  Barbados 687-8, 696
  British Virgin Islands 412
  Dominican Republic 307-8, 311, 319
  St Lucia 643
  St Vincent & the Grenadines 671
  Trinidad & Tobago 756-8, 770
  Turks & Caicos 125
Klein Bonaire 56
Klein Knip 809
Kleine St Michiel 808, 809
Kralendijk 792-7, **794-5**

## L

La Baie Orientale 447
La Boca 311
La Ciénaga 314-15
La Désirade 572-3
La Habana, see Havana
La Sagesse Nature Centre 713
La Saline 271
La Soufrière (Guadeloupe) 564-5
La Soufrière (St Vincent) 659
Lac Azueï 270
Lac Bay 798
Lac Cai 798
Ladder Bay 477
Lagún 809
Lake Antoine 715
Lambert Bay 402
Lance aux Épines 712-13
Landhuis Groot Santa Martha 808-9
Landhuis Kenepa 809
languages 844-52, see also individual countries
Las Cuevas Bay 747
Las Galeras 303-6
Las Terrenas 306-10, **308**
Layou River 589
Le Chameau 570
Le Galion 447-8
Le Moule 559-60
Le Souffleur 572
Leeward Hwy 659-60
Leeward Road 762-3
legal matters 824
Leinster Bay 376
leishmaniasis 840
Les Cayes 271-2

Les Salines 622
lesbian travelers, see gay & lesbian travelers
L'Esterre 718
Levera Beach 715
l'Habitation Fond St-Jacques 616
Liberta 528
Lighthouse Beach 95
l'Îlet du Gosier 555
literature, see books
Little Bay 544
Little Cayman 208-10, **208-9**
Little Dix Bay 405
Little Harbour 409-10
Little Hawksbill Cay 98
Little Tobago 56, 767
Little Water Cay 123
Loblolly Bay 412
Loma Quita Espuela 316
Long Bay (Antigua) 530
Long Bay (Jamaica) 234
Long Bay (Negril) 247
Long Bay (St-Martin) 444
Long Bay (Tortola) 400
Long Bay (Virgin Gorda) 407
Long Island 102
Lorient 462
Lower Bay 664
Lucaya 79-86, **85**
Lucayan National Park 86
Luquillo 343

## M

Macabou 621
Macouba 615
Macoucherie Distillery 589
Madamas Bay 748
Magens Bay 367
Maho 441
Maho Bay 376
Mahoe Bay 407
Mahogany Beach 235
Maison de la Forêt 561
malaria 840
Malcolm Roads 121
Malendure Beach 565-6
Malgretout 640
Malibu Beach Club & Visitor Centre 682-3
Malmok Beach 791
Mamiku Gardens 643
Man of War Bay 768
Man of War Island 534
Manaca Iznaga 170
Manchebo Beach 791

manchineel trees 822
Barbados 697
Martinique 622, 624
St Vincent & the Grenadines 662, 671
Mangazina di Rei 797-8
Manzanilla Beach 752
maps 824
Maracas Bay 747-8
Maria Islands Nature Reserve 643
Marie-Galante 570-2, **548**
Marigot 442-3, **443**
Marigot Bay 638-9
marine life 48-9
marine parks, see national parks & reserves
Marley, Bob
music 45-6, 220
museums 225, 238
Marsh Harbour 88-90
Martha Brae 246
Martin's Bay 693-4
Martinique 603-27, **605**, **11**
accommodations 622-3
arts 606
business hours 624
climate 604
culture 606
embassies 624
environment 606-7
food 607
history 604-5, 614
internet resources 624
language 625
money 625
music 606
safe travel 624
travel to/from 625-6
travel within 626-7
visas 625
Mary's Point ruins 477
Mata Grande 314-15
Matura 753-4
Mayaro 752
Mayreau 667
Meads Bay 426-7
measures 816, see also inside front cover
medical services 839, see also health
merengue music 283, 290, 320
Mero Beach 589

metric conversions, see inside front cover
Middle Caicos 129-30
Middleham Falls 595
Milot 274
Miriam C Schmidt Botanical Gardens 488
mobile phones 826
Molinière Bay 710
monasteries, see convents & monasteries
money 28-9, 824-5, see also individual countries
Mont Pelée 613, 614, 615-16, 623
Montego Bay 239-45, **240-1**
Montego Bay Marine Park 242
Montserrat 540-5, **542**
Morgan Lewis Sugar Mill 691
Morne Coubaril Estate 640
Morne de Lurin 463
Morne Fortune 633
Morne Rouge 615
Morne Rouge Bay 712
Morne Trois Pitons National Park 595-6
Morne-à-l'Eau 560-1
motion sickness 838
motorcycle travel 835, 836
Mt Alvernia 102
Mount Gay Rum Visitors Centre 683
Mt Irvine Beach 762
Mt Scenery 476, 478
Mt St Benedict 746
Mt Standfast 689
mountain biking, see cycling
Mountain Trunk Bay 407
Mudjin Harbor 129
Mullet Bay 441
Mullins Beach 689
museums, see also galleries
Asociación Cultural Yoruba de Cuba 145-8
Barbados Museum 682
Bob Marley Museum 225
Curaçao Maritime Museum 804
Horatio Nelson Museum 507-8
Indian Caribbean Museum 750-1
Maison de la Canne 618
Monumento Ernesto Che Guevara 165
Musée de la Banane 616
Musée du Rhum 563
Musée du Rhum St James 616
Musée Paul Gauguin 612-13
Musée Schoelcher 553
Musée Volcanologique 613

Museo de la Revolución 148
Museo de las Américas 332
Museo de las Casas Reales 288
Museo del Hombre Dominicano 289-90
Museo del Ron 145
Museo Histórico Municipal 170
Museo Mundo de Ambar 288
Museum Kura Hulanda 803-4
National Museum & Art Gallery 740
Nevisian Heritage Village 511
Nidhe Israel Museum 682
Nine Mile Museum 238
Pirates of Nassau 69
Pompey Museum 69
Reggae Xplosion 235
Sint Eustatius Museum 486
Turks & Caicos National Museum 116
music 12-13, 45-6, **12**, **13** see also Marley, Bob; individual countries; individual music styles
music festivals
BVI Music Festival 400, 414
Merengue Festival 290, 320
Moonsplash 431
Reggae Sumfest 242, 823
St Kitts Music Festival 514
World Creole Music Festival 599
World Steel Band Festival 772
Mustique 664-5

**N**
Nail Bay 407
Nariva Swamp 752
Nassau 66-76, **68**, **71**
accommodations 72-4
attractions 69-72
drinking 75
entertainment 75
food 74-5
safe travel 67-9
national parks & reserves, see also gardens & parks
Arikok National Wildlife Park 790-1
Asa Wright Nature Centre 746-7
Bahía Mosquito 344
Barbados Marine Reserve 689
Barkers National Park 204
Bloody Bay Marine Park 55, 194, 209
Blue Mountains-John Crow National Park 231
Bonaire Marine Park 55, 56, 799

Booby Pond Nature Reserve 209
Bosque Estatal de Guánica 350
Brimstone Hill Fortress National Park 505, 9
Buccoo Reef 761
Buck Island Reef National Monument 381
Cabrits National Park 591
Caroni Bird Sanctuary 750
Chaguaramas 744-6
Chalk Sound National Park 121
Christoffel National Park 810
Columbus Landfall National Park 116
Copper Mine National Park 405
East Bay Islands National Park 128
El Yunque 343
Exuma Cays Land & Sea Park 98
Farley Hill National Park 691
Flamingo Pond 410-11
Fort George Land & Sea National Park 123
Gorda Peak National Park 407
Grafton Caledonia Wildlife Sanctuary 762
Grand Etang National Park 714-15
JR O'Neal Botanic Gardens 396
Little Tobago 56, 767
Little Water Cay 123
Lucayan National Park 86
Maria Islands Nature Reserve 643
Montego Bay Marine Park 242
Morne Trois Pitons National Park 595-6
National Trust Parrot Reserve 207
Northern Forest Reserve 590
Northwest Point Marine National Park 121
Parc National La Visite 270
Parc National Macaya 272
Parc Nationale Historique La Citadelle 274
Parque de las Cavernas del Río Camuy 342
Parque Ecológico Punta Cana 297
Parque Nacional Alejandro de Humboldt 183
Parque Nacional Los Haitises 317
Parque Nacional Viñales 160-3
Península de Guanahacabibes 163-4
Peterson Cay National Park 86
Pigeon Island National Park 638
Pigeon Pond & Frenchman's Creek Nature Reserve 121

Pointe-à-Pierre Wildfowl Trust 751
Princess Alexandra National Park 123
Rand Nature Centre 83
Reserva Científica Loma Quita Espuela 316
Réserve Cousteau 565
Royal Palm Reserve 250
Saba Marine Park 55, 56-7, 478
Sage Mountain National Park 400
St Vincent Parrot Reserve 659
Shete Boka National Park 810
Soufriere Bay 57, 596-7
Statia Marine Park 55, 57, 489
Three Mary Cays National Park 128
Tobago Forest Reserve 765
Virgin Islands National Park 372
Washington-Slagbaai National Park 798
Natural Bridge 790
Natural Pool 790
nature reserves, see national parks & reserves
Necker Island 404
Negril 246-50
Nelson, Horatio 507-8, 510
Nelson's Dockyard 529
Netherlands Antilles 779
Nevis 506-12, **507**
New Providence 64-77, **65**
newspapers 816
Newton Ground 505
Nine Mile 238
Nonsuch Bay 530
Norman Island 404
North Caicos 127-9
North Friar's Bay 504
North Shore (Antigua) 526-7
North Shore (St John) 374-6
North Side 205-6
North Sound 407
Northern Forest Reserve 590
Northern Range 747
Northwest Point 121
Northwest Point Marine National Park 121
Nueva Gerona 160
Nylon Pool 761

**O**
Ocho Rios 235-8
Oistins 687
Old Road 528
Old Road Town 504
Olde Town 544

opening hours 819, see also individual countries
Oppenheimer's Beach 375
Oranjestad (Aruba) 781-9, **782-3**
Oranjestad (Sint Eustatius) 485-91, **487**
Orchid Beach 344
Orient Beach 447
Owen Island 210
Owia 659
Oyster Pond 448

**P**
painting 45, 265, 361
Palm Beach 791
Palm Island 669
Palmetto Point 534
Paradise Beach (Carriacou) 718
Paradise Beach (Paradise Island) 77
Paradise Cove 87
Paradise Island 76-7
Parc Archéologique des Roches Gravées 564
Parc National La Visite 270
Parc National Macaya 272
Parc Nationale Historique La Citadelle 274
Paria Bay 748
Paria Falls 748
parks, see gardens & parks
Parlatuvier 764-5
Parque de las Cavernas del Río Camuy 342
Parque Ecológico Punta Cana 297
Parque Histórico Militar Morro-Cabaña 159
Parque Nacional Alejandro de Humboldt 183
Parque Nacional Los Haitises 317
Parque Nacional Viñales 160-3
Parque Ojos Indígenas 297
passports 829, 830
patois 846
Paynes Bay 688-9
Península de Guanahacabibes 163-4
Península de Samaná 300-10
Penlyne Castle 231
people 43, 44
Peter Island 404
Peterson Cay National Park 86
Petit Carenage Bay 718
Petit Martinique 719-20
Petit Piton 640-1
Petit St Vincent 669
Petit-Canal 560

INDEX

Petite Anse 572
Petites Cayes 446
Petites-Anses 570
Philipsburg 438-40, **439**
phone cards 826
phone codes 826-7
photography 825-6
Pic Paradis 444
Pico Duarte 314-15
Pigeon 565-6
Pigeon Island 565-6
Pigeon Island National Park 638
Pigeon Peak 768
Pigeon Point 756-8
Pigeon Pond 121
Pigeon Pond & Frenchman's Creek
    Nature Reserve 121
Pinar del Río Province 160-4
Pine Cay 123
Pink Beach 799
Pink Sands Beach 93, 95
Pinney's Beach 509
pirates 30, 31
    Aruba, Bonaire & Curaçao 785
    Bahamas, the 60, 69, 70, 84, 99
    Blackbeard 60, 358, 364
    Bonny, Anne 250, 361
    British Virgin Islands 391
    Cayman Islands 205, 212
    Haiti 272
    internet resources 32
    Jamaica 230, 250
    Kidd, Captain 99
    Montbars 'the Exterminator' 462
    Morgan, Captain 272
    Pirates of Nassau museum 69
    Pirates Week 212
    Rackham, 'Calico' Jack 250, 358,
        361
    Read, Mary 250, 361
    St-Barthélemy 462
    Trinidad & Tobago 728
    US Virgin Islands 358, 361
Pirate's Bay 768
*Pirates of the Caribbean*
    Bahamas, the 84, 97, 99-100
    Dominica 592
    St Vincent & the Grenadines
        659-60, 668
Pitch Lake 751
Pitons, the 640-1

Pitons Waterfall 640
Plage de l'Anse Mitan 618
Plage de Malendure 565-6
Plage Labadie 273
planning 27-32
    itineraries 30, 33-40
plantations
    Annaberg Sugar Mill Ruins 375
    Betty's Hope 530-1
    Caféiere Beauséjour 562
    Château Dubuc 616-17
    Landhuis Groot Santa Martha 808-9
    l'Habitation Fond St-Jacques 616
    Morne Coubaril Estate 640
    Plantation Mont Vernon 446-7
    St Nicholas Abbey 691
    Sunbury Plantation House 694
    Wades Green Plantation 127
    Wallblake House 423
    Whim Plantation 383
plants 49
Playa Ancón 170
Playa Bariguá 181
Playa Blanca 181
Playa Bonita 310
Playa Brava 346
Playa Cabarete 311
Playa Cabo Engaño 297
Playa Canoa 810
Playa del Macao 297
Playa El Cortecito 297
Playa Encuentro 311
Playa Flamenco 346
Playa Frontón 304
Playa Isla Verde 332-3
Playa Kalki 809
Playa Knip 809
Playa Lagún 809
Playa Limón 297
Playa Luquillo 343
Playa Madama 304
Playa Maguana 181
Playa Rincón 303-4
Playas del Este 159
Playita 304
Pleasant Prospect 762-3
Plum Bay 444
Plymouth 763
Point Salines 712
Point Udall 382
Pointe de la Grande Vigie 560
Pointe des Châteaux 558-9
Pointe du Bout 618-19
Pointe-à-Pierre Wildfowl Trust 751
Pointe-à-Pitre 551-5, **553**

Pointe-Noire 561-2
Ponce 348-50, **349**
Port Antonio 232-3
Port d'Enfer 560
Port Elizabeth 661-4
Port of Spain 735-44, **736-7**
Port Royal 230-1
Port Salut 272
Port-au-Prince 266-9, **267**
Portsmouth 590-2
postal systems 826
Presqu'île de Caravelle 616-17
Prickly Pear 428, 431
Princess Alexandra National Park 123
Princess Margaret Beach 662
Protestant Cay 379
Providenciales 120-7, **122-3**
Public 460
public holidays 823
Puerto Rico 324-56, **326**, 11
    accommodations 351
    arts 327, 360-1
    business hours 352
    climate 325
    culture 327
    embassies 353
    environment 327-8
    food 328
    history 325-7
    internet resources 353
    language 353, 846
    money 354
    safe travel 352
    travel to/from 354-5
    travel within 355-6
    visas 354
Pumpkin Bluff 127-8
Punta Cana 296-300

**Q**
Queen Elizabeth II Botanic Park 205
Quill, the 485, 486, 489-90

**R**
rabies 840-1
radio 816
rafting, *see* white-water rafting
Rand Nature Centre 83
Rastafarianism 45
    Dominica 580, 583
    Jamaica 219
    St Lucia 631
    St Vincent & the Grenadines 652
    Trinidad & Tobago 729
Red Beach 344

**000** Map pages
000 Photograph pages

INDEX

Red Hook 368-70
Reduit Beach 635-7
regattas 44-5
    Antigua Sailing Week 536
    BVI Spring Regatta 413-14
    Family Island Regatta 98-9
    Foxy's Woodenboat Regatta 414
reggae
    festivals & concerts 242, 249,
        431, 823
    museums 235
    music 46, 220
religion 45, see also Rastafarianism
    Santería 45, 145-8
    Vodou 45, 264, 265, 631
Remedios 168-9
Rendezvous Bay 427-8
Reserva Científica Loma Quita Espuela
    316
Réserve Cousteau 565
reserves, see national parks & reserves
responsible travel 29-30, see also
    volunteering
    Anguilla 422
    climate 831
    diving 54-5
    Dominican Republic 282-3, 303
    photography 825
    Saba 472
    St Vincent & the Grenadines 653
    St-Barthélemy 457
    Trinidad & Tobago 731
    US Virgin Islands 385
Richmond Beach 659
Rincon (Bonaire) 797
Rincón (Puerto Rico) 350-1
Rio Grand Valley 233
Río Yaque del Norte 315
River Antoine Rum Distillery 715
Road Town 395-9, **397**
Rocher du Diamant 620
rock climbing
    Aruba, Bonaire & Curaçao 790, 793
    Cuba 161-2, 183-4
    Saba 479
Rocklands Bird Feeding Station 246
Rockley 685
Rodney Bay 635-7
Rolle Town 97
Rose Hall Great House 245
Roseau 584-9, **586**
Route de la Trace 614-15
Route de la Traversée 561
Roxborough 767
Royal Battery 488

Royal Palm Reserve 250
rum 51
    museums 145, 563, 616
    shops 790
rum distilleries
    Appleton Rum Estate 252
    Bacardi Rum Factory 342
    Callwood Rum Distillery 400
    Cruzan Rum Distillery 383
    Distillerie Bielle 572
    Distillerie Poisson 572
    Distillery Damoiseau 559-60
    Domaine de Bellevue 572
    Macoucherie Distillery 589
    Malibu Beach Club & Visitor Centre
        682-3
    Mount Gay Rum Visitors Centre 683
    Musée du Rhum St James 616
    Pyrat Rums 424
    Rhum JM distillery 615
    River Antoine Rum Distillery 715
    Trois-Rivières Distillerie 621
Rum Point 206
Runaway Bay 525-6
Runaway Ghaut 544

**S**
Saba 469-81, **471**, 8, 10
    accommodations 478
    arts 472, 474
    business hours 479
    climate 470
    culture 472
    environment 472
    food 472-3
    history 470-1, 779
    internet resources 480
    money 480
    travel to/from 480-1
    travel within 481
    visas 480
Saba Marine Park 55, 56-7, 478
Sacré-Coeur de Balata 615
safe travel, see also manchineel trees
    Antigua & Barbuda 536
    Aruba, Bonaire & Curaçao 803, 811
    Bahamas, the 67, 103-4
    Barbados 696-7
    British Virgin Islands 396, 413
    children 820
    crime 821-2
    Cuba 184-5
    drugs 254, 771, 824
    Dominica 599
    Dominican Republic 285, 319

    gay & lesbian travelers 823
    Grenada 721
    Guadeloupe 552, 574
    Haiti 266-7, 275
    hiking 818
    hitchhiking 836
    Jamaica 223, 235, 239, 254
    Martinique 624
    Montserrat 545
    Puerto Rico 352
    St Kitts & Nevis 514
    St Lucia 645
    St Vincent & the Grenadines
        662, 671
    St-Martin/Sint Maarten 449-50
    Trinidad & Tobago 738-9, 771
    Turks & Caicos 131
    US Virgin Islands 385
Sage Mountain National Park 400
sailing, see boat travel, boat trips,
    yachting
St, see also St-, Ste-, Sint
St Croix 377-84, **359**
St George Village Botanical Garden 384
St George's 707-10
St John 370-7, **359**
St John's (Antigua) 523-5, **524**
St John's (Saba) 476
St Kitts 499-506, **497**, 9
St Kitts & Nevis 495-516, **497**, 9
    accommodations 512
    books 513
    business hours 513-14
    climate 496
    culture 498
    embassies 514
    environment 498
    food 498-9
    history 496-7, 498
    money 514
    music 514
    safe travel 514
    travel to/from 515-16
    travel within 516
    visas 515
St Lawrence Gap 686-7
St Lucia 628-49, **630**
    accommodations 644
    arts 631
    books 645
    business hours 645
    climate 629
    culture 629-31
    embassies 645
    environment 631-2

St Lucia *continued*
food 632
history 629
internet resources 646
money 646
music 631, 634
safe travel 645
travel to/from 647-8
travel within 639, 648-9
visas 647
St Nicholas Abbey 691
St Paul's 505
St Thomas 362-70, **359**
St Vincent 654-60, **655**
St Vincent & the Grenadines 650-74,
   **651**, **655**
accommodations 670
arts 652-3
business hours 671
climate 651
culture 652
embassies 671
environment 653
food 653-4
history 651-2
internet resources 671-2
money 672
music 652-3
safe travel 662, 671
travel to/from 673
travel within 673-4
visas 672
St Vincent Botanic Gardens 657
St Vincent Parrot Reserve 659
St-Barthélemy 454-68, **456**
accommodations 464
arts 457
books 465
business hours 466
climate 455
culture 457
embassies 466
environment 457
food 457-8
history 455-7
internet resources 466
money 466
music 460, 466
travel to/from 467-8
travel within 468
visas 467

Ste-Anne (Grande-Terre) 556-7
Ste-Anne (Martinique) 621-2
Ste-Luce 620-1
Ste-Marie 563
Ste-Rose 563
St-François 557-8
St-Jean 460-1
St-Louis 571-2
St-Martin 441-8, **436**
St-Martin/Sint Maarten 434-53, **436**
accommodations 448
business hours 449
climate 435
culture 436-7
embassies 450
environment 437
food 437
history 435-6, 779
internet resources 450
money 450
safe travel 449-50
travel to/from 451-2
travel within 452-3
visas 451
St-Pierre 613-14
Salt Cay 57, 119-20
Salt Island 404
Salt Pond 659
Salt Pond Bay 376
Salt Water Pond 207
Salto de Baiguate 315
Salto de Jimenoa Dos 315
Salto del Caburní 170
Salto Jimenoa Uno 315
Saltwhistle Bay 667
Salybia 754
Samaná 300-3
San Fernando 751
San Juan 328-42, **330**, **334-5**
accommodations 334-7
attractions 329-33
drinking 339-40
entertainment 340
food 337-9
travel to/from 341
travel within 341-2
San Nicolas 791
sanctuaries, *see* aquariums & zoos,
   national parks & reserves
Sandy Bay 659
Sandy Beach 685
Sandy Ground (Anguilla) 424-5
Sandy Ground (St-Martin) 444
Sandy Island (Carriacou) 719
Sandy Island (Grenada Island) 715

Sans Souci 273-4
Santa Clara 165-8
Santería 45, 145-8
Santiago de Cuba 173-80, **176-7**, 12
Santo Domingo 284-96, **286-7**
accommodations 290-2
attractions 285-90
drinking 293
eating 292-3
entertainment 293-4
shopping 294-5
travel to/from 295
travel within 295-6
Sapodilla Bay 121
Sauteurs 716
Savannah Bay 405
Scarborough 765-6
schistosomiasis 574, 624, 645, 841
Scotland Bay 745
Scotts Head 57, 597
sea kayaking, *see* kayaking
Secret Beach 344
Secret Harbour 369
Seguin 270
Settlement, the 411-12
Seven Mile Beach (Grand Cayman)
   196-204, **198-9**
Seven Mile Beach (Jamaica) 247
Sharpe, Sam 244
Shell Beach 460
Shermans 690
Shete Boka National Park 810
Shoal Bay East 428-9
Shoal Bay West 427-8
Silver Sands 687-8
Simpson Bay 440-1
Sint Eustatius 482-94, **484**
accommodations 490-2
books 486
business hours 492
climate 483
culture 485
food 485, 491
history 483-5, 779
money 492
travel to/from 493
travel within 493-4
visas 493
Sint Maarten 437-41, **436**
Site de l'Alma 615
Smuggler's Cove 400
snorkeling, *see* diving & snorkeling
soccer 730
solo travelers 826
Sopers Hole 399-400

INDEX

Soufriere (Dominica) 596-7
Soufrière (St Lucia) 639-43
Soufrière Bay 57, 596-7
Soufrière Hills Volcano 544
Soup Bowl 692-3
South Caicos 130
South Friar's Bay 504
Spanish language 849-52
Spanish Point 534
Spanish Town 405-7
Speightstown 690
Speyside 767-8
sportfishing, see fishing
sports 43-5, see also cricket
    baseball 43, 44, 282, 293-4
    soccer 730
Spring Bay 405
Staniel Cay 98
Statia, see Sint Eustatius
Statia Marine Park 55, 57, 489
steel pan 520, 730-1, 744, 13
Stingray City 199-200
Stocking Island 97-8
Store Bay 756
Sulphur Springs 640
Sunbury Plantation House 694
surfing 819
    Aruba, Bonaire & Curaçao 810
    Bahamas, the 91, 95, 103
    Barbados 688, 692-3, 696
    British Virgin Islands 400, 402,
        413
    Dominican Republic 311
    Guadeloupe 558, 559, 560, 574
    Jamaica 234, 253
    Martinique 616, 617
    Puerto Rico 351, 352, 11
    St-Barthélemy 458, 461, 463, 465
    Trinidad & Tobago 747, 748, 753,
        762, 770
    US Virgin Islands 367, 385
sustainable travel, see responsible
    travel
synagogues
    Barbados Synagogue 682
    Honen Dalim 487
    St Thomas Synagogue 365
    synagogue ruins 487

**T**
Tarpon Lake 209
Tartane 616
telephone services 826-7
Ten Bay 95
Terre-de-Bas 570

Terre-de-Haut 566-70, **568**
Terres Basses 443-4
Three Mary Cays National Park 128
Thunderball Grotto 98
time 827
tipping 825
Titou Gorge 595
Tobago 754-69, **755**
Tobago Cays 669
Tobago Forest Reserve 765
Toco 753
Tombeau des Caraïbes 614
Topes de Collantes 170
Tortola 395-403, **392-3**
tourist information 827
Trafalgar Falls 594-5
tramping, see hiking
transportation 829-36
travel to/from the Caribbean islands
        829-33, see also individual
        countries
travel within the Caribbean islands
        833-6, see also individual countries
traveler's checks 825
trekking, see hiking
Treasure Beach 250-1
Treasure Cay Beach 89
Trellis Bay 402
Trinidad (Cuba) 169-73
Trinidad (Trinidad & Tobago) 732-54,
        **733**
Trinidad & Tobago 726-76, **727**,
        **733**, **755**
    accommodations 769
    arts 730-1
    books 730, 747, 771
    business hours 771
    climate 727
    culture 728-9, 752
    embassies 771
    environment 731
    food 731-2
    history 727-8
    internet resources 772
    language 735
    money 772
    music 730-1, 772, 13
    safe travel 738-9, 771
    travel to/from 774
    travel within 774-6
    visas 773
Trinité 617
Trois-Îlets 618
Trois-Rivières 564
Trois-Rivères Distillerie 621

Tropic of Cancer Beach 97
Trou Caïman 270
True Blue Bay 712
Trunk Bay 375, 405
Turks & Caicos 111-134, **112**
    accommodations 130
    arts 114
    books 131
    business hours 131
    climate 112
    culture 113-14
    environment 114
    food 114-15
    history 113
    internet resources 132
    itineraries 112
    language 846
    safe travel 131
    travel to/from 133-4
    travel within 134
    visas 133
Turks Islands 115-20, **112**
Turtle Beach 235
turtles
    Barbados 689
    Cayman Islands 204
    Puerto Rico 346
    St Lucia 644
    Trinidad & Tobago 753-4
TV 816
Twin Bay 665
typhoid 841
Tyrol Cot Heritage Village 691
Tyrrel Bay 719

**U**
Union Island 667-9
US Virgin Islands 357-89, **359**
    accommodations 384
    books 385
    business hours 385
    climate 358
    culture 360
    embassies 385
    environment 361-2
    food 362
    history 358-60
    internet resources 386
    money 386
    language 846-7
    music 361
    safe travel 385
    travel to/from 387-8
    travel within 388-9
    visas 386-7

INDEX

**V**
vacations 823
vaccinations 837, 838
Valle de Tetero 314-15
Valley Church Beach 527
Valley, the (Anguilla) 422-4
Valley, the (Virgin Gorda) 405-7
Valombreuse Floral Park 563
Vessup Beach 369
Victoria 716
video systems 816, 825-6
Vieques 343-6
Villa Beach 657-8
Viñales 160-3
Virgin Gorda 403-7, **392-3**
Virgin Islands National Park 372
visas 828, *see also individual countries*
  passports 829, 830
Vitet 462-3
Vodou 45, 264, 265, 631
volunteering 827
  Puerto Rico 346
  Sint Eustatius 485, 489
  Trinidad & Tobago 753-4, 758
  US Virgin Islands 372

**W**
Wades Green Plantation 127
wakeboarding 311
walking, *see* hiking
Wallilabou Bay 659-60
Wallilabou Falls 660
Washington-Slagbaai National Park 798
Water Island 369
waterfalls
  Annandale Falls 713
  Argyle Falls 767
  Cascada El Limón 301, 306, 9
  Cascade aux Écrevisses 561
  Concord Falls 716
  Damajagua 313
  Dunn's River Falls 235
  Emerald Pool 593-4
  Falls of Baleine 660
  Middleham Falls 595
  Paria Falls 748
  Pitons Waterfall 640
  Salto Jimenoa Uno 315
  Trafalgar Falls 594-5
  Wallilabou Falls 660
  YS Falls 252

Waterlemon Cay 376
Waterloo Temple 750
weather 27-8, 821, *see also* hurricanes,
  *individual countries*
websites, *see* internet resources
weights 816, *see also inside front cover*
Welchman Hall Gully 691
Well's Bay 477
West Bay 204-5
West End (Anegada) 410-11
West End (Anguilla) 427-8
West End (Tortola) 399-400
Westerly Ponds 207
Westpunt 809
whale-watching
  Dominica 587, 590, 599
  Dominican Republic 301, 302-3,
    319
  St Vincent & the Grenadines 660
  Turks & Caicos 119
wildlife 48-9
wildlife reserves, *see* aquariums &
  zoos, national parks & reserves
Whim Plantation 383
Whitby Beach 127-8
White Bay 409
White Island 719
white-water rafting
  Dominican Republic 315, 316
  Jamaica 233, 246
Willemstad 802-7, **800-1**
William Thornton Estate 399
windsurfing 810, 819
  Antigua & Barbuda 526
  Aruba, Bonaire & Curaçao 786,
    791, 798, 810
  Barbados 687-8, 696
  British Virgin Islands 399, 402,
    413
  Cayman Islands 211
  Dominican Republic 304, 307-8,
    311, 319
  Guadeloupe 555, 558, 574
  Martinique 618
  St Kitts & Nevis 509, 513
  St Lucia 643
  St Vincent & the Grenadines 671
  St-Barthélemy 461, 463, 465
  Trinidad & Tobago 756-8, 770
  Turks & Caicos 124, 130
  US Virgin Islands 369, 385

Windward 718
Windward Beach 510-11
Windward Hwy 659
Windward Rd 766-7
Windwardside 473-6, **471**
Winnifred Beach 234
women travelers 647, 826, 828
  Antigua & Barbuda 538
  Aruba, Bonaire & Curaçao 812
  Barbados 699
  British Virgin Islands 415
  Dominica 600
  Grenada 723
  Puerto Rico 354
  St Kitts & Nevis 515
  St Vincent & the Grenadines 672
  St-Martin/Sint Maarten 451
  Trinidad & Tobago 774
  Turks & Caicos 133
  US Virgin Islands 387
work 828
World Heritage sites 29
  Bonaire Marine Park 55, 56, 799
  Brimstone Hill Fortress 505, 9
  Castillo de San Pedro del Morro
    175
  Citadelle, the 273-4
  Fuerte San Cristóbal 331
  Fuerte San Felipe del Morro 331
  Habana Vieja 144-5, **142-3**
  Morne Trois Pitons National Park
    595-6
  Parque Nacional Alejandro De
    Humboldt 183
  Trinidad 169-73
  Valle de los Ingenios 170
  Viñales 160-3
  Willemstad 802-7, **800-1**
  Zona Colonial 285-9, **286-7**
Worthing 685-6
Wreck of the Ten Sails Park 205

**Y**
yachting 384, 413, 416, 834-6, *see
  also* boat trips, regattas
yellow fever 841-2
YS Falls 252

**Z**
Zeelandia 488
zoos, *see* aquariums & zoos